A Dictionary of
Contemporary World History

From 1900 to the present day

THIRD EDITION

 SEE WEB LINKS

Many entries in this dictionary have recommended web
links. When you see the above symbol at the end of an entry
go to the dictionary's web page at http://www.oup.com/uk/
reference/resources/contemporaryworldhistory, click on
Web links in the Resources section and locate the entry in
the alphabetical list, then click straight through to the
relevant websites.

Jan Palmowski is Senior Lecturer in European Studies
and Head of the School of Humanities, King's College,
London (University of London).

A Dictionary of

Contemporary World History

From 1900 to the present day

THIRD EDITION

JAN PALMOWSKI

OXFORD
UNIVERSITY PRESS

OXFORD
UNIVERSITY PRESS

Great Clarendon Street, Oxford OX2 6DP

Oxford University Press is a department of the University of Oxford.
It furthers the University's objective of excellence in research, scholarship,
and education by publishing worldwide in

Oxford New York

Auckland Cape Town Dar es Salaam Hong Kong Karachi
Kuala Lumpur Madrid Melbourne Mexico City Nairobi
New Delhi Shanghai Taipei Toronto

With offices in

Argentina Austria Brazil Chile Czech Republic France Greece
Guatemala Hungary Italy Japan Poland Portugal Singapore
South Korea Switzerland Thailand Turkey Ukraine Vietnam

Oxford is a registered trade mark of Oxford University Press
in the UK and in certain other countries

Published in the United States
by Oxford University Press Inc., New York

First published as the Dictionary of Twentieth Century World History 1997
Reprinted with corrections 1998
Second Edition 2003
Reissued with new covers 2004
Third Edition 2008

Typeset by SPI Publisher Services, Pondicherry, India
Printed in the U.S.A.

ISBN 978-0-19-929567-8 (Hbk.)

Book Club Edition

Contents

Acknowledgements for the First Edition   vii

Acknowledgements for the Second
and Third Editions   vii

Preface to the Second and Third Editions   viii

Preface to the First Edition   ix

**A Dictionary of Contemporary
World History**   **1**

Maps   759
  Austria-Hungary and its successor
    states   761
  The Ottoman Empire, 1912–14   762
  The British Empire, 1914   764
  The French Empire, 1914   765
  The Soviet Union and its
    successor states   766

To the Memory of
H. C. G. Matthew FBA,
First Editor of the *New Dictionary of National
Biography*

Acknowledgements for the First Edition

A book of this size and this complexity could only have been written with the extensive and generous help of others. I am particularly grateful to: Martin Meenagh (for his contributions on the USA), Stephen Johnson (on Japan), Richard Grayson (on the UK), Joseph Coohill (on the Republic of Ireland). The entries relating to these countries benefit enormously from their expertise, though I accept full responsibility, of course, for their content. I am also extremely indebted to C. Annesley, whose alertness has contributed much to the accuracy of this book.

I should also like to thank all those who have diligently and unflinchingly helped in correcting or checking various parts of the dictionary, especially T. Connolly and F. DeAngelis (Canada), C. Defrance (France), A. Barenco (Italy), W. Palmowski (Germany), and S. Knott (women's history). I am also grateful to William Wagner (USSR), John Davis (UK), and Michael John (general comments) for their invaluable suggestions. I am also grateful to Christ Church, Oxford, for providing me with an ideal work environment in which to write this book.

Last, but by no means least, I want to thank my friends without whose constant support, encouragement, and enthusiasm this book might never have been written. They alone have made this period of intense writing an enjoyable one, while they put up admirably with my constant mutterings about 'the dictionary'. In this sense, the book is very much a team effort, so that I should like to acknowledge my gratitude to Tara, Franco, Matt, Robin, Tore, Norunn, Joe, Adriano, and, above all, to Cressida.

Acknowledgements for the Second and Third Editions

While I wrote the second and third editions of this book, I was sustained by the unlimited understanding, patience, and kindness of Heather Williams. Despite her own commitments, she has made writing this book a uniquely happy experience. I am grateful as ever to my parents. More than can be intimated here, they have provided the selfless and invaluable practical, intellectual, and emotional support that has made this book possible. At a practical level, this book in its various editions could simply not have been written without my father. From my childhood onwards, he consistently stimulated my interest in World history and politics. In our discussions he has continued to inspire me through the soundness, intelligence, and thoughtfulness of his views. For the third edition, I would like to thank Helen Popp for her help at a crucial juncture in preparing the manuscript. I am also extremely grateful to Katherine and Leo Martin, without whose support and practical help the third edition could never have been written.

   This work is dedicated to the memory of Colin Matthew, the first editor of the
Dictionary of National Biography. He had an extraordinary understanding of
modern history and the individual and institutional forces shaping it. This
appreciation, together with his wisdom, humanity, and dedication to students,
have been sorely missed since his early death in 1999. Colin was a bedrock of
inspiration to those who worked with him, and I am forever indebted to him for
the faith which he placed in me early on in my career, which includes encouraging me to write this book.

Preface to the Second and Third Editions

The *Dictionary of Contemporary World History* is a thoroughly revised and updated
edition of the *Dictionary of Twentieth-Century World History*, which was completed in
1996. Its predecessor's aim to present comprehensive and explanatory entries
with the highest standards of accuracy also guides this new book. True to the
original aim of providing unrivalled coverage for a dictionary of this kind, this
third edition contains over 150 entries compared to the first edition. These
explore and analyse personalities that have had a significant impact on world
politics, such as George W. Bush, Lula (the President of Brazil), Nicolas Sarkozy,
Gordon Brown, Angela Merkel, and José Zapatero. They discuss concepts such as
climate change, the War on Terrorism, AIDS, and globalization. They inform
about events such as the London and Madrid Bombings, the Tsunami, September
11, and the genesis of the euro. Finally, they present new international organizations such as the WTO and the International Criminal Court. One major
improvement in this respect is a greatly enhanced section on the EU, its founding
treaties and its constitutional development. This reflects its growing political and
economic importance in Europe and the world at large.
   In addition to the new entries, around 1,300 entries contained in the original
dictionary have been checked for accuracy, and in addition over 600 entries have
been thoroughly updated and revised. The history of each country has been
expanded significantly, to enable the reader to relate current political events to
historical developments. Individual biographies of statesmen such as Tony Blair,
Hilary Clinton, Vladimir Putin and Helen Clark have been enriched significantly.
Particular attention has also been paid to ongoing developments in places such
as Iraq, Afghanistan, Israel, Palestine, Timor Leste, Northern Ireland, and
Sudan (Darfur). Changes in treaties and laws pertinent to issues such as
land claims, immigration, and British devolution have been fully considered.
Transformations of international organizations such as the African Union,
NATO and the WEU are also discussed. Finally, changes have been
made to reflect shifts in the debate among historians and political analysts,
for instance on issues such as nationalism, human rights and the impact of
Roe v. *Wade* in the USA.
   The *Dictionary of Twentieth-Century World History* was designed for the student
and scholar who needed accurate information about particular events and
ideas, and for any reader interested in contemporary history and current affairs.
The *Dictionary of Contemporary World History* addresses a further group of readers,

those who wish to take the entries as their cue for further research. For this purpose, internet addresses have been added. These are normally official sites which contain more information about particular organizations. Personal websites have usually not been included, nor have websites been included that do not contain English content. All entries in this book cover events up to 4 August 2007.

Preface to the First Edition

This dictionary is written both for a general readership and for students of history, politics, and international relations. Its first objective is to provide an accurate and comprehensive account of facts and developments. At the same time, it shies away from a purely descriptive account, in order to present a balanced view of causes and motivations. This book is as much about *why* things happened the way they did, as about *what* happened.

Any dictionary of this length inevitably has to be selective about the choice of entries, and this book is no exception. While it was not possible therefore to include every personality or event, every effort has been made to make the choice of entries as logical and consistent as possible. In particular, the choice of entries is based on two central criteria:

1. To make coverage genuinely global. There is a detailed and comprehensive entry for every sovereign country in the world, including, for example, the newly independent states of the former Yugoslavia and Soviet Union. There are also detailed entries for historical 'regions' such as Kurdistan, Chechnya, and the Basque Territory. The attention given to African, Latin American, and Asian countries is, perhaps, unique for a dictionary of this kind, providing an indispensable background in past events to their current affairs.

2. To make the choice of entries as comprehensive as possible. For instance, the book includes a detailed account of every twentieth-century Prime Minister of Great Britain, the Republic of Ireland, Israel, South Africa, and Canada, as well as every President of the USA. It contains an entry on every Prime Minister of Australia, India, and New Zealand who was in office for two years or more, and on the more important of those whose administration lasted only weeks or months. In countries where governments have been traditionally short-lived (e.g. Japan, France, Italy), the dictionary provides a full description of important statesmen.

Two categories of entry set the dictionary apart from others of its length. First, there is a full and separate treatment of treaties, worldwide organizations, and events ranging from the oil-price shock to World War II. Second, articles are included on the development of central ideas (e.g. socialism, Marxism, and monetarism) and religion, which had a major impact on the political development of the twentieth century.

In short, this dictionary offers comprehensive coverage of the statesmen, military leaders, movements (e.g. civil rights movement, emancipation of women, abortion) and events that have shaped national, regional, or world history. It presents the ideas that have been primary political influences on the course of twentieth-century history. And it gives an account of the principal political movements, and of the trends that have had an important impact on politics.

Cross References

These are used frequently, again in an effort to make this book as clear and easy to use as possible. They are used judiciously rather than exhaustively. Cross references are marked by a *before each relevant heading: for instance, the entry for the Indian National *Congress will be found under Congress, the term by which it is commonly known. On the whole, adjectives and sovereign states are not cross-referenced, except for those which the reader might not otherwise expect to find under a separate heading: adjectives such as *fascist, *corporatist, etc., and newly formed states such as *Bosnia and *Azerbaijan. At the end of some entries, the reader is referred to other entries that are related in theme or content.

Dates

To provide as much information as possible, additional information about people appearing in the text who do not have a separate entry is given in brackets after their name. Birth and death dates are indicated by the appropriate abbreviation, e.g. for the French explorer of the Congo, Savorgnan de Brazza (b. 1852, d. 1905). Alternatively, the dates given indicate the period in office, e.g. the Colombian 'military dictatorship under Rojas Pinilla (1953–7)'.

Terminology and Orthography

The text is in British English throughout, though terms that are particular to individual countries have been kept. For instance, unless otherwise indicated, in each entry referring to Canada, the 'House of Commons' refers to the Canadian lower House of Parliament, not to that in London. Similarly, the Australian House of Representatives is not to be confused with those in the USA and New Zealand.

I have used contemporary names for entries of current personalities or countries (e.g. the history of Rhodesia can be found under the entry for Zimbabwe), while historical terms have been maintained: it would have been foolish, for example, to rename the 'Burma Campaign' the 'Myanmar Campaign'.

A use of all accents or particular letters would have made some Korean or Vietnamese entries unintelligible to the non-specialist. Therefore, I have restricted the use of accents to those that are immediately familiar in English, i.e. those used in Spanish, German, French, and Portuguese.

Concerning the entries for China, I have adopted the system of Pinyin spelling now used by the majority of Chinese historians (e.g. Mao Zedong and Guomindang instead of Mao Tsetung and Kuomintang), except for those names that are still more commonly known in the old Wade–Giles system (e.g. Chiang Kai-shek instead of Jiang Jieshi). To avoid confusion, there are headings in both systems, with the reader being referred to the Pinyin entry where necessary.

A

Aaland Islands

Some 6,500 islands in the Gulf of Bothnia, between Finland and Sweden. They were part of Sweden until 1809, when, together with Finland, they were annexed by Russia. After the collapse of the Russian Empire in 1917, they were administered by Finland. Despite popular demands to be governed by Sweden, Finnish sovereignty was confirmed by the *League of Nations in 1921. At the same time, the islands were granted considerable autonomy, since when Swedish has been the official language. In 1945, the islands' assembly again voted to come under Swedish sovereignty, but the islands' constitutional status remained unchanged.

Abacha, Sani (b. 20 Sept. 1943, d. 8 June 1998). Nigerian dictator 1993–8

Born in Kano of the Hausa people, he was educated at the local government college before entering the army in 1962. He rose through its ranks to become major-general in 1984, and was part of the ruling Supreme Military Council (1984–5). A close colleague of *Babangida, he supported his military coup in 1985 and was made Chief of Staff. Abacha became Minister of Defence in 1990. Following Babangida's electoral defeat by *Abiola in 1993, he staged a coup against Babangida and became President himself on 18 November 1993. Despite waves of protest strikes, he outlawed all democratic political institutions, pacifying some of the strikers through withdrawing a number of the draconian economic policies he had introduced, such as a 600 per cent increase in the price of petrol. Abacha managed to defy growing international pressure for an end to his brutal regime. Western sanctions remained ineffective as long as they excluded Nigeria's vital export commodity, oil. He clung on to power despite domestic and international pressure, and died in office from a heart attack.

Abbas, Ferhat (b. 24 Oct. 1899, d. 24 Dec. 1985). Algerian nationalist

A student of chemistry, he founded a Muslim students' association in 1924. Abbas fought in the French army from 1939, but in 1942 produced a Manifesto which called for Algerian autonomy from France. He joined *Ben Bella's *Front de Libération Nationale in 1956, and after the outbreak of the *Algerian War of Independence founded the Algerian government-in-exile in Tunis (1958). Upon Algerian independence he became president of the National Constituent Assembly (1962–3) and provisional head of state. As the leader of the moderate nationalists, Abbas soon fell out of favour with Ben Bella. He was exiled in 1963, but was allowed to return shortly before his death.

Abbas, Mahmoud (b. 26 Mar. 1935). Palestinian President 2005–

Born in Safed, he went to Syria in 1948, and studied both in Damascus and in Moscow. After his return he co-founded al-*Fatah, and from 1968 he was part of the ruling circle of the *PLO, under the leadership of *Arafat. He represented the PLO at the talks that led to the *Oslo agreement of 1993. Trusted by Israel and the international community, he was effectively sidelined by Arafat, who strove to concentrate all power in his hands in the last years of his life. After Arafat's death, Abbas became chairman of the PLO in 2004, and he was sworn in as President of the *Palestinian National Authority in early 2005. Also referred to as 'Abu Mazen', Abbas struggled to assert his authority over more radical groups inside Fatah and other groups who continued their attacks against Israel. Following the 2006 elections, Abbas entered a power-sharing agreement with *Hamas in 2007. This broke apart months later, when Hamas effectively gained sole control over Gaza. He remained in control of the *West Bank.

Abboud, Ibrahim (b. 26 Oct. 1900, d. 8 Sept. 1983). Sudanese general and politician

Educated at Gordon College, he became a soldier and, after distinguished service with the British army in World War II, became a general in 1954. He was made Commander-in-Chief of the Sudanese army upon independence in 1956. Abboud overthrew the country's democratic government in 1958, and thereafter led the military government. His military genius was not matched by political astuteness, and he was forced to resign in 1964.

Abd al-Aziz ibn Saud (b. 24 Nov. 1880, d. 9 Nov. 1953). King of Saudi Arabia 1932–53

Born in Riyadh of the Wahabi dynasty, he was forced into exile in Kuwait in 1902. From there, he organized and led a successful Bedouin revolt which enabled him to recapture Riyadh.

He then conquered the Turkish province of Al Hasa, and was recognized by the British as Emir of Nejd and Hasa in 1915. He then challenged *Hussein ibn Ali, whom he eventually defeated, annexing Azir in 1923, and taking the Holy City of Mecca in 1925. He proclaimed himself King of Hejaz and Nejd in Mecca on 8 January 1926, a country which covered most of the Arabian peninsula. In 1932, he renamed his kingdom Saudi Arabia. A devout Muslim, he laid the foundations of the country's subsequent development (and the royal household's fortune) by granting the first concession to oil exploration in 1933, and by creating the Arabia-American Oil Company (ARAMCO) in 1944. He maintained a good relationship with the USA and the UK, which he supported in World War II.

Abd al-Ilah ibn Ali ibn Hussein (b. 1912, d. 14 July 1958). Regent of Iraq

Born in Hejaz as the grandson of *Hussein ibn Ali, he became regent of Iraq for his 4-year-old cousin *Faisal II, after the death of his brother-in-law, King Ghazi. Strongly pro-British throughout his life, in 1941 he was expelled by a group of pro-German officers. He was reinstated by the British, since when he was regarded as a pawn of Britain and the USA. After the war, he attempted to democratize the political system, but failed to create democratic stability. He relinquished office in 1953 but continued as chief adviser to King Faisal until both were killed in the Iraqi Revolution of 1958.

Abd al-Krim (Muhammad ibn Abd al-Karim al-Khattabi) (b. 1882, d. 5 Feb. 1963). Moroccan nationalist leader

Born in Agadir, he became a newspaper editor and rose through the ranks of the Spanish administration of northern Morocco to become chief justice in 1915. He became increasingly hostile to the Spanish and French occupation of Morocco, however. He was imprisoned by the Spanish in 1917, and after his release he organized a rebellion by his tribe, the Ait Waryaghar. He inflicted a series of heavy defeats upon the Spanish, and established the Republic of the Rif in 1921. He was defeated by a joint Franco-Spanish army in 1926, imprisoned, and sent to detention on the island of La Réunion until 1947, when he was allowed to return to France. On the way he escaped to Cairo, where he set up the Maghreb Bureau or Liberation Committee of the Arab West. After Moroccan independence (1956) he refused to return, since he did not consider the new government to represent the interests of the Rif.

Abdication Crisis (UK)

This crisis in the British establishment was provoked by King *Edward VIII's desire to marry a twice-divorced American, Wallis Simpson. He made this announcement to senior politicians and churchmen on 16 November 1936. Prime Minister *Baldwin, the Cabinet, the Archbishop of Canterbury (Cosmo Lang), and the Dominions' representatives were all vehemently opposed to passing the special legislation necessary, partly on the grounds that marriage to a divorcee would be inconsistent with the King's role as head of the Church of England. One compromise proposed by Edward was a 'morganatic marriage', whereby Wallis Simpson would not acquire his rank: he could become King, but she would not become Queen. This was also rejected by the political and religious leaders. The British press did not cover the crisis until 3 December, by which time the abdication was virtually certain, as the political parties all agreed that the King should accept the advice of his ministers. Edward announced his abdication on 11 December, and was succeeded by his brother *George VI.

Abdul Rahman Putra (Al-Haj Ibni Al-Marhum Sultan Abdul Hamid Halim Shah), Tunku (b. 8 Feb. 1903, d. 6 Dec. 1990). Prime Minister of Malaya/ Malaysia 1957–63, 1963–70

Son of the 24th Sultan of Kedah, he studied at Cambridge and qualified as an English barrister. Upon his return to Malaya in 1931 he entered the civil service, where he continued to work during the Japanese occupation. He co-founded the *United Malays National Organization, and succeeded Dato Onn bin Jafaar (b. 1895, d. 1962) as leader in 1952. Recognizing that independence could only be achieved through cooperation between the various ethnic groups, he organized an alliance with the Malayan Chinese Association, and then the Malayan Indian Congress. Following the alliance's victory in the 1955 elections, he became Chief Minister and Minister for Home Affairs. He negotiated independence, and became Malaya's first Prime Minister.

In 1962–3 he presided over the formation of the Federation of Malaysia, which he led as Prime Minister, successfully securing the support of both the Chinese and the Indian communities through pragmatic compromise. During the general elections in May 1969 there were widespread ethnic riots in the capital between Chinese and Malays. Faced with the breakdown of his attempt to rule on the basis of harmonious

Chinese–Malay relations, he resigned in January 1970. Through active political journalism he remained an influential figure in Malaysia during the years of his retirement.

Abdullah Bin-Abd-al-Aziz Al Saud
(b. 1926). King of Saudi Arabia 2005–

Born in Riyadh as the son of *Abd-al Aziz ibn Saud, he was educated at the court. In 1962 he became commander of the National Guard, and in 1982 he became Crown Prince to King *Fahd. When Fahd suffered a stroke in 1995, he became Saudi Arabia's regent in all but name. He led a drive against corruption, though his greatest challenge came in 2001, when Osama *Bin Laden, who had received Saudi funding, attacked the US on *September 11. Although an ally of the USA, he did not allow the US to engage in the *Iraq War from Saudi Arabian soil. Since then, he has steered a difficult course. Cracking down on Islamic terrorists received little public support in a country infused with conservative Islamic views.

Abdullah ibn Hussein (b. 1880,
d. 20 July 1951). Emir of Transjordan 1921–48, King of Transjordan/Jordan 1948–51

Son of *Hussein ibn Ali, Sherif of Mecca, with his brother *Faisal he led the *Arab Revolt of 1916. In 1921 he was made Emir of the province of Transjordan, a territory created by the *Sykes–Picot Agreement and made a British protectorate in 1923. He spent the next decades creating a sense of identity and unity in his quite arbitrarily defined kingdom, establishing state institutions such as a parliament, a constitution, and a police force through the creation of the *Arab Legion. He became King upon his country's independence from Britain in 1948. During the first Arab–Israeli War (1948–9), he used the Arab Legion to occupy the *West Bank and East Jerusalem, which he united with Transjordan as the *Hashemite Kingdom of Jordan in 1950. After he engaged in secret negotiations with Israel, he was assassinated by an Arab nationalist.

Abdullah II bin Al Hussein (b. 30 Jan.
1962). King of Jordan 1999–

Born in Amman, he was the oldest son of King *Hussein and his second, English-born wife. Educated at Sandhurst, he studied at Oxford and Georgetown University before joining the Jordanian army, where in 1994 he became the commanding officer of its elite troops. In January 1999 he was appointed Crown Prince, at the expense of his uncle, who had held that position for over 30 years. His father died two weeks later, and on 7 February he became

King. Although relatively inexperienced, his army background and support proved to be a major asset as Abdullah established himself both as the leader of the royal family and within the population at large. He continued his father's policy of promoting the peace process in the Middle East. He also tried to introduce economic liberalization without offending too many entrenched interests whose anger might endanger Jordan's stability.

Abe, Shinzo (b. 1954). Prime Minister of
Japan 2006–

Born in Nagato as the grandson of Prime Minister Nobusuke *Kishi, he graduated in political sciences from Seikei University and took up a position at Kobe Steel Company. He became an assistant to his father, Shintaro Abe, at the Foreign Ministry in 1982, and in 1993 he entered the House of Representatives for the *Liberal Democratic Party (LDP). In 2003, he became Secretary General of the LDP, and in 2005 *Koizumi appointed him to the pivotal role of Chief Cabinet Secretary. Abe succeeded Koizumi to become Japan's youngest Prime Minister since World War II. Abe was less adept at dealing with his ministers and the party establishment. He also suffered from a scandal over pensions, and was weakened by the party's disastrous showing in the 2007 elections to the upper house.

Abiola, Moshood Kashimawo
Olawale (b. 24 Aug. 1937, d. 7 July 1998).
Nigerian politician

Born in Abeokuta of the Yoruba people, he studied at the University of Glasgow (1961–3) before becoming a business manager, advancing to become vice-president of ITT Africa and Middle East, as well as chairperson of ITT Nigeria, 1971–88. He joined the social democratic National Party of Nigeria (NPN) in 1979 and became its chairman in his home state of Ogun. He was chosen to contest the 1993 presidential elections against *Babangida. When his victory was clear, the military government annulled the elections and imprisoned him. He died of heart failure days before he was to be released from prison under a compromise negotiated by the *UN.

Abkhazia

A Caucasian territory which was part of the Soviet Union as an Autonomous Soviet Republic within Georgia. In April 1991 it became part of the independent Republic of Georgia, against the will of the Muslim Abkhazian population (17.8 per cent of the total population) and its Russian minority (14.3 per cent). Helped by a contingent of

Muslim volunteers from neighbouring autonomous Russian republics such as *Chechnya, the rebels managed to repel the Georgian troops, weakened already by civil war. Georgia had to concede defeat, and negotiations focused on extensive autonomy for a territory over which Georgia had lost all control. Negotiations between the Abkhazian government and Georgia proved futile, and a fragile peace was supervised at the border by *UN observers and Russian troops. In 2006, the self-declared president of Abkhazia, Sergei Bagapsh, demanded that Georgia accept Abkhazia's independence, which was backed by Russia.

Aborigines and Torres Strait Islanders (Australia)

The original inhabitants of Australia, whose existence there is thought to go back some 40,000 years. They were semi-nomadic hunters whose value systems included common use, and a spiritual appreciation of the land. Their population is estimated to have been between 300,000 and 700,000 before White settlement began in 1788. Aborigines were quickly reduced in numbers, owing to loss of land (and water resources), adoption of European habits such as drinking alcohol, diseases against which they had not developed immunity (smallpox, influenza, etc.), and a declining birth rate. Moreover, violence between Europeans and Aborigines also led to the death of around 2,500 Whites and 20,000 Aborigines. By the early twentieth century their numbers had diminished to less than 50,000. During the 1930s, sparked off by celebrations of the 150th anniversary of the first European settlements, campaigns developed for an end to social and legal discrimination against Aborigines and Torres Strait Islanders. Campaigners also demanded targeted government aid in areas of health, education, and employment. Official policy changed in the 1950s. Rather than segregating Aboriginal groups from the rest of society the government attempted to integrate them. In the following decade, Aborigines and Torres Strait Islanders began to emphasize their right to assimilate themselves while maintaining their own culture. In 1967, they were granted full citizenship, and 90 per cent of (White) Australians voted in a referendum to transfer responsibility for Aboriginal affairs from the individual states to the federal government.

Since 1972, land has been returned to the Aborigines and Torres Strait Islanders, in central Australia and the Torres Straits respectively. In the central issue of *land claims as in other matters, the federal government usually spearheaded action on behalf of Aboriginal rights, often against fierce resistance from the individual states unwilling to concede jurisdiction over their territory. Their claims for land titles were recognized for the first time in 1992, and in 1994 they were promised considerable ownership of land. The number of Aborigines and Torres Strait Islanders had risen to 410,000 (4.5 per cent of the overall population) in 2001. Aborigines and Torres Strait Islanders continued to be the most disadvantaged section of Australian society, making up almost 20 per cent of the prison population. In 2001, life expectancy was 18 years below that of Australian Whites, average income was at 62 per cent of Whites, and their unemployment rate constituted three times the national average. Their protests against continued discrimination in public life were championed by the Australian *Labour Party. However, under John *Howard the government was much less sympathetic towards specific indigenous claims. Howard abolished a specialized government agency dealing with indigenous affairs, and refused to sign a public treaty of reconciliation which contained an apology for land appropriations.

(⊕) SEE WEB LINKS

- Official statistical information relating to Aborigines and Torres Strait Islanders.

abortion

The premature termination of pregnancy by removal of the foetus from the womb. It has been strongly opposed by many religions which emphasize the sanctity of human life from the day of conception. By contrast, its legalization has been demanded by 'pro-choice' groups which stress each individual mother's right to choose whether or not to proceed with a pregnancy. The issue of abortion has become a touchstone for the influence of religion in the state. Abortion is still illegal in Arab countries, where *Islam is the state religion, and in Ireland, where the influence of the Roman *Catholic Church is still strong.

The issue has been particularly divisive where the relationship between religion and the state has been ambiguous, if not in theory, then in practice. It has been a crucial issue in countries such as Poland, which has sought to redefine the role of the Catholic Church in state and society after the collapse of communism in 1989. In Germany, five years after reunification (1995), laws were drawn up which amounted to a compromise between a more religiously observant western half and a completely secularized eastern half. In the USA, a Supreme Court judgment,

Roe v. *Wade* of 1973, ruled in favour of a 'right to choose' as an implied constitutional 'right to privacy'. However, the problem has continued to polarize society between Roman Catholics and fundamentalist Christians on the one hand and 'pro-choice' groups on the other. Christian groups have become increasingly influential in the *Republican Party, while pro-choice advocates have been largely reliant on the *Democratic Party for the defence of the present system. Abortion has become a central issue in US politics.

By contrast, in more secularized societies the subject causes only sporadic controversy. Within the European Union, Spain and Ireland do not allow abortion unless the mother's health is at risk, while Portugal has voted in a referendum to relax its ban on abortion in 2007. Apart from that, most EU countries allow abortion for up to 12–14 weeks after conception. In the Netherlands, abortion is legal for up to 24 weeks after conception, and in Britain, abortion has been allowed for up to 24 weeks after conception (reduced from 28 in 1990) on social or medical grounds.

Abu Dhabi, see UNITED ARAB EMIRATES

Abyssinian War (1935–6)
The conquest of Ethiopia (formerly Abyssinia) by Italian forces was born out of *Mussolini's desire to strengthen his domestic position through the establishment of an Italian East African Empire. Mussolini also wanted to avenge Italy for its previous humiliating defeat by the Ethiopian forces at Adowa in 1896 during an earlier attempt to occupy the area. Following a border clash at the Abyssinian oasis of Walwal, Mussolini rejected all attempts by the *League of Nations to mediate, and invaded Abyssinia on 2 October 1935. Some six months later, the ill-equipped Ethiopian army succumbed to the Italian use of airforce, tanks, and poison gas, and on 5 May 1936 *Badoglio captured the capital, Addis Ababa. The Italian aggression caused international outrage, but the inability of the League of Nations to agree to more than limited sanctions against Italy demonstrated the essential ineffectiveness of the League as well as the concept of *appeasement. The war also exposed some serious deficiencies in the Italian army, which were largely ignored by Mussolini and others who were deluded by the fact of the victory.

Acheson, Dean Gooderham (b. 11 Apr. 1893, d. 12 Oct. 1971). US Secretary of State 1949–53
Born in Middletown, Connecticut, he was educated at Yale and Harvard Law School. He served as a personal assistant to *Supreme Court Justice Louis *Brandeis between 1918 and 1921, and built a successful New York law practice thereafter. Having briefly served as Under-Secretary of the Treasury in 1933, he became Assistant Secretary of State for economic affairs for President F. D. *Roosevelt in 1941. In 1944 Acheson became a key figure in promoting the establishment of the *Bretton Woods conference. As Under-Secretary for President *Truman (1945–7), he urged international control of atomic power in the Acheson–Lilienthal Report of 1946. He helped formulate the *Truman Doctrine of US support for nations threatened by *Communism, and was instrumental in creating the *Marshall Plan.

As Secretary of State Acheson helped in the creation of *NATO, but he was criticized by Republicans in *Congress for what they regarded as his failure to pursue a more vigorously anti-Communist policy in China; and his policy towards South Korea was seen as having invited the North Korean offensive in 1950. He was a strong supporter of the French in *Indochina and of the Republic of China in Taiwan. In 1961, he once again became an important influence on US foreign policy as an adviser to President *Kennedy. In 1967–8, he became opposed to the *Vietnam War despite his earlier staunch support, and called publicly upon President *Johnson to end it. His memoirs, *Present at the Creation*, won the 1970 Pulitzer Prize in history.

Action Française
A French ultra-right-wing movement with traits of *Fascism co-founded by *Maurras at the height of the *Dreyfus Affair in 1898. The movement's newspaper (1908–44) carried the same name. Its parliamentary representation remained relatively weak, but it became very influential in that it made anti-republicanism and *anti-Semitism respectable in intellectual circles. Banned in 1936, from 1940 most of its members supported the *Vichy government.
FASCISM

Adams, Gerard (Gerry) (b. 6 Oct. 1948). Republican politician in Northern Ireland
Born and educated in Belfast, he worked as a bar manager, and joined the Republican movement in 1964. He was imprisoned twice (1971, 1978) on suspicion of being a leader of the *IRA, but both times was released on grounds of insufficient evidence. He was successively elected to parliament for *Sinn Féin (1983–92), but never took up his seat in the House of Commons, since he objected in principle to British rule in *Northern Ireland. He became President of the party in

1984. In 1988 and 1993, he held meetings with *Hume to discuss proposals for talks on the future of Northern Ireland. He came to appreciate that, after conducting a terrorist campaign for more than 20 years, the IRA had not come closer to fulfilling its aim of a British withdrawal from Northern Ireland. After a flurry of secret negotiations with British government representatives, he persuaded the IRA to announce a ceasefire, in order to meet the British condition of a renunciation of violence before negotiations. In consequence, he acquired a pivotal role as a spokesman for the nationalist Catholic community—a role which was recognized on 17 March 1995, when he met US President *Clinton in Washington. Following a breakdown of negotiations, the ceasefire was resumed in 1997, and a compromise was reached at the *Good Friday Agreement. He was elected to the Northern Ireland Assembly, whereupon he became one of two Sinn Féin members of the Northern Ireland executive. Upon the suspension of the Assembly in 2002, Adams continued to work for peace, convincing the IRA to destroy its weapons. According to international monitors, this process was completed in 2006, which removed a major obstacle to the peace process. Despite this, the continued hostility of radical Protestant leaders such as Ian *Paisley meant that he was represented in the talks leading to the *St Andrews Agreement by his deputy, Martin McGuinness. Nevertheless, boosted by steady growth in the political support of his party, Adams continued as the leading figure of Sinn Féin and the IRA.

Adams, Sir Grantley Herbert (b. 28 Apr. 1898, d. 28 Nov. 1971). Leader of Barbados 1946–58, and of the Federation of the West Indies 1958–62

Educated in Barbados, he studied at Oxford University, became a lawyer, and returned to Barbados in 1925. Elected to the House of Assembly in 1934, he co-founded the Barbados Labour Party (BLP) in 1938. As leader of the government (1946–58) he agitated for full internal self-government, which was granted in 1958. He also supported the creation of the short-lived Federation of the *West Indies, whose only Prime Minister he became. He spent the remaining years of his life as leader of the BLP in opposition. He was knighted in 1967.

Addams, Jane Laura (b. 6 Sept. 1860, d. 21 May 1935). US social reformer

Born in Mayesville, South Carolina, she graduated from Rockford College in 1881. With her friend Ellen Gates Starr, she opened Hull House in Chicago in 1889, a settlement house for immigrants and workers modelled on *Toynbee Hall in London, with the aim of attacking urban poverty. One of the leading activists of the *Progressive movement, she was a pioneer in the new discipline of sociology, advocating better labour and housing conditions, and campaigning for child labour regulation by law. She later had considerable influence over the planning of neighbourhood welfare institutions throughout the USA. As part of her commitment to social reform, Addams was a prohibitionist and fought against gambling and prostitution. She became a leading figure in the women's suffrage movement, and promoted the influence of women in high political circles. Addams pursued her goal of political equality also by becoming a leading member of the *NAACP in 1909. During World War I, her activism for pacifism grew, and in 1919 she helped to found the Women's International League for Peace and Freedom. In 1931, she became the first American Woman to receive the *Nobel Peace Prize.

Adenauer, Konrad (b. 5 Jan. 1876, d. 19 Apr. 1967). Chancellor of West Germany 1949–63

Early career Born in Cologne, he joined the *Centre Party in 1906, and was Lord Mayor of Cologne 1917–33. Deposed by the *Nazis, he was reinstated by the American administration in 1945, though the British soon discharged him for 'incompetence'. Elected *CDU leader in the British Zone in 1946, he was elected chairman of the parliamentary council which drafted the Constitution in 1948. Adenauer was narrowly elected Chancellor of the Federal Republic of Germany (FRG) in 1949, but won the subsequent elections of 1953, 1957, and 1961 with a handsome majority.

Foreign policy At a time when the majority of Germans sought reunification with the German Democratic Republic (GDR: East Germany) as their first priority, Adenauer pursued the goal of Western integration, even if that made unification less likely in the short run. For this reason, Adenauer accepted the *Schuman Plan which led to the *ECSC, and he supported the creation of the *European Defence Community even if this entailed the rejection of the *Stalin Note. In a crucial further concession to France, Adenauer agreed to the *Saarland referendum held in 1955. In that year, full sovereignty was finally achieved, and West Germany was admitted into *NATO.

The culmination of his policy of reconciliation with France came in the Franco-German friendship treaty of 22 January 1963. This signalled the start of a 'special' relationship between the two countries, e.g. through cultural exchanges and regular, twice-yearly consultations between the French President and German Chancellor. A further milestone of Adenauer's policies of normalization came in 1955, when in a visit to Moscow he negotiated the release of the remaining 10,000 German prisoners of war, and the initiation of diplomatic relations with the USSR. Through the *Restitution Agreement he initiated the beginning of a long process of reconciliation between Germans and Jews.

Domestic policy These successes abroad were complemented by dramatic achievements in domestic policy. The Equalizations of Burdens Act provided compensation for those who had lost their possessions in the war, especially the German immigrants from the East. This contributed inestimably to reducing tensions between Germans who had been affected by the war in very different ways. Adenauer also reaped the rewards of Germany's rapid economic recovery which set in with the start of the *Korean War, and which were greatly helped by the liberal policies of his Finance Minister, *Erhardt. Perhaps his most popular measure was the introduction of a generous pension scheme, just ahead of the 1957 elections.

Adenauer was increasingly criticized for his autocratic and obstinate style of leadership. This had been crucial in the first years of government, but was increasingly out of place by the early 1960s. He was thus forced to resign by his coalition partners, the *Liberal Party. Through his successful policies, Adenauer integrated a heterogeneous population, and integrated many former *Nazi adherents into the democratic process. In this way, he created the conditions for the establishment of the first successful democracy on German soil.

affirmative action (USA)

Initiated as US government policy by President *Johnson in 1965, when he created the Office of Federal Contract Compliance and the Equal Employment Opportunity Commission. Through these bureaus, affirmative action was designed to reduce social inequalities in US society by requiring all federal government contractors as well as public institutions to give consideration to racial minorities and, from 1971, to women. In 1978 the policy was given an ambiguous verdict by the *Supreme Court in *Bakke* v. *University of California*. The court confirmed the

policy as constitutional while deciding at the same time that the use of quotas to favour minorities violated the Fourteenth Amendment to the Constitution, which secured the citizens' equal protection before the law. In the case of *United Steel Workers of America* v. *Weber* (1979), the Supreme Court went further by deciding that in training programmes, preference to Blacks could be given as long as this did not bar Whites from advancement.

During the 1980s and particularly the 1990s, popular opposition to affirmative action increased, and was reflected in a series of Supreme Court rulings in the mid-1990s which limited or narrowed its scope. In 1996, California voters adopted Proposition 209, which abolished any preference in its hiring policies on the basis of race, sex, colour, ethnicity, or national origin. In response, employers such as the University of California, which had always been at the forefront of affirmative action, introduced a new system of admission based on 'comprehensive review'. This took into account a candidate's educational opportunities at high school, and in this way employed more sensitive measures of discrimination ensuring continuous above-average access to minorities candidates.

In *Grutter v. Bollinger* (2003), the Supreme Court confirmed that race and ethnicity could be one of a number of criteria in deciding on university admissions, though it forbade universities, in this case the University of Michigan, to apply a rigid points system. Under the presidency of George W. *Bush, the attorney general has put considerable pressure on individual universities to withdraw affirmative action programmes.

CIVIL RIGHTS ACTS (US); CIVIL RIGHTS MOVEMENT

Afghanistan

A poor, mountainous central Asian country which has struggled to find stability, between persistent interference from outside powers on the one hand, and the domestic religiousness of the population which opposed the formation of a secular state on the other.

Early history (up to 1919) In the nineteenth century, Afghanistan managed to maintain its independence largely because of its strategic importance between an expanding Russian Empire and a *British Empire keen to preserve its dominance over, and extend its control beyond, the Indian subcontinent. In 1879 Afghanistan was forced to concede nominal British sovereignty, though Britain never exerted much control over its internal affairs, which continued to be dominated by the relationship between its ethnically and religiously heterogeneous social groups.

Monarchical rule (1919–73) With the country formally independent from 1919, King Amanullah introduced a number of reforms designed to introduce Western norms and practices into a traditional, Islamic society. Islamic dress was forbidden in favour of European dress, polygamy abolished, and universal education for men and women introduced. This caused enormous resistance and he was forced to abdicate in 1929. He was succeeded by Nadir Shah and, in 1933, his son Zahir Shah. They reversed many of their predecessor's reforms, and shied away from any attempt at social or economic change.

Zahir Shah entangled his country in tense relations with the newly founded state of Pakistan in 1947, when he claimed the Pathan state from Pakistan. In the tradition of his predecessors, Zahir Shah used the country's geopolitical position to maximum benefit, this time to attract large-scale foreign aid from the Soviet Union and the USA during the *Cold War without giving any reciprocal commitments. He ruled with the help of his cousin General Mohammad Daoud as Prime Minister (1953–63), and in 1964 transformed the country into a constitutional monarchy, with the first elections being held in 1965.

Political and civil unrest (1973–2002) On 19 July 1973, when Shah was abroad, Daoud asserted full control, deposed the King, and declared Afghanistan a republic, with himself as President. He nationalized a number of industries, a measure which alienated important sections of the community. He failed to establish a permanent political base, and was deposed on 27 April 1978 by a Communist 'Armed Forces Revolutionary Council' (Khalq). Daoud was assassinated and the Democratic Republic of Afghanistan proclaimed. The new regime suffered from considerable infighting, until the accession to power of Babrak Kemal in 1979. The failure of Kemal's new regime to establish its authority quickly, and the unpopularity of its Communist, secular reforms, led to the eruption of the tension that had been building up for some time.

Anarchy was subdued by the invasion of the Soviet army in December, at Kemal's request. This gave the diverse groups, ranging from *Islamic fundamentalists, the *mujahidin,

and tribal factions, to intellectuals, a common enemy. Helped by the country's rugged terrain, and especially by large military aid from Pakistan, Arab states, and, above all, the USA, the oppositional groups managed to sustain the war until the USSR pulled its troops out in 1989. Out of a population of around thirteen million in 1979, one million are estimated to have died in the civil war, with almost five million becoming refugees (around one million within the country, over two million into Pakistan, and over one million into Iran).

Kemal was replaced with the more conciliatory Mohammad Najibulla (b. 1947, d. 1996) in 1987, but he failed to gain the necessary endorsement from the mujahidin, and retired in 1992. The mujahidin's victory over their opponents exposed their own divisions, leading to a state of complete anarchy. In 1993 a new group emerged, the *Taliban. Supported by Pakistan, they aimed to erect a theocratic state based on *Islamic law. They pushed back the major mujahidin faction, the *Northern Alliance, until they controlled four-fifths of the territory in 1999. Although slighted by the international community, the Taliban regime supported itself through the drugs trade, as three-quarters of all opium was harvested in Afghanistan.

Contemporary politics (since 2002) The Taliban developed close connections to Osama *Bin Laden, whose *Al-Qaeda network helped support the regime while using Afghanistan as a training ground for terrorist activities in return. Following the *September 11 attacks, and the subsequent refusal of the Taliban to extradite Bin Laden, Taliban fighters were attacked by the US from the air. After weeks of bombardment, Taliban rule imploded, and opposition movements took control over the entire country.

The US supported a new government headed by Hamid *Karzai. Karzai was unable to impose his authority over the regions, which continued to be controlled by opposing warlords. This allowed al-Quaeda and Taliban forces to reestablish their presence in the remote south of the country. Within Kabul, Karzai's authority was protected by a multinational UN force of around 5,000 troops. In January 2004, the tribal grand council approved a constitution which declared Afghanistan an 'Islamic Republic'. Owing to *Taliban resurgence in the south, *NATO forces became increasingly active, taking over command of military operations in 2006.

AFL (American Federation of Labor)

A confederation of so-called 'craft' unions to represent skilled trades, founded in 1886 after mass disorders culminating in the Haymarket Square riot in Chicago. From its formation until his retirement in 1924 the AFL was decisively shaped by its President, Samuel Gompers, who stood for 'pure and simple' unionism. He summed up his approach simply with one word, 'More'. He wanted a pragmatic organization of skilled workers committed to collective bargaining for better wages and conditions. The AFL reflected this, as each of the Federation's thirteen craft unions was self-governing and extended membership only to skilled workers. The growing numbers of semi-skilled workers in mass-production industries who were outside the AFL's definition of craft at first found their champion in John L. *Lewis, leader of the more militant United Mine Workers.

When Lewis failed to convince the AFL of the need to promote industry-wide unions in steel, automobiles, and chemicals, he formed (1936) the **Committee (later Congress) of Industrial Organizations (CIO)**, its members seceding from the AFL. In 1955 these two rival organizations were reconciled as the AFL-CIO under George Meany and Walter *Reuther. The *Teamsters were expelled from the new organization in 1957. In 1968, the United Auto Workers under Reuther seceded; they were brought back in 1981, and six years later the Teamsters rejoined. With fifty-four affiliated trade unions and ten million members in 2007, it remained the recognized voice of organized labour in the USA, although in common with the rest of the industrial world, *trade union membership had declined sharply from the 1960s.

(🌐) SEE WEB LINKS

• The official home page of the AFL-CIO.

Aflaq, Michel (b. 1910, d. 23 June 1989).
Arab nationalist politician

Born in Damascus (Syria) as a Greek *Orthodox Christian, he became a schoolteacher. In the 1930s, he developed the idea of Arab unity, which would be free from foreign (especially Western *capitalist) influence. To this end, in 1943, together with Salah-al-Din al-Bitar, he founded the *Ba'ath (Arab Renaissance) Party. After an unsuccessful career in Syrian politics, in 1953 his party merged with the Arab Socialist Party to form the Arab Socialist Renaissance Party. In 1959, he published *In the Ways of the Ba'ath*, which outlined the movement's ideology, now with strongly anti-*Zionist overtones. The movement staged successful coups in Syria (1963) and Iraq (1969), but these Ba'athist regimes were more interested in the maintenance of their own power than in Arab unity.

PAN-ARABISM

African National Congress, see ANC

African Union (AU)
An international organization founded as the Organization of African Unity (OAU) on 25 May 1963 in Addis Ababa. It currently comprises fifty-three African states. Morocco left the OAU in 1984, in response to the OAU's recognition of Sahara as being represented by the Saharan freedom movement POLISARIO. The aim of the OAU was to further African cooperation and solidarity, oppose all forms of colonialism and *apartheid, and defend *human rights. However, it operated on the principle of non-intervention in its members' domestic affairs, so that it became relatively ineffective. At the Lomé Summit in 2000, the OAU decided to transform itself into a more effective African Union, which was accomplished at the Durban Summit in 2002. With a structure loosely modelled on the EU, the AU is ruled by an Assembly made up of Heads of States. This is assisted by a Commission as well as permanent representatives of the nations. It envisaged setting up a pan-African parliament, as well as an African Court of Justice, as well as a common currency. Due to the continuing heterogeneity, it was doubtful whether the AU's more ambitious goals could succeed. The AU has become important almost immediately, however, as it authorized forces to act as peacekeepers in Burundi and Sudan.

PAN-AFRICANISM

(🌐) SEE WEB LINKS

• The AU's home page.

Afrikaner
A term originally used to describe a person born in South Africa rather than Europe; in the twentieth century it was used to denote a White person whose first language was **Afrikaans**. Afrikaners descended largely from the **Boers** ('farmers'), mostly Dutch, but also French and Germans who immigrated before the advent of British rule in the Cape, 1806. While a minority assimilated, many retained their distinct culture, their Calvinist (Dutch Reformed) faith, and their language, which became more and more distinct from written Dutch. Afrikaner identity was emphasized by the emergence of Afrikaner *nationalism. This was partly a response to the development of Afrikaans into a written language towards the end of the nineteenth century, partly to the British occupation of the Transvaal in 1879–85, and partly to the *South African War (1899–1902), when the Afrikaner states (the Transvaal and the Orange Free State) were annexed by the British.

Afrikaner political identity was formed and expressed by the *National Party (NP) and the *Afrikanerbond. It was further strengthened by general approval of *apartheid, which was partly inspired by a sense of religious destiny. Although Afrikaners could muster only a little more than 50 per cent of the White population, they managed to dominate South African politics and society after 1948 through a much clearer sense of unity and cultural identity than non-Afrikaners. This unity came under strain as pressures to change the apartheid system grew during the 1980s, leading to the formation, for instance, of the *Conservative Party. Afrikaner culture and values were challenged even further by the end of apartheid. Following the establishment of a multi-racial democracy in 1994, Afrikaans became only one of eleven officially recognized South African cultures. The Afrikaner community was weakened further by emigration of some of its wealthiest members, as around 20,000, mostly Whites, left the country in the year 2000 alone.

Afrikanerbond

A South African organization founded as the secret Afrikaner Broederbond (Brotherhood) designed to promote *Afrikaner interests. Originally established in 1918 as a cultural organization under the name of Jong Suid-Afrika (Young South Africa), it established an effective public front to further its interests in 1929, the Federasie van Afrikaanse Kultuurverenigings (Federation of Afrikaner Cultural Organizations). Increasingly political, it sought to achieve its aims through the growing *National Party (NP), despite the hostility of *Hertzog and *Smuts, who forbade state employees to join. *Malan's acceptance of its influential support played a significant part in uniting Afrikaner opinion behind him, which led to his surprise election victory in 1948. Thereafter, every NP leader (and South African premier until 1992) was a member, which ensured its success within the top ranks of the *apartheid state. Following the end of apartheid, it changed its name in 1994, and opened up its membership to all races and to women. The purpose of the Afrikanerbond was now to defend a political minority, the Afrikaners and their cultural values, in a multicultural South Africa dominated by the *ANC.

(⊕) SEE WEB LINKS

• The home page of the Afrikanerbond.

Agadir

A port in Morocco which became the focus of the **second Moroccan crisis** (July–November 1911). In response to the French occupation of the Moroccan city of Fez, which broke the agreement over Moroccan neutrality reached after the first *Moroccan Crisis, a German gunboat, the *Panther*, was sent to *Agadir, ostensibly to protect German commercial interests in Morocco. In practice, the '**Panther's Leap**' amounted to a German appeal to be taken seriously as a colonial power in a period that marked the high noon of *imperialism. Ultimately, the Germans agreed to recognize Morocco as a sphere of French influence, in return for French territorial concessions in the Congo (added to the German colony of Cameroon). It marked a further milestone in the build-up of the international tensions that precipitated World War I. More specifically, it convinced the British of German naval aggression and the resulting direct threat to the *British Empire.

Aguinaldo, Emilio (b. 23 Mar. 1869, d. 6 Feb. 1964). Founder of the Philippine Republic

Born in Cavite, he studied at the Colegio de San Juan de Letran. He became hostile to Spanish rule, and after leading a successful attack on a Spanish garrison at the outbreak of the revolution against Spain (1896–7), he became acknowledged as one of the nationalist leaders. As such, he was elected president of the revolutionary government. When this was defeated by the Spanish and he was forced into exile, he accepted US help, and in 1898 returned to found the Philippine Republic on 23 January 1900. He turned against the US forces, who soon defeated him and made him swear allegiance to the USA, an act which marked the decline of the Filipino resistance movement. He retired into private life, though in 1935 he stood unsuccessfully for President. Accused in 1945 of collaboration with the Japanese in World War II, he was arrested but never went on trial. On his release he was appointed a member of the Philippines Council of State, and devoted the rest of his life to improving US–Philippines relations.

Ahern, Bartholomew Patrick ('Bertie') (b. 12 Sept. 1951). Prime Minister of Ireland 1997–

Born in Dublin, he studied in Dublin and at the London School of Economics and became an accountant. He entered the Dáil Éireann (parliament) in 1978, and in 1986 he became Lord Mayor of Dublin. He was the Minister of Finance from 1991, but following the resignation of Charles Haughey he lost the leadership contest of *Fianna Fáil against Albert *Reynolds. He succeeded Reynolds as leader of the party in 1994, and after his party's excellent performance in the 1997 elections he proceeded to form a minority government with the Progressive Democrats. He followed his predecessors in supporting the Northern Ireland peace process, and was one of the signatories of the *Good Friday Agreement. He presided over an unprecedented economic boom, and in 2002 he became the first sitting Prime Minister in more than 30 years to be re-elected. Ahern became a respected statesman at EU level. When Ireland held the EU presidency in 2004, he managed to obtain agreement from all EU governments on the treaty establishing a European *Constitution. Confounding his critics, Ahern led his party to a record third successive victory in 2007.

Ahidjo, El Hadj Ahmadou (b. Aug. 1924, d. 30 Nov. 1989). Prime Minister of Cameroon 1958–60, President 1960–82

Born at Garua as the son of a chief of the Fulani people, he became a radio operator in the post office. He was elected to the French Cameroon Territorial Assembly in 1947 and became leader of the Union Camérounaise (UC). Ahidjo came to represent Cameroon at the Assembly of the *French Union in Paris (1953–6), and succeeded André-Marie Mbida as Prime Minister, aged only 34. President after independence in 1960, he tried to create a united country through integrating all other political movements into the UC, so that dissension and conflict was internalized in the party which he controlled. He further sought to unite the country (and increase his personal control) through political centralization. The *human rights violations committed by his government also contributed to the stability of the country and of his personal position. He surprised his country by retiring in 1982. His subsequent attempt to continue his influence in the political process led to a power struggle with his successor, *Biya, which he lost. He retired to Senegal.

Ahmadi Nejad (Ahmadinejad), Mahmoud (b. 1956). President of Iran 2005–

Born in Garmsar, he studied engineering in Tehran at the Science and Technology University, and obtained a Ph.D. in 1997. He became a university teacher while also becoming active in politics, founding the Islamic Association of Students at his university in 1979. A Provincial Governor from 1993–7, he became Mayor of Tehran in 2003, and in 2005 he became the first secular President of the Islamic State. Ahmadi Nejad succeeded the more moderate *Rafsanjani, and took on a confrontational stance against

Israel and the USA. He accelerated Iran's programme to develop nuclear weapons capabilities, and reinforced Iranian help for insurgents against US forces in neighbouring Iraq.

AIDS (Acquired Immune Deficiency Syndrome)

An illness that became widespread during the early 1980s, though its origins are still unclear. It is caused by the HIV virus, which gradually destroys a person's immune system until he or she develops AIDS. There is no final cure for AIDS, which makes the body vulnerable to diseases like pneumonia, cancer, or fever. However, drugs have been developed in recent years which dramatically slow down the reproduction of the HIV virus in the body, and in this way extend the life expectancy of the individual.

According to UNAIDS, by 2006 around forty million people were affected with the virus worldwide, with around twenty-five million living in sub-Saharan Africa alone. There, HIV infection had reached epidemic proportions in sixteen countries. In Botswana, around 40 per cent of pregnant women were infected with the virus in 2006. After 2000, infection levels stabilized owing to much better education and the large-scale supply of retroviral drugs. Owing to the scale of the problem, however, the majority of those infected with HIV did not receive these drugs. Over 20 per cent of the adult population in South Africa, Namibia, Lesotho, and Swaziland continued to be infected by 2006, with Swaziland being the country with the world's highest infection levels. This raised important issues of equity, as almost all research on the disease is devoted to strands of HIV most common in the United States and Europe. Through its concentration, the HIV virus also became a crucial demographic issue, as life expectancy in the most affected countries dropped to pre-1950 levels. According to UNAIDS, a high prevalence of HIV infections led to Zimbabwe having the world's lowest life expectancy rate, at 34 years.

SEE WEB LINKS
- The home page of the joint UN programme on HIV/AIDS.

airships

The first airship was built in 1900 by Count Ferdinand Zeppelin (b. 1838, d. 1917). Following successful trials, he was commissioned to build 100 airships (**Zeppelins**) for the German military, which used them for reconnaissance and bombing flights during *World War I. In Britain, airships were built after World War I, but they were abandoned in favour of flying boats in the wake of the explosion of the hitherto largest airship, the *R101*, on its maiden voyage to India in 1930. The Germans continued to use the Zeppelins until the *Hindenburg*, the body of which contained 200,000 cubic metres of hydrogen, exploded above New York in May 1937.

Akihito (b. 23 Dec. 1933). 125th Emperor of Japan 1989–

Emperor Akihito's early life was unconventional by the standards set by his predecessors. His early school career at the peers' school, the Gakushûin, was disrupted by World War II, in which he was forced to spend long periods outside Tokyo to escape Allied bombing raids. After 1945, the future ruler of Japan was tutored by Elizabeth Vining, an American *Quaker and children's author. His marriage to Michiko Shôda, following a much-publicized romance begun on the tennis courts, was also largely unprecedented in that Crown Princess Michiko was the first commoner to marry into the imperial house. During his time as Crown Prince Akihito participated in numerous royal visits, cementing Japan's ties with the rest of the world. On his accession to the throne, he emphasized his commitment to the principles enshrined in the *Japanese Constitution, his rule being known as the Heisei period ('perfect peace'). In 2001, his son, Crown Prince Naruhito, ensured the imperial succession as Crown Princess Masako gave birth to a baby girl. In 2006, his younger son, Prince Akishino, and his wife, Princess Kiko, gave birth to a son, who under current laws would succeed Crown Prince Naruhito.

Alanbrooke of Brookeborough, Alan Francis Brooke, 1st Viscount (b. 23 July 1883, d. 17 June 1963). British field marshal

Born in Bagnères-de-Bigorre (France) of an Ulster family. Educated at the Royal Military Academy, Woolwich, he served in Ireland and India, before serving with the Royal Artillery in France during World War I. In the interwar period he was heavily involved in the education of soldiers at the School of Artillery and the Imperial Defence College. He also worked in the War Office, before taking over the preparation of the anti-aircraft corps in 1938. In 1940, as commander of the *British Expeditionary Force, he was instrumental in the evacuation of British troops at *Dunkirk. A strong influence on Churchill, he became chief of the Imperial General Staff in 1941 and chairman of the Chiefs of Staff Committee in 1942. He supported forcefully the *North

African campaigns and subsequent campaigns in southern Europe. This diverted German troops away from the heavily fortified French coast, and thus laid the ground for the eventual success of the Allied *D-Day landings at Normandy. He retired in 1946.

Albania

A Balkan country which, in order to evade persistent foreign intervention, became the most isolated European state in the second half of the twentieth century.

Early history (up to 1945) From 1878, a growing nationalist movement sought independence from the *Ottoman Empire, which had encompassed Albania since the fifteenth century. A series of popular uprisings culminated in the declaration of independence on 28 November 1912, which was recognized by the major European powers in 1913. After the outbreak of *World War I a year later, Albania's southern half was occupied by Italian troops to check Greek expansionism. The whole country was formally declared an Italian protectorate in 1917. Plans by Italy, Yugoslavia (then the Kingdom of Serbs, Croats, and Slovenes), and Greece to partition Albania came to naught in the face of fierce Albanian resistance, led by Ahmen Zogu (later King *Zog I). *Giolitti withdrew the Italian forces in 1920, and in 1921 Albania's independence was recognized (its border with Greece was recognized in 1923).

King Zog tried to reduce his country's economic and military dependence on Italy, but on 7 April 1939 *Mussolini, spurred by *Hitler's annexationist policies, invaded Albania. Zog fled the country, and the Italian King Victor Emmanuel III was declared King over Albania instead. Albania subsequently fought on the side of Italy and Germany, but when Italy changed sides and joined the Allies, the Albanian parliament dissolved its link with Italy in October 1943. The Albanian government, now dependent on *Nazi Germany for support, was challenged by various resistance movements. The most important of these were the Communist *partisans led by *Hoxha, who had fought against the Fascist domination of Albania since November 1941.

The Hoxha era (1945–85) Following the collapse of German rule in the area, Hoxha established a popular front and proclaimed a

People's Republic on 11 January 1946. Albania became a fiercely Stalinist state, as land was expropriated and industrialization introduced. In contrast to other Communist countries it did not abandon its rigorous *Stalinism after the death of Stalin, which soon brought Hoxha into conflict with the new USSR leadership. Diplomatic relations between the two countries were abandoned in 1961, and in 1968 Albania left the *Warsaw Pact. For a while, Hoxha sought to compensate for the breakdown of this relationship with the maintenance of good relations with China, but this phase ended in 1977, when even China under *Mao became too 'liberal'.

Democratization (from 1985) Following Hoxha's death in 1985, Ramiz Alia (b. 1925), gradually moved his country out of its total international isolation. In 1990, political reform was begun through the admittance of an opposition party (Democratic Party of Albania). Led by Sali Berisha, it won the parliamentary elections of March 1992. Under Berisha's rule, the economy continued to be stifled by political and economic corruption. In 1997, the Socialist Party of Albania came to power, but it, too, was plagued by allegations of political and economic corruption. In 2005, a coalition led by the conservative Berisha returned to power, Albania entered an Association Agreement with the EU, but despite impressive rates of economic growth, membership of the EU remained a distant prospect.

Alcalá Zamora y Torres, Niceto (b. 6 July 1877, d. 18 Feb. 1949). President of Spain 1931–6
Born in Priego de Córdoba, he became a lawyer and an active Liberal. In 1917, he became Minister for Development, and, in 1922, Minister of War. He joined the opposition during *Primo de Rivera's dictatorship, and on 17 August 1930 was a co-sponsor of the Pact of Sebastian, which called for an end to the monarchy and the establishment of a republic. When this was achieved after the municipal elections of 1931, he became Prime Minister of the provisional republican government and drew up the Constitution of the Second Republic. He was succeeded as Prime Minister by *Azaña, who ensured his election as President. In this post, Alcalá Zamora called two elections, in 1933 and 1936, to secure a popular majority for a government. After an official review of his actions, he was impeached for his dissolution of 1936, which the report argued should have occurred two years previously. His impeachment constrained his successor, Azaña, to a much more limited role, despite the crisis of the *Spanish Civil War. He was a widely respected

head of state, and his dismissal was a severe blow to the fragile republic. In 1941, *Franco sent him into exile, which he spent in Buenos Aires.

Alemán Valdés, Miguel (27 Sept. 1902, d. 14 May 1983). President of Mexico 1946–52
Born in Sayula, Jalisco, he became a qualified lawyer who became state Governor of Vera Cruz in 1936 and Minister of the Interior under President *Ávila Camacho. The first civilian President since the Revolution (1911), he reorganized the ruling Partido de la Revolución Mexicana (PRM) into the Partido Revolucionario Institucional (*PRI). He inaugurated a programme of industrialization and economic development, while protecting the nascent industries with high import tariffs. He also laid the foundations for Mexico's tourist industry, which subsequently developed into a crucial hard-currency earner for the economy. He was never particularly popular, largely because of alleged government corruption.

Alessandri (Palma), Arturo (b. 20 Dec. 1868, d. 24 Aug. 1950). President of Chile 1920–4, 1925, 1932–8
Born in Linares to Italian immigrants, he graduated in law from the University of Chile in 1893 and entered politics in 1897, acting on behalf of the nitrate miners. The first politician to appeal to urban middle- and working-class voters, the charismatic 'Lion of Tarapacá' was elected President on the promise of the legalization of *trade unions and the introduction of social welfare reforms. These measures were blocked by the conservative Congress. In 1924 the army intervened, and shortly afterwards Alessandri went into exile. He was brought back by the army in 1925, now on a mission to restore law and order, which he did partly through the brutal suppression of strikes. He was in office just long enough to oversee the passing of a new Constitution. This extended the suffrage, separated church and state, guaranteed religious liberty, and introduced compulsory primary education. He resigned again in October 1925 and went to Italy. Re-elected in the wake of the Great *Depression, he introduced successful liberal economic reforms, but the working classes saw their real earnings diminish. As a result, he lost his labour support and did not stand for re-election. He was elected to the Senate in 1946.

Alessandri Rodríguez, Jorge (19 May 1896, d. 31 Aug. 1986). President of Chile 1958–64
Son of Arturo *Alessandri, he entered politics when his father was President. He

worked as an engineer during the 1930s and was Minister of Finance (1948–50). Alessandri won the 1958 presidential elections by a narrow margin against *Allende and *Frei, with only 31.6 per cent of the vote. Despite his personal popularity, he proved unable to bridge the social divisions within Chilean society. His orthodox liberal economic policies had some success, notably in bringing inflation down from over 25 per cent in 1958 to 8 per cent in 1961. Nevertheless, a growing trade deficit caused suspicions among foreign investors and a withdrawal of much-needed capital. He also failed to address the problem of urban poverty owing to continuing migration from the land to the cities. He did not stand for re-election in 1964, and in 1970 was narrowly defeated by *Allende.

Alexander I (b. 17 Dec. 1888, d. 9 Oct. 1934). King of Serbs, Croats, and Slovenes 1921–9, King of Yugoslavia 1929–34

Born in Cetinje, the son of Prince Peter Karadjordjevic (r. 1903–21) of *Serbia was educated in Geneva and St Petersburg. He returned to Serbia in 1909. He distinguished himself in the *Balkan Wars, and in 1914 became Prince Regent of Serbia owing to his father's ill health. After *World War I he ruled the newly unified Kingdom of Serbs, Croats, and Slovenes, and in 1921 became King upon the death of his father. He found it extremely difficult to balance the desires of the Serbs, Croats, and other minority peoples for autonomy with his own desire for a Greater Serbia, and the emphasis on Serbian predominance throughout the kingdom. Faced with domestic instability resulting from ethnic conflict in parliament, he dissolved the chamber and established a royal dictatorship (6 January 1929). To reduce tensions between the different communities he changed the country's name to Yugoslavia, but in practice continued to promote Serb interests. He was assassinated on a state visit to France, by Macedonian and Croatian *Ustase terrorists.

Al-Fatah, see FATAH, AL-

Alfonsín, Raúl (b. 12 Mar. 1927). President of Argentina 1983–9

Member of the *Radical Union Party (UCR) from 1945, he was a lawyer as well as a member of the Chamber of Deputies during two brief periods of civilian rule. He became leader of the UCR in 1981, and in 1983 was elected as an erstwhile opponent of military dictatorship and the *Falklands War. He succeeded in stabilizing his country's fragile democracy, despite a number of attempted military coups, which was possible owing to popular aversion to a return to authoritarian rule. By contrast, he was unable to lead his country to economic recovery. When he lost the elections to his opponent, *Menem, he caused a general surprise by resigning five months before Menem was due to take over, leaving the economy in a state of near-collapse. He became a Senator, and supported President Duhalde's efforts to restore the economy after the economic breakdown of 2001/2002.

Alfonso XIII (b. 17 May 1886, d. 12 Feb. 1941). King of Spain 1886–1931

Born nearly six months after his father's death, he assumed the crown from his mother, who had acted as regent, upon reaching the age of majority. Alfonso proved to be a weak ruler who was unable to provide his country with the stability and integration it so desperately needed. His acquiescence in the dictatorship of *Primo de Rivera meant that he was unable to survive the latter's resignation. He left the country after the Republicans' victory in the 1931 elections, but he did not formally abdicate until 1940, in favour of his son. His grandson, *Juan Carlos, returned to Spain and acceded to the throne in 1975, providing a fragile political system with the visionary leadership which Alfonso had been unable to give.

Algeciras, Conference of (Jan.–Apr. 1906)

An international conference to resolve the first *Moroccan crisis of 1905. From the conclusion of the Anglo-French *Entente Cordiale, which had effectively established Morocco as a French sphere of influence, Germany became increasingly worried about its growing diplomatic isolation. On 31 March 1905 the German Emperor, *Wilhelm II, landed at Tangier in order to display his support for Moroccan independence and neutrality. He also attempted to arouse British opposition to France and thus split the Entente. The conference of Algeciras (Spain) did, indeed, confirm Moroccan independence, though this was to be guaranteed by France and Spain. French control was therefore assured, while English support for France strengthened the Entente. The outcome thus represented a double defeat for German diplomacy. Morocco officially became a French protectorate in 1912.

Alger Hiss Trials (USA, 1949–50)

Alger Hiss was a Harvard-educated lawyer who had worked at the highest levels for the US State Department. In 1948 he became

the focus of an anti-Communist investigation under the direction of the Committee on Un-American Activities set up by the US House of Representatives. Hiss was originally suspected of having passed secret information to the Soviet Union in the 1930s. Since the statute of limitations prevented the charge of espionage, he was charged with perjury for having denied on oath that he had passed secret documents to Whittaker Chambers, a self-confessed Communist Party courier. Hiss maintained his innocence. In his first trial there was a hung jury, but in the second he was found guilty. At both trials high government officials testified on his behalf. The defence challenged Chambers's sanity and alleged that the *FBI had tampered with evidence to obtain a conviction. Hiss was sentenced to five years in prison. He was released in 1954 and returned to private life as a lawyer, and in 1975 he was readmitted to the Massachusetts Bar.

The trials epitomized some of the anxieties of the *McCarthy era. At the time, much of the evidence remained unproven, though since then most commentators have agreed that he did commit perjury, and that he did pass on documents to the Soviet Union. The trial also established the reputation of Richard *Nixon, who pursued Hiss with great energy, and who made much of Hiss's position as part of a privileged Ivy League-educated elite.

Algeria

Africa's second largest country was shaped, first, by French colonial rule, and then by an autocratic regime trying to avert the rise of Islamic fundamentalism.

The colonial era (1830–1962) Algeria's colonization began with the French occupation of Algiers in 1830. In 1848, it was given an administrative structure to parallel that of metropolitan France through the creation of three *départements*, Algier, Oran, and Constantine. In 1882 Algeria formally became part of metropolitan France, even though the Algerian population enjoyed no political or civil rights. In 1919 members of the indigenous elite were offered full French citizenship if they renounced their Muslim faith and customs. This was part of a general attempt to integrate the African state into what were regarded to be superior French

culture and customs. The French colonists took possession of the areas suitable for agrarian cultivation, with Algerian peasants working on their farms for minimal wages.

During World War II, Algeria was ruled by the *Vichy government. The successful landing of *Allied troops in French North Africa in November 1942 enabled de *Gaulle to set up his headquarters and the 'Committee of National Liberation' in Algiers on 3 June 1943. Led by *Abbas, Algerian nationalists demanded more rights, eliciting French promises (formally made in 1947) of full Algerian participation in the politics and government of the country. The promise was not fulfilled, however. France was preoccupied with its own attempts at constitutional and social renewal, and the emerging Fourth Republic in mainland France proved too weak to impose its will upon the conservative and intransigent French Algerian colonists. At the same time, the French government was hindered by its inability to rely fully on the loyalty of its military commanders in Algeria, who often sided with the colonists.

After independence (from 1962) Brutal acts of repression against the Muslim population led to the *Algerian War of Independence (1954–62). It devastated the country, through material destruction and loss of life during the war. The economy suffered further owing to the subsequent exodus of most of the colonists, who took their capital and their skills with them. Under the leadership of *Ben Bella, the colonists' farms were nationalized and given to peasant self-government. This socialist experiment failed to increase production and had to be abandoned under *Boumédienne, who came to power after a coup in June 1965. While Boumédienne continued to espouse the principles of *socialism, he shifted economic policy from the development of agriculture to the establishment of an industrial base, e.g. through the nationalization of companies. This was accompanied by a policy of religious and cultural nationalism which emphasized Algeria's Arabic ethnicity and its Muslim traditions, rather than its colonial history.

During the 1970s, Algeria came to rely heavily on its oil revenues. When the price of oil began to fall from 1981, Algeria's foreign debt burden increased dramatically. Boumédienne's successor, *Chadli, was thus forced to introduce market-oriented economic reforms. As dissatisfaction with economic austerity measures increased, it became evident that the regime's policy of fostering Algerian *nationalism had backfired. Popular resentment against the government spurred the growth of *Islamic fundamentalist opposition. In 1989, Chadli revised the Constitution and allowed the formation of political parties. He also permitted the organization of Islamic fundamentalists as the Islamic Salvation Front (Front Islamique du Salut, FIS), despite their pledge to destroy the current system of government if elected. After the first round of parliamentary elections (26 December 1991), the FIS gained 188 out of 435 parliamentary seats, though it had gained only 25 per cent of the popular vote. Chadli subsequently resigned, his power passing to a transitional state council consisting of five members. On 9 February 1992 the council banned the FIS, and proclaimed a state of emergency. The 1990s were thus marked by civil war, which *Bouteflika, who became president in 1999, tried hard to end. Bouteflika passed a series of amnesty laws while pursuing rigorously those militia groups who did not accept them. Bouteflika sidelined the opposition in 2004, when he was re-elected, but his autocratic style made it harder for him to appease the warring factions in the civil war. By 2007, the civil war had claimed over 150,000 lives.

Algerian War of Independence
(1954–62)

On 1 November 1954, hostilities broke out between the Christian colonists of French descent and Algerian Muslim nationalists who were organized into the *Front de Libération Nationale (FLN) under *Ben Bella. Despite its initial inferiority, the brutality of the well-armed French and colonists' troops soon brought the FLN agrarian mass support. The FLN continued to rely on guerrilla attacks, which spread to Algiers in late 1956. In turn, the war radicalized the settlers and the military's hardline policies in Algeria, so much so that the governments of the Fourth Republic lost control over them. The fact that the French considered Algeria to be an integral part of the French state only intensified the fundamental sense of crisis in France. It triggered the collapse of the Fourth Republic and the return of de *Gaulle to end the Algerian war and create a new, more stable Republic. De Gaulle lost little time in doing both. His personal authority was sufficient to re-establish the army's allegiance in Algeria, despite the resistance of *Salan's *Organisation de l'Armée Secrète. He ordered negotiations with Ben Bella, which led to the *Evian Agreements. Independence was declared on 3 July 1962.

Algiers Agreement, see IRAN–IRAQ WAR

Allende (Gossens), Salvador (b. 26 July 1908, d. 11 Sept. 1973). President of Chile 1970–3

The son of wealthy parents, he qualified as a doctor in 1932. In 1933 he helped found the Socialist Party of Chile, and he was its general secretary (1943–70). After three unsuccessful attempts, Allende won the 1970 presidential elections as leader of an alliance of Socialists and Communists, which made him the first avowed *Marxist to win a Latin American presidency in a free election. Yet, his narrow 'relative' majority (winning 36.3 per cent of the popular vote) gave him a dubious mandate for the decisive reforms he embarked on. He nationalized the copper mines and a host of other, mostly foreign-owned, businesses without compensation. This incurred the wrath of foreign governments, and brought foreign investment almost to a standstill. Allende promoted consumption rather than investment, through the introduction of a pay rise and price freeze. These measures promoted a thriving economic black market, and the economy got increasingly out of control. In addition, an ill-prepared but nevertheless aggressive land reform resulted in the breakup of the hacienda estates, aggravating social and economic chaos in the countryside. Mindful of their private property, the elites and the middle classes supported his overthrow by General *Pinochet (backed by the *CIA), in which Allende died in the burning presidential palace.

Alliance (New Zealand)

A Social Democratic Party created in December 1991 by a number of groups including the *Democrats, in order to provide a more effective opposition to the social reforms undertaken by *Bolger's *National Party. In the 1993 elections it gained 18.3 per cent of the popular vote, but because of the first-past-the-post electoral system, it only gained two seats in parliament. This under-representation of its voters was a major cause for the introduction of a proportional representation system (MMP). The NZ Alliance gained thirteen seats (10.3 per cent of the vote) in 1996, and ten seats (7.7 per cent) in 1999. It became the junior partner in a coalition with the *Labour Party, though some of its left-wing demands on government, as well as debates about its response to *September 11, led to a split. Its leader, Jim Anderton, defected, and led the **Progressive Coalition** into the 2002 elections. These produced a dismal showing for both factions, with the Alliance gaining no representatives, while the two Progressive Representatives supported the Labour government. Jim Anderton became the sole MP returned for the Progressive Party in 2005, whereupon he entered a coalition with Labour, becoming Minister of Agriculture.

(⊕) SEE WEB LINKS

- The official website of the Alliance Party.
- The official website of the Progressive Party.

Alliance for Progress

A US initiative under President John F. *Kennedy, formalized in August 1961 when the countries of Latin America (bar Cuba) and the USA signed a Charter at Punta del Este in Uruguay. Its aim was 'the maintenance of democratic government', mainly through assistance in social and economic development. The $18 billion programme was funded almost equally by loans, from banking and investment houses in the USA, and the US government. It resulted in modest development of schools and hospitals, but soon lost impetus. Its fundamental problem was that at the time, social, economic, and political progress rarely coincided. In fact, economic progress often served to reinforce existing social imbalances and dictatorial regimes. Also, the Alliance was weakened by continuing US interference in the domestic affairs of its neighbours, most notably in Cuba in 1961–2, and the Dominican Republic in 1965, as well as through continuing *CIA activities.

Allied Powers

A term for the co-belligerents who fought against the *Central and *Axis Powers in World War I and World War II respectively. Strictly speaking, in World War I the Allies comprised those countries who had created a formal alliance of cooperation, principally the *British Empire and France. The USA and other countries (Brazil, Bolivia, China, Tibet, etc.) entered the war without entering any official pact, and were thus officially known as Associate Powers of the Allies. In World War II, around 50 countries entered the war on the side of the Allies, though some (e.g. in Latin America) never sent any troops into battle. During the war itself, Britain, the USA, and the USSR were the dominant Allies ('the Big Three'), and coordinated the progress of the war and its aftermath at meetings in *Tehran, *Yalta, and *Potsdam. After the war, France was accepted as a fourth main ally. The term 'the Allies' has been applied to military coalitions led by the US since, notably in the *Gulf War and the war against the *Taliban in Afghanistan of 2001–2.

al-Qaeda ('the Base')

A terrorist organization founded in 1988. Its members were originally recruited from the *Islamic fundamentalist resistance fighters who fought against the Soviet invasion of Afghanistan in the 1980s. Headed by Osama *Bin Laden, it is a highly secret organization whose effectiveness has been ensured by the idea of compartmentalization. This means that its different divisions in over 30 countries (which included Kenya, Pakistan, Somalia, the Sudan, and the Philippines) have had little detailed knowledge of each other's activities. In 1998 it was held to be responsible for an attack on the US embassy in Kenya, killing 213 people, and on the US embassy in Dar-es-Salaam, killing eleven. The organization then organized the attack on USS *Cole* in Aden in 2000.

Sustained by volunteers and money coming from Egypt, Saudi Arabia and other predominantly Arab states, the al-Qaeda network is sustained by a belief that the US epitomizes values that are opposed to *Islam, and which must be fought by a holy war. The organization was behind the *September 11 attacks, after which it became the prime target in the *War on Terrorism led by President George W. *Bush. Al-Qaeda's fighters were the backbone of the *Taliban regime in Afghanistan, and when the Taliban fell, many al-Qaeda fighters were captured by *Northern Alliance forces and other tribal groups. Some were handed over to the US forces, which transported them to special imprisonment in *Guantanamo Bay, where the US government denied them protection under the US Constitution as well as the 1949 Geneva Convention relative to the Treatment of Prisoners of War.

Al-Qaeda cells continued to be active, Two and a half years to the day after the September 11 attacks, they caused the *Madrid Bombings (2004), while in 2005 they were responsible for the *London Bombings. With the London Bombings, al-Qaeda demonstrated its capacity to recruit Muslims of British nationality, which made it even more difficult for security forces to track down al-Qaeda's members. Al-Qaeda continued to support the Taliban, and its increasingly successful fight against *NATO forces in Afghanistan.

Alsace-Lorraine

The Alsace is a territory west of the River Rhine which became part of France 1648–97 and borders Lorraine in the north. Lorraine came under French influence during the sixteenth century and became part of France during the seventeenth. After the French Revolution of 1789, Alsatians were content to live within France, despite the fact that they were largely Protestant and German-speaking. They joined the fierce opposition of the people of Lorraine to the German annexation which followed Germany's victory over France in 1871. The two territories were combined and administered from 1879 by a powerful Governor who was a direct appointee of the imperial government in Berlin. Arbitrary decrees by the German administration, misbehaviour by the German army (as at Saverne (*Zabern)), and efforts at 'Germanization' furthered the resentment. The vast majority welcomed the return of French rule in 1918. In many ways subsequent French efforts at eliminating Alsatian peculiarities such as the German language and traditional customs were even more draconian than German rule, so that resentment turned toward the French. Following the experience of *Nazi rule, 1940–5, the people of Alsace and Lorraine have thrived under French rule since 1945, and there has been a natural decline of the Alsatian German dialect.

Alto Adige, see SOUTH TIROL

Ambedkar, Bhimrao Ramji (b. 14 Apr. 1893, d. 6 Dec. 1956). Indian politician
Born in Mhow into the Mahar caste of 'untouchables', he won a series of scholarships and graduated from Columbia University with a Ph.D., and with a D.Sc. degree from the University of London in 1923, when he was called to the Bar. Back in India, he founded the Bahishkrit Hikarini Sabha in July 1924, an organization which campaigned for the rights of the 'untouchables'. To this end, he embarked upon a number of specific campaigns (*satyagraha), while also leading the fight for the Depressed Classes in the Bombay Legislative Assembly (1926–34). Meanwhile, in the legal profession he advanced to become Perry Professor of Jurisprudence at the Government Law College in 1935. A representative at the *Round Table Conferences, he clashed with *Gandhi over the latter's rejection of a separate vote for the 'untouchables'. The resulting Poona Pact of 1932 was a compromise which reserved seats for 'untouchables' in the legislature. It was a formula that he still felt prolonged their social and political isolation. Nevertheless, it became an enduring feature of Indian political life. He founded the Scheduled Castes Federation in April 1942, and in 1945 established the People's Education Society. Ambedkar participated in the independence negotiations in 1947 and, as *Nehru's Law Minister, successfully drafted India's constitution. After resigning from the government in 1951, he failed to gain re-election in 1952 and 1953. Frustrated by the ostensible impossibility for

'untouchables' to gain equality in India, he urged his followers to join him in *Buddhism.

America First Committee (1940–1)
A broad isolationist front which formed the political nexus for Americans who wished not to intervene in the Franco-British war with *Nazi Germany which began in 1939. It was associated with Republicans, particularly those linked with the American Midwest. It also garnered the support of some Democrats, pacifists, socialists, and independents, and some representatives of ethnic groups such as German Americans.

American Federation of Labor, see AFL

American Indian Movement (AIM)
A militant organization emerging from the growth of a pan-American Indian identity in 1968 to advance American Indian cultural, legal, and property claims. Some of its members occupied Alcatraz Island in San Francisco Bay (1969–71), offering to buy the island for cheap jewellery worth $24—the sum for which Manhattan Island had been bought from the Indians in 1626. Similarly, the Washington offices of the Bureau of Indian Affairs were occupied in 1972, as was the village of Wounded Knee in 1973, scene of the last great US–Indian battle in 1890.
    In 1970 President *Nixon formally repudiated the paternalistic policy of assimilation and adopted that of Indian self-determination. Since then the AIM has achieved numerous grants of land to Indian tribes and the return of ancestral burying grounds, while Native American cultural awareness has steadily increased. It has suffered, however, from competing rival groups representing American Indian interests, such as the National Tribal Chairmen's Association and the National Congress of American Indians. For its early policy of illegal occupation of property, one of its founders, Dennis Banks, was a fugitive from justice between 1975 and 1984. Despite the support during his period on the run of such governors as Jerry Brown of California and Mario Cuomo of New York, he received a three-year sentence for political violence and riot.

(●) SEE WEB LINKS
• The home page of the AIM.

American Indians

Assimilation (1880s–1920s) The first major shift in attitudes amongst Whites towards American Indians came about with the publication of Helen Hunt Jackson's book

A Century of Dishonor in 1881. A scathing attack on previous government policy towards Indians, the book encouraged the formation of the Indian Rights Association and aroused public awareness over the treatment of Native Americans. In the first campaign to improve the situation of Native Americans, reforms aimed at assimilating American Indians to White culture. Boarding schools sought to resocialize children to new White ways of life. Traditional religious practices were outlawed, and tribal customs were suppressed. The 1887 Dawes Severalty Act divided the hitherto common land of the reservations into individual landholdings, in an attempt to impose White patterns of landholding.

The new language of reform clothed the continuing exploitation, as Indians often received fractions of the lands they had held collectively, with the rest of the lands allocated to companies and White settlers. The 1887 Act robbed the American Indians of around 14 per cent of their remaining land, a total of 17 million acres (around 68,800 km^2). Between 1887 and 1934, American Indians lost a total of 86 million acres (348,000 km^2). The remaining land was unable to support their population, which after centuries of decline began to grow again from a low point of around 250,000 in 1900. Many Indians moved into urban areas, and incidences of intermarriage increased.

Recognition of distinctiveness (1930s–60s) According to the Snyder Act (1924) all Indians born in the USA were granted full citizenship. The attempt to force American Indians to assimilate and to destroy their culture was only halted by the Indian Reorganization Act, passed in 1934 as part of the *New Deal. It reversed the 1887 Act by consolidating Indian reservations through the public purchase of land for the Native American peoples. It recognized tribal authority, which was encouraged to adapt to modern developments, and supported a return to Indian education. After World War II, a Federal Indian Claims Commission was established, together with a Bureau of Indian Affairs. Under *Eisenhower, the government reversed these developments by encouraging a move of Indians away from the poverty-stricken and unsanitary conditions of the reservations, to the cities. The controversial programme, which relocated around 100,000 Indians, offered possibilities for greater education and employment opportunities, but also entailed the prospect of further cultural assimilation.

Assertiveness (from the 1960s) American Indians benefited greatly from President *Johnson's *Great Society. In 1966, the Bureau of Indian Affairs was headed, for the first time in a century, by an American Indian, marking further recognition by the government of Indian concerns. At the same time, during the 1960s, better education and American Indian uprootedness in the cities caused a change of identity away from the individual tribe to a pan-Native American consciousness. This led to the increasingly articulate and militant formulation of demands for Native American rights and land claims, which found expression in books such as *Custer Died for your Sins* (1969) by Vine Deloria Jr, and the foundation of the *American Indian Movement in 1968. In response, *Nixon appointed a Mohawk-Sioux, Louis R. Bruce, as Commissioner for Indian Affairs, and spearheaded a return to New Deal policies of encouraging tribal autonomy, realized through President *Ford's Indian Self-Determination Act of 1975.

American Indians continued to be one of the most disadvantaged sections of US society, whose income was well below the national average. Compensation for land claims was granted only on a piecemeal basis. More important to the fortunes of many tribes was legislation in 1988 allowing the opening up of gambling halls on lands owned by American Indians. This has led to the opening of some of America's most profitable and prosperous casinos, although these benefited American Indians highly unevenly.

American Popular Revolutionary Alliance, see APRA

American Samoa

This eastern part of the Pacific islands of Samoa came under US control in 1899. Under the formal government of the US navy, it remained effectively governed by Samoan chiefs, who rejected unification with Western *Samoa under mistrusted New Zealand rule. Following the closure of the US naval base, its administration passed from the navy to the US Department of the Interior in 1951, as an unincorporated territory. American interest in the Samoans' welfare only began after *UN accusations of neglect, whereupon US spending increased tenfold (1959–63). In 1976 the American Samoans finally accepted self-government (which they had rejected in 1972). Political life has been characterized by the absence of political parties, and the relatively strong political power of local chiefs in the second chamber, the Senate.

American Virgin Islands, see VIRGIN ISLANDS OF THE UNITED STATES

Amin, Idi (b. 1925?, d. 16 Aug. 2003). President of Uganda 1971–80
Probably born in Koboko, he joined the (British) King's African Rifles in 1946 as a cook. He soon became a soldier, and exercised his physical strength as a boxer and rugby player. He took part in the British campaigns to prevent the independence of Burma and then of Kenya, where he helped crush the *Mau Mau rebellion. Despite early signs of his brutality, he rose quickly to become commander of the Ugandan army in 1966. At a time when his corruption became ever more evident, he led a coup against *Obote in January 1971. He rejected his predecessor's socialist policies, which earned him applause from the USA and UK. His initial domestic popularity soon diminished, as his regime of terror led to widespread, sporadic anarchy. He was not directly responsible for all the violence, but encouraged it through his seemingly arbitrary executions, as well as the incitement to nationalist hatred of Asians and Jews. Claiming areas of Tanzania as part of a 'Greater Uganda', he attacked Tanzania in 1978. His forces were soon forced to retreat, however, as the Tanzanians advanced to the capital (Kampala) and reinstated Obote. He lived in exile in Saudi Arabia. It is estimated that some 250,000 Ugandans were tortured and killed during his regime.

Amnesty International
This international pressure group for the release of prisoners of conscience was founded by Peter Berenson in London on 28 May 1961. It has also been active against forms of punishment which it regards as inhumane, such as torture or capital punishment. It campaigns through the provision of legal aid and direct pressure, notably through publishing acts of injustice against individuals and through getting its members to protest to the governments concerned in letter-writing campaigns. It received the *Nobel Peace Prize for its work in 1977. By 2007, it claimed 1.8 million members in 150 states.

(((⊕)) SEE WEB LINKS)

• The official website of Amnesty International.

Amritsar Massacres (1919, 1984)
Two massacres occurred in Amritsar, in the Indian province of Punjab, which has a central significance for *Sikhs as the site of their Golden Temple (Hari Mandir), containing the sacred Sikh scripture, the Granth Sahib. On 13 April 1919, following nationalist riots against the *Rowlatt Bills which had led to the death of five Englishmen, Gurkha troops under the command of Brigadier R. H. Dyer fired on peaceful, unarmed nationalist crowds gathered in the Jallianwala Bagh, an enclosed park, They killed 379 people and wounded over 1,200. The massacre led to growing resentment of British rule in India. Dyer was given an official, if belated, censure.

In 1984, the Golden Temple was seized by a group of militant Sikhs, who used it as a base for attacks to campaign for an independent, Sikh-dominated *Punjab. The holy site was stormed on the orders of the Indian Prime Minister, Indira *Gandhi, in defiance of the consequences of this act of sacrilege to the Sikhs. In revenge, Gandhi was assassinated by a militant Sikh, which in turn led to angry massacres of Sikhs by Hindus.

Amsterdam, Treaty of (1997)
A follow-up treaty to the Treaty of European Union at *Maastricht, it strengthened the institutions of the European Community. It extended the number of areas in which the *European Parliament took part in the legislative process according to the cooperation procedure with the *European Council. It also extended *Qualified Majority Voting in the *European Council, and it extended the purview of the European Community by integrating aspects of justice and home affairs such as immigration. It also integrated the *Schengen Agreement into the EU. Despite these changes, the Treaty failed to fulfil its brief to make the decisive reform of the EU's institutions in preparation for the EU's enlargement by up to twelve new members from eastern, central, and southern Europe. In consequence, a new *Intergovernmental Conference was instituted for 1999, to lead up to the Treaty of *Nice.

Amur River Society (Kokuryûkai)
A Japanese ultra-nationalist organization often mistranslated as the '**Black Dragon Society**', which, before 1945, promoted Japan's conquest of east Asia. It was established as a successor to other groups in 1901 by Uchida Ryôhei with the support of leading figures on the ultra-nationalist fringe. This was an influential but small grouping of activists which promoted Japan's expansion into Manchuria and the war with Russia. The Society was able to forward its policies both with the support of sympathizers among

Japan's ruling establishment and through the more direct actions of its members, who combined espionage, agitation, assassination, and scholarship at home and abroad to pursue their objectives.

anarchism

Developed into a consistent, individualistic theory by Pierre Joseph Proudhon (b. 1809, d. 1865), it started as a movement which rejected large-scale property and the state. Instead, anarchists supported decentralized, local/communal forms of authority, and promoted the self-help of workers. In a change of emphasis, at the turn of the century many anarchists focused on the revolutionary ideas of Bakunin to create a new social order through violent action and terrorism. This led to the assassinations of the Austrian Empress Elizabeth (1898), the Italian King Umberto I (1900), and US President *McKinley (1901). In the early twentieth century, anarchists achieved some influence through *syndicalism in France, despite their repression by the French government following the murder of the President, Sadi Carnot, in 1894. In Spain, anarchists participated in the government from November 1936 until May 1937. Anarchism disappeared after the fall of the Spanish Republic, and the rise of *Mussolini in Italy. In the USSR, most anarchists turned into Communists after the *Russian Revolution.
   COLLECTIVISM

anarcho-syndicalism

A term which described principally trade union movements or political parties whose actions and ideals were based on *anarchism and *syndicalism. In particular, they advocated direct, militant action by their largely working-class members, rather than using the established agencies of the state (e.g. parliament) or of property (e.g. industrial arbitration).

ANC (African National Congress)

Resistance (until 1990) This was established in 1923 through the renaming of the South African Native National Congress, itself founded in 1912 as the first national native African political organization. Until the 1940s, it was led by an elite of highly educated Christian Blacks who hoped by persuasion and lobbying to make the White political elite reduce discrimination against Blacks. When the introduction of successive racial laws and the increase of *Afrikaner *nationalism exposed the ineffectiveness of the ANC's moderation, a new generation including

Nelson *Mandela and Oliver *Tambo formed the ANC Youth League in 1944, which aimed to secure equality not through the charity of Whites but through the strength of the Blacks. The ANC cooperated with the South African Indian Congress (SAIC) in 1947, its militancy increasing further with the start of *Malan's *apartheid regime in 1948.

The defiance campaign launched in 1952, in which the ANC and the SAIC called for a boycott of identity cards, *bantustans, and other expressions of apartheid, provided the ANC for the first time with a mass membership. None the less, under *Luthuli's leadership it remained too moderate for its more radical members, who broke away under *Sobukwe to form the *PAC. The latter organized a march against identity cards which led to the *Sharpeville Massacre, whereupon the ANC was banned (8 April 1960). In response, Mandela and others continued the struggle through the establishment of a military wing together with the South African *Communist Party, **Umkhonto we Sizwe (Spear of the Nation)**, which for two years led a campaign of bombing state property. Its leaders, including Mandela, were soon arrested, and for the next decade morale was low.

An exodus of several thousand young Blacks, most of whom had been recruited as fighters by the ANC in Zambia and Mozambique, was triggered by the *Soweto riots. More importantly, under its president, Tambo, the ANC gradually built up an international anti-apartheid campaign which, together with the vociferous protests of leaders such as Winnie *Mandela and Desmond *Tutu in South Africa itself, increased South Africa's international isolation and emphasized the leading role of the ANC in the struggle.

Contemporary politics (since 1990) The ANC was legalized as part of *de Klerk's drive for a solution to South Africa's racial problems in February 1990, to coincide with Nelson Mandela's release from prison. Under the latter's effective leadership, it rapidly became the most authoritative movement representing South African Blacks, a position which was confirmed in the 1994 elections, when it gained over 60 per cent of the popular vote. Despite its strong links with the *Communist Party, which had matured in common resistance to the regime since the 1940s, after 1990 the ANC became extremely pragmatic, accepting the need for capitalism and foreign investment. Although from the 1990s the ANC's unity and moderation were guaranteed by the unquestioned authority of its leaders, it faced continuous challenges by radical supporters in Black townships who demanded immediate economic betterment. Under *Mbeki's leadership from 1999, the ANC tried to internalize dissent by entering a coalition with the Inkatha Freedom Party. It also promoted government spending on health and education, as well as improving the conditions in townships.

The ANC commanded a virtual monopoly of power nationally, and in all provinces apart from the Western Cape. This led to widespread corruption, which resulted in growing public criticism. These developments coincided with a growing power struggle for Mbeki's succession in 2009. In 2005, Mbeki dismissed his former ally, Jacob Zuma, from office, though in 2006 Zuma was declared not guilty of rape in the courts.

((⊕)) SEE WEB LINKS

• The home page of the ANC.

Andean Group (Grupo Andino, or officially, Acuerdo de Cartagena)

An agreement signed at Cartagena in 1969 between Bolivia, Colombia, Ecuador, Peru, Venezuela, and Chile (which left in 1977). Its aim was to enhance the economic competitiveness of its members relative to the more developed economies of Latin America. In 1984 a new Andean peso was established to reduce dependency on the US dollar. The removal of tariff barriers during the 1990s was largely unsuccessful. The union has been largely ineffective owing to the political and economic instability of its members. In 1995 Peru and Equador were involved in a border war, and in 2006 Venezuela under *Chávez withdrew its membership, though Chile became an associate member that year.

LATIN AMERICAN INTEGRATION ASSOCIATION

((⊕)) SEE WEB LINKS

• The official website of the Andean Community.

Andorra

A tiny state (453 km², 175 square miles) in the Pyrenees between France and Spain, whose Constitution is based on a treaty of 1278, which shares power between the Spanish Bishop of Seo de Urgell and the French President (as the legal successor to the original signatory, the Count de Foix). Until 1993, these were represented by two Governors who had almost total control. The assembly, the 'general council of the valleys', was elected by restricted franchise (only third-generation Andorrans had the vote), and it had no legislative powers, merely an advisory role. The new Constitution of 12 December 1993 retained its titular heads of state, but otherwise established the co-principality as a sovereign state. The franchise was extended, political parties were allowed, and the assembly became the principal legislative body. The assembly was dominated by the Liberal Party of Andorra, whose leaders, Marc Froné Molne (1995–2005) and Albert Pintat Santolària (since 2005) served as Head of Government.

Andreotti, Giulio (b. 14 Jan. 1919). Prime Minister of Italy 1972–3, 1976–9, 1989–92

As a law student at the University of Rome, where he met *Moro and Montini (Pope *Paul VI), he became President of the Italian Catholic University Federation. Subsequently, as a protégé of *De Gasperi since 1944 he rose quickly within the *Christian Democratic Party (DC). He was Minister of the Interior (1954), of Finance (1955–8), of Treasury (1958–9), of Defence (1959–66), and of Industry (1966–9), and formed his first government in 1972. His second tenure of office was more successful as a result of a pact with the Italian *Communist Party, which promised to tolerate his government in return for concessions from the DC. At the same time, his government struggled to find a solution to the terrorist crisis which peaked with Moro's assassination. He was Foreign Minister in 1983–9. His last period as Prime Minister was marked by old-fashioned power-broking between the parties within his five-party coalition, leading Andreotti to abandon the cautious government reforms begun by his predecessors during the 1980s. His personality and his success epitomized the postwar Italian political system, marked by compromise, pragmatism, and an inability to overcome corruption. In fact, he stood trial from 1993 on charges of corruption (*Tangentopoli) and membership of the *Mafia. He was cleared of the charges in 1999, and a later retrial confirmed the verdict.

Andropov, Yuri Vladimirovich (b. 15 June 1914, d. 9 Feb. 1984). General Secretary of the Communist Party of the Soviet Union 1982–4

Born in Naguskaia near Stavropol, Andropov joined the *Communist Party in 1939 and became a high-ranking member of the Communist Youth League during World War II. Involved in Karelian partisan activities during the war, from 1945 he quickly rose within the Karelian Communist Party, and was appointed ambassador to Hungary 1957–62. In this capacity, he warned *Khrushchev of a possible revolution and advised the dismissal of *Rákosi, but then supported the ruthless suppression of the *Hungarian Revolution. He was also Secretary of the Party Central Committee department in charge of coordinating Soviet relations with its Communist neighbours. By this time, he had acquired a reformist reputation, while his appointment to head the *KGB (1967–82), whose effectiveness he improved with ruthless and clinical aplomb, endeared him to the heart of conservatives. He thus prevailed over *Brezhnev's acolyte, *Chernenko, and succeeded Brezhnev as General Secretary of the Communist Party. His term in office was too short to have a major impact on the country, despite efforts to increase efficiency in party and economy. Perhaps his most lasting contribution was his promotion of *Gorbachev to positions of power.

Anglican Communion

Autonomous, episcopal, Protestant churches in fellowship with the **Church of England**. The origins of the Communion go back to 1534, when the British parliament rejected the role of the papacy and recognized the King, Henry VIII, as the 'Supreme Head in Earth of the Church of England'. Subsequently, most of the English population became members of the new church. Sister churches were soon established in Ireland, Scotland, and Wales, and throughout the *British Empire in subsequent centuries. The twentieth century has seen the emergence of a consciousness from a body of loosely connected churches as a world-wide Protestant church. Nevertheless, the members of the Communion continued to emphasize the importance of consensus and discussion instead of the establishment of a unitary, authoritarian structure.

The Communion recognizes the leadership of the Archbishop of Canterbury, who presides over the decennial Lambeth Conference (since 1857), the principal meeting of Anglican bishops. However, his leadership is more titular than real. The recommendations of the Lambeth Conferences are not binding to the individual parts of the Communion, so that its coherence and unity is dependent on consultation and consensus. During the twentieth century, its relationship with the Roman *Catholic Church improved, and communion was established between the Church of England and the Lutheran churches in the early 1990s. The Communion has around seventy-three million members, principally in Britain, Nigeria, Uganda, Australia, and North America. In 2003 the Communion split over the ordination of a practising homosexual as Bishop of New Hampshire (USA). This triggered threats of schism led by the Anglican Church of Nigeria, which refused to recognize fellowship with those Anglican provinces that recognized homosexuals in the ministry, and provided leadership to American parishes who felt similarly.

(()) SEE WEB LINKS

• The official website of the Anglican Communion worldwide.

Anglo-Irish Agreement, see FITZGERALD, GARRET

Anglo-Japanese Alliance (20 Jan. 1902)

An agreement for an initial period of five years, in which the UK and Japan agreed to remain neutral if either was involved in a war with a third power. If either was involved in a war with two other countries, then the other would assist. They also recognized each other's special interests in China, whilst the UK recognized Japan's interests in Korea. It was renewed in 1905, when each agreed to support the other if it was attacked by another country.

Anglo-Russian Entente (31 Aug. 1907)

An agreement between the UK and Russia, which sought to settle disputed questions between the two countries regarding their interests in areas affecting India. Russia agreed that Afghanistan was a British sphere of interest; Tibet was recognized as neutral; Persia was divided into three zones, the northern Russian sphere being separated from the southern British zone by a neutral area. The agreement settled long-standing differences between the two countries, and Britain had made its vital Indian interests more secure by making concessions in less important areas. Since France had already concluded an alliance in 1894, the Entente paved the way for the eventual alliance against Germany which emerged in World War I.

Angola

A country in south-western Africa which, despite its wealth in mineral resources, has experienced great economic hardship as a result of almost perpetual civil war since independence.

Colonial rule (up to 1974) Portuguese colonization began in the late sixteenth century, though the entire country was only brought under full control in 1885. Portuguese settlement began on a large scale only after World War I. In a country without a tradition of private property, any land that was not explicitly owned was taken over by Portugal and partly given to the settlers. Growing dissatisfaction with colonial exploitation led to a popular uprising in 1961, which was contained only three years later. Already by 1956 the first resistance movement had been formed, the **MPLA** (Movimento Popular de Libertação de Angola, Popular Movement for the Liberation of Angola). This was followed in 1962 by the foundation of the **FNLA** (Frente Nacional de Libertação de Angola, National Liberation Front of Angola), from which emerged a third movement led by **Jonas Malheiro Savimbi** (b. 1934, d. 2002) in 1966, the **UNITA** (União Nacional par a Independência Total de Angola, National Union for the Complete Independence of Angola). The mounting resistance to Portuguese rule did trigger some concessions from the colonial power, notably the abolition of forced labour for the indigenous population in 1962. At the same time, Portuguese attempts at integrating Angola into the 'motherland' through the introduction of Portuguese culture failed. After the end of military rule in Portugal in 1974, Angola was hastily released into independence in 1975.

Civil war (1975–2002) There ensued a struggle for political dominance between the three competing guerrilla organizations, which was complicated by foreign interference. The MPLA was supported by Cuban troops and Soviet aid, whereas UNITA, operating in the south, was supported by the US and South Africa. The FNLA, operating in the north, was supported also by the US, as well as by neighbouring Congo. As a result of the civil war, and the exodus of the majority of the skilled labour force to Portugal, the economy collapsed in 1975. The MPLA soon gained the upper hand, and in February 1976 proclaimed a socialist People's Republic. Nevertheless, it remained unable to overcome the armed resistance of both the FNLA and UNITA. The situation was complicated by frequent attacks by South African troops against *SWAPO bases in the south. Following the initial establishment of a planned economy, market forces were gradually introduced. Angola finally joined the third *Lomé Convention in 1985, and in 1987 President Eduardo *dos Santos announced economic reforms and the promotion of private property.

As it became clear that neither side could win in the civil war, on 22 December 1988 South Africa, Angola, and Cuba signed a peace treaty brokered by the *UN. This stipulated withdrawal of the 50,000 Cuban troops and the South African troops from Angolan and neighbouring Namibian soil. On 2 May 1991, the MPLA and UNITA agreed to fuse their armed forces and hold of a general election in November 1992. UNITA refused to accept the outcome of these elections, which gave the MPLA an absolute majority, and in the resulting violence in 1993 over 30,000 people died. New elections were agreed in May 1994, and despite continued heavy fighting, on 20 November 1994 both parties signed a peace treaty. The fragile peace process that ensued was brought to an end by UNITA's refusal to hand over some of their territories to government control. The civil war that returned in 1998 led to over three million people being displaced from their homes. Bolstered by military spending that took up over 40 per cent of the budget, the government took control over most of Angola, while Savimbi's death in action in February 2002 weakened UNITA still further. UNITA disbanded officially in August, thus ending 27 years of Civil War.

Recent developments (Since 2002) The onset of peace allowed the government to profit from growing exports in diamonds and crude oil. By 2006, Angola had advanced to become Africa's largest oil producer after Nigeria. Widespread corruption, however, prevented the majority of the population from experiencing the economic benefits of Angola's wealth in mineral resources.

Anguilla

A small island in the Caribbean, it came under British sovereignty in 1650 and was administered from the island of St Christopher (St Kitts) from the nineteenth century. In 1956, it became part of the colony of *St Christopher and Nevis, but when this gained independence in 1967 Anguilla rebelled, asking for continued British protection. Its political and constitutional system was finally settled in 1982, when it became a British Dependent Territory with a Governor appointed by the British Crown. From 1984 it was governed by the centre-right Antigua National Alliance (ANA) under Emile R. Gumbs, who was succeeded in 2000 by Osbourne Fleming of the ANA.

Annan, Kofi (b. 8 Apr. 1938). UN Secretary-General 1997–2006

Born in the Ghanaian town of Kumasi, he studied economics, and in 1962 entered the civil service of the *UN. He interrupted his time there in 1971, when he obtained a master's in management at the Massachussetts Institute of Technology. He rose through the ranks of the UN, and in 1993 became Under-Secretary for Peace Management. He served as the UN special envoy in former *Yugoslavia, where he gained much respect from the nations involved in the peacekeeping efforts there. He succeeded the controversial *Boutros Gali, and launched internal reforms of the UN's vast bureaucratic apparatus, which were only partially successful. While this helped overcome a central criticism especially of the USA, Annan also urged greater support for less developed nations, particularly in Africa. He spoke out passionately about the *AIDS crisis there. Annan gained popularity through his diplomatic skills, his personal integrity, and his independence, and was re-elected to a second term in 2001. Under Annan, UN peace-keeping missions expanded markedly, including successful missions in Timor Leste, Kosovo, and southern Lebanon. However, he also presided over setbacks, notably his inability to prevent the *Iraq War as well as the genocide in Sudan. He was succeeded by *Ban Ki-Moon.

Anschluss ('political union')

*Hitler's annexation of his native Austria to the *Third Reich on 12–14 March 1938. Following the dissolution of *Austria-Hungary after World War I, the Allies forbade Austria's unification with Germany, even though it had been part of the German Confederation until 1866 and the Austrians had voted for it in a referendum in 1918. In his drive to create a greater German Empire, and to reverse the terms of the *Versailles Treaty, Hitler used the first opportunity to march his troops into Austria once he was assured of *Mussolini's acquiescence. Austria was passive in this episode, but it was not exactly a victim either. Despite the fears of many liberal, left-wing, and Jewish Austrians, the Anschluss was received with approval and even enthusiasm by most Austrians.

Antarctica

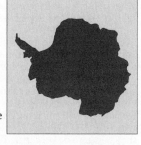

The Antarctic continent was first charted by James Cook in 1773–4, though it was not fully explored until the twentieth century. In a race to reach the South Pole, the Norwegian Roald Amundsen was the first to arrive on 15 December 1911. The ill-fated British expedition led by Captain Robert Falcon Scott (b. 1868, d. 1912) did not arrive there until 18 January 1912. (The myth of Scott's amateurism against Amundsen's professionalism has been largely refuted, since temperatures on Scott's route were 40°F below the expected average.) Most of Antarctica's territory was claimed by Britain (British Antarctic Territory) in 1908, New Zealand (Ross Dependency) in 1923, Australia (Australian Antarctic Territory) in 1933, France (Adélie Land) in 1938, Norway (Queen Maud Land) in 1939, Chile (Antarctic Peninsula) in 1940, and Argentina (Antarctic Peninsula) in 1942. These claims have not been recognized by either the USA or the Soviet Union (Russia).

The Antarctic Treaty signed in 1959 by twelve nations, including Britain, the USA, the Soviet Union, France, and Japan, guaranteed the continuation of peaceful research, the banning of military or nuclear activity, and the establishment of a system of mutual inspection. The treaty was valid for 30 years. In 1991, the Antarctic Treaty was extended by the Antarctic Environmental Protocol, which was signed in Madrid and became effective in 1998. Ratified by 26 countries, it banned the exploitation of the continent's mineral resources for another 50 years, and kept it free from direct environmental pollution. Its ice masses on the edges have been particularly vulnerable to the advance of global warming. By contrast, most of its area has seen little change because even with an increase in overall temperatures, the climate has remained below melting point at all times of the year.

(((⊕))) **SEE WEB LINKS**

• The website of the British Antarctic Survey.

anthrax

A disease caused by the bacillus *anthracis*, which most commonly occurs in warm-blooded animals and the soil on which they tread. In sufficient quantities its spores can be lethal to humans. As it is easily reproduced in biological laboratories, it has found a military use as a weapon of biological warfare. Exactly one week after the *September 11 attacks on the US, a letter was posted in Trenton, NJ, containing lethal spores of anthrax. In the following weeks, a series of letters were posted, one of them to the Senate majority leader, Tom Daschle. None of the addressees were affected, but a number of postal workers were slow to receive attention, and died from exposure to the spores. The attacks heightened a sense of insecurity and vulnerability in a society still in shock from the September 11 attacks, even though the two incidents were almost certainly unrelated.

Anti-Ballistic Missile Treaty (1972), see
DISARMAMENT

anticlericalism (Europe)
The opposition to the secular influence of the Church, usually the Roman *Catholic Church. It was a major theme in the domestic politics of several European countries during the late nineteenth century, such as in Germany 1871–87 and beyond, Spain in 1873, and the Netherlands and Belgium during the 1880s and 1890s. It proved a central factor in French politics from the French Revolution of 1789, and provided a crucial stimulus for the *Radical Party, 1902–6 and beyond. During the twentieth century it was an important issue in Spain, as the powerful Catholic Church was largely hostile to the Republican regime of 1931–9. In a sense, Communist regimes have been anticlerical as they tried to reduce if not eliminate the influence of religion upon society, though this policy often lacked popular support. As European societies became more secular during the twentieth century, anticlericalism largely ceased to be a dominant political issue in the later decades of the century.
    SECULARIZATION

Anti-Comintern Pact (25 Nov. 1936)
A treaty between Germany and Japan (joined by Italy the following year) in which they declared their common hostility to Communism. It formed the basis of the coalition formed by the **Tripartite Pact** on 2 September 1940, in which the three countries joined forces in their fight against the *Allies in World War II.
    AXIS POWERS

Antigua and Barbuda

A country consisting of the Caribbean islands of Antigua, Barbuda, and the uninhabited Redonda, which came under British sovereignty in 1632. Apart from 1971–6, it was governed by **Vere Cornwall Bird** (b. 1909, d. 1999) and his Antigua Labour Party (ALP) (founded 1938) from 1946. Universal adult suffrage was introduced in 1951, and in 1967 it

became an independent country in 'association' with Britain. Antigua and Barbuda gained full independence on 1 November 1981. The 1980s were marked by considerable tensions within the ALP caused by corruption allegations against, and hostilities between, Bird and two of his sons in the government. After winning the 1994 elections with a reduced majority, the country's leadership passed to Bird's younger son, Lester, who had campaigned against government corruption for some time. Unsurprisingly, Lester Bird proved unable to overcome the corruption which had become connected so closely to his family. The 2004 elections were won by the oppositional United Progressive Party, leading to the Bird family's loss of power.

Anti-Party group, see KHRUSHCHEV,
NIKITA

anti-Semitism

Modern anti-Semitism (since 1870s) Whilst Christian hostility towards Jews dates back to the first century, modern anti-Semitism denotes hostility towards the Jewish race or, more popularly, towards Jewish culture and traditions. Its origins go back to the late 1870s, when earlier, sporadic outbreaks of anti-Jewish feelings became a permanent phenomenon in European society. In the writings of early anti-Semites, such as the German Wilhelm Marr or the Frenchman Ernest Renan, Jews were identified as a separate race. From this perspective, even if individuals converted from Judaism to Christianity or assimilated to current cultural values they continued to be considered Jewish. Throughout history, Jews had been made the scapegoats for economic and other misfortunes, but from the late nineteenth century Jews also became identified by conservative populists as the harbingers of progress, industrialization, and international capital, who destroyed the values and livelihoods of an idealized rural peasant society.

One of the most striking characteristics of modern anti-Semitism especially before World War II was its strength in countries such as Poland and France, where conservatives linked to the Roman *Catholic Church were united principally by anti-Semitism in their opposition to economic and social change. In France, this broad coalition of forces resistant to change came together as a result of the *Dreyfus Affair, which at the same time revealed the extent of popular (as well as official) anti-Semitism. In Russia, where Jews had settled relatively recently, they began to be prosecuted in *pogroms, with the support of officials eager to please the anti-Semitic Tsars Alexander III and

Nicholas II. Partly in response to the pressures of modernization, anti-Semitism developed in Germany and Austria, too. It was fuelled by widespread Jewish immigration from Eastern Europe into a number of urban centres which already had considerable populations of highly assimilated Jews. In the Vienna of *Hitler's years as an apprentice (1909–13), anti-Semitism had been made acceptable in public discourse during Karl Lueger's mayorality (1897–1910), since he was an anti-Semite supported by the growing Austrian Christian Social Union.

Germany and the Holocaust In Germany, anti-Semites remained on the political fringe before 1918, though it was during the *German Empire that the foundations for the extraordinary rise of anti-Semitism in politics and society were laid. The conclusion of the *Versailles Treaty, the ensuing widespread economic misery of the Weimar Republic, and its political weakness made many Germans very receptive to the anti-Semitism of the right wing (and of the emerging *Nazi Party in particular). Many of the Republic's most ardent supporters, most affluent business leaders, and many influential politicians (such as *Rathenau) were Jewish, and became easy scapegoats. What was most striking about the German Third Reich under Hitler was the brutality with which anti-Semitism was brought to its most horrendous and extreme conclusion through the murder of over five million Jews in *concentration camps during *World War II.

Since World War II These horrors ensured that for the first decades after the war anti-Semitism became publicly unacceptable not only in Germany (where the denial of the *Holocaust became a criminal offence), but throughout most of Europe and elsewhere in the world. At the same time, anti-Semitism was thinly disguised in the USSR, where it was partially encouraged by the state during the 1950s and early 1960s because of fears the Jews might look towards Israel rather than the Soviet Union as their ultimate authority. From the 1980s, in some Western European countries, anti-Semitic parties such as the *Front Nationale in France and the Austrian *Liberal Party generated considerable electoral appeal, which was the result more of inherent xenophobic popular moods against immigrants. Furthermore, the appeal of such parties was based on general popular prejudices against Jews rather than on the racial anti-Semitism (with its implications of assumed Jewish racial inferiority) which was current before and during World War II. Since 1945, such

anti-Semitism remained the preserve of violent neo-Fascist groups.
JEDWABNE MASSACRE

Antonescu, Ion (b. 14 June 1882, d. 1 June 1946). Romanian dictator 1940–4
Born in Pitesti, he became a professional soldier and served as a colonel in World War I. After the war he continued to advance in rank. In 1933 he became army Chief of Staff. He was Minister of Defence, 1937–8. In 1940, *Carol II appointed him Prime Minister with dictatorial powers. Hoping initially to rule with the *Iron Guards to enlist some popular support, he destroyed the Guards when they got out of hand, and created a full-blown military dictatorship. In June 1941 he joined World War II when Germany attacked the Soviet Union. His troops were victorious at first, recapturing Bessarabia and the *Bukovina. They captured Odessa, which without undue modesty he renamed Antonescu. However, his position changed after 150,000 of his troops were lost in the decisive battle of *Stalingrad. Thereafter, he concentrated in vain on preventing eventual Soviet domination, pinning his hopes on a speedy Anglo-American advance in the West. Shortly after the *Red Army crossed into Romania, he was deposed on orders of King Michael I, whereupon Romania changed sides. He was tried and shot as a war criminal.

ANZAC (**A**ustralian and **N**ew **Z**ealand **A**rmy **C**orps)
Formed in World War I, it was associated primarily with its landing at *Gallipoli on 25 April 1915 and the following unsuccessful battle of attrition, in which it lost more than 10,000 soldiers. Subsequently, the term has been used as shorthand for Australian and New Zealand forces during the rest of World War I and World War II. Since 1916, 25 April has been commemorated as ANZAC Day in Australia and New Zealand. The Gallipoli campaign, in which Australians and New Zealanders had no national interest, epitomized the general senselessness and brutality of war.

ANZUS
A defensive military alliance concluded in 1951 by **A**ustralia, **N**ew **Z**ealand, and the **US**. It served to reassure Australia and New Zealand against the double threat of US-sponsored Japanese rearmament, on the one hand, and the spread of *Communism in Asia as manifested in *Mao's victory in China and in the outbreak of the *Korean War, on the other. The military alliance with the USA was a consequence of the British defeat at

*Singapore in 1942, which had shown that Britain could no longer guarantee the defence of her former Empire. The alliance was effectively ended in 1984, when New Zealand refused nuclear vessels from the USA and elsewhere entry to its ports.

Aotearoa

The Maori name for *New Zealand meaning 'land of the long, white cloud'. The use of this term has been encouraged by Maori groups, but it is also increasingly adopted by New Zealanders of non-Maori (usually European) descent ('pakehas').

apartheid ('apartness')

Origins A racial policy which dominated South African culture, politics, society, and economics during the twentieth century. Policies of segregation were progressively introduced in the different parts of the country before the creation of South Africa, and were continued by the unified state from 1910. These policies enjoyed the support of every Prime Minister and every White political party. Apartheid became a cornerstone of the politics of the *National Party (NP) governments from 1948, taking segregation to new, unprecedented levels. Its official justification was that each race (White, mixed-race (Coloured), Indian, and Black (Bantu)) would prosper most if it developed separately. Harmony would be possible through the races living peacefully side-by-side, while tension would result from them being mixed together in the same environment, competing for the same resources.

History In fact, apartheid served to maintain the political and economic supremacy of the White minority, which comprised less than 20 per cent of the total population. By keeping other races apart, poor, and uneducated, the system was designed to prevent them from developing a sense of solidarity and demanding the same rights and benefits which the Whites enjoyed from South Africa's natural wealth and industrialization. The enactment of apartheid was made possible through the 1950 Population Registration Act, which made compulsory the carrying of a pass to identify the racial group of each holder. In 1951, the Bantu Authorities Act was the first of a series of acts designed to create separate and distinct areas in which Blacks would live separately, without intruding into White neighbourhoods (see *bantustans). The 1952 Native Law Amendment Act established the close control of the movement of urban Blacks in particular. The 1953 Bantu Education Act for the first time created a national education system for Blacks. By taking education away from the independent churches this increased state control over Blacks, and consolidated an inferior education system for Blacks. Discrimination in the workplace was enhanced, and sexual relationships between Whites and non-Whites were forbidden.

In 1953 '**petty apartheid**' began, whereby public amenities (restaurants, lavatories, beaches, post offices, etc.) were set apart for Whites. This was relaxed and gradually abolished under *Vorster and P. W. *Botha. Apartheid itself, however, did not come to an end until 1993, after a referendum in the previous year in which two-thirds of White South Africans approved its abolition. This was caused by a combination of the protest of the Black majority led by the *ANC, international isolation, and the burden of a vast security apparatus on the resources of a White minority whose relative size was declining. (Comprising almost 23 per cent of the population in 1921, Whites made up 12.8 per cent of the population in 1994, as a result of a comparatively low birth-rate.) In 1996, the *Truth and Reconciliation Commission was established to deal with the moral and social effects of apartheid.

Apollo program (USA)

The launch by the USSR of the first orbital satellite, Sputnik, in 1957, and the fact that the first man in space was a Soviet citizen, Yuri Gagarin, had dented US national pride. Rather than build a space station, President *Kennedy decided that the USA could demonstrate its technological lead over the Soviets during the Cold War and show its power to the world with a moon mission. In May 1961 he announced to *Congress a plan to land men on the moon by 1970. By 1966, the USA had completed several orbital missions to the moon and had landed an unmanned probe on that body. The programme was set back in 1967 by the death of three astronauts, Roger Chafee, Edward White, and Virgil Grissom, who were preparing for a launch exercise at Cape Canaveral, Florida. In 1968, Apollo 8 carried three men in orbit around the moon; on 20 July 1969, Apollo 11 carried Michael Collins, Edwin 'Buzz' Aldrin, and Neil Armstrong to the moon. The latter two became the first men to set foot on the moon, Armstrong going first.

In the course of the next six moon missions, lasting until 1972, only the near-disaster in space of the Apollo 13 mission excited public interest to the same degree. On that mission, three astronauts and the *NASA control centre at Houston nursed a damaged spacecraft back from the moon's orbit to land safely on earth. In 1975, the Apollo programme ended with a joint Soviet–US link-up in earth orbit. Since 1975, no human being has left earth orbit, with NASA concentrating on unmanned space missions to explore the galaxy, and the Space Shuttle programme.

(⊕) SEE WEB LINKS

• The home page of NASA.

appeasement

A policy of giving in to hostile demands of another nation to avoid war, primarily associated with British and increasingly also with French foreign policy between the two World Wars. From 1933 to 1939 this allowed *Hitler to violate the Treaty of *Versailles by remilitarizing the Rhineland and to regain control over the *Ruhr District, annex Austria (*Anschluss), and invade Czechoslovakia.

CHAMBERLAIN, NEVILLE; MUNICH AGREEMENT

APRA (Alianza Popular Revolucionaria Americana, American Popular Revolutionary Alliance)

Founded in Mexico in 1924 by the Peruvian exile *Haya de la Torre. Its ideals were influenced by the ideals of *socialism and of the Mexican Revolution. It supported land reform, the nationalization of foreign-owned companies, and the safeguard of Indian rights and culture. Contrary to Haya's objectives, the movement failed to spread across Latin America, but it did become the leading democratic party in Peru. There, its progress was continuously hampered by the military, most glaringly in 1962, when they prevented the elected Haya from taking up the presidency.

APRA exercised considerable influence over the writing of the 1979 constitution, which introduced e.g. a universal suffrage without educational qualifications. In 1985, its candidate, Alan García Perez (b. 1949), finally managed to become president. His attempt to meet Peru's economic crisis through government spending proved disastrous, and APRA's support plummeted from 50 per cent in 1985 to 19.2 per cent (1990). It boycotted the following elections in protest against the 1992 political coup by President Fujimori. APRA regrouped for the corrupt 2000 elections, and at the free elections in 2001 it became the second largest party in parliament, and in 2006 its candidate, Alán, García Pérez, was elected to the Presidency.

Aquino, Benigno 'Ninoy' (b. 1932, d. 21 Aug. 1983). Filipino opposition leader
Originally a journalist from a well-connected political family, he married Corazón M. *Aquino in 1954. Soon known as the 'wonder boy' of Filipino politics, he entered politics and became Mayor in 1955, Governor in 1961, and Senator in 1967. His meteoric rise was stopped by his imprisonment in 1972, when President *Marcos declared martial law. Despite being sentenced to death in 1977, he was allowed to leave for the USA in 1980 to undergo heart surgery. Though himself firmly committed to non-violence, he was assassinated on Marcos's orders immediately on his return to the Philippines.

Aquino, (María) Corazón (b. 25 Jan. 1933). President of the Philippines 1986–92
Born in Talac as Corazón Cojoangco. In 1946 her family moved to the USA, where she received much of her education, graduating from Mount Saint Vincent College in 1953. In 1954, she married the journalist Benigno 'Ninoy' *Aquino, who became a prominent critic of President *Marcos. Upon her husband's murder, she succeeded him as opposition leader, launching a defiant and successful campaign for the 1986 elections.

Aquino came to power despite Marcos's refusal to yield, due to the extent of her popular support, and her support in the army. In office, she fought successfully against Communist resistance movements, and made peace with Muslim secessionists, as well as the Cordillera People's Liberation Army. In order not to endanger the weak democracy, she did not carry out any major social or economic reforms. For instance, for fear of alienating the powerful landowning elites she refrained from land reforms, even though this might have alleviated some of the distress of the mass of landless labourers. She did not run for re-election, and was succeeded by her favoured candidate, *Ramos. Following her retirement, she actively supported the cause of democracy and *human rights throughout Asia.

Arab Federation

A political federation between the *Hashemite Kingdoms of Jordan and Iraq, founded on 14 February 1958 in response to the formation of the aggressively *pan-Arab *United Arab Republic. The relatively loose union was effectively dissolved by the Iraqi coup of 14 July 1958, in which its leader, *Faisal II, was murdered.

Arab League

An association founded in 1945 by Egypt, Saudi Arabia, Syria, Transjordan (Jordan),

Iraq, Lebanon, and Yemen, originally to promote political cooperation among Arab countries. Since then, it has been joined by Libya (1953), Sudan (1956), Morocco (1958), Tunisia (1958), Kuwait (1961), Algeria (1962), South Yemen (1967), Qatar (1971), Bahrain (1971), Oman (1971), the United Arab Emirates (1971), Mauritania (1973), Somalia (1974), the *PLO (1976), Djibouti (1977), and the Comoros (1993). In 1950, its aims were extended to military, and in 1957 to economic, cooperation. It has largely failed in its aim to promote Arab unity, because of long-standing conflicts between some of its members (e.g. Syria and Iraq), the rejection of Iraqi leadership claims over the organization, and the different political systems in the various member states.

Following the *Camp David agreement, Egypt's membership was suspended in 1979, and its full status was not restored until general Arab moves towards an agreement with Israel in 1989. The League was fundamentally undermined by the *Gulf War, when the majority of its members fought under the leadership of the USA against a fellow Arab state. As a result, it did not have a summit meeting for a decade, until unity was found again in 2001, in support of the Palestinians. However, the Arab League was again thrown into disarray by the response to *September 11 and President *Bush's *War on Terrorism. While denunciation of the attacks was universal, US action against *Bin Laden in Afghanistan was less popular. In particular, the League was uncertain how to respond to a broadening of the War on Terrorism to its own members, notably Iraq.

PAN-ARABISM

(⊕) SEE WEB LINKS

• The official website of the Arab League.

Arab Legion

Originally founded in 1921 as a police force for the British *League of Nations *Mandate of Transjordan, it contained a force of 1,000 volunteers under the command of Colonel Frederick Peake. In the 1930s, under Major John Glubb it became a highly disciplined military force which played a significant part in campaigns in the Middle East in World War II. In 1948-9, with a strength of over 7,000 volunteers, it won and held East *Jerusalem and the *West Bank territories, which *Abdullah ibn Hussein proclaimed part of the Kingdom of Jordan in 1949. Glubb resigned in 1956, by which time the Legion had become the nucleus of the Jordan Arab Army.

Arab Revolt (1916)

A revolt against Turkish rule in the Middle East. In July 1915 *Hussein ibn Ali, Sherif of Mecca, negotiated with Britain about rising up against the *Ottoman Empire, a German ally during World War I, which ruled the Middle East at the time. In return, the British High Commissioner in Egypt, Sir Henry McMahon, promised that Britain would support Arab independence once Turkish control had come to an end. The revolt began in June 1916, when an Arab army of some 70,000 men, financed by Britain and led by *Faisal I, moved against Turkish forces. They captured Aqabah and cut the **Hejaz railway**, a vital strategic link through the Arab peninsula which ran from Damascus to Medina. This enabled British troops to advance into Palestine and Syria. With the capture of Damascus (1 October 1918) Turkish hold on the Middle East ended. Despite their promise to support Arab independence, the British took charge of governing Transjordan, Iraq, and Palestine as a *Mandate themselves, while France took control of Syria and the Lebanon. As a further affront, the *Balfour Declaration directly contradicted the British commitment to the Arabs through the promise to support an independent Jewish state in Palestine.

Arab–Israeli War, Fourth, see YOM KIPPUR WAR

Arab–Israeli War, Second, see SUEZ CRISIS

Arab–Israeli War, Third, see SIX DAY WAR

Arafat, Yasser (b. 24 Aug. 1929, d. 10 Nov. 2004). Palestinian leader 1969–2004

Early career Born in Jerusalem (according to other sources born on 21 March 1929 in Cairo), he participated in the war against Israeli independence (1948–9). As a student of electrical engineering in Cairo from 1951 he founded the General Union of Palestinian Students. He fought in the *Suez Crisis in the Egyptian army, and then went to work as an engineer in Kuwait, 1957–65. There, he co-founded and led the al-*Fatah movement, which from 1969 became the leading movement within the *PLO. In February 1969 he became president of the PLO's executive council.

PLO leader (from 1969) Arafat's subsequent career was marked by a series of political and military miscalculations, as impressive personal comebacks oscillated with repeated failures to seize the right moment and consolidate his gains. Under his leadership, the PLO was expelled from Jordan (1970–1), Beirut (1982), Damascus and Tripoli (1983), and south Lebanon (1988). These expulsions contributed to splits in the movement, divisions which deepened as Arafat became more pragmatic in his search for a negotiated peace settlement with Israel. In 1990 he became isolated in his support for Saddam *Hussein in the *Gulf War, while his support for the *August coup in the USSR was peculiarly out of touch.

Arafat's survival as Palestinian leader is, therefore, a testament to his unrivalled sensitivity towards Palestinian opinion at the grass roots—about what it would, at the end of the day, accept. A dreadful public speaker, he was always helped by his opponents' underestimation. Ultimately, his dogged pursuit of international recognition, and his renunciation of violence in 1988, finally convinced Israel that he was the country's best hope of achieving a peace with the Palestinians. He negotiated the *Oslo Accords and the *Gaza–Jericho Agreement, and subsequently struggled to maintain his authority given the strong opposition from more radical groups such as *Hezbollah and *Hamas.

Leader of the PNA (1996–2004) In 1996, Arafat scored an important victory when he was elected President of the newly created *Palestinian National Authority (PNA) with a high voter turnout, despite the campaign by his rivals to abstain. While he governed an extremely poor and disparate territory, he did little to create structures that would offer hope to a war-torn and impoverished population.

Arafat found it difficult to lead a population impatient for Palestinian independence and ready for more violence, while also dealing with an Israeli government which since *Rabin's assassination had lost its assuredness in dealings with the PLO. He agreed to the *Wye accords in 1998, but these were never implemented in full. Arafat refused a peace deal brokered in the dying days of the *Clinton administration and the *Barak government, because it did not involve complete Palestinian control over East Jerusalem. This helped bring down Barak, who was replaced by Arafat's archenemy, *Sharon. Sharon put Arafat under house arrest in March 2002, in an attempt to clamp down on the *Intifadah. Given the heterogeneity of the Palestinian movement, Arafat remained an important point of approach for the US and the EU. Sharon was forced to give up the siege of Arafat's headquarters. In April 2003 Arafat was forced to concede powers to a Cabinet, but he remained the ultimate source of political authority inside Palestine until his death.

Arbenz Guzmán, Jacobo (b. 14 Sept. 1913, d. 27 Jan. 1971). President of Guatemala 1951–4
Son of a Swiss immigrant, he joined the army and in 1944 co-sponsored a military coup, after which he joined a junta to oversee the establishment of a democracy. As President, he granted unprecedented political and civic freedoms. He carried out cautious economic reforms, mainly heeding the advice of the *World Bank. However, the land reform that followed, and especially the expropriation of lands held by the powerful United Fruit Company (UFC), triggered the open hostility of the US government (its Secretary of State, *Dulles, was a shareholder in the UFC). With US help, a group of insurgents began an uprising, while air raids undertaken by *CIA pilots induced the army to depose him.

Arcos Raid

A raid on the offices of a British-registered Soviet trading company, Arcos Ltd. It took place on 12 May 1927, with 200 police officers searching the company's premises in London, on suspicion that the company was a front for Communist subversion, and that it was holding a British army signals manual. No evidence of subversion was found, however. Still, partly to cover *Baldwin's embarrassment over the incident, diplomatic relations with the Soviet Union were broken off in what marked the height of British insecurity about the perceived spread of *Communism following the *General Strike. Relations were only restored by *MacDonald's Labour government in October 1929.

Ardennes offensive (16–24 Dec. 1944)
The last desperate counter-attack by the Germans in *World War II, also known as the **Battle of the Bulge**. In an effort to prevent the Allies' advance into German territory, Field Marshal von *Rundstedt was ordered by *Hitler to launch an attack through the hilly, wooded country of the Ardennes in northern Luxembourg and Belgium. Despite taking their opponents by surprise, the lack of equipment, fuel, air support, and experienced soldiers meant that the Germans did not even come near their target of Antwerp. The advance ground to a halt after eight days, most notably at Bastogne. Allied counterattacks led by *Montgomery and *Bradley cleared the Ardennes by 16 January 1945. The hopeless offensive had resulted in 120,000 German casualties.

Argentina

By 1914 one of the world's wealthiest countries, when it had a per capita income similar to that of the German Empire or Switzerland, it has been marked by a steady relative industrial decline ever since, as a result of its chronic political instability. From the 1970s, what is potentially the wealthiest country in Latin America has been plagued by endemic unemployment and mass poverty.

Early history (1853–1943) A federal republic since 1853, it extended its territory south through the colonization of Patagonia during the last two decades of the nineteenth century. The emergence of the steamship enabled it to become a major grain-exporting country at that time, and new methods of refrigeration and preservation led to a booming export industry in beef.

Through the *Radical Party, the increasingly prosperous and numerous middle classes demanded political participation. In an effort to split their alliance with the underprivileged, the conservative regime granted universal suffrage in 1912. Under *Yrigoyen, this led to a period of rule by the Radicals (1916–30) in which industrialization began and government was increasingly characterized by party politicization and participation. Challenged by the growing viability of the popular democracy, the army and conservative elites staged a coup and removed Yrigoyen from office in 1930.

Peronism and military rule (1943–83) The military took over power directly in 1943. In the following years the populist Secretary of Labour, Juan *Perón, built up substantial support among the working classes. These formed the basis for his victory in the presidential elections of 1946, and underpinned the *Peronist movement, which remained a major political force after his death. Perón managed to overcome some of the country's economic problems, but after the death of his first wife, Evita *Perón, he lost touch with the people, and in 1955 was forced to go into exile. The tripolar tensions between a strong military, a strong but divided Radical party, and a popular Peronist movement led to a succession of weak governments and military dictatorships unable to cope with the country's economic and social problems.

From the late 1960s onwards, the emergence of a revolutionary left-wing movement resulted in growing political violence, providing the occasion for Perón's come-back. In a state of near civil war, the Peronist candidate Héctor Cámpora was elected President in May 1973, making way for Perón to be re-elected President in September 1973. Perón died the following year but was succeeded by his third wife, Isabelita *Perón, who failed to hold the disintegrating country together. Yet another military coup followed in 1976. To combat the escalating political violence and to cope with the strong forces of left-wing opposition (particularly the trade unions), the military committed countless acts of terrorism against its opponents and in violation of *human rights: at least 10,000 people disappeared between 1976 and 1983. Against the background of yet another recession, and of increasingly widespread discontent about the military regime, President *Galtieri attempted to restore the military's popularity through an invasion of the Malvinas (Falkland) Islands in 1982.

Democratization (from 1983) Overcome by superior British troops in the ensuing *Falklands War, the military was forced to resign its political power and allow democratic elections. These were won by *Alfonsín in 1983, who successfully strengthened the fragile democracy while failing to cope with its fundamental economic problems. However, it was the Peronist government under *Menem from 1989 that brought about medium-term economic and political stability. Menem persuaded the armed forces to accept a cut of 60 per cent in the number of officers and non-commissioned officers. His unique talent for achieving compromise enabled him to persuade different groups, including the trade unions, to make some economic concessions. This did achieve some social and economic stability, and contributed to Menem's popularity. However, the concern for social consensus including labour prevented much-needed structural reform such as a reduction in public-sector pay and employment, as well as the diminution of trade union influence.

Menem's successor from 1999, Fernando de la Rúa, was faced with the bankruptcy of national finance, which was exacerbated by a severe contraction of the economy. Unable to realize austerity measures amidst corruption allegations against his government, the staunch opposition of trade unions, and pressure from the *IMF, de la Rúa resigned in December 2001. This sparked off a public crisis, as the month of December 2001 saw a succession of five Presidents. Eduardo Duhalde subsequently managed to create a fragile hold on the presidency. Although neither the state nor the economy emerged from the crisis with any credit, in the context of Argentinian history it was remarkable that the Argentinian military did not make any efforts to intervene.

Contemporary politics (since 2003) Duhalde was succeeded in 2003 by the fellow Perónist Nestor Kirchner, though Duhalde remained highly influential within the Peronist Justice Party, leading to subsequent inner-party struggles between the two rivals. The economy began to show significant growth of almost 9 per cent each year between 2003 and 2007, which allowed Argentina to repay all debts owed to the *IMF in 2004. Nevertheless, the economy was affected by a high inflation rate, while large parts of the working and middle classes continued to live below the poverty line.

Arias Navarro, Carlos (b. 11 Dec. 1908, d. 27 Nov. 1989). Prime Minister of Spain 1973–6
Born in Madrid, he studied law there and joined the civil service at the Ministry of Justice. From 1944 he became, successively, Governor of León, Santa Cruz de Tenerife, and Navarre. He became Director of General Security in 1957, and was Mayor of Madrid (1965–73). As Prime Minister, his main task was to provide for a gradual political liberalization to ensure a peaceful transition of power between the ailing *Franco and *Juan Carlos. He managed this with some success. However, after Franco's death he remained tainted by his long association with him. Impatient with the speed of his reforms, Juan Carlos replaced him with the energetic *Suárez.

Arias Peace Plan, see ARIAS SÁNCHEZ, OSCAR

Arias Sánchez, Oscar (b. 13 Sept. 1941). President of Costa Rica 1986–90, 2006–
A student of law in San José, he studied politics in London and Essex, where he obtained a doctorate. After returning to San José to teach political science, he was Minister of Planning 1972–7. In 1979 he was elected president of the social democrat Partido de Liberación Nacional (PLN, Party of National Liberation).

In 1987, Arias distinguished himself as the author of the **Arias Peace Plan**, officially known as **Esquipulas II**, for which he received the *Nobel Peace Prize in the same year. It followed decades of tension between and within the Central American states, fuelled by the *Cold War as the US and the Soviet Union jostled for influence in each of the countries. The Plan was based on the premise that regional peace could only be established without interference from the superpowers. Free elections and other measures to stabilize democratic government in Central America were to be guaranteed collectively by the participating states. Despite the Costa Rican belief in the importance of a regional solution, there can be no doubt that the Plan could only work because the improved relations between the USA and the USSR under *Gorbachev reduced the superpowers' interest in the region.

The success of the Arias Peace Plan was facilitated by the defeat in the 1990 general elections of the Nicaraguan *Sandinistas, who had been the central cause of US involvement in the region. Peace was restored to Nicaragua in the following years (1990–4), and to El Salvador in 1992. Arias was re-elected after the Constitutional Court ruled that presidents could be re-elected for a second period in office. He promised to revive the economy, and ratify a controversial Free Trade agreement with the USA.

Aristide, Jean Bertrand (b. 15 July 1953). President of Haiti 1991–6, 2001–4
Born in Port Salut, he became a priest of the Salesian order. He was a committed preacher of *liberation theology, but the more the political content of his sermons grew, the more he was opposed by the church hierarchy and his order, and the more venerated he was by the people. He was suspended from the priesthood in 1987 and, following the creation of his own popular Lavalas ('landslide') movement, was elected President with 67 per cent of the popular vote in 1990. Taking office on 7 February 1991, he was deposed by a military coup on 30 September 1991 and went into exile in the USA. There, his socialist leanings ensured that he was supported by US public opinion only with some ambiguity, but President *Clinton none the less ordered a (peaceful) invasion to enable Aristide to return on 15 October 1994. On 7 February 1996, he was succeeded by René Prevál of his Lavalas movement, who had been elected with almost 90 per cent of the vote. Amidst general allegations of widespread corruption, Aristide was elected for a second non-consecutive term in 2001. The elections were boycotted by the opposition, and international aid was frozen. Aristide survived a domestic coup attempt, but sporadic violence against his rule continued, and in 2004 he left the country.

Armenia

A Caucasian republic which finally gained its independence on 20 October 1991, just before the formal disintegration of the Soviet Union.

Foreign rule (to 1991) At the beginning of the twentieth century, Armenia was occupied by Turkey and Russia. Its population declined in the first genocidal massacres of the twentieth century, carried out by Turks and Kurds (1895–7, 1909, 1915–17). In 1915–17, over 500,000 Armenians are estimated to have died as Ottoman Turks resettled over 1.5 million Armenians in Syria and Mesopotamia. A Republic of Armenia was declared on 28 May 1918 in an attempt to profit from the collapse of the *Ottoman Empire, as well as the *Russian Civil War. However, Armenia's eastern areas were reoccupied by the Turks in 1920. Russian occupation was accepted in the rest of Armenia, with Russians seen as a guarantor against further invasion by the dreaded Turks. Armenia became part of the USSR in 1922, and in 1936 it became a distinct republic within the USSR. Throughout the Soviet period, its claim for sovereignty over the Armenian enclave of Nagorno Karabakh in neighbouring *Azerbaijan caused periodic friction.

After independence (1991) Following independence in 1991, Armenia soon became involved in the violent clashes between Armenians in Nagorno Karabakh and Azerbaijani authorities. Armenian forces occupied Nagorno Karabakh as well as some strategic Azerbaijani territory in 1993. Partly as a consequence of the war, which cut Armenia off from Azerbaijani oil supplies, Armenia's economy, devoid of mineral resources or fertile soil, collapsed. By 1994, Gross Domestic Product had fallen to 33 per cent of its 1990 levels, while inflation stood at over 4,000 per cent. Despite nominal independence, therefore, Armenia continued to remain dependent on Russia, which took 60 per cent of its exports while obtaining the right to leave army contingents stationed at the Turkish border. In 1998, President Ter-Petrosian was forced to resign following his tacit support of an *OECD proposal to settle the status of Nagorno Karabakh. He was succeeded by Robert Kokharyan. His re-election in 2003 was marred by allegations of electoral fraud. Kokharyan tried to reduce Russian influence by opening the country to EU and US aid, and introducing a constitutional reform in 2005. This enhanced the power of parliament and gave citizenship rights to the large Armenian diaspora living abroad. Refusing to ease its grip over the country, Russia increased the price of its gas deliveries in 2006, causing acute economic hardship.

Armenian genocide (1915–16)

At the height of World War I, the *Young Turk government of the *Ottoman Empire suspected its Armenian population of harbouring sympathy for the Russian enemy. Armenians serving in the Ottoman army were taken into camps and killed, as were Armenian political leaders and intellectuals. The mass of the population were rounded up and marched off to concentration camps, where many of them died of hunger, thirst or disease. In 1920–3, when the Ottoman Empire invaded parts of Armenia, Armenians were subject to further mass killings.

It is estimated that up to 1.5 million out of a population of 2.5 million Armenians died. As genocide is defined as a purposeful extermination of an entire people or race, the mass killing of Armenians has been widely accepted as a genocidal act (whose denial became punishable by law in France). Since the founders of the Turkish Republic participated in the Young Turk movement, this is still a hotly contested issue in Turkey, with most Turks (including the Turkish government and most Turkish academics) denying that the genocide ever happened, underlining instead that this was a relocation move necessitated by the realities of war. The Armenian genocide is commonly referred to as the twentieth-century's first genocide, though that term should be applied to the German attempted extermination of the Herero people in its South-West African colony in 1904.

Aruba

A small island state off the Venezuelan coast, it came under Dutch control in 1634 and was part of the *Netherlands Antilles until 1985. It received self-government on 1 January 1986 with the promise of independence in 1996. In 1990, this was postponed indefinitely owing to disagreements about Dutch involvement in its post-independence affairs. Situated off the Venezuelan coast, its economy has been primarily sustained by oil refining and shipping, as well as tourism.

Arusha Declaration (Tanzania)

A programme developed in 1967 by *Nyerere, which sought to adapt the principles of *socialism to the conditions of Tanzania. Taking the communal life of the Arusha tribe as a model, the village (*Ujamaa) was to be the country's principal administrative, productive, and political unit. All capital stock and properties were owned by the village. The aims of this policy were to increase the country's economic self-sufficiency and reduce its dependence on agricultural imports, and to establish equality of individual income. At the same time its aims were moral: to encourage self-sacrifice and community spirit. It did bring about a greater equality of income, but failed to increase agricultural production, which suffered from a lack of personal incentive to increase yields.

ASEAN (Association of South East Asian Nations)

Founded in 1967 by Indonesia, Malaysia, the Philippines, Singapore, and Thailand (and joined by Brunei in 1984, Vietnam in 1995, Laos in 1997, Myanmar in 1997, and Cambodia in 1998) to promote political, economic, and social cooperation. With the notable exception of Singapore, these economies had been lacking in capital and industry, but were rich in labour and natural resources. They came to export their natural resources to Japan and the newly industrialized countries of Hong Kong, Singapore, Taiwan, and South Korea, while the latter responded through exporting manufactured goods and investing in their oil, mining, and forestry industries. In the late 1970s, the ASEAN countries changed their economic policy by developing low-cost, labour-intensive, and export-oriented industries with considerable success, very much as their wealthier Asian neighbours had done before them. These initiatives led to high annual growth rates of 6–8 per cent. ASEAN countries continued to rely heavily on the export of their commodities, and were thus badly hit by the general fall in commodity prices during the 1980s. At the same time, most countries experienced considerable structural difficulties caused by mass migration from rural areas into the cities by people wanting to work in the new industries. Asean was expanded to comprise all ten south-east Asian nations by 1998, so that attention shifted to the integration of the new, poor member states into an economic free trade area. By 2005, tariffs had been eliminated or reduced for most goods traded between member states.

((⊕)) SEE WEB LINKS

• The official website of ASEAN.

Asquith, Herbert Henry, 1st Earl of Oxford and Asquith (b. 12 Sept. 1852, d. 15 Feb. 1928). British Prime Minister 1908–16

Early career Born in Morley (Yorkshire), he overcame a difficult childhood, when he was orphaned at the age of 8, to attend Oxford University and become a barrister. A *Liberal, he was elected to parliament in 1886 for East Fife and soon caught general attention as a brilliant debater. He was appointed Foreign Secretary in the Liberal governments of 1892–5, despite having held no previous post in government. He lost some ground in his party during the *South African (Boer) War, as he did not share the sentiments of those Liberals who were opposed to the conflict. However, his defence of free trade when Joseph *Chamberlain raised tariff reform once more raised him to prominence, and he became Chancellor of the Exchequer in 1905 under *Campbell-Bannerman. He had much success in this office: in 1907 he introduced a new system of income tax rates which discriminated between earned and unearned income. In 1908, he introduced old-age pensions.

In office Asquith took over from Campbell-Bannerman as Prime Minister in 1908, and, in the row over *Lloyd George's People's Budget, twice led the party to electoral victory in 1910. This gave him the popular mandate to overcome the resistance of the House of Lords to pass the *Parliament Act (1911). Having won the constitutional battle which had eluded all his Liberal predecessors, he continued to face considerable political challenges, notably rising *trade union power and the growing *suffragette movement. His biggest prewar challenge, however, concerned the question of Irish Home Rule (i.e. Irish autonomy). This measure had been deeply unpopular within Britain, and had greatly contributed to the weakness of the Liberal Party between 1886 and 1905. Asquith eventually steered through a moderate, but still controversial, bill on Home Rule in 1912–13. This was given the Royal Assent on 18 September 1914, though it was never enacted because of the start of World War I. Asquith led Britain into World War I in the face of strong pacifist sentiments within his own party. He was further weakened by his rather lacklustre style of government. A munitions shortage precipitated the formation of a coalition government with the *Conservative Party in May 1915.

Liberal Party decline This failed to revive his popularity, and in December 1916 he resigned rather than accept demands from colleagues that he establish a war committee to coordinate Britain's war effort without chairing it. He was succeeded by Lloyd George, whose bitter rival he became. Asquith lost his seat in 1918, but was returned to parliament in 1920, with the Liberal Party divided between his supporters and those of Lloyd George. He worked with Lloyd George in response to the Conservative endorsement of tariffs, but they were divided again over the *General Strike. Despite his intellectual brilliance and his remarkable legislative record, Asquith's career ended in disappointment owing to his failure to reunite and revive a dying Liberal Party.

Assad, Bashar al- (b. 11 Sept. 1965). President of Syria 2000–

Born in Damascus as the second son of Hafez al-*Assad, he studied medicine at Damascus University, specializing in ophthalmology. Following the death of his older brother in a car accident, he was groomed for his father's succession. He joined the military in 1994, rising to the rank of colonel in 1999. Upon his father's death, he moved cautiously to initiate economic and political reform, but he was careful not to offend entrenched political elites. Assad continued to try and exert pressure on Israel to return the *Golan heights even after being forced to withdraw troops from Lebanon, by forging a close partnership with Iran and supporting *Hezbollah.

Assad, Hafez al- (b. 6 Oct. 1930, d. 16 Oct. 2000). President of Syria 1971–2000

Early career Born in Qardaha into the Alawi sect, he became an officer in the airforce. He joined the *Ba'ath Party in the 1950s, and became part of a group of nationalist officers who organized the successful coup of 1963. He was appointed commander of the airforce, and in 1965 moved up to the leadership of the Ba'ath Party. In the internal struggles of the party, he became a leader of the military faction, which he supported in the 1966 coup. He was rewarded with the appointment of Minister of Defence, though he came to oppose the doctrinaire rigidity of President Jadid. He took power in a coup in 1969, and consolidated his power in another coup in 1971. In 1971 Assad established the People's Council, by which he was elected President

(confirmed in a plebiscite the following month).

In office Together with his bitter rival, *Hussein II of Jordan, and his more erratic ally, *Gaddafi, Assad became one of the most skilful politicians of the Arab world. At home, he secured his regime through the application of ruthless methods against the opposition, which came mainly from *Islamic fundamentalists objecting to his secularism and his Alawi origin. Espousing state *socialism and nationalization, he sought assistance from the Soviet Union in his opposition to US-sponsored Israel, though he was always careful not to become too reliant on the USSR. He sought to increase pressure on Israel by supporting various Islamic groups in Lebanon. He was rigorously opposed to any conciliation with Israel which might have endangered his claim for the *Golan Heights. This explains his hostility to *Sadat's *Camp David Accords, his opposition to *Arafat's *PLO for its moderation, and his rejection of the *Oslo Accords.

Assad's greatest diplomatic achievement came in 1990, when he used his support for the *UN in the *Gulf War quietly to secure his authority in Lebanon, since when he acted as the effective arbiter and guardian of that country. The last years of his reign were characterized by low-level contacts with Israel over the Golan Heights, and an attempt to improve relations with the West. In 1999 he replaced his brother, Rifaat al-Assad, in the office of Vice-President with his son, Bashar al-*Assad, who succeeded him after his death.

Assam

A constituent state of the Republic (Union) of India, to which it is linked by a narrow corridor through the lower Himalayas. Conquered by the British by 1838, it was developed into a plantation economy. A large Hindu and Muslim labour force was imported to this end. Assam suffered from some of the worst ethnic and communal tensions after Indian independence in 1947. These were aggravated by Indian administrative reorganizations aimed at destroying Assam as a single entity, and by the influx of around two million Muslims from neighbouring East Pakistan (now Bangladesh) in the Pakistan Civil War (1970).

Atatürk ('Father of the Turks'), Mustafa Kemal (b. 12 Mar. 1881, d. 10 Nov. 1938). Founder and President of the Republic of Turkey 1923–38

Early career Born in Saloniki, he became an officer in the army of the *Ottoman Empire, and soon began to concern himself with his country's internal divisions and weaknesses. He participated in the *Young Turk Revolution of 1908, and distinguished himself in the defeat of the Italian army at Tripoli (1911), and as the defender of the *Dardanelles in World War I. In 1919, he became army commander in Anatolia. There, at the port of Samson on the Black Sea, in May 1919, he began his campaign to liberate the country from continuing Allied military control and Greek occupation in the west. In the following months Kemal rallied the various movements for Turkish liberation around his leadership, so that on 23 April 1920 he was able to convene a Turkish Grand National Assembly, which elected him Chairman and head of government.

In office His victorious army reclaimed the Greek-occupied areas in Asia Minor in 1922. In 1923 he concluded the Treaty of *Lausanne, whereby Turkey's European possessions were extended, international control of Istanbul ended, and its control over Asia Minor and parts of *Armenia confirmed. He then dissolved the Ottoman Empire and proclaimed the Republic of Turkey. In the fifteen years of his rule, he carried out a remarkable programme of 'Westernization'. The Roman alphabet replaced Arabic writing, the state became exclusively secular, monogamous marriages were introduced, and education was secularized. In foreign policy, he committed his country to international neutrality. He strengthened the new state through reforms in army and administration, but twice failed to introduce a multi-party democracy, as he discovered that this would produce a majority for those parties which opposed his reforms and thus threaten his state. His energy, drive, and authority ensured that his reforms created a lasting foundation for the Turkish state. In 1934 he was given the title 'Atatürk' by the Turkish Grand National Assembly.

Atlantic, Battle of the (1939–45)

The name given by *Churchill to the maritime struggle for supply routes to the UK across the Atlantic and northern European waters during *World War II. It involved aircraft, surface raiders, and mine-laying craft, but it has become principally associated with German U-boats (*Unterseeboote*, submarines). Under Admiral Dönitz, the Germans developed the technique of sending out packs of U-boats, which defied British underwater detection devices by attacking on the surface by night. The first 'wolf-pack' attack sank 32 ships (18–19 October 1940). The development of long-range submarines carried the war to the US coast and the Caribbean, so that by 1942 the Allies lost an average of 96 ships per month.

By the spring of 1943, the Allies had improved their radar systems, and were able to take the battle to the submarines with the help of special escort aircraft carriers and destroyers. They proved immediately effective, leading to the loss of over 40 German submarines in May 1943. As a consequence, on 24 May 1943 Dönitz abandoned the U-boat campaign to destroy as much Allied tonnage as possible. He limited his now fragile submarines to disrupting Allied traffic on the Atlantic, and binding enemy aircraft and navy to protect the convoys. Effectively, the Battle of the Atlantic had been decided. From destroying a maximum tonnage of 8,245,000 with the loss of 85 submarines in 1942, in 1943 the Germans destroyed 3,611,000 at a cost of 287 submarines, until in 1944 the Germans managed to sink a mere 458,000 at a cost of 153 U-boats.

Atlantic Charter (1941)

A declaration of principles of international political conduct that should come into effect after *World War II. It was composed at a meeting between the British Prime Minister, *Churchill, and the US President, *Roosevelt, on the British battleship *Prince of Wales* moored off the Newfoundland coast, at a time when the USA had not yet entered the war. It stipulated freely chosen governments, free trade, freedom of the seas, and disarmament of current aggressor states. It condemned territorial changes made against the wishes of local populations, and proposed the establishment of an international security system. Both Britain and the USA renounced all territorial ambitions. Fourteen other nations fighting the *Axis Powers, including the Soviet Union, declared their support for these principles. The Charter provided an ideological basis for the UN (*UNO) Charter of June 1945. The more immediate aim of the two signatories was to tie the USA more closely to Britain, in the face of *isolationist opposition, by underlining that Britain was fighting *Nazi Germany in the defence of the values that underpinned the USA itself.

atomic bomb, see NUCLEAR BOMB

Attlee, Clement Richard, 1st Earl Attlee (b. 3 Jan. 1883, d. 8 Oct. 1967). British Prime Minister 1945–51

Early career Born in London, he was educated at Haileybury and read history at Oxford. After leaving university, he went to London to study law and qualify as a barrister. During this time, voluntary work at *Toynbee Hall in the poor East End of London encouraged him to become a socialist. He joined the *Fabian Society in 1907, and the *Independent Labour Party in 1908. He also worked as a lecturer at the London School of Economics. In 1914, at the outbreak of war, he joined the army. He served at Gallipoli and on the Western Front, and rose to the rank of major.

On his discharge from the army in 1919, Attlee returned to London, became Mayor of Stepney, and was endorsed as the *Labour Party candidate for Limehouse. He was elected to parliament in 1922, and became Ramsay *MacDonald's Private Secretary. As Under-Secretary at the War Office in the first Labour government (1924), he became noted for his diligence and attention to detail. In 1927, he was appointed to the *Simon Commission of Inquiry examining British rule in India. Owing to his involvement in this, he was not immediately made a minister when Labour returned to power in 1929, although he became Chancellor of the Duchy of Lancaster in 1930, and Postmaster-General in 1931.

Attlee opposed MacDonald's formation of the *National Government of 1931, and became *Lansbury's deputy in a severely shrunken parliamentary party. In 1935, on the retirement of Lansbury, he was elected Labour leader. From May 1940 he held high office in the coalition government of Winston *Churchill as Lord Privy Seal, Deputy Prime Minister (from 1942), and Dominions Secretary. He chaired many crucial Cabinet committees, and gained a reputation as a skilful manager of disagreements and disputes among colleagues. This experience became vital after 1945, when Labour won the general election, as he had to lead a Cabinet of diverse talents and conflicting opinions.

Prime Minister In foreign policy, *decolonization began with the granting of independence to India, Pakistan, and Burma in 1947. British withdrawal from *Palestine allowed the creation of Israel in 1948. At the same time, Attlee's attempts to maintain friendly relations with the Soviet Union were increasingly unsuccessful.

It is the achievement of his government in domestic affairs for which he is best remembered. Despite a war debt of $20,000 million, the government implemented the proposals of the *Beveridge Report, and pursued the economic policies advocated by *Keynes. It passed the National Insurance Act of 1946, and introduced a *National Health Service. Nationalization was expanded to include the Bank of England, along with key industries such as gas, coal, electricity, and railways. Full employment was rigorously pursued, whilst the government relocated industries and planned new towns. Attlee's generous policies of public spending at a time of record public debt could only succeed through maintaining tight control over public consumption. The maintenance of wartime rationing, and the perceived slowness of his government's policies of house-building, resulted in his government's increasing unpopularity. At the 1950 general election Labour gained a majority of only five seats. The government soon faced fierce opposition over its austerity programme, while entry into the *Korean War necessitated the diversion of financial resources to rearmament. In October 1951, Labour lost the election to the *Conservative Party. Attlee was suffering from poor health by this time, but he remained leader of the opposition until 1955, when he went to the House of Lords.

An unassuming, uncharismatic, and deeply uninspiring figure, he was described as a 'sheep in sheep's clothing' (Churchill). However, his prominence within the Labour Party arose from his very efficiency and modesty; during the 1930s, in a deeply divided party, he was seen by neither faction as a threat and he was able to communicate with all of them. In this sense, the success of his governments resulted from his ability to coordinate his ministers, many of whom were as diverse as they were brilliant. He resigned as leader of the Labour Party in 1955, having transformed it into a stable pillar of the British political system.

BEVAN, ANEURIN; BEVIN, ERNEST; MORRISON, HERBERT

August coup (19–21 Aug. 1991)
A coup attempt against the reformist Soviet leader *Gorbachev. It was led by people who had personally benefited from the Gorbachev regime, such as Vice-President *Yanaev and the Minister of Defence, Yazov, but who wanted to exploit the widespread resentment in the army and the state bureaucracy. They were opposed to many of Gorbachev's reforms, in particular the impending restructuring of the Soviet Union in a manner that would have weakened central control in favour of the national republics. They imprisoned Gorbachev in his holiday cottage in the *Crimea, with Yanaev taking over in Gorbachev's stead. A defiant *Yeltsin immediately transformed the Russian parliament, the White House, into a centre of resistance, and declared the new leaders' orders void.

The coup failed owing to popular support for Yeltsin, who was also backed by many loyal sections of the army. Yeltsin was also helped by international support, especially from the USA, whose *CIA was able to record and decode the entire communication between the coup leaders. Instead of halting reform, the coup drastically accelerated it: the Baltic States (Estonia, Latvia, and Lithuania), which had been occupied by Soviet troops during the coup, immediately declared their full independence, followed within days by virtually every other non-Russian constituent republic of the USSR. Moreover, the radical Yeltsin emerged as a hero, who had pushed the more hesitant Gorbachev into the sidelines.

Aung San Suu Kyi Daw (b. 19 June 1945). Burmese opposition leader

The daughter of Burmese national hero *Aung San, she studied at Rangoon, New Delhi, and Oxford. She held a number of posts in the *UN, and in 1972 married a British academic, Michael Aris, settling down to a quiet private life. In 1988 she returned to Burma to care for her dying mother, and became involved in the turbulence of 1988, with its strong pro-democracy demonstrations. She was elected Secretary-General of the new National League for Democracy, which she directed to become a mass movement committed to non-violent change. She was arrested in 1989 and put under house arrest, though her party won the 1990 elections in a landslide victory. She was awarded the *Nobel Peace Prize in 1991, upon the nomination of V. *Havel. Released from her confinement on 10 July 1995, her actions continued to be closely circumscribed by the military regime. She was largely forbidden to move outside the capital, Rangoon. Her contacts with the opposition throughout Myanmar (as Burma was now called) and with the outside world were severely restricted (in 1998, she was thus prevented from visiting her dying husband in Oxford). From 2000, she was almost permanently under house arrest, though she remained the spiritual leader of the opposition.
MYANMAR

Aung San U (b. 13 Feb. 1915, d. 19 July 1947). Burmese nationalist leader

Born in Natmauk, he became a student at Rangoon University in 1935, where he became involved in politics as the organizer of the 1936 student strike. Leader of the All Burma Students' Union (1936–8), he joined the nationalist movement Dobama Asiayone, and was its secretary (1938–40). He was also the general secretary of the Communist Party of Burma (1939–40). He went into exile in 1940. After a period of military training under the Japanese, he returned to Burma in 1942.

He became leader of the Japanese-sponsored Burma National Army, which actively assisted the Japanese advance through the country. He served as a minister in the Ba Maw puppet government, but became increasingly disillusioned, and defected to the Allies in the closing weeks of World War II. He formed the Anti-Fascist People's Freedom League in 1944 and led a postwar Council of Ministers. The architect of Burmese independence, and of its new constitution, he was denied the honour of leading the country into independence in 1948. He was assassinated together with five other members of his interim government by his political rival, U Saw. In 1988, his struggle for freedom and justice was taken up by his daughter, *Aung San Suu Kyi.
MYANMAR

Auschwitz

The largest *concentration camp ever, its main sites consisted of the labour camp Auschwitz and the extermination camp Auschwitz-Birkenau in occupied Poland. Owing to its proximity to the industrial areas of Upper *Silesia, a forced labour camp was established in June 1940. In spring 1941 the chemical conglomerate IG Farben set up a large factory there to benefit from the camp's cheap labour. IG Farben produced, among other things, the poisonous gas Cyclon B, whose effectiveness was 'tested' for the first time in the new camp at Birkenau on 900 Soviet prisoners of war in September 1941. Subsequently, mostly Jews, but also homosexuals, gypsies, and other groups which the German *Nazis wanted to exterminate, were murdered there before the camp's liberation in January 1945.

Upon their arrival from all over German-occupied Europe, the prisoners were sorted according to their fitness for work. The majority, mostly women, children, and the elderly, were sent to the gas chambers for immediate extermination, while around 20 per cent were sent to the labour camps until they, too, were too weak to work and were exterminated. A total of 405,000 people were admitted to the labour camps, of whom more than 260,000 died. Those sent to the extermination camps were never registered, but are estimated to have been between one and a half and two million people. The camp was vacated and destroyed by the Germans on 1 November 1944. Around 60,000 prisoners were sent on a march westwards and large numbers died of illness and exhaustion. On 27 January 1945, the advancing Russians liberated around 5,000 frail inmates who had been left behind.

Australia

Overview A country whose society, economy, and politics until the 1960s were dominated first by its closeness to Britain as part of the *British Empire and *Commonwealth. Thereafter, Australians began to recognize more clearly the country's geopolitical closeness to Asia. Australia comprises the erstwhile British colonies of New South Wales (which became self-governing in 1855), Victoria (1855), Tasmania (1856), South Australia (1856, including the *Northern Territories), Queensland (1859), and Western Australia (1890). These former colonies became states within a federation as the Commonwealth of Australia in 1901, created by a British Act of Parliament.

Since then, national politics have been characterized by two developments. First, the federal government, supported by a House of Representatives and a Senate, initially had relatively few powers compared with the individual states. Federal institutions gradually increased their role against that of the individual states when they assumed responsibility for the national crises of the Great *Depression and the two World Wars. Second, the federal government was originally restricted by the role of the British government, which remained responsible for Australia's defence and foreign policies. Australia received its formal independence over all policy matters through the Statute of *Westminster in 1931, but it pursued an independent foreign policy only from 1942. In that year, the defeat of the British in *Singapore and the Japanese invasion of Dutch East India (Indonesia) demonstrated that its security was bound up with the USA, not with the UK.

The country's electoral system, modelled mainly on that of Britain, has produced a stable governmental system. At the same time, the increase of federal powers, which was sometimes achieved at great political cost, led to a considerable flux within the national party system. The Australian *Labor Party was significantly weakened by splits to form the *National Labor Party in 1917, and the *Democratic Labor Party in 1957. It also suffered from the defections of many of its most effective leaders, such as *Hughes, *Lyons, and *Lang. Meanwhile, despite the relative stability of the Country Party (*National Party since 1982), the main

conservative opposition to Labor has had to regroup three times, forming the *Nationalist Party (1917–32), the *United Australia Party (1932–44), and the *Liberal Party (since 1945). Ultimately, Labor's splits proved to be more debilitating than conservative regroupings, so that for most of the century federal government was held by conservatives (1901–8, 1909–10, 1913–14, 1917–29, 1932–41, 1949–72, 1975–83, 1996–).

The impact of both World Wars (1914–45) As part of the British Empire, Australia made a significant contribution towards the Allied victory in World War I. Yet as the need for troops in Europe increased, the pressing question of compulsory military service overseas caused deep divisions within society, and was rejected twice in a referendum. Owing to the organizational talents of *Monash, the returning troops were decommissioned without great disruption. After the war, an economic boom coupled with significant levels of immigration caused general optimism which led many to believe that Australia would become an immigrant country second only to the US in population, power, and wealth. These hopes were shattered by the Great Depression, when *Scullin's inability to control his own Labor Party's response exacerbated general discontent, expressed in the rise of Communist and right-wing paramilitary groups, such as the *New Guard. Calm was restored by the more disciplined and stable Lyons government, which dominated Australian politics during the 1930s.

Led by *Menzies and *Curtin (from 1941), Australia mobilized all its economic and manpower resources to support the British during World War II. However, Australian leaders were soon disappointed and frustrated by the British use of these troops without keeping them informed, let alone consulted. They withdrew some of the troops stationed in Egypt to defend Australia against a possible Japanese attack, though the possibility of such an attack was significantly exaggerated by Curtin in order to win approval for his drastic war measures.

The post-war period (1945–96) After the war, Australia's new relationship with the USA was underlined by the conclusion of a military alliance (*ANZUS), as well as Australian participation in the *Korean and *Vietnam Wars. Under *Calwell and *Chifley, there began a slight shift in the traditional immigration policy in favour of immigration from southern and eastern Europe. It was the Menzies governments from 1949 that laid the foundations of the

Table 1. **Australian Prime Ministers Since 1901**

Edmund *Barton	1901–3	Robert *Menzies	1939–41
Alfred *Deakin	1903–4	Arthur W. Fadden	1941
John *Watson	1904	John *Curtin	1941–5
George *Reid	1904–5	Francis M. Forde	1945
Alfred *Deakin	1905–8	Ben *Chifley	1945–9
Andrew *Fisher	1908–9	Robert *Menzies	1949–66
Alfred *Deakin	1909–10	Harold Holt	1966–7
Andrew *Fisher	1910–13	John McEwen	1967–8
Joseph Cook	1913–14	John Gorton	1968–71
Andrew *Fisher	1914–15	William McMahon	1971–2
William Morris *Hughes	1915–23	Gough *Whitlam	1972–5
Stanley Bruce	1923–9	Malcolm *Fraser	1975–83
James Henry *Scullin	1929–31	Robert *Hawke	1983–91
Joseph Aloysius *Lyons	1932–9	Paul *Keating	1991–6
		John Winston *Howard	1996–

modern Australian state through the expansion of university and secondary school education, and the creation of a system of social security.

The years 1965–75 formed a decisive watershed in politics, society, and government. Changing attitudes to *Aborigines and Torres Strait Islanders led to the recognition that these formed an integral part of Australia's heritage and society, and this was manifested in their acquisition of full Australian citizenship in 1967. Furthermore, attitudes towards immigration changed, leading to the scrapping of the racist *White Australia Policy and an influx of Asian immigrants. Finally, Australia's traditional trading patterns, whereby most of its imports came from the UK as finished goods, while most of its exports went to the UK as primary (agricultural and mineral) goods, ended with Britain's entry into the EEC. As Australian goods were subsequently liable to EEC import duties, it focused its trading activities on its Asian neighbours.

All these factors sparked off a gradual growth of Australian *nationalism away from Britain. This was confirmed by the dismissal of *Whitlam in 1975, which called into question the role of the Governor-General representing the head of state, the British monarch (Queen *Elizabeth II). In contrast to *Fraser, who lost support because of the economic recession up to 1982, *Hawke and *Keating proved particularly adept at formulating this change in consciousness, vociferously defending Australian interests on the world stage.

Contemporary politics (since 1996)

On 2 March 1996 Australians rejected Keating's more flamboyant style in favour of *Howard's more sturdy focus on tackling the country's problems of youth unemployment and excessive social spending. As Australia celebrated its centenary, it thus experienced a sustained period of economic growth, which became a hallmark of the Howard era.

Under John Howard, economic liberalization was coupled with rigid policies on immigration and domestic security, with Australia adopting among the toughest anti-immigration and anti-terrorism laws. Australian troops became more active overseas, leading the *UN mission to create the state of Timor Leste. Australia also deployed troops in Afghanistan (from 2002) and Iraq (from 2003). The challenges of terror attacks in Asia and worldwide after *September 11 encouraged Australia to pursue an assertive regional policy, pushing its claims for hegemony in the south-east Pacific region. Australia provided unprecedented assistance to its neighbours, pledging record aid to areas devastated by the 2004 *tsunami, and helping stabilize the Solomon Islands, Papua New Guinea and Timor Leste through co-operation agreements.

((())) SEE WEB LINKS

• The official website of the Australian government.
• Sponsored by Charles Sturt University, this site contains weblinks on Australian topics.

Austria

A small German-speaking Alpine republic which struggled to find its own national identity before 1945, and which since then has been characterized by a strong inclination towards consensus-oriented politics.

The interwar years (1918–38) The Austria that emerged after World War I contained only around 14 per cent of the territory of *Austria-Hungary. Chancellor Renner (1918–20) sought to stabilize the new republic through social legislation, while at the same time expressing the wish for an eventual link (*Anschluss) with Germany. Despite this, social unrest was a feature almost from the beginning. The state was weak, mainly as a result of a heavy debt burden from the war. It was thus unable to cope with the impact of the demobilization of troops, which resulted in large-scale social dislocation. Matters were made worse by the loss of important economic areas such as the industrial Czech lands, and of access to the sea through *Trieste. An entirely new domestic economic structure had thus to be created.

The federal Constitution became effective on 1 October 1920. In that year, the reformist Social Democratic Party of Austria (SPÖ) lost power to a bourgeois party coalition. Backed by a conservative, inefficient bureaucracy, the government failed to stabilize the economy, whose collapse was prevented by a series of credit agreements, mainly with the US. At the end of a period of international economic recovery, industrial production was still only at 80 per cent of the prewar levels, while unemployment remained at 25 per cent. In view of the economic and social difficulties, political differences became increasingly marked during the 1920s, and led to an upsurge in political violence between supporters of the Communists, Social Democrats, and *Fascist organizations. The collapse of Austria's largest bank in the wake of the Great *Depression, the Östereichische Creditanstalt für Handel und Gewerbe (May 1931), appeared to many a final admission of defeat for the republic. In response, changes to the Constitution increased the executive powers of the President.

Authoritarianism and Nazism (1930s–1945) Political polarization continued unabated and in 1932 the local and state elections were won by the Austrian *Nazi Party, which was under the tutelage of its German sister party. In response, *Dollfuss dissolved parliament and instituted a dictatorial regime, based on a People's Front. His Fascist policies (authoritarianism, conservative moral values, *corporatism rather than democracy), which led to a brief civil war against the socialists in early 1934, were continued by *Schuschnigg, who was increasingly unable to resist domestic and German pressure towards union with Germany after *Mussolini had accepted it in principle in 1936.

Under *Seyss-Inquart, Austria was finally 'invited' to join in a union with Germany, and on 12 March 1938, German troops marched into Austria to consummate the *Anschluss. Hitler was jubilantly received into his native country, while membership figures for the Nazi Party, which surpassed those in Germany, suggest that support for the *Third Reich was, indeed, very high. The levels of *anti-Semitism had also been remarkably similar in both countries. As World War II dragged on, and Austrian cities were bombarded, while Austria itself was increasingly run by a German administrative elite, many people became disillusioned, and resistance movements began to form.

Allied occupation (1945–55) In 1945, Austria was occupied in four zones by the *Allies (USSR, USA, UK, and France), who encouraged the readoption of the 1920 Constitution under the leadership of Renner, and the formation of political parties. Renner had persuaded the Allies to regard Austria not as a perpetrator, but as Nazism's 'first victim', a perception that became a founding myth for post-war Austria. On 25 November 1945 the first parliament was elected, which resulted in an absolute majority for the conservative Austrian People's Party (Österreichische Volkspartei, ÖVP). Through large-scale nationalizations of heavy industry, banks, and energy suppliers, and through *Marshall Aid, the economy was soon on the path to recovery. In 1955, the country finally received full sovereignty through the conclusion of the *Austrian State Treaty.

Consensus politics (1950s–80s) During the 1950s and 1960s, the government was made up of the country's two largest parties, the the ÖVP and SPÖ. This period inaugurated the system of 'Proporz' (proportionality), whereby important positions in administration and public life were awarded to members of both parties, a harmonious arrangement that stood in stark contrast to the polarization of the inter-war period.

Austria was governed by the SPÖ under *Kreisky during the 1970s, who carried out an ambitious programme of social and penal reform. The SPÖ lost its absolute majority in 1983, and henceforward governed with the *Liberal Party (FPÖ). In 1986, the latter elected Jörg Haider to the leadership, who transformed the party into a neo-Fascist party. The SPÖ responded by forming a new coalition with the ÖVP. The two established political parties faced the challenge not only of a blossoming FPÖ, which received over 20 per cent of the vote in the 1994 and 1995 elections, but also of the fragmentation of the political system through the formation of two new small parties, the Greens and the Liberal Forum.

EU membership (since 1995) In an attempt to revive the country's stagnant economy, in a referendum two-thirds approved membership of the European Union (effective from 1 January 1995). In 2000 the FPÖ won further seats, so that with 52 seats in parliament it was as strong as the ÖVP, against 65 seats for the SPÖ. Wolfgang *Schüssel thus formed a coalition with the FPÖ, which caused international consternation, and led to the imposition of temporary diplomatic sanctions within the EU. This was an unprecedented step designed to ensure the maintenance of the EU's values on human rights. In domestic politics, the government instituted a tax reform to stimulate demand, which encouraged further economic growth at a time of rising demand for exports. As a result, GDP increased by over 4 per cent in 2000, with unemployment declining to below 6 per cent.

Contemporary politics (since 2000)
In fact, despite the xenophobic outbursts of the FPÖ, Austria was one of the great winners of the EU's eastern enlargement, as its GDP increased by around 1 per cent, attributable solely to growing trade with the prospective and new member states from 2000. New elections in 2002 confirmed the coalition, with Schüssel leading the ÖVP to one of its best election results. In subsequent years, the FPÖ split, with Jörg Haider leaving the party and creating a new party, the BZÖ. Following the 2006 elections, a grand coalition between SPÖ and ÖVP was formed again, with Alfred Gusenbauer becoming the new Chancellor.

The new coalition showed that the FPÖ had not managed to undermine the system of proportionality completely. The popularity of the populist right resulted from deep unease about migration and EU expansion to the east. At the same time, Austria was the EU's greatest winner from the EU's eastern enlargement in 2004, as its GDP increased by over 1 per cent every year solely as a result of Austrian businesses capitalizing on new markets. Not least for this reason, Austria had developed into a very successful economy, with the Austrian economy even surpassing that of its large northern rival, Germany.

Austria-Hungary

A dual monarchy since 1867, the two countries retained complete control over their own internal affairs, but were linked by a ministerial council responsible for common affairs (e.g. defence). They were ruled by the house of Habsburg, whose head was simultaneously Emperor of Austria and King of Hungary (*Francis Ferdinand I, r. 1848–1916; Charles I, r. 1916–18).

The internal set-up was complicated by the vast size of the two kingdoms, which included a host of distinctive nationalities which became increasingly assertive. This development was not addressed in either country, since it was held that even small concessions to *nationalist movements would encourage them and lead to the disintegration of the Empire. In the Austrian part, legislators hoped to compensate for the growth of nationalism through a liberal economic and social policy designed to achieve economic prosperity and satisfaction with the state. In fact, however, this added social polarization to national fragmentation, and led to the eclipse of the Liberals by the Social Democrats and the Christian Socialists under the *anti-Semitic Karl Lueger. Hungary was largely unaffected by structural economic change before 1914, so that the social polarization did not occur. However, whereas the problem of nationality was simply not addressed in Austria, it was made much worse in Hungary through a policy of 'Magyarization', i.e. enforcing Hungarian culture and language upon other peoples.

Both parts, therefore, had developed a political and constitutional paralysis, compounded by administrative chaos. World War I proved to be an illusory escape, and the Empire imploded in 1918. True to US President *Wilson's *Fourteen Points, an attempt was made in the Treaty of *St Germain to enable each nationality to become a viable nation-state. This led to the emergence of *Czechoslovakia, Romania, and ultimately Yugoslavia. In addition, many Poles were included in Poland, while the Trentino and *South Tirol became part of Italy. The rump states of Hungary and Austria survived, though their small size encouraged large-scale resentment and the rise of *Fascism in subsequent years.
MAP 1

Austrian State Treaty (15 May 1955)

The treaty, signed by the Soviet Union, the USA, Britain, and France, formally recognized the second Austrian Republic and agreed that occupation forces would withdraw within five months. Unlike in Germany, whose eastern half the Soviet Union had integrated into its Communist sphere of influence, the USSR agreed to vacate its Austrian zone of occupation, in return for *reparation payments, and Austrian adherence to a strict policy of neutrality.

Aventine Secession (Italy; 1924–6)

A term derived from the withdrawal of the Roman population to the Aventine Hills in protest against the Patriciate in 493 BC. It denotes the anti-Fascist parliamentary opposition to *Mussolini of around 100 parliamentary deputies who left their seats on 27 June 1924 in protest against the Fascist assassination of *Matteotti. However, the parliamentarians failed to persuade the King to take action against Mussolini, who responded by annulling their seats, forcing their leaders to emigrate, and outlawing the participating opposition parties.

Ávila Camacho, Manuel (b. 24 Apr. 1897, d. 14 Oct. 1955). President of Mexico 1940–6
Born in Teziutlán, Puebla, his election to the presidency was determined by the outgoing President *Cárdenas, under whom he had served as Minister of War. More moderate than his predecessor, his land reforms favoured less the *ejidos* (communally owned farms) than individual families. He supported the moderate working classes through the establishment of a social security system which, though embryonic at first, was steadily extended to the industrial labour sector by subsequent presidents. Although he was sympathetic to the *Allies, his suspicion of the USA, which at first prevented Mexican entry into World War II, was only overcome after the repeated German sinking of Mexican ships in 1942.

Awami ('People's') League
A political party in East Pakistan (Bangladesh) founded in 1949 by Husain Shahid Suhrawardy. Originally a consciously Muslim party, the Awami League (AL) was soon opened to non-Muslims in an effort to heal the religious divisions bedevilling the country. It became the dominant party in East Pakistan, where it defeated the Muslim League in the 1954 elections. Under the leadership of *Mujibur Rahman since Suhrawardy's death in 1963, it won the 1970 elections with an overwhelming victory. As the main instigator of Bangladeshi independence, the AL dominated politics until the 1975 coup. Suffering subsequent intermittent bans, the party nevertheless continued as the main opposition party (largely to the Bangladesh Nationalist Party, BNP), under its leader, Sheikh Hasina Wajid, the daughter of Mujibur Rahman. The AL won the 1996 elections, and, with Sheikh Hasina Wajid as Prime Minister, it improved relations with India and introduced a number of austerity measures demanded by the *World Bank. These measures met bitter popular protest organized by the BNP, and even before the 2001 elections the government was practically unable to govern. It suffered a devastating election defeat in the 2001 general elections, but it continued its opposition to the BNP, boycotting parliament again in 2005–6.

((⊕)) SEE WEB LINKS
• The official website of the Awami League.

Awolowo, Obafemi (b. 6 Mar. 1909, d. 9 May 1987). Nigerian statesman
Son of a peasant of the *Yoruba people, Awolowo was a newspaper reporter and trade union leader until he went to London, where he qualified as a lawyer in 1944. During this time, he wrote *Path to Nigerian Freedom*, in which he argued for internal autonomy of each Nigerian tribe within a loose federation. Back in Nigeria, he founded the Action Group to preserve Yoruba culture in 1951. He became Premier of Western Nigeria in 1954. In 1963 he was imprisoned for allegedly conspiring to overthrow the federal government, but he was released in 1966 by *Gowon, whom he supported in the *Biafran War against the Ibo people. In 1978 he founded the Nigerian Unity Party and stood for President. He was defeated and his party banned in 1983.

Axis Powers
A term used from October 1936 to describe cooperation between the *Fascist regimes of Italy and Germany, and the creation of a Berlin–Rome Axis 'round which all European states can also assemble'. Japan joined a month later, on signing the *Anti-Comintern Pact. A full military and political alliance between Italy and Germany (the 'Pact of Steel') followed in 1939, and this became a **Tripartite Pact** in 1940. After Italy's entry into World War II in 1940, the term was applied to those countries that joined the Tripartite Pact and supported Germany in the war. Hungary, Romania, and the puppet state of *Slovakia joined the Pact in November 1940, while Bulgaria joined in March 1941. Yugoslavia's entry on 25 March 1941 did not prevent its invasion by Italian and German troops on 6 April 1941, though membership was continued by the 'Independent State of *Croatia'.

ayatollah
A religious leader among the Imamis, the major tradition of the Muslim *Shi'ites. As exemplified by *Khomeini, the holding of this title became almost a prerequisite for leading the theocratic state established in the 1979 Iranian Revolution. (Khomeini's successor to the political leadership, *Rafsanjani, was not an ayatollah himself, but had been a pupil of Khomeini.)

Ayub Khan, Muhammad (b. 14 May 1907, d. 19 Apr. 1974). President of Pakistan 1958–69

Early career Born in Rehana (North-West Frontier Provinces) as the son of a junior officer in the British Indian Army, he went to study at Aligarh University, and then joined the army. After spending a couple of years at the Royal Military College, Sandhurst, he was commissioned into the British Indian Army in 1928. After distinguished service in World War II, he was given command of the military forces of East Bengal (later Bangladesh) in 1948 and in 1950 was appointed to become the first Commander-in-Chief of the Pakistan army. He found it difficult to gain political support to carry out the military reforms he considered necessary. As Minister of Defence 1954–6 he became further disillusioned with the political process, and concluded that Pakistan was not ripe for a full working democracy.

In office On 7 October 1958 he forced the President, Iskandar Mirza, to impose order through martial law, with himself taking effective power as Chief Martial Law Administrator. He then assumed the presidency shortly afterwards, on 27 October 1958. With considerable public support, he instituted a system of 'basic democracies' through the 1962 constitution, whereby political activity was encouraged at the local level through the creation of union councils in the villages, while democracy in national politics was largely abolished. Thriving on large amounts of US aid, the stability which he created for a decade spurred economic growth. However, his popularity was shattered by the country's failure to win a costly *Indo-Pakistan War in 1965. Increasingly confronted by demonstrations and an opposition movement led by Zulfikar *Bhutto, and weakened by personal illness, he was persuaded by the military to resign in favour of General *Yahya Khan.

Azaña y Díaz, Manuel (b. 10 Jan. 1880, d. 3 Nov. 1940). President of Spain 1936–9
Born in Alcalá de Henares, he graduated with a doctorate in jurisprudence from the University of Madrid in 1900. After working in the Ministry of Justice, Azaña turned to writing and journalism. In 1925 he created Acción Republicana in opposition to *Primo de Rivera, and in 1930 became co-sponsor of the Pact of San Sebastian to abolish the monarchy. He emerged as Minister of War in the newly formed Republican government of 1931, and within days reformed the military by releasing more than half of the officer corps from their duty. He was also a chief architect of the removal of the Roman

*Catholic Church's control of health, education, and welfare. As Prime Minister (1931–3) he granted Catalan autonomy. He was briefly Prime Minister after the *Popular Front's victory in 1936, and became President on 10 May 1936. He failed, however, to reconcile the various factions of the government, and was unable to rally greater international support for the Republican forces. He also had an uneasy relationship with his Prime Ministers, *Largo Caballero and *Negrín. He resigned after fleeing to Paris, on 5 February 1939. He died in poverty in Bordeaux.

Azerbaijan
A Caucasian country which was steadily conquered by both Russian and Persian armies in the eighteenth and nineteenth centuries. During the

*Russian Civil War, the northern part declared its independence on 28 May 1918 as an Islamic republic. However, by 1920 it was reconquered by Russia, and in 1922 it became a constituent part of the Soviet Union as part of the Transcaucasian Socialist Soviet Republic. In 1936 the Transcaucasian Republic split, with Armenia, Azerbaijan, and Georgia becoming separate republics within the USSR. Since then, there has been constant friction between the Islamic majority and the Christian Armenian minority in **Nagorno Karabakh**, which wanted to be part of Armenia. In the wake of the collapse of central Soviet authority, this erupted into a violent conflict which was only interrupted in 1994–5 by a ceasefire between Armenians and Azerbaijanis. The ceasefire continued to hold into the new millennium, with Armenia occupying Nagorno Karabakh. More than one million Azerbaijanis were displaced as a result of the hostilities. Azerbaijan has been independent since 20 October 1991, and with the Baku oilfields it controls probably the world's greatest single oil reserves. Large-scale corruption, organized crime, and a weak government led to a striking inability to profit from its potential mineral wealth. Azerbaijan was ruled, throughout the 1990s, by Heydar Aliyev. He was succeeded, in 2003, by his son Ilham, who won subsequent elections against a fragmented opposition, and, allegedly, with the help of electoral fraud.

Azhari, Ismail al- (b. 1902, d. 26 Aug. 1969). Prime Minister of Sudan 1953–6, head of state 1964–9

Born in Omdurman, he graduated from Gordon College to become a mathematics teacher. He joined the Graduates Congress, which campaigned for independence, in 1938, and became its President in 1940. In 1942, he broke away to found the more militant Ashigga Party, which campaigned for the end of British colonial rule, in association with Egypt. Leader of the National Unionist Party since 1952, he became Prime Minister in 1953. Rising nationalist feeling against union with Egypt persuaded him to seek independence, so that on 1 January 1956 he led Sudan into independence on its own. He was forced to resign after a split in his party in 1956, when he became leader of the opposition. He was elected to head a civilian government in 1966, but was deposed by *Nimieri's coup in 1969.

Azikiwe, Benjamin Nnamdi (b. 16 Nov. 1904, d. 11 May 1996). President of Nigeria 1963–6

Born in Zungeru, he studied in the USA (Howard University, Lincoln University, Pennsylvania University), and became a successful newspaper editor/owner both in Nigeria and the Gold Coast (now Ghana). In 1944 he founded the nationalist National Council of Nigeria and the Cameroons (NCNC). His newspaper articles in the *West African Pilot*, signed Zik, exerted a powerful influence throughout the 1940s and 1950s on emerging Nigerian *nationalism. He led his party in the constitutional conferences leading up to independence, and was Premier of the Eastern Region, 1954–9. Azikiwe was the country's first indigenous Governor-General upon independence in 1960, and became its President when it became a Republic. He was deposed in 1966 by a military coup, which ousted civilian government. Sympathetic to the Ibo cause, he supported the attempt to create an independent state of *Biafra, but sought a compromise when it became clear that the federal forces were winning the war. He became leader of the Nigerian People's Party and was unsuccessful in a bid for the presidency in 1979.

Aznar López, José María (b. 25 Feb. 1953). Prime Minister of Spain 1996–2004

Early career Born in Madrid, in his youth he became associated with the anti-democratic and anti-royalist elements within the *Falange. He obtained a law degree at the University of Madrid in 1975, and became a government tax inspector. In 1975 he joined the right-wing Popular Alliance (AP), a party composed primarily of former supporters of *Franco. He was elected to parliament in 1982, and was the AP's general secretary 1982–7. He was regional president of Castille and León, until in 1989 he became Vice-President of the newly named Partido Popular (*Popular Party, PP). As President of the PP from 1990, he was initially on the right of the party, but soon realized that he needed to move to the centre ground, then occupied by the popular *González. He thus accepted many of his opponent's past policies, and focused instead on the need to reduce government corruption and provide it with a new impetus.

In office On this platform he won the 1996 election, albeit with a slender majority. Although possessing less charisma than his more flamboyant predecessor, Aznar turned his apparent rectitude and competence into major political assets. He helped his party to its best electoral performance ever in the 2000 elections. Aznar was committed to resolving the issue of *Basque separatism by tough action against the terrorist organization ETA, while outlawing its political wing, Herri Batasuna. He also opposed greater regional autonomy for Spain's regions, notably Catalonia. Perhaps his most important legacy in domestic politics consisted of continued strong economic growth, as Spain grew by over 3 per cent per year (1996–2004), while unemployment fell from 18 to 11 per cent. In foreign policy, Aznar entered a close relationship with George W. *Bush and Tony *Blair. In 2003, Spain became Bush's most important European ally next to Britain and Poland in the *Iraq War, with Spain sending over 1,000 troops to the defeated Iraq.

With the significant exception of his foreign policy, Aznar was extremely popular, but he threw his party into disarray when he announced that he would not seek a third term in office. Following the *Madrid Bombings, in which his government was duplicitous about the perpetrators, Aznar was unable to prevent the defeat of his party in the 2004 elections.

B

Baader-Meinhof group

An *anarchist West German terrorist movement, founded by Andreas Baader (b. 1943, d. 1977) and Ulrike Meinhof (b. 1934, d. 1976), which aimed to show that terrorist attacks would reveal the true repressive nature of the West German state. Despite the imprisonment of its leaders by 1975, the movement continued its actions through the abduction of the *CDU leader of Berlin in 1975, and a series of killings in 1977, including the murder of the Federal Chief Prosecutor, Siegfried Buback. A turning point came in the hijacking of a German civilian aircraft to Mogadishu on 13 October 1977. This ended in disaster for the terrorists as a German special unit freed the hostages on 18 October. Baader and two other terrorist leaders were found shot in their cells, presumably having committed suicide, around seventeen months after Meinhof had taken her own life.

Ba'athism

In 1943 the Ba'ath Arab Socialist (Renaissance) Party was founded by Michel *Aflaq and Salah al-Din al-Bitar in Syria. It regarded all current borders as random results of Western *imperialism and had Arab unity as its central goal. This *nationalism was combined with a commitment to *socialism. Its ideological influence climaxed perhaps during the years 1958–61, when Egypt and Syria united to form the *United Arab Republic. The failure of this experiment shows that Ba'athism has been unable to finally overcome the national egotism of individual Arab states. None the less, the Ba'ath rhetoric of *pan-Arabism has remained highly influential, particularly in Syria and Iraq, where the Ba'ath Party is still the party of government.

Babangida, Ibrahim Gbadamosi (b. 17
Aug. 1941). President of Nigeria 1985–93
Of the Fulani people. Babangida was born in Minna, and received secondary school education. After military training in India, the UK, and the USA, he rose through the ranks of the Nigerian army to become Chief of Staff in 1984. He became President after initiating a successful military coup on 27 August 1985. He tried to achieve political stability through establishing constitutional change to suit the various ethnic groupings, but he was unable to accept the consequence of this process,

when he lost the presidential elections to *Abiola. Annulling the elections, he set up a government under Adegunle Oladeinde Shonekan, until both were forced into exile by another military coup. In 2006, Babangida announced his candidacy for the 2007 Presidential elections, but he withdrew when he was not supported by the ruling People's Democratic Party.

Bachelet Jeria, Michelle (b. 29 Sept
1951). President of Chile 2006–
The daughter of a socialist critic of Pinochet, she grew up in exile in the German Democratic Republic, returning to Chile in 1979. She completed her medical degree, and joined the socialist party. She joined the Ministry of Health and in 2000 was appointed Minister for Health in the *Lagos government. She then became Defence Minister, where she had to deal carefully with a military stung by its recent loss of power. She won the 2005 elections, and became Latin America's first woman president. During her first year of office she had to cope with a series of difficulties, including the resignation of several government ministers following public protests at government inefficiency.

Baden-Powell, Robert Stephenson Smyth, 1st Baron Baden-Powell of Gilwell (b. 22 Feb. 1857, d. 8 Jan. 1941).
Founder of the Boy Scout and Girl Guide movements
Born in London, he was educated at Charterhouse, and joined the army in 1876. He became internationally famous for organizing the defence of **Mafeking** in the *South African War, when it was besieged for 217 days (October 1899–May 1900). During this time he developed ideas about the value of discipline, self-respect, and fitness, and the importance of public service. He experimented with these ideas through running a boys' camp in Poole, Dorset, in 1907. This, and the publication of his *Scouting for Boys* in 1908, proved so popular that he established the **Boy Scouts** in 1908, and the **Girl Guides** in 1909. The two movements spread rapidly on a national and international scale, as they emerged at a time of general concern within industrialized countries about the poor health of the young growing up in large, unhealthy, and seemingly corrupt cities. As Chief Scout of the World from 1920,

he continued to promote the cause of the two movements for the rest of his life.

Badoglio, Pietro (b. 28 Sept. 1871, d. 1 Nov. 1956). Italian general

A professional soldier, he fought at Adowa (1896) and in Libya (1911). He led the successful assault on the Austrian stronghold of Monte Sabotino in 1916, but was subsequently at least partly responsible for the disastrous defeat at *Caporetto (1917). Nevertheless, he finished World War I as deputy Chief of Staff, and served as army Chief of Staff 1919–21. Assured by his loyalty to the new *Fascist state, *Mussolini made him chief of the general staff of the armed forces in 1925, and marshal of Italy in 1926. He was made Governor of Libya in 1929, and in 1935 he took charge from *De Bono of the struggling army in the *Abyssinian War. In realistic appreciation of the current strength of the Italian army he opposed its participation in the *Spanish Civil War, and even more so its entry into World War II. He resigned following Italy's invasion of Greece in 1940. After Mussolini's deposition by the *Fascist Grand Council he was invited to form a new government on 26 July 1943. He concluded an armistice with the Allies on 3 September 1943, and declared war on Germany the following month. Nevertheless, his government lacked authority because of the *CLN's refusal to cooperate with him until April 1944. Unable to overcome its distrust, he resigned in June 1944, following the liberation of Rome, and was replaced by *Bonomi.

Baghdad Pact (Feb. 1955)

A treaty between Turkey and Iraq, which was at first aimed against militant *Kurdish groups. It became a more comprehensive regional security treaty when it was joined later in the year by Pakistan, Iran, and the UK. It became ineffective after the Iraqi Revolution of 1958. Iraq withdrew formally in 1959. In that year, the USA joined what became *CENTO.

Bahamas, Commonwealth of the

Made a British colony in 1717, the archipelago of around 700 islands lies south-east of Florida. For centuries domestic politics was largely determined by the merchant elite of its capital, Nassau, until the introduction of male suffrage with property qualifications in 1959. The vote was extended to women (1962), and the Progressive Liberal Party (PLP) under **Lynden Oscar Pindling** (b. 1930) proceeded to win the first general elections held under universal suffrage. The colony gained internal self-government in 1964, becoming fully independent on 10 July 1973. In the 1980s, Pindling and the PLP were involved in a number of corruption scandals including allegations of involvement in the drugs trade. Furthermore, Pindling (who was knighted in 1983) tried to spend his way out of an economic recession, forcing the country to take on a massive foreign debt. As a result, he lost the 1992 elections to Hubert Ingraham of the conservative Free National Movement (FNM). In 2001, the country imposed tougher rules on its financial services sector. This reduced the incidence of money-laundering, but increased its reliance on tourism to make up for its trade deficit. The 2002 elections were won by Perry Gladstone Christie (PLP), but Ingraham returned to power in 2007.

Bahrain

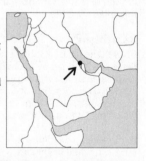

An independent state comprising 33 islands in the Persian Gulf, with a combined area of 691 km^2 (267 sq. miles). Ruled by the Al Khalifa dynasty since 1782, it was a British protectorate, 1861–1971. Iranian claims on the islands were rejected by the *UN in 1970. Despite British encouragement to join the United Arab Emirates, Bahrain opted for complete independence on 14 August 1971. Tensions mounted within its native population, whose religion was divided between the *Sunni (35 per cent) and the *Shi'ite (65 per cent) traditions of *Islam, after the Iranian Revolution (1979) brought to power an *Islamic fundamentalist Shi'ite government.

From 1961 to 1999, Bahrain was ruled by the Emir, Sheikh Isa ibn Sulman al Khalifa. He took absolute powers in 1975, after he dissolved the first parliament because of its alleged left-wing tendencies. In 1981, an abortive Iranian-supported *coup d'état* led to a security pact with Saudi Arabia, whose population follows the Sunni tradition. In 1995 there were renewed clashes as the Shi'ite population demonstrated against the economic decline, which they claimed had affected them disproportionately. From 1999 Bahrain was ruled by Sheikh (from 2002: King) Hamad Ibn Isa Al-Kahlifa. He lifted the state of emergency, decreed an amnesty for his political opponents, and instigated a referendum which approved of his plans to transform the country into a constitutional monarchy by 2004. Democratization was linked to a decline in oil revenues. The Al-Kahlifa family retained firm control over the important government positions, but lower oil revenues than its Arab neighbours and a diverse Muslim population forced the government to become more responsive to public opinion.

Baker v. *Carr* (USA, 1962)

The first of a series of *Supreme Court decisions which undermined the custom of manipulating legislative apportionments at state and federal levels for political or racial purposes. Electoral boundaries had been drawn up to discriminate against Americans of Color. This decision ruled that population was the only acceptable basis for representation in the United States. Crucially, the Court ruled that the apportionment of seats was not simply a political question, but that it did fall within the purview of the judiciary.

Balaguer y Ricardo, Joaquín Videla

(b. 1 Sept. 1907, d. 14 July 2002). President of the Dominican Republic 1961–2, 1966–78, 1986–96

Born in Villa Navarette, he was the protégé of *Trujillo, and became his Foreign Minister (1954) and Vice-President (1957–60). President after Trujillo's assassination in 1961, he lost the 1962 elections and went into self-imposed exile in the USA, where he founded the moderate Partido Reformista (Reform Party). Strongly supported by the USA, he was elected President following his return after the 1965 civil war, Balaguer governed with methods similar to the Trujillo regime. By 1974, the parties of the left had become completely disorganized, while 4,000 opponents had been murdered by government forces. He lost the 1978 elections, whose result he was forced to accept by US President *Carter. Although he became partly deaf and mostly blind, the divisions within the other parties enabled his return in 1986. His subsequent policies of generous public spending followed by economic stringency failed to revive the economy. In 1994, he was confirmed in office for the seventh and last time.

Balbo, Italo (b. 6 June 1896, d. 28 June 1940). Italian Fascist

After participating in World War I he became a leader of the *Fascist *blackshirts. He organized the *March on Rome in 1922, and in 1923 was appointed head of the Fascist militia. He became the central innovator of the Italian air force first as Under-Secretary (1926–9), then as Chief Minister (1929–33). As Governor of Libya from January 1934 he attempted to modernize the colony to turn it into an integral part of Italy. Although opposed to *Mussolini's pro-German and *anti-Semitic policies, he remained loyal to the regime and led the Italian forces in the *North African Campaigns in World War II. He died when his aeroplane was shot down accidentally by Italian batteries.

Baldwin, Stanley, 1st Earl Baldwin of Bewdley (b. 3 Aug. 1867, d. 14 Dec. 1947). British Prime Minister 1923–4, 1924–9, 1935–7

Early career Born in Bewdley (Worcestershire), educated at Harrow and Cambridge. He worked for his father's iron manufacturing company for twenty years, an experience which impressed upon him the need for a good relationship between workers and owners. He also developed a love for the English countryside, which enabled him to portray himself in later years as a representative of 'deep England'.

Baldwin entered parliament in 1908 as a *Conservative, inheriting his father's Bewdley seat. He made little impact until he became Bonar *Law's private secretary in 1916, and Financial Secretary to the Treasury in 1917. In 1921, he entered the Cabinet as President of the Board of Trade in *Lloyd George's coalition government. He rose to prominence when he spoke against continuing Conservative support for Lloyd George in October 1922.

In office Following a general election, Baldwin was selected by Bonar Law to be Chancellor of the Exchequer, and became Prime Minister in 1923, when the latter resigned because of ill health. He soon launched the Conservative Party into an unsuccessful election campaign in favour of tariffs, but achieved a large majority at a further election in 1924. His premiership was marked by the return to the *Gold Standard, the *General Strike, and a programme of social legislation introduced by Neville *Chamberlain. Throughout this time, he tried to articulate a brand of 'New Conservatism', which emphasized moderate reforms in order to reduce class tensions. He lost the election of 1929, in spite of having given the 'flappers' (women aged 21–30) the vote the year before. He faced strong opposition from Conservatives calling for 'Empire Free Trade' (a system of tariffs involving preferential treatment for the Empire), and narrowly survived various threats to his leadership.

With Ramsay *MacDonald, Baldwin formed the *National Government in 1931, serving as Lord President of the Council (i.e. as second-in-command), Baldwin was crucial in gaining Conservative support for the 1935 Government of India Bill, which gave measures of self-government to India. He succeeded *MacDonald as Prime Minister in 1935. His last ministry was marked by the *Abdication Crisis, and rising tensions in international affairs. In 1935 he approved of the Hoare-Laval proposal to allow Italy to annex part of Ethiopia, but later withdrew his support, when Italy went on to annex the whole country. In response to this, and the rise of *Hitler, Baldwin initiated plans for rearmament, although he was conscious of the need to proceed gradually owing to public fears of an arms race. He resigned as Prime Minister in 1937 and moved to the House of Lords. Despite his mixed legislative and administrative record, his dominant position in British politics for almost fifteen years (1923–37) was based on his image as a trustworthy politician, who understood the needs of the ordinary person.

Balewa, Alhaji Sir Abubakar Tafawa
(b. Dec. 1912, d. 15 Jan. 1966). Prime Minister of Nigeria 1957–66

Born in Tafawa Balewa Town, he became a teacher, and in 1945–6 went to the UK to attend the London Institute of Education. After returning to Nigeria he was elected to the Northern Region House of Assembly. In 1947 he became a member of the Central Legislative Council and in 1949 co-founded what became Nigeria's largest political party, the Northern People's Congress (NPC). He joined the federal government in 1952, and became the first Prime Minister of the Federation of Nigeria, a post which he retained when the country became independent in 1960. Despite his efforts, he was unable to unite the divided country, or to establish some sense of law and order. He was himself re-elected in 1964 in rigged elections, which led to arguments with *Azikiwe. A three-month period of near-anarchy preceded the 1966 army coup, in which he was killed.

Balfour, Arthur James, 1st Earl Balfour and Viscount Traprain
(b. 25 July 1848, d. 19 Mar. 1930). British Prime Minister 1902–5

Early career Born in Whittinghame, East Lothian, he was educated at Eton and Cambridge, entering parliament in 1874 for the *Conservative Party to represent Hertford. Initially associated with a rebellious group of Conservative MPs called the 'Fourth Party', he became Chief Secretary for Ireland (1887–91). His time there was successful from the point of view of British politics, even though in Ireland his repression of the Home Rule movement gained him the nickname of 'Bloody Balfour'. He became leader of the House of Commons in 1891, and succeeded his uncle, Lord *Salisbury, as Prime Minister in 1902.

In office Thereafter, Balfour began to display the lack of political judgement that became his hallmark. His 1902 Education Act enraged Nonconformists who were faced with having to pay for the upkeep of Anglican schools through rates (taxation), and galvanized their previously dormant support for the *Liberal Party. Furthermore, he was unable to prevent the deep splits within his party following Joseph *Chamberlain's *tariff-reform campaign from 1903. In foreign affairs, he created the Committee of Imperial Defence and helped establish the *Entente Cordiale with France in 1904.

In opposition In 1906, the Conservatives were heavily defeated at the polls, and Balfour then used the House of Lords, described by *Lloyd George as 'Mr Balfour's Poodle', to attempt to block Liberal legislation. Since he lacked his uncle's command and knowledge of the Lords, however, his policy backfired as the Lords' intransigence was used by *Asquith to crush their absolute veto over non-financial legislation, thereby virtually annulling the importance of this bastion of Conservatism. He resigned the leadership of a demoralized and defeated Conservative Party to Bonar *Law in 1911.

Perhaps Balfour's biggest positive contribution to British political life came when, relieved of the responsibility of leadership, he was able to use his formidable intellectual skills on specific policies and departments. He returned to office in 1916 as Foreign Secretary in Lloyd George's wartime government, when he issued the *Balfour Declaration. He was a prominent British representative at the *Paris Peace Conference in 1919, and participated at the *Washington Conference of 1921–2. As Lord President of the Council in 1925–9 he was a strong supporter of the concept of dominion status, and the Statute of *Westminster of 1931 owed much to his inspiration.

Balfour declaration
The name given to Britain's pledge to support the establishment of a Jewish national home

in Palestine. It was contained in a letter of 2 November 1917 from Arthur *Balfour to the leading British *Zionist, Lord Rothschild. The letter pledged that such a home should be established 'without prejudice to the civil and religious rights of the non-Jewish people [Arabs]' in *Palestine. The declaration aimed to forestall more far-reaching promises by the Germans and ensure British influence over the area. The statement represented a fundamental contradiction in British policy because at the same time, Britain had pledged to recognize the leaders of the *Arab Revolt as rulers of Palestine. Nevertheless, the Balfour Declaration was confirmed by the Allies, and became the basis of Britain's *Mandate for Palestine, granted by the *League of Nations in 1920. Subsequent attempts to reconcile the Balfour Declaration with pledges to the Arabs were at the root of Britain's future problems in Palestine.

Balilla (Opera Nazionale Balilla, ONB). Italian Fascist youth movement

Constituted on 3 April 1926, it was organized in three main sections, the Balilla (8–15-year-old boys), the Avanguardie (15–18-year-old boys), and the Piccole Italiane (for girls). Its purpose was to organize and educate a new, 'Fascist' generation loyal to *Mussolini. However, it struggled to become the predominant national youth movement, especially given the continued popularity of the youth organizations of the Roman *Catholic Church. In 1928 all other youth organizations were outlawed, but even afterwards it is doubtful whether it succeeded in its mission of Fascist indoctrination, despite its predominance. In 1937, it was renamed **GIL (Gioventù Italiana del Littorio)**.

HITLER YOUTH

Balkan Pact (1934, 1954)

An attempt to reduce the tensions in the Balkans which had been evident for half a century. In February 1934, a defensive pact was signed by Yugoslavia, Romania, Greece, and Turkey. From the start, its aim to restore stability and cooperation to the entire region of the Balkans proved futile, as a resentful Bulgaria refused to join, due to its claims over *Macedonia which had become part of Greece and Serbia. The pact became the basis for the Balkan Entente which joined the signatory states in a permanent council. It was too weak to provide any united resistance to German and Italian invasion during *World War II. Indeed, the Balkan states were deeply divided in their response to the War, between opposition (Greece), cooperation (Romania and Bulgaria), neutrality (Turkey), and

internal divisions (Yugoslavia). After World War II, a second Balkan Pact between Yugoslavia, Greece, and Turkey was formed in 1954. This became ineffective within a few months because of mounting Graeco-Turkish tensions over *Cyprus.

Balkan Wars (1912–13)

In March 1912, the First Balkan Entente was formed through a system of bilateral treaties between *Serbia, *Montenegro, Bulgaria, and Greece, mainly to prevent *Austria-Hungary benefiting from the disintegration of the European areas of the *Ottoman Empire. In October 1912, the Entente attacked the Ottoman Empire. After a series of successful battles, in the Peace of London (May 1913) the Empire lost most of its European possessions. Serbia doubled its territory, Albania became an independent state, Greece gained much of Macedonia, while Bulgaria obtained access to the Aegean Sea. Nevertheless, Bulgaria was unhappy with its share of the spoils. In June 1913 it attacked Serbia in the Second Balkan War. Bulgaria was soon defeated in a coalition which included Greece, Montenegro, and Romania. In the Peace of *Bucharest (August 1913), Bulgaria lost the *Dobrudja to Romania, and virtually all of *Macedonia to Serbia and Greece, which also secured its authority over Crete. Altogether, the two wars increased the tensions in the Balkans: a victorious Serbia gained self-confidence and the status of a regional power, while harbouring resentments at not having gained access to the Mediterranean. Moreover, Bulgarian resentments ensured its participation in *World War I on the side of the *Central Powers.

Ban Ki-Moon (b. 13 June 1944). UN Secretary-General, 2007–

Born in Changju, Ban studied at Seoul University and at Harvard, before joining the Korean foreign diplomatic service. In this position he worked with the UN Mission at the Foreign Office, and later became First Secretary at Korea's permanent mission to the UN in New York. Ban also served as ambassador to Austria. In 1996 he became foreign policy adviser to the Korean president, and in 2004 he was appointed Foreign Minister. A skilled negotiator seasoned in difficult diplomatic missions through his work with North Korea, Ban was seen to be less political than his predecessor, *Annan, and more an administrator who would focus on the UN's internal reform.

Banaba (Ocean Island), see KIRIBATI

Banda, Hastings Kamuzu (b. 14 May 1906, d. 25 Nov. 1997). President of Malawi 1966–94

A medical doctor born in Kasungu, he co-founded and led the Malawi Congress Party (MCP) in opposition to White rule in the *Central African Federation (1953–63). Emerging as the clear winner from the country's first elections in 1961, he became Prime Minister upon Malawi's independence on 6 July 1964. He became President in 1966 after the abolition of the power of the British Crown in Malawi, and declared himself president for life in 1971. He succeeded in establishing total control over the political system. In addition, he owned the two largest economic enterprises in the country, whose profits made him the country's richest man, financed the MCP, and provided funds for bribes and other illegal transactions. A frail man, he was forced by international pressure to concede democratic elections in 1994, which the MCP lost. He was subsequently charged with the murder in 1983 of three of his ministers and one deputy, who had been speculating on Banda's successor. He was acquitted in December 1995.

Bandaranaike, Sirimavo Ratwatte Dias (b. 17 Apr. 1916, d. 10 Oct. 2000). Prime Minister of Ceylon (Sri Lanka from 1972) 1960–5, 1970–7, 1994–2000

Born in Balangoda, she married Solomon *Bandaranaike in 1940. She became involved in politics only upon her husband's assassination, becoming president of the Sri Lanka Freedom Party in May 1960. Despite her inexperience, the wave of sympathy was so strong that months later she was made the world's first woman Prime Minister. She developed her late husband's neutralist policies further to the left, bringing the main *Marxist group out of opposition and into her government in 1964. In opposition, she formed the United Front together with the Marxists and other left-wing groups, leading to her re-election. She severed the country's ties with Great Britain and proclaimed a new, *socialist constitution. The United Front collapsed in 1975, amidst signs of economic decline and civil unrest. She lost the 1977 elections, and in 1980 was expelled from parliament for her abuse of power. While she continued to command considerable respect, this was not enough to ensure success in her bid for the presidency in 1988. She became Prime Minister once again in 1994, after her daughter, Chandrika Bandaranaike Kumatunga (b. 1945), had been elected President. She coordinated government policy, whose main lines were determined by Kumatunga. She died on election day, hours after casting her vote in the elections.

Bandaranaike, Solomon West Ridgeway Dias (b. 8 Jan. 1899, d. 26 Sept. 1959). Prime Minister of Ceylon 1956–9

Born in Columbo, he was educated there and in Oxford, and became a lawyer. He became active in politics in the 1920s, and founded the Maha Sinhala Party in 1937, in a successful bid to create a power base among Sinhalese and Buddhist groups. He brought his movement into the United National Party (UNP) and was Minister of Health and Local Government (1948–51). In 1951, he left the UNP to found the Sinhalese Socialist Sri Lanka Freedom Party, which attracted support from the political centre, as well as Sinhalese and Buddhist interest groups. He thus won the 1956 election, and was now compelled to realize his election promises to special interest groups. His fulfilment of the Buddhist demand to make Sinhalese Ceylon's official language without concessions to the *Tamil minority proved fateful, as it aggravated decisively the tensions between the two communities. He was a promoter of *non-alignment in foreign policy, and of *socialism in domestic policies; his assassination ensured his lasting reputation in Ceylonese (Sri Lankan) politics.

Bandung Conference (17 Apr. 1955)
The first international conference of independent Asian and African countries held in the Indonesian city of Bandung, which called for the neutrality of the lesser developed countries in the current *Cold War, in the interest of world peace. It inaugurated the *non-alignment movement, whose principal tenets were non-aggression, respect for sovereignty, non-interference in other countries' internal affairs, equality, and peaceful coexistence.

Bangladesh
A south Asian country predominantly inhabited by Muslims, which has the world's greatest population density (except for city-states like Singapore).
Its agriculture, subject to recurrent poor harvests through either drought or floods, has been unable to feed its increasing population.

Its geography is entirely dominated by the Ganges delta, so that most of its territory is but a few feet above sea level, with water as the most important source of communication. The large-scale felling of forests to make space for the expanding population has led to greater erosion and a much greater vulnerability to the seasonal monsoon rains, with those in 1988 and 1991 leading to as many as one million dead between them.

Colonial history (up to 1947) Under British influence since 1763, the eastern part of Bengal formed part of the British colony of India until 1947, when India became independent and split into two parts: that granted to the Hindu majority (currently India), and that given to the Muslim minority. This became independent as West Pakistan (currently Pakistan) and, in the east of the subcontinent, East Pakistan, comprising eastern Bengal, separated from the predominantly Hindu-populated western part of Bengal.

East Pakistan (1947–71) East and West Pakistan (terms officially in use since 1956) were joined in the Union of Pakistan, even though the two parts shared relatively few traditions. As a remnant of the colonial period, East Pakistanis found little representation in the government, administration, or the higher ranks of the military of the country. These differences were epitomized in the introduction of the Urdu language as the official language of Pakistan, even though few Bengalis in East Pakistan could speak it. Demands for autonomy, articulated through the *Awami League, were magnified by the (West-dominated) government's refusal to grant any recognition to East Pakistan grievances. In the 1970 elections the Awami League gained 160 out of 162 seats in East Pakistan, but continued West Pakistani refusal to grant autonomy aggravated the hostility between the two parts. The Pakistani military intervened against public demonstrators, and in the brief but brutal civil war that followed, East Pakistan gained its independence as Bangladesh, largely thanks to the active intervention of the Indian military.

Independence (from 1971) Bangladesh's first Prime Minister, the popular *Mujibur Rahman, attempted to create a socialist economy, through establishing friendly relations with the Soviet Union. He also nationalized industries and other economic assets, most of which had been owned by inhabitants of Pakistan. These policies halted delivery of Western aid due to the *Cold War, and discouraged foreign investors. Economic

problems were compounded by shortcomings in Mujibur's administration and the growth of public corruption. His attempt to bolster his increasingly contentious position by assuming presidential powers and creating a one-party state in 1975 was ended by his assassination in August that year. Subsequently, the army retained a very strong role in the government of the country.

Bangladesh was led from 30 November 1975 by the spirited and pragmatic General Zia-ur Rahman, who ruled the country until 1981. He founded the Bangladesh National Party (BNP), which won a relatively fair election held in 1979 with an absolute majority. Zia was assassinated in a failed coup in 1981, whereupon the army took power under General Ershad. Throughout the rest of the decade, he was opposed by the Awami League under Mujibur's daughter, Sheikh Hasina Wajid, and the BNP led by Zia's widow, Khaleda *Zia.

When Ershad was toppled by popular demonstrations in 1990, Zia's BNP won the ensuing elections of 1991, whereupon she became the country's first Prime Minister to complete her term in office. This did not indicate a return to political calm, however. The Awami League walked out of parliament in 1994 and subsequently confined its opposition to paralysing the country through general strikes. In 1996, the Awami League came to power after tumultuous elections, but the continued opposition of the BNP and its *Islamic fundamentalist allies prolonged the polarization of domestic politics.

Contemporary politics (since 2001) In 2001 the BNP and its allies were returned in a landslide election victory, with Khaleda Zia becoming Prime Minister again. Bitter political strife made it difficult for the government to control widespread lawlessness and violence, which was compounded by a series of bomb attacks carried out by Muslim fundamentalist groups (2005, 2006). Mohammad *Yunus announced his entry into politics and the creation of a political movement in 2007, but weeks later the military backed Fakhruddin Ahmed to become caretaker Prime Minister. Ahmed announced elections for 2008, and attempted to overcome the deadlock between, and corruption within, the country's major political forces.

Bantustan

Separate Black homelands in South Africa whose creation from 1951 formed the cornerstone of *apartheid as realized by the

*National Party and the relentless *Verwoerd. They built on the existing 'reserves' for Blacks (Bantus), which had been established to segregate them from Whites in 1913 and in 1936. The 1951 Bantu Authorities Act set up a hierarchical structure of authority in each reserve, which corresponded to different ethnic groups. Tribal chiefs who did not cooperate were deposed. The 1959 Bantu Self-Government Act provided mechanisms for these territories to achieve self-government, which was granted in 1963 for the first time to the **Transkei**, the largest single homeland territory.

Thereafter, self-governing homelands were encouraged to opt for independence, since the more Blacks belonged to an independent homeland, the fewer could claim South African nationality. Thus, the 1970 Bantu Homelands Citizenship Act ruled that all Blacks would assume the nationality of one of the homelands, even if they had never set foot in it. This would ensure that, in the long run, there would be no Black South Africans. Transkei accepted independence in 1976, followed by **Bophuthatswana** (1977), **Venda** (1979), and the **Ciskei** (1981). As creations of apartheid, these 'countries', whose territories were widely interspersed throughout the eastern part of South Africa, were not internationally recognized. With the notable exception of Bophuthatswana, their governments were corrupt, and their single most important 'independent' revenue came from the ability to run casinos, as gambling was forbidden in South Africa.

In reality, Bantustans were vast slum areas without industry or fertile soil for agriculture. The majority of their populations depended on jobs in South Africa (e.g. 65 per cent of the working population in Bophuthatswana), while most of their governments' income depended on direct transfer payments from the South African government (e.g. 80 per cent in Transkei, 1985). The 'independent' bantustans were reintegrated into South Africa in 1994, sometimes, as in the case of Bophuthatswana, against the will of the local governing elites.

Bao Dai (b. 22 Oct. 1913, d. 2 Aug. 1997). Emperor of Vietnam 1926–45

Born as Prince Vinh Thuy, he adopted his title ('Protector of Grandeur') upon accession to the throne. Represented by a regent in his absence, he studied in France until 1932. Bao Dai cooperated with the French colonial authorities, though it was his compliance with the Japanese from 1940 which discredited him in the eyes of many

Vietnamese. He was deposed by *Ho Chi Minh's *Vietminh, and left for Hong Kong in 1946. After the return of the French colonial authorities to Vietnam, he agreed to become leader of a French puppet state in Vietnam in 1949. Following the *Geneva agreements, this became South Vietnam in 1954, of which he became President. However, he lacked the charisma, integrity and the authority to become accepted by his people. In 1955 he was deposed by his Prime Minister, *Ngo Dinh Diem, and retired to France.

Baptist Church

One of the largest evangelical Protestant churches which stresses the authority of the Holy Scripture, adult baptism, and the autonomy of local congregations. It originated in sixteenth-century Anabaptist movements whose leaders came to England as they were persecuted elsewhere in Europe. During the nineteenth century, Baptists spread rapidly in both Britain and the USA, where they became the largest religious community in many southern states. There, Black Baptist congregations grew after the Civil War and contributed significantly to Black culture. Around two-thirds of African-American church membership is Baptist. Many Baptist ministers came to be at the forefront of the *civil rights movement during the 1950s and 1960s, most notably Martin Luther *King. In the US, Baptists are organized in four Conventions, of which the Southern Convention has been a particularly vociferous opponent of the legalization of *abortion. There are over thirty-five million Baptists worldwide, whose unity is promoted through the Baptist World Alliance in Washington DC (founded 1905).

(((●))) SEE WEB LINKS

• The home page of the Baptist World Alliance.

Barak, Ehud (b. 12 Feb. 1942). Prime Minister of Israel, 1999–2001

Born in Mishmar Hasharon of Polish immigrants, he joined the military in 1959 and advanced quickly through the ranks of the army. In 1972 he made the headlines through his daring and successful storming of a Belgian airliner in Tel Aviv after it had been hijacked by the *PLO. Further such commands followed, including the risky *Entebbe raid. He advanced to the military command in the 1980s, and became chief of military intelligence. He left the military in 1995, and became Minister of the Interior under *Rabin. A few months later he succeeded *Peres as Foreign Minister. One year later, following *Netanyahu's election victory which was seen as a defeat of the old guard of the *Labour Party, he was elected leader of the opposition.

As Israel's most-decorated general, the electorate entrusted him with negotiating peace with *Arafat in the 1999 elections, when he defeated Netanyahu decisively in 1999. His government, however, enjoyed only a very uncertain majority in parliament. He withdrew the army from southern Lebanon after almost twenty years of occupation. He also rekindled the *Wye accord, and resumed negotiations with the Palestinians. However, growing violence by *Hamas in the *Intifadah led many Israelis to question his judgement. After a series of defections from his government he called new elections, which he lost to *Sharon. Barak was subsequently sidelined in the party. In coalition with *Olmert's *Kadima, Labour shared responsibility for the disastrous war against *Hezbollah in 2006. In 2007, Barak won the elections for the party leadership against the Defence Minister in that war, Amir Peretz. Barak thus returned to government, as Defence Minister and Deputy Prime Minister.

Barbados

The most easterly island in the Caribbean Sea. Settled by the British from 1627, it became a Crown Colony in 1652. Its economy long depended on sugar plantations operated with the use of African slaves, who were not emancipated until 1834, when slavery was abolished, and 1838, when slaves were set free. Partly as a result of the decline of the sugar industry, there were widespread riots and disorder in 1937-8, with bitter racial antagonism emerging. In response, the economy of Barbados was diversified, and in 1950 universal adult suffrage was introduced. The first elections held under the new suffrage in 1951 confirmed the predominance held by the Barbados Labour Party (BLP) in the country's political sphere since 1938. Under the leadership of *Adams, Barbados joined the short-lived *West Indian Federation (1958-62). Eventually, Barbados was granted full independence as a member of the *Commonwealth on 30 November 1966. Since the 1960s, power has alternated between the BLP and the Democratic Labour Party (DLP). Led by Errol Walton Barrow (b. 1920, d. 1987), the DLP gained a majority for the first time in 1961 and remained in power until 1976. The DLP reclaimed power in 1986. In 1987 Lloyd Erskine Sandiford of the DLP was elected Prime Minister, but the failure of his policies to stimulate the stagnant economy produced a dramatic election victory for the BLP in 1994. Led by Owen Arthur, the BLP was re-elected in 1999 and 2004. In this period, the economy grew barely at all, but was diversified, from agriculture (notably sugar) to greater income from tourism.

Barbarossa (22 June 1941 – Dec. 1941)

Origins The codename for the largest military campaign in history, the German invasion of the Soviet Union in *World War II. Planned from late 1940 (despite *Hitler's previous warnings about the dangers of a two-front war), it was originally scheduled to begin on 15 May 1941. However, it was postponed after German troops had to come to the rescue of Italian forces which were being defeated in the Balkans and North Africa.

The course of the campaign The German attack on the USSR occurred seven weeks later than originally planned; an important delay which gave the Germans even less time to achieve their ambitious plans before the onset of the harsh Russian winter. A total of 3.05 million German soldiers (75 per cent of its army), assisted by 65 per cent of its own air force, as well as Romanian and Finnish troops, attacked 4.7 million *Red Army soldiers stationed in the European part of the USSR. Under the overall command of Field Marshal von Brauchitsch, the Army Group North under von Leeb advanced against Leningrad, the Army Group Centre under von Bock pressed against Moscow, while Army Group South under von *Rundstedt proceeded against the *Crimea.

German *Blitzkrieg tactics produced swift results, and within six months the German army had advanced to the outskirts of Leningrad and Moscow, while occupying the *Ukraine and the Crimea. Yet the Army Groups North and Central failed in their objectives to take Leningrad and Moscow respectively, while the German army had failed to break the Red Army.

Outcome Some (though not all) German military leaders, and, above all, Hitler himself, had underestimated the strength of the Soviet army. The German leadership had counted on a collapse of *Stalin's regime, which did not occur. The Soviet army was reinforced by fresh troops from the east, released there after the conclusion of the Japanese-Soviet non-agression pact of 13 April 1941. As the war progressed, the Red Army became better equipped with superior arms, tanks, and planes. Finally, the German military leadership made tactical mistakes partly owing to Hitler's direct intervention. His orders to broaden Germany's attack to include the *Crimea and Leningrad needlessly stretched German resources and diverted them away from an attack on the political and infrastructural centre of Moscow. By January 1942, the German army had lost almost 30 per cent of its soldiers, with a total of 900,000 casualties. The Barbarossa offensive thus failed, and ground to a halt in December 1941. Indeed, some of its gains were lost to a Soviet counter-attack (December 1941–January 1942). Despite further German victories in the summer offensive of 1942, the campaign turned decisively in Stalin's favour after the German defeat at *Stalingrad in the winter of 1942–3.

Barroso, José Manuel (b. 23 Mar. 1956). President of the EU Commission, 2004–
Born in Lisbon, he studied law and European studies, before writing a doctorate on the impact of *European integration on Portuguese politics. He lectured at Lisbon and Geneva Universities, and in 1985 entered the Portuguese parliament for the centre-right Social Democratic Party. He advanced to become Minister for Foreign Affairs, and in 2002 he led his party to an election victory, becoming Prime Minister. Since Barroso had become prominent within the European People's Party, the EU party association of Christian Democrats, Barroso was proposed as Commission President by *Merkel. As the European Parliament's majority party, the European People's Party had emphasized that they would only accept a President who reflected their majority, Barroso was duly appointed.

After the disappointment of the *Prodi-led Commission, Barroso was successful in drafting a response to French and Dutch rejection of the European *Constitutional Treaty, which was agreed among EU leaders in 2007. Presiding over an enlarged commission of record size, he was surprisingly effective, not least by establishing good relations with the European Parliament, and cultivating excellent connections with a number of EU leaders, notably Angela *Merkel.

Barthou, Jean Louis (b. 25 Aug. 1862, d. 9 Oct. 1934). Prime Minister of France 1913
An adept moderate right-wing member of the Chamber of Deputies since 1889, he held a large number of ministerial appointments before and after World War I. Hostile to Germany and suspicious of *Briand's policies, he had the opportunity to realize some of his demands for a tougher stance towards Germany as president of the *Reparations Committee 1922-6. As a result of this vigilant stance, he led French hostility towards the aggressive *Nazi regime in Germany in 1933 and 1934. He prepared an anti-Fascist alliance with the Soviet Union, which was concluded by *Laval in 1935 after Barthou's death. Barthou was assassinated during a state visit of the Yugoslav king, *Alexander I. This deprived France of its last major politician ready to stand up to *Hitler and eased the way for politicians like *Blum to follow British policies of *appeasement toward Germany.

Barton, Sir Edmund (b. 18 Jan. 1849, d. 7 Jan. 1920). Prime Minister of Australia 1901–3
Born in Glebe, Sydney, he studied classics at the University of Sydney and was admitted to the Bar on 21 December 1871. A free trader, he was elected to the New South Wales Legislative Assembly in 1879, whose Speaker he became in 1883. He resigned in 1887, and subsequently concentrated his efforts on promoting the cause of an Australian Federation. He took over the leadership of the federal movement in New South Wales in 1891, and was gradually accepted as leader of the federal movement in all Australia. Barton was the first of forty-nine candidates to be elected to the Australasian Federal Convention. Following an arduous campaign to convince his home state to join, he led a delegation to explain the proposed Constitution to Joseph *Chamberlain and the imperial government in London in 1900. The Commonwealth of Australia was thus proclaimed on 1 January 1901, with Barton becoming its first Prime Minister.

Baruch, Bernard Mannes (b. 19 Aug. 1870, d. 20 June 1965). US financier and political adviser
Born in Camden, South Carolina, to a poor Jewish family, by 1914 he had made a personal fortune on the New York stock exchange. He became the respected adviser of presidents from *Wilson to *Kennedy, preferring to be an *éminence grise* to running for elective office. In World War I he served under President Wilson on the Council of National Defense. As chairperson of the War Industries Board 1917-19, he exercised enormous power over the US wartime economy. He served as US economic adviser at the *Paris Peace Conference after the war. During World War II he was special adviser to President Franklin *Roosevelt on manpower mobilization and

postwar planning. In 1946 he was appointed to the UN Atomic Energy Commission, which proposed a World Atomic Authority with full control over the manufacture of atomic bombs throughout the world—a proposal rejected by the Soviet Union.

Basic Treaty (*Grundlagenvertrag*),
see GERMAN QUESTION

Basques

Contemporary history A people living mostly in the Basque territory ('Euskadi') which is situated along the western Pyrenees and the eastern end of the Bay of Biscay. Since 1514, its (smaller) northern part has been part of France, while its southern part covers today's Spanish provinces of Álava, Guipúzcoa, Navarra, and Viscaya. Cut off by the mountains from outside culture and population migrations before the tenth century, Basques kept their culture and their language, which is not related to any other language in the world. The distinctive Basque culture was recognized by the rulers of Castile until the nineteenth century, when the Basques' privileges were removed by the Spanish court. However, the country's wealth of iron ore meant that, except for Catalonia, it was the only Spanish region where industrialization started before the twentieth century. Consequently, it developed into one of Spain's richest regions, which was conducive to the resurgence of Basque *nationalism.

In the *Spanish Civil War, it remained loyal to the republican *Popular Front government, for which it suffered extensively under *Franco, who subsequently discriminated against the Basque population and forbade the use of their language. In response, a guerrilla organization, **ETA** (Euzkadi ta Azkatasuna, 'Basque Territory and Freedom') was formed in 1959 to gain independence by military means. After *Franco's death the Basques received extensive autonomy, and the first Basque Autonomous Parliament and President were elected in 1980. From that date, the Basque government was formed by the moderate Basque Nationalist Party (PNV, Partido Nacionalista Vasco/ Euzko Alberdi Jeltzalea), which tried to extend the province's already extensive autonomy. The Basques received powers over taxation, the police, energy, education, and culture.

Separatist conflict (since 1970) ETA had become too committed to the principle of full independence, and thus continued its terrorist campaign regardless of the political concessions granted by the Spanish government. Since 1970, ETA has carried out over 800 assassinations. In 1998, it declared an unlimited ceasefire to promote a political solution to the conflict. A year later, however, in late 1999, the organization resumed its campaign of violence. The brutality of ETA led to a decline in popular support for its political arm, as the Herri Batasuna ('United People') gained but seven out of 75 seats in the 2001 regional elections. Herri Batasuna was banned in 2002, though in subsequent elections radical nationalists supported the little-known Communist Party, which became their political mouthpiece. After the election of *Zapatero, who was more open to regional autonomy than his predecessor, *Aznar, ETA declared a permanent cessation of violence to begin a peace process in March 2006. Dissatisfied with the speed of progress, ETA ended the peace process by planting a bomb attack in Madrid on 30 December 2006.

Batista y Zaldívar, Fulgencio (b. 16 Jan. 1901, d. 6 Aug. 1973). Cuban dictator 1933–40; President 1940–4, 1952–8
A professional soldier, he led a successful revolt against President Carlos Manuel de Céspedes in 1933 and subsequently determined Cuban politics until 1958. He governed through a series of puppet regimes until 1940, when he took power directly. He continued to exert a decisive influence on Cuban politics behind the scenes after his official retirement into exile in 1944. In 1952, he returned to lead another military coup to re-establish a one-party dictatorship. His corrupt and brutal methods cost him the support of the middle classes and ultimately of the army. He was deposed by *Castro and fled to exile in the Dominican Republic on 31 December 1958.

Bay of Pigs (17 Apr. 1961)
A *CIA-backed invasion attempt by Cuban exiles to overthrow *Castro's new Communist regime at Cochinos Bay (Bay of Pigs). Following increasing tensions between the USA and Cuba, an ill-advised and inexperienced President *Kennedy finally gave the go-ahead for the long-prepared invasion. The exiles proved no match for Castro's forces. In addition, the American assumption that the invasion would generate a popular rebellion was completely unfounded. Instead, it proved to be a major boost to Castro's authority, who could claim that all his warnings about US interference and support for the discredited *Batista were true. Moreover, it convinced *Khrushchev of Kennedy's weakness in office, which he subsequently sought to exploit by the building

of the *Berlin Wall and the *Cuban Missile Crisis.

Bayar, Mahmud Jelâl (b. 16 May 1884, d. 21 Aug. 1986). President of Turkey 1950–60
Born in Umurbey, he took up work in a bank and other employment. He joined the *Young Turk movement in 1907, and in 1919 the resistance movement led by Kemal (*Atatürk). He was a member of the last parliament of the *Ottoman Empire, and joined the Turkish Grand National Assembly on its foundation in 1920. He became Minister of the Economy in 1921, and Minister of Reconstruction in 1924. Again Minister of the Economy (1932–7), his policies of promoting both private enterprise and developing important state industries contributed greatly to the success of the first five-year plan of 1933. Together with *Menderes he founded the Democratic Party in 1945 and, when it won the 1950 election, he became the country's first civilian President. Despite his office, which required him to remain neutral and above day-to-day political events, he was heavily partisan and supported his party particularly as its popularity faded. He was deposed in an army coup and sentenced to death for violation of the constitution. He escaped the fate of his colleague, Menderes, as his sentence was commuted to life imprisonment. He was released from prison in 1964, and retired from politics.

BBC (British Broadcasting Corporation) (UK)
The public broadcasting organization which now controls much of British radio and television. The British Broadcasting Company Limited, as it was originally known, was formed in 1922, by 200 shareholders and manufacturers. It established a system of paid licences for those who owned radio receivers, and it opened transmitters in London, Manchester, Newcastle, and Birmingham. The British Broadcasting Corporation was established by a royal charter in 1926 (operating from 1 January 1927), to provide radio (and later television) programmes for an initial ten years, funded by a system of licences for all radio owners. The charter was renewed periodically, most recently in 2005.
The BBC initially broadcast one radio service, the National Programme, and some regional services. A single Home Service replaced these in 1939, and the Forces Programme was added in 1940. In 1945, this latter station was replaced by the Light Programme, and the Third Programme was added in 1946. The BBC's World Service was established in 1932 as the Empire Service, broadcasting BBC programmes around the world. It gained particular significance through its broadcasts to occupied Europe during World War II, and to countries with press censorship (e.g. the Soviet Union, China) since. The BBC thus became a model for, and patron of, broadcasting services established throughout the former *British Empire (e.g. Canadian Broadcasting Corporation, South African Broadcasting Corporation, etc.) and elsewhere (e.g. the German public broadcasting services, established after 1945).

(🌐) **SEE WEB LINKS**

• The website of the BBC.

Beatty, David, 1st Earl Beatty (b. 17 Jan. 1871, d. 11 Mar. 1936). British admiral
Born in Stapeley, Cheshire, he became a cadet in the Royal Navy in 1884. His service in Egypt and during the *Boxer Rebellion in China (1900) earned him rapid promotion. In 1913, the First Lord of the Admiralty, Winston *Churchill, ensured that he was given command of the navy's battle-cruiser squadron. His major role was in the 1916 Battle of *Jutland. He was then appointed Commander-in-Chief of the British Grand Fleet, and received the German Grand Fleet's surrender at Scapa Flow in November 1918. As First Sea Lord (1919–27) he reduced the navy to peacetime strength. Together with *Jellicoe, his role at Jutland has been severely criticized, as he was accused of being rash, and of failing to train his command adequately.

Beauvoir, Simone de (b. 9 Jan. 1908, d. 14 Apr. 1986). French philosopher
Born in Paris, she was a materialist existentialist philosopher, left-wing activist, and, from the 1970s, a feminist. Her best-known book, about the oppression of women, *The Second Sex* (1949) insisted that womanhood as we know it is a social construct; she wrote 'One is not born, but rather becomes a woman'. In the USA and in France, de Beauvoir was mentor to those who arrived at feminism via the 1960s student movements for social change.
De Beauvoir only formally identified with feminism in 1971, when she signed a petition for legalized abortion with 343 other French women who openly declared that they had had *abortions. In 1972, she explained this change of heart: 'we must fight for the situation of women, here and now, before our dreams of socialism come true'. De Beauvoir's private life came to be admired as much as her writings. She never married, nor lived with, nor bore the child of her long-term partner, the philosopher Jean-Paul Sartre, although a biography appearing after her death depicted

her as more dependent on him than outsiders had imagined.

Beaverbrook, Lord (William Maxwell Aitken) (b. 25 May 1879, d. 9 June 1964). Conservative politician

Born in Maple, Ontario (Canada), Max Aitken was elected as a Unionist MP in 1910, shortly after his arrival in the UK, and was effective in the two world wars as Minister of Information in 1918, and especially as Minister of Aircraft Production in 1940. He is best known for his newspaper empire, including the *Express* and *Evening Standard* newspapers which gained record circulation. He used these to exercise political influence, for example through the promotion of Empire Free Trade (1929–31), a system of trade giving preferential treatment to goods coming to Britain from the Empire. Beaverbrook's real, rather than perceived, influence is questionable. He failed to prevent the fall of *Lloyd George, and his constant and fierce opposition to *Baldwin did not stop the latter from being undisputed Conservative leader for fourteen years.

Bechuanaland, see BOTSWANA

Beck, Józef (b. 4 Oct. 1894, d. 5 June 1944). Polish Foreign Minister 1932–9

Born in Warsaw, as a protégé of *Pilsudski he played an important part in his government after 1926. As Foreign Minister, and especially after Pilsudski's death in 1935, he determined the country's controversial policy of trying to remain on equally good terms with both its aggressive neighbours. He concluded non-aggression pacts with the USSR (1932) and Germany (1934), rather than allying Poland with one of these powers against the other. Ultimately, both powers equally disregarded Poland's sovereignty in the *Hitler–Stalin Pact, and carved up the country between them in September 1939. To what extent this outcome was the result of Beck's policies has remained subject to intense debate, though it is doubtful if any policy could have kept *Hitler out of Poland for long. Beck fled to Romania, where he was interned until his death.

Begin, Menachem (b. 16 Aug. 1913, d. 9 Mar. 1992). Prime Minister of Israel 1977–83

Born in Brest-Litovsk in White Russia (later Poland), he graduated in law from the University of Warsaw. He was soon active in the radical Revisionist *Zionist Movement, whose Polish president he became in 1939. After the outbreak of World War II Begin was imprisoned by the USSR, and was interned in Siberian labour camps until 1941. He joined

the Polish army in exile and was sent to *Palestine until demobilization in 1943. As commander of the *Irgun Zvai Leumi, he became involved in various terrorist attacks against the British, including the destruction of the King David Hotel. On the creation of Israel he founded the Herut (Freedom) Party, which he represented in parliament (the Knesset) from 1949. During the *Six Day War in 1967 he joined a National Unity government and in 1973 helped to form the right-wing *Likud bloc.

Likud won the elections of 1977, whereupon Begin became Israel's first non-socialist Prime Minister. During his leadership, US military and financial assistance rose to new heights, in return for his acceptance of *Sadat's overtures for peace. In 1978, he signed the *Camp David Accords, which ended hostilities with Egypt, Israel's most populous neighbour, also requiring it to relinquish its vast occupied territories in the Sinai peninsula. For this, he was awarded the *Nobel Peace Prize. His decision to invade the Lebanon in 1982 proved to be misguided, however. It failed to meet its objective of destroying the *PLO, aroused widespread international condemnation, and inflicted heavy casualties on the Israeli army. He resigned in 1983 despite his undented domestic popularity.

Belarus

A territory formerly also known as **Belorussia** (White Russia) which had been under Polish and Lithuanian domination for centuries, until

it came under Russian control in the late eighteenth century. As a result, it has had comparatively few national traditions of its own.

Foreign rule (until 1991) When the Tsarist Empire collapsed after the *Russian Revolution of 1917, independence was proclaimed briefly in July 1917, until the territory became a Soviet Republic during the *Russian Civil War. It was occupied by Polish troops in the *Russo-Polish War, and then partitioned in the Peace Treaty of Riga (18 March 1921), with its western areas becoming part of Poland, while the east became a founding Soviet Republic of the USSR in 1922. The western parts were reclaimed for good after the Soviet invasion of eastern Poland, in accordance with the *Hitler–Stalin Pact. It was devastated by the German army, during whose occupation around two million people, mostly, but not exclusively, Jews, were killed. After World War II the poor country benefited economically from its membership of the USSR, as it was industrialized despite its lack of mineral resources. It became a sovereign state amidst the collapse of the USSR, in the wake of the *August coup, on 26 August 1991.

Independence (since 1991)

Following independence, a tug of war developed between the reformist President, Stanislav Shushkevich, and a parliament that had retained its Communist composition of the Soviet era. Shushkevich was deposed by a no-confidence vote in 1994, and was replaced by Aleksandr Lukashenka (1994–) on an anti-corruption platform. This did not end the confrontations with parliament, whose composition remained the same after the 1995 elections were made void through their low voter turnout. Of the former Soviet republics, Belarus has remained most closely attached to Russia: in a 1995 plebiscite, Russian was reintroduced as an equal language with Belorussian, and the old Soviet Belorussian flag was readopted. In 1999 it entered into a formul union with Russia. Lukashenka's pro-Russian policy became increasingly contentious among the population, and discontent was fuelled further by his autocratic governing style. Lukashenka suppressed the opposition by curtailing freedom of speech and closing down independent media outlets. The Orange Revolution in neighbouring Ukraine boosted the domestic opposition movement, but in the 2006 elections it failed to topple Lukashenka, who maintained power through corruption and vote-rigging. At the same time, Lukashenka was not without popular support, as real income and growth rates grew in the early years of 2000. Lukashenka's dictatorial regime made him a *persona non grata* in the EU, the USA and other democratic countries.

Belgium

A heterogeneous European country whose differences have been accentuated by economic and cultural transformation, and the impact of two World Wars.

Early history (up to 1945)

It became independent in 1830. Primarily to prevent possible military attacks from France or the Netherlands, its neutrality was guaranteed by Britain in 1839. In the nineteenth century it was the first continental European country to be industrialized, partly because of its proximity to industrializing Britain, and partly because of the abundance of coal in the south. Its economic weight buttressed the domination of the French-speaking (Walloon) south over the Flemish-speaking majority in the north, whose wealth derived from agriculture and commerce. To ensure the country's continued industrial expansion, King Leopold II (r. 1865–1909) acquired the Congo territory in 1881–5, which was transferred to the sovereignty of the state in 1908. Despite its neutrality, Belgium was attacked by the Germans in 1914 in order to circumvent the French fortifications along the Franco-German border. This triggered the entry of the UK and the entire *British Empire into the war and transformed it into World War I. In the next four years it saw some of the heaviest fighting of the war, particularly at *Ypres and *Passchendaele. In response to increasing protests from the Flemish population, Flemish was accepted as an equal official language to French in 1922. During World War II, it again saw some heavy fighting, and was the place of the last, desperate *Ardennes offensive by the Germans in 1944.

Post-war history (1945–1980s)

In the years after the war there erupted a major constitutional crisis around the figure of *Leopold III, who was accused by many of collaborating with the Germans. He abdicated only in 1951, after a general strike called by the Socialists had prevented his return. In marked contrast with other former *Nazi-occupied areas, this episode was symptomatic of a wider debate about *collaboration with the Germans which left deep scars in Belgian society, as the population of Wallonia accused many Flemish-speaking Belgians of sympathizing with the occupiers and even helping them. The country jettisoned its principle of neutrality to join *NATO and the *Benelux union, and subsequently became one of the central protagonists of *European integration. In 1960, Belgium conceded that it no longer possessed the strength to exploit the Congo in the face of growing resistance, and hurriedly withdrew from the colony.

As Belgians became emphatically European, their own national identity was increasingly under question. The structural difficulties of heavy industry, which had been the backbone of Wallonia's prosperity, shifted the economic advantage to the Flemish north. Flanders continued to prosper through trade and commerce, and was a favoured location for new industries owing to its ready access to the sea. The growing economic, social, and emotional gulf between the two parts also led to political instability, heightened in the 1970s. In addition to the emergence of a number of regional parties, the Flemish and Walloon sections of the Christian Democrats, the Socialists, and the Liberals split to form separate parties.

Federalism (from the 1980s) In an effort to address its growing divisions, the country was built into a federal state in three stages (1980, 1988, 1993). By 1993, there were parliaments for the Walloon region, the Flemish region, and the bilingual city of Brussels. The federal regions were given authority over around 40 per cent of public expenditure for matters in their purview, i.e. education, culture, health, economic, and labour policy. In these areas, they were also empowered to conclude international treaties. Further powers to the regions in matters of agriculture, transport, and foreign aid were granted in 2001. The contrast between the Flemish part and Wallonia was exacerbated by the growth, in the Flemish part, of separatist and xenophobic parties from the mid-1990s, most notably the Vlaams Blok (Flemish bloc). Advocating Flemish independence and racist immigration policies, it polled over 20 per cent of the vote in Belgium's Flemish cities, polling most votes in Belgium's second city, Antwerp, in the 2000 and 2004 regional elections. The Vlaams Blok was found guilty of racism by Belgium's high court, whereupon it changed its name to Vlaams Belang (Flemish concerns) in 2004. In federal politics, a major political shift occurred in 1999, when the Christian Democrats lost the leading role in politics which they had occupied throughout the century, owing to a series of corruption scandals. The Liberals headed a new 'rainbow' coalition including Socialists and Greens. The gain of regional parties in the 2004 elections further weakened the federal government relative to the regions. These events prompted the royal family, one of the few accepted symbols of national unity, to make unprecedented political interventions by speaking out against divisive separatist tendencies. The 2007 elections were won by the Christian Democrats, whose leader, Yves Leterme, was open to yet further regional autonomy for Flanders.

Belize

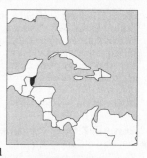

A country in Central America on the Gulf of Mexico settled by British shipwrecked sailors in 1638, and under British protection since 1782. It was used for the exploitation of high-grade timber and the maintenance of the supply of slaves and cheap labour to Jamaica. A British colony since 1862, it became a Crown Colony in 1871. Mexico renounced its claims to Belize in 1893, but in 1940 Guatemala renewed its demands to incorporate the territory. Belize received partial self-government in 1954 and was subsequently led by **George Price** (b. 1919), leader of the social democratic People's United Party (PUP). Home rule was granted in 1964, but full independence was delayed by the need to retain British links as a guarantee against Guatemalan pretensions.

Independent as a constitutional monarchy within the *Commonwealth, from 1981, Belize continued to host a contingent of British troops. In 1984, Price's continuous rule for 30 years was ended by a landslide election victory for the conservative United Democratic Party (UDP), though Price was re-elected Prime Minister in September 1989. He sought to improve the country's standing among its neighbours, and thus in 1991 he obtained membership of the *OAS. Price also established diplomatic relations with Guatemala, which nevertheless refused to give up its territorial claims on many areas of Belize. The UDP returned to power in 1993, but it was the government of Said Wilbert Musa of the PUP (from 1998) which in 2000 had to cope with the devastating effects of Hurricane Keith on the country's infrastructure and economy.

Bello, Alhaji Sir Ahmadu (b. 12 June 1910, d. 15 Jan. 1966). Nigerian statesman

Born in Rabbah, near Sokoto, he was the great-grandson of Usman Dan Fodio, the founder of the Fulani Empire in the nineteenth century. As Sardauna of Sokoto ('leader of war', a traditional military title), he co-founded the Northern People's Congress (NPC), and in 1954, when the Federation of Nigeria was formed, he became Premier of the Northern Region. Upon independence in 1960, his party combined with *Azikiwe's National Council of Nigeria and the Cameroons (NCNC) to control the new federal parliament. Bello's deputy in the NPC, *Balewa, was federal Prime Minister, while Bello himself continued to lead the party in the north. In 1966, when the army seized power, Bello was one of the political leaders who were assassinated.

Belorussia, see BELARUS

Ben Ali, Zine el-Abidine (b. 3 Sept. 1936). President of Tunisia 1987–

Born in Hamam-Sousse, he graduated from the French military academy of Saint-Cyr, and received further military training in France and the USA. He rose to become Tunisia's most senior general, and in 1978 was appointed by *Bourguiba to become Director-General of National Security. After serving as ambassador to Poland (1980–4), he returned to become Minister of National Security, and Minister of the Interior in 1986. Though an active Muslim, in these posts he was mainly concerned with combating the growing militant *Islamic fundamentalist movement.

A month after his appointment as Prime Minister, Bourguiba was found incapable of continuing office, whereupon Ben Ali assumed the presidency according to paragraph 57 of the Constitution. Despite constitutional changes, he remained careful to control political liberalization in order to contain the spread of the Islamic fundamentalist movement. He was re-elected with over 99 per cent of the vote in 1994 and 1999, though the absence of free elections made the level of his real support difficult to ascertain. Following changes to the constitution, he was allowed to run again in 2004, when he won again with 95 per cent of the vote.

Ben Bella, Mohammed Ahmed (b. 25 Dec. 1916). President of Algeria 1963–5

Born in Maghnia close to the Moroccan border, Ben Bella served in the French army during World War II. He then turned against the French and in 1947 became leader of the militant wing of the Algerian nationalist movement, the 'Special Organization'. Imprisoned by the French in 1950, he escaped to Cairo in 1952 and subsequently founded the *Front de Libération Nationale (FLN), which became the main Algerian nationalist force during the *Algerian War of Independence. In 1956, he was captured and imprisoned after the French government persuaded a Moroccan aeroplane to land in Algiers. Released in 1962 to conduct the *Évian Agreements which won his country independence, he became Prime Minister in September, before becoming President with extended powers in April 1963. Ben Bella established a socialist Arab republic, but was reluctant to exchange his country's economic reliance on France for the Soviet Union. He hoped to secure his power with the establishment of a one-party state, but was ousted in a coup by his defence minister, *Boumédienne, on 19 June 1965. Ben Bella spent the next fourteen years under house arrest. He was allowed to move to France in 1979, but returned to Algeria in 1990, creating a new political party, the Movement for a Democratic Algeria. During the 1990s, he promoted political reconciliation to end the civil war.

Benedict XVI (Josef Ratzinger) (b. 16 Apr. 1926). Pope 2005–

Born in Bavaria, he joined an auxiliary anti-aircraft corps in the last months of the war. Ordained to the priesthood in 1951, he made a name for himself as a liberal theologian who advised the Archbishop of Cologne at the Second *Vatican Council. The impact of the liberalism of the 1960s moved him towards increasingly conservative theological positions, and in 1977 *Paul VI appointed him Cardinal at the diocese of Munich. At the election of *John Paul II, Ratzinger is thought to have been instrumental in the election of the first non-Italian pope since the sixteenth century. In John Paul II appointed him Prefect of the Congregation of the Faith at the Vatican, 1981, a position in which he was responsible for the observance of the Pope's dogmatic conservatism, which he shared. In this position, he came into close contact with all the cardinals of the Church. In 2005, it did not come as a surprise that the College of Cardinals agreed speedily to elect him Pope. In this position, he emphasized the significance of personal faith and Christian values in a fast-changing world. Benedict also reasserted the pre-eminence of Catholicism within Christianity.

Benelux Customs Union

Effective from 1 January 1948 between **Bel**gium, the **Ne**therlands, and **Lux**emburg, to complement the economic and monetary unions between Belgium and Luxemburg established in 1921 and 1944 respectively. An economic union followed in 1960. In contrast to the European Union, it is not a supranational orgnization, as the three members retain their full sovereignty in all common areas of policy. However, close co-operation and consultation has not only increased the movement of goods and capital between the three countries, but it has also given them added weight and experience in their support for the process of *European integration.

(SEE WEB LINKS)

- The official website of the Benelux Customs Union.

Beneš, Edvard (b. 28 May 1884, d. 3 Sept. 1948). President of Czechoslovakia 1935–8, 1945–8.

Born in Kozlány (Bohemia), he was educated in Prague and at the Sorbonne (Paris), and became a lecturer in economics at Prague University before World War I. In 1914 he fled from Prague to Paris, where he helped *Masaryk to form the Czechoslovak National Council. He became the leader of the Czech National Socialist Party, and was Czech delegate at the *Paris Peace Conference. As Foreign Minister (1918–35) he sought to stabilize the young state through international treaties. The *Little Entente was created in 1921 to prevent the restoration of the Habsburg King Charles in Hungary. The Czechoslovak–French treaty of 1924 was designed to guarantee the country's independence. As one-time Prime Minister (1921–2), and one of Masaryk's closest allies, he was the natural successor to the presidency following Masaryk's resignation. A pragmatist as well as a nationalist, he grudgingly accepted Slovak demands for recognition of their distinctiveness, and was even prepared to surrender the *Sudetenland in return for peace with Germany. Ultimately, however, he resigned in solidarity with the entire Cabinet over the *Munich Agreement.

Beneš went into exile and taught in the USA until the outbreak of war, when he became head of the Czechoslovak government-in-exile in 1939, first in Paris, and then in London. He had no ideological prejudices against *Stalin, and believed that after the war there would be a 'convergence', whereby the USSR would become more *capitalist, and Western Europe more *socialist. This explains his willingness to accept the growing power of the Czechoslovak Communist Party under *Gottwald in his postwar government, and his failure to mobilize opposition against the Communist takeover of the state in February 1948. Indeed, he agreed to stay on as President, resigning only on 6 May 1948.

Bengal

The culturally relatively homogeneous eastern part of the Indian subcontinent around the Ganges–Brahmaputra deltas. Under effective British rule since 1757, the nawab dynasties of Bengal, Orissa, and Bihar were united into a single province and ruled from Calcutta. In 1905 the Viceroy, Lord *Curzon, proposed a division into East Bengal (majority Muslim and to be united with *Assam) and the richer West Bengal (to include Orissa and Bihar). His action was violently opposed, especially among Hindus. In 1911 Britain accepted Indian criticism and reunited East and West Bengal. *Assam became a separate province again, while the new provinces of Bihar and Orissa were formed. With independence the division of the Indian subcontinent between Hindus and Muslims resulted in the division of Bengal, with East Bengal becoming part of Pakistan. In 1971, East Bengal gained independence as Bangladesh.

Ben-Gurion, David (b. 16 Oct. 1886, d. 1 Dec. 1973). Prime Minister of Israel 1948–53, 1955–63

Born David Gruen at Plonsk, in Russian Poland, he became a *Zionist and emigrated to *Palestine in 1906. He became active in the trade union movement and in journalism until he went to the University of Constantinople (1912–14) and obtained a law degree. Expelled by the *Ottoman authorities for his renewed work in the trade unions, he joined the *Jewish Legion. After World War I, he became one of the organizers of the *Mapai (Israel Workers' Party) and of the Jewish Federation of Labour (*Histadrut), for which he served as general secretary (1921–35). In 1935 he became chairman of the *Jewish Agency, thus effectively becoming the leader of the Jewish community in Palestine. He opposed the radical actions of the *Irgun under *Begin, which he felt undermined British goodwill towards an independent Jewish state. Instead, he organized the influx of large refugee movements, which made a Jewish state more viable and more inevitable.

In 1948, Ben-Gurion became Prime Minister of the newly founded state of Israel, and remained in government until 1963, except for two years of chosen retirement. Under his leadership, Israel survived the initial threat to its existence, when it was attacked by its Arab neighbours (1948–9). He also ensured that Israel was able to withstand subsequent Arab hostilities. Through agricultural and social reforms, Ben-Gurion established the foundations of the new state and created a stable country. This achievement was particularly remarkable in the light of Israel's culturally and socially heterogenous population which had immigrated from all over the world, with most people having suffered from persecution. He founded a new party known as Rafi in 1965, and remained in parliament (Knesset) until 1970.

Benin (Dahomey)

A heterogeneous state which has nevertheless generated a relatively stable political system after independence.

Early history (up to 1989) Occupied by French troops in 1894, the west African country became part of the colony of *French West Africa in 1904. Under French rule, the differences between its fifty tribes in the north and south increased, since along the southern coast there emerged an educated, politicized elite. With political representation in France from 1945, it became an overseas territory in 1946. It received limited self-government in 1957, and in 1958 became an autonomous republic under the name of Dahomey, within the *French Community.

Independent since 1960, Dahomey was plagued by political instability during the 1960s, caused by social, educational, and ethnic disparities within the population. Civilian government alternated with military rule (there were altogether five military coups), until *Kérékou assumed the presidency in 1972. He declared *Marxism-Leninism as his principle of government in 1974, and in 1975 proclaimed a new constitution, established a one-party state, and changed his country's name to the People's Republic of Benin. He introduced agrarian and educational reforms to reduce the social and economic inequalities between north and south.

Democratization (from 1989) In 1989 popular protests against his economic austerity measures forced Kérékou to concede political liberalization. The subsequent elections in March 1991 were won by the leader of the opposition, Nicéphore Soglo (b. 1934), with a two-thirds majority. Despite a number of reforms, economic performance remained poor, largely owing to structural problems such as high debts and an illiteracy level of 77 per cent. Owing to the discontent caused by the poor economy, Soglo surprisingly lost the 1996 presidential elections to Kérékou. Benin has been a major exporter of cotton, and in the 1980s began the exploration of relatively minor off-shore oil reserves. In 2000, it hosted the *Cotounu agreements. Kérékou remained in office until 2006, when the constitution barred him and his rival, Soglo, from standing for office due to old age. Yayi Boni, the former head of the West African Development Bank, was elected President on promises of promoting economic growth and combating corruption.

DECOLONIZATION; IMPERIALISM

Bennett, Richard Bedford, 1st Viscount Bennett (b. 3 July 1870, d. 26 June 1947). Prime Minister of Canada 1930–5

Born at Hopewell Hill (New Brunswick), he studied law at Dalhousie and practised in Calgary. Elected to the Alberta legislature as a *Conservative in 1909, he became an MP in 1911. Disappointed at not being appointed to the federal government under *Borden, he stood down in the 1917 elections. He became Minister of Justice under *Meighen in 1921, despite his failure to re-enter parliament until 1925. A brilliant parliamentary speaker, he became leader of the Conservative Party in 1927. He won the general election of 1930 on a promise to overcome the *Great Depression, but once in office he proved indecisive and unable to develop a coherent programme. He was instrumental in persuading the British to replace their traditional policy of free trade with the system of Imperial Preference, formalized by the *Ottawa Agreements of 1932. Apart from this, his actions were considered half-hearted and ineffective. Despite the announcement of proposed major social reforms in a Canadian *'New Deal' in 1935, he lost the elections of that year to *Mackenzie King. He remained leader of the Conservative opposition until he retired to England in 1938, embittered by his continuing unpopularity at home.

Ben-Zvi, Yitzhak (b. 6 Dec. 1884, d. Apr. 1963). Hebrew scholar, President of Israel 1952–63

Born in Poltava (Ukraine), he became an active *Zionist. He narrowly escaped the 1906 *pogroms there and left for *Palestine. Exiled by the Turks in 1915, he joined *Ben-Gurion in the USA and returned to Palestine in 1918 to become a member of the *Jewish Legion, fighting alongside the British. A co-founder of the *Histadrut (General Federation of Jewish Labour) he was also a member of the self-governing National Council for Palestine Jews (Vaad Leumi), rising to become its chairman from 1931, president from 1944. He was one of the signatories of Israel's Declaration of Independence on 14 May 1948, and entered the first parliament (Knesset) in the same year. He was President of Israel from the death of *Weizmann until his own death.

Beria, Lavrentii Pavlovich (b. 29 Mar. 1899, d. 23 Dec. 1953). Head of the Soviet Security Systems 1938–53

Born in Merkehuli (Georgia), in 1917 he joined the *Bolsheviks while a student and, after *propaganda activities in *Azerbaijan and *Georgia he became head of the Georgian secret police (*Cheka) in 1921. He continued to rise within the Georgian Communist Party, whose First Secretary he became in 1931. From 1934 he was also a member of the Central Committee of the Soviet *Communist Party. In 1938, he was appointed by his fellow Georgian *Stalin to take charge of the *NKVD secret police as head of internal affairs, and to organize Soviet prison camps. His appointment, which marked the end of the *Great Purge, was at first greeted with relief. However, he introduced much greater efficiency and sophistication to the internal security machine, which he used mercilessly to increase his own power, and that of Stalin. In consequence, prison camps expanded to record numbers. His position became increasingly unassailable, so that during World War II he was Stalin's deputy as head of state and as head of the defence committee. After the war, Beria played an important part in the build-up of the security systems of Eastern European states, which helped greatly to tie these countries closer to the Soviet Union. He also gave them a helping hand in their *Stalinist purges after 1948 (*Slánski, *Rajk). After Stalin's death, he failed to take over the leadership himself, and was instead outmanoeuvred by *Khrushchev, who had him imprisoned and shot.

Berisha, Sali (b. 11 July 1944). Albanian President 1992–7, Prime Minister 2005–
Born in Tropoje, he joined the Communist Party and became a cardiac surgeon. Berisha moved to lead the opposition in 1989, and in 1992 became President after a landslide election victory. His manipulation of election results led to widespread popular unrest, forcing him to resign in 1997. In 2005, he returned to lead the opposition, this time against the electoral manipulation of his successors, the socialists. Following his election victory, he became Minister President in 2005. Berisha supported economic liberalization as well as closer integration of his country into the EU.

Berlin

The German capital which came to epitomize the *Cold War. It surrendered to the Russian troops on 2 May 1945, but according to the *Yalta Conference was divided into four sectors which were administered separately by the four victorious Allied powers, France, the UK, the USA, and the USSR. Even though in subsequent years most powers were passed on to the civilian local authorities, the four

powers continued to hold sovereignty over the city until 1990.

Despite an initial commitment to cooperation, relations between the Western Allies and the USSR deteriorated rapidly., Matters came to a head when reform of the West German currency was also carried out in Western Berlin. In an attempt to assert its control over all of Berlin, the USSR closed all roads, canals, and railway lines leading into the western part of the city. In response, the American and British air forces organized the Berlin Airlift (24 June 1948–12 May 1949). In almost 200,000 flights (one flight about every three minutes) the Allies supplied the western half of the city with 1.5 million tons of goods and enabled the city to survive, forcing the USSR to give up after eleven months. This impressive display of resolve in the first direct confrontation of the Cold War effectively guaranteed the security of the western half of Berlin against any further attempted encroachments from the USSR or East Germany. As living standards improved in West Germany (and West Berlin) in the following years, and as dissatisfaction with the East German regime grew, more and more East German citizens moved to West Germany by crossing into West Berlin.

In response, East Germany erected the Berlin Wall (13 August 1961) to stop this exodus particularly of young and skilled people. West Berlin became surrounded by a complex system of watchtowers, manned with guards ready to shoot to kill, minefields, and underground corridors to enable quick movement of the border guards. It is estimated that 125 people were killed in the attempt to cross it. The fall of the Berlin Wall on 9 November 1989 became the most potent symbol of a new world order that emerged with the collapse of *Communism in Eastern Europe. Since the status of Berlin had been at the heart of the division of Germany, the event also paved the way for German reunification. Berlin once again became the capital of Germany, and the united city became the epitome of many of the difficulties between the Eastern and Western halves of Germany.
GERMAN QUESTION

Berlin–Baghdad railway

An enterprise to build a railway from Baghdad to Constantinople (which was connected to Berlin by rail), begun in 1903 with substantial German financial involvement. It became controversial because it potentially challenged British and Russian involvement in Persia and the Middle East. In recognition of this the

German government was always lukewarm about the project, but through skilful negotiations it managed to gain Russian acceptance in 1911, and British approval as late as June 1914. Hence the scheme is notable less for the minor irritation which it caused to international relations than for the demonstration that German diplomacy in the years before World War I could be low-key, tactful, and successful. After many interruptions the railway was finally completed in 1940.

Berlinguer, Enrico, see COMMUNIST PARTY, ITALY

Berlusconi, Silvio (b. 29 Sept. 1936). Prime Minster of Italy 1994, 2001–2006

Early career The son of a bank clerk, he studied law and then made his fortune in the construction industry, where he was involved in the building of new satellite towns, notably in Milan during the 1970s. At that time, he was also a good friend of the Milanese Socialist leader, the future Prime Minister *Craxi. He became involved in the entertainment business in 1979 and quickly built up an unrivalled national media empire. His holding company, Fininvest, owned several national television channels, radio stations, newspaper and publishing houses, supermarkets, building contractors, and financial service providers. This made him one of the twenty richest people in the world, and the richest and (arguably) the most influential person in Italy. At a time when the established parties collapsed owing to allegations of corruption and incompetence (*Tangentopoli), he seized the political initiative and founded the *Forza Italia. This quickly gained popular support because of Berlusconi's reputation for managerial competence and efficiency, and his promise to cleanse the political system of all corruption and scandal.

In office Forza Italia won the national elections of March 1994 and formed a controversial coalition with the neo-*Fascist Aleanza Nazionale (National Alliance) and the autonomist *Lega Nord. As Prime Minister, Berlusconi was unsuccessful in his attempts to reform the social welfare system, largely because of his inability to achieve a popular consensus for them. His image already dented through his association with Craxi and rumours about involvement in his company's corruption, he resigned after seven months in office on 22 December 1994. In opposition, he faced numerous charges of corruption, though he was able to face off a number of attempts to convict him.

After the perceived failure of the *Olive Tree government to introduce sufficient social and economic reforms, he won a resounding parliamentary victory in 2001. He formed Italy's longest-serving government since World War II, which again included the National Alliance and the Lega Nord. The government's stability did not just result from a stable parliamentary majority, but also from an unwillingness to tackle important, but controversial, reform. In foreign policy, Berlusconi entertained friendly relations with George W *Bush, though Berlusconi's support for the *Iraq War was highly controversial. By contrast, Berlusconi was less interested in the EU, so that Italy's EU presidency in 2003 developed into a blueprint of ineffective leadership. In 2005, Berlusconi changed Italy's electoral laws, so that a party alliance with only a small majority would obtain extra seats to allow it to form a stable government. Although this had been passed to help him secure another stable period of government, it in fact helped his opponent, as *Prodi won the elections of 2006 by a tiny majority. Berlusconi became opposition leader, and was charged again with corruption.

Bermuda

A British Crown Colony since 1684, its population consists of 65,000 people who live on twenty of its around 360 islands. It boasts the  oldest parliament in the New World, which dates back to 1620. Owing to its strategic location in the mid-Atlantic, it served as a British naval base 1797–1957, while in 1941 the USA was granted a 99-year lease on some islands for use as a naval and airforce base. Universal adult suffrage was introduced in 1944, and in 1968 Bermuda was granted self-government. There were sporadic riots during the 1970s, when politics and society were dominated by the racial relations between its inhabitants, of whom 30 per cent are of White and 70 per cent of Black or mixed origin. A second crucial issue of greater permanence has been that of full independence. It is supported by the Black Progressive Labour Party (PLP) but rejected by the dominant multiracial United Bermuda Party (UBP), which emphasizes the cost of independence and the income generated through the British navy and British tourism.

In a referendum of 16 August 1995, 74 per cent rejected independence. In the 1998 elections to the House of Assembly, the PLP gained a majority for the first time in its history. Led by Jennifer Smith (1998–2003), Alex Scott (2003–2006), and Ewart Brown, the PLP focused on improving the economy and improving social policy. The party thus attempted to position itself for the 2008 elections against a rejuvenated UBP led by Michael Dunkley.

Bernadotte, Folke, Count (b. 2 Jan. 1895, d. 17 Sept. 1948). Swedish international mediator

Born in Stockholm, the nephew of King Gustav V of Sweden, he was involved in work for humanitarian causes for most of his life, particularly on behalf of the *Red Cross. During World War II, he managed to establish good contacts with *Himmler. This enabled him to save around 30,000 people (among them around 20,000 Scandinavians) from *Nazi *concentration camps. In return, he was asked by Himmler to arrange peace talks with the Allies in 1945, to *Hitler's great irritation. As president of the Swedish Red Cross since 1946, he was asked by Trygve *Lie to act as a mediator in *Palestine in 1948 for the *UN. He was murdered by Israeli terrorists determined to prevent the partition of Palestine.

Bernstein, Eduard (b. 6 Jan. 1850, d. 18 Dec. 1932). Revisionist German socialist leader

A member of the German *SPD since 1872, he became head of the party newspaper in 1881. He was the co-author of the party's Erfurt Programme, and in 1899 he published his major book on the nature of social democracy, *Die Voraussetzung des Sozialismus und die Aufgaben der Sozialdemokratie*. In it, he rejected the SPD's traditional goal of social revolution, in favour of a pragmatic approach which aimed at a reform of the current capitalist system to the immediate benefit of the working classes. He was an MP (1902–6, 1912–18, and 1920–8), though during 1917–20 he had been a member of the new Independent Socialist Party (USPD). He was the major influence behind the party's transformation from the ideals of *Marxism to an acceptance of the Empire, and he endorsed the Weimar Republic from 1918.

Besant (née Wood), Annie (b. 1 Oct. 1847, d. 20 Sept. 1933). British reformer

Born in London, and originally an evangelical Christian, she separated from her clergyman husband in 1873 and joined the National Secular Society a year later. She began promoting birth control in 1877, and during the early 1880s was attracted to *socialism.

She had become a *Fabian by 1885, and a *trade-union organizer, most notably being involved in the 'match-girls' strike' of 1888. In the early 1890s, she became a leading exponent of the religious movement of theosophy (emphasizing an individual spiritual awareness of God), and went to live in India. There, she founded what later became the Benares Hindu University of India. In 1916 she helped to form the All India Home Rule League. She became a hero for the Indian cause when she was interned for three months in 1917, and briefly became the president of the Indian *National Congress (1918–19). She published a number of books on theosophy.

Betancourt, Rómulo (b. 22 Feb. 1908, d. 28 Sept. 1981). President of Venezuela 1945–8, 1959–64

Born in Guatire near Caracas, he was exiled in 1936, and again in 1939 for opposition to the military regime. He returned in 1941 to found the left-wing Democratic Action party (Acción Democrática), which soon attracted popular support. After a military coup he was made President, whereupon he inaugurated a programme of social reform which included land redistribution and the imposition of greater controls over oil companies. Exiled again in 1948, he came back ten years later and was elected President. His main achievement was to establish and strengthen the new democracy. In particular, he was able to control and curtail the influence of the armed forces, and he oversaw the writing of the new Constitution in 1961.

Bethlen of Bethlen, István Count (b. 8 Oct. 1874, d. 1947?). Prime Minister of Hungary 1921–31

Born into an aristocratic family in *Transylvania, he was first elected to the Hungarian parliament in 1901. A committed counter-revolutionary, he helped to support Admiral *Horthy's activities in deposing Béla *Kun and became Prime Minister in April 1921. With his belief in the need to preserve feudal aristocratic privileges, he ended land redistribution. Bethlen gained the support of the Roman *Catholic Church by giving it substantial control over education, and confirmed his political position through merging the popular smallholders' party with his own Christian Social Party. He also reintroduced the open ballot in the country districts in order to restore landowner control over the vote of their tenants. Eventually, he also received the support of the army by allowing it to ignore some of the restrictions imposed upon it by the Treaty of *Trianon. He tried hard to promote modern agricultural and industrial techniques, and foreign investment. His regime came unstuck as a result of the Great *Depression, with the collapse of production and exports followed by a banking crisis in 1931. He resigned in the face of growing unrest. He managed to hide from the German troops occupying the country in 1944, but was discovered by the Soviet forces who followed. The Red Army took Bethlen to Moscow, where he died.

Bethmann Hollweg, Theobald von
(b. 29 Nov. 1856, d. 2 Jan. 1921). Chancellor of Germany and Minister President of Prussia 1909–17

From 1899 the chief commissioner (Oberpräsident) of the Prussian province of Brandenburg, he became Prussian Minister of the Interior (1905) and German Secretary of State for Home Affairs (1907). Bethman Hollweg tried to avoid the failure of his predecessor, von *Bülow, to build a parliamentary majority for his government. As Chancellor, therefore, he tried to seek the consent of parliament as little as possible, with the result that urgently needed reforms, most importantly of the country's finances, could not take place. This political stalemate, and Germany's increasing inability to find the necessary finances to keep up with the arms race, contributed directly to the sense of crisis that led Germany into World War I. More directly, his contribution to the outbreak of the war lay in his unconditional support of Austria after the assassination of the Archduke Francis Ferdinand at *Sarajevo in 1914, in the hope that any ensuing war would be restricted to Russia. From 1916 Bethmann Hollweg was forced to acquiesce in *Hindenburg's direction of the war.

Bethune, Mary McLeod (b. 10 July 1875, d. 18 May 1955). US civil rights activist

Born in Myseville, South Carolina, she was an early feminist and African-American activist who studied at Scotia College and the Moody Bible Institute. She founded a female teaching academy in 1904 at the age of 29, which became Bethune-Cookman College (Florida), nineteen years later. She chaired the National Association of Colored Women in 1926 and, between 1935 and 1949, the National Council of Negro Women. She was a prominent federal administrator for youth under the *New Deal Youth Administration and was close to Eleanor *Roosevelt.

Bevan, Aneurin ('Nye') (b. 15 Nov. 1897, d. 6 July 1960). British politician

Born in Tredegar, Monmouthshire, he started work in a coalmine at the age of 13. He was active in the South Wales Miners' Federation, and was elected to Parliament as *Labour Party MP for Ebbw Vale in 1929. Angered by *MacDonald's failure to deal with unemployment, Bevan briefly considered supporting *Mosley, but instead became an outspoken socialist critic of government policies. From 1939 until 1940, he was expelled from the party for advocating a *Popular Front against *Fascism, and remained vocal during the war, as a critic of Labour's subordinate attitude to *Churchill.

As Minister of Health under *Attlee, (1945–51), he was responsible for a programme of house-building, and, most importantly, in 1948, for the creation of the *National Health Service. In doing this, he tackled resistance from members of the medical profession by allowing private practice to continue. In 1951 he became Minister of Labour, but resigned over *Gaitskell's imposition of charges for adult false teeth and spectacles, in order to help pay for Britain's contribution towards the *Korean War. The informal Bevanite group, opposed to high defence spending and the party's concessions to capitalism, then formed within the party. In 1955 Bevan failed to defeat Gaitskell in the party leadership election, but in 1956 he became Shadow Foreign Secretary after he had criticized Eden's activities in the *Suez Crisis. In 1957 he opposed those in the Bevanite group who demanded unilateral renunciation of the hydrogen bomb, thus dividing the left of the party. He was a brilliant and inspirational speaker in debates and on the platform. His wife, Jennie Lee, was also a Labour MP and minister.

Beveridge Report (UK)
William *Beveridge's 1942 report on *Social Insurance and Allied Services* was a full-scale review of social services in Britain. Its main proposal was a universal social insurance scheme to cover areas such as unemployment benefits and family allowances. This aimed at universal protection from poverty by creating a financial safety net. The report also emphasized the importance of full employment. It was greeted with great enthusiasm, and sold over half a million copies, but the wartime coalition decided only to plan to implement it, rather than carry out its recommendations in full. The report was debated in the House of Commons in February 1943, when James Griffiths led a Labour revolt against government reluctance to implement it. This was important in convincing the electorate that the *Labour Party would best create a just society after the war, and prepared

the ground for *Attlee's surprise victory against *Churchill in 1945. Its recommendations formed the foundation of British social and economic policy from 1945 until the advent of *Thatcherism in 1979.

Beveridge, William Henry, 1st Baron Beveridge of Tuggal (b. 5 Mar. 1879, d. 16 Mar. 1963). British economist and social reformer

Born in Rangpur, Bengal, he was educated at Charterhouse and Oxford. He then held a fellowship at University College, Oxford, until 1909, while his involvement with *Toynbee Hall as Sub-Warden laid the foundation of a deep commitment to the social problems of unemployment, malnutrition, and old age. He was also, during 1906–8, a leader-writer on social affairs with the *Morning Post*. In 1909, Beveridge joined the Board of Trade as Winston *Churchill's personal assistant, becoming closely involved in the drawing-up of social legislation, such as the establishment of labour exchanges and the National Insurance Act (1911). From 1919 to 1937 he was director of the London School of Economics, and was Vice-Chancellor of London University (1926–8). In 1937, he returned to Oxford as Master of University College. During those years he also served on numerous public committees, e.g. as chairman of the Unemployment Insurance Statutory Committee (1934–44). He again served as a civil servant from 1940, in the Ministry of Labour; but, after disagreements there with Ernest *Bevin, he became chairman of the interdepartmental committee on social insurance and allied services. In this post, in 1942 he produced his most important work, the *Beveridge Report, a full-scale review of social services in Britain. He was elected as Liberal MP for Berwick-upon-Tweed in 1944, in order to support the report in parliament. He lost his seat in 1945, and entered the *Lords as a Liberal in 1946. He then concentrated his prolific energy in writing on historical, social, economic, and philosophical matters.

Bevin, Ernest (b. 7 Mar. 1881, d. 14 Apr. 1951). British Minister of Labour 1940–5, Foreign Secretary 1945–51

Born in Winsford (Somerset), he began work in Bristol as a van driver, and considered becoming a *Baptist minister, before emerging as a leader of dock-workers. He became assistant secretary of the Dockers' Union in 1911, and then persuaded eighteen unions to merge to form the Transport and General Workers' Union in 1922. His union supported the miners in the *General Strike

of 1926, but he was also active in negotiations for a settlement. As chairman of the *TUC (Trades Union Congress) general council from 1937, he was a crucial figure when war broke out in 1939, and in 1940, he was appointed Minister of Labour and National Service by *Churchill. This involved entering parliament as MP for Central Wandsworth. Bevin was tremendously successful in expanding and organizing a labour force to meet wartime production. In 1945, *Attlee appointed him Foreign Secretary, in which post he was influential in creating *NATO in 1949. He secured the US *Marshall Plan for Britain, but he was unable to make *Palestine's transformation into Israel an easy one for Britain. He was Lord Privy Seal from March 1951 until his death.

Bharatiya Janata Party (BJP)

In 1976, a coalition of Indian parties formed as the **Janata Morcha** (People's Movement). This was in response to the authoritarian rule of Indira *Gandhi in the 'Emergency' of 1975–7. It consisted of five different parties: Bharatiya Lok Dal, Congress (O), Congress for Democracy, Jana Sangh, and the socialists. Led by Morarji *Desai, it gained a majority in the 1977 elections, thus ending the *Congress party's monopoly of national power. The Janata Morcha ended Gandhi's emergency legislation, and restored civil liberties and free speech. However, it was weakened by constant rifts between its component fractions, and lost in 1979 against the resurgent Mrs Gandhi. One of its component groups reorganized itself as the Bharatiya Janata Party (BJP) in 1980. In the 1990s this emerged as the principal rival to the Congress Party. Led by *Vajpayee, it became the governing party in 1998. The BJP gained popular support against the secularism of Congress, on a platform of Hindu nationalism. It lost power unexpectedly in the 2004 elections, whereupon the party became disoriented and plagued by scandals.

(⊕) SEE WEB LINKS

• The official website of the BJP.

Bhave, Vinoba (b. 11 Sept. 1895, d. 15 Nov. 1982). Indian leader

Born in Gagoda (Maharashtra) of a high-caste Brahmin family, Bhave became an ardent disciple of *Gandhi in 1916. Interned regularly in the 1920s and 1930s for his non-violent opposition to British rule, he was imprisoned (1940–4) for his opposition to Indian participation in World War II. After Gandhi's assassination in 1948 he was regarded as the leading exponent of Gandhism. In 1948 he founded the Sarvodaya Samaj to work among Indian refugees, and in 1958 he began the Bhoodan or land-gift movement, with the object of acquiring land for redistribution among landless low-caste villagers. At first his object was to acquire individual plots, but later he sought to transfer ownership of entire villages to village councils, walking some 45,000 miles in his campaign. While it did lead to a substantial redistribution of land, most of the land gifts were unproductive and uneconomic. He also led the Shantri Sena volunteer movement for conflict resolution and economic and social reform.

Bhopal

The capital city of the state of Madhya Pradesh in India. On 3 December 1984 it was the scene of the worst industrial accident in history, when 45 tons of the toxic gas methyl isocyanate escaped from a plant owned by the US corporation Union Carbide. Probably 2,500 people died within twenty-four hours, while an estimated 50,000 or more victims suffered greater or lesser lung disease and other complications. Efforts by the Indian government to obtain adequate compensation for the victims because of Union Carbide's sub-standard safety levels were only partially successful, mainly because of the intricacies of the legal system in the USA, where the trials were held.

Bhumibol, Adulyadej (b. 5 Dec. 1927). King (Rama IX) of Thailand 1946–

Born in Massachusetts, where his father, Prince Mahidol of Songkhla, studied medicine, he succeeded his brother, Ananda Mahidol, to the throne, and was crowned in 1950 upon finishing his studies in Switzerland. Following the abolition of the absolute monarchy in the 1932 revolution, the King retained a largely ceremonial role as head of state, and as Commander-in-Chief. The world's longest reigning monarch became an important integrative national symbol, and a moderating force in the country's stormy political history, which was characterized by varying degrees of military rule.

Bhutan

A small buffer state in the eastern Himalayas between India and China. Under the patronage of British India since 1774,

British control over its foreign and to some extent also its domestic politics passed over to India after independence in 1949. Apart from its relations with India, it remained in isolation, preserving its social and economic traditions against economic change. Hence, despite some constitutional reform in 1968, in practice it continued to be ruled by a theocratic elite of monks belonging to the Lamaist monastic tradition and a king (Maharaja), Jigme Singhye Wangchuck, from 1972. One of the poorest countries in the world, its backward agriculture, which employs 90 per cent of the country's working population, remains characterized by subsistence farming. In the 1990s, social tensions emerged with the growth of a community of Nepalese origin, which demanded equal political, social, and economic rights. In the late 1990s, the ruling elite's policies of discrimination against the Nepalese minority were slightly relaxed, not least through a royal amnesty in 1997. In the early years of 2000, Jigme Singhye Wangchuck carefully introduced democratic institutions. A new constitution provided for a constitutional democracy, with parliamentary elections to be held for the first time in 2008. In 2006, Jigme Singhye resigned to make way for his son, Jigme Kesar Namgyal Wangchuk. As part of the country's democratization process, private newspapers were allowed in 2006.

Bhutto, Benazir (b. 21 June 1953). Prime Minister of Pakistan 1988–90, 1993–6

Early career Born in the Sind Province as the daughter of Zulfikar Ali *Bhutto, Benazir studied history and politics at Harvard and Oxford, where she became the first foreign president of the Oxford Union Society. She returned upon her father's assumption of the Presidency in 1977, and advised him briefly on foreign policy issues. When her father was deposed in July 1977, she was placed under house arrest. After spending two years in exile in Britain (1984–6), Bhutto returned to Pakistan and, with her mother, became chairwoman of the Pakistan People's Party (PPP). After an unsuccessful attempt to come to power on a wave of populist support in 1987, she reformed the PPP by moving it to the right, and by bringing the party's administration firmly under her control. This enabled the PPP to emerge from the 1988 elections with a simple majority.

In power As Prime Minister, Bhutto aimed for Pakistan to improve relations with India, return to the *Commonwealth, and, without losing the support of the army, reduce involvement in Afghanistan. After a year in office she was accused of abetting corruption and failing to eradicate any of the country's domestic problems, which were compounded by the presence of some three million Afghan refugees. She was dismissed in 1990, and lost the subsequent elections. Three years later, she staged a spectacular comeback in the elections. Cleared in the courts of the corruption allegations, the main challenge of her term in office was the growth of *Islamic fundamentalism, which forced her to concede the introduction of Islamic law (shariah) in one of the areas of the North-West Frontier province. Corruption charges resurfaced, notably in connection to the role of her husband, whom she had appointed to the post of Investment Minister and who had apparently taken bribes.

She was dismissed by President Farooq Leghari in 1996, and was defeated in the following elections of 1997. While her husband was imprisoned in 1996, she left the country in 1999 and from that time was a fugitive from Pakistani justice.

Bhutto, Zulfikar Ali (b. 5 Jan. 1928, d. 4 Apr. 1979). President of Pakistan 1971–3, Prime Minister 1973–7

Early career Born in Larkana (Sind) into a wealthy landowning family, he studied law at Berkeley and Oxford, becoming a barrister in Karachi in 1953. He came to the attention of *Ayub Khan, who brought him into his government, first as Minister of Fuel, Power, and Natural Resources (1958), then as Foreign Minister (1963). Rejecting too close relations with the US, he pursued a policy of greater neutrality (against Ayub Khan's own inclinations) in favour of greater cooperation with the Soviet Union and China. He persuaded Ayub Khan to precipitate the second *Indo-Pakistan War in September 1956 by sending troops into Indian Kashmir. He opposed the subsequent *Tashkent Agreement, in which India and Pakistan compromised in their dispute over *Kashmir. Expelled from the government in 1966, Bhutto founded the People's Party of Pakistan (PPP) in 1967.

In power Bhutto won the 1970 elections in West Pakistan with 81 out of 138 allocated seats, but refused to discuss the demands of the *Awami League, which had gained an overwhelming mandate with 160 out of the 162 seats allocated to East Pakistan. This ultimately led to the separation of East Pakistan as Bangladesh in 1971. In its wake, he was appointed as Pakistan's first civilian President. He nationalized a large number of industries, and introduced a new Constitution in 1973. Despite his formidable political skills and his powerful personality, his power was based throughout on the support of the military. He called a surprise election in 1977, which he was only able to win by large-scale electoral fraud. It led to serious riots which the army quelled, deposing Bhutto in the process. Vastly overestimating his own popularity and strength, Bhutto continued to be defiant against the new regime, insisting that *Zia-ul-Haq would not dare touch him. He was wrong. He was sentenced to death and executed for the alleged murder of a political opponent.

Biafran War (1967–70, Nigeria)
A Nigerian civil war caused by irreconcilable ethnic tensions. In 1966, an army coup brought to power a military regime headed by an Ibo (from the south), who was himself deposed by a group of northern military officers under the leadership of *Gowon, in order to forestall Ibo domination. Many of the Ibo people were murdered in retaliation, which made them feel even more acutely their disadvantaged position in the Nigerian polity. In response, on 30 May 1967, the erstwhile Military Governor, Colonel *Ojukwu, declared the independence of the Ibo-dominated Eastern Nigeria as the Republic of Biafra. It had few chances of survival, as the Nigerian state was determined to regain control of this area of vital oil reserves. Despite desperate efforts, international recognition was only forthcoming from four African countries, as well as Haiti. By 1968, Port Harcourt and Enugu, the Biafran capital, had come under Nigerian control, making Biafra land-locked. Surrender was announced on 12 January 1970. The war caused the starvation and death of perhaps a million Ibo people.

Bidault, Georges (b. 5 Oct. 1899, d. 26 Jan. 1983). Prime Minister of France 1946, 1949–50, 1958
He joined the French *Résistance in 1941, and succeeded Jean Moulin as leader of the National Resistance Council in 1943. After liberation in 1944 he co-founded the Christian Democrat *MRP, whose chairman he was (1949–52). As Foreign Minister (1944–6, 1947–8, 1953–4), he was responsible for the transition in 1947 of French policy towards Germany, from de *Gaulle's initial hardline stance to *Schuman's conciliatory attitude. His opposition to de Gaulle became more vociferous in 1959, when he opposed his policies to end the *Algerian War of Independence. He became president of the Rassemblement pour l'Algérie Française (Union for French Algeria) and an executive member of the *Organisation de l'Armée

Secrète. In 1963 he went into exile in Brazil and then Belgium, but returned in 1968.

Bierut, Boleslaw (b. 18 Apr. 1892, d. 12 Mar. 1956). President of Poland 1945–52, Chairman of the Council of Ministers 1952–4

Born near Lublin, he became a printer and joined the Polish Communist Party in 1920. In 1933, he was sentenced to seven years' imprisonment for his party activities. He was released early, however, and in 1938 he went to Moscow. He returned in 1943 to work with the Communist resistance there. As chairman of the Communist National Council for the Homeland from 1944, he organized the Communist takeover of Poland, which had been facilitated greatly by the *Warsaw Rising. A colourless, anti-intellectual, and uninspiring bureaucrat, his main virtue was his obedience to *Stalin, whose directions he obeyed without fail. He died at the XX Communist Party Congress in Moscow, which happened to trigger the demise of *Stalinism which he had promoted so earnestly.

Bikini Island, see MICRONESIA

Biko, Steve (Bantu Stephen) (b. 18 Dec. 1946, d. 12 Sept. 1977). South African political activist

In 1965 he won a scholarship to study medicine at the University of Natal (Durban) and soon became involved in the multiracial National Union of South African Students (NUSAS). He came to believe that effective resistance to the *apartheid regime could only come under Black leadership in Black organizations. He founded the Black South African Students Organization in 1969, whose first president he became. Under the influence of the US *Black Consciousness movement, he developed the theory that Blacks had to become conscious of their own identity as a precondition for political emancipation. A brilliant and charismatic speaker, the rhetoric he employed was radical and, at times, violent. At the same time, his actual programme was relatively liberal. Thus, he derived most of his following from educated circles of the Coloureds (mixed race) and Blacks, but failed to extend his support to the Black townships. He left university in 1972, and in 1973 the South African government confined his freedom of movement to his native King William's Town. Arrested several times (1976–7) he was arrested on 19 August 1977 for moving outside his restricted area. He died from a brain haemorrhage and other injuries caused by police brutality while in police custody.

Bildt, Carl (b. 15 July 1949). Prime Minister of Sweden 1991–4

Born in Halmstad, Bildt was born into a family of Danish aristocratic origin and of good political connections since the days of Gillis Bildt (Prime Minister 1888–9). He studied political science at Stockholm University. He became chairman (1973–4) of the student's union of the Moderate Party, whose political fortunes were greatly improved under the leadership (1971–81) of his father-in-law, Gösta Bohman. A member of the Riksdag (parliament) since 1979, he served as Under-Secretary of State (1979–81). As party leader from 1986, he rebuilt his party and pledged it to a reform of the *welfare state. As head of a four-party government coalition, he tried to reduce the influence of the state in economy and society, while continuing to press for the country's membership of the European Union. In June 1994, he signed Sweden's accession treaty to the EU. Owing to rising unemployment and other economic difficulties, he lost the 1994 elections, and in 1995 he became active as negotiator for the European Union in the *Bosnian Civil War. Bildt co-chaired the *Dayton peace talks, and in 1999 he was appointed the *UN Secretary General's Special Envoy to the Balkans. Bildt returned to Swedish politics in 2006, when he became Minister of Foreign Affairs.

Bin Laden, Osama (Bin Ladin, Mujahid Usamah) (b. 1957). Most Wanted Terrorist

Raised in Medina and Hejaz, he was the nephew of one of Saudia Arabia's wealthiest business men. He went to Afghanistan in 1979, to assist fellow Muslims in a 'holy' struggle (jihad) against the Soviet occupying forces. In addition, Bin Laden became effective at raising money for the Afghan cause. He became head of the *al-Qaeda organization in 1988, and was believed to be responsible for the killing of eighteen US servicemen during the US action in Somalia. As he became increasingly hostile to the Saudi monarchy, which he considered beholden to the USA, his Saudi Arabian citizenship was withdrawn in 1991. Bin Laden turned his wrath against his former allies, the USA, in the belief that a jihad should be declared against the Judaeo-Christian values it epitomized. For his cause, he was believed to have amassed a fortune of hundreds of millions of dollars. This, and the willingness of his followers to die in the jihad, made him such a potent foe of the US and of Western civilization. Video evidence captured his admission of responsibility for the *September 11 attacks, which sparked the US *War on Terrorism.

It also turned the US security apparatus against him, though his whereabouts remained elusive.

Bird, Vere Cornwall, see ANTIGUA AND BARBUDA

Biya, Paul (b. 13 Feb. 1933). President of Cameroon 1982–

Born at Mvomeka, he was educated in Yaoundé (1954–6) and in Paris (1956–62) before returning to Cameroon. He held various positions in *Ahidjo's government, and became his Secretary-General and Minister of State in 1968. In 1975 he became Prime Minister, and in 1982 he succeeded Ahidjo upon his retirement. Ahidjo's desire to maintain a position of influence in the country caused a power struggle, which Biya won. The hardships caused by a severe economic crisis forced him to introduce a programme of democratization in 1992. Re-elected several times with the help of electoral fraud, he continued to preside over one of the world's most corrupt governments.

BJP, see BHARATIYA JANATA PARTY

Black and Tans

An auxiliary force of the Royal Irish Constabulary, comprising of British ex-soldiers. It was established in January 1920 to supplement the regular force, which was under increasing pressure from the activities of Irish republicans. It gained its name from its distinctive uniforms which, owing to a shortage of police uniforms, included items of army clothing. The Black and Tans adopted a policy of harsh reprisals against republicans, killing many people in raids, and destroying property. In December 1920, they burnt down the County Hall in Cork, in retaliation against *IRA attacks, and earlier in the year, on 21 November, twelve people had been killed when they fired into a football crowd. They were often accused of brutality, and were withdrawn after the Anglo-Irish Treaty of 1921.

Black Consciousness

An awareness of the identity, aspirations, and commonality of the Black peoples of the world by those of African origin. In the 1920s it developed rapidly in the USA, where Marcus *Garvey became a cult figure, while the Harlem Renaissance of the 1920s brought Blacks into positions of considerable artistic and musical visibility. During the 1930s in Africa and the Caribbean the writings of Aimé Césaire and Léopold-Sédar *Senghor helped to cultivate 'négritude'—the belief that the Black

African has a distinct cultural heritage which has to be conserved against colonial pressures towards Europeanization. On both sides of the Atlantic there has been a nostalgia for the 'beauty and harmony of traditional African society', based on emotion, intuition, and spontaneous social interaction, as against the rationalistic tradition of European hellenism. In the 1950s and 1960s Black Consciousness spawned a variety of movements in the USA such as the *Black Power movement, and intersected with non-integrationist movements within the African-American community such as the *Nation of Islam.

Black Dragon Society, see AMUR RIVER SOCIETY

Black, Hugo Lafayette (b. 27 Feb. 1886, d. 25 Sept. 1971). US Supreme Court Justice 1937–71

Born in Harlan, Alabama, Black graduated from the University of Alabama Law School in 1906, and qualified as a lawyer. He entered politics as a Democrat, and became a US Senator in 1927. A strong supporter of Franklin *Roosevelt in the 1930s, he was nominated and confirmed as a Justice in 1937. Although for two years he had belonged to the *Ku Klux Klan, and continued to support it during the 1920s, he became a highly influential liberal voice in the *Supreme Court's decisions, upholding the right of free speech as absolute. His written opinions banned public-school prayers as contrary to the separation of church and state. They also, mandated reform of electoral practices designed to undermine Black rights in the south. Black also required legal representation for defendants in serious cases to be paid for by the state. The one illiberal decision associated with his name concerned his validation of the dispropriation and relocation of Japanese Americans during World War II (in the case of *Korematsu* v. *USA*, 1944). He also refused to extend First Amendment protection to 'sit-in' demonstrators during the civil rights and anti-Vietnam war protests. He died a week after retiring from the court.

Black Monday (19 Oct. 1987)

The worst stock-market collapse since the *Wall Street Crash, when the average share index (Dow Jones) on the New York Stock Exchange (Wall Street) fell by more than 20 per cent, leading to similar levels of decline in other stock markets around the world. It was caused mainly by overconfidence in the economy during the mid-1980s, which had led to a disproportionate inflation in share prices.

Black Power (USA)

Originating as a movement in the 1960s, it was developed into a coherent ideology by Stokely Carmichael and Charles Hamilton in their book *Black Power* (1969). It called upon African Americans to take pride in their culture and their descent. By exhibiting a greater sense of solidarity and community, they could create a distinctively Black economic and political base that would increase the bargaining power of African Americans in their claim for full equality in US society. Organizations closely associated with the Black Power movement, such as the Student Nonviolent Co-ordinating Committee and the Congress of Racial Equality, had been instrumental in the movement's original aim of integration.

As these goals were seen to be unfulfilled, Black Power adopted an increasingly assertive and confrontational rhetoric. The most prominent of the Black Power groups became the Black Panther Party for Self-defense, which urged the self-help of black communities through the organization of youth centres, health clinics, and so on. It also advocated the organization of paramilitary self-defence units. The violence associated with such Black Power groups led many Whites to turn against the civil rights movement in the 'White backlash' of the late 1960s and 1970s. Black Power was opposed by the leaders and members of the *civil rights movement such as Martin Luther *King. The Black Power movement destroyed any hopes for the Black unity which it advocated, but its actions did result in a significant increase in cultural awareness among many young African Americans.

Black Thursday (24 Oct. 1929), see WALL STREET CRASH

Blackshirts (*camicie nere*)

The colloquial name given to the members of *Mussolini's paramilitary Squadre d'Azione (**'Action Squad'**) after the black shirts of their uniform. They were founded in 1919 to fight socialist and Communist groups in the streets and disrupt their meetings, as well as to maintain law and order within the *Fascist movement itself.

MVSN; BROWNSHIRTS; SA

Blair, Anthony Charles Lynton
('Tony' Blair) (b. 6 May 1953). British Prime Minister, 1997–2007

Early career Born in Edinburgh, he was educated at Fettes and at Oxford. After qualifying as a lawyer, he was called to the Bar in 1976, and elected as *Labour MP for Sedgefield in 1983. As Shadow Home Secretary under John *Smith from 1992, Blair successfully developed Labour's image as a party which was strict on law and order, an area that had hitherto been a strong asset of the *Conservative Party. His youthful image, and his ability to unite the reformist elements within the party, secured his succession to the party leadership in 1994, after Smith's sudden death. He accelerated his predecessor's drive for the modernization of the party: within a year he had successfully completed an unprecedented programme of internal party reform which culminated in the amendment of Clause IV of its constitution, removing the commitment to nationalization. Blair was elected in a landslide, as Labour obtained 419 seats (+148) against the Conservatives' 165 (−161).

First term (1997–2001) Perhaps the most notable achievement of the first Blair administration was constitutional reform. Home Rule was granted to Scotland, which received its own parliament, and to Wales, which received a National Assembly. London was granted its own assembly and a directly elected Mayor, and first steps were taken towards a reform of the unelected House of Lords through the abolition of the representation of hereditary aristocrats by right. Blair was also successful in his handling of the *Northern Ireland peace process, since unlike his predecessor, *Major, he was not beholden to the parliamentary strength of the *Ulster Unionists. Blair was positively inclined towards the EU, and supported institutional reform as well as a reduction in EU spending. However, under pressure from his powerful Chancellor of the Exchequer, *Brown, he declined to adopt the *euro.

Blair was extremely careful not to alienate the middle classes whose votes had carried him to power. He kept his promises of keeping income taxation at its low levels, and reduced social spending on unemployment benefits. His moderate policies, his personal charm, and his touch at expressing popular opinion were all heightened by the weakness of the leadership of his *Conservative rivals. For this reason, Blair achieved what no Labour leader had managed before him: he avoided a devaluation of the currency in his first term in office, and he was re-elected to a second consecutive term, in a second landslide victory in 2001.

Second term (2001–5) Reversing some of his fiscal conservatism, Blair staked much political capital on investment in the *National Health Service, education and infrastructure. Annual spending on the NHS increased by 7.5 per cent in real terms, while

Blair not only increased spending on education, but he also introduced university fees, a highly controversial move within his own party. Overshadowing all domestic reform was Blair's controversial decision to commit 45,000 British troops to participating in the *Iraq War. Blair justified his actions by vastly exaggerating the threat posed by Iraq. Britain's involvement in the Iraq War proved deeply unpopular. The Hutton and Butler enquiries of 2004 absolved Blair of misleading parliament, but the public's perception that Blair had not been truthful about the war eroded his personal popularity. Blair won the 2005 election, with a reduced majority of 67 seats, and backed by just 35.3 per cent of the popular vote. Blair, who had announced that he would not seek a further term in office, became the only Labour leader to win three elections in a row.

Third term (2005–7) Blair continued to be dogged by the occupation of Iraq, as growing discontent within the army leadership became known in public. His commitment to further public reform became difficult to realize owing to his reduced majority and an increasingly rebellious parliamentary party. In 2005, Blair proved his leadership abilities in his response to the *London Bombings, demonstrating compassion for the victims, a determination to pursue tough and controversial anti-terrorism measures, and an appeal against racism. With Gordon Brown, Britain took the lead among industrial nations in cancelling the debt of African states. Blair also pushed towards a new international agreement on preventing climate change that moved beyond the *Kyoto Protocol and included the USA, China, and India. In part because of the continuing failure to stabilize Iraq, Blair was under growing pressure from his own party to resign. Blair did make way for Gordon Brown, but not before overseeing the successful implementation of the *St Andrews Agreement and the return to peaceful self-government in Northern Ireland,

Blitzkrieg ('lightning war')
The description of the rapid German campaigns in which Poland, the Low Countries, and France were occupied at the beginning of World War II. In England, the term was shortened ('Blitz') and adapted to describe the German air raids on London, Coventry, and other industrial cities in 1940–1.

Bloc Québécois (BQ) (Canada)
A party founded by *Bouchard in 1990 to represent the *Quebec separatist movement in the federal parliament. Supported by the

*Parti Québécois (PQ), it gained 54 seats in the 1993 elections. Owing to the dismal electoral performance of the *Conservative Party, it became the official opposition, which gave it an extra platform to campaign for the independence of Quebec. Together with the PQ, it presented the issue of sovereignty in a referendum in the province in 1995, which it narrowly lost. It lost its status as the official opposition in 1997, when it gained 44 seats. Led by Gilles Duceppe from 1997, the BQ's representation stabilized at over 50 seats in subsequent federal elections. From 2006, it lent its support to *Harper's minority government on a number of issues. Even though the *Conservatives had a very different electoral base, the BQ shared common ground on the issue of more provincial rights against the federal government.

(🌐) **SEE WEB LINKS**

• The official website of the Bloc Québécois.

Bloody Sunday, see NORTHERN IRELAND

Blue Shirt Society
A secret Chinese organization within the *Guomindang (KMT). It was formed on 1 March 1932 in response to the Japanese invasion of Manchuria (*Manchukuo) by members and graduates of the Whampoa Military Academy. Often mistaken for a *Fascist organization, its aim was to strengthen China through political and economic reform, as envisaged by *Sun Yat-sen. Organized in various circles, the biggest of which was the Chinese Renaissance Society, it demanded a strong, sovereign central government, led by a reformed KMT movement. This should implement land reforms such as farming cooperatives and reductions in land rent, guiding China's commercial development through authoritarian policies until China was sufficiently stable to sustain a democracy. The Blue Shirt Society initiated various mass campaigns during the 1930s but, together with other KMT factions, it was disbanded by the party's Extraordinary National Conference in 1938.

Blum, Léon (b. 9 Apr. 1872, d. 30 Mar. 1950). Prime Minister of France 1936–7, 1938, 1946–7
Of a Jewish family from the *Alsace, the journalist was drawn into politics by the *Dreyfus Affair. As secretary from 1916 he was instrumental in reforming the *Socialist Party (SFIO) towards pragmatism, and in 1936 he became the first Socialist Prime Minister at

the head of a *Popular Front government. The government broke up because of financial difficulties and his refusal to intervene in the Spanish Civil War. A second period in office lasted for only a month, again because of his financial policies. Arrested by the Vichy government in 1940 and charged with causing France's defeat, his skilful defence obliged the government to call off his trial (1942). From 1943, he was interned in several German *concentration camps. Back in office at the head of a caretaker government, he helped write the Constitution of the Fourth Republic

BARTHOU, JEAN LOUIS

Boer ('farmer'), see AFRIKANER

Boer War (1899–1902), see SOUTH AFRICAN WAR

Bokassa, Jean Bédel (b. 22 Feb. 1921, d. 5 Nov. 1996). President of the *Central African Republic 1966–79

Born in Bobangui, he joined the French army in 1939, advancing to the rank of captain by 1961. He became Chief of Staff in the newly created Central African Army in 1964, and on 1 January 1966 assumed the presidency after a successful coup. He established a ruthless dictatorship, channelling up to a third of the annual state budget into his private fortune. He proclaimed himself emperor in 1976, and crowned himself in a lavish ceremony in 1977. To the later embarrassment of *Giscard d'Estaing, France supported his idiosyncratic regime until 1979. International opposition grew, however, on account of his friendly relations with *Gaddafi, and in response to his personal involvement in the brutal murder of 100 schoolchildren. He was deposed in a coup carried out by the French military, but escaped abroad. Sentenced to death twice, he was pardoned upon his return to the Central African Republic in 1988, when his sentence was commuted to lifelong imprisonment with hard labour.

Bolger, James Brendan ('Jim') (b. 31 May 1935). Prime Minister of New Zealand, 1990–7

Early career Born in Taranaki as the son of Irish immigrants, he became a farmer. In 1972 Bolger became a Member of Parliament for the *National Party, rising quickly to become parliamentary under-secretary in 1975, and Minister of Fisheries and Associate Minister of Agriculture in 1977. In 1978, he held the portfolios of Labour and Immigration, in which position he liberalized the country's relatively rigid labour laws. After the National Party's election defeat in 1984, he became a

prominent spokesperson for his party, and in 1986 he became chairman of the National Party and leader of the opposition. Following another election defeat against *Lange's *Labour Party, he shifted the party from its previous interventionist stance to one which endorsed the radical liberalization of the economy. Fostering an image of solid reliability (as against the charismatic Lange), he led his party to a landslide victory in the 1990 general elections, ruthlessly exploiting Labour's internal divisions.

In office Arguing that the country could no longer afford its comprehensive welfare system, Bolger revolutionized social policy from universal to means-tested assistance designed to benefit only the very poorest sections of society. Pensions were no longer automatically guaranteed, rents in state-owned accommodation were raised to market levels, and expenditure on university education was drastically cut. He was re-elected in 1993, albeit with a small majority, which enabled him to continue his reforms. At the same time, he tried very hard to come to an agreement with the *Maoris about their land claims resulting from the Treaty of *Waitangi. He struck a more populist note in his outspoken condemnation of the French resumption of nuclear testing at Mururoa in 1995. He was succeeded by Jenny *Shipley, and in 1998 was appointed ambassador to Washington.

Bolivia

A Latin American country torn by internal violence and political instability for much of its contemporary history.

International conflicts (up to 1941) From the foundation of the Republic of Bolivia (1884), tin mining constituted a major source of export earnings. The resulting profits did not benefit the population in general, however, but three families and their dependants (the 'tin barons'), who used their influence to determine the politics of the country. During this time, sharecropping agriculture was extended, which destroyed the native Indian culture in these areas and increased the number of landless labourers. In three wars, Bolivia lost more than half of its territory: its coastline was lost to Chile (1879–83), substantial areas of rubber forest to the east were lost to Brazil (1902-3), while in the *Chaco War (1932-5) a large territory to the south was lost to Paraguay. The large debts incurred by this last war, together with the effect of the Great *Depression, led to a deep economic recession.

The dominance of the military (1941-85) In 1941, the National Revolutionary Movement (Movimiento Nacionalista Revolucionario, MNR) was founded under the leadership of *Paz Estenssoro. Originally a small organization supported by a few hundred university graduates and disappointed Chaco veterans, it joined the government in 1943 as a result of its good connections with the military. During the following three years it developed mass support amongst the middle classes, tin miners, agricultural labourers, and farmers, all of whom were radicalized by the brutal military oppression of strikes and unrest.

In a coup in 1946, complete military rule was re-established, but Paz Estenssoro returned to Bolivia following his election victory in 1952. Almost immediately, the mines were nationalized, universal suffrage introduced, and land reform implemented. This brought about not only social revolution but a political one as well, depriving the old elites of their power bases. The period was known as 'La Violencia', as sporadic domestic violence and unrest caused the loss of hundreds of thousands of lives. In response to this, after twelve years of MNR rule Paz Estenssoro was deposed in a coup by the military, which governed the country almost without interruption for the next eighteen years. Bolivia returned to civilian rule only in 1982, though freedom of manoeuvre remained constricted by the continuing domination of the military, which staged two abortive coups in 1984 and 1985.

Democratization (1985-2001) Following the collapse of world tin prices, President Paz Estenssoro (1985-9) tried to deal with the complete breakdown of the country's tin-mining industry through drastic economic liberalization. The programme, which has been maintained by his successors, yielded considerable economic benefits such as the reduction of inflation, but at a high social cost in one of Latin America's poorest countries after Haiti. Bolivia's predominant political and economic problem from the 1980s onwards has been its economic reliance on the production of cocaine, equivalent to around 25 per cent of its agricultural output. In the early 1990s cocaine was the country's biggest export good, with exports amounting to 50-100 per cent of the value of all legal

Bolivian exports altogether. More than 15 per cent of the working population was employed directly or indirectly by the coca industry, with cocaine exports amounting to a national income of $750 million (according to *The Economist*, 1997). In 1998, the government signed an accord with the United States to substitute cocaine farming by the growing of alternative agricultural crops. Subsequently, the destruction of large cocaine-farming areas at a time of widespread agricultural poverty caused massive popular discontent.

Contemporary politics (since 2001) In 2001 President Hugo Bánzer retired due to ill-health, and was succeeded by Jorge Quiroga Ramirez. Ensuing elections in 2001 produced a protest vote against the establishment, with the indigenous representative of the coca farmers, Evo Morales, obtaining the second largest vote at 20.9 per cent. Morales won the following elections, in the wake of an economic and political crisis in 2004-5. The first indigenous Bolivian to be President, Morales nationalized oil and gas production as a way of fulfilling his pledge better to share the revenues from Latin America's second largest gas reserves among the indigenous population. In 2006, Congress also approved Morales's request for a constitutional assembly. Morales formed close alliances with other left populist regimes, notably *Chávez in Venezuela, and *Castro in Cuba.

Bolsheviks ('the majority')
The radical group of the Russian Social Democratic Party. It derived its name from the 1903 party congress, when it won the vote about the composition of the editorial board of the party newspaper, *Iskra*, against the future *Mensheviks ('the minority'). The term disguises the fact that *Lenin's faction actually lost the most important vote at the congress, the issue of party membership, with the definition proposed by the future Mensheviks being accepted by a majority.

The relationship between the Bolsheviks and the Mensheviks oscillated between cooperation and opposition, until in 1912 the Bolsheviks formally constituted themselves as a separate party under Lenin's leadership. By this time, they advocated violent revolution, in contrast to the Mensheviks' more gradualist approach to change. The Bolsheviks accepted Lenin's fundamental belief in the need for an elite leadership which would guide the proletariat to revolution and, ultimately, to *Communism. With their leaders (Lenin, *Zinoviev, and *Stalin) in exile, they were surprised by the *Russian (February) Revolution of 1917. Even after that, it took all of Lenin's political skills and his personal authority to forge a common response to the provisional government, and to organize the October Revolution. Once in power, the party leadership quickly established a hierarchical and authoritarian system of government, while seeking to establish the new Communist state through *Cheka terror and the *Russian Civil War. Once the Bolsheviks had established their control over all of Russia, they adopted the official title of *Communist Party of Russia (and then Soviet Union), though the synonymous name of Bolsheviks continued to be in use until 1952.

Bonar Law, Andrew, see LAW, ANDREW BONAR

Bonomi, Ivanoe (b. 18 Oct. 1873, d. 20 Apr. 1951). Italian anti-Fascist leader
One of the leading proponents of a reformist, pragmatic *socialism which he advocated in *Le vie nuove del socialismo* (The New Paths of Socialism, 1907). None the less, he remained in the minority with his views, such as advocating that the *Socialist Party join coalition governments in order to gain real influence in the Italian state. Following his opposition to the Socialist Party's condemnation of Italy's conquest of Libya he was expelled from the party in 1912. A strong supporter of Italy's entrance into World War I, Bonomi served as Minister of Public Works 1916–17, Minister of War 1920–1, and Prime Minister 1921–2. Following *Mussolini's accession to power he retired from public life, but in late 1942 took up contact with anti-Fascist resistance circles. After Mussolini's fall and the conclusion of an armistice with the Allies on 8 September 1943, Bonomi was chosen to lead the *Committee of National Liberation, which united all anti-Fascist parties. He resigned in June 1945 after the end of World War II in Europe, but became president of the Senate in 1948.

Bophuthatswana, see BANTUSTAN

Borden, Sir Robert Laird (b. 26 June 1854, d. 10 June 1937). Prime Minister of Canada 1911–20
Born at Grand Pré (Nova Scotia), he was admitted to the Nova Scotia Bar in 1878 and became a prominent lawyer in Halifax. In 1896, he was elected to parliament as a *Conservative. As Conservative Party leader from 1901 he successfully rebuilt his party. In 1911 he engineered a broad alliance between various enemies of *Laurier to bring down his government. Remembered particularly for his leadership during World War I, he introduced

national direct taxation (1916) and nationalized some of the railways (1917). Most controversially, when voluntary enlistment for service in the war proved insufficient, he introduced conscription through the Military Service Act (1917). In return for the Canadian contribution to the war effort, he insisted in 1917 that Canada become more independent of British sovereignty, as an 'autonomous nation of an Imperial Commonwealth'. He pressed this claim also as the leader of the Canadian delegation to the *Paris Peace Conference, where the autonomous status of Canada and the other Dominions was internationally recognized. He remained a respected international figure after his retirement in 1920, and was a strong advocate of the *League of Nations.

Boris III (b. 30 Jan. 1894, d. 28 Aug. 1943). King of Bulgaria 1918–43
As Crown Prince he commanded Bulgarian troops on the Macedonian front in World War I, and was defeated by *Franchet d'Esperey's Allied troops. He became King on the abdication of Ferdinand I, at a time when the monarchy was weak. He kept a low profile, and only gradually increased his powers as various radical dictatorships failed one after the other. By 1934 he had come to control public affairs, and in 1935 he instituted a royal dictatorship. He tried to keep out of the growing European conflict, despite his country's military and economic dependence on Germany, and despite his original sympathies with *Mussolini. Faced with military submission to Germany or joining the war on Germany's side, he chose the latter, as this allowed him greater independence. On 1 March 1941, the country joined the Tripartite Pact. However, he did not send his troops to fight against the Soviet Union, nor did he allow the deportation of Jews to *Nazi *concentration camps. The sudden death of this skilful visionary left his country directionless and greatly facilitated the Communist takeover in 1944.

Bormann, Martin (b. 17 June 1900, d. 1 May 1945). Secretary to Hitler 1943–5
Born in Halberstadt, he entered the *Nazi Party in 1928 and rose quickly through its ranks to become deputy Rudolf *Hess in 1933,whom he succeeded as head of the party machine, the Chancery, in 1941. Bormann became a key figure in the closing years of the *Nazi regime. As *Hitler's secretary he became the *Führer's right-hand man, controlling access to him and even the flow of information. He almost certainly died in Berlin when it was captured by the *Red

Army, though his body has never been found. In the *Nuremberg Trials, he was sentenced to death *in absentia*.

Bose, Subhas Chandra (b. 23 Jan. 1897, d. 18 Aug. 1945). Indian nationalist

Born in Cuttack (Orissa) as a Bengali kayasth, he studied at Calcutta (where he was expelled for his Indian nationalism) and Cambridge. Popularly known as Netaji ('revered leader'), he entered the Indian Civil Service, but resigned almost immediately in the wake of *Gandhi's announcement of his non-cooperation campaign in 1921. Gandhi sent him to Calcutta, where he came under the tutelage of Chittaranjan Das. In 1924, Netaji became chief executive officer of the Calcutta Corporation. He was imprisoned later that year for his political activism (until 1927). In 1928 he became secretary of the Indian National *Congress (INC). He was made president of the INC in 1938, but in 1939 he was forced to resign, largely because he had become more radical than Gandhi himself. Imprisoned and then placed under house arrest early in World War II, he escaped and went to Germany. Having failed to gain support there, Netaji travelled to Japan, where he announced the formation of an Indian National Army to drive the British from India. He recruited Indian prisoners of war and formed a provisional government-in-exile, though his army was defeated in Burma. He was reported to have died in an air crash over Taiwan.

Bosnia

The northern half of the state of *Bosnia-Hercegovina since 1580. The term is generally used as an abbreviation for the entire state since its independence in 1992.

Bosnia-Hercegovina

A state in the Balkans composed of some of Europe's most diverse ethnic, cultural and religious populations.

Early history (up to 1992)

A heterogeneous country consisting of Bosnia in the north and Hercegovina in the south, whose population is divided into Muslims (around 40 per cent), Orthodox Serbs (32 per cent), Roman Catholic Croats (18 per cent), as well as a host of ethnic minorities, mainly Montenegrines, Albanians, and Slovenes. Bosnia and Hercegovina were united in 1580 as part of the *Ottoman Empire. As the Ottoman hold over the Balkans progressively weakened, the territory came under the administration of *Austria-Hungary in 1875-8, and was annexed by Austria in 1908. The annexation by Roman Catholic Austria was widely resented. One of the new organizations opposed to Austrian rule, 'Young Bosnia', participated in the *Sarajevo assassination of Archduke Francis Ferdinand in 1914.

The territory became part of the Kingdom of Serbs, Croats, and Slovenes after 1918, which in 1929 became Yugoslavia. During the years of German and Italian occupation in World War II it was home to the *Chetnik resistance movement. After the war it became part of Yugoslavia again. As Yugoslavia's most heterogeneous state it had much less influence in *Tito's state than Serbia or Croatia, while its economic development lagged behind that of its neighbours.

Independence (from 1992)

Inspired by the domestic developments in Slovenia and Croatia, democratic elections were held in 1990, whereupon a coalition government between Muslims, Serbs, and Croats was formed under the nationalist Muslim President *Izetbegovic. It proclaimed its independence from Yugoslavia on 3 March 1992, against fierce opposition from the Serb minority which, under the leadership of *Karadzic, proclaimed the Serb Republic of Bosnia-Hercegovina. The country was torn apart in the *Bosnian Civil War (1992-5), at the end of which the *Dayton Agreement created a fragile state consisting of two halves, a Bosnian Serb half, and a loosely organized Muslim-Croat Federation. Peace was restored, though another wave of migration ensued, as neither ethnicity dared live under the control of another. Meanwhile, the stability of the new state was overwhelmingly dependent on the deployment of 60,000 *NATO troops under US leadership.

Bosnia-Hercegovina was henceforward governed by a parliament and a three-member Presidium consisting of a Bosnian, a Serb and a Croat. It was subdivided into two relatively autonomous republics of roughly equal size, the Bosnian-Croat Federation with its seat in *Sarajevo, and the Serb Republic (Republika Srpska) with its seat in Banja Luka. The complex governmental structure was made all the more inoperable by the relative success of the nationalist parties especially, but not exclusively, in the Serb Republic. As a result, many of the major decisions that institutionalized the sovereignty of the unloved state were forced through by the UN High Representative, over the heads of the various intransigent popular representatives.

Contemporary issues (since 2002) Although foreign military presence was reduced to 20,000 troops by 2002, the integrity of the state was far from established. At the same time, the complex state structure and the international community supporting it became discredited by a bankrupt economy with up to three quarters of the population unemployed, and the establishment in many areas of organized crime. The tenth anniversary of the Dayton Agreement in 2005 coincided with international pressure to overcome the unworkable heterogeneity of state institutions, and to create structures for a common army, an integrated police force, and a more effective parliament, as well as a more centralized common executive. These reforms were only partially successful. A police reform was introduced in 2005, while the 2005/6 army reforms allowed Bosnia to join the *NATO Partnership for Peace progrmame. However, a constitutional reform to transform politics failed in 2006, as it failed to gain the necessary support in parliament. The efforts to create a more workable federated state were also undermined by moves in the Serbian part of Bosnia to achieve independence.

Bosnian Civil War (1992–5)
The longest and most violent European war in the second half of the twentieth century. It was caused by the opposition of the orthodox Serbian minority in Bosnia-Hercegovina to the country's secession from Yugoslavia, as demanded by its Muslim majority. Supported by substantial military assistance from Serbia, the Bosnian Serbs scored successive wins over a Muslim army severely weakened by an international arms embargo. In the areas which came under its control, the Bosnian Serbs carried out a brutal programme of 'ethnic cleansing', whereby Muslims and Croats were expelled (and, in many cases, murdered) in order to create ethnically homogeneous areas under Serb control, and to present the Bosnian Muslims and the international community with a *fait accompli*. As brutality and inhumanity escalated, rape became commonplace, while prisoners of war and innocent civilians were kept in ill-disguised *concentration camps. In this way, the Bosnian Serbs controlled around 70 per cent of the country's area by the beginning of 1995.

Several factors began to change in the Bosnian Muslims' favour. They were strengthened by an alliance with the Bosnian Croat minority, which led to the creation of the Muslim-Croat Federation on 31 May 1994. More importantly, despite continuous European mediation through the *UN and the deployment of a UN peacekeeping force, it was only the intervention of the USA in August 1995 against continued Serb aggression which led to Serbian agreement to negotiations. This led to the 1995 *Dayton Agreement, which re-established a united country which would pursue a common foreign and defence policy, but which had two largely autonomous halves, the Muslim-Croat Federation based in *Sarajevo and the Serb part of Bosnia-Hercegovina. Out of an original population of around 4.4 million (1991), virtually the entire population was uprooted, as around three million people became internal refugees migrating from areas under hostile control, and 1.3 million fled to other European states. As ethnic tensions within Bosnia-Hercegovina continued, more than one million refugees had still not returned to their homes by 2002.

Botha, Louis (b. 27 Sept. 1862, d. 27 Aug. 1919). First Prime Minister of the Union of South Africa 1910–19

Early career A prosperous farmer from Vryheid (Transvaal), he was the youngest member of the Eerste Volksraad (Parliament) in 1896. He became a successful general in the *South African War, winning one of the most astounding Boer victories at Colenso, 15 December 1899. He came to support the Peace of Vereeniging, realizing that as the war could not be won given British numerical superiority, it was better to give in to an honourable peace which protected *Afrikaner interests. The practical and pragmatic politician formed a close partnership with the more intellectual and philosophical *Smuts, and together they envisioned a South Africa with extensive state self-government and reconciliation between the South Africans of English descent and Afrikaners. He became Prime Minister of the Transvaal in 1907. His conciliatory stance towards English-speaking South Africans alienated many conservative Afrikaners, but mollified the English-speakers, so that he became the natural choice for the first Prime Minister of the Union of South Africa.

In office Botha founded the South African Party (SAP) in 1911 with the policy of reconciliation with Britain, though it was this policy which split the party in 1913, when *Hertzog left to found the *National Party. In World War I he led his country in support of Britain, though his invasion of South-West

Africa (*Namibia) was also motivated by opportunities for territorial gain. At the same time, the decision triggered an Afrikaner rebellion in 1914, whose suppression caused deep and lasting resentment of him among many Afrikaners. Bitter rifts between the Afrikaners who were more sympathetic to Germany, and the South Africans of English descent who demanded more involvement in the war for the sake of the *British Empire, further weakened his authority. In the 1915 elections, he failed to get an absolute majority, the SAP gaining only 5 per cent more votes than the National Party. He attended the *Paris Peace Conference in 1919, and gained a *League of Nations *Mandate for the South African administration of South-West Africa. Just after his return he died of a heart attack.

Botha, Pieter Willem (b. 12 Jan. 1916, d. 31 Oct 2006). Prime Minister of South Africa 1978–84, President 1984–9

Early career Born in Paul Roux (Orange Free State), he abandoned his university studies and moved to Cape Province in 1936 to become a full-time officer of the *National Party. He entered parliament in 1948, becoming Minister of Defence in 1966. Following *Vorster's resignation he became Prime Minister, largely owing to the disunity among the Transvaal members of the National Party.

In office He became President under a revised Constitution which gave him extensive powers. While he appreciated the difficulties arising from the growing economic, cultural, and military isolation of his country because of the *apartheid system, he was also frightened by the potential erosion of National Party support at the hands of more radical proponents of apartheid, who in 1982 formed the *Conservative Party. Hence, his racial reforms were careful and partial. He abolished the pass laws compelling Blacks and Coloureds to carry identity cards, and conceded limited Coloured and Indian (though not Black) representation in parliament. He also conceded the idea of Namibian independence in 1988, which ultimately took place in 1990. His autocratic style and his increasingly evident inability to find a solution to the country's racial problems, plunged the country more and more into international isolation. While recuperating from a heart attack, he was replaced by *de Klerk. The 'Great Crocodile' refused to cooperate with the *Truth and Reconciliation Commission, which he considered illegitimate. For this, he was given a 12-month suspended jail sentence and a fine of 10,000 Rand.

Botswana

One of Africa's most stable countries, which has plentiful mineral resources, relative wealth, but which is also threatened by demographic crisis.

Colonial rule (before 1966) A landlocked country in southern Africa, which was occupied by British troops in 1884 and named **Bechuanaland**. In 1885, its northern half was declared a British protectorate, while the southern part became a British Crown Colony. Despite South Africa's initial desire to incorporate the territory, it remained under British sovereignty, though in 1961 it was given some degree of home rule. In 1962, the Bechuanaland (later Botswana) Democratic Party (BDP) was founded by *Khama, and became the predominant political party. Khama became President upon independence in 1966.

Independence (from 1966) Since the desert state relied heavily on agricultural imports and was entirely surrounded by South African-ruled Namibia, South Africa, and Rhodesia, it was very vulnerable to the international boycott first against Rhodesia (until 1979), and then against the *apartheid regime in South Africa. Despite several border attacks on the capital (Gaborone) by the South African army in search of *ANC members, Botswana continued to provide a sanctuary for resistance to apartheid. As a result of widespread drought its agricultural sector, which employed almost 50 per cent of the population, experienced a sharp decline during the 1980s. This prompted large-scale structural reforms under Khama's successor, *Masire, also from the BDP, in order to increase employment and reduce infrastructural, economic, and technological dependence on South Africa. Economic problems, as well as corruption scandals involving MPs from the BDP, led to heavy losses by that party in the elections of 15 October 1994, when it gained 53.1 per cent of the popular vote.

Under the leadership of Festus G. Mogae (from 1998), the BDP was re-elected with a clear majority in 1999 and 2004. In the late 1990s, Botswana's wealth in diamond mines ensured rapid economic growth of over 10 per cent per year. On the other hand, Botswana has the world's highest proportion of *AIDS sufferers. In 2006, almost 40 per cent of the population were infected by HIV, with average life expectancy declining to 37 years.

Bouchard, Lucien (b. 22 Dec. 1938). Premier of Quebec 1996–2001
Born at Saint Cœur-de-Marie (Quebec), he studied law at Laval University, and was a successful private lawyer for twenty years. Following his appointment as ambassador to Paris (1988), he was elected to the House of Commons as a member of the *Conservative Party and became a member of *Mulroney's Cabinet. Convinced by the failure of the *Meech Lake Accord that Quebec had no future within Canada, he founded the *Bloc Québécois (BQ) in 1990, which he led in 1993 to become the second largest parliamentary party nationwide, thus becoming leader of the official opposition. The fiery orator used this platform whenever possible to advance the cause of independence, and his charismatic intervention in the 1995 Quebec referendum secured a large number of pro-sovereignty votes. To further the goal of separation, he resigned from the federal BQ to become Premier of Quebec in January 1996, and lead the *Parti Québécois (PQ). He was unable to increase support for separatism and, owing to the province's difficult economic situation, was increasingly forced to introduce unpopular cuts in public spending. As a result, the PQ started to perform badly in provincial elections, and in 2001 he resigned following the BQ's bad showing in the national elections. Bouchard returned to practising law.

Boumédienne, Houari (b. 23 Aug. 1927, d. 27 Dec. 1978). Chairman of the Revolutionary Council 1965–77, President of Algeria 1977–8
Born as Mohammed Bou Kharrouba in Guelma (eastern Algeria), he studied in Paris, Tunis, and Cairo, where he met *Ben Bella. Having joined the *Front de Libération Nationale in 1955, he became Chief of Staff of the Algerian government-in-exile (1960). Two years later, he supported Ben Bella's accession to power, joining the government as Minister of National Defence. In 1965 Boumédienne led a coup against Ben Bella whose policies he considered too Western. He tried to create an industrial base to make Algeria economically more independent from France. To this end Boumédienne founded national industries and nationalized existing ones, such as the oil industry in 1971. Within the *UN and the *non-aligned movement he championed a new dialogue between the industrialized northern and the less developed southern countries of the world, with countries such as Algeria as a mediator. He gradually improved relations with France, though relations with Morocco deteriorated because of his substantial support of the *Western Saharan independence movement, POLISARIO. He died in office.

Bourguiba, Hubib ibn Ali (b. 3 Aug. 1903, d. 6 Apr. 2000). President of Tunisia 1957–87
Born in Tunis, he studied jurisprudence in Paris and on his return in 1921 joined the moderate nationalist party, the Tunisian Constitutional Party (Destour). In 1934 he formed a more extreme group, the Neo-Destour Party, which he had just enough time to organize effectively before his imprisonment by the French in 1934. Released by the *Popular Front government in 1936, he was again arrested in 1938. Despite his release by the *Vichy government, he rejected collaboration with *Fascism and returned to work for greater autonomy after the return of the *Free French to Tunisia in 1943. In 1945, he left the country for four years to rally international support for independence. Negotiations during 1950–1 failed, but after violent protests in Tunisia the French government returned to the conference table.

In 1956, Bourguiba became Tunisia's first Prime Minister, and in 1957 he became President. He embarked upon a programme of secularization to carry out what he considered the modernization of the society. At the same time, he increased his hold on the party, making himself president for life in 1975. Despite his authoritarianism, as the liberator of Tunisia the charismatic leader retained strong levels of popular support. After failing a series of medical tests, he was declared unfit for office and replaced by *Ben Ali.

Bouteflika, Abdelaziz (b. 2 Mar. 1937). Algerian President, 1999–
Born in Morocco, he joined the *Front de Libération Nationale (FLN) in 1956. Following independence he served as Foreign Minister (1962–79) under *Ben Bella and *Boumédienne. After living abroad he returned to Algeria, and in 1999 won the elections at the head of the FLN. His overwhelming election victories in 1999 and 2004 in a country torn by civil war resulted in charges of electoral fraud. He was partially successful in overcoming the civil war by appeasing a number of Islamist groups, but proved unable to bring about a comprehensive peace settlement.

Boutros Ghali, Boutros (b. 14 Nov. 1922). UN Secretary-General 1992–7
From one of the best-known Egyptian families, he studied jurisprudence and

political science and in 1948 received a doctorate from the Sorbonne University. He was appointed professor of international law at Cairo University, and as editor of a number of journals he became a well-respected observer of public affairs. After the *Six Day War in 1967 he advocated reconciliation between Israel and Egypt, and in 1977 President *Sadat appointed him Minister of State in the Foreign Ministry, where he became one of the principal architects of the *Camp David Peace Accord of 1978. He was appointed Deputy Prime Minister in May 1991, seven months before his election to become the first *UN Secretary-General from the African continent and from an Arab country. He was a strong advocate of the unsuccessful UN intervention in the Somali Civil War in 1992. Thereafter, regional conflicts in the *Bosnian Civil War, Cambodia, Haiti, and Rwanda stretched the UN's military and financial resources to the limit, leading him to propose an independent task force under his command. He was increasingly criticized for his partiality, not least by the US, who led the opposition against his reappointment. He was succeeded by Kofi *Annan, and became the Secretary-General of the Community of Francophone Countries.

Boxer Rebellion (China)

A Chinese nationalist uprising, in protest against the growing foreign encroachment into Chinese sovereignty. It took place against the background of foreign acquisition of bases on Chinese soil (such as *Hong Kong and *Macao), and the attempts of foreign *imperialist powers to monopolize trade in the country. There was considerable resentment against the advent of 'foreign' Christianity through missionaries. The protest was triggered by the secret Society of Righteous and Harmonious Fists, popularly known as 'Boxers', which had strong links to the anti-Western Imperial Court. In addition to attacks on missionaries, they occupied the foreign legations in Beijing (Peking). On 19 June 1900, they killed the German minister, Freiherr Clemens von Ketteler. Popular unrest followed in a number of cities, most notably in Tientsin.

The rebellion was brought under control when a foreign six-nation expeditionary force freed the legations on 14 August. Some units then looted Beijing, while a separate punitive expedition was carried out by the Germans to avenge Ketteler's death. In 1901, the foreign powers imposed harsh terms on the imperial government in the Peking Protocol (1901). China was obliged to pay a compensation of the then staggering sum of £67 million ($330 million) in annual payments over 39 years. In addition, China was forced to allow foreign troops on its soil. This humiliation further increased Chinese *nationalism, while fully exposing the weakness and incompetence of the Qing Manchu dynasty. These were prerequisites to the growth of the nationalist movement under *Sun Yat-sen, and the eventual *Wuchang Revolution.

Boy Scouts, see BADEN-POWELL, ROBERT STEPHENSON SMYTH

Bradley, Omar Nelson (b. 12 Feb. 1893, d. 8 Apr. 1981). US Chairman of the Joint Chiefs of Staff 1949–53

Born in Clark, Missouri, he graduated from the US Military Academy in 1915. He did not see action in World War I, but he rose steadily in rank to become commander of US forces in Tunisia and Sicily in World War II. He went on to command the US land forces at *D-Day and the subsequent US advance through France. After the *Ardennes campaign, as commander of the 12th Army Group of some one million men he swept through Europe to link up with Soviet forces on the Elbe in 1945. From 1948, he was responsible for the build-up of *NATO and for formulating US global military strategy. He supported the US involvement in the *Korean War. However, he deeply distrusted General *MacArthur, whose plans to take the Korean War into China he famously criticized as leading to 'the wrong war, at the wrong place, at the wrong time, with the wrong enemy'.

Brains Trust (USA)

A name given to the panel of advisers set up by *Roosevelt in 1932. The original team advised Roosevelt as New York Governor, presidential candidate, and President elect on economic and financial matters. It included Ray Moley, Rex Tugwell, and Adolf Berle, who all became prominent federal policy-makers and administrators during the New Deal. The phrase exemplifies the popular touch and reliance on experts which characterized the Roosevelt presidency before 1937.

Brandeis, Louis Dembitz (b. 13 Nov. 1856, d. 5 Oct. 1941). US Supreme Court Justice 1916–38

Born in Louisville (Kentucky), he was a brilliant law student, holding the highest academic average in the history of Harvard when he graduated there in 1878. An advisor to President *Wilson, he became the first

Jewish *Supreme Court Justice. Brandeis brought a *Progressive rationalism to the Supreme Court which is memorialized in the phrase 'Brandeis brief', used to describe a submission to court containing economic, statistical, and sociological arguments. He had a strong populist and anti-corporate bent, while being a fervent advocate of the law's duty to enforce civil liberties.

Brandt Reports (1980, 1983)

Two reports by an international commission convened by the *UN on the state of the world economy, which had met since 1977 under the chairmanship of Willy *Brandt. In the reports, the commission urged an immediate redress of the inequalities of prosperity between the wealthy countries of the northern, and the poorer countries of the southern, hemispheres. This was to be achieved, for example, through changes in the economic system (lower tariffs) and a redistribution of wealth from north to south. More specifically, the reports recommended the annual payment of development aid of a minimum of 0.7 per cent of GDP by 1985, and 1 per cent by the year 2000. This was regularly exceeded by the Scandinavian countries, with Norway, for example, giving 1.15 per cent of its GDP in 1992. Most other developed countries, however, never undertook serious efforts to meet this target, with Switzerland giving 0.46, the UK 0.31, Japan 0.3, and the US 0.2 per cent of GDP in 1992. At the same time, the report has been criticized for an exaggerated emphasis on economic aid, and too little concern for structural reforms to be undertaken in the poorer countries themselves.

Brandt, Willy (b. 18 Dec. 1913, d. 8 Oct. 1992). Chancellor of West Germany 1969–74

Early career Born Ernst Karl Frahm, he joined the *SPD in 1930 and fled to Norway, where he became a journalist and published under the name Brandt. He acquired Norwegian nationality in 1938, but escaped to Sweden following the German invasion of Norway in 1940. Brandt returned to Germany in 1945, rejoined the SPD in 1947, and reacquired German citizenship in 1948. He was a member of the Berlin city parliament 1950–66, and of the West German parliament from 1949 to 1957 and from 1969. As Lord Mayor of Berlin (1957–66) he proved an inspiration to Berliners when the *Berlin Wall was built. Recognizing that the German Democratic Republic (GDR) was not a short-term phenomenon that could be ignored, Brandt worked for a fundamental change in German internal relations to relieve the lot

of individuals suffering from the German division. He became Foreign Secretary in 1966, and, after leading his party to its first election victory since 1945, he became Chancellor in 1969.

In office Brandt's term in office was marked by a radically new approach to the *German question, in particular through his policy of recognition and cooperation with the Eastern European states of the USSR, Poland, and in particular East Germany (GDR). His policies not only proved to be a new departure for German internal relations, but also introduced a new phase in the *Cold War globally. In recognition of this achievement, he was awarded the *Nobel Peace Prize in 1971. In domestic politics, Brandt took over at a time of deep social divisions caused by the student protest movement. Under the slogan 'Daring more democracy', Brandt's government, with the support of the *Liberal Party, dramatically increased funding for universities, and introduced co-decision in university administration. His ministers reformed many of Germany's penal laws, liberalized laws on sexual behaviour, and instigated a change in abortion legislation. Many of Brandt's social reforms were stopped by the onset of the *oil price shock in 1973, which made them financially unfeasible. Soon thereafter, his secretary was uncovered as an East German spy. Brandt resigned as Chancellor, though he remained SPD Chairman until 1987. In this position, he retained a significant influence on his party, and his lack of support for *Schmidt contributed to the collapse of the SPD-led government in 1982. From 1977 to 1989 he chaired the North–South Commission, which produced the *Brandt Reports.

Although Brandt was Chancellor for a relatively short period, his government was crucial in two ways. Its domestic policies paved the way for the ultimate political integration of the radical left active in the student protest movements. Brandt's policy towards the GDR served as a new basis for the policies of every West German government towards the GDR until 1989. This improved the lives of the citizens in the GDR, while increasing contact with West Germany helped keep alive East German desires for reunification.

Bratianu, Ionel (b. 20 Aug. 1864, d. 26 Nov. 1927). Prime Minister of Romania 1909–11, 1914–18, 1918–19, 1922–6

Born in Florica as the son of Ion C. Bratianu (b. 1821, d. 1891), a leading National Liberal Romanian politician, he became leader of the Romanian Liberal Party in 1909. At the outbreak of World War I he maintained neutrality, but in 1916 Bratianu was persuaded to enter the war on the side of the Allies in the hope of territorial gains. He miscalculated the strength of the Bulgarian and German forces, which entered Bucharest in December 1916. Nevertheless, he successfully represented his country at the *Paris Peace Conference, where he gained most of the territory he demanded. Bratianu devised a new Constitution in 1923, which created a centralized state. He encouraged the often conflicting goals of protection, industrialization, and restrictions of foreign ownership. The country became one of the most protectionist states in Europe, with tariffs being used to finance industrialization. He hoped to strengthen the political system through forcing the abdication of Crown Prince *Carol. However, his policies created strong discontent in the countryside, which became fertile ground for the support of the Fascist parties. He retired in 1926.

Braun, Wernher von (b. 23 Mar. 1912, d. 16 June 1977). German rocket scientist Appointed director of the rocket research station at the test site of Peenemünde, Braun developed the first automatically steered long-distance rocket called the A4, later renamed the **V2**. In 1943, the improvement of his rockets received the full support of *Hitler, who hoped that this *Wunderwaffe* (miracle weapon) would swing the balance in a war which saw the Germans in retreat on all fronts. Between 8 September 1944 and 27 March 1945, more than 1,000 of these rockets, each carrying a ton of explosives, were launched against England. However, their real impact upon the British war effort was negligible. After the war, Braun became a US citizen. As director of the US Ballistic Missile Agency, he took a leading part in the development of the rocket carriers which were used in the US Saturn and Apollo missions.

Brazil

Latin America's largest country, whose economic and social disparities prevented the development of a stable democratic government for much of its contemporary history.

First Republic (1889–1930) Brazil's federal constitution, which was closely modelled on that of the USA, was destabilized by the disparity of its federal states. Most notably, São Paulo had gained virtual autonomy as the most dynamic state: its population trebled in 1890–1920, it contracted a foreign debt larger than that of the national government, and it produced more than a third of Brazil's total output. As a result, the President usually came from São Paulo or the next most important state, Minas Gerais. The franchise was restricted to the literate population, which amounted to around 3 per cent of the population before 1930. As a result, power remained in the hands of elites whose composition varied depending on the social and economic structure of each state. Finally, effective government was made difficult through the lack of national communications, which in turn encouraged the power of the state elites.

After World War I, the Republic came under increasing criticism from educated groups, who saw widespread corruption as proof that it had become too liberal too soon. The Republic was equally criticized by Democrats largely centred in São Paulo, who demanded more liberal constitutionalism to counter the influence of the agrarian elites in most other states. The military reacted to the government's inability to respond to the Great *Depression with a coup supported largely by dissatisfied sections of various state elites, thus ending the First Republic and installing *Vargas as President of a provisional government in 1930.

The Vargas era (1930–45) Initially, Vargas was concerned with securing his own power base, which was particularly challenged by a revolt of the Democrats in the state of São Paulo. The government forces were successful in crushing the rebellion, but Vargas compromised by calling a Constituent Assembly in 1933. The new Constitution of 1934 was very similar to that of the First Republic, albeit with reduced state powers. Vargas was elected President in the same year. The political crisis of the early 1930s and the new Constitution lessened the political power of the traditional landed elites (especially coffee growers) whose earnings from agriculture, the source of most of Brazil's exports, were hit at the same time by the Great *Depression. The middle and lower-middle classes in the cities responded to the political and economic crisis by mass organization, so that by 1935 around 25 per cent of the electorate was organized in political movements. Of the two central political movements that emerged, the

Communist-led *Popular Front (Aliança Libertadora Nacional, ALN) was suppressed in 1935 by Vargas, who thus endeared himself to the elites by responding to their fear of *Communism. Instead of cooperating with the neo-Fascist Integralists, however, in 1937 he responded to their growing claims for participation in government with a further coup.

With it, Vargas established the **Estado Nôvo (New State)**. Unlike the Fascist regimes of *Hitler and *Mussolini, however, he never developed an ideology backed by a mass movement, but instead ruled with a number of technocrats who modernized the country. To maintain its power, the regime resorted to torture and imprisonments, but here, too, it did not engage in the excesses of *Nazism or Italian *Fascism. In recognition that participation in World War II on the side of the democratic USA would inevitably lead to demands for a return to democracy, he called for new elections in 1945. Although he emerged victorious, the army deposed him and called new elections in December 1945.

The Second Republic (1946–64) The Constitution of the Second Republic, passed in 1946, was very similar to the Constitution of 1934, and marked a return to liberal guarantees of individual liberties. President *Dutra reversed Vargas's policy of industrialization, preferring to promote agricultural exports, especially of coffee. Back in power in 1951, Vargas became unable to cope with the economic problems of mounting debts, a worsening balance of trade, and inflation. As a popularly elected leader, he was torn between the opposing demands of different sections of society, and in the end satisfied nobody. He committed suicide in 1954, and after a number of caretaker administrations he was followed by *Kubitschek, who stabilized his power by keeping the military content with large arms purchases, and generating general enthusiasm through an ambitious programme of economic growth. This was achieved, however, with high external borrowing, while corruption became ever more widespread. His populist successor, *Goulart (his immediate successor, Jânio Quadros, resigned after six months in office), was too weak and indecisive to carry out the necessary economic squeeze imposed by the *IMF. Instead, he increasingly tried to appeal to an anti-establishment alliance of peasants and workers.

Military rule (1964–85) Another coup in 1964 ensured military rule which was to last until 1985. An initial period of economic liberalization under Castello Branco (1964–7), which included the creation of a central bank, produced moderate results and ultimately did not lead to economic recovery. The high social costs of these reforms led to general unrest under Artur Costa e Silva (1967–9), which was brutally suppressed. The economy did improve from 1968, and in the following years grew by an average of 10 per cent. A potent sign of economic maturity was the fact that manufactured goods replaced coffee as the country's main export earner. Nevertheless, unrest did not subside fully, and continued in the form of guerrilla warfare against the government, which the latter only managed to suppress in 1974. Under *Geisel, preparations were made for an eventual return to civilian rule, but the introduction of full democracy was hampered by the unlikelihood of a military-backed candidate winning any free election. Geisel's problems were compounded by the onset of another recession triggered by the *oil price shock of 1973 which not only depressed export earnings, but kept interest rates at a record high. By 1982 Brazil was the world's largest debtor, with total obligations of up to $100 billion. President *Figueiredo reintroduced democratic government, first through the direct elections of state Governors in 1982, and then by the democratic election of a new President in 1985.

Democratization, 1985–2002 The renewed period of democratic rule began with the death of the President elect, Tancredo Neves, who was succeeded by Vice-President elect *Sarney. Despite short-term economic growth, he failed in his social reforms, as the annual inflation rate (1987–93) oscillated between 366 and 2,567 per cent. Sarney was successful in overseeing the passing of a new Constitution in 1988. Sarney's successor, Fernando Collor de Mello (b. 1949), was not much more successful in introducing any of the badly needed social or economic reforms. In particular, he failed to reduce the inequality of landownership, and he proved unable to replace the semi-corporatist structures established by Vargas with more effective mechanisms for wage bargaining.

Since 1992, domestic policy has been overshadowed by various corruption scandals, the most prominent of which forced Collor de Mello to retire on 29 December 1992, to be succeeded by Itamar *Franco. Franco did manage to restore some economic stability, and was succeeded by his Minister of Finance, Fernando Henrique Cardoso in 1995, under whom the economy continued to improve. Cardoso pursued a policy of rigid austerity, which kept the inflation rate low and enabled

Brazil to overcome its previously growing reliance on foreign debt. The policies of rigorous reduced federal spending, however, aggravated social inequality, in a country already characterized by one of the most unequal income distributions in the world, with 66 per cent of the population malnourished.

Contemporary politics (since 2002) Politically, Brazil continued to be riven by large-scale corruption scandals involving its elites at federal and state levels, while continuous police brutality undermined public confidence in the state still further. This provided the background for the election of the left-wing populist Luiz Inácio da Silva (*Lula) in 2002. Contrary to the hopes of many of his supporters, Lula continued liberal economic policies. Under his leadership, Brazil began to repay debt ahead of schedule, including all its obligations to the *IMF. However, at $260 billion Brazil's national debt retained a stranglehold on public finances. Lula was thus unable to fulfil his pledges for greater financial aid to the poor, as over one-third of the population continued to live below the poverty line.

Brazzaville Bloc

One of the first post-colonial associations to encourage economic and political cooperation. It emerged in 1960 from a conference in the Congolese capital of Brazzaville, and consisted of the newly independent countries of former *French Equatorial Africa and *French West Africa (except Guinea and Mali). The Bloc was short-lived, being superseded in 1961 by the **Organization of Cooperation of the African and Malagasy States**, which eventually led to the foundation of the OAU (*African Union) in 1963.

Brazzaville Declaration (1944)

Issued after a meeting between the leader of the *Free French, de *Gaulle, and representatives of the French colonies in Africa, it was designed to provide a basis for the relationship between France and her colonies. Independence or autonomy were rejected, but colonial assemblies, economic reforms, equal rights for all citizens, and greater native participation in colonial administration were proposed. Even though these concessions were extremely limited, their implementation was impeded to varying degrees by the French settlers in these territories.

Brest-Litovsk, Treaty of (3 Mar. 1918)

The first peace treaty of World War I, concluded between Germany, *Austria-Hungary, and Russia. Although first proposed in December 1917, *Trotsky skilfully prolonged discussions in the hope of *Allied help, or of a socialist uprising by German and Austrian industrial workers. Neither happened and the German army resumed its advance. *Lenin finally ordered his delegates to accept the German terms, which were now even tougher than before. In return for peace on the Eastern Front, Russia lost Finland, Estonia, Latvia, and Lithuania, west Belorussia (*Belarus), Poland, the *Ukraine, and parts of the Caucasus. It thus lost almost half of its European territories, with around 75 per cent of its heavy industries. Russia was also obliged to pay 6 billion gold marks in *reparations. The treaty was annulled by the Allies on 11 November 1918, after the German defeat. Nevertheless, Russia only managed to reclaim the Ukraine and its Asian territories after the *Russian Civil War.

Bretton Woods Conference (July 1944)

An international financial conference of representatives of forty-four countries which met in the town of Bretton Woods, New Hampshire. In an attempt to establish a more successful international financial system than the *Gold Standard, which had been the determinant of currency values until the 1930s, the conference devised a system of exchange rates which were pegged to the US dollar. It also established an International Bank for Reconstruction and Development (the *World Bank) and the International Monetary Fund (*IMF) to finance short-term imbalances in international trade. After an initial collapse in 1947, the Bretton Woods system of fixed exchange rates survived in modified form until August 1971, when the USA left the agreement. In the face of increasing capital mobility and the consequent inability of national governments to control the exchange rate, the system of fixed exchange rates was finally abandoned in 1976.

ERM, EURO

Brezhnev, Leonid Ilich (b. 19 Dec. 1906, d. 10 Nov. 1982). First (General) Secretary of the Communist Party of the Soviet Union 1964–82

Early career Born in Dneprodzerzhinsk (Ukraine), where he graduated from the Metallurgical Institute in 1935. A member of the Soviet *Communist Party, he became Secretary of his local party organization, and served in World War II as a senior political officer in the *Red Army. After the war, he became First Secretary of the Communist Party in Moldova, and in 1952 joined the Central Committee of the Soviet Communist Party. He was put in charge of agricultural policies in Kazakhstan in 1955, but returned in 1957 to join the Presidium of the Central Committee, responsible for the development of heavy industry.

In power Brezhnev became head of state in 1960, and assumed control over state and party in 1964, when he succeeded *Khrushchev as First Secretary of the party. A more steady leader than either the brutal *Stalin or the erratic Khrushchev, he left no doubt as to his intention of preserving and extending Soviet influence through ordering his troops to intervene in the Czechoslovak *Prague Spring of 1968. He justified this through the **Brezhnev doctrine** of limited sovereignty, whereby a socialist state was justified in interfering in the affairs of another in order to uphold *socialism.

Brezhnev presided over a period of economic stagnation caused by his country's ever-increasing technological backwardness, and the crippling cost of keeping up with the arms race. He agreed to some measures of *disarmament, as well as the *Helsinki Accord, though he lacked the flexibility to make the country's Communist system viable in the long run. His inability to adapt to changing circumstances was best portrayed when in December 1979 he ordered his troops to enter Afghanistan in a last (and ultimately unsuccessful) attempt to impose Communist rule in a country regardless of internal or international opinion. After his death, the system limped on for another three years until the leadership of *Gorbachev, who found that it had become moribund beyond reform.

Briand, Aristide (b. 28 Mar., 1862, d. 7 Mar. 1932) Prime Minister of France 1909–11, 1913, 1915–17, 1921–2, 1925–6, 1929
A deputy for the *Socialist Party from 1902, he joined the *Radical government as Minister of Public Instruction and Worship in 1906, where he was responsible for the introduction of sweeping *anticlerical measures. He succeeded *Clemenceau as Prime Minister in 1909 and betrayed his former socialist beliefs by breaking a strike of railwaymen in 1910. A member of most governments 1906–32, Briand is best remembered as the driving force behind French foreign policy, 1920–32, when he sought to achieve *disarmament and European stability through a system of collective security, for which the establishment of good relations with Germany was crucial. With his colleagues *Stresemann and Austen *Chamberlain he engineered the *Locarno Treaty in 1925. For their efforts at international reconciliation, which were extremely contentious in both France and Germany, the three men won the *Nobel Peace Prize. He was also the moving spirit behind the *Kellogg-Briand Pact of 1928.

brinkmanship

A term first employed by *Dulles to describe the Cold War strategy employed by both superpowers at varying times after 1945 of confronting the opponent power even at the risk of war ('going to the brink') when national interests were at stake. The strategy was most famously employed during the *Cuban Missile Crisis in 1962, but the danger of thermonuclear war implicit in the policy was thereafter recognized by the Kennedy administration. Both Kennedy and his successors resiled from the strategy.

Britain, Battle of (Aug.–Oct. 1940)

A name coined by *Churchill for the series of air battles between the Royal Air Force (RAF), commanded by *Dowding, and the German *Luftwaffe* over Britain during *World War II. It represented an attempt by Germany to gain air superiority before launching an invasion of Britain. After the fall of France in June 1940, the *Luftwaffe* attacked British shipping in the English Channel. On 12 August, it began attacks on airfields and aerodromes in southern England. German losses were heavy, with seventy-five aircraft being shot down on 15 August. Eventually, owing to its sustained heavy losses, Germany lost confidence in launching an invasion. On 7 September, the offensive was diverted to the bombing of British cities in a desperate attempt to destroy British morale. Finding that day-bombing resulted in heavy German casualties, the *Luftwaffe* switched to night-bombing on 1 October. By this time, it was clear that British air power had not been destroyed, and on 12 October the planned invasion was postponed indefinitely. The RAF was heavily outnumbered by the *Luftwaffe*, but it lost about 788 fighter planes, compared with the 1,292 lost by Germany. Throughout, radar, which was being used by the British for the first time in battle, was crucial in tracking German aircraft.

British Empire

The colonies, protectorates, and territories brought under British sovereignty from as early as the sixteenth century. In the late nineteenth century, some in Britain still harboured dreams of expanding the Empire, such as *Rhodes and *Milner, who wanted to create a unified Cape-to-Cairo dominion in Africa. However, the *South African (Boer) War (1899–1902) damaged Britain's confidence in its Empire. In many areas, control had never advanced beyond *indirect rule. Nevertheless, the twentieth century has been a story of the gradual end of the Empire. This did not look likely following World War I, when Britain secured control of a number of former German and Turkish territories, as *Mandates from the *League of Nations. At that point, the Empire was at its greatest ever size, with over 600 million people ruled from London.

At the 1907 *Imperial Conference, Australia, Canada, New Zealand, South Africa, and Newfoundland were recognized as self-governing **'Dominions'** (Eire/Ireland was added in 1922). From 1909, the British gradually gave Indians some self-government (*Government of India Acts) and in 1931, under the Statute of *Westminster, the Dominions became 'autonomous communities within the British Empire'. Despite reforms in India, the non-white peoples of the Empire found their aspirations for self-government thwarted. Only after 1945 did *decolonization begin, when Britain found its status in the world greatly reduced by the costs of World War II. India became independent in 1947, African colonies followed in the late 1950s, and with the bulk of the Caribbean colonies gaining their independence in the 1970s, the process was largely complete by 1980. From the 1920s, the term *Commonwealth was often used to describe the Empire, and this was formalized after World War II.

MAP 3

British Expeditionary Force (BEF)

The name given to British troops deployed for immediate conflict in the first half of the twentieth century. As a result of *Haldane's army reforms in 1906–7, a territorial reserve army was created in Britain, and it was advised that this, along with the regular army, should be made ready for dispatch overseas in an emergency. When World War I was declared on 4 August 1914, both regular and reserve troops were sent to France under Sir John French, as the BEF. As German troops advanced into France, the BEF moved up the German flank towards Belgium, before it was defeated at the Battle of Mons (23–4 August). After a steady retreat, it took part in the first Battle of *Ypres (20 October-17 November). Estimates suggest that by the end of November, survivors from the original force averaged no more than one officer and thirty men, in each battalion of about 600 men.

In World War II, an expeditionary force was again mobilized and sent to France in September 1939, as Britain's contribution to its alliance with France. It comprised 152,000 men and, from 4 September, was situated along the Belgian border. By May 1940, it numbered 394,165 men, and was also stationed along the Franco-German border. On 10 May, when Germany attacked, the BEF moved towards Belgium, but was soon forced to withdraw from *Dunkirk. A number of other evacuations took place in May and June, leaving behind 64,000 vehicles and other important equipment. Altogether, it lost 68,111 killed, wounded, or captured.

British North Borneo, see SABAH

British South Africa Company

A company founded by *Rhodes on 13 July 1889 after the conclusion of a treaty with the Matabele King Lobengula which secured him the mineral rights in Matabeleland and the Matabele-dominated Shonaland. Rhodes's interest in the area was sparked off by rival *Afrikaner interests moving into the area. The BSAC was loosely modelled on the British India Company following the British government's refusal to become directly involved in the colonization of the area. After the submission of the Matabele on 14 January 1894, it governed and administered what became Rhodesia until 1923, when it became the colony of Southern Rhodesia (now Zimbabwe) with limited self-government under direct British authority. In 1890, it also established its authority over Northern Rhodesia (now known as Zambia), over which it had to resign its authority to the British government in 1923.

British Union of Fascists (BUF), see
MOSLEY, SIR OSWALD ERNALD

British Virgin Islands

The smaller part of the Caribbean Virgin Island group, they came under British sovereignty in the seventeenth century, and were part of the British colony of the Leeward Islands until 1956. Since then they have been administered as a United Kingdom Dependent Territory, with effective local self-government guaranteed by the 1977 constitution. Banking and tourism have become the major economic activities, accounting for around three-quarters of the Gross Domestic Product in 2001. In 2002, residents were granted full UK and EU citizenship.

VIRGIN ISLANDS OF THE UNITED STATES

Brooke, Alan Francis, see ALANBROOKE OF BROOKEBOROUGH, VISCOUNT

Brooke, Basil Stanlake, 5th Baronet and 1st Viscount Brookeborough (b. 9 June 1888, d. 18 Aug. 1973). Prime Minister of Northern Ireland 1943–63

Born in Colebrooke, Co. Fermanagh, and educated at Winchester and the Royal Military College, Sandhurst. A minister in the government of *Northern Ireland during the 1930s, he replaced J. M. Andrews as Prime Minister in May 1943. He modernized the government in membership and policy, and after the war was heavily involved in the application of the *Attlee government's welfare reforms to Northern Ireland. In the 1950s, he presided over an economic expansion, which led him to overestimate his grip on the province. He failed to appreciate the strength of Catholic feeling against his government, which was compounded by his decision to oppose the selection of Catholics as candidates for his *Ulster Unionist Party. He was replaced by Terence *O'Neill in 1963.

Brown, Gordon (b. 18 July 1952). British Prime Minister, 2007–

Early career Born in Kirkcaldy (Scotland), he graduated from Edinburgh University with a first-class degree, and obtained a doctorate. He was a lecturer at Edinburgh University and then Caledonian University, and after a brief spell working for TV he entered the House of Commons at *Westminster in 1983. He formed close associations with a group of fellow Scottish MPs, notably John *Smith. His influence in the Scottish *Labour Party became the backbone of his political strength, but this was insufficient in his bid for the Labour leadership in a three-way contest in 1994. He formed an alliance with Tony *Blair in order not to split the moderate vote, and Blair duly won the leadership elections. The terms of this alliance were never made public, and have been subject to intense speculation. They ensured, however, Brown's unprecedented influence over Blair before and after Labour came to power in 1997.

Chancellor of the Exchequer (1997–2007) Brown became the first Labour Chancellor who managed to avoid panic in the financial and currency markets. He achieved this by handing over the autonomy to set interest rates to the Bank of England within days of taking up his position. Brown directed three victorious election campaigns for the party, in 1997, 2001 and 2005. This pivotal role, and the fact that his allies became increasingly numerous and powerful in Blair's

successive Cabinets, ensured that he served as arguably the most influential Chancellor of the Exchequer in British history. Despite, or because of, Brown's importance to the Blair governments, the two men never enjoyed an easy relationship. Brown was pivotal in convincing Labour MPs to demand Blair's resignation in 2007, while Blair was never entirely comfortable with Brown succeeding him.

Prime Minister (from 2007) After he had finally succeeded Blair as Prime Minister, Brown was keen to cultivate the image of an honest, incorruptible leader. While emphasizing the difference in style, Brown continued many policies, while putting greater emphasis on the provision of affordable housing. In foreign policy, he maintained Britain's special relationship with the US.

Brown v. Board of Education of Topeka, *Kansas* (USA, 1954–5)

One of five cases and two decisions in which the US Supreme Court under Justice *Warren revealed its liberal inclinations by unanimously reversing precedents dating from the case of *Plessey v. Ferguson*. On 17 May 1954, the Court ruled that racial segregation in the provision of publicly funded schooling was contrary to the provisions of the Fourteenth Amendment of the Constitution and therefore illegal and inherently unequal. The ruling marked the beginning of a comprehensive legal attack, culminating in the end of racial segregation in the southern states. The case was also a milestone in the history of the *NAACP, whose activism in promoting the ruling's enforcement was critical in the way it was applied. The case was argued by J. T. *Marshall, and in the second ruling on 13 May 1955 produced the phrase 'desegregation with all due speed' on the part of the Justices. The case constituted a civil rights landmark, and marked the beginning of the second reconstruction period in American race relations that would project full social integration of African Americans into the centre of the American political agenda.

Brownshirt

Name for a member of the *SA which derives from the organization's brown uniform.
BLACKSHIRTS

Bruce, Stanley, 1st Viscount Bruce of Melbourne (b. 15 Apr. 1883, d. 25 Aug. 1967). Prime Minister of Australia 1923–9

Born at St Kilda (Victoria) and educated in his native Melbourne, he spent his formative years in England, studied at Cambridge, and became a barrister. Bruce served in the British forces at Gallipoli and in France during World War I. He returned to Australia in 1917, and was elected to the House of Representatives for the *Nationalist Party (1918–29) and the *United Australia Party (1931–3). He served briefly as federal Treasurer before succeeding *Hughes as Prime Minister and Minister of External Affairs, leading a coalition government with *Page's Country Party (*Nationalist Party). He sought to further Australia's links with Britain, mainly through attracting (primarily British) immigration, industrial investment, and trade. Job creation could not keep up with immigration, so that unemployment grew and trade-union hostility increased. He lost his seat in the 1929 elections, and in 1933 became Australia's high commissioner in London (until 1945), acting also as Australia's chief representative at the *League of Nations. Thereafter, he served as chairman of the World Food Council of the *UN Food and Agriculture Organization (1946–51). Created Viscount Bruce of Melbourne in 1947, he became the first Chancellor of the Australian National University in Canberra in 1951.

Brundtland, Gro Harlem (b. 20 Apr. 1939). Prime Minister of Norway 1981, 1986–9, 1990–6

Early career Born in Oslo as the daughter of a former government minister, she studied medicine in Oslo and at Harvard and became a Medical Officer of Health in Oslo. A member of the Labour Party, she served as Minister for Health and Social Security (1965–7), and Minister for the Environment (1974–9). She became deputy leader of her party in 1975, but did not enter the Storting (parliament) until 1977.

In office She was elected party leader in 1981, when she also became the country's first woman Prime Minister. She led a minority government during her first two periods in office, but nevertheless managed to introduce several controversial economic reforms to reduce the country's budget deficit. She received a worldwide reputation as a leading spokeswoman on issues regarding the environment, the equality of women, and international cooperation. In her report as chairwoman of the *UN World Commission on Environment and Development (1987) she introduced the concept of **sustainable growth**. This discounted a country's industrial growth by its social, environmental, and cultural costs, so that it described the optimal rate of growth at which environmental and other negative side effects are kept to a minimum. Her report was widely received, and triggered the 1992 environmental conference in Rio de Janeiro. She was also a driving force behind the 1995 UN women's conference in China. She was a passionate advocate of Norway's participation in the process of *European integration. However, her application for entry into the EU was rejected in a referendum in 1994. Despite this political blow, her popularity remained high at home and abroad. She stepped down in 1996, and two years later she became the Director-General of the *World Health Organization.

Brunei

A small country on the island of Borneo, it was made a British protectorate in 1888. It was occupied by the Japanese during World War II (1941–5). While the Sultanate of Brunei had been an independent and at times powerful force before the arrival of the British, it was mainly the discovery of large on-and offshore oil and gas deposits which prompted it to remain under British protection and not join the Federation of Malaysia in 1963. It received partial home rule in 1959, though the Constitution was suspended and a state of emergency declared in 1962, which has been in force since. Ruled by Sultan Haji Hassan al-Bolkiah (b. 1946) since 1967, it received complete autonomy in 1971, and became independent on 1 January 1984. In 1998, the country was hit by a major financial scandal involving the collapse of the Brunei Investment Authority run by the Sultan's brother, Jefri Bolkiah, involving the loss of several billion US dollars. Brunei's wealth has continued to be predominantly based on oil and gas exports (almost 90 per cent of all exports in 2006), even though the government has tried to diversify the domestic economy to reduce the country's dependence on food imports.

Brüning, Heinrich (b. 26 Nov. 1885, d. 30 Mar. 1970). German Chancellor 1930–2
A leader of the Christian *trade union movement from 1920, he became an MP for the *Centre Party in 1924 and soon established himself as a financial expert. As Chancellor he ruled largely with the help of exceptional legislation from the President, *Hindenburg, against the parliamentary majority. This enabled him to pursue a revision of the *Versailles Treaty with much

greater ruthlessness, accepting a worsening economic crisis in order to convince the Allies of the impossibility of fulfilling Germany's *reparations obligations. In this aim he was ultimately successful, but only at the cost of effectively suspending the democratic Constitution. With the country's major institutions, especially parliament, thus emasculated, it became easier for *Hitler to be appointed as Chancellor in 1933. In 1934 Brüning fled to the Netherlands; he settled in the USA in 1935, where he became a professor at Harvard in 1939.

Brusilov, Aleksey Alekseevich (b. 31 Aug. 1853, d. 17 Mar. 1926). Russian general
Born in Tiflis, he was commissioned as a cavalry officer into the Russian Imperial Army, and fought against Turkey and Japan before World War I. In June 1916 he launched an offensive against *Austria-Hungary between the Pripet Marshes and the Carpathians, capturing some 250,000 prisoners at Lutsk. The offensive cost even more Russian lives and came to a halt because of a failure of Russian supply lines. Yet it forced the Germans to withdraw men from the Somme and prompted Romania to enter the war on the Allied side. One of the frontline generals to convince *Nicholas II to abdicate, he became the Supreme Commander of the Russian army after the *Russian Revolution of February 1917, though he was replaced in July 1917. He stayed loyal to the *Bolsheviks after they took power, serving as an adviser to the *Red Army in the *Russo-Polish War (1919–21), and becoming an inspector of the cavalry.

Brussels, Treaty of (17 Mar. 1948)
Signed by the UK, France, the Netherlands, Belgium, and Luxemburg, the treaty committed its members to collective self-defence against any armed attack for fifty years. Signed less than three years after the end of World War II, it provided a further security guarantee in the face of the eventual creation of an independent West German state. The implicit purpose of the Treaty was to demonstrate that Western European states were willing to contribute to their own military defence. This helped President *Truman's efforts in convincing the US *Congress to participate in a European military alliance.
NATO

Bruton, John (b. 18 May 1947). Prime Minister (Taoiseach) of the Irish Republic 1994–7
Born in Dublin, educated at University College and King's Inns Dublin, he was first elected to Dáil Éireann (the Irish parliament) in 1969 as its youngest member. He quickly became

opposition spokesman for *Fine Gael (Agriculture 1972–3, 1977–81). He served as Finance Minister (1981–2, 1986–7), Leader of the House (1982–6), Minister for Industry and Energy (1982–3), and Minister for Industry, Trade, Commerce, and Tourism (1983–6). On 20 November 1990 he succeeded Alan Dukes as leader of Fine Gael. Although his party lost the 1994 elections, when its strength in the Dáil declined from 55 to 45 seats, he managed to form a coalition 'Government of Renewal' with *Labour, which had doubled its strength in the Dáil, and the Democratic Left. His government has been noted for the legalization of divorce, and for tough legislation on crime. Bruton continued the efforts of his predecessor, *Reynolds, at finding a negotiated settlement that would bring peace to *Northern Ireland. In the 1997 elections, Fine Gael gained nine seats, but his coalition lost overall, as Labour lost half its parliamentary strength. He was succeeded by Bertie *Ahern. In 2004, he became the EU Commission Head of Delegation in the USA, effectively the EU's ambassador to the United States.

Buck, Sir Peter (b. 15 Dec. 1880?, d. 1 Dec. 1951). New Zealand politician
Born in Urenui as the son of a White father of Irish descent and a *Maori mother. After his mother's early death, he was raised by her relatives and was given the name Te Rangi Hiroa. He was educated at Te Aute College, and graduated with a medical degree from Otago University in 1905. He soon became involved in the *Young Maori movement of *Ngata and *Pomare. He set out to work for the improvement of Maori sanitation, hygiene, and health as a government Medical Officer for Maori Health (1905–9). He became a Member of Parliament (1909–14), and was Minister of the Maori Race and the *Cook Islands (1912–14). He narrowly failed to be re-elected to a non-Maori seat in 1914, and embarked upon a successful military career in World War I. Thereafter, he resumed his public health work as Government Director of Hygiene (1919–27). During this time, his research into Maori anthropology established him as a leading scholar in the field, so that in 1927 he took up an appointment at the Bernice Bishop Museum of Ethnology in Honolulu (Hawaii), whose president he became.

Buddhism
A world religion which saw a significant revival in the twentieth century in south and south-east Asia and in Japan, as well as growth in Europe and the USA. An eightfold path (right understanding, intention, speech, conduct, occupation, effort, mindedness, and concentration) leads ultimately to nirvana,

when the soul is released from the cycle of birth and death. Buddhists are divided into two mainstream branches. The Little Vehicle, comprising about 38 per cent of Buddhists, looks upon Buddha's teaching as that of a self-redeemed human being. It is predominant in Sri Lanka, Burma, Thailand, Cambodia, Laos, and Vietnam. The Great Vehicle, by contrast, comprises around 56 per cent of Buddhists and recognizes Buddha as a divine incarnation. It is most common in Nepal, China, Japan, and Korea. Zen Buddhism developed in Japan and, with its strong emphasis on mysticism, was particularity influential in the USA during the 1960s and again during the 1980s through the New Age movement. Lamaism is also a form of Buddhism, albeit with a strong sense of religious hierarchy absent in other forms of Buddhism. Lamaism is still the predominant religion in *Tibet, and its leader, the *Dalai Lama, is also recognized as the exiled ruler of Tibet.

Bukharin, Nikolai Ivanovich (b. 9 Oct. 1888, d. 13 Mar. 1938). Communist ideologue
Born in Moscow, he studied economics at Moscow University, 1907–10. A prominent member of the *Bolsheviks since 1906, Bukharin was arrested in 1909 and 1910, before being exiled to Siberia in 1911. He escaped to Germany and subsequently became an important ally of *Lenin, whom he met in 1912, as well as *Stalin, whom he helped write his first major article on *Communism (1913). In 1915 he went to Sweden to link up with Bolsheviks still in Russia. Expelled from there, he went to the USA to join *Trotsky in editing the Russian daily newspaper, *Novyi Mir* (New World).

After returning to Russia in 1917 Bukharin played an active part in the *Russian (October) Revolution, in which he led the Bolshevik insurrection in Moscow. He opposed Lenin's conclusion of the Treaty of *Brest-Litovsk, pushing instead for the extension of the Russian Revolution abroad. As editor of the main party newspaper, *Pravda* (Truth), from 1917, and as the author of the standard texts on communism of the early 1920s, the *ABC of Communism* (with Preobrazhensky, 1919) and *Historical Materialism* (1922), he was a major force in the spread of Communist *propaganda. He defended vigorously the *New Economic Policy, and opposed the collectivization of agriculture. Despite his personal integrity, Bukharin supported the terror campaigns to increase the hold of the Communist Party over society, arguing that 'executions are a method of educating humanity'.

After the advent of *Stalin, whom he had at first supported, Bukharin became a victim of terror himself. He was officially expelled from the *Politburo in 1929, but remained influential as a Communist theoretician, and became editor of the newspaper *Izvestia* (1934–6). Ultimately, his opposition to Stalin and his policies ensured his indictment in the *Great Purge. He was arrested in 1937, sentenced to death for an invented plot to kill Lenin, and executed. He was rehabilitated by the Supreme Court of the USSR in 1988.

Bukovina
Meaning 'Beech-Tree Country', it is a disputed area in the Carpathian foothills. It was part of Austria and then *Austria-Hungary from 1775, inhabited mostly by Ukrainians. After World War I it became part of Romania. Northern Bukovina was occupied by the Soviet *Red Army in June 1940, as part of the *Hitler–Stalin Pact. When Romania joined Germany's attack on the Soviet Union, its troops reoccupied the territory. It finally came under Soviet control in 1944, and was formally recognized as part of the Soviet Union in 1947, when it became part of Ukraine.

Bulganin, Nikolai Aleksandrovich (b. 11 June 1895, d. 26 Feb. 1975). Soviet statesman
Born in Nijni Novgorod, he fought in World War I and joined the *Communist Party at the time of the *Russian Revolutions in 1917. He contributed to the *Russian Civil War as a member of the secret police, *Cheka. He was chairman of the Moscow City Soviet (i.e. mayor) (1931–7), and became Deputy Prime Minister in 1938. Bulganin held a number of high political offices in the *Red Army during World War II, and in 1944 was appointed Deputy Defence Minister. He became Defence Minister in 1947, and Deputy Prime Minister in 1949. He became Prime Minister under *Khrushchev in 1955, but in 1957 fell from grace for his close links with the 'anti-party' opposition to Khrushchev under *Molotov and *Malenkov. He was dismissed from the Presidium in 1958, worked for the Stavropol Economic Council, and retired in 1960.

Bulgaria
A Balkan country distinguished by close cultural ties to neighbouring Turkey, Greece and Macedonia.

Territorial decline (1878–1918) A part of the *Ottoman Empire since 1393, it achieved autonomy in 1878. In 1908, Prince Ferdinand of Saxe-Coburg used the weakness of the Ottoman government under the *Young Turk movement to proclaim independence, and have himself crowned Tsar (King). It bore the brunt of the first *Balkan War (1912–13), in which it was victorious. Unhappy with its subsequent territorial gains, it turned against its former allies in the second Balkan War (1913), and its army was quickly defeated. In consequence, it lost most of *Macedonia to Greece and Serbia, as well as the south of *Dobrudja to Romania. It was the last state to join World War I on the side of the *Central Powers in September 1915, in an attempt to reclaim its lost territories. As it was completely exhausted, it was also the first Central Power to conclude an armistice on 29 September 1918. In the Treaty of *Neuilly, it lost its remaining parts of Macedonia and access to the Aegean Sea, though these losses were relatively small compared to those of the other former Central Powers.

Years of conflict (1918–44) After a transitional period of political turmoil, marked by the decline of the old discredited parties, the 1919 general election was won by the Bulgarian Agricultural National Union (BANU), under the populist Stambolisky. He created an agrarian dictatorship in a country where the majority of the population consisted of agrarian smallholders. Stambolisky failed, however, to integrate the growing number of militant right-wing movements, which toppled him in 1923. The new government used a further coup attempt by the Communists as an excuse to eliminate completely by 1925 not just the Communists, but left-wing politics in general. Policies became more relaxed after the appointment of Andrei Liapchev as Prime Minister in 1926. He was unable to deal effectively with the effects of the Great *Depression. In the ensuing elections, the hitherto ruling Democratic Alliance gained around 30 per cent of the vote, while the centre-left People's Bloc received 47 per cent. The new government was hardly more effective at improving the economy, which resulted in another coup on 19 May 1934. The new rulers, backed by the army, were unsure as to the direction of the new government. This confusion left a power vacuum which allowed King *Boris III to take control through his protégé, Koseivanov.

Boris wanted desperately to avoid another war, and to keep a distance from Italy and Germany. Thus, in 1937 he concluded a friendship treaty with Bulgaria's former foe, Yugoslavia. However Hitler's plans to attack Greece through Bulgaria left Boris with little option but to enter the conflict. He only declared war on Britain and the USA in December 1941, and never declared war on the USSR. His death led to political vacuum, with matters turning for the worse when the USSR declared war on Bulgaria on 5 September 1944. To make the confusion complete, the Bulgarian government declared war on Germany on 8 September. Bulgaria thus managed to be at war simultaneously with all the belligerents, Germany, the USA, Britain, and the USSR. On the same day, the *Red Army advanced on Bulgaria.

Communist rule (1944–90) A Communist-inspired coup by the 'Fatherland Front' on 9 September 1944 created a new government. From now on, Bulgaria was in the Soviet sphere of influence, and the Communists moved quickly to eliminate all opposition. Under *Dimitrov, the People's Republic was declared, and in 1948 the last step towards total control was taken through the forced union between the Communist and Social Democratic Parties. For the next 40 years the Bulgarian state was a mirror image of its admired ally, the Soviet Union. Under *Chervenkov, *Stalin's policies of terror and economic misplanning were carried out with enthusiasm and gusto, while *Zhivkov became a most loyal follower of *Khrushchev and *Brezhnev respectively. Indeed, there were unsubstantiated rumours of plans to make Bulgaria the sixteenth Soviet republic.

Political dependence on the Soviet Union was complemented by accelerating economic dependence, since Bulgaria lacked major mineral deposits and investment capital. Efforts to industrialize the country proved disastrous in the long run, as the need for raw material imports increased its debts, while the small size of its domestic market made it even more dependent on foreign imports and exports. Cut off from Western markets, its attempted technological revolution in the 1970s proved to be a disaster. Growing discontent in the 1980s, made worse by the economic slump in response to the *oil price shock of 1979, was deflected through *nationalism, concentrating specifically on the sizeable Turkish minority (around 10 per cent of the population). Its religious (Muslim) customs were forbidden, the use of the Turkish language was disallowed, and Turks had to adopt Bulgarian names. As a result of this Bulgaria fell into international disrepute, worsened by its development as a centre of the drugs trade and an abode for terrorists. Growing opposition at home and abroad, against a general background of the collapse of *Communism throughout Eastern Europe, culminated in demonstrations and led to the dismissal of Zhivkov on 10 November 1989.

Democratization (1990-) The Communists ended their monopoly of power in early 1990, and on 3 April 1990 the party changed its name to the Bulgarian Socialist Party (BSP). The ensuing elections produced a victory for the reformed Communists, whose enormous party organization had remained intact. In an attempt to spread the responsibility for the reforms ahead, the BSP elected as President the leader of the oppositional Union of Democratic Forces (UDF). Elections in 1991 produced a hung parliament, which increased further the political instability of the country. Owing to the disunity among the fifteen parties within the UDF, however, early elections in December 1994 produced an absolute majority for the BSP, with the UDF returning to power in 1997. Continued popular dissatisfaction with the political parties, and the popular reluctance to embrace the social consequences of the government's economic reforms, produced the spectacular return of the Monarch in 2001. Heading a 'National Movement Simeon II', former Tsar Simeon (b. 1937, r. 1943–46) returned to Bulgaria and was elected Prime Minister with the promise of a spiritual and economic renewal. Almost nonexistent economic growth and political instability continued to frustrate Bulgaria's efforts to be accepted as a candidate for membership of the European Union. It failed to be admitted in the first wave of the EU's eastern enlargement in 2004, owing to continued widespread corruption and deficits in Bulgaria's judicial system. Led by Prime Minister Sergei Stanishev of the BSP from 2005, Bulgaria entered the EU in 2007, albeit under strict conditions. The difficulty of pursuing large-scale domestic reform was compounded by considerable domestic political instability, as an electorate disappointed by continued hardship continued to be vulnerable to populist political movements.

Bulge, Battle of the, see ARDENNES OFFENSIVE

Bülow, Bernhard Heinrich Martin Fürst von (b. 3 May 1849, d. 28 Oct. 1929). Chancellor of Germany and Minister President of Prussia 1900–9

Born near Hamburg, he entered the diplomatic service in 1874, became an ambassador in Rome in 1894, and Minister of State for Foreign Affairs in 1897. As Chancellor, he conducted an expansionist foreign policy, while at home he raised tariffs in 1902 to protect domestic agriculture and industry. Bülow fell out with the increasingly dominant *Centre Party over colonial policy in 1906. In an effort to free the government from the influence of the Centre, he created the 'Bülow Bloc' in 1907, allying all parties together excluding the *SPD and Centre. However, the Bloc's members, some of whom had opposed each other since the beginning of the Empire, proved too diverse to manage crucial policy matters such as constitutional and fiscal reform. Greatly weakened by the *Daily Telegraph Affair, Bülow was deprived of parliamentary support after the Bloc's collapse in 1909. He was succeeded by *Bethmann Hollweg.

Bunche, Ralph (b. 7 Aug. 1904, d. 9 Dec. 1971). UN diplomat

Born in Detroit and educated at Harvard, he taught political science at Harvard and Howard Universities. In 1944, he published a major book on race relations, *An American Dilemma*. During World War II he served with the US Joint Chiefs of Staff and the State Department, joined the *UN Secretariat in 1946, and served on the Palestine Peace Commission in 1947. Following the assassination of Count *Bernadotte in 1948 he carried on negotiations with such skill that he was able to arrange an armistice between the warring Arabs and Jews. For this he was awarded a *Nobel Peace Prize, the first awarded to an African American. He served as director of the Trusteeship Division of the UN 1948–54 and then, until his death, as Under-Secretary for Political Affairs. As such he was responsible for UN peacekeeping ventures in Suez (1956), the Congo (1960), and Cyprus (1964).

Burger, Warren Earl (b. 17 Sept. 1907, d. 25 June 1995). Chief Justice of US Supreme Court 1969–86

Born in St Paul, Minnesota, he initially sold insurance during the day and studied law at night school. He went on to teach and practise law until appointed assistant US Attorney-General by *Eisenhower in 1953. In 1956 he became a Federal Appeal Court Justice and developed a reputation as hard-line on crime. This led Richard *Nixon to nominate him Chief Justice of the *Supreme Court in 1969, upon the retirement of Earl *Warren. Despite his conservative image, he disappointed many on the right by consolidating Warren's court initiatives and opening the law to issues such as *abortion, gender discrimination, *affirmative action, and welfare rights. His opinion in *United States v. Nixon* forced *Nixon to hand over tape recordings to congressional investigators in the *Watergate scandal. This incriminating evidence ultimately forced the President to resign.

Burkina Faso

Colonial rule (up to 1960)

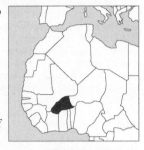

A landlocked country in western Africa, which was seized by the French in 1896. As the colony of **Upper Volta** it was integrated into *French West Africa in 1919, but in 1932 it was divided up and its components were added to the colonies of the Soudan, the Côte d'Ivoire, and Niger. Reconstituted as one territory within the *French Union in 1947, it joined the *French Community in 1958 as the autonomous Republic of Volta (renamed Upper Volta in 1959) before achieving independence on 5 August 1960.

Independence (from 1960) Following the corrupt and authoritarian rule of the first President, Maurice Yaméogo (b. 1921), politics were marked by instability. Major tension developed between the left (*trade unions, parties, and a radical wing of the army leadership) and the right (the Roman *Catholic Church, parts of the military, and politicians favourable towards France). Following a military coup in early 1966 General Lamizana assumed the presidency. Political parties were disallowed (1974–6), but in 1977 Lamizana devised a new Constitution which was accepted by a plebiscite, whereupon he became democratically elected in May 1978. He was deposed by a bloodless military coup on 25 November 1980. After two further coups power was assumed by Thomas Sankara (b. 1950) on 5 August 1983, who changed the country's name to Burkina Faso.

Sankara inaugurated a unique reform programme which aimed at improving the living standards of underprivileged sections of society, particularly women and peasants. He battled against corruption and reduced the proportion of state expenditure taken up by salaries in the public sector from 70 to 40 per cent. This challenged many entrenched interest groups, which supported a coup against him on 15 October 1987 in which he lost his life. His erstwhile colleague, and leader of the coup, Captain Blaise Compaoré (b. 1951), pursued more moderate policies and re-established a nominal democracy. He

was confirmed in office in the presidential elections of 1991, 1998 and 2005. International observers judged these to have been relatively fair, but the opposition accused him of corruption, political violence, and electoral fraud. One of the world's poorest countries with an annual Gross Domestic Product per head of around $200, in 2000 Burkina Faso was granted debt relief of US$400 million by the *IMF and the International Development Agency. In 2002 it qualified for the *HIPC Initiative.

Burma, see MYANMAR

Burma Campaigns

(Jan. 1942–May 1945)

The longest campaign involving troops from the *Commonwealth and the *British Empire during *World War II. On 19 January 1942 two Japanese divisions advanced into Burma, accompanied by *Aung San's Burma National Army. They captured Rangoon (8 March) and quickly reached Lashio at the southern end of the Burma Road, thus cutting off the supply link from India to China. In May they took Mandalay, forcing the British forces to withdraw to the Indian frontier. Attempts to regain the Arakan (October 1942 to May 1943) failed. Meanwhile, in February 1943 *Wingate led 3,000 Chindit troops behind Japanese lines. They suffered heavy casualties, but provided an important boost to British morale.

In 1944 the Allies repelled a Japanese attempt to advance into northern India, inflicting upon the Japanese army the biggest defeat in its history. In October an offensive was launched by British and Commonwealth troops, and US-supported Chinese Nationalists under General *Stilwell. The Burma Road was reopened in January 1945. By now a discontented Aung San had contacted *Mountbatten and in March his troops switched sides to join the Allies. As General Slim's 14th Army advanced down the Irrawaddy, a force of Indian, Gurkha, and west African forces moved through the jungle of the Arakan, supported by air-drop and amphibious operations. The Japanese headquarters at Akyab fell in January, while inland Mandalay fell to Indian and British troops, after fierce fighting, on 20 March.

Rangoon was attacked by land and sea and fell on 2 May, and by 17 May Burma had been recaptured.
MYANMAR

Burundi

A small state in central Africa whose history has been greatly affected by ethnic conflict between the Hutu and Tutsi tribes.

Colonial rule (up to 1962) Burundi was subjected and annexed to the German colony of German East Africa in 1890. After World War I it came under Belgian sovereignty, and was administered as a *League of Nations *Mandate and, from 1946, as a *UN *trust territory. Belgian rule entrenched traditional social structures, whereby power and privilege belonged to a minority of mostly Tutsi landowners, professionals, and government officials. By contrast, the underprivileged and often landless peasants belonged to the Hutu (Bantu) tribe, which made up 85 per cent of the population.

After independence in 1962 the tensions between the two tribes escalated and often erupted in violent massacres (1965, 1972, 1988, 1993, 1995–6). They were fuelled by events in neighbouring Rwanda, with its similar social structure, and the periodic influx of Rwandan refugees in times of crisis. This was compounded by a growing competition for scarce food resources. Burundi is one of the poorest and most densely populated African countries, with an average annual population growth of 3 per cent.

In 1966 the King, who had become a political pawn of the influential Tutsi aristocracy, was deposed and a military regime installed. A Hutu rebellion was brutally suppressed in 1972, and in 1976 a further coup brought to power a new military regime under J.-B. Bagaza, whose followers were again Tutsi. His proposed new constitution, establishing a one-party state, was approved in a referendum by 99 per cent in 1981. He was deposed in 1987 in a coup that brought to power Pierre Buyoya, a Tutsi. Free elections in June 1993 resulted in the victory of the Democratic Front of Burundi (FRODEBU), whose leader, Melchior Ndadaye, became Burundi's first Hutu President.

Ndadaye was murdered in October 1993, with Buyoya being implicated. This marked the start of a civil war, which by 1996 had claimed some 150,000 lives and caused the migration of around 700,000 Hutu refugees, who fled from the largely Tutsi-dominated army. The war also transformed large areas of the country in the north and west into virtual no-go areas. A fragile government coalition between the Hutu and the Tutsi parties in parliament was unable to stop the violence, as Hutu militias continued to fight against the persistent predominance of Tutsis in state institutions and government offices.

Contemporary politics (since 2000) In 2000 Nelson *Mandela brokered a peace deal, which led to the working out of a fragile political compromise even while the civil war continued unabated. Parliament would be composed of 60 per cent Hutus and 40 per cent Tutsi, an allocation that was maintained after 2005, when a five-year transitional period had come to an end. A new constitution was accepted for a further five years, with Pierre Nkurunziza, a Hutu, elected President in 2005. Apart from the economic stabilization of one of the world's poorest countries, Nkurunziza's greatest challenge consisted of formulating a reconciliation process allowing Hutus and Tutsis to come to terms with their recent past.

Bush election victory (2000)

Following a highly divisive election campaign, in the 2000 presidential elections George W. *Bush won over Vice-President Al *Gore with a small majority of votes in the electoral college, but with a minority of the popular vote. The most controversial element of the victory, however, concerned the decisive vote count in the state of Florida, which either candidate needed to win for a majority in the electoral college. After the first count, Bush was declared the winner by a majority of 500 out of five million votes. After the first recount, this majority was significantly reduced, but with the overseas votes (largely from the military) now factored in, Bush was again declared the winner by just over 500 votes. Confusion arose because different counties used different counting methods and different voting forms. In a number of pro-Gore counties, many voting machines were old and failed to record the marks of election ballots. Attention focused on individual counties that appeared to under-represent Gore's vote.

Gore's legal team tried to effect manual recounts. The state political authorities, headed by Bush's brother, Governor Jeb Bush, and George W. Bush's legal team sought to avoid this at a political level and in the courts. The Florida Supreme Court was inclined to allow widespread recounts, but on 11 December 2001, the US *Supreme Court decided that the state Supreme Court was interfering in the political process. This action effectively put an end to Gore's challenge, and the latter conceded defeat. The case marked an unprecedented and highly controversial intervention in the political realm by the Supreme Court, which before had only been prepared to intervene in the political arena under conditions of unanimity among the judges, as happened at *Watergate. The votes have been subjected to several recounts by newspapers and other organizations. These have failed to produce conclusive evidence about who actually won the most votes in Florida, though there has been a slight bias in favour of Bush.

Bush, George Herbert Walker (b. 12 June 1924). 41st US President 1989–93

Early career Born in Milton, Massachusetts, he was the second son of Prescott Bush, a banker and US Senator from 1953 to 1963. He served with distinction in World War II as a pilot and graduated from Yale with a BA in economics. Despite his East Coast patrician heritage, he moved to Texas and became extremely successful in the oil industry. He was elected to the US *Congress as a *Republican in 1966, after being beaten in the 1964 Senate contest in Texas. Bush was again defeated as a Senate candidate in 1970, and was appointed US ambassador to the *UN in 1971. Two years later he became the Chair of the Republican National Committee which called on *Nixon to resign after *Watergate. He was appointed by President *Ford in 1974 to the US Liaison Office in China, and became Director of the *CIA, 1976–7. He was defeated by *Reagan in the 1980 *primary elections and became his running mate, serving as Vice-President 1981–9. In July 1985 Bush became the first Acting President in US history when *Reagan invoked the Twenty-Fifth Amendment before undergoing a surgical operation.

Presidency Bush won the 1988 elections for President, on a tough anti-crime platform and a pledge of 'no new taxes', with 54 per cent of the popular vote. He capitalized on his ample foreign policy experience by successfully launching a series of foreign policy initiatives. He proclaimed a 'New World Order' on the basis of the end of the *Cold War, launched a military operation against Panama, sent US troops into Somalia under the auspices of the *UN, and brought together the worldwide coalition under US leadership which won the *Gulf War. The latter initiative in particular sent his popularity to an all-time high of an

almost 90 per cent approval rating in 1991. However, in 1990, he had agreed with a *Democrat-dominated *Congress to a budget deficit reduction plan which involved some tax rises, thereby breaking his electoral pledge. This, and the economic recession which overtook his administration in 1992, cost him the support of the Republican right wing which had enthusiastically supported Reagan. He lost the 1992 elections to Bill *Clinton. His son Jeb became Governor of Florida in 1998, while his elder son, George W., was the first son since John Quincy Adams (b. 1767, d. 1848) to succeed his father to the Presidency in 2001.

Bush, George Walker (b. 6 July 1946). 43rd US President 2001–

Early career Born in New Haven, Connecticut, he graduated with a BA from Yale, and enlisted in the National Guard, which allowed him to avoid service in Vietnam. Bush obtained an MBA from Harvard Business School, and returned to Midland, Texas, where he had spent part of his childhood. He had mixed success in the oil business, but made a fortune through his investment in the Texas Rangers baseball team. Having failed in 1978 to become a Representative in the US Congress, his candidacy for the governorship of Texas in 1994 came as a surprise. Even more striking was his victory against the popular incumbent, Ann Richards. This was enabled by a conservative programme opposing *abortion rights and gun control.

Bush excelled at working together with the Democrat-dominated legislature, focusing on education reform and tax reforms to stimulate business. As Governor, he moved to the centre ground, reinventing himself as a 'compassionate conservative'. His willingness to be identified with the right wing of the party and his own evangelicalism allowed him to move to the centre without alienating the right wing of the *Republican Party. After consistently high opinion poll ratings from 1998 onwards, he became the Republican candidate for the Presidency. His friendliness towards business interests allowed him to collect substantial campaign donations against the formidable machine of his Democratic opponent, Vice-President *Gore. During the race, he came across as affable and congenial, against the more wooden and cold image of his opponent. He was elected President in a most controversial election by a minority of the popular votes cast. The contest was decided by the electoral votes of Florida, which Bush won by a few hundred votes after one recount and several high court challenges (culminating in a controversial US *Supreme Court decision) about the ways in which ballots were counted.

First term of office The first son since John Quincy Adams to succeed his father to the Presidency, Bush left much of the organization of his administration to his running mate, Dick *Cheney. The administration's first months in office were highly controversial. The President's energy policies were seen as pandering to business rather than the national interest, while his tax cuts were considered by many economists as being too sweeping and ill-targeted. His popularity, the lowest of any president in his first months in office, soared after the *September 11 attacks. Bush caught the national mood when declaring *War on Terrorism, which toppled the *Taliban in months, at almost no human cost to the Americans.

Bush pursued controversial economic policies. His 2001 and 2003 tax cuts of up to $2 trillion over ten years projected a growing budget deficit, as did the 2002 budget: This passed the largest increase in regular military spending (by 15 per cent) for 20 years, up to a total of $379 billion. Bush was boosted by unprecedented levels of popular support. This allowed him to realize much of his political agenda, which included the biggest shake-up of government administration for 50 years through the creation of the Department of Homeland Security. Bush also enacted educational reform and moved to appoint right-wing district judges.

To a greater degree than many of his predecessors, Bush became involved in foreign policy, against his original intentions. Much to the confusion of American and European foreign policy elites, Bush conducted a personal style of foreign policy based less on diplomacy than on personal rapport and trust. As a result, he bore lasting personal resentments against the French President, *Chirac, and against the German Chancellor, *Schröder, for their refusal to back his campaign for regime change in Iraq. Bush appeared vindicated by the spectacularly swift US occupation of Iraq in the *Iraq War. His declaration of 1 May 2003, however, that major combat operations were over, proved ill-advised, as US troops continued to be subject to hostile attacks thereafter. In 2003, more US soldiers were killed in November (81) than in April (73) at the height of the war.

Second term of office Bush narrowly won a second term in office, this time with a popular majority of votes. In foreign policy, he became more conciliatory towards those countries which had opposed the Iraq War in an unsuccessful attempt to generate international help for the reconstruction of Iraq. In domestic politics, most of his major initiatives failed, notably his plan to privatize social security. His administration made serious blunders in its response to Hurricane *Katrina shortly after his re-election. Most importantly, his second term was overshadowed by the continued occupation of Iraq, which became increasingly controversial within the USA. As US troops continued to be subject to attacks while Iraq appeared to get no closer to self-government, voters expressed their dissatisfaction in the mid-term elections. Facing a hostile Congress for his final two years in office, Bush increased US presence in Iraq in early 2007, even though this move was controversial inside his own party.
BUSH ELECTION VICTORY

Bush v. Gore, see BUSH ELECTION VICTORY; SUPREME COURT (USA)

Busing (USA)
Following the move to end *segregation in public facilities during the later 1960s, children were taken by bus from Black or Hispanic neighbourhoods usually to what had been White suburban schools and vice versa. This was to secure racially integrated schooling as demanded by the *Brown v. Board of Education ruling. The desegregation movement had mainly affected the southern states, where busing was first introduced against strong opposition from White families. But it was also used in many northern cities like Boston where de facto segregation also existed. In 1971 the *Supreme Court approved the principle of busing, but in 1972 *Congress ordered that further schemes should be delayed. Busing remained a controversial issue, but its use steadily declined as a means of racial integration.
CIVIL RIGHTS ACTS (USA); GEORGE WALLACE

Bustamante, Sir William Alexander
(b. 24 Feb. 1884, d. 6 Aug. 1977). Prime Minister of Jamaica 1962–5
Born in Blenheim (Jamaica), he studied in the USA and lived in Cuba and Panama before returning to Jamaica in 1934 to become a *trade-union organizer. In 1938 he founded the right-wing Bustamante Industrial Trade Union. In that year, he was successfully defended by Norman *Manley from charges of sedition. He organized a general strike in 1939, and in 1943 founded the conservative Jamaica Labour Party (JLP). He became Chief Minister of Jamaica, 1944–55. Originally an opponent of greater autonomy ('self government means slavery'), he changed course and ignited Jamaican patriotism to

campaign for independence from the Federation of the *West Indies. The first Prime Minister upon independence, he retired because of ill health.

Buthelezi, Gatsha Mangosuthu
(b. 27 Aug. 1928). South African politician

Career under apartheid Born in Mahlabatini (Zululand) as the grandson of King Dinizulu. Admitted to Fort Hare University in 1948, he joined the *ANC Youth League, where he met *Sobukwe and *Mugabe. Expelled for ANC activities in 1951, he became chief of the Buthelezi tribe in 1953, and was made chief executive officer of the newly established Kwa Zulu Territorial Authority in 1970. In 1975, he founded **Inkatha yeNkululeko yeSizwe (Freedom of the Nation)**, an organization committed to non-violence which soon emerged as the predominant political movement of the Zulu people. In 1976 he consolidated his role as chief spokesman for the Zulu by becoming Chief Minister of Kwa Zulu, but subsequently rejected independence for his poor nation. He consistently demanded the release of Nelson *Mandela, though relations between them worsened during the 1980s. Buthelezi opposed international sanctions to end *apartheid, arguing that the system could only be ended through the internal logic of a liberal economy. This stance stood in stark contrast to the *socialist rhetoric of the ANC. It gave him a growing international platform as a 'legitimate' spokesperson for the South African Blacks at the expense of the ANC, particularly among the right-wing governments of Europe and the USA.

Since the demise of apartheid (1990) Buthelezi's authority was fundamentally weakened by Mandela's release in 1990 and the subsequent revelation that Inkatha had received payments from the South African government (though he denied knowledge of this). In an attempt to halt his own marginalization in South African politics through Mandela's authority, he assumed a stubborn stance in the negotiations for a new constitution. He founded the **Inkatha Freedom Party** in 1990, which won the state elections for the new territory of KwaZulu-Natal in 1994. In that year, he also agreed to become Minister for Home Affairs in Mandela's government, despite continuing tensions between the Inkatha and the ANC, particularly in KwaZulu-Natal.

On 20 September 1994 Buthelezi was dismissed by the Zulu King Goodwill Zwelithini from his office of Chief Minister of KwaZulu-Natal. Nevertheless, he managed to retain some influence over the province through being elected President of the Upper House (Chamber of Chiefs), which could delay provincial legislation. In 1998, he was found guilty by the *Truth and Reconciliation Commission for being responsible of violent attacks of his followers against members of the ANC and other opponents. Buthelezi remained Minister of Home Affairs until he fell out with the ANC in 2004.

Butler, Richard Austen ('Rab'), Baron Butler of Saffron Walden (b. 9 Dec. 1902, d. 8 Mar. 1982). British Chancellor of the Exchequer 1951–5

Born in Attock (Punjab, India) and educated at Cambridge, he was elected to parliament in 1929 as a *Conservative. In 1932, he became Under-Secretary of State for India, and after a period at the Ministry of Labour, he became an Under-Secretary at the Foreign Office in 1938. Despite his support for *appeasement and the *Munich Agreement, Butler remained in government under *Churchill, who promoted him to become President of the Board of Education in 1941. He was then responsible for the 1944 Education Act, which built the framework for postwar education in England, through the introduction of free secondary schooling open to all who passed the '11-plus' examinations. In opposition (1945–51), as chairman of the Conservative Research Department he was influential in persuading the Conservative Party to accept the principles of the *welfare state introduced by *Beveridge and *Attlee's government.

During the subsequent years of Conservative government, he became Chancellor of the Exchequer (1951–5), Home Secretary (1957–62), and Foreign Secretary (1963–4). In these posts, he was associated with dissolving the *Central African Federation, persuading the Treasury to build more prisons, presiding over periods of increased living standards, and reluctantly restricting immigration from the *Commonwealth (*immigration legislation (UK)). Despite his prominence and seniority within the party, he lacked political killer instinct and failed three times to gain the Conservative leadership, losing it to *Eden (1955), *Macmillan (1957), and *Douglas-Home (1963). He became Master of Trinity College, Cambridge, in 1964, but continued sporadic political activity in the House of Lords after 1965.

Byrnes, James Francis ('Jimmy')
(b. 2 May 1882, d. 24 Jan. 1972). US Secretary of State 1945–7

From a modest background in Charleston, South Carolina, he trained as a lawyer and built up a practice to become a public prosecutor in 1908. In order to meet the age requirement for his first job, he falsified his date of birth as 1879, and continued to use it thereafter. He sat in the House of Representatives as a Southern Democrat (1911–25), and in the Senate, (1931–41). Although on the right of his party he strongly supported President *Roosevelt's *New Deal, Byrnes, cooled towards it after Roosevelt's attempted purge against conservative Democrats during 1937–8. However, he still supported Roosevelt's campaign for a third term in 1940. Briefly a *Supreme Court Justice, he became director of the Office of War Mobilization 1943–5 and was then appointed Secretary of State by President Truman. A strong believer in the *UN, he helped to ensure economic recovery in Germany and was reluctant to accept the division of that country. No enthusiast for the *Truman Doctrine, he was succeeded by George *Marshall and was later elected Governor of South Carolina in 1951, where he supported racial *segregation.

C

Cabinet Mission Plan (16 May 1946)
The last viable attempt to come to a peaceful
solution to Indian independence and
partition. The Indian elections of 1945–6 were
won in the Hindu-dominated constituencies
by the nationalist Indian National *Congress
(INC), and in the Muslim-dominated areas by
the *Muslim League. This raised the issue of
whether independence was to result in a
united India (as favoured by the INC), or one
divided into Hindu and Muslim areas (as
demanded by the Muslim League). On 23
March 1946, three representatives of the
*Attlee Cabinet, Lord Pethick-Lawrence,
Stafford *Cripps, and A. V. Alexander, went to
India to find a solution. Their plan envisaged a
three-tier government structure for a united
India, with the lowest being the provincial
level. The second tier would have created
three zones consisting of the Muslim-
dominated areas of the north-west and the
north-east, and the Hindu-dominated rest of
the subcontinent. Finally, the third tier bound
these structures together into a loose
federation. To lay to rest Muslim fears against
Hindu domination, it provided also that after
fifteen years, each individual zone was free to
leave the union. Originally accepted by both
parties, it was effectively scuppered by
*Nehru's careless remark shortly afterwards,
whereby he denied some of the Muslim rights
negotiated so painstakingly, especially the
right of the Muslim-dominated zones to
secede after fifteen years. This killed off any
residual goodwill with *Jinnah, and led to the
overhasty and acrimonious division between
India and Pakistan.

Cabral, Amilcar (b. 12 Sept. 1924, d. 20
Jan. 1973). Guinea-Bissau revolutionary
Born in Bafata (Guinea-Bissau) of a father from
Cape Verde and a mother from Guinea-Bissau.
He studied agronomy at Lisbon University and
entered the colonial government of Guinea-
Bissau in 1950. On 19 September 1956, he
founded the Partido Africano da
Independência da Guiné e de Cabo Verde
(PAIGC, African Party for the Independence of
Guinea and Cape Verde). He campaigned for
the unification of Guinea-Bissau and Cape
Verde. Cabral was adamant that the struggle
for independence should not only lead to
political *decolonization, but also to the end
of foreign control of culture, society, and
economy. He worked actively for the

coordination of independence movements in
Portuguese-controlled African countries.
Following his assassination his brother, Luìs,
became the country's first President.

**Caetano, Marcello José das Neves
Alves** (b. 17 Aug. 1906, d. 26 Oct. 1980).
Prime Minister of Portugal 1968–74
Born in Arganil, he studied law and in 1933
became professor of constitutional and
administrative law at the University of Lisbon.
A close associate of *Salazar, he helped to
draft the 1933 constitution. As Minister for
Colonies (1944–7) he encouraged further
economic, political, and administrative
integration of the colonies with metropolitan
Portugal. He was President of the Chamber of
Estates (1949–55), and Deputy Prime Minister
in 1955. He left politics in 1959 to become
Rector of Lisbon University. When Salazar had
a stroke in 1968 he returned and became
Prime Minister. He introduced liberal reforms
in the economic sphere, but held back from
political reform. Ultimately, he became
hostage to his intransigence towards the
colonies, as the Portuguese were exhausted by
unwinnable colonial wars. He was deposed in
a military *coup*, and went into exile in Brazil.

Cairo Conference (22–6 Nov. 1943)
A prelude to the *Tehran Conference it was
attended by US President *Roosevelt and the
British Prime Minister, *Churchill. Also
attended by *Chiang Kai-shek, its principal
aim was to decide on policy for the Far East
during *World War II. This included the
demand for unconditional surrender by Japan,
and the return of Taiwan and Manchuria to
China (*Manchukuo). The participants also
demanded Japanese withdrawal from its
colonies of Korea and Taiwan and from its
*League of Nations *Mandates, which
included much of *Micronesia. These
resolutions were incorporated into the Cairo
Declaration of 1 December 1943.

Calderón Hinojosa, Felipe (b. 18 Aug.
1962). President of Mexico, 2006–
Born in Morelia, he graduated with a BA in law
and an MA in economics before obtaining a
masters in public administration at Harvard.
He joined the National Action Party (Partido
Acción Nacional, PAN) and became its youth
leader in 1986, and its president in 1996. He
narrowly won the 2006 election, which was

contested by his left-wing populist opponent, Andrés Manuel López Obrador. In office, he stepped up a campaign against drugs trafficking, vowing to destroy the gangs whose attacks cost the lives of more than 2,000 people in 2005.

Caliphate Movement, see KHILIFAT MOVEMENT

Callaghan, Leonard James, Baron Callaghan of Cardiff (b. 27 Mar. 1912, d. 26 Mar. 2005). British Prime Minister 1976–9

Early career Born in Portsmouth, he grew up there, and worked as a clerk in the Inland Revenue before joining the Royal Navy during World War II. Callaghan was elected as *Labour Party MP for Cardiff South in 1945, and became Parliamentary Secretary in the Ministry of Transport in 1947. In opposition, he gained experience of a variety of issues, first shadowing foreign affairs, then becoming Labour's Treasury spokesperson. He lost the 1963 leadership election to *Wilson, who made him Chancellor of the Exchequer (1964–7) in his government. Faced with strong pressure on the pound, he implemented policies such as the creation of a prices and incomes board, cuts in public spending, and, finally in 1967, the devaluation of the pound. In the wake of this humiliating measure, he became Foreign Secretary (1967–70), where he had to deal with the emerging *IRA violence in *Northern Ireland, and calls for immigration restrictions (*immigration legislation (UK)).

In office After Labour's return to power in 1974 Callaghan became Foreign Secretary, and in 1976 he succeeded Wilson as Prime Minister. He was handicapped by the lack of an overall parliamentary majority, economic recession caused by the 1973 *oil-price shock, and his unwillingness (and inability) to overcome *trade-union hostility to his economic austerity measures. The disastrous outcomes of the referendums on Scottish and Welsh devolution respectively triggered a successful vote of no confidence in parliament in March 1979, which was followed by a general election. However, it was the large-scale trade-union strikes of 1978–9, popularly remembered as the 'Winter of Discontent', that destroyed the party's popular image and foiled its political prospects for over a decade. His party was routed at the 1979 general elections, and he resigned as party leader in 1980.

Calles, Plutarcho Elías (b. 25 Sept. 1877, d. 19 Oct. 1945). President of Mexico 1924–8

An elementary school master from Sonora, he rose through the ranks of the army, supporting first *Madero and then *Carranza, and became Governor of his home state in 1917. As Obregón's successor to the presidency, he succeeded in putting the new political system on a more solid footing. Most importantly, he quelled the *Cristeros (Christers) Revolt, an alliance of traditional elites, committed to the old economic system under *Díaz, and Roman Catholic opponents to the new secular state. After leaving office he remained the predominant figure in Mexican politics, and in 1929 sought to unite and confirm the new political establishment through the creation of the National Revolutionary Party (PNR), which later became the *PRI. In 1935 the new President, *Cárdenas, refused to accept Calles's dominance and sent him into exile. He was allowed to return from the USA in 1941.

Calwell, Arthur Augustus (b. 28 Aug. 1896, d. 8 July 1973). Australian politician

Born and educated in Melbourne, he joined the state civil service of Victoria in 1913. He joined the *Labor Party in 1914 and advanced through its ranks to become president of the Victorian Labor Party in 1931. Entering federal parliament in 1940, he became Minister for Information in 1943, but his most important legacy came from his time as the first Minister for Immigration (1945–9). Given the pressing need for immigrants, he sought to preserve the traditional emphasis on a 'White' Australia, through aggressive campaigns to attract not only British, but for the first time also continental and especially southern European immigration. The deputy leader of the Australian Labor Party from 1951, he served as its leader (in opposition), 1960–7.
WHITE AUSTRALIA POLICY

Cambodia (Kampuchea)

A country sandwiched between Vietnam and Siam (Thailand), it was subject to the domination of these two countries from the fifteenth century until 1884, when it became a French protectorate. In the twentieth century, Cambodia continued to be subject to the influence of both countries, and especially Vietnam.

Colonial rule (up to 1950s) In 1887 Cambodia was incorporated into French *Indochina. Of the different Indochinese territories, Cambodia was the most docile, not least because of its long history of foreign domination. The French built an infrastructure and created a rudimentary education system. In 1941, the *Vichy French colonial government welcomed the Japanese, and appointed the young *Sihanouk King.

After World War II, Sihanouk cautiously welcomed back the French troops. Cambodia was involved in the subsequent *Indochina War, mainly through the *Vietminh-supported Khmer Issarak (Free Khmers). Resistance to the French also came from the National Assembly, created after Cambodia had become an autonomous member of the *French Union in 1946. France granted independence in 1953, and confirmed it in the 1954 *Geneva Agreements. In 1955, Sihanouk abdicated in favour of his father, and focused on politics instead. As Prime Minister, he founded his own movement, the Sangkum Reastr Niyum, and pursued moderately *capitalist policies. He also sought to remain neutral, which enabled him to draw on competing Soviet and US assistance in the light of the *Cold War and the escalating conflict in Vietnam.

Khmer Rouge (1960s–1970s) The *Vietnam War made Sihanouk's neutralism untenable, as Cambodia was used by *Vietminh and *Vietcong forces as a supply route from North to South Vietnam, receiving its share of US carpet bombing in consequence. Encouraged by the North Vietnamese, the radical Communist *Khmer Rouge began to wage a civil war against the government, which continued after Sihanouk was deposed in a coup by the pro-American *Lon Nol. His Khmer Republic was defeated by the United Front, a somewhat odd alliance between the Khmer Rouge and Sihanouk, though the real power in the newly proclaimed Democratic Kampuchea was *Pol Pot.

Pol Pot tried to realize a unique, authoritarian vision of *Communism which relied on certain elements of *Maoism. He attempted to dissolve the cities and forced people to work in agricultural communes, abolishing money and introducing a barter economy, and killing everyone who did not appear supportive of the new order. Encouraged by his Chinese allies, in 1977 he also started an ill-judged war with Vietnam. The Vietnamese forces entered Pnomh Penh and forced his retreat in January 1979, though he continued to offer stubborn resistance in the countryside. Within a decade, almost two million people had died, as a result of civil war (750,000 dead and over three million refugees) and subsequent genocide (over one million dead).

Since the Khmer Rouge (1979–) A new Communist government was formed under Heng Samrin, which focused on restoring basic food supplies—a difficult task, since more than half of the country's cultivable area was mined. With mixed success, the government also attempted to overcome the social and economic trauma of the Khmer Rouge regime. However, the government was opposed by Khmer Rouge guerillas, who continued their armed struggle with the help of Vietnam. The Communist government was also opposed by the Coalition Government of Democratic Kampuchea (CGDK). Created in 1982, the CGDK was chaired by Sihanouk, and became the internationally recognized government in exile. The complex political situation began to unravel with the financial and military exhaustion of the Vietnamese at the end of the Cold War. The Vietnamese army withdrew in 1989, and in 1991 four of the parties involved in the conflict concluded a peace treaty, under *UN mediation.

Sihanouk became President once again, and in 1993 he was made King. He had two co-Minister Presidents, but in 1998 the Communist Minister President, Hun Sen, deposed his royalist colleague, Prince Ranariddh, on charges of contacts with the Khmer Rouge. The coalition between Communists and royalists continued, however, and the ensuing political stabilization was helped by the surrender of the last Khmer Rouge units in 1999. The government thus stabilized with Sihanouk being succeeded by his son, Norodom Sihamoni, in 2004, but stabilization came at the expense of freedom of expression, as many of those critical of the regime were imprisoned.

Cambrai, Battle of (World War)

The first successful tank battle in history. On 20 November 1915, the new Tank Corps broke the German line with 500 British tanks and captured 10,000 prisoners. The British failed to consolidate their gains, allowing a German counter-attack early in December to regain their line and take as many British prisoners.

Cameron, David William Duncan (b. 9 Oct. 1966). UK Conservative Leader, 2005–

Born in London, he was educated at Eton and Oxford, where he obtained a first-class degree. Cameron became employed at the *Conservative Party's research department, and became closely involved in speech writing and policy formation in the *Major era. Cameron became head of corporate

communications at Carlton Television before
returning to politics in 2001, as MP for the safe
Oxfordshire seat of Witney. Helped by his
intimate knowledge of the party, he rose
quickly through the ranks, and was appointed
Shadow Minister for Education in 2005.
Nevertheless, he entered the 2005 leadership
contest as an outside candidate, but overtook
all other candidates with a ten-minute speech
at the Conservative Party conference which
mesmerized the party.

After becoming leader, Cameron worked
hard at transforming his party and moving to
the centre ground. The party adopted a new
symbol, with a green tree symbolizing the
party's new commitment to the environment.
Cameron also vowed not to reduce Labour's
spending on the *National Health Service,
while shocking many in his own party with
his liberal attitude towards the family, which
included backing adoption by homosexual
couples.

Cameroon

Separating
central and
western Africa,
Cameroon is a
heterogeneous
country which
comprises over
200 ethnic
groups.

**Colonial rule
(up to 1961)** The territory came under
German influence in 1884, and was confirmed
as a German colony in 1911. It was occupied
by British and French troops in 1916, and in
1919 was divided into a smaller, western part
administered by the British, and an eastern
part administered by the French, both as
*League of Nations *Mandates. Britain
integrated the western part into its colony of
Nigeria, while France tried to transform the
east into a separate colony. In 1946, the
*UN established both parts as *trust
territories and ordered France and Britain to
prepare them for independence. This was
granted to the east on 1 January 1960, and the
west was reunited with it on 1 October 1961,
after a referendum.

Independence (since 1961) Despite
independence, President *Ahidjo continued
to rely on French military assistance to
combat the militant rebels of the Union des
Populations du Cameroun (Union of the
Populations of Cameroon). He created a one-
party state in 1972, and abolished the federal
structure which had given each part of the
country its separate parliament. The unitary
state led to discrimination against the English-
speaking minority. While he secured his
regime with dictatorial powers, Ahidjo's rule
was characterized by relative stability and
prosperity, facilitated by revenues from oil
exports, and a diverse agricultural base which
gave it relative independence from food
imports.

Ahidjo was succeeded by *Biya, under
whose government falls in the prices of its
most important export goods (oil, coffee,
cocoa) rendered the government unable to
pay for its inflated public sector, and obliged it
to take up a large foreign debt. It became
dependent upon the intervention of the *IMF,
which forced the state to privatize many of its
companies, to freeze public-sector pay, and
to reduce the number of state employees. A
consequent wave of public protests was met
by political liberalization. In elections which
were boycotted by some of the opposition
parties, Biya was re-elected in 1992. In that
year, his Rassemblement Démocratique du
Peuple Camérounais (RDPC, Democratic
Union of the People of Cameroon) won 88 out
of 180 seats in parliament. In 1997 the RDPC
entered a coalition with the other major
French-speaking party, the Union Nationale
pour la Démocratie et le Progrès. Under Biya's
rule, Cameroon engaged in a bitter border
dispute with its neighbour, Nigeria.

Contemporary politics (since 2006) The
country benefited from debt relief granted to
the world's poorest countries in 2006, but its
economy continued to suffer from high levels
of corruption. In 2006, Nigeria accepted an
International Court ruling that the Bakassi
peninsula, which was rich in mineral
resources, was part of Cameroon, with
administration to be handed over in 2008.

Camp David Accords (Sept. 1978)

Two peace resolutions between Israel and
Egypt, negotiated during a thirteen-day
conference between *Begin and *Sadat,
under the crucial leadership of *Carter, at the
retreat of the US President, Camp David. The
first provided a general framework for Middle
East relations, and specified ways in which
reductions in Israeli military presence in the
occupied areas of the *West Bank and *Gaza
Strip would lead to a comprehensive peace
settlement. Since the accords were violently
opposed by the other Arab states, as well as by
the *PLO, it proved to be of little consequence.
More important was the second accord which
provided a framework for the conclusion of a
peace treaty between Egypt and Israel. The
former vowed to recognize Israel and refrain
from military attack, while the latter agreed
to a gradual return of the occupied Sinai
peninsula to Egypt. This served as a prelude to

a peace treaty, which was agreed by both countries in 1979. For the Camp David Accords, Begin and Sadat received the *Nobel Peace Prize.

Campaign for Nuclear Disarmament, see CND

Campbell, Avril Kim (b. 10 Mar. 1947). Prime Minister of Canada 1993

The first woman Prime Minister in Canadian history was born at Port Alberni (British Columbia). After obtaining degrees from the University of British Columbia and the London School of Economics, she became a member of the provincial legislative assembly in 1986, entering the House of Commons for the Progressive *Conservative Party in 1988. Campbell became Minister of Justice and Attorney-General in 1990, and Minister of Defence in 1993. Following *Mulroney's resignation, she won the party leadership and became Prime Minister. Campbell failed to revive the party for the general elections three months later, plunging it into deeper unpopularity through her disorganized campaign and unguarded comments. The party's parliamentary strength fell from 154 to just two seats and she lost her own seat to the *Liberal Party.

Campbell-Bannerman, Sir Henry

(b. 7 Sept. 1836, d. 22 Apr. 1908). British Prime Minister 1905-8

Born in Glasgow, and educated at the Universities of Glasgow and Cambridge. He was elected as MP for Stirling Burghs in 1868, and gained a reputation as a radical Liberal. He served as a junior minister and in 1884 the patient conciliator became Chief Secretary for Ireland. He entered Cabinet as Secretary for War in 1886 and 1892-5. Almost by default, he came to lead the *Liberal Party in the House of Commons from 1899. His charming, unthreatening personality enabled him to form a cohesive parliamentary party despite bitter internal disputes, mainly through avoiding controversial policy commitments. During the *South African (Boer) War, he managed to overcome Liberal controversies through focusing not on the cause, but on the conduct of war. Underestimated not just by his own colleagues, but also by *Balfour, he won the 1906 elections after the latter had resigned in 1905. As Prime Minister, however, he continued to avoid debates which might split the Liberal Party, most notably the issue of Irish *Home Rule. As a result, his short term of office did not match that of his successor, *Asquith, in its reforming zeal. He retired because of ill health, and died shortly afterwards.

Canada

The world's second largest country by area, it has distinguished itself through multi-culturalism, a commitment to international peacekeeping, and fraught relations among its federal states.

Overview Canada emerged from the British colonies of British North America as a self-governing Dominion through the British North America Act of 1 July 1867, consisting of a confederation of the mostly French-speaking province of Quebec, and the predominantly English-speaking provinces of Ontario, Nova Scotia, and New Brunswick. The growth of British colonists outside Quebec, who now formed a majority in the Canadian population, ensured that government would be dominated by English-speakers. Quebec benefited from being part of Canada because it was too weak economically to be independent. As part of Canada, Quebec maintained control over its own cultural and

Table 2. **Canadian Prime Ministers Since 1896**

Wilfred *Laurier	1896–1911	Lester B. *Pearson	1963–8
Robert L. *Borden	1911–20	Pierre E. *Trudeau	1968–79
Arthur *Meighen	1920–1	Charles Joseph *Clark	1979–80
William Lyon *Mackenzie King	1921–6	Pierre E. *Trudeau	1980–4
Arthur *Meighen	1926	John *Turner	1984
William Lyon *Mackenzie King	1926–30	Brian *Mulroney	1984–93
Richard B. *Bennett	1930–5	Kim *Campbell	1993
William Lyon *Mackenzie King	1935–48	Jean *Chrétien	1993–2003
Louis S. *St Laurent	1948–57	Paul *Martin	2003–6
John G. *Diefenbaker	1957–63	Stephen *Harper	2006–

educational affairs, securing its heritage and language against US encroachment.

Throughout its history Canada's existence has been fundamentally shaped by its southern neighbour, the USA, which became the world's wealthiest and most powerful nation during the twentieth century. After the decline of British influence from World War I, two factors became the fundamental determinants of Canada's twentieth-century history: the internal threat of tensions between its English- and French-speaking populations, and the constant need to preserve cultural, economic, and national identity against the United States.

To make Canada viable as an independent state, in the early twentieth century *Laurier encouraged westward expansion and European settlement there, to the detriment of the *native peoples, whose rights were largely ignored. Laurier authorized a second transcontinental railway line to link Manitoba with the Pacific in 1903. Finally, in 1905, the provinces of Manitoba and British Columbia were linked by the creation of the provinces of Saskatchewan and Alberta.

The era of two World Wars (1914–48) Canadian ambiguities towards the US surfaced in 1911, when Laurier's plans to liberalize trade between the two countries gave rise to fear of US goods flooding the Canadian economy, and brought down his government. Laurier was succeeded by the Conservative *Borden, who steered the country through World War I. Canada participated automatically through the British declaration of war on behalf of the *British Empire. This involvement was relatively uncontroversial as long as it concerned the recruitment of volunteers. However, as in Australia and Ireland, social discord erupted on the issue of compulsory military service overseas. This was fundamentally opposed by the French-speaking Canadians, who felt no principled loyalty toward the British Empire. The 1917 *Military Service Act, therefore, deeply divided Canadian society as well as the political parties, and it required a unionist government including some Liberal defectors to enact conscription.

The *Liberal Party recovered under *Mackenzie King, who became Canada's longest-serving Prime Minister in the twentieth century (1921–48), discounting brief interludes by the Conservatives *Meighen (1926) and *Bennett (1930–5). World War I heightened Canada's self-confidence as a nation. In the *Paris Peace Conference and the *League of Nations Canada was not represented by Britain, but participated in its own right. Canada's

international autonomy was formally recognized by the Statute of *Westminster (1931), when it gained control over all its affairs, including foreign and defence policy. Its economic dependence on the USA was exposed, however, by the Great *Depression. Canada was affected as severely as the USA, but its leaders were unable or unwilling to pass effective measures to combat the economic slump. Ultimately, recovery depended greatly on the success of *Roosevelt's *New Deal.

Owing to pressure from *Woodsworth and the growth of the *Cooperative Commonwealth Federation, Mackenzie King overcame his relative legislative passivity to inaugurate the beginnings of a welfare state before and during World War II. In World War II, Canada took an active part on Britain's side, though its participation was no longer automatic. Once again, conscription became the most contentious issue, raising questions about Canada's allegiance to the Crown, the status of Quebec, and the power of the state.

Post-war Canada (1948–90) However, the welfare state was mainly legislated by Mackenzie King's successors, the Liberals *St Laurent and *Pearson, and the *Conservative *Diefenbaker. Under Canada's *Medicare system, health care provision became universal by the 1960s, setting Canada further apart from the economic and social liberalism of the USA. A further distinctively Canadian feature was its active support of, and identification with, the *UN, and particularly its peacekeeping operation, which was championed rigorously by Pearson.

After a decade of prosperity, the Liberal Party of Quebec launched the *Quiet Revolution in 1960, which became the catalyst for renewed and increasingly popular demands for the sovereignty of *Quebec, as underlined by the growth of the separatist *Parti Québécois. Since the 1970s, Canadian domestic politics have been dominated by the debate about the role of Quebec within the Canadian confederation. In a 1980 referendum, 60 per cent of Quebeckers rejected sovereignty, partly because of the assurances of *Chrétien and *Trudeau that a new, comprehensive, and lasting constitutional settlement would be worked out which would take into account the French-speaking population's concerns. However, Quebec's aspirations were insufficiently recognized in the 1982 settlement of the *Canadian Constitution, while other provinces refused to grant Quebec the special status accorded to it in the *Meech Lake Accord of 1987, worked out by *Mulroney.

In 1995, a referendum in Quebec for independence failed by a margin of 1 per cent. Thereafter, the separatist tide turned. In the 1998 provincial elections, the federalist Liberal Party gained a majority of the popular vote. In that year also, the Supreme Court ruled that the province did not have the right to declare independence unilaterally, and that such a decision would have to respect the concerns of Canada's other provinces, as well as the *First Nation minorities inside Quebec.

The Liberal era (1990s–2005) Whereas the decade up to 1994 was dominated by the Conservatives under Mulroney and *Campbell, the Conservative Party was routed in the 1994 elections, which ushered in more than a decade of Liberal Party rule. Under the Liberals, Canada addressed a major constitutional issue successfully, the *land claims of the *Canadian Indian peoples, the *Inuit and the *Métis. Different native peoples were given self-rule, covering vast areas in the mineral-rich north of the country. Thus, *Nunavut was created as a Territory of Canada in 1999.

Chrétien presided over unprecedented economic stability. Aided by high prices for Canada's rich mineral resources, including oil, Canada experienced strong economic growth and persistent budget surpluses. Chrétien's political domination was assured not just by the economy, but also by the fragmentation of the opposition. The oil-rich western province of Alberta became increasingly assertive politically, voting overwhelmingly for the right-wing *Reform Party. Given the weakness of the Conservative Party, the Reform Party became Canada's principal opposition party in 1997. However, it never managed to create a popular appeal beyond Alberta, so that it was ultimately forced to merge with the traditional Conservative Party in 2003. Chrétien was succeeded by Paul *Martin, whose governments were shaken by a series of corruption scandals.

Contemporary politics (since 2006) In 2006, the Conservatives finally regained power, with Stephen *Harper leading a minority government. Harper reduced taxation and improved Canada's relations with the USA, which had been affected by Canada's refusal to join the *Iraq War. Harper openly challenged Canada's ability to fulfil its obligations under the *Kyoto agreement; while Canada had committed itself to a 6 per cent reduction of greenhouse gas emissions (1990–2012), its emissions had increased by almost 25 per cent (1990–2005). Harper was unable to introduce major political transformations for as long as he did

not command a majority in the House of Commons.

In a bid to reduce Quebec separatism, Parliament recognized Quebec as a distinct nation within a united Canada in 2006.

Canadian Constitution, patriation of

The 'bringing home' of the Constitution to Canada from Britain, whose parliament had retained the notional right of accepting or rejecting changes to the Canadian constitution. The issue was raised during the 1980 referendum on sovereignty for *Quebec, in which *Trudeau argued successfully for a redefinition of Quebec's status if the Quebeckers voted to remain within Canada. With his lieutenant, *Chrétien, Trudeau set about not only bringing home to Canada all the rights still in Britain, but also defining once and for all the roles of the Canadian federal state and of its provinces, which had been in dispute ever since the creation of Canada on 1 July 1867.

After eighteen months of protracted negotiations between Trudeau and the provincial premiers, a compromise was reached. Moreover, a new Canadian Charter of Rights and Freedoms to replace *Diefenbaker's Bill of Rights was announced, which became law on 17 April 1982. Though legally binding, these agreements were rejected by Quebec. As the province encompassing the vast majority of French speakers, Quebec insisted on the principle of 'duality', whereby Canada was divided into separate English- and French-speaking parts, both of which had to agree to constitutional change. By contrast, the other provinces agreed that constitutional change would have to be supported by a substantial majority in federal parliament, and among the provinces. According to this reasoning, Quebec was thus not accorded any special constitutional status. As a result, the agreement failed in its original purpose, that of pacifying separatist demands in Quebec. To the contrary, it fuelled separatism by failing to incorporate the province's demands into the Canadian constitutional framework.

MEECH LAKE ACCORD

Canadian Indians

Overview A term used to refer to the aboriginal people of Canada who are neither *Inuit nor *Métis, and encompassing a wide variety of distinct peoples. Linguistically, Canadian Indians can be broken up into ten language families, ranging from Algonquian (with over 115,000 speakers in 1986) to Haida and Kutenai (with 200 speakers each in 1986). Legally, Canadian Indians are said to be 'status' Indians or 'nonstatus' Indians. Nonstatus Indians are those who, especially by intermarriage, have lost the legal rights granted to status Indians by the federal government. In 1987 there were approximately 360,000 status Indians in Canada.

Early policies (1900–45) The twentieth century saw many changes in the lives of all of Canada's native peoples. Throughout the first quarter of the twentieth century several Canadian Indian groups signed treaties with the federal government, by which they surrendered their title to large tracts of lands in return for certain federal rights and benefits, such as exemption from most federal and provincial taxes. By 1929 treaties had been signed covering most of the territory in Ontario, Manitoba, Saskatchewan, and Alberta. This period also saw the continued numerical decline of the native population due mainly to disease and the loss of traditional food supplies.

Aided by missionaries who often acted as mediators between the native peoples and government officials, a self-consciousness slowly emerged among some of the peoples during the 1920s, in protest against their treatment. In British Columbia, for example, the Allied Tribes of British Columbia was set up in 1915, and the Native Brotherhood of British Columbia in 1931. However, this evolution of protest was slowed down by the Great *Depression, which caused particular distress in the reservations and led many Indians to leave them for the cities.

The post-war era (1945–98) After World War II, the Canadian Indians became more vociferous in demanding a restoration of their rights. More important for the change in government policy was that their marginalization and discrimination became publicly less acceptable among the majority of Canadians descended from immigrants. A redefinition of Indian status was attempted in 1951, but rejected as insufficient by the Indian peoples demanding the settlement of their *land claims. In the 1960s, the government became active in creating employment opportunities in the reservations, and in preserving Indian cultures. Yet the Indian peoples' hopes were further dashed by a 1969 White Paper, which once again failed to address adequately the issue of their land claims.

In response, the native peoples created a network of pressure groups, which were often supported by the government, to enable them to formulate a coherent and united set of proposals. In 1982 they successfully lobbied for the insertion of a clause stating their land claims in the Constitution Act (*Canadian Constitution, patriation of). In 1983, a House of Commons Special Committee recommended the creation of Indian self-government within the provincial and national framework.

The economic and educational situation of Canadian Indians improved vastly after World War II. Their average income has increased, though it is still two-thirds of that of an average Canadian of immigrant descent. Their education is now almost equivalent to that of a White Canadian, and overall discrimination in Canadian society has declined markedly. In 1991 the Royal Commission on Aboriginal Peoples was launched, which became the most comprehensive and expensive government investigation to date. It found that traditional Canadian law had failed the native peoples, and that each people should receive and administer its own system of justice according to its own traditions and values.

Contemporary politics (since 1998) In 1998, the *Liberal government under *Chrétien formally apologized for the treatment of Canadian Indians and other aboriginal Canadians in the past. The government proceeded to respond to the Royal Commission recommendations. To improve life expectancy for Canadian Indians and other aboriginal peoples, which was seven years below that of White Canadians in 2001, Paul *Martin agreed in 2005 to transfer $5 billion over five years to help improve aboriginal Canadians' standard of living. This agreement was not honoured by Martin's successor, Stephen *Harper, who reduced government transfers to Canadian Indians. The *Conservatives' reduced commitment to the rights of Canadian Indians was manifested further in 2006, when Canada was one of only two nations not to sign the *UN Declaration on the Rights of Aboriginal People.
FIRST NATIONS; NUNAVUT

Canadian Labour Congress (CLC)

A *trade union emerging in 1956 from a fusion between the Trades and Labor Congress of Canada (est. 1883) and the Canadian Congress of Labour (est. 1940). In 1961, it joined forces with the *Cooperative Commonwealth Federation to found the *New Democratic Party, which it continued to support. It is the central organization of English-speaking trade unionists in Canada, representing almost 100 individual unions with a combined membership of 2.4 million members in 2006.
CONFÉDÉRATION DES SYNDICATS NATIONAUX

 **SEE WEB LINKS**

• The official website of the CLC.

Canaris, Wilhelm (b. 1 Jan. 1887, d. 9 Jan. 1945). German admiral and resistance leader

Having joined the German navy in 1905, he rose to become admiral and chief of the military counter-intelligence in 1935. Although he was right-wing politically, he became an opponent of the *Nazi regime and was involved in the organization of the *resistance movement in 1938. He became reluctant, however, to contemplate an attack on *Hitler, and thus lost touch with the inner circles of the resistance in 1941. Nevertheless, because of his association with them he was imprisoned in the wake of the *July Plot and executed at the Flossenbürg *concentration camp.

Cape Verde

An island state in the Atlantic, occupied by Portugal from 1595. Most indigenous farmers lost their land during the Portuguese *Estado Novo from 1926. After independence on 5 July 1975, it was governed by the Partido Africano da Independência da Guinée de Cabo Verde (African Party for the Independence of Guinea and Cape Verde), which strove for the unification of the country with Guinea-Bissau. When this was rendered impossible by a military coup there (1980), the party was renamed the Partido Africano da Independência de Cabo Verde (African Party for the Independence of Cape Verde, PAICV), turning its attention to domestic economic and social reform.

The PAICV introduced free elections in 1991, which were duly won by the opposition, the Movimento para Democracia (Movement for Democracy, MPD), supported by the majority of the population living abroad. The MPD's new dominance of the country's political system was confirmed in the 1995 parliamentary elections, which it won with an overwhelming majority. Despite attempts to promote capitalism and economic diversification, into tourism for example, the country's economy still depended on foreign aid, which amounted to around 70 per cent of its total foreign income in the 1990s. In 2001, the PAICV gained an absolute majority in the National Assembly. In the presidential elections, Pedro Pires of the PAICV won by a margin of only thirteen votes. Pires was re-elected in 2006, with the PAICV also winning a parliamentary majority. Cape Verde had a more stable economy than many of the poorer African countries, but its agriculture suffered from a chronic water shortage, which, during the 1990s, often transmuted into a severe drought.

Capitalism

An economic system characterized by the private ownership of production and the regulation of supply and demand through the price mechanism in a free market, as described by Adam Smith (b. 1723, d. 1790) in his book *Inquiry into the Nature and Causes of the Wealth of Nations* (1776). The term has been used by *Marxists to describe an epoch in the evolution of history from a feudal to an ideal, Communist society. However, the longevity of capitalism has been proven by the ultimate failure of Communist countries to replace the free market with the central planning of supply and demand, and their inability to create sufficient incentives for individual enterprise apart from private property.

KEYNESIANISM; MONETARISM; GLOBALIZATION

Caporetto, Battle of (World War I; 24 Oct.–18 Nov. 1917)

A counter-attack by the forces of *Austria-Hungary and Germany. It was encouraged by the return of soldiers after victory at the Eastern Front, and directed against the Italian forces. In two years of warfare, these had only managed to advance ten miles into Austrian territory, up to the town of Caporetto (Kobarid, *Slovenia). Led by *Ludendorff, the advance of the *Central powers threatened to outflank the entire front, forcing General Cadorna to retreat. Fighting continued until mid-November, when river flooding brought it to an end. The Italians regrouped on a line running north of Venice along the River Piave, 70 miles (110 km) into Italian territory. The front was later strengthened by British, French, and US reinforcements. Around 45,000 Italians lost their lives, with 300,000 being taken prisoner. Even though ultimately the Italians emerged victorious from World War I, the defeat of Caporetto continued to be felt as a national humiliation and was consistently used in *Fascist propaganda by *D'Annunzio and *Mussolini.

Cárdenas, Lázaro (b. 21 May 1895, d. 19 Oct. 1970). President of Mexico 1934–40

A general in the Mexican army, he was instrumental in the foundation (with *Calles) of the National Revolutionary Party (Partido

Nacional Revolucionario, PNR), which became the dominant political party linking the political establishment with the popular masses. Upon becoming President he immediately showed that he was to be his own man through sending into exile the hitherto predominant personality in Mexican politics, Calles. He proceeded to realize many of the more radical aspirations of the 1917 constitution, particularly through distributing twice as much land as all his predecessors combined since 1917. A subsequent decline in productivity notwithstanding, this measure gained him enormous popularity. This was enhanced when in 1938 he nationalized the largely US-owned oil refineries, in response to their refusal to comply with an order of the Mexican Supreme Court for them to pay better wages to Mexican workers. Cárdenas reformed the PNR into the Mexican Revolutionary Party (Partido de la Revolución Mexicana, PRM) in 1938, which subsequently consisted of four sectors representing peasants, labour, the military, and the middle classes. After his term in office he continued to be a popular and influential figure in Mexican politics, and was Minister for National Defence, 1943–5.

PRI

Cardinal Principles (China)

The guiding principles of *Deng Xiaoping's regime, announced in 1979 in response to the Democracy Wall Movement. These were 'Keep to the socialist road; uphold the people's democratic dictatorship; uphold the leadership of the Communist Party; and uphold *Marxism-Leninism and *Mao Zedong Thought'. Despite the pragmatism of the new leadership on liberalism in economic matters, these hardline principles served as a stern reminder that political liberalization was out of the question. They provided the basis and justification of the political repression under Deng.

TIANANMEN SQUARE

Caribbean Community and Common Market (CARICOM)

Formed in 1973 to extend the goals of the Caribbean Free Trade Association (CARIFTA) from economic liberalization to economic integration. Its members are Antigua and Barbuda, the Bahamas, Barbados, Belize, Dominica, Grenada, Guyana, Haiti, Jamaica, Montserrat, St Christopher and Nevis, St Lucia, St Vincent and the Grenadines, Surinam, and Trinidad and Tobago. Anguilla, Bermuda, the British Virgin Islands, the Cayman Islands and the Turks and Caicos Islands are associate members. The Bahamas

are members of the Community, but not of the Common Market, while the Dominican Republic, Haiti, and Surinam act as observers. CARICOM's aims are (a) to coordinate foreign policy; (b) to cooperate in such areas as health, education, sport, and tax administration; (c) to harmonize economic policies such as taxation and import duties.

CARICOM has assisted growth in trade among its members, not least by the successful establishment of a Common External Tariff. Its members also established the Caribbean Court of Justice, which deals with trade disputes between member states while also acting as a High Court for Barbados and Guyana. Nevertheless, the aim of a single market, espoused from 2000, continued to be a distant prospect. Freedom of movement of persons was still restricted, while the poorer and smaller members remained sceptical about allowing freedom of land purchases by nationals of other member states. CARICOM has been hampered in its development by the economic disparity of its members, their strong economic ties to third countries such as the UK and the USA, and their reluctance to surrender any sovereignty in favour of common policies.

(⊕) SEE WEB LINKS

• The official website of CARICOM.

Carmona, António Oscar de Fragoso

(b. 24 Nov. 1869, d. 18 Apr. 1951). President of Portugal 1928–51

Born in Lisbon, he graduated from the Royal Military College of Portugal in 1888 and by 1922 held the rank of general. He took part in the military *coup* in 1926 and became Prime Minister, with *Salazar as his Finance Minister. Two years later he had himself elected President. In 1932, he appointed Salazar Prime Minister. Carmona then became more of a figurehead, responsible primarily for maintaining the crucial relationship between the regime and the military. He left the day-to-day management of the *Estado Novo to the civilian Salazar. In the last years of his life, his influence declined, mainly because of his old age and declining health.

Carol II (b. 15 Oct. 1893, d. 4 Apr. 1953). King of Romania 1930–40

As crown prince, he was forced by a liberal regime to renounce the succession to the throne on the pretext of his relationship with a mistress, but in reality because of his anti-liberal views. He returned from exile in 1930 and was accepted as king by the new right-wing government of Iuliu Maniu (b. 1873,

d. 1953), albeit with considerable reluctance. In response to the co-operation of the popular National Peasants' Party and the *Iron Guard, he argued that constitutional rule had become practically impossible, and created a royal dictatorship in 1937. His new constitution, which abolished all political parties and created a *corporatist state, was accepted in a plebiscite in 1938. Carol ventured to keep the country out of World War II, restricting the country's role to that of *Nazi Germany's major supplier of oil. To maintain this policy, he acquiesced in *Stalin's demands and ceded Bessarabia and *Bukovina to the Soviet Union on 28 June 1940. A few weeks later, as a result of the second *Vienna Award, Romania lost the most important areas of *Transylvania to Hungary. On 7 September 1940 the territorial carnage came to an end with the cession of southern *Dobrudja to Bulgaria. Nationalist opinion was unable to stomach this, and he was forced to abdicate. He died in exile in Lisbon.

Carranza, Venustiano (b. 29 Dec. 1859, d. 21 May 1920). President of Mexico 1917–20
Son of a landowner, he was active in politics from 1880 and became Governor of Coahuila, the home state of Francisco I Madero, in 1910. He eventually supported Madero in his revolutionary struggle against *Díaz. When President Madero was assassinated by one of his generals, Huerta (b. 1854, d. 1916), Carranza became the leading constitutionalist leader in the Revolution through his command over a large army. He became provisional President after forcing Huerta's resignation in 1914. Initially without a clear social programme, he restored order through appealing to the masses with promises of a land reform, and the creation of favourable labour laws. On the battlefield he defeated the armies of his most formidable opponent, *Villa, in 1915, which rendered the latter unable to mount a national military challenge. His position thus secured, he called a constitutional convention in 1916. The eventual 1917 Constitution was far more radical and socialist than Carranza himself had envisaged. As it stipulated that a president's six-year term was non-renewable, he attempted to realize the appointment of a successor who would be his mouthpiece. He failed and was forced to flee by his military commander, Obregón, who probably ordered his assassination on his way into exile.

Carrington, Peter Alexander Rupert, 6th Baron (b. 6 June 1919). British Foreign Secretary 1979–82
Born in London, he was educated at Eton and the Royal Military College, Sandhurst, and was awarded the Military Cross in World War II. He took his seat in the House of Lords in 1945, and held a variety of ministerial posts, until he became Secretary of State for Defence in 1970. He was Secretary for Energy in 1974, and Chairman of the *Conservative Party, 1972–4. As *Thatcher's Foreign Secretary, he resigned after he had failed to predict an Argentine invasion of the Falkland Islands, despite detailed information (see *Falklands War). From 1984 to 1988, he was Secretary-General of *NATO, and in 1992 he served as an observer for the *Council of Europe in the Balkans.

Carson, Edward Henry, Baron Carson of Duncairn (b. 9 Feb. 1854, d. 22 Oct. 1935). Irish Unionist leader
Born in Dublin, and educated at Portarlington School, and Trinity College, Dublin. He qualified as a lawyer and was called to the Irish Bar in 1877. For his legal skill, he was awarded the distinction of QC (Queen's Counsel) in Ireland (1889) and England (1894). He was elected as Conservative MP for Dublin University in 1892, and held this seat until 1918, when he became MP for Belfast Duncairn. Carson was Solicitor-General for Ireland in 1892, and for England 1900–6. He was Attorney-General under *Asquith in 1915–16. Under *Lloyd George, he was First Lord of the Admiralty in 1917, and a member of the War Cabinet in 1917–18. He is remembered principally as a formidable opponent of Irish Home Rule, and later as an advocate of Ulster remaining part of the United Kingdom. In 1912, in Belfast, he organized the signature of a covenant, in which thousands pledged that Ulster would not recognize the authority of any Dublin parliament. This gave popular backing to the *Ulster Volunteer Force, a private army of 80,000, whose threat of civil war was only averted by the outbreak of World War I. Thereafter, he reluctantly agreed to Home Rule for southern Ireland as long as *Northern Ireland remained under the British Crown. He entered the House of Lords in 1921.

Carter Doctrine
A policy announced by President *Carter in his State of the Union Address on 23 January 1980, which declared that 'Gulf oil reserves were of vital interest to the US and the US would therefore be justified in preventing outside domination of the region by military intervention'. It formed the basis of *Bush's response to the Kuwait crisis in the *Gulf War 1991.

Carter, James Earl ('Jimmy') (b. 1 Oct. 1924). 39th President of the USA 1977–81

Early career Born in Plains, Georgia, he graduated with high honors from the Naval Academy as a nuclear engineer, and became a successful farmer. Carter was elected a State Senator and, in 1971, he became Governor of Georgia. He was successful at streamlining the state government administration, and actively promoted the advancement of minorities. Carter appeared to come from nowhere to win the Democratic nomination for presidency, and then won narrowly against the unpopular *Ford. He projected an unpretentious, open image, and his reputation for moral rectitude became a crucial asset for a nation still shocked by the *Watergate scandal.

Presidency Carter's election strategy which banked on him being an outsider to the political establishment in Washington became a crucial liability during his presidency. He failed to establish a working relationship with *Congress and found little support for his policies, such as the energy strategy which he proposed as a solution to the oil crisis of the 1970s. His administration was plagued by economic stagnation and inflation, which was above 10 per cent in 1978. In foreign affairs, Carter had two lasting successes. He secured the return of the *Panama Canal against initial congressional opposition, while generally under his presidency the US took a relatively non-interventionist stance in Central America. Even more remarkably, he achieved the *Camp David agreement which established lasting peace between Israel and Egypt. Carter thus achieved the most enduring act of reconciliation in the Middle East in the twentieth century.

In other important areas, however, Carter's foreign policy was hampered by the contradictory appointments of the conciliatory Cyrus Vance as secretary of state, and the hawkish Zbigniew Brzezinski as national security adviser. He failed to get the SALT II agreement ratified by the Senate (see *Disarmament), while the Soviet invasion of Afghanistan in 1979 started a new phase of the *Cold War and brought the relationship between the two superpowers to a nadir. The *Iran hostage crisis, compounded by a bungled rescue attempt authorized by Carter, dealt the final blow, precipitating a collapse in public regard for his abilities. His complaint that America was suffering from a 'malaise' only made the optimism of Ronald *Reagan seem all the more attractive. Although he beat off a strong challenge from Edward *Kennedy for the 1980 Democratic nomination, he lost the subsequent presidential election.

In 2002, Carter was awarded the *Nobel Peace Prize for his work as a mediator and head of the Carter Center in Atlanta. He had become involved in promoting low-cost housing developments, served as a *UN election monitor in less developed countries, and served on various peace missions, e.g. to Uganda (1999), Sudan (1995) Haiti (1994), and Nicaragua (1990).

⊕ SEE WEB LINKS

• The home page of the Carter Center.

Casablanca Conference (14–24 Jan. 1943)

A conference convened in the Moroccan port of Casablanca, on territory controlled by the *Free French. With de *Gaulle present, it was led by the British Prime Minister, *Churchill, and US President *Roosevelt, in order to agree on further strategies in the common conduct of *World War II. There was to be an increase in US bombing of Germany. Plans were agreed for the forthcoming invasion of Sicily and for the transfer of British forces to the Far East on the defeat of Germany. Roosevelt issued a statement, with which Churchill concurred, insisting on Germany's unconditional surrender. It was de Gaulle's first international conference and thus signalled his international acceptance as leader of the anti-*Vichy forces. Nevertheless, the French leader resented the conference being held on 'his' territory without prior consultation.

Casement, Roger (b. 1 Sept. 1864, d. 3 Aug. 1916). Irish nationalist

Born in Sandy Cove (Co. Dublin) and educated at Ballymena Academy in Co. Antrim, he went to Africa in 1884 and joined the colonial service there in 1892. His reports on the inhuman treatment of native workers in the Belgian Congo (1904) and in the rubber plantations of Peru (1912) earned him an international reputation as a humanitarian. He was knighted for this work in 1911, but was forced to retire from foreign service due to the adverse effects of the tropics on his health.

Casement became active in the Gaelic League and other Irish nationalist movements, joining the Irish Volunteers in 1913. During World War I, he went to Berlin (October 1914) to try to enlist Irish prisoners of war in an Irish rising against Britain. He failed to form a brigade, but eventually persuaded the Germans to send 20,000 guns to Co. Kerry on the ship *Aud* in April 1916, intended to support the planned *Easter Rising. Casement worried that the supply was inadequate. He followed in a U-boat and landed at Banna Strand, Tralee, Co. Kerry, on 20 April and tried to get a message to Dublin to halt the rising. Casement was captured and taken to London for interrogation. While he was there, the Easter Rising broke out in Dublin. Casement was charged with high treason, convicted, and sentenced to death. A large campaign was mounted to have the sentence revoked, but copies of his diaries (which contained homosexual references and passages) were circulated to discredit him. This worked, the campaign failed, and Casement was hung at Pentonville gaol. His remains were returned to Ireland in 1965 and he was reinterred in Glasnevin Cemetery on 1 March after a state funeral.

Casey, Richard Gavin Gardiner, Baron (b. 29 Aug. 1890, d. 17 June 1976). Australian Governor-General 1965–9

Born in Brisbane, he was educated at the Universities of Melbourne and Cambridge. Casey served in the Australian Imperial Force during World War I at *Gallipoli and in France. Casey returned to Melbourne to take up his father's business interests in 1919, and he befriended *Bruce, whose political agent he became upon his appointment as Australia's liaison officer in London in 1924. He returned to Australia in 1931 and was elected to the House of Representatives for the *United Australia Party. He became *Lyons's adviser on international affairs, and in 1940 became the first Australian representative to a country outside the *Commonwealth, the USA. He became a member of the British War Cabinet from 1942, and in 1944 was appointed Governor of Bengal. Returning to Australian politics in 1946, he became federal president of the *Liberal Party in 1947, entering parliament in 1949. As Minister for External Affairs (1951–60) he focused Australian foreign policy on its hitherto neglected relations with its Asian neighbours, away from the traditionally exclusive emphasis on the UK and the Commonwealth. He accepted the peerage as Baron Casey of Berwick (Victoria) and the City of Westminster in 1960. In 1965 he became the first Australian appointed as Governor-General by a non-Labor government.

Cassin, René (5 Oct. 1887–20 Feb. 1976). French politician

Born in south-western France, he became a professor of law in Lille (1920) and then in Paris (1929). Cassin was a French delegate to the *League of Nations, 1924–38. He joined de *Gaulle and became a prominent member of the *Free French. Cassin was a member of the Council of State (1944–60), but is best remembered as the principal author of the *UN Declaration of *Human Rights in 1948. He became a member of the European Court of Human Rights in 1959, and was its President 1965–8. In 1968, he was awarded the *Nobel Peace Prize.

Castle (née Betts), Barbara Anne, Baroness Castle of Blackburn (b. 6 Oct. 1910, d. 3 May 2002). British Secretary of State for Employment (1968–70)

Born in Bradford, she was educated at Bradford Girls' Grammar School, and Oxford. In the 1930s, she worked as a journalist, and was involved in local politics in London. In 1945, she was elected as Labour MP for Blackburn, and rose to prominence as a left-winger in the 1950s, a supporter of Nye *Bevan. She was chairwoman of the *Labour Party in 1958–9, entered the Cabinet as Minister of Overseas Development when *Wilson won the 1964 general election, and was Minister of Transport (1965–8). As Secretary of State for Employment and Productivity (1968–70), she proposed to weaken excessive *trade-union power through a compulsory twenty-eight-day conciliation period, and a universal membership ballot prior to strike action. Unsurprisingly, this was strongly opposed by the powerful trade unions, championed by *Callaghan, who effectively scuppered the plans. Secretary of State for Social Services in Wilson's last Cabinet, she was dropped by Callaghan when he became Prime Minister in 1976. She became a Member of the *European Parliament in Strasburg (1979–89), and entered the House of Lords in 1990.

Castro Ruz, Fidel (b. 13 Aug. 1927). Prime Minister of Cuba 1959–76; President 1976–

Early career A trained lawyer who assisted the poor, he was imprisoned after leading an abortive revolt on 26 July 1953. Released after a general amnesty in 1955, he went to Mexico, where he gathered and trained a group of about eighty resistance fighters, including his brother, Raul, and *Che Guevara. They returned to Cuba secretly on 2 December 1956, and subsequently waged guerrilla warfare against the hated *Batista dictatorship. Castro called for an all-out popular insurrection against the regime in March 1958. Throughout this period of guerrilla warfare and after, his authority was based on unrivalled leadership skills, charisma, and fabrication of myth. His 1953 group of fighters became the romantic '26 July movement', while his guerrilla campaign from 1956 onwards transformed him into some latter-day Robin Hood in the popular image.

In power After his triumphant entry into Havana as the great liberator on 9 January 1959 he thrived on his ability to stand up to the USA, which had backed Batista and the country's corrupt wealthy elites. This image was greatly enhanced by clumsy *CIA attacks on his life (such as the dispatch of explosive cigars for his use) and the abortive US-sponsored *Bay of Pigs invasion in 1961. As a legend in his own time, therefore, he has been able to remain leader of his country despite numerous economic failures. Castro's authority survived unscathed the collapse from 1989 of Communist Eastern Europe and the USSR, which had sustained significant parts of the Cuban economy. Although in the 1990s he did not change his anti-American stance, he did soften his anti-US and anti-capitalist rhetoric in an effort to overcome his country's international isolation, especially from Canada and the European Union. Incapacitated by a mysterious illness since 2006, he nevertheless remained unchallenged as (nominal) Cuban leader. Indeed, his fame reached a new peak in old age, as a number of leftist popular leaders in Latin America, notably *Chávez and the Bolivian president, Evo Morales, declared him their idol.

Catholic Church, Roman

The largest Christian denomination, comprising around 800 million members, which looks to the infallible authority of the Pope in matters of doctrine, and his supreme guidance in all spiritual affairs. In addition to the Scriptures, its structure and teaching has drawn from the tradition of the Church Fathers, which developed from the early Christian communities under the guidance of St Paul and St Peter. The Pope heads the Church as he derives his legitimacy from the apostolic succession going back to St Peter as the first 'Pope' of the early Church.

After Vatican I (1870) The history of modern Catholicism goes back to 1860/70, when it faced two major threats. The first was the challenge of industrialization and demographic change, which uprooted many communities and alienated many people from the Church. The second, more immediate,

challenge was the loss of the Papal States to a unified Italy. The loss of the Pope's secular powers turned out to be a blessing in disguise, however. Following the First Vatican Council (1869-70), the Church emphasized papal spiritual authority throughout the worldwide Church (ultramontanism). In particular, the Pope's role was strengthened through the declaration of papal infallibility. This claim to worldwide authority, even if it was restricted to spiritual matters, brought about the hostility of *liberalism, with its emphasis on the supremacy of state institutions, as well as *socialism.

Ultimately, this new centralism strengthened the authority of the Church, while the revival of popular forms of religious practice (such as the veneration of saints) further increased its appeal. In contrast to other Christian Churches, Roman Catholics were also relatively quick to respond to the new problems caused by industrialization and urbanization through the establishment of new parishes in working-class areas, and the organization of workers in Catholic *trade unions, clubs, and societies. At the same time, Roman Catholics were active in missionary work in Africa and Asia, so that during the first half of the twentieth century the Church expanded its worldwide membership, while avoiding the same decline in membership levels in Europe as many Protestant Churches after World War I.

During World War II, under Pope *Pius XII the Church was torn between its own mission to be a universal Church and the need to condemn the atrocities of *Nazi Germany. In the end, the Church was heavily criticized for taking the former stance, so that it was left to individual priests and bishops in Germany and Austria and occupied countries to speak out against *Hitler, at the risk of their own lives. The Church has been subsequently criticized for its refusal to speak out for Jews before 1945, and because it was not until the papacy of *John Paul II that it acknowledged the special sufferings of Jews, although it never formally apologized.

After World War II, the Church was confronted with the *Cold War, and took a confrontational stance against the newly

Table 3. **Popes of the Roman Catholic Church Since 1878**

Leo XIII	1878–1903	*John XXIII	1958–63
Pius X	1903–14	*Paul VI	1963–78
Benedict XV	1914–22	*John Paul I	1978
Pius XI	1922–39	*John Paul II	1978–2005
*Pius XII	1939–58	*Benedict XVI	2005–

established Communist regimes of Eastern Europe. This led to discrimination against Catholics in most Communist countries except in Poland, where religious observance was so strong as to force the Communist government there to come to an accommodation with the Church.

After Vatican II (1965) Perhaps the most important event for the Catholic Church in the postwar era was the election of Pope *John XXIII, a compromise candidate elected only after twelve electoral rounds. Through his charity and humanity he infused the Catholic Church with a greater desire for unity and harmony, which was institutionalized in the Second *Vatican Council (1962–5). Under his successor, *Paul VI, the reforms to make the Church more up to date continued, while Pope John Paul II continued to emphasize the Church's progressive and radical positions on social issues and international relations (e.g. through condemning the *Gulf War). This was accompanied by a decidedly conservative stance on issues of morality (e.g. on birth control) and theology (rejection of *liberation theology). Finally, the Church took a more liberal stance on ecumenism, not so much with Protestants as with Orthodox Churches of eastern Europe.

Through his long reign, his strong personality, and his charisma, John Paul II, who himself had appointed all but three of the cardinals who were entitled to vote for his successor, had left a deep imprint on the Church. He was succeeded by one of his closest allies, Cardinal Ratzinger, who as *Benedict XVI concentrated on internal reform, an area of relative disinterest to his predecessor.

( ) SEE WEB LINKS
• The official website of the Papacy.

Catt, Carrie Chapman (b. 9 Jan. 1859, d. 9 Mar. 1947). US suffragist
Born at Ripon, Wisconsin, she was present at the founding of the National American Woman Suffrage Association in 1890. As its president (1900–4 and 1915–20), she saw the fulfilment of women's suffrage in the US with the passing of the Nineteenth Constitutional Amendment in 1920. In that year she co-founded the League of Women Voters. An isolationist, Catt was also associated with the American pacifist movement. In 1915, she founded the Woman's Peace Party (together with Jane *Addams). She chaired the Commission on the Cause and Cure of War between 1925 and 1932. In contrast to Addams, however, after the war she partly turned her attention away from the issue of international peace. She devoted her efforts to the International Woman Suffrage Alliance (later the International Alliance of Women),

which she had co-founded in 1904 and which she continued to lead with energy until 1925. Opposition to *Fascism and the *Nazis caused her to abandon her pacifism in the 1930s.

Cavaco Silva, Aníbal António (b. 15 July 1939). Prime Minister of Portugal, 1985–95

President of Portugal 2006– Born in Boliqueime, he studied economics at the Universities of Lisbon and York (England), where he received a doctorate. He joined the Democratic People's Party in 1974, and the conservative Social Democratic Party in 1976. In 1980 he became Minister of Finance, and in 1985 led his party to an election victory, heading a minority government. In 1987, he was elected with an absolute majority of votes (50.2 per cent), for the first time in Portuguese history. He repeated this achievement in 1991, when he was re-elected with 50.4 per cent of the popular vote. His government therefore produced a crucial stability in a system which had seen more than ten changes of government in as many years, and helped the republic to settle down to an essentially two-party system, dominated by a party for the centre-right and one for the centre-left. In 1995, he lost the elections against a revitalized Socialist Party. He lost the 1996 presidential elections, but was successful in 2006.

Cavell, Edith (b. 4 Dec. 1865, d. 12 Oct. 1915). English nurse
Born in Swardeston, Norfolk, and educated at home, in Somerset, and in Brussels. In 1906, she co-founded a school in Brussels to train nurses according to British techniques. She stayed in Brussels during World War I with the permission of the German authorities, nursing both Allied and German wounded. She also assisted British and French soldiers to escape to neutral Holland. When this was discovered, she was arrested for espionage, tried, and executed. She was regarded as a martyr in the Allied countries, and even the German Emperor *Wilhelm II, who was not usually noted for his political tact, recognized the execution to have been a major political mistake.

Cayman Islands
A Caribbean island group south of Cuba, which came under British sovereignty in 1670. Administered from Jamaica, it joined the

Federation of the *West Indies in 1959, and upon its breakup became a separate colony in 1962, receiving the status of a United Kingdom Dependent Territory. Under this arrangement, the inhabitants became relatively prosperous, as it attracted the registration of around 20,000 banks, insurance companies, and other businesses. Despite autonomy, the islands were exposed to substantial pressure from the British government to tighten their control over the services sector. This intensified after *September 11, amidst concerns that money-laundering through the Cayman Islands encouraged global terrorism. From 2002, political representatives were unable to agree with the British government on a new constitution that would have granted a Bill of Rights. In 2004, the legislative assembly passed a controversial citizenship law which compelled most foreign workers to leave the island after seven years, before becoming eligible for citizenship,

CDU (Christlich-Demokratische Union, Christian Democratic Union)

A German political party founded in 1945 as a broad interdenominational *Christian Democratic party. In Eastern Germany, it was subjected to Communist control by 1948, from which it only managed to liberate itself in 1990, when it emerged as the largest party from East Germany's first and last free national elections.

In West Germany (Federal Republic of Germany, FRG), together with its Bavarian sister party, the *CSU, the CDU narrowly won the first national elections of 1949. The CDU/CSU won the 1953 elections with 49.9 per cent of the popular vote, and in 1957 they won an absolute majority (50.2 per cent), an unrivalled achievement. It provided West Germany's first three Chancellors: *Adenauer, *Erhard, and *Kiesinger. During this time, the party put into practice the **social market economy**. This was a *capitalist economic system in which the state actively regulates the framework in which market forces operate in an effort to minimize their negative side effects such as monopolies and the creation of social inequality. The CDU tied Germany politically and militarily to the West, as the FRG joined *NATO in 1955 and took a lead in *European integration from the 1950s. Defeated in the 1969 elections by the *SPD, the CDU was led by *Kohl from 1973, under whom the party ruled in coalition with the *Liberal Party (1982–98).

The CDU has sought to be a 'people's party', representing all sections of society, though it has been traditionally strong in Roman Catholic and rural areas. It has been more popular among businessmen, the self-employed, professionals, and white-collar employees than among manual workers. From the 1998 elections onwards, the party polled below 40 per cent of the vote, which indicated the party's difficulties in integrating an increasingly heterogeneous population defined by concerns different from the party's original Christian, middle-class values. Under the leadership of Angela *Merkel, the party formed a grand coalition with the SPD in 2005.

(⊕) SEE WEB LINKS

• The official website of the CDU.

Ceausescu, Nicolae (b. 26 Jan. 1918, d. 25 Dec. 1989). President of Romania 1967–89

Early career Born in Scornicesti in rural Romania, he moved to Bucharest and soon became politically active, joining the Communist Party in 1936. He became a protégé of *Gheorghiu-Dej and was put in charge of building up a Communist youth organization. He worked underground until the entry of Soviet troops in 1944 and the establishment of the Communist Romanian Republic in 1948. He entered the *Politburo in 1955, and in 1965 succeeded Gheorghiu-Dej as First Secretary (later Secretary-General) of the Communist Party. He was President of the State Council (1967–74) and, when his position had become unassailable, conferred upon himself the title of President in 1974.

In power He installed a brutal regime of terror, backed by his loyal security police, the notorious *Securitate*. In common with dictators such as Saddam *Hussein, he elevated the members of his large family to high and strategic positions in state and society. Most famously, he made his wife, Elena, Deputy Prime Minister and Minister of Culture. He successfully played a double game of persuading the West that he was an independent agent at a distance from the USSR, while assuring *Brezhnev that his control over party and state was as great as ever. He thus became a favoured Communist leader for Western states, and even received a knighthood from the British government.

At home, however, the economic problems caused by the 1973 and 1979 *oil-price shocks, which turned Eastern Europe's command economies from bad to worse, were compounded by the megalomanic building and industrial projects he envisaged after the 1977 earthquake. His obsession with increasing the birth-rate imposed strict penalties on *abortions. Too many of those families who had fulfilled the target of bearing five children found that they did not have the physical or economic means to raise them, so that thousands of children were raised in underdeveloped orphanages. With the collapse of *Communism elsewhere in Eastern Europe, not even his *nationalism, which he had fostered to ridiculous proportions, saved his much-hated regime from collapse. With his wife, he fled the growing unrest, but was captured, and, after a brief trial, executed.

CENTO (Central Treaty Organization)

The successor to the *Baghdad Pact, which was reorganized to take account of the new anti-Western regime that had come to power in Iraq. It included the UK, Turkey, Iran, and Pakistan, and accorded the US observer status. Its primary function was to provide a link between the Asian *SEATO and the European *NATO military alliances in defence against Soviet expansionism in the context of the *Cold War. It was dissolved in 1979, following the Iranian Revolution.

Central African Federation

Founded in 1953, it united Northern Rhodesia (Zambia), Southern Rhodesia (Zimbabwe), and Nyasaland (Malawi) in order to create a counterweight to the regionally dominant South Africa. The hopes of its main proponent, *Welensky, to create a multiracial single entity, were not fulfilled as the federation remained dominated by the White minority of Southern Rhodesia. This fuelled the independence movements in Northern Rhodesia under *Kaunda, and in Nyasaland under *Banda. The federation fell apart when Northern Rhodesia and Nyasaland gained autonomy in 1963, and independence in 1964.

Central African Republic

In one of the world's poorest countries, economic recovery has been hampered by a poor infrastructure, drastic income inequality, and persistent economic crisis.

Early history (up to 1979) A landlocked colony of France since 1894, it became part of *French Equatorial Africa in 1910 as the territory of Ubangi Shari. It was an Overseas Territory of the *French Union in 1946, and became an autonomous member of the

*French Community in 1958 under the 'founder' of the nation, Barthélemy Boganda (b. 1910, d. 1959). Boganda was succeeded by David Dacko (b. 1930, d. 2003), who led the country into independence on 13 August 1960, but who remained heavily reliant on French support. On 1 January 1966, he was deposed in an army coup by Jean-Bédel *Bokassa.

Bokassa established a ruthless and authoritarian government, ruling the country as his private fiefdom to enrich himself. He proclaimed himself Emperor in 1976, and, in a farcical ceremony on 4 December 1977, crowned himself as Bokassa I, thus emulating his role model, Napoleon Bonaparte.

Even though his crowning ceremony was not attended by any Western leaders, Bokassa's rule was only made possible by tacit Western, and especially French, support. As the brutality of the regime and its links with Libya became an increasing embarrassment to the French under *Giscard d'Estaing, French troops intervened in 1979 and restored Dacko to power.

Contemporary history (since 1979) Dacko did not enjoy popular support, and was deposed in another military coup in 1981 under General André Kolingba (b. 1935). Kolingba was opposed by Ange-Félix Patassé, who from his exile in Togo founded the Mouvement pour la Libération du Peuple Centrafricain (Movement for the Liberation of the Central African People). As his country was as dependent as ever on French and other foreign aid, Kolingba was forced to give in to international demands for democratization. The 1993 elections were won by Patassé, who became the country's first freely elected President on 22 October. Despite the adoption of a new Constitution in 1995, Patassé was re-elected in 1999 amidst allegations of electoral fraud. The opposition's charges against the government were fuelled by the government's failure to pay its employees. This led to a widespread breakdown of public order in 2000, and the mutiny of sections of the army. Following an unsuccessful coup attempt in 2001, François Bozizé led a successful coup in 2003, and was confirmed as President in a relatively fair election in 2005. Bozizé's main challenge came from abroad, as three of the country's neighbours (Congo, Chad and Sudan) were engaged in violent civil wars, which destabilized the border regions through the presence of foreign rebels and refugees.

Central American Common Market (CACM)

An agreement from 1960 between Guatemala, Honduras, El Salvador, Nicaragua, and Costa Rica (which joined in 1962) to create a common market, promote industrialization, and establish a customs union. It resulted in a growth in trade among its members and a considerable increase in foreign capital investment during the first part of the 1960s. However, slower economic growth, increasing debts, and growing economic heterogeneity as a result of partial industrialization led to tensions culminating in the *Football War of 1969. Subsequent efforts at a reformulation of priorities towards economic development during the 1970s were hampered by domestic unrest in Nicaragua and El Salvador, whose civil wars in the 1980s brought the development of the CACM to a complete standstill. Only once these conflicts had been resolved, at the end of the 1980s, were efforts at closer economic and political integration resumed. This was spearheaded by an agreement between Guatemala, Honduras, and El Salvador to create a Free Trade Area from 1 January 1993. In 2004, its goals were superseded through the creation of the *Central American Free Trade Area (CAFTA).

Central American Free Trade Area (CAFTA)

The second largest free trade area on the American continent. Agreed in 2004, it included the United States, the Dominican Republic, Costa Rica, El Salvador, Honduras, Nicaragua, and Guatemala. It proved very controversial owing to the large wealth differential between the USA and the other participants, causing fears that the weaker economies would be swamped by US goods. Following his election victory in 2006, *Arias Sánchez announced that Costa Rica would ratify CAFTA. By contrast, another veteran re-elected to the presidency, *Ortega, announced that Nicaragua would reject CAFTA in favour of co-operation with Venezuela under the leadership of *Chávez.

Central Intelligence Agency, see CIA

Central Powers

The term used for the co-belligerents in World War I, Germany and *Austria-Hungary, as they were engulfed by their opponents, Russia to the east, and Britain, France, Belgium, and Luxemburg to the west. It is often extended to include their partners, the *Ottoman Empire and Bulgaria.

Centre Party (Zentrumspartei)

(Germany)

A party representing the interests of the Roman Catholic minority in Germany. It gradually emerged from the Revolutions of 1848/9, though it did not function as a national party until after German unification in 1871. From the 1880s onwards, and to a more limited extent after 1918, it could count on the electoral support of the majority of Catholics, which gave it a fundamental stability and thus a pivotal role in increasingly fragmented parliaments. As the failure of the *Bülow Bloc showed, it became virtually impossible to govern without the parliamentary support of the Centre in the long run.

Despite its commitment to the monarchy, after World War I the party quickly accepted the Weimar Republic and became its central pillar next to the *SPD. Towards the end of the Republic, under *Brüning's leadership, it hoped to overcome the problems of the parliamentary democracy through cooperation with conservative elites. Brüning's willingness to rule against the parliament signalled the end of parliamentary democracy. In 1933 most centre parliamentarians voted for the *Enabling Act after accepting *Hitler's guarantees for civil and religious liberties. The party was dissolved in 1933, and refounded in 1945, albeit with little electoral success since most of its former members joined the *CDU.

Centro Cristiano Democratico (Christian-Democratic Centre), see
CHRISTIAN DEMOCRATIC PARTY, ITALY

CGT (Confédération Générale du Travail). French trade union

Founded in 1895, the CGT adopted the *syndicalist Charter of Amiens in 1906, which rejected affiliation to the current left-wing parties in order to seek class warfare through direct action. Its leadership became increasingly reformist, so that the frequent strikes it organized were mostly to achieve more immediate aims such as better pay and working conditions. This trend was reinforced in September 1921, when its more radical members split to form the Confédération Générale du Travail Unitaire (CGTU), thus reflecting the division in the political labour movement between *Socialist Party and *Communist Party in December 1920. It reunited again on the eve of the *Popular Front government in 1936. The CGT emerged from World War II, during which many of its members were active in the *Résistance, under the control of the *Communist Party. It was unable to prevent the breakaway of the more moderate CGT-Force-Ouvrière in 1948. Even though the CGT has remained the biggest French trade union with about one third of all trade union membership, its membership began to decline sharply from the 1990s, from 1.8 million in 1992 to 700,000 in 2007.
TRADE UNIONS

Chaco War (1932–5)

A war between Bolivia and Paraguay about the disputed Gran Chaco territory, an extensive but infertile and inhospitable lowland plain at the foot of the Andes. In the mistaken belief that the area might be harbouring large oil reserves, Bolivia constructed a strategic fort in an area previously occupied by Paraguay. In response, Paraguayan forces reoccupied the site. Misled by the superiority of their armed forces in numbers and equipment, the Bolivians declared war, but this superiority counted for little in a terrain unsuitable for an all-out offensive war. In the eventual peace, Paraguay gained most of the disputed territory while Bolivia gained access to the River Paraguay and hence to the South Atlantic coast. The war cost the lives of 50,000 Bolivians and 35,000 Paraguayans and, coupled with the Great *Depression, inflicted irreparable economic damage.

Chad

A large, sparsely inhabited, landlocked country in central Africa, which has been racked by civil war since independence.

Colonial rule (until 1960) Under French influence since 1900, it became part of *French Equatorial Africa in 1910. The territory was largely neglected by the French colonial authorities, so that by 1933 there were still only eighteen qualified teachers in a country more than twice the size of France. The first secondary school was not established until after World War II.

The country suffered from tensions between its more populous and economically active south, inhabited largely by tribes following animistic religions, and the more sparsely populated north, whose inhabitants were mainly Muslims (predominantly of Arabian descent) living in hierarchical social structures dominated by tribal chiefs. The French administration had favoured the northern populations over the more anarchic southern population groups, which caused the latter's bitter resentment. During the 1950s the southern population became increasingly powerful. Chad became an autonomous territory within the *French Community in 1958, and achieved independence on 11 August 1960.

Independence (since 1960) Chad's first President, François Tombalbaye (b. 1918, d. 1975), came from the south. His attempt to infringe some of the traditional powers of the northern chiefs led to a series of local revolts, which culminated in a civil war (1966–8). The government collapsed, but was saved by French intervention in 1968. Tombalbaye had no intention of becoming more conciliatory, or less corrupt than he had been since taking office. His nationalist policies, which included the prosecution of Christian missionaries and the requirement to change all European names into African ones, failed to impress the population.

Tombalbaye was deposed in a military coup in 1976, which led to a power vacuum and the eruption of a civil war between various ethnic factions. One of the most powerful leaders from the north of the country, Goukouni Oueddai, called for the help of 10,000 Libyan troops in 1980. Despite this, his *CIA-backed rival, Hissène Habré (b. 1936), was able to assume power in 1982. Following the renewed advance of Libyan troops to help Goukouni, France sent its troops to assist Habré, so that the country was effectively divided between a Libyan-controlled northern half and a French-dominated southern half. A ceasefire was agreed in 1987, and civilian rule was gradually restored. Habré failed to attract significant popular support because of the brutality of his regime. A commission of enquiry set up after he was deposed in 1990 found that Habré was responsible for around 40,000 deaths, and 200,000 cases of torture.

Contemporary history (since 1991) Under Habré' successor, Idriss Déby (b. 1956), human rights violations continued, albeit on a smaller scale. In 1998, Youssouf Togoimi left the government to found the oppositional Mouvement pour la Démocratie et la Justice au Tchad (Movement for Democracy and Justice in Chad, MDJT). It organized a rebel movement which operated from the north against government forces. Déby was unable to contain the rebels, despite several attempts from 2001 at agreeing a cease-fire. In 2000, the *World Bank assisted in the construction of a pipeline into neighbouring Cameroon, allowing Chad to export its oil from the Doba region. Contrary to World Bank stipulations, however, the revenues from the sale of oil were not used to combat the poverty in one of the world's poorest countries. Instead, Déby increased military spending, as a new front opened up in the civil war in 2005, with the formation of the Front Uni pour le Changement Démocratique (United Front for Democratic Change, FUCD), which controlled large parts of eastern Chad.

Chadli, Benjadid (b. 14 Apr. 1929).
President of Algeria 1979–92

Born into a peasant family in Bouteldja,
he joined the movement for Algerian
independence in 1955. As a protégé of
*Boumédienne, he quickly advanced within
the ranks of the *Front de Libération
Nationale to succeed his mentor as its general
secretary in 1979, when he also became
President and Defence Secretary. He had to
cope with an overexpanded socialist state
sector, which could no longer be financed
with declining oil revenues following the
collapse of the world oil price from 1981. In
response, he introduced market forces into
the economy, though his attempts to reduce
state expenditure were met with increasing
popular hostility. This was fuelled by the rise
of *Islamic fundamentalism, which became
particularly dangerous when he allowed its
articulation in a political party, the Islamic
Salvation Front (Front Islamique du Salut, FIS).
Following the victory of the FIS in the first
round of multi-party elections in December
1991, the military forced him to resign, on 14
January 1992, suspending the second round
and declaring a state of emergency.

Chamberlain, (Arthur) Neville (b. 18
Mar. 1869, d. 9 Nov. 1940). British Prime
Minister 1937–40

Early career Born in Birmingham, the son of
Joseph *Chamberlain and half-brother of
Austen *Chamberlain. From 1890, he spent
seven years unsuccessfully running his
father's sisal plantation in the Bahamas. He
returned to Birmingham, and was involved in
business, before becoming Lord Mayor of the
city in 1915. Lloyd George asked him to
become Director-General of National Service
in 1916, but he resigned a year later after
disagreements with Lloyd George. He was
elected as Conservative MP for Birmingham
Ladywood in 1918 (moving to Edgbaston in
1929), became Paymaster-General under
Bonar *Law in 1922, and served briefly as
Chancellor of the Exchequer in 1923.

A successful and efficient Minister of Health
(1924–9), he reformed the Poor Law,
promoted council-house building, and
developed local government. Despite these
reforms, his openly dismissive attitude
towards the *Labour Party meant that he
gained few friends on the opposition benches
of the House of Commons. In 1931 he was a
key figure in the negotiations resulting in the
formation of the *National Government, and
then, as Chancellor of the Exchequer (1931–
7), he steered the British economy back
towards prosperity, and finally introduced

measures of protection unsuccessfully
championed by his father for so long.

Prime Minister In May 1937 Chamberlain
succeeded *Baldwin as Prime Minister. His
hope for a large programme of social reform
was ended, however, by the prominence of
international affairs and the necessity for
rearmament, which had already begun. His
policy of 'appeasement', which was popular at
the time, was to accommodate the European
dictators in order to avoid war, which he
regarded as potentially disastrous for all,
especially the *British Empire. At three
meetings with Hitler, at Berchtesgaden, at
Godesberg, and at *Munich, he conceded
Czechoslovak territory to Germany. In spite of
this he did not save *Czechoslovakia from
German invasion in March 1939. Like many of
his colleagues, he was reluctant to negotiate
seriously with the Soviet Union, but did
pledge military support to Poland in March
1939. When Germany invaded Poland later in
the year, Chamberlain had little choice but to
declare war. In May 1940, following a disaster
for British forces in Norway, his own party
rebelled against him and he was forced to
resign in favour of Winston *Churchill,
whom he wholeheartedly supported until his
death later in the year.

For many years, Chamberlain was vilified as
being responsible for many of the policies
which facilitated World War II. More recently,
some historians have explained his policy as an
understandable reaction to Britain's weakness,
and to a realistic appreciation of the cost
involved in another world war. Even so, it is
clear that right up to August 1939 he hoped
and believed in the possibility of coming to a
peaceful arrangement with Hitler, at a time
when the aggressive nature of Germany had
been evident at least since the *Anschluss.

Chamberlain, Joseph (b. 8 July 1836, d. 2
July 1914). British politician

Born in London, he left school at the age of 16,
and went to work in Birmingham in 1854. He
quickly established a considerable income
through manufacturing screws, and this
enabled him to become active in politics.
He achieved national prominence as an
outspoken critic of the 1870 Education Act,
though his reputation as a radical *Liberal
derived from his time as Mayor of Birmingham
(1873–6), when his innovative application of
the 'municipal gospel' led to the
municipalization of water and gas, as well as
the destruction of slums through large-scale
street clearances. His success in Birmingham
was also based on the development of an
effective political organization, which he

sought to translate to the national level through the establishment of the National Liberal Association in 1877.

Despite his lack of experience, Chamberlain became President of the Board of Trade (1880–5), and of the Local Government Board (1885–6). He left the *Liberal Party in opposition to Home Rule for Ireland and co-founded the Liberal Unionists, who subsequently worked with the *Conservative Party. In coalition with the latter, he was Colonial Secretary (1895–1903). He resigned, however, in order to campaign openly for the abandonment of free trade through *tariff reform. Free trade was so deeply entrenched in the English system of government that the main effect of his campaign (and his main impact on the twentieth century) was to split the Conservatives and Liberal Unionists and render them incapable of government for two decades, just as he had done with the Liberals in 1886.

PROTECTIONISM

Chamberlain, Sir (Joseph) Austen
(b. 16 Oct. 1863, d. 16 Mar. 1937). British Foreign Secretary 1924–9

Early career Born in Birmingham, he was the half-brother of Neville *Chamberlain, and the son of Joseph *Chamberlain, who groomed him for a political career. He was educated at Rugby and studied at Cambridge before entering parliament in 1892 as Liberal Unionist (later *Conservative) MP for East Worcestershire. As a loyal mouthpiece of his father, he was made Chancellor of the Exchequer (1903–5) to represent Joseph's views in government, from which Joseph had resigned in order to pursue his *tariff-reform campaign. Austen's identification with this deeply divisive issue, however, precluded him from the leadership in 1911, as he was seen by some as an unconventional upstart in the mould of his father. He served as Secretary of State for India (1915–17), but resigned over alleged blunders in the *Mesopotamia campaign, for which he accepted ministerial responsibility. A minister without portfolio from 1918, he again became Chancellor of the Exchequer in 1919 and leader of the Conservative Party in 1921, but loyalty to *Lloyd George led to his refusal to replace him as Prime Minister. When the *Conservative Party opposed the continuing of its coalition with Lloyd George in 1922, Chamberlain resigned as leader, thus becoming only one of three Conservative leaders in the twentieth century never to be Prime Minister.

Foreign Secretary Chamberlain made peace with the party during 1923, for which

*Baldwin made him Foreign Secretary in 1924. His main aim was to encourage France to adopt a more conciliatory stance towards Germany, in order to assist *Stresemann in his aim to revise by peaceful means the Treaty of *Versailles. Together with *Dawes, Chamberlain succeeded in rescheduling Germany's *repatriation payments, for which he received the *Nobel Peace Prize. He also had an important role in securing the *Locarno Treaties of 1925, which secured Germany's entry into the League of Nations and achieved some geopolitical stability in western Europe. Like his father, his political career was hampered by his adherence to fair trade and his mercantile Birmingham roots. Attempts to shake off these deficiencies also hindered him, leading him to an exaggerated sense of honour and loyalty.

Chamorro, Violeta Barrios de (b. 18 Oct. 1929). President of Nicaragua 1990–7
Daughter of a wealthy landowner, she married the editor of the liberal daily newspaper *La Prensa*. After the assassination of her husband (presumably on the orders of Anastasio *Somoza Dabayle), she took over the editorship and became a leading opponent of the dictatorship. After Somoza's fall she joined the Sandinista junta, but left in April 1980 to become the leading critic of the Sandinistas through her newspaper, which provided some freedom of opinion during the Sandinista government. Heading a diffuse coalition of fourteen parties, she was the surprise winner of the 1990 elections against President *Ortega. She managed to maintain a careful balance between appeasing both the Contra rebels and Ortega's Sandinista movement which still controlled the bureaucracy and the army. From 1993 she was forced to govern with a Sandinista parliamentary majority, and in 1995 she eventually agreed to a constitutional reform as demanded by parliament.

Chanak Crisis (Sept.–Oct. 1922)
The Treaty of *Sèvres in 1920 had allocated European Turkey, as well as the city of Smyrna (Izmir), to Greece. Constantinople and the *Dardanelles Straits continued to be neutral and occupied by British and Allied troops. Unhappy with the treaty, *Kemal defeated the Greeks and occupied Smyrna, and threatened to advance to Constantinople. To prevent this, British troops at Chanak on the Dardanelles were reinforced. After a tense military confrontation Kemal accepted a compromise, to be negotiated at the Treaty of *Lausanne in 1923. As a result of this, Turkey gained full control over eastern Thrace and

Constantinople (later Istanbul). Meanwhile, the incident served as a pretext for *Conservatives in Britain to topple *Lloyd George as Prime Minister, alleging that he had been irresponsible in bringing Britain to the verge of war.

Chang Hsüeh-liang (b. 4 July 1901, d. 14 Oct. 2001). Chinese warlord

Born in Taishan County (Liaoning), son of the *warlord Chang Tso-lin, he graduated from the Military Institute and soon distinguished himself in his father's army. In 1926, he reluctantly fought *Chiang Kai-shek's *National Revolutionary Army during its *Northern Expedition. Known as the 'Young Marshal', he inherited control of Manchuria in 1928 when his father was murdered by officers of the Japanese *Guandong Army. Fully appreciating the danger from Japan's expansionism in the region, he sought to develop his territory economically (e.g. through the building of railways), educationally (through the foundation of the Northeastern University), and through a military build-up. At the same time, he accepted the authority of the *Guomindang government in Nanjing (Nanking). With many of his troops dispatched at Chiang Kai-shek's demand, he was powerless to prevent the Japanese invasion into Manchuria in 1931 (*Manchukuo). He remained an important ally to Chiang, and successfully urged him to form an anti-Japanese alliance with the Communists, mainly by placing him under house arrest until he agreed. Chiang never forgave him for this, and had him arrested soon afterwards. He was taken to Taiwan in 1949, and lived under house arrest until Chiang's death. Released in 1990, he moved to Hawaii in 1995, where he died.

Chappaquidick, see KENNEDY, EDWARD MOORE

Charles, Prince of Wales (Charles Philip Arthur George) (b. 14 Nov. 1948)

The eldest son of *Elizabeth II, he was educated at Gordonstoun and Cambridge. Since 1968, when Queen *Elizabeth decided to modernize the image of the royal family, Charles has been a prominent public figure. He was invested as Prince of Wales on 1 July 1969, in a televised ceremony at Caernarfon Castle, and in 1970 became the first heir to the throne to receive a university degree. From 1971 to 1976, he served in the Royal Navy and the RAF. Various roles were discussed for him, the most important perhaps being that of Governor-General of Australia, a country of which he has always been very fond. These

schemes came to naught, and instead he sought to create a progressive and useful public role for himself, becoming an outspoken promoter of social, ecological, cultural, and architectural concerns. He launched the Prince's Trust in 1976 to provide young people with grants for individual projects, and since then has inaugurated, promoted, or led a host of other initiatives to help poor individuals, new small businesses, and disadvantaged communities. His work in this and other areas was often overshadowed by his unhappy marriage to Lady Diana Spencer—their wedding took place on 29 July 1981. Especially after their formal separation in December 1992, the two engaged in a public battle to discredit each other. They were divorced on 28 August 1996. In 2005, Charles married his long-time love, Camilla Parker Bowles, who became the Duchess of Cornwall.

(((⊕))) SEE WEB LINKS

• The official website of Prince Charles.

Charlottetown Accord, see CLARK, CHARLES JOSEPH

Charter '77

A document signed by 243 people, most of whom were intellectuals. Addressed to the Czechoslovak government, it protested against the violations by the state against the basic *human rights guaranteed by the *UN and the *Helsinki Conference, to both of which Czechoslovakia had subscribed. The group of signatories was led by Professor Jan Patocka, *Havel, and Jiry Hajek, a former Communist minister. It was delivered to the government in 1977, and had attracted 2,500 signatures within ten years, despite the prosecution and discrimination which public support for the document attracted. The impact of the Charter '77 movement remained in some ways limited, owing to its restricted social base. On the other hand, the articulate oppositional movement became well-known inside and outside the country, so that many of its leaders were at the forefront of the political discussions surrounding the collapse of the Communist regime in 1989.

Chavez, César Estrada (b. 31 Mar. 1927, d. 23 Apr. 1993). US labour union organizer

Born on a farm near Yuma, Arizona, of Mexican emigrant parents, he spent his childhood living and working in *Chicano migrant labour camps in Arizona and California. After serving in the US navy he returned to California and began to organize migrant farm labor. In 1962 he created the National Farm Workers' Association (NFWA), which in 1971 became the United Farm Workers of America (UFW). From 1965 he led a five-year grape-pickers' strike in California, which won much public support. During the early 1970s the UFW was competing with the *Teamsters for members, but in 1977 it won an agreement to have the sole right to organize field labour. During the 1980s Chavez somewhat compromised his reputation by his preoccupation with faith healing and holistic religion. An abundance of labour also reduced the UFW's bargaining power, and its membership declined dramatically. Chavez is remembered as one of the most prominent Chicanos in US history, who did much to boost the position and self-esteem of American Chicanos.

Chávez Frías, Hugo (b. 28 July 1954). Venezuelan dictator 1998–

Early career Born in Sabaneta, he studied history and politics, and became an officer in the Venezuelan army. As a major of a parachuting regiment, he led an unsuccessful coup against the President in 1992. After two years in prison, Chávez was released under an amnesty. He became active in politics as a populist, spending much time in the slums of Caracas to appeal to the mass of Venezuela's poor.

In power In 1998 he was elected President, and after taking office he proceeded to establish dictatorial powers. He instituted the creation of a constitutional assembly, whose Constitution was accepted in 1999 and greatly increased his position. To strengthen his position against an obstinate parliament which he was trying to abolish, he had himself confirmed in a further election in 2000. In April 2002, a coup attempt led by some army generals and conservative elites ousted Chávez briefly. He regained control over the army, and used the disunity among his opponents to re-establish political control.

Chávez promoted an active foreign policy in opposition to US influence in Latin America. Helped by the country's vast oil and gas reserves, which he sold on to allies at preferential rates, and claiming his position as ideological heir to Fidel *Castro, Chávez sought to make Venezuela the predominant regional power. He supported and created an alliance with other left-wing populist movements, notably in Nicaragua (*Ortega), Brazil (*Lula) and Bolivia under Evo Morales.

Chechnya

Early history (up to 1991) A Caucasian territory whose inhabitants have resisted Russian rule almost since its beginnings in the late eighteenth century. It was eventually pacified by the Russians only in 1859, though sporadic uprisings continued until the collapse of Tsarist Russia in 1917. Together with Ingushnya, it formed part of the Soviet Union as an Autonomous Soviet Republic within Russia from 1936. Continuing uprisings against Russian/Soviet rule, notably that of 1934, caused the anger of *Stalin. In retaliation, he dissolved Chechnyan autonomy in 1944, and ordered the deportation of the ethnic Chechnyan population to central Asia, in which half of the population died. They were not allowed to return to their homeland until 1957, when *Khrushchev restored an autonomous status for Chechnya. Thereafter, the striving for independence among the devout Muslim population, nurtured by the collective memory of repression, continued.

Civil war (1991–7) After the *August *coup* of 1991, which the Chechnyan leadership failed to condemn, popular support swung behind Mussayev Dudayev (b. 1944, d. 1996), a Soviet air force commander turned national activist. Elected President in October 1991, he declared independence from the Soviet Union as well as Russia on 1 November 1991. Thereafter, the Russian government attempted to influence events in Chechnya indirectly, through the military and financial assistance of groups opposed to the Chechnyan government. A civil war between supporters and opponents of Dudayev developed, until the Russian President *Yeltsin ordered his troops to invade the territory on 11 December 1994. Despite the much better equipment of the Russian troops, the ensuing war turned into a military disaster, whereby Russian elite troops failed to gain complete control over a country the size of Connecticut. In 1996, the Russian government agreed a peace deal which gave the Chechens almost complete autonomy. The twenty-month-long civil war cost the lives of 80,000 people, with 240,000 injured.

Contemporary politics (since 1997) In 1997, Alan Mashadov was elected President, and in that year Islam was declared the state religion. With Russian forces having completely withdrawn, crime was rampant, and officials from Russia and other parts of the world were increasingly in danger of abduction or murder. Mashadov introduced Islamic Law in early 1999, while at the same time losing control over Chechen bandits who started to attack Russian targets outside Chechnya. On 30 Sept 1999, Russian forces began a merciless war against Chechnya to reassert Russian authority. Over a five-month long campaign, Chechnya was brought under Russian control, at the cost of tens of thousands of lives, the displacement of over 200,000 Chechnyan refugees, and numerous *human rights violations committed by both parties. Thereafter, the territory was governed by a Russian administration, which was supported by a heavy military presence. The army continued to be subject to persistent attacks committed by Chechen guerrilla fighters. In turn, the Chechen population was subject to Russian raids for evidence of rebel activity. Both sides continued to operate through methods of torture and other human rights abuses, with Mashadov, who had continued to lead Chechen resistance, killed in 2005.

Cheka

An abbreviation for Chrezvychaynaya Komissiya (All-Russian Extraordinary Commission for the Suppression of Counter-Revolution and Sabotage). This secret police force was instituted without official status by *Lenin in December 1917 and run by *Dzerzhinsky, a Pole. Its purpose was to protect and establish the Communist Revolution (*Russian Revolutions, 1917) through terror. Its headquarters, the Lubyanka prison in Moscow, contained offices and places for interrogation under torture and for execution. In 1922 Cheka became GPU and later OGPU (United State Political Administration), under the supervision of the Ministry of the Interior. Its successor was the *NKVD.

Chen Duxiu (Chen Tu-hsiu) (b. 8 Oct. 1879, d. 27 May 1942). Chinese Communist leader

Born at An-ch'ing (Anhwei Province) of wealthy parents, he sat the civil service (chü-jen) examination before going to Japan to further his studies. Following the 1911 Revolution Chen founded the New Culture Movement, which he promoted with the nationwide magazine, *The New Youth*. This offered a platform for a large number of intellectuals and thinkers urging enlightened progress. In 1917, he was appointed dean of the college of letters at Beijing University. He became increasingly critical of republican institutions, which were riven with factionalism and corruption. He turned towards *Marxism-Leninism, and became a co-founder of the Chinese *Communist Party in 1921. He built up an independent and effective organization and provided widely accepted autocratic but moderate leadership, until the withdrawal of *Stalin's support. Chen was dismissed in 1927, and expelled from the party in 1929. He became a *Trotskyist, but was imprisoned 1932–7, after which he retired.

Chen Yi (Ch'en I) (b. 1901, d. 6 Jan. 1972). Chinese general

Born at Loshan (Sichuan province), he studied in St Germain and Grenoble (France) 1919–21, where he met *Zhou Enlai. On his return he joined the newly formed Chinese *Communist Party (CCP) as well as the *Guomindang. At Zhou Enlai's invitation he went to the Whampoa Military Academy in 1926. When the coalition between the Guomindang and the CCP ended in 1927, he escaped to join *Mao Zedong and *Zhu De in *Jianxi. Chen soon became a leading figure in the Communist army. He did not take part in the *Long March, but organized instead the 22nd Red Army to pursue guerrilla warfare in central and southern China. In the *Sino-Japanese War he became commander of the New 4th Army, which by 1947 comprised over 200,000 men. He thus played a central role in the Communist victory in the *Chinese Civil War. On the establishment of the People's Republic he became Mayor of reoccupied Shanghai and was then chosen by his old friend, Zhou Enlai, to become Foreign Minister (1958–66). He was deposed in the *Cultural Revolution and stripped of all his offices.

Cheney, Richard ('Dick') B. (b. 30 Jan. 1941), US Vice-President, 2001–

Born in Lincoln, Nebraska, he was raised in Wyoming and graduated from the University of Wyoming. He joined the *Nixon administration in 1969, but he first made his name when he succeeded Donald *Rumsfeld as Gerald *Ford's able Chief of Staff (1975–6). From 1977–89, he was Representative for Wyoming in *Congress, and from 1989 to 1993 he served under George *Bush as Secretary of Defense. In 2000, he was asked by George W. *Bush to direct the search for a running mate, and on the strong recommendation of George Bush Sr. he ended up with the job himself. Cheney became by far the most active and influential Vice-President in US history, overseeing day-to-day policy as well as the administration's political appointments. Cheney had made a fortune from the oil business and continued to enjoy strong links with business. This came to haunt him after the collapse of *Enron, a giant energy supplier, which raised suspicions that he had framed the administration's energy policy under undue influence from affected companies. Cheney and his staff also became subject to investigations during 2005–7 for allegedly passing on to the newspapers the name of a CIA agent whose husband had been a prominent critic of the administration over the *Iraq War. A formidable intellect, Cheney was popular with conservatives, but his abrasive, dismissive manner never endeared him to the wider public.

Chernenko, Konstantin Ustinovich
(b. 14 Sept. 1911, d. 10 Mar. 1985). General Secretary of the Communist Party of the Soviet Union 1984–5

Born in Novoselovo, he joined the *Communist Party in 1930 and, after serving in the *Cheka border guards (1930–3) became a party official working on organization and *propaganda. After activity in his native Krasnoyarsk area, he became head of the propaganda department of the Moldovan Communist Party Central Committee in 1958, where he met the local party leader, *Brezhnev, with whom he established an excellent relationship. Despite his mediocrity, his subsequent rapid rise was commensurate with that of Brezhnev, until he himself joined the party's Central Committee (1971) and the *Politburo (1978). Brezhnev clearly groomed his trusted lieutenant to succeed him, though in 1982 the party leadership went to the much more gifted *Andropov instead. When Andropov died, Chernenko was chosen mainly in order to stall the inevitable rise of *Gorbachev. His death marked the final end of the Brezhnev era, and removed all obstacles to Gorbachev's final rise to power.

Chernobyl
A Ukrainian town near Kiev, which was the site of the world's worst peacetime nuclear disaster. On 26 April 1986, inadequately prepared tests in block 4 of the graphite-moderated nuclear power station led to the outbreak of fire in the reactor. The fire was not completely put out for weeks. The rogue generator itself was buried in concrete, while other parts of the nuclear power station continued to function. The catastrophe resulted in 31 immediate deaths. One year into *Gorbachev's leadership, the disaster was dealt with in the usual Soviet manner, and thus epitomized how entrenched old traditions were, and just how far reform would have to go to effect real change. The catastrophe was long denied, with traditional May Day parades in Kiev and elsewhere suggesting business as usual. The accident itself was met with typical bureaucratic incompetence, whilst provisions to prevent contamination were virtually non-existent. Once Western scientists had produced undeniable evidence of the disaster, it was admitted. An evacuation of around 135,000 people living in a radius of 30 km took place. Altogether an estimated 600,000 people have suffered from the effects of the radiation,

while agricultural produce in large parts of Finland, Scandinavia, Poland, and Romania, and to a lesser extent Germany and Britain, was also contaminated.

Chervenkov, Vulko
(b. 6 Sept. 1900, d. 21 Oct. 1980). Secretary-General of the Bulgarian Communist Party 1949–54

Born at Slatiza (near Sofia), he joined the Communist Party in 1919. He went to the Marx-Engels Institute in Moscow, where he became an instructor, and an agent for *Comintern. During World War II, he worked for the Bulgarian section of the Soviet broadcasting service. He returned to Bulgaria in 1946, and in 1949 his good connections inside (he was *Dimitrov's brother-in-law) and outside (notably *Stalin) ensured his rise to the head of the party and the state. Known as 'little Stalin' for his adoration of the Soviet dictator, he set about purging the party of moderate elements, expelling almost 100,000 people. He nationalized industries and agriculture, and expelled around 150,000 ethnic Turks, ostensibly for their resistance to his policies. His overwhelming domination in state and party came under fire after the death of Stalin in 1953. In 1954, *Zhivkov replaced him as general secretary of the party, and in 1956 dismissed him from the office of Prime Minister. He was relieved of all offices in 1961, and expelled from the party in 1962.

Chetniks
Serbian nationalist guerrillas who fought to protect the Serbian minorities in *Macedonia in the late nineteenth century. The name was then adopted by nationalist guerrillas fighting initially with British support during *World War II against the German and Italian occupying forces. Their operations were concentrated in *Bosnia and the Serb-inhabited areas of *Croatia. However, they became embroiled in a bitter struggle with *Tito's Communist *partisans, in which they were overcome towards the end of 1944. Once Croatia moved towards independence from around 1990, new Serbian guerrilla units formed under the name, fighting against Croatian control of areas with a substantial Serb population.

Chiang Ch'ing, see JIANG QING

Chiang Ching-kuo
(b. 18 Mar. 1910, d. 13 Jan. 1988). President of the Republic of China (Taiwan) 1978–88

Born in Fengwah, he studied at the University of Shanghai, and was then sent by his father, *Chiang Kai-shek, to study at the *Sun Yat-sen University in Moscow. Following a decline in relations between his father and

*Stalin, he was only allowed to leave the country with his Russian wife in 1937. Thereafter, he was groomed by his father to succeed him. He followed his father to Taiwan, and held a number of increasingly important posts within the government and the National Party, including Minister of Defence (1965–9) and Deputy Prime Minister (1969–72). He became Prime Minister in 1972, and immediately embarked upon a programme of political reform. He instigated an anti-corruption drive, introduced a (gradual) political opening, and supported the appointment of more Taiwanese to positions of importance in government and the National Party, making *Lee Teng-hui his deputy. As President, he continued promoting economic *liberalism, investment, and education which became the basis of the country's spectacular economic growth. He was a popular leader, not just for his policies, but also for his approachable and low-key manner.

Chiang Kai-shek (b. 31 Oct. 1887, d. 5 Apr. 1975). President of the Republic of China (Taiwan since 1949) 1928–49, 1950–75

Born at Feng Hwa (Chekiang) as the son of a poor salt merchant, he attended the Chinese Imperial Military Academy and later lived in Japan, where he received military training. He returned to China in 1911 as a supporter of *Sun Yat-sen. He became Sun's loyal lieutenant, and was entrusted with running the Military Academy at Whampoa on 3 May 1924. The academy was to play a vital role for the *Guomindang and the *National Revolutionary Army, and Chiang recruited from it his favoured officers. In 1926 he succeeded Sun Yat-sen as Commander-in-Chief of the National Revolutionary Army, and launched the successful *Northern Expedition (1926–8) to unify the country.

Chiang's *National Government, established in Nanjing (Nanking) in 1928, lasted until 1937 and succeeded in unifying much of China. Financial reforms were carried out, and communications and education improved. A New Life Movement tried to reassert traditional Confucian values to combat Communist ideas. At the same time, he was forced to accept the loss of Manchuria to the Japanese (*Manchukuo), and he failed to come to a lasting arrangement with the *Communist movement, despite his attempts at ruthless suppression. His government was constantly at war with provincial *warlords, with the Japanese, and with the Communists in their rural bases. Kidnapped at *Xi'an by *Chang Hsüeh-liang in 1936, he agreed to co-operate with the Communists against the Japanese in the *United Front.

In the ensuing *Sino-Japanese War, *Nanjing was lost in 1937, and Chiang lost control of the coastal regions and most of the major cities, retiring from Nanjing to Chongqing (Chungking). None the less, his prestige was at its peak towards the end of the war in 1945. He attended the *Cairo Conference, and achieved a place for the Republic of China as a permanent member of the *UN Security Council in 1945. This explains his refusal to come to an agreement with *Mao Zedong, and resume his old fight against the Communists. Despite generous US aid he lost the *Chinese Civil War, largely because of his strategic cautiousness, and his inability to contain indiscipline and corruption within his own army.

In 1949, he retreated to Taiwan, where he ruled as the head of the Republic of China until his death. He remained in firm control of the party, which he frequently purged, and continued his habit of appointing those who were politically trustworthy over those with outstanding ability. By the late 1950s, he probably gave up his hope of reconquering mainland China, hoping to defeat it ideologically instead, through the introduction of *capitalism. He left behind an economically advanced and dynamic society, though it remained for his successor and son, *Chiang Ching-kuo, to establish social and political consensus.

SONG QINGLING

Chiapas Rebellion (Mexico)

An armed uprising of Mayan Indians in the Mexican state of Chiapas which erupted on 1 January 1994. They demanded greater autonomy from the federal government, the preservation of their own distinctive culture, and the introduction of social reforms. Exploiting the myth of *Zapata, they were organized in the Zapatista National Liberation Army (Ejército Zapatista de Liberación Nacional, EZLN). The rebellion was brought under control by the superior government forces in January 1994, albeit with serious *human rights violations. In March, the government agreed with EZLN representatives on a series of reforms. However, on 12 June 1994 a peace agreement between the EZLN and the government was rejected by a majority of the Mayan Indian population. The truce was broken following the installation of the state Governor, a member of the nationally dominant Institutional Revolutionary Party (*PRI). On 19 December 1994, EZLN forces occupied 38 villages, and tensions were only reduced with the Governor's resignation. Subsequent peace talks were slow to progress, however, with the EZLN insisting on nationwide reforms, against government offers of regional reform. In February 1996, the state agreed to grant limited autonomy to the indigenous Mexicans, guaranteeing bilingual education and the preservation of indigenous culture. The agreement was not passed into law. The new President, *Fox, finally realized greater cultural autonomy for the indigenous population of Chiapas. The new laws, which necessitated a change in the constitution, were passed in 2001. Although these fell short of the EZLN's demands, the organization's leaders began to operate within the political system, and constructed a political movement from 2006.

Chicanos (USA)

Originally the descendants of Mexicans living in the area of the USA occupied in the Mexican–American War of 1846-8. In the 1950s the name was gradually adopted by Mexican Americans, who as the country's second largest minority group began to develop a distinctive consciousness. Chicano cultural organizations were formed, while successful trade union activity under *Chavez led to some improvements in pay and working conditions in the 1960s and 1970s. Meanwhile, the 1970s brought some educational advances with the establishment of bilingual and bicultural courses. Despite this, their group identity remained brittle, as many considered themselves merely as sojourners, there to make money to take home to Mexico. In 2000, 21.5 million Chicanos were recorded as living in the US, though this census figure revealed little about their self-identification as Mexican Americans apart from other Hispanic American groups.

Chichester-Clark, James Dawson, Lord Moyola (b. 12 Feb. 1923, d. 17 May 2002). Prime Minister of Northern Ireland 1969-71

Educated at Eton, he entered the Irish Guards in 1942, and served as aide-de-camp (1947-9) to the Governor-General of Canada, Earl Alexander. He left the army in 1960 as a major, and was elected an *Ulster Unionist MP in the *Stormont that year. He served as Minister of Agriculture under *O'Neill from 1967, and succeeded him as Prime Minister in May 1969. He immediately issued an amnesty for those convicted of, or charged with, political offences since October 1968. During his premiership, far-reaching policies included reform of the police and the creation of an ombudsman to investigate allegations of discrimination against Catholics. However, serious rioting continued in Londonderry and Belfast. In the end, he was forced to ask for British troops to help maintain order. The period was marked by the emergence of the *IRA as a threat to order, while Chichester-Clark urged the British government to increase the numbers of troops in Northern Ireland, and to saturate areas dominated by the IRA with security forces.

Chifley, Joseph Benedict ('Ben') (b. 22 Sept. 1885, d. 13 June 1951). Prime Minister of Australia 1945-9

Born in Bathurst (New South Wales), he became a railway engine driver and in 1920 joined the state general committee of the Australian Federated Union of Locomotive Enginemen. After three unsuccessful attempts he was finally elected to the House of Representatives in 1928. He briefly became Minister for Defence in 1931 until he lost his seat that year, returning to Bathurst local politics. In 1935, *Casey's advocacy ensured Chifley's appointment to the Royal Commission on Monetary and Banking Systems. This made him familiar with the intricate system of government finance, and convinced him of the need to nationalize all banking, which he advocated in a minority report. Chifley also used his time outside parliament to rebuild Labor support at the grass roots in New South Wales. His efforts were rewarded by Labor's landslide victory there in 1941, when he returned to parliament. Despite the high cost of World War II, as Secretary to the Treasury (1941-9) he actually managed to reduce Australia's foreign debt significantly. He also became Minister for Postwar Reconstruction in 1942, when he devised many social policies that became law in the postwar period.

Succeeding his friend *Curtin as Prime Minister in 1945, Chifley supported *Calwell's immigration policies, and introduced the Conciliation and Arbitration Act of 1947 to regulate industrial arbitration. Although he encouraged, for example, the building of public housing, his social policies were relatively careful. Having been deeply influenced by the Great *Depression, to him the stability of the economy was paramount over social welfare schemes. The latter became particularly difficult to introduce, as buoyant domestic demand and high wage claims were already fuelling inflationary pressures. He tried to establish control over the Australian financial system, principally through the establishment of a central bank. When aspects of this measure were successfully challenged in the High Court, he responded by introducing legislation to nationalize all banks. In a two-year battle, this was also rejected by Australian and London High Courts. Unsuccessful in the introduction of a national health service in the face of doctors' resistance, and unpopular through his stern economic policies (such as the maintenance of petrol rationing), he lost the 1949 elections to *Menzies.

Chile

A Latin American country rich in mineral resources, which has been characterized by relative economic prosperity and institutional stability.

Democratization (1880s–1930s) In the War of the Pacific (1879–83), Chile acquired its northern territories rich with nitrates and copper, whose exports became the basis of almost half a century of economic expansion. While many mines were owned by British (nitrates) and US capital (copper), a substantial amount of the profits accrued to Chilean owners. In Chile, in marked contrast to Brazil, the commercial and industrial elite was closely related to the traditional elites of the large landowning estates (haciendas). Attracted by booming industry, an increasing number of people left the countryside to seek jobs in the cities, forming a substantial urban proletariat. In the absence of legal, political, or economic workers' representation, this proletariat provided support for *anarchist and *syndicalist movements. The establishment reacted with the introduction of preventive welfare reforms, Arturo *Alessandri realized the political potential of actually integrating these groups into the political establishment. He appealed specifically to the urban middle and working classes with a programme of legalizing *trade unions, which could then be controlled by the government. Alessandri was elected President in 1920 and soon introduced a labour code and a social welfare programme. However, these were blocked by a Senate representing the conservative establishment.

The impasse was resolved in 1924 through military intervention which deposed Alessandri. Ultimately, the leading figure to emerge from this crisis was General *Ibáñez, who in 1927 broke with the Chilean democratic tradition by establishing a dictatorship. Civil liberties were suspended and labour leaders imprisoned. His regime did not survive the Great *Depression and its catastrophic effects on Chile. After an

interlude in which the country found itself close to anarchy, from 1932 Alessandri restored stability and democracy. His tough economic policies coupled with increased world demand for Chilean exports led to a period of recovery. None the less, the 1939 elections brought victory to the Radical Pedro Aguirre Cerda, at the head of the only *Popular Front government outside Europe. His successor, the Radical Juan Antonio Ríos (1942–6), tried to keep Chile neutral during World War II because of fear of Japanese invasion of its long, exposed coastline. Despite protests from the country's large community of German origin, Ríos finally bowed to US pressure and joined the opposition to the *Axis Powers in 1943.

Political polarization (1940s–1973) The government of the Radical President *González Videla contained three Communists initially, but he soon broke with them and outlawed the increasingly popular Communist Party in 1948. Videla was succeeded by General Ibáñez, who nurtured an image of being 'above' politics, even if in reality he was backed by the centre-right. In a desperate effort to overcome the country's lack of foreign currency and runaway inflation, he accepted the help of the *IMF in return for drastic economic austerity measures. His unpopularity became such that he did not stand for re-election, and in 1958 Jorge *Alessandri was elected President. He, too, pursued an orthodox economic policy, but there was little progress in solving the country's growing social problems—rural poverty and exodus, bad housing, ill-nourishment, and lack of education. In 1964, the conservatives successfully supported the Christian Democrat leader Eduardo *Frei, in order to avert the real danger of a Communist victory at the polls. Frei's ensuing reforms, such as the partial nationalization of the copper mines and land reform in favour of *cooperatives, turned out to be ineffective.

As a result, 1970 finally saw the free election of the world's first *Marxist President, *Allende. He immediately nationalized copper mines and other foreign-owned industries, introduced wage rises and price freezes, and expropriated the haciendas. By 1973 this had caused serious economic dislocation, while public order became increasingly difficult to maintain. In addition, he encountered fierce opposition from the USA, whose *CIA had long been an important supporting agency for the right wing.

The Pinochet era (1970–88) On 11 September 1973, the new army Commander-in-Chief, *Pinochet, staged a military coup which many believed to be inevitable at the time. Against hopes for a speedy return to democracy, he established a fiercely repressive regime, suppressing any hint of opposition. His neo-liberal economic policies increased poverty, but also increased foreign investment, reduced foreign debt, and stabilized the inflation rate. He confirmed his position in two plebiscites in 1978 and 1980, but lost a further one in 1988, called in response to rising international pressure on him to liberalize his regime. He accepted the verdict, but was to remain Commander-in-Chief until 1998.

Democratization (since 1988) Pinochet was succeeded by two Christian Democrats, Presidents Patrício Aylwin (1990–4) and *Frei Ruiz-Tagle (1994–2000).They continued their predecessor's economic policies and achieved stable inflation, declining foreign debt, and overall increases in income. This enabled the country in the late 1990s to steer clear of the economic collapse that befell neighbouring Argentina, and the political collapse of neighbouring Peru. In 2000, Ricardo *Lagos Escobar became Chile's first socialist President since Allende, and he was succeeded, in 2006, by Michelle *Bachelet Jeria. The socialist Presidents also maintained liberal economic policies. Chile's economy benefited from a boom in world demand for Chile's mineral resources, of which copper was the most important. Throughout the period, the key political question concerned the public reckoning with the crimes committed under the Pinochet regime. Pinochet himself was put up for trial, but died before he could be sentenced. Meanwhile, constitutional changes agreed in 2005 further reduced the political power of the military. This further stabilized the political system, which was dominated by two stable party alliances, the centre-left Concertatión (which had a majority in both houses of parliament from 2005), and the centre-right Alianza.

Chiluba, Frederick T. (b. 30 Apr. 1943). President of Zambia 1991–2002
Born at Kitwe, he worked on a sisal plantation and rose to become a financial manager. As a convinced socialist he was educated in Moscow and the German Democratic Republic (East Germany) before returning to become active for the trade union ZCTU (Zambia Copper Trade Union), whose president he became in 1974. In 1981 he refused *Kaunda's offer to join his Cabinet as Minister of Labour, and was subsequently imprisoned for a short period. He resigned from his post in the ZCTU in 1990 in order to lead the newly founded Movement for a Multi-party Democracy (MMD). In the elections of 31

October 1991 Chiluba was elected President with 64.4 per cent of the popular vote. Having gradually abandoned his Communist views, he rejected Kaunda's socialist policies and liberalized the economy. His privatization programme, which involved the sale of 251 state-owned companies, exposed him to allegations of corruption. He was unable to generate enough support for a constitutional change that would allow him a third term in office. In the end, he stepped down after ensuring that he was succeeded by Levy *Mwanawasa. In 2006, he was charged with embezzlement during his time as President, but he was too ill to face trial.

China
An Asian country characterized by relatively weak, bureaucratic rule at the centre, which made it difficult for those vying for power to establish control over the entire country during the first half of the twentieth century.

The Imperial era (up to 1911) During the nineteenth century, the government relied on the power of local landlords to collect taxes from a mass of poor, and often propertyless, peasants, who made up over 80 per cent of the population. In marked contrast to Europe, a sharp increase in population (1800: 300 million; 1880: 450 million) was not accompanied by improvements in agricultural productivity through more efficient farming methods. There was no industrialization, either. Most commerce was subject to state monopoly, so that enterprising urban commercial classes largely failed to develop. Given the lack of mechanical innovation in economics and the military, it was relatively easy for foreign powers to force the Imperial Court into allowing them to occupy bridgeheads such as as *Hong Kong or *Macao, from which they could penetrate the Chinese market.

Protest against this humiliating domination by foreign powers led to the *Boxer Rebellion in 1899–1901. While the Imperial Court was, eventually, moved to carry out some reforms, such as the abolition of the ancient, Confucian civil service exams, most reform proposals were vetoed by the Empress Dowager, Cixi. Incensed by the corruption and impotence of the Imperial Court, the growing poverty in the countryside, and the foreign intrusion into a country with an unrivalled cultural and political heritage, nationalist groups began to form.

The Republic of China (1911–49) Most of these groups united behind *Sun Yat-sen, who directed the republican movement from exile abroad, until the *Wuchang Revolution of 1911. Sun was elected President, but retired in

favour of *Yuan Shikai, who had been
instrumental in persuading the last Emperor,
*Pu Yi, to abdicate, and who commanded the
country's strongest military forces. Instead of
consolidating the newly established Republic
of China, however, Yuan made himself
Emperor, exiling the Republic's other leaders,
including Sun. After Yuan's death in 1916, Sun
struggled to reunite the disorientated
republican movement. Central power
degenerated in a country where local power
was more determinant than ever, in the era of
*warlords. Sun began to realize that he could
only gain authority over China by
refashioning his political force, the
*Guomindang (KMT), and its military
counterpart, the *National Revolutionary
Army (NRA), in order to break the power of
the landlords nationwide. He reorganized the
KMT along Leninist lines, with the active help
of *Comintern. He was also happy to accept
the help of the Chinese *Communist Party
(CCP), founded in 1921. Sun died in 1925.

Sun's successor, *Chiang Kai-shek, was
never able to unite all the disparate wings of
the nationalist, republican movement behind
him. Chiang had a promising start, as he set
out to unite the country under the KMT in the
*Northern Expedition in 1926, which reached
Beijing in 1928.

Civil war (1927–49) In 1927, Chiang
committed the fundamental error of dividing
the movement by seeking to annihilate the
CCP. This became a critical source of
weakness to his *National government,
which he established in Nanjing in 1927. The
area under his control never extended beyond
around one-third of China. Substantial areas,
around *Jianxi during 1931–4, and *Yan'an
during 1935–47, were subject to CCP control.
His obsession with overcoming the CCP
diverted his attention from Manchuria, where
in 1932 the Japanese established the puppet
state of *Manchukuo.

Owing to persistent warfare, government
expenditure on warfare reached more than 70
per cent of the total budget. As a result, the
KMT government suffered from chronic
budget deficits and inflation, despite
considerable economic and infrastructural
reforms. The KMT government also failed to
establish a permanent popular base. Chiang
continued to rely heavily on landowners and
warlords for military and financial support,
which rendered him unable and unwilling to
carry out any major, albeit much-needed,
social reforms. By contrast, the CCP gained
considerable administrative and military
experience at its base in Jianxi. Almost
annihilated during the *Long March, under
the leadership of *Mao Zedong it established

a mass peasant membership, mainly through
successful land reforms and strict party
discipline.

As both movements agreed to cooperate
against Japanese aggression, for which
purpose they created a *United Front in 1937,
Communist influence spread inexorably from
their base in the north, while Chiang's forces
bore the brunt of the Japanese military
onslaught of the *Sino-Japanese War.
Cooperation between the KMT and the CCP
effectively ended in 1943, while the United
Government formally fell apart in 1945. The
two sides clashed in the *Chinese Civil War, at
the beginning of which around one million
Communist soldiers faced three million KMT
troops. Despite early KMT victories, Chiang
fought a losing battle, as those areas that came
under the control of his troops remained loyal
to the Communist cause. By contrast, as
inflation and mismanagement reached new,
unprecedented peaks, Chiang lost the support
of important sections of society in his own
areas, such as the commercial classes in the
towns. After the victory of *Huai-Hai, the KMT
government collapsed. Chiang and his
troops retreated to *Taiwan, where they
maintained a KMT government waiting to
return to the mainland. Mao Zedong
proclaimed the People's Republic of *China
on 1 October 1949.

China, People's Republic of

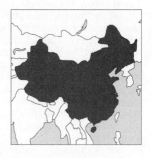

The world's
most populous
country has
undergone
dramatic
transformation
from one of
the world's
poorest
countries in the 1950s to one of the most
powerful states in the early years of the
twenty-first century.

The Maoist period (1949–1970s) The
People's Republic was established on
mainland *China on 1 October 1949 by *Mao
Zedong. In the first decade of its existence,
together with his loyal deputy, *Zhou Enlai,
Mao sought to establish the control of the
Chinese *Communist Party over the entire
country, as well as over *Tibet, which was
occupied in 1950. This involved not just
political control, but also the realization of a
Communist economy, society, and culture.
The power of the gentry was broken through
expropriation and the redistribution of the
majority of the farmland to around 75 per cent

of peasant households. Given the mass of peasants, this meant the creation of extremely small and inefficiently sized properties. Collectivization was encouraged, and encompassed almost 60 per cent of peasant households by 1954. In 1955 an impatient Mao quickened the pace of communist reform, so that by 1957 all farms were collectivized, while in the cities all commercial and industrial enterprises had been nationalized. Apart from the destruction of traditional social relationships, perhaps the most significant innovation of those years was the creation of legal sexual equality. While traditional codes between men and women were not eradicated overnight, the 1950 marriage laws, for example, gave women equal status.

By 1957 Mao was satisfied that a proletarian society had been created. He chose to show this in the *Hundred Flowers campaign, which created a brief atmosphere of intellectual liberalization. Ultimately, however, the campaign confirmed the regime's hostility to intellectuals in general, and its critics in particular. In the first decade of its existence, China relied heavily on the economic and diplomatic support of the USSR, particularly after its confrontation with the USA in the *Korean War. This influence led to an economic development modelled on the Soviet Union, so that resources were put almost exclusively into industrial growth, at the expense of agriculture. The severe consequences of this policy had become evident by 1958. Economic growth had averaged 7 per cent per annum, mainly as a result of economic reorganization, and was now reaching a natural limit. Moreover, investment was focused on the cities, resulting in discontent among peasants, who were, after all, the social and ideological backbone of the Communist Party.

Under increasing criticism from followers of *Liu Shaoqi, Mao launched the *Great Leap Forward. In attempting to create self-sufficient communities, he sought to mobilize new labour resources (e.g. women) in the countryside, while employing the newly created labour surplus in the building and running of communal industries. Industrial output increased dramatically, and China was flooded with industrial goods of shoddy quality for which there was no demand. By contrast, there was a dramatic decline in agricultural production, which decreased by a staggering 26.3 per cent (1958–60), causing the starvation of millions of Chinese.

The early 1960s were devoted to a period of normalization organized by Liu's supporters, with Mao taking a back seat. Mao reasserted his total control, however, in the 'Great Proletarian *Cultural Revolution', which resulted in a dramatic purge of the CCP, as well as economic and cultural elites. The reassertion of Mao's authority was further facilitated by the fall of *Lin Biao.

Economic liberalization, 1976– The death of Mao in 1976 formed a watershed in the history of the People's Republic. The Cultural Revolution was brought to an end, and the *Gang of Four was arrested by *Hua Guofeng. Most important was the rapid re-emergence of the pragmatic *Deng Xiaoping, whose leadership was established by late 1978. He liberalized academic debate, and introduced unprecedented economic reforms. Industrial enterprises received a stimulus through being allowed to keep some of their profits, while certain private industries and foreign investment were encouraged. In the countryside, too, individual responsibility and accountability were reintroduced in a fundamental shift away from the collective ideal. Under Deng, the Chinese economy began an uninterrupted period of growth over three decades. Economic liberalization, however, did not mean that the Communist Party was willing to contemplate political plurality, with the government brutally suppressing demonstrations in the *Tiananmen Square Massacre of 1989.

Deng was succeeded by *Jiang Zemin, who continued to suppress any political opposition. Impressive annual growth rates of around 10 per cent led to increasing social stratification, rather than a general increase in the standard of living, which was eroded by rising inflation (22 per cent in 1994). Domestically, the prestige of the CCP (and of Jiang) was bolstered by the incorporation of *Hong Kong and *Macao into mainland China. International recognition was manifested by China's entry into the *WTO in 2001, and its commission to host the 2008 Olympic Summer Games.

Contemporary politics (since 2002) In 2002, *Hu Jintao succeeded Jiang Zemin as Chairman of the CCP. At home, Hu was concerned to address the negative side-effects of China's growth. The government channelled much greater investment into infrastructure and education in the countryside, as rural areas had largely been left behind by the dynamism of the urban economy. This was only partially successful: it did increase income in the countryside, but income in the cities increased even further. Perhaps of even greater import were the environmental consequences of China's development. China is predicted to overtake the USA as the world's largest emitter of greenhouse gases, with hundreds of thousands already dying from the effects of environmental pollution. China also faced a critical shortage of clean water, while pollution increased the discrepancy between the arid north and the south affected by frequent flooding. In 2006, the government embarked on a large-scale initiative to invest $160 billion in environmental protection, including the development of renewable energy sources.

By 2006, China had overtaken the USA as the world's second largest exporter of industrial goods. As the world's fourth largest economy with the largest reserves of foreign currency, it also required rapidly expanding fuel resources. For these reasons, China became a major actor on the world stage. It exerted growing influence in Africa, providing loans with none of the strings attached by bodies such as the *IMF. Deriving much of its oil from Angola, Sudan and Iran, China also prevented effective UN resolutions against these countries. China also exerted its influence more aggressively within Asia, underlining its position not least by stark increases in military expenditure—over 10 per cent in 2004 and 2005, according to official figures.

Chinese Civil War (1946–9)

A war that evolved from the collapse of the *United Front in 1945. As Japan surrendered, Chinese *Communist Party (CCP) and *Guomindang (KMT) forces moved quickly to occupy the areas vacated by the Japanese, with CCP control concentrated in the north and north-east. Following the breakdown of negotiations led by George *Marshall, fighting broke out in February 1946. Supported by the US military, the KMT forces scored a number of early victories. Ultimately, the Communists' superior popular base and organization prevailed. The KMT forces lost around 500,000 men in battles (1947–8), and another 500,000 in the decisive confrontation at *Huai-Hai. In the following months, the Nationalist government collapsed, and was evacuated to Taiwan in December 1949, where its leader, *Chiang Kai-shek, re-formed a nationalist government in 1950. On the Chinese mainland, the Communist People's Republic of China was established on 1 October 1949, under the leadership of *Mao Zedong.

Chinese People's Political Consultative Conference (CPPCC)

Originally a gathering of anti-*Guomindang groups, not all of whom were Communists. It met for the first time on 21 September 1949 in order to draw up a Constitution for the People's Republic of China; the Constitution was proclaimed in 1954.

Thereafter, it met at regular intervals, and served as a useful instrument for the Communist Party to integrate and size up the non-Communist forces in the country.

Chinese Revolution (1911), see WUCHANG REVOLUTION

Chirac, Jacques René (b. 29 Nov. 1932). President of France 1995–2007

Early career Born in Paris, Chirac graduated from the prestigious École Normale d'Administration, entered the state bureaucracy, and became *Pompidou's Private Secretary in 1965, and a parliamentary deputy in 1967. He became Minister for Parliamentary Relations (1971–2), and Minister for Agriculture (1972–4). After a brief spell as Minister for the Interior, he became Prime Minister in 1974 as a reward for his support for the presidency of *Giscard d'Estaing. The two men increasingly disagreed, however, and in 1976 he resigned. Later that year, he relaunched the *Gaullist party, now named the RPR (Union for the Republic), to support his own ambitions to become President. He became Mayor of Paris in 1977, a city which subsequently became his power base. He failed in the first round of the 1981 presidential elections, and during his brief spell as Prime Minister in 1986–8 he became so unpopular against the venerable *Mitterrand that he lost the 1988 presidential elections to the latter.

Presidency In 1995, Chirac became President and relaunched a Gaullist foreign policy through underlining his commitment to the *nuclear bomb, and voicing initial concerns about *European integration. Meanwhile, his two central but conflicting goals of fighting unemployment and the budget deficit resulted in considerable tax increases while showing few early signs of success. He experienced the worst plunge into unpopularity of any President of the Fifth Republic in his first year of office. He called parliamentary elections in 1997, but these were won by the *Socialist Party under Lionel *Jospin. In the following period of *cohabitation, Chirac lost control over government policies except for the traditional presidential briefs on foreign and EU policy.

During the late 1990s, a growing number of financial irregularities committed by the Paris Mayor's office under his direction came to light. Chirac successfully defended his presidential prerogative not to testify, and a direct link to any corruption could never be proved. This greatly appeared to dent his chances for re-election against his rival, Jospin, himself a model of probity. However,

Chirac wrongfooted his opponent by conducting an election campaign primarily on the issue of law and order. He won in the first round, and since he stood in the second round against Le *Pen, he was re-elected by a huge republican majority of over 80 per cent. He appointed *Raffarin as his interim Prime Minister, and created a new movement, the *UMP, which won an absolute majority in parliament. In 2003, his resolute hostility to military intervention in Iraq was pivotal in foreclosing UN sanction of the US-led invasion of Iraq. For this he received overwhelming popular support from the French people. His popularity soon declined, however, owing to his determination to introduce pension reforms for the public sector. Chirac's government was unable to improve the country's growing unemployment rate, which plunged his government to ever-new depths. Chirac called a referendum on the European *Constitution, which many voters used as an opportunity to vent their dissatisfaction with the government's economic policies. Thereafter, Chirac's standing had declined to such an extent that he was unable to prevent the nomination of his rival, *Sarkozy, as the UMP's candidate for the presidency.

Chisholm, Shirley Anita (b. 30 Nov. 1924, d. 1 Jan. 2005). US politician
The first African-American woman to enter the House of Representatives. Born in Brooklyn, New York, she graduated with a BA from Brooklyn College, and an MA from Columbia University. Running as a *Democrat, Chisolm entered the New York State assembly as a Brooklyn member in 1965. Four years later she entered the US House of Representatives, and sought the Democrat presidential nomination in 1972. Despite winning the endorsement of the *Black Panthers she picked up little support, and remained a member of Congress. She retired from public life in 1983.

Chissano, Joaquim Alberto (b. 22 Oct. 1939). President of Mozambique 1986–2005
Born in Malehice, he was one of the first African pupils at a secondary school in Maputo (then Lourenço Marques) before studying medicine in Portugal. He took part in the foundation of *FRELIMO in 1962, and in 1963 was elected to its central committee. He was Secretary to the President (1966–9), and Chief Representative in Tanzania (1969–74). He became *Machel's principal lieutenant, and was Prime Minister of the transitional government of Mozambique (1974–5) before becoming Foreign Minister.

Like Machel, he was a devotee of *Marxism-Leninism. However, when he succeeded his friend to the Presidency, he was much more pragmatic. His greater political astuteness was displayed in 1987, for example, when he made it a priority to visit US President *Reagan. He introduced some economic liberalization, and started to negotiate with *RENAMO to end the civil war. This was achieved by 1994, when he was re-elected President in a democratic election monitored by 2,500 international observers. He was re-elected in 1999. Constitutionally barred from another term in office, he declined to stand again. By this time, widespread disillusionment had settled in, as mass poverty in one of Africa's poorest countries continued, with most of the proceeds from economic growth flowing to a small proportion of the population.

Chou En-lai, see ZHOU ENLAI

Chrétien, (Joseph Jacques) Jean (b. 11 Jan. 1934). Prime Minister of Canada 1993–2003

Early career Born at Shawinigan, Quebec, he studied law at Laval University and was admitted to the Quebec Bar in 1958. He became a member of the House of Commons for the *Liberal Party in 1963, serving in various ministries including National Revenue (1968), Indian Affairs (1968–74), Industry, Trade, and Commerce (1976–7), Finance (1977–9), as well as Energy, Mines, and Resources (1982–4). In 1980, he campaigned actively for the government in the Quebec referendum against sovereignty, supporting *Trudeau's promise of a lasting constitutional settlement which would meet the province's aspirations. He was then put in charge of the constitutional negotiations (1980–2) which led to the patriation of the *Canadian Constitution. However, this failed to satisfy many Quebeckers, who never quite forgave him for what they considered his broken promise.

Prime Minister He returned from political retirement in 1990, when he was asked to lead a disunited and demoralized Liberal Party. He became leader of the opposition, and in 1993 his steady leadership, as well as the exhaustion of the *Conservative Party after a long spell in government, ensured a comfortable victory for the Liberals. In his first years in office, Chrétien was faced with the growth of Quebec separatism, fuelled by the popularity of the charismatic *Bouchard. The government narrowly averted defeat in a referendum on Quebec independence in 1995, not least by generous funding of the 'no' campaign.
   Chrétien pursued a policy of economic liberalization and the reduction of the

national debt. Helped by his Finance Minister, Paul *Martin, the government achieved a budget surplus in the early years of 2000. To benefit from the divisions within the fragmented opposition, Chrétien called two early elections in 1997 and 2000, both of which he won handsomely. In 2002 he faced great pressure for his resignation. Even though his popularity was boosted by his decision not to support the USA in the *Iraq War, he was forced to resign in 2003 to make way for his rival, Paul Martin. Chrétien did not hide his disdain for his successor. Illegal funding of the Liberal Party under Chrétien's leadership did much to undermine his successor, and bring about his downfall in 2006.

Christian Democratic Party (Democrazia Cristiana, DC) (Italy)

Founded in July 1943 from the remnants of various groups which had been outlawed in Fascist Italy, the Italian *Popular Party, the Florentine group *Catholic Action, the Lombardian Guelf movement, and the Italian Federation of Catholic Students. Under its first leader, *De Gasperi, it acquired a heterogeneous mass base and quickly developed into Italy's main conservative party and a central pillar of the Italian political order. As such, it was the pivotal constituent of each of the 50 governments 1945–92, despite the gradual erosion of its popular support from around 48 per cent in 1948 to 29.7 per cent in 1992.

During the 1950s, official Roman Catholic influence within the party declined, even though clerical influence remained considerable throughout. In 1962, under the influence of *Moro, the party moved to the political centre through expressing its willingness to cooperate with the *socialist parties, which became the basis of many coalition governments from 1963 until the early 1990s. Following the revelation that several leading members of the DC belonged to a secret masonic lodge, in 1981 the Republican leader Giovanni Spadolini became the first Prime Minister who was not a member of the party, unlike most of his ministers. The declining fortunes of the DC in general elections weakened its influence during the 1980s, when the party was only able to govern in coalition with three or even four other parties (except for the Fanfani caretaker government in 1987).

Against the more forceful *Craxi and Spadolini, the DC's leaders were relatively weak and weakened by internal party divisions. Under *Andreotti, the party failed to transform itself into a more vibrant political force, its own immobility reflecting that of the political system which it had always represented. Thus, when Andreotti and other DC leaders were implicated in the country's corruption scandals (*Tangentopoli) from 1992, the DC, exhausted from 45 years in government, collapsed. It was dissolved and two new parties formed in January 1994, the cetre-left **Partito Popolare Italiano (Italian People's Party)**, which became allied to the *Olive Tree coalition, and the centre-right, **Centro Cristiano Democratico (Christian-Democratic Centre)**, which came to form part of *Berlusconi's right-wing bloc House of Liberty.

Christian Democrats

Moderate right-of-centre parties which in many European and some Latin American countries have been the dominant right-wing parties since World War II. Before World War II, the absence of conservative parties committed to the respective political systems they were operating in had led to fundamental domestic instability in Germany, Italy, France, and countries in Latin America. The success of the Christian Democrats as a moderate political force dedicated to upholding the political order was thus a major contributor to the post-war stability of Europe.

Originally, their social and moral values were rooted in Christianity, while their openness to economic liberalism and (in Europe) to *European integration ensured considerable middle-class and commercial support. The processes of secularization and *globalization from the 1960s eroded many of the traditional milieus from which the Christian Democrats derived their support. From the 1990s, they had to contend with rival populist right-wing movements. These in part eclipsed the traditional Christian Democrats, as in Italy, and in part supported them, as in Austria or the Netherlands. Only in a few countries such as Germany did the Christian Democrats appear to be strong enough to integrate such populist movements and remain the sole broad-based right-wing political movement at the national level.

CDU (GERMANY); CHRISTIAN DEMOCRATIC PARTY (ITALY); FORZA ITALIA; BERLUSCONI; HAIDER

Christmas Island (Kiritimati), see
KIRIBATI

Chu Teh, see ZHU DE

Church of England, see ANGLICAN
COMMUNION

Church of Scotland

The Presbyterian Church in Scotland, also known as the 'Kirk', to which the majority of

Scots belong. During the eighteenth and nineteenth centuries it was split between the official, conservative, Moderators' Church of Scotland and a more evangelical Free Church of Scotland. In 1921 the former was disestablished from the Crown and in 1929 the two rival churches were reunited as the Church of Scotland. It derives its theology from the sixteenth-century Calvinism of John Knox. Over the centuries, the Church of Scotland contributed to the high levels of Scottish education and mission work. Attempts to unite it with the Church of England were defeated in 1959 and 1971. In England and Wales the Presbyterian United Reformed Church (formed in 1972) is allied to it.

(⊕) SEE WEB LINKS

• The official website of the Church of Scotland.

Churchill, Sir Winston Leonard Spencer (b. 30 Nov. 1874, d. 24 Jan. 1965). British Prime Minister 1940–5, 1951–5

Early career Born in Blenheim Palace, Oxfordshire, the son of Lord Randolph Churchill and his American wife Jenny (née Jerome). He was educated at Harrow, where he did not do well, and his thirst for adventure led him first to the Royal Military College at Sandhurst, and then into a commission in the 4th Hussars in 1895. Churchill fought at the Battle of Omdurman in 1898, and, having resigned his commission in 1899, became a renowned war correspondent during the *South African (Boer) War. Captured by the *Afrikaners, he escaped, and returned to the UK to stand as *Conservative candidate for Oldham in 1900. He won the seat, yet joined the *Liberal Party in 1904 in support of free trade, becoming Liberal MP for Manchester in 1906, and from 1908, for Dundee.

Ministerial office Churchill had also become convinced of the need for social reform, and put this into practice as a Liberal minister. He was Under-Secretary of State for the Colonies (1906–8), and then President of the Board of Trade (1908–10), when he introduced measures to improve working conditions, and established labour exchanges. As Home Secretary (1910–11) he was criticized for overreacting to events by calling in troops to combat industrial disputes, and for personally directing the police at the siege of Sidney Street. He was also criticized, unfairly, for the response to the Tonypandy Riots (1910). At the Admiralty from 1911 until 1915, he continued reforms begun by Admiral Fisher. Churchill resigned after being blamed for the *Gallipoli campaign, and served briefly on the Western Front with the Royal Scots Fusiliers. He returned from France in 1917 at *Lloyd George's behest, and became Minister of Munitions. In 1918 he moved to the Ministry for War and Air, and was Colonial Secretary in 1921–2.

When the Lloyd George coalition fell in 1922, he began to drift back to the Conservative Party. He had been closely associated with Britain's intervention in the *Russian Civil War, and was increasingly concerned that *Bolshevism was a threat in Britain. His outspokenness against all socialists may have contributed to him losing his Dundee seat in 1922, which at least enabled him to begin writing his story of World War I in *The World Crisis* (1923–31).

Churchill was elected under the title 'Constitutionalist' as MP for Epping in 1924, which effectively marked his return to the Conservative Party. As Chancellor of the Exchequer in Baldwin's Conservative government (1924–9), he was associated with the return to the *Gold Standard, despite the tendency of an increasing number of countries to abandon it. His prominent role in organizing the government's measures against *trade unions in the 1926 *General Strike earned him the enmity of the *Labour Party and substantial sections of the working population. Churchill also opposed many of the measures of expenditure that the Royal Navy claimed were necessary for it to be adequately prepared for war.

On the backbenches Churchill was out of office from 1929 until 1939, partly because he was seen as unreliable, hot-headed, and reactionary by many Conservative colleagues. These sentiments were confirmed for some when he vigorously opposed the measures of Indian self-government put forward by the *National Government, and supported *Edward VIII during the *abdication crisis. His reputation partly explains why many people ignored his warnings in the 1930s about the need to rearm, and the dangers posed by *Hitler's rise to power in Germany.

World War II His association with rearmament made him the ideal choice as First Lord of the Admiralty, in Neville *Chamberlain's wartime government, formed in September 1939. In May 1940 he became Prime Minister and Defence Minister of a coalition government of Conservative, Liberal, and Labour members. As a war leader, Churchill was superb in maintaining popular morale, particularly at a time when Britain was alone in resisting German conquest, until the entry of the USSR and the USA into the war in 1941. He attached a high priority to close relations with the USA, but was often wanting in his consultation with the leaders of his *Commonwealth allies, whose troops he liked to dispatch as he deemed necessary. In August 1941, with President Franklin D. Roosevelt, he was instrumental in drawing up the *Atlantic Charter. Wary of Soviet expansionism, Churchill was concerned that the USA should not concede too many of *Stalin's demands as the war drew to a close: he is often said now to have overestimated the extent to which Britain could influence America.

Having won the war, many observers (including, perhaps, Churchill himself) were surprised that he lost the 1945 elections to the relatively bland *Attlee. This was largely because of the popularity of the *Beveridge Report, and the public sense of social change necessitated by the turbulence of the war, for which Labour seemed better equipped.

Second term in office Although leader of the opposition (1945–51), he left much of the actual work to *Eden. Instead, he travelled widely, and spoke on international affairs. He also wrote his six-volume *The Second World War* (1948–54), for which he received the Nobel Prize for Literature in 1953. He returned as Prime Minister in 1951, by now with failing health. Churchill devoted most of his attention to maintaining the 'special relationship' between Britain and the USA, which granted him honorary US citizenship. Otherwise, he was detached from the day-to-day running of his office, leaving much of the foreign policy to Eden, and most domestic and economic policy to *Butler, whom he disliked personally. He suffered a stroke in 1953 and resigned two years later.

Despite his rhetoric of glory, Churchill in fact presided over the demise of Britain as a world power. It is difficult to see how he could have prevented this, given Britain's involvement in a war of such proportions. Ultimately, there is little doubt that his undogmatic, enthusiastic, and charismatic leadership in the face of extreme adversity made him perhaps the greatest Englishman of the twentieth century.

CIA (Central Intelligence Agency)
(USA)

Early history An intelligence agency established by the 1947 National Security Act to collect, coordinate, and analyse foreign intelligence in the executive office of the President. The CIA grew out of the wartime Office of Strategic Services and the postwar Central Intelligence Group. During the 1950s it developed four subdirectorates: Intelligence, Operations, Science and Technology, and Administration. Under Director Allen Dulles (1953–61) its role was widened to include covert action projects, whereby clandestine projects against non-friendly states would be planned and financed. It thus masterminded the actions against Prime Minister *Mossadeq of Iran in 1953 and President *Arbenz of Guatemala in 1954. The CIA was also deeply involved in the *Congo Crisis of 1960.

Following the fiasco of the *Bay of Pigs operation in Cuba in 1961 *Kennedy sought to control the CIA's covert action projects, though he continued to use it to develop clandestine plans to eliminate *Castro. Kennedy was rumoured to have expressed a wish to dismantle the CIA, but he died before showing his hand.

Challenges (from the 1960s) Kennedy was not very successful in the reforms which he did institute; the CIA intelligence on Vietnam was riddled with inaccuracy, and the CIA role in Latin America during the 1960s and 1970s helped to poison US relations with that part of the world. Although successful in its efforts to depose President *Allende of Chile in 1973, the CIA failed to provide satisfactory intelligence for the *Yom Kippur War or the Turkish invasion of *Cyprus in 1974. CIA equipment and materials also found their way into the hands of the *Watergate burglars.

During the 1980s, the CIA was implicated in illegal activities in the *Iran–Contra scandal, though it was directed in its role by key staff at the National Security Council. The overall success of the CIA has been difficult to evaluate, as failures attracted more attention than successes. However, the remarkable success of the CIA at breaking the Russian army code contributed to the failure of the *October Putsch in 1993. The CIA faced stinging allegations for failing to track town Osama *Bin Laden during the 1990s, and for misinterpreting signals that foreshadowed the *September 11 attacks. The CIA faced a number of re-organizations which led to low morale inside the organization. Eventually, in May 2002 President George W. *Bush announced the creation of the **Department of Homeland Security**. This was to take over the role of the CIA and the FBI in preventing terrorist acts against US citizens in the *War on Terrorism.

((⊕)) SEE WEB LINKS

• The home page of the CIA.

Ciano, Count Galeazzo (b. 18 Mar. 1903, d. 11 Jan. 1944). Italian Fascist leader
Born in Livorno, he obtained a degree in law from Rome in 1925, and entered the diplomatic service. Not surprisingly, his career

was significantly boosted by his marriage to Edda, *Mussolini's eldest daughter. In 1933 he became the head of Mussolini's press office, and in 1935 he was promoted to Minister of Press and Propaganda. He left in the same year to join the *Abyssinian War, and in 1936 was appointed Foreign Minister. Despite his lack of experience and the absence of a power base within the *Fascist movement, he managed to put his own stamp on Mussolini's foreign policy, advocating the intervention in the *Spanish Civil War and the conquest of Albania. He also managed to persuade Mussolini to remain neutral at the outbreak of World War II, though when Italy did join in 1940 his influence declined rapidly, following the disastrous Italian invasion of Greece (1940–1). He was demoted to ambassador to the Pope in February 1943, and supported the decision of the *Fascist Grand Council to depose Mussolini on 25 July 1943. However, he was captured by the Germans and executed in the Republic of *Salò. His diaries 1935–43 provide an important insight into the internal workings of Fascist Italy.

CIO, see AMERICAN FEDERATION OF LABOR

CIS (Commonwealth of Independent States)

An international organization founded in 1991 to create a framework for regular consultation among the successor states of the Soviet Union. It was joined by twelve member states (excluding the Baltic States of Estonia, Latvia, and Lithuania), though its 1993 charter for a common economic and foreign policy was not signed by three of them (Ukraine, Moldova, Turkmenistan). Chaired by the Russian President, *Yeltsin, and his successor, *Putin, the CIS was weakened by the frailty of the members' economic and political systems, as well as intense mistrust of Russia's overwhelming predominance in size and population. It was further weakened by Russia's own geopolitical interests, which in Georgia and Moldova were directed towards the destabilization of fellow CIS members.

Ciskei, see BANTUSTAN

Civil Rights Acts (USA)

There have been ten major US Civil Rights Acts, nine of which were passed in the period 1957–91. The Acts were aimed at equalizing the political conditions of African Americans and White Americans. The 1957 Act began the modern cycle by creating the Civil Rights Commission, the Civil Rights Division of the US Justice Department, and the procedure whereby federal courts could enforce the voting rights of US citizens against

obstructions without jury trials of obstructers. Whereas before, White Americans who had prevented African Americans from voting were often acquitted by all-White juries, from now on voting-rights offenders were no longer tried by jury. This was followed by a 1960 Act which introduced criminal sanctions for racial violence and which reinforced voting-rights protection by the courts.

The landmark of civil rights legislation was the 1964 Act. In it, the federal government acquired powers to bar racial segregation and discrimination in federally funded programmes, and establishments serving interstate commerce. Racial discrimination in employment was outlawed and an Equal Opportunities Commission created to promote *affirmative action. This also benefited women, who were now protected by law from discrimination based on gender. A Voting Rights Act was passed in 1965 which implemented the Twenty-Fifth Amendment outlawing voting restrictions based on poll taxes and literacy tests, and which resulted directly in a threefold increase in African-American registration in the southern states.

A 1968 Act, passed in the wake of the *King assassination, outlawed racial discrimination in all but 10 per cent of the then housing space (sale and rental), and struck against racialist agitation and violence against civil rights workers and demonstrations. A 1970 Act reinforced the provisions of the 1965 **Voting Rights Act**, extending its scope for five years, establishing uniform federal election residence requirements, and lowering (unconstitutionally) the voting age to 18 in all elections. In 1991, a bill allowing class action suits against employers statistically biased against women or ethnic minorities was passed over President *Bush's veto, but in 1994 the Supreme Court decided that the law did not enforce an employer's liability retroactively, and only had force from 1991.

civil rights movement (USA)

After the *Plessey v. Ferguson ruling of 1896 had entrenched further the legal, social, economic and political discrimination of African Americans, a growing number of White liberals and African-American activists founded the *NAACP (1908). Progress was slow, despite the emergence of cultural leaders and political activists such as Marcus *Garvey and W. E. B. *Du Bois. The civil rights movement found it difficult to unite behind a common strategy, and to gain political support amongst sufficient numbers of White voters.

A turning point was reached in World War II, when the economic and military mobilization for the war effort relied on

African Americans. This raised hopes and expectations for greater civil rights equality in the postwar period, and when these were not fulfilled, the movement became more militant. At the same time, the *Supreme Court became a crucial, if not unambiguous, ally in realizing civil rights, starting with its decision in *Brown* v. *Topeka*, Kansas (1954).

In December 1955 the arrest of Rosa Parks, who had defied a rule of segregation on the bus system in Montgomery, Alabama, caused a year-long boycott of the entire system. Further boycotts followed throughout the late 1950s and early 1960s. These boycotts were galvanized by support from Martin Luther *King, who co-founded the Southern Christian Leadership Conference and the Student Non-Violent Co-ordinating Committee. His charisma empowered the civil rights movement through religion and a sense of calling, while his insistence on peaceful action divided White opposition.

Eventually, the civil rights movement began to win the political argument. In September 1957 federal troops were sent to Little Rock, Arkansas, to enforce school desegregation. *Congress passed a *Civil Rights Act establishing a federal agency of six commissions to investigate complaints. A further Act was passed in 1960. During 1960–1 there were student sit-ins forcing desegregation of lunch counters, cinemas, supermarkets, libraries, and other public facilities. Freedom Riders, racially integrated groups of travellers, went south and there were some 3,600 arrests. In August 1963 some 250,000 people took part in the peaceful *March on Washington, where they were addressed by King, who outlined his vision of an equal society ('I have a dream'). The Civil Rights Act of July 1964, which was introduced by *Kennedy and skilfully guided through Congress by *Johnson, was the most far-reaching bill of its kind, forbidding racial discrimination in employment, education, or accommodation. In 1965 this was followed by the Voting Rights Act, which aimed at ending voter discrimination. The movement, which had always held on to a common agenda only with great difficulty, fragmented from the mid-1960s. This was accelerated by King's death, but at its heart was a disagreement on how to define and acquire non-political civil rights, as discrimination continued in areas like housing, employment, the law, and access to high-quality education.

Clark, Charles Joseph ('Joe') (b. 5 June 1939). Prime Minister of Canada 1979

Born at High River, Alberta, he went to the University of Alberta, becoming national *Conservative student president before taking a master's degree in political science. He worked for the party until he was elected to the House of Commons in 1972. Despite his position on the progressive wing, he emerged as leader of a party riven with internal divisions in 1976. He formed a minority government in May 1979, when he became the country's youngest Prime Minister, and the first to come from the western provinces. His major policy proposals, such as the privatization of the national petroleum company, Petro-Canada, were ill-considered given his weak parliamentary position. Following the parliamentary rejection of his austere budget he lost a vote of confidence in December 1979, which paved the way for the *Liberal election victory under *Trudeau in 1980.

Clark was an effective leader of the opposition, but as a progressive never commanded the full support of his entire party, which replaced him with *Mulroney in 1983. Under Mulroney, Clark became Minister of External Affairs. As Minister for Constitutional Affairs from 1991, Clark put together a constitutional package in the aftermath of the failure of the *Meech Lake Accord. The resulting **Charlottetown Accord** (1992) was defeated in a referendum by six provinces and one territory, and Clark announced that he would not run in the 1993 election. He returned to active politics in 1998, when he was elected to head the Progressive Conservative Party. He regained his seat in the House of Commons in 2000, but his party obtained a meagre thirteen seats. In 2002 he announced his resignation as party leader for 2003. Clark opposed the merger between the Progressive Conservatives and the Canadian Alliance in 2003, sitting as an independent Progressive Conservative until the 2004 elections, in which he did not stand for re-election.

Clark, Helen (b. 26 Feb. 1950). Prime Minister of New Zealand, 1999–

Early career Born in Hamilton into a wealthy farming family, she studied political science and graduated from the University of Auckland with a Ph.D. In 1973 she became a lecturer at the University of Auckland, and in 1981 she became the first woman member of the *Labour Party to be elected to parliament, as an MP for Mt Albert. She rose quickly within the parliamentary party, and became Minister for Conservation and Minister of Housing (1987–9). In 1989 she served briefly as deputy Prime Minister until Labour's defeat in the 1990 elections. She replaced Mike Moore as Labour leader from 1993, and from then on worked hard to overcome a dry, intellectual image. Clark presided over a disastrous election defeat in 1996, but the party recovered in the 1999 elections.

In office In addition to being Prime Minister, she also held the portfolio for Arts, Culture, and Heritage. Her coalition government with the Alliance party was two seats short of a parliamentary majority, so that she was reliant on the support of the Green Party. She called early elections in 2002, but despite a strong showing by Labour she was unable to secure the absolute majority she had bargained for. She won the 2005 elections by a narrow majority, and became the first Labour Prime Minister since 1945 to hold three successive terms in office. Once again, she led a minority government, relying on shifting support from the Green Party, the Maori Party and the United Future party. In her period of office, Helen Clark tried to combine social policies (such as the introduction of the four-week statutory annual holiday) with a market-oriented approach. She promoted a reduction in New Zealand's emission of greenhouse gases to comply with the *Kyoto Protocol, for instance by supporting biofuels. She also increased government spending on public transport by 750 per cent since taking office.

CLC, see CANADIAN LABOUR CONGRESS

Clean Government Party (Japan), see KÔMEITÔ

Clemenceau, Georges (b. 28 Sept. 1841, d. 24 Nov. 1929). Prime Minister of France 1906–9, 1917–20
Mayor of Montmartre at the time of the Paris Commune (1870–1), he became a member of the Chamber of Deputies and leader of the *Radicals in 1876. Although a brilliant speaker, his sharp, destructive, and negative temperament earned him few friends. He lost his seat in 1893 owing to his links with the Panama scandal, but his attacks against the right wing during the *Dreyfus Affair launched his political comeback, and he became a Senator in 1902. His first period in office as Prime Minister is best known for his savage repression of labour unrest, which earned him the hostility of the *Socialist Party and left him little time for social reform. Despite general dislike for 'the tiger' (as he was known), he was called back to lead a war-weary France, a task which he again performed by crushing all opposition, though this was only possible because he was supported by the majority of the French population. After World War I, his main objective was to ensure that Germany would never be able to start another war. He had to resign after the *Versailles Treaty was heavily criticized in France for its supposed leniency towards Germany.

climate change

History Climate change has been integral to the planet's historical development. The earth has been affected by ice ages which recurred between long intervals, with the last ice age receding when average temperatures rose again 20,000 years ago. The fundamental elements of today's geography in northern Europe, northern Asia, North America, southern Latin America, and southern New Zealand are a product of the land masses moved by the ice. A more minor drop in temperatures occurred in the sixteenth and seventeenth centuries. It is believed that such changes in temperature have been caused by changes in the earth's relative position to the sun.

Causes The impact of humans on climate change has been more recent, and began with accelerating pace with the industrial revolution from the late eighteenth century. Industrial production, as well as motorized transportation, produced carbon-rich emissions which have also been called 'greenhouse gases'. As the energy generated by the planet is released into the atmosphere, some of it is bound by greenhouse gases so that they warm up the earth's atmosphere. The more greenhouse gases are released, the less heat is lost beyond the atmosphere, and the warmer the planet becomes.

Although the greenhouse gas emissions generated by pollution were relatively small at first, they grew exponentially as more countries industrialized, as consumption of energy per capita increased, and as the population grew from 1.6 billion in 1900 to over 6 billion people in 2000. From 1900 to 2000, this led to an average global temperature increase of 1 degree centigrade. There is an acceleration to this change, with a 0.4 degree centigrade increase produced between 1980 and 2000 alone. In this period, carbon dioxide emissions by the USA, by far the largest producer of greenhouse gases in the world, doubled.

Effects As a result, the UN-sponsored Intergovernmental Panel on Climate Change (IPCC) predicted a dramatic rise in the global temperature by 2100, unless contrary measures were taken. The effect of these emissions on climate change reached a critical dimension by 2000, so that for the period up to 2100 the IPCC predicted that global warming would have a dramatic impact. This would include increased incidence of death among older age gropus and the urban poor, increased damage from natural catastrophes such as flooding, soil erosion, and avalanches, and decreased crop yields overall. As a result of melting icecaps, especially in the Arctic, sea levels were predicted to rise, which would endanger island states in the Pacific. It would also affect coastal areas throughout the world, especially in low-lying deltas such as the Ganges delta in Bangladesh; a rise of the sea level by 40 cm would mean that the average annual number of people affected by flooding would rise fivefold, from over 40 million to almost 250 million. Increased temperature would also vastly expand the desert areas of Africa, thus reducing the continent's economic potential still further.

Policy responses A major problem in avoiding human-produced climate change was its international dimension, since pollution fell within national jurisdiction, but affected the welfare of the entire planet. In response, the *Kyoto Protocol represented a landmark agreement to reduce the emissions of greenhouse gases. In 2007, the EU as the world's most closely integrated international organization decided further unilateral steps towards reducing greenhouse emissions. International efforts continued to formulate a successor to the Kyoto Protocol which would be more far-reaching and which would include the USA (responsible for about a quarter of the world's pollution) and China, the largest-growing polluter.

(((♁))) SEE WEB LINKS

• The home page of the Intergovernmental Panel on Climate Change (IPCC).

Clinton, Hillary Rodham (b. 26 Oct. 1947). US Senator, 2001–
Born at Park Ridge, Illinois, in 1947 and originally a *Goldwater *Republican, Hillary Rodham studied at Wellesley College and Yale Law School. She became a distinguished and successful lawyer associated with children's rights. She practised law in Arkansas and headed various state committees whilst her husband, Bill *Clinton, was Governor of that state. Clinton gave up her legal practice to become First Lady in 1993, but maintained a prominent policy role by chairing the Task Force on National Health Reform which produced proposals for the reform of the US health care system that were defeated in a venomous congressional battle in 1994. Clinton attracted strong criticism for her liberalism, her prominence in politics, and her association with the *Whitewater charges. She saved her husband's career twice, by

standing by him publicly after he admitted sexual relations with Paula Jones in 1992, and after the *Lewinsky Affair.

In 2000 Clinton became a politician in her own right, when she was elected to the Senate for the State of New York. In her first years as a Senator, Clinton consciously avoided the controversial national policy agendas which had been her passion as the President's wife, preferring instead to build up a reputation of looking after her constituents' interests. This was rewarded in 2006, when she was re-elected with 67 per cent of the popular vote, a remarkable achievement even in a Democrat-leaning state. Clinton pointed to this success as evidence that she had overcome the polarization of her husband's presidency, and that she could appeal to centrist and Republican voters. As by far the best known active Democratic politician in the USA, she announced her candidacy for the presidential race in 2008.

Clinton, William Jefferson ('Bill')
(b. 19 Aug. 1946). 42nd US President 1993–2001

Early careeer Born William Jefferson Blythe at Hope, Arkansas, after his father died he changed his name to that of his later stepfather. He rose from poor beginnings to become a student of international relations at Georgetown University, a *Rhodes Scholar, a Yale law student, and a law professor. At the age of 30, he was appointed Arkansas Attorney-General, and two years later he became Governor of Arkansas. He was defeated in his 1980 re-election campaign, but returned to the Governor's mansion in 1984, where he stayed until his election to the Presidency. Within the *Democratic Party, he co-founded the pragmatic, somewhat populist Democratic Leadership Council. Under his direction, this organization of moderate Governors and officeholders associated with the south lobbied to move the party closer to the political centre. He announced his candidacy for the Presidency at a time when the incumbent, George *Bush, was enjoying record popularity ratings. After winning over a relatively weak field in the primaries, he chose Al *Gore as his running mate. This added gravitas and experience to Clinton's charisma. He aimed his campaign at suburban and centrist voters, particularly through his conservative positions on crime and welfare. He was elected in a three-way race with 43.2 per cent of the popular vote, on a platform predominantly concerned with economic matters and health care reform.

Presidency Once in office, Clinton pushed through some important legislation, notably the ratification of the *NAFTA agreement, as well as the Brady Bill on gun control. His popularity declined during the first two years, largely because of his failure to build coalitions in *Congress. Eager to please everyone, and an outsider in the Washington political establishment, he was often seen as indecisive and divisive. He also wasted much political capital on relatively controversial and ultimately unsuccessful policies. For instance, his attempt to lift the ban on homosexuals in the military angered the *Republican establishment, while his failure fuelled the disappointment of his own liberal supporters. Two years into his Presidency the *Democrats lost control of both Houses of Congress to the *Republicans, who emphasized their probity and effectiveness in alleged contrast to the president.

Ironically, Clinton was at his most successful when he dealt with a hostile *Congress, proving time and again the winner in escalating confrontations. He won a stand-off with Congress about federal spending (1995–6), and avoided impeachment over the *Lewinsky Affair. However, the increasing acrimony generated by these confrontations hindered much of his domestic legislation. In domestic politics, his major achievement was the balancing of the federal budget after the profligacy of the *Reagan administration, though Clinton was helped by a buoyant economy. Stifled in domestic politics by Congress, Clinton directed surprising energy abroad. He intervened peacefully in Haiti to end the dictatorship there in 1993. He also played a key role in the *Dayton Agreement concerning *Bosnia-Hercegovina, and in continuing efforts to establish a peace process between the *PLO and Israel. Clinton's mediation was also crucial in the *Northern Ireland peace process. A man of great intellect and outstanding charm, Clinton ultimately was his own worst enemy, as his personal and human weaknesses prevented him from realizing his more ambitious political visions.

After leaving the Presidency, Clinton proved surprisingly adept at adjusting to the role of private citizen, leaving the political limelight to his wife, Hillary *Clinton. Bill Clinton devoted his energies to causes such as the fight against AIDS and the construction of medical facilities in Rwanda, while also giving political advice to his wife.

CLN (Committee for National Liberation)

The *Comitato di Liberazione Nazionale* was the central organization which coordinated the resistance movements in German-occupied Italy, established on 9 September 1943. In all, around 250,000 partisans were active in the Italian resistance, while the CLN itself was dominated by many politicians from the pre-Fascist era. In the initial period after the armistice in 1943, relations between the royal government and the parties active in the CLN were very poor. The other parties of the CLN did not follow the Communists and enter *Badoglio's government until 22 April 1944. The CLN formed the nucleus of the political system that emerged after *World War II, as the three main parties of postwar Italy emerged from it: the *Christian Democratic Party, the *Socialist Party, and the *Communist Party.

CLNAI (Committee for the Liberation of Upper Italy)

The *Comitato di Liberazione Nazionale per l'Alta Italia* coordinated the Italian resistance movements in the various regions of German-occupied northern Italy from November 1943. In January 1944, it was invested with extraordinary powers of government in northern Italy by the *CLN (Committee for National Liberation). By the summer of 1944, over 80,000 people were active in the resistance, and despite heavy casualties this grew to over 100,000 by April 1945. The CLNAI organized urban insurrections which led to the liberation of Florence in August 1944, and the surrender of Turin and Naples (amidst heavy casualties) in April 1945. It failed to gain the political recognition it desired from the Allies, so that it was forced to disband immediately upon the liberation of northern Italy. In June 1945, the predominant Action Party within the CLNAI was able to insist upon its candidate, Ferrucio Parri, to replace *Bonomi as leader of the government. Parri's government gave a constant impression of incompetence, and he was replaced by *De Gasperi in December 1945 to inaugurate over 40 years of *Christian Democratic predominance in Italian politics.

Clynes, John Robert (b. 27 Mar. 1869, d. 23 Oct. 1949). British Labour leader 1920–2
Born in Oldham, and educated at elementary school. He began work in a textile mill at the age of 10, and became an active trade unionist. He joined the *Independent Labour Party in 1893, and became an MP for North-East Manchester in 1906. He opposed Labour's entry into the *Asquith coalition in 1915, but served under *Lloyd George from 1917. Clynes was elected as chairman of the parliamentary *Labour Party in 1921, leading it in the 1922 general election. He lost this post in the same year to Ramsay *MacDonald, but in the first two Labour governments was Lord Privy Seal (1924) and Home Secretary

(1929–31). He lost his seat in 1931, but returned to the Commons in 1935, remaining there until his retirement in 1945.

CND (Campaign for Nuclear Disarmament)

Created in 1958 under the presidency of Bertrand *Russell, CND advocated the abandonment of British nuclear weapons. Support for the CND split the *Labour Party, which voted in 1960 for unilateral disarmament, only to reverse its stand in 1961. Frustration at lack of progress led to the creation by Russell of a splinter group in 1962, the Committee of One Hundred. Created to counter attempts to pin responsibility on a single invidiual, it aimed at inciting mass civil disobedience. From 1963 to 1980 the CND all but disappeared, but it revived in the 1980s in reaction to the deployment of US cruise missiles in Britain. Again, the Labour Party's support for the CND became very controversial and contributed to the breakaway of the *Social Democrats in 1981. It also contributed to the lack of Labour's electoral credibility among most voters during the 1980s. Following the end of the *Cold War, CND has lost much of its support.
DISARMAMENT AND ARMS CONTROL; NUCLEAR BOMB

((())) SEE WEB LINKS

- The official website of CND.

CNI (*Centre Nationale des Indépendants*), see UDF

Coates, Joseph Gordon (b. 3 Feb. 1878, d. 27 May 1943). Prime Minister of New Zealand 1925–8

Early career Born in Pahi (near Auckland), he worked on his father's farm before being elected to parliament in 1911 as an 'independent Liberal', though from 1912 he sided with the oppositional Reform Party which represented the country's farming interests. He saw distinguished service in France during World War I, and upon his return was made Postmaster-General, Minister of Telegraphs, and Minister of Justice. One of the most able ministers of *Massey's Cabinet, he made a considerable contribution towards the successful reintegration of the soldiers returning from the war. As Native Minister (1921–5) he became the first politician of European descent to champion *Maori rights, staying in close contact with *Ngata. He was also an energetic Minister of Works (1920–6) and of Railways (1923–8), being responsible for

considerable improvements in the country's infrastructure.

In power Coates succeeded Massey as Prime Minister, and was returned with a substantial majority in the 1925 elections. He failed to cope with the country's economic problems, however, and was unable to prevent the country sliding into an economic recession. He lost the 1928 elections and set about rebuilding the party.

Coates reluctantly agreed to join *Forbes in a coalition government to respond to the Great *Depression. As Deputy Prime Minister Coates engineered the major economic policies of the government. At the *Ottawa Conference he secured agreement for open access to the British market, he lowered the exchange rate (to increase exports), and he established the Reserve Bank (1933) to increase monetary control. This earned him little gratitude from an electorate impoverished by the economic slump. Following an electoral defeat in 1936, he had to accept the merger of the Reform Party with the *National Party, after which he was relegated to the sidelines. However, from 1940 until his death he was a member of the War Cabinet, in charge of the important Ministry of Armed Forces and War Coordination. The efficiency and skill he displayed in this function marked the most distinguished period of his career.

Cod Wars (1958–61, 1973, 1975–6)

The popular name given to the antagonism between Britain and Iceland over fishing rights. They resulted from Iceland's unilateral extension of its fishing limits from 12 to 50, and then to 200 miles. Especially in 1975–6, Icelandic gunboats harassed, and sought to arrest, British trawlers entering these zones. In 1972–4, Britain obtained favourable judgments from the International Court of Justice, and subsequently sent Royal Navy frigates to escort its trawlers. A compromise was agreed in 1976, whereby twenty-four British trawlers could fish within an agreed 200 mile zone.

cohabitation ('coexistence') (France)

A term denoting the coincidence in France of a president from one party and a prime minister from another. Under the Constitution of the *Fifth Republic, the president had a strong role and could determine the contours of government policy. This became difficult in the 1970s, when under *Giscard d'Estaing and *Chirac the president and his prime minister came from two different, but still right-wing, parties. It became even more problematic during the

1980s and 1990s, when president and prime minister came from opposing political camps. This dramatically reduced the powers of the president. As the prime minister became primarily responsible for all aspects of policy formation, the president's role became restricted to matters of EU and foreign policy. The reduced role of the president was reflected in a constitutional amendment of 2001, when the president's term was reduced from seven to five years. The French elections of 2002 brought the longest period of cohabitation to an end, as Chirac's *UMP obtained an absolute parliamentary majority.

Cold War

A term coined by *Baruch in 1947 to describe the emerging tensions between the Soviet Union, and the Eastern European states under its influence on the one hand, and the USA and its Western European allies on the other. The tensions had been apparent ever since the division of occupied Germany into four zones and the beginning of Soviet administration in Eastern Europe, and was intensified by the *Marshall Plan, which the Soviet Union forbade the countries under its control to accept. The Cold War can be subdivided into three periods:

1. The first, most hostile phase began after the *Potsdam Conference, included the Greek Civil War (1946-9) and the *Berlin Blockade in 1948, and reached a first climax with the *Korean War (1950-3). There was a slight relaxation after *Stalin's death in 1953, but it continued until the *Cuban Missile Crisis of 1962. This brought the two superpowers of the USA and the USSR to the brink of a nuclear war, and thus caused a change of attitude which led to first efforts at *disarmament.

2. Despite the fact that indirect confrontation between the USSR and the USA never stopped, such as during the *Vietnam War, tensions began to ease during the 1960s. This development culminated in *Brandt's 'Ostpolitik' (*German question) beginning in 1969, the *Helsinki Conference (1973-5), and the Conference on Security and Cooperation in Europe after 1975.

3. The phase of *détente ended in 1979 with the Soviet invasion of Afghanistan, the suppression of the Polish *Solidarność Movement from 1980, and the deployment of Soviet nuclear ballistic missiles (SS20) in Eastern Europe, to which *NATO responded with the deployment of US Pershing missiles in Western Europe. Tensions declined with the coming to power of *Gorbachev in the USSR, as he appreciated that his country's deteriorating economic position meant that it could never keep up with the USA in the arms race which had developed by then. In 1988,

the USSR declared officially that it would no longer interfere in another country's affairs. The late 1980s saw the steady improvement of relations between the USSR and the USA, and in 1991, following the collapse of the Soviet Union, US President *Bush officially declared the Cold War over.

SDI; BRINKMANSHIP; NUCLEAR BOMB

collaboration (France)

The act of co-operating with the German authorities in France during World War II. It was the public policy of the *Vichy government, whose leader *Pétain announced his readiness to 'enter into the way of collaboration' in October 1940. In the French territory under German occupation, considerable numbers of French bureaucrats, police officers, and other public officials also collaborated, although their number is uncertain. In recent years, the compliance of many ordinary French people with the occupying forces—partly out of conviction, but mostly to avoid repression—has been established by historians. To make a clean break after the Liberation in 1944, it was rumoured that over 100,000 collaborators were executed, though the real figure was less than 10,000. Many public officials, especially lawyers and bureaucrats needed for the country's reconstruction after the war, were kept in office. Few of the collaborators in business and commerce were punished, and some Vichy officials were even elected to the Chamber of Deputies after 1945.

collectivism

A loose term originally developed by Bakunin (b. 1814, d. 1876), in the context of *anarchism, to extol the virtues of self-governing associations as opposed to individualism on the one hand, and the supremacy of the state on the other. At the end of the nineteenth century, collectivism came to describe the primacy of the public good over individual interests, in order to ensure equality of opportunity. In Scandinavian countries, and in countries such as Britain and France after World War II, this ideal led to the public ownership of utilities, subsidies, and regulation of industries which provided goods that were considered necessities for the public good. In other countries, collectivism took quite different forms. In Communist countries, it led to the establishment of industrial and agricultural cooperatives, while a rather more radical attempt at communal living was made by the *kibbutz movement in Israel. The criticism of such collectives was that common ownership did not provide incentives for individual achievement and hence they tended to be

inefficient. With the collapse of
*Communism in Eastern Europe, and the
prevalence of neo-liberal economic doctrine
emphasizing individual thrift, the collective
idea underwent a general decline from the
1980s.

Collins, Michael (b. 16 Oct. 1890, d. 22
Aug. 1922). Irish soldier and politician
Born in Woodfield, Clonakilty, Co. Cork, he
went to London in 1906 to work as a clerk.
While there he joined the nationalist Gaelic
Athletic Association and the Irish Republican
Brotherhood. He returned to Ireland in 1916
and joined in the *Easter Rising in Dublin. He
was imprisoned until December, after which
he became prominent in *Sinn Féin and
Volunteer movements. He became Minister of
Home Affairs and later Minister of Finance
after Sinn Féin's 1918 electoral victory and the
establishment of Dáil Éireann, the Irish
parliament (not yet recognized as sovereign).
His greatest success was as an originator of
modern guerrilla tactics, particularly in
intelligence, which he perfected during the
War of Independence (1919–21) against
Britain. Collins became a reluctant member of
the delegation to London, which resulted in
the Anglo-Irish Treaty of 6 December 1921.
This established the Irish Free State but
retained six Ulster counties under British rule.
Collins became Chairman of the Provisional
Government, an interim government
awaiting the official establishment of the Free
State in December 1922. The partition
resulted in a civil war between those in
Ireland who accepted the treaty and those
who did not, lasting until 1923. Collins was
Commander-in-Chief of the National
(pro-treaty) Army, and was killed during an
ambush at Béal na mBláth, Co. Cork.

Colombia

A Latin
American
country in
which relative
institutional
and economic
stability has
coexisted with
fundamental
social conflicts,
lawlessness,
and endemic civil war.

Before 1948 The Constitution of 1885 ended
bitter struggles between centralists and
federalists by establishing a central presidential
system, which the Conservatives sought to
strengthen whilst in power, (1886–1930).

Nevertheless, they were unable to stop the US-
assisted breakaway of Panama as an
independent country in 1904. During the
period of Conservative rule, foreign investment
was encouraged, and coffee became the main
export commodity. The Liberals (1930–46)
continued the policy of industrial expansion,
but also introduced social welfare legislation.
Their tolerant stance towards opposition
groups on the left threatened the hegemony of
the traditional Liberal and Conservative elites.
When the Conservatives came to power in 1946
they dissolved Congress and banned the left-
wing opposition parties while marginalizing
the Liberals.

La Violencia (1948-58) In an increasingly
volatile atmosphere, the murder of the
populist leader Jorge Eliécer Gaitán sparked
off the **bogotazo** of 9–10 April 1948, one of
the most destructive riots in Latin American
history. The bogotazo in turn triggered off
widespread violence in the countryside,
which became known as '**la violencia**'. One of
the most bitter civil wars in the twentieth
century, it cost the lives of over 200,000
people and displaced around 800,000. Despite
the institution of a military dictatorship under
Rojas Pinilla (1953–7), 'la violencia' only ended
when Conservatives and Liberals agreed on a
system of power-sharing in all levels of
government and administration, with the
President coming from each party in turn.

Civil war (since the 1960s) This hegemony
was increasingly challenged by the rise of new
opposition parties, and the formation of left-
wing guerrilla movements, notably the
Fuerzas Armadas Revolucionarias de
Colombia (Revolutionary Armed Forces of
Colombia, FARC) established in 1964, and the
Ejército de Liberación Nacional (National
Liberation Army, ELN) established in 1965.
Following the establishment of free
presidential elections in 1974, the political
system continued to be dominated by the
Conservative and Liberal elites. Since the
presidency of the Conservative B. Betancur
(1982–6), the state has successfully made
peace with most guerrilla movements by
integrating them into the system. This was a
necessary precondition for attacking the
power of the drug barons, who controlled
extensive areas of the country and whose
illegal exports of drugs yielded more capital
than the export of coffee. In 1991, a new
Constitution was passed which gave more
power to the state and legal institutions to
help them in the battle against the drug
cartels, a battle which had already cost the
lives of more than 80,000 people (1986–90).
On 19 June 1994, the Liberal Ernesto Samper
Pizano was elected President. While he was

successful in arresting further drug barons, there was increasing evidence of state corruption and public officials accepting bribes from the drug barons. In this atmosphere, Colombia became the country with the highest incidence of murder in the world, with homicide being the single greatest cause of death among male adults (on average more than 100 per day in 1995).

Samper was succeeded by Andreas Pastrana of the Social Conservative Party. Responding to US pressure, he sought to realize 'Plan Colombia' to fight the drug cartels by destroying coca and opium fields with pesticides from the air and through improved international cooperation. Despite these attempts, coca and opium production increased by over 20 per cent in 1999 alone, with production capacity increasing to 7.5 tonnes of heroin and 75 tonnes of metric opium. The high stakes in the drug war fuelled the civil war.

Contemporary politics (since 2002) At the 2002 presidential elections, voters ran out of patience with the established parties' efforts to deal with the civil war, and elected the hardline independent, Alvaro Uribe, with an absolute majority in the first round. Uribe was re-elected in 2006, and commanded a majority in both houses of parliament. He was successful in stabilizing the economy, signing a free trade agreement with the USA in 2006. His hardline policies were effective at convincing some rebel groups to give up their armed struggle, though the major left-wing rebel groups continued their armed resistance.

Colombo Plan

Based on an Australian initiative at a meeting of *Commonwealth ministers in Colombo in January 1950, the Plan was originally intended as a means by which richer Commonwealth countries, the UK, Canada, Australia, and New Zealand, could assist the poorer members in south-east Asia. However, the Australian Prime Minister, *Menzies, lobbied for US financial involvement by which he hoped to prevent *Communism from spreading to the recipient nations, very much akin to the *Marshall Plan. As a consequence, US financial support came to exceed that of any of the Commonwealth countries, and in turn non-Commonwealth countries such as South Korea were included in the list of recipient nations.

colonels' coup (Greece), see GREEK COLONELS

Comecon (Council for Mutual Economic Assistance)

A trading bloc which linked the planned economies of the Communist world. It was established on 25 January 1949, in response to the integrative power the *Marshall Plan exerted on Western economies. Its original members were Albania (until 1962), Bulgaria, Czechoslovakia, Hungary, Poland, Romania, and the Soviet Union. East Germany joined in 1950, Mongolia in 1962, Cuba in 1972, and Vietnam in 1978. Yugoslavia had associate status from 1965. It functioned as a bilateral trading system in which the USSR supplied primary goods, as well as oil and gas, in return for finished goods from the other member states. Increasingly, there was an emphasis on closer integration of the various economies, a measure which effectively increased the economic control of the USSR. It collapsed with the implosion of *Communism in Eastern Europe, and was formally dissolved on 28 June 1991.

Comintern

An acronym for the Communist International founded in March 1919 in Moscow, in an effort to coordinate the actions of the Communist Parties worldwide. Also known as the **Third International**, it followed the pattern established by the First (1864) and Second (1889) Internationals, which had sought to harmonize the working-class movements of Europe, increasingly in common opposition to *imperialism and *nationalism. With the *Bolsheviks and then the Soviet *Communist Party being by far the largest and most powerful Communist Party, Comintern was throughout dominated by the Soviet leadership. Especially during *Stalin's time, it was used as an international arm of the Soviet Communist Party. Because of its intrinsic aggressiveness, Stalin was forced to abolish it in 1943 as a concession to the *Allies during World War II. In 1947, it was revived as **Cominform** (Communist Bureau of Information), which was joined by the Communist Parties of Yugoslavia (until 1948), Bulgaria, Poland, Romania, Hungary, Czechoslovakia, France, and Italy. Again, it was used mainly as an instrument to secure Stalin's control, and was dissolved in 1956 by *Khrushchev as part of his campaign against *Stalinism.

Comité National Français, see FREE FRENCH

Committee for National Liberation, see CLN

Common Agricultural Policy (CAP)

The central policy area of the European Union (EU) from its inception as the EEC in 1957 (*European integration). From the beginning,

Table 4. **Commonwealth of Nations**

Date joined	Country	Date joined	Country
1931	Anguilla[†]	1964	Malta
1931	Australia	1964	Zambia
1931	Bermuda[†]	1965	British Indian Ocean Territory[†]
1931	British Antarctic Territory[†]	1965	Gambia
1931	British Virgin Islands[†]	1965	Singapore
1931	Canada	1966	Barbados
1931	Cayman Islands[†]	1966	Botswana
1931	Channel Islands[†]	1966	Guyana
1931	Cook Islands[†]	1966	Lesotho
1931	Falkland Islands and Dependencies[†]	1968	Mauritius
1931	Gibraltar[†]	1968	Nauru
1931	Hong Kong[†]	1968	Swaziland
1931	Isle of Man[†]	1970	Fiji (expelled 1978)
1931	Montserrat[†]	1970	Tonga
1931	New Zealand	1970	Western Samoa
1931	Niue[†]	1972	Bangladesh
1931	Norfolk Islands[†]	1973	Bahamas
1931	Pitcairn Islands[†]	1974	Grenada
1931	Ross Dependency[†]	1975	Papua New Guinea
1931	St Helena[†]	1976	Seychelles
1931	South Africa (left 1961)	1978	Dominica
1931	Tokelau[†]	1978	Solomon Islands
1931	Turks and Caicos Islands[†]	1978	Tuvalu
1931	United Kingdom	1979	Kiribati
1936	Australian Antarctic Territory[†]	1979	St Lucia
1947	India	1979	St Vincent and the Grenadines
1947	Pakistan (left 1972)	1980	Vanuatu
1948	Sri Lanka	1980	Zimbabwe (suspended from 2002)
1957	Ghana	1981	Antigua and Barbuda
1957	Malaysia	1982	Belize
1960	Nigeria	1982	Maldives
1961	Cyprus	1983	St Christopher and Nevis
1961	Sierra Leone	1984	Brunei
1961	Tanzania	1989	Pakistan (re-entry)
1962	Jamaica	1990	Namibia
1962	Trinidad and Tobago	1994	South Africa (re-entry)
1962	Uganda	1995	Cameroon
1963	Kenya	1995	Mozambique
1964	Malawi		

[†] indicates non-sovereign states.

member states agreed on a coordinated policy which guaranteed a stable standard of living for the relatively inefficient European agricultural sector through subsidies and the guarantee of quotas. The system led to vast overproduction and the creation of so-called butter mountains and wine lakes. Much of the overproduced grain was sold to less developed countries at dumping prices, thus destroying the livelihood of many local farmers. To overcome the problem, farmers were paid to set some of their land aside from cultivation. This, together with the occurrence of a series of bad harvests in the early 1990s, led to a virtual elimination of the EU's excess food supplies. Nevertheless, expenditure on the CAP still constituted 50.2 per cent of total EU expenditure in the 1995 budget. Reform of the CAP remained a deeply contentious and intractable issue in EU reform, and its resolution was not achieved in the

*Amsterdam and *Nice Treaties. EU enlargement in 2004 and 2007 added central and eastern European countries with large and inefficient agricultural sectors to the EU, making further reform even more difficult.

Commons, House of (UK), see
PARLIAMENT (UK)

Commonwealth of Nations

An international organization composed of independent states, all of which were part of the *British Empire. It was constituted by the Statute of *Westminster, in which the British Dominions (New Zealand, Australia, South Africa, Canada, Newfoundland, Eire) were recognized as 'autonomous communities', bound together by the British Crown. Since 1947, when India chose to remain within the Commonwealth, it has consisted of an increasing number of republics. The role of the British monarch, who is the head of only seventeen out of a total of 53 member states, is thus confined to that of head of the Commonwealth. Given that its member states have little in common apart from a historical tie to the UK (with the exception of Mozambique), it has rarely been able to influence world affairs, except perhaps for its leadership on the international imposition of sanctions upon South Africa (which only the UK opposed). Of the former members of the British Empire, Burma did not join upon gaining independence, Ireland left in 1949, South Africa in 1961 (but rejoined in 1994), Pakistan in 1972 (rejoined in 1989), and Fiji in 1987. In 2002, its unity was tested over whether to impose sanctions on *Mugabe's regime in Zimbabwe. Despite its relatively loose structure, the regular meeting of the heads of state, representing 30 per cent of the world's population, served as a unique global forum for industrialized and developing nations.

See TABLE 4.

((()) SEE WEB LINKS

• The official website of the Commonwealth Secretariat.

Communauté Française (1958–60), see
FRENCH COMMUNITY

Communism

A political ideology which aims for an ideal society characterized by common ownership and communal life. Despite earlier theories about such a society, Communism was first developed into a consistent and comprehensive ideology by Karl Marx (b. 1818, d. 1883) and Friedrich Engels (b. 1820, d. 1895).

They sought to describe how current industrial societies would inevitably overcome *capitalism through revolution to create a classless society, in which there would exist no private property, and where services were rendered 'from each according to his ability, to each according to his need'. Through followers such as *Lenin, *Stalin, *Mao, and *Tito, Communism became the dominant ideology of Eastern European countries (1945–89), the USSR, China, and various states in Africa and Latin America. While each of these leaders based their Communism on Marx's vision of revolution and a classless society, they developed individual ideological variants of Communism to adapt *Marxism to the society and economy within which they operated.

COMMUNIST PARTIES; MAOISM; MARXISM-LENINISM; STALINISM; TROTSKYISM; GRAMSCI

Communist Parties, India

A small Communist Party was formed clandestinely in India in the early 1920s, attracting support from anti-British intellectuals, and in the cities of Bombay and Calcutta. In contrast to the Communist movements in *Indochina and China, it failed to win mass support from the peasantry. It affiliated to the Indian National *Congress (INC), with which it had an ambiguous relationship, alternating between rejection and support. They united in their opposition to World War II, but in 1941, after Germany's invasion of the Soviet Union, the party became one of the few nationalist groups to support the war, in opposition to the INC. The Communist Party further triggered the INC's enmity in 1947, when it supported the establishment of an independent Muslim state (Pakistan). Marginalized by the INC, the party attempted to gain more power through a campaign of violence (1948–51), most notably the unsuccessful agrarian revolt in Telengana in Andhra Pradesh, which was suppressed by the Indian army.

The Indian Communist Party returned to legal politics in 1951. Between 1957 and 1959, it formed its first government at state level, in Kerala. Elsewhere, however, it still failed to attract mass support. In 1964 it split, into the pro-Russian Communist Party of India (CPI), and the pro-Chinese Communist Party of India (Marxist) (CPM). The latter was the more powerful and militant wing, being strong in both West *Bengal and Kerala. Since 1977 it has been the dominant partner of a coalition in West Bengal, while in Kerala an alliance, CPI and CPM, has alternated in power with the *Congress Party. Since 1999, the CPM has been returned as the largest splinter group, with 43 out of 545 seats in the Lok Sabha

(Lower House) in 2004. From 2004, it extended its influence as it supported the government of the *Congress Party. While the CPI and the CPM have thus been integrated into the political process, more extreme splinter groups, such as the *Naxalites, have been suppressed because of their continued terrorist campaigns.

Communist Party, China (CCP)

Early history (1921–49) Founded in Shanghai on 1 July 1921 by *Li Dazhao and *Chen Duxiu, it was a response partly to international developments, most notably the *Bolshevik *Russian Revolution of 1917, and partly to domestic events. Most important of these were the spread of Communist and left-wing ideas during the *May Fourth Movement (1919), and the current political anarchy in a country dominated by local *warlords. In 1922 it accepted the direction of *Comintern, and followed its orders to cooperate with the *Guomindang (KMT) of *Sun Yat-sen. Initially, the party was slow to take off, with around 1,000 members in 1925. Building on *trade union organization and *nationalism, the party had recruited around 50,000 members by 1927, to the concern of the KMT leader, *Chiang Kai-shek, who came to identify the Communists as his biggest rival. Chiang thus set out to destroy the CCP, by means of brutal massacres in Shanghai and elsewhere in April 1927.

On the run from the KMT in the cities, the CCP sought refuge in the countryside, and established its base in *Jianxi in 1931. Here, it grew into a mass party with around 300,000 members, while it gained vital experience in government and party organization. It also developed an effective army, hardened by five attacks from Chiang's *National Revolutionary Army in an effort to exterminate the Jianxi *Soviet. In 1934, around 100,000 Communist Red Army soldiers embarked upon the epic *Long March of 6,000 miles, during which *Mao Zedong finally asserted his leadership, aided by his lieutenant, *Zhou Enlai. Mao arrived with around 8,000 soldiers at *Yan'an. Whereas the time at Jianxi and the Long March transformed the party from a fledgling urban movement to a party with a mass peasant base, the time at Yan'an was not only one of regeneration and growth. It was also a pivotal time for the party's ideology and mythology. It was here that the roots of Mao's leadership cult developed, while a leadership elite formed which continued to lead the party into the 1990s. An idea of revolutionary dynamism and change, as well as strict party discipline, developed among this elite which was at the root of later purges, most notably the *Cultural Revolution. At the end of the *United Front in 1945, the party could claim a membership of around one million. This number had tripled by the end of the *Chinese Civil War, when the People's Republic of China was established.

In power (since 1949) From 1949, party primacy was established throughout the country. Despite a series of purges, most notably in the *Hundred Flowers campaign, and the *Great Leap Forward, party membership grew to 17 million in the 1960s. This made it more cumbersome and bureaucratic, while the number of committees and subcommittees also reduced Mao's scope for control of the party. As a result, millions of party members were purged in the Great Proletarian *Cultural Revolution, though even greater numbers were admitted to the party.

The CCP managed to overcome the shock of the death of Mao and Zhou Enlai with relative ease, mainly because power remained in the hands of the gerontocracy. While under *Hua Guofeng and then *Deng Xiaoping the leadership displayed a considerable sense of economic pragmatism, their commitment to stern party rule remained unchanged, as was displayed most brutally at the *Tiananmen Square Massacre of 1989. The liberalization of the economy, coupled with heavy-handed administration and low salaries of party officials, predisposed much of the party hierarchy to corruption. A number of scandals came to light, the worst of which involved the discovery in late 1999 of a smuggling ring in Xiamen involving goods worth $20 billion, which implicated hundreds of party and local government officials. The CCP had 66 million members by 2002.

Communist Party, Cuba (Partido Comunista Cubano, PCC)

Established in 1925 as the Popular Socialist Party (Partido Socialista Popular), its influence grew quickly, particularly within the emerging *trade unions. Following *Batistá's accession to power in 1933 it came to a subsequently embarrassing arrangement with the dictator whereby the PCC would support him, e.g. during the 1940 presidential elections, in return for being allowed to enter the realm of electoral politics. In 1965 the party assumed its current name after being taken over by *Castro's revolutionary movement (1958). Despite the establishment of a Communist dictatorship in 1959, compared to other Communist regimes the PCC remained unusually weak. This was partly the result of weak and undeveloped membership, with only around 50,000 members in 1965, 58 per cent of whom were members of the military. In addition, the PCC's ideology and structure remained highly focused on its leader, Castro, while its organization and political role were left undefined until its first party congress in 1975. From then, its importance grew significantly as a body of discussion and consultation, thereby diminishing the pressure on Castro as the economy began to stagnate from the late 1980s.

Communist Party, France (Parti Communiste Français, PCF)

Early history (up to 1947) Founded in December 1920, when at the Congress of Tours the more radical members left the *Socialist Party, a move which marked the division of French left-wing politics. Under the influence of the Soviet *Communist Party, in its early years it was increasingly *Stalinist. As a result of its own sectarianism, its membership dwindled until 1934, when it decided to cooperate with the *Socialists in response to the growth of *Fascism, especially in Germany. This paid off in the 1936 elections, when its representation in parliament increased from eleven to 72. Subsequently, it supported *Blum's *Popular Front government (although it did not participate in it directly), and tolerated subsequent governments until *World War II. Hitherto the most consistent opponents to Hitler, the PCF was thrown into confusion by the pacifist line dictated by Moscow following the *Hitler–Stalin Pact. However, after the German invasion of the USSR in 1941 it became one of the pillars of the *Résistance. In 1945, it received 26 per cent of the vote, and it participated in the governments of 1944–7.

Contemporary history (since 1947) In May 1947, a major shift in the French political system occurred as the party was isolated from government, in response to increasing anti-Communist sentiments arising from the *Cold War. This isolation lasted throughout the 1950s and most of the 1960s. Under the leadership of *Marchais, the party adopted more pragmatic policies and officially renounced the goal of a proletarian revolution, thereby turning towards *Eurocommunism. During the 1970s it was supported by around 20 per cent of the vote, and despite previous antagonisms the party was invited by the *Socialist Party to help form a coalition government in 1981. During the 1980s the Socialists encroached upon Communist support, which declined to around 10 per cent of the vote. This precipitated an identity crisis which was heightened by the collapse of *Communism in Eastern Europe in 1989.

In 1995 the veteran Marchais resigned as party leader, and was replaced by Robert Hue. For the 1997 elections, the party increased its share of the vote from 9.2 per cent to 9.9 per cent, but it gained 38 seats (up from 23) and was able to join a governmental coalition led by the *Socialist Party. Joining the government brought problems of its own, however, as distinctiveness of the PCF vis-à-vis the Socialist and Green parties then became less pronounced. In the 2002 elections its vote declined to unprecedented lows, as the party obtained 21 seats, with Hue not even salvaging his own seat in parliament.

Communist Party, Germany

The German Communist Party (Kommunistische Partei Deutschlands, KPD) was founded in 1919 by the *Spartakist group under *Luxemburg and *Liebknecht. It acquired a mass following after the merger with the independent Socialist Party in 1920. The KPD was able to increase its support from 3.5 million to almost six million votes in 1932, but immediately upon coming to power, *Hitler had the Communists harassed, prosecuted, imprisoned, and even killed.

After World War II, the KPD was quickly re-established with Soviet help. However, it soon became apparent that the KPD did not command a majority in Soviet-occupied Germany. In 1946, the Communist authorities forced a merger between the KPD and the *SPD in the Soviet Zone to form the **SED** (Sozialistische Einheitspartei Deutschlands, Socialist Unity Party). In response to these events, in West Germany the KPD soon became isolated and its support dwindled into insignificance. It was banned in 1956. In 1968 the (West) German Communist Party (Deutsche Kommunistische Partei, **DKP**) was founded, which, despite considerable East German financial support, failed to gain electoral success.

Meanwhile, in East Germany, the SED quickly brought other parties under state control so that it won every election until the fall of the *Berlin Wall in 1989. In response to East Germany's imminent first democratic elections in March 1990, the SED changed its name to the **PDS** (Partei des Demokratischen Sozialismus, Party of Democratic Socialism). It transformed itself into a radical socialist party with claims to express the grievances of the former East German population in a political system that was dominated by Germans from the West. Subsequently, the party was able to poll between 15 and 25 per cent in East German local and state elections.

The PDS entered a government coalition with the SPD from 1998, and an SPD/PDS coalition came to power in Berlin in 2001. The PDS failed to gain any significant electoral support in the western German states however, which put its ability to enter the national parliament, with over 5 per cent of the national vote, in doubt. To overcome its isolation as a regional party, the PDS engaged in a merger of independent socialists who had formed in opposition to *Schröder's social reforms. Under its new name 'The Left' (Die Linke), the party gained more than 8 per cent in the 2005 federal elections.

(⊕) SEE WEB LINKS

• The official website of The Left Party.

Communist Party, Indonesia

Founded as the Partai Komunis Indonesia (PKI) on 23 May 1920, it emerged from the Social Democratic Association of the Indies. A member of *Comintern since December 1920, its members were soon expelled from the *Sarekat Islam (1921), whereupon it conducted a series of campaigns in the countryside. It was almost eclipsed following severe Dutch repression of its uprisings in Banten and West Sumatra in November 1926 and January 1927 respectively. After Japanese occupation it became one of the main challengers to *Suharto's rule, when it grew to become one of the largest Communist Parties outside China and the Soviet Union. In the early 1960s, it claimed over three million members in Java alone. *Sukarno's implicit acceptance of the PKI, as well as the PKI's advocacy of radical land reform and expropriation, made the military under *Suharto extremely nervous. The 1965 *coup* attempt occurred with alleged PKI involvement, and it was banned in 1966, with tens of thousands of its members ruthlessly killed.

Communist Party, Italy (Partito Comunista Italiano, PCI)

Early history Founded on 21 January 1921, following a breakaway of the extreme left in protest against the reformism of the Italian *Socialist Party. Led by the Neapolitan engineer Amadeo Bordiga (b. 1899, d. 1970), the party's development was severely constrained by the rise of *Mussolini, so that by 1923 the PCI had only 9,000 members. The leadership passed to the more pragmatic *Gramsci, under whom membership rose to almost 25,000 members by 1925, which ensured that it was able to provide the main opposition to Mussolini by 1926. In that year its leadership was either exiled or imprisoned,

and, owing to the lack of a mass base in Italian society, it was unable to offer much resistance to Mussolini until the end of the Fascist era.

The PCI was quick to organize itself in a liberated Italy from 1944, and with its new emphasis on pragmatism and its commitment to operate within the existing political framework, it had attracted over 1.5 million members by 1945, and supported *De Gasperi in government. Under the influence of the *Cold War, the PCI was frozen out of government in 1947, and henceforth resumed its opposition to the political system and its allegiance to the USSR. Following the Soviet invasion of Hungary in 1956, however, the PCI finally abandoned its close links to Moscow. It promoted an independent, *Eurocommunist stance which aimed at an Italian road to *socialism, rather than Communist world revolution. The party's commitment to pragmatic politics was emphasized by **Enrico Berlinguer** (b. 1922, d. 1982), who established the PCI as an influential force in the mainstream of Italian politics, e.g. through its agreement in 1976 to tolerate *Andreotti's *Christian Democrat-led government. From 1979 the PCI became the leading opposition to the broad coalition governments that emerged.

Contemporary politics (since the 1990s) As a result of its position outside government circles throughout the 1980s and early 1990s, with the breakup of the old party system in 1992–3 it was relatively untainted by political scandals. The PCI's successor parties, the reformed **PDS** (**Partito Democratico della Sinistra**, Democratic Party of the Left, which in 1999 was named the **DS**) and the more orthodox **RC** (**Rifondazione Comunista**, New Communist Foundation), became the largest parties on the left with 115 and 40 seats respectively in 1994. Furthermore, as a result of electoral alliances designed against *Berlusconi's *Forza Italia, the PDS won the local and regional elections of 1993, becoming the leading party in the *Olive Tree coalition of Romano *Prodi, which won the 1996 parliamentary elections. Between 1996 and 2001, the Olive Tree coalition was weakened significantly by the RC's opposition to a number of reform measures in the Senate. It was the RC's opposition to the budget which caused Prodi's resignation in 1998. The DS and the RC lost heavily in the 2001 elections, but revived in the 2006 elections, when the Olive Tree coalition, which included the RC, gained a majority in parliament. The strength of the DS became apparent as its candidate, Giorgio Napolitano, became President in 2006, while its party leader, Massimo D'Alema, became foreign minister in Prodi's government.

Communist Party, Japan (Japan Communist Party, JCP)

Early history (until 1955) Japan's oldest political party, established 15 July 1922, emerged from a split in the *anarcho-syndicalist movement, and was formed from among those active in labour unionism, as well as socialists and radicals. At first, it resembled more an intellectual study group than an effective political force. Indeed, its early leaders, including Yamakawa Hitoshi (b. 1880, d. 1958), demonstrated a concern that theory should not become an obstacle to action. During the prewar period, the party's activities were undermined by state repression, and also because the organization was seldom free from internal bouts of factionalism, most often manifested as regular shifts in the party line. By 1933 a series of police actions had ensured that the party's leaders were either detained or in exile.

After the war, Japan's Communists emerged from their prison cells and returned from abroad with a high reputation for having been one of the few political groups that had opposed Japanese militarism. Although the Communists were initially closely associated with the democratization of Japan, the Occupation's (*SCAP) decision to curtail its reforms in 1947 did much to define the JCP as an opposition force. Further harm was caused to the party's standing by its decision to move from the peaceful and gradual revolutionary line proposed by Nosaka Sanzô to a disastrous policy of armed revolution from 1950 on prompting from Moscow. Once more, internal conflict and a state crackdown forced the organization underground, from which it did not emerge until 1955.

Contemporary history (since 1955) Under the leadership of Party Secretary Miyamoto Kenji in the late 1950s, the party began to re-emphasize parliamentary methods. During the period of high economic growth, an invigorated JCP experienced a rapid increase in its organizational strength. At the time it also developed a party line that came to resemble *Eurocommunism, ostensibly independent of both the USSR and China. In this period, the Communist Party constituted a dynamic political organization which posed a real challenge to the *Liberal Democratic Party. By 1970 its membership was the largest of any Japanese political party, with a total of 300,000 cardholders, while the party newspaper, *Akahata*, claimed a readership of two million. The successes of the 1970s, where the JCP performed well in local and national elections, contrasted with its performance during the 1980s and 1990s when its organization and election results

declined. The JCP's position has been weakened by internal squabbling as well as ideological shifts following the collapse of Communism in Eastern Europe in the 1980s. In the 2005 elections, the JCP obtained only nine out of 480 seats in the House of Representatives.

Communist Party, South Africa

Founded in 1921, it attempted to raise the class consciousness of the White proletariat before accepting Moscow's orders to work for the establishment of a multi-racial 'native' republic by 1931. Its membership remained small, however, and its significance derived from its cross-fertilization with the *ANC from the 1940s, providing many of its leaders and much of its ideology. Banned in 1950, it regrouped as the clandestine **South African Communist Party** and together with the ANC set up an armed wing, Umkhonto we Sizwe (Spear of the Nation) in 1961. It was effectively destroyed by the security police by 1963, and subsequently was run from exile, again in close cooperation with the ANC. The alliance held after both organizations were released from their ban in 1990. While not tying the ANC to an anti-capitalist programme, it has provided the ANC with important *trade-union support.

(((●))) **SEE WEB LINKS**

- The official home page of the South African Communist Party.

Communist Party, Soviet Union

Early history (before 1945) The party emerged from the *Bolsheviks as the Communist Party of Russia in 1921, but was renamed the Communist Party of the Soviet Union in 1925. It had branches in each state of the Union, apart from Russia itself. Throughout its existence, it operated on the principle of *Marxism-Leninism, as a party led by a small elite. Since it constituted the USSR's only official political party, the party leadership automatically formed the leadership of the state. With around 730,000 members just after the *Russian Civil War in 1921, initially its membership was relatively selective, as Lenin considered the Russian peasantry and working classes too 'uncultured' to provide many useful members. Membership figures fluctuated sharply. To eliminate fellow travellers, the party was periodically purged, the first major purge ridding the party of around 250,000 members (1921–2). Most of the party hierarchy (apart from *Stalin himself) was eliminated during the *Great Purge. As the only Communist Party in control of a state before 1945 (apart from Mongolia), the Soviet

Communist Party became an example for other Communist movements worldwide, which it sought to control through the establishment of the *Comintern. During World War II, the party trained Communist leaders of other countries, whom it encouraged to set up Communist Parties after the Soviet model in their home countries after 1944.

After Stalin (1953–85) The effective monopoly of the party's principal authority among Communists around the world (and inside the Soviet Union), was shattered with Stalin's death and *Khrushchev's anti-Stalinist campaigns, when the party's brutality and fallibility was openly admitted. This led to the formation of *Eurocommunism in Western Europe, and growing resistence to the predominance of the Soviet party among Eastern European Communist movements, most apparent during the *Hungarian Revolution, the *Prague Spring, and the *Solidarność protests in Poland. Meanwhile, under the leadership of *Brezhnev within the Soviet Union, increasing emphasis was put on mass recruitment, as party membership became the *sine qua non* for holding any responsible position in public, cultural, economic, or educational life.

Decline (from 1985) From the leadership of *Andropov, who, after *Chernenko's brief tenure, was succeeded in 1985 by *Gorbachev, party discipline was strengthened through anti-corruption drives. This led to the exchange of up to 80 per cent of the party hierarchy in some central Asian republics. Paradoxically, the reforms also led to the drastic decline of the importance of party membership, as expertise and know-how were valued more than party allegiance. The party was also badly shaken by *Gorbachev's political reforms which increased the role of the state relative to the party. Increasingly riven by controversies over the pace of change, it began to disintegrate in 1990, losing over four million members 1990–1.

The end of the party came with the *August coup of 1991, after which the party was outlawed in Russia and all other component states of the Soviet Union. Nevertheless, in each state a successor party was created, and became a major political force. In Russia, the Communist Party of the Russian Federation emerged as the largest party inside the *Duma in 1995 and 1999, though its representation declined considerably in 2003.

Communist Party, Spain (Partido Comunista Español, PCE)

Established in April 1920, mostly by members of the *Socialist Workers' Party (PSOE)

dissatisfied with their party's moderation in its acceptance of gradual reform instead of outright Communist revolution. It faced severe repression under *Primo de Rivera, but reorganized after 1931 and worked to uphold the new republic against *Fascism and threats from other right-wing parties. The PCE participated in the formation of the *Popular Front after the 1936 elections had given it a 3 per cent share of the national vote. Its fortunes changed in the face of adversity during the *Spanish Civil War, when Communist movements throughout Europe, and the Soviet Union in particular, became the main allies of the Republican government through arms and food supplies, as well as the *International Brigades. Under the defiant leadership of Dolores *Ibarruri Gómez, membership of the party quintupled to 250,000 within a year. After the war, it was banned during the *Franco regime, though it continued to be much more active against the dictatorship than the Socialists. After 1975, the PCE received almost 10 per cent of the vote, though from 1982, when it received 4 per cent of the vote, it was eclipsed by the PSOE under the alluring and pragmatic *González, who managed to unite the vote of the left behind him.

Comoros

An African state of islands in the Indian Ocean, which has struggled to establish a stable political balance between its constituent islands.

Contemporary history (up to 1997) The main islands of the Comoros are Grande Commore, Anjouan, and Moheli. A fourth island, *Mayotte, voted twice against independence and has remained a French territory. The other three islands were under French influence from the 1880s, and were declared a French colony in 1912, administered from Madagascar. They became a French Overseas Territory in 1946, and were granted administrative autonomy in 1961.

Independence was achieved on 6 July 1975, and Ahmed Abdallah Abderrahman was elected President. He was deposed, and replaced by Ali Soilih in 1976, who proclaimed a secular, socialist republic. Foreign mercenaries led by Robert Denard overthrew Ali Soilih in 1978, and reinstalled Ahmed Abdallah. In 1989 the latter was assassinated

Table 5. **Concentration camps 1933–1945**[a]

	Opened/liberated[b]	No. of Prisoners	No. of Dead
Forced Labour Camps			
Dachau	Mar. 1933/Apr. 1945	210,000	32,000
Sachsenhausen	Aug. 1936/Apr. 1945	200,000	45,000
Buchenwald	June 1937/Apr. 1945	240,000	43,000
Flossenbürg	May 1938/Apr. 1945	100,000	30,000
Mauthausen (Austria)	June 1938/May 1945	200,000	120,000
Ravensbrück	May 1939/Apr. 1945	130,000	50,000
Neuengamme	June 1940/May 1945	106,000	55,000
*Auschwitz (Poland)	June 1940/Jan. 1945	410,000	340,000
Gros-Rosen	Aug. 1940/Feb. 1945	125,000	40,000
Natzweiler (Alsace)	May 1941/Sept. 1944	50,000	25,000
Stutthof (Poland)	Sept. 1939/Jan. 1945	115,000	65,000
Bergen-Belsen	Apr. 1943/Apr. 1945	100,000	70,000
Mittelbau-Dora	Aug. 1943/Apr. 1945	60,000	20,000
Vaivara (Estonia)	Sept. 1943/Oct. 1944	20,000	10,000
Kraków-Plaszów (Poland)	Jan. 1944/Jan. 1945	50,000	50,000
Extermination Camps			
*Auschwitz-Birkenau (Poland)	Nov. 1941/Jan. 1945	3,000,000	1,500,000
Chelmno (Poland)	Dec. 1941/Jan. 1945	200,000	200,000
Sobibor (Poland)	May 1942/Nov. 1943	250,000	250,000
Lublin/Majdanek (Poland)	Apr. 1943/July 1944	500,000	260,000
Treblinka (Poland)	July 1942/Nov. 1943	750,000	750,000
Belzec (Poland)	Mar. 1943/June 1943	600,000	600,000
Transit Camps[c]			
Herzogenbosch (the Netherlands)	Jan. 1943/Sept. 1944	35,000	2,000
Kaunas (Lithuania)	Sept. 1943/July 1944	3,000	2,000
Theresienstadt (Czechoslovakia)	Nov. 1941/Apr. 1945	140,000	35,000

[a] The figures given here are only rough estimates, especially in the case of the extermination camps.
[b] Some of the camps were destroyed by the retreating Germans before they were reached by the Allies.
[c] Many of who survived the transit camps died after being transported to the extermination camps.

by Denard's mercenaries, who made Ali Soilih's half-brother, Mohamed Djohar, President. This caused the French to intervene and force Denard's group to leave the islands. Djohar readmitted political parties, but was widely accused of corruption in the 1990 elections. These had been held after being postponed four times, against a background of popular unrest. Djohar was deposed in a coup in 1995, and in March 1996, the veteran politician Mohammed Taki Abdoulkarim was elected President. The islands continued to be heavily reliant on French aid, which amounted to over 30 per cent of their Gross National Product in the 1990s.

Contemporary politics (since 1997) In 1997 the islands of Anjouan and Moheli seceded from Comoros, as they felt disadvantaged politically, while their inhabitants were discriminated against and even persecuted on the main island of Grande Comore. Following Abdoulkarim's death in office in 1998, the interim president was deposed in a coup in 1999, in which Assoumani Azali assumed the Presidency. In 2000, over 90 per cent of the population of Anjouan confirmed their desire for independence. In 2001 the different sides agreed to a fragile compromise which granted the breakaway islands internal autonomy within a new federal Constitution of the Comoros. The Presidency rotated between the leaders of the three islands, with the Anjouani Islamist Ahmed Abdallah Mohamed Sambi elected in 2006.

concentration camps

These large prison camps were first used in Cuba (1896), and in the Boer War, when around 160,000 Boers were interned, around 30,000 of whom died. However, it was in *Nazi Germany that they were systematically used, first to imprison opponents of the regime but increasingly also during the *Holocaust to imprison and murder those whom Nazi ideology considered 'undesirable'. The vast majority of victims in the concentration camps were Jews, but those imprisoned and murdered also included *Jehovah's Witnesses, priests, homosexuals, gypsies, and the mentally ill. Since *Hitler's ideology was founded and focused upon the hatred of Jews and *Bolsheviks (i.e. Communists), two groups which he considered to be synonymous, the German attack on the Soviet Union in 1941 heralded a new phase in the mass murder of Jews in all of German-occupied Europe. New camps were built, including six 'extermination camps', whose sole purpose was the killing of Jews. The German drive to kill all Jews was given its final sanction in the **Wannsee Conference** of 20 January 1942. Although the mass killing of Jews was already under way, a number of *SS leaders and high-ranking Nazi officials met in Berlin to approve the *Endlösung* (final solution) to what they considered to be the 'Jewish problem', in effect their mass murder. In the following years, the Nazis were ruthlessly effective at carrying out their plans. It is estimated that of a total of around seven million interned persons, only around 500,000 people survived.

AUSCHWITZ; WARSAW GHETTO; WARSAW RISING; see TABLE 5.

Confédération des Syndicats Nationaux (Confederation of National Trade Unions)

The major Canadian trade union representing French-speaking workers. Founded in 1921 as an overtly Catholic, anti-socialist trade union (Canadian Catholic Federation of Labour), it became increasingly radical in the 1960s, when it adopted its new name. In 2006, it represented over 300,000 members, supporting not just economic welfare, but also political sovereignty for *Quebec.

CANADIAN LABOUR CONGRESS (CLC)

(⊕) SEE WEB LINKS

- The official website of the Confédération des Syndicats Nationaux.

Conference on Security and Cooperation in Europe (CSCE)

An organization with thirty-four members that emerged on 1 August 1975 from the *Helsinki Conference in an attempt to carry on the dialogue between Eastern and Western Europe. The CSCE marked the high point of a thaw in the *Cold War during the 1970s. It was signed by the Soviet Union and its satellite states because it represented a de facto recognition of its sphere of influence. However, as an unintended consequence, *human rights citizens' movements such as *Charter '77 began to form in order to demand the realization of the commitments undertaken by their governments. The long-term effect of the CSCE, therefore, was the undermining of the legitimacy of the Communist states of Eastern Europe. After the Helsinki conference, until 1990 the CSCE was the only forum at which all the (*Communist and *capitalist) states of Europe (as well as the USA and Canada) met at regular intervals, notably in Belgrade (1977–8), Madrid (1980–3), Vienna (1986–9), and Helsinki (1992). It underwent a major reorganization in 1992, when it became an agency of the *UN. Reformed as the **Organization for Security and Co-operation in Europe (OSCE)** from 1995, it had 55 member states in 2007. Its members were committed to human rights through election monitoring, peace-keeping, and the promotion of international trade. A relatively loose forum, it served principally as a forum for exchange between members.

(⊕) SEE WEB LINKS

- The official website of the CSCE.

Confrontation (Konfrontasi) (1963–6)

A diplomatic and military confrontation between Indonesia and Malaysia, which was precipitated by the formation of Malaysia in 1963, which the Indonesian President *Sukarno opposed as a 'neocolonialist' action on the part of Malaya. Effectively aiming to unite the new Malaysian territories of *Sabah and *Sarawak with the rest of Borneo under Indonesian rule, he launched a guerrilla war in these areas in April 1963. It served as a catalyst for greater federal unity in Malaysia, whose troops were assisted by British, Australian, and New Zealand contingents. It also led to increased disaffection in the Indonesian army, which contributed to

Sukarno's downfall. His successor, *Suharto, ended all hostilities.

Congo

A country in western central Africa, which has struggled to achieve political stability after independence.

Contemporary history (up to 1979) Congo came under French control through the explorer Savorgnan de Brazza (b. 1852, d. 1905) in 1880. It acquired its present borders as the Congo Français (French Congo) in 1887. It became part of *French Equatorial Africa in 1910, administered from its own capital, Brazzaville. In 1946 it received greater autonomy and its first political rights. In 1956 all adults were enfranchised. They voted overwhelmingly to join the *French Community as an autonomous republic in 1958, and on 20 September 1960 Congo became fully independent.

Between 1963 and 1979, five new constitutions were passed. This political instability was nourished by the existence of an unusually well educated, articulate population for whom the weak economy had little employment, and which in its frustration could be easily mobilized against the current regime. Congo witnessed frequent coups or coup attempts. A coup in 1963 brought Massamba-Débat to power. He was deposed and replaced by Marien Ngouabi in 1968. Massamba-Débat then instigated the murder of Ngouabi in 1977, and was himself killed soon afterwards.

The Sassou-Nguesso era (since 1979) Denis *Sassou-Nguesso came to power after a coup in 1979. Economic policies became more pragmatic, as Western aid and technology was increasingly preferred to that from the USSR or China. Inefficient policies led to a virtual collapse of the economy in the late 1980s, however, and necessitated a drastic economic restructuring. In four years, 1985–9, state expenditure was reduced by two-thirds. The 1993 elections were won by Pascal Lissouba (b. 1931), though they were never recognized by Sassou-Nguesso and the opposition owing to accusations of electoral fraud. A civil war erupted between supporters of Sassou-Nguesso, who was supported by militias from neighbouring Zaïre and French oil interests, and the government. In 1997, Sassou-Nguesso's troops forced Lissouba to flee. Sassou-Nguesso established a transitional

government, and proceeded to strengthen his own political powers while attempting to reintegrate the erstwhile warring factions back into society. In 2001 a Constitution was proclaimed which strengthened the powers of the President.

Congo Crisis (1960–5)

A state of near-anarchy triggered by the sudden independence of the Democratic Republic of Congo from Belgium on 30 June 1960. In the months before independence, Belgian authority collapsed. Armed police attacked their senior (Belgian) officers, while there were many attacks against European property. As the police forces became ineffective, rivalries between many of the different tribes erupted again, and strikes were a frequent occurrence. Despite the instalment of *Kasavubu as President and *Lumumba as Prime Minister, central authority failed. Most threatening to the young state was the declaration of independence by the Katanga Province under its Governor, Moïse *Tshombe. He was supported by White mercenaries hired by the Belgian mining company, Union Minière du Haut-Katanga. The army leader *Mobutu led a *coup* in September, ousting Lumumba and handing him over to the forces in Katanga, where he was murdered. Under the direction of *Hammarskjöld, the *UN sent troops in 1962 to restore order, but these left in 1964. Tshombe won the elections of 1965, but was dismissed by Kasavubu in October 1965. One month later, Kasavubu was in turn deposed by Mobutu, whose army then managed to restore order and defeat the Katangese troops.

Congo, Democratic Republic of (Zaïre)

A central African state rich in mineral resources which has suffered from weak and corrupt central governments over the twentieth century.

Colonial history The territory was founded in 1885 as a personal possession of the Belgian King Leopold II as the Congo Free State, on the basis of treaties signed between his agents and over 400 local chiefs in the area. Leopold's insistence that the cost of the economic development of the area should be borne by the colony itself led to the ruthless

exploitation of the territory by European
firms, who were allowed to force the local
population to work for them. Responding to
the international public outcry when this
became known, the Belgian state annexed the
territory in 1908 and took over from the
personal government of the King to create the
Belgian Congo.

Harsh rule by the colonial government
persisted. It remained 'paternalist' even after
World War II: indigenous people were trained
for subservient positions, and the growth of
educated, articulate local elites was prevented.
Despite the ban on political organizations,
independence movements began to form in
1955, such as the Mouvement National
Congolais (Congolese National Movement)
under Patrice *Lumumba. To the surprise of
many Belgians, these gained unstoppable
momentum from the autonomy status
granted to the states of neighbouring *French
Equatorial Africa, particularly the Congo,
in 1958.

Civil war Overwhelmed by colonial and
international pressures, the Belgian
government agreed to independence on 30
June 1960, when the Democratic Republic of
Congo was proclaimed (named **Zaïre** from
1971 to 1997). Without a developed social or
national elite, with inexperienced leadership,
and with few developed ties between over 400
different peoples, the country immediately
sank into chaos. Ethnic tensions made the
democratic formation of a national party
impossible. The withdrawal of skilled labour,
which had been entirely foreign, caused
economic chaos, while the army, devoid of
indigenous high-ranking officers, was in
disarray. At the request of the government,
the *UN sent in troops to restore order.
Matters were complicated by the declaration
of independence on 11 July 1960 (*Congo
Crisis) by the prosperous region of Katanga,
whose economy provided 60 per cent of the
state's income.

The Mobutu era The civil war was eventually
overcome in 1965, when *Mobutu declared
himself President and transformed the
country into an authoritarian, single-party
state. His policy of fostering *nationalism
created a hostile climate for foreign
investment, which caused tremendous
problems in an economy dependent on
foreign technology for the exploitation of its
vast mineral resources. By 1995 Zaïre's
economy had still not progressed beyond its
levels of output in 1958, before independence.
Gross National Product declined by an annual
average of 9 per cent, 1988–93. By contrast,
there had developed a small, wealthy elite of
some 5,000 people who controlled the

political and military machine, led by
Mobutu.

Civil war (1996–2003) The increasingly
fragile dictator was unable to prevent the
spread of the civil war from 1996, as his
government troops were faced by a well-
organized opposition. Its leader, *Kabila, took
the capital in May 1997 and declared himself
President. Kabila struggled to establish control
over the entire country and end the civil war,
which was fuelled by numerous African
nations fighting for their own share in
Congo's mineral wealth. Troops from
Namibia, Zimbabwe and Angola sided with
the government, while forces from Rwanda,
Burundi and Uganda helped the rebel forces
control the country's eastern half. Meanwhile,
the rebel forces were themselves split into
different factions, with opposition against
Kabila providing the single common element.
What was described as 'Africa's First World
War' (M. Albright) claimed over three million
lives between 1998 and 2003.

Contemporary politics (2003–) Kabila was
assassinated in early 2001, and was succeeded
by his son, Laurent. Following a peace deal
brokered by *Mbeki, Laurent Kabila formed
an interim government in June 2003, which
included leaders from the rebel factions.
Fighting continued in the east, and in June
2003, an international European and African
force led by France and sanctioned by the UN
arrived in the north-eastern town of Bunia. In
2005, a new Constitution was accepted in a
referendum, and presidential elections were
held in 2006. Guaranteed by *EU troops, the
elections were relatively peaceful and fair,
with Kabila winning in the second round
against his political opponent, Jean-Pierre
Bemba. The end of the civil war brought some
annual growth of around 6 per cent, but the
majority of the country's population
continued to live in abject poverty.

Congress, Indian National

Early history (up to1967) The principal
Indian political party, founded in 1885 as an
annual meeting of educated Indians wanting a
greater share in the government of India. The
decision of Viceroy *Curzon to split *Bengal
in 1905 resulted in the precipitation of more
extremist policies under the leadership of Bal
Gangadhar Tilak. From 1920, under the
leadership of Mohandas *Gandhi, the
Congress developed from a party of the
educated middle classes to one with urban
and rural mass support. The party conducted
campaigns of civil disobedience throughout
the 1920s. In 1937 it won 70 per cent of the
total popular vote in the provincial elections,
held under the *Government of India Act

(1935). In 1939 it withdrew from provincial government in protest over the British declaration of war on India's behalf without prior consultation. Many of its leaders were imprisoned (1942–5), during the 'Quit India' campaign (see *Satyagraha), They were eventually released from prison in order to negotiate independence.

Under Jawaharlal *Nehru the party continued to dominate the politics of the republic as a broad political movement combining *nationalism, *Fabian *socialism, a commitment to make India economically self-reliant, and the desire to break down the caste system. The breadth of its support has been both the party's strength and its weakness, as Congress has been unusually reliant on strong and charismatic leadership which was acceptable to all sides. The death of Nehru marked the beginning of a gradual process of decline, which could not be reversed under the strong but controversial leadership of Nehru's daughter, Indira *Gandhi (1966–77, 1979).

Contemporary history (since 1967) In protest against Indira Gandhi's poor performance in the 1967 elections, and her headstrong leadership of the party in general, Congress split, into the Congress (O) (for 'Old'), and Congress (I) (for Indira). While Congress (O) withered away, the more dynamic and authoritarian Congress (I) continued as India's dominant political party, though it was weakened by further splits in the 1970s. In 1975, Indira Gandhi imposed a state of emergency after she had been convicted of electoral corruption in 1975. As a result, Congress (I) lost power to the *Janata Alliance Party in 1977.

Owing to divisions in the Janata Alliance Party, Congress (I) returned to power in 1980. After Indira Gandhi's assassination in October 1984 the splits between factions largely healed and the leadership of the Congress (I) Party passed to her son Rajiv *Gandhi, who became Prime Minister. Following his assassination in May 1991, the party leadership passed to P. V. *Narasimba Rao, whose government ruled on a very slender majority until its defeat in 1996. Given the party's lack of direction since the death of R. Gandhi, and because of internal disagreements, the party offered the leadership to Sonia *Gandhi, the Italian-born wife of the late Rajiv. In 1999, the party lost its third parliamentary elections in a row.

Contemporary politics (since 2004) In 2004, the party staged a spectacular comeback, with an election victory few had predicted. If Gandhi had been a burden to the party in 1999, in 2004 she was its unmitigated asset. With Manmohan *Singh as Prime Minister,

Congress continued most of the economic policies of the preceding *Bharatiya Janata Party government, with Gandhi firmly established as undisputed party leader.

(⊕) SEE WEB LINKS

- The official website of the Indian National Congress.

Congress of the United States

Rights and responsibilities The federal legislature of the USA, Congress is a bicameral body, provided for by Article 1 of the US constitution. The House of Representatives, whose members serve a two-year term, originates all revenue bills (i.e. federal taxes and duties), can initiate other bills, and must give majority approval to all legislation; it is presided over by a Speaker elected from the majority party. The Senate, a third of the members of which are elected every two years for six-year terms, must ratify all treaties and approve senior presidential appointments, and also give majority approval to all legislation. The Senate is presided over by the US Vice-President, who has a casting vote if the vote is evenly split. If, as in some nineteenth-century elections, a presidential election were to result in no candidate gaining a majority in the electoral college, the congressional delegations acting on a state-by-state basis would elect the President.

Congress alone can declare war, is responsible for raising and maintaining the armed services, for the regulation of commerce, patents, and copyrights, and for the establishment of post offices and federal courts. During the twentieth century much of the effective work of Congress has been done through powerful standing committees, whose proceedings since 1951 have been nationally televised. While the Presidency has moved between the *Democrat and *Republican parties, Congress has tended to be Democrat-controlled through most of the century.

Executive dominance Tension between the powerful presidential executive and determined congressional legislature has been a continuous feature of US government, whichever party had the majority. In 1973 the *War Powers Act reclaimed some congressional control over US foreign commitments, since it restricts to 60 days the time a President can unilaterally commit US troops overseas. Under George W. *Bush, the executive's role in wartime served as a rationale for greatly expanding the power of the presidency at the expense of Congress. Following *September 11, the prison camp at *Guantanamo Bay, secret phone tappings of US citizens, and covert investigations of banking transfers were all ordered by the executive without consultation with Congress.

Contemporary issues In recent years, a major issue for Congress elections has been that of campaign finance. Through a system of 'soft finance', special interest groups could endorse particular candidates without limits to campaign spending. To avoid the in-built advantage to incumbent candidates, and to reduce the leverage of interest groups on politicians, in 2002 Congress passed the McCain–Feingold Bill on Campaign Finance, which limited campaign and soft-money donations. At the same time, the Bill fuelled fears that this would limit the pool of candidates to those rich enough to run without the backing of special interests.

(((()))) SEE WEB LINKS

- The official website of the US Senate.
- The official website of the US House of Representatives.

Conrad von Hötzendorf, Baron Franz

(b. 11 Nov. 1852, d. 25 Aug. 1925). Chief of Staff of the Austro-Hungarian army 1906–17 Born in Penzing (Vienna), the professional soldier became a close friend of the Archduke Francis Ferdinand. Appointed in 1906, he did much to reorganize the imperial army and was responsible for its mobilization after the Archduke's death in *Sarajevo. A biography by Günther Kronenbitter (2003) showed that Hötzendorf was well aware that war constituted a massive gamble. He was motivated to push for war not least because he hoped this would make him a hero, and persuade the love of his life, a married woman, to divorce her husband for him. In 1915 he took the field and defeated the Russian army in Galicia. He was dismissed, however, by the new Emperor Charles I. In June 1917 he commanded the army and was defeated at Asiago in Italy. He then retired and wrote his memoirs.

Conservative Party, Canada

Early history (up to 1920) The Conservative Party emerged from the Liberal-Conservative government in Upper Canada of Sir John A. Macdonald (b. 1815, d. 1891) in 1854. After the creation of the Canadian Confederation in 1867 it was the principal party of government until 1896 (though it was briefly out of government, 1874–8). Its support was based on a coalition between the establishment of *Anglicans in Ontario and the Roman *Catholics in Quebec. The party originally advocated protective tariffs for Canadian goods, a close link with the *British Empire, and a strong federal government. Given the latter emphasis, the Conservatives neglected provincial government, which enabled their rivals, the *Liberal Party, to build up grass-roots support there. The Conservative Party was in disarray after Macdonald's death, but was rebuilt by *Borden, who defeated *Laurier by emphasizing Canadian patriotism linked to Britain. His majority was extremely fragile, and from 1917 he could govern only with the support of Liberal defectors who joined him in a Unionist government to realize the controversial conscription for overseas service. Though the issue divided both Liberals and Conservatives, it was the latter who were responsible for this and other wartime measures, earning the party the lasting hostility of the French Canadian electorate.

The twentieth century In the 1920s *Meighen tried to rebuild broad conservative support, a task complicated by the formation of the **Progressive Party** in 1920, which attracted significant support in the west, Ontario, and New Brunswick. With the Conservative Party unable to win much support in Quebec either, it only came third in the 1921 elections. Under *Bennett's leadership it won the 1930 elections, albeit under the extreme conditions of the Great *Depression, which *Mackenzie King had failed to tackle. Unable to find a coherent response to the economic crisis either, it lost the elections in 1935. It changed its name to the Progressive Conservative Party in 1942, following the defection of several Progressive members. This failed to translate into more support, since it became once again the principal proponent of conscription during World War II.

The party, which was increasingly dominated by Ontario interests, failed to win an election until *Diefenbaker's victory in 1957. His programme was based more on rhetoric and charisma than on substance, so that Conservative support quickly declined again, his government collapsing in 1963. Outpaced by *Trudeau, the Conservatives spent the following two decades in the political wilderness, despite a brief minority government under *Clark. The Conservatives only managed to return as a serious party of government under the leadership of *Mulroney, who revived Conservative support in his native Quebec and elsewhere through his personal charisma and his control of party organization. He remained party leader and Prime Minister until 1993, and was briefly succeeded by Kim *Campbell. After a disastrous election campaign the party was routed in the 1993 elections, when only two candidates won seats in the House of Commons.

Contemporary politics (since 2000) Under the leadership of the veteran Clark, the party obtained but twelve seats in 2000. As a result, party members saw little alternative to merging with the Canadian Alliance in 2003 to form the Conservative Party. With strongholds in the eastern and the western part of Canada, the party increased its parliamentary representation in the 2004 elections, and in 2006 it formed a minority government under the leadership of Stephen *Harper. Harper pursued moderate policies, benefiting from a divided Liberal Party.

(⊕) SEE WEB LINKS

• The official website of the Conservative Party of Canada.

Conservative Party, South Africa

Established in 1982 by **Andries Petrus Treurnicht** (b. 1921, d. 1993), who had been expelled from the *National Party (NP) for his negative stance to P. W. *Botha's moderate reform of *apartheid, earning him the nickname 'Dr No'. As former leader of the influential Transvaal section of the NP, Treurnicht had considerable standing in the *Afrikaner communities of the Transvaal and Orange Free State. In the 1987 elections, the Conservative Party (CP) became the biggest party of opposition with twenty-two parliamentary seats, increasing its representation to 39 seats in 1989, with just over 30 per cent of the votes cast. However, its fortunes underwent a dramatic decline after *de Klerk's decision to hold a referendum on the abolition of apartheid in 1992, which the White population approved with an overwhelming majority, against the opposition of the CP. It did not participate in the 1994 multi-racial elections out of protest.

Conservative Party, UK

The dominant political party in twentieth-century British politics. Despite the absence of an ideology about what exactly it wants to conserve, it has been able to gather support around the issues of patriotism and allegiance to the Crown, support for the Established (*Anglican) Church of England, and the maintenance of the constitutional integrity and union of the United Kingdom. The absence of set beliefs beyond these general tenets has imbued the party with a sense of flexibility and pragmatism which, since the leadership of Lord *Salisbury (1886–92, 1895–1902), has given it an ability constantly

to re-evaluate its ideas and its leadership, and to adapt them to changing social circumstances. Within the above parameters, therefore, it has successfully pursued whatever policies would best keep it in power.

Early history (up to 1933) A rare exception to the rule occurred under the unhappy leadership of *Balfour (1902–11), who was unable to contain party divisions under Joseph *Chamberlain's disastrous *tariff reform campaign. Furthermore, Balfour's inability to control the intransigence of the House of Lords led to a major constitutional reform in the 1911 *Parliament Act, which deprived the British establishment of a crucial bastion of political influence.

The party recovered under the leadership of Bonar *Law and Austen *Chamberlain, and under *Baldwin it dominated British politics in the interwar period in a way that was surpassed only by the Conservative governments from 1979 to 1997. This position was buttressed by the weakness of the progressive opposition, whose vote was divided between various *Liberal parties and the *Labour Party. It was also enabled by the party's traditionally strong organization. Through the establishment of the Primrose League and local Conservative Associations, many of which became major centres of socialization, the party was able to harness the support of a large proportion of newly enfranchised women, and up to half of the working-class vote. Ever mindful of the costs and consequences of another war, under Neville *Chamberlain it rigorously pursued *appeasement. When this failed, the party shifted to support *Churchill, who had been controversial in his own party before.

World War II (1933–45) The party led Britain through *World War II, in a wartime coalition which included Labour ministers such as *Attlee. Churchill's wartime popularity prevented the party from detecting a major ideological shift in the electorate, which demanded a new postwar order along the lines of the *Beveridge Report. The party was, therefore, taken aback by its disastrous loss in the 1945 elections, but immediately adapted to the new circumstances by accepting the public desire for *Keynesian demand management, the nationalization of some state-run services such as the railways, and *social welfare institutions such as the *National Health Service.

Political hegemony (1951–97) It won the 1951 elections with opportunistic proposals to end rationing and to build more public housing. Success in these social areas helped the party overcome the disaster of *Eden's precipitation of the *Suez Crisis of 1956. Thereafter, under *Macmillan, the party's pragmatism overcame its patriotism in agreeing to the rapid *decolonization of the *British Empire in Africa, most of which was complete by the time *Douglas-Home left office in 1964. That it was the Conservatives, the traditional party of the Empire, who undertook this measure greatly eased the domestic tensions that otherwise might have occurred (and did occur at this time, e.g. in France).

After a recuperative time in opposition (1964–70), the party regained power under *Heath, a singularly pro-European leader who took Britain into membership of the EEC (*European integration). Another concession of pragmatism over patriotism, this weakened further the country's connection with the *Commonwealth. After narrowly losing two elections in 1974, Heath was replaced as party leader by *Thatcher in 1975, who became Prime Minister in 1979.

Thatcher perfected the party's sense of pragmatism and response to electoral demands. However, she did so in a way that was wholly radical, and offended many of the traditional conservative tenets. Her market-orientated policies, which greatly increased the amount of poverty in the country, incurred the wrath and vocal opposition of the Church of England. She used the state institutions at her disposal (e.g. the civil service, *parliament) to minimize opposition and maximize her control without regard for precedence or custom. The grocer's daughter was a profoundly anti-establishment figure, despising privilege or birthright if it stood in her way.

When the party recognized that a fourth election victory would be unobtainable for her, it replaced her with the more conciliatory *Major, who narrowly won the 1992 election. That election marked an important generational change for the party, as a host of young, right-wing Conservatives entered parliament who had become politically active during the Thatcher years, and who generally espoused the values of *Thatcherism. This increased the party's divisions further. Even Thatcher had been at a loss to find a clear line between the opposing goals of pragmatism and patriotism with regard to further British participation in the European Union. This fundamental contradiction became more apparent under Major, whose greatest achievement was perhaps to have avoided an open party split on the issue, though at the cost of weakening his government permanently. Major's government was fatally wounded by Britain's exit from *ERM in 1992,

and the subsequent devaluation of the pound. The Conservatives had lost their greatest asset against Labour, the public perception of economic competence.

Political opposition Major suffered a resounding defeat at the hands of Tony *Blair in 1997, and Major was succeeded by William Hague (b.1961). Hague had been a compromise candidate, but his relative youthfulness turned out to be anything but an advantage, as he struggled to command loyalty from the party faithful. Hague was unable to find any popular policy alternatives to Blair, and his focus on opposition to the EU failed to broaden the party's appeal sufficiently to avoid another election defeat by a landslide in 2001. Unable yet again to agree to a successor, the party chose the obscure and uncharismatic Iain Duncan Smith, before he in turn was replaced by Michael Howard. Under the former Home Secretary, who was a seasoned politician with excellent debating skills, the party reduced the Labour majority at the 2005 elections. Nevertheless, Howard resigned and was replaced in 2006 by David *Cameron. Under Cameron, the party shifted to the centre ground, building a substantial lead over the Labour Party in the polls.
POLL TAX

⊕ SEE WEB LINKS

• The official website of the Conservative Party.

Constantinople Agreement (Mar.–Apr. 1915)

A number of secret assurances given by Britain and France. In their concern to prevent Russia from concluding a separate peace with Germany, they promised that Constantinople and the *Dardanelles would be incorporated into the Russian Empire. This concession had eluded Tsarist Russia despite its efforts for over a century. In 1918 the *Bolsheviks published the agreement, deeply embarrassing the *Allies. Knowledge of the agreement also strengthened *Atatürk's determination and moral right to regain Constantinople for the new Turkish Republic, even at the risk of war with the Allies.

Constitution for Europe, Treaty establishing a

A treaty which emerged in 2004 from the document adopted by the European *Constitutional Convention. It had been highly contentious among the EU's member states. Poland and Spain were very reluctant to agree to new simplified voting procedures within the *Council of Europe which would have reduced their influence. In the end, the *Intergovernmental Conference (IGC) agreed to a revised text which included a new preamble. The IGC also made it more difficult for the larger member states to outvote their smaller neighbours.

The Constitutional Treaty was rejected by referendums in France and the Netherlands in 2005. In 2007, the European Council agreed to replace it with a treaty which no longer contained references to state-like symbols, but which contained many of the original Treaty's reforms.

Constitutional Convention, European

A forum convened in March 2002, with a brief to devise a draft constitutional makeup of the EU. This was to recognize the dramatic growth of the EU since the 1980s, as *European integration both became much deeper (e.g. through the *euro) and wider (through the accession of twelve new member states in central and eastern Europe). The Convention had been asked to reflect on a reformed structure for Europe, but it soon focused on establishing a Constitutional Treaty. The Convention was directed by a nine-member Praesidium headed by a Chairman, *Giscard d'Estaing, and two Vice-Chairmen (Guiliano Amato and Jean-Luc Daehane). In addition to the Praesidium, the Convention was composed of three delegates per member state representing the executive and legislature. It also included three representatives of each of the thirteen applicant member states, though these were not allowed to vote. In addition, the Convention included sixteen members of the *European Parliament and two representatives from the *European Commission. The Convention agreed on a Draft Treaty establishing a Constitution for Europe (18 July 2003). It proposed the adoption of a Charter of Fundamental Rights, a reduction in the number of commissioners, and more powers for the European Parliament. The Draft Treaty was submitted to an Intergovernmental Conference, which approved the document with a number of amendments.

Constitutional Friends Association,

see SEIYÛKAI

containment

A key foundation of US policy during the *Cold War, describing the policy of preventing the extension of *Communism by means of regional military pacts (such as *NATO, *SEATO, *ANZUS, or *CENTO), clandestine operations (notably through the *CIA), nuclear deterrence, and the disbursement of overseas aid and investment.

Conté, Lansana (b. 1934), President of Guinea, 1984–

Born in Dubréka, he joined the army in 1955, and fought in Algeria before returning to Guinea upon independence in 1958. He joined the Guinean army and rose through its ranks to become commander in 1975. In 1984, he assumed power in a coup. Conté managed to stay in power through corruption and by suppressing opposition. He benefited from his country's mineral wealth, which allowed him to build up a system of extensive patronage.

Continuation War (1941–4)

A war precipitated by the Finnish attack on the Soviet Union in the wake of *Hitler's attack on the Soviet Union. The Finnish army used the current weakness of the *Red Army to advance and take possession of its territories lost after the *Winter War. In 1944, it was forced to withdraw before the advancing Red Army, and *Mannerheim quickly sued for peace. The borders from 1940 were restored, and the Petsamo region was ceded to the Soviet Union.

Contras, see NICARAGUA

Cook Islands

A group of fifteen fertile Polynesian islands discovered by Captain Cook in 1773. Owing to pressure from the New Zealand government they were declared a British protectorate in 1888, and were handed over to be annexed by New Zealand in 1901. During and after World War II, resistance against New Zealand rule mounted, within the islands and from the international community through the *UN. They were granted internal self-government in 1965. Until 1978 they were governed by Albert Henry, who was found guilty in 1979 of bribery, nepotism, corruption, and misuse of public funds. He was succeeded as leader of the New Cook Islands Party (CIP) by his cousin, Geoffrey Henry, who was confirmed in office in 1994. In 1999, however, the CIP suffered a heavy electoral defeat at the hands of Terepai Maoate of the Democratic Alliance Party, which formed a coalition with the New Alliance Party. The Democratic Alliance Party won the 2004 elections, but split thereafter, with the Demo Tumu Party emerging under Jim Marurai, who became Premier.

Cook, Sir Joseph (b. 7 Dec. 1860, d. 30 July 1947). Prime Minister of Australia, 1913–14

Born in Staffordshire (England), he became a coalminer in 1873, and emigrated to New South Wales in 1887. He was elected to the state Legislative Assembly in 1891, where he became the leader of the parliamentary

*Labor Party in 1893. Against Labor's wishes he accepted *Reid's offer to become Postmaster-General (1894), and became increasingly alienated from his Labor roots. A representative in federal parliament from 1901, he led the Free Traders from 1908, and in the 1913 elections led the Liberals to victory. His slender majority in the House of Representatives, and the hostility of the Senate, precluded the enactment of any major legislation. He became deputy leader of the *Nationalist Party in 1917, and served as Australian High Commissioner in London (1921–7).

Coolidge, John Calvin (b. 4 July 1872, d. 5 Jan. 1933). 30th US President 1923–9

Early career He was born to a middle-class family in Plymouth, Vermont, studied at Amherst, Massachusetts, graduated with a BA in 1895, and became a Massachusetts barrister in 1897. Active in municipal politics in Northampton, he became Mayor in 1909. Coolidge was elected as a *Republican to the State House in 1906, to the State Senate in 1911, and to the Lieutenant-Governorship in 1915. He became Governor after the election of 1915. Tough action in response to a police strike in Boston in 1919 made him a national figure, and he won election as Vice-President on his law-and-order credentials in 1920. Following the death of President *Harding in 1923, he became President.

In office His integrity in office and firm action against corrupt officers of the Harding administration, combined with national prosperity, caused him to be re-elected in 1924. The national debt fell and taxes were cut whilst relations were re-established with Mexico and improved with Latin America. However, Coolidge's laissez-faire attitude to governance—his hands-off approach earned him the nickname 'Silent Cal'—frustrated many who wanted a more activist Presidency. In particular, this approach was conducive to the speculation and amassing of debt that marked the economic boom of the 1920s. Although he was believed to be a certain candidate for President in 1928, Coolidge refused to run for the nomination and left office—and public life—in early 1929. On a personal level he was deeply affected by the death of his youngest son, Calvin Jr, in 1924, an event which caused recurrent attacks of depression.

Cooperative Commonwealth Federation, Canada (CCF)

A political party backed by farming interests, intellectuals concerned with social welfare, and some representatives of industrial labour, founded in Calgary in 1932 as a response to the Great *Depression. It advocated the introduction of a *welfare state and the nationalization of key industries. The party enhanced its appeal during World War II, when it benefited from hopes for a better postwar society. In 1943 it came second in the Ontario provincial elections, and in 1944 the CCF won the provincial elections in Saskatchewan, where it governed until 1964. During that time a pioneering universal health service (*Medicare) was established, as well as an intercity bus company and public petrol distribution. Nationally, it gained 15.6 per cent of the popular vote in the 1945 general elections, but because of the *Cold War, support for its socialist policies declined. The CCF merged with the *Canadian Labour Congress in 1961 to form the New Democratic Party. Its most important legacy to Canadian history lies in the realm of welfare. Its growing support during World War II galvanized the ever-pragmatic *Mackenzie King to expand the welfare state.

SOCIAL CREDIT PARTY; UNION NATIONALE

cooperative organizations

Early history Businesses which are owned and run jointly by their employees and customers. Their purpose is to ensure fair working and trading conditions rather than the maximization of profit, in marked contrast to capitalist enterprise. They tend to be particularly appealing in areas undergoing rapid social and economic change where low wages, job insecurity, and low consumer protection are the norm. They developed in England from the late eighteenth and early nineteenth centuries as (a) consumer cooperatives to provide cheap food, (b) producers' cooperatives to provide work in cases of strikes, and (c) utopian cooperatives where alternatives to *capitalism were tried out, most famously Robert Owen's Rochdale Pioneers of 1844.

In 1864 a federation of cooperative societies, the Co-operative Wholesale Society (CWS), was formed in Britain, which developed as a manufacturer and wholesale trader, opening factories and developing its own farms. The cooperative movement has also exerted some political and economic influence through the *Labour Party and the *trade union movement. In the USA the first cooperatives were mainly agrarian, established in the early nineteenth century to open up the prairies. In Canada, they became influential in rural areas from the 1860s, when over 1,200 cooperatives were set up. The Co-operative Union of Canada was formed in 1909.

Contemporary history During the twentieth century the breakup of private estates in both Communist and capitalist societies through land reforms and split inheritance has resulted in the extensive development of farming cooperatives which provide the individual farmer with the expensive technology and know-how to run his/her small plot of land efficiently and to gain competitive prices for his/her products. In addition, as a result of rapid urbanization during the nineteenth and twentieth centuries, housing cooperatives developed which remain an important provider of affordable housing in most industrially developed countries. Finally, credit cooperatives and credit unions have developed in many countries to provide small investors, other types of cooperatives, and trade unions with their financial wherewithal. These have developed into large institutions in some European countries, while in the USA there existed around 8,600 credit unions by 2007.

Copenhagen Criteria (EU)

Criteria established by the EU at the European Council meeting in Copenhagen in 1993. Since the collapse of the Soviet Union during 1989–91, eastern European states began pushing to be admitted into the EU. At Copenhagen, EU member states agreed on the criteria which any state that wished to join the EU, whether from eastern Europe or not, should fulfil. These consisted of: (1) stable political institutions and the guarantee of human rights and the rule of law; (2) economic stability and the existence of a robust market that could cope with economic integration with the EU; and (3) an acceptance of the Community Acquis, the body of EU law that has developed since the beginning of *European integration in the 1950s. In addition to these criteria, the EU stipulated that its own institutions needed to be prepared to accept new members. The Copenhagen Criteria appeared to provide objective benchmarks for new member states and thus provided great incentives for potential candidate states to engage in political, legal and economic reform. At the same time, however, the decision on whether candidate states for membership fulfilled the Copenhagen Criteria was a political one, so that the Criteria were far from fully objective in their application.

Coral Sea, Battle of the (4–8 May 1942)

The first major naval battle between Japan and the USA in *World War II. It involved a US force under Admiral Fletcher, which consisted of two aircraft carriers and seven cruisers, against three Japanese carriers and six cruisers. The battle, which was largely fought by aircraft, originated in the Japanese preparations to land at Australian New Guinea. On the Japanese side, all three carriers were immobilized (one was sunk), together with three heavy cruisers, one light cruiser, and two destroyers. The US lost the carrier *Lexington* and one destroyer. This US victory averted the danger of a Japanese invasion of the USA, and prepared the ground for the decisive US victory at *Midway Island.

Corfu Incident (Aug. 1923)

On 27 August an Italian general and four members of his staff, on an international mission to determine the Greek–Albanian frontier, were found murdered in Corfu. To increase his reputation of military strength, *Mussolini used this as a pretext to capture this strategically placed island at the mouth of the Adriatic in 'retaliation' on 31 August. Greece appealed to the *League of Nations, which referred the dispute to its Council of Ambassadors. Greece was ordered to pay 50 million lire in 'compensation', and under pressure from Britain and France, Italy finally withdrew its forces on 29 September.

Corfu Pact (20 July 1917)

An agreement between the Serbian Prime Minister, Nicola Pasic (b. 1846, d. 1926), and the leader of South Slav refugees, Ante Trumbic (b. 1868, d. 1938). Concluded at the seat of the Serbian government-in-exile on the island of Corfu, at a time when Serbia was overrun by the troops of the *Central Powers, it provided for a unified state of Serbs, Croats, Slovenians, and Montenegrins after the war. It became the basis of the Kingdom of Serbs, Croats, and Slovenes set up after 1918, which became Yugoslavia in 1929.

Corporatism

An ideology which sees a political community as composed of various economic and functional groups, syndicates, or corporations, which then represent the interests of their members. It was developed in *Fascist Italy where all officials within syndicates and corporations were members of the party. In this way, the state greatly increased its control over economy and society. After 1945, corporatism has tended to involve the direct participation of economic interest groups in policy-making in areas 'relevant' to the concerns of the various interests.

Cosgrave, Liam (b. 30 Apr. 1920). Prime Minister (Taoiseach) of the Irish Republic 1973–7

Born in Dublin, the son of William T. *Cosgrave, he was educated at King's Inns, Dublin. He then served in the army, and was elected to Dáil Éireann (the Irish parliament) in 1943 as a *Fine Gael member. He was chairman of the committee of the Ministers of the Council of Europe in 1955, and led the first Irish delegation to the *UN General Assembly in 1956. He became leader of Fine Gael in 1965, and in 1973 became Taoiseach and leader of the National Coalition Government. The deteriorating situation in *Northern Ireland occupied much of his administration's attention, and an attempt at compromise (the Sunningdale Agreement of December 1973) met with little success. After his election defeat of 1977, he was succeeded as party leader by *FitzGerald.

Cosgrave, William Thomas (b. 6 June 1880, d. 16 Nov. 1965). President of the Executive Council of the Irish Free State 1922–32

Born in Dublin, he attended the first *Sinn Féin convention in 1905. He fought in Dublin in the *Easter Rising of 1916, was captured, and sentenced to death (commuted to life imprisonment), but was released in the general amnesty in December. He was elected a *Sinn Féin member for Carlow-Kilkenny to the first Dáil Éireann (the Irish parliament, not yet recognized as sovereign) in 1919. He supported the Anglo-Irish Treaty of 1921 which led to the autonomy of southern Ireland, as well as the creation of a separate *Northern Ireland. He became President of the second Dáil in 1922, and succeeded *Collins as Chairman of the Provisional Government. In December 1922, he became effectively Prime Minister, as the first President of the Executive Council of the Irish Free State. He founded Cummann na nGaedheal (a pro-treaty political party), which he led until 1933. In that year, he merged his party with two others to form *Fine Gael, and Cosgrave became its president in 1935. He remained its leader (and therefore leader of the opposition to *Fianna Fáil governments) until 1944.

Costa Rica

The second smallest Central American state, it is often referred to as the 'Switzerland of Central America' owing to its geography, its political stability, and the absence of a standing army.

The Second Constitution (1871–1949) The working of the 1871 Constitution was considerably helped by the existence of a relatively homogeneous and educated farming population. The political order was challenged in 1917 by the establishment of a military dictatorship by the Minister of War, Federico Tinoco Granados, but US hostility and domestic opposition forced a return to democracy in 1918. It was the only Central American country to maintain a democratic government throughout World War II, though a serious challenge to its system appeared when the government tried to annul the 1948 elections. After a popular uprising led by *Figueres, stability was restored and a Third Constitution was passed in 1949.

The Third Constitution (since 1949) Based on its predecessor, the new Constitution abolished the army, introduced universal suffrage, and strengthened the presidential democracy. Since then, the dominant political force has been the centre-left social democratic Partido de Liberación Nacional (Party of National Liberation, PLN), which attempted to reduce US influence without provoking the US government or scaring US investors. Thus it allowed, for example, the stationing of US-backed Contras for the Civil War in *Nicaragua in the 1980s while promoting its own solutions for the region's stability. This culminated in the Arias Peace Plan, for which its author, President *Arias, received the *Nobel Peace Prize. From 1983, the centre-right Partido Unidad Social Cristiana (United Christian Social Party, PUSC) emerged, which subsequently became the second major national party. It obtained power under President Rafael Calderón Fournier (1990–4) and Miguel Ángel Rodríguez Echeverría (1998–2002). Under President J. M. Figueres (PLN, 1994–98) and Echeverría, the government was struggling to fight the drugs trade, which used the country for transit. In 2002 Abel Pacheco of the PUSC was elected to the Presidency.

Contemporary politics (since 2006) Shaken by a series of corruption scandals as well as strong labour unrest in the country, the PUSC lost dramatically in the 2006 elections, with the centre-left Partido Acción Ciuadadana (PAC) becoming the second party in parliament, behind the PLN. The presidential elections that year were narrowly won by Oscar *Arias Sánchez, who promised a series of market reforms to revive an economy hit by high foreign debts and low world prices for its major exports, bananas and coffee.

Costello, John Aloysius (b. 20 June 1891, d. 5 Jan. 1976). Prime Minister (Taoiseach) of the Irish Republic 1948–51, 1954–57

Born in Dublin and educated at University College Dublin, he was called to the Bar in 1914, and held various government offices serving as Attorney-General of the Irish Free State, 1926–32. He entered Dáil Éireann (the Irish parliament) in 1933. When *Fianna Fáil failed to secure a majority, Costello (although not leader of his own party, *Fine Gael) was asked to form a compromise coalition government, commencing 18 April 1948. This Inter-Party Government (1948–51) saw the formal establishment of the Republic of Ireland on 18 April (Easter Monday) 1949. In May 1951 the government fell over the lengthy debate on the 'Mother and Child' healthcare scheme (which was strongly opposed by the *Catholic Church), and other controversies. Costello formed a second coalition government in May 1954. This second term tried to react to a renewal of *IRA activity in Northern Ireland, but failed. A motion of no confidence was moved, and the government resigned in January 1957.

Côte d'Ivoire, see IVORY COAST

Cotounu Agreement

A successor to the *Lomé Agreements, signed on 23 June 2000 in Cotounu, Benin, between the European Union and 73 states in Asia, the Caribbean, and the Pacific (ACP). It aims at the gradual complete liberalization of trade between the signatory states by 2020, while the poorest ACP states are given complete tariff-free entry to the EU market in 2005. Cotounu was more far-reaching than its predecessors in the economic sphere, but it also inaugurated a new era of political cooperation. For the first time, the European Union used its agreement with the ACP states to encourage and monitor *human rights, political stabilization, and the rule of law.

GLOBALIZATION; HIPC INITIATIVE

Coty, René (b. 20 Mar. 1882, d. 22 Nov. 1962). Last President of the Fourth French Republic 1953–9

A lawyer, he was a *Radical member of the Chamber of Deputies from 1923 until he became a Senator in 1935. He was a Deputy again (1945–8) and, despite his earlier support of *Pétain, he served as Minister for Reconstruction (1947–8). Although he held strong anti-Communist and colonialist views, during his period of office as President, *Indochina gained independence. In response to the *Algerian War of Independence he facilitated a return to power of de *Gaulle as leader in his stead.

Coudenhove-Kalergi, Count Richard Nicolas von (b. 16 Nov. 1894, d. 27 July 1972). Austrian diplomat

Born in Tokyo, he was educated in Vienna, which was long his home. In his book *Paneuropa* (1923) he urged the formation of 'a European organization to fill the void left by European anarchy'. In 1924 he funded a secretariat in Vienna which organized a Pan-European Congress in October 1926. In a second congress in Berlin (1930), he urged the formation of a United States of Europe to overcome the political instability of interwar Europe. In 1938, he emigrated to Switzerland and then the USA. In 1946 he helped organize the Congress of The Hague which led to the formation of the *Council of Europe. A consistent advocate of closer *European integration, he was honorary Secretary of the European Movement, 1952–65.

Council of Europe

An association of European states independent of the European Union. It was established on 5 May 1949 in London, and committed to the principles of *human rights, individual freedom, and the rule of law, as well as safeguarding the political and cultural heritage of Europe. With a membership of forty-one European states by 2002, it is served by a Committee of Ministers, a Parliamentary Assembly at Strasbourg, the European Court of Human Rights (ECHR), and the European Commission of Human Rights. Although without legislative powers, agreements between its members have covered the suppression of terrorism, the legal status of migrant workers, and the protection of personal data. The judgments of the ECHR in Strasbourg have been non-binding on its member states, but they have been incorporated into national law by many member states. Through the ECHR, the Council has therefore been surprisingly effective at realizing its human rights agenda across most of the European continent.

EUROPEAN INTEGRATION

(((🌐))) SEE WEB LINKS

• The official web page of the Council of Europe.
• The home page of the European Court of Human Rights.

Country Party, see NATIONAL PARTY OF AUSTRALIA

Coupon Election (UK)

The British general election of December 1918. Its name comes from the 'coupon', a letter of commendation from party whips, which was issued to Liberal and Conservative candidates who supported the continuation of the wartime coalition under *Lloyd George. The election had been called after the armistice of 11 November 1918, so that Lloyd George could go to the *Paris Peace Conference with the authority of a new *parliament. Following an agreement between the *Conservative Party and Lloyd George, around 150 Liberals were granted the Coupon. Basking in the endorsement of the man who had won the war, the Conservatives gained 335 seats, and the Coalition ('Coupon') Liberals 133. The main *Liberal Party, led by *Asquith, won only twenty-eight seats, whilst *Labour won sixty-three. This represented a triumph for the Conservative Party, and made Lloyd George dependent on its support. The Liberals never recovered from the blow, and Labour had become the official opposition in parliament for the first time.

Craig, Sir James, Viscount Craigavon

(b. 8 Jan. 1871, d. 24 Nov. 1940). Prime Minister of Northern Ireland 1921–40

Born in Tyrella (Co. Down), he was educated at Merchiston, Edinburgh. He was Unionist MP for Down East from 1906 until 1918, when he campaigned against Home Rule (autonomy) for Ireland. He became the first Prime Minister of *Northern Ireland in 1921, and initially used the rhetoric of conciliation, seeking to reach an agreement with nationalist leaders. By the 1930s, he had come to see the *Stormont as a bastion to defend Protestant privilege in Northern Ireland, and those years saw the consolidation of sectarian rule in the province. On his death in 1940, he was succeeded by J. M. Andrews, who was only in office until 1943, when he was replaced by Basil *Brooke.

Craxi, Bettino (b. 24 Feb. 1934, d. 19 Jan

2000). Prime Minister of Italy 1983–7

Born in Milan, he joined the *Socialist Party at the age of 18 and became so involved in politics that he never finished his law degree at university. He joined the party's Central Committee at the age of 22, and became provincial party secretary in 1965. A member of the Chamber of Deputies since 1968, he became Deputy Party Secretary in 1969 and Party Secretary in 1976, when a deeply divided party entered a period of crisis. Under his leadership, the Socialist Party gave up its inactive position between the *Communists and the *Christian Democrats in favour of participating in government with the latter at the expense of the former. His high media profile and popularity contributed to his becoming Italy's first Socialist Prime Minister, though during his tenure of office he remained above all a power-broker interested in his own and his party's fortune rather than political or fiscal reform. Amid corruption allegations (*Tangentopoli) he escaped to Tunisia, and on 29 July 1994 he was sentenced *in absentia* to eight and a half years' imprisonment for having accepted 7 billion lire ($4.4 million) from the corrupt Milanese Banco Ambrosiano for the Socialist Party coffers.

Crerar, Henry Duncan Graham (b. 28

Apr. 1888, d. 1 Apr. 1965). Canadian general

Born at Hamilton (Ontario), he went to the Royal Military College of Canada, was commissioned into the artillery in 1910, and served in World War I. Appointed chief of the General Staff in 1940, he became commander of the 1st Canadian Corps in 1941. After fighting in Italy, he landed with the 1st Canadian Army in Normandy on *D-Day, and commanded the army throughout its advance towards Germany in the *Normandy and *North-West Europe campaigns. More successful as a chief of staff than as a commander, he retired in 1946, having been made a full general in 1944.

Cresson, Edith (b. 27 Jan. 1934). French

Prime Minister 1991–2

The daughter of a finance inspector and wife of a high-ranking executive, she was an organizer of the youth in the *Socialist Party (1974–9) and a member of the Agricultural Commission of the European Parliament (1979–81), before joining all Socialist Cabinets of the 1980s, with responsibility for agriculture (1981–3), trade (1983–4), industry (1984–6), and European affairs (1988–90). Her appointment as the first woman Prime Minister of France was applauded as a radical step, but she soon became extremly unpopular, partly because of her stringent economic policies, and partly for her tactless outbursts, e.g. against the English (as singularly prone to homosexuality) and the Japanese (describing them as 'ants'). In charge of the portfolio for Science, Research and Development in the European Union from 1995, she was one of the members of the *European Commission accused of corruption and nepotism. She appointed personal friends to public positions, such as hiring her dentist as a co-ordinator of EU *AIDS research programmes. This became a public scandal, and ultimately led to the resignation of the entire Commission in 1999.

Crete

A strategically placed Greek island in the Mediterranean, almost equidistant from

Europe, Africa, and Asia Minor. It was part of the *Ottoman Empire from the late seventeenth century, and became a part of Greece under the Treaty of London only in 1913, following a series of repeated uprisings. Owing to its strategic importance as a stepping-stone on the way to North Africa, in 1941 it was attacked by German troops. Despite strong resistance by Greek and *Commonwealth forces the Germans successfully made the first airborne invasion in military history. A bloody twelve-day battle followed, during which some 18,000 *Allied troops were captured.

Crimea

A peninsula in the Black Sea off the Ukrainian coast. An autonomous republic of the Soviet Union, it was occupied by the Germans in 1941–4. Thereafter, most of its original population, the Tartars, were deported for their collaboration to central Asia; they were officially rehabilitated only in 1967, and not allowed to return until 1989. It became part of the Ukrainian Soviet Republic in 1954. Throughout the Soviet period the Crimea enjoyed formidable Russian investment as the prime holiday resort of the Russian and Soviet apparatchiks. By 1989 its population was over 60 per cent Russian, and resisted independence from Russia as part of the Ukraine. It was granted extensive autonomy in 1991, with a separate parliament and President. Subsequently, its domestic affairs were characterized by extensive corruption, with the area's Ukrainian and Tartar minorities bitterly complaining against discrimination throughout the 1990s. This was but one complicating factor in the ongoing conflict with the Ukraine about the Russian majority's attempts to gain even greater sovereignty, leading the Ukraine periodically to suspend the rights of the Crimean parliament.

Cripps, Sir (Richard) Stafford (b. 24 Apr. 1889, d. 21 Apr. 1952). British Chancellor of the Exchequer 1947–50

Born in London, he was educated at Winchester and studied at University College, London. He was called to the Bar in 1911, and during World War I he served in the *Red Cross in France, and then as a scientist in an explosives factory. After suffering from ill health, he resumed his career as a barrister in 1919.

Cripps joined the *Labour Party in 1929, and was made Solicitor-General in 1930, becoming an MP for East Bristol. He responded to the economic crisis of 1931, and the subsequent formation of the *National Government, by moving to the left of the Labour Party. His advocacy of a *Popular Front saw him expelled from the party in 1939. *Churchill made him ambassador to Moscow in 1940, and when Russia was attacked by Germany in 1941, Cripps's profile rose as the government sought to promote its Russian ally. He returned to the UK to be Lord Privy Seal in the War Cabinet in 1942, and was soon responsible for securing firm Indian support for the war against Japan. During 1942–5, he was Minister of Aircraft Production, and in 1945, he was readmitted to the Labour Party.

Cripps served as *Attlee's President of the Board of Trade (1945–7), and as Minister for Economic Affairs (1947), before becoming Chancellor of the Exchequer (1947–50). In the latter post, he was forced to devalue the pound in 1949, which at the time was seen as a great blow to British prestige in general, and to the Labour government in particular. He was associated with the austerity policies which aimed at limiting consumption in order to promote production and exports: these included rationing, strict taxation, and wage controls. Thus he managed to pay for the new and costly *National Health Service and other social spending despite record levels of public debt, and laid the ground for the country's subsequent economic recovery.

Cristero (Christers) Revolt (1927–9)

A widespread popular rebellion which was largely confined to the Mexican states of Colima, Jalisco, Michoacán and Morelos. It was led by members of the old pre-revolutionary elites, but gained its popular impetus under the banner of Roman Catholicism which was opposed to the new, secular state as established by the 1917 constitution. The revolutionary state under *Calles and his successors proved too weak to defeat the movement, and was forced to accept a compromise whereby the Church was allowed to conduct religious instruction.

ANTICLERICALISM

Croatia

A Balkan state which for most of the twentieth century formed the second largest component of Yugoslavia, and which struggled for ten years after  Yugoslavia's breakup to form stable democratic institutions.

Early history (up to 1992) Croatia came largely under Hungarian sovereignty within *Austria-Hungary in 1867. A Croatian *nationalist movement began to develop in response to Hungarian efforts to 'Magyarize' the country through the introduction of the Hungarian culture and language. At the *Corfu Pact its popular leaders agreed to a united Kingdom of Serbs, Croats, and Slovenes, which came into existence in 1918. However, Croatians soon rejected renewed foreign domination, this time by the Serbs, who were seen to occupy the most important and privileged positions in the new state. The traditions of Catholic Croatia, whose history and culture had been tied closely to that of Venice and Austria, came into increasing conflict with the predominance of the more Eastern-oriented Serbian culture, language, and *Orthodox Church, which had been historically tied to the *Ottoman Empire.

Resentment led to the growth of the *Ustase terrorist movement, which was responsible for the assassination of King *Alexander I. When Yugoslavia was overrun by German and Italian troops in World War II, the Ustase declared the puppet Independent State of Croatia, in which it brutally persecuted, gaoled, and murdered Serbs, Jews, and other minorities. In 1945, the *Fascist dictatorship of *Pavelic came to an end after a brutal civil war which was won by *Tito's Communist *partisans. The refounded state of Yugoslavia sought to calm Croatian fears of renewed Serb dominance, and was superficially successful through a combination of constitutional guarantees and coercion. However, Croatian protests for greater liberties in the spring of 1971 were brutally suppressed.

After Tito's death, resentment against Serbian dominance grew, and came into the open after the collapse of *Communism in central and eastern Europe in 1989, posing a fundamental challenge to the existence of the Yugoslav Communist regime. Democratic elections were held in 1990, which were won by *Tudjman, who introduced liberal economic reforms and hastened his country's process towards independence from Yugoslavia, which was finally declared on 7 October 1991.

Democratization (1992–2003) A bitter civil war ensued against the Croatian Serb minority, who were helped by the Yugoslav, Serb-dominated army. The latter were principally agitated by the popular memory of Croatian aggression during World War II, and occupied around a third of the territory as a result. The civil war was shortened by the civil war in *Bosnia, and in 1995 Croatian troops regained most of the territory lost to the Serbs. After the *Dayton Agreement, the Croatian government continued to refuse full cooperation with the International Criminal Tribunal for the Former Yugoslavia in The Hague. A number of high-profile arrests were made, however, and new evidence of Croatian *human rights violations did come to light.

Following *Tudjman's death, elections in January 2000 led to a dramatic victory for the Social Liberal and Social Democrat alliance, and a change in government for the first time since Croatia's independence. Under Ivica Raćan of the People's Party, the new government now cooperated fully with the War Crimes Tribunal in The Hague. It also sought to overcome its international isolation through signing an Association agreement with the EU in order to prepare a path for an application for membership. Against protests of the nationalist opposition, the government guaranteed the integrity of the state of Bosnia-Hercegovina, and it pledged the repatriation of 200,000 Serbs to their homes in Croatia. Croatia joined the *WTO in 2000, and later that year the government solidified Croatia's democratic structures by introducing constitutional changes to strengthen the authority of parliament vis-à-vis the President.

Current issues (2003–) Exhausted and divided by the transformations it had introduced, the People's Party lost the 2003 elections to the Croatian Democratic Union (HDZ). Under Ivo Sanader, the reformed centre-right party led a minority government which continued to pursue the path of Western integration. In 2004, Croatia was accepted as a candidate member of the EU, and in 2005 membership negotiations were begun.

Croce, Benedetto (b. 25 Feb. 1866, d. 20 Nov. 1952). Italian philosopher, historian, and politician

Born in Abbruzzi, he studied law in Rome, but soon became interested in philosophy. In his first essay, published in 1893, he re-established the separation between art and science, and categorized the study of history as an art. As he elaborated in his *Teoria e storia della storiografia* (The Theory and History of Historiography, 1917), the writing of history was a function of intuition, imagination, and thought, and hence principally related to the discipline of philosophy. He became the leading exponent of Italian new idealism against the positivism predominant in the late nineteenth century. During 1903–46, he was also a prominent literary figure as editor of the review *La critica*. He served as Minister of Public Instruction in *Giolitti's last government (1920–1), and as a historian he subsequently became the most prominent apologist for the Giolittian era. He first regarded *Mussolini with tolerant detachment, but openly opposed *Fascism from 1925 following the *Matteotti Crisis and the ensuing *Aventine secession. In 1943, he refounded the Liberal Party, which failed, however, to transform itself into a major political force in the following years.

Crosland, (Charles) Anthony Raven

(b. 29 Aug. 1918, d. 19 Feb. 1977). British Labour politician

Born in St Leonard's-on-Sea, Sussex, he studied at Oxford, and fought in World War II, as a member of the Parachute Regiment. He returned to academic life after the war as an economist at Oxford, but left in 1950 to become Labour MP for South Gloucestershire. He made his name with the publication of *The Future of Socialism* (1956), which was the leading inspiration to revisionists in the *Labour Party. In it, he claimed that increasing equality should be Labour's main aim, and that nationalization was not vital in achieving this. Instead, he focused on *Keynesian demand management as the best way of spreading the benefits of an increasingly affluent Britain. As Secretary of State for Education during 1964–7, he closed most grammar schools, believing them to be anti-egalitarian. Instead, he developed the comprehensive state school system. During 1967–70 and 1974–7, he occupied a number of Cabinet posts, and was Foreign Secretary from 1976 until his sudden death in 1977. He bequeathed to the Labour Party the idea that *socialism must update itself in order to remain relevant to people's everyday needs.

CSCE, see CONFERENCE ON SECURITY AND COOPERATION IN EUROPE

CSU (Christian Social Union) (Germany)

A Bavarian conservative sister party of the *CDU, which does not exist outside Bavaria. Founded in 1945, it has always formed the state's government except for the period 1954–7. It tends to be more conservative than the CDU, and has stood for federalism, the protection of the family, and high standards in education. As a coalition partner of the CDU at the national level, the CSU has had considerable influence on national politics, especially in the Ministries of the Interior and Agriculture, providing successive ministers during its years in government. The CSU has been particularly influential in national politics under the leadership of the controversial *Strauss (1961–88) and Edmund Stoiber (1993–2007). Priding itself on being Europe's

most successful democratic party, the CSU has won an absolute majority in the state parliament since 1962, while in 2003 it even obtained a two-thirds majority in parliament, with over 60 per cent of the popular vote.

(⊕) SEE WEB LINKS

• The official website of the CSU.

Cuba

The largest Caribbean island. Immediately to the south of the USA, its affairs have been dominated by its relationship with its American neighbour.

Early history (up to 1959) Following the American entry into the Cuban War of Independence from Spain (1895–1901), the Republic of Cuba was finally proclaimed in 1902. At the same time, Cuba became essentially a US protectorate under the terms of the **Platt Amendment,** whereby Cuba had to consent to US intervention whenever the USA deemed it necessary for 'the protection of life, property, and individual liberty'. The Amendment was frequently invoked until its repeal in 1934, by which time the USA had already established its political influence (e.g. through the backing of the dictator *Batista) as well as its economic dominance. By 1959 over 60 per cent of Cuban sugar went to the USA, while American investment controlled 90 per cent of the country's mines as well as the entire energy industry. The income which US investments provided was unequally divided between a small elite, a growing middle class in the towns, and a large rural population living in poverty.

Communism (since 1959) From 1956 the 'strong man' in Cuban politics since 1933, General Batista, was challenged by a growing revolutionary movement led by *Castro, which in early 1959 managed to gain power. Castro's immediate efforts to annul US influence through the nationalization of US companies, and to export Communist revolution to all of Latin America, soon gained him the enmity of the Western superpower. He managed to withstand attempts at destabilizing his regime, such as a total economic blockade beginning in 1962, the *Bay of Pigs invasion, and the *Cuban Missile Crisis. This struggle exposed his country more and more to Soviet military, economic, and political influence. After the failure of Castro and his principal aide, *Che Guevara, to find a unique Cuban way to *socialism during the 1960s, the country became increasingly integrated into the Soviet economic system.

As a member of *Comecon from 1972, Cuba exported sugar and fruit to the Eastern Bloc countries, in return for Soviet oil, industrial goods, and military equipment. Soviet methods of central planning were adopted, while during the 1970s Castro's rule became institutionalized: the judiciary was reorganized in 1973, the first congress of the *Communist Party of Cuba met in 1975, and a Constitution was proclaimed in 1976. The regime proved very successful in eliminating illiteracy, increasing life expectancy, and furthering social equality.

The problems of the relatively stagnant economy were compounded by the collapse of the Soviet Union in 1991. As a result of Cuba's previous over-reliance on the Soviet Union, in 1989–93 domestic output declined by 34 per cent. Owing to the bad sugar harvest of 1993, the country was unable to meet its contractual deliveries to Russia, which stopped all supplies of oil in response. To cope with an increasingly desperate situation, even the orthodox Castro was forced to allow the emergence of private markets and to encourage foreign investment in certain areas, notably the sugar industry and tourism in the 1990s.

Contemporary politics (since 2000) In the early years of the twenty-first century, Cuba's economic prospects improved, the result of a deal with Venezuela. Venezuela provided oil on generous terms, with Cuba sending 20,000 qualified medical staff there in return. In 2004, Cuba secured the economic assistance of China. This allowed the regime to reverse some of its earlier decisions to liberalize the economy, and to crack down on political opponents in 2003. This led to a temporary breakdown in relations with the EU, though relations were resumed after political prisoners were released in 2005.

Cuban Missile Crisis (Oct. 1962)
A superpower confrontation precipitated when the US government learnt that Soviet ballistic missiles with atomic warheads capable of hitting the USA were being installed in Cuba. President *Kennedy reinforced the US naval base at Guantanamo, ordered a naval blockade against Soviet military shipments to Cuba, and demanded that the Soviet Union remove its missiles and bases from the island. On 27 October there seemed a real danger of nuclear war, as the rival forces were placed on full alert. The crisis was heightened as Soviet merchant vessels, thought to be carrying missiles, approached the US blockading forces.

On 28 October the Soviet ships were ordered by *Khrushchev to turn back. The Soviet Union agreed to US demands to dismantle the rocket bases in return for a pledge not to attack *Castro's Cuba, and the removal of some obsolete US Jupiter missiles in Turkey. The naval blockade was lifted on 20 November. One outcome of the crisis was the establishment of a direct, exclusive line (the 'hot line') of communication, to be used in an emergency, between the President of the United States and the leader of the Soviet Union. Another was the retreat from *brinkmanship and an easing of the *Cold War.

Cultural Revolution (1966–76)
A dramatic purge of the Chinese *Communist Party. Party functionaries, as well as officeholders in the economy, education, and cultural institutions, were removed from their offices in an ostensible attempt to rid Chinese society of 'bourgeois' influences. The Cultural Revolution was officially announced on 8 August 1966, when people were encouraged to denounce their neighbours for not being genuine Communists. Words of Chairman *Mao became the sole rule of conduct, and all established patterns of behaviour became subject to question. Altogether around three million people were thus denounced, and tens of thousands died in imprisonment. By 1967, matters had escalated to near anarchy as student *Red Guards terrorized the streets, and from 1968 the military was called in to restore order.

The Cultural Revolution ended officially only with Mao's death. It was primarily an urban phenomenon, affecting around half of China's urban population. It caused great disruptions in the Communist Party itself, as over 70 per cent of government and party leaders at regional and provincial levels were replaced. Around half a million people died as a consequence of the Revolution, which produced deep divisions within the Communist Party and in much of urban China. From Mao's point of view, the Revolution served its purpose, as it allowed him to reassert absolute control over the party hierarchy. Most of his opponents, critics (most notably State Chairman *Liu Shaoqi), and sceptics were removed from office.

Curragh Incident (1914)
A 'mutiny' of officers on the Curragh plain near Dublin, the location of a British military headquarters. It resulted from the possibility that the army might have to quell an insurrection by Protestants in *Northern Ireland, fighting against Irish Home Rule and in favour of the country remaining an integral

part of the United Kingdom. Apparently on the instruction of Colonel John Seeley, the Secretary of State for War, the commander, General Sir Arthur Paget allowed those officers to resign who were unwilling to fight against the Irish Protestants. General Hubert Gough and fifty-eight of his seventy-one officers gave in their resignations. The War Office then agreed not to coerce Ulster into Home Rule, and reinstated the officers. *Asquith saw the incident as a threat to discipline and requested the resignations of Seely, the Chief of Staff (Sir John French), and the Adjutant-General (Sir Spencer Ewart). The latter officers were soon reinstated. The incident was not technically a mutiny, but was a rare occasion when the British army (successfully) exerted pressure on government policy within the United Kingdom.

Currie, Sir Arthur William (b. 5 Dec. 1875, d. 30 Nov. 1933). Canadian general . Born at Strathroy (Ontario), he served in the Canadian militia before being appointed commander of the 2nd Canadian Infantry Brigade in 1914, without any previous experience of military leadership. By June 1917, he had been appointed commander of the Canadian Corps. In 1918, he was one of the most important leaders of the final Allied offensive, which ultimately forced Germany to surrender. He became inspector-general of the Canadian militia (1919–20), and in 1920 became Principal and Vice-Chancellor of McGill University. Currie received criticism for the heavy casualties caused by his campaigns, and for using regimental money in 1928 for his own personal expenses in a libel action. Nevertheless, he is remembered as Canada's most successful general of World War I.

Curtin, John Joseph (b. 8 Jan. 1885, d. 5 July 1945). Prime Minister of Australia 1941–5 From an Irish Catholic family in Creswick (Victoria), Curtin joined the Victorian Socialist Party upon its foundation in 1906. He became secretary of the Timber Workers Union (1911) and its first federal president in 1914, though in 1915 he had to resign his posts, having become an alcoholic. After drying out, he was appointed organizer of the Australian Trades Union Anti-Conscription Congress in 1916 before moving to Perth to become editor of the trade union's *Westralian Worker*. His views gradually became more reformist and conciliatory, and in 1928 he entered the federal parliament, where he became known as an outstanding debater. After losing the 1931 elections he returned to journalism, but regained his seat in 1934. Promising to refrain from alcohol, he was elected leader of the Australian *Labor Party in 1935 by one vote,

thus becoming the first party leader from Western Australia.

As Prime Minister, he led Australia through the most difficult years of World War II. In opposition to the British, he rejected *Churchill's demands that Australian troops should be subject to British war priorities. In consequence, he withdrew many Australian units from North Africa to defend Australia against a possible Japanese attack. He also came to look primarily towards the USA, rather than the UK, for protection against the Japanese, angering Churchill by stating: 'Australia looks to America, free of any pangs as to our traditional links or kinship with the United Kingdom'. After Labor was returned with a record 50 per cent of the vote in 1943, with his chief lieutenant, *Chifley, he proceeded to devise a new postwar order. The most important step had already been taken through the conversion of income tax into a purely federal tax in 1941. After 1943, widows' pensions and maternity allowances were introduced. He died in office.

Curzon, George Nathaniel, Marquess of Kedleston (b. 11 Jan. 1859, d. 20 Mar. 1925). British Foreign Secretary 1919–23 Born in Kedleston, Derbyshire, he was educated at Eton and Oxford. He entered parliament in 1886, and in 1898 was appointed Viceroy of India. For seven years, Curzon presided over reforms of education and agriculture, and the extension of the country's railways and canals. However, his partition of *Bengal in 1905 was controversial, and he resigned after clashing with the Commander-in-Chief in India, *Kitchener, over control of the Indian army. In 1915, he became a member of Asquith's coalition Cabinet as Lord Privy Seal; in 1916, he was made Lord President of the Council, a post he continued to hold in *Lloyd George's War Cabinet. As Foreign Secretary, his influence was limited due to the interference of Lloyd George, although his name was given to the *Curzon Line—the proposed boundary between Poland and Russia in 1920. He hoped to become Prime Minister in 1923, but was passed over in favour of *Baldwin. He continued as Foreign Secretary in Baldwin's first government, but was mortified when he lost this office to Austen *Chamberlain in Baldwin's second government in November 1924. He then served as Lord President of the Council until his death.

Curzon Line
The border between Soviet Russia and Poland established by the *Paris Peace Conference on

8 December 1919, and later named after the British Foreign Secretary *Curzon. According to the principle of national self-determination, it incorporated into Poland all those areas with a Polish majority. The Poles demanded a border further to the east, to include areas that had been Polish until the Polish partitions of the eighteenth century. This caused the *Russo-Polish War, as a result of which, in the Peace of Riga (18 March 1921), they secured a border much further to the east, enlarging their territory by about one-third. Following the *Hitler–Stalin Pact, Poland was divided between the USSR and Germany in September 1939 roughly along the Curzon Line, and it became the basis for Poland's eastern border after 1945.

Cyprus

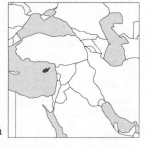

The third largest island in the Mediterranean, strategically situated off Turkey and Syria. Its contemporary history has been dominated by the tensions arising out of its geographical closeness to Turkey, and the Greek origins of much of the population.

Colonial rule (up to 1960) Ruled by the *Ottoman Empire from 1571, Cyprus was overwhelmingly inhabited by Greeks. The island was occupied and administered by the British from 1878, and formally annexed by them at the beginning of World War I (1914), an act that was recognized in the Treaty of *Lausanne of 1923. A British Crown Colony from 1925, it served as an important military base during World War II and the *Suez Crisis. In the 1950s the movement against foreign rule and for union (Enosis) with Greece picked up momentum, against the background of *decolonization worldwide. It was led by Archbishop *Makarios III, the head of the Cypriot *Orthodox Church. A second movement, *EOKA, started a violent campaign against British rule in 1955. Britain was eager to retain some influence on the strategically important island, so that in 1959 it offered independence and membership of the *Commonwealth instead of union with Greece. This was accepted by Makarios, who proclaimed independence in 1960. It entered the *Commonwealth in 1961, and the UK retained sovereignty over its two military bases there.

Separation (from 1974) Since independence, the central question in Cypriot politics has been the relationship between the Greek majority and the Turkish minority living on the island. The latter began to form self-governing enclaves, while the Greeks (almost 80 per cent of the population) dominated the island's political life. In a desperate bid for greater domestic popularity, the *Greek colonels instigated a coup against Makarios in 1974, in order to achieve Enosis. As this fundamentally threatened the rights of the Turkish minority, Turkish troops invaded the island's north-eastern half on 20 July 1974. Subsequently, over 200,000 Greeks were expelled from the Turkish-occupied areas, and replaced with members of the Turkish army and settlers from mainland Turkey.

Separated from the Greek areas by the 'Blue Line' running across the island, the Turkish Federated State of Cyprus was founded on 13 February 1975, but was not recognized by the *UN or the international community. Renamed the Turkish Republic of Northern Cyprus, it was governed by President Rauf Rasit Denktash (b. 1924) from 1976 to 2005. In the Greek part of Cyprus, Makarios returned to power until his death in 1977. His successors have continued to claim unity for the whole island, even though as a result of the events of the 1970s the Greek and Turkish inhabitants of Cyprus had little in common in ethnic, religious, cultural, or linguistic terms.

Relations between the two parts remained tense, while under its head of state, Glafkos Klerides (1993–2003), the unoccupied part of the island was brought under Greek military protection in 1993. Owing to its isolation, Northern Cyprus experienced a stagnant economy in the 1990s, which increased its dependence on transfer payments from Turkey. Whereas Northern Cyprus was slow to develop its tourist industry, the southern Republic of Cyprus experienced steady economic growth.

Contemporary politics (since 2004) In 2004, the Republic of Cyprus entered the EU, an event which triggered new diplomatic efforts to bring about the island's unification. Under Kofi *Annan, the UN exerted unprecedented pressure on Klerides and Denktash to agree on a plan to unify the island in a loose federation of the Turkish and the Greek parts. Both leaders reluctantly agreed to put this to a referendum. It was approved in the Turkish part, as the population was lured by automatic entry into the EU and an end to its economic and international isolation. With guaranteed entry into the EU, however, the leaders of the Greek part of Cyprus were in little mood for compromise, with the Greek population rejecting the deal in 2003.

Turkey's refusal to recognize the Republic of Cyprus continued to affect relations between Turkey and the EU. Meanwhile, in 2005 the electorate in the Turkish part confirmed the pro-EU Mehmet Ali Talat as President and successor to Denktash. The Greek Cypriots, by contrast, were led, since 2003, by Tasssos Papadopoulos, who remained sceptical about the UN-sponsored plans for unification.

Czech Republic

The economically, culturally, and politically dominant part of *Czechoslovakia, which became independent on 1 January 1993.

The Havel era (up to 2003) The Czech economy was hit doubly hard by the transition from a planned to a capitalist economy and by separation from *Slovakia, which reduced the amount of mutual trade by 50 per cent. Nevertheless, under the neo-liberal *Klaus it adapted to capitalism with unusual speed, so that by 1995, around 80 per cent of the Gross Domestic Product came from the private sector. Domestic politics were frequently marked by public clashes between Klaus and the president *Havel. Havel tried hard to maintain a social and conciliatory spirit in the country despite the growth of competitive market forces. Owing to a number of corruption scandals and internal party friction within the Democratic Citizens' Party (ODS), Klaus and his government resigned in 1998. The ensuing elections were won by the Social Democrats under Miloš Zeman, who formed a minority government with the tacit support of the ODS. In 2000, an attempt by the two large parties to change the election laws at the expense of smaller parties was foiled by Havel, who feared a threat to political pluralism. Economically, the transition towards liberal markets fell behind that of Poland and Hungary, as economic growth and privatization slackened.

Contemporary politics (since 2003–) After a series of inconclusive votes owing to the enmity between the political camps, Havel was succeeded as President by his rival, Klaus. The Czech Republic entered the EU on

1 January 2004. Klaus presided over a growing stalemate in the political system, as the two major political camps achieved parity in popular support. Zeman was succeeded by Vladimir Spidla in 2002, who led a centre-left coalition commanding 101 out of 200 seats. The following elections in 2006 produced a relative victory for the ODS, but its centre-right coalition was only able to command 100 seats. After seven months, the leader of the ODS, Mirek Topolánek, was finally able to form a government, with the help of the centrist Christian Democrats and the Green Party. Topolánek supported the cautious approach of President Klaus towards further EU integration, and conducted a pro-American foreign policy.

Czechoslovakia

An east-central European country marked by persistent tensions between its constituent nationalities, and domination by its overbearing neighbours.

The liberal period (1918–1939) Following the collapse of the *Austro-Hungarian Empire, Czechoslovakia was proclaimed on 28 October 1918, and confirmed at the *Paris Peace Conferences, on 10 September 1919. It consisted of the economically advanced historical regions of Moravia, Bohemia, and parts of *Silesia, which made up the Czech lands, and the industrially backward Slovakia, including parts of the even poorer Karpathia. The new state was thus extremely heterogeneous, consisting of 66 per cent Czechs and Slovaks, 22 per cent Germans, 5 per cent Hungarians, and 0.7 per cent Poles. This fact alone obliged the new state to pursue an extremely liberal policy in order to reconcile its minorities. This trend was reinforced by its enlightened, intellectual leadership under Thomas *Masaryk and *Beneš, and supported by the well-developed and stable middle classes of the Czech lands.

During the 1920s the country experienced a much greater degree of stability than all its neighbours. Through the *Little Entente, and a friendship treaty with France, the country hoped to buttress its position in foreign affairs. Nevertheless, after the Great *Depression it became even more difficult to insulate the country from the rise of *Fascism and authoritarianism which developed among its neighbours. In particular, the German *Nazi movement whipped up opposition amongst the Germans in the *Sudetenland (in north-western Bohemia), who came to demand more autonomy ever more aggressively. Grievances were also growing in the Slovak half of the country. Since the educated middle classes were overwhelmingly Czech, the Slovaks found themselves vastly under-represented in the political and administrative system, so that there, too, demands for greater autonomy emerged.

World War II (1939–45) Czechoslovakia was not overcome by internal collapse, but by the *Munich Agreement, whereby the Sudetenland was annexed by Germany, and the lands inhabited by the Polish (i.e. *Teschen) and Hungarian minorities were annexed by Poland and Hungary respectively. On 14–15 March 1939, *Hitler's armies invaded the rest of the Czech lands and created the protectorate of Bohemia and Moravia, which became relatively autonomous, with a puppet President (*Hácha). The Germans brutally suppressed the Czech intelligentsia and middle classes. Following the murder of *Heydrich, the German rule of terror climaxed in the retaliatory destruction of the village of Lidice. However, although German suppression and brutality were undoubtedly severe, they remained at a level comparable with Nazi rule in occupied Western Europe. They were not remotely as brutal as in Poland or the occupied Soviet Union, partly because of Nazi reliance on the Czech workforce in the armaments industry. After *World War II, the government in exile under Beneš returned to the country.

Communist rule (1945–90) The first break with the country's prewar traditions of *liberalism and toleration came in June 1945, when it became the first Eastern European country outside Nazi Germany and the USSR to carry out 'ethnic cleansing', expelling the German and Hungarian minorities from the country. In the elections of May 1946, the Communist Party under *Gottwald became the largest party, with 38 per cent of the vote. Amidst signs of Communist decline afterwards, Gottwald staged a coup in February 1948, and established a Communist one-party state. This was accelerated through a series of *Stalinist purges, culminating in

the *Slánski trial. The country had thus firmly come into the fold of Moscow, and adhered to the extremes of Stalinism even after *Stalin's death. *Human rights violations by the state and a dependent judiciary continued, while the economy, which had suffered comparatively little damage during the war, was disastrously mismanaged, leading to an economic crisis in the early 1960s.

Growing unrest and protests led to the appointment of the reform-minded *Dubček as First Party Secretary in January 1968. However, his attempts to strengthen *Communism through political and economic liberalization went further than other Communist leaders such as *Ulbricht and *Brezhnev were willing to allow, thus threatening the status quo in Eastern Europe. The period of reform called the *Prague Spring was violently ended on 20 August 1968, when the *Warsaw Pact troops arrived in Czechoslovakia and entered Prague.

There followed two decades under *Husák, in which Communist political orthodoxy was re-established with a mixture of tight press censorship and an attempt to mollify opposition with economic benefits. The latter proved extremely difficult, as economic growth remained slow during the 1970s and 1980s, This was caused in part by the 1973 and 1979 *oil price shocks, central economic planning, and the failure to invest in new technologies in a country reliant on its traditional heavy industry. Husák's inability to contain the opposition became apparent in the establishment of the *Charter '77 movement, which provided an inspiration to dissident movements elsewhere in Eastern Europe.

Democratization (1989–93) Charter '77 provided leadership once Communist regimes were tumbling in neighbouring countries. In the *Velvet Revolution of December 1989, the Communist government collapsed, and a government under the leading Charter '77 dissident *Havel was formed. However, the new political leadership was unable to prevent a growing sense of *nationalism in Slovakia, which had already begun under the Communist leadership. Unable to reach an agreement on a federal or confederate link between the two parts, the country peacefully split into the independent Czech and Slovak Republics on 1 January 1993.

D

Dad's Army, see HOME GUARD

Dahomey, see BENIN

Daily Telegraph Affair
On 28 October 1908 an interview appeared in the British newspaper *Daily Telegraph* in which the German Emperor *Wilhelm II mourned that he was the only anglophile German, and claimed that during the *South African (Boer) War he had not only prevented a continental alliance against England, but that English victory was achieved on the basis of battle plans which he himself had drawn up for his grandmother Queen Victoria. This claim caused an uproar in Britain, while in Germany it raised serious constitutional questions about the role of the Emperor in German politics, especially his meddling in current affairs. While the German parliament's censure of the Emperor demonstrated its increased self-confidence, its failure to press home this advantage to limit the Emperor's political rights also revealed its continued weakness in the Empire's constitutional system.

Daladier, Édouard (b. 18 June 1884, d. 10 Oct. 1970). Prime Minister of France 1933, 1934, 1938–40
A *Radical in the Chamber of Deputies (1919–40) and the National Assembly (1946–58), he was Minister of War and Defence 1932–4 and 1936–40. Having already participated in fifteen Cabinets, he was immensely popular when he became Prime Minister once again in 1938. Given the renewed threat of a European war, he was able to command a relatively solid parliamentary majority which enabled him to introduce a public works programme and, against bitter trade-union opposition, an increased working week. He steered the Radical Party towards the right, away from the *Popular Front. He pursued the policy of *appeasement with Germany, and signed the *Munich Agreement in 1938. He had to resign after ineffective and badly coordinated French efforts to help the Finns in the *Winter War. However, he stayed on as Minister of War until the defeat, when he was imprisoned by the *Vichy government. He was tried unsuccessfully at *Riom, and spent the last two years of the war in a German prison. After the war, he became again a

leading influence within his party, but since its support had declined considerably, he was unable to join another ministry.

Dalai Lama
The title of the abbot of the Dge-lugs-pa (Yellow Hat) order of Tibetan Buddhist monks, who is revered as the incarnation of the angelic bodhisattva Avalokiteshvara. The order was founded by the first Dalai Lama, Gendun Druba, in 1400. The 'Great Fifth' Dalai Lama, Losang Gyatso, unified the country in 1642 and thus became Tibet's secular as well as spiritual ruler. Subsequently, Tibet was ruled by successive Dalai Lamas in a monastic bureaucracy from Lhasa. The Fourteenth Dalai Lama, Tenzin Gyatso, was born in 1935 and enthroned in 1940. He was unable to stop the invasion by the People's Republic of China in 1950. After trying in vain to cooperate with the new Communist rulers, he left the country in 1959, together with around 100,000 followers, and set up a government-in-exile in India. He campaigned tirelessly to keep the plight of Tibetans in world attention, and was awarded the *Nobel Peace Prize in 1989.
BUDDHISM

🌐 SEE WEB LINKS

• The official website of the Dalai Lama.

D'Annunzio, Gabriele (b. 12 Mar. 1863, d. 1 Mar. 1938). Italian writer and political adventurer
A well-known writer, he entered the Chamber of Deputies in 1897 where his support oscillated between the extreme right and the extreme left. He left politics in 1900 and entered the most productive period of his life, partly inspired by his eventful and well-publicized affair with Eleonora Duse. Because of debts he left Italy in 1910 but returned to serve in World War I, where he became a war hero with a daring and distinguished record in the army, the navy, and, especially, the air force. Appalled by the Italian failure to secure the disputed city of *Fiume at the *Paris Peace Conference, he staged a coup and took control of the city. He established an authoritarian right-wing city-state and managed to defy the Italian authorities for sixteen months, until he was eventually forced to abandon the city by *Giolitti in January 1921. He retired and became a cultural figurehead in *Fascist Italy.

Danquah, Joseph Kwame Kyeretwi Boakye (b. 21 Dec. 1895, d. 4 Feb. 1965). Ghanaian nationalist leader

Born in Bepong, he became a law clerk at 17 and then secretary to his brother, a tribal chief. He studied law at the University of London from 1921, and in 1926 qualified as a lawyer at the English Bar. In 1927, upon completion of his doctoral thesis, he returned to the Gold Coast (now Ghana) to establish a law practice. In 1931 he set up a daily newspaper, the *Times of West Africa*, which gained immense popular influence and established him as a moderate leader of the nationalist movement for independence.

Danquah was elected to the Legislative Council in 1946, and in 1947 founded the colony's first political party, the United Gold Coast Convention, offering *Nkrumah the post of general secretary. Imprisoned for incitement to violence in 1948, he became a leading figure in constitutional negotiations from 1949. Increasingly hostile to Nkrumah, he failed to be elected to the Legislative Assembly in 1954 and 1956. He was imprisoned 1961-2 and again in 1964 for criticism of Nkrumah's dictatorial methods. He died in prison.

Danzig

A disputed city between Poland and Germany since the twelfth century. Against the protest of its citizens, 95 per cent of whom were German, it was declared a Free City under the protection of the *League of Nations by the Treaty of *Versailles, in order to give the newly independent state of Poland, which was virtually land-locked, access to a neutral port. In 1933, the city elected a *Nazi majority to its parliament, and following Germany's invasion of Poland it was reintegrated into German territory in 1939. After the war, the city became an integral part of Poland under the name of **Gdansk**, and those Germans that had not left the city already were expelled. During the 1980s, the city's dockyards became the home of the protest movement *Solidarność. Polish sovereignty over the city was finally recognized by Germany in 1990.

Dardanelles

A 61 km (38 mile) strait between the Aegean Sea and the Sea of Marmara, and part of the strategic waterway that links the Black Sea and the Mediterranean. The strait has constituted a vital supply route for Russia, connecting its only winter ports to the outside world. During World War I, the British decided to force their way into the Dardanelles and thus reach the Turkish city of Constantinople by sea. In preparation for the attack, the Turkish coastal defences were bombarded between 19 and 26 February 1915, though they were still able to inflict heavy losses on the Anglo-French fleet as it tried to make its way through the strait. Altogether, one-third of the capital ships were sunk, so that the naval campaign was aborted to concentrate on the land attack at *Gallipoli. Since World War I, access to the straits has been regulated by a succession of international treaties, the last being the *Montreux Convention of 1936.

Darfur

A semi-arid region in western Sudan, in which Arab nomads and Black African populations have competed for precious resources such as grazing land. In 2003, African groups began to rebel by launching attacks against government installations, accusing the government of discriminating against them in favour of Arabs. The Arab Janjaweed militias formed in response. Supported by the government military, its bands have sought to expel Africans from their homes, raping and killing many residents. By 2007, around two million people had been expelled from their homes, with 200,000 living in refugee camps in neighbouring Chad. Around 300,000 had died in the conflict. In 2006, a peace deal was signed that involved the disarming of the Janjaweed militia, with the *African Union sending troops to ensure peace. However, fighting continued, with the Janjaweed militia continuing to fight in armed conflict. Despite an agreement in 2006 that the region be pacified under the supervision of troops from the *African Union, fighting continued. In 2007, the UN authorized the largest peace mission in its history, to be operational by the end of the year.

Darlan, François (b. 7 Aug. 1881, d. 24 Dec. 1942). French admiral

A distinguished naval commander in World War I, he was appointed admiral and Commander-in-Chief in 1939. His instinct to *collaborate with the Germans during the *Vichy government was intensified by the British destruction of much of his fleet at *Mers el-Kebir in July 1940. As Vice-Premier (1941–2) he was effectively in charge of the Vichy government, when he tried unsuccessfully to carve out a greater role for the French military and navy in the context of the *Third Reich. Following the Allied successes in the *North African campaigns which led to their attack on Algiers on 8 November 1942, and the German occupation of Vichy France, he reluctantly changed sides, though he was murdered soon afterwards.

David Hotel, King, see IRGUN

Dawes Plan, see REPARATIONS

Dayan, Moshe (b. 20 May 1915, d. 16 Oct. 1981). Israeli general and Minister of Defence, 1967–74

Born in *Kibbutz* Degania, he studied at the Hebrew University of *Jerusalem, where he joined the *Haganah. In 1941, he became a member of its elite corps, the Palmah Assault Forces, and took part in a joint assault with the British against the *Vichy forces in Syria, where he lost his left eye. He distinguished himself in the Israeli War of Independence (1948–9), and thereafter rose to become Chief of Staff in 1953. He commanded the armed forces during the Sinai War of 1956, but retired from the army in 1958 in order to take up a political career. A *Mapai (Israel Workers' Party) Member of Parliament (Knesset) from 1959, he became Minister of Agriculture under *Ben-Gurion, with whom he left the party in 1963 to join his new Rafi party. He resigned his ministry in 1964, but due to his general popularity *Eshkol was forced to appoint him Minister of Defence in 1967. He was one of the principal leaders of the *Six Day War, taking much of the credit for its success even though that was due more to the quiet *Rabin. His reputation suffered, however, when the army proved ill-prepared for the *Yom Kippur War of 1973. He was left out of Rabin's Cabinet in 1974, but served as Foreign Minister under *Begin, when he played an important role in the peace negotiations with Egypt leading up to *Camp David. He resigned in 1979 over policy differences and founded his own party, which did not survive him.

Dayton Agreement (21 Nov. 1995)

A peace deal brokered by US President *Clinton and his Secretary of State, Warren Christopher, between the Presidents of *Bosnia (*Izetbegovic), Yugoslavia (*Milošević), and *Croatia (*Tudjman), after six days of intense negotiations in Dayton (Ohio). It provided for a nominally united Bosnian state, which was effectively divided between a decentralized Bosnian–Croat Federation and a centralized Serb Republic. In order to ensure the stability of the peace, to supervise the relationship between the former enemies, and to encourage their cooperation, under US leadership *NATO committed 60,000 troops, under the auspices of the *UN. The agreement restored a fragile peace, but also contained significant shortcomings; for example, Bosnians who found themselves living in areas that would be under Serb control burnt their homes rather than leave them to the former enemy, and vice versa. The agreement itself was nothing new and had been under discussion for two years. That it took the active involvement of the USA to implement it, demonstrated the continued US predominance in world politics, unrivalled even by the combined efforts of the European Union.

D-Day (6 June 1944)

A pivotal battle in *World War II. Although German troops were already on the defensive against the *Red Army in the east, *Stalin had continually urged the Western *Allies to open up a front in the west. D-Day breached the heavily fortified French coastline in Normandy. The Germans had expected such an invasion to take place further to the east. The date was also unexpected, since the German forecasts indicated bad weather for this day. An armada of over 2,500 ships crossed the Channel to transport 130,000 soldiers from the USA and the *British Empire. The troops from the British Empire landed on the beaches to the west, and the US troops landed on three beaches to the east, encountering fierce resistance at Omaha Beach. Owing to overwhelming superiority in the air, the *Allies managed to land an additional 20,000 troops behind enemy lines, which were crucial in blocking the German flow of reinforcements. Once the beachheads were established, supplies of soldiers and equipment could be sent from England. Although the initial advance towards Caen was slower than expected and took a month to complete, D-Day started off the *Normandy Campaign, the liberation of France, and the final phase of the war.

De Bono, Emilio (b. 19 Mar. 1866, d. 11 Jan. 1944). Italian Fascist

A commander of the 9th Army Corps during World War I, he turned to *Fascism in 1922 and participated in the *March on Rome. He was in charge of public security (1922–4), but had to resign following *Matteotti's assassination. He became Governor of Libya in 1925, and Minister for Colonies in 1929, in which office he lead the invasion of Ethiopia in 1935 only to be quickly replaced by *Badoglio. Increasingly sceptical of *Mussolini's leadership, in 1943 he joined the majority of the *Fascist Grand Council when it voted to depose him. He was captured by Mussolini's supporters in the Republic of *Salò and executed.

De Gasperi, Alcide (b. 3 Apr. 1881, d. 19 Aug. 1954). Italian Prime Minister 1945–53

Early career Born in the Trentino (which was then part of *Austria-Hungary), he graduated from the University of Vienna in 1905. He became politically active in the Italian Catholic Social Movement and in 1911 he entered the Austrian parliament as a representative of the Trentine Popular Party, which stood for local autonomy. Following Italy's acquisition of Trentino after World War I, he became active in the Italian *Popular Party and was elected to the Chamber of Deputies in 1921. An outspoken opponent of the *Fascist movement, he took part in the *Aventine Secession, which lost him his parliamentary seat in 1926. He was arrested in 1927, but after his release in 1929 he took refuge in the Vatican, where he advanced from a cataloguer to secretary of the Vatican Library.

In office After the liberation of Rome in 1944 he became active in the newly founded *Christian Democratic Party (DC), and in December 1945 he became the party's first Prime Minister. In his long (especially by Italian standards) period of office, he laid the foundations for an Italian republic committed to *NATO and oriented towards US friendship, a relatively liberal financial policy, and a social policy directed at social compromise. Increasingly he also became a strong advocate of *European integration. By contrast, he failed to introduce fundamental administrative or judicial reforms, for example. His tenure of office inaugurated the DC's uninterrupted participation in national government until its dissolution in 1994. He resisted any attempt for the DC to become a confessional (Roman Catholic) party, even though he was happy to accept the Church's support in general elections. At the same time, he steered the DC along a violently anti-Communist course, from which it liberated itself only in the 1970s under *Andreotti. He resigned in July 1953 after he failed to gain an absolute majority for the DC and its allies in the parliamentary elections, though he remained party secretary until his death.

de Gaulle, Charles, see GAULLE, CHARLES DE

de Klerk, Frederik Willem (b. 18 Mar. 1936). President of South Africa 1989–94

Early career Born in Johannesburg, he entered the *National Party (NP) youth organization (Jeugbond), proceeded to study law and became an attorney in Vereeniging in 1961. A Member of Parliament for the NP since 1972, he became a Cabinet minister in 1978. As leader of the pivotal Transvaal section of the NP (from 1982), he became leader of the NP following P. W. *Botha's stroke on 2 February 1989. He took part in 'encouraging' Botha to resign and became

President himself on 15 August 1989. A pragmatic politician, he accepted the need to come to an agreement with the Black majority of the country, particularly as long as it was still represented by a unified and relatively moderate leadership.

The end of apartheid (from 1990) In a dramatic speech opening the South African parliament in Cape Town on 2 February 1990, de Klerk announced a radical change in government policy on *apartheid, announcing a 'new South Africa' based on the principle of racial equality. Almost immediately he ordered the release of Nelson *Mandela and other political prisoners (11 February 1990), simultaneously lifting the ban on the *PAC, *ANC, and the *Communist Party. He entered negotiations with Mandela and other Black leaders such as *Buthelezi about the transition towards a multi-racial democracy. In 1992 he called a referendum among White South Africans in which two-thirds approved an end to the apartheid system, which was duly implemented. In 1993 he received the *Nobel Peace Prize, together with Mandela.

In the first free, universal election in South Africa's history, under his leadership the NP won 20.4 per cent of the popular vote, thus becoming the country's second biggest party after the ANC. He achieved this result through managing to appeal to many people of mixed race ('Coloureds') and exploiting their fears about the ANC's inexperience in government. With *Mbeki he became Deputy Prime Minister, but he subsequently failed to extend the NP's popular base to the Black communities. In 1996, he led his party out of the coalition of 'National Unity' with the ANC to become leader of the opposition. In 1997 he retired from politics, stating that he was too implicated in the former apartheid regimes to lead his party to a fresh start.

de Valéra, Éamon (b. 14 Oct. 1882, d. 29 Aug. 1975). Irish Premier 1932–48, 1951–4, 1957–9; President 1959–73

The foremost Irish politician of the twentieth century, under whose leadership Ireland achieved full political independence from the UK.

Early career Born in New York, he was sent to Ireland to be raised by his maternal grandmother after the death of his father. Educated at University College Dublin, de Valéra began a career as a mathematician and college lecturer. He joined the Irish Volunteers, a nationalist military force, in 1913, and commanded a battalion in the *Easter Rising of 1916. Along with other leaders, he was captured, tried, and sentenced to death. His sentence was commuted to life imprisonment, but he was released on 16 June 1917. In October 1917 he was elected president of *Sinn Féin. He was arrested by the British for his opposition to extending conscription to Ireland, but escaped in 1919.

Political leadership De Valéra was elected president of the first Dáil Éireann (the native Irish parliament, not yet recognized as sovereign). During the War of Independence against Britain he was active raising funds in the USA (1919–21). He was closely involved in the peace talks with the British, but rejected the eventual settlement, which saw the division of Ireland. In the ensuing civil war between supporters and opponents of the settlement (1922–3), de Valéra led those who opposed the treaty. In 1923, he called an end to the conflict by suspending IRA activity. In April 1926, he founded a new republican party, *Fianna Fáil, whose president he became.

In office He continued to lead Irish opposition to British institutions, refusing to take up his seat in the Dáil Éireann over the required loyalty oath to the British Crown until 1927. Fianna Fáil were brought into power for the first time on 9 March 1932 and he became President of the Executive Council (Prime Minister) of the Irish Free State (1932–7). His first administration abolished the loyalty oath. Taking advantage of the *Abdication Crisis in 1936, he set about removing all references to the British Crown in the Free State Constitution (retaining the King only for external relations). The new Constitution of Éire came into operation on 29 December 1937.

De Valéra continued in office, with the title of Taoiseach (Prime Minister) of Éire (1937–48). He insisted on Irish neutrality during World War II, made easier by the fact that the British government had returned control of ports to the Republic in the Anglo-Irish Agreement of April 1938. He argued that this neutrality was necessary for the new nation to assert its independence. This angered *Churchill, who denounced him in a radio address on 13 May 1945. De Valéra's famous response on 17 May 1945 drew much praise in Ireland and elsewhere. The war period left the Irish economy in trouble, and he was defeated in the 1948 election, replaced by John A. *Costello. Back in power as Taoiseach of the Republic of Ireland 1951–4, de Valéra and Fianna Fáil were unable to revive the economy and were replaced by Costello again. De Valéra's final government during 1957–9 saw some economic reform. As President, he became the oldest serving head

of state in the world. He died in Dublin, and was buried in Glasnevin cemetery.

Deakin, Alfred (b. 3 Aug. 1856, d. 7 Oct. 1919). Prime Minister of Australia 1903, 1905–8, 1909–10

Born at Collingwood, Melbourne, Deakin studied law in Melbourne and in 1878 was admitted to the Bar, though he was never a passionate lawyer. He started a career in journalism, and in 1880 was elected to the Victorian parliament as a Liberal. He held a number of posts in various coalition governments (1883–90), and was an active member of the opposition between 1890 and 1900. From 1887, he became increasingly involved in the campaign for an Australian Federation, and in 1900, along with *Barton, he joined the delegation presenting the case for a federal Australia to the British government.

As Prime Minister, Deakin took care to strengthen the federation, e.g. through the realization of a uniform tariff, the ordering of a survey of a transcontinental railway line, and the building of a separate Australian navy. Especially during his second term, with the support of *Labor, he also introduced a number of reform measures, such as old-age pensions. His regulation to ensure minimum wage levels established the concept of a basic wage in 1907. Deakin hoped to stop the progressive decline of the Liberals against Labor through a 'fusion' of non-Labour groups into an enlarged *Liberal Party, with whose support he led his third government. However, he was heavily defeated in 1910, and retired from politics in 1913. Of his writings the most revealing about contemporary political life are the posthumously published *The Federal Story* (1944) and the edited *Federated Australia: Selections from Letters to the Morning Post, 1900–1910* (1968).

HARVESTER JUDGMENT

Déat, Marcel (b. 7 Mar. 1894, d. 5 Jan. 1955). French Fascist

He left the *Socialist Party (SFIO) in 1933 to co-found the Socialist Party of France. In 1938, he supported the *Munich Agreement, and in 1939 opposed entering war over the city of *Danzig. During the 1930s, he turned increasingly towards *Fascism, and during the German occupation he became one of the leading opponents of what he considered to be Marshal *Pétain's 'moderation'. He founded the **Popular National Assembly (RNP)** in January 1941 but was unable to rally all French Fascists behind it. He failed to win German support for his aim, but was made Minister of Labour in March 1944 instead.

After the war he fled to an Italian monastery, so his death sentence was never carried out.

Debré, Michel (b. 15 Jan. 1912, d. 2 Aug. 1996). Prime Minister of France 1959–62
Part of de *Gaulle's *Free French Cabinet during World War II, he was a Senator from 1948–58 and subsequently a Deputy in the National Assembly. He supported de *Gaulle's return to power in 1958, confident that he would be able to restore French rule in Algeria by winning the *Algerian War of Independence. Despite de *Gaulle's subsequent termination of French rule in Algeria, he remained one of his faithful followers. As Minister of Justice in 1958 he was in charge of preparing the Constitution of the Fifth Republic. As its first Prime Minister, he also had an important role in the negotiations of the *Évian Agreements. Thereafter, he was Minister of Economics and Finance (1966–8), of Foreign Affairs (1968–9), and of Defence (1969–73). He ran unsuccessfully against the neo-Gaullist J. *Chirac to become the right wing's main contender in the 1981 presidential elections.

Debs, Eugene Victor (b. 5 Nov. 1855, d. 20 Oct. 1926). US socialist
Born at Terre Haute, Indiana, he started work for the US railroad system at 14, and soon became a prominent advocate of labour organization. He became the founding president of the American Railroad Union in 1893 and was imprisoned in 1894 for 'conspiracy' over the unsuccessful boycott and strike of the Pullman Palace Car Company. While in prison he became a socialist and, after his release, was elected president of the Socialist Party of America in 1900. A highly effective public speaker, he was socialist candidate for President five times between 1900 and 1920. Debs was sentenced to imprisonment again, under the 1917 Espionage Act, for his anti-war speech in 1918, in which he discouraged recruitment to the US armed services. He was released in 1921 on the order of President *Harding, but his citizenship was never restored. He spent the rest of his life as a newspaper editor.

Declaration of Human Rights, see HUMAN RIGHTS

decolonization
The gradual dismantling of *imperialism which began after World War I as Germany had to give up its colonies and the British Dominions were granted virtual independence by the Statute of *Westminster in 1931. It accelerated greatly after World War II, when the weakness of the traditional

Table 6. **Decolonization during the twentieth century**

Country (colonial name)	Colonized	Independent	Colonial power
Algeria	1830–70	1962	France
Angola	1491	1975	Portugal
Bangladesh	18th century	1971	East Pakistan until 1974
Belize (British Honduras)	1782	1981	UK
Botswana (Bechuanaland)	1885	1966	UK
Burkina Faso (*French West Africa)	1896	1960	France
Cambodia	1863	1953	France
Cameroon	1884	1960/1	Germany; UK/France from 1916
Central African Republic (*French Equatorial Africa)	1894	1960	France
Chad (*French Equatorial Africa)	1910	1960	France
Congo (*French Equatorial Africa)	1888	1960	France
Congo, Democratic Republic of (Belgian Congo)	1885	1960	Belgium
Côte d'Ivoire (*French West Africa)	1893	1960	France

Table 6 (Cont.)

Country (colonial name)	Colonized	Independent	Colonial power
Ethiopia (Abyssinia)	1936	1941	Italy
Gabon (*French Equatorial Africa)	1886	1960	France
Gambia	1843	1965	UK
Ghana (Gold Coast)	1850	1957	UK
Guyana (Guiana)	1796	1966	UK
Hong Kong	1843	1997	UK
India	18th/19th century	1947	UK
Indonesia (Dutch East Indies)	1602	1949	The Netherlands
Jamaica	1655	1962	UK
Kenya	1895	1963	UK
Laos (French *Indochina)	1893	1954	France
Lesotho (Basutoland)	1868	1966	UK
Libya	1912	1951	Italy
Macao	1557	1999	Portugal
Madagascar	1896	1960	France
Malawi (Nyasaland)	1891	1964	UK
Malaysia (Malaya)	1867	1963	UK
Mali (Soudan/*French West Africa)	1904	1960	France
Malta	1814	1964	UK
Mozambique	1508	1975	Portugal
Myanmar (Burma)	1886	1948	UK
Namibia (Southwest Africa)	1884	1990	Germany; South Africa from 1920
Niger (*French West Africa)	1921	1960	France
Nigeria	1861	1960	UK
Pakistan (India)	19th century	1947	UK
Papua New Guinea (New Guinea)	1884	1975	Germany; Australia/UK from 1914
Philippines	1898	1946	USA
Sierra Leone	1808	1961	UK
Singapore	1867	1965	Part of Malaya until 1965
Somalia	1885/1905	1960	Italy
Sri Lanka (Ceylon)	1796	1948	UK
Surinam	1667	1975	The Netherlands
Tanzania (East Africa/ Tanganyika)	1885	1961	Germany; UK from 1919; United with Zanzibar 1964
Togo	1884	1960	Germany (France from 1914)
Trinidad and Tobago	1797	1962	UK
Tunisia	1883	1956	France
Uganda	1896	1962	UK
Vietnam (French *Indochina)	1862–87	1954	France
Zambia (Northern Rhodesia)	1899/1911	1964	UK
Zimbabwe ((Southern) Rhodesia)	1891	1980	UK

imperial powers (especially Britain, France, Belgium, and the Netherlands) had been exposed by their inability to survive against *Hitler and defend their colonies without US help. Marginalized by the two superpowers, the USA and the USSR, European powers had no choice but to relinquish their imperial role, though many countries, most notably France (*Indochina, Algeria), Belgium (Congo), the Netherlands (Indonesia), and Portugal (Angola, Mozambique) did so with great reluctance.

MAPS 3 and 4

Delors, Jacques (b. 20 July 1925). President of the EC Commission 1985–94

Following a university degree in economics he worked for the Bank of France (1945–61), while also being active in the Christian *trade-union movement. Delors joined the French *Socialist Party in 1974 and became *Mitterrand's spokesperson for economic affairs. Following the latter's election victory in 1981, he became his powerful minister of economics and finance. Under his presidency of the European Commission the EC changed beyond recognition. He was the architect of major structural reforms which entailed an overhaul of the EC's finances and agricultural policies, as well as the introduction of *qualified majority voting. With the backing of *Kohl and Mitterrand, Delors promoted *European integration through the *Single European Act and the *Maastricht Treaty. He enjoyed considerable popularity in continental Europe, and was widely tipped to become a candidate in the French presidential elections of 1995, as polls indicated that he stood by far the best chance of winning. However, he decided to retire and has since been active promoting the ideals of the Maastricht Treaty.

Demirel, Süleyman (b. 6 Oct. 1924). Prime Minister of Turkey 1965–71, 1975–7, 1979–80, 1991–3; President 1993–2000

Born in Islamköi, he studied civil engineering at Istanbul Technical University and became a civil servant. He joined the right-wing Justice Party, whose chairman he became in 1964. As Prime Minister, he supported his agricultural constituencies, e.g. through major state investment in infrastructure. At the same time, he fostered good relations with the business community through his encouragement of private investment and free trade. He resigned in 1971 when the military demanded a number of policies under threat of intervention. Demirel remained the leader of his party and, together with *Ecevit, dominated Turkish politics throughout the 1970s. He was deposed by the military in 1980 and temporarily imprisoned. He was released in 1983, but was forbidden to take part in any political activity for ten years. He nevertheless instigated the Grand Turkey Party in 1983, but the party was not allowed to contest elections since it was seen as a direct successor to the now outlawed Justice Party. Demirel tried once more with the formation of the True Path Party (DYP), which he came to lead officially after the ban on political activity was lifted in 1987. He won the 1991 elections, and in 1993 was elected President by parliament. He became so popular that the Prime Minister, *Ecevit, tried to have the consitution changed to allow him a second term of office. This failed to get the necessary parliamentary majority, and he was succeeded by Ahmed Necdet Sezer.

Democratic Alliance, South Africa

Established in April 1989 as the Democratic Party, it sought to unite White liberal opposition to the *National Party (NP) through a merger of the *Progressive Federal Party, the National Democratic Movement, and the Independent Party. After the end of *apartheid, it played an important mediating role in the negotiations between the *National Party and the *ANC for a transition to a multiracial democracy. As the NP became more attractive to liberal voters and the major party representing the interests of Whites, the DP lost some of its identity as the major party of liberal opposition, gaining seven seats with 1.7 per cent of the popular vote in 1994. Nevertheless, it played a disproportionate role in the subsequent constitutional debates, campaigning for a liberal, non-interventionist state. This paid off in 1998, when it benefited from internal squabbles in the National Party to become the country's largest opposition party, with 9.6 per cent of the vote and 36 seats. In 2000, it formed effectively the senior partner to the demoralized NP as the two parties merged to become the Democratic Alliance (DA). A number of members broke away in 2001 to re-form the NP, but in the 2004 elections, the DA remained the principal opposition party, with 50 parliamentary seats. From 2007 the party was led by the energetic Mayor of Cape Town, Helen Zille.

((⊕)) SEE WEB LINKS

• The home page of the Democratic Alliance.

Democratic Labor Party, Australia

A political party emerging from the Australian *Labor Party in 1957, sparked off by *Evatt's handling of the *Petrov affair, when some right-wing members left the ALP in 1955 in opposition to what they considered its

Communist, dogmatic leanings. Supported by the Catholic Social Movement and *Mannix, its overreliance on the Catholic vote and its fixation upon the single issue of anti-Communism meant that the party was unable to gain more than a few Senate seats, even though at times it held the balance of power there. It was unable to send any representatives to parliament from 1974.

Democratic Movement (France), see UDF.

Democratic Party, New Zealand
Founded in 1953 as the **Social Credit Political League**, which followed the social credit ideas of C. H. Douglas, whereby a recession was caused by a lack of purchasing power within the population. In 1966, it gained 14.4 per cent of the popular vote, though because of New Zealand's first-past-the-post electoral system it only gained one seat. It split in 1972, and in 1985 acquired its current name. Its major significance in New Zealand politics derived from its function as an expression of protest against the two established parties dominating the system, the *Labour and *National Parties. In addition, the discrepancy between its popular share of the vote (over 20 per cent in 1981) and its parliamentary representation (two seats in 1981) sparked off a debate on the electoral system, which led to the adoption of proportional representation after a referendum in 1991. Its share of the vote declined from the mid-1980s, and it lost its parliamentary representation in 1987. In 1991, it merged with four other groups to form the *Alliance.
  SOCIAL CREDIT PARTY, CANADA

Democratic Party of Japan
Created in 1996, it consisted of many former members of the Social Democratic Party (*Socialist Party) as well as other oppositional splinter groups. It sought to provide a more effective opposition against what it considered the increasingly corrupt rule by the ruling *Liberal Democratic Party (LDP). It vowed to promote a transparent and just government, social fairness, pacifism, and the devolution of power to the local level. The DP quickly developed into Japan's largest opposition party, gaining 127 seats in the 2000 elections to the House of Representatives, and 177 benefited from *Abe's unpopularity in 2007, when it became the strongest party in the Upper House in 2007.

(SEE WEB LINKS)

• The official website of the Democratic Party Japan.

Democratic Party, USA
History The oldest democratic political party in the world. Known in the 1790s as the Democratic-Republican Party, Democrats split in 1860 over the questions of slavery and the US Civil War. They reunited after the Civil War, gaining support from the ever-expanding west and from the immigrant working classes of the industrialized north-east, while retaining the loyalty of the deep south. In the early twentieth century the party adopted many of the policies of the *Progressive movement and its candidate for President, Woodrow *Wilson, was elected in 1912.

Although in eclipse during the 1920s, it re-emerged in the years of the Great *Depression, with policies to end unemployment and stimulate industry. It captured both *Congress and the Presidency, with Franklin D. *Roosevelt the only President to have been elected four times. Since then the Democratic Party has tended to dominate the House of Representatives and has generally held the Senate as well, supporting civil rights, social welfare, and Third World aid.

Following the *civil rights movement and desegregation in the 1950s and 1960s, the Democratic Party lost much of its support from the *Dixiecrat southern states. The Democratic presidencies of John F. *Kennedy and Lyndon B. *Johnson saw fruitful partnerships between Congress and President. The *Vietnam War, however, badly divided the party in 1968. Under the Republican President *Nixon, Democrats retained control of Congress and won the election of President *Carter in 1976. During the 1970s and 1980s, following *Nixon's and *Reagan's adoption of *Goldwater's 'new republicanism', the Democratic Party lost the support of large sections of the middle and upper classes, becoming increasingly identified with the poorer population of the big cities and small farmers. As a result, defections of urban workers to the *Republican Party undermined the strength of the party in presidential elections during the 1970s and 1980s.

Contemporary politics A key problem for the Democrats from the 1980s was the diversity of their coalition, comprising many different ethnic groups and social movements each requiring support from party representatives. Related to this was a reputation for 'big government' policies. This concern was reduced during the *Clinton presidency, as he managed to balance the budget, in marked contrast to his Republican predecessors and successor. Clinton also managed to capture the allegiance of the 'soccer moms'. These had formed the core of floating voters attracted to *Reagan's Republicans, as Clinton emphasized fiscal rectitude, economic growth, and investment in education.

Led by Al *Gore (2000) and John Kerry (2004) in recent presidential campaigns, Democrats proved extremely adept at generating mass support, not least among Black voters. However, they were outsmarted by their Republican adversaries, who proved even more capable of mobilizing their voters concerned by Christian values. In 2004, Howard Dean was appointed Director of the Democratic National Committee. Howard adopted the '50 state strategy', on the basis that to form a majority in Congress, Democrats needed to be campaigning not just in the states that currently looked winnable, but also in Republican bastions like the south and the midwest.

(⊕) SEE WEB LINKS

• The official website of the Democratic Party USA.

Democratic Unionist Party (DUP), Northern Ireland

Formed in 1971 by Ian *Paisley and Desmond Boal, the party is committed to *Northern Ireland remaining part of the UK. The party stood firmly against Protestants sharing power with the Catholic minority in the 1970s, and is opposed to British membership of the European Community (*European integration). A more radical proponent of Protestant interests than the *Ulster Unionist Party (UUP), it has consistently opposed talking to ministers from the Irish Republic, and it rejected the *Downing Street Declaration of 1993. From the 1970s to the 1990s the DUP tended to win three seats in Westminster elections, with about 20 per cent of the Northern Ireland vote in British general elections.

The DUP's popularity was boosted by its rejection of the *Good Friday Agreements, whereby it capitalized on Protestant fears of compromise. It trebled its representation in Westminster to nine MPs in 2006. In the Northern Ireland elections of 2003 it also eclipsed the UUP, becoming the strongest party with 30 seats. Within Northern Ireland, the party continued its hostile rhetoric against *Sinn Féin, but it found itself in a difficult position after the *IRA had destroyed its weapons. Paisley engaged in talks with Sinn Féin which led to the *St Andrews Agreement. On the basis of this, its representation in the Assembly increased even further after the 2007 elections, with 36 seats. After protracted negotiations, the DUP joined Sinn Féin in a historic government of reconciliation as the majority party.

(⊕) SEE WEB LINKS

• The official website of the DUP.

Deng Xiaoping (Teng Hsaio-p'ing)
(b. Aug. 1904, d. 19 Feb. 1997). Chinese leader 1978–97

Early career Born at Guang'an (*Sichuan), he studied with *Zhou Enlai in France (1920–5), where he joined the Chinese *Communist Party (CCP) (1924). He studied briefly in Moscow before returning to China in 1926. He led several uprisings against the *Guomindang, and was the political commissar of the Communist 7th and 8th Armies. A devout follower of *Mao Zedong, he went to *Jianxi in 1931, and took part in the *Long March. In the *Sino-Japanese War, his rise to prominence continued as a political commissar in the 8th Route Army and the 129th Division, until in 1945 he joined the CCP Central Committee. Owing to his experience in battle, he played an important part in the Communist success in the *Chinese Civil War, notably in the *Huai-Hai campaign. In 1949 Deng was First Secretary of the party's south-west bureau, and in 1954 he was made Secretary-General of the Chinese Communist Party, with a seat in the *Politburo. He was a central figure in the growing ideological and then political alienation between China and the Soviet Union.

In the *Cultural Revolution, Deng was deprived of all posts and forced to recant his alleged 'reactionary-bourgeois' tendencies. Zhou Enlai reinstated his old friend, and Deng became Vice-Premier of the State Council in 1973. His renewed advance peaked when he practically ran the government during Zhou's illness. He was dismissed after Zhou's death in 1976, becoming a victim of the *Gang of Four.

After the arrest of the Gang of Four, he was reinstated once again in July 1977. He now became the strong man in Chinese politics, outmanoeuvring the more ideological *Hua Guofeng by appropriating Mao's slogan of 'Practice as the sole criterion of truth'. With this pragmatist platform, his leadership was confirmed at the Third Plenum of the 11th CCP congress in December 1978.

In power Deng played down the memory and teachings of Mao Zedong, and emphasized instead the need for socialist modernization. He encouraged individual enterprise and economic growth while insisting on the continued political domination of the CCP. Deng did not hesitate to suppress all opposition, most notably at *Tiananmen Square in 1989, while granting his people an unprecedented amount of personal freedom in other spheres. In foreign policy, he combined a high degree of pragmatism with *nationalism. He was a pivotal influence in the taking up of diplomatic relations with the USA in 1979, and normalized Sino-Soviet relations in 1989. At the same time, he was insistent on the return to the People's Republic of China of all territories under outside control. He thus negotiated the incorporation into China of *Hong Kong and *Macao, while continuing to call for unification with Taiwan. Deng was the most important leader of the People's Republic of China after Mao. He became increasingly affected by Parkinson's disease, and was succeeded by *Jiang Zemin.

Denikin, Anton Ivanovich (b. 4 Dec. 1872, d. 8 Aug. 1947). Russian general

Son of a serf, he joined the Imperial Army when he was 15 and by 1917 had reached the rank of general. He served in the provisional government after the *Russian (February) Revolution in 1917. Once the *Bolsheviks seized power in October 1917 he assumed command of a counter-revolutionary army. His forces gained control of a large part of southern Russia, and in May 1919 he launched an offensive against Moscow. His *White Army forces were defeated by *Trotsky's *Red Army at Orel. He retreated to the Caucasus, where in March 1920 his army disintegrated. He fled to the USA.

Denison, Flora MacDonald (née Merrill) (b. Feb. 1867, d. 23 May 1921). President of the (Canadian) National Suffrage Association 1911–14

Born in Hastings County, Canada West (later Ontario), she ran a dressmaking business and participated in the Toronto women's suffrage movement from 1906. She became widely known through her column in the *Toronto Sunday World* (1909–13). Always on the radical edge of the movement, in 1914 she had to resign because of her support for the English militant *suffragettes. She was horrified by World War I, which she felt needed to be followed by a spiritual renewal among Canadians, part of which would involve giving women equal rights. In the last years of her life, she became a theosophist.

Denmark

Scandinavia's southernmost country has benefited from remarkable social consensus, a profitable agricultural base, and a strong parliamentary tradition.

Contemporary history up to 1945 Defeat in the Prussian–Danish War of 1864, and the consequent loss of the duchies of Schleswig and Holstein, led to a major domestic political crisis, which the Conservatives tried to use to shore up their power. The Liberals, on the other hand, sought to strengthen the state through the introduction of parliamentary government, so that government would be dependent on parliamentary rather than royal approval. This came into effect after the landslide Conservative defeat in 1901. Subsequent coalition governments between Liberals and Social Democrats, which dominated politics until 1920, introduced considerable social legislation such as a progressive income tax, and the encouragement of *trade union membership. In 1915, an already liberal franchise was made almost universal. Denmark remained neutral in World War I, and in the ensuing *Versailles Treaty gained northern Schleswig, a majority of whose population spoke Danish.

During 1920–4 and 1926–9 Denmark was governed by a coalition of middle-class parties to the exclusion of the Social Democrats. In that period, the country faced severe economic difficulties, as it had one of the highest unemployment rates in Europe (over 17 per cent, 1921–9). In 1929, the Social Democrats finally became the country's dominant party. Similar to the Swedish *Social Democrats, under Thorvald Stauning (Prime Minister 1933–9) their response to the Great *Depression was the introduction of *Keynesian demand management. In the Kanslergade Agreement of 1933, they established a consensus between agriculture and industry. The currency was devalued by 20 per cent, agricultural debts were restructured, and agricultural taxes were reduced. The recovery of the export-oriented agricultural sector would then pay for social welfare reforms in the cities, and create jobs in industry. After the outbreak of World War II, Denmark affirmed its neutrality, and was the only Scandinavian country to conclude a non-aggression treaty with *Hitler in late 1939. Still, it was invaded on 9 April 1940. King Christian X remained in Copenhagen, while Danish resistance led the Germans to declare a state of emergency on 29 August 1943.

After World War II The country was subsequently transformed from a primarily agricultural to a mainly industrial economy with an important and prosperous, but none the less subsidiary, agricultural sector. In the postwar period, the political system was characterized by the existence of a relatively large number of parties, each of which established a fairly well-defined regional and social base. In some ways, this strengthened the still dominant Social Democratic Party, which became the linchpin of a political system characterized by multi-party coalitions and minority support in the Folketinget (parliament). The prevalence of minority governments encouraged consensual politics. In 1953 the Constitution was revised to allow female succession to the throne, establish a unicameral legislature, and include the territory of *Greenland as an integral part of the kingdom. The last measure was reversed in 1979, when Greenland was granted internal autonomy.

A founding member of *EFTA since 1960, Denmark left EFTA to join the EEC in 1973. It did, however, retain a decided scepticism towards the idea of further *European integration; for example, it took two referendums to get the Maastricht Treaty approved in 1993. Under the first Prime Minister from the Conservative Party (Konservative Folkeparti, KF) since 1901, *Schlüter, Denmark became the first Scandinavian country to embark upon reforms of its generous social welfare system. Schlüter's new priorities of low inflation and low public debt even at the cost of a relatively high rate of unemployment were eventually accepted by the Social Democrats, who resumed government under Poul N. Rasmussen in 1993. Rasmussen was re-elected in 1998, but thereafter broke his election promise not to cut the basic state pension. Cuts in unemployment benefit increased the government's unpopularity further, and in 2000 it lost a referendum on Denmark's entry into *EMU.

Contemporary politics (since 2001) In a general election marked by xenophobia, Fogh Rasmussen of the Venstre won the 2001 elections. He formed a government tolerated by the far right anti-immigration Danish People's Party, and, following his re-election in 2005, formed a coalition with the more moderate KF. Under Rasmussen, Denmark adopted tough anti-immigration laws. The economy prospered through steady growth and low unemployment, while Denmark engaged in a pro-US foreign policy, sending its own troops to support the US in the *Iraq War.

Department of Homeland Security,
see CIA

Depression, the Great (1929–32)

Causes The worst recession in world history, which was triggered off in the USA, then by far the most important economy in the world.

In part, US prosperity in the 1920s had been very fragile, as 5 per cent of the population received a third of all income, whereas over 70 per cent of the population received an annual wage which was less than was considered necessary to live in decent comfort. Hence, the large rises in consumption were effected by only a very small section of the population, and this became problematic as soon as its demands for consumer goods (such as cars, radios, etc.) were satisfied. In addition, the banking system was structurally weak and very badly regulated, with a large number of small banks (over 30,000) in the 1920s. Finally, high US tariffs on imports led to a huge imbalance between exports and imports, so that foreign countries could only afford to buy US exports with the help of US loans. The combination of these factors led to the *Wall Street Crash, but they also explain the severe depression that followed. Banks collapsed, domestic consumption collapsed, and because US investors needed to recall their foreign assets quickly US exports also collapsed.

International impact In Europe, the withdrawal of US funds, on which especially the continental European economies had come to depend, caused a fully fledged financial panic in 1931. The liquidation of foreign assets brought the largest Austrian commercial bank, the Creditanstalt, to the brink of insolvency, forcing the Austrian government to freeze all its remaining assets. This created a panic across central Europe, as investors rushed to the banks to retrieve their own investments before these were frozen too. For Germany, the economic and financial crisis led US President Hoover to announce on 21 June 1931 a one-year moratorium for *reparation payments. In Britain, the fact that its banks had given substantial loans to the now collapsing economies of central Europe, together with the lack of German reparation payments at the time of a large budget deficit, led to pressure on the value of the pound which forced the final abandonment of the *Gold Standard. This was tantamount to an admission by the formerly dominant economic power that it was no longer able to lead the world economy.

Effects The depression led to a sharp increase in tariffs and hence to a substantial reduction in international trade, so that during the 1930s the trade in manufactured products between Germany, France, and the UK declined to half of the level of 1913. Unemployment reached record levels of around 20 per cent worldwide, but declined thereafter to around 10 per cent in 1937, a

figure still considerably higher than in 1928. In the US, the depression led to greater economic involvement of the state, through *Roosevelt's *New Deal. Most importantly, in the countries worst hit by the recession (in central Europe and in South America) the ensuing hardship and misery provided a receptive and fertile ground for the aggressive, chauvinistic, romantic-authoritarian rhetoric of far-right movements.
FASCISM

Desai, Morarji Ranchhodji (b. 29 Feb. 1896, d. 10 Apr. 1995). Prime Minister of India 1977–9
Born in Bhadeli (Gujarat) he was a civil servant in Bombay (1918–30) before becoming a disciple of *Gandhi, spending a total of ten years in British prisons for civil disobedience. He made his reputation as Finance Minister of Bombay Province (1946–52), before becoming its Chief Minister (1952–6). Desai joined the Indian government in 1956 as Minister of Commerce and Industry, and was then Minister of Finance (1958–63), overseeing a series of five-year plans which led to a doubling of industrial output in ten years. After *Nehru's death (1964) he was a contender for the succession, but his austere style failed to win him support in the *Congress Party against Indira *Gandhi. He came to oppose her bitterly, in return for which he was imprisoned during the Emergency, 1975–7. In 1977 he was the obvious candidate to lead the *Janata opposition to Mrs Gandhi, and he won the election of that year. His government restored parliamentary democracy. As Prime Minister he failed to deal with the economic and factional problems confronting him. An austere and principled man (and a great believer in the strength to be derived from drinking his own urine), he suffered from his inability to compromise, often threatening to fast himself to death if he did not get his way.

desegregation (USA)
The abolition of racial *segregation.
BROWN V. TOPEKA; CIVIL RIGHTS MOVEMENT; BUSING

détente
A term generally used to describe the decline of tensions between two countries or parties. In particular, it describes the second phase of the *Cold War from 1962 until 1979, when the USA and the USSR established better diplomatic relations and direct lines of communication. Serious attempts were made at *disarmament. In particular, *Brandt's Ostpolitik (*German question) as well as the *Conference on Security and Cooperation in

Europe, beginning with the *Helsinki Conference, provided for enhanced *human rights within Eastern Europe. They also improved relations between Eastern European countries under Soviet influence and the countries of Western Europe and North America.

Díaz, (José de la Cruz) Porfirio (b. 15 Sept. 1830, d. 2 July 1915). President of Mexico 1877–80, 1884–1911
Born in Oaxaca de Juárez, the professor of law was in 1867 one of the principal architects of the overthrow of the French-backed Emperor Maximilian (b. 1832, d. 1867). Ten years later he organized a coup in which he declared himself President, after which he ruled for thirty-four years (1880–4 through a puppet president). By quashing all opposition he stabilized a country which had been in almost constant turmoil since independence in 1821. Through his programme of economic liberalization the economy underwent significant transformation. Largely with the help of foreign capital, oil resources were explored, railways built, and mining encouraged. In agriculture, small farmers were bullied into selling their land to large landowners, a measure which increased agricultural efficiency, but which also created tremendous social problems through leaving the majority of all farmers landless by 1910. By 1911, the economic problems had also cost him the support of much of the middle classes. This rendered him vulnerable in the Mexican Revolution, which was triggered by the opposition of members of the elite led by Francesco I. *Madero. He died in exile in Paris.

Dictation Test, see WHITE AUSTRALIA POLICY

Diefenbaker, John George (b. 18 Sept. 1895, d. 16 Aug. 1979). Prime Minister of Canada 1957–63
Early career Born at Neustadt (Ontario), he grew up in the North-West Territories and in Saskatchewan, and served in World War I. He was admitted to the Saskatchewan Bar in 1919, and in 1924 opened a practice in Prince Albert. A distinguished lawyer by 1929, when he was appointed a King's Counsel, he had an unsuccessful political career until he became leader of the Saskatchewan Conservative Party, which failed to win a single seat in the 1938 election. In 1940, he was elected to the House of Commons, where he gained a reputation for his parliamentary skills.

In office Diefenbaker became leader of the Progressive *Conservative Party in 1956, which he led to a surprise victory in 1957, later confirmed by a landslide election victory in 1958. He introduced the franchise to the *native peoples, and legislated for a Canadian Bill of Rights. He also sought to develop the northern areas of Canada. A strong believer in international organizations such as the *UN, he was instrumental in forcing South Africa's withdrawal from the *Commonwealth in 1961. Following the 1962 elections his government commanded only a minority. This was caused by uneasiness about the economy and his opposition to the deployment of US nuclear weapons on Canadian soil. Despite a formidable personal performance on the campaign trail he narrowly lost the 1963 elections. As leader of the opposition, Diefenbaker became a fierce and celebrated critic of *Pearson's Liberal government. He was replaced as party leader in 1967, but remained in parliament until his death.

Diem, Ngo Dinh, see NGO DINH DIEM

Dien Bien Phu
A village in North Vietnam, strategically close to the Laotian border, and site of a decisive battle in the French-*Indochina War.
In November 1953, the French Commander-in-Chief, Henri Navarre, ordered his forces to occupy Dien Bien Phu, in an attempt to prevent the *Vietminh troops from crossing the border into Laos. The French came under siege by numerically vastly superior Vietminh forces on 7 March 1954, who captured the village on 7 May 1954. Of the French garrison of 16,500 men, little more than 3,000 survived the siege or subsequent imprisonment. By contrast, over 25,000 Vietminh troops died. While not a disastrous loss in military terms, it was none the less a severe blow to French morale. With defeat coming days before the Geneva conference (*Geneva Agreements), it demonstrated that the French would never be able to overcome the numerically superior Vietminh armies.

Dieppe Raid (19 Aug. 1942)
An amphibious raid on the French coast during *World War II to destroy the airfield, port, and radar installations of Dieppe. Some 1,000 British commando and 5,000 Canadian infantry troops were involved. There was considerable confusion as landing-craft approached the two beaches where they met heavy fire. The assault was a failure and the order was given to withdraw. In one morning of fighting, almost 3,400 Canadians and more than 500 British soldiers and officers were killed or captured. German coastal defences sank one destroyer, thirty-three landing-craft, and shot down 106 aircraft. The raid, which had been postponed once and had virtually no chance of success at the outset, raised serious questions among the Canadian public about British use (or misuse) of Canadian troops in battle. For the *Allies, the raid offered many useful lessons for later landings in Italy and France, not least the need for meticulous planning and total security. By contrast, it was a warning to the Germans, who strengthened their extensive coastal defences on the French North Sea and the Atlantic.

Dimitrov, Georgi Mikhailovich (b. 18 June 1882, d. 2 July 1949). Prime Minister of Bulgaria 1946–9
Born at Radomir, Dimitrov became a printer and followed his father and brothers into *trade-union activity. In 1902 he joined the Social Democratic Party, which he left in 1903 to join a more radical movement which later became the Communist Party. After completing an eighteen-month gaol sentence, he left for Moscow, where he was groomed to become an effective Communist Party leader. He returned to lead the abortive 1923 uprising against King *Boris III. As head of the Bulgarian sector of *Comintern in Berlin from 1929, he was accused of responsibility for the *Reichstag fire, but was acquitted after conducting a brilliant defence. He spent World War II in Moscow. In 1945 he returned to Bulgaria to become head of the provisional government. He created a legal and constitutional framework which led to the establishment of the Bulgarian People's Republic in 1946. His ruthless policies of sovietization were an important contributor to Bulgaria's subsequent servility to the Soviet Union. By contrast, his unrealistic plan for a federation of Balkan states collapsed when Yugoslavia broke with the Soviet Union in 1948.

Diouf, Abdou (b. 7 Mar. 1935). President of Senegal 1981–2000
Born in Louga, he was educated at the University of Dakar, and graduated in law from the University of Paris. Upon his return to Senegal he became the protégé of President *Senghor, and became secretary-general of the President's office in 1964. He was made Prime Minister in 1970, and succeeded Senghor to the Presidency in 1981. While being less of an ideologue than his predecessor, he was a much better and more efficient administrator. He also liberalized political life. In 1981, he responded to the call of his Gambian colleague, *Jawara, for military assistance against a coup, and

subsequently became engaged in the formation of a union between the two countries (Senegambia). In 1985 he became the head of the OAU (*African Union). Economic difficulties as a result of falling prices for Senegal's main exports and the failure of the union with Gambia in 1989 gave rise to a serious opposition movement, though he continued to be sufficiently popular to be re-elected in 1993. Diouf faced a united opposition in the 2000 presidential elections, and obtained only 41 per cent of the vote in the second round against Abdoulaye Wade. In 2002, he succeeded *Boutros Ghali as Secretary-General of the organization of French-speaking countries, the Francophonie.

disarmament

Attempts to achieve disarmament by international agreement began at the Conferences of The Hague in 1899 and 1907, both of which failed to achieve significant outcomes. After World War I, the *League of Nations convened a conference of 60 nations during 1932–4. Its failure was caused partly by French caution, but more especially by Germany's withdrawal in October 1933. After World War II, the UN (*UNO) established a permanent disarmament commission in 1952. During the height of the *Cold War, progress was slow, and in 1957 the Soviet Union left the commission.

The *Cuban Missile Crisis of 1962 brought the two superpowers, the USA and the USSR, to the brink of a nuclear war. This manifested the real possibility of all-out war whose nuclear devasation would leave no winner. Both sides realized that a further escalation of the Cold War had to be avoided, and this led to the partial **Nuclear Test Ban Treaty** of 5 August 1963, signed by the USA, the Soviet Union, and the UK, banning nuclear weapons tests in the atmosphere, in outer space, or under water.

These countries signed the **Nuclear Non-Proliferation Treaty** of 1 July 1968, committing themselves not to aid other countries in the development of nuclear weapons. By 1994, this treaty had been ratified by 154 nations, though it was never signed by China or France, both of which had developed nuclear weapons by then. The treaty may have slowed down the spread of nuclear weapons, but it could not prevent it, as Israel, and possibly South Africa, developed nuclear weapons on their own in the 1980s. The original treaty expired in 1995.

The end of the Cold War led to hopes of substantial nuclear disarmament, which were partly realized. Some countries such as the Ukraine agreed to their nuclear weapons

being destroyed. In September 1996 a new Nuclear Test-Ban Treaty was signed by the five traditional nuclear powers (China, France, Russia, UK, and USA), which was due to come into effect within three years, once it was signed by all powers with the capability to build nuclear weapons. Nevertheless, actual disarmament turned out to be less drastic than many had hoped. Geo-political tension continued in the area of the former Soviet Union, between India and Pakistan, in Korea, and in the Gulf region. As a result, Pakistan and India succeeded in reaching nuclear weapons capabilities in the 1990s, with North Korea and Iran attempting to build nuclear weapons in the early years of the twenty-first century.

Strategic Arms Limitation Talks between the USSR and the USA to limit long-range missiles and bombers began in November 1969, which led to the **SALT I** agreement of 26 May 1972. This limited the deployment of anti-ballistic missiles and froze the number of intercontinental ballistic missiles for the next five years, or until further SALT negotiations had been concluded. After six years of renewed talks, the **SALT II** treaty, which brought about only a minimal reduction in the number of missile launchers and other weapons, was concluded. Owing to the Soviet invasion of Afghanistan in December 1979, SALT II was never ratified by the US Senate.

Strategic Arms Reduction Talks (START) began on 29 June 1982 in Geneva, were abandoned in 1983, but were resumed in 1985 after *Gorbachev became the Soviet leader. The first START treaty, signed in July 1991 by Gorbachev and *Bush, reduced each country's long-range missile launchers to 1,600, and warheads to 6,000. In December 1992 Bush and the Russian President *Yeltsin signed a second START treaty which almost halved the number of warheads on each side.

Meanwhile, the **Mutual and Balanced Force Reduction Talks (MBFR)** in Vienna between members of *NATO and the *Warsaw Pact, which started on 30 October 1973, was concerned with limiting ground forces in central Europe. As both sides were unable to overcome their mutual distrust, the talks ended on 2 February 1989 without agreement.

By contrast, the **INF (Intermediate-range Nuclear Forces) Treaty**, signed on 8 December 1987 by President *Reagan and Soviet leader Gorbachev, was notable not only for the substantial reduction in nuclear arms, but also for the innovative verification procedures it prescribed, such as on-site inspection of nuclear stock at short notice. It reduced US stockpiles by 436 nuclear warheads, and

Soviet ones by 957 missiles equipped with a total of 1,565 warheads by 1991.

In 2002, the **Anti-Ballistic Missile Treaty** expired after twenty years. It was not renewed by President George W. *Bush, who preferred instead to proceed with the creation of a nuclear shield over the US as part of National Missile Defence. In response, Russia abandoned the START II treaty of 1993, which had been superseded by an agreement on further missile reductions between Bush and *Putin earlier in the year.

NUCLEAR BOMB

Dixiecrat (USA)

A popular name in the USA for a *Democrat in a southern state opposed to *desegregation. In 1948 the States Rights Democratic Party was founded by diehard Southern Democrats opposed to President *Truman's renomination as Democrat candidate, on account of his stand on civil rights. Instead, they ran Senator Strom Thurmond of South Carolina as their presidential candidate. After Truman's victory they abandoned their presidential efforts, but continued to resist civil rights programmes in *Congress. Many Dixiecrats moved to support the *Republican Party in the 1960s and 1970s. A short-lived Dixiecrat American Independent Party was formed for the 1968 elections, with the Alabama Governor George *Wallace as candidate for President. The triumph of desegregation was also marked by the dissolution of the traditional southern wing of the Democratic Party. Where once there had been a 'solid south' which was staunchly Democrat, by the 1980s the south was dominated by Republican Senators, Congressmen, and Governors. Consequently, the Dixiecrats belonged to history as well. Thurmond joined the Republican Party in 1964, and became the longest-serving member of the US Senate in history (1954–2002).

Djibouti

A small African country strategically situated at the mouth of the Red Sea. Under French influence since 1859, it was declared a protectorate as French Somaliland in the 1880s. The French ruled through skilfully exploiting the tensions between the dominant ethnic groups, the Afar and the Issa. After World War II it became a French Overseas Territory, but in 1967 the population voted against unification with Somalia. Instead, it opted for independence in a referendum on 8 May 1978, and on 22 June 1978 an independent republic was declared.

In practice, Djibouti has remained one of the most dependent countries in the world. With virtually no exports of its own and an unemployment rate of over 40 per cent, it has become almost entirely reliant on foreign aid. Economic activity has centred on the capital's harbour, which is strategically placed at the mouth of the Red Sea, and which serves as the main entrepôt for Ethiopian trade. Owing to its strategic location, Djibouti hosts a large French military presence, and it provides the only African base for the US military.

The country's first President, Hassan Gouled Aptidon (from the Issa people), founded the Rassemblement Populaire pour le Progrès (RPP, Popular Union for Progress) in 1979 and banned all other parties (1981). Owing to growing ethnic tensions leading to civil war, he agreed to the introduction of a multi-party democracy. In 1992, the RPP again won all the seats in the legislative assembly, though Aptidon admitted two members of the rebel group, Front pour la Restauration de l'Unité et de la Démocratie (Front for the Restoration of Unity and Democracy, FRUD) into the government. In 1999 Aptidon was succeeded by a joint candidate of the FRUD and the RPP, Ismail Omar Guelleh. The chamber of deputies consisted of 33 Issa representatives, and 32 Deputies of the Afar people. In light of the reconciliation between the two people, a number of radical rebel splinter groups gave up their arms in 2001. Guelleh was re-elected in 2005, with the cooperation between FRUD and RPP leaving no room for an official opposition.

Djindjić, Zoran (b. 1 Aug. 1952, d. 12 Mar 2003). Prime Minister of Serbia, 2001–3

Born in Bosanski Šamac, he became a student of philosophy in Belgrade. After a brief spell in prison following the 1974 purges, he continued his studies in Germany. After obtaining his doctorate there, he returned to Yugoslavia to teach philosophy at the University of Belgrade and Novi Sad. In 1990, he co-founded the Democratic Party (DP), and in the elections of that year he entered the Serbian parliament. As leader of the DP from 1994, he worked to unite the opposition, whose candidate he became at the Belgrade local elections in 1996. When the state was unsuccessful at annulling the elections, Djindjić became the first freely-elected mayor of Belgrade since 1945. His support in the local assembly crumbled, however, and at the end of 1997 he was forced to resign. In December 2000, the opposition alliance, of which he was a prominent member, won the elections to the Serbian parliament. As Prime Minister, he was determined in the pursuit of political, administrative and economic reform. He ordered the extradition of *Milošević, and began to fight against corruption and graft. Djindjić was assassinated by members of criminal groups and nationalist security forces.

DKP, see COMMUNIST PARTY, GERMANY

Dobrudja
The disputed Black Sea littoral at the mouth of the Danube. It became part of the *Ottoman Empire in 1417, but in 1878 the northern half became part of Romania. Meanwhile, the south was claimed by the newly independent state of Bulgaria, but was annexed by Romania in 1913. During World War I, it witnessed heavy fighting between Romanian and Austrian troops. Briefly part of Bulgaria in 1918, it was annexed again by Romania in 1919. In 1940 it reverted to Bulgaria, whose sovereignty over the southern part of Dobrudja was confirmed in 1947.

Doi Takako (b. 30 Nov. 1928). Chairwoman of the Japan Socialist Party 1986–91
Japan's first female leader of a mainstream political party who became the first woman to hold the office of Speaker in the House of Representatives. A lecturer in constitutional law at Dôshisha University in Kyoto, she was persuaded to stand as a Japan *Socialist Party (JSP) candidate in the 1969 House of Representatives elections in Kobe's second constituency. She became a notable figure through her ability to avoid factional squabbles, concentrating instead on issues such as foreign affairs, the environment, and women's rights. She was elected vice-chairwoman of the party in 1983. As chairwoman, she was able to project a popular and charismatic persona which appealed directly to the electorate. The combination of her personal popularity and a discredited *Liberal Democratic Party (LDP) allowed the JSP to win a plurality of seats in 1989. The opposition parties combined won a majority of seats in the House of Councillors election. This was the first time that the ruling party had lost control of either House of the Diet since 1955. This feat was followed by a good, although less spectacular performance for the JSP in the 1990 House of Representatives election. Even though she had been responsible for such unprecedented electoral successes, Doi stepped down as party chairwoman in 1991, partly because of poor results in the local elections of that year. She remained the focus

for the pacifist wing of her party until her reluctant acceptance of the speaker's chair in the lower house in 1993. Throughout her career, she retained an immutable attachment to the pacifist principles enshrined in the *Japanese constitution.

Doihara Kenji (b. 8 Aug. 1883, d. 23 Dec. 1948). Japanese general
Born into a service family, Doihara rose to become a general in the *Guandong Army. With *Ishiwara, he is remembered as one of the architects of the Manchurian Incident of 1931, which involved the military takeover of north-eastern China. In addition, he played an important part in negotiating the Doihara-Quin Agreement (June 1935), which paved the way for the withdrawal of the *Guomindang from northern China, the partition of the country, and the establishment of a puppet state in Manchuria (*Manchukuo). After 1945 Doihara was indicted as a Class A war criminal. During his trial he refused to give testimony and was later hanged.

Dollfuss, Engelbert (b. 4 Oct. 1892, d. 25 July 1934). Chancellor of Austria 1932–4
Born in Texing (Lower Austria) as the illegitimate child of a farmer's daughter, he briefly studied theology and then law at the University of Vienna before participating in World War I, in which he won eight decorations for bravery. The war hero and devout Catholic became a Member of Parliament for the right-wing Christian Social Party. As Minister of Agriculture from 1931, his success in coping with the *Great Depression made him a natural choice for the chancellorship.
    At a time when the country was riven with strife, which often erupted into street fights, he fought hard to contain the main protagonists of the general unrest, the Communists and the Nazis. In 1933 he created an authoritarian dictatorship by dismissing parliament and outlawing the Communist and Nazi Parties. He tried to maintain popular support through the foundation of a Patriotic Front. In practice, his policies closely resembled those of *Fascism, and he received support from *Mussolini. In 1934, he added the more moderate members of the working classes to the list of his enemies, as he reacted to a demonstration of socialist workers by ordering the army to attack a large socialist housing estate in Vienna, which was defeated after five days of bitter fighting. Despite his lack of popular support, he proclaimed a Fascist Constitution in May 1934, but in July he was murdered by

Austrian Nazis in a miscalculated attempt to trigger *Hitler's intervention and thus force the Anschluss.

Dominica

An island state in the Lesser Antilles, which came under British sovereignty in 1805. Following the introduction of universal suffrage in 1951, its politics were dominated by the centrist Dominica Labour Party (DLP). In 1978 it became an independent republic within the *Commonwealth. The DLP split in 1979 and lost the subsequent elections to the right-wing Dominica Freedom Party, whose leader, **Mary Eugenia Charles**, became the first woman Prime Minister in the Caribbean. Her conservative and anti-*trade union economic policies became increasingly controversial.

The 1995 elections were won by the Dominica United Workers' Party under the former general manager of the Dominica Banana Marketing Corporation, Edison James. James was largely credited with orchestrating a buy-out of the marketing and shipping of his country's bananas, in conjunction with St Lucia, St Vincent, and Grenada, thus giving these islands control over their main agricultural product for the first time. After more than twenty years in opposition, the DLP regained power in the 2000 elections, but its leader, Roosevelt Douglas, died after a few months in office. He was replaced by Pierre Charles, who embarked on a campaign against the corruption of public officials. Charles died suddenly in 2004, and was succeeded by Roosevelt Skerrit, who led the DLP to an increased majority in the 2005 elections. Dominica was severely affected by the *WTO decision to force the EU to end its preferential system of importing Caribbean bananas, Dominica's major export good.

Dominican Republic

The second largest Caribbean country has suffered from fundamental political instability, social inequality, and, lately, from mass immigration from neighbouring Haiti.

The Trujillo dictatorship (1931–61)

Between its independence in 1844 and US occupation (1916–24), the Dominican Republic experienced over a hundred coups, revolutions, and uprisings. This weakened its body politic to such an extent that in 1931 *Trujillo could establish the most complete dictatorship in Latin American history. He came to control the country not only through the army and the police, but also through his 'acquisition' of the economy. By 1961, his firms produced 80 per cent of industrial output and employed 45 per cent of the country's active labour force. In addition, the state, over which he also exercised total control, employed a further 15 per cent of the labour force, so that a large majority of Dominicans were directly dependent on him for their income. Since the progress of the country's economy was immediately relevant to his own wealth, the economy did improve under his government through the payment of debts, the establishment of a balance of payments surplus, improvements in communications, and the establishment of a small but important industrial base. However, his leadership remained controversial: he granted exile to various deposed Latin American dictators, and exterminated up to 20,000 Haitians living in the country in 1937. By 1960, he began to lose his grip on his country, with the USA withdrawing its support. He was assassinated with the complicity of the *CIA in 1961.

The Balaguer era (1960s–90s) After a brief period of democratization the country plunged into civil war with a coup against the democratically elected President, Juan Bosch (1962–3). This was not ended until the 'Act of Reconciliation' of 3 September 1965, which had been partly brought about by the military intervention of the US marines in April 1965. The following elections were won by the US-backed Joaquín *Balaguer, a former associate of Trujillo. He established another regime of terror, but stabilized the economy initially through massive US aid to stave off bankruptcy. After the 1970s, he benefited from high world sugar prices.

In 1978, Balaguer was finally forced to accept the election of Antonio Guzmán, who in turn proceeded to establish a corrupt personal rule, which wiped out virtually all the recent economic gains. He committed suicide in 1982, and after the government of Salvador Jorge Blanco, Balaguer was re-elected (albeit with the help of electoral fraud) in 1986, 1990, and 1994. During this time, *human rights and political freedoms were largely respected, though the economy failed to show significant signs of improvement.

Contemporary politics (since 1996) In August 1996 the 89-year old Belaguer was replaced by Leonel Fernandez of the centrist Liberation Party, who narrowly won the fair elections held on 30 June 1996. His privatization policies were highly contested, but they did yield substantial economic growth (GDP growth of 8.3 per cent, 1998–9). The following elections of 2000 were won by Hipólito Mejía Domínguez of the Dominican Revolutionary Party (Partido Revolucionario Dominicano). Mejía was committed to increasing welfare payments to alleviate mass poverty exacerbated by mass immigration from neighbouring Haiti. However, state spending and inflation grew substantially, while Mejía was also accused of corruption. Mejía was succeeded in 2004 by Fernandez, who returned to his liberal economic policies to stabilize the economy.

Dominions, see BRITISH EMPIRE

domino theory
The name given in 1954 to the opinion of President *Eisenhower that the states of south-east Asia were like a row of dominoes which might all fall to *Communism if Communists managed to 'knock one down'. It was translated into an article of faith during the *Democratic *Kennedy and *Johnson administrations. Their strategists were haunted by the political costs incurred by the Democratic administration when China fell to Communism in 1949. Belief in the domino theory had crucial implications for the *Vietnam War. It gave successive administrations reason to increase military involvement in south-east Asia, and provided decision-makers and journalists with an apparent rationale to justify such efforts.

Dönitz, Karl (b. 16 Sept. 1891, d. 24 Dec. 1980). Hitler's successor
During World War I he commanded a U-boat, and in 1936 he was put in charge of developing the German U-boat fleet. As Commander-in-Chief of the German navy from 1943 he had a distinguished military record. *Hitler came to trust him more than his army or air force generals, with whom he always had an uneasy relationship. In his political testament, which became effective after his suicide on 30 April 1945, Hitler designated Dönitz as his successor, even though Dönitz had never been a prominent *Nazi functionary. Dönitz failed in his efforts

to negotiate a separate settlement with the Western Allies to enable him to continue the fight against the *Red Army. He did achieve, however, an armistice in north-western Europe (4 May), while Germany did not officially surrender until 8 May 1945. This delay enabled the safe arrival in northern Germany of around 100,000 refugees from Eastern Europe. As the Allies needed a 'legitimate' chain of command that was recognized by all Germans, Dönitz and his Cabinet were not imprisoned until 23 May 1945. He was sentenced to ten years' imprisonment at the *Nuremberg Trials.

dopolavoro ('after work')
One of the more popular institutions of *Fascist Italy, whose official title was Opera Nazionale Dopolavoro. It consisted of a national recreational network of clubs, bars, sports facilities, libraries, and holiday centres. It included almost three million members by 1936, though after the outbreak of World War II it became a less prominent factor in the Italian state.

dos Santos, José Eduardo (b. 28 Aug. 1942). President of Angola 1979–
Born at Luanda, he joined the Angolan resistance movement, the MPLA (Popular Movement for the Liberation of Angola), in 1961. In that year, he was forced into exile to the Congo, and in 1963 went to Moscow, where he attended university. He then returned to join the MPLA government-in-exile, and became Minister of Foreign Affairs upon independence in 1975. In 1979, he became President. Although originally a dogmatic Marxist, he became more progressive during the 1980s as he recognized that the country's economic problems could not be overcome unless the Civil War was ended. He led his country through a bitter civil war, and in 2002 he prevailed over his rival, Jonas Savimbi, who was killed by government troops. In subsequent years, dos Santos was criticized by the political opposition for delaying democratic elections.

Douglas, William Orville (b. 16 Oct. 1898, d. 19 Jan. 1980). US Supreme Court Justice 1939–75
The second youngest *Supreme Court appointee, and longest-serving justice in US history, and one of the most colorful and controversial. He was born poor in Maine, Minnesota, where he was afflicted with polio. Raised in Washington State, he became a distinguished scholar and lawyer, initially graduating from Whitman College in 1920 before obtaining an LLB from Columbia

University in 1925. He served as chairperson of the Securities and Exchange Commission, and was appointed to the Supreme Court in 1939 by Franklin *Roosevelt. On the Court, the four-times married Douglas was concerned with personal freedom, civil liberties, and the regulation of business during wartime. In *Griswold* v. *Connecticut* (1965), he famously emphasized a constitutional principle to privacy. He faced calls for his impeachment when he temporarily stayed the *Rosenberg executions in 1953. House Minority Leader *Ford again called for his impeachment in 1970 because of what he considered the absence of 'good behavior' in Douglas's alleged 'involvement with pornographic publications and espousal of high-style hippie-yippie style revolution'. In the end he was forced to resign after being partially paralysed by a stroke. He cultivated a persona as an activist defender of the weak, and lived to see his name given to a national park in his beloved Washington State.

Douglas-Home, Sir Alexander Frederick, 14th Earl of Home, Baron Home of the Hirsel (b. 2 July 1903, d. 9 Oct. 1995). British Prime Minister 1963–4

Born in London, educated at Eton and Oxford. He was elected as Conservative MP for South Lanark in 1931, and, in 1937, became Neville *Chamberlain's Parliamentary Private Secretary. He accompanied Chamberlain on the visit to *Hitler which led to the *Munich Agreement. He lost his seat in 1945, regained it in 1950, but left the House of Commons in 1951 for the House of Lords, to succeed his father as Earl of Home. During 1951–5, he was Secretary of State for *Scotland, presenting the Conservative case for union against the growing strength of *nationalism there. In 1955, under *Eden, he became Secretary of State for *Commonwealth relations, holding the post until he was made Foreign Secretary by *Macmillan in 1960.

In 1963, he was a surprise choice to succeed Macmillan as Prime Minister, partly because the latter wanted to prevent *Butler from succeeding him. It was considered inappropriate for the Prime Minister to be in the House of Lords, so he renounced his peerage and was elected to the Commons again. His short government is remembered for its policy of monetary expansion, under Reginald Maudling as Chancellor of the Exchequer, and for accepting the Robbins Report on the expansion of higher education. He took over the leadership of the *Conservative Party when it was tired from twelve years in office and suffered from bad opinion-poll ratings. He managed to increase the party's prospects considerably, yet ultimately his old-fashioned, aristocratic appearance stood little chance against the appeal of the young and innovative profile of the *Labour leader, Harold *Wilson. He served again in the Cabinet, as *Heath's Foreign Secretary (1970–4), and then returned to the House of Lords.

Doumer, Paul (b. 22 Mar. 1857, d. 7 May 1932). President of France 1931–2

He became a *Radical member of the Chamber of Deputies in 1888, Secretary of Finance in 1895, and from 1896 to 1902 he served as Governor-General of *Indochina, where he modernized the colonial administration. He became a nationalist symbol after he lost three sons in World War I. He was Secretary of Finance again between 1921–2 and 1925–6. He was murdered by a Russian *émigré*, Gorgoulov.

Doumergue, Gaston (b. 1 Aug. 1863, d. 18 June 1937). French President 1924–31

A *Radical member of the Chamber of Deputies (1893–1910), he became a Senator in 1910, then Prime Minister and Foreign Secretary in 1913–14. In 1924, he was the first Protestant to become President of France. In 1934, he came back from retirement to head a government of national union as Prime Minister in order to respond to the *Stavisky scandal.

Dowding, Hugh Caswall Tremenheere, Baron Dowding of Bentley Priory (b. 24 Apr. 1882, d. 15 Feb. 1970). British air chief marshal

Born in Moffat, Dumfriesshire, he was educated at Winchester and the Royal Military College, Sandhurst. He joined the Royal Artillery, but learnt to fly in 1913 and during World War I became a member of the newly formed Royal Flying Corps, eventually reaching the rank of brigadier. In the interwar period, he served in Iraq and Palestine, and was also involved in training. Most importantly, as Commander-in-Chief of Fighter Command from 1936, he oversaw the development of new fighter aircraft (mainly the Spitfire and Hurricane), developed new strategies of air defence, and recognized the importance of nascent radar technology. In May 1940 he prevented the deployment of Fighter Command in France, thus preserving Britain's defences against the imminent German attack. When this happened in August 1940, he coordinated the British aircraft in the Battle of *Britain. He was replaced in November 1940, as he was not considered to possess the necessary personal skills nor the military vision.

Downing Street Declaration (15 Dec. 1993)

A resolution signed by the Irish Taoiseach, *Reynolds, and the British Prime Minister, *Major, following months of secret negotiations driven principally by Reynolds and *Hume. The declaration stated 'that it is for the people of Ireland alone, by agreement between the two parts respectively, to exercise their right of self-determination on the basis of consent . . . to bring about a united Ireland, if that is their wish'. Thus, for the first time the British government declared officially that it had no inherent strategic, political, or economic self-interest in *Northern Ireland. The declaration laid out plans for negotiations for the future of Northern Ireland, in which all parties were welcome to participate, including former terrorist organizations which laid down their arms and committed themselves to peaceful agitation. The *IRA responded on 31 August 1994 with a cessation of violence, without indicating whether this was permanent. Despite the efforts by *Hume and the encouragement of *Clinton, progress was slow. An impatient wing of the IRA resumed its bombing campaign in February 1996. However, the Declaration provided the basis for efforts to find a peace settlement in Northern Ireland, and ultimately led to the *Good Friday Agreement.

Dresden Raid (13–14 Feb. 1945)

The main air raid on the city of Dresden during *World War II. The city had been considered safe because of its unique architectural beauty, and its relative strategic unimportance. It was carried out by over 800 British bomber planes under the command of Bomber *Harris. This main thrust was followed by two further daylight attacks by the US 8th Air Force. The city was known to be overcrowded with some 500,000 refugees, but it was felt that the inevitably high casualties might in the end help to shorten the war. Several hundreds of thousands were wounded and around 100,000 people are estimated to have been killed.

Dreyfus Affair (France)

A crisis that shook French politics and society to their foundations. In December 1894 Captain Alfred Dreyfus (b. 1859, d. 1935), a Jewish officer from *Alsace on the General Staff of the French Army, was convicted of treason by a military court for passing on military secrets to the Germans. Since the leaking of information continued, the new chief of the French intelligence service, Colonel Picquart, established that the culprit was not Dreyfus, but one Commandant Esterházy. The army refused to reopen the case, and Picquart received a posting to Tunisia. His successor began to manufacture evidence to prove Dreyfus's guilt, but meanwhile so many questions had been raised in public that a trial of Esterházy became inevitable. The latter's acquittal in a farcical trial spurred the famous novelist Émile Zola into action. He attacked the army's actions against Dreyfus in an open letter under the title *J'accuse* ('I accuse') on 13 December 1898. Yet it was not until a change of President (Loubet for Faure) and of Prime Minister (Waldeck-Rousseau for Dupuy) that a retrial became possible. In August 1899, Dreyfus was still found guilty, but 'with extenuating circumstances', and his sentence was reduced to ten years. In response, Dreyfus received a presidential pardon, but it was not until 1906 that he was fully rehabilitated and reinstated in the army.

The affair revealed the deep *anti-Semitism that permeated every social strata in France and led to widespread disturbances at the height of the affair, in 1898. For the following decades, it polarized French society, which had just begun to overcome its political divisions, into a right wing hostile to the Republic and supported by popular Catholicism, which rallied around anti-Semitism, and a left wing which had (generally) advocated Dreyfus's acquittal, and which rallied behind the Republic.

Drnovšek, Janez (b. 17 May 1950). Prime Minister of Slovenia, 1992–2000, 2000–2, President 2002–

Born in Celje, he graduated with a doctorate in economics. He became director at a local bank before entering the diplomatic service. In 1984, Drnovšek became a Slovenian deputy in the Yugoslav parliament. In 1989, he was appointed Slovenia's representative in the Yugoslav State Council, whose chairman he became in 1990. He resigned shortly thereafter, when the Yugoslav army moved into Slovenia. In 1992 he became chairman of the Liberal Democratic Party, and in April he presided over a transitional government which was confirmed by Slovenia's first free elections in December 1992. In subsequent years, Drnovšek benefited from the popularity of his economic and political reforms. These had stabilized the democracy and ensured a level of prosperity which contrasted sharply with the economic difficulties of the other former Yugoslav republics. As a result, Slovenia was the only state of former

Yugoslavia to be admitted to *NATO and the EU by 2004. In 2002, he won the Presidential elections with 56 per cent of the vote.

Drummond, Sir James Eric (Earl of Perth) (b. 17 Aug. 1876, d. 15 Dec. 1951). First Secretary of the League of Nations 1919–33

The private secretary to Prime Minister *Asquith (1912–15) and then to Foreign Secretaries *Grey (1915–16) and *Balfour (1916–18), he was part of the British delegation at the *Paris Peace Conference (1918–19). Following his long tenure as first secretary of the *League of Nations, during which time the organization was successful in mediating between belligerent nations but unable to prevent war, he was appointed British ambassador to Rome until the outbreak of World War II.

Druze

An Islamic sect founded in the eleventh century by Fatimid Caliph al-Haki bi-Amr Illah, who has since been regarded by its members as an incarnation of divinity. The community has been organized hierarchically, along feudal lines, and has traditionally resided around Mount Lebanon. Tensions arose during the nineteenth century, when Christian *Maronites were settling in the area. This culminated in 1860, when the Maronites were attacked and massacred by jealous Druzes, thus provoking French forces in Syria to intervene. Many Druzes migrated to the Houran Mountains in southern Syria, which became the new major Druze area of settlement (Jabal Druz). They enjoyed considerable autonomy under the French *Mandate in Syria, and after the departure of the French, Jabal Druz became a Syrian province. Meanwhile, in Lebanon they formed around 5 per cent of the population. They traditionally provided the Minister of Defence under the Lebanese communal constitution. However, their rivalry with the Maronites never subsided, and was reinforced in the 1950s, when they supported *Nasser's *pan-Arabism. Under the leadership of Kamal Jumblat (up to 1977; b. 1917, d. 1977) and his son Walid Jumblat (since then; b. 1949)), they became more radicalized, and formed a militia movement. At times in coalition with other Islamic groups, they scored considerable military successes against the divided and disorganized Maronite Phalange led by *Jumayyil. They were uncomfortable with the *Taif Accord of 1989, but tolerated the new government, mainly as a result of Syrian pressure.

Du Bois, William Edward Burghardt (b. 23 Feb. 1868, d. 27 Aug. 1963). US sociologist and civil rights leader.

Born in Great Barrington, Massachusetts, he graduated from Fisk University, Tennessee, in 1888 and in 1895 received a doctorate from Harvard. As a professor at Atlanta University (1897–1914) he became a recognized scholar in the field of race relations. His book *The Souls of Black Folk* (1903), a sophisticated description of the Afro-American people achieved through blending sociology, history, and popular memory, established him as leader of a movement for civil rights. In this book he challenged current ideas (developed by Booker T. Washington) that Blacks should aspire to White values of thrift and enterprise, while (at least initially) accepting White supremacy. In 1905 he founded the Niagara Movement, which demanded full civil rights for African Americans, and in 1909 he was a founder of the *NAACP. After active work with NAACP (1909–34) he returned to Atlanta, where he wrote another important work, *Dusk of Dawn: An Autobiography of a Race Concept* (1940), which charted the development of modern racial theory.

In contrast to his advocacy of immediate African–American integration in the US, Du Bois also advocated Black nationalism elsewhere. He was a pioneer of *pan-Africanism and co-organizer of various Pan-African Conferences around the world between 1919 and 1927. In 1945 he organized the Pan-African Conference in Manchester, where he worked closely with Kwame *Nkrumah. During the 1950s he moved left ideologically, and in 1951 he was indicted (but acquitted) as 'an unregistered agent of a foreign power'. In 1961 he joined the Communist Party and received a Lenin Peace Prize from the Soviet Union. He moved to Ghana, where he became a citizen and where he died.

Duarte, José Napoleón (b. 23 Nov. 1925, d. 23 Feb. 1990). President of El Salvador 1980–2, 1984–9

A co-founder of the Christian Democrat Party in 1960, he supported the reformist military *coup* of 15 October 1979 and continued to work with the military junta even after the parties to the left, notably the Socialists and Communists, broke away in 1980 to form the oppositional left-wing Frente Farabundo Martí de Liberación Nacional (FMLN, National Liberation Front). During the ensuing civil war (1981–92) his dependence on military support continued even in his second term in office, which he served as an elected President largely because the FMLN parties had boycotted the elections. He was unable to mediate in the war, or to stop the *human rights abuses of the military and its associated death squads.

Dubček, Alexander (b. 27 Nov. 1921, d. 7 Nov. 1992). First Secretary of the Czechoslovak Communist Party 1968
Born in Uhrovek (*Slovakia), he grew up in the Soviet Union. He joined the Slovak Communist Party upon his return in 1938, and was active in the Slovak resistance throughout World War II. After 1945, he was a minor party official until in 1951 he joined the Central Committee of the Slovak Communist Party. A member of the Central Committee of the Czechoslovak Communist Party from 1958, he became increasingly opposed to *Novotny's hardline policies, arguing that the Communist Party needed to reform itself in order to ensure its survival. As *de facto* leader of the country from January 1968, he embarked upon the period of reform known as the *Prague Spring, with the aim of creating 'socialism with a human face'. He failed to appreciate the extent to which his policies were unacceptable to the hardline *Brezhnev. His programme came to an abrupt halt in August 1968 with the invasion by Soviet, East German, and Polish troops. He was briefly sent as an ambassador to Turkey, and finally ended up working in forestry. He retired, but reappeared before jubilant crowds in 1989 after the collapse of *Husák's Communist regime. He was elected Parliamentary President on 28 December 1989, and was confirmed in that office by the new freely elected parliament on 27 June 1990.

Duce, Il ('the leader')
The title adopted by *Mussolini to describe his authoritarian, unconstitutional position as head of the *Fascist movement and the ruler of Italy (1922–43).

Dulles, John Foster (b. 25 Feb. 1888, d. 24 May 1959). US Secretary of State 1953–9
Born in Washington, DC, he was educated at Princeton and the Sorbonne, Paris, before obtaining an LLB degree at George Washington University. Dulles became a successful New York lawyer and was invited to attend the *Paris Peace Conference in 1919. He returned to private practice between the wars. Through his association with the unsuccessful Republican candidate for the presidency, Thomas Dewey, he had become a leading Republican spokesperson on foreign affairs by 1944. By and large, he supported President *Truman's bi-partisan approach to foreign policy after World War II. Thus he was called on to draft the Peace Treaty of *San Francisco with Japan in 1951.
As Secretary of State under *Eisenhower, Dulles became a keen protagonist of the *Cold War. He built up *NATO and was largely responsible for *SEATO. He advanced beyond the *Truman Doctrine of *containment by urging that the USA prepare a massive nuclear arms buildup as a deterrent to Soviet aggression, which could be used to support the policy of *brinkmanship. He helped formulate the *Eisenhower Doctrine of 1957, but his more aggressive anti-Soviet impulses were checked by President *Eisenhower. Complementing his anti-Communism was a deep commitment to Western *European integration, a conviction bolstered by his friendship with Jean *Monnet.

Duma
A Russian council or assembly. In 1906, Tsar *Nicholas II became one of Europe's last autocratic rulers to concede a popular assembly, in an attempt to pacify popular opinion after the *Russian Revolution of 1905. The first (10 May–22 July 1906) and the second (5 March–17 May 1907) State Dumas were quickly dissolved. A new restrictive franchise produced a more conservative majority, so that the third Duma lasted for five years (1907–12), being involved in judicial, educational, and administrative reforms. The fourth Duma, which sat until the *Russian Revolutions of 1917, was less effective, particularly after the outbreak of World War I, for most of which time it was suspended. The Duma's ability to legislate much-needed reforms was constrained by a second chamber, the State Council, which was a much more conservative body.
The term was adopted for the popularly elected Russian assembly created by *Yeltsin's federal Constitution of 1993. The State Duma was no stronger than its predecessor, since it was constrained by the fragmentation of parties and the consequent difficulty of finding stable majorities. Under *Putin, the Duma was able to reclaim some of its importance, though its powers against the executive were relatively limited.

Dumbarton Oaks Conference (Aug.-Oct. 1944)
A number of meetings held at Dumbarton Oaks, Washington, DC. Attended by representatives of the USA, Britain, the Soviet Union, and China, it prepared for the foundation of the *United Nations at San Francisco the following year. One of the main items under discussion was the role of the Security Council, and its relationship to the discredited *League of Nations.

Dunkirk Evacuation (27 May–4 June 1940)
Following the end of the *Phoney War in *World War II, German tank forces advanced rapidly through Belgium and

northern France. They encircled over 200,000 British troops, 140,000 French soldiers, and a contingent of the remnant Belgian army around the port of Dunkirk. Believing that victory was assured, *Hilter ordered a brief two-day halt to the German advance on 23 May, in order to wait for reinforcements. This allowed the British, under the command of General Gort, to carry out plans for an evacuation by sea, in which most of the troops were safely transported to England by an armada of over 850 hurriedly gathered vessels. Although disaster was averted, it represented a tremendous blow to the British army, which had to leave all its heavy equipment behind.

Dunkirk, Treaty of (4 Mar. 1947)

A defensive pact between France and Britain against an attack from Germany. Apart from attempting to revive the *Entente Cordiale of 1904, it also pledged economic cooperation and consultation between the two countries. The pact was enlarged in March 1948 by the Treaty of *Brussels, when the *Benelux countries joined.

Duplessis, Maurice Le Noblet, see

UNION NATIONAL (CANADA)

Dutch East Indies, see INDONESIA

Dutch Guyana, see SURINAM

Dutra, Eurico Gaspar (b. 18 May 1885, d. 17 June 1974). President of Brazil 1946–51

A conservative general in the Brazilian Army, he was an early supporter of *Vargas and served as Minister of War until 1945, when he participated in the *coup* to depose him. He was elected President with the support of the nationalist right-wing Social Democratic Party (Partido Social Democrático) in 1946. He had a more democratic Constitution adopted during his first year in office and promoted economic nationalism and industrialization. Despite the structural problems emerging in Brazilian politics and society, his government was marked by relative quiet since the country was still enjoying the prosperity obtained during World War II.

Duvalier, François (b. 14 Apr. 1907, d. 21 Apr. 1971). President of Haiti 1957–71

A medical doctor by profession, which earned him the nickname 'Papa Doc', he became President with the support of Black nationalist groups (the *noiristes*). He was backed by the Black business community, and successfully gathered popular appeal through claiming supernatural powers in the voodoo tradition practised by over 70 per cent of the

population. In a manipulated plebiscite of 1964 he was confirmed president for life. Despite opposition from the Roman *Catholic Church and other institutions, and despite continued poverty in his country, he managed to retain power until his death, largely through establishing one of the world's most ruthless regimes in the second half of the twentieth century. He was succeeded by his son, J.-C. *Duvalier.

Duvalier, Jean-Claude (b. 3 July 1951). Dictator of Haiti 1971–86

Nicknamed 'Baby Doc', as the son of 'Papa Doc' whom he succeeded as president for life at the age of 20, he claimed to instigate a programme of economic reform but in fact he pocketed most of the international aid provided for it. Modest economic growth during the 1970s was followed by a sharp economic downturn during the 1980s. He was increasingly unable to keep the support of vital sections of the Black middle class, particularly after his marriage in 1980 to the extravagant daughter of a businessman of Mulatto (i.e. mixed-race) descent, and he became even more corrupt. A popular uprising and lack of US support forced him into French exile on 7 February 1986. Despite taking with him around a hundred million US dollars, he was reported to be bankrupt in 1993.

dyarchy

A system of government formally introduced into British India by the 1919 *Government of India Act. Government of the thirteen Indian provinces was to be on a dual basis: a reserved area of finance, police, and justice, which remained under the control of the Governor; and a transferred area, such as local government, education, and health, under the control of Indian ministers chosen from the elected members of a legislative council. Introduced by the Secretary of State for India, Edwin Samuel Montagu on the basis of the **Montagu-Chelmsford Proposals** (1918), it left the most important areas of government outside the purview of Indian influence. Nevertheless, it represented an important step towards Indian self-determination and eventual independence.

Dzerzhinsky, Feliks Edmundovich (b. 11 Sept. 1877, d. 20 July 1926). Soviet politician

Born in Dzerzhinovo, near Minsk, as the son of a Polish nobleman, he became a revolutionary for the Lithuanian-Polish *Marxist parties in 1896. He was subsequently arrested six times, and was eventually released after the February Revolution, 1917. He became one of the principal organizers of *Lenin's October Revolution (*Russian Revolutions, 1917), and in December 1917 founded perhaps the most ruthless organization of state terror of its day, the *Cheka. Through the establishment of prison camps and the use of torture, hostages, and assassinations, he played a central part in breaking domestic opposition to *Communist rule. In addition, as People's Commissar (i.e. Minister) for Transport, he promoted industrialization while remaining sensitive to the need for sound agricultural policies. He became chairman of the Supreme Council of the National Economy in 1924. He died of heart failure.

E

East Timor, see TIMOR LESTE

Easter Rising (24 Apr. – 1 May 1916)
An armed insurrection against British rule in
Ireland. The secret Military Council of the
Irish Republican Brotherhood intended it to
be a national rebellion on Easter Sunday, 23
April. But a series of organizational and
planning blunders meant that supporting
arms organized by *Casement did not arrive.
The rising was called off, but Patrick *Pearse
and others decided to proceed nevertheless,
on Easter Monday. The confusion meant that
the nationwide rising failed, while the Dublin
one proceeded. Volunteers led by Pearse and
members of the Irish Citizen Army led by
James Connolly occupied the General Post
Office in Sackville Street, which became the
headquarters of the rising. Pearse announced
the Proclamation of an Irish Republic, reading
out the document and posting it around the
GPO. Various other parts of central Dublin
administration were attacked and occupied,
including the Four Courts, Liberty Hall, City
Hall, and various strategic hospitals and
factories. The British army counter-attacked
fully on 25 April, recovering several important
buildings, and cordoning off many of the
rebels' communication avenues. British
reinforcements began to arrive from Belfast
and other postings, and on 27 April the British
started shelling the GPO and the Four Courts.
Pearse and his rebels retreated from the
burning GPO to Moore Street on 28 April, and
on 29 April they surrendered. Rebels were
captured, imprisoned, and tried. Martial law
was proclaimed and the rising's leaders court-
martialled. Pearse and fourteen other leaders
were executed between 3 and 12 May.
Although the rising itself was a dismal failure,
Pearse and his fellow leaders quickly entered
popular mythology as martyrs for Irish
nationhood. The harsh British reaction to the
rising prompted such widespread anti-British
feelings as to make continued British rule in
Ireland impossible within five years.

Ebert, Friedrich (b. 4 Feb. 1871, d. 28 Feb.
1925). President of Germany 1919–25
Born in Heidelberg, he became a saddler, and
joined the *SPD in 1889. From 1893 Ebert
edited a party newspaper, and in 1900 he
became leader of the SPD in the parliament of
the city-state of Bremen. Elected to the
national parliament in 1912, he became
chairman of his party in 1913.
  Upon the collapse of the Empire Ebert was
appointed Chancellor on 9 November 1918,
partly because of his hostility to the current
workers' revolts throughout Germany. On 10
November he established a pact with the army
leader, General Groener. With the tacit
support of the bureaucratic elites, this
enabled him to squash the revolution and
establish a democracy. In return he had to
grant the army and bureaucracy almost
complete autonomy. The persistence of these
old power structures fundamentally
weakened the new *Weimar Republic
throughout its existence.
  Ebert was elected President by the National
Assembly on 11 February 1919, and tried (in
vain) to secure a better treatment of Germany
at the *Paris Peace Conference. He was due to
face a popular presidential election in 1922,
but, owing to Germany's volatile domestic
situation, parliament voted to extend his
period in office. Constantly exposed to
personal attacks from rightist groups, in 1924
he was forced to defend himself in court
against the accusation of treason during the
war, when he had participated in a strike of
munitions workers. In a judgment that
exemplified the right-wing bias of the
judiciary, his accuser was found guilty of
lying, but Ebert was not cleared of treason.
The trial strained his health, and he died soon
afterwards.

Éboué, Félix (b. 28 Dec. 1884, d. 17 May
1944). French colonial administrator
Of West Indian origin, he was educated in
Paris and in 1908 was sent to Ubangi Shari
(now the Central African Republic), where he
served in the French colonial service. He was
appointed acting Governor of Martinique in
1932, Governor of Guadaloupe in 1936, and
Governor of Chad in 1938. In World War II he
supported the *Free French and was
appointed by de *Gaulle Governor-General of
*French Equatorial Africa. He became the first
coloured person to be interred in the
Panthéon in Paris.

EC (European Community), see
EUROPEAN INTEGRATION

Ecevit, Bülent (b. 28 May 1925, d. 11 May
2006). Prime Minister of Turkey 1974, 1977,
1978–9, 1998–2002
Born in Istanbul, where he studied, in 1953
the writer joined the left-of-centre Republican
People's Party, and between 1961–5 served as
Minister of Labour under the party leader,
*Inönü. He became the party's general
secretary in 1966, and in 1971–2 toppled
Inönü, whom he accused of compliance with
the military regime, to become party
chairman himself. Nevertheless, he endorsed
and took responsibility for the military
occupation of north-east Cyprus in 1974. After
the 1980 army coup he was banned from
active politics for ten years, though the ban
was lifted in 1987. He became chairman of the
Democratic Left Party, founded by his wife
two years earlier, which eventually managed
to get into parliament in 1991. It gained 14.65
per cent of the popular vote in 1995. His
leadership experience became an asset in the
political crisis of 1998–9, after the ruling
Welfare Party had been banned by the
Constitutional Court. He formed an interim
government, and won the ensuing
parliamentary elections of 1999, in which his
Democratic Left Party increased its
representation from 76 to 136 seats. Ecevit
cooperated well with the military, which he
supported in the fight against *Islamic
fundamentalists as well as the separatists in
*Kurdistan. Exhausted by pursuing
fundamental political and institutional
reform in a fragile political coalition, his party
began to fall apart in the face of his refusal to
heed growing calls for his resignation. As ill-
health contributed to the erosion of his
political authority, he was swept from office
in the 2002 elections by *Erdogan.

Echeverría Álvarez, Luis (b. 17 Jan.
1922). President of Mexico 1970–6
A professor of jurisprudence, he was general
secretary of the ruling Institutional
Revolutionary Party (Partido Revolucionario
Institutional, *PRI), 1957–68. As Minister of
the Interior (1964–70) he was responsible for
the brutal suppression of the student riots
around the 1968 Olympic Games in Mexico
City. Yet he realized the need to reduce social
tension through reforming the grossly
unequal income distribution in Mexican
society. As President, he improved the rural
infrastructure to benefit the peasants, and for
the urban population introduced strict price
controls for food, which amounted to a de
facto state subsidy. Increased state spending
could only be met through increased

borrowing, which caused inflation. Yet a
stubborn commitment to maintain the
exchange rate of an increasingly overvalued
peso against the US dollar resulted in a
tremendous capital flight which reached
panic proportions during the last months of
his presidency and finally forced the peso's
devaluation by almost 100 per cent. To restore
his popularity, less than two weeks before the
end of his presidency he expropriated
northern landlords for the benefit of landless
peasants. His hopes of becoming *UN
Secretary-General never materialized.

Economic and Social Council
A principal organ of the *UN which consists
of 54 members elected by the General
Assembly to investigate any social or cultural
topic, and which has thus established
commissions, e.g. on population growth,
human rights, drugs, and women's rights.

(((🌐))) SEE WEB LINKS

• The home page of the Economic and Social
Council.

Economic Community of West
African States (ECOWAS)
An international economic community
founded in 1975, largely on the initiative of
Nigeria and Togo. Other members were Benin,
the Ivory Coast, Ghana, Guinea, Guinea-
Bissau, Cape Verde (since 1977), Liberia, Mali,
Mauritania, Niger, Senegal, Sierra Leone, and
Upper Volta. It aimed at the gradual
establishment of free trade between its
member states (originally within fifteen
years), as a prelude to eventual political
integration. From the beginning it was
plagued by the overwhelming economic
predominance of Nigeria, and by rivalries
between various members. Individual
member states were also in other, competing
political and economic blocs, which made
integration no easier. Finally, ECOWAS was
weakened by the domestic instabilities of
many member states. On the whole,
therefore, it was only moderately successful at
realizing freedom of trade and freedom of
movement, and it failed to bring about further
political integration. Nevertheless, the
community has contributed to a stabilization
of the region, with ECOWAS sending peacekeeping troops to end conflicts in Sierra Leone
(2002) and Ivory Coast (2003).

(((🌐))) SEE WEB LINKS

• The official website of ECOWAS.

ECOWAS, see ECONOMIC COMMUNITY OF
WEST AFRICAN STATES

ECSC (European Coal and Steel Community)

An alliance originating in proposals made by Jean *Monnet and announced by Robert *Schuman on 9 May 1950, which called for the placement of coal and steel production in West Germany and France under joint control. This surrender of national sovereignty in sensitive economic areas which had been at the heart of the armaments industry in the two World Wars helped significantly overcome Western European security concerns in the immediate postwar world. It led to the creation of the ECSC through the Treaty of Paris on 18 April 1951 (effective from 1952), which comprised Belgium, France, Italy, Luxemburg, the Netherlands, and West Germany. It was governed by a High Authority, which in turn came under the control of a Council of Ministers delegated from each member state. The High Authority was further advised by a general assembly made up of parliamentarians from the member states. Finally, the clauses of the Treaty of Paris were guarded by a High Court. The ECSC formed the nucleus of *European integration. Its institutions provided models for the *European Commission, the Council of Ministers, the *European Parliament, and the *European Court of Justice.

Ecuador

The world's largest producer of bananas, the Latin American country has benefited from significant oil reserves, though these have not reduced the social inequality among the population.

Military domination (up to 1979)

Independent since its separation from greater Bolivia in 1830, Ecuador's politics have been marked by tension between the conservative landowners of the interior and the more liberal business community of the coastal plain. Their consensus, underpinned by the prosperity of the cocoa boom from the 1870s, collapsed with the decline of cocoa as the country's main export after 1920. There followed a period of political and economic instability, compounded by a military attack by Peru in 1941, which resulted in the loss of almost two-fifths of its territory. Between 1944 and 1972 government alternated between relatively weak military rule and civilian rule,

with the charismatic José Maria *Velasco Ibarra emerging as the most important figure. Military rule, re-established in 1972, was at first facilitated by a rise in oil prices which increased hard-currency earnings from its newly discovered resources.

The social reforms begun by the military in 1972 remained too modest to change significantly Ecuador's large social imbalances. In 1974, 2.2 per cent of the landholding companies cultivated 50 per cent of the land, while two-thirds of all agricultural ownership was restricted to holdings of twelve acres or less. In fact, by 1976 the majority of the population was worse off than before the oil price boom, and in 1979 the military government was forced to give way to a democratically elected government under a new constitution.

Democratization (1979–2002) Despite continuing economic difficulties and an attempted military coup in 1986, the political situation remained relatively stable. At the same time, large-scale poverty persisted (over 40 per cent of the urban population lived in extreme poverty in the early 1990s), and economic stringency measures introduced by the government in 1994 caused such widespread protests as to necessitate a state of emergency.

The drop in the price of oil in 1998, coupled with declining prices for banana exports, caused a dramatic economic collapse. Ecuador defaulted on its debts, and, to stave off inflation, adopted the US dollar as its currency in 2000. This policy of deflation, coupled with the introduction of new taxation and lower state spending as dictated by the *IMF, increased further the economic hardship experienced by the majority of the population. It led to a sustained political crisis, with ministers unwilling to accept the necessary responsibility for government action. The crisis was compounded by evidence of widespread endemic corruption among members of Congress, government ministers, and successive Presidents.

Contemporary politics (since 2002) In 2002, Lucio Gutierrez was elected President. Facing a hostile Congress, Gutierrez tried to gain political leverage by replacing all except four of the 31 Supreme Court justices with more compliant appointments. This was declared unconstitutional, and triggered mass protests. In 2005, Gutierrez was impeached by Congress, and replaced by his former vice president, Alfred Palacio. Palacio also tried to take on Congress, by initiating constitutional change. Owing to his lack of a popular majority inside and outside parliament, however, Palacio was also unsuccessful. The elections of 2006 were won by the left-wing populist Raffael Correa, who began to strike up political alliances with *Chávez and *Castro.

ecumenical movement

A movement whose name derives from the Greek *oikoumenē* ('the whole inhabited world'). Its aim is to unite all believers in Christ, transcending all divisions of denomination. The beginnings of the modern movement culminated in the World Missionary Conference in Edinburgh in 1910, which led to the establishment of an International Missionary Council and to further interdenominational meetings. The institution of a World Council of Churches was held up by World War II, but in 1948 it met for the first time in Amsterdam, with the participation of representatives from 147 churches from forty-seven countries. As a result of more liberal attitudes within the Roman *Catholic Church from the papacy of *John XXIII, Catholic observers were sent to the Assembly of the World Council of Churches for the first time in 1961. Under John XXIII and his successor, Pope *Paul VI, the conflict between the *Eastern Orthodox Churches and Western Catholicism was bridged. There have been constant set-backs, for example the controversy between the Church of England (*Anglican Communion) and the Roman Catholic Church over the ordination of women for the priesthood during the early 1990s, and the failure of Anglican-Methodist unity in 1972. However, there has been continued progress and dialogue between the denominations. This was witnessed by the establishment of more regional church councils and of a communion between the Anglican and Lutheran Churches in the early 1990s.

Eden, (Robert) Anthony, 1st Earl of Avon (b. 12 June 1897, d. 14 Jan. 1977). British Prime Minister 1955-7

Early career Born in Windlestone, Co. Durham. After finishing at Eton he served on the Western Front in World War I and was awarded the Military Cross. After the war, he resumed his education at Oxford, and became Conservative MP for Warwick and Leamington in 1923. During 1926-9, Eden served as Parliamentary Private Secretary to the Foreign Secretary, Austen *Chamberlain. He became an Under-Secretary at the Foreign Office in 1931, and in 1935 entered the Cabinet as Minister for *League of Nations Affairs. Later that year, he replaced Samuel Hoare as Foreign Secretary. Initially, he supported the policies of

*appeasement pursued by the government, but when Neville *Chamberlain replaced *Baldwin as Prime Minister in 1937, Eden found that his department was being increasingly interfered with.

Eden had the good fortune to resign in February 1938, just before the signing of the *Munich Agreement, so that his career was untainted by the episode. His resignation was triggered by the government's recognition of Italy's conquest of *Abyssinia, while the underlying cause was his struggle with Chamberlain over control of policy. Subsequently, he was critical of the government's foreign policies, and did not regain office until war broke out, when he became Dominions Secretary. Made Foreign Secretary by *Churchill in 1940, he emerged as the second-in-command within the *Conservative Party.

In office After defeat in the 1945 elections, Eden became increasingly impatient with Churchill's refusal to resign, especially as Churchill left the running of day-to-day politics to him, basking in his glory as a war hero. Again Foreign Secretary from 1951, his appeal to Churchill to resign became ever more pressing, though he was unable to succeed him until 1955, a year in which he led the party to a clear election victory. However, the fiasco of the *Suez Crisis made his early resignation inevitable. Though not a military disaster, it was his complete failure to foresee and then acknowledge international outrage at Britain's actions which resulted in a resounding diplomatic and national humiliation. In this sense, his long and successful involvement in foreign policy for three decades proved more of a liability than an asset, leading him not to understand that Britain was no longer the world power it had been when he first took office.

Edward VII (Albert Edward) (b. 9 Nov. 1841, d. 6 May 1910). King of Great Britain and Ireland and Dependencies Overseas, Emperor of India 1901-10

Born in Sandringham, Norfolk, the second child of Queen Victoria. He waited many years to become King, and when he did so, he refurbished many of the monarchy's ceremonial aspects. He also asserted his right to be consulted over political decisions. His claims were disregarded by Prime Ministers, but he did have a role in foreign affairs. Many saw him as influential in securing the *Entente Cordiale and the *Anglo-Russian Entente, through his influence on European royal families and dignitaries.

Edward VIII (Edward Albert Christian George Andrew Patrick David) (b. 23 June 1894, d. 28 May 1972).

King of Great Britain and Northern Ireland and Dependencies Overseas, Emperor of India 1936 Born in Richmond, Surrey, he served in the Royal Navy in 1907–10. He was a staff officer in World War I. As Prince of Wales (from 1911) he made a series of tours of the Empire and became increasingly concerned about levels of poverty in Britain. His public appearances made him a popular member of the royal family. Despite his general popularity, in the *abdication crisis he was forced to renounce the throne and emigrate after insisting on marrying a twice-divorced American, Wallis Simpson. They married in 1937 and settled in France. As Duke of Windsor, he visited Germany later that year, which caused some embarrassment to the royal family. In 1940, the government feared that he might be kidnapped by Germany, and he left Europe, becoming governor of the Bahamas (1941–5). He then lived in France, but was buried at Windsor in 1972, as was the Duchess of Windsor after her death in 1986.

EEC, see ROME, TREATY OF; EUROPEAN INTEGRATION; EU

EFTA (European Free Trade Association)

Established in May 1960 on a British initiative in response to the establishment of the EEC. It was a free trade area without the EEC's commitment to further political union, whose original members were Austria, Britain, Denmark, Norway, Portugal, Sweden, and Switzerland. Though subsequently joined by Liechtenstein, Finland, and Iceland, the EFTA was too small and its members too diverse to be able to compete successfully with the EEC. In 1973, the UK and Denmark left to join the EEC, followed by Portugal (1986), Austria (1995), Finland (1995), and Sweden (1995). From 1994, EFTA (with the exception of Switzerland) states were linked to the European Union in the European Economic Area. This created extensive freedom of goods and services between member states, but it did not give EFTA states the right to decision-making within the European Union. Since 1995, then, EFTA has been a very heterogeneous and loose alliance of four disparate member states (Liechtenstein, Switzerland, Norway, and Iceland).
  EUROPEAN INTEGRATION

(⊕) SEE WEB LINKS

• The official website of EFTA.

Egypt

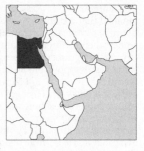

The most populous country of the Arab world with strategic control over the *Suez Canal, its relative economic poverty has prevented Egypt from exercising a leading position in the Arab world.

British influence (up to 1952) Part of the *Ottoman Empire from 1517, it became practically autonomous under the rule of the Khedives (governors) during the nineteenth century. Domestic unrest prompted Egypt's occupation by British forces in 1882 to protect its interest in the Suez Canal, which served as a vital link of the trade route between Britain and India. It was declared a British protectorate in 1914, though increasing nationalist resistance, which after World War I found its political expression in the *Wafd party led by *Saghlul Sa'd, forced the British to introduce a constitutional monarchy in 1923. Egypt was given internal autonomy, though the continuation of a substantial British military presence effectively gave Britain a veto in Egyptian affairs. This fuelled further nationalist agitation under the new leader of the Wafd party, *Nahhas, who was instrumental in formalizing Egypt's relationship with Britian in the Anglo-Egyptian Treaty of 1936. By this, British occupation was formally ended and Egypt's independence recognized, though a British military presence would continue along the Suez Canal. The treaty also allowed for the expansion of British forces in times of war. This allowed the British to use Egypt as a base for repelling *Rommel's advance in the *North African campaigns. In response, nationalist sentiment and popular agitation reached new heights.
  After the war, King *Farouk I and his ministers distinguished themselves by their weak and corrupt leadership. This became evident when the armed forces were humiliated during the war against the newly independent state of Israel (1948–9).

The Nasser era (1952–70) Continued nationalist hostility to the British armed forces precipitated the coup by the *Free Officers group on 22–3 July 1952, led by *Neguib. The monarchy was abolished in

1953, and in 1954 *Nasser assumed power. He held that a complete break with the country's imperial past could only be undertaken through fundamental political, economic, and social reform. Nasser outlawed all political opposition, and replaced the traditional political and administrative elite with his followers. Through extensive land redistribution he significantly reduced the hitherto glaring income inequalities of Egypt's predominantly agrarian population. His programme of 'Arab *socialism' sought to direct industrial output, which was to be facilitated by the nationalization of the country's largest banks and key industries. The most important part of this programme, the nationalization of the Suez Canal in 1956, sparked off the *Suez Crisis, which increased further his reliance on the support of the USSR. It also solidified his reputation as a strong Arab leader, though this was damaged in 1967 when Egypt took part in the *Six Day War. The disastrous outcome for Egypt forced the closure of the Suez Canal until 1975 and put the Sinai peninsula as well as the *Gaza strip under Israeli control.

Contemporary history (1970–2001) Nasser remained in power until his death in 1970 and was succeeded by *Sadat, who restored national pride through the *Yom Kippur War of 1973. This strengthened his authority to such an extent that he was able to carry out a complete reversal of Nasser's policies. The economy was liberalized, foreign capital investment encouraged, and formerly close links to the USSR severed. Most significantly, he was the first Arab leader to sign a peace agreement with Israel (at *Camp David) in 1978, thus anticipating by more than a decade the mutual recognition between Israel and most Arab states. Peace with Israel also yielded a return of the Sinai peninsula, whose oil resources became an important factor in the Egyptian economy in the 1980s.

Following Sadat's assassination, *Mubarak continued Sadat's policies. Mubarak eventually, from 1987, succeeded in breaking Egypt's diplomatic isolation from the Arab community, which had been the consequence of the Camp David Agreement. On 26 May 1989 Egypt was readmitted into the *Arab League. Egypt's economy at this time was crippled by foreign debts, rapid urbanization, and a large population growth. The *Gulf War, in which Egypt committed troops to the allied forces, heightened its economic problems owing to the interruption of trade with Iraq, and the repatriation of over 700,000 Egyptians who had worked in Iraq or Kuwait before the war.

From the 1990s, the main political concern for Mubarak was presented by increasing popular support for *Islamic fundamentalism, which challenged the authority of Mubarak's secular regime. In the elections of 1995 and 2000, Mubarak was forced to resort to substantial corruption to secure a parliamentary majority for his National Democratic Party, and deny the *Muslim Brotherhood substantial representation. In 1998, Egypt completed a stabilization programme involving privatization and the reduction of public debt. This had stimulated economic growth throughout the decade, and led to a cancelling of half of Egypt's debt with the *IMF. From 1997, Egypt was a growing target of terrorist attacks especially against tourists, attacks that were frequently financed by Osama *Bin Laden.

Contemporary politics (since 2001) Of the terrorists directly implicated in the *September 11 attacks, a disproportionate number came from Egypt, pointing to the continuing popularity of radical Islamic fundamentalism beneath the apparent stability of Mubarak's regime. Under pressure from the USA under George W. *Bush, Mubarak agreed to a careful and limited democratization without endangering his grip on power, by allowing more open debate around the presidential and parliamentary elections. In 2005, this led to a greatly increased representation of the Muslim Brotherhood in parliament. Mubarak was re-elected in elections generally characterized as rigged.

Eichmann, Karl Adolf (b. 19 Mar. 1906, d. 31 May 1962). Nazi war criminal
Originally a salesman from Solingen (*Ruhr District), he joined the *SS security service under *Heydrich in 1934. In 1939, he was put in charge of Jewish affairs and became one of the central figures responsible for the 'final solution', the mass killings of Jews in *concentration camps, begun in 1941. In 1945, he fled from US captivity to Argentina, where the Israeli security service, Mossad, traced him and deported him to Israel in 1960. In one of the most prominent trials against Nazi criminals since the *Nuremberg trials, he was sentenced to death and hanged. For many observers, including Hannah Arendt, Eichmann became the epitome of the unrelenting Nazi perpetrator feigning powerlessness in the face of superior orders.

Einaudi, Luigi (b. 24 Mar. 1874, d. 30 Oct. 1961). President of Italy 1948–55
Born in Carrù, he graduated from Turin University, where he was professor of economics, (1902–48). In 1908 he became

editor of the *Riforma sociale*, and began writing for the newspapers *La stampa* and *Corriere della sera*. As an economist, he fell foul of *Mussolini's regime for attacking not only *Communist, but also *Fascist economics. As a result, he was forced to emigrate to Switzerland in 1943. He returned to liberated Italy in 1944 and became president of the national bank, the Banca d'Italia. Through his liberal economic policies in this position and as Budget Minister under *De Gasperi he made a substantial contribution to the stabilization of the lire, for which he is best remembered. In 1948 he was the first to be elected to the largely ceremonial post of President of the Republic.

Einstein, Albert (b. 14 Mar. 1879, d. 18 Apr. 1955). Theoretical physicist
Born in Ulm (Germany) of Jewish parents, he was educated in Munich and Zurich. In 1905 he formulated his first special theory of relativity and in 1909 became a professor of physics in Zurich. In 1912 he put forward a theory of photochemical equivalence and was made director of the Kaiser Wilhelm Institute in Berlin (1914–33). In 1916 he published *Die Grundlagen der allgemeinen Relativitätstheorie*, in which his general theory of relativity revolutionized the previous Newtonian theory of the universe. For his observations, which were confirmed at a total eclipse in 1919, he was awarded the *Nobel Prize for Physics.

In 1933 he fled Hitler's *anti-Semitism and became a US citizen, teaching at Princeton. In 1939 he warned President *Roosevelt of German research into the possibilities of an atomic bomb, and thus initiated the bureaucratic process which led to the US development of atomic weapons code-named the *Manhattan Project. After 1945, he became increasingly alarmed at the potential threat to mankind through atomic warfare. Together with Bertrand *Russell, he helped establish the Pugwash conferences of scientists against a nuclear war, which started in 1957. He became an icon of scientific genius for the twentieth century. His public image as a humane scientist was also based on his revulsion at the technology his discoveries led to, and a strong commitment to political and personal liberty.

Éire, see IRELAND, REPUBLIC OF

Eisenhower Doctrine (USA)
Following the *Suez Crisis of 1956, President *Eisenhower proposed to give US economic and military aid to Middle East governments who felt their independence threatened, and to guarantee such regimes against invasion or Soviet subversion. In 1957, *Congress authorized the provision of $200 million for the purpose. In 1958 the USA sent 5,000 troops to Lebanon to support President Camille *Chamoun (b. 1900, d. 1987), who feared revolution. It was based upon the central (and flawed) assumption that *pan-Arab *nationalism was necessarily inspired by the Soviet Union. It lapsed in the last years of the Eisenhower adminstration from 1959.

Eisenhower, Dwight David ('Ike') (b. 14 Oct. 1890, d. 28 Mar. 1969). 34th US President 1953–61

Early career Born in Denison, Texas, he grew up in Kansas and graduated from the Military Academy in West Point in 1915. During World War I he commanded a tank-training unit and had numerous assignments between the wars, including service with Douglas *MacArthur in the Philippines. In 1942 General George *Marshall selected him over 366 more senior officers to be commander of US troops in Europe. As a lieutenant-general he went on to command Operation Torch in November 1942, the Allied landing in North Africa (*North African campaigns). In December 1943 he was appointed Supreme Commander of the Allied Expeditionary Forces. As such he was responsible for the planning and execution of the *D-Day landings and subsequent campaigns in Europe. His tact, optimism, and command of bureaucratic politics enabled him to secure inter-Allied collaboration and to avoid confrontation. After the war he retired to the USA, where he was courted by *Republicans at the same time as Democrats. The latter feared Truman's defeat, and offered him the 1948 *Democrat nomination for President, which he refused. In 1951 he was persuaded to return to active service as supreme commander of *NATO, a command he held for fifteen months, finally retiring from the army in June 1952.

Presidency Eisenhower was elected President as a Republican in November 1952, with Richard *Nixon as Vice-President. In July 1953 he fulfilled his promise to seek an end to the *Korean War by signing an armistice. The first Republican President since 1933, Eisenhower considered himself a 'dynamic conservative', attempting to encourage business through tax cuts and the decrease of federal control in the economy, while expressing a concern for social welfare. His administration became a bystander in the right-wing 'witch hunt' of Senator *McCarthy, and he has since been criticized for his public neutrality during the episode. Eisenhower's record on *civil rights was moderate, culminating in the important

decision to appoint Earl *Warren to the
Supreme Court. He was also responsible for
the relatively moderate 1957 *Civil Rights Act.
In 1957 he used federal troops to quell
segregationist violence at Little Rock,
Arkansas.

In foreign policy, Eisenhower increased US
political commitment in *Indochina
following the defeat of France at *Dien Bien
Phu, though he resolutely opposed the
sending of US troops into the area. With
*Dulles as Secretary of State, the NATO and
*ANZUS pacts were extended by the *SEATO
Pact of 1954. Keenly interested in foreign
affairs throughout his Presidency, he was
embarrassed in May 1960, when he publicly
denied that a US high-altitude reconnaissance
*U-2 plane was shot down over Soviet
territory. The Soviets proved him wrong by
producing evidence, and publicly exposed his
lie. In the 1960 presidential contest between
*Nixon and John F. *Kennedy, he refused to
throw his full support behind his Vice
President (Kennedy was elected by a narrow
margin).

El Alamein, Battles of (1942)

In June 1942 the British took up a defensive
position on the Mediterranean at El Alamein,
some 50 miles (80 km) from Alexandria, in an
effort to stop the advance of the German Afrika
Korps. During the first battle (30 June–25 July
1942) *Rommel's forces were effectively
halted. A front was established between the sea
and the salt marshes of the Qattara Depression.
General *Montgomery, who had been
appointed to command the 8th Army in
August, launched an offensive on 23 October.
After heavy artillery preparation, about 1,200
tanks advanced. Rommel was handicapped by a
fuel shortage and had only about 500 tanks in
effective use. He never regained the initiative.
On 4 November he ordered a retreat,
withdrawing back into Libya. This battle
marked the beginning of the end of Germany's
*North African campaign in *World War II.

El Salvador

The smallest and
most densely
populated
Central
American
country, it has
suffered under
the tensions
arising from
glaring social
and economic
inequality.

Authoritarian rule (up to 1979) The
instability which marked El Salvador's
political system following its independence
from Spain in 1821 was not overcome until
1903, when a newly created oligarchy of
coffee-plantation owners came to monopolize
power. This facilitated the expansion of its
large coffee estates at the expense of small
peasants. The social tension thus created
culminated in a peasants' uprising during
1931–2, which was suppressed by the
military. Subsequently, the coffee-growing
oligarchy relinquished its political power to
the military in return for the latter's support
of its economic monopoly. In the following
decades, economic modernization and
population growth stood in increasing
contrast to the continued economic
predominance of *las catorce*, the fourteen
families owning most of the land. Tensions
mounted during the 1970s, when the defeat of
the military's presidential candidate could
only be averted through large-scale
repression. After a military coup of reforming
officers on 15 October 1979, a coalition of
Christian Democrats, Socialists, and
Communists joined the military government,
only for the left-wing groups to leave it three
months later.

**Civil war and democratization (1980s and
1990s)** In response to the assassination by
government agents of the Roman Catholic
Archbishop, Oscar A. Romero, the opposition
parties joined in March 1980 to form the
left-wing Frente Farabundo Martí de
Liberación Nacional (FMLN, National
Liberation Front). In January 1981 civil war
broke out between the FMLN and
government forces, which received crucial
support from a USA worried about a potential
spread of *Communism in the region. The
stalemate between the two sides, the end of
the *Cold War, and the conclusion of a
regional peace agreement negotiated by
*Arias, enabled the signing of a peace
settlement on 16 January 1992. Political,
social, and judicial reforms were subsequently
enacted, the military reduced, and the FMLN
guerrillas disbanded.

In the elections of 20 March 1994, the
FMLN became the largest opposition party,
while the majority of the ruling right-wing
Alianza Republicana Nacionalista (ARENA,
National Republican Alliance) under
Armando Calderón Sol (b. 24 June 1968)
was confirmed. The FMLN became the
largest parliamentary party in the 2000
elections, after the presidential elections of
1999 confirmed the ARENA candidate,
Francisco Flores Pérez.

Contemporary history (since 2000) The country continued to be torn by the question of reconciliation between those implicated in the civil war, with an amnesty in 2002 failing to settle the issue. In an effort to create a more stable economy and overcome widespread poverty, Pérez introduced the US dollar as a national currency to stabilize the economy in 2001. This imposed strict budget discipline on the state, and rendered it unable to make generous transfer payments to the poorer sections of the population. Economic growth continued to be low in the early years of 2000, with annual GDP growth of between 1 and 2 per cent. Widespread poverty and dramatic income inequalities encouraged widespread crime. However, under the government of ARENA's Tony Saca Gonzalez from 2004, crime in a counry with one of the world's highest murder rates grew further. According to Amnesty International (2006), 3761 murders were committed in 2005, an increase of 34 per cent over the previous year.

Elizabeth II (Elizabeth Alexandra Mary)
(b. 21 Apr. 1926). Queen of Great Britain and Northern Ireland and Dependencies Overseas, Queen of Australia, Canada, New Zealand, and other independent Caribbean and Pacific countries 1952–

Born in London, she served in the Auxiliary Territorial Service during World War II, and in 1947 married Prince Philip of Greece. She became Queen in 1952, at the age of 25, her lavish coronation in 1953 becoming a symbol of national revival following the austerity of the 1940s. In an age when the monarch has little political influence, she has devoted much of her reign to ceremonial functions and to tours of the *Commonwealth and other countries. She has held weekly audiences with her Prime Minister, and shown a strong personal commitment to the Commonwealth. The serenity and distance with which she has performed her role won general respect and acclaim, but was curiously at odds with the free use of the media by her son, Prince *Charles, from the early 1990s. In that decade, she was affected by the often tumultuous personal lives of her children. In the early 1990s her role as head of state of a number of Commonwealth countries such as Australia became increasingly challenged. Nevertheless, her personal popularity was affirmed in the Golden Jubilee celebrations that marked the 50th year of her rule.

(⊕) SEE WEB LINKS

• The official website of the British monarchy.

Ellice Islands, see TUVALU; KIRIBATI

Ellis Island (USA)
An island in New York Bay off Manhattan Island. Long used as an arsenal and a fort, from 1892 until 1943 it served as the main US centre for immigration control. From 1943 until 1954 it was a detention centre for deportees, until it became part of the Statue of Liberty National Monument in 1956. More than twelve million immigrants passed through Ellis Island.

(⊕) SEE WEB LINKS

• The home page of the Ellis Island Immigration Museum.

Empire, British, see BRITISH EMPIRE

Emu, see WOOMERA ROCKET RANGE

Enabling Act (*Ermächtigungsgesetz*)
(23 Mar. 1933)

A law which according to the constitution of the German Weimar Republic enabled the government to rule by decree without parliamentary consent in cases of emergency. It had to be passed by a two-thirds majority in parliament, with at least two-thirds of all MPs voting. The law was used in 1923 to overcome the country's hyperinflation and cope with the occupation of the *Ruhr. While this helped stabilize the Republic then, the Enabling Act undermined it ten years later as the legal foundation of *Hitler's assumption of dictatorial powers during the *Third Reich. Following his failure to secure an absolute majority in the elections of 5 March 1933, Hitler persuaded most of the other parties to vote for an enabling law by giving them the hope that they might be able to have influence after its execution. Apart from the *Communist Party (KPD), which had already been outlawed, only the *SPD voted against the measure. To keep the appearance of legality, the Act was renewed in 1937, 1939, and 1943.

encyclical
A circular letter sent by a bishop to every church within his jurisdiction, and more particularly a letter by the Pope to Roman *Catholic parishes worldwide. Unlike church dogma, encyclicals are not infallible pronouncements, but Catholics are expected to follow them, while the declaration of the papal view limits the freedom of theological discussion.

Before 1961 The most important encyclicals include Pope Leo XIII's *Rerum Novarum* (1891) which formulated the social ideals of Catholicism in an industrializing world. The more conservative Pius X wrote against modernism (*Pascendi Domini Gregis*, 1907) and Protestantism (*Borromaeus*, 1910), while his successor, *Pius XI, revised Catholic social teaching through *Quadrigesima Anno*, 1931, in which he warned that that which could be accomplished by subordinates should not be done by higher levels such as the state. This founded the principle of subsidiarity, which became an important organizational principle for the EU from the 1990s. Pius XI also wrote the German encyclical *Mit brennender Sorge* (1937), in which he (finally) distanced the Roman Catholic Church from the *Nazi Party.

Since John XXIII Catholic social teaching was revised in *Mater et Magistra* (1961) by *John XXIII, which accepted some beneficial aspects of *socialism, e.g. its universal promotion of human dignity. Rather controversially especially among Roman Catholics in Western Europe and North America, *Humanae Vitae* (1968) by *Paul VI condemned *abortion and contraception. Of the encyclicals of *John Paul II, *Laborem Exercens* (1981) appeals for mutual understanding in the workplace, and *Mulieris Dignitatem* (1988) affirms the equality of women with men in the Church despite the insistence on a male priesthood. *Veritatis Splendor* (1993) attempts a redefinition of Catholic moral teaching in a fast-changing world of opportunity and technology, and *Fides et Ratio* (1998) explores the relationship between faith and human reason. John Paul II's encyclicals were strongly influenced by Cardinal Ratzinger, whose first encyclical as *Benedict XVI, *Deus Caritas Est* (2005), considered the essence of Christian love.

Enewetak Island, see MICRONESIA

England

The largest constituent country of the *United Kingdom, comprising 54 per cent of its territory, and 83 per cent of its population. It has traditionally dominated British politics. Scottish, Welsh, and Irish nationalist movements have developed largely in protest against English domination of their own affairs, which explains why a movement for greater English autonomy from the UK has never developed. Its territorial integrity has remained largely intact since 1066, while the growing power of *parliament, notably the House of Commons since 1360, reinforced the power of the capital. As a result of both of these factors, England became a highly centralized country whose traditional regional identities were underdeveloped by European standards. The cultural diversity that does exist, most notably the difference between northern and southern England, was more an expression of an economic diversity marked by the traditional industrial structures of the north, and a south dominated more by new industries, commerce, and finance. In other words, cultural diversity and regional differences have been reinforced, and impacted upon, by class identities. As devolution was realized for Scotland and Wales in 1999, the relative weakness of regional identities in and across England became a fundamental political problem. It precluded the establishment of a federal structure for the UK, in which separate parliaments for *Northern Ireland, *Wales, and *Scotland would be matched by parliaments for English regions of similar size and economic weight.

Enron

One of the most rapidly growing energy and financial services companies during the 1990s. Founded in 1985 and based in Houston, Texas, its dramatic growth was predicated on the deregulation of the energy markets in the 1980s, and a move into the futures markets for energy contracts. On 16 October 2001 Enron disclosed a loss of $618 million in the past quarter. On 8 November 2001 it admitted that it had falsified its earnings since 1997. The company's shares, which the company directors sold just before the announcements at about $80 per share, collapsed in the wake of these announcements, and Enron had to file for bankruptcy. The failure to report Enron's true financial position and the shredding of evidence put into doubt the future of one of the world's largest accounting firms, Arthur Anderson. It also threatened political repercussions, as a number of *Democrat and *Republican leaders, including *Cheney and George W. *Bush, had had close links with the company.

Entebbe Raid

On 27 June 1976, an Air France aircraft was hijacked and forced to land at the Ugandan airport of Entebbe. The hijackers of the Popular Front for the Liberation of Palestine demanded the release of over fifty Arab terrorists in return for the release of their (mostly Jewish) hostages. On 3 July 1976, in a spectacular raid an Israeli commando unit under the command of *Barak was flown in from Israel and made a surprise attack on the airport. It freed the hostages and returned them to Israel, despite vigorous attacks from the Ugandan air force. The raid humiliated Idi *Amin, who had supported the terrorists, and boosted Israel's military confidence, still badly shaken from the *Yom Kippur War. It served also as a reminder of Israel's vulnerability, at a time when Western opinion showed greater recognition of Palestinian grievances.

Entente Cordiale (1904)

The Anglo-French treaty of April 1904. It was a colonial agreement, in which France recognized British interests in Egypt, whilst Britain recognized French interests in Morocco. The Entente also settled disputes over Newfoundland, Madagascar, and Siam. The agreement greatly reduced tensions between Britain and France. It led to cooperation in the *Moroccan Crisis of 1905, and paved the way, from 1906, for talks between British and French military figures for military cooperation against Germany.

TRIPLE ENTENTE

EOKA (National Organization of Cypriot Fighters)

A guerrilla organization loosely linked to the Enosis (Union) movement in Cyprus. It organized five years of guerrilla warfare from 1954 to 1955, demanding an end to British military rule, and the union between the island and Greece. Its commander was Colonel Georgios Grivas, whose terrorist attacks were aimed mostly at the British army. After independence in 1960 it continued to operate underground, as EOKA-B, with its attacks now directly aimed against *Makarios III and independent rule for the island. It sought to bring about union when it carried out a coup in 1974 with the encouragement of the *Greek colonels. This brought about a Turkish invasion of the north-eastern part of the island, however, and made union of the whole island with Greece even more difficult.

Equatorial Guinea

Formerly the Spanish colonies of Fernando Póo (Bioko) and Mbini on the west coast of Africa, since independence the country has suffered from mass poverty and human rights abuses by its autocratic regimes.

Contemporary history (up to 1991) The mainland was not effectively occupied by Spain until 1926. It was declared independent on 12 October 1968 following a campaign led by Macias Nguema (b. 1924), who became the first President. Nguema imprisoned or murdered most members of the opposition, and established a brutal dictatorial regime, during which 120,000 people went into exile. This culminated in 1978 with the outlawing of the Roman *Catholic Church, to which over 80 per cent of the population belonged. In 1979 Nguema was overthrown and executed by his nephew, Colonel Teodore Obiang Nguema Mbasogo (b. 1942). Continuing his uncle's *human rights violations, Obiang created a new unity party, the Partido Democrático Guinea Ecuatorial (PDGE, Democratic Party of Equatorial Guinea), and in the early 1990s introduced a notional process of democratization.

Contemporary politics (since 1991) A new Constitution in 1991 introduced in theory a multi-party democracy, though new parties would be required to pay a ridiculously high deposit. As a result, the 1993 parliamentary elections were boycotted by the opposition, and hence duly won by the PDGE. On 24 May 1995, the President of the oppositional Partida del Progreso (Progressive Party) was tried and convicted for treason, and sentenced to 28 years' imprisonment. Obiang won elections from 1996, his PDGE also winning the elections held from then on into the early years of 2000. Harassment of the opposition and a curtailment of freedom of speech continued. The economy was boosted by the growth of oil exploration, which accounted for almost all of the country's exports at the beginning of the twenty-first century. The improvement in the country's overall economy did little to lift the appalling conditions of the mass of the population in one of the poorest countries in the world. According to the UN Human Development Index, average life expectancy fell from around 50 years in 2001 to under 44 years in 2005.

Erdogan, Recep Tayyip (b. 26 Feb 1954).

Turkish Prime Minister, 2003–

Born in Istanbul, the observant Muslim graduated from a state-sponsored Islamic school, and studied economics. He became a prominent politician of the religious Welfare Party, and was elected Mayor of Istanbul in 1994. A popular and pragmatic politician, he was imprisoned and banned from holding political office in 1998, for reading an Islamic poem at a political rally. After his release from prison, and the ban of the Welfare Party, he founded the Justice and Development Party (AKP), which aimed at pursuing religious principles in a secular state. The AKP won a landslide election victory in 2002, and after a constitutional amendment he was allowed to become Prime Minister a few months later. A popular politician, Erdogan presided over a revival of the economy. In 2007, he led the AKP to a resounding election victory, when it obtained 47 per cent of the popular vote.

Erhard, Ludwig (b. 4 Feb. 1897, d. 5 May 1977). West German Economics Minister 1949–63; Chancellor 1963–6

A professor of economics and economic adviser to the US administration in Germany from 1945, Erhard is generally remembered as the 'father of the German economic miracle'. He served as the economics director of the English- and American-controlled zones of Germany from March 1948, and then as West German Economics Minister. In these positions, he realized a social market economy, a *capitalist economy in which the state maintained a strong role in the provision of social welfare and market regulation. Defying strong domestic opposition and the wishes of the Allies, Erhard successfully abolished wage and price controls in 1948. His 'ordo-liberal' policies aimed at creating a stable market economy, as well as strong institutions to guard against the abuse of market power.

Erhard made a major contribution to the success of the fragile West German political system. Through his successful economic policies, average economic growth was around 8 per cent per annum. This translated into rapidly improving living conditions and the beginning of a consumer society from the late 1950s.

As Chancellor, Erhard's foreign policy was less focused on France and more directed towards the USA. In domestic politics, Erhard found it difficult to establish his authority, with his predecessor, Adenauer *constantly sniping at him from the background. Ironically, it was the economic crisis of the mid-1960s, as well as growing disagreements with his junior coalition partner, the *Liberal Party (FDP), which led to his resignation in 1966.

Eritrea

One of the world's poorest countries, the east African country on the Red Sea became Africa's youngest nation upon independence in 1993.

Foreign rule (up to 1993) By 1889 Italy had occupied the region and declared it a colony. Under Italian administration, medical and agricultural improvements were made. However, Italian rule became extremely harsh after the establishment of *Mussolini's Fascist dictatorship, when Eritrea became a prime exercise ground for 'theories' of racial discrimination within *Fascism. It also served as a base for the Italian campaigns against Ethiopia during 1895–6 and 1935–6. It came under British military administration in 1941, and was transferred to the *UN in 1952.

As a compromise between Ethiopian designs for incorporation and Eritrean demands for independence, the UN decided to make it a federal region of the Ethiopian Empire. Against UN intentions, the Ethiopian leadership under *Haile Selassie and then under the Communist military decided to integrate the territory firmly into the Ethiopian state, and to deny it any recognition of distinctiveness. This sparked off a violent guerrilla war against the Ethiopian armed forces, which the latter were unable to continue after the collapse of Soviet military aid in 1989. In 1991, the Eritrean People's Liberation Front (EPLF) combined with the rebel forces of the *Tigré to advance into Ethiopia and take its capital, Addis Ababa. It installed a new regime under the Tigréan leader Meles Zenawi (b. 1955), who granted the EPLF's wish for independence after a referendum had shown almost 100 per cent of Eritreans in favour.

Contemporary politics (since 1993) The EPLF's leader, Isaias Afwerki (b. 1945), became the country's first President upon independence on 24 May 1993. He transformed the EPLF into a political party in February 1994, named the People's Front for Democracy and Justice. Afwerki and Zenawi continued to work together, reaching agreements of cooperation in 1994, and establishing a free-trade area between the two countries in 1995. Relations with Ethiopia began to worsen, however, first at an economic level. This spilled over into the military arena, and in 1998 a war broke out between them as Eritrea accused Ethiopia of infringements of its border. The war cost the lives of about 100,000 people, and the displacement of 20 per cent of the Eritrean population. Already one of the world's poorest countries, Eritrea was brought to ruin by the war, as the state could not fulfil fundamental needs such as education and basic medical care. A fragile peace was brokered by the *UN in December 2000, with a commission examining the border disputes between the two countries. Its recommendations were rejected by Ethiopia, which claimed the border town of Badme. Eritrea suffered financially from sustaining a costly military, and relied heavily on international aid and money transfers from Eritreans living abroad.

Erlander, Tage Fritiof (b. 13 June 1901, d. 21 June 1985). Prime Minister of Sweden 1946–68

Born in Ransäter (Värmland), he graduated from Lund University in 1928. He worked as the editor of an encyclopaedia, but in 1933 was elected to the Riksdag (parliament) as a *Social Democrat. He was an Under-Secretary in the Social Department (1938–44), then Minister without Portfolio, and Minister of Education (1945). He was the party's surprise choice to succeed Per Albin Hansson as party leader and Prime Minister. He continued his predecessor's development of Sweden's model *welfare state. Erlander introduced an extremely high rate of very progressive taxation in 1947 which was designed to reduce income inequalities and put large funds for redistribution into the hands of the state. In response, pensions were increased, and a child allowance scheme introduced, while other measures such as statutory holidays were in place by 1955. Erlander was able to overcome initial economic difficulties by capitalizing on the disunity among the opposition parties. He was able to sustain his model of a *socialism that he took to be the middle way between *Communism and *capitalism, owing to his political craftsmanship, his pragmatism and common sense, and the blossoming of the economy. Erlander was succeeded by *Palme, and wrote his memoirs in six volumes (1972–82).

ERM (European Exchange Rate Mechanism)

A system of fixed exchange rates among a majority of member states of the European Community (*European integration), established in 1979. Originally, the central banks of member states were obliged to intervene if the value of a particular currency changed by more than 2.5 per cent against the determined exchange rate with any other currency. Despite numerous realignments, the ERM arguably provided for some stability in the money markets. Since 1993, it has been less effective, as the permissible deviation of most currencies from their predetermined value was then raised to 15 per cent. Nevertheless, it continued to operate, as all applicant member states' currencies needed to prove the stability of their currencies within the ERM before they were allowed to join the *euro.

The British pound entered the ERM only in 1990. After desperate attempts by the British government to support the value of the currency, it was forced out of the ERM on 17 September 1992, an episode that proved a tremendous embarrassment for the British Prime Minister, John *Major.
GOLD STANDARD; BRETTON WOODS

Ermächtigungsgesetz, see ENABLING ACT

ERP (European Recovery Program), see MARSHALL PLAN

Erzberger, Matthias (b. 20 Sept. 1875, d. 26 Aug. 1921). German Finance Minister 1919–20

An MP of the *Centre Party from 1903. Initially he supported World War I, but in 1917 he was instrumental in bringing about a peace resolution in the German parliament which called for negotiations to end the war. Partly because of this, and partly because as a Minister of State from October 1918 he was one of the signatories of the German armistice, Erzberger became a hated figure among the German right. His most enduring legacy was the comprehensive fiscal reform which strengthened the income of the federal Weimar Republic at the expense of its states and localities. He was murdered by two right-wing ex-army officers.

Eshkol, Levi (b. 25 Oct. 1895, d. 6 Feb. 1969). Prime Minister of Israel 1963–9

Born Levi Scholnik at Oratovo (Ukraine), he went to *Palestine in 1914 and became a farm labourer. When the British entered Palestine in 1917 he enlisted in the *Jewish Legion. With *Ben-Gurion and *Ben-Zvi he was a founder of the *Histadrut (General Federation of Jewish Labour), as well as of the *Mapai (Israel Workers' Party) in 1929. He rose to prominence mainly as Ben-Gurion's lieutenant. As such, he became Minister for Agriculture and Development in 1951, and Minister of Finance in 1952. In this position, Eshkol presided over a period of considerable economic growth. Despite successfully leading Israel through the *Six Day War in 1967, he was relatively conciliatory towards the other Arab states, and refused to annex formally the occupied territories in the *West Bank, apart from the eastern part of *Jerusalem. Just before his death, he managed to reunite various socialist groups to form the *Labour Party.

Esquipulas II, see ARIAS SÁNCHEZ, OSCAR

Estado Novo (New State)

The official name of the Portuguese dictatorship, which was established by *Carmona in 1926 and came to bear the imprint of *Salazar (1928–68). Its central features were economic stringency and conservatism (which prevented industrial expansion), social conservatism and maintenance of good relations with the Roman *Catholic Church, authoritarianism, and the maintenance of its colonies at all cost, tying them closer to metropolitan Portugal through administrative integration and the promotion of emigration to the colonies. After the replacement of *Caetano in 1974, the Estado Novo collapsed concurrently with the colonial empire.

Estonia

The wealthiest of the Baltic states, Estonia has enjoyed a close cultural and linguistic relationship with Finland.

Early history Colonized by the Teutonic Order of Knights from 1346, Estonia became dominated by a German landowning elite, which maintained its social and economic position during Swedish occupation (1561–1721) and for most of the subsequent period of Russian rule. From 1855, when they could finally acquire land, Estonians in increasing numbers became independent and prosperous farmers. Migration also increased the Estonian population in the cities during this period. Clumsy attempts to introduce the Russian language and culture backfired. As a result of these factors, from the 1880s an articulate, self-confident Estonian *nationalism developed, and this accelerated after the *Russian Revolution of 1905. After 1914, the independence movement was increasingly dominated by *Bolsheviks, but during the German occupation in World War I a nationalist government was established.

The First Republic (1920–40) After Germany's collapse in 1917, the government successfully fought the Communists, with foreign (particularly Finnish) help. After the proclamation of a republic in 1920, a land reform expropriated the wealthy landowners

and thus increased support for the state among the mass of the peasant population. Its relative homogeneity (88 per cent were Estonians) led to an atmosphere of toleration, as Estonians could afford to appreciate the cultural distinctiveness of Russian, German, Swedish, and Jewish minorities. Remakably, Estonia allowed every minority that consisted of more than 3,000 people to constitute itself into a corporate body, and elect a representation with responsibility for clubs, schools and other cultural affairs. The country suffered serious economic and social dislocations during the Great *Depression, which led to the increasing popularity of Fascist movements. To prevent their takeover, the President and leader of the Agrarian Party, Konstantin Päts, dissolved parliament and declared martial law in 1934. The authoritarian regime created new representative bodies, in which opposition was possible, and left the rights of the minorities untouched.

Soviet rule Under the terms of the *Hitler–Stalin Pact, Estonia was overrun by the *Red Army in June 1940, and incorporated into the USSR on 6 August 1940. As in the other Baltic States (Latvia, Lithuania), the Soviet regime hoped to weaken its national spirit though large-scale deportations of Estonia's intelligentsia. Further deportations after the country was reclaimed from German occupation (1941–4) reduced the Estonian population within its own country to some 60 per cent. Nevertheless, *Gorbachev's reformist policies of *glasnost sparked off demands for independence, which was declared on 30 March 1990, and recognized by *Yeltsin on 28 August 1991.

Renewed independence (since 1991) The wealthiest among the Baltic republics (all of whose average income per head had been among the highest in the USSR), Estonia's economy stabilized by 1995 after undergoing a traumatic period of transition, though economic progress was still hindered by the prevalence of *Mafia-like gangster organizations. Initially, government policy against minorities was relatively harsh, but in 1995, a suggestion by the European Union was accepted whereby all residents who had lived there for a minimum of five years could become citizens if they so wished. The elections of March 1995 produced a victory for the ex-Communist Coalition Party and Rural Union. Subsequent elections in 1999 and 2003 were won by a centre-right coalition, which was presided over by a quick succession of Prime Ministers who struggled to introduce anti-corruption measures against entrenched political and economic interests. Under Prime

Minister Andrus Ansip since 2005, Estonia continued its economic growth, having joined the EU in 2004.

ETA (Euzkadi ta Azkatasuna), see
BASQUES

Ethiopia

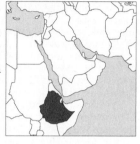

A country in north-east Africa originally known as Abyssinia, which managed to withstand imperial colonization until well into the twentieth century.

The imperial era (up to 1974) Ethiopia's history has been characterized by great linguistic and ethnic diversity, involving around 80 different peoples. These were unified under Emperor Menelik II (r. 1889–1913), who managed to strengthen his state sufficiently to withstand an attempt at colonization by Italy. He beat the Italian forces in 1896, thus producing the first European military defeat in Africa. Thereafter, Menelik concentrated on developing his country through the establishment of secular secondary education and the improvement of the infrastructure, establishing postal and telegraph services. He was succeeded by his grandson Lej Iyasu (1913–16), who was deposed for his alleged laxity in Christian devotion.

Power passed to Menelek's daughter, Empress Zewditu (1916–30), who ruled with her nephew Ras Tafari Mekonnen as her regent. The latter was crowned Emperor as *Haile Selassie I upon Zewditu's death in 1930. His efforts to hasten his country's economic development were accelerated during the period of Italian occupation which followed the *Abyssinian War, when schools and roads were built with the brutal use of Ethiopian forced labour. After World War II, the reinstated Emperor faced the difficult tasks of pacifying the various peoples, ridding the country of the British occupation forces which had reinstated him, and continuing to attract Western aid. As ruler of the only fully independent African country in 1945 (apart from Liberia), he became an important African leader in the era of *decolonization which began with the independence of Ghana in 1957, and the establishment of the *French Community in 1958. Nevertheless, corruption and internal administrative inefficiency

continued, while living standards hardly increased.

Communist rule (1974–91) A severe drought in 1973 led to an army revolt, which Haile Selassie countered with the appointment of a short-lived liberal administration headed by Endel Katchew Makonnen. Both men were deposed in September 1974 by a group of radical officers who, after several years marked by internal power struggles, established a Communist regime. From 1975, Ethiopia was governed by a Provisional Military Administrative Council (Ethiopian abbreviation: Derg), which instituted perhaps the most radical social and economic reform in Africa. All land was nationalized, and each family was given a maximum of ten hectares (25 acres) for cultivation. Most of the economy was nationalized, while sweeping attempts were made to reduce the country's illiteracy rate.

This economic rupture, compounded by never-ending civil war in *Eritrea and *Tigré, led the country to a complete breakdown, with large-scale famines in 1984 and 1987. From 1984 to 1988, 600,000 people were forcibly removed from the north to the south, in order to facilitate the war against the Eritrean guerrillas. Unable to continue the fight without military help from the crumbling Soviet Union, the Communist army collapsed in front of the advancing rebel forces of Eritrea and Tigré in 1991. The latter occupied the capital, Addis Ababa, and installed a new regime under the Tigréan leader, Meles Zenawi.

Contemporary politics (since 1991) Zenawi inaugurated a limited process of democratization and devolution of power to provincial authorities. Eritrea was released into independence, and each of the provinces was given the right to secede from Ethiopia if this was established as the popular will by a referendum. A new Constitution was passed on 8 December 1994, and on 7 May 1995 Zenawi was elected President with 90 per cent of the popular vote in an election which international observers deemed fair, despite contrary claims from the opposition.

In 1998 Ethiopia was attacked by neighbouring Eritrea, though Ethiopian forces repelled the attack and occupied the west of Eritrea. A peace was brokered on 12 December 2000, which established a 25 km wide de-militarized zone along the border inside Eritrea. The war constituted a huge burden on the economy, as public debts amounted to ten times the value of all annual exports. The economic situation was worsened by the collapse in the world price of Ethiopia's main export staple, coffee. Meles Zenawi was confirmed in office in 2000 and 2005, with the opposition mounting violent protests against what it claimed were unfair elections.

EU (European Union)

Created by the Treaty of *Maastricht, it was made up of three pillars: (1) the European Community (EC), whose legislation was proposed by the *European Commission and agreed between the *European Council and the *European Parliament, and guarded by the *European Court of Justice; (2) the Common Foreign and Security Policy (3) Justice and Home Affairs. The second and third pillars have been subject to intergovernmental decisions taken by the European Council. The absence of strong Community institutions in the decision-making processes of the second and third pillars led to their relative ineffectiveness. As a consequence, the Treaty of *Amsterdam transferred a number of crucial policies on immigration and border control from the third to the first pillar. In response to the attacks of September 11, the EU tried, with limited success, to coordinate immigration and anti-terrorism policies. *European integration continued with the enlargement of the EU to 25 members in 2004, and 27 in 2007. In its relatively short history, the EU has thus seen a remarkable trend towards deepening common policies and widening its membership. As a result, popular resistance to an EU dictated by the heads of government was manifested by the referendums against the Treaty establishing a *Constitution for Europe in 2005, and growing public hostility to further enlargement, which would include Turkey.

See TABLE 8.

(⊕) SEE WEB LINKS

• The official website of the European Union.

Eupen-Malmédy

A German-speaking territory of around $1,000 \text{ km}^2$ (390 sq. miles), it was part of the Austrian Netherlands until it became part of Prussia under the terms of the Congress of Vienna (1814). After World War I the prosperous area was awarded to Belgium in 1919. During 1940–5, it formed part of *Nazi Germany. It was finally confirmed as Belgian territory in a German-Belgian agreement of 1956. The region was part of the Wallonia region, which from 2001 became a federal state within Belgium. Within Wallonia, however, Eupen-Malmédy maintained considerable autonomy with its own government.

EURATOM, see ROME, TREATY OF

euro

The single currency adopted by eleven states of the European Union in 1999.

Rationale The single currency grew out of the recognition that in a context of *globalization and free capital flows, individual governments could only exert limited influence on the outcomes of monetary policies. This had become evident during the 1980s and early 1990s, when the national central banks of the European Community (EC) member states were forced to shadow the decisions of the German central bank without having any influence over its decisions. For this reason, the European Central Bank (ECB) was created, largely on the successful model of the German central bank, so that the ECB was relatively well-respected by the financial markets from the start. This, in turn, has meant that the low interest and inflation rates previously enjoyed by Germany were extended to the entire euro-zone.

Creation Further to the creation by 1993 of a single market through the *Single European Act, the *Maastricht Treaty of 1992 instituted the European Monetary Union (EMU). During a transition period, in which monetary policies were to be harmonized further and economic convergence was to be achieved, a European Currency Institute was created in 1994. The Institute coordinated monetary policies, as all the future members' national central banks had achieved autonomy from national political interference. The convergence criteria used to decide whether an applicant could be accepted for membership were: (1) a national budget deficit below 3 per cent of GDP; (2) total public debts below 60 per cent of GDP, or moving towards that target; (3) an inflation rate no more than 1.5 per cent above the countries with the lowest rate; (4) a stable national currency against the other members of the *ERM for at least two years. A Stability and Growth Pact was adopted in 1997, which created penalties for members who had been accepted into the single currency but who were subsequently failing to meet the first three criteria.

Contemporary history (since 1998) On 1 July 1998 Austria, Belgium, Finland, France, Germany, Ireland, Italy, Luxembourg, the Netherlands, Portugal, and Spain were admitted to the final stage of EMU. On 1 January 1999, the euro was formally adopted. The member states' currencies were locked in their exchange rate, while the successor of the ECI, the European Central

Bank (ECB) in Frankfurt, took all decisions about the interest rate. In 2001 Greece became the twelfth member of the euro-zone, and on 1 January 2002 euro bank notes and coins were introduced to replace the old national denominations. In 2007, Slovenia became the thirteenth state (and the first from former Eastern Europe) to enter the euro-zone,

(⊕) SEE WEB LINKS

• The official website of the European Central Bank.

Eurocommunism
The practice of Western European Communist Parties, notably in Italy and France, to behave independently of directions from the Soviet Communist Party, and to pursue pragmatic policies to further *socialism within existing capitalist countries instead of working towards a proletarian revolution as predicted by the doctrine of *Communism.

COMMUNIST PARTY, ITALY; COMMUNIST PARTY, FRANCE

European Coal and Steel Community, see ECSC

European Commission
Established by the Treaty of Rome in 1957, the European Commission's principal role has been that of the 'guardian of the founding treaties' of the EU. A unique, supranational body whose seat is in Brussels, its composition has changed with each wave of enlargement. Before the EU's eastern enlargement in 2004 and 2007 the commission was composed of twenty commissioners from the fifteen member states of the EU. Since 2007, it has comprised 27 commissioners, one from each member state. The commission heads the civil service of the European Union, which was composed of about 17,000 employees in 2000, and which deals with issues ranging from regional policy, agriculture, culture, energy, employment, environment, enlargement, to foreign affairs. As such, the commission has obtained a unique position within the European Union, as the only body with detailed information on all areas within its

purview across all member states. Moreover, it was responsible for over 150 diplomatic representations of the EU throughout the world.

The Commission's power has been further enhanced by its executive functions. Throughout its history it has jealously guarded its power of initiative, whereby it alone can initiate European legislation to come before the *European Council and the *European Parliament. Moreover, by passing directives, regulations, and decisions to implement legislation, the commission has gained enormous practical influence upon the economics, society, and environment of the EU member states. Beyond its regular powers, the Commission's influence as a driving force of *European integration has been largely contingent upon the political adeptness of its members, especially its President. Its most influential period was under the Presidency of Jacques *Delors (1985–95). It enjoyed a lower profile under its subsequent Presidents, Jacques Santer (1995–9; b. 1937) and Romano *Prodi (1999–2004), with its influence increasing again under Manuel *Barroso.

(⊕) SEE WEB LINKS

• The official website of the European Commission.

European Community (EC), see
EUROPEAN INTEGRATION

European Council
A governing body of the *EU, it was established by the Paris summit in 1974. It is composed of the heads of government of the EU member states (and the heads of state in the case of France and Cyprus), and has met at least three times a year to discuss common issues. Its main purpose has been to provide opportunities for informal meetings to help solve major issues standing in the way of *European integration. To guard this informality, national advisers and the press have been kept at arm's length at these meetings, leading to accusations of a lack of transparency. Nevertheless, the council has developed into one of the pivotal institutions of the EU, since its decisions could be directly

Table 7. **Presidents of the European Commission**

Walter Hallstein	1958–67	Gaston Thorn	1981–85
Jean Rey	1967–70	Jacques *Delors	1985–95
Franco Malfatti	1970–72	Jacques Santer	1995–99
Sicco Mansholt	1972–73	Romano *Prodi	1999–2004
François-Xavier Ortoli	1973–77	José Manuel *Barroso	2004–
Roy *Jenkins	1977–81		

implemented by the national governments of the member states. It was formally recognized by the *Single European Act, and has been given further recognition by the Treaty of *Maastricht. The European Council is not to be confused with the Council of Ministers, a regular meeting of government ministers of the EU member states dealing with day-to-day policy issues.

(⊕) SEE WEB LINKS

• The official website of the European Council.

European Court of Justice (ECJ)

Created in its present form by the Treaty of Rome in 1957, it emerged originally from the *ECSC. Its role has been to pronounce over supranational law common to all members of the EEC and its successors, the European Community and the *EU. In this role, it has often been described as a 'motor' for *European integration, since it created a quasi-constitutional legal order that was at best implied in the founding treaties of the EEC and its successors. In 1963, the ECJ established the doctrine of direct effect in its *Van Gend en Loos* decision, which stated that European Community law was directly applicable to citizens of European member states. This was followed by the 1964 *Costa v. Enel* pronouncement of supremacy, which stated that European Community law took precedence over national law. With the importance of the ECJ thus established, the 1970s saw a large upsurge in ECJ pronouncements, which were made with reference to Art. 177 of the Treaty of Rome. This stipulated that national and regional courts could refer legal decisions directly to the ECJ for an opinion on their compatibility with European law, without first referring the matter to a higher national court. The 1980s saw a number of challenges in the supreme courts of EC member states to the principle that EC law was supreme over national law even on constitutional matters. But by the late 1990s all supreme courts had accepted the constitutional status of EU law, albeit not unconditionally. The activism and success of the ECJ led to lively discussions as to whether a European *Constitutional Convention was desirable, or even necessary. The ECJ with its seat in Luxemburg is not to be confused with the European Court of Human Rights (ECHR) with its seat in Strasbourg.

(⊕) SEE WEB LINKS

• The official website of the ECJ.

European Economic Community

(EEC), see EUROPEAN INTEGRATION; ROME, TREATY OF

European Free Trade Association, see EFTA

European integration

The formation of European states into the world's closest regional association, which has assumed many of the characteristics of statehood.

Early history (up to 1957) The attempt to promote economic and political union in Europe emerged initially from a desire after World War II to integrate European powers so closely as to make another war between them impossible. It was also influenced by the need of Western European states to respond to the *Cold War while binding in West Germany and enabling its rearmament. A further central motive emerged from the 1980s in the concern about the internationalization and globalization of trade and politics, in which the relatively small European states could only have an influential voice if they acted in coordination with each other.

The European Coal and Steel Community (*ECSC) was established by the Treaty of Paris on 18 April 1951, to create a common market for coal and steel between the signatories, Belgium, the Federal Republic of Germany, France, Italy, Luxemburg, and the Netherlands. Through the common control of those industries which were deemed crucial for war production, German and French politicians such as Robert *Schumann and Jean *Monnet intended to prevent the unilateral rearmament of any of its member states, and especially to avoid renewed unilateral German rearmament.

Encouraged by the economic and political success of the ECSC, the six member states proceeded to sign the Treaty of *Rome in 1957. This established the European Economic Community (EEC), which from 1967 was transformed into the European Community (EC).

The 1960s and 1980s The EEC excluded Europe's most powerful economy of the immediate postwar years, the United Kingdom. The UK was not involved in the negotiations leading up to the Treaty of Rome because it still conducted most of its trade with its Empire, and because the *Eden government and its civil service failed to appreciate the will of the other European states to go ahead without it. Following the

Treaty of Rome, the UK founded a looser economic association (*EFTA), but decided to apply for membership during the 1960s, only to be turned down twice (1963, 1967) because of the veto of the French President, de *Gaulle. After de Gaulle's resignation in France, the EC was expanded by the first wave of enlargement to include Denmark, the Republic of Ireland, and the UK as new members, with effect from 1 January 1973. Earlier, Norway had withdrawn its application after a referendum had shown that a majority of its population opposed entry. (This outcome was confirmed in a renewed referendum in 1994.) Under the government of Harold *Wilson, a referendum was held in the UK on 5 June 1975, and produced a two-thirds majority in favour of continuing membership of the EC.

In 1974 the Paris Summit convened by *Giscard d'Estaing made a number of changes that proved to be decisive. It instituted the *European Council, and it transformed the *European Parliament into a directly elected body with effect from 1979. The 1960s and the 1970s also saw dramatic progress in European legal integration through the rulings of the *European Court of Justice. Finally, 1979 saw the creation of the *ERM.

Deepening integration (1980s–90s) The 1980s were notable for four developments. (1) In 1984, Margaret *Thatcher gave up her obstinate attitude in the European Council in return for a settlement on the size of a rebate on British overpayment into the European budget. This crisis, however, strengthened the resolve of other member states to increase the application of *Qualified Majority Voting to make decision-making more effective. (2) A second wave of integration saw the accession of Greece in 1981, and Portugal and Spain in 1986. This created further impetus for institutional reform, and changed the geopolitical outlook of the EC. The accession of countries that had recently overcome dictatorships also demonstrated the EC's ability to stabilize and promote the economic and political systems of poorer, more fragile member states. (3) The recovery following the *oil price shocks of the 1970s demonstrated the relative inability of fiscal policies to overcome supply-side shocks. During the 1970s and 1980s, the German central bank had established itself as the EC's key central bank. Whatever the political preferences of other members, its decisions became increasingly determinate over the monetary policies of other member

states, which greatly strengthened the will to coordinate monetary and commercial policies more formally. (4) This led to the *Single European Act in 1986, and ultimately gave rise to demands for European Monetary Union (EMU). German resistance against this was removed by German unification in 1990, because it gave its political leadership under *Kohl sufficient strength in domestic politics to realize this aim against domestic and institutional opposition.

The *Maastricht Treaty was perhaps the most radical milestone in European integration. It created the *European Union, and set out a timetable for the introduction of a single currency, which was named the *euro at the Madrid Summit in 1995. Followed by the Treaties of *Amsterdam and *Nice, the 1990s led to fundamental institutional reform and to a dramatic extension of areas of common EU concern. In other words, from the Single European Act on, European integration was less and less about the 'negative' removal of barriers, and more and more about 'positive', active harmonization. As this affected individual citizens much more, integration since 1986 has led to growing public scepticism, if not outright hostility, in many member states. During the 1990s, then, public opinion became a much more prominent factor in European integration, and at times even threatened its progress, as the negative outcome of the Irish referendum on *Nice showed in 2001.

Widening integration (1995–2007) From 1995, the EU enlarged in three waves. In 1995, Austria, Sweden and Finland became members. Following extensive accession negotiations, ten new states in eastern and central Europe, as well as Malta and Cyprus, joined in 2004. Bulgaria and Romania joined in 2007, albeit with stringent conditions to encourage these countries to carry out further domestic reforms. The enlargement rounds of 2004 and 2007 increased the EU's economic and cultural diversity. In many of its new member states, the EU had helped stabilize a number of fragile political systems because membership had been a common goal across the political divides. At the same time, the economic discipline demanded of the new member states eroded support for established parties in many of them, as accelerating growth did not translate into a general improvement in living standards. The new size of the EU required a dramatic institutional restructuring and simplification of working procedures in a union in which unanimous decisions between member states were still the norm. In response, a *Constitutional Convention tried to create a new institutional and legal framework for the EU, which culminated in the Treaty establishing a *Constitution for Europe (2004). This was rejected by France and the Netherlands in 2005.

Contemporary issues Having begun to station troops outside the EU's frontiers in Bosnia and Congo, the EU's member states established Battle Groups from 2007, which were ready to be deployed at short notice for peacekeeping operations. In response to the attacks of *September 11 as well as the *London and *Madrid Bombings, member states also agreed significant measures for the prevention of cross-border crime. The EU was also a crucial partner in realizing the *Kyoto Protocol, committing itself in 2007 to a 20 per cent reduction in greenhouse gas emissions by 2020. At a 2007 summit, EU leaders decided to replace the constitution by a Treaty to render the EU's institutions more effective, with the aim to have it ratified by 2009.

WEU; LOMÉ CONVENTION; COUTOUNU AGREEMENT

European Parliament

An elected institution of the European Union with its seat in Strasbourg. Originally, its members were appointees of the parliaments of the EC member states, but since 1979 they have been elected directly every five years by universal suffrage. Treaties signed in 1970 and 1975 gave the European Parliament (EP) important powers over budgetary and constitutional matters, and through the Single European Act of 1986 it assumed greater powers through the cooperation procedure: accordingly, a number of decisions made by the *European Council needed to have the assent of the EP. This right was extended by the *Maastricht Treaty, which gave the European Parliament equal legislative powers through the right of co-decision in substantial areas of legislation. On issues affecting the common market, for instance, the EP now had the upper hand in its search for a compromise with the Council.

The EP's powers have been extended in the Treaties of *Amsterdam and *Nice. However, it was still hampered by the requirement that all decisions under the co-decision procedure had to be approved by an overall majority of members. This prevented the emergence of traditional political fault-lines, as the need for large majorities precluded the establishment of traditional opposition and governing

camps. This, and the inability to impose taxation, have made the parliament relatively obscure and seemingly insignificant to its voters. As a result, since 1979, voter participation in European elections has declined steadily. However, declining voter participation affected most mature democratic systems. Overall, the EP continued to enjoy legitimacy as the only democratically elected organ of the EU.

EUROPEAN INTEGRATION

((())) SEE WEB LINKS

• The official website of the European Parliament.

European Recovery Program (ERP),

see MARSHALL PLAN

European Union, Founding Treaties of, see EU; EUROPEAN INTEGRATION; ROME, TREATY OF; SINGLE EUROPEAN ACT; MAASTRICHT, TREATY OF; AMSTERDAM, TREATY OF; NICE, TREATY OF

Evatt, Herbert Vere (b. 30 Apr. 1894, d. 2 Nov. 1965). Australian Labor leader 1951–60

Born in East Maitland (New South Wales), Evatt taught at the University of Sydney before developing a law practice that specialized in civil liberties. He resigned a safe *Labor seat (which he held since 1925) to become the (then) youngest justice of the Australian High Court (1930–40). He returned to politics in 1940 following his election to the House of Representatives. He became the second most senior minister in the *Curtin and *Chifley Cabinets as Attorney-General and Minister for External Affairs (1941–9). Concerned to strengthen Australia's links with its regional neighbours, he negotiated the *ANZAC pact. He also became involved in the setting up of the *UN, presiding over its General Assembly during 1948–9. A man with tremendous intellectual qualities but without much political judgement, he took over from *Chifley as leader of the *Labor Party, but did not have the charisma or the authority to prevent the party's third split since World War I over the *Petrov Affair. He retired from politics in 1960 and served for two years as Chief Justice of New South Wales.

DEMOCRATIC LABOR PARTY

Évian Agreements (18 Mar. 1962)

A peace treaty signed in the French spa town of Évian by *Pompidou (for France) and *Ben-Bella (for the *FLN) which brought peace and independence to Algeria, after a ceasefire had been in operation since

21 February 1962. Subsequent referendums in Algeria and France ratified the agreements with overwhelming majorities, despite threats from colonialist terrorist organizations, and the *Organisation de l'Armée Secrète.

Table 8. **Members of the European Union (by date of entry)**

1957	Belgium	1995	Austria
1957	France	2004	Cyprus
1957	Germany	2004	Czech Republic
1957	Italy	2004	Estonia
1957	Luxemburg	2004	Hungary
1957	Netherlands	2004	Latvia
1973	Denmark	2004	Lithuania
1973	Ireland	2004	Malta
1973	United Kingdom	2004	Poland
1981	Greece	2004	Slovakia
1986	Portugal	2004	Slovenia
1986	Spain	2007	Bulgaria
1995	Sweden	2007	Romania
1995	Finland		

F

Fabian Society

Established in 1884 by predominantly middle-class intellectuals to spread and apply socialist ideas to Britain through democratic and gradual, non-revolutionary means. Its name was derived from the Roman general Fabius Maximus Verrucosus, whose military successes in the second Punic War were the result of his preference for piecemeal skirmishes rather than an all-out battle against the Carthaginians (217 BC). The Fabians, who included Sidney and Beatrice *Webb, George Bernard Shaw, and later Ramsay *MacDonald and Clement *Attlee, criticized the current order not so much as unjust, but as inefficient and wasteful. A bureaucratic elite should administer a centrally planned economy to eliminate the inefficiencies inherent in a liberal economic order, and thus avoid failures such as unemployment and poverty. Though generally attached to the *Labour Party (it helped found its predecessor, the Labour Representation Committee, in 1900), it also had considerable influence on the Edwardian 'new' *Liberal Party, for example in its claim that the state had a responsibility to create a minimal provision of social welfare to enable each individual to reach his or her highest potential. It continued to exist as a left-wing political pressure group.

(⊕) SEE WEB LINKS

• The official website of the Fabian Society.

Facta, Luigi (b. 16 Nov. 1861, d. 5 Nov. 1930). Last President of the Italian Council of Ministers 1922

Born near Turin, he became a Member of Parliament in 1892 and came to hold various ministerial posts in the *Giolitti ministries. As *de facto* Prime Minister from February 1922 his efforts to stop *Mussolini's advance through secret negotiations and then through force were at best unconvincing. Following the latter's *March on Rome his government collapsed on 28 October 1922 to make way for Mussolini's *Fascist takeover.

Fahd ibn Abd Al-Aziz al Saud (b. 1921). King of Saudi Arabia 1982–2005

The fourth son of *Abd-al-Aziz ibn Saud to become King, he was Minister of Education (1953–62) and Minister of the Interior (1962–75) before becoming Crown Prince to his brother, King Khalid. A playboy in his youth, he was regarded as progressive. Nevertheless, he maintained the country's religious and social conservatism, and focused his energies on dealing with an economy that was badly damaged by the decline in oil prices during the 1980s. He was much criticized at home and in the Arab world for his moderation against Israel, but the good relations with the West which this yielded stood him in good stead as the country was threatened by a spillover of the *Iran–Iraq War. Even more importantly, he was able to rally US support to defend him against Saddam *Hussein's aggression in the *Gulf War. Fahd suffered a stroke in 1995, whereupon his power effectively passed on to his half-brother, *Abdullah Bin-Abd-al-Aziz Al-Saud.

Fair Deal (USA)

The term used to describe the domestic programme of US President *Truman in January 1949. Following his unexpected victory in the 1948 presidential election, Truman hoped to advance beyond the *New Deal to introduce measures on civil rights, fair employment practices, education, public health insurance, extended social security benefits, support for low-income housing, price and rent control, and farm subsidies. The programme also proposed guaranteed full employment and an increased minimum wage. A coalition of *Republicans and conservative Southern *Democrats (*Dixiecrats) blocked most of the measures in Congress until financial and personal scandals involving members of the administration, the Communist takeover in China, and the outbreak of the *Korean War undermined Truman's political capital. Nevertheless, he did manage to secure some advances in housing (through the 1949 Housing Act) and social security.

Faisal I (b. 20 May 1883, d. 8 Sept. 1933). King of Iraq 1921–33

Son of *Hussein ibn Ali, he took part in the *Arab Revolt of 1916. He worked closely with T. E. *Lawrence, and with his northern Arab army he entered Damascus in September 1918. Faisal was proclaimed King of Syria, but had to abandon his claim when at the *Paris

Peace Conference Syria became a French *League of Nations *Mandate. Forced into exile by the French, he was compensated by the British with its new Mandate of Iraq, of which he became King. He subsequently displayed considerable skill and astuteness in carefully responding to the strong Arab nationalist sentiments in his country, while maintaining a good relationship with Britain. Thus he managed to create working state institutions, promulgating a constitution in 1925. His greatest success came when he gained de facto Iraqi independence and admission into the League of Nations (1930–2).

Faisal II (b. 2 May 1935, d. 14 July 1958). King of Iraq 1939–58

The grandson of *Faisal I, he succeeded his father, King Ghazi, at the age of 4, though he did not take up formal power from his regent, *Abd al-Ilah, until 1953. Educated in England with his cousin *Hussein of Jordan, in February 1958 he became head of the *Arab Federation of Jordan and Iraq, which was formed in response to the *United Arab Republic of Syria and Egypt. Devoid of the political instinct or the charisma of his cousin Hussein, he was ousted in a pro-*Nasser military *coup*, when he and his uncle were murdered and the Republic of Iraq was proclaimed.

Faisal ibn Abd al-Aziz (b. Nov. 1906, d. 25 Mar. 1975). King of Saudi Arabia 1964–75

Son of the first ruler of Saudi Arabia, *Abd al-Aziz ibn Saud, he was appointed Viceroy of the Hejaz in 1926, and in 1934 led a victorious campaign against Yemen. He became effective ruler of Saudi Arabia in 1958, owing to the incompetence and later ill health of his brother King Saud ibn Abd al-Aziz, who was deposed in 1964. As such he had to deal with the main consequences for his country of its immense oil revenues. Faisal created a strong, modern army, a comprehensive network of communications, an extensive education system, and a free, well-equipped health service. At the same time, he remained culturally and politically conservative, opposing revolution even in the name of *Islam. An opponent of Israel, he granted financial assistance to both Jordan and Egypt after the disastrous *Six Day War of 1967. As the main supplier of US oil, he used his influence to reduce support for Israel. He took a key role in the *OPEC negotiations of December 1973 which precipitated the world *oil-price shock. He was shot by a disgruntled nephew and succeeded by his brother Khalid.

Falange Española Tradicionalista (FET)

A Spanish *Fascist organization founded as the Falange Española in 1933 by José Antonio Primo de Rivera, son of General *Primo de Rivera. Through its manifesto adopted in 1934, the Twenty-seven Points, it espoused political illiberalism and authoritarianism, and a belief in a national community devoid of class conflict and linked by *nationalism. Through paternalist social values it successfully enlisted and reinforced the power of the Roman *Catholic Church. After a slow start, it developed into a mass movement after 1936 and the outbreak of the *Civil War. It was hijacked by *Franco, who needed a political movement to back his military campaign, and thus the FET came into being on 18 April 1937.

The FET served as an indispensable link between Franco's regime and the population. It gained almost one million affiliated members in 1942, but, despite this, never had decisive influence over Franco, who refused the demand of many Falange members to join Germany in World War II, and who carefully balanced the influence of the FET with that of other interests. After 1943, and especially after 1945, the *Fascist elements of the FET were progressively reduced, and its more acceptable elements, such as its link with the Catholic Church, emphasized. The Twenty-seven Points were replaced in 1958 with a vague programme advocating the hardly controversial issues of peace, cooperation, and unity. Devoid of any ideology and purpose after Franco's death, the FET was dissolved in 1977.

Falklands War (2 Apr.–14 June 1982)

The war over the sovereignty of the Falkland Islands in the South Atlantic. These had been first discovered by the British in 1592, and became home to a British settlement in 1833. Argentina also claimed them (as the **Malvinas**) on the basis of a Spanish settlement dating back to the 1760s, and their geographic location around 600 km (385 miles) off the Argentinian coast. Argentina revived its claim after 1945, and from 1965 it negotiated with Britain through the *United Nations. By the 1970s, Britain appeared to be willing to transfer sovereignty to Argentina. One solution was 'leaseback', whereby Argentina would be given sovereignty, but Britain would administer the islands. However, the Falkland Islanders wished to remain under British rule, and negotiations broke down in 1982. In late March 1982 the Argentine President, *Galtieri, sent three warships to South Georgia (a dependency of the Falklands), in order to deflect Argentinian attention from the poor economic and *human rights record of his regime. This was followed by an invasion of the Falkland Islands on 2 April.

Negotiations were attempted by the *UN, the USA, and Peru, but despite international pressure (backed by UN Resolution 502) calling on Argentina to withdraw, Galtieri stood firm. By 5 April, a British task force was ready to depart to the Falklands, eventually numbering twenty warships, along with supporting vessels and 6,000 troops. Having sailed 13,000 km to the South Atlantic, it easily recaptured South Georgia on 25 April, and began to attack East Falkland. On 7 April, Britain had declared a 200-mile 'exclusion zone' around the Falklands; in one of the most controversial acts of the war, on 2 May the Argentinian cruiser, *General Belgrano*, was sunk (at the cost of 370 lives) despite the fact that it was sailing away from the Falklands. There were commando landings on West Falkland on 14 May, and the main British invasion was launched on the night of 20/21 May, at Port San Carlos on East Falkland. Extensive fighting took place between 21–7 May, by which time a bridgehead had been established. The major battle between the opposing land forces took place at Goose Green on 28 May. After this, despite Argentine counter-attacks at Fitzroy and Bluff Cove, British troops made steady progress and recaptured Port Stanley on 14 June.

The war cost 225 British and approximately 750 Argentinian lives. The Argentinian defeat resulted in the fall of Galtieri, and it helped to portray Margaret *Thatcher as a strong and decisive leader. Britain has since refused to reopen discussions over sovereignty, but after the accession of *Menem relations with Argentina have been normalized.

Fanfani, Amintore (b. 6 Feb. 1908, d. 21 Nov. 1999). Prime Minister of Italy 1954, 1958–9, 1960–3, 1982–3, 1987

A professor in economic history at the Catholic University of Milan (since 1936), Fanfani joined the *Christian Democrats (DC) out of his commitment to social reform in 1945, and became a member of the Constituent Assembly in 1946. He served as

Minister of Labour (1947–50), of Agriculture (1951–3), and of the Interior (1953–4). As Party Secretary of the DC (1954–9 and 1973–5), he was responsible for a considerable improvement in party organization and party membership. As Prime Minister he steered his party to the left and was responsible for the cooperation with the *Socialist Parties, which formed the basis of the DC governments from 1963 to 1974. His influence within the party dwindled thereafter, so that he was unable to prevent the DC accepting the help of the *Communist Party in government under *Andreotti in 1976. His last two periods as Prime Minister were brief, as he was chosen because of his seniority to head a pre-election caretaker government. He joined the Senate in 1968 and served as its president, 1976–82 and 1985–87.

Farinacci, Roberto (b. 18 Oct. 1892, d. 28 Apr. 1945). Italian Fascist

He gained a degree in law and then became politically active as a moderate and pragmatic socialist. A supporter of Italy's entry into World War I, he co-founded the *Fascist movement in 1919 and organized the Fascist party in and around Cremona, which became his subsequent power base. Since *Mussolini detested him personally and feared that his extremist ideas would offend the old Italian order which he tried to accommodate, Farinacci only gained a brief spell in office as the party's general secretary (1925–6). After 1936 he supported an alliance with Germany and later advocated *anti-Semitic policies in Italy. He voted against Mussolini's dismissal by the *Fascist Grand Council on 25 July 1943, and loyally served him in the Republic of *Salò. He was captured and executed by partisans.

Farouk I (b. 11 Feb. 1920, d. 18 Mar. 1965). King of Egypt 1936–52

Educated in England, his early popularity subsided when schemes for land reform collapsed owing to endemic corruption. He was in no hurry to help the British in World War II, which he saw as an opportunity to rid Egypt of British domination. In 1942, however, he had to give in to the British and appoint his political enemy, *Nahhas of the *Wafd party, as Premier. He dismissed Nahhas in 1944, but was too corrupt and uninterested in the day-to-day running of politics, which soon deteriorated into chaos. His appointment of his brother-in-law as president of the Officer's Club proved the last straw, prompting the army, under the leadership of *Nasser and *Neguib, to depose him.

Farrakhan, Louis, see NATION OF ISLAM

Fascism

A *totalitarian ideology which is opposed to
*Communism, *liberalism, and democracy.
The term was derived from the Latin *fasces*, a
bundle of rods with a projecting axe which
constituted the insignia of consular authority
in ancient Rome. The symbol was first applied
by an Italian anti-socialist militia, Fascio di
Combattimento, in 1919, and was applied by
*Mussolini to his movement after his rise to
power in 1922. A number of movements in
interwar Europe modelled themselves on
Mussolini's movement and have been
frequently referred to as Fascist, such as
*Franco's *Falange in Spain, the Croatian
*Ustase, or *Hitler's *Nazi Party. The basis for
these Fascist movements was an extreme form
of *nationalism which contrasted some
glorified (mystical) past with current
problems. These were usually held to be
caused by all those that were considered to be
apart from the 'national community', in
particular foreigners and domestic minorities
such as gypsies and Jews. The wide appeal of
these largely irrational, emotive, and
prejudicial arguments during the interwar
years was encourged by large-scale economic
crises and the failure of the political systems
in many European countries to cope with
them. Fascists encouraged domestic industrial
self-sufficiency (not least to improve the
nation's prospects in wartime), and tried
with some success to regulate economic
supply and demand. In contrast to
Communism, however, Fascism was not
principally opposed to private property,
despite the existence of some anti-*capitalist
tendencies. Fascism was anti-liberal and
anti-democratic, and once in power it was
reliant on an authoritarian state machine in
order to remain in power.

   Since the end of World War II there have
been a number of neo-Fascist popular
movements in Europe. Most recently,
however, the term has been popularly used to
denote movements like the French *Front
Nationale, the far-right *Liberal Party in
Austria, and the neo-Fascist part of the Italian
National Alliance, which formed part of Silvio
*Berlusconi's governments. They were
distinguished more by their distinctive
populism and their xenophobia, which often
included *anti-Semitic rhetoric. These
populist movements generated strong
support across social classes. However, the
label of Fascism has usually been applied
wrongly to these movements, since the actual
content of their policies differed widely. They
ranged from a defence of liberalism in the
Netherlands, to an ostensible defence of
French republican values in France.

Fascist Grand Council (Italy)

Founded on 15 December 1922, it was set up
by *Mussolini to disguise his own
authoritarian control over the Italian state. It
constituted an important instrument of
patronage, as the ambition of loyal supporters
was satisfied through a seat on the council.
Nominally the highest organ of the *Fascist
state, it had little executive power and could
do little against Mussolini's will. Nevertheless,
its mere existence pointed to the fact that
Mussolini was never in control of his own
party in the way that *Hitler was in total
control of the German *Nazi Party. This was
fateful for Mussolini at the meeting of the
Fascist Grand Council on 24–5 July 1943, when
for once it did act against Mussolini's will,
voting with seventeen against seven votes to
support the motion from Count Grandi(b.
1895, d. 1988) for Mussolini's dismissal.
Arrested the following day, Mussolini was
eventually liberated by the Germans and
became head of their puppet state of *Salò.

Fascist movement, Italy

In 1919, *Mussolini founded the Fasci di
Combattimento, a movement which
combined militant *nationalism with
vociferous demands for political and social
renewal. In particular, it demanded
progressive taxation, an eight-hour working
day, and workers' councils. Despite a slow
take-off, the movement was helped by official
toleration of its strident anti-socialist actions
(including street fights against socialists). In
consequence, it gained the support of
bureaucrats, journalists, and industrialists. It
also managed to extend its social base from
just the petty bourgeoisie to attract rural
support, mainly in northern Italy. In the
elections of April 1921 it gained 35 out of 535
parliamentary seats. To improve the
movement's organization Mussolini founded
the **Partito Nazionale Fascista (PNF)**, which
had attracted 320,000 members by May 1922.
The growing strength of the movement, as
well as Mussolini's assurances of respect for
the Church and the monarchy, gave it added
weight in a frail political system riven by party
divisions and weak leadership. With his
*March on Rome Mussolini presented a *fait
accompli* to a political establishment more
unwilling than unable to stop him.

   Mussolini was appointed Prime Minister on
30 October 1922 in a coalition government
dominated by non-Fascists. An enabling law of
2 December 1922, the creation of the *Fascist
Grand Council, and the institutionalization of

the Fascist militia began the erosion of the liberal state. Following changes in the electoral laws, the PNF and its allies won the elections of 1924 with a two-thirds majority. The murder of *Matteotti resulted in a crisis within the movement, which was torn between its radical and moderate elements. Mussolini responded with the establishment of a *totalitarian Fascist state, in which power was concentrated in his hands, and where the Fascist movement came to dominate virtually all aspects of Italian life. All other political parties were banned, while the Fascist party attempted to control society through outlawing all other social organizations except its own (such as the *dopolavoro and the *balilla). *Trade unions were banned, and the judiciary came under Fascist control.

By contrast with *Nazi Germany, the effectiveness of Italian *Fascism and its organizations was significantly limited because of (a) the power of the Roman Catholic Church, with which Mussolini dared not interfere too much, (b) the relative autonomy of the army, and (c) the institution of the monarchy. The latter, bestowed legitimacy on him while in office, but in withdrawing its support the monarchy was ultimately responsible for Mussolini's fall in 1943.

Fatah, al- (acronym for Palestine National Liberation Movement)

A militant Palestinian organization, founded in Kuwait by *Arafat in 1958 to fight for the restoration of *Palestine to the Arabs. It began its paramilitary operations in 1964, and assumed the leadership of the *PLO in 1968. It was almost completely destroyed when it was expelled from Jordan by *Hussein in 1970–1, though it recovered and remained the principal group within the PLO, providing a basis for Arafat's leadership. In the first Palestinian Council elections consequent upon the second stage of the *Oslo Accords ('Oslo B', 1995), the movement gained 55 out of 86 seats in January 1996, thus strengthening further Arafat's position in Palestine itself, as well as vis-à-vis Israel and the outside world. Members of the al-Fatah movement became involved in policing the territory, and took a prominent role in the second *Intifadah from 2000. In this period, it recruited a growing number of young fighters (probably numbering over 10,000) ready to fight against Israeli occupation of Palestinian lands.

Fatah lost control of the Palestinian Council elections of 2006, when its rivals, *Hamas, gained absolute control of the Council. Following a brief civil war in 2007, it lost control over *Gaza, whereupon its control was reduced to the *West Bank.

Faulkner, (Arthur) Brian Deane, Baron Faulkner of Downpatrick (b. 18 Feb. 1921, d. 3 Mar. 1977). Prime Minister of Northern Ireland 1971–2

Born in Helen's Bay, Co. Down, he was educated in Dublin and Belfast. He worked in his father's business during World War II, and became a member of the *Stormont government for the *Ulster Unionist Party (UUP) in 1949. As Minister for Home Affairs (1959–63), he was influential in defeating the IRA's campaign begun in 1956. As Minister of Development under *Chichester-Clark, he appeared to be a modernizer, an impression he underlined by including (for the first time ever) a Catholic in his Cabinet upon becoming Prime Minister in March 1971. However, his term of office saw huge increases in sectarian violence, and he angered nationalists by introducing internment without trial in August 1971. In March 1972, he lost office when direct rule was imposed from Westminster. His subsequent support for power-sharing between Protestants and Catholics lost him the support of the UUP, leading him to resign as leader in 1974. He retired from politics in 1976.

FBI (Federal Bureau of Investigation) (USA)

Origins The investigative branch of the US Department of Justice. Established by Attorney-General Charles J. Bonaparte in 1908, a nascent Bureau of Investigation was used against radicals and immigrants by Attorney-General Palmer during the *Red Scare.

The Hoover era It was reorganized in 1924, following systematic violations of the Constitutional Bill of Rights, and J. Edgar *Hoover was appointed Director. In response to the kidnapping of Charles Lindbergh's son, the Bureau was again reorganized in 1935 and became an independent agency, acquiring its present name. Hoover embarked on a much-publicized campaign against prominent mobsters, and used the publicity to build up the reputation of the Bureau. Hoover worked not only to further the efficiency of the FBI, but also to promote its independence and unaccountability. He treated the Bureau as his personal fiefdom, and used the files on prominent individuals, Congressmen, Senators, and Presidents accumulated during his time in office to blackmail and pressure his way through Washington.

The FBI was active in anti-Communist operations, beginning with President *Roosevelt's request in 1936 that it 'survey'

Communist and Fascist organizations. In 1946 it launched an anti-Communist offensive through agents in corporate personnel departments and *trade unions and its formidable publicity machine. Later, in the 1950s, the FBI was essential to *McCarthyism and the prosecutions of *Alger Hiss, the *Rosenbergs, and many others. Hoover established the COINTELPRO program, which was aimed at political radicals and resulted in dozens of illegal wiretaps and break-ins. Ultimately, this gave *Nixon the idea for the 'plumbers', the team of operatives who broke into the *Watergate buildings. The FBI's reputation began to fall in 1971, when the COINTELPRO was revealed.

After Hoover Since Hoover's death, efforts have concentrated on increasing the FBI's public accountability, and improving anti-racketeering activities. Hoover's immediate successor was never confirmed because of the *Watergate scandal; he was succeeded by William Webster, who held the job until 1987. Subsequently, Director William Sessions was dismissed after allegations that he took financial advantage of his position, and he was replaced by Louis Freeh in 1993. Freeh increased the FBI's activities abroad, which resulted in the indictment of the terrorists responsible for the 1996 bombing of a US military base in Saudi Arabia. However, the FBI was severely criticized for blunders in the prosecution of Timothy McVeigh (responsible for the *Oklahoma Bombing).

Current developments In 2001, one week before the *September 11 attacks, Robert S. Mueller III became the new Director. With the attacks, the FBI was faced with new challenges, of solving what happened (and why the FBI did not prevent the attacks from happening), of establishing and bringing to justice those responsible, and of making sure no further terrorist attacks would occur. These responsibilities were complicated by a series of *anthrax attacks, which presented yet a further, qualitatively new challenge to the FBI. A number of its functions were integrated into the Department of Homeland Security, which George W. *Bush created in part as a consequence of the FBI's perceived failures in the *War on Terrorism.

(((•))) **SEE WEB LINKS**

• The home page of the FBI.

FDP (Freie Demokratische Partei), see LIBERAL PARTY (GERMANY)

Federal Bureau of Investigation, see FBI

Federal Reserve System (USA)

Origins A regulatory body of the US banking sector, set up by the 1913 Federal Reserve Act in an effort to stabilize the hitherto relatively unregulated US banking system. It comprised twelve federal reserve banks, which were all owned by private banks, but which had the power to issue federal reserve notes as currency. They were supervised by a Federal Reserve Board consisting of the Secretary of the Treasury, a Controller of the Currency, and five members of a Board of Governors appointed by the President. The regional banks had the power to alter regional interest rates, expand or contract the money supply, and expand or contract credit. The system still contained many weaknesses. The relationship between the regional banks and the center remained ill-defined, and thousands of small banks continued to operate relatively freely.

After the Wall Street Crash (1929) By 1929, only about one third of all banks were members of the Federal Reserve System (FRS). The FRS was thus unable to respond effectively to the Great *Depression after the 1929 *Wall Street Crash. Its reorganization was thus a central issue in the *New Deal. The Banking Act of 1933 reorganized and strengthened the central Board of Governors, who were given control over interest rates, reserve requirements, and all activities of the twelve federal reserve banks. The successes of the US postwar boom owe much to the Federal Reserve System, which had supported the war through a policy of cheap money. From the 1950s, the Federal Reserve System received autonomy in setting interest rates, and in the late 1970s it responded to the *oil price shocks by pursuing a policy of monetary stability and low inflation. This inaugurated a period of monetary stability which characterized the 1980s and 1990s, interrupted only by an economic downturn in the late 1980s. The Federal Reserve System has enjoyed much greater freedom than other central banks such as the *European Central Bank, since it is not bound by any predetermined economic targets.

Federated States of Micronesia, see MICRONESIA

feminism, see WOMEN'S MOVEMENT

Fianna Fáil (Ireland)
The main Irish political party since the early twentieth century, whose Irish Gaelic name is translated as 'Soldiers of Destiny'. It was founded by *de Valéra on 16 May 1926, and is often referred to as the 'Republican Party'. Its

initial goals were the ending of the partition of Ireland, the preservation and revitalization of the Irish language, the redistribution of large farms to small farmers, and Irish economic self-sufficiency. Although initially made up of militant nationalists and *Sinn Féin members and still opposed to the acceptance of partition, Fianna Fáil agreed to enter Dáil Éireann (the Irish parliament) on 11 August 1927. The party newspaper, the *Irish Press*, was founded in 1931.

The first Fianna Fáil government was formed on 9 March 1932, headed by de Valéra. The de Valéra governments lasted until 1948, during which time the oath of allegiance to Britain was abolished, the new constitution of the republic was written and adopted (1937), and Ireland asserted and maintained neutrality during World War II. Returning to power in 1951–4, the Fianna Fáil government passed the Social Welfare Act and other social legislation. The 1957–66 governments (under de Valéra 1957–9 and *Lemass 1959–66) were noted for their economic reform and success. Under *Lynch, the party formed the governments of 1966–73 and 1973–7, which saw further state economic activity and Irish membership of the European Economic Community. Charles *Haughey led the party in government 1979–81, 1982, 1982–7. Albert *Reynolds served briefly as party leader (1992–4), and was succeeded by Bertie *Ahern.

In the absence of left-right ideological divisions in traditional European, Latin American, or Australian terms, Fianna Fáil has styled itself more strictly republican and nationalist than its main rival, *Fine Gael. In the 1990s, it suffered from corruption allegations against Haughey, but under Ahern's steady leadership it returned to government in 1997. It extended its majority in 2002, when it narrowly missed an absolute majority of seats in parliament.

(((●))) SEE WEB LINKS

• The official website of Fianna Fáil.

fifth column

A term coined during the Spanish *Civil War. As four columns advanced on Madrid, the fifth was described as consisting of collaborationists within the city. During World War II the term was applied to *Nazi collaborators in occupied countries, such as *Quisling, who had assisted the German occupation from within.

COLLABORATION (FRANCE)

Figueiredo, Joao Baptista de

(b. 15 Jan. 1918, d. 24 Dec. 1999). President of Brazil 1979–85

After a career in the Brazilian army, in which he rose to the rank of general, he was one of the planners of the 1964 military *coup*. He was chief of National Intelligence until 1979, when he was appointed President by *Geisel, whose social and populist gestures he sought to continue. Military rule was further relaxed, until in 1984 he oversaw the election of the first civilian as President in twenty-one years (with effect from 1985).

Figueres (Ferrer), José (b. 25 Sept. 1906, d. 8 June 1990). President of Costa Rica 1953–8, 1970–4

Active in Costa Rican politics as a member of the social democrat Partido de Liberación Nacional (PLN, Party of National Liberation), he led a civilian uprising in 1948 against the incumbent government's attempt to annul the election of the PLN's candidate for the presidency. He remained in power for the following months and introduced structural reforms to weaken the country's powerful institutions, abolishing the army and nationalizing the banks. In addition, he carried out welfare and educational reforms, and introduced universal suffrage. His efforts to strengthen democracy climaxed in the 1949 constitution, which has been the basis of the country's political stability ever since. After stepping down from the leadership of his country in 1949, he was twice elected President. In his two periods in office, Figueres continued in his efforts to enhance the country's democratic traditions. His son served as President between 1994 and 1998.

Fiji

A group of some 330 islands in the Melanesian archipelago, whose politics, culture, and society have been characterized by bitter ethnic rivalry.

Contemporary history The islands became a British Crown Colony in 1874, when British settlers immediately began to import Indians to work on sugar plantations on an indenture system. In the first forty years of British rule, Indian settlers received no political rights, so that political and administrative power became entrenched among native Fijians. During World War II, Fiji was an important supply station for US forces. Self-government was granted in 1948, and independence gained in 1970, with the British monarch remaining the titular head of state.

As before independence, politics were dominated by the ethnic conflict between the Indian population (44 per cent in 2006) represented by the Labour Party, and the Fijians (51 per cent) represented by the conservative Alliance Party. The Fijians remained in control of 80 per cent of the land and dominated the political system. In 1987, T. Bavadra led the Labour Party to victory in the elections, but on 14 May 1987 he was deposed by the military composed mainly of Fijians. After a further coup, led by Sitiveni Rabuka, Fiji was declared a republic, whereupon it was expelled from the *Commonwealth (17 October 1987). In 1990, a constitutional amendment guaranteed the Fijians thirty-seven of the seventy parliamentary seats, compared with twenty-seven for the Indians (the rest being distributed among other ethnic groups). Rabuka returned to power in 1992, and in 1998 instituted a new constitution.

Contemporary politics (since 1999) The new constitution generated Fiji's first democratic elections, in 1999, leading to the victory of Mahendra Chaudry and the Labour Party. Chaudry was deposed the following year by a coup led by the Fijian businessman, Georges Speight. Although the coup was unsuccessful, it led to the assumption of power by the military. A new government under Laisenia Qarase of the United Fiji Party won the 2001 elections, and was returned in 2006. Qarase was an outspoken defender of Fijian rights, against the Indian community represented by Chaudry. Qarase's proposal to pardon the coup leaders of 2000 angered the military, however, which overthrew Qarase later that year. The coup leader, Commodore Voreqe Bainimarama, confirmed the octogenarian president, Ratu Josefa Iloilo, and promised the organization of new elections.

Final Solution, see CONCENTRATION CAMPS

Fine Gael

Ireland's second political party, originally called the United Ireland Party but soon known by its current Irish Gaelic name (translated as 'Tribe of the Gaels'). It was founded in 1933 in a merger of Cummann na nGaedheal, the National Guard, and the National Centre. Fine Gael is the successor of the 'pro-treaty' parties in Irish politics, but found itself out of government for most of its history until 1973. Although the principal opposition to the *Fianna Fáil governments, Fine Gael was the main party in the coalition governments of 1948–51 (which saw the establishment of the Irish Republic in 1949) and 1954–7 (which failed to deal adequately with a renewal of IRA violence, and fell). After 1973, Fine Gael saw greater success in government. In the so-called National Coalition Government, it formed an alliance with the *Labour Party, 1973–7.

A new generation of leaders, under Garret *FitzGerald, returned Fine Gael to power in 1981–2 and 1982–7, emphasizing economic development and cooperation with Britain over *Northern Ireland. It formed the Government of Renewal in coalition with Labour and the Democratic Left under *Bruton from 1994 to 1997. Fine Gael has traditionally been associated with industry, business, commerce, the professions, and substantial farmers. It has considered itself more constitutionally nationalist and conciliatory than its main rival, Fianna Fáil. The party's support declined dramatically in the 2002 elections, when it gained but 31 seats, mainly to the benefit of smaller parties and the Fianna Fáil which gained 81 seats. Led by Enda Kenny, it attempted to rebuild itself into a major political challenger. However, Kenny was unsuccessful at the 2007 elections to convince the elections to convince the electorate that it was time for change.

(((⊕))) **SEE WEB LINKS**

• The official website of Fine Gael.

Finland

A Nordic country which successfully maintained its autonomy against an often overbearing Russia (Soviet Union), with which it shared most of its land borders.

Occupation and early independence (up to 1945) Finland was ceded by Sweden to Russia in 1809, when it became an autonomous member of the Russian Empire. In an attempt to integrate the country more closely into its Empire, towards the end of the nineteenth century, Russia tried to introduce its language and culture, as well as military conscription. In 1899, Russia formally removed the country's autonomy. This led to a growth of Finnish *nationalism and increasing resistance to Russian rule. Many Finns readily took part in the *Russian Revolution of 1905, whereupon autonomy was restored. In 1906 a unicameral legislature was established, and a universal franchise introduced. Under the leadership of *Mannerheim, the Finns seized the opportunity presented by the *October Revolution of 1917 to declare their independence from Russia on 6 December 1917. To fight the *Red Army and the Finnish Communist guard, a 'white guard' was organized. A republican Constitution was declared on 21 June 1919, and in 1920 Russia accepted Finnish independence.

Finland became a member of the *League of Nations, and in 1921 it received sovereignty over the *Aaland Islands. Over the next two decades the politics of the country were markedly unstable, as governments had to deal with recurrent tensions between the vociferous Swedish minority and the Finnish population. A relatively poor country, it was less successful in its response to the Great *Depression than its western neighbours in Scandinavia. In 1917–39, it saw 23 changes of government.

The country's main concern, however, remained its volatility due to its 1,000 mile-long border with the unstable USSR. It built a defensive fortification along its south-eastern border with the USSR, but this was only able to halt temporarily the advance of the Red Army when it finally attacked in the *Winter War of 1939–40. Finland suffered significant territorial losses as a result, which it tried to regain in the *Continuation War (1941–4), when it followed Germany in its attack on the Soviet Union. It was again overwhelmed by the weight of the Red Army.

Neutrality (1945–91) The Soviet Union accepted Finland's independence as long as it remained a neutral state with a capitalist economy. Under its Presidents, Paasikivi and Kekkonen, a social democratic *welfare state was established, much along the lines of the Swedish model. Despite its official neutrality, however, the country was de facto within the Soviet sphere of influence. In 1948 Finland concluded a defensive military alliance and a friendship treaty with the Soviet Union, which was last renewed in 1983. This was complemented by a mutual trade agreement in 1950. This policy preserved the country's independence and brought it considerable prosperity: among Western countries, it had a near-monopoly on certain trades with the Soviet Union. Friendship with the Soviet Union was also dictated by domestic conditions, as the Communist Party was the strongest party in Finland until 1958. Finland became an associate member of *EFTA, and conducted a free-trade agreement in industrial goods with the EEC. These

agreements only served to reinforce the country's primary function as an entrepôt between Western *capitalist economies and the Communist countries of the East.

Finland was greatly affected by the collapse of the Eastern Bloc countries and *Comecon after 1989, which destroyed the basis of the Finnish economy and resulted in the country's biggest economic crisis since World War II. Unemployment soared to over 15 per cent, and despite drastic cuts in social security payments, the currency continued to devalue.

Contemporary history (since 1995) In an effort to produce a major restructuring of the economy, it jettisoned its policy of neutrality, and became a full member of the European Union on 1 January 1995. Subsequently, Finland became the most enthusiastic of the Nordic members of the EU, adopting the *euro from its start in 1999. A new Constitution became effective in 2000, which strengthened the powers of the parliament vis-à-vis the President. In that year, Tarja Halonen of the ruling Social Democrats became the country's first female president. She was re-elected in 2006.

Finnish–Russian War, see WINTER WAR

First Nations (Canada)
A term which describes the three original (aboriginal) inhabitants of Canada, *Canadian Indians, *Inuit, and *Métis. In 1997, Canada's supreme court ruled that First Nations were entitled to compensation for the lands taken away from them by European colonists. This was followed by an official apology, in 1998, by the Canadian government for the maltreatment of First Nations in Canadian history. A compensation fund of CAN$ 350 million was created, while a number of First Nations peoples were given self-governing autonomy in their lands.

First World War, see WORLD WAR I

Fisher, Andrew (b. 29 Aug. 1862, d. 22 Oct. 1928). Prime Minister of Australia 1908–9, 1910–13, 1914–15
Born in Ayrshire (Scotland), in 1879 he was elected district secretary of the Ayrshire Miner's Union, which collapsed after an unsuccessful ten-week strike in 1881. Fisher emigrated to Queensland in 1885, and within months became manager of a new colliery. In 1891, he founded a local branch of the new *Labor Party at Gympie, and became its first president. Elected as Gympie's representative

in the Queensland Legislative Assembly, he was one of the few within his party to support a federated Australia. Elected to the first federal parliament in 1901, he became a leading member of the federal Labor caucus (faction). Fisher maintained strong links with the grass roots, succeeding *Watson as party leader in 1907.

Fisher withdrew his support from *Deakin to form his own government, in which he strove towards more power for the Australian federal state, at the expense of both the British Empire and the individual states. In 1910, he was the first Labor prime minister to be voted into office. His government established a central bank, extended invalidity pensions, and provided maternity allowances. He was less successful in wresting power from the individual states. After narrowly losing the 1913 elections, his support for World War I won him a resounding victory in 1914. He resigned in 1915 due to ill health and his personal opposition to the impending issue of compulsory military service. He became Australian high commissioner in London until 1920, and finally retired to London in 1922.

Fitt, Gerard ('Gerry'), Lord Fitt of Bell's Hill in the County of Down (b. 9 Apr. 1926, d. 26 Aug. 2005). Northern Irish politician

Born in Belfast, he worked in a barber's shop, and then served in the British merchant navy (1941-53). He was elected as a Republican Labour MP for West Belfast in 1966, and brought the plight of Catholics in Northern Ireland to the notice of many in the British House of Commons. In 1970, he became the first leader of the *Social Democratic and Labour Party (SDLP). He consistently opposed the *IRA, and usually supported the *Labour Party in the Commons. He resigned as SDLP leader in 1979, claiming that he was more of a socialist than a nationalist. He stood as an Independent Socialist in 1983, but lost his seat to Gerry *Adams. He entered the House of Lords in the same year.

FitzGerald, Garret (b. 9 Feb. 1926). Prime Minister (Taoiseach) of the Irish Republic 1981-2, 1982-7

Born in Dublin, he gained a doctorate at University College Dublin (UCD) and a BL at King's Inns. A lecturer in Political Economy at UCD (1959-73), he became a Senator in 1965, and was elected a *Fine Gael member of the Dáil Éireann (parliament) for Dublin South-East in 1969. FitzGerald served as Minister for Foreign Affairs (1973-7), and in 1977 succeeded Liam *Cosgrave as party leader. In his first period as Taoiseach, he set up an Inter-

Governmental Council on *Northern Ireland with the British Prime Minister, Margaret *Thatcher. He lost the March 1982 elections, but was returned to office in the December 1982 general election, with another Fine Gael-*Labour coalition. On 15 November 1985 FitzGerald signed the **Anglo-Irish Agreement** with Thatcher, which for the first time gave the Republic a consultative role in Northern Ireland, yet recognized the right of the majority in Northern Ireland to decide the province's political allegiance. This failed to bring a solution to the violence there, as it was fiercely rejected by the Ulster Unionists, but did not go far enough for the *IRA. FitzGerald's political career is notable both for his willingness to understand Unionist loyalities, his work with Thatcher, and his attempts to make the Irish constitution more attractive to Ulster Protestants.

Fiume (Rijeka)

A port on the Adriatic which was claimed both by Yugoslavia and Italy. After World War I the formerly Austrian port was given to Yugoslavia, despite vociferous Italian protests. In defiance of the Treaty of *St Germain, the adventurist *D'Annunzio and his followers occupied the city, transformed it into a city-state and established an authoritarian government, 1919-21. In 1924 it was acquired by Italy in an agreement with Yugoslavia, though after World War II it became part of Yugoslavia once again. As part of Croatia, it became part of an independent Croatian state in 1991.

FLN, see FRONT DE LIBÉRATION NATIONALE

FLQ, see FRONT DE LIBÉRATION DU QUÉBEC

FNR (Fédération Nationale des Républicains Indépendants), see UDF

Foch, Ferdinand (b. 2 Oct. 1851, d. 20 Mar. 1929). French marshal

After fighting in the Franco-Prussian War (1870-1), he joined the General Staff as an artillery specialist. In World War I, he led the 9th French Army in the Battle of the *Marne (1914), and distinguished himself in the military planning of the Battle of the *Somme (1916). In 1917, he became Chief of Staff to the French Commander-in-Chief, *Pétain, and in 1918 he was appointed Supreme Commander of all Allied forces on the Western Front. After the war he took part in the negotiations of the *Versailles Treaty, but heavily criticized what he considered to be *Clemenceau's leniency towards the Germans, and even advocated the breakup of Germany to undo the country's unification of 1871. He also criticized Clemenceau's failure to impose a French military occupation of the Rhineland up to the *Ruhr. He is the only French person to have been created an honorary field-marshal by the British army and to be commemorated by a statue in London.

Food and Agriculture Organization (FAO)

A specialized agency of the *UN. It was established in October 1945, with its headquarters in Rome from 1951, and became one of the largest and most successful UN agencies. With the aim of raising the standard of nutrition worldwide, it researched and collected information about agricultural problems, gave information and technical advice on improvements to food distribution. By encouraging the *Green Revolution and other initiatives, it provided important technical advice to poorer countries on how to increase production in agriculture, fisheries, and forestry.

(●) **SEE WEB LINKS**

• The home page of the FAO.

Foot, Michael (b. 23 July 1913). British Labour leader 1980–3

Born in Plymouth, he was initially a *Liberal, but joined the *Labour Party after working in Liverpool's poverty-stricken areas whilst at Wadham College, Oxford. He entered journalism, and was one of the writers of *Guilty Men* (1940), a devastating critique of *appeasement. In 1945, Foot was elected MP for Plymouth Devonport, which he lost in 1955. He was returned to parliament for Ebbw Vale in 1960, succeeding his political hero, *Bevan. A leading member of the left of the party, he had gained a reputation as a platform orator. As a result, he was popular in internal party elections, but did not gain ministerial office until 1974, when he became Employment Secretary. In 1976, he stood against James *Callaghan for the party leadership, but lost in the third ballot. He became a surprisingly effective Leader of the House, taking responsibility for steering through legislation despite the goverment's lack of an overall majority. In 1980, Foot became Labour leader, when the party responded disastrously to *Thatcherism by steering to the left, rather than to the centre. He supported unilateral disarmament and the *CND, which convinced many that the party had become unfit to govern. This, and his opposition to *European integration, led to the defection of the *Social Democratic Party, dividing the left throughout the 1980s. He

resigned after leading the party to a crushing defeat at the 1983 elections, but remained active in politics.

Football War, see SOCCER WAR

Forbes, George William (b. 12 May 1869, d. 17 May 1947). Prime Minister of New Zealand 1930–5

Born in Lyttleton (near Christchurch), he became involved in the Cheviot Settlers' Association. A staunch leaseholder, *Seddon appointed him to the Royal Commission on Land Tenure and Settlement in 1905, and in 1908 he became a *Liberal member of the House of Representatives. He was Liberal whip from 1912 to 1922, and in 1925 became party leader. The party contested the 1925 elections as the 'National Party', but was unable to secure more than nine seats. His career took a further turn for the worse when, after the creation of the new United Party, he had to step down as leader to make way for *Ward.

In 1928, Forbes became Deputy Prime Minister for the ailing Ward, whom he succeeded in 1930. In 1931, he formed a coalition with *Coates of the *Reform Party to cope with the Great *Depression. Full of integrity, but lacking imagination or charisma, most of his Cabinet's important legislation was carried out by his political rival Coates, rather than by himself. Against bitter resistance from the *Labour Party, his government abolished the twin pillars of the former Liberal Party, the graduated land tax and compulsory arbitration in labour disputes. He was unsympathetic to the grievances caused by the economic depression and his austere economic policies, maintaining that unemployment benefits should be cut since they were demoralizing. He was heavily defeated in the 1935 general elections, and resigned as party leader later that year.

Forces Françaises Libres, see FREE FRENCH

Ford, Gerald Rudolph (b. 14 July 1913, d. 26 Dec 2006). 38th US President 1974–7

The only unelected President of the USA, he was selected as Vice-President by Richard *Nixon in 1973 following the resignation of Spiro Agnew.

Early career Born Leslie Lynch Key in Omaha, Nebraska, his name was changed to that of his stepfather after his mother moved to Michigan and remarried. He was a gifted football player who became assistant coach at

Yale, and he graduated from Yale Law School in 1941. He served on an aircraft carrier in World War II in the Pacific, and after the war in 1945 returned to Michigan to practise law. He was elected to the US House of Representatives as a *Republican in 1948, and became House Minority Leader in 1965.

Presidency In 1973, upon the resignation of Spiro *Agnew owing to accusations of tax evasion and bribery, President *Nixon, himself in desperate need of shoring up support in *Congress in the growing *Watergate investigation, appointed the affable Ford as his Vice-President. When Nixon himself resigned ten months later, Ford became the first unelected President of the USA. Amongst his first acts as President following Nixon's resignation was to pardon his predecessor for any crimes which he might have committed. This act was deeply unpopular, and implicated Ford in the traumas of Watergate. Ford was also hurt by his inability to overcome the economic problems caused by the first *oil price shock of 1973. This was not helped by his inability to get his fiscal proposals through Congress, after the Democrats achieved a landslide majority in the congressional elections of 1974. In foreign policy, Ford presided over the end of US involvement in the *Vietnam War in 1975. He also prepared the ground for a re-negotiation of the Panama Canal Treaty, completed by his successor. His campaign for re-election was damaged by a strong challenge from Ronald *Reagan in the primaries, a campaign that bitterly divided the party. He narrowly lost the elections to Jimmy *Carter.

Although not spectacularly successful through any particular measure, Ford's assured and steady presidency soothed a nation traumatized by the Watergate scandal. With the passage of time, criticisms of his pardon of president Nixon diminished, as it allowed the office of the President to recover relatively quickly without the bitterness of Watergate lingering on in the courts.

Ford retired in 1977 to California, where he helped his wife Betty to recover from illness, and alcohol and drug dependency, as well as pursuing various part-time businesses and academic jobs. In the final years of his life, the moderate Republican became a critic of George W. *Bush, even though his most trusted advisers when he was President, Dick *Cheney and Donald *Rumsfeld, were closely associated with the Bush presidency.

Foreign Legion, French

A French volunteer force founded in Algeria in 1830 to defend and enlarge the *French Empire. Originally it consisted of French officers and foreign foot-soldiers, for whom the legion's attraction was its disinterest in the recruits' past, a significant bonus for those with a criminal record. It established a reputation for its particularly tough military discipline, though its importance diminished after the *Algerian War of Independence, after which its headquarters were transferred to Corsica. It was last active in the Lebanon in 1982 to supervise the withdrawal of the *PLO from Beirut. It continued to maintain bases in Djibouti and *French Guyana. In 2000, it started to admit women.

Forza Italia ('Let's go Italy') (Italy)

A political movement formed in 1994 by Silvio *Berlusconi. Founded in the wake of the collapse of the traditional Italian party system, notably the *Christian Democrats, it sought to create a strong political force on the centre right. Intensely un-ideological, the movement has been largely a vehicle to promote the political ambitions of its founder. In elections later that year, the 'Pole of Freedom' coalition, spearheaded by Forza Italia, won, and Berlusconi formed his first government. Berlusconi was unable, however, to form a stable government, not least because Forza Italia's position vis-à-vis its coalition partners was relatively weak. Berlusconi used his subsequent years in opposition to strengthen his movement. In the 2001 elections Forza Italia obtained 29.5 per cent of the vote, while its right-wing alliance, the House of Liberties, won a total of 49.6 per cent. Despite concerns about its political value system, Forza Italia was accepted into the European People's Party, the union of centre-right parties represented in the *European Parliament. The House of Liberties narrowly lost the 2006 elections, when it polled 25,000 votes less than the *Olive Tree coalition.

Four Freedoms (USA)

F. D. *Roosevelt's *human rights ideals, proclaimed during his third term and intended to emphasize the distinction between the *Allied and *Axis powers. These 'four freedoms' to which Roosevelt committed the USA were freedom from fear, freedom from want, freedom of worship, and freedom of speech. Roosevelt used the term to popularize the specific policy of lend-lease intended to aid the British against *Hitler, but the idea had grown naturally out of the rhetoric of his third presidential campaign in 1940. The *Atlantic Charter committed the Allies to the four freedoms.

Fourteen Points (USA)

President *Wilson's peace programme for the end of World War I, announced on 8

January 1918 in a speech to *Congress. It demanded freedom of the seas, equality of trade conditions, reduction of armaments, adjustment of colonial claims, evacuation by Germany of Russian territory and Belgium, the return to France of *Alsace-Lorraine, recognition of nationalist aspirations in eastern and central Europe, freedom for subject peoples in the *Ottoman Empire, independence for Poland, and the establishment of a 'general association of nations'. These aims set the context for the *Paris Peace Conference, with disputes arising, for instance, about which nationalist aspirations were to be realized. Many of these contradictions were not resolved—indeed, the creation of new nation-states created new national minorities. Moreover, at Versailles Britain and France, which had never formally agreed the Fourteen Points, insisted on punitive action going well beyond the demands made by Wilson (*reparations). An association of nations was realized in the *League of Nations, but it remained a weak and imperfect organization, not least because of the refusal by the USA to join.

Fox Quesada, Vincente (2 July 1942).
President of Mexico, 2000–6

Born in Mexico City, his family moved to the state of Guanajuato when he was a child. He studied business administration in Mexico City and obtained a diploma in upper management. He joined the Coca-Cola company in 1964, and eventually became the youngest person to be the company's president for Mexico and Latin America. In 1987 he entered politics by joining the oppositional Catholic Party of National Action (Partido Acción National, PAN), and in 1988 he entered Congress. After an unsuccessful bid in the gubernatorial elections for his home state, Guanajuato, in 1991, he was elected Governor there in 1995. The telegenic and charismatic Fox used a popular campaign to bypass the PAN's elite and obtain his nomination for the presidency in 2000. This campaign increased his popularity throughout the country, and he became the first oppositional candidate to win the Presidency for over 70 years. He was only partially successful in ending the impasse over ending the *Chiapas Rebellion, and in introducing a fundamental tax reform, since he did not command a majority in the legislature. Nevertheless, under his guidance Mexico was relatively successful at stabilizing the economy, by reducing state spending and overcoming inflation. Fox was succeeded by Felipe *Calderón.

France

Historically the country with the greatest political influence on the European continent, France has sought to redefine its European role through leadership of the EU.

The Third Republic (up to 1940) The Third Republic, emerged into the twentieth century under the shadow of the *Dreyfus Affair. This brought about a fundamental realignment of French politics, with the formation of an *anti-Semitic right-wing alliance. This was countered by the unification of various parties on the left to form a united *Socialist Party under the leadership of *Jaurès and *Guesde in 1905. This left the *Radical Party in a crucial position, a party which strongly influenced public policy through its *anti-clericalism, and which would defend the Republic at all cost. Radical governments under *Clemenceau and *Briand crushed strikes and pursued policies hostile to the increasingly successful socialist and *Communist parties. Torn by social and cultural conflict before 1914, the Republic nevertheless survived World War I, not least owing to Clemenceau's austere but inspiring leadership during the closing stages of the war.

After World War I, the overriding foreign-policy objective became the containment of Germany, to ensure that it could never start another war against France. Relations with Germany were strained by the *Versailles Treaty, which regulated Germany's territorial losses and *reparation payments, Although Germany considered these too harsh, they were criticized in France for the opposite reason, as being insufficiently severe. For this reason, *Poincaré ordered, in 1923, the French occupation of the *Ruhr, an act which proved unsuccessful in increasing German reparations payments but which was very costly to the French state. Under *Briand, relations with Germany subsequently improved, though the rise of Fascism first in Italy and then in Germany gave a new sense of crisis and urgency to a country weakened by the absence of firm political leadership. The left rallied in 1936 to form the *Popular Front government, though the presence of the Communist Party in government, as well as

Table 9. **Presidents and Prime Ministers of the French Republic**

Presidents

General Charles de *Gaulle	1959–69
Georges *Pompidou	1969–74
Valéry *Giscard d'Estaing	1974–81
François *Mitterrand	1981–95
Jacques *Chirac	1995–2007
Nicolas Sarkozy	2007–

Prime Ministers

Michel *Debré	1959–62
Georges *Pompidou	1962–8
Maurice Couve de Murville	1968–9
Jacques Chaban-Delmas	1969–72
Pierre Messmer	1972–4
Jacques *Chirac	1974–6
Raymond Barre	1976–81
Pierre *Mauroy	1981–4
Laurent Fabius	1984–6
Jacques *Chirac	1986–8
Michel Rocard	1988–91
Edith *Cresson	1991–2
Pierre Beregovoy	1992–3
Edouard Balladur	1993–5
Alain *Juppé	1995–7
Lionel *Jospin	1997–2002
Jean-Pierre *Raffarin	2002–5
Dominique de Villepin	2005–7
François Fillon	2007–

unprecedented social legislation, further alarmed and alienated many supporters of the right from the Republic. Given the social and cultural divisiveness of the Great *Depression, politicians like *Daladier had little option but to follow the British policies of appeasement which culminated in the *Munich Agreement of 1938.

World War II (1939–45) In September 1939 France entered *World War II against Germany. In spring 1940, the Germans attacked France, and on 22 June 1940 Marshal *Pétain sued for peace. France was divided into an occupied zone covering three-fifths of its territory, and an autonomous area which became known as the État Français (French State), or *Vichy France, governed by Pétain himself. The Vichy state hoped (largely in vain, as it turned out) to win concessions from the Germans through *collaboration. By contrast, those who refused to be led by Pétain and who could escape from mainland France joined de *Gaulle, who by 1943 had become the leader of the *Free French. The liberation

of France began with the Allied *D-Day landings in Normandy on 6 June 1944, and on 25 August 1944, Paris was liberated, with the Vichy state collapsing soon afterwards. To de *Gaulle's dismay, the Constituent Assembly of 1945 rejected his ideas for a strong executive Presidency in the next republic.

The Fourth Republic (1945–58) Instead, like its predecessor until 1940, the Fourth Republic had a weak President who was merely a figurehead, and its governments were extremely unstable, lasting for an average of just over six months. Under the guidance of *Schuman and *Monnet, the Republic presided over rapid economic recovery and a redirection of French foreign policy, trying to contain Germany through cooperation and *European integration. This reorientation was linked to an extremely painful process of *decolonization. France could only accept *Indochina's independence after losing the nine-year *Indochina War in 1954. The country's global role was undermined by the *Suez Crisis in

1956, and it had to cope with increasing challenges for independence from its colonies in *French West Africa and *French Equatorial Africa. Most traumatic of all, however, was the *Algerian War of Independence, as Algeria was considered an integral part of France at the time. With the fragmented political elites of the Fourth Republic unable to overcome the crisis, de Gaulle was asked to return as head of state in 1958 and given a free hand to redesign the constitution.

The Fifth Republic (since 1958) In the Fifth Republic, the president was given a seven-year term of office, the right to call new parliamentary elections, and a strong role in the execution of policies. As a result, the political system became more stable, due to the emergence of only a few parties with broad appeal, i.e. the Communist Party, a united Socialist Party, the *UDF, and the *Gaullists. Partly triggered by this new-found stability and ostensible rigidity, the widespread *student revolt of 1968 challenged the existence of the new state, but on 30 May de Gaulle recovered his nerve and the demonstrations died down. De Gaulle resigned in 1969, to be succeeded by *Pompidou, his erstwhile right-hand man. Following Pompidou's death from cancer in 1974, *Giscard d'Estaing, a non-Gaullist, was elected President. He was faced with an economic recession as a result of the *oil price shocks of 1973 and 1979, the unpopularity of his own distant and seemingly aristocratic style of government, and a resurgent left.

Giscard d'Estaing lost his quest for re-election in 1981 to *Mitterrand, the first Socialist President of his country. A number of radical Socialist policies of his Prime Minister, *Mauroy, brought the country close to financial ruin. Mitterrand lost the Socialist majority in the National Assembly and had to contend with the Gaullist leader, *Chirac, as his Prime Minister, 1986–8. Chirac proved to be more unpopular than Mitterrand, and the latter won a second term of office in the 1988 presidential elections. Under Mitterrand, France became particularly committed to the goal of *European integration.

In 1995 the French finally elected Chirac to the presidency. Through his Prime Minister, *Juppé, Chirac proceeded to introduce reforms to reduce government spending. Equally controversial was a drastic law against illegal immigration. The 1997 Assembly elections, which were won by the Socialists under *Jospin, inaugurated a further period of *cohabitation. It proved surprisingly

successful, as France experienced a strong economic boom. Meanwhile, the established parties became embroiled in scandals involving corruption and illegal personal and party donations.

Contemporary politics (since 2002) The veteran Chirac ironically benefited from the voters' disillusionment with the political elite, as his popular touch ensured his victory in the 2002 presidential elections. With the Socialists and the left disoriented and divided, Chirac's new right-wing movement, the *UMP, won an overwhelming victory under the unassuming *Raffarin. Chirac inaugurated an assertive foreign policy, refusing to lend support to the *Iraq War. The popularity which this brought Chirac soon dissipated, however. In 2005, a wave of social unrest spread through the suburbs of Paris and other towns, reminding the country of the social exclusion suffered by many immigrants and long-term unemployed. Unemployment remained relatively high, with France's share of world exports declining. Concerns at the social and economic effects of globalization were voiced in 2005, when French voters rejected in a referendum the European *Constitution, seen by many as too neo-liberal.

In 2007, Nicolas *Sarkozy succeeded Chirac as President. The first President not to have experienced World War II, Sarkozy was also unusual as he had never graduated from the elite school of national administration. Sarkozy initiated an assertive and independent foreign policy, though he also valued the EU and the Franco-German alliance. In domestic politics, he introduced far-reaching social, educational, and economic reforms.

FRENCH EMPIRE

Franchet d'Esperey, Louis Félix (b. 25 May 1856, d. 8 July 1942). French marshal Born in Algeria, he was commissioned into the French army, serving in *Indochina and in China. In 1914 he was commanding general of the French 5th Army, and in September halted the German advance in the first Battle of the *Marne. After his failure to stop the German offensive of March 1918, he was sent to Salonika, from where he launched a campaign against Bulgaria. In the speediest advance of the war, he managed to reach the Hungarian capital of Budapest by the time war ended. He served in North Africa after the war, and on retirement entered politics. Despite his right-wing inclinations he refused to join Marshal *Pétain in the *Vichy regime.

Francis Joseph I (b. 18 Aug. 1830, d. 21 Nov. 1916). Emperor of Austria 1848–1916, King of Hungary 1867–1916

He succeeded to the throne of Austria amid the revolutions of 1848, which shaped his conservative and anti-democratic outlook. In 1867, with the formation of the Dual Monarchy, he became also King of Hungary. He subsequently opposed all *nationalist demands from the multitude of peoples in his Empire. He was suspicious of parliamentary institutions, trusting instead in the virtues of a (fictitiously) efficient, centralized bureaucracy. Ironically, this contributed greatly to the further articulation of nationalism and the various peoples' identities, which weakened the Empire the more they were ignored. Despite this, there is no doubt that in his stoic belief in the institution and dignity of the monarchy, he remained the Empire's strongest (and perhaps only effective) symbol of unity. He suffered many personal tragedies: his brother Maximilian was shot in Mexico; his son committed suicide; his wife was assassinated in 1898; and his nephew was assassinated at *Sarajevo. He was succeeded by his great-nephew Charles I.

Franco Bahamonde, Francisco (b. 4 Dec. 1892, d. 20 Nov. 1975). Spanish dictator 1939–75

Path to power Born in El Ferrol (Galicia) into a naval family, he graduated from the Toledo Military Academy in 1910. Quickly establishing a reputation for courage and leadership, he was put in charge of the elite Spanish Legion in 1920 and, after taking part in the defeat of *Abd al-Krim, was promoted to become Spain's youngest general. He became commandant of the Saragossa Military Academy in 1928, though it was closed by the new republican leaders in 1931, who disliked his monarchist tendencies. After the victory of the centre-right parties in October 1933, he returned to favour and was made Commander-in-Chief in 1934, and Chief of the General Staff in 1935. After the victory of the *Popular Front, he was 'relegated' to the Canary Islands. In 1936, he became the leader of a nationalist military insurrection that spread from Morocco to the Spanish mainland. During the *Spanish Civil War, he set forth to strengthen his powers through obtaining mass support of a popular movement, the *Falange.

In power A committed opponent of democracy, *socialism, and *liberalism, he instituted an authoritarian, *corporatist regime after his victory on 1 September 1939,

always carefully balancing the interests of important groups, notably the landowning elites, the military, and parts of the bourgeoisie.

Unlike *Mussolini, Franco refused to enter *World War II on *Hitler's side, mainly because the latter did not offer adequate concessions in return. This enabled him to survive after World War II, though to overcome international ostracism he had to abandon *Fascism. He relied increasingly on the Roman *Catholic Church, e.g. through his appointment of ministers from *Opus Dei, to maintain a traditionalist and patriarchal society in the countryside. At the same time, this goal of maintaining a traditionalist society was effectively undermined by his reluctant pursuit of economic liberalism after 1959, caused by the country's near-bankruptcy. Always maintaining that his authoritarian regime merely continued a tradition of Spanish monarchical rule dating from the fifteenth century, he groomed the young pretender to the Spanish throne, *Juan Carlos, to succeed him. Weakened for some time by Parkinson's disease, he died after a heart attack, and was indeed succeeded by Juan Carlos; his dictatorial regime, however, crumbled, defeated not least by the materialism and secularism that had resulted from his own policies.

Franco, Itamar Augusto (b. 28 June 1931). President of Brazil 1992–4

An engineer from Bahia, he became mayor of his home town Juiz da Fora in 1967, and in 1974 was elected into the State Senate of Minas Gerais. In 1988 he presided over the committee investigating the corruption charges against *Sarney, and in 1989 made a crucial contribution to Fernando Collor de Mello's successful presidential campaign. In return, he became Vice-President, but he soon broke with Collor and left his party. He took charge of the affairs of state following Collor's suspension on suspicion of corruption in October 1992, and became President upon his resignation on 29 December 1992. To reduce the country's endemic hyperinflation (2,567 per cent in 1993), he carried out a currency reform and introduced the *real*, whose value was pegged to the US dollar. He sought to strengthen the country's democratic and liberal base through constitutional reform (24 May 1994), which limited the President's term of office to four years and for the first time granted native Indians a degree of self-government.

franc-tireur, see RÉSISTANCE, LA

Frank Trial (USA)

In September 1913 Leo Frank, the Jewish superintendent of a pencil factory in Atlanta, Georgia, was found guilty of the murder of a 13-year-old female employee, Mary Phagan. His death sentence was commuted to one of life imprisonment by Georgia Governor John Slaton who expressed doubts about Frank's guilt. Slaton's decision was unpopular throughout Georgia, resulting in acts of anti-Semitic public protest and vandalism. On 16 August 1915 a vigilante group belonging to the *Ku Klux Klan removed Frank from his cell and, on the morning of the 17 August in front of a large crowd, hanged him from a tree until he died. New evidence emerged in 1982, and the Georgia Board of Pardons and Paroles posthumously pardoned Frank in 1986. The case evidenced the existence of *anti-Semitism in the judicial system and elements of the American public at large.

Fraser, John Malcolm (b. 21 May 1930). Prime Minister of Australia 1975–83

Born and raised in Melbourne, he studied at Oxford and upon his return was elected to the federal parliament in 1955 for the *Liberal Party. Fraser was appointed Minister for the Army in Harold *Holt's government (1966–7), the time of Australia's controversial involvement in the *Vietnam War. Under Gorton, he served as Minister for Education and Science (1968–9) and Minister for Defence (1969–71), until he resigned due to differences with Gorton. In March 1975 he became Liberal leader and his Liberal/Country coalition won the December election.

Commanding a majority in both Houses of Parliament until 1980, he was less reformist than his predecessor, *Whitlam. Fraser improved the relationship between the federal government and the individual states, and confronted the bellicose *trade unions with an austere economic policy. Strikes decreased dramatically, and inflation was reduced to below 10 per cent in the late 1970s. He promoted the exploitation of Australia's mineral resources, so that Australia benefited from the rise of commodity prices in 1979. He sought to improve Australia's relationship with its Asian neighbours, and in 1979 persuaded *Thatcher to accept an independent, multi-racial Zimbabwe. The country plunged into another recession after 1979, caused by the second *oil-price shock and compounded by the overvaluation of the Australian dollar which reduced agricultural and mineral exports further. He called an election to exploit *Labor's perceived disarray, but lost after Labor rallied unanimously behind its new leader, *Hawke.

Fraser, Peter (b. 28 Aug. 1884, d. 12 Dec. 1950). Prime Minister of New Zealand 1940–9

Early career Born in Fearn in the Scottish Highlands, he went to London in 1907, where he became influenced by the ideas of the *Independent Labour Party. Unemployed in 1910, he emigrated to New Zealand, where he arrived in 1911. He joined the Socialist Party, and later that year became president of the Auckland General Labourers Union. He led a number of unsuccessful strikes and was active in the seamen's and coalminers' strike of 1912–13, getting arrested. As Secretary of the Social Democratic Party from 1913, he was closely involved in the establishment of the Joint Conference of 1916, where the *Labour Party was created. Later that year, he was imprisoned for twelve months for his opposition to conscription.

In 1918, Fraser was elected to the House of Representatives, where he became a brilliant performer. The once-militant party member gradually became more pragmatic, accepting, for example, by the late 1920s the undesirability of the nationalization of land, and the benefits of industrial arbitration. Becoming after 1935 Minister of Education, of Health, of Marine, and of Police, he was particularly well-known for his educational reforms. Fraser performed the functions of Prime Minister for the ailing *Savage from August 1939, whom he succeeded after his death.

In office He led the country during World War II, despite a critical parliamentary opposition and a suspicious trade-union movement. He cooperated closely with *Curtin's Labour government in Australia, though the two men disagreed about use of their forces given the threat of a Japanese attack, with Fraser accepting US advice that it was best to retain the New Zealand forces in Europe and leave the home defence to the USA. He received international distinction for his role in the establishment of the *UN. Even though he had been a supporter of much greater powers for the organization, he was instrumental in drafting its policies on former colonies which were to be prepared for independence as *trust territories. He only narrowly won the 1946 general election against a revived *National Party under *Holland. Thereafter, his pragmatism made him increasingly out of touch with the party rank and file. Against strong opposition among his own supporters, he held a referendum which agreed to compulsory military training in peacetime. Worn out and divided, his party lost the 1949 general elections.

Free French (Forces Françaises Libres)

Those French military and civilian forces outside mainland France occupied by the Germans or ruled by the *Vichy government, which continued the fight on the side of the *Allies during World War II. They were led by de *Gaulle and his Council for the Defence of the Empire (later **Comité National Français**, French National Committee). During the first years, support for the most junior general in the French army, de *Gaulle, against the celebrated veteran of *Verdun, Marshal *Pétain, was very slow. Indeed, initial encouragement from the British was only lukewarm, while the Americans were even more suspicious of de Gaulle's intentions. However, by 1943 it had become clear that there was no realistic alternative to de Gaulle's political astuteness, particularly as he had just managed to establish his authority in the *Résistance* movement in France itself. On 25 August 1944 the Free French, who had been renamed as the French Fighting Forces (Forces Françaises Combattantes) on 19 July 1942, were permitted by the Allies to be the first to enter Paris. The following day, de Gaulle staged a triumphal procession which confirmed his position as liberator and leader of France.

Frei Montalva, Eduardo (b. 16 Jan. 1911, d. 22 Jan. 1982). President of Chile 1964–70

From a wealthy Catholic family, he graduated in law from Chile Catholic University in 1932, where he subsequently became professor of labour law. He became a leader of the anti-Fascist Catholic movement, the Falange Nacional, which in 1957 became the Partido Demócratico Cristiano (Christian Democratic Party). As its leader he won the 1964 presidential elections with the overambitious slogan 'revolution in liberty'. The programmes he initiated included extension of education and social welfare, agrarian reform, and the 'Chileanization' (i.e. partial nationalization) of the copper industry, whose controlling interests had until then been held by US companies. His reforms were too much for the conservatives, and too little for the left. Frei was succeeded by *Allende.

Frei Ruiz-Tagle, Eduardo (b. 24 June 1942). President of Chile 1994–2000

Eldest son of President E. *Frei, he studied engineering and in 1988 sold the shares of his business to turn to politics. Elected Senator in 1989, he became chairman of the Christian Democratic Party (PDC) in 1991 and was elected President on 11 December 1993 with 58 per cent of the vote. Officially President from 11 March 1994, he sought to stabilize the country's fragile democracy without

upsetting the powerful military, still led by *Pinochet. His appointment as Senator for life in 2000 gave the ruling centre left coalition a majority in the Senate.

Freikorps (Germany)

Independent paramilitary units which numbered 250,000 men by 1919. Their formation was encouraged by the German High Command to keep order in the German border regions and to circumvent the restrictions placed upon the number of regular army soldiers by the *Versailles Treaty. They were instrumental in crushing the Revolution of 1918 as well as other revolts, notably the *Spartakus revolts. They became a destabilizing factor since most of them were hostile to the Weimar Republic. Under pressure from other powers, the *Freikorps* units were disbanded in 1920, though many continued to exist unofficially.

FRELIMO (Frente de Libertaçao de Moçambique, Mozambique Liberation Front)

A resistance movement established in 1962 to fight against Portuguese colonialism in Mozambique. It emerged as a union of various independence movements which had been encouraged by *Nkrumah and Eduardo Chivambo Mondlane, a professor at Syracuse University (US). The latter was chosen to become its leader, and on 25 September 1964 it launched its guerrilla campaign against the Portuguese. Armed by the USSR, China, and other Eastern Bloc countries, it controlled more than one-fifth of the country by 1974 and inflicted increasingly heavy losses upon the colonial troops. Independence came suddenly in 1974, and caught the movement almost completely unawares. Led by *Machel since 1968, it became the country's single party, so that the leader of FRELIMO was President as well as head of the armed forces. Efforts to end the civil war led to the country's democratization and the holding of free elections on 27–9 October 1994, in which the former guerrilla movement, *RENAMO, was allowed to participate. FRELIMO won the elections, gaining 129 out of 250 seats. Its leader (since 1986), *Chissano, was confirmed President with 53.3 per cent of the popular vote. FRELIMO presided over remarkable economic growth, which reached up to 10 per cent per year, and its parliamentary majority was confirmed in the elections of 1999 and 2004.

French Community (Communauté Française) (1958–60)

A successor to the *French Union, it consisted of France and most of her west African colonies. The latter gained considerable self-government, though France remained responsible for foreign, economic, and financial policies, as well as for defence. The Community ceased to be effective when its African members gained independence. It still exists in name, and its members have sought close cultural and economic links with France on an individual basis, e.g. through linking their currencies to the French currency (since 1999 the *euro).

French Empire

The French acquisition of overseas territories began in the seventeenth century, though the last continuous period of expansion began with the occupation of Algiers in 1830. In the following decades, France occupied the rest of Algeria as well as other territories in the Pacific and in Africa (Senegal). France undertook its most ambitious acquisitions after 1870, when it added Madagascar and *Indochina to its Empire. By 1914, the colonies made up 95 per cent of French territory, and 54 per cent of her population. The Empire expanded even further after World War I, when it acquired most of the former German colonies of Cameroon and Togo, in addition to the *League of Nations *Mandates of Lebanon and Syria. After World War II, the power vacuum left by the withdrawal of the Japanese occupying forces in Indochina led to the Declaration of Independence by the Communist-led *Vietminh in 1945. The French had little choice but to acquiesce in 1954, following defeat at *Dien Bien Phu in the *Indochina War. When in that same year hostilities broke out against French rule in Algeria, it became clear that the French would be unable to stop the disintegration of the Empire, despite attempts such as the creation of the short-lived *French Community to stall this process. None the less, France not only retains strong links with her former colonies, but also still has a considerable number of overseas territories. In addition to the French *Antarctic territory, its overseas territories (territoires d'outre-mer) with limited self-government consist of *French Polynesia and *New Caledonia in the Pacific. Territories with more autonomy (collectivités territoriales) are the North American island of Saint-Pierre-et-Miquelon (off the coast of Newfoundland) and the African Island of *Mayotte. By contrast, the African island of Réunion, the Caribbean islands of *Martinique and *Guadeloupe, and *French Guyana (in South America), are legally and politically an integral part of France (départements d'outre-mer).

DECOLONIZATION; FOREIGN LEGION; MAP 4

French Equatorial Africa

An administrative amalgamation of French colonies in central-west Africa formed in 1910, from which the modern states of the Central African Republic, Chad, Congo, Gabon, and most of Cameroon (added to the territory in 1920) emerged. It included some of the most underdeveloped parts of the *French Empire, but experienced rapid economic progress during World War II, in which it became the initial stronghold of de *Gaulle's *Free French opposition to the *Vichy regime. Led by *Eboué, its infrastructure was improved, its administration overhauled and political participation increased. Legal reforms were introduced, freedom of association established, and forced labour abolished by 1946. In that year, it was transformed into a colonial federation, but the new structure failed to produce the degree of uniformity necessary to prevent its breakup in 1958, when its constituent parts joined the *French Community.

DECOLONIZATION

French Guyana, see GUYANE FRANÇAISE

French Polynesia (Polynésie Française)

A collection of some 130 islands in five archipelagos, spread out in an area of two million km^2 (772,200 sq. miles) of the Pacific Ocean. It was governed as a French colony from 1903, but in 1945 its inhabitants acquired French citizenship. As overseas territories (territories d'outre-mer) from 1959 they were given limited autonomy, which was extended in 1977 and 1984. From 1963, it acquired a central importance for the French nuclear-testing programme, which has subsequently been carried out underground at the island of Mururoa. Despite riots sparked off by the renewed tests ordered by *Chirac in 1995, the majority of the islands have repeatedly rejected independence, as French financial assistance and military spending have ensured a standard of living for the islanders which is almost double that of some of their Polynesian neighbours.

FRENCH EMPIRE

French Union

A reorganization in 1946 of the *French Empire to implement the *Brazzaville Declaration. It proved unacceptable to both African and Indochinese nationalists, especially as it established little in the way of self-government. It broke up following the independence of *Indochina in 1954 and the creation of the *French Community in 1958.

French West Africa

Following the establishment of French settlements on the African west coast in 1659 and a gradual extension of the French West African territory during the nineteenth century, it was created a colonial territory under a Governor-General in 1904. In 1942, it switched its allegiance from the *Vichy government to de *Gaulle. In 1946 it became an overseas territory of the *French Union, but as a result of strong nationalist pressures in the constituent colonies, Senegal, Ivory Coast, Mali, Niger, Benin, and Mauritania were given greater autonomy as part of the *French Community in 1958 (to achieve independence in 1960), while Guinea insisted on immediate independence, also in 1958.

Frente Sandinista de Liberación Nacional (Sandinistas), see SANDINO, AUGUSTO CÉSAR

Freyberg, Sir Bernard Cyril, 1st Baron (b. 21 Mar. 1889, d. 4 July 1963). New Zealand general

Born in London, his parents moved to New Zealand in 1891. He returned to London to volunteer for service in World War I, in which he was wounded nine times, and was awarded several medals for bravery, including the Victoria Cross. He remained a professional soldier in the British army, but in 1939 took over command of the New Zealand Division in the Middle East. He was briefly Commander-in-Chief of the abortive *Allied operations in Crete in 1941 and commanded the New Zealand Division in Greece, Africa, and Italy. He was Governor-General of New Zealand, 1946–52.

Friedan, Betty (b. 4 Feb. 1921, d. 4 Feb 2006). US feminist

Born in Peoria, Illinois, her first book, *The Feminine Mystique* (1963), is seen as marking the beginning of the second wave of feminism in America (*Women's movement). A suburban mother of three who had graduated from Smith University some twenty years before, Friedan's frustrations and insights struck a chord with women across the USA. The book criticized what Friedan saw as a concerted campaign, since the end of World War II, to convince American women that they could only achieve happiness through marriage and motherhood. It was this 'happy homemaker' ideology that was the 'feminine mystique'. In contrast to Simone de *Beauvoir in France, Friedan was highly practical. She founded the National Organisation of Women in 1966, and was its first president until 1970. Two of her subsequent books deal with feminism and the women's movement, *It Changed My Life* (1976) and *The Second Stage* (1981). She won numerous awards, including the Eleanor Roosevelt Leadership Award in 1989.

Front de Libération du Québec (Quebec Liberation Front)

A terrorist organization founded in 1963 with the aim of realizing independence for the Canadian province of *Quebec. It caused over 200 bombings (1963–70), but split into two groups in 1969, consisting of twelve members each. In 1970, it abducted the British Trade Commissioner James Cross and the Quebec Liberal minister Pierre Laporte, murdering the latter after seven days. *Trudeau responded by invoking the *War Measures Act, whereupon almost 500 people were arrested, including 150 suspected of links with the FLQ. Some of the movement's leaders fled to Cuba and then to France, but all were eventually brought to trial. The FLQ ceased to operate in 1971.

Front de Libération Nationale (FLN)

An Algerian radical Muslim independence movement founded by *Ben Bella in 1952. Despite strong differences of opinion between its military, political, and religious wings, the movement remained united during the *Algerian War of Independence and became the only political party after Algerian independence until 1989. Faced by the subsequent growth of the fundamentalist Islamic Salvation Front (Front Islamique du Salut, FIS), its role was secured through the declaration of a state of emergency in 1992, as a result of which the FLN became dominated by the military.

Front National (France)

A French neo-Fascist party, founded in 1972 by Jean-Marie *Le Pen. It has advocated under the banner of 'France for the French' the deportation of immigrants, whom it blames for rising crime, unemployment, and welfare costs. Le Pen has also been reported as making very strong *anti-Semitic statements. Hence, while his opposition to immigration is anti-Arabic, he has supported the Arab countries against Israel. Such contradictions have not harmed the party's prospects. It broke through in the 1984 European elections, when the party took about 11 per cent of the popular vote. In the elections during the following decade, it polled around 10 per cent, though in the French presidential elections of 1995, Le Pen gained almost 19 per cent of the votes. In these last elections, the party was able for the first time to gather substantial support outside the industrial areas of the north and areas with a large immigrant population in the south, for example in prosperous *Alsace. In 1998, a split emerged between Le Pen and a group of ambitious nationalists led by Bruno Megret, who tried to assert the leadership of the movement. Megret was unsuccessful, and in 1999 founded his own nationalist party, the National Republican Movement (MNR, Mouvement National Republicain). Despite these divisions, Le Pen's charisma and his ability to address popular dissatisfaction with the governmental elite ensured an unprecedented success at the 2002 presidential elections, when he beat the Prime Minister, *Jospin, into third place. As a result of the complex French electoral system, however, the Front National did not get a single deputy elected into the National Assembly at the subsequent parliamentary elections of 2002. Le Pen stood again in the 2007 presidential elections, receiving much help from his daughter, Marie, who acted as the party's vice-president.

Front National (World War II), see RÉSIST-ANCE, LA

Fuad I, Ahmad (b. 26 Mar. 1868, d. 28 Apr. 1936). King of Egypt 1923–36
Younger son of Khedive Ismail (b. 1830, d. 1895), who had sold the Egyptian Suez Canal shares to Britain in 1875. He was chosen by the British to become Sultan of Egypt in 1917 owing to his friendly views towards the *British Empire. As King under the new constitutional monarchy from 1923 he tried to pursue an autocratic government and was locked in constant battle with the *Wafd party, though he also resented constraints imposed upon him by the British.

Führer ('leader')
*Hitler's title, adopted from that of *Mussolini (Il Duce).

Fujimori, Alberto Kenya (b. 28 July 1938) President of Peru 1990–2000

Early career Born in Lima, the son of Japanese immigrants studied agrarian science and maths, and eventually became head of an agricultural college. In response to the catastrophic state of the Peruvian economy and the ever-increasing power of the *Sendero Luminoso guerrillas, he founded the Cambio 90 (Change 90) movement, and four months later was the surprise winner of the elections of 10 June 1990.

In power Initially, his tough economic measures further increased domestic unrest, but they proved extremely successful. They reduced annual inflation from 7,000 per cent in 1990 to 22 per cent in 1994, and reversed the economic decline with a growth rate of 7 per cent in 1993. Furthermore, Fujimori managed to contain the guerrillas. With the help of the army he led a coup in April 1992 in order to replace the officials in the state bureaucracy and judiciary with his own followers, and to rewrite the 1979 Constitution, not least to allow his re-election. Nicknamed 'El Chino' (the Chinaman) because of his oriental looks, he won in the first round of the presidential elections on 9 April 1995 with 64.8 per cent of the popular vote. He ignored a constitutional ban on running for a third period in office, and rigged the 2000 elections amidst growing popular, parliamentary, and judicial hostility.

Shortly after his victory in these rigged elections, Fujimori was forced to flee to Japan, as his main backers among the secret service were charged with corruption. Despite the absence of a bilateral extradition agreement, Peru demanded from Japan the extradition of Fujimori. Japan refused, however, pointing out that Fujimori enjoyed the protection of Japanese citizenship.

Fukuda Takeo (b. 14 Jan. 1905, d. 5 July 1995). Prime Minister of Japan 1976–8

Early career After graduating from Tokyo University's Faculty of Law in 1929, Fukuda Takeo followed the elite course to enter the Ministry of Finance as a career bureaucrat. In this, the most powerful of Japan's civil service ministries, Fukuda headed the budget and banking bureaux in the late 1940s. As a senior government official he was implicated in the Shôwa Denkô scandal, although the courts cleared him of all charges in 1958. Fukuda's Diet career began in 1952 and he progressed rapidly as an associate of *Kishi Nobusuke. He came to serve in senior party positions within the *Liberal Democratic Party to become Minister of Agriculture in 1959. Under *Ikeda Hayato's premiership Fukuda was a voice of dissent within the party, and he openly criticized government economic policy for its inflationary effects.

In power Fukuda's support for *Satô Eisaku's election to the premiership was rewarded with his appointment as Minister of Finance in 1965. Although Fukuda was widely expected to succeed Satô, he did not win the premiership until 1976. Nevertheless, Fukuda was a leading figure in the governments of most of the 1970s, and as Minster of Finance in *Tanaka Kakuei's Cabinet he was responsible for the government's attempts to control inflation in the wake of the first *oil price shock. After 1978, Fukuda continued a campaign of rivalry with Ôhira Masayoshi who had replaced him as Prime Minister, and battles between the two threatened to split the ruling party towards the end of the decade. After 1980 Fukuda retired from the forefront of politics, although he remained an influential party broker. One of the achievements of his brief premiership was the negotiation of the peace settlement with China.

Fulbright, James William (b. 9 Apr. 1905, d. 9 Feb. 1995). US Senator 1945–75
Born in Sumner, Missouri, he was raised in Fayetteville, Arkansas. He was educated at Arkansas University and at Oxford, and went on to become a distinguished lawyer specializing in antitrust litigation. Fulbright was elected to the House of Representatives as a *Democrat in 1942, and to the Senate in 1944. An opponent of isolationism as well as of *McCarthyism, he was chairperson of the Senate Foreign Relations Committee from 1959 until 1974. An active critic of US interventionist policies in the 1960s and 1970s, he criticized the 1965 intervention in the Dominican Republic. He abandoned his earlier support for the *Vietnam War, and urged that *Congress should have more control over the President's powers to make war. A *Rhodes Scholar himself, in 1946 he sponsored the Fulbright Act, which provided federal funds for the exchange of students and teachers between the USA and other countries.

FYROM (Former Yugoslav Republic of Macedonia), see MACEDONIA

Gabon

A country on the west coast of central Africa whose leadership has benefited from rich oil reserves and a long tenure of office.

History (up to 2003) Under French influence from 1853, it was integrated into *French Equatorial Africa in 1910. It became an autonomous member of the *French Community in 1958, and acquired complete independence on 17 August 1960. In 1967, its first president, Léon Mba, was deposed in a coup by Omar Bongo (b. 1935), who has continued to rule the country in an authoritarian manner, despite introducing façades of democracy. Thus, a new constitution was proclaimed in 1991, and other political parties were allowed, but only with the help of large-scale electoral fraud did he win the general elections of 1993. In 2003, the constitution was changed, lifting any restrictions on the number of times the president could be re-elected. Bongo's position was made tenable through the tacit acquiescence of Western leaders, particularly in France, who did not want to see their investments or exports (e.g. of arms) in danger.

Contemporary politics (since 2003) Most of the wealth coming in from its oil exports went either to foreign-owned companies or to its corrupt leadership and bureaucratic machine. The economy has suffered from its over-reliance on oil exports, high foreign debt, and its dependence on foreign (and especially French) aid. Oil reserves have declined since the 1990s, exposing the vulnerability of an economy with high unemployment and insufficient economic diversification.

Gaddafi, Muammar al- (b. Sept. 1942).
Libyan leader 1969–

Born into a nomadic family near Sirte (Fezzan), he was expelled from school in 1961 for his political activities, to which his admiration for *Nasser had led him. He enlisted in the army in 1963 and, following the example of Nasser's Free Officers, movement, he eventually founded the Free Unitary Officers group which deposed King Idris I and established the Libyan Arab Republic. He fervently believed in the ideal of Arab unity, which led him to propose short-lived federations with Syria and Chad. A charismatic orator, he maintained power through vastly improving the economic conditions for the majority of the population.

Libya became perhaps the only oil-producing country in Africa and Latin America where the revenues of oil exports are relatively widely distributed among the population. Gaddafi's popularity was enhanced through his use of nationalist and Islamic rhetoric which appealed to the country's cultural and religious traditions. His support of terrorist groups in Egypt and other countries during the 1980s transformed him into an internationally destabilizing figure. He became perhaps the world's most reviled leader, until that distinction passed on to Saddam *Hussein in 1990. From the 1990s, he worked hard and successfully to distance himself from the terrorist organizations he had done so much to encourage. He brokered a peace deal between government and rebels in the Philippines in 2001, and helped secure the release of Western hostages captured in the Philippines and in the Sahara desert (2003).

Gaitskell, Hugh Todd Naylor (b. 9 Apr. 1906, d. 18 Jan. 1963). British Labour leader 1955–63

Born in London, and educated at Winchester and Oxford, he worked in adult education, and became a lecturer in economics at University College, London, in 1928. During World War II, he was a civil servant, in the Ministry of Economic Welfare, and was elected to parliament for Leeds South in 1945. He served as Minister of Fuel and Power (1947–50). As Chancellor of the Exchequer in 1950–1 he imposed the prescription charges covering half the cost of adult spectacles and dentures, which he felt necessary in order to pay for rearmament; he was opposed by *Bevan, who resigned from the Cabinet. He was by this time the most prominent figure on the right of the *Labour Party, and when he succeeded *Attlee as party leader in 1955, he soon confronted the left-wing 'Bevanites' by opposing unilateral nuclear disarmament (1960–1), and by seeking, unsuccessfully, to revise the Labour Party constitution's Clause IV (which committed the party to nationalization) at the 1959 party conference. Although of undoubted intellect and ability, he never managed to reconcile fully the left wing of the party to his leadership.

Gallipoli campaign (25 Apr. 1915–9 Jan. 1916)

A failed military offensive in *World War I on the southernmost peninsula on the European side of the *Dardanelles. Following the failure of a naval advance through the Dardanelles, British and *ANZAC forces decided to land at Gallipoli, and from there attack the forts guarding the Dardanelles and the entrance to Constantinople. On 25 April a French corps attacked the Turkish positions at Gallipoli from land bases in Asia Minor. British and Australian troops under General Ian Hamilton landed at Cape Helles, at the tip of the Gallipoli peninsula, while Australian and New Zealand troops, under General William Birdwood, landed at Ari Burnu (later renamed Anzac Cove). Security had been so lax that the Turks under the German General Liman von Sanders were expecting them, and offered strong resistance. British and ANZAC troops desperately tried to advance up the steep hillsides, despite heavy casualties. On 6 August a further landing was made at Suvla Bay, to the west. This was a much more suitable site, but the Allies did not press their advantage, enabling Turkish troops to move into the hills above them. Trench warfare ensued until an evacuation was finally ordered. Some 36,000 Allied troops were killed, including 8,587 Australians. A further 82,000 were wounded or taken prisoner. The campaign failed due to inadequate and confused planning, and had been controversial from the start. Many had argued that it merely deflected efforts from the war's main and decisive theatre of operations, the Western Front.

Galtieri, Leopold Fortunato (b. 15 July 1926, d. 12 Jan 2003). Argentinian general and dictator 1980–2, President 1982

The Commander-in-Chief of the army, he took part in the coup which re-established the military dictatorship in 1976. He became President in a period of economic crisis when inflation exceeded 100 per cent per annum, industry produced at half of its capacity, and real income was less than it had been ten years before. He chose to revive the army's fortune by sending his forces to occupy the Falkland Islands, which subsequently led to the *Falklands War. Its disastrous outcome in 1982 and his subsequent resignation inaugurated a period of democratic rule for his country, and twelve years' imprisonment for himself starting in 1986, though he was later pardoned. In 1997, he was indicted for *human rights violations against Spanish civilians by a Spanish judge, but Argentina refused to extradite him to stand trial.

Gambia

A west African country plagued by poor soil and a lack of mineral resources.

Contemporary history (up to 1994) In 1843 the British declared the area around the town of Bathurst (now Banjul) a British colony and in 1888 extended their control up the River Gambia into the interior, claiming the entire area as a British protectorate. It was mainly governed through *indirect rule by local chiefs and, by the same token, was largely neglected by British investment. After the British had long resisted the formation of political parties, they had to consent to a degree of politicization as a necessary prelude to independence. In 1962, Dawda *Jawara became Prime Minister. He negotiated the country's independence on 18 February 1965.

Gambia was the last country in western Africa to gain independence, as it had been deemed too poor for *decolonization. Jawara established a republic in 1970, and became the country's first President. Gambia retained many of its traditional local hierarchical structures, and was thus politically stable for a time. It entered a political union with Senegal in 1982, but this was revoked in 1989. Jawara was re-elected for a fifth successive term in 1992, having overcome two coup attempts by the army in 1980 and 1981.

Contemporary politics (since 1994) Jawara was ousted from power in a successful military coup on 23 July 1994, led by Yayah Jammeh. Jammeh suspended the Constitution until 1998, banned all political parties, and reintroduced the death penalty in 1995. Jammeh was re-elected amidst allegations of electoral fraud with 53 per cent of the popular vote in 2001. Economic and administrative mismanagement have prevented the effective tackling of the country's long-term problems. The country continued to be over-reliant on the harvesting of peanuts, which accounted for almost 70 per cent of its exports in 2006. After severely curtailing the freedom of the press, Jawara was re-elected in 2006 in elections that were generally regarded as unfair.

Gandhi, Indira (b. 19 Nov. 1917, d. 31 Oct. 1984). Prime Minister of India 1966–77, 1980–4

Early career The only child of Jawaharlal *Nehru, she was educated in India and in non-British schools in Europe. In 1939 she joined the Indian National *Congress. In 1942, she married a member of the Congress Party, Feroze Gandhi (no relation to Mohandas *Gandhi), which many objected to on the grounds that it was an intercommunal marriage. She was imprisoned shortly afterwards for her wartime activities, but was released within a year. She became her father's principal aide, serving as president of Congress (1959–60), and was devastated when he died in 1964 (her husband had died in 1960). She served as Minister for Broadcasting and Information in 1964 in *Shastri's Cabinet.

In office Although conciliatory at first, she became involved in a major confrontation with the rest of the party establishment after the bad performance of Congress in the 1967 elections. This led to the 1969 split of the party, in which her followers took on the name of New Congress, or Congress (I) for Congress Indira.

Gandhi rapidly gained popularity through her *nationalism, which led to the third *Indo-Pakistan War in 1970, and her populism, which led her to promise the scientific eradication of poverty in India. Re-elected in 1971 with an overwhelming majority, her programme was badly shaken by the 1973 *oil-price shock. In response to mounting criticism, she became increasingly authoritarian. In 1975 she was even convicted of electoral fraud. In response, she gaoled many of her opponents under the Emergency provisions of the constitution. Her controversial and unorthodox policies at this time included a forced sterilization campaign to reduce the country's birth-rate. Despite the continuation of the Emergency until 1977, the opposition parties of the *Janata Alliance gained enough strength to win the 1977 elections.

Gandhi was re-elected in 1980, when she was faced with yet another international economic crisis. Devastated by the death of her son and designated successor, Sanjay (b. 1946, d. 1980), she prepared her only other son, Rajiv *Gandhi, for her succession. Her good relations with Moscow cooled markedly during this period, owing to the Soviet Union's invasion of neighbouring Afghanistan. The main problem of her second term in office, however, was widespread separatist violence in the seven tribal states (including *Assam). Her order to storm the Golden Temple against *Sikh extremists in *Amritsar provoked her assassination by Sikh terrorists.

Gandhi, Mohandas Karamchand
(b. 2 Oct. 1869, d. 30 Jan. 1948). Indian national and spiritual leader

Known in Hindu as *mahatma* (great soul), Gandhi was the spiritual and moral founder of modern India.

South Africa (1893–1915) Gandhi was born at Porbanda (Gujarat) into a well-to-do family from a trader caste. He read for the Bar in London (1888–9), despite the lack of a university education. On his return to Bombay his first years as a lawyer were not blessed with unqualified success, and in 1893 he was sent to Natal (southern Africa) to help in the case of an Indian client. Just before his intended return in 1894, he became involved in the protest movement against the disenfranchisement of and withdrawal of civil rights from the Asian immigrant community. A leader of the protests for the next two decades, it was here that he developed the basis of his political and philosophical consciousness.

At the heart of this was his belief in the 'inner voice' present within each individual, which was the voice of God. Truth could only be obtained by listening to the inner voice, and this was only possible through focusing on the self, and the denial of all corrupting outside influences. Personally, he began an austere life marked by chastity, simplicity, and hours spent on the spinning wheel, in an attempt to return to his Indian roots and defy Western, 'alien', industrially produced textiles. His faith in the inner voice also formed the basis of his political beliefs, which were founded upon religious tolerance, non-violence, and an intense cultural *nationalism hostile to the imposition of values and cultures on foreign peoples.

In 1904, Gandhi founded the Phoenix settlement, which aimed to realize these ideals in common life. Through his personality, his writings, and his political campaigns, he first united the disparate Indian community in South Africa. He then stepped up his campaign through a peaceful march into the Transvaal, and through other acts of defiance against the authorities. Finally, his campaign was successful, and the

South African government backed down in 1914.

Early political activity in India (1915–22) Gandhi returned to India on 9 January 1915, and took part in a number of specific agitations. Through his non-violent protest (*satyagraha*, or 'truth force'), he led all these to a successful conclusion. Based on this experience, on his reputation from South African and subsequent campaigns, and his sheer personality, during 1919–20 he was able to convince the Indian National *Congress (INC) to start a campaign of non-cooperation. This was a reaction to the *Rowlatt Act, the *Amritsar Massacre, and Muslim concerns at the abolition of the *Khilafat in the *Ottoman Empire, with British compliance. The confirmation of the non-cooperation policy at the INC's Nagpur Session in 1920 was an unqualified personal triumph, and marked the beginning of Gandhi's hold over the INC and the Indian nationalist movement in general. The immediate campaign was called off on 24 February 1922 because of its escalation into violence. Gandhi was imprisoned, but released in 1924. In the following years he retreated somewhat, but even in times of withdrawal he remained the real leader of the INC, though his formal control was always minimal.

Growing nationalism (1922–45) Gandhi's next burst of energy came in response to the establishment of the *Simon Commission, which led to his demand of Dominion status for India. When this was ignored, he initiated another civil disobedience movement, choosing the symbolic issue of the Salt Law, which hit the poor particularly hard, as the focus of his campaign. He led the *Salt March in 1930, which received enormous national attention and support. He was then sent to represent the INC at the second *Round Table Conference in London in 1931. Against *Ambedkar's opposition, he was hostile to its decision for separate political representation for the Depressed Classes as divisive for the Hindu community. He thus negotiated the **Poona Pact** of 1932, a compromise which reserved seats for the Depressed Classes, while maintaining a united electorate. Indeed, during the 1930s, Gandhi became increasingly concerned with the Depressed Classes and the untouchables, whom he called *harijans* ('children of God'). In World War II, he opposed *Bose's attempt to use Britain's weakness for the cause of independence, despite the unpopularity of his cause among the INC rank and file. He did, however, launch another wave of protests against the British involvement of India in the war without Indian consent, through his 'Quit India'

campaign (1940–2). He was imprisoned again in 1942, and released in 1944.

Path to independence (1944–48) After World War II, he was relegated to the political sidelines, while the negotiations for independence and separation were led by *Nehru and *Jinnah. The decline of his actual influence was partly due to his elevation to mythical status within his own lifetime. In the main part, however, it was because he was his own worst enemy as a practical politician. His strengths of charismatic leadership, wisdom, and integrity predestined him to unite and lead the nationalist movement when its main task was defiance. He was less suitable to develop and lead protracted, pragmatic policies, owing to his constant self-doubts and his reluctance to compromise on his ideals. His ideals of unity, harmony, and religious tolerance were increasingly out of harmony with the majority of the Indian population, and its leadership.

Deeply disturbed by the division of India and the communal violence that accompanied it, he withdrew to Delhi and on 11 January 1948 embarked upon a final fast to protest against the persecution of Muslims in the city. Nehru's Cabinet quickly established better relations with Pakistan, while the violence in Delhi ended. Gandhi broke off his fast a week later, only to be assassinated soon afterwards by a young Hindu radical outraged by his benevolence towards Muslims. His importance was summed up by Nehru, who said that his death meant 'the loss of India's soul'. On the night of the murder, Nehru declared that 'The light has gone out of our lives and there is darkness everywhere.'

Gandhi, Rajiv (b. 20 Aug. 1944, d. 21 May 1991). Prime Minister of India 1984–9 Despite being the eldest son of Indira *Gandhi and the grandson of Jawaharlal *Nehru, he showed no interest in politics. He married an Italian (Sonia *Gandhi) and became a pilot for Air India. After the death of his brother, Sanjay (b. 1946, d. 1980), who had been groomed to succeed his mother, he entered politics and immediately became secretary-general and president of the *Congress (I) party. He succeeded his mother upon her assassination, and distinguished himself with a less firm and more conciliatory style. He called an election in November 1984, which he won with an unprecedented majority (400 out of 500 seats in the Lok Sabha, the Lower Chamber). Using this mandate, he sought to reduce some of the long-standing provincial conflicts, notably in the *Punjab, *Assam, and Mizoram. Especially in the Punjab, *Sikh violence soon returned, while the resurgence of violence in the two other provinces by the end of the 1980s further dented his popularity. He was also weakened by charges of corruption in his administration. In foreign policy, he improved relations with the USA, but incited the anger of the *Tamil Tigers by his intervention in Sri Lanka in 1987. He lost the 1989 elections, though Congress remained the largest party. Gandhi's popular campaigning style brought his party to the verge of another victory in the 1991 elections, at the height of which he was assassinated by a suicide bomber from the Tamil Tigers. He was succeeded by *Narasimha Rao.

Gandhi, Sonia (b. 9 Dec. 1946). Indian politician

Born in Orbassano, Italy, she became an interpreter. In 1968, she married Indira *Gandhi's son, Rajiv *Gandhi, and moved to India. She moved into public life when her husband became Prime Minister, in 1984. Following his assassination in 1991, she faced calls to head the Indian National *Congress, despite her Italian descent. Party leader from 1998, her inexperience became a liability to the party, which lost the 1999 elections. In 2004, however, she led the Congress to a surprise victory. Although not Prime Minister because of her Italian descent, she occupied a pivotal position in Indian politics owing to her control of her party's agenda.

Gang of Four

A group that rose to political prominence during the *Cultural Revolution in China (1966–76). It comprised *Mao Zedong's wife, *Jiang Qing, Wang Hogwen, Yao Wenyuan, and Zahng Chungquiao. They were radical adherents to the idea of the Cultural Revolution, and wielded their greatest influence from 1969, by which time they had been made members of the *Politburo (in the cases of Jiang, Yao, and Zahng) and the Party Central Committee (Wang) respectively. In the early 1970s, the Gang of Four became the main driving force in the Cultural Revolution. Its influence climaxed in early 1976, when it achieved the removal of its greatest enemy, *Deng Xiaoping, from all his posts. However, the Gang's greatest strength, its influence on, and access to, Mao, was also its greatest weakness. Jealously resented among the other members of the party, their power collapsed less than a month after Mao's death, when they were arrested on the orders of *Hua Guofeng. In a public trial, they were sentenced to death in the case of Jiang and Zahng (later commuted to life imprisonment), life imprisonment for Wang, and twenty years' imprisonment for Yao.

Garvey, Marcus Moziah (b. 17 Aug. 1887, d. 10 June 1940). Jamaican and African-American activist

Born and educated in Jamaica, in 1914 he founded the Universal Negro Improvement Association (UNIA), which aimed to encourage racial pride and Black unity through the slogan 'Africa for the Africans at Home and Abroad'. He failed to attract a following and in 1916 went to New York to campaign for the repatriation of African Americans who could take over and govern former German colonies. By 1919 UNIA claimed a following of up to a million. The enterprising Garvey had, by 1919, founded a newspaper, *Negro World*, a Negro Factories Corporation, and a shipping line called *Black Star Line*. Despite these successes, Garvey was a deeply divisive figure, as his blue-collar movement was opposed by more integrationist, middle-class Black leaders such as William *Du Bois and the *NAACP. Garvey mismanaged his movement's finances and was convicted of attempted fraud in 1923. After serving part of a five-year prison sentence, he was deported to Jamaica. He died in obscurity in London.

GATT (General Agreement on Tariffs and Trade)

A series of meetings and agreements launched in the spirit of *Bretton Woods by 23 nations in 1947 (with effect from 1 January 1948) to create a harmonious economic world order. In particular, they aimed to reduce tariffs, which had been so harmful to the international economy during the interwar period, as much as possible. Since its foundation, there have been eight rounds of negotiations, which resulted in the reduction of trade barriers. On 15 April 1994, after eight years of negotiations, the last GATT agreement to conclude the Uruguay Round was signed by the 110 member states. This would gradually implement a reduction in national subsidies, for example on agricultural products, and the reduction of trade tariffs for most finished and unfinished goods. In 1995, GATT was transformed into a permanent organization, the *WTO.

PROTECTIONISM; GLOBALIZATION

Gaulle, Charles de (b. 22 Nov. 1890, d. 9 Nov. 1970). President of Free France 1940–4, President of France 1958–69

Military career Born in Lille, de Gaulle graduated from the military academy of Saint-Cyr, and took part in the *Russo-Polish war as a military adviser to the Poles. He rose through the ranks of the military and was appointed Under-Secretary at the Ministry of Defence on 6 June 1940. Upon the French surrender to the Germans he fled to London where in a radio broadcast on 18 June 1940 (which was little noticed at the time) he called for the continuation of the fight, and proclaimed himself the legitimate representative of his country in opposition to Marshal *Pétain and the *Vichy government. As the self-proclaimed leader of the *Free French, he became the head of the Comité Français de la Libération Nationale (CFLN, French Committee of National Liberation), effectively the French government-in-exile, in June 1943.

His pride, determination, stubbornness, and his unswerving belief in his own destiny as the saviour of his country enabled him to become a symbol of French resistance. These attributes also made for strained relations with *Churchill and *Roosevelt, both of whom found it difficult to accept his claim for France to be recognized as an equal fourth *Allied superpower. None the less, they gave him the privilege of entering Paris at the head of his own troops on 25 August 1944, and at *Yalta they decided to accept France as an equal ally in the postwar administration of Germany.

Political career De Gaulle headed various provisional governments until 1946, when he resigned in opposition to the proposed constitution of the Fourth Republic, especially the weak role the President was to receive. He founded his own political movement of *Gaullism, the RPF (Rassemblement du Peuple Français), in 1947, but withdrew from political life in 1953 following the party's inability to achieve a majority. In the political crisis caused by the Algerian War of Independence, President *Coty asked him to take over, initially as Prime Minister, on 29 May 1958.

Together with Michel *Debré he worked out a new constitution, which created the office of a US-style president who could appeal to the people directly by plebiscite, elected for seven years. It was accepted in a referendum on 28 September 1958, and de Gaulle was elected President on 21 December 1958. He ended the Algerian War of Independence through the *Évian Agreements, though he was lucky to survive several assassination attempts by the *Organisation de L'Armée Secrète. He sought to unite the French public through the conduct of a patriotic and independent foreign policy, in which he aspired for French leadership in Europe. He insisted on the development of a nuclear deterrent, which at the time was considered a quintessential underpinning of superpower status (*nuclear bomb). France left the *NATO high command in 1966. His claim to world

influence led him to conduct an independent foreign policy, proclaiming, in 1967, his support of the *Quebec separatists (Vive le Québec libre). At the same time, together with *Adenauer, he inaugurated a 'special relationship' with Germany, whose backing he considered essential for French leadership in Europe. Re-elected in 1965, his position was severely shaken by the *student revolt in May 1968. Although unknown at the time, de Gaulle fled to Baden-Baden to go into exile in Germany on 29 May, but was persuaded by General Masu to return and face the crisis. On 28 April 1969 he resigned following the negative result of a plebiscite on planned reforms of the Senate and regional government.

Gaullism

A French political movement with a diffuse ideology. Although it has developed into a movement on the political right, it contains elements drawn from across the political spectrum, from the *Action Française to the *Socialist Party (SFIO). It seeks to realize the aims of de *Gaulle, particularly achieving unity among the French people through a patriotic and independent foreign policy. In 1947 de Gaulle founded the **RPF (Rassemblement du Peuple Français**, Union of the French People), which he hoped would gather enough popular support for his constitutional idea of a strong presidency. By 1952 it was clear that the RPF had failed, whereupon it was disbanded and de Gaulle was left in the political wilderness.

Upon his return to office in 1958, de Gaulle founded the **UNR (Union pour la Nouvelle République**, Union for the New Republic), whose leader, *Pompidou, became Prime Minister in 1962 in a coalition government with *Giscard d'Estaing. Renamed the UDR (Union des Democrates pour la Ve République, Union of the Democrats for the Fifth Republic) in 1968, the movement was relaunched by *Chirac as the **RPR (Rassemblement pour la République**, Union for the Republic) in 1976. The Gaullists held the major offices of power until 1974, when *Giscard d'Estaing became President, though he appointed Chirac as Prime Minister. They did not recapture the presidency until 1995, under Chirac. Towards the end of his first term, Chirac had become unpopular owing to divisions within his own party, and allegations of corruption. Chirac led the initiative to merge the RPR and a number of smaller parties on the right to form the *UMP in 2002, which allowed him to win a second term that year.

Gaza–Jericho Agreement (13 Sept. 1993)

A follow-up treaty to the *Oslo Accords, in which the details of Palestinian autonomy were concluded. It provided for the establishment of Palestinian autonomy in the *Gaza Strip and the *West Bank after a maximum transition period of five years. More immediately, it contained a detailed plan for the withdrawal of Israeli troops from the Gaza Strip and Jericho, which were the first areas to be granted Palestinian self-rule. In the following nine months, Israeli troops were to withdraw from virtually all areas of Arab settlements in the *West Bank, where control would be exercised by an elected Palestinian council. Three years into the transition period at the latest, negotiations were to begin on outstanding controversial issues, the most contentious of which remained the status of East *Jerusalem. The implementation of the Agreement was prevented by the assassination of *Rabin and the election of Benjamin *Netanyahu as Prime Minister, who upon taking office refused to withdraw troops from any areas that were still under Israeli occupation.

Gaza Strip

A narrow strip of the Mediterranean coast around the town of Gaza which was part of the British *Mandate of Palestine between 1920 and 1947. In 1947, the *UN allocated it to Arabs, whereupon it was occupied by Egyptian troops. In 1955 Israeli troops raided the strip and left 36 Egyptians dead, thus exposing the weakness of Egyptian control over the area. In the *Suez Crisis (1956) it was quickly occupied by the Israeli army, which returned it to Egypt in 1957. It was reoccupied by Israel during the *Six Day War in 1967, and in subsequent years neglect, overcrowding, and the lack of industry and natural resources (40 per cent unemployment in 1994) led to a deterioration of the living conditions there. In 1994, it became one of the first areas to receive Palestinian self-rule under *Arafat. Under Palestinian rule, conditions failed to improve, despite generous foreign aid, in particular from the EU. It is estimated that unemployment even increased, while Arafat's *Palestinian National Authority became accused of mismanagement and the embezzlement of funds by individual members. In 2005, Israel withdrew its settlers and its armed forces from Gaza. However, attacks on Israel from the Gaza Strip continued, as did military action from the Israeli army inside the Gaza Strip. *Hamas increased its control, and in 2007 it assumed control

after a brief civil war against the *Fatah movement.

Gdansk, see DANZIG

GDR (German Democratic Republic), see GERMANY, GERMAN QUESTION

Geddes Axe (1922)

Proposals for spending cuts in Britain, made by Sir Eric Geddes. He had been Director-General of Munitions and Railways in World War I, and Minister of Transport (1919–21). In 1921, at *Lloyd George's behest, he took the chair of a committee which would suggest reductions in public expenditure. The report of the Geddes Committee, dubbed the 'Geddes Axe', recommended savings of £86 million. The Axe effectively scrapped plans for the introduction of compulsory education after the age of 14 in continuation schools, and ended planned housing reforms. There was to be the abolition of a wide range of government posts and some departments such as transport, plus reductions in salaries for police, teachers, and others. The report provoked an outcry and some recommendations were rejected, so that the eventual reduction in the 1922 budget was £64 million. Education had initially been marked for savings of £18 million—the final figure was around £6 million, but it still suffered, especially through the cutting of continuation schools. However, the Axe was aimed mainly at the armed services, whom Geddes had successfully portrayed as profligate spenders.

Geisel, Ernesto (b. 3 Aug. 1907, d. 12 Sept. 1996) President of Brazil 1974–9

Born in Bento Gonçalves (Rio Grande do Sul), he enlisted in the Brazilian army and in 1930 helped bring *Vargas to power, continuing to support him until 1945. In 1964 he formed part of the military junta which took over the government. The chief of the military Cabinet 1964–7, he was president of the supreme military court 1967–9. As President of Brazil from 1974, he appreciated the popular dissatisfaction with the regime and sought to reconcile the public through concessions such as a relaxation of censorship. Despite his promises for a return to democracy, however, he imposed his successor, *Figueiredo, upon the military and the whole country.

General Assembly, see UNO

General Strike, British (3–12 May 1926)

Following World War I, Britain's coalmining industry faced severe problems from overseas competition, and ageing equipment due to a chronic unwillingness to invest in new technology. The industry depended for its survival on cheap labour, which inevitably led to much discontent from miners over working conditions and wages. Matters came to a head in July 1925, when the government stopped its subsidies for the industry, originally introduced during World War I, which threatened to lead to a reduction in wages. Impending strike action was averted when the government continued the subsidy temporarily until the report of *Samuel's Royal Commission on the Coal Industry. The report, which appeared on 11 March 1926, recommended a reorganization of the industry, including the amalgamation of smaller pits, and better working conditions. However, it also proposed an immediate reduction in wages and an increase in the length of the working day.

Negotiations took place throughout March and April, but no solution was found. Under the slogan, 'Not a penny off the pay, not a minute on the day', the miners went on strike on 1 May. On the same day, the Trades Union Congress (*TUC) agreed to hold a general strike in support of the miners on 3 May. In last-minute negotiations, conducted without the miners' authorization, the TUC pledged to accept pay cuts if the government would enforce the rest of the Samuel Report. but this could not be agreed.

The General Strike duly began on 3 May. The country was brought to a standstill. *Baldwin's government declared a state of emergency and placed troops in areas where trouble might erupt. The TUC had agreed to maintain vital food supplies, but other services were kept running by middle- and upper-class volunteers. In the face of resolute government action, the TUC called off the strike on 12 May. The miners, however, continued striking until November, when the suffering of their families forced them to accept reduced wages. The government's response, in 1927, was to pass the Trade Disputes Act. This made general strikes illegal, and the payment of the political levy to the *Labour Party became a matter of individual 'opting-in' of union members. The Act was repealed in 1946, under *Attlee's Labour government.

General Strike, Winnipeg, see
WINNIPEG GENERAL STRIKE

Geneva Agreements (20 July 1954)
The conclusion of the Geneva conference, convened on 7 May 1954 to negotiate peace settlements for war-torn Korea and French *Indochina. It had been attended by the foreign ministers of France, Britain, the USA, the Soviet Union, and the People's Republic of China, together with representatives from Laos, Cambodia, North Vietnam, and South Vietnam. While no solution was found for Korea, all troops were to be withdrawn from Laos and Cambodia, where elections were to be held. In Vietnam a cease-fire line was to be drawn along the 17th Parallel. This did not formally separate the country, but divided the country *de facto* into the Republic of Vietnam (South Vietnam) under *Ngo Dinh Diem in Saigon, and the Democratic Republic of Vietnam (North Vietnam) under *Ho Chi Minh in Hanoi. As both countries claimed to represent the whole country, and strove for unification even by violent means, the agreements did not provide for a lasting peace. They did, however, provide a mechanism for the withdrawal of French colonial forces, to be replaced by an increasing number of US military advisers in the south.

Geneva Conventions
A series of international agreements on the treatment of victims of war. The first was the result of the work of Henri Dunant (b. 1828, d. 1910), founder of the International *Red Cross movement, and laid down basic rules for the treatment of wounded soldiers and prisoners of war, the protection of medical personnel, and the safeguard of civilians. The second convention extended the care of the Red Cross to wounded at sea in 1899 (revised in 1906). In 1929 a third convention agreed on international standards for the treatment of prisoners of war, to be supervised by the Red Cross. Finally, the fourth convention of 1946 concerned the protection of civilians in time of war. Further amendments and additions have been made since, and a total of around a hundred treaties of international humanitarian law have been concluded under the aegis of the Red Cross. Whereas these treaties were signed and ratified by different member states, the four conventions had been ratified by all 194 states in the world by 2007.

(((●))) SEE WEB LINKS

* The website of the International Red Cross dedicated to international humanitarian law.

Genscher, Hans-Dietrich (b. 21 Mar. 1927). German Foreign Secretary 1974–92
Born near the East German city of Halle, he moved to West Germany in 1952, where he became an MP in 1965. From 1968–74 he was deputy leader, then leader of the German *Liberal Party (FDP). Genscher served as Minister of the Interior in 1969, but is best

remembered for his long tenure as Foreign Secretary, during which time he stood for a pragmatic policy towards East Germany. He contributed to the change of government of 1982, when he switched his party's support from the *SPD to Helmut *Kohl's *CDU. His popularity peaked when he helped negotiate German reunification in 1990. In his last year in office Genscher was heavily criticized for his overhasty push to recognize the new states of former *Yugoslavia. Following his retirement he remained much respected within his party and his country.
GERMAN QUESTION

Gentile, Giovanni (b. 27 May 1875, d. 15 Apr. 1944). Italian idealist philosopher and Fascist
Born in Sicily, he graduated from the Scuola Normale Superiore di Pisa in 1897, and subsequently met *Croce, with whom he formed a close intellectual partnership. He taught at the University of Naples from 1903 and began to publish for Croce's review, *La critica*. By 1907 Gentile had begun to formulate his idealist philosophical position which he subsequently elaborated with work on critical philosophy. In 1914, he became professor of theoretical philosophy at Pisa, and in 1917 he moved to the University of Rome. In marked contrast to Croce, he became a careful supporter of *Mussolini and joined his first government as Minister of Education (1922–4). There, he carried out an educational reform which introduced religious teaching in primary schools, and state examinations for teachers and pupils. He also established separate middle schools for technology and the humanities. He resigned over the murder of *Matteotti.

In 1925 Gentile became general editor of the *Enciclopedia italiana* (Italian Encyclopaedia) in which he, rather controversially, sought to give a scholarly and conclusive definition of *Fascism. (The article was signed by Mussolini himself, who pretended to be its author.) In 1925 he joined a Manifesto of Fascist Intellectuals in support of Mussolini, and subsequently he repeated his public support for him, even following the proclamation of the Republic of *Salò. He was executed by partisans on 14 April 1944.

George V (George Frederick Ernest Albert) (b. 3 June 1865, d. 20 Jan. 1936). King of Great Britain and Ireland (from 1920 Northern Ireland) and Dependencies Overseas, Emperor of India 1910–36
Born in London, he served in the Royal Navy in 1877–92. Immediately upon accession to the throne, he was faced with the reform of the House of Lords through the Parliament Bill,

whose passage he assisted after *Asquith had received an electoral mandate on the issue in 1910. He chose *Baldwin as Bonar *Law's successor, and encouraged *MacDonald to form a *national government in 1931. Despite his fierce patriotism, he found himself compelled to change the royal family's name from the German Saxe-Coburg-Gotha to *Windsor. He discovered the benefits of radio and initiated Christmas radio broadcasts to the nation and Empire. His public popularity surfaced during the celebrations of his Silver Jubilee in 1935.

George VI (Albert Frederick Arthur George) (b. 14 Dec. 1895, d. 6 Feb. 1952). King of Great Britain and Northern Ireland and Dependencies Overseas 1936–52, Emperor of India 1936–47
Born in Sandringham, Norfolk, he served in the Royal Navy (1909–17), and in the newly formed Royal Air Force (1918–19). He never expected to become King, but was thrust into the position when his brother, *Edward VIII, abdicated (*abdication crisis); in developing his public profile, he had to overcome a serious speech impediment. He would have preferred *Halifax to replace Neville *Chamberlain in 1940, but was soon impressed by *Churchill. His main impact on the war effort was to boost public morale by remaining in London during the Blitz, with his wife, Elizabeth Bowes-Lyon, and his daughters, *Elizabeth and Margaret. He created the George Cross and the George Medal, to acknowledge the bravery of civilians.

Georgia
A Caucasian state of relative prosperity in the USSR, which since independence has been marked by political instability, territorial disputes, and economic fragilty.

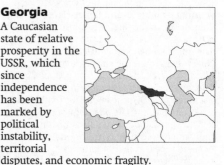

Early history (up to 1991) Georgia was a protectorate of the Russian Empire from 1783. Russian attempts to impose its own culture and language upon the Georgians led to a series of uprisings in the nineteenth century, which were brutally suppressed. It declared its independence at the outbreak of the *Russian Civil War (1918), but was subjected again by the *Red

Army in 1921. In 1922 it joined the USSR as part of the Transcaucasian Soviet Republic (together with *Armenia and *Azerbaijan), becoming a separate Soviet Republic in 1936. *Gorbachev's reformist policies revived *nationalist hopes for independence, which were expressed at the parliamentary elections in 1990, won by the oppositional 'round table' party coalition. Under its leader, Zviad Gamsakhurdia, it became independent in April 1991.

Post-independence politics (1991–2003) Gamsakhurdia's government became increasingly corrupt, until the opposition of the National Guard and civic unrest bordering on civil war forced him out of office in 1992. His successor, *Shevardnadze, struggled to overcome the continued resistance offered by Gamsakhurdia's supporters. Too weak to maintain control over the separatist republic of *Abkhazia, Shevardnadze was only able to restore some order within Georgia itself with implicit Russian assistance. This followed his agreement to allow the continued presence of 20,000 Russian troops, and the Russian use of its Black Sea port of Poti. Georgia was also in desperate need of Russian economic assistance, as in 1994 its Gross Domestic Product had declined to 25 per cent of its 1991 levels. Thereafter, the economy stabilized, as inflation was brought under control and state spending reigned in. The state nevertheless struggled to establish its authority against economic corruption, a thriving black market and rampant tax evasion. In 2000, the Justice Minister, Mikhail Saakashvili, led a campaign against government corruption. He was forced to resign, and became leader of the opposition movement.

Contemporary politics (since 2003) Following rigged elections in favour of Shevardnadze in November 2003, Saakashvili led a peaceful 'rose revolution' which toppled the president. Saakashvili was elected President in January 2004 in fair elections. He reformed the police by raising pay, and pacified the separatist region of Adjaria. However, Abchasia and Ossietia continued to defy his authority, while his fight against corruption slowed down markedly as he continued in office.

German Democratic Republic, see GERMANY

German Question

Traditionally, this is the question of how Europe's most populous state at the centre of the European continent should be defined. Germany had never comprised a cohesive political entity before 1871, and many Germans lived in communities outside the German states. As Germans sought to define themselves as a nation-state, the question arose whether Germany should be defined culturally, through religion and/or language, a definition that included Germans living in pockets of Russia and Romania. An alternative definition focused on Germany's geographical characteristics, even if this excluded a large number of Germans living outside its natural boundaries. Germany formed a state defined by geography and geopolitics in 1866/71. The new state excluded Austria, with which it had shared a common cultural and political history.

After World War II, the concept received a new relevance as there were now two German states which tried to justify their existence in competition with each other. East Germany (the **German Democratic Republic, GDR**) emphasized the Communist ideology of its regime, and insisted that it was the first post-capitalist German state and the only part of Germany which had drawn the correct lessons from the *Third Reich. Until the same socialist conditions obtained in West Germany (the Federal Republic of Germany, FRG), the GDR was an independent, sovereign state. From the 1960s, the GDR even constructed a distinctive GDR-nationhood, though this was rejected by the overwhelming majority of the population. In contrast, West Germany claimed that it alone was the legal continuation of the German state, and insisted that its constitution and citizenship were valid for all Germans, including those living in the GDR.

West Germany developed the **Hallstein Doctrine** (1955), formulated by Walter Hallstein (b. 1901, d. 1982), according to which it refused to take up diplomatic relations with any country (except the Soviet Union) that recognized the East German state. The doctrine effectively prevented the diplomatic recognition of the GDR in the non-Communist world until 1969. In that year, the new German Chancellor, *Brandt, changed West German policy vis-à-vis the GDR, based on the idea of cooperation with, rather than hostility to, the GDR.

As a precondition to that aim, Brandt's new **Ostpolitik** (Eastern Policy) began with the Moscow Treaty of 12 August 1970, in which West Germany de facto recognized the postwar annexations of German territory by the USSR and Poland. On 7

December 1970 the Warsaw Treaty was signed, in which West Germany again guaranteed the inviolability of Poland's western border. These treaties paved the way for an agreement on 3 September 1971 between the Allied powers, still sovereign over *Berlin, in which the Soviet Union (and implicitly the GDR) recognized the Allied presence in West Berlin and guaranteed free access to the city through East Germany. Finally, in the **Basic Treaty (*Grundlagenvertrag*)** of 21 December 1972, the FRG and the GDR accepted each other's existence while West Germany continued to look forward to the self-determination of the German people in its entirety. The treaty paved the way for the admission of both German states into the *UN in 1973. Despite fierce initial hostility by the *CDU, the SPD's policy towards the GDR was accepted by the CDU when it came to power in 1982. Following reunification in 1990, the German question was finally settled, as Germany formally recognized its eastern border with Poland.

Germany

Europe's most populous state whose instability caused two World Wars, and whose stability since 1949 has greatly contributed to the solution of the *German question and the success of *European integration.

The German Empire (1871–1918) Before 1900 the German Empire, unified by Bismarck in 1866/71, experienced a process of singularly rapid industrial transformation which created unusually large social and political tensions. In addition, in the federal nation-state created by Bismarck the constituent states, rather than the Empire, controlled most of the revenues. Without their consent, the Empire could not increase its own revenue substantially. As a result, Germany could not keep up with the arms race that developed, partly as a result of Germany's own *imperialist ambitions and its consequent building of a large navy at the instigation of Admiral *Tirpitz. This sense of crisis explains why Emperor *Wilhelm II and his Chancellor, *Bethmann Hollweg, felt compelled to incite World War I: they were convinced that if there had to be war, the

chances of winning it would be higher the sooner it broke out.

World War I (1914–18) The initial consensus in favour of supporting the war was relatively short-lived, and soon the political parties began to demand domestic reform, particularly in *Prussia. In 1917, parliament passed a motion demanding peace negotiations. By then, however, the country was run in a virtual dictatorship by Generals *Hindenburg and *Ludendorff, who instilled in most Germans a belief and confidence in ultimate victory. Defeat in World War I came as a complete shock to most Germans, as did the territorial losses and the *reparation payments imposed upon them by the *Versailles Treaty, under the humiliating charge that Germany had been the sole aggressor.

The Weimar Republic (1918–1933) These factors became a great burden for the new democracy that began to form after the popular unrest of 1918 had forced the Emperor to abdicate. This democracy is known as the Weimar Republic, so named after the city of the German poets Goethe and Schiller in which the National Assembly convened to write the new Constitution. The Assembly established universal suffrage and unrestricted proportional representation. Given the social, cultural and political fragmentation of the population in subsequent years, this made it increasingly difficult to establish stable parliamentary majorities.

Another problem for the Weimar Republic was that it depended on the bureaucratic and military elites of the former Empire, neither of whom felt any commitment to the democracy. After years of crisis, marked by the decommissioning of millions of soldiers, the payments of *reparations, the *Kapp Putsch in 1920, the murder of *Erzberger and *Rathenau, and the events of 1923 (which saw the occupation of the *Ruhr, hyperinflation, and the *Hitler Putsch), the Republic gained some stability during the *Stresemann era. However, after the world economic crisis caused by the *Wall Street Crash in 1929, millions of disaffected people voted for *Hitler's *Nazi Party from 1930, and Germany became ungovernable, with Chancellors *Brüning and von *Papen governing against parliament, under emergency laws that made them responsible to the President only. In the end, President von *Hindenburg appointed Hitler Chancellor in the misguided confidence that Hitler could be controlled by others in the Cabinet.

Table 10. **German leaders since 1900**

Emperor

*Wilhelm II	1888–1918

Presidents of the Weimar Republic

Friedrich *Ebert	1919–25
Paul von *Hindenburg	1925–34

Leader of the *Third Reich

Adolf *Hitler	1933–45

German Democratic Republic (East Germany)

COMMUNIST PARTY LEADERS:

Wilhelm Pieck	1949–50
Walter *Ulbricht	1950–71
Erich *Honecker	1971–89
Egon Krenz	1989

PRIME MINISTERS:

Hans Modrow	1989–90
Lothar de Maizière	1990

Federal Republic of Germany (West Germany)

CHANCELLORS:

Konrad *Adenauer	1949–63
Ludwig *Erhard	1963–6
Kurt *Kiesinger	1966–9
Willy *Brandt	1969–74
Helmut *Schmidt	1974–82
Helmut *Kohl	1982–98
Gerhard *Schröder	1998–2005
Angela *Merkel	2005–

The Third Reich (1933–45) Hitler's appointment as Chancellor on 30 January 1933 and his acquisition of dictatorial powers through the *Enabling Law marked the beginning of the *Third Reich. Hitler sustained and increased his popularity by ending record unemployment (largely through a massive programme of rearmament), and restoring order and security on the streets. Hitler realized a succession of major foreign policy triumphs such as the *Saarland return to the Reich in 1935, the *Anschluss with Austria (1938), and the annexation of the *Sudetenland (1938) and of the Czech lands (1939). These successes led most Germans to overlook the fact that this sense of national unity was acquired at the expense of minorities such as gypsies, homosexuals, *Jehovah's Witnesses, priests, the mentally ill, and especially Jews, who were officially degraded as second-class citizens by the *Nuremberg Laws. Jews and other opponents of the regime were thrown into *concentration camps, while the persecution of Jews reached new heights with the *Kristallnacht of 1938.

Following the conclusion of the *Hitler-Stalin Pact, Hitler started his pursuit of more 'living space' (*Lebensraum*) with the invasion of Poland on 1 September 1939, which unleashed World War II. In 1941, Hitler started an all-out offensive against the Soviet Union, and in the wake of the initial *Barbarossa campaign the Nazis embarked upon the *Holocaust, the extermination of up to six million people, mainly Jews, in concentration camps such as *Auschwitz. Despite sporadic *resistance to Hitler, most notably through the *July Plot of 1944, the *Third Reich could only be overcome by the subjection of Germany through the Allied invasion which forced German capitulation on 8 May 1945.

The division of Germany (1945–9) Germany was divided into four zones, governed by the Soviet Union in the east, Britain in the north,

France in the west and the US in the south. All German territories east of the Rivers *Oder and Neisse were placed under Polish and Soviet administration. Despite initial endeavours at cooperation, which only succeeded in a few circumstances such as the *Nuremberg Trials, the Soviet zone became administered increasingly separately from the other three.

East Germany (1949–90) The **German Democratic Republic (GDR)** was founded in the Soviet eastern zone on 7 October 1949, in response to the foundation of the FRG (see below). Led by *Ulbricht, who transformed it into a Communist satellite state of the Soviet Union, the GDR's economy suffered from its transformation into a centrally planned economy, and from the dismantling of industries by the Soviet Union. Disenchantment with the dictatorial regime and the slow economic recovery compared to West Germany sparked off an uprising of over 300,000 workers on 17 June 1953, which was crushed by Soviet tanks. However, the country's viability continued to be challenged by the exodus of hundreds of thousands of East Germans to West Berlin every year. To enable East Germany's continued existence, the *Berlin Wall was built on 13 August 1961 as a complement to the existing impenetrable border between East and West Germany. In the following decades, authoritarian Communist rule, severe travel restrictions, the world's largest secret police apparatus (the *Stasi), and economic prosperity relative to its eastern neighbours provided the GDR with a relative degree of stability.

The Soviet-style rule of *Honecker, Ulbricht's successor, from 1971, became undermined by the advent of *Gorbachev as Soviet leader, when the East German leadership became more orthodox than the Soviet original. Matters came to a head in the summer of 1989, when Hungary opened its borders with Austria, thus enabling thousands of East German tourists to escape to the West. Meanwhile, Gorbachev's visit to the 40th anniversary celebrations of the GDR sparked off weekly mass protests, first in Leipzig and Berlin, and then throughout East Germany. Honecker had to resign, and in the confusion that followed, the Berlin Wall was opened by the GDR authorities on 9 November 1989. As East Germans used the opportunity to flee to West Germany in droves, the continuance of the GDR as a separate state became untenable. On 22 July 1990 the East German parliament reintroduced the five states that had existed 1945–52, each of which acceded to West Germany. On 3 October 1990 the GDR ceased to exist and Germany was unified.

West Germany (since 1949) The **Federal Republic of Germany (FRG)** was founded on 23 May 1949, and after a narrow election victory *Adenauer became its first Chancellor. Aided by a rapid economic recovery masterminded by *Erhard, the new democracy won general acceptance and support. This stability was further strengthened by Adenauer's policy of integration into the Western alliance, e.g. through *European integration and the joining of *NATO, which enabled the speedy gain of full sovereignty for the new state from the Western allies. Adenauer was succeeded by Erhard in 1963, but following disagreements with his coalition partner, the *Liberal Party (FDP), he resigned in favour of *Kiesinger, who headed a 'grand coalition' between the SPD and *CDU.

After the 1969 elections the Liberals decided to support the SPD for the first time, which enabled its party leader, *Brandt, to become Chancellor. He inaugurated a new, conciliatory approach towards East Germany of dialogue and compromise, which henceforth became the basis of German internal relations. This policy was even maintained by *Kohl after he took over from Brandt's successor, *Schmidt, in 1982, as a result of which relations with East Germany, though always fragile, improved markedly during those years. Indeed, Kohl recognized the opportunity presented by the disintegration of East Germany for German unification more clearly than most other West Germans, many of whom had abandoned the goal of reunification long before.

German political unification was completed by 1990. For the rest of the decade, the economic effects of unification continued to loom large. Transfer payments from western to eastern Germany augmented already high burdens of debt and taxation without achieving their goal of economic recovery in the eastern states. These factors contributed to sluggish economic growth and persistently high structural unemployment, especially in the eastern states. In 1998, *Schröder was elected Chancellor to head the country's first coalition between Social Democrats and the *Green Party.

Contemporary politics (since 1998) Following the move of the capital from Bonn to Berlin, the red-green coalition epitomized a transformation of the FRG. It pursued social and cultural change, such as the legalization of same-sex unions. In foreign policy, the government committed troops to multinational military peacekeeping operations in Bosnia, *Kosovo (1999), and Afghanistan (2002). At the same time, *Schröder's refusal to participate in any *Iraq

War soured relations with the US, but brought him great domestic popularity. Schröder presided over a flagging economy, and from 2003 carried out far-reaching social reforms. These split his own party, forcing him to call an early election in 2005, which he lost. The new government was formed by a grand coalition between the CDU and the SPD, under the Chancellorship of *Merkel. The economy finally began to improve, with Merkel becoming a respected statesman in foreign policy and within the EU.

Gestapo (Geheime Staatspolizei, Secret State Police)

The internal security police of the Nazi regime. Under the leadership of *Himmler from 1936, it came to form the most important branch of the security service (*Sicherheitsdienst*) of the *SS.

Ghana

The first British Black African colony to gain independence in 1957 and thus a model of *decolonization, and the first African country to adopt *capitalist economic reform in 1983.

Colonial rule (up to 1957) A west African state under European influence since 1471, the territory came under British rule in 1850 and was declared the British Colony of the Gold Coast in 1874. After 30 years of warfare against the rebellious Asante people, it was finally pacified in 1900. After 1920 economic growth based on mining and cocoa -farming, combined with high standards of education, produced demands for home rule. Achimota College, one of the first secondary schools for Africa, was founded in Accra in 1925. (A university college was established in 1948.) In 1946, Ghana became the first British colony in Africa whose legislative assembly consisted mostly of Africans. Serious rioting in 1948 caused the British to speed up the drafting of a new Constitution, though *Danquah and *Nkrumah demanded self-government and independence. Nkrumah was elected Prime Minister in 1952, and led the country to independence on 6 March 1957.

Contemporary history (1957–2000) Foreshadowing the developments in most other newly independent African colonies, Ghana soon degenerated into a showcase of postcolonial instability. A Western-style democracy upon independence, Ghana became a socialist dictatorship until the overthrow of Nkrumah in 1966. He was replaced by an anti-socialist, pro-capitalist military regime, which in turn was replaced in 1969 by a civilian government led by the conservative Busia. The latter was deposed by the military in 1972, which governed through a National Redemption Council (Supreme Military Council as from 1975). This tried to establish its nationalist credentials through promoting the country's economic and cultural self-sufficiency.

In 1979 a military coup was led by Jerry John *Rawlings. He subsequently purged the military and government administration of corruption, executing three former leaders (I. K. Acheampong, A. A. Afrifa, F. W. K. Akuffo) and other senior officers. He introduced civilian rule, but when he was beaten in the elections he soon re-established his own authority in a coup on 31 December 1981. By this time, the once-prosperous colony was all but bankrupt. From 1970 to 1982 Gross Domestic Product declined by 30 per cent per capita, export revenues declined by 50 per cent, and average real income declined by 80 per cent. Revenues from its main export staple, cocoa, declined almost fourfold. Education and literacy levels declined, and the state social security system withered away.

Rawlings appealed to the *World Bank for help, and in 1983 he introduced a series of economic reforms. These produced one of the highest rates of economic growth in Africa, though this was achieved at an immense social cost of unemployment and poverty. In the early 1990s, therefore, it appeared as though the prescriptions of the *IMF and the World Bank to overcome the indebtedness of developing countries were working. However, it was soon apparent that economic and political liberalization, far from complementing each other, appeared to be mutually exclusive. After devising a new democratic constitution in 1992, Rawlings was only able to win the ensuing elections by 'bribing' the electorate with large government spending. The economic damage which this caused lasted until the 1996 elections.

Contemporary politics (since 2000) In late 2000 the oppositional New Patriotic Party won both the parliamentary and the presidential elections, with John Kufuor becoming President in 2001. Kufuor was re-elected in 2004, as he steered the country towards GDP growth rates of 10 per cent per year, and a declining inflation rate. Under his leadership, Ghana also qualified for debt relief under the *HIPC initiative.

Gheorghiu-Dej, Gheorghe (b. 8 Nov. 1901, d. 19 Mar. 1965). General Secretary of the Communist Party of Romania 1945–55, First Secretary 1955–65

Born in Bîrlad (Moldavia), the electrician took employment with the railways, where he became engaged in *trade-union and political activity. He joined the Communist Party in 1930. For his alleged part in a railway strike in 1932 he was sent to prison, where he created a close-knit group of Communist leaders, which included the young *Ceausescu. After the Soviet takeover he was released and accepted as leader. With Soviet help, he worked until 1948 to establish Romania as a Communist state. Thereafter, in a second phase of his leadership he consolidated his own position and authority within the party. Carrying out *Stalinist purges with gusto, he gradually dismantled all internal opposition within the party. This led to the creation of an unusually personalized regime, in which important posts were filled by loyal protégés. In a final phase of his leadership, he successfully created greater distance from the Communist leadership in Moscow. This was done through skilful exploitations of the internal divisions that had opened up between Yugoslavia, Albania, and China, on the one hand, and the other *Comecon states, on the other. He died in office.

Ghetto, see WARSAW GHETTO

Giap, Nguyen Vo, see VO NGUYEN GIAP

Gibraltar

A peninsula on the Spanish coast, whose possession allows control over the Gibraltar Straits linking the Atlantic and the Mediterranean. Under Spanish control since 1462, it was conquered by the British navy in 1704, became a British possession in 1713, and a Crown Colony in 1830. It was an important base for the Royal Navy from the eighteenth to the twentieth centuries. Claimed by Spain, it received self-government in 1964. Negotiations between Britain and Spain about the status of Gibraltar broke down in 1966, and in a 1967 referendum 95 per cent of Gibraltarians voted against becoming part of Spain. In a frustrated gesture, and to force the population into submission, *Franco closed the border in 1969. As a condition for British agreement to Spanish membership of the EC, some border traffic was allowed in 1982, with the border being fully reopened in 1985. In the early 1990s it suffered from the end of the *Cold War, which led to the closure of some Royal Navy docks. Furthermore, its indirect membership of the European Union led to the British enforcement of stricter banking laws in 1996, damaging its reputation as a liberal tax haven.

In 2001 the British and Spanish Foreign Ministers began negotiations over the future of Gibraltar. This led to fierce resistance by the head of the Gibraltar government, Peter Caruana of the Gibraltar Social Democrats, who feared that Britain would seek to hand over the colony to Spain against the wishes of Gibraltarians. Caruana organized a referendum for autumn 2002, calculating that an overwhelming popular rejection of joint sovereignty would increase pressure on the British government to abandon its talks with Spain. Britain and Spain nevertheless agreed to lift travel restrictions in 2006, including the introduction of direct flights between Gibraltar and Spain.

Gierek, Edward (b. 6 Jan. 1919, d. 21 July 2001). First Secretary of the Polish Communist Party 1970–80

Born in Porabka Nowy Sacz (Austrian *Silesia), in 1923 he emigrated with his mother to France, where he joined the French *Communist Party. During World War II he operated in Belgium among groups of Polish underground resistance fighters. In 1948, Gierek returned to Silesia, now part of Poland, and was appointed to the Polish Communist Party *Politburo in 1959. In 1970 he succeeded *Gomulka as First Secretary.

Gierek sought to calm popular discontent by increasing wages and introducing a 'popular' style of government through travelling widely and listening to complaints. Yet the substance of the regime and its policies remained unchanged. Most devastating was his heavy borrowing in precious hard currency, ostensibly to modernize industry and make it competitive, but in reality to keep the loss-making and ineffective economic system afloat. Burdening the country with long-term debt could at best be a short-term solution. When the inevitable happened and the economy worsened while drastic price increases were introduced, mass strikes began which led to the formation of *Solidarnosc. In the face of this overwhelming protest, Gierek was dismissed from office. His memoirs, containing an apologia for his policies, were entitled *An Uninterrupted Decade* (1990).

Gilbert Islands, see KIRIBATI

Giolitti, Giovanni (b. 27 Oct. 1842, d. 17 July 1928). Prime Minister of Italy 1892–3, 1903–5, 1906–9, 1911–14, 1920–1

A law graduate from the University of Turin (1860), he became a civil servant and served, amongst other positions, in the legislative high court until he entered the Chamber of Deputies as a Liberal in 1882. He became Minister of the Treasury 1889–90. As Prime Minister he won the 1892 elections but was forced to resign over a banking scandal. As Minister of the Interior 1901–3 he emerged as the main force behind a 'new liberalism' which attempted to adapt classical liberal traditions to the changed social conditions of early twentieth-century Italy, when the consequences of industrialization were beginning to make themselves felt in many northern cities. Thus, he was responsible for an increase in the parliamentary franchise, and the acceptance of the bargaining powers of *trade unions. He also launched Italy's entry into the high noon of *imperialism through the conquest of Libya in 1911. He opposed Italy's entry into World War I, and afterwards called for a complete overhaul of the Italian state. During his fifth ministry he resolved the *Fiume affair, and ended the workers' occupation of factories in 1920. He also supported *Croce's attempts at educational reform. However, Giolitti was unable to stop the escalating violence between the *blackshirts and socialist and Communist bands. To provide himself with a new mandate, he called new elections in May 1921, which he lost. He tolerated the *Fascist movement at first, but became increasingly critical of *Mussolini after the murder of *Matteotti.

Gioventù Italiana del Littorio (GIL), see BALILLA

Girl Guides, see BADEN-POWELL, ROBERT STEPHENSON SMYTH

Giscard d'Estaing, Valéry (b. 2 Feb. 1926). President of France 1974–81

Born the son of a French official in the occupied German city of Koblenz, he became a parliamentary Deputy in 1956. As leader of a group of Independent Republicans, he occupied a central political role from 1962 to 1968, when the *Gaullists needed his support to form a government. He was Minister of Finance 1961–6 and 1969–74. Elected President in part because the Gaullists failed to agree upon a strong candidate themselves, he at first impressed with a populist style. His liberal policies included lowering of the voting age to 18 and the legalization of *abortion within the first ten weeks of pregnancy. He pursued the goal of improving social equality through the introduction of comprehensive secondary schools. His popularity decreased owing to difficulties at coping with the 1973 *oil-price shock. Although strengthened to some extent by the foundation in 1978 of the *UDF (Union pour la Démocratie Française), he was increasingly weakened by his rocky relationship with the Gaullists led by *Chirac. This relationship deteriorated even further in 1976, when he dismissed Chirac from the office of Prime Minister and appointed the UDF's Raymond Barre (b. 1924) instead. He lost his bid for another term in office as a result of public impatience with his increasingly patricianly and distant style, a renewed economic crisis, and a rejuvenated left led by *Mitterrand. He continued to exert considerable influence as an elder statesman and president of the UDF until 1996, and remained an influential critic of *Chirac thereafter. His career experienced a renaissance in 2002, when he became the chair of the *Constitutional Convention of the EU.

glasnost (openness)

Along with *perestroika, it was the central policy of the Soviet leader Mikhail *Gorbachev which encouraged a more open debate about the state of the Soviet Union and its history. Opening the lid on decades of repression, it created a critical public as Soviet publishers, newspapers, and television stations gradually expanded the limits of their criticism. Ultimately, it made possible Gorbachev's own downfall as he, too, became subject to a hostile and dissatisfied public, and it enabled the breakup of the Soviet Union, the purpose and legitimacy of which became increasingly challenged.

Glemp, Jozef (b. 18 Dec. 1929). Primate of Poland 1981–

Born in Inowroclaw, he was ordained a priest in 1956 and obtained a doctorate in civil and canon law at the Lateran and Gregorian Universities in Rome. He became *Wyszynski's secretary in 1967, and was appointed Bishop of Warmia in 1979. He succeeded Wyszynski in 1981, and subsequently tried to mediate between *Solidarność and the government led by *Jaruzelski. In this way, Glemp inadvertently acquired a greater political role for himself and the Roman *Catholic Church. After the fall of *Communism, he tried desperately to halt the growing secularization of society. He opposed, for instance, liberalization of legislation on *abortion. Glemp supported the continued political involvement of the Church, in favour of market reforms and accession into the EU.

globalization

Overview The growing interconnectedness between political, social, and economic systems beyond national or regional borders. The international regulation of politics, and the global conduct of commerce and finance, is as old as the establishment of individual states. New developments towards the end of the twentieth century were characterized by: (1) the accelerating pace of communication through the worldwide web and satellite systems. (2) the spread of more global cultures of consumerism and popular culture; (3) the internationalization of domestic problems, e.g. through migration and social movements; (4) the apparent victory of capitalism after 1989, as a result of which the world (exceptions like North Korea notwithstanding) was organized according to similar principles of political economy; (5) a culture of dramatic innovation and fluctuation at the workplace, which caused a great sense of dislocation as jobs and social systems were no longer secure.

Contemporary history Globalization has worked in complex ways. Instead of signalling a victory of cosmopolitan internationalism, it promoted local identities and nationalist movements, which provided comforting, traditional contexts in a world of rapid change. Globalization accounted for the international repercussions of national crises as diverse as the Asian economic crisis of 1997, the *Bosnian Civil War, and the *War on Terrorism. And yet, in each case only national actors proved sufficiently effective in overcoming these challenges. Conversely, the importance of national actors transformed, but did not replace, the role of international actors, notably the *UN. The position especially of the UN, but also of bodies like the *African Union and the *EU as independent arbiters in international and domestic conflicts has become more important than ever.

Despite the opportunities it has provided for economic growth and prosperity, globalization has had ambiguous results. The diminution of national barriers has enabled dramatic economies of scale amongst the wealthier nations, which have benefited both from the comparative advantages of their economies, and from the fact that the global economic system has been most conducive to their economic systems. The USA has been the principal beneficiary of the globalization of its economic and political models. Western Europe, and its response to globalization in the form of the EU, has benefited greatly also. Parts of Asia such as the south-east have also gained, as they were able to adapt to capitalism and the communications revolution towards the end of the twentieth century. On the whole, and with huge variations, Latin American countries have neither gained nor lost particularly from the accelerated pace of globalization. By contrast, Africa has suffered dramatically since its component states acquired independence from the late 1950s. With the possible exception of South Africa and Egypt, it has been completely left behind by the advent of a global economy, with many of its domestic conflicts fuelled by international—especially oil—companies. Its populations have suffered disproportionately from diseases such as *AIDS, while a disproportionate number of people have remained uneducated and undernourished. Despite initiatives such as the *HIPC, overall most of Africa has suffered rather than benefited from globalization.

Goa

A small Portuguese colony on the Indian subcontinent between 1510 and 1961. Neglected by the Portuguese, it was incorporated into India after brief military action. It became a state of the Union in May 1987, with three elected Members of Parliament.

Goebbels, Joseph (b. 29 Oct. 1897, d. 1 May 1945). Nazi propaganda minister 1933–45 After finishing his studies in literature, art history, and philosophy with a doctorate, he joined the *Nazi Party in 1924, and was made the party leader of the Berlin and Brandenburg area in 1926, when he demonstrated his exceptional talents for demagoguery. In 1929 *Hitler made him the party head of *propaganda. As Minister of Public Enlightenment and Propaganda, he created a cult around Hitler and the myth of his infallibility through skilful use of the new means of mass communication, radio and film. Whereas until 1939 he was careful to demonstrate the new glory of Nazi Germany to Germans and the international community alike, after the defeat of *Stalingrad in early 1943 he successfully aroused stiff defiance and a stubborn belief among Germans that ultimately Hitler would overcome the enemy.

He committed suicide after witnessing Hitler's own suicide hours before.

Goering, Hermann (b. 12 Jan. 1893, d. 15 Oct. 1946). German Nazi leader

A successful fighter pilot during World War I, he became the commander of Baron von *Richthofen's fighter-plane squadron. Goering joined the *Nazi Party in 1922 and was wounded during the *Hitler Putsch of 1923, though he managed to escape to Austria. He returned in 1926, and became an MP in 1928 and Speaker of parliament in 1932. In 1933 he became Minister without Portfolio and also Minister President of *Prussia, a position which he used to crush all opposition to *Hitler within the state. His responsibilities included the rearmament of the air force (*Luftwaffe*), becoming supreme commander in 1935. In 1936, he was put in charge of the economy and was responsible for carrying out Hitler's orders to prepare it for war within four years. Though immensely influential and considered Hitler's natural successor in the early years of the *Third Reich, he lost influence during the war. The air force failed to prevent incessant air raids on German cities, though this did little to diminish his pomposity or his drug addiction. He was sentenced to death at the *Nuremberg Trials but committed suicide before his execution.

Golan Heights

A mountainous area in south-east Syria, just along the Israeli border. Over 6,000 feet (2,000 metres) high, they are of enormous strategic importance as they make possible the military control of northern Israel up to Haifa and beyond, as well as southern Syria up to Damascus. They were occupied by Israel after the *Six Day War from 1967, the population of around 130,000 was expelled, and new Jewish settlements were founded to claim the area permanently for Israel. They are an important source of water, and provide 50 per cent of the water supply for Israel's deserts. The Heights were annexed in 1981, though this was not internationally recognized. After Israel's recognition of the *PLO, their occupation by Israel remained the biggest stumbling block to a lasting peace with Syria. Negotiations were taken up in 1999, but ended inconclusively following the breakdown of the *Oslo Accords and the *Wye Agreement. From the mid-1990s, the Israeli government encouraged Jewish settlers to move to the Golan Heights. By 2006, around 20,000 Jewish settlers lived next to 20,000 Arabs.

Gold Coast, see GHANA

Gold Standard

A financial system in which the currency was pegged to the price of gold, so that one currency unit always bought the same amount of gold. Since the amount of gold in supply and demand was relatively constant, currency values were fixed, as were exchange rates. After it had been introduced in the UK in 1821, it was used by most economically advanced countries until the period between the two World Wars. However, a fixed currency does not necessarily reflect the real value of a currency, which is determined by inflation and interest rates. This growing disparity had already put a strain on the Gold Standard before 1914. Owing to the explosion of government activity during the First World War, governments needed to print money very quickly. This forced up interest rates and inflation, causing the Gold Standard to collapse in most European countries. Despite tremendous national debts after the war, efforts were made to reintroduce the Gold Standard, such as in the UK (1925–31) and France (1926–36). However, since government activity continued to expand, through the provision of social welfare and the active regulation of the economy, the Gold Standard became increasingly untenable. It was abandoned by the USA under President *Roosevelt in 1933.

  BRETTON WOODS; ERM; EURO

Goldstein, Vida Mary Jane (b. 13 Apr. 1869, d. 15 Aug. 1949). Australian feminist and suffragist

Born at Portland (Victoria) of a suffragist mother, she was educated privately and ran a coeducational primary school with her sisters, 1892–8. During this time, she became engaged in social work and in activity for the women's suffrage movement. In 1899, she was recognized as the leader of the radical women's movement in Victoria, and in 1902 she was elected secretary to the International Woman Suffrage Conference in the USA. Australian women were enfranchised in 1902, whereupon she became the first woman in the *British Empire to stand for election to national parliament. She concluded from her defeat that women needed better organization, which she pursued through the Women's Political Association and her newspaper, the *Women's Sphere*. She failed in four subsequent attempts to enter federal parliament, not just because of her sex. Voters were unimpressed by her failure to register with any party, her radicalism (e.g. her committed advocacy of pacifism during

World War I), and her unusual opposition to the *White Australia Policy. She nonetheless exerted much influence, advocating many advances in social welfare not just for women, such as the realization of equal property rights for men and women, and the *Harvester Judgment which established the principle of a minimum wage.

Goldwater, Barry Morris (b. 1 Jan. 1909, d. 29 Aug. 1998). US Senator 1953–65, 1969–87
Born at Phoenix, Arizona, he became a Senator for his home state and was *Republican candidate for President in 1964. Goldwater was identified with the radical right in the 1950s and 1960s and was the first important national figure to represent a prominent new republicanism. This included the demand for lowered taxes, *brinkmanship with the Soviet Union, and reduced government. Although he suffered a crushing defeat at the hands of Lyndon *Johnson in 1964 (losing 44 states and taking only 38 per cent of the popular vote), ultimately it was this new conservatism which underpinned the Republican presidencies of Richard *Nixon, Ronald *Reagan, and George *Bush.

Gomulka, Wladyslaw (b. 6 Feb. 1905, d. 1 Sept. 1982). First Secretary of the Polish United Workers' Party (and Polish leader) 1956–70
Born in Krosno (Austrian *Silesia), he became an active *trade unionist and joined the Polish Communist Party on its foundation in 1918. He was a member of the party's central committee from 1931. Gomulka was gaoled for his party activities (1932–4, 1936–9), and spent World War II working for the Polish underground resistance. In 1943, he became First Secretary of the Polish Workers' Party, and in 1945 was appointed *Bierut's deputy, responsible for the German territories under Polish administration. Unlike Bierut, he advocated the adaptation of *Marxism-Leninism to Polish conditions rather than the blind implementation of *Stalinism. This took him out of favour with Stalin and Bierut in 1948, when he was dismissed, but at the same time it enhanced his credibility to succeed Bierut once Stalinism was discredited in Moscow. His 'Polish way' to *Communism entailed a relatively free agricultural sector, toleration of the independence of the Roman *Catholic Church, and relatively great personal freedom (e.g. foreign travel). While emphasizing Poland's autonomy against the USSR, Gomulka was happy to send troops to suppress the *Prague Spring in 1968. In the end, however, the economy remained stifled and inefficient

through economic mismanagement and lack of incentive. His increase of the price of foodstuffs in 1970 caused widespread riots, leading to his replacement by *Gierek.

González Márquez, Felipe (b. 5 Mar. 1942). Prime Minister of Spain 1982–96
Early career Born in Seville, he studied law in Seville and Louvain (Belgium), where he joined the social democratic movement. He became a professor of labour law, and active in the outlawed Spanish *Socialist Party in 1965, advancing to become its executive secretary in 1970. In 1974, he became first secretary of the restored Partido Social Obrero Español (PSOE, Socialist Workers' Party of Spain), which was legalized after *Franco's death in 1975. He built up a strong party organization with close links to the *trade unions. At the 1977 elections the PSOE became the second largest party in parliament. A relentless critic of *Suárez, he benefited from the latter's inability to cope with the country's economic problems, from numerous and increasing divisions among the right, and from the uncertainties hanging over the political system after the military coup attempt of 1981.

In office Thanks to his overwhelming charm and charisma, the PSOE won an absolute majority in 1982. Under his leadership, the party won the elections of 1986 and 1990 with absolute majorities, while from 1994 he was forced to rule with the help of the Catalan and *Basque nationalists. He successfully sought to integrate the country into the EEC, and subsequently became one of the major proponents of further *European integration. As such, he benefited from his friendship with the socialist veteran, *Brandt, and from increasingly good relations with *Kohl. He promoted further autonomy for the various regions, so that by 22 February 1983, there were seventeen autonomous regions with their own parliamentary institutions. He liberalized the country's social laws (e.g. on *abortion), and improved labour conditions through the introduction of a forty-hour working week.

In the mid-1980s, González tried to consolidate the improvement of the economy (and reduce state debt) through a tighter fiscal policy, which triggered the opposition of much of the labour movement. Throughout his government, he has sought to end the violence of the Basque terrorist organization, ETA, through the dual strategy of tough police action and negotiations. Excessively brutal police action against ETA and allegations of a subsequent cover-up led to growing opposition to his increasingly autocratic style of leadership in the 1990s. He lost the 1996 elections to *Aznar owing to the unpopularity and the exhaustion of the PSOE after fourteen years of rule. Yet he had lost none of his personal appeal, which alone ensured a very respectable showing for his party, against all predictions.

Good Friday Agreement (10 April 1998)

An agreement on *Northern Ireland which proved the centrepiece of a fragile and often interrupted peace process begun under John *Major in 1993. It prescribed a complex system of government for Northern Ireland, which received internal self-government under a First Minister. The members of the Northern Irish government were to receive the support of the Protestant and Catholic deputies, and important legislative decisions were also to be supported by at least 40 per cent of the Catholic and Protestant deputies respectively. The United Kingdom repealed the Government of Ireland Act of 1920 which determined the partition of Ireland. In return, the Irish people voted to repeal Article 4 of the Irish Constitution, which determined the eventual unification of Ireland. For the first time, the Republic of Ireland gained a direct say in the affairs of Northern Ireland, through membership of the 'Council of the Isles' which would also contain representatives of *Wales, *Scotland, and the Isle of Man. The Good Friday Agreement was approved in Northern Ireland with over 70 per cent of the popular vote, including a majority of both Protestants and Catholics.

The agreement was possible because Tony *Blair's clear majority in parliament, and the fewer historic ties between *Labour and the Protestant *Ulster Unionist Party made Blair appear less biased to the Catholic minority. At the same time, Bill *Clinton's acceptance of Gerry *Adams strengthened the latter's hand against the IRA, and allowed him to declare a cease-fire while keeping the majority of the IRA behind him.

Unfortunately, some of the most controversial questions were left in the Agreement, notably the question of the decommissioning of arms (largely a Protestant concern) and the reform of the police force, the Royal Ulster Constabulary (a Catholic concern). Failure to agree on these issues led to a suspension of the Northern Ireland Assembly in 2000 and from 2001. Genuine progress on the decommissioning of arms was only made following the *September 11 attacks. As part of the *War on Terrorism, the US was in no mood to tolerate the continuation of illicit arms depots by the IRA. Under threat from the withdrawal of US

funds, and in order to encourage the resumption of self-rule, Sinn Féin agreed to the destruction of its weapons in 2001, which an independent commission declared to be complete in 2005. The *Democratic Unionist Party demanded a dissolution of the IRA, however, thus blocking the resumption of parliamentary self-rule. The Agreement was revived in 2006 by the *St Andrews Agreement.

Good Neighbor Policy (USA)

A term used to describe the US Latin America policy of Secretary of State Cordell *Hull during the first term of President F. D. *Roosevelt. Based on the principle that no country has the right to intervene in the affairs of another, it reversed the *Roosevelt Corollary. It was implemented by the withdrawal of US marines from such countries as Haiti and Nicaragua and the abrogation of the Platt Amendment, which had given the US government a quasi-protectorate over Cuba. While it created much better relations between the USA and Latin America, the USA continued to follow Latin American affairs closely, and US influence reached a new high during and after World War II.

PAN-AMERICANISM

GOP (Grand Old Party), see REPUBLICAN PARTY

Gorbachev, Mikhail Sergeevich (b. 2 Mar. 1931). General Secretary of the Communist Party of the Soviet Union 1985–91

Early career Born in Privolnoye near Stavropol (northern Caucasus) of a peasant family, the successful pupil and farm worker was sponsored by his local party to be educated at Moscow University in law and then at the Stavropol Agricultural Institute. He was active in the Communist Youth League (Komsomol), and joined the *Communist Party in 1952. He graduated from Moscow in 1955 with the highest marks, and returned to Stavropol, where he began a rapid rise within Komsomol and the regional Communist Party. In 1970, he became regional first secretary of the party.

In 1971 Gorbachev became a member of the Central Committee of the Soviet Communist Party. There, he was noted not just for his intelligence, but also for his sternness and his reliability. In 1979, he became a non-voting member of the *Politburo, and in 1980 he became a full member of the country's highest political body, in charge of agriculture. He failed to make a particular impact in this post, but he did come to the attention of *Andropov. As party leader, Andropov put Gorbachev in charge of the entire economy. Though the more senior *Chernenko was chosen in 1984 to succeed Andropov, he was able to expand his responsibilities to include party matters and ideology, as well as foreign policy. Despite considerable opposition on account of his relative youth, he became leader of the party on 11 March 1985.

Soviet leader Gorbachev used his early popularity to bring like-minded reformers into the Politburo within a few years, thus steadily increasing his own power base. He first concentrated his reformist efforts on foreign relations, where he replaced the long-serving Andrei Gromyko (b. 1909, d. 1989) with his own protégé, *Shevardnadze, as Foreign Minister in 1985. Relations with the USA, which had been at a low ebb since the Soviet invasion of Afghanistan in 1979, were improved, and he enjoyed more frequent meetings with a US President (i.e. *Reagan and *Bush) than any other Soviet leader.

In domestic politics, Gorbachev had a more difficult start. His clumsy handling of the *Chernobyl disaster of April 1986 was still very much in line with his predecessors' grasp of public relations. In the summer of 1986, he embarked on his twin strategies to reform the Communist state, *glasnost (opening) and *perestroika (restructuring). Moreover, the Supreme *Soviet, which used to lie dormant for most of the year, was given an enhanced role more like that of a parliament, whose members were chosen in contested elections (though they were still members of the Communist Party). With many of his old-guard opponents thus deselected, these reforms consolidated his own power. At the same time, his domestic popularity began to fall as the economic situation deteriorated. Gorbachev had freed the economy of old regulations, but had shied away from drastic capitalist reform. As a result, the economy found itself in a state of limbo between the old Communist world and Western *capitalism, an uncertainty that led to the worst of both worlds. He was also unsettled by the growth of *nationalism among the different ethnic peoples of the Soviet Union, unleashed by glasnost. It was a development whose ferocity he had clearly not foreseen, as his violent repression of the independence movements of the Baltic States (Estonia, Latvia, and Lithuania) showed.

The break-up of the Soviet Empire While he aroused the disappointed anger of radical reformers like *Yeltsin, and the determined self-assertion of the country's national minorities, Gorbachev also angered hardliners and the military, partly through his reforms at home, but also because of their effects abroad. Having modelled their political systems closely upon that of the Soviet Union for forty years, it became impossible for the Eastern European hardline leaders such as *Honecker or *Husák to prevent demands for glasnost and perestroika in their own countries, hard though they tried. In contrast to its previous role, the Soviet army was forced to stand by idly as the Soviet Empire in Eastern Europe collapsed in 1988–9. His promotion of peaceful political transition in Eastern Europe brought him the award of the *Nobel Peace Prize in succession to dissidents like *Walesa; to the military and Communist hardliners, this was the final confirmation of a world gone mad.

Gorbachev's dependence on *Yeltsin to break the *August coup revealed the true decline of his popularity. It was Yeltsin who negotiated the breakup of the USSR into the *CIS, which undermined Gorbachev's function as head of state of the USSR. He resigned on 25 December 1991, a week before the USSR ceased to exist. Thereafter, he continued to enjoy popularity in the West on numerous lecture tours, but his bad showing in the 1996 Russian presidential elections, in which he gained 0.51 per cent of the popular vote, was another confirmation of his genuine domestic unpopularity.

Gore, Albert Jr ('Al') (b. 31 Mar. 1948). US Vice-President 1993–2001

Born at Carthage, Tennessee, into a political family (his father was a non-racialist US Senator who had voted against southern segregation), he studied religion and law at Vanderbilt University and Harvard. After service in Vietnam he was first elected to *Congress in 1976, into the House of Representatives. As Senator for Tennessee (1985–93) he was associated with environmental issues and foreign affairs. He ran for the *Democrat nomination for President in the 1988 *primary elections. His telegenic looks were not complemented by his uninspiring, 'wooden' speaking style, and he lost the nomination to Michael Dukakis. Following an accident which severely injured his son he decided not to run for President in 1992, but was persuaded to serve as the vice-presidential nominee alongside Bill *Clinton.

Gore contributed greatly to Clinton's success, as his war service and his reputation for solidity and moral conservatism in a crucial way made up for Clinton's lack of these attributes, whilst his intellect and youth reinforced these qualities in Clinton. One of the most influential Vice-Presidents in US history, he won his party's nomination for the 2000 election campaign. Al Gore scored the second highest number of votes ever polled for a candidate in US history to date (after Ronald Reagan in1984). However, he had to concede reluctantly to a *Bush election victory because his rival, George W. *Bush, had a majority in the electoral college.

Ironically for someone who had been hampered by his inability to connect to the public, Gore became a popular figure after his vice-presidency, as a tireless campaigner against global warming and for the *Kyoto accord. Gore's documentary, *An Inconvenient Truth* (2006), became a box-office success and won an Oscar for best documentary.

Gottwald, Klement (b. 23 Nov. 1896, d. 14 Mar. 1953). President of Czechoslovakia 1948–53

Born in Dedice (Moravia), he fought in the *Austro-Hungarian army in World War I. He became a founder member of the Czechoslovak Communist Party in 1921. A proponent of its radical wing, he joined its Central Committee in 1925, and became its General Secretary in 1929. He made the party more amenable to *Stalin, but lost a lot of popular support for the party as a result. He spent World War II in Moscow, and returned in 1945 to form a national front government, whose leader he became in 1946. Though initially dominant, the Communists lost support following Soviet refusal to allow Czechoslovak acceptance of *Marshall Aid. Gottwald thus led a *coup* in February 1948, which firmly entrenched Communist power. Unable to stand up to *Stalin, he agreed to wide-scale purges culminating in the *Slánski trial, which vastly increased Soviet control over the Czechoslovak Communist Party.

Goulart, João (b. 1 Mar. 1918, d. 6 Dec. 1976). President of Brazil 1961–4

Born in Rio Grande do Sul, he became a lawyer and joined the nationalist right-wing Social Democratic Party. He was Minister of Labour (1953–4), and served as *Vargas's Vice-President 1955–61. An incompetent politician whose prominence rested largely on the patronage of Vargas, he was unable to avoid his country's economic decline as indicated by an annual inflation rate of over 100 per cent and economic growth of merely 2 per cent. His period in office saw the polarization of Brazilian society into various hostile factions and interest groups. Opposed by most Governors of the federal states, his challenge to the elites through the

nationalization of oil refineries and other populist measures triggered a little-resisted military *coup* in 1964.

Government of India Acts (1919, 1935)
Two British Acts of *Parliament which determined the structure of government in India. They were created with the aim of appeasing Indian *nationalism and preventing India's eventual independence. In this sense, their outcome was completely the opposite of what had been intended. The controversy surrounding them agitated the Indian National *Congress (INC) even more, while their provision of greater Indian participation in government gave Indians the administrative and political experience for successful independent statehood. The Government of India Act (1919) established a bicameral legislative parliament for all British India, but without the power to restrain the Viceroy's executive. In the provinces, the Act aimed to prepare Indians for 'responsible government' through the system of *dyarchy.

This system of dyarchy was abolished by the Government of India Act (1935, implemented 1937), which gave the provincial assemblies full responsibility for government. It also removed Aden and Burma from the administration of British India. Finally, it proposed that the Indian Empire be transformed into a federal dominion, which would have included the princely states, though this section of the Act was never implemented. Though heavily criticized at the time, provincial assemblies gave the INC and the *Muslim League a crucial platform, and provided them with the opportunity to demonstrate their popularity for the first time in the 1937 popular elections. The 1935 Government of India Act remained the basis of government after independence, until the adoption of a new Constitution in India (1950) and Pakistan (1956).

Gowon, Yakubu (b. 19 Oct. 1934). Nigerian head of state 1966–76

Born in Lur Pankshim, he was a graduate of Zaria Government College and joined the Nigerian army. He attended the Royal Military College at Sandhurst (UK) and Camberley Staff College, and was appointed lieutenant-colonel in 1963. Not implicated in the *coup* of 15 January 1966, he became leader of the government following a second *coup* on 29 July 1966. He was immediately faced with the *Biafran War, which he had won by 1970. Keenly aware of the importance of international support, he had invited foreign observers to monitor his troops' conduct of the war. To make unity viable in the long run he insisted that the Biafra region was not to be punished, and Biafran soldiers be treated with respect. In 1970, he announced plans for an eventual return to civilian rule by 1976, though this was delayed in 1974. In 1976, while he was abroad, he was deposed in a bloodless *coup*. He has since lived mostly in England, graduating with a doctorate in political science from the University of Warwick.

Gramsci, Antonio (b. 22 Jan. 1891, d. 27 Apr. 1937). Italian Communist

Career Of Albanian origin, he was born in Cagliari and educated locally until 1911, when he received a scholarship at the University of Turin. He joined the Italian *Socialist Party (PSI) in 1913. In late 1915, he was writing for the national socialist newspaper, *Avanti!*, and by the end of World War I he had already established some of the tenets of his political views. Influenced by *Croce, he rejected positivism, determinism, and reformism, and emphasized the importance of the cultural struggle instead. Following Italy's domestic political disorder after World War I he hoped a socialist state would be established through the factory councils which paralysed the economic and political life of Turin, but which were ultimately crushed by *Giolitti.

Gramsci joined the Italian *Communist Party upon its foundation, but soon found himself in opposition to the rigid determinism of its general-secretary, Bordiga. Supported by instructions from Moscow, in 1922 he began to improve Communist organization and to encourage anti-Fascist cooperation among the left-wing parties, in opposition to Bordiga's intentions. By 1926, he was firmly in control of the party, though he failed in his efforts to hinder the establishment of a Fascist authoritarian state. In the same year, all non-Fascist parties were banned, while he was arrested on 8 November 1926. He died in prison.

Writings Gramsci's seminal importance to Communist ideology derives from his *Prison Notebooks* (1928–37), in which he reflected on why the Communist world revolution had failed to materialize. He argued that, contrary to traditional Marxist assumptions, in liberal democracies governments ruled mostly with general support. In other words, owing to historical, cultural, and religious factors which shaped people's perceptions, they were actually content with their own oppression. As a Marxist response, he advocated a sustained Communist campaign against the whole breadth of bourgeois institutions, leading to the eventual overthrow of the state and the establishment of a new socialist culture. Despite his insistence on the need for the masses to be guided by the Communist Party, he none the less advocated much greater mass involvement in the Communist movement. The party's most important task was to combine Communist theory and practice, i.e. to seek the combination of intellectual assiduity and revolutionary zeal (the 'pessimism of the intellect and optimism of the will'). His ideas had a tremendous influence on the Communist parties which operated in relative independence from Moscow, e.g. in Italy, France, and various South American countries.

MARXISM; TROTSKYISM; EUROCOMMUNISM

Grand Old Party (GOP), see REPUBLICAN PARTY

Great Britain

The largest of the British Isles, it is composed of *England, *Wales, and *Scotland. It is popularly (though incorrectly) used as a synonym for the *United Kingdom of Great Britain and *Northern Ireland (Ireland until 1922).

Great Leap Forward (1958–60)

An attempt by *Mao Zedong to galvanize Chinese agriculture, and thus release forces for the growth of heavy industry envisaged by the first five-year plan (1953–8). Agriculture was to be revolutionized, e.g. through the reorganization of collectives of a few hundred households into communes with around 50,000 people each. Private plots were abolished to encourage work in state agriculture. Through these efficiency drives, millions were released to work in industry, in order to fulfil Mao's pledge to increase steel production by 15 per cent every year, in order to overtake British steel production by 1973. The campaign backfired, with disastrous consequences. Given the intense pressure to report productivity increases, reported efficiency gains were more apparent than real. The building of around one million backyard furnaces by around sixty million people was nothing short of economic folly, and led to the production of unwanted goods of shoddy quality. In total, agriculture was deprived of around 20 per cent of its labour force within two years. By 1960, grain output had declined by over 40 per cent. Compounded by a series of natural catastrophes, this set off the greatest famine in twentieth-century history. In 1960 alone, an estimated ten million people died, while in total, between sixteen and twenty-seven million people died of hunger.

Great Purge (1936–8, USSR)

After coming to power in 1924 against *Lenin's wishes, *Stalin confirmed his position as leader of the *Communist Party and the Soviet Union by using terror against his opponents, through exile, imprisonment, and execution. While his position had thus become relatively secure in the late 1920s, the hardships of the first five-year plan increased opposition to Stalin, both within the party and within the country at large. At the 1934 party conference many began to turn their attention towards *Kirov as an alternative, more moderate leader. Shortly afterwards, Kirov was murdered, presumably on the orders of Stalin himself. Stalin used this incident to round up many of his opponents, while placing many of his supporters in key positions: *Khrushchev became Moscow party secretary, *Vyshinsky was made chief prosecutor, and *Yezhov became head of the *NKVD. With the reorganization of the forced labour system through the formation of GULAG (Main Administration of Corrective Labour Camps) in place from 1930, everything was ready for the Great Purge itself (or 'Yezhovshchina' after Yezhov) to begin in summer 1936.

Brutality climaxed as Stalin put his authority beyond question. On the surface, it was marked by televised, 'educational' show trials of senior Communists such as *Zinoviev, *Kamenev, and *Bukharin, all of whom were forced under torture to confess invented charges, sentenced, and executed. In this way, almost 70 per cent of the Communist Party Central Committee and 50 per cent of the Party Congress were executed or died in labour camps; 35,000 *Red Army officers were tried, among them 80 per cent of its colonels, 90 per cent of its generals, and all of its deputy commissioners of war. The total number of dead is unclear, but lies probably in the middle of the range of estimates between one and ten million people. With the party, military, economy, and society completely exhausted, it ended in late 1938, though Stalin's terror continued in other forms until his death.

Great Society (USA)

The name bestowed by Lyndon *Johnson on his vision of an American society with fair educational, health, and social provision for all. Johnson developed the theme in the 1964 election campaign, which he won by a landslide against Barry *Goldwater. Johnson presented a programme to *Congress comprising a 'war on poverty', medical insurance underwritten by the state for all old people and a majority of younger people, particularly the poor, housing developments,

and educational provision. It redefined government responsibility for these goals through the creation of the Office of Economic Opportunity and the Department of Housing and Urban Development. Some of the most important legislation concerned education. The Elementary and Secondary Education Act of 1965 proposing a more effective funding formula for schools, while the Higher Education Act sought to encourage College access irrespective of social background. This legislation was accompanied by the introduction of large, publicly funded health programmes for the poor, Medicaid and *Medicare. Other lasting changes included the introduction of food stamp provisions for the poor, while the federal government also became involved in culture through the National Endowments for the Arts and the Humanities and the Public Broadcasting Act.

The 'Great Society' programme was accompanied by lasting *civil rights legislation. However, many of these reforms cost Johnson much political capital, as the *Watts riots and other civil disturbances helped cause a White backlash against the perceived privileges of welfare recipients. Most importantly, the *Vietnam War devastated Johnson's political reputation and absorbed national attention and funds. Much of Johnson's legislation came under attack in subsequent decades, and it is not clear that his vision of a 'Great Society' was ever achieved. However, his domestic record was remarkable for its sheer scope, as well as for the President's ability to drive his legislation through *Congress.

Great War, the, see WORLD WAR I

Greater East Asian Co-prosperity Sphere

A blueprint for Asia proposed by the Japanese government during World War II, both in an attempt to excite Asian *nationalism and to justify its military conquests in the region. Japan's promotion of a sphere from which the European powers were to be excluded was viewed by the *Allies as thinly disguised *propaganda to serve Japan's aggressive purposes in the region. However, for some Asian nationalists, Japan's establishment of a new order in Asia did win some sympathy, and a number of groups, particularly in Burma and Indonesia, cooperated with the Japanese in the belief that this would enable them to become free from European colonialism. In *Indochina the *Vichy French authorities collaborated, with the Indochinese nationalist movement (*Vietminh) turning more towards Communism. In Malaya the Communist Malayan People's Anti-Japanese Army was opposed to occupation from the start, as was the Philippine *Hukbalahap movement. In Burma and Indonesia early cooperation gradually turned into opposition, as the use of forced labour and the requisitioning of supplies produced resentment. The idea of a Greater East Asian Co-prosperity Sphere itself did not have universal applicability. At the Greater East Asian Conference in November 1943, delegates from Japan's allies in China, *Manchukuo, Burma, and the Philippines were invited to Tokyo to discuss Asia's future. Noticeably absent, however, were such countries as Korea, which Japan regarded as an integral colony.

Greece

The cradle of European civilization, Greece has seen its modern history being shaped by long-time geopolitical fragility, which gave way, from the late 1970s, to political stability and economic growth through *European integration.

Territorial transformations (up to 1923) Independent since 1829, it aimed at territorial extension to claim historic Greek provinces. In the late nineteenth century, a policy of extensive infrastructural, military, and economic investment, as well as gains in administrative efficiency, plunged the state into large international debt. At the same time, this provided the basis for its victory in the two *Balkan Wars (1912–13), as a result of which Greece doubled its territory. During World War I a fundamental constitutional, political, and social conflict erupted about the stance Greece should take. While the Germanophile King, Constantine I, insisted on his country's strict neutrality, his liberal government advocated joining the war on the side of the *Allies. The King dismissed his ministers, who proceeded to form an alternative government in opposition to him. Given this domestic instability, external pressures from the Allies and the *Central Powers made neutrality increasingly difficult to maintain. In 1916, Allied troops entered Greece in support of the liberal government, and forced the King into exile.

After World War I, under the Peace Treaty of *Sèvres, Greece gained its greatest territorial expansion in the nineteenth and twentieth

centuries, when it came to occupy significant areas of Asia Minor. It was forced to surrender these in the campaign of Kemal (*Atatürk) in the Greco-Turkish War of 1921–2. The Treaty of *Lausanne resulted not just in territorial losses to Turkey. A population 'exchange' led to the expulsion of most Turks living on Greek territory, while in return Greece was faced with the integration of over one million Greeks expelled from Turkey. It achieved this integration through a large redistribution of land. This destroyed large landholdings and created a large group of small landowners, who continued to be the backbone of the Greek economy for the remainder of the century.

Between two World Wars (1920–49) In the interwar years, politics continued to oscillate between monarchial government, restored 1920–4, and republican government, reintroduced 1924–35. In 1935, following the election victory of the royalist parties in 1933, a plebiscite resulted in the reintroduction of the monarchy. The royalist leader, *Metaxas, became provisional head of government before being granted dictatorial powers. Even though the country had been riven with political instability compounded by the Great *Depression, Metaxas managed to re-establish some stability. Indeed, Metaxas's reforms were effective enough to enable Greece successfully to repel *Mussolini's invasion in 1940. Unfortunately, this triggered an invasion by German (together with Italian and Bulgarian) troops in 1941. The brutality of the occupation forces led to the quick growth of the active resistance movement, *ELAS.

Towards the end of the occupation, as victory came closer, the resistance movement was increasingly split between its Communist and non-Communist wings. This erupted into a bloody civil war following the defeat of the Germans in 1944, a conflict fuelled by the tensions between the US and the USSR in the emerging *Cold War. The war, which was in full force 1946–49, led to the Communists' eventual defeat. This was brought about by the end of Yugoslav assistance to the Communists, and by *Truman's determination to fund lavishly the Greek anti-Communist forces in order to stop Soviet expansionism as laid out in the *Truman Doctrine.

Political instability (1949–74) In subsequent years Greek politics remained unstable, with the role of the monarchy unresolved and as contentious as ever, and an even stronger role for the victorious military. Relations with its Communist neighbours continued to be uneasy, while its relationship with Turkey was fraught with tension. The only way the

Greek government, under the major influence of *Karamanlis, Georgios *Papandreou, and, later, Andreas *Papandreou, managed to cope with these difficulties was through rapidly expanding the state to embrace and bring into its fold the various polarized social groups. By contrast, Communists and other groups deemed to be 'extremist' were excluded from this social pact, partly through illegal and corrupt means. This system managed to keep social and political polarization beneath the surface, but did not tackle the role of the monarchy or the army. Differences over the rights of the crown led to a series of constitutional conflicts with Kings Paul I and Constantine II from 1963.

Disagreement about the power of the monarchy in the military, and impending army reforms designed to reduce the military's role as supreme actor on the political scene, led to an army coup in 1967, and the establishment of the *Greek colonels' government. Their administration was even more inefficient than that of their predecessors, while their flagrant *human rights violations increased internal opposition. In 1974, the government made the disastrous decision to annex *Cyprus through a coup against *Makarios III, which was foiled by the invasion of Turkish troops there. In response, the Greek colonels were forced to make way for the reintroduction of democratic rule under Karamanlis. In retaliation against King Constantine's initial support for the Greek colonels, 69.2 per cent voted in a plebiscite of 8 December 1974 for the abolition of the monarchy.

European integration (from the 1970s)
With army and monarchy thus discredited, politics entered a more stable phase. Karamanlis continued to dominate politics in the 1970s, successfully steering Greece towards entry of the EEC in May 1979 (effective from 1 January 1981).

Under Andreas Papandreou's government, however, the funds flowing in from the EEC, as well as the USA, were not used to introduce greater efficiency into the economy. Unlike Spain or Portugal, which had similar economic structures at the time, the 1980s did not see an expansion of the country's industrial base. The economic realm reflected the dominance in the political sphere of patronage and nepotism, stifling private initiative. As the economy remained in the control of around two dozen families, a black economy developed which by 1996 produced perhaps as much as half of the country's wealth.

Contemporary politics (since 1996) In January 1996 Papandreou was succeeded by the commercial lawyer Costas Simitis (b. 1936). He aimed at integrating the country more closely with the West, while introducing badly needed political and economic market reform. Simitis received a popular mandate for these reforms in elections in 1996 and (with a reduced majority) in 2000. Economic growth had picked up to over 3 per cent per year 1998–2000. Moreover, Simitis's reforms had been sufficiently successful for Greece to meet the criteria for entry into *EMU. For this reason, Greece was the twelfth country to enter into the *euro-zone on 1 January 2001. In the late 1990s, there was a marked improvement in relations with Turkey. While disputes about territorial borders and Cyprus remained, a number of agreements were reached to allow Turkey to apply for membership of the EU. In 2004, Simitis was succeeded by Kostas Karamanlis, a nephew of the former Prime Minister. Greece continued to have strong economic growth rates, though Karamanlis struggled to reduce unemployment and public debt.

Greek colonels
The military regime of Greece, 1967–74. It was brought about by a military coup on 21 April 1967, ostensibly in order to secure Greece against a Communist takeover. They filled the government, administration, and military with their own supporters, who were ill-qualified to run the country. Administrative chaos was papered over by repression, censorship, and the violation of *human rights. The divisions within the military junta were exposed in 1973, when the leader of the regime, Georgios Papadopoulos, was deposed in a coup of 1973 by Brigadier Dimitrios Ionanides. Harassed by international pressure and internal demonstrations, he attempted in 1974 to stir nationalist support in his attempt to overthrow Archbishop *Makarios III of Cyprus. This led directly to the Turkish invasion of the island and its subsequent division. The regime became untenable, forcing Ionanides to ask *Karamanlis to supervise a return to democratic rule.

Green Party, Germany
Founded as a national party in 1980 following the merger of local environmental groups, it won 5.6 per cent of the popular vote in the national elections of 1983. It has been represented in the German parliament ever since (with the exception of 1990–4), vying with the *Liberal Party to be the third

strongest party nationwide. In 1993 it merged with the East German Greens and the Bündnis "90, a party which emerged out of the *Neues Forum in 1990. As a result of its participation in several German state governments from 1985, the party's policies have become more pragmatic, while its continued strength has forced the other German parties to formulate their own environmental policies to an unusual degree. The party's pragmatism paid off in the 1998 elections, when it gained 47 parliamentary seats. As a junior partner in the government of *Schröder, the party reversed many of its earlier policies, including the military engagement of German troops overseas. Owing to the unpopularity of the Schröder government, the party lost support in the federal and state parliaments, so that by 2007 it was no longer part of any governing coalition.

(((⊕))) SEE WEB LINKS

• The official website of the Green Party, Germany.

Green Revolution

A term used to describe the increased agricultural productivity due to new agricultural methods such as pesticides, irrigation, and better tools. As part of the Green Revolution, more resistant crops were developed, such as the rice variety IR-36, produced by the UN International Rice Research Institute in 1976, which became one of the world's most widely grown crops in the 1980s. While the Green Revolution increased the food supply for a growing population in the developing world, it also increased income inequality through favouring capital-intensive farming methods.

Greenland (Kalaalit Nunaat, 'Land of the People')

The world's largest island, inhabited by a total of around 56,000 people (2000), came under Norwegian authority in 1261, though its Viking settlements were subsequently abandoned. It was resettled by Europeans from 1721, and in 1776 it came under the direct control of the Danish state. It remained under Danish authority after the separation between Denmark and Norway in 1815, but was subject to rival Norwegian claims. Only in 1933, after an abortive Norwegian attempt at annexation in 1931, was the matter settled in

Denmark's favour by the International Court of Justice in the Hague.

Greenland's position between North America and Europe became strategically important during World War II, when the USA founded a number of air force bases there (1941) in support of the Battle of the *Atlantic. Throughout the *Cold War, its *NATO air force bases were to be an important source for the island's economy (next to fisheries). Danish efforts in 1953 to make it an integral part of Denmark remained deeply unpopular, as did other Danish attempts at 'modernization'. Autonomy was eventually granted in 1979, with a parliament (Landsting) having control over internal matters. Concern over fishing rights led to a referendum in which the majority of the population voted to terminate membership of the EEC (which had been automatic from Denmark's entry in 1973), with effect from 1 January 1985. Despite the desire of the largely Inuit population for independence from Denmark, Danish aid continued to be a crucial factor for Greenland's economy. In 1998, direct Danish transfer payments amounted to 125 per cent of the total value of its exports, or two-thirds of the Greenland government's total revenues.

Greenpeace

The world's largest environmental campaign organization, with 2.8 million supporters registered in forty countries worldwide. It was founded in 1971 in British Columbia (Canada) to organize protests against US nuclear testing at Amchitka Island, Alaska. It has campaigned against nuclear testing, whaling, and the dumping of toxic and radioactive waste. Its methods have been direct and spectacular to attract maximum media attention, but always non-violent. Despite this, in 1985 its ship *Rainbow Warrior was sunk by French intelligence agents off New Zealand.

(((⊕))) SEE WEB LINKS

• The official website of Greenpeace.

Grenada

An island state in the eastern Caribbean which came under British sovereignty in 1763. It became the administrative centre for the Windward Islands Colony (including St Lucia, St Vincent, and Dominica)

in 1885. Universal adult suffrage was introduced in 1951, and in 1958 Grenada became a member of the Federation of the *West Indies. When the latter was dissolved in 1962, it became an independent state 'associated' with Britain in 1967, before it became fully independent on 7 February 1974. In 1979 the Labour government was overthrown by Maurice Bishop, who ruled at the head of a People's Revolutionary Government. Following his assassination in 1983, the USA intervened, as President *Reagan was concerned about the advance of *Communism on the island. Constitutional government was resumed in 1984, first by Herbert Blaize (b. 1918, d. 1989) of the conservative New National Party (NNP) coalition, and then (in 1990) by Nicholas Brathwaite of the National Democratic Congress. In the elections of 20 June 1995, however, the NNP recovered to gain a parliamentary majority under Keith Mitchell, which it extended in the 1999 elections, when it won all the seats in parliament. Grenada continued to be heavily reliant on tourism, with agricultural exports (bananas and a quarter of the world's nutmeg production) being the most important export goods. Mitchell, who oversaw a significant rise in prosperity, was re-elected with a reduced majority in 2003. In 2004, the island's buildings and infrastructure were severely damaged by a hurricane.

Grey, Edward, 3rd Baronet and 1st Viscount Grey of Falloden (b. 25 Apr. 1862, d. 7 Sept. 1933). British Foreign Secretary 1905–16

Born in London, and educated at Winchester and Oxford. He entered parliament in 1885 for the *Liberal Party, representing Berwick upon Tweed. In the government of Lord Rosebery, he served as under-secretary to the foreign office. As a Liberal Imperialist, he strongly supported Britain's effort in the *South African (Boer) War, but *Campbell-Bannerman still appointed him as Foreign Secretary in 1905. Grey was responsible for the *Anglo-Russian Entente of 1907, and for negotiating an end to the Balkan War of 1912–13. In 1914 he persuaded the British Cabinet to go to war, because Germany had violated Belgian neutrality. He lost office in 1916, when *Lloyd George formed a new government. After the war, he was a prominent supporter of the *League of Nations.

Griffith, Arthur (b. 31 Mar. 1871, d. 12 Aug. 1922). Irish journalist and statesman

Born in Dublin, he became a printer, but soon was active in republican politics, joining the Gaelic League and the Irish Republican Brotherhood. After a brief stint in South Africa (1896–8), he returned to Ireland to edit *The United Irishman*. In 1904 he published *The Resurrection of Hungary: A Parallel for Ireland*, arguing for passive resistance to British rule and the establishment of a native Irish government and judicial system. In 1905 he developed these separatist ideas under the banner *Sinn Féin ('we ourselves'), emphasizing national self-reliance. This threw him into direct opposition to John *Redmond and the Irish Parliamentary Party in Westminster, and to those who supported the Home Rule Bill of 1912. Griffith did not take part in the *Easter Rising of 1916, but was imprisoned under martial law for his republican journalism and remained in Reading gaol until 1917. The reaction to the execution of the Rising's leaders helped Griffith's *Sinn Féin become the major republican political movement during the Irish War of Independence. As Acting President of Dáil Éireann (the Irish parliament, not yet recognized as sovereign), he was the head of the Irish delegation to London to negotiate the end of the war. Unhappy with the treaty of 6 December 1921, which partitioned Ireland, he agreed to it as a temporary settlement that would lead to eventual unification. Griffith became president of Dáil Éireann on 10 January 1922, and in the ensuing civil war led the Free State government against the anti-treaty forces under *de Valéra until his sudden death in Dublin from a brain haemorrhage.

Gronchi, Giovanni (b. 10 Sept. 1887, d. 17 Oct. 1978). President of Italy 1955–62

One of the founders and leaders of the *Popular Party, he joined parliament after World War I. A member of *Mussolini's first government, he resigned in protest over the *Matteotti murder and led his party into the *Aventine Secession. In 1943 he helped found the *Christian Democrats (DC) and became one of their representatives in the *CLN. On the left wing of the party, he was Minister for Industry and Trade (1944–6), and in 1948 was elected president of the Chamber of Deputies. He was a widely respected Italian President, and continued to exert considerable influence after his retirement.

Grundlagenvertrag (Basic Treaty),
see GERMAN QUESTION

Guadeloupe

A group of islands in the Caribbean which have been under French sovereignty since 1635. It received the status of a French Overseas Department in 1946, and was recognized as a French region in 1974. It is legally an integral part of France, which provides most of its national income through trade, financial aid and public-sector salaries. The islands are represented in Paris by four Deputies in the National Assembly, as well as two Senators.

Guam

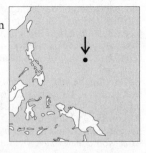

A Pacific island in *Micronesia. A US territory since 1898, it was an unincorporated territory governed by the US navy until 1950, except for the period 1941–4, when it was occupied by the Japanese. Civilian rule was established in an Organic Act of 1950, and in 1971 it received its first elected Governor, followed by a non-voting delegate to the US House of Representatives in 1972. It became autonomous in 1982. From 1995, it was headed by a *Democrat Governor, Carl Gutierrez, but he was replaced in 2003 with a *Republican, Felix Camacho.

Guandong (Kwantung) Army

The Japanese army in Manchuria which came into being after the *Russo-Japanese War, when Japan had assumed control over the southern tip of the Liaotung peninsula (including Port Arthur), which it renamed the Guandong Leased Territory in 1906. Together with the Japanese control over the Manchurian Railways, the Territory was administered by a Governor-General. This office was held by a military general, who simultaneously commanded the local army, until in 1919 it was occupied by a civilian, but without control over the Guandong Army. Subsequently, the army enjoyed an increasing amount of autonomy from political control, and even from the Japanese military establishment. Its leaders from 1928 and 1929 respectively, *Ishiwara Kanji and Itagaki

Seishiro, transformed it into an effective fighting force. Before even the radical Japanese command could order restraint, the Guandong Army proceeded to occupy Manchuria on 18 September 1931, declaring a puppet state of *Manchukuo in 1932. Thereafter, its strength grew from around 200,000 to a maximum of 700,000 troops. It retained much of its autonomy during the *Sino-Japanese War, and was dissolved at the end of World War II.

Guantanamo Bay

A bay in south-western Cuba, in which US marines landed in 1898 during the Cuban War of Independence. With independence from Spain achieved, Cuba was forced to accept the Platt Amendment in 1901, which gave the US a permanent right to intervene in Cuba's home affairs. In 1903 the Cuban government had little alternative but to accept the presence of the US Navy in Guantanamo, and the two sides agreed on a lease of the base. In 1934 the Platt Amendment was repealed, but in return the status of Guantanamo Bay was confirmed until both treaty signatories agreed on a change of status. Since *Castro was never prepared to risk his revolution by giving the US a pretext for open warfare, the US presence in Guantanamo persisted even after Castro's revolution in 1959.

Guantanamo Bay subsequently became a colony of about 6,000 people, sustained by heavy subsidies from the US government, which used the area as a front-line training ground for its marines. In 2002 it became important as a place of imprisonment for suspected *al-Qaeda terrorists. Since the bay was not formally part of the USA, this gave the administration of George W. *Bush full jurisdiction over their fate, without protection by the Bill of Rights enforced by the US *Supreme Court. However, in *Rasul v. Bush* (2004), the Supreme Court held that, although Cuba retained ultimate sovereignty over the territory, for the duration of the US lease the US had full jurisdiction over Guantanamo Bay. This meant, in practice, that prisoners had the right to challenge their detention in US courts. In response, the US government decided that prisoners would have access to military commissions, which in 2006 the Supreme Court struck down as inadequate. In response, the Bush administration promoted the Military Commissions Act to try terrorist suspects, which immediately became subject to renewed legal challenges.

Guatemala

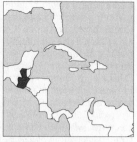

A Central American country characterized by the strength of its indigenous culture, and the continuing influence of the armed forces.

Contemporary history (up to 1993)

Independent from Spain since 1821 and an independent republic since 1839, Guatemela was governed by a host of liberal populist dictatorships from 1871. These were supported by an alliance of local coffee and banana plantation owners and the powerful US-owned United Fruit Company (UFC). Economic difficulties during World War II weakened the authority of the dictatorial system. A military rising of 20 October 1944 was followed by a brief period of democratization which reached its climax during the presidency of Colonel *Arbenz Guzmán (1951–4). He carried out a much-needed land reform which included the nationalization, with compensation, of 15 per cent of UFC-owned lands.

Arbenz Guzmán's overthrow by a US-backed military coup restored the alliance between the military and the agrarian elite, which became determined to preserve the social and economic status quo at all costs. In response, guerrilla groups emerged in 1960 to start a civil war. In 1965, a new Constitution was adopted in a decade marked by a series of military coups and counter-coups. Guatemala finally returned to civilian government, but political domination continued to be exercised by the military until 1986. Given continued widespread poverty, illiteracy, and ill health among the population, growing popular dissatisfaction could only be met by severe repression. The acts of violence committed during the 25 years of the civil war cost the lives of an estimated 200,000 people. The social and political turmoil also affected the economy, with 72 per cent of the mainly indigenous rural population living below the poverty line in 1989.

Contemporary politics (since 1993)

Peace negotiations were begun in May 1993 and were concluded in 1996. On 7 January 1996, Alvaro Arzu of the National Advancement Party was elected President with 52.3 per cent of the popular vote, against Alfonso Portillo, who was backed by the former military dictator, General Efrain Rios Montt. Nevertheless, the army remained the real power behind the scenes, and Portillo was elected in 1999, with Montt becoming parliamentary president. Politics and society continued to be extremely fragile, as army atrocities committed during the civil war—such as the murder in 1982 of 3,000 indigenous Maya people—came to light. Given the continued political power of the army, which was responsible for 93 per cent of the murders committed in the civil war, it proved extremely difficult to realize effective reconciliation. Montt's immunity was lifted in 2004 and he was put under house arrest. In 2004, Óscar Berger was elected President, after his predecessor, Portillo, left the country on charges of corruption.

Guesde, Jules (Bazile) (b. 11 Nov. 1845, d. 28 July 1922). French socialist

Born as Jules Bazile, he supported the Paris Commune of 1871 and went into exile after its failure, where he became converted to *Marxism. After his return to France in 1876, he founded the Parti Ouvrier Français (POF, French Workers' Party) in 1880 which rejected social reform as a dangerous palliative that would stave off the inevitable demise of the capitalist system. After his election as Deputy for Roubaix in 1893 he became more pragmatic. In 1905 he agreed to the merger of the socialist parties to form a united *Socialist Party (SFIO). The SFIO subscribed to the *Marxism of Guesde, but in practice followed the more moderate ideas of his rival *Jaurès.

Guevara, Ernesto 'Che' (b. 14 June 1928, d. 9 Oct. 1967). Latin American revolutionary

An Argentinian physician, he became a revolutionary following the *CIA-conducted overthrow of the left-wing *Guzmán regime in Guatemala in 1954, of which he was a member. He fled to Mexico and joined Fidel *Castro, whom he helped overthrow the *Batista regime in 1959. After serving as Minister for Industries (1961–5), he went to Bolivia in an attempt to export the Cuban revolution to other Latin American countries. However, he failed and was captured and executed by Bolivian government forces. Guevara's writings, and especially his confident and aggressive *Communism which was hostile to the USA, but also independent from the Soviet Union, inspired a generation of radicals and student leaders in the 1960s and 1970s.

Guides, see BADEN-POWELL, ROBERT STEPHENSON SMYTH

Guild Socialism

A short-lived but influential British labour movement. Founded in 1906 by Samuel Hobson, it called for revolutionary change in the organization of British industry through giving workers, organized in monopolistic guilds authorized by the state, control of industry. After World War I it established a National Guild League, which split when many members joined the newly formed Communist Party. Ideological differences followed and the movement had come to an end by 1923.

Guinea

A west African country rich in mineral resources, which has been plagued by wide-ranging corruption and misguided economic policies.

Contemporary history (up to 1984) A country in western Africa which came under French influence in 1880. Founded as the colony of Rivières in 1882, it became the colony of French Guinea in 1893. It joined the *French Union in 1946, but later rejected membership of the *French Community, becoming the first French African colony to gain independence on 2 October 1958. Owing to its rejection of French influence, it made up for the sudden withdrawal of French assistance by seeking help from Communist countries. In return, its exports went almost exclusively to the USSR, which caused a shortage of hard currency and foreign investment. In order to secure his near-total grip on power, President *Touré organized purges at regular intervals, in which those who voiced dissent were dispossessed or imprisoned.

The Second Republic (since 1984) The one-party state collapsed a week after Touré's death in 1984, when a military coup brought General Lansana *Conté to power. He gradually introduced market-oriented reforms, such as the privatization of state companies, a reform of the banking system, and agrarian reform. The austerity measures which he introduced led to considerable popular resentment, despite the decline of the inflation rate and the creation of an economic growth rate of 6 per cent. Following an abortive coup against him in 1985 by his erstwhile colleague, Diarra Traorré, the

development towards democratic institutions was temporarily suspended. Eventually, Conté introduced a new Constitution in 1991, and allowed the foundation of political parties. In the first free elections since independence on 11 June 1995, his Parti de l'Unité et du Progrès (Party of Unity and Progress) gained the majority of seats in parliament. He was accused of massive electoral fraud in 1995 and in the 1998 elections, when he was re-elected. The country's economy was bolstered by its reserves in gold and diamonds and by its coffee crops. However, many of the profits enriched a tiny social and political elite, while the economic conditions for the masses were made more difficult by the presence of over 500,000 refugees from Sierra Leone and Liberia. Conté's failing health led to political instability by 2006 which had disastrous economic consequences. Inflation spiralled to the world's third highest rate, at 25 per cent, while the government became unable to ensure regular payment to state employees.

Guinea-Bissau

One of the world's poorest countries, the west African state has been plagued by corrupt and unstable governments, few natural resources, and a particularly uneven income distribution.

Colonial rule (up to 1974) A west African state between Senegal and Guinea, it came under Portuguese influence in 1588, and in 1879 became the colony of Portuguese Guinea. It was transformed into a Portuguese overseas territory in 1951. Resistance began to form under A. *Cabral, who founded the Partido Africano da Independência da Guiné e de Cabo Verde (PAIGC, African Party for the Independence of Guinea and Cape Verde) in 1956. The PAIGC demanded independence for both Portuguese Guinea and neighbouring Cape Verde from Portuguese rule. It quickly gained popular support in both territories, and in 1963 began armed resistance to the Portuguese authorities.

Contemporary politics (since 1974) Upon independence on 10 September 1974, President Luìs Cabral (b. 1931) introduced socialist and anti-colonialist policies, with the support of Cuba and the USSR. Economic difficulties and resistance to political union with Cape Verde (many of whose immigrants were already resented because of their political domination within Guinea-Bissau) led to a coup which toppled Cabral in 1980. General Joao Bernardo *Vieira was installed as President, and restored civilian rule in 1984. He opened the country to foreign investment and carried out economic reforms in conjunction with the *IMF. Despite these, it remained one of the world's poorest countries, with an average annual inflation rate of 70 per cent (1985–93).

The first free elections took place on 3 July 1994, and resulted in a comfortable majority for Vieira's ruling party, the PAIGC. Vieira was deposed in a military revolt led by Antsumane Mané, whose forces managed to bring the country under his control from 1998 to 1999. The elections in late 1999 resulted in only 25 seats for the PAIGC, which came behind the Partido para a Renovação Social (PRS) with 37 seats, and the Resistência da Guiné-Bissau with 27 seats. Kumba Yala of the PRS was elected President. Yala struggled to impose his authority on Mané, who led a renewed— but this time unsuccessful—revolt. Mané was shot in November 2000. Yala was deposed in a coup in 2003, but returned in 2005 to run for President. Ultimately, these elections were won by another deposed ex-President, Vieira. The political instability did little to generate much-needed economic growth, or to reduce dramatic income inequalities among the population.

GULAG, see GREAT PURGE

Gulf War (First), see IRAN–IRAQ WAR

Gulf War (Second) (1990–1)
As soon as Kuwait gained independence from the British in 1961, Iraq claimed the territory as its own, and subsequently the border between the two countries remained disputed. Kuwait not only hosted the world's third largest oil reserves, but its geographical position makes Iraqi access to the Persian Gulf extremely difficult. On 17 July 1990 the Iraqi President, Sadam *Hussein, accused Kuwait of overproduction and thus depressing the price of oil. Furthermore, he claimed that Kuwait was exploiting the Rumalla oilfields which were already on Iraqi territory. Despite negotiations, tensions between the two countries mounted, and on 2 August around 100,000 Iraqi troops invaded Kuwait. On 8 August, Hussein formally annexed Kuwait and on the same day US President *Bush announced the dispatch of troops to Saudi Arabia to protect its borders against

Iraq. At the same time, an international boycott against the Iraqi economy, which had been decided on by the *UN two days earlier, became effective.

In the following months, the US force in Saudi Arabia was augmented to 500,000 troops, and was supported by an international force including 65,000 soldiers from Saudi Arabia, 43,000 from the United Arab Emirates, and 35,000 from the UK. Following Iraq's failure to respond to a UN ultimatum to withdraw its troops from Kuwait by 15 January 1991, the UN forces led by the US general Norman Schwarzkopf started the 'mother of all battles' (Hussein) with a massive bombing campaign against strategic Iraqi targets as well as the merciless bombing of Iraqi troops. This ensured that the Allied ground attack, which began on 24 February, was swift and entailed minimal Allied casualties. The UN forces continued to advance north, until Hussein accepted a cease-fire on 28 February. The official US estimate of casualties included 343 allied soldiers, around 110,000 Iraqi soldiers, around 10,000 Iraqi civilians, and up to 5,000 Kuwaiti civilians.

Guomindang (Kuomintang, KMT)
Early history (1912–49) Also known as the Chinese Nationalist Party, its origins go back to the end of the Qing dynasty. In April 1912 Song Jiaoren and *Sun Yat-sen reorganized and merged several revolutionary organizations into the Chinese Revolutionary Party. Outlawed by *Yuan Shikai in 1913, Sun set up a government in Guangzhou (Canton) of the 'Republic of China' in 1917 as a rival to the regime in Peking. In 1918, he himself was forced to leave for Shanghai, where he transformed the Chinese Revolutionary Party into the Guomindang on 10 October 1919. He was able to return to Guangzhou in 1920. Having sought Western aid in vain, he received support from the Soviet *Communist Party, and in 1923 entered an alliance with the Chinese *Communist Party (CCP). The party was reformed on Leninist principles of democratic centralism, which remained the party's organizational principle until the 1990s. Communists were admitted into the party, which held its first conference in January 1924. It claimed leadership in the nationalist struggle to unite the country and to rid it of all foreign influence. Its ideology was based on the 'Three People's Principles': nationalism, people's rights, and people's livelihood.

Under *Chiang Kai-shek's leadership from 1925, it was encouraged and strengthened by the successful conduct of the

*Northern Expedition, which allowed the KMT to form a government in Nanjing (Nangking). Boosted by this. Chiang dissolved the alliance with the CCP in April 1927. Success in the Northern Expedition, however, also strengthened the KMT's military wing, the *National Revolutionary Army. As the party grew, Chiang lost his ability to control its various factions, though his leadership remained undisputed. Apart from internal friction, the KMT was also weakened by constant warfare, first against the Communists, and then against the Japanese. After World War II, it resumed its fight against the Communists in the *Chinese Civil War. By 1949, the KMT was defeated by a well-organized Communist movement and by popular resentment against the corruption within the KMT's own ranks.

Taiwan (from 1949) The leaders of the KMT retreated to Taiwan, where it remained the ruling party claiming to represent the whole of China. It retained its authoritarian, Leninist structure, being dominated by a clique of KMT officials originally from the mainland. Its rigid policies were only carefully relaxed under Chiang's successor from 1975, his son *Chiang Ching-kuo, who chose a native Taiwanese, *Lee Teng-hui, as his deputy. Tensions within the party continued, however, since Chinese members continued to have a disproportionate influence over the party. In 2000, the KMT's candidate, Vice-President Lien Chan, lost the presidential elections to Chen Shui-bian. It opposed Chen's drives towards formally declaring independence from mainland China, and underlining this claim by emphasizing Taiwan's cultural distinctiveness. The KMT was unable to stop a growing popular identification with Taiwanese culture, and narrowly lost the 2004 presidential elections.

Gusmão, José Alexandre ('Xanana')
(b. 20 June 1946). President of East Timor, 2002–7
Born in Laleia (Manatuto), he visited a Jesuit school and completed his military service in the Portuguese army. He became a journalist, and went to Australia to work for the East Timorese independence movement, the Frente Revolucionára do Timor Leste-Independente (Fretlin). Following the Indonesian invasion of East Timor in 1975, he became Fretlin's military commander, but in 1992 he was betrayed, captured, and imprisoned. There, his status was elevated by a number of visits by world leaders, including Nelson Mandela in 1997. He was released in 1999 and accepted by the Indonesian

government as a spokesperson for the East Timorese, and became a leader in the ensuing transition to independence. He was elected the first President of East Timor with 82 per cent of the popular vote. He was succeeded by Jose Ramos Horta, a former Prime Minister.

Gustavson Lake, see LAND CLAIMS, NATIVE

Guyana

A country on the north-east coast of South America, which has suffered from a relative absence of mineral resources and which, despite debt relief under the *HIPC initiative, has been one of Latin America's poorest countries.

Contemporary history (up to 1992) Guyana became a British colony in 1831. Its sugar plantation owners responded to the abolition of slavery in 1834 with the importation of some 340,000 Indians to work on the plantations. Political agitation began in 1922 with the foundation of the Guyana Labour Union, the first *trade union of the Caribbean. Agitation for political reform led to the granting of Crown Colony status and the enfranchisement of women in 1928. Unrest continued, but further reform was postponed by World War II.

The 1953 general elections were won by the Indian Cheddi Jagan (b. 1918, d. 1997), who had founded the People's Progressive Party (PPP) together with the Black barrister, Forbes Burnham (b. 1923, d. 1985), in 1950. As the PPP became avowedly *Marxist, Burnham split from the largely Indian-supported PPP to form the People's National Congress (PNC). Fearing Marxist PPP rule, the British postponed the date for independence from 1963 to 1966 and introduced proportional representation which would be more favourable to the PNC. Burnham did win the 1965 elections, and was Prime Minister until his death in 1985, albeit with the help of an increasingly repressive regime and rigged elections. He transformed Guyana into a 'cooperative' republic (as it was officially named in 1970) in an attempt to base the state neither on *Communism nor on *capitalism, but on self-help and cooperative communities. However, through corruption, mismanagement, and the decline of world prices for Guyana's main exports, sugar and bauxite, the experiment failed.

Contemporary politics (since 1992)
Guyana's GDP per head was among the lowest in Latin America, while in 2000 foreign debt stood at about 300 per cent of its entire annual GDP. The poor economic conditions and social tensions finally resulted in a change of power in 1992, when the PPP, which was favoured by the country's majority of Indian descent, came to power. In 2006, Bharrat Jagdeo of the PPP, who had succeeded Jenni Jagan in 1999, was re-elected President. The former Minister of Economics vowed to reduce rampant crime and violence. He also struggled to cope with Guyana's continued economic fragility, indigenous land claims, and border disputes with neighbouring Surinam.

Guyane Française

The largest remaining French overseas territory, situated on the north-east coast of Latin America. A French colony from 1816, after the abolition of slavery colonists brought in Asian immigrants to work on the plantations. The territory became famous for its notorious penal settlement on the offshore Devil's Island, which was closed down in 1947. A Department of France since 1875 with representatives in the French parliament, its society and culture came to be closely linked to that of France. It was divided into two Departments in 1930, which in 1946 gained official recognition as equal overseas Departments. Apart from a brief period in the 1960s, demands for independence have found relatively little support, as around 70 per cent of its national income has been provided by France. Around a quarter of its income, for instance, derives from its satellite-launching centre run by the European Space Agency. With over two-thirds of its exports going to France, its GDP was around eight times that of neighbouring Guyana. A large influx of Maroons (Blacks from the bushlands) fleeing the political unrest in their native Surinam arrived from 1989, and now constitute over 10 per cent of the population.
FRENCH EMPIRE

H

Haakon VII (b. 3 Aug. 1872, d. 21 Sept. 1957). King of Norway 1905–57
Formerly Prince Charles of Denmark, he was elected by the Norwegian Storting (parliament) to the throne in 1905, when Norway and Sweden separated. He tried to coordinate a policy of neutrality for Norway, Denmark, and Sweden during the two World Wars. When the Germans did invade in 1940, he met them at the head of the Norwegian troops. Rather than accept *Quisling's *Nazi government, he escaped to London as the constitutional head of the government-in-exile, and encouraged his countrymen to resist the occupying forces. He returned to Norway in 1945. Known for his simple, modest lifestyle, and admired for his integrity, the 'People's King' was an important symbol of unity and statehood in the first half of the twentieth century.

Haganah ('Defence')
A Jewish defence force in *Palestine which was first established in 1920 as a secret organization to defend Jewish settlements from Arab attacks. It became gradually accepted by the British authorities as a supplementary police force, coming under the control of the *Histadrut, the General Federation of Jewish Labour. During the period of Arab-Jewish unrest (1936–9) it acquired a general staff and developed close links with the *Jewish Agency. During World War II it contributed units to the British 8th Army, but it was also involved in organizing illegal Jewish immigration from Europe. It condemned the terrorist activities of the *Stern Gang and *Irgun, and in 1947, when the British prepared to leave Palestine, it took on the defence of Jewish Palestine against Arab troops. Some 60,000 strong, it formed the nucleus of the army of the new state of Israel.

Hague Peace Conferences, see
DISARMAMENT

Haig, Douglas, 1st Earl Haig of Bemersyde (b. 19 June 1861, d. 30 Jan. 1928). British soldier
Born in Bemersyde, Berwickshire, he was educated at Clifton College, then moved on to Oxford and the Royal Military College, Sandhurst. He joined the Royal Hussars in 1895, and first saw active service in the Sudan.

He also served in the *South African (Boer) War, and was Chief of Staff of the Indian army (1909–11). In *World War I, he commanded the 1st Army Corps at *Ypres and *Loos. In 1915, Haig became Commander-in-Chief of the *British Expeditionary Force, succeeding John French. He was committed to the doctrine of destroying the enemy through a decisive offensive. Winning a battle was not so much a factor of innovative or superior tactics, but of superior strength, willpower, and resources. His belief in the value of the cavalry demonstrated his failure to appreciate the realities of modern, twentieth-century warfare. Full, frontal attacks against the entrenched Germans resulted in the loss of around 400,000 men at the battle of the *Somme, while these tactics at *Passchendaele in 1917 resulted in similar losses. He had more success in his final campaign (September-November 1918), which ended the war more quickly than many had predicted, though victory resulted perhaps more from the genius of Marshal *Foch.

Haile Selassie (b. 23 July 1892, d. 27 Aug. 1976). Emperor of Ethiopia 1930–74
Born in Harar as a great-nephew of Emperor Menelik II, he was baptized Ras Tafari Makonnen as a Coptic Christian. When his aunt, Waizeru Zewditu, became Empress in 1916, he became her regent and effective ruler of the country. He managed to control the opposition, and continued Menelik's reforms, such as the encouragement of missionary schools. Keen to establish his country as a modern state, Haile Selassie led Ethiopia into the *League of Nations in 1923. He was crowned King in 1928 and, upon his aunt's death, Emperor in 1930. He continued attempts at political reform, and created a military academy. He was forced into exile in London during the Italian occupation of the country (1936–41). After his restoration he received massive aid from the *UN, Britain, and the USA, which enabled him to create schools, colleges, medical services, and an army. He also became a well-known and influential international figure, for example within the UN and the Organization for African Unity (*African Union). However, warfare against Eritrean independence organizations and internal ethnic opposition forces preserved his country's

poverty. After a drought in 1973, the effects of which were compounded by inefficient administration of relief, he was deposed on 13 September 1974. He died (presumably murdered) under house arrest.

Haiti

Latin America's poorest country, on the western third of the Caribbean island of Hispaniola, has suffered from the marked absence of civil society structures which could support a stable political system.

Early history (up to 1957) Haiti achieved independence from France through a slave rebellion in 1804. The political system degenerated gradually into a state of virtual anarchy until an occupation by US troops in 1915. The US pursued a policy of extending its influence in the Caribbean, and was concerned about the significant German influence at a time when World War I had broken out. Despite the partial modernization of the economy due to US investment, growing nationalist pressure in Haiti, and *Roosevelt's *Good Neighbor Policy in particular, led to a withdrawal of US troops in 1934, though direct US fiscal control continued until 1947. In subsequent decades, power passed from the mixed-race Mulatto minority to representatives from the Black majority, which made up 95 per cent of the population. This process was completed by the election of François *Duvalier in 1957.

The Duvalier dictatorship (1957–86) Duvalier established a ruthless authoritarian regime and methodically reduced the influence of the USA. He also diminished the influence of the military, the Roman *Catholic Church, the business community, and the trade unions. After his death, his son, Jean-Claude *Duvalier, promised to follow his father's political 'revolution' (as he put it) with an economic one. However, his economic policies failed. This eroded the support for his regime of key groups such as the Black business community. Furthermore, the visit of Pope *John Paul II in 1983 restored some of the self-confidence of the Church, which subsequently became a principal voice of opposition. Given the increasing poverty of the population which contrasted with the corruption of the regime, Duvalier preserved

his power through terror exercised by his personal death squads, the *Tonton Macoute*. As violence escalated, US hostility to the regime grew.

Contemporary politics (since 1986) Duvalier was finally forced into exile on 9 February 1986, though subsequent efforts at democratization were stopped by a military coup on 19 June 1988. Following the overthrow of the military regime, US pressure led to the first truly democratic elections in Haitian history on 16 December 1990, which were won by *Aristide. He was deposed by another military coup in October 1991 and fled to the USA. Given the accelerated rate of Haitian emigration to the USA, President *Clinton decided in favour of a military intervention in September 1994 in order to restore Aristide to power, though skilful last-minute negotiations by *Carter and *Powell led to a voluntary withdrawal from power of the Haitian military junta.

  Throughout the 1990s, the economy continued to be hampered by political uncertainty and administrative incompetence, with the economy declining in real terms. On 19 September 1994, 15,000 US troops landed in Haiti to restore order and help in the establishment of civil authority and a civilian police force. Subsequently, US forces were gradually displaced by an international force consisting mainly of soldiers from neighbouring Caribbean countries and Canada under the authority of the *UN. With opposition parties boycotting the elections, on 17 December 1995, René Prevál from Aristide's Lavalas movement was elected with 87.9 per cent of the popular vote to become President on 7 February 1996. In 2000, the presidential elections were won by Aristide with over 90 per cent of the vote. However, the opposition accused the government of massive electoral fraud, and in early 2001 it appointed a rival President of its own, Gerard Gourgue. Unable to overcome growing unrest in the country, Aristide fled Haiti in 2004. An interim government took charge, with Prevál winning the 2006 elections. The government was unable, however, to restore order to the country, as brigands proclaiming their loyalty to Aristide or to his opponents controlled much of the country, including the capital.

Haldane, Richard Burdon, 1st Viscount Haldane of Cloan (b. 30 July 1856, d. 19 Aug. 1928). British Liberal and Labour politician

Born in Edinburgh, he was educated there apart from a brief spell at the German University of Göttingen in 1874. He was called to the Bar in 1879, and entered parliament in 1885 for the *Liberal Party, representing the constituency of East Lothian. As Secretary of State for War (1905–12) he carried out fundamental army reforms. He created a small expeditionary force, equipped for instant action, along with a reserve territorial force. An Imperial General Staff was made responsible for all military strategic planning. In 1912, he became Lord Chancellor, but *Asquith dismissed him in 1915 following an unjustified press campaign which claimed he was pro-German. Following the war he supported the *Labour Party, and was once again made Lord Chancellor in 1924. His main domestic concern was education: Haldane co-founded the London School of Economics with Sidney and Beatrice *Webb, was President of Birkbeck College, and an active supporter of the Workers' Educational Association.

Halifax, Edward Frederick Lindley Wood, 3rd Viscount and 1st Earl of (b. 16 Apr. 1881, d. 23 Dec. 1959). Viceroy of India 1926–31; British Foreign Secretary 1938–41

Born in Powderham Castle, Devon, he was educated at Eton and Oxford. He was elected to parliament in 1910 for the *Conservative Party to represent Ripon. He served in World War I as a cavalry officer. He was made President of the Board of Education under Bonar *Law in 1922, and was Minister of Agriculture in *Baldwin's second government from 1924. In 1926, he was sent to India as viceroy, having been given the title of Lord Irwin. It was this name that he gave to his famous **Irwin Declaration** of 1929; this made concessions to the increasingly active Indian nationalists, by announcing a *Round Table Conference to discuss India's future, and by pledging that Britain aimed to give India *Dominion status. He also agreed to negotiate with Mohandas K. *Gandhi, whom he had imprisoned after the *Salt March. He was replaced as viceroy in 1931, and became Chancellor of Oxford University in 1933. He had returned to the government in 1932, partly to assist its Indian reforms, and eventually became Foreign Secretary in 1938. In that post, he was a noted advocate of *appeasement, accepting the *Anschluss of Germany and Austria, and the separation of the *Sudetenland from *Czechoslovakia following the *Munich Agreement. In 1939 he refused an invitation to Moscow, and thus lost any chance of concluding an anti-German agreement with the Soviet Union. He supported *Chamberlain's view in September 1939 that there was no alternative to war. Despite *George VI's preference for him, he

did not form a government in May 1940 since he did not command the support of the Conservative Party, which opted for *Churchill instead. Halifax served as ambassador to the USA in 1941–6. He was a devout High *Anglican throughout his life.

Hallstein Doctrine, see GERMAN QUESTION

Halsey, William Frederick (b. 30 Oct. 1882, d. 16 Aug. 1959). US admiral

Born in Elizabeth, New Jersey, he graduated from the US Naval Academy in 1904, served in World War I, and rose steadily to the rank of admiral. In 1941, when he was commander of the Pacific Fleet aircraft carriers, he and his fleet were fortunately out of harbour when the Japanese attacked *Pearl Harbor. In 1942 he led a spectacular raid against the Japanese-occupied Marshall and Gilbert Islands, and during the campaign of the Solomon Islands he was given command of the South Pacific area. In October 1944, he commanded the US 3rd Fleet at the battle of *Leyte Gulf, the largest naval engagement in the Pacific up to that time. In 1945 he led the seaborne bombing offensive against Japanese cities. He retired from the navy in 1947.

Hamaguchi Osachi (b. 1 Apr. 1870, d. 26 Aug. 1931). Prime Minister of Japan 1929–31

Prior to his political career Hamaguchi had served as an official in the Ministry of Finance. As the successor to the government of *Tanaka Giichi, Hamaguchi's *Minseito party administration proved unable to cope with the turbulence in domestic and international affairs. The policies of the Minister of Finance, Inoue Junnosuke, imposed austerity on the economy which deepened the 'Shôwa Depression'. Foreign policy was equally unpopular, especially after the Foreign Minister, Shidehara Kijirô, accepted an inferior position for the Japanese navy towards the other powers in the Pacific in negotiations for the London Treaty of 1930. In the welter of domestic criticism that followed, Hamaguchi was attacked by a rightist youth and died later of his wounds. The Hamaguchi Cabinet came to be seen as having contributed greatly to the loss of support for party government in prewar Japan.

Hamas ('Enthusiasm')

Early history An islamic Palestinian guerrilla organization formed in the *Gaza Strip, where it was radicalized under conditions of poverty, unemployment, and Israeli military rule. Led by Sheikh Ahmad Jasin, it became well financed through annual donations from

Iran of around $30 million, and managed to recruit around 8,000 guerrilla fighters. Together with *Hezbollah it led the *Intifadah and became one of the leading radical Palestinian organizations: almost half of the Palestinians in Israeli prisons are members of the organization. It opposed the *Gaza-Jericho agreement and the subsequent rule of the rival *PLO in the Gaza Strip, where it still enjoyed overwhelming support. Hamas not only opposed Israeli domination of *Palestine, but also built hospitals and schools and was thus seen by much of the population as a positive influence as well. Hamas fighters continued their attacks against Israeli military and civilian targets. This led to a radicalization of the Israeli electorate, whose confidence in compromise achieved, for example, in the *Oslo Agreements was undermined as the violence increased. At the same time, Arafat was unable to stop Hamas effectively, owing to the support it enjoyed in the Gaza Strip.

Contemporary politics (from 2006) Owing to the inability of *Fatah to use foreign aid to combat general poverty, the Palestinian electorate returned Hamas with a majority in the Palestinian Council elections of 2006. Fatah formed a new government headed by Ismail Hanija, but frequently clashed with the Palestinian President, Mahmoud *Abbas, who also led the Fatah movement. Meanwhile, relations with Fatah worsened through bitter fighting between armed supporters of both groups. In 2007, both groups agreed to form a unity government, though this did not overcome the rivalry between Hamas and Fatah.

Hammarskjöld, Dag Hjalmar Agne Carl (b. 29 July 1905, d. 18 Sept. 1961). UN Secretary-General 1953–61
Born at Jönköping in Sweden, he studied at Stockholm University, where he later became professor of economics 1933–6. He then entered government service and was deputy Foreign Minister 1951–3. Succeeding Trygve *Lie as *UN Secretary-General, he showed great skill and impartiality in his adept handling of the *Suez Crisis. Under his direction, the UN gained a central role in the *decolonization of Africa. He initiated and directed the UN's involvement in the *Congo Crisis, through making controversial use of Article 99 of the UN Charter, which he believed allowed the Secretary-General to take initiatives independent of approval by the Security Council or the General Assembly. His death in an air accident on a flight from the Congo was suspected to have been engineered by the powerful mining interests which opposed his use of UN troops to maintain the

unity of the Congo. He was awarded the *Nobel Peace Prize posthumously.

Hara Takashi (b. 9 Sept. 1856, d. 4 Nov. 1921). Prime Minister of Japan 1918–21
The protégé of Inoue Kaoru, also known as Hara Kei and Hara Satoshi. Hara was to win a position for himself independent of the oligarchs who had ruled Japan since the Meiji Restoration, establishing the power of the party in politics. Hara's early career included time spent as a journalist and as a senior official in the consular service in China and ambassador to Korea. As a leading member of the *Seiyûkai, he entered the Diet in 1900 and served in several Cabinets as Minister of Communications and head of the powerful Home Ministry. In 1914, Hara succeeded Saionji Kinmochi as party president and four years later he became the first commoner to hold the premiership. He was an expert at building up the party machine, largely through the funnelling of patronage provided by big business to the grass roots. A combination of strong electoral performances and the brilliant skills Hara displayed as a political schemer allowed Japan's political parties to win power from the bureaucracy and the old political establishment. Hara's policies, as well as his emphasis on domestic economic well-being, brought him into conflict with the entrenched interests in the bureaucracy. He was assassinated by a right-wing fanatic.

Hardie, (James) Keir (b. 15 Aug. 1856, d. 26 Sept. 1915). Chairman of the British Labour Party 1906–8, 1909–10
Born in Legbrannock (Scotland), Hardie had a background as a miner and trade unionist. He founded the Scottish Labour Party in 1888, and in 1892 he was elected to parliament for the London constituency of West Ham, founding the *Independent Labour Party shortly afterwards. A devoted pacifist and internationalist, he supported the plight of the unemployed and defended the *suffragettes. He was not a good organizer, but was passionately devoted to the cause of the Labour movement, so that he (unsuccessfully) opposed *MacDonald's 1905–10 strategy of working with the *Liberal Party. Hardie was not always the most influential figure in the *Labour Party, but he is still remembered as someone who helped make Labour a national political force.

Harding, Warren Gamaliel (b. 2 Nov. 1865, d. 2 Aug. 1923). 29th US President 1921–3

Early career Born at Corsica, Ohio, into an established Ohio family, he studied at Ohio

Central College (1879–82). He made his name as a publisher and editor of the *Marion Star* newspaper. Harding held a variety of state offices as a *Republican before winning election to the US Senate in 1914. His handsome appearance, conservatism, inoffensiveness, and uplifting speaking style earned him the Republican presidential nomination as a compromise candidate in 1920. One of his critics described Harding's speeches as 'an army of pompous phrases moving across the landscape in search of an idea' (William Gibbs McAdoo). Conducting the election campaign from the porch of his home, he won it through his reassuring programme, predicated upon a return to 'normalcy' after the upheaval of the *Wilson years.

Presidency In office, he demonstrated a lack of grip which allowed associates from Ohio whom he had appointed without reflection to indulge, without his knowledge, in corrupt practices. One such practice led, after Harding's death, to the *Teapot Dome affair. Shortly after his death from a heart attack, revelations of the misdemeanours of his appointees led to a rapid decline in his reputation.

Hariri, Rafiq al- (b. 1944, d. 14 Feb. 2005). Prime Minister of Lebanon, 1992–8; 2000–4
Born in Sidon, into a poor family, he studied at Beirut American University and in 1966 emigrated to Saudi Arabia, whose citizenship he acquired. He founded his own construction business, and became active in banking and real estate. One of the world's wealthiest men, his fortune is estimated at around $4bn. He tried to mediate a peaceful solution to the Lebanese civil war in the 1980s, and was instrumental in securing the *Taif Accord of 1989. In 1992, he was asked to lead the government. In his first two terms in office, he stabilized the currency, and spent much energy (and some of his personal fortune) in rebuilding Beirut. He was confirmed in office in 1996, but in 1998 he was dismissed by the President owing to personal disagreements. In 2000, however, candidates supporting him won the general elections on the promise of economic improvements. In response, the President, Émile Lahoud, asked Hariri to form another government. His second period in office was characterized by his rivalry with the Syrian-backed Lahoud. Hariri proposed the privatization of state-owned companies to reduce state debt, a move which Lahoud opposed. Hariri ultimately resigned. He was killed in a car bomb attack a few months later,

a move widely believed to have been instigated by Syria.

Harper, Stephen (b. 30 Apr. 1959). Prime Minister of Canada, 2006–
Born in Toronto, he graduated with an MA in economics from the University of Calgary. He entered the House of Commons in 1993 for the *Reform Party, but left politics in 1997. In 2002, he re-entered politics after being elected leader of the Canadian Alliance, which had been created by the Reform Party to broaden its appeal. The following year, he guided the Alliance into a merger with the Progressive Conservatives to form the *Conservative Party, whose leader he became. Harper capitalized on the *Liberal Party's corruption scandals to lead the Conservatives back to government, after more than twelve years in opposition. Harper improved relations with the US, reduced the Goods and Services Tax, and tried to take the initiative in dealing with the status of Quebec by proposing its recognition as a nation within Canada.

Harris, Arthur Travers ('Bomber Harris') (b. 13 Apr. 1892, d. 5 Apr. 1984). Head of British Bomber Command 1942–5
Born in Cheltenham, he joined the Royal Flying Corps in 1915, after having fought as a soldier in South-West Africa. He rose through the service to become Commander of 5 Group (Bomber Command) in 1939, when *World War II broke out. Harris consistently advocated the value of area bombing, believing that the total destruction of Germany would force the surviving Germans to surrender without the necessity of a full-scale invasion. Although this strategy received the support of *Churchill, it remained controversial. It has since been shown that the bombing of selected targets such as transport systems, industrial installations, and oil refineries proved far more effective in hindering the German war effort. He has also been criticized over his role in the bombing of *Dresden in February 1945, in which 100,000 civilians were killed and a city with a rare historical heritage was flattened.

Harvester judgment (1907)
A landmark court ruling in Australia by Justice Henry B. Higgins (b. 1851, d. 1929), which established principles of a minimum wage, and became a major component of industrial relations until the 1960s. Higgins decided against an application for exemption from excise duty under the Excise Act of 1906 made by a manufacturer of harvesting machines, Hugh V. McKay (b. 1865, d. 1926), on the

grounds that he payed 'fair and reasonable' wages. Higgins pronounced that McKay's wage of 6 shillings per day was not enough, calculating that an average household of two adults and three children needed at least 7 shillings per day to maintain a decent life in a 'civilized' community.

Hasan al-Banna, see MUSLIM BROTHER-HOOD

Hashemite dynasty
A notable Arab family whose members are direct descendants of the founder of *Islam, the Prophet Muhammad. By the nineteenth century, its leaders were the Emirs of Mecca under the Turks. The last of these was *Hussein ibn Ali, who became King of the Hejaz, but was ousted by *Abd al-Aziz ibn Saud in 1924. His eldest son Ali briefly replaced him before also being forced into exile by Saud. His other sons *Abdullah and *Faisal became Kings of Transjordan and Iraq respectively. The Iraq branch ended in 1958 with the murder of *Faisal II, but the dynasty continued in Jordan under *Hussein ibn Talal and his son, *Abdullah II.

Hashimoto Ryûtarô (b. 29 July 1937, d. 1 July 2006). Prime Minister of Japan 1996–8
The son of a former Cabinet Minister, he was first elected to the Diet (the House of Representatives) at the age of 25, a rare achievement in Japan's gerontocratic political system. This distinction marked the beginning of an outstanding political career, especially in the field of health and welfare policy. In 1995 he succeeded Kôno Yôhei as president of the *Liberal Democratic Party. The directness with which he pronounced his views on a number of controversial issues suggested that he would prove to be a decisive leader when he took his turn as Premier in January 1996. However, in the early days of his coalition government, suffering many of the same difficulties as his predecessor, he proved unable to overcome the legislative morass caused by continuing financial scandals in Japan. He was unable to find a response to the Asian economic crisis from 1997. His popularity declined, and he resigned following bad results for the Liberal Democratic Party in elections to the Upper House.

Hassan II (b. 9 July 1929, d. 23 July 1999). King of Morocco 1961–99
Born in the royal palace at Rabat, he studied law in Bordeaux and was soon active in the court of his father, Mohammed V. He accompanied him into exile in 1953, and in 1957 became crown prince. He was Commander-in-Chief of the armed forces. Thus groomed in political and military affairs, he succeeded his father in 1961. Between 1965 and 1977, he ruled by decree, and overcame several coup attempts (1971, 1972, 1973). He relaxed his authoritarian rule (without ever relinquishing his grip on politics) after occupying the Western Sahara, and thus united the country's nationalist forces behind him. However, the long guerrilla war that followed exhausted his army and his country's economic resources, which he had worked hard to improve. He was able to resist domestic pressures mounting in the 1990s for democratization, mainly through the loyalty of the army. Hassan's continued defiance of the *UN was enabled by tacit support from the USA and France, which welcomed his pro-Western stance. He was the first Arab leader to denounce Saddam *Hussein's invasion of Kuwait in 1990, and was the third Arab leader to create diplomatic links with Israel on 1 September 1994. He instituted moderate political reforms a few years before his death, which were continued by his son, *Mohammed VI.

Hatoyama Ichirô (b. 1 Jan. 1883, d. 7 Mar. 1959). Prime Minister of Japan 1954–6

Early career Following family tradition, Hatoyama pursued a political career from a young age, representing his Tokyo constituency at the local and national level to become part of the prewar political establishment. Before 1945, he was a member of three administrations and leader of the *Seiyûkai. The reputation he developed as an enemy of intellectual freedom during his terms as Minister of Education in the Inukai (1931–2) and Saitô (1932–4) Cabinets remained with him after 1945. As Japan embarked on its war in Asia, Hatoyama withdrew from politics after actively criticizing the economic policies of the government.

Postwar politics Hatoyama returned to public life following the Japanese surrender as the founder and first president of the Liberal Party (Jiyûtô), but was purged by the occupation authorities just when the Liberals emerged as the largest party in the 1946 Lower House elections. He was forced to relinquish control of his party to his deputy *Yoshida Shigeru. On Hatoyama's return to politics in the early 1950s, Yoshida refused to make way for his former boss and the two leaders became involved in acrimonious rivalry leading to splits within the party. In 1954, Hatoyama led his followers out of the Liberal Party to join others on the centre-right in forming the Democratic Party (Minshutô). This new party went on to unseat Yoshida and win the premiership for Hatoyama later in the same year. When conservative groups united in 1955 as the *Liberal Democratic Party, he became its first president and retained the premiership. Regarded by many as an arch-conservative and enemy of postwar democratic reforms, Hatoyama was also the politician who presided over the formal conclusion of hostilities with the USSR in October 1956, despite the opposition of many within the conservative camp.

Haughey, Charles James (b. 16 Sept. 1925, d. 13 June 2006). Prime Minister (Taoiseach) of the Irish Republic 1979–81, 1982, 1987–92

Born in Castlebar, Co. Mayo, and raised in Dublin, he studied at University College Dublin, and King's Inns. He began a career as an accountant, and joined the *Fianna Fáil party in 1948. He married the daughter of Sean *Lemass in 1951, and was elected to Dáil Éireann (the Irish parliament) in 1957. Haughey became Minister for Justice in 1961. He contested the party leadership in 1966, but withdrew in favour of Jack *Lynch, under whom he became Minister for Finance in 1966. Haughey was forced to resign on 6 May 1970 after being accused of complicity in smuggling arms for militant nationalists into the Republic of Ireland. A trial for this conspiracy found him (along with Agriculture and Fisheries Minister Neil Blaney) not guilty.

Haughey was re-elected to the executive of Fianna Fáil in 1972. He was Minister for Health and Social Welfare 1977–9, and succeeded Lynch as Prime Minister on 11 December 1979. Alternating in power with *FitzGerald, he won a convincing victory in 1987. During this government, Ireland increased its involvement in European Community affairs, and several national boards and commissions (such as the Department of the Marine and the Independent Radio and Television Commission) were established. Criticized for his autocratic leadership style and his failure to stop the party's decline in the polls through more energetic leadership, he resigned as party leader and Taoiseach in February 1992. From 2000, Haughey was at the centre of corruption allegations involving illicit payments of US$13 million. Further details about tax evasion amounting to 7 million *euros, and his flamboyant lifestyle, came to light in the last years before his death.

Havel, Václav (b. 6 Oct. 1936). President of Czechoslovakia 1989–92; President of the Czech Republic 1993–2003

Early career Born in Prague, he was refused a place at university on account of his 'bourgeois descent'. Instead he worked as a laboratory assistant and a taxi-driver, attending evening classes at Prague Technical University. He then obtained entry into a theatrical academy, qualifying in 1967 and becoming a stage-hand and technician. He had already begun serious writing in 1961 with *Hitch-Hiking*, followed by plays such as *The Garden Party* (1963), *The Message* (1965), and *Difficult Understanding* (1968). At this time, he openly called for a return to the liberal intellectual democratic traditions of interwar *Czechoslovakia. Following his signature of *Charter '77, as whose spokesman he acted intermittently, he spent several terms in prison, the last of which was in early 1989. By that time, he had become the leading spokesman for more *human rights and political liberalization.

In office He was chosen President by the Czechoslovak Assembly when Husák resigned in December 1989, and elected by popular vote in 1990. However, he found it difficult to cope with the day-to-day administrative tasks of government. More importantly, in his concern for social justice he disagreed with his more energetic ministers led by *Klaus over the speed of economic change and the introduction of *capitalism. Refusing to preside over the division of Czechoslovakia into the *Czech Republic and *Slovakia, he resigned in 1992. He was elected President of the new Czech Republic on 26 January 1993. He continued to assume the role of moral and social conscience of a country experiencing radical economic liberalization. At home and abroad, he was respected for his efforts to bring reconciliation between Czechs and their neighbours. He was also influential in formulating a vision of the *EU that placed the Czechs and other countries in central and eastern Europe in the mainstream of European culture. Havel was constitutionally barred from a renewal of his second term in office. Despite his poor health, he returned to writing after retirement.

Hawke, Robert James Lee (b. 9 Dec. 1929). Prime Minister of Australia 1983–91

Born in Bordertown (South Australia), he studied economics and law at Perth and as a *Rhodes Scholar in Oxford, joining the Australian *Labor Party in 1946. A research scholar at the Australian National University (1956–8), he then became a research scholar for the Australian Council of Trade Unions (1958–69) before becoming its president in 1970. He joined the national executive of the Labor Party in 1971, but did not become a member of the House of Representatives until 1980. He joined the party's parliamentary executive, and on 5 March 1983 was unanimously elected to the party's leadership.

Succeeding *Fraser as Prime Minister on 11 March 1983, Hawke based his long tenure on a careful maintenance of an internal balance of power within Labor, between broad left, centre left, and right. Anxious to appease business, he achieved a government-sponsored compromise between business leaders and *trade unions, inaugurating a six-year-long spell of industrial peace. Criticized for being less radical than the *Whitlam government, his pragmatic policies effectively seized the middle ground in Australian politics, which was maintained by *Keating after him and which ensured Labor's long tenure in office. He was helped by a dramatic economic recovery (1983–5), though his liberalization of the banking system caused a massive increase in Australia's (private) foreign debt. A renewed decline in economic growth from the late 1980s, and increasing hostility to his long grip on power, eventually led to his replacement by Keating.

Haya de la Torre, Victor Raúl (b. 22 Feb. 1895, d. 3 Aug. 1979). Peruvian politician

Born in Trujillo, he became active in student politics, and in 1923 founded the popular University of Peru. Expelled for his opposition to the dictator Leguía, he went to Mexico (1923–30), where he founded the American Popular Revolutionary Alliance (*APRA) in 1924. With his party he came to lead the popular opposition to the Peruvian ruling elites. Back in Peru, he lost the 1931 rigged presidential elections and spent the subsequent decade in hiding. He briefly returned as Minister without Portfolio in 1945, but was forced into exile by the renewed military takeover of 1948. He returned from Mexico in 1957 and successfully contested the 1962 presidential elections, though he was prevented from taking office by the military. His stature as Peru's leading democratic politician was recognized in 1978, when he became head of the constituent assembly responsible for the development of a new constitution.

Hay–Buneau–Varilla Treaty, see PANAMA

Hayek, Friedrich August von (b. 8 May 1899, d. 24 Mar. 1992). Political economist

One of the leading liberal thinkers of the twentieth century. Of Austrian origin, he taught in Vienna until 1933, when he moved to the London School of Economics. In 1938 he acquired British citizenship. In 1950 he became a professor at the University of Chicago, and from 1962 he taught at Freiburg University in Germany. In 1974 he received the Nobel Prize for Economics. In his most famous book, *The Road to Serfdom* (1944), Hayek warned against the state taking over duties that can be performed by the individual, as this would always have negative and unforeseen side effects. Although he admitted that any civilized society had to live by a given set of rules, he resolutely opposed any degree of state interventionism in the economy and in society. Hayek was one of the most cogent opponents of *Keynes, and proved very influential among liberal thinkers and economists, not least in the new democracies of eastern Europe.

Heath, Edward Richard George ('Ted') (b. 9 July 1916). British Prime Minister 1970–4

Early career Born in Broadstairs, Kent, he was educated at Chatham School and Oxford, where he won a music scholarship. His early travels through the European mainland instilled in him a strong dislike and suspicion of *Fascism, which led him to oppose *appeasement. At the same time, it gave him a deep understanding of, and commitment to, a common European cultural heritage, which became the basis for his pro-European attitudes. After a distinguished military career in World War II, he was elected to parliament for the *Conservative Party to represent Bexley in 1950.

Heath was a member of the Conservative whips' office in 1952–5, and then became chief whip until 1959. Having worked hard to keep the party together during the *Suez Crisis, he was then Minister of Labour (1959–60), Lord Privy Seal (1960–3), and President of the Board of Trade (1963–4). In 1961–3, he was prominent as Britain's chief negotiator for entry into the European Economic Community (EEC). When *Douglas-Home resigned as party leader in 1965, Heath became leader in the first election for the post ever held. He was chosen for his youthful dynamism, which the party hoped could match that of his political rival, *Wilson. As party leader, he tried to reinvigorate the Conservative agenda by proposing tax cuts, union reforms, membership of the EEC, and the general reduction of government involvement in industry.

In office Heath became Prime Minister after winning the 1970 general election.

He succeeded in the task that was most dear to him, obtaining British entry into the EEC, which occurred on 1 January 1973. Domestically, though, he faced many difficulties. He responded to the growing *IRA campaign in *Northern Ireland and the intransigence of the Protestant majority over Catholic participation in business and politics with the imposition of direct rule from London. Meanwhile, despite his earlier intention to disengage government from industry, Heath was forced to rescue a number of key industries which were failing because of Britain's increasing economic difficulties.

Heath's main difficulty, however, was his relationship with *trade unions. Unable to negotiate a moderate wage settlement, he imposed an incomes policy in an attempt to deal with inflation. This led to a national coal strike in 1972, and strikes in the coal, power, and transport industries during the winter of 1973–4, culminating, in January-March 1974, in a three-day week caused by power shortages. In February 1974, Heath was forced to call a general election. He hoped to win, thus restoring his authority over the unions; the Conservatives gained more votes than *Labour, but fewer seats, and Harold *Wilson formed a minority government. Heath lost a subsequent election in October 1974, and was replaced as party leader in 1975 by Margaret *Thatcher. He remained in parliament until 2001, and over the years he became strongly critical of the Conservatives' drift against *European integration and towards monetarist economic policies.

Hejaz railway, see ARAB REVOLT

Helsinki Conference (30 July–1 Aug. 1975) The concluding meeting in a series of conferences held since 1973 in an attempt to reduce political tensions in Europe. It was attended by political leaders from thirty-five nations, with representatives from the Communist Eastern European states, Western Europe, the USA, and Canada. The concluding Helsinki Final Act contained three central commitments. First, it outlined a number of ways to prevent accidental confrontations between Eastern and Western Europe, i.e. between the *Warsaw Pact and *NATO. Second, it proposed a series of measures for economic and technological cooperation. Third, it obliged its participants to accept international conventions on *human rights, and generally to promote better understanding between the countries. The conference, and its offspring, the *Conference on Security and Cooperation in Europe, acknowledged a role for universal

human rights in domestic and international affairs. It represented a major breakthrough in communication between East and West, even if from 1979 *Cold War tensions increased again after the Soviet invasion of Afghanistan.

CHARTER '77; DISARMAMENT

Henlein, Konrad (b. 6 May 1898, d. 10 May 1945). Nazi leader of the Sudetenland 1938–45
From the *Sudetenland, an area in outer Bohemia inhabited by around three million people of German origin, he founded the Sudeten-German Party, which claimed Czech atrocities against the German minority. This served as *Hitler's excuse for his invasion of Czechoslovakia in 1938, and his annexation of the Sudetenland to Germany. Hitler appointed Henlein leader under the title of *Reichskomissar* (1938), and *Gauleiter* and *Statthalter* in charge of the Sudetenland (1939–45). Henlein committed suicide whilst in American imprisonment.

Herriot, Édouard Marie (b. 5 July 1872, d. 26 Mar. 1957). Prime Minister of France 1923–4, 1926, 1932
Herriot was *Radical Mayor of Lyons from 1905 until his death, except for the period of World War II. Despite his intimate knowledge of the political system, as Prime Minister he failed to address the country's financial problems, and relied on nationalist gestures instead. Following the abortive occupation of the *Ruhr in 1923 his acceptance of the *Dawes Plan signalled the French acknowledgement that Germany could not be pressured into *reparation payments by force, but only by diplomacy. He was president of the Chamber of Deputies (1936–40), but was arrested in 1942 and taken to Germany in 1944. Herriot served as president of the National Assembly 1947–54, whereupon he became its honorary president.

Hertzog, James Barry Munuik (b. 3 Apr. 1866, d. 21 Nov. 1942). Prime Minister of South Africa 1924–39

Early career Born in Soetendal (Cape Colony), his belief in the value of the Dutch-derived *Afrikaner language and culture was strengthened during his studies in the Netherlands, where he studied for a doctorate in law at the University of Amsterdam (1889–92). He returned to open a law practice in Pretoria, and in 1895 was appointed a judge in the Orange Free State (OFS). He became first a legal adviser and then a general of the OFS forces in the *South African War, and reluctantly became one of the signatories of the Peace of Vereeniging (31 May 1902). A co-founder of the Orangia-Unie party in 1906, in the first postwar government he became responsible for education, where he became controversial for his support of the Afrikaans language. He took part in the negotiations for South African union, and as a cultural leader of the Afrikaans-speaking people was included in Louis *Botha's first Cabinet. He opposed Botha's conciliatory attitude towards the English, however, and in early 1913 he was excluded from the Cabinet, whereupon he left the South African Party (SAP) to form the *National Party (NP). He opposed entry into World War I, and continued to appeal to Afrikaner *nationalism in demanding the right to secede from the *British Empire.

In office His party won the 1924 elections, and thereafter realized an enhanced status for his country within the British Empire (1926), introduced a new flag (1927), and elevated Afrikaans to the status of an official language (1925). He gained an absolute majority in the 1929 elections, but the Great *Depression, and his decision to leave the *Gold Standard in 1932, caused severe divisions in the NP.

In 1933, he agreed to join forces with *Smuts, with most of the NP and with the SAP, to form the *United South African National Party in 1934, despite the ferocious opposition of *Malan. Perhaps Hertzog's time in office is best known for his relentless and eventually successful campaign for the stepping-up of racial segregation, sealed by the passing of the Native Trust and Land Act and the Representation of Natives Act (1936). These became the basis of the *apartheid system. He was forced to resign because of his opposition to South Africa's entry into World War II.

Herzl, Theodor (b. 2 May 1860, d. 3 July 1904). Creator of modern Zionism
Born in Budapest, he was an assimilated Jew who became a journalist in Vienna, and was the Paris correspondent of the newspaper *Neue Freie Presse*, 1891–5. The *Dreyfus case sparked off his interest in *anti-Semitism and how it could be overcome. He published a book, *Der Judenstaat* (The Jewish State, 1896), in which he argued that the only effective response to centuries of anti-Jewish discrimination would be the foundation of an independent Jewish state in *Palestine. He devoted the rest of his life to propagating the idea, for which purpose he founded the World Zionist Organization, convened at the first World Zionist Congress in Switzerland in 1897.

Herzog, Roman (b. 5 Apr 1934). President of of Germany 1994–9
Born in Landshut (Bavaria), Herzog studied law and became an academic, and was given a chair in jurisprudence in 1965. An active Protestant, he joined the *CDU in 1970 and moved to the Rhineland Palatinate, where he became a close ally of the state's Minister President, *Kohl. He became a minister of the Rhineland Palatinate and then of Baden Württemberg, and in 1983 Kohl nominated him to Germany's supreme court, the Federal Constitutional Court. He became its President in 1987. As German President, Herzog confounded concerns that he might be too right-wing by speaking out for atonement for the German past and the better integration of the Eastern states. Perhaps his greatest achievement came in 2000, when, as Chair of the first European Convention, he oversaw the successful acceptance of the Charter of Fundamental Rights. This success led directly to a greater acceptance of the Convention model for reaching complex decisions in the EU, and the creation of the European *Constitutional Convention.

Hess, Rudolf (b. 26 Apr. 1894, d. 17 Aug. 1987). Hitler's deputy 1933–41
He joined the *Nazi Party in 1922, and following the *Hitler Putsch he served his prison sentence together with Hitler, whose dictations for his book *Mein Kampf* he wrote down. Hess became Hitler's private secretary in 1925, and Minister without Portfolio in 1933. He made a major contribution to the emergence of the cult around Hitler, which was popularized by the *propaganda of J. *Goebbels. On 10 May 1941, he flew to Scotland on his own initiative to try to conclude a separate peace with the British. He was imprisoned and sentenced at the *Nuremberg Trials to lifelong imprisonment, which he spent at the Spandau Prison, being from 1966 its sole inmate. After repeated Soviet refusals of a pardon, he committed suicide.

Heuss, Theodor (b. 31 Jan. 1884, d. 12 Dec. 1963). First President of West Germany 1949–59
Heavily influenced by the social and liberal ideas of Friedrich Naumann (b. 1860, d. 1919), the university lecturer entered the left-liberal Freisinnige Vereinigung in 1903, and the Deutsche Demokratische Partei in 1918, for whom he became an MP, 1924–8 and 1930–3. In 1945–9 a member of the Württemberg state parliament, he became the *Liberal Party (FDP) leader in 1948. Heuss greatly influenced the writing of the West German Basic Law (constitution), and in 1949 he was elected the

country's first President. He worked passionately for the reconciliation of all sections of German society, and his popularity helped greatly to reconcile many Germans to the new democratic system.

Heydrich, Reinhard (b. 7 Mar. 1904, d. 4 June 1942). Nazi police general

One of the most ruthless *Nazis, Heydrich joined the *SS in 1931, and in 1933 became chief of the Bavarian security services. In 1934 he took an important part in the Röhm Putsch against the *SA. In the same year he became chief of the *Gestapo, before being promoted to chief of the internal security service (*Sicherheitsdienst*) by H. *Himmler. Appointed general of the police in 1941, he became responsible for the execution of the 'final solution'. As he had also been appointed deputy 'protector' of Bohemia in 1941, he was murdered by a Czech in Prague. In retaliation, **Lidice**, a Czech village, was destroyed by the SS and *Gestapo on 10 June 1942. All male inhabitants (over 160) were shot, the 192 women were deported to the *concentration camp at Ravensbrück, where 52 of them died, and 96 children were deported to be 'Germanized' in SS camps.

Hezbollah ('party of allah')

Origins A radical *Islamic fundamentalist party and guerrilla organization. It emerged in response to Israel's occupation of Lebanon (1982–4), and was primarily committed to the expulsion of the Israeli military from southern Lebanon. For this purpose, it committed regular attacks on military targets, as well as civilian targets in northern Israel. Ultimately, it was pledged to the destruction of the state of Israel, and the erection of a theocratic Islamic Palestinian state. In response to the *Gaza-Jericho agreement of 1993, it joined a radical Arab alliance to fight the subsequent Middle Eastern peace process, which it managed to put at serious risk in 1996, when its attacks on northern Israel triggered heavy Israeli bombardment of southern Lebanon.

Contemporary politics (since 2005)
Hezbollah not only contributed to the Israeli withdrawal from Lebanon, it also gained popular support through the running of social services. As a result, Hezbollah gained over a quarter of all seats in the Lebanese Assembly in 2005. Its political influence increased further following the murder of *Hariri, which was blamed on Hezbollah even though the organization denied involvement. Meanwhile, its paramilitary groups continued to arm, largely with the aid of Syria which

wanted to keep up pressure on Israel to end Israeli occuption of the *Golan Heights. Indeed, following the withdrawal of Syrian troops in 2005, Hezbollah fighters constituted a strong military presence in southern Lebanon.

In 2006, Hezbollah abducted two Israeli soldiers in order to trade them for Hezbollah prisoners in Israel. However, Israel struck back, attacking Hezbollah fighters in southern Lebanon. In a month of fighting, Israel damaged much of Hezbollah's military infrastructure, but Hezbollah was not defeated, firing rockets into northern Israel until the end. Following a UN-brokered ceasefire, southern Lebanon was occupied by an international force, whose remit was to keep the peace and to prevent the illegal provision of arms to Hezbollah.

Himmler, Heinrich (b. 7 Oct. 1900, d. 23 May 1945). Leader of the SS

Born in Munich, he studied agriculture and took part in the *Hitler Putsch of 1923. He joined the *SS in 1925, and headed it from 1929. After the *Nazis took power in 1933, he managed to submit the German police to SS control. Himmler created a security network which eliminated most of the German opposition and murdered millions of Jews, eastern Europeans, and other groups that did not conform to his fanatic image of a 'pure, Aryan' German race. During the last months of World War II he sought to negotiate a peace with the Western *Allies so as to be able to continue fighting the Soviet Union. After Germany's capitulation he dressed up as a policeman, and was imprisoned by the British. He committed suicide when he was recognized.

Hindenburg, Paul von Beneckendorff und von (b. 2 Oct. 1847, d. 2 Aug. 1934). President of Germany 1925–34

He retired as supreme commander of the German armed forces in 1911, but re-entered the army in 1914. After his legendary victorious campaign on the Eastern Front which included the battle of *Tannenberg, he became with *Ludendorff the head of the German Supreme Command in 1916. In this position he became a quasi-dictator of military, political, and economic affairs. After the war he retired again until his election as German President with the support of the right. In 1932, he was the only person whose standing was so high that he could beat *Hitler in the elections for President, this time with the support of the *SPD and the *Centre. He has often been accused of being unwilling and/or

unable to stop the rise of Hitler, whom he
appointed Chancellor in 1933. Yet despite
the fact that the *Nazi party had become
the biggest party in parliament by 1932, he
refused at first to appoint Hitler as Chancellor,
preferring the appointments of von *Papen
(1 June–17 November 1932) and then
K. von Schleicher (3 December 1932–28
January 1933).

Hindu Mahasabha

An Indian political party established in 1913
to bring together various Hindu movements
opposed to British concessions to the
*Muslim League. With its main strength in
areas with a large Muslim community (Punjab
and Bengal), it campaigned for the Hindu
character of India, and encouraged the
conversion of Hindus from *Islam. Its
aggressive attitudes towards Muslims led to
strained relations with the Indian National
*Congress, which fundamentally restricted
the growth of the movement. Under its leader,
V. D. Sarvarkar, it became an important
influence in the foundation of the Jana Sangh
(*Janata Party) after independence in 1947.

Hinduism

The oldest world religion, to which most
Indians adhere. All gods are manifestations of
Brahma, the supreme being of the Hindu
pantheon, who is part of a trinity with Vishnu,
the all-preserver, and Siva, the mystic,
miracle-working deity. Into Brahma, the
ultimate world-spirit, the reincarnated,
purified individual spirit is finally absorbed.
The oldest extant scriptures are the
eighth-century BC Sanskrit texts, the
Upanishads, from which the systems of Hindu
law and social structure are derived, including
the caste system. Of later texts the
Mahabharata remains extremely influential,
within which is the Bhagavadgita (c.300 BC),
where Krishna, the lord of creation, teaches
self-mastery through the Yoga, which aims at
the harmonization of body, soul, and spirit.
   Perhaps the greatest modern Hindu
reformer was Mohandas K. *Gandhi, who
based his campaign on the deep roots of
Hinduism. His *satyagraha ('holding fast to the
truth'), emphasized non-violent methods of
protest, while he also his practised yoga,
meditation, fasting, and non-violence to any
living thing, ahimsa. At the same time, Gandhi
was concerned to reform some fundamental
aspects of Hinduism, in particular the
rejection of the caste of the untouchables,
whom he addressed as harijans ('children of
God'). This pointed to a fundamental problem
of modern India, namely the tension between
the old Hindu caste systemand traditional

subservience of women on one hand, and the
requirements of a modern secular state with
equal responsibilities toward all its citizens
on the other. The insistence on non-violence
also clashed with frequent involvement in
wars with religious undercurrents, notably
the *Indo-Pakistan Wars and civil war in Sri
Lanka.

HIPC (Heavily Indebted Poor Countries) initiative

Proposed by the *World Bank and the *IMF in
1996, and extended by a meeting of finance
ministers of the G7 meeting in Cologne in
1999. It proposed debt relief for the 42 poorest
countries which had 'unsustainable debts' if
they met a number of criteria, which included
stable government structures and stable
budgets in which the gains from debt relief
would be invested in education and social
spending. Although welcomed by many non-
governmental organizations, it was criticized
as not being the breakthrough claimed by
politicians. The classical criteria for economic
stability were criticized, as they had not
worked in the past. The G7 criteria for the
'sustainability' of debt (according to ability to
pay, not the need to develop) have also been
criticized. Finally, the mechanisms by which
countries were to qualify were accused of
being heavy-handed and slow. Nevertheless,
by 2007, 29 countries had successfully
qualified for full debt relief under the HIPC
initiative. According to data provided by the
World Bank, total debt relief for these
countries amounted to some $62 billion. In
these countries, an average of 2 per cent of
GDP was diverted from debt relief to fighting
poverty. Nevertheless, the countries were not
relieved of all of their debt, and many states
continued to struggle with servicing their
debt burdens.

((⊕)) SEE WEB LINKS

- Data from the World Bank on the state of the HIPC.
- Data from a think tank monitoring the progress of the HIPC.

Hirohito (b. 29 Apr. 1904, d. 7 Jan. 1989).
124th Emperor of Japan 1926–89
After World War II, the question of
responsibility for Japan's decision to attack its
neighbours was to remain a source of
controversy for Emperor Hirohito and much
attention has focused on the early years of his
reign. After attending the peers' school,
Gakushûin, he took a tour of Europe in 1921 to
see for himself the role of constitutional
monarchy in Great Britain, Belgium, Holland,
and Italy. In the same year Hirohito was

appointed regent because of the illness of his father. Known as the Shôwa Emperor, the extent to which Hirohito could exercise influence over political developments in Japan at this time is a matter of debate, although it seems clear that the removal of his support for *Tanaka Giichi's Cabinet was instrumental in its downfall. Moreover, his forthright opposition to the coup attempted by army officers in the 26 February Incident (1936) did much to facilitate its suppression. Nevertheless, the imperial house has provided evidence that Emperor Hirohito was unable to block Japanese aggression until he insisted on the surrender in August 1945. After the surrender, Hirohito became integral to the US occupation's successful programme for the democratization of Japan. Crucial to this process was his renunciation of divinity in his New Year radio message of 1946. Under the new *Japanese constitution, the Emperor's sovereignty was made subject to that of the people. In private life Hirohito avoided much controversy, devoting much of his time to marine biology.

Hiroshima

A Japanese city in southern Honshu. During *World War II, it had remained undamaged by the US bombing campaign of 1944–5. The site of extensive armaments industries was chosen as the target for the first atomic bomb attack on 6 August 1945. This resulted in the virtual obliteration of the city centre, some 80,000 immediate deaths, with another 60,000 dying within a year. Radiation effects continued for decades. The attack, together with that on *Nagasaki, led to Japan's unconditional surrender and the end of World War II.

MANHATTAN PROJECT; NUCLEAR BOMB

Hirota Kôki (b. 14 Feb. 1878, d. 23 Dec. 1948). Prime Minister of Japan 1936–7
Hirota's origins were humble, but after a brilliant academic career as a student at Tokyo University, he had become a career diplomat, serving as ambassador in Moscow. Heading a government formed in the aftermath of the 26 February Incident (1936), Hirota, in his dual role as Foreign Minister, concluded the Tripartite Anti-Comintern Pact with Germany in 1936 and Italy in 1937 (*Axis). He was thus held directly responsible for Japan's later decision to go to war with China first and then the USA and Great Britain. His decision to allow serving military officers to represent the army and navy Cabinet posts also bolstered the political influence of the military. After stepping down from the premiership, Hirota managed to retain the foreign portfolio

(1937–9) and his influence was maintained during the war years as a senior member of the political establishment. Although Hirota always maintained that he preferred conciliation to conflict, he played an instrumental part in Japan's Asian war. On that charge he was found guilty and sentenced to hang by the *Tokyo Trials for war crimes.

Histadrut (General Federation of Labour, Israel)
A trade union established in Haifa in 1920 in order to organize workers in their quest for better pay and working conditions. It became the most important Jewish grass-roots movement, and provided invaluable support for *Mapai and the *Jewish Agency. In the absence of a Jewish state, it assumed widespread responsibilities for its members' health care and protection against poverty, while it provided crucial economic services such as banking, the marketing of members' products, etc. It maintained many of these functions after the creation of the state of Israel, in which it assumed a position of overwhelming economic importance, thanks to its alliance with *Mapai and the *Labour Party, which dominated Israeli politics until 1977. As a result, it became Israel's biggest employer, owning the country's largest bank and its largest health insurance fund. The organization declined sharply from the 1980s, losing a majority of its membership. The Histadrut had had its social and cultural base amongst European Jewish immigrants, and proved unable to appeal to the influx of citizens from other parts of the world, notably Africa and the Middle East.

(⊕) SEE WEB LINKS
• The official website of Histadrut.

Hitler, Adolf (b. 20 Apr. 1889, d. 30 Apr. 1945). The world's most ruthless dictator.

Background Born in the Austrian town of Braunau, as the son of a customs official conceived out of wedlock, he left middle school without qualifications in 1905 and subsequently failed twice to get into a Viennese art school for lack of ability. During these years of unfulfilment he probably developed his racial ideas as well as his hatred of Jews and eastern Europeans, whom he blamed for his personal misery and whom he came to regard collectively as his greatest enemy. He went to Munich to evade the draft into the Austrian army in 1913, but upon the outbreak of World War I he volunteered into a Bavarian regiment. He failed to rise in rank beyond corporal, but was awarded the Iron Cross for military bravery.

Political beginnings and creed

Directionless once again after 1918, he joined the *Nazi Party as its fifty-fifth member in 1919 and became its leader in 1921. Amidst a host of other nationalist groups which operated in Munich, Hitler's party soon became one of the most prominent. Following the abortive *Hitler Putsch he used his nine months (1924) in prison to write a book, *Mein Kampf* (*My Struggle*, published in two volumes, 1925, 1926) in which he laid out his central ideology, which had two key characteristics. The first was his racial ideology, especially his belief in the superiority of the 'Aryan' (German) race. For the benefit of this race, he aimed at expanding its 'living space' (*Lebensraum*) at the expense of the Slavs to the east, whom he considered 'inferior'. A precondition of this would be the revision of the *Versailles Treaty and the revival of Germany as an economic, political, and military world power. A second, and related, characteristic was the aim to create a 'national community' in Germany which would break down all barriers of class. In accordance with his racial ideology this could only be achieved through the 'removal' of Jews and other minorities (of sexual orientation, race, religion, etc.). Although these ideals were clearly extreme in the contemporary climate, they nevertheless fed into the prejudices that were rapidly developing in Weimar Germany.

Ascent to power

After his release from prison he resolved to gain power by legal means. Eventually, this attempt to gain 'respectability', together with the youthful and promising image which the party presented under the influence of its *propaganda leader, *Goebbels, paid off. In the elections that were held in 1930 during the Great *Depression, the *Nazi Party was catapulted from the political fringe to the second largest party nationwide. As the general sense of crisis deepened, Hitler's popularity increased, and on 30 January 1933 he was finally appointed Chancellor at the head of a government which contained only three members of the Nazi Party (out of ten ministers).

Securing power

After four months, in which he used the *Reichstag fire as a pretext for persecuting *Communist Party and *SPD members, and in which he passed the *Enabling Act, Hitler had succeeded in assuming dictatorial powers. His position was strengthened by the Röhm Putsch on the *SA, which ensured the cooperation of the military, and the death of *Hindenburg in 1934, which enabled him officially to take over as *Führer of the country. He virtually eliminated unemployment through a massive rearmament programme and, at the first signs that his popularity was declining, he began the expansionist policies which would spark off World War II. The remilitarization of the *Rhineland in 1936 was followed by the *Anschluss, as well as the annexations of the *Sudetenland and the Czech lands. These moves were condemned abroad, but no power dared challenge Hitler's actions. As a result of these military and diplomatic successes, Hitler believed even more firmly in his own destiny and invincibility.

World War II

After concluding the *Hitler–Stalin Pact, Hitler attacked Poland on 1 September 1939. Britain and France had made clear that such a step would bring them into war. As a result, Hitler attacked France and the Low Countries, as well as Denmark and Norway in 1940, bringing them under his control in the *Blitzkrieg. Despite the widening of the war, which expanded to North Africa and the Balkans, Hitler remained preoccupied with his colonial fantasies of the east. On 22 June 1941 he launched the *Barbarossa campaign against the Soviet Union. On 19 December 1941, the former corporal took charge of the military planning of the war himself, while at the same time he became increasingly paranoid and reclusive. The start of the 'total war' in 1941 coincided with the attempt to realize Hitler's second aim in *Mein Kampf*, the start of the 'final solution' in Germany and the occupied territories. This meant the deportation of millions of Jews prior to their mass murder in *concentration camps such as *Auschwitz. Although in the absence of a written order for the 'final solution' the exact timing is still highly controversial, it is clear that the 'final solution' was part of the radicalisation of war. With the conquest of Poland, the number of Jews living under German control had risen sixfold. As some German troops systematically rounded up Jews in conquered villages and shot them in mass graves, in the autumn of 1941 Jews in Poland and elsewhere were forced to move into Ghettos, from where they would be transported to the concentration and extermination camps.

Defeat

In the end, Germany's military mistakes, its inferior equipment, and the strong resurgence of the Red Army proved decisive in the Barbarossa campaign, and Hitler's own mistakes added to this. Military withdrawal was hastened by the German inability to prevent *D-Day, so that German troops were fighting a three-front war in the east, south and west. Hitler's dictatorship ended with the total military, economic, and moral collapse of Germany. Remarkably, so charismatic was his rule that right up to the bitter end, most Germans remained loyal. Rather than facing the consequences, he decided to commit suicide with his companion Eva Braun, whom he had finally married only hours earlier.

Hitler Putsch (8–9 Nov. 1923)

An abortive coup attempt by *Hitler. With the support of *Ludendorff, he tried to seize power in the Bavarian capital of Munich as a prelude to a March on Berlin akin to *Mussolini's *March on Rome. After initial hesitation, the Bavarian government ordered police to suppress the coup attempt, and sixteen people died. In the ensuing trials Ludendorff was acquitted, and Hitler was sentenced to five years' imprisonment, though he was released after nine months.

Hitler Youth

Founded in 1926 as the youth organization of the *SA, it had around 100,000 members by 1933. Given the *Nazi aim of controlling all cultural aspects of the *Third Reich, and the desire to indoctrinate especially the young as the future bearers of responsibility, it was developed into a national mass organization. All other youth organizations (apart from Roman Catholic ones) were forbidden. From the ages of 10 to 14, children were expected to join separate groups for boys or girls respectively, while those aged between 14 and 18 were encouraged to join the Hitler Youth proper for boys, and the League of German Maidens for girls. In 1936, these youth organizations were given official sanction as an educational institution alongside the school and home. Membership became compulsory in 1939, when it reached almost nine million members. As many children joined only with the minimum degree of commitment required, it is unclear to what extent the Hitler Youth was successful in inculcating the young with a Nazi world-view.

Hitler–Stalin Pact (23 Aug. 1939)

Also referred to as the *Molov-*Ribbentrop pact after its two principal signatories, the foreign ministers of the Soviet Union and Germany. Both countries agreed not to attack each other or support a third power which attacked either of them. The pact came as a surprise to contemporaries, since it was signed by fierce ideological opponents. Taking note of German expansionism since the *Anschluss, *Stalin hoped to avoid a confrontation with *Nazi Germany. To *Hitler, by contrast, it guaranteed a free hand

for his intended conquest of Poland at the beginning of *World War II. In the event of British and French intervention, it allowed Germany to avoid a war on two fronts.

Of much greater significance than the official pact was its secret protocol. It divided eastern and central Europe into a German and a Soviet sphere of influence within which each power was free to undertake military invasions without retribution from the other power. Throughout its existence, the Soviet Union denied the existence of the Secret Protocol, which was supplemented by two further secret protocols determining the borders between the German and Soviet spheres of influence. From the day of its signing, the pact proved an ideological embarrassment to Communists who defined themselves as anti-Fascists. It became a dead letter when Hitler surprised Stalin through the *Barbarossa campaign.

Ho Chi Minh (he who enlightens) (b. 19 May 1890, d. 3 Sept. 1969). President of the Democratic Republic of Vietnam 1945–69

Rise to power Born Nguyen Tat Thanh as the son of a local scholar in Kim Lienh (central Annam), he was educated at the National Academy (Quac Hoc). In 1911, he travelled to Europe as a ship's steward. In 1918 he went to work as a socialist journalist in Paris, and in 1920 he became a founding member of the French *Communist Party. Expelled from France in 1923, he went to Moscow and then to south China in 1924, where he recruited Vietnamese exiles to *Communism, under the banner of the Communist Youth League of Vietnam. This was transformed in 1930, under his direction, into the Communist Party of *Indochina, which was fiercely repressed after uprisings in 1930–1. At this time he was in Hong Kong, where he was briefly imprisoned, before returning to Vietnam to build up the Communist Party into the main oppositional force to French colonial rule. Back in China from 1938, together with other Communist exiles such as *Vo Nguyen Giap he founded the *Vietminh Front in 1941. In 1943 he again returned in secret to Vietnam, where he began to recruit Vietminh guerrilla fighters and to organize resistance to the Japanese, adopting the name Ho Chi Minh.

In power Upon the defeat of the Japanese in 1945 he proclaimed the Democratic Republic of Vietnam on 2 September, of which he became President and (until 1955) Prime Minister. The new state was never recognized by the French, who now sought to re-establish colonial control. Helped by his military commander, Vo Nguyen Giap, he won the ensuing *Indochina War through his capacity to inspire and generate popular support. By his authority alone he managed to convince the more radical members of his party to accept the compromise of the *Geneva Agreements, which left him only in control of Vietnam north of the 17th Parallel. In this territory, he established a socialist regime, while striving to undermine the South Vietnamese government in any way possible. He managed to keep the support of both the Soviet Union and China as he led the country through the first years of the *Vietnam War. Though stern and authoritarian, he was known as 'Uncle Ho' among his people. Saigon was renamed Ho Chi Minh City in 1975.

Hobhouse, Leonard Trelawny (b. 8 Sept. 1864, d. 21 June 1929). British Liberal theorist

Born at St Ive, near Liskeard, Cornwall, he was educated at Marlborough and Oxford. He taught philosophy at Oxford (1890-7), publishing his first book, *The Labour Movement*, in 1893. This contained the first statement of his views on *collectivism, which made an impact on the *Liberal Party in the 1890s through 'New Liberalism'. Its proponents argued that the state should take a more active role in combating poverty through the collective provision of welfare schemes, in order to enable each individual to reach her/his highest potential. These ideas were best developed in his *Liberalism* (1911). In 1897-1902, Hobhouse worked on the *Manchester Guardian* as a leader-writer, promoting closer links between the *Liberal Party and the Labour movement. Apart from his immensely important contribution to British Liberal thought, his other major contribution to British intellectual life concerned his work in the development of sociology as a separate intellectual discipline in Britain. In 1903, he co-founded the Sociological Society, and in 1907, he became the first professor of sociology at London University. Hobhouse was a consistent advocate of the enfranchisement of women. He campaigned for better relations with Germany, but supported the British war effort once World War I had commenced. As the war went on, he drifted leftwards, urging Britain to modify its war aims, and looking forward to the establishment of a *League of Nations. He continued to criticize the class antagonisms of the *Labour Party, and the postwar divisions of the Liberals, although throughout the 1920s he advised and consulted with members of both parties.

Hobson, John Atkinson (b. 6 July 1858, d. 1 Apr. 1940). British economist

Born in Derby, and educated in Derby and at Oxford. In the 1880s and 1890s he taught classics at various schools, and was a lecturer in Oxford and London. From the publication of his first work, *The Physiology of Industry* (1889), he was a prominent advocate of progressive taxation, as a way of developing welfare schemes and tackling poverty. He also argued that redistribution of wealth throughout all levels of society was necessary, since the economy needed large numbers of people to be able to consume its products if it were to thrive. The absence of consumption caused not only unemployment, but also *imperialism, as the owners of capital were forced to look for new markets. Together with *Hobhouse, his views were influential on the *Liberal Party in developing 'New Liberalism', which sought to adapt the classic tenets of individual *liberalism to a modern, industrial society. His most famous work was *Imperialism: A Study* (1902), which partly reflected his distaste for Britain's part in the *South African (Boer) War. Despite this devastating critique of *capitalism, for many years he pinned his hopes on gradual reforms through Liberal governments, though he was close to Ramsay *MacDonald and other leaders of the *Labour Party.

Hoffa, James Riddle ('Jimmy') (b. 14 Feb. 1913, d. 30 July 1975). US trade union activist

Born at Brazil, Indiana, he devoted his life to trade union activism, and was elected president of the *Teamsters Union in the US in 1957. He quickly became one of the most famous and infamous of trade union leaders in American history. He expanded the union's membership, secured many advantages for his members, and worked towards the creation of a comprehensive transport union. However, his methods—which involved a great deal of accommodation with organized crime and corruption—attracted the interest of Robert F. *Kennedy, who, as Attorney-General of the USA (1961-4), pursued Hoffa in the hope of bringing criminal charges. In March 1967 Hoffa was finally convicted and sentenced to thirteen years' imprisonment. In 1971 his sentence was commuted to parole on President *Nixon's orders, albeit with the stipulation that for the remainder of his sentence he was not to engage in trade union activity. Nevertheless, in 1975 he seemed poised to recover his status as leader of the Teamsters when he disappeared in mysterious circumstances. He has been presumed dead.

Holland, see NETHERLANDS, THE

Holland, Sir Sidney George (b. 18 Oct. 1893, d. 5 Aug. 1961). Prime Minister of New Zealand 1949–57

Born in Greendale (Canterbury), he served in World War I and became a successful businessman thereafter. In 1935 he followed his father into the House of Representatives and in 1940 became leader of the *National Party due to their desperate search for a vigorous and youthful leader. After a brief period in the War Cabinet, he set about rebuilding his divided party, which eventually came to power in 1949. As Prime Minister, he gradually relaxed the state controls on enterprise established during the war. In 1950, he abolished the Upper House and the Legislative Council. In 1951, he used the bitter strike by the Waterside Worker's Union to call a general election, which he won with a comfortable majority.

Holland shifted the National Party to the left, whereby it endorsed pragmatic conservatism, for example through strengthening much of the social welfare legislation which had been introduced by the *Labour Party. In foreign policy, he committed troops to fight in the *Korean War, and welcomed the creation of *ANZUS and *SEATO, which New Zealand joined. Despite his emphasis on the need for closer relations with the USA and its Asian neighbours, he remained strongly committed to the country's links with Britain and the *Commonwealth, supporting *Eden in the *Suez Crisis. He retired owing to ill health.

Holocaust
The term denotes a victim who has been burnt completely. It is used to describe the *Nazi genocide of the Jewish people in *concentration camps such as *Auschwitz during World War II.

Holyoake, Sir Keith Jacka (b. 11 Feb. 1904, d. 8 Dec. 1983). Prime Minister of New Zealand 1957, 1960–72

A successful farmer from the area north of Wellington, he entered New Zealand politics in 1932 as an MP for the *Reform Party and spokesman for farmers' interests. In 1936 his party amalgamated with the United Party to form the *National Party. He was Deputy Prime Minister and Minister of Agriculture under Sidney *Holland (1949–57). When Holland had to retire in September 1957 because of ill health, he briefly took over as Prime Minister and Minister of Native Affairs, but he lost the election in December. He won the 1960 general elections, however, when he

also became Minister of External/Foreign Affairs (1960–72). Holyoake was a leading *Commonwealth opponent of Ian *Smith's establishment of a racist White government in Rhodesia, and of the *apartheid regime in South Africa. Firmly committed to the country's military alliance with the USA through *ANZUS, he supported US involvement in the *Vietnam War, and was responsible for the participation of New Zealand troops there. He was bitterly opposed to, but unable to prevent, British entry into the EEC (*European integration), though he did manage to retain some preferential treatment for New Zealand products. He acted as Minister of State, 1975–7, and retired from party politics to become Governor-General (1977–80).

Home Guard ('Dad's Army') (UK)
Originally formed as the Local Defence Volunteers on 14 May 1940, in response to the German invasion of the Low Countries. It was principally raised to combat possible German parachute landings. Over a quarter of a million men had volunteered by 15 May, and local units were formed immediately. It was renamed the Home Guard in July 1940, and equipped with khaki uniforms. Initially dress was varied and in the absence of guns, its members equipped themselves with old swords, pikes, and pitchforks. Known as 'Dad's Army', most of its members were men who were too old to serve in the forces, together with boys of 17 and 18. In 1942 compulsory enrolment was introduced, and by the summer of 1943 its numbers reached two million. It was disbanded in December 1944. Despite considerable doubts as to its effectiveness, it made a very positive impact upon British morale in the early years of the war.

Home, Lord, see DOUGLAS-HOME, SIR ALEXANDER FREDERICK

Honduras
One of Central America's poorest societies, which has been struggling to come to terms with a legacy of social injustice and civil war.

Contemporary history (up to 1982) Perhaps the perfect example of a Central American 'banana republic', by the late 1920s 90 per cent of its exports consisted of bananas from the plantations of three giant US companies. At that point, the companies determined not only the country's economy but also its infrastructure, politics, and social spending. Their authority was further enhanced by the support of the US government, which frequently interfered in domestic politics (seven military interventions 1903–37). Even though they continued to retain a crucial role in domestic life, the influence of the banana companies was reduced by two central factors. First, they were hit by a slump in prices following the Great *Depression, and the spread of plant diseases during the 1930s. In 1942–3, banana exports stood at 10 per cent of their peak in 1929–30, with GDP in 1943 only at 36 per cent of its 1930 level. Second, the country was modernized dramatically under the government of Juan Manuel Gálvez (1949–54), when the banana companies were taxed efficiently for the first time, an independent infrastructure was established, an independent central bank was founded (1950), and sanitary works were instigated.

These policies of modernization were continued by Gálvez's three successors until they were halted in 1963 by a military whose own privileges had become threatened by the reforms. Military rule was characterized by high administrative incompetence during the 1960s, while the military itself was almost defeated in the 1968 *Soccer War. Despite increasing levels of corruption during the 1970s, the economy began to show some gradual improvement. After the establishment of a Constituent Assembly in 1980, a new Constitution was passed and in January 1982 civilian rule was resumed.

Democratization (1982–2000) During the 1980s, US influence increased even further through its use of Honduras as the main refuge for the Nicaraguan Contras, and the establishment of a direct US military presence there. Virtual US domination of Honduran foreign policy was ended only towards the late 1980s, when the civilian government decided to endorse the peace plan of *Arias Sánchez in opposition to current US policy. The domestic economy was hit by the subsequent decline of US spending in Honduras. At the same time, the civilian government also became more confident against the dominant military establishment. Under the liberal president Carlos Roberto Reina Idiaquez (1994–98), compulsory military service was abolished in April 1995, while the first military officers were charged with *human rights abuses in July 1995. Honduras continued to struggle with the human rights legacy of the civil war under his predecessor, Carlos Flores Facussé.

Contemporary politics (since 2000) Former military generals became subject to prosecution after the Supreme Court declared in 2000 that unjustified imprisonments and capital punishment committed during the civil war were not covered by the amnesty of 1987. In 2005 Honduras qualified for debt relief under the *HIPC initiative, though with coffee and bananas continuing to be its major export commodities, the country suffered from widespread poverty. In 2006, José Manuel Zelaya was sworn in as President. He vowed to continue the fight against the criminal gangs responsible for high murder rates and extensive drug trafficking.

Honecker, Erich (b. 25 Aug. 1912, d. 29 May 1994). Leader of East Germany 1971–89

Early career Born in Neunkirchen, *Saarland, he joined the Communist Youth League in 1926, and the *Communist Party in 1929. Following the *Nazi takeover in 1933 he went underground, but was captured in 1935 and sentenced to ten years' imprisonment in 1937. Liberated by the *Red Army in 1945, the Soviet commanders of Eastern Germany put him in charge of building up the Communist youth movement, the FDJ (Freie Deutsche Jugend, Free German Youth), whose leader he remained until 1955. A member of the Communist Party's Central Committee since 1945, he joined the *Politburo in 1958 and replaced *Ulbricht as its First Secretary in 1971.

In office As leader of East Germany (the German Democratic Republic, GDR) Honecker's political priority was to provide the individual with the wherewithal to realize her or his fulfilment within socialism. This included not just political stability and economic growth, but also an emphasis on consumer goods and leisure activities. Of particular importance to Honecker was the building of new flats. Wages were increased, and the five-day working week accepted. If these policies were daring when they were envisaged at the start of his time in office, they became completely unrealistic after the *oil price shock of 1973. Imports became more expensive, as did the energy deliveries in oil and gas which the GDR was forced to import from the USSR. To maintain the increased standard of living for the population, therefore, the GDR was forced to borrow heavily on the international money markets.

By the early 1980s Honecker's policies had rendered the GDR practically bankrupt. The country was sustained by West German credit payments, notably in 1983 and 1984. However, the election of *Gorbachev in 1985 exposed a final Achilles heel for the GDR. An artificial state since its creation which had failed to legitimize itself through its political system, it was sustained by Soviet military support. Honecker was unwilling and unable to follow the policies of *glasnost and *perestroika. After unprecedented popular demonstrations sparked off by Gorbachev's visit to the country in 1989, which increasingly challenged the nature of the Communist regime itself, Honecker was forced to resign on 18 October 1989. By that time, Honecker had completely lost touch with his citizens and their anger. After German reunification, he stood trial for manipulating elections and for being responsible for those who died at the *Berlin Wall, but in 1993 he was released because of ill health.

Hong Kong

British sovereignty (up to 1997) A territory on the south coast of China, situated on the mouth of the Pearl River, opposite *Macao. The British occupied the island of Hong Kong in 1841, declaring it a Crown Colony in 1843. To it were added Kowloon and Stonecutters Island in 1860. The British acquired the New Territories, which became its biggest area by far, on a 99-year lease in 1898. Its population quadrupled from 1900 to 1941, owing to continuous unrest and warfare in mainland China, until the Japanese overran the British forces stationed there in December 1941. British control was re-established after the Japanese surrender in 1945, but the struggling colony only began to prosper from 1949, when *Mao's victory in the *Chinese Civil War prompted the influx of capital and cheap labour from China.

Over the decades, the area was transformed into one of the world's fastest-growing economies, with full employment, growth rates averaging 10 per cent, and a booming stock market. In 1966 and 1967, riots against the authoritarian government, into whose affairs Britain hardly intervened, caused a moderate opening-up of the colony's administration, though this was restricted to the consultation of elites rather than democratic government. Under Governor Sir Murray MacLehose, an extensive housing scheme was introduced for the first time, and social services were improved.

In 1984, an agreement between the UK and China was reached over the future of the New Territories, the lease on which expired on 1 July 1997. The entire colony of Hong Kong would revert to Chinese control, but retain considerable autonomy as a Special Administrative Region, which would retain its *capitalist economy for at least fifty years. Details were put down in a Basic Law, which fell short of the colony's expectations of guarantees against arbitrary Chinese rule. Concerns about impending Communist rule, which reached a climax in response to the *Tiananmen Square Massacre of 1989, led to a series of unprecedented political reforms. A Human Rights Ordinance was passed in 1990, capital punishment was abolished, and the Legislative Assembly was opened to greater democratic representation.

Contemporary politics (since 1997) Under Chinese rule since 1997, Hong Kong's economy was transformed into a high-skilled economy which benefited from its access to China's industrial base. Many of the political reforms of the final years of British rule were repealed by the Chinese, with Hong Kong being governed by a Chief Executive appointed in Beijing. Between 1997 and 2005, this post was filled by the unpopular Tung Chee Hwa, who appeared to be unable to respond to the concerns of Hong Kong's political classes. Following his resignation, Tung was replaced by his deputy, Donald Tsang.

Hoover, Herbert Clark (b. 10 Aug. 1874, d. 20 Oct. 1964). 31st US President 1929–33

Early career A gifted administrator and self-made millionaire with an extensive knowledge of mining engineering, he was born at West Branch, Iowa, and graduated with an AB in engineering from Stanford in 1895. He directed the Belgian relief operations in 1917–19 and became Commerce Secretary in the *Harding administration after being passed over for the *Republican presidential nomination in 1920. In 1928, he won his campaign against the Democrat Al Smith, the first serious Catholic candidate for the presidency.

Presidency Almost immediately upon coming into office, Hoover was faced with the *Wall Street Crash. Hoover was deeply suspicious of government interference in the economy. Instead, he hoped to create inducements for private industry to stimulate growth, and encourage investment through extra lending from the private sector. In 1932 he authorized the creation of the Reconstruction Finance Corporation to provide extra loans for banks. He authorized the building of the Colorado Dam project in Nevada (now named after him), but vetoed a similar programme for job creation and electricity generation in Tennessee. He also endorsed the Smoot–Hawley Tariff, which sought to protect US domestic markets from foreign competition. Unfortunately, the Tariff increased the price of imports at a time of low liquidity, and contributed materially to a slump in world trade.

Hoover's name has been, perhaps somewhat unfairly, associated with the Great *Depression. His insistence that 'prosperity was just around the corner' caused his reputation to plummet, against the evidence of growing jobless queues and pending economic crisis. In 1932, an angry 'Bonus Army' of about 20,000 veterans gathered in Washington demanding premature payment of their bonuses. The dispersal of their temporary camp by troops commanded by Douglas *MacArthur, who used excessive violence, fuelled the impression of Hoover as heartless. After leaving office, Hoover chaired several important commissions on the reorganization of the federal government and executive for Presidents *Truman and *Eisenhower.

Hoover, John Edgar (b. 1 Jan. 1895, d. 2 May 1972). Director of the FBI 1924–72
Born in Washington, DC, Hoover studied law and received his LLM Degree from George Washington University in 1917. He entered the Federal Department of Justice, and in 1921 became assistant director of the Bureau of Investigation (*FBI from 1935). As its director from 1924 he improved the Bureau's reputation by vigorous selection and training of personnel. Under his direction, the FBI pioneered techniques in forensic science. During the 1930s his widely publicized arrests of certain criminals, while not ending syndicate crime, earned the FBI a reputation for integrity.

Hoover's increasingly authoritarian style and his almost complete autonomy became more and more controversial. Most damaging of all was his antipathy to Black activists and to the *civil rights movement, evident in his harassment of Martin Luther *King. He also passed on incriminating material obtained illegally to *McCarthy and the House Committee on Un-American Activities. He died in office after a career marked by the abuse of power rooted in files on thousands of politicians and prominent individuals with which he destroyed careers and refined the business of blackmail. These files disappeared on his death, thought to have been destroyed

by his secretary, Helen Gandy, or his partner, Clyde Tolson.

Horn, Gyula (b. 5 July 1932). Prime Minister of Hungary 1994–8
Born in Budapest, he joined the Communist Party as a teenager, after his father had been murdered by the *Gestapo for his Communist convictions. He studied economics in the USSR, and returned to join the Ministry of Finance and, in 1959, the Foreign Ministry. He took part in the repression of the *Hungarian Revolution, and in the subsequent purges. He joined the foreign policy unit in the Politburo in 1971, and became Secretary of State in the Foreign Office in 1985. Despite his orthodox and committed Communist past, he became Foreign Minister in the reformist Communist government (now under the name of Hungarian Socialist Party, MSZP) of 1989–90. His decision to open Hungary's border with Austria on 27 June 1989 led to the fall of the *Iron Curtain and, ultimately, to the collapse of the *Berlin Wall. In 1990, he negotiated the withdrawal of Soviet troops by 1991. He became leader of his party after its heavy losses in the 1990 general elections, and guided it to an overwhelming victory in 1994. Despite its absolute majority in the new parliament, he entered a coalition with the Liberal Party to increase the government's popular base for its radical economic reforms. These proved very unpopular, and he suffered a heavy election defeat at the hands of Viktor *Orbán.

Horthy de Nagybánya, Nikolaus Miklós (b. 18 June 1868, d. 9 Feb. 1957). Regent of Hungary 1920–44
Born in Kenderes, he graduated from the Imperial Naval Academy of *Fiume, and by 1918 he had advanced to become Commander-in-Chief of the *Austro-Hungarian navy. Lacking purpose in a post-1918 Hungary which had become land-locked after World War I (confirmed at the Treaty of *Trianon), his resentment was heightened by the new *Bolshevist regime of Béla *Kun. In response, he spearheaded the Nationalist Army in its overthrow of the regime, and was declared regent in January 1920. In response to the country's growing political polarization, and particularly to a popular, radical right wing, his rule became increasingly dictatorial during the 1930s. He placated the new tendencies, for example, by allowing the rise of official *anti-Semitism. Although personally on bad terms with *Hitler, he was dazzled by the latter's initial military successes during 1939–40, so that he joined in the *Nazi attack on Hungary's

former ally, Yugoslavia, on 11 April 1941. In 1944 he tried unsuccessfully to negotiate a separate peace with the Allies. For this he was imprisoned after the German invasion of Hungary, to be released by the Allies in 1945. He died in exile in Portugal.

Houphouët-Boigny, Félix (b. 18 Oct. 1905?, d. 7 Dec. 1993). President of the Ivory Coast 1960–93

Born in Yamoussoukro, he was one of the first Africans in the French colony to graduate in medicine. His first wife was of royal descent, and in 1940 he himself was appointed regional chief of the Akuwe people. He became prominent through the foundation of the Association of Customary Chiefs, and his presidency of the Syndicat Agricole Africain (African Agricultural Trade Union), a movement founded in protest against racial discrimination among planters. Houphouët-Boigny represented the Ivory Coast in the French Constituent Assemblies (1945–6) and the National Assembly (until 1958), where he successfully introduced a measure calling for the abolition of all forced labour throughout the French colonies. Back home, he was supported by the Parti Démocratique de la Côte d'Ivoire (Democratic Party of the Ivory Coast). At first allied with the Communist Party, he broke with it in 1950 and cooperated with the French to build up the country's economy. After holding several ministerial posts in France he returned to the Ivory Coast when it was offered self-government within the *French Community. With full independence in 1960 he became President of the new Republic. An astute and pragmatic politician, he maintained power mainly by playing off various contenders for his position against each other. In addition, his pro-Western (particularly pro-French) capitalist policies created a powerful elite, whose welfare was tied to his survival in power. He died in office.

House of Commons (UK), see PARLIAMENT (UK)

Howard, John Winston (b. 26 July 1939). Prime Minister of Australia 1996–

Early career Born in Sydney, Howard studied law at the University of Sydney and became a solicitor at the supreme court of the state of New South Wales in 1962. In 1974, he became a member of the House of Representatives for the *Liberal Party. Following the fall of *Whitlam's government, *Fraser appointed him Minister for Business and Consumer Affairs (1975–7) and then Treasurer

(1977–83). In opposition again from 1983, Howard served as deputy leader (1983–5), and leader of the opposition (1985–9), though with his solid but uninspiring personality he was unable to pose a threat to the popular *Hawke.

Prime Minister Howard re-emerged as leader of the opposition in 1995. This time, despite being personally much less popular than the fiery *Keating, his image of seriousness and reliability at a perceived time of economic crisis was successful. In the 1996 elections his Liberal/ *National Party coalition emerged with a 40-seat majority. Although not a supporter of the abolition of the monarchy, he did introduce a referendum on constitutional change in 1999, but this was narrowly defeated. He took steps to liberalize Australia's labour market, thereby inviting confrontation with the country's strong *trade unions. His strict economic policies contributed to strong economic growth, which continued even after economic recession in the Pacific Rim region after 2000. This led to a dramatic reduction in public debt, which was halved, and a fall in the unemployment rate to around 5 per cent in 2006.

Responding to the growing attractiveness of the populist *One Nation Party to his supporters, Howard lurched to the right in the 2001 elections, and successfully campaigned for policies of strict immigration controls. His immigration policies, which included the creation of internment camps on Nauru and on offshore islands, were popular with voters, even if they were severely criticized by *human rights groups. Howard sent troops to Afghanistan (2002) and Iraq (2003), bolstering Australian presence further during 2005–6 despite public criticism. Boosted by strong, uninterrupted economic growth and benefiting from his experience against a weak opposition, Howard led his party to a fourth successive election victory in 2004. Howard became the longest serving Prime Minister in Australian history after *Menzies.

Hoxha, Enver (b. 16 Oct. 1908, d. 11 Apr. 1985). Albanian leader 1945–85

Born in Gjirokastër (southern Albania), he studied in France and Belgium and became a teacher. During the Italian occupation of Albania he founded the Communist Party on 8 November 1941 and built up a Communist *partisan resistance movement. After the defeat of the *Fascist occupation forces (1944) he came to head a *popular front government, which he used to entrench Communist Party power and establish a one-party state. A fierce *Stalinist, he broke with his erstwhile comrade *Tito, ordering the execution of all his opponents and those identified as 'Titoists' in 1948. He then broke with the USSR after *Khrushchev had renounced Stalinism in 1961, and with China in 1977. He rendered his country subject to complete isolation, while his regime brutally quashed all opposition: e.g. in 1976 all religious activity was prohibited and all mosques and churches closed. He died in office, leaving a country which had declined to become one of the poorest in the world.

Hu Jintao (b. 1942). Chairman of the Chinese Communist Party (CCP), 2002–

Born at Jinxi, he studied engineering and worked for the government on projects in the Gansu province. He became Communist party secretary in that province in 1985, and in 1988 he was appointed party secretary for Tibet, where in the following year he brutally suppressed popular demonstrations, declaring martial law. Appointed to the standing committee of the CCP's Politbureau in 1992, Hu became the leader of the central party academy in 1993, and in 1998 he was appointed Deputy President of the People's Republic. Hu succeeded *Jiang Zemin in 2002 as party chairman, and in 2004 he took over Jiang's last important office, as head of the army. Hu tried to direct economic growth to prevent overheating and the further rise of social inequality, which was already one of the highest in the world. Hu rigorously opposed political liberalization, as the use of internet and other modes of communication were tightly controlled.

Hu Yaobang (b. 1915, d. 15 Apr. 1989). Chinese Communist leader

Born in Liuyang (Hunan province), he became active in the *Communist Party Youth League at *Jianxi in 1933. He took part in the *Long March, and he was trained at the Anti-Japanese Military and Political Academy in 1936. Over the next decade, he obtained a distinguished military record, and became a close ally of *Deng Xiaoping. He liberated Sichuan from the *National Revolutionary Army and stabilized Communist rule there until in 1952 he was appointed head of the Communist Youth League. In 1958 he joined the Communist Party's Central Committee. His ascent was stopped by the *Cultural Revolution, and again by the *Gang of Four in 1976. After the latter's fall he became an important ally of *Deng Xiaoping in carrying out his reformist policies. His new role as Deng's most trusted lieutenant was confirmed in 1981, when he became chairperson of the Communist Party's Central Committee. In 1987 he was dismissed from his post for having gone too far in his liberal reforms, and for his failure to contain student protests.

His death triggered weeks of unrest, culminating in the *Tiananmen Square massacre on 4 June 1989.

Hua Guofeng (Hua Kuo-feng) (b. 1920). Chinese Premier 1976–80

Born in Shanxi province, he joined the *Long March in 1936, and served for twelve years under *Zhu De in the 8th Route Army. He became Deputy Governor of Hunan province (1958–1967) and survived the *Cultural Revolution strengthened, as chairman of the Hunan Provincial Revolutionary Committee. He became a member of the *Politburo in 1973, and succeeded *Zhou Enlai as Premier. On the death of *Mao Zedong he defeated the *Gang of Four in October 1976, becoming Chairman of the Central Committee. However, his power declined in proportion to the rise of his rival, *Deng Xiaoping. In 1981 he was replaced as Chairman of the Central Committee by one of Deng's protégés, *Hu Yaobang.

Hua Kuo-feng, see HUA GUOFENG

Huai-Hai campaign (China)

A decisive campaign in the *Chinese Civil War, fought in the valley of the River Huai in the Shandong and Jiangsu provinces, November 1948–January 1949. In September 1948 *Chen Yi had swept south and captured Jinan (Chinan) with its garrison of 80,000 Nationalist troops under General Tu Li-ming, who then withdrew to defend the railway town of Xuzhou (Hsuchow). A series of engagements followed. Chen defeated Huang Po-tao around the railway town of Nianzhuang (6–22 November), and advanced towards Xuzhou, which fell on 1 December. The decisive battle against Tu followed from 6 December to 6 January 1949 around Yungchung. Chen won and captured 327,000 Nationalist prisoners, including Tu. In a separate move, the Communist general Liu Bocheng moved against the Nationalist forces in their stronghold of Ch'inglungchi to the north-east. It fell on 22 January, leaving the way open for an advance on Nanjing (Nanking) and Shanghai, which fell in the spring. The Chinese Communists had conquered China, much sooner than even they had anticipated. Nationalist losses in this campaign amounted to over half a million.

Huggins, Godfrey (Martin), Viscount Malvern (b. 6 July 1883, d. 8 May 1971). Prime Minister of Southern Rhodesia 1933–53, Central African Federation 1953–6

Born in Kent (England), he studied medicine and joined a medical partnership in the Rhodesian capital of Salisbury in 1911. Elected to the Southern Rhodesian Legislative Assembly in 1924, he left the ruling Rhodesia Party in 1931 and in 1932 became leader of the Reform Party, which in 1933 merged with sections of the Rhodesia Party to form the United Party. An admirer of *Smuts, Huggins advocated the 'two-pyramids system', a modified system of racial segregation which allowed Blacks self-administration for sanitation and education in their segregated reserves. He came to realize that the system became untenable as economic progress created an increasingly complex and interwoven economy and society, which led to the creation, for example, of a Black middle class. His increasing moderation was bitterly opposed by the White conservatives within and outside his party. He pushed for a union with Nyasaland (Malawi) and Northern Rhodesia (Zambia) in order to create a stable economy balanced by agriculture and mining. This was to provide an imperial 'bastion' against the growth of *Afrikaner *nationalism in South Africa, and of Black African independence movements in western Africa. He finally managed to persuade the British government to create the Central African Federation, whose Prime Minister he became until his retirement to his farm near Salisbury (now Harare).

Hughes, Charles Evans (b. 11 Apr. 1862, d. 27 Aug. 1948). Chief Justice of the US Supreme Court 1930–41
Born in Glenn Falls, New York State, Hughes studied for an LLB at Columbia in 1884, became a successful member of a New York City law firm, and in 1906 was elected state Governor. From 1910 until 1916 he served as a member of the federal *Supreme Court, but resigned to run in 1916 as the *Republican candidate for President. Defeated by *Wilson, he became Secretary of State (1921–5) under Presidents *Harding and *Coolidge. In this position, he supported US cooperation with the *League of Nations, negotiated a separate peace treaty with Germany, and hosted the Washington Conference of 1921–2, which achieved some restrictions on naval expansion.
Hughes's career was crowned by his years as Chief Justice. He enhanced the efficiency of the federal court system, and gave firm support to the freedom against state actions guaranteed to the citizen under the First Amendment. He was largely responsible for defeating a plan of President *Roosevelt in 1937 to 'pack' the court by adding to it extra liberal justices to counter sitting members over 70 years of age who refused to retire. At the same time his court supported a number

of *New Deal proposals, such as the Social Security Act.

Hughes, William Morris (b. 25 Sept. 1864, d. 28 Oct. 1952). Prime Minister of Australia 1915–23

Early career Born in London of Welsh origin, he emigrated to Australia in 1884, and finally settled in Balmain (Sydney) in 1890. He soon became active in the Labor movement (Australian *Labor Party), and was elected to the parliament of New South Wales in 1894, where he proved to be a clever tactician and effective orator. Despite his opposition to the establishment of the Australian Federation on the actual terms, he became involved in federal politics and was elected to the House of Representatives in 1901. Following his qualification as a barrister in 1903 he became Attorney-General in *Fisher's Cabinets from 1908, supporting the latter in reducing the power of the individual states.

Prime Minister Hughes used the exigencies of World War I to strengthen the powers of the federal government. He misjudged opinion within the general public and in his own party by advocating conscription for overseas military service in 1916. For this, he was expelled from the Labor Party, together with other proponents such as *Watson. With his followers, he merged with the opposition to form the *Nationalist Party, which won a resounding victory in the 1917 elections, though in this new environment, cut off from his political grass roots, Hughes never commanded the authority or adulation which he had enjoyed with Labor. Nevertheless, his position was still strong enough to survive another defeat on the conscription issue in December 1917.
At the *Paris Peace Conference Hughes successfully advocated Australia's interests, securing control over German New Guinea (now Papua New Guinea) and the maintenance of a *White Australia policy. After performing badly in the 1922 elections he was forced to resign by the refusal of *Page to support him.

Late career Increasingly critical of the *Bruce–Page ministry, he brought down the government in 1929, leading to its defeat in the ensuing general elections. In return, he was expelled from the Nationalist Party and attempted to form a new party, the *Australia Party, but in 1934 he joined the *Lyons ministry as member of the *United Australia Party (UAP). Forced to resign in 1935 owing to his open disagreement with the government over its handling of Italy's invasion of Abyssinia, he returned as minister in 1937. In

1941, he became leader of the UAP, but soon found it easier to cooperate with the Labor government than with his own party. Expelled from his party yet again in 1944, he joined the *Liberal Party in 1945, and remained in the House of Representatives until his death.

Hukbalahap (Huk) movement
(Philippines)

A left-wing guerrilla movement consisting of two successive groups, the People's Anti-Japanese Army, which was the main focus of the resistance movement during World War II, and the People's Liberation Army, which emerged from the former and was predominantly active from 1946 to 1952. It was composed largely from tenant organizations formed before World War II against the great capitalist estate owners and local elites. During the war, these organizations were formed into an effective resistance movement, largely through the efforts of the Huk leader on Luzon (the largest Philippine island), Luis *Taruc. By the end of the war it virtually controlled central Luzon, the 'breadbasket of the Philippines'. When Taruc was refused a seat in the Congress although elected (April 1946), he retreated to the jungle and began terrorist activities against the great estates as head of the People's Liberation Army (PLA). By 1950 the PLA was waging more or less open war against the landlord elite. Although only loosely allied to the Philippine Communist Party, against the background of the *Cold War and the *Korean War, the PLA was increasingly combated with US help as a Communist revolt. Taruc surrendered in 1954, thanks partly to the persuasion of young B. *Aquino.

Hull, Cordell (b. 2 Oct. 1871, d. 23 July 1955). US Secretary of State 1933–44

Born in Overton County, Tennessee, he studied at the National Normal University, Lebanon, Ohio, and Cumberland University Law School, and became a lawyer. He entered state politics as a *Democrat in 1892. He was elected to *Congress in 1906, lost his seat in 1920, but returned to the House in 1923 until he became a Senator in 1931. He resigned to become Secretary of State for F. D. *Roosevelt.

Hull established the *Good Neighbor Policy with Latin America and sought to revive world trade by getting *Congress to pass the Reciprocal Trade Agreements Act (March 1934), a forerunner of *GATT. His efforts markedly improved relations with Latin America in the run-up to World War II. Hull was a staunch supporter of China in its war against Japan. As soon as war was declared, he

began work on creating a postwar peacekeeping body, initiating a Moscow Conference for Foreign Ministers in 1943 from which was to develop the plan for a *United Nations. He was never actively involved in the day-to-day planning and decision-making of the war, as President Roosevelt allegedly considered him 'too cautious'. He retired in 1944 in ill health. He won the *Nobel Peace Prize in 1945.

human rights

Overview On 5 December 1948 the UN (*UNO) General Assembly passed a Declaration of Human Rights, the first ever recognition that the safeguard of basic freedoms and human rights, regardless of race, sex, language, or religion, was an international concern. Passed unanimously, with the USSR and five Eastern European countries, as well as Saudi Arabia and South Africa, abstaining, its clauses were not legally binding, though they have become the basis of international law. In 1976 it was complemented by an international covenant on social, economic, and cultural rights (signed by 149 states by 2004) and an international covenant on civil and political rights (signed by 152 states by 2004). These stipulated the right to live, the freedom of expression and religion, the protection of minorities, and the prohibition of torture. An additional protocol of 15 December 1989 condemning capital punishment had only been accepted by 50 states by 2004. Moreover, over twenty individual agreements have been signed thus far, including the prohibition of genocide (12 January 1951), the condemnation of *apartheid (18 July 1976), and opposition to the discrimination against women (3 September 1981).

Under the authority of the Security Council of the UN, a number of courts were established to deal with international human rights abuses. In 1993 the International Criminal Tribunal for the Former Yugoslavia was set up in The Hague, whose most prominent case from 2002 involved the former Serb leader, *Milošević. An International Criminal Tribunal for Rwanda was set up in 1994. In 2002, the UN helped create the *International Criminal Court, though it operated as an independent authority.

The state of human rights By their very nature, human rights have been universal. This gave them their moral power, since opposition to human rights was hard to justify, as the regimes of Soviet Europe were to find out after they had subscribed

to the maintenance of human rights at
*Helsinki. However, this universality also
proved to be their weakness. They could
be universally claimed and defined, and
hence consensus about what human
rights constituted was impossible to achieve.
The only point of agreement was that
universal rights have not been realized.
In the face of *globalization, the gap between
rich and poor has increased since the
1990s. According to the 2001 UN
Development Report, 1.2 bn. people had
less than $1 per day to live on, and
2.8 bn. people lived on less than $2 per day.
2.4 bn. people had no access to basic
sanitation, and over 850 million people were
illiterate. There were about 50 million
refugees in 2000, with reports of over
300,000 people being tortured, missing,
or executed (though the true figure for this
was likely to be much higher). In 2000,
an estimated 300,000 children below the age
of 18 fought as soldiers in civil wars and
international conflicts.

((())) SEE WEB LINKS

- The official UN web page on human rights.
- The official website of the United Nations
  Development Programme.
- The home page of Human Rights Watch, an
  independent pressure group monitoring
  progress on human rights.

Hume, John (b. 18 Jan. 1937). Nationalist
politician in Northern Ireland
Born in Londonderry, he studied at St Patrick's
College, Maynooth, and became a teacher. He
rose to prominence in 1968 through his
involvement in the civil rights movement, as
vice-chairman of the Derry Citizens' Action
Committee. In 1969 he was elected for Foyle
as an independent member of the *Stormont
parliament. A founder member of the
*Social Democratic and Labour Party
(SDLP) in 1970, he became its leader in 1979.
He was elected to the *European Parliament
in the same year. In 1983 he was elected to
the British House of Commons, and since
then he has taken the lead in trying to
arrange talks between all groups in *Northern
Ireland. He conducted talks with Gerry
*Adams in 1988 and 1993. After the
*Downing Street Declaration, he was one of
the principal influences on the British
government's position not to give up on *Sinn
Féin despite repeated IRA bomb attacks
during the mid-1990s. This was rewarded by
the accelerating pace of negotiations from
1997, which led to the *Good Friday
Agreement. Hume was strongly urged to
succeed Mary *Robinson as Irish President,

but he chose instead to retire from politics. He
resigned his seat in the Northern Irish
Assembly in 2000, and in 2001 he resigned as
leader of his party. He did, however, remain as
a Member of the British and European
Parliament. In 1998, he was awarded the
*Nobel Peace Prize together with David
*Trimble.

Humphrey, Hubert Horatio (b. 27 May
1911, d. 13 Jan. 1978). US Vice-President
1965–9
From a modest family in Wallace, South
Dakota, Humphrey started training as a
pharmacist, but soon became interested in
politics and graduated in political science
from the University of Minnesota (BA,
1939) and Louisiana State University (MA,
1940). Back in Minneapolis, he became a
director of a worker-education programme
for the Works Progress Administration set
up by F. D. *Roosevelt's *New Deal, and
became active in local politics as a
*Democrat. After becoming Mayor of
Minneapolis in 1945 Humphrey was elected
to the Senate in 1948, where he developed a
reputation for brilliant debating skills as well
as for the highest integrity. He spearheaded
the campaign for a strong commitment to
civil rights in the 1948 Democratic Party
platform.
   A presidential candidate in 1960, he became
a strong supporter of John F. *Kennedy and
was elected Vice-President in 1964, in
Johnson's landslide election victory. As such
he supported US involvement in the
*Vietnam War. Defeated in the presidential
election of 1968, he returned to the Senate,
where he served until he died. He was
regarded as one of the most significant
political figures of the USA in the postwar
period, both for his influence and
effectiveness in the Senate itself and in the
Democratic Party at large. In 1977 he
sponsored the Humphrey–Hawkins Act,
which he had first proposed in 1975, and
which sought to establish national goals of
low unemployment and low inflation. It
defined a right to work for all Americans
which no President after *Carter attempted to
implement.

Hundred Flowers campaign (1956–7)
A campaign whose title was taken from the
ancient phrase 'Let a hundred flowers bloom,
let a hundred schools of thought contend', in
an attempt to encourage intellectual criticism
of party and state. Trusting that most
intellectuals had been successfully converted
to *Communism, the ruling Chinese
Communist Party under *Mao Zedong and

*Zhou Enlai ostensibly wanted to strengthen the state through constructive criticism. After a timid start, a barrage of criticism was unleashed in May 1957, as not only intellectuals, but also students and other groups criticized the party hierarchy and the state. This triggered a quick government clamp-down on its critics, many of whom were sent to gaol. The campaign thus anticipated an effective party purge by inducing those who were critical of the party to disclose themselves.

Hungarian Revolution (23 Oct.–4 Nov. 1956)

The process of de-Stalinization which was begun in February 1956 at the XXth Congress of the Soviet *Communist Party created an atmosphere of hope and patriotism in Hungary, a country that had been plagued by violent repression and arbitrary purges since the trial of *Rajk in 1949. *Khrushchev forced the hated *Stalinist party leader *Rákosi to resign in July.

The appointment of the almost as repressive Ernó Geró proved to be an own goal, and fuelled popular protest against the leadership. On 23 October 1956, the confused secret police answered a demonstration by university students for democratization and the return of *Nagy as Communist Party leader by opening fire on the crowd. The incident became a victory for the students, as the panicking guards then surrendered their arms. Geró declared martial law, and requested the installation of Soviet tanks in the streets of Budapest. On 25 October, Hungarian policemen fired on a crowd of demonstrators and killed 300 people. An enraged population stampeded into the Communist headquarters.

On 28 October, a cease-fire was established, Soviet tanks were withdrawn, and a new government under Nagy was formed. Political prisoners were released, and political parties were legalized. Nagy announced his country's withdrawal from the *Warsaw Pact. He was betrayed, however, by his Minister of State, *Kádár, who fled towards the advancing Soviet troops and officially requested their intervention on 3 November 1956. The next day, Nagy was overthrown by an invading army of over 150,000 *Warsaw Pact troops and 2,000 tanks. He was imprisoned and executed in secret, while Kádár created a regime that lasted for more than thirty years.

Hungary

A central European country marked by deep political instability during the first half of the twentieth century, which became an economic model to its eastern neighbours from the 1960s.

Creation (1918–20) Hungary was a constituent part of the dual monarchy of *Austria-Hungary from 1867, until Count *Károlyi declared it an independent republic on 16 November 1918. The new state was politically and economically extremely fragile. Defeated in World War I, it faced the demobilization of 1,200,000 soldiers, and a crippling state debt. More problematic was the fact that its army had been forced to withdraw from those areas that were inhabited by a majority of Romanians, Slovaks, and Serbs. This did not just wound national pride but also created havoc, as hundreds of thousands of Hungarian refugees flooded into the country. Factories were cut off from supplies and their traditional markets, while agriculture was hit by several hundred thousand deserters who had hidden in the woods and now raided farms for food. The territorial losses were confirmed by the Treaty of *Trianon on 4 June 1920, whereby Hungary lost 68 per cent of its territory, and 59 per cent of its former population. One-third of Hungarians then lived outside Hungary.

The interwar period (1920–32) Politics, culture, and the economy were therefore dominated by a national question, with demagogues and politicians making competing promises to restore at least some of the land which Hungary had lost. Károlyi's hope of retaining the old Hungarian territory through a confederation of autonomous states was given the cold shoulder by the Romanians, Slovaks, and Serbs, who had had enough of Hungarian rule. Indeed, the advance of the Romanian army into Hungary's historic heartland, *Transylvania, triggered such unrest that Béla *Kun was able to topple the government and declare a Communist regime.

In a rare example of a Communist takeover on a wave of *nationalism, Béla Kun could ill afford to make concessions to the Romanians. This increased further the suspicions of the Allies, who were already extremely unhappy about the establishment of a Communist regime in central Europe. Aided by French and Romanian armies, a nationalist government under *Hórthy came to power in the country's third revolution in a year, on 18 November 1919. After an initial burst of reactionary and *anti-Semitic laws (1920), the Prime Minister, *Bethlen, stabilized the state through the introduction of a restricted franchise. He also enlisted the support of the Roman *Catholic Church, the landowners, and, increasingly, the army and middle classes. Nevertheless, the country's economic position remained precarious, and Bethlen was forced to resign in the wake of the Great *Depression and the 1931 banking crisis.

From Fascism to Communism (1932–48) In 1932–6 there was an attempt to create a Fascist state by the near-comic Gyula Gömbös, a man of mixed Swabian and Armenian descent, who for his admiration and imitation of *Mussolini was nicknamed 'Gömbölini'. His major achievement was the conclusion of a trade treaty with *Nazi Germany in 1934, which was a major contributor to the country's economy. This provided a further motive for the growing popularity of *Fascism, which was helped by the gains of the *Vienna Agreements, the country's first success at regaining some of its lost territories. Despite *Teleki's efforts, the country went to war alongside Germany on 11 April 1941, when it attacked Yugoslavia. On 27 June, after the *Kosice attack, it declared war on the USSR.

On 19 March 1944, German troops occupied Hungary to force the creation of a more German-friendly government. The *Red Army advanced into the country from December, and on 22 December 1944 the USSR created an alternative provisional Hungarian government. By 4 April 1945 the country was under Soviet control. In the following three years the country was transformed into a *Communist state, through the harassment of non-Communist opposition, and the forced merger of the Communist Party and the Social Democrats to form the Hungarian Worker's Party on 12 June 1948.

Communist rule (1949–89) This prepared the ground for the declaration of a Communist 'People's Republic' on 20 August 1949. Soviet control over the party was intensified by a series of purges under the hardline Rákosi, which began in 1948–9 with the imprisonment of *Rajk. Over-investment in heavy industry at the expense of consumption, in a country devoid of the necessary raw materials, further heightened

dissatisfaction, not only in the cities. Incomes in agriculture dropped, so that in 1953 incomes were at 30 per cent of their levels in 1949. With the death of *Stalin the repressive system became untenable, and Rákosi was replaced by the moderate *Nagy in 1953. Rákosi's return to power in 1955 defied completely the popular mood in the country, and ultimately led to the *Hungarian Revolution of 1956.

The Revolution's defeat led to the exodus of around 200,000 Hungarians, who feared the creation of a repressive neo-Stalinist regime under *Kádár. Once his authority was secure internally and against encroachments from the USSR, Kádár gradually relaxed his policies towards minorities. In economic policy, he created room for some private initiative, allowing peasants small plots of land. The result was that on 3.5 per cent of the cultivated land 33 per cent of the food was cultivated, which made Hungary the only *Comecon country that was self-sufficient in its food production. Nevertheless, the country's industrial production remained largely inefficient. Like its *Comecon neighbours, it was ultimately unable to overcome the effects of the *oil price shocks of 1973 and 1979. To maintain its citizens' standard of living, the state was forced to subsidize industry through loans raised from Western banks. By the middle of the 1980s, a debt of over $20 billion had accumulated while new loans were no longer forthcoming. Smothered by its own inherent contradictions, the economy declined rapidly, accelerating further economic reforms (e.g. of the banking system in 1987).

Democratization (1990s) The economic circumstances of the 1980s initiated a public debate about the future of the economic (and, by implication, the political) system. On 27 September 1987, an opposition movement formed, the Hungarian Democratic Forum (MDF). In May 1988, Kádár was replaced. In addition, the Communists reformed themselves into a Social Democratic Movement (MSP, later MSZP). In the elections of 1990 the MSP was eclipsed by a bourgeois bloc led by the MDF, which gained 42.5 per cent of the popular vote. Under the new Prime Minister, József Antall (b. 1932, d. 1993), a state property agency carried out a programme of privatization, encouraging joint ventures. By 1993, 45 per cent of the GDP came from the private sector. The transition to a market economy created economic and social problems of unemployment and inflation. This resulted in the comeback of the MSZP, which under the leadership of *Horn increased its representation in parliament from 33 to 209 seats in the 1994 elections, gaining an absolute majority. Together with the Liberal Federation of Free Democrats (SZDSZ), the new government continued a drastic programme of cuts in state expenditure, higher taxation, and a devaluation of the currency. This did succeed in reducing inflation and encouraged the country's structural transformation, but the fiscal parsimony only stimulated economic growth towards the end of the parliamentary session.

Contemporary politics (since 2000) The 1998 elections were won by the right-wing Young Democrats–Bourgeois Party (FIDESZ–MPP) under *Orbán. The economy continued to revive, so that Hungary became considered as a model candidate for EU membership. In 1999 it joined *NATO, and in 2004 it became a member of the EU. With a keen eye for populist measures, Orbán passed a new citizenship law in 2001, which granted a special status to Hungarians living outside its borders, in neighbouring countries. Despite the domestic popularity of this law, Orbán's government faced increasing difficulties because of the scandals affecting its coalition partner, the Small Peasants' Party (FKgP).

Orbán narrowly lost the 2002 elections to the MSZP and the SZDSZ, which formed a new centre-left coalition government under the leadership of Peter Medgyessy (b. 1942) of the MSZP. Medgyessy was succeeded by Ferenc Gyurcsány in 2004. His government became the first to be confirmed in a free election in 2006, but it came under severe strains when Gyurcsány was secretly recorded as saying that he had lied about the state of the economy before the election. The effect of the scandal was compounded by severe economic reforms which Gyurcsány announced after the elections, which reduced public spending so that Hungary could qualify for the adoption of the *euro.

MAP 1

Husák, Gustáv (b. 10 Jan. 1913, d. 18 Nov. 1991). First Secretary of the Czechoslovak Communist Party 1968–88; President of Czechoslovakia 1975–89
Born in Dúbravka (near Bratislava), he joined the Communist Party in 1932, when he was a law student at the University of Bratislava. He practised as a lawyer until 1942, when he started to work for the underground party full-time, and became a pivotal figure in the Slovak uprising of 1944. He rose quickly in the party ranks, became Minister for Agriculture (1948–9), and a member of the national party's Central Committee in 1949. In 1951 he became a victim of *Gottwald's *Stalinist purges, and was sentenced to life imprisonment for the heinous crime of 'Slovak bourgeois nationalism'. He was released in 1960, and rehabilitated in 1963. Husák worked in the Slovak Academy of Sciences and on various committees, until in 1968 he became Deputy Prime Minister of Czechoslovakia. He supported the *Warsaw Pact invasion to end the *Prague Spring on 20 August 1968, whereupon he became the effective state leader, even though he did not officially replace *Dubček until 1969.

His rule was marked by economic, ideological, and political orthodoxy, which anaesthetized the vast majority of the population, whose hopes had been so raised by the Prague Spring, into passive submission. Old age did not create a taste for adventurism, and he stubbornly resisted the reformist impulses of *Gorbachev. This attitude was shared by the party high command, which replaced him as party leader in 1988 with another hardliner, Milos Jakes. In one of the more gratifying ironies of history, he was replaced as President by his complete intellectual and ideological opposite, *Havel, whom he had tried so hard to silence through incarceration and discrimination.

Hussein ibn Ali (b. 1853?, d. 4 June 1931). King of the Hejaz 1916–25
A member of the *Hashemite family, he was made Sherif of Mecca under Turkish rule in 1908. In June 1916 he began the *Arab Revolt, proclaiming himself to be King of the Hejaz and, from November 1916, King of the Arabs. He was able to bring most of the Hejaz under his control, though this was less on the basis of his own strength, than on the British policy in Arabia, which restrained his much stronger rival, *Abd al-Aziz ibn Saud, from challenging him during the course of World War I. Thereafter, however, his power was steadily eroded by the military advances of Abd al-Aziz. After losing Mecca he abdicated and went into exile. One of his sons, Abdullah, was King of Transjordan (1920–51), while another was made King of Syria (1920) and then of Iraq (1921–33) as *Faisal I.

Hussein ibn Talal (b. 14 Nov. 1935, d. 7 Feb. 1999). King of Jordan 1952–1999
Grandson of *Abdullah ibn Hussein, he was educated at the Victoria College (Alexandria), Harrow, and the Royal Military College, Sandhurst. His schizophrenic father was removed from the throne by parliament on 11

August 1952 and, after a hasty conclusion of his education, he returned to succeed him in May 1953. His rule was marked by a notable success in blending Islamic traditionalism and Western *capitalism. He gained a lot of authority from his lineage as heir to the *Hashemite dynasty and thus his direct descent from the Prophet Muhammad. This also encouraged him as a leader of Arab unity, though he was always careful to emphasize the principle of a universal voice of independent Arab states, rather than an Arab superstate. At the same time, he was extraordinarily pro-Western in relying on the USA and the UK for military and economic assistance.

Hussein created an extensive education system and, despite the relative poverty of his country, steadily improved its healthcare provision. In the 1950s and 1960s, he had to maintain a careful relationship with his extremist Arab neighbours, Syria, Iraq, and Egypt, whose more radical *pan-Arabist regimes sponsored several unsuccessful coups against him. He suffered a humiliating and devastating defeat during the *Six Day War, losing the *West Bank to Israel. Thereafter, Palestinian guerrillas, notably the *PLO, regrouped in Jordan. These began to form a state within a state, which triggered a civil war when he expelled them in 1970–1. He met Israeli representatives in secret negotiations throughout the 1970s and 1980s but, ever-mindful of the large Palestinian minority in his country, he was only able to sign a Peace Treaty with Israel in 1995, after the latter had recognized the *PLO. Shortly before his death he ensured his succession by his son, *Abdullah II, at the expense of his eldest brother, Hassan.

Hussein, Saddam (b. 28 Apr. 1937, d. 30 Dec 2006). President of Iraq 1979–2003

Rise to power Born in Tikrit, Hussein joined the *Ba'ath Socialist Party in 1957 and became involved in its underground activities. Imprisoned in 1956, he fled to Syria and Egypt following a coup against Prime Minister Abdul Karim *Qassem in 1959. He returned to Iraq in 1963, and became a leader of the Ba'ath party, advancing to the post of assistant General Secretary of its Iraqi section in 1966. He took part in the July 1968 revolution led by General Bakr, as a prominent member of its 'civilian' wing. In 1969, he became deputy chairman of the Revolution Command Council, the country's new ruling body. From that time onwards, he was the effective strong man in Iraqi politics, though he did not formally assume the presidency until 1979. In this he

was helped by his total command of the party machinery, especially since his party purges of 1969–71.

Dictatorial rule Hussein's rule was marked by a singularly pragmatic ruthlessness. Never hesitant to have his opponents executed, he made peace with them when necessary (the Kurds in *Kurdistan 1970, 1991; Iran 1975, 1990), and attacked them with singular brutality when expedient (the Kurds in 1974, 1988–91; Iran in 1980). He reinforced his hold on army, government, and party through nepotism, placing his family members in control of strategic posts. Finally, he strengthened his position through an intense personality cult, using themes of Arab *nationalism, anti-*Zionism, and Islamic rhetoric to elevate himself to a supreme position. In this way, he managed to survive his two great miscalculations: his unleashing of the *Iran–Iraq War (1980–8), and the *Gulf War (1990–1). Following the latter conflict, Hussein continued to attract the wrath of the United States and the *UN, as he refused to allay fears that he was producing weapons of mass destruction.

Demise Hussein complied only reluctantly with UN resolution 1441, which called for full Iraqi co-operation in UN-led weapons inspections. This did not improve his standing with George W. *Bush, who had already identified Iraq as one country in an 'Axis of Evil'. In the ensuing *Iraq War, Hussein was toppled as he had lost control of Baghdad by 9 April 2003. His intransigence against the USA was a third miscalculation which he ultimately did not survive. Hussein escaped to his home region around Tikrit, where he was captured on 13 December 2003. Hussein was kept in US military imprisonment, and during 2005–6 he was tried by an Iraqi court for the massacre of 148 Shi'ite Muslims in the village of Dujail in 1982, a case that was relatively easy to prove. Hussein was sentenced to death, and hanged by the Iraqi authorities.

Hyderabad
Formerly a princely state in India. Following an agreement with Lord *Curzon in 1902, the Nizams of Hyderabad became rulers of the largest princely state in British India. During the 1920s and 1930s they continually resisted demands from the state congress for more responsible government, and in 1947 the Nizam declared Hyderabad an independent state. The state congress, supported by the Indian National *Congress, started civil

resistance, and a period of political chaos was ended in September 1948 by the Indian army. The Nizam then accepted pressure that Hyderabad join the Union, with himself as princely Governor. In 1956 Hyderabad ceased to exist as it was subdivided between Andhra Pradesh, Mysore, and Bombay. At that time, the Nizam became a plain citizen of India.

hydrogen bomb, see NUCLEAR BOMB

Ibáñez (del Campo), Carlos (b. 3 Nov. 1877, d. 28 Apr. 1960). Chilean President 1927–31, 1952–8

Of wealthy parents, he had a successful career in the army and in 1924 took part in a military coup against President Arturo *Alessandri. When Alessandri briefly returned to power he became his Minister of War before seizing power himself in 1925. Elected President in 1927, he at once imprisoned or exiled his political opponents. He initiated a series of reforms, notably of the police, and introduced public works. However, Chile's economy collapsed during the Great *Depression, forcing his resignation. In 1937, he briefly returned from exile to lead a series of abortive Fascist uprisings. Against the background of widespread disillusionment with party politics, he was elected as the 'general of hope' in 1952. To everyone's surprise his regime was conciliatory, encouraging economic growth and seeking to end corruption. It won the support of the more progressive middle class and of the trade unions, promulgating a Labour Code. He was succeeded by Alessandri's son, José.

Ibarruri Gómez, Dolores (b. 9 Dec. 1895, d. 12 Nov. 1989). Spanish Communist

Born in Gallarta, she was raised in a poor mining family, and took work as a seamstress and cook. After marrying the socialist Julian Ruiz in 1915 she became active in the socialist movement. In 1919 she published an article in the mining journal *El Minero Vizcaíno* signed 'La Pasionaria', a name by which she became popularly known. In 1920, she co-founded the *Communist Party. As a member of the party's national executive, she was frequently in gaol under the dictatorship of *Primo de Rivera. After the establishment of the Second Republic in 1931, she moved to Madrid. She campaigned tirelessly and effectively for the party, and organized its women's movement. In return, in 1933 she was elected the party's president. During the *Civil War she became a legend in her lifetime, as she used her formidable rhetorical skills to exhort the Republican troops with courage and defiance. She organized thousands of women for the war effort. After *Franco's victory she left for Moscow, where she lived as the figurehead leader of the outlawed Communist Party. She returned to Spain after Franco's death, and led the party's return to parliament in 1977.

She remained the nominal leader of her party until her death.

Ibn Saud, Abd al-Aziz, see ABD AL-AZIZ IBN SAUD

Iceland

A Nordic country which, despite its small population and its inhospitable climate, has succeeded in achieving a remarkably high standard of living.

Danish rule (up to 1944) Under Danish sovereignty since 1380, Europe's second largest island acquired limited autonomy from Denmark in 1874, when its Assembly, the Althing, gained legislative powers. Moves to achieve independence were finally successful in 1918, when Iceland gained full sovereignty, though its head of state continued to be linked to the Danish crown. Owing to its important strategic location, during World War II Iceland was occupied by British and US troops in 1940 and 1941 respectively. Taking advantage of the German occupation of Denmark at the time, Iceland severed its ties with the Danish King in 1944, when it was declared a Republic, with Sven Björnsson becoming the first President (1944–52).

Contemporary history (1944–2000) After World War II, it became an important base for *NATO, which it joined in 1949. Traditionally, its economy depended on fisheries, which accounted for around 80 per cent of its exports. As its coastal waters became exploited by foreign fishing fleets, it gradually extended its fishing limits, up to 200 miles around the island. This led to a series of *Cod Wars, culminating in the temporary breakdown of diplomatic relations with the UK in 1976. In 1980 Vígdis Finnbogadóttir (b. 1930) was elected the first woman President. In the early 1990s, fishing quotas had to be reduced to prevent further decline in fishing stocks. This led to substantial underemployment among its fishermen, and caused a period of economic stagnation which was not overcome until the end of the decade.

Contemporary politics (since 2000)
Iceland's reliance on fishing, which accounted for over 70 per cent of its exports in 2001, has been the main stumbling block in repeated negotiations about membership of the European Union. Despite its lack of formal membership, however, from 1997 it enjoyed virtual free trade with the European Union. In 2001 it entered the *Schengen Agreement.

Ichikawa Fusae (b. 15 May 1893, d. 11 Feb. 1981). Japanese women's rights campaigner
Ichikawa's pedigree as a Japanese political activist was long and varied. In her twenties she worked as a journalist and also helped establish the New Women's Association (Shin fujin kyôkai) with Hiratsuka Raichô and Oku Mumeo in 1921. After visiting the US (1921–4), she returned to Tokyo to participate in the establishment of the local office of the *International Labour Organization. She also became a leading figure in the League for the Achievement of Women Suffrage (Fusen kakutoku dômei). The League was dissolved in 1940 in compliance with the demands of the wartime regime. After the surrender and the emancipation of women that followed, Ichikawa became an enthusiastic supporter of the postwar democratic reforms.

Ichikawa found herself purged by the occupation authorities in 1947 because of her involvement with the prewar regime and was unable to participate in any political activity until 1950. In the House of Councillors elections of 1955 she entered the Diet. As a nationally recognized politician, Ichikawa was a consistent champion of *women's emancipation and political fairness. During the 1950s she sponsored legislation which outlawed prostitution, while in the 1970s she was a leading critic of big business's financial support for the corrupt politics of the *Liberal Democratic Party. Viewed by many as an icon of Japanese citizens' movements, Ichikawa was an enduring example of what could be achieved without money in Japanese politics.

Ikeda Hayato (b. 3 Dec. 1899, d. 13 Aug. 1965). Prime Minister of Japan 1960–4
Following a career in the pivotal Ministry of Finance as a civil servant, in 1949 he was elected to the House of Representatives; and as a member of *Yoshida Shigeru's Liberal Party, he entered the Cabinet as Minister of Finance (1949–52). During this time, his role as the planner of Japan's economic recovery was so important that he was the only member of the government to retain his job in Yoshida's Cabinet reshuffle. Ikeda also played

a secret and key part in the peace negotiations with the USA, which led to the Peace Treaty of *San Francisco in 1951. On succeeding *Kishi Nobusuke as Prime Minister, Ikeda contrasted the confrontational policies of his predecessor with his low-key but highly popular 'income doubling plan', which promoted the expansion of the Japanese economy. Often perceived by his contemporaries as a dour bureaucrat whose elite background gave him little understanding of the needs of ordinary Japanese, Ikeda is now remembered as one of the chief architects of Japan's rapid economic growth in the postwar era.

Iliescu, Ion (b. 3 Mar. 1930). President of Romania 1989–96, 2000–2004

Early career Born in Olenita, he joined the Communist Party at the age of 15 and studied at Moscow University to become an electrical engineer (1950–3). Back in Romania, in 1956–60 he became chairman of the Communist Students' League and, after further work for the Communist Party, he became first secretary of the Youth League (1967–70), and then Secretary for *Propaganda, 1971. In the same year he fell out with *Ceausescu and was demoted to the provinces. In 1979 he was appointed head of the National Water Council, with a seat in Ceausescu's Council of State. He was widely tipped as a successor to Ceausescu, but perhaps because of this he was dismissed in 1984, deprived of party membership, and made director of a publishing company. A student colleague of *Gorbachev, he advocated the introduction of reform (*perestroika) in 1987.

In power On 22 December 1989 Iliescu resurfaced to become head of the National Salvation Front (NSF). In elections on 20 May 1990 he was confirmed as President with 85 per cent of the vote, and in October 1992 with over 60 per cent of the vote, after considerable intimidation and violence. He was weakened by a split of the NSF in 1992, and thereafter presided over the Democratic National Salvation Front. This did little to endanger his position, as he continued to profit from the ongoing fragmentation and disunity of his opposition. He was succeeded in office by Emil Constantinescu. In 2000, he was re-elected, but in 2004 he was constitutionally barred from a further term in office.

IMF (International Monetary Fund)
One of the central institutions to emerge in 1945 from the *Bretton Woods Conference, it was designed to stabilize the international

economy. Its central tasks were defined as economic surveillance, financial assistance, and technical assistance. The IMF could help member countries which faced a liquidity or balance-of-payments crisis, through the provision of short-term loans. Its role changed significantly with the onset of *decolonization, as the countries in greatest need of economic assistance were now the new states in Asia and Africa. The IMF's significance was further enhanced with the retreat of Communism from these continents in the 1980s, and the collapse of Communism in Eastern Europe and the former Soviet Union. As a result of these developments, the number of countries within the purview of the IMF increased once again, so that by 2007 it had 185 member states.

The power of the IMF derives from its principle of conditionality, whereby credits to overcome liquidity problems are conditional upon domestic structural economic reforms. This has given the IMF enormous economic, cultural, and political power over debt-ridden countries with no choice but to accept its conditions. At the same time, the IMF's role was challenged by other lenders such as China, which invested some of its surplus currency reserve in loans to states in Africa and Latin America. This increased Chinese influence in these countries, while the loans did not come on condition of financial accountability and sustainability, thus undermining the IMF's principle of conditionality. Heavily under pressure to cancel world debt, the IMF and its sister institution, the *World Bank, have granted substantial debt relief under the *HIPC initiative.

((⊕)) SEE WEB LINKS

• The official website of the IMF.

immigration legislation (Australia), see
WHITE AUSTRALIA POLICY

immigration legislation (Canada)
The first Canadian census of 1871 gave the number of White Canadians as 3.7 million, of whom 2.1 million were English-speaking and 1.1 million French-speaking, the rest coming from diverse European nations. As Canada's territory expanded through the creation of new provinces in the west, it tried to attract more immigrants, whose numbers exploded during the *Laurier government. There were 16,835 immigrants in 1896, compared to 331,288 in 1911, a number which rose to 400,000 just before World War I. Despite the open encouragement of immigrants, the influx of Chinese was restricted in 1885, owing to fears that they would undercut

wages in the labour market. Immigration was restricted during World War I, in the wake of the Great *Depression, and during World War II.

A non-discriminatory immigration policy was gradually introduced from 1962, while the 1978 Immigration Act sought further to refine guidelines for immigration. While aiming for 10 per cent of immigrants to be refugees, it encouraged the establishment of foreign businesses and capital in Canada, in order to create demand for immigrant labour. Immigration has been subject both to federal and provincial legislation. In 1968, *Quebec established its own immigration policies which sought to encourage the influx of French -speakers. Quebec was particularly concerned about the size of its francophone population given its low birth-rate compared to the rest of Canada. Moreover, immigration was distributed unevenly in the different provinces, with Ontario and, since the 1970s, Alberta and British Columbia attracting disproportionate amounts of domestic and international immigration. By 2006, Canada was accepting around 250,000 immigrants per year, with a total population of around 32.5 million.

immigration legislation (New Zealand)
New Zealand had an estimated population of around 1400,000 Maori people, and 2,000 Whites, in 1839. Immigration began in the 1840s as companies and settlers sought to make the country a viable White colony. The discovery of gold in 1861 attracted a large number of immigrants, including some from China. In order to restrict their entry, a poll tax was introduced for them in 1881, which was not repealed until 1944. Between 1945 and 1966, 17 per cent of those who immigrated did so with direct help from the New Zealand government. Until the 1964 Immigration Act, people born in the British Isles and wholly of European descent were admitted freely. Immigration policies focused on the United Kingdom and Australia, so that during the 1960s, over 80 per cent of the population were of British or Irish descent. In 1964, all immigrants were required to have entry permits, which were awarded generally without discrimination.

In 1991, the criteria for immigration were changed. A points system giving preference to business and professional immigrants was introduced, as were yearly immigration targets. In 1995 and 2002, the government raised the English requirement for immigrants, and in 2003 immigration was targeted further at high-skilled employees. Even though immigrants from the British Isles continued to constitute the largest single group of immigrants, they now made up less than one-third of all immigrants. At the same time, the government tried to stop a significant exodus of skilled labour to Australia, which attracted 20,000 people in 2004 alone.

immigration legislation (UK)

Contemporary history (up to 2000) The first restriction of immigration in Britain was the 1905 Aliens Act, which responded to concerns that victims of anti-Jewish *pogroms in Russia, Poland, and south-east Europe might come to Britain in large numbers. The Act empowered the Home Secretary to refuse entry to anyone who could not prove that they had the means to support themselves, but it did not end rights to political/religious asylum, or apply to immigrants from the *British Empire. The Act was replaced by the more powerful Aliens Restriction Act (1914), giving the Home Secretary complete authority over foreign immigration. This was renewed by the 1919 Aliens Restriction (Amendment) Act, which in turn was replaced by the 1920 Aliens Order. This was renewed every year until it was succeeded by the 1971 Immigration Act (see below). Despite these pieces of legislation, Britain has not consistently sought to restrict immigration. Unlike other parts of the Empire, Britain's 1914 and 1948 Nationality Acts affirmed that there was no colour bar to British citizenship.

After the war, the 1947 Polish Resettlement Act helped 120,000 Poles who were in the British services during the war stay in Britain. Furthermore, immigration from the West Indies was encouraged. Anti-Black riots in Nottingham and Notting Hill (London) in 1958 led to widespread concerns about growing levels of racism. In 1962 the Commonwealth Immigrants Act made entry subject to having a job in Britain, or holding special skills that were 'useful' to the country. This ended the tradition of considering all *Commonwealth citizens as British citizens with equal rights. Further restrictions on Commonwealth citizens followed, until the 1971 Immigration Act unified the systems regarding alien (non-Commonwealth) and Commonwealth immigration.

The British Nationality Act (1982) established three different categories of citizenship, each giving different rights of residence, ranging from full to none. In 1986, the government introduced visa controls on people visiting Britain from Bangladesh, Pakistan, India, Nigeria, and Ghana. Most recently, the 1990 British Nationality (Hong Kong) Act responded to fears that when Hong Kong was taken over by China in 1997 many of its citizens would come to Britain. Under the legislation, a maximum of 225,000 people were allowed to enter.

Contemporary politics (since 2000) In 2000, a new Immigration and Asylum Act was passed, which improved provisions for existing immigrants, while making it more difficult to seek asylum. Between 1998 and 2000, the number of asylum seekers rose by over 50 per cent. Britain also became very attractive for illegal immigrants, since upon entry these were difficult to trace in a country without identity cards. Since Britain was outside the *Schengen Agreement, illegal immigrants could not be returned to the country of transit.

immigration legislation (USA)

Early history From the 1890s, immigration to the US became more diverse, and included large numbers of eastern and southern Europeans. It also became more visible, as most immigrants settled in the cities to take up low-skilled jobs in trade and industry. In response, a strongly assimilationist culture emerged. Expressed through the metaphor of the melting pot, it aimed at harmonizing the growing heterogeneity of immigrants. Accordingly, immigrants were to be integrated by a common emotional, cultural, and civic ideal of the US.

Legislation While certain immigration restrictions had already been passed in the nineteenth century, *Congress passed the Emergency Quota Act in 1921, which limited immigration and introduced an ethnic bias towards northern Europeans to the US immigration system. This was followed by the 1924 National Origins Act. Immigration then fell drastically, though this was at least in part the result of the recovery of the world economy in the 1920s, and the severity of the Great *Depression in the USA. Thus, immigration fell from around 4.1 million between 1921–30 to 528,000 between 1931–40. In the aftermath of World War II, legislation was passed to cover the refugees from eastern Europe through three displaced persons Acts of 1948–51. Shortly afterwards, Asian immigration restrictions were eased by the 1952 *McCarran–Walter Act.

In 1965, Congress sought to reform immigration procedures by setting a finite number rather than ethnic quotas as the basis for immigration to the USA. This effectively discouraged northern and western Europeans from immigrating. A 1986 law attempted to restrict the number of illegal aliens in the USA (the Simpson–Mazzoli Act), but this measure was undermined by the unwillingness of employers and the federal government to comply with its procedures, which sought to limit jobs to Americans.

Contemporary issues New demands by right-wing populists and left-wing trade unions for tougher restrictions emerged in the 1990s. At that time, anti-immigrant feeling grew in tandem with fears that the free-movement provisions of the *NAFTA treaty would encourage more illegal immigrants from Canada and Mexico. The 2000 census data provided further evidence of the breakdown of the 'melting pot' ideal since the 1960s. Americans increasingly defined themselves through their ethnic and cultural diversity. By 2004, Mexico had become by far the largest country of immigration, with 170,000 arrivals, while 80,000 had arrived from Caribbean countries, and 61,000 from Central American states. Whereas 70,000 had arrived from India and over 50,000 had come from China and the Philippines each, immigration numbers from Europe were low, with the UK sending 15,000 immigrants, more than any other European country.

Imperial Conferences

Meetings between the Prime Ministers of the United Kingdom and the British Dominions. These were held in London with the exception of the 1932 conference. The conferences replaced the colonial conferences which had begun in 1887, as it had been agreed in 1907 that the colonies inhabited by a White majority would be called 'Dominions', and that they would have significant measures of authority in their domestic affairs. The first imperial conference was held in 1911. In 1918, an Imperial War Conference discussed war strategies and the supply of raw materials. The 1921 conference included representatives from India, and it became increasingly clear that the Dominions desired total independence over external as well as internal affairs. The 1923 conference discussed imperial preference (*tariff reform) at length, as well as disarmament and issues arising from the *Chanak Crisis. The conference of 1926 discussed *Balfour's formula for defining the relationship between Britain and the *British Empire, which resulted in the 1931 Statute of *Westminster. At the 1930 conference, the world economic crisis dominated discussions, with the result that the *Ottawa Conference of 1932 finally established a system of tariffs. The final conference was held in 1937, following *George VI's coronation. It discussed the worsening international situation, and overwhelmingly supported *appeasement.

Since World War II, regular *Commonwealth Conferences have been held.

Imperial Preference, see OTTAWA AGREEMENTS; TARIFF REFORM

Imperial Rule Assistance Association (Taisei Yokusankai)

An organization intended to form a totalitarian political regime in wartime Japan, established on 12 October 1940 and dissolved after the Japanese surrender in 1945. It was set up by the Prime Minister, *Konoe Fumimaru, in order to replace existing political parties and groups, and to absorb all in a single organization that could be used to mobilize the domestic population and facilitate the prosecution of Japan's war in Asia. While recognized parties were dissolved in preparation for the IRAA in 1940, the organization never possessed the monolithic character of its counterpart in *Nazi Germany. For example, the IRAA's attempts to bring under its control established business and financial interests met with strong resistance throughout the war period. Opposition to the IRAA was also voiced on the principle that such an organization undermined the constitution of imperial rule. A measure of its efficacy came during the 1942 general elections, when candidates who had not received its endorsement were able to stand and win seats in the Imperial Diet. Its formal machinery was vast, reaching down to the local level in an attempt to involve every Japanese subject in its activities. IRAA campaigns included a drive to increase productivity and decrease consumption. As the war progressed the IRAA became increasingly an organization through which the Home Ministry exercised its control, despite the army's attempts to use it for its own purposes.

imperialism

The tendency to strive for control of other countries or regions as colonies or dependencies. Imperialism reached a peak in 1914, when 79 per cent of the world's land surface was under the control of a few colonial powers (mostly European, but also states such as Japan and the USA). Even though the underlying motives of imperialism are still unclear, there are three major theories of imperialism.

1. The first notes the economic interests of European capitalists in an expansion of their markets, a view taken by many Marxists. For example, the Belgian Congo became a market for Belgian goods and an important provider of raw materials for Belgium in return. However, with a number of notable exceptions (such as India, or *French West Africa) very few imperial ventures yielded a high rate of return on investment.

2. The second, more important reason for imperialism concerns events outside Europe, in the colonies themselves. According to this theory, individual soldiers or administrators proceeded to extend their country's sphere of influence and created a situation which the home government then had to accept. The most famous example of this is perhaps the desire of Cecil *Rhodes to extend British sovereignty over Rhodesia (now Zambia and Zimbabwe). Similar instances led to the French expansion from Senegal to the Soudan (now Mali), and the expansion of the Russian Empire. Another example of a 'local' cause was a power vacuum in an area, which was then filled for strategic reasons by European states, as happened in the colonization of Egypt, Tunisia, or *Indochina.

3. The third and most potent set of arguments refer to non-economic circumstances in Europe and the USA. One theme has been the rivalry between European states, which was a major factor in German colonial expansion from the 1880s onwards. Another was the use of imperialism by state leaders as a machiavellian technique to deflect attention from domestic problems, for example in Portugal, France, and Italy (Abyssinia, Libya). Finally, there developed a genuine belief in the superiority of Western culture (as exemplified by men such as Rudyard Kipling and Rhodes), supported by a missionary zeal to spread the Christian religion. In the case of Britain, almost as important as its imperial territories was its 'informal empire', territories which were not nominally under British control, but which were heavily dependent on British commercial, financial, or military patronage. Since 1914, most countries in Africa and Asia have become independent. However, in a process of what Kwame *Nkrumah has termed 'Neocolonialism', most African countries remain economically, militarily and technologically dependent on the interference and goodwill of developed countries.

DECOLONIZATION; MAPS 3 and 4

Independent Labour Party (ILP) (UK)

One of the organizations which formed the Labour Representation Committee (LRC). It was a socialist organization founded in Bradford in 1893, initially led by Keir *Hardie. Other early members included Ramsay *MacDonald and Philip *Snowden. When the LRC became the *Labour Party in 1906, it formed an uneasy alliance with the ILP. The latter disaffiliated from the Labour Party in 1932, seeing it as too reformist. In the later 1930s, many Labour politicians saw it as an electoral liability because of its sympathy towards *Communism, and its pacifism. Chaired by James Maxton (b. 1885, d. 1946) from 1926, it became increasingly centred on Glasgow, winning its only seats (four) there in 1935. After Maxton's death, its representation in parliament dwindled from three in 1945 to none in 1950. It did not put forward any candidates after 1959. Its role in local government, and its discussion of foreign affairs, had influenced Labour's early years, and it had brought many middle-class idealists into the Labour Party.

Independent Republican Party, France (FNR), see UDF

India

Known as the 'Jewel in the Crown' of the British Empire at the beginning of the twentieth century, India experienced a traumatic partition before independence, when it became the world's largest democracy.

Colonial rule India had come under British colonial rule by 1850, after a drawn-out process of territorial conquest, acquisition, and contracts with existing rulers which had been drawn up over a period of 250 years. British rule was asserted by the suppression of the Indian mutiny (1857–8). Perhaps the most intriguing question of the first half of the twentieth century with regard to Indian history is why and how a small colonial British elite could govern the world's second most populous country, then containing around 450 million people.

The most important factor, and a central tenet of Indian history even after independence, was its unrivalled diversity. Despite its predominantly Hindu population, 25 per cent were Muslim, while Christians and Buddhists remained small but important minorities. Moreover, its diverse peoples and tribes used over 1,600 different languages and dialects, and over 200 different scripts. The gradual encroachment of the English into the subcontinent had allowed them to adapt their system of government to the prevailing local conditions. In the British *Raj around two-fifths of India was still ruled by autonomous or semi-autonomous princes who paid only formal allegiance to the British crown. In addition, particularly in the twentieth

Table 11. **Viceroys and Prime Ministers of India since 1899**

Viceroys

Lord *Curzon (George)	1899–1905
Lord Minto (Gilbert John Elliot-Murray-Kynynmond)	1905–10
Lord Hardinge (Charles)	1910–16
Lord Chelmsford (Frederick John Napier Thesiger)	1916–21
Earl of Reading (Rufus Daniel Rufus Isaacs)	1921–6
Lord Irwin (Edward Frederick Lindley Wood: *Halifax)	1926–9
Lord Goschen (temporary)	1929
Lord Irwin	1929–31
Lord Willingdon (Freeman Freeman-Thomas)	1931–4
Sir George Stanley (temporary)	1934–6
Lord Willingdon	1936–43
Lord *Wavell (Archibald)	1943–7
Lord *Mounbatten	1947–8
C. R. Rajagopalachari	1948

Prime Ministers

Jawaharlal *Nehru	1947–64
Lal Bahadur *Shastri	1964–6
Indira *Gandhi	1966–77
Moraji *Desai	1977–9
Charan Singh	1979–80
Indira *Gandhi	1980–4
Rajiv *Gandhi	1984–9
Vishwanath Pratap Singh	1989–90
Chandra Shekhar	1990–1
P. V. *Narasimha Rao	1991–6
Shri Atal Bihari *Vajpayee	1996–2004
Deve Gowda	1996–7
Inder Kumar Gujral	1997–8
Shri Atal Bahari *Vajpayee	1998–2004
Manmohan *Singh	2004–

century, the British were happy to point to the growing Muslim/Hindu tensions, and to present themselves as the indispensable neutral arbiter between these communities.

Another important fact about British rule was that the British never settled in India in great numbers. For the British, India's main function was to export such goods as spices, tea, coffee, raw cotton, and silk, and to provide a large market for British manufactured goods. As a result, a European administrative system and a legal system based on English law were introduced. In addition, the colonial rulers created a public sphere through books, education, and newspapers. These changes were imposed upon India. There was no Indian parliament that could have approved them. Nevertheless, they were implemented overwhelmingly by Indians, and were quickly adapted to Indian conditions, so that the legal or administrative systems soon became semblances of their former selves. These reforms, as well as extensive commerce with England, created a substantial Indian middle class. Meanwhile, the British had neither the power nor necessarily the inclination to change popular culture, except for a few traditional rites such as the live burning of widows, at the side of their dead husbands. Its ban in the 1830s was enforced with great difficulty. Thus, British rule in India functioned largely because of the implicit or explicit consent of the educated and commercial classes that benefited from it, and because of British administrative skill.

The growth of nationalism (1885–1930s) The creation of a public sphere, a Western education system, and protection by the rule of law was increasingly at odds with the absence of a parliament or any form of Indian political representation. It was this demand for Indian participation in government which led to the foundation of the Indian National *Congress in 1885, which developed into the central Indian nationalist organization.

Nationalist feelings were excited by Lord *Curzon's partition of *Bengal, because it suggested the division of the Indian nation into Muslims and Hindus, and because it was made without prior consultation with Indians. In response to the unrest, a very limited change came through the Morley–Minto reforms (Indian Councils Act) of 1909. For the first time a small number of elected Indian representatives were admitted to the imperial and provincial parliaments. Controversially, the Act also granted separate representation to Muslims and Hindus, thus reflecting a nascent feeling of Muslim cultural distinctiveness expressed in the foundation of the *Muslim League (1906). After World War I, it was again not the demand for independence as such, but the British denials of the civil liberties (through the *Rowlatt Act), the concept of which they themselves had introduced, which led to the radicalization of Congress under its new leader, Mohandas K. *Gandhi, from 1920.

Gandhi appreciated the profound truth that it was not so much British might as Indian compliance which enabled colonial rule. He was determined to raise Indian self-consciousness and self-confidence through the *svadeshi* ('of our own country'), in which he campaigned for Indian self-sufficiency in order to attack the British in the most sensitive area, commerce. This was complemented by his *satyagraha* campaigns of peaceful resistance and non-cooperation with the British. Each of the three *satyagraha* campaigns demonstrated the growing strength and authority of Gandhi and his Congress.

Partition (1930s–1947) Despite belated administrative reforms, such as the granting of the *Government of India Acts (1919, 1935), and the *Round Table Conferences, it became clear that the British could not remain in the country for long. While a revolt by the radical nationalists led by *Bose could be prevented with some difficulty, during World War II there occurred an important shift within Indian nationalism. Under *Jinnah's leadership, the hitherto fledgling Muslim League was propelled to represent the vast majority of the Muslim community, on the basis of its Pakistan (Lahore) declaration of 23 March 1940 which demanded separate Muslim homelands. After the war, the final attempt by the *Cabinet Mission Proposal to achieve a compromise between Congress and the Muslim League ended in acrimony because of *Nehru's insistence on the sovereignty of the (Hindu) popular majority. The tension was reflected in widespread communal violence, particularly in the north, where Muslims and Hindus coexisted. It led to the hasty partition of India, completed on 15 August 1947, when India and Pakistan became independent.

The Constitution of India (1947–1960s) Independence had been negotiated largely by Gandhi's lieutenant, *Nehru, who came to dominate Indian affairs until his death in 1964, and even afterwards through the leadership of his daughter and his grandson respectively. His able ministers, especially *Patel and *Ambedkar, had drafted a Constitution by 1950, which integrated 562 formerly autonomous princely states into the Union of India. India became a leading country of *non-alignment in foreign policy, though in practice this meant playing both superpowers against each other when it came to technological aid or arms purchases.

Under Nehru and his successors, Congress remained the political force committed to Indian unity and the defence of its territorial integrity. This was threatened from without, notably by Pakistan and China, and led to a series of *Indo-Pakistan Wars, and an *Indo-Chinese War in 1962. Indian unity was also challenged from within, as certain states such as *Assam, *Kashmir, and *Punjab demanded more autonomy. Nehru inaugurated an ambitious programme of industrialization in a series of centrally devised five-year plans, which was continued by his successors, L. B. *Shastri, and, from 1966, by Nehru's daughter, Indira *Gandhi.

Political and economic transformation (1970s–80s) India strove for economic self-sufficiency, and in large measure succeeded. This was thanks to its wealth in mineral resources, its pre-existing economic infrastructure, and technological innovations such as the *Green Revolution in agriculture. The contrast remained striking between the country's overall economic progress and the enormous levels of individual poverty that remained. The first root cause for this was India's caste system, whereby, according to the *Hindu faith, people born into a certain structure should remain there, i.e. those born poor were doomed to die in poverty. The second hindrance to India's development has been its rapid population growth, which caused its population to increase by 25 per cent per decade. Most of India's economic growth from the 1950s to the 1980s was occasioned by, and spent on, demographic growth.

Indira Gandhi continued her party's long-standing fight against the caste system. She tried to curb population growth through the introduction of contraception, and even forced sterilization. Together with her other authoritarian policies, this proved so unpopular that it allowed a loose *Janata coalition to wrest power from Congress in 1977. Under M. *Desai, the coalition had just enough time to restore democratic rule before Congress returned to power, after a brief interim government of Charan Singh (1979–80), first under Mrs Gandhi (1980–4) and then under her son Rajiv *Gandhi (1984–9). The two Gandhis encouraged economic liberalization, which did restore a period of growth, but the government's austerity measures encouraged further regional autonomy movements, and led to a *Sikh rebellion in *Amritsar in 1984, and to disruptions in other states. There was a change of government in 1989, to an alliance of oppositional groups under Vishwanath P. Singh. He remained in office for one year, and was succeeded by the short-lived government of Chandra Shekhar, both of which governments were overwhelmed by their inability to control communal violence.

Economic revival (1990s) In 1991, Congress returned under *Narasimha Rao, who changed the country's policy of non-alignment to a slight opening towards the USA. His policies of privatization fostered renewed resentment, and led to charges of corruption. A supremely able politician whose skill was inversely proportional to his charisma, he governed until 1996 despite continuous unpopularity. He lost the elections of May 1996, against a heterogeneous opposition led by the National Front coalition and the *Baharatiya Janata Party (BJP). Under an unstable minority government supported by Congress, the National Front tried to exclude the BJP from government.

In 1998, the BJP increased its parliamentary strength and took over power under *Vajpayee. His charismatic, assured style of government assuaged international fears about the religiously inspired party. Vajpayee did, indeed, pursue a more determined religious-nationalist agenda. This strengthened his position at home, but it also challenged India's fragile internal religious and ethnic balance. In February 2002, it encouraged bloody unrests of Hindus against the substantial Muslim minority in Uttar Pradesh and elsewhere throughout India which the government struggled to bring under control. In the international context, India's new assertiveness included the carrying out of nuclear testing in 1998. This confirmed India's nuclear capability, but led to an international credit and technology boycott, and triggered similar trials in Pakistan.

Contemporary politics (since 2001) India's international isolation was broken after the *War on Terrorism in Afghanistan, when India sought to call attention to the Pakistani guerrilla fighters in Kashmir which it considered to be terrorists. After a gun attack on the Indian parliament in December 2001, India went to the brink of war with its western neighbour until Pakistan took measures against those responsible for the incident. Under Vajpayee, India's economic growth continued to outpace population growth, thus leading to an overall increase in wealth. However, incomes continued to be distributed highly unevenly. Misreading the public mood, Vajpayee called early elections in 2004, but he was beaten by an energized Congress led by Sonia *Gandhi which appealed to the poor. Congress returned to government, with Manmohan *Singh becoming Prime Minister. The new government introduced unemployment insurance to the rural population, while stimulating growth in other sectors of the economy.

India Acts, see GOVERNMENT OF INDIA ACTS

Indian army

By 1902, when *Kitchener became Commander-in-Chief in India, it was established practice that most regiments of the British army stationed a battalion in India. In 1903 the three armies of Madras, Bombay, and Bengal were united and the Indian army proclaimed by the Viceroy, Lord *Curzon. Those officers holding the King's Commission were British; they were assisted by sepoy officers holding the Viceroy's Commission. Kitchener reorganized this army and established a staff college to recruit and train more Indian officers. From 1917 Indians became eligible for the full King's Commission. The Indian army served in Iran, Mesopotamia, *Palestine, and Egypt, as well as on the Western Front during World War I. In 1922 it was again reorganized, reducing the cavalry regiments and creating an Auxiliary (Territorial) Force. During the 1920s it steadily recruited and trained more Indian personnel into specialist units such as engineers and signals, while the number of British battalions stationed in India was steadily reduced. In World War II, the army served in North Africa, Italy, and Burma.

In July 1947 it was reorganized into the Indian and Pakistani armies, and its British officers were repatriated. In both countries, the army retained an important role, though it was also an important source of grievances. For instance, the army continued to recruit sections in the population whom the British had considered 'reliable'. India began to build up the largest volunteer army in the world, with a peacetime strength of over one million men. Its army was considered to be better equipped and better organized than that of Pakistan. This caused concern that in the event of a military conflict, Pakistan would seek to compensate for its inferiority in a conflict with conventional forces through a nuclear attack. Paradoxically, despite the relative weakness of the Pakistan army relative to its Indian rival, its political influence was much higher. Even at times of civilian leadership its influence remained pivotal.

indirect rule

Britain's method of administering many of its colonies. It was first developed during the nineteenth century in India, where two-thirds of the country was ruled by native princes. Its most notable proponent was Frederick *Lugard, who developed indirect rule in Nigeria during 1912–19, and expounded the idea in his *Dual Mandate in British Tropical Africa* (1922). As colonies were developed, it was applied elsewhere in Africa, and in Malaya. The policy was most successful in monarchical or hierarchically structured societies, where Britain could back an existing ruler or a ruling caste. In more fragmented or unstable societies, indirect rule became more difficult to apply as it was not always clear whom the British should support.
  BRITISH EMPIRE

Indochina

A French colony from 1887, when the Indochinese Union was formed consisting of Cambodia (a colony since 1884), Annam (a protectorate since 1884), Tonkin (a protectorate since 1884), and Cochin-China (a colony since 1867). To this was added the protectorate of Laos in 1893. The royal houses of Laos, Cambodia, and Vietnam (Tonkin and Annam) were retained within a federal system, with the Governor-General in Hanoi controlling finance and defence. Cochin-China, with its capital of Saigon, was administered directly by a French prefect. A French educational system was developed and a French university established in Hanoi.

Struggle for independence (from 1930s) Resistance to colonial rule was concentrated in the provinces of Annam and Tonkin, where a host of nationalist movements developed in the 1920s. Still, the Nghe Tinh Revolt (1930–1) in central Vietnam developed relatively independently of these political formations. The peasant rebellion was brutally suppressed, with some 10,000 killed and 50,000 deported.

  In September 1940 the Japanese obtained military and commercial concessions from the *Vichy administration, with free use of ports and airfields. As a result, though never formally under Japanese occupation, the Japanese military became the prime target of nationalist organizations, led by the *Vietminh from 1943. On 9 March 1945 the Japanese ambassador Matsumoto gave Governor-General Decroux an ultimatum, which he ignored. The next day 750 French officials were imprisoned, of whom 400 died. Cambodia, Laos, and Vietnam proclaimed themselves independent. On 19 August *Ho Chi Minh's forces entered Hanoi, forcing Emperor *Bao Dai to abdicate. France recognized the autonomy of the states of Vietnam, Cambodia, and Laos on 6 March 1946, as part of an Indochinese Federation within the *French Union. After the *Indochina War, France finally accepted the full independence of Cambodia and Laos, and withdrew completely from Vietnam.

Indochina War (1946–54)

A war caused by French efforts to reassert control over its former colony of *Indochina, following its exposure to Japanese forces during World War II. During that war, the Communist-dominated *Vietminh forces of *Ho Chi Minh had developed into the main opposition to the Japanese. Upon Japanese defeat, Ho Chi Minh proclaimed the independent Democratic Republic of Vietnam. Other parts of Indochina, Laos and Cambodia, had also declared their independence. They were recognized by France on 6 March 1946 as autonomous states within the *French Union.

  Conflicts soon erupted between the Democratic Republic of Vietnam and French colonial authorities. After a dispute regarding rights to levy import duty, the French administration demanded the withdrawal of all Vietminh forces from the port of Haiphong. When this was not met, the French bombarded the town's Vietnamese quarter, killing over 6,000 civilians. The French failed to rally all non-Communist forces behind the weak *Bao Dai, while their tanks and superior equipment made little headway in jungle warfare. The confrontation soon proved to be beyond the French, who appealed to the USA for help. Impressed by the *domino theory, the USA complied and bore 78 per cent of the military costs by 1954. By this time, the Vietminh, supported by a majority of the peasants, controlled virtually all the rural areas, while the French retained control of the cities. The French were by this time eager to withdraw, especially after losses at *Dien Bien Phu. In the summer of 1954, they left behind a country divided along the 17th Parallel. French colonial forces had suffered almost 100,000 casualties in the war, though it is likely that losses among the Vietminh forces far exceeded this number.

Indo-Chinese War (20 Oct.–22 Nov. 1962)

A war caused by China's refusal to accept the Indo-Chinese border drawn along the *McMahon Line in 1914. It became a current issue with China's annexation of *Tibet in 1950. A number of border clashes led to the 'cartographic war' (1960–2), when both sides argued their claims on the basis of different maps. Following India's decision to defend vigorously the territories it regarded as its own, the Chinese quickly advanced into *Assam. The Chinese withdrew on 21 November, but retained the Ladakh salient. It was a devastating defeat for the *Indian army, triggering the resignation of the Minister of Defence, Krishna Menon. It prompted a series of army reforms, and led to extensive investment in foreign (intitially US) armaments technology.

Indonesia

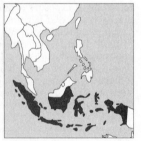

A heterogeneous country comprising some 13,000 islands. Following brutal colonial rule, the country's wealth in mineral resources was squandered by corrupt leaders, leaving behind a difficult legacy for a fledgling democracy.

Foreign rule (up to 1949) Indonesia was colonized by the Dutch from 1602 in order to control the spice trade. As the Netherlands lost its pre-eminence as a seafaring nation, the **Dutch East Indies**, as it was known, became a cornerstone not just of Dutch *imperialism but also of Dutch commercial and economic prosperity. From 1901, a series of reforms introduced better educational and health provisions for the indigenous population, as well as some access to local government. In 1916 a Volksraad (People's Council) was established, to which the indigenous population sent fifteen out of the 39 representatives (30 out of 60 from 1931). Nevertheless, colonial rule was still very much geared to Dutch requirements. The emergence of a substantial indigenous commercial middle class was hampered further by the existence of a prosperous Chinese immigrant community.

The political and economic impotence of the native Indonesian population caused much resentment, and led to the formation of the *Sarekat Islam in 1912 as the country's first nationalist movement. This was followed by a host of other, often more radical, movements. The Sarekat Islam was soon eclipsed by the Indonesian *Communist Party, founded in 1920, and the radical Partai Nasional Indonesia (PNI, Indonesian Nationalist Party) under *Sukarno in 1927 (it adopted this current name in 1928). These parties were brutally suppressed by the colonial authorities. Meanwhile, the rise of nationalist groups triggered the evolution of radical, racist settlers' groups, looking to South Africa for inspiration by virtue of its independent colonial status and race relations. The most important of these groups was the Vaderlandse Club (Patriotic Club), founded in 1929, and the *Nazi Nationaal-Socialistische Beweging (National Socialist Movement), which won a considerable following during the Great *Depression.

The country was invaded in 1942 by the Japanese, who brought great suffering to the Dutch colonial population, while many Indonesian nationalists cooperated willingly. Thus strengthened by Japanese rule, Sukarno declared Indonesian independence on 17 August 1945. This was not recognized by the Dutch, who returned to bring considerable parts of the country under their control in two Police Actions in 1947 and 1948. In addition, Sukarno's republic was threatened by the Communist declaration of east Java as a *'Soviet' state. However, the Dutch forces were outnumbered and overstretched, so that despite considerable brutality (which remained a taboo subject in the Netherlands into the 1990s), the Dutch finally had to concede independence on 27 December 1949.

The Sukarno era (1949–67) The country's disparate geography often made communication very difficult and provided superb hideouts for opposition groups. In fact, owing to Indonesia's ethnic, cultural, linguistic, and religious heterogeneity, democratic government remained all but an illusion. Instead, a strong military remained Sukarno's most important consideration, as he proceeded to extend his power until he became President for life in 1963. Crucially, Sukarno managed to attract the displeasure of the army, mainly on three counts. First, his policy of neutrality and friendly relations with Communist China and the Soviet Union appeared often ambiguous and ill-advised, particularly at a time when the Communists continued to pose a significant domestic threat for the state. Secondly, while his incorporation by military force of *Irian proved a success, his military conflict with Malaysia, known as the *Confrontation, backfired. It dragged on, weakened the army in its fight against Communist rebels inside the country, and reduced its international standing even further. Finally, the Communist uprising of 1965, partly inspired by the military's engagement with Malaysia, and Sukarno's half-hearted response to it, spelt his end.

The Suharto era (1967–98) With the help of the army, *Suharto assumed control over the government in 1967–8, and suppressed the Communists. He ended the Confrontation, and steered the country towards a strongly pro-*capitalist course, with good relations with the USA and Japan. During the 1970s, Suharto was able to preside over strong economic growth, helped largely by high oil prices (Indonesia has large oil reserves). Unfortunately, most of the economic spoils went to members of the military and government protégés. There were also expensive, unsuccessful, and environmentally catastrophic attempts to settle large parts of the population (around five million people) in sparsely inhabited areas of the country, and to provide them with arable land through the deforestation of rainforest. In 1975 the army invaded *Timor Leste (East Timor), and formally annexed it in 1976.

In the 1980s the economy suffered from a decline in world commodity prices (including oil). The government was thus punished for its failure to establish a manufacturing base in the previous decade. Suharto maintained a tight reign and introduced a series of economic austerity measures which led to resumed economic growth. These policies also led, however, to growing hardship among the mass of the population, which suffered from poverty and an unofficial unemployment rate of around 40 per cent in the early 1990s.

Democratization (from 1998) Suharto's decision in 1998 to increase energy prices by over 50 per cent led to mass protests, and ultimately forced Suharto to resign. His successor, Bacharuddin Habibie, was the choice of the military and political establishment. He was unable to stem the growth of the opposition movement, which in 1999 won the first democratic elections. The Indonesia Democratic Party—Struggle (PDI-P), headed by *Sukarnoputri, emerged as winners. She was unable to form a government against the resistance of the army, and instead became Vice-President to Bacharuddin Habibie. In this period of political weakness the army was unable to

intervene effectively in Timor Leste, which gained its independence in 2002. Habibie also became involved in a series of corruption scandals, and was forced to resign in 2001. He was succeeded by Sukarnoputri. In 2001, regional autonomy was instituted through an administrative reform, and in 2002 the process of democratization was continued when direct popular elections for the presidency were introduced. However, central authority continued to be undermined by a variety of guerrilla movements fighting for greater autonomy in Irian Jaya, Kalimantan, and Aceh.

Contemporary politics (since 2004) Soon after the first-ever democratic presidential elections in 2004 were won by S. B. *Yudhoyono, Indonesia was hit by the *tsunami, which killed over 120,000 people. Indonesia received over $4 billion in reconstruction aid, which lessened the storm's economic impact. Nevertheless, Yudhoyono continued to struggle to enhance economic growth and reduce the unemployment rate, which stood at around 10 per cent. In 2005, Yudhoyono achieved a remarkable success by signing a peace agreement with the rebels in the province of Aceh.

Indonesian Communist Party, see
COMMUNIST PARTY, INDONESIA

Indo-Pakistan Wars
A series of conflicts which erupted out of the tense relations between India and Pakistan that followed their acrimonious separation in 1947. During 1947–9, there were military clashes, mainly as an outflow of the communal violence between Hindus and Muslims in both countries. The most important dispute arose around the states of *Hyderabad and *Kashmir. Despite Pakistan's support of the Muslim prince in this Hindu state, Hyderabad joined the Union of India in 1948. Conflict over the case of Kashmir, situated between India and Pakistan, with a Muslim population and a Hindu ruler, led to its eventual partition. The second Indo-Pakistan War occurred between 6 and 23 September 1965, again over Kashmir. It was precipitated by Pakistan, but ended in stalemate, and was resolved by the *Tashkent Agreement of January 1966. The third Indo-Pakistan war occurred during 1970–1, when the *Indian army successfully intervened in East Pakistan to help the independence movement there in its fight against the regular army of (West) Pakistan. Thereafter, the greater military sophistication of both armies, as well as the development of nuclear

weapons on both sides, has drastically reduced the feasibility of short, sharp confrontations. Thus no further wars between the countries followed, though this was not matched by an improvement in relations.

Industrial Workers of the World (IWW)

A revolutionary *anarcho-syndicalist trade union in the USA, founded in 1905. Nicknamed 'the Wobblies', it attempted to attract migrant, unskilled workers in addition to the existing membership made up largely of militant western miners. Its membership peaked at around 60,000 in 1912, but after conducting an unsuccessful silkworkers' strike in Paterson, New Jersey, in 1913, its influence declined. The IWW was also fundamentally weakened by perennial controversies between its moderate, social-democratic wing, and its militant, anarchist wing.

IWW had a relatively marginal influence in the employment market. Nevertheless, it has retained an important place in socialist mythology because of its attempt, for the first time, to speak for the inarticulate sections of the working classes, to cross boundaries of race as well as class, and because of its charismatic leadership (the most notable leader being William D. ('Big Bill') Haywood, b. 1869, d. 1928).

INF (Intermediate-range Nuclear Forces) Treaty (8 Dec. 1987), see
DISARMAMENT

Inkatha yeNkululeko yeSizwe (Free-dom of the Nation), see BUTHELEZI,
GATSHA MANGOSUTHU

Inönü, Ismet (b. 14 Sept. 1884, d. 25 Dec. 1973). Prime Minister of Turkey 1923–4, 1925–37, 1961–5; President of Turkey 1938–50
Born **Mustafa Ismet** in Izmir, he was commissioned into the *Ottoman army in 1903. Mustafa became a prominent participant in the rebellion of the *Young Turks in 1908, and became a member of the General Staff during World War I. He took a leading part in the Turkish-Greek War of 1921–2, where he gained a famous victory at Inönü in 1921. An increasingly close ally of Kemal (*Atatürk), as Foreign Minister he negotiated the favourable terms of the Treaty of *Lausanne in 1923. He was the first Prime Minister of the new Turkish Republic. In this office, and as Atatürk's successor as President, he did more than anybody else to confirm and strengthen Kemal's legacy of a secular, Westernized state. Perhaps most importantly,

for the most part he kept the country out of World War II, which it could have ill-afforded given his efforts at economic and social reform. He finally created a multi-party system in 1945, and subsequently lost the elections of 1950. He remained head of his party, the Republican People's Party, until 1972, and was Prime Minister following the army coup of 1960.

Inter-American Treaty of Reciprocal Assistance (Rio de Janeiro Treaty) (Sept. 1947)
A security agreement signed and ratified by all of the 21 American republics, which formalized and extended the informal security pact against Germany and Japan during World War II in response to the emerging *Cold War. A pact against aggression from outside and within the alliance, it was regarded by most members as a multilateral mechanism for the maintenance of peace and stability across the region. The US, however, considered this to be another bloc against the spread of *Communism.

The treaty was invoked in a number of regional conflicts, such as those between Nicaragua and Costa Rica in 1949, 1955, and 1959. At the same time, it has also been used to justify US intervention in the member states' domestic affairs, such as those in Grenada (1983) or Panama (1989). Since 1948 it has been complemented by the formation of a political alliance, the *OAS.

Intergovernmental Conference (IGC)
A conference of government representatives of the member states of the EU. It is convened to deliberate on amendments to the Treaty of *Rome. There is no time limit to IGCs, but they usually take between one and two years in order to reach a viable consensus, since every change to the Treaty of Rome can only come into effect if agreed by consensus and ratified by every member state. The most important IGCs since the Treaty of Rome prepared the *Single European Act (1985–6), the *Maastricht Treaty (1991–2), the Treaty of *Amsterdam (1996–7) the Treaty of *Nice (1999–2000), and the Treaty establishing a *Constitution for Europe (2003–4).

International Atomic Energy Agency
An autonomous organization of the *UN which assists in the peaceful and safe use of nuclear energy. Established in 1957 with an original membership of 81 nations, the IAEA assisted moves towards *disarmament, notably the non-proliferation of nuclear weapons. The IAEA came to occupy a pivotal

role as neutral arbiter to assess the nuclear threat emanating from potential nuclear powers. In the run-up to the *Iraq War, its assessment that there was no evidence that Iraq had nuclear weapons was not accepted by George W. *Bush. However, following the invasion the US had to accept the IAEA's earlier assessment, which enhanced the IAEA's reputation. It continued to occupy an important role in assessing the nuclear threat emanating from Iran and North Korea. In 2005 the organization and its director from 1995, Mohamed el-Baradei, were awarded the *Nobel Peace Prize.

International Bank for Reconstruction and Development,
see WORLD BANK

International Brigades
International groups of volunteers fighting for the Spanish Republic in the *Spanish Civil War, three-quarters of whom were Communists keen to fight the growth of *Fascism. Welcomed by the *Popular Front government, they consisted of a total of almost 60,000 combatants, drawn from over fifty nations. A majority were working people, though the Brigades became best-known through the participation of writers and other intellectuals, such as W. H. Auden, George Orwell, and Ernest Hemingway, whose book *For Whom the Bell Tolls* remains perhaps the best-known representation of the horrors faced by members of the International Brigades in particular, and of the Civil War in general. In 1996, Spain honoured the surviving members of the International Brigades by granting them Spanish citizenship.

International Court of Justice
The judicial court of the *UN, founded in 1946. Based in the Dutch capital of The Hague, it arbitrates between consenting nations based on international law. It has been relatively ineffective, as it could only spring into action if both the accuser and the accused agreed to the ICJ's involvement and its judgment. The ICJ is one of the five principal organs of the UN, whereas the International Criminal Tribunals for the Former Yugoslavia (est. 1993) and Rwanda (est. 1994) were instituted under the authority of a different organ, the Security Council. *Human rights violations became the subject of another court, the *International Criminal Court set up in 2002.

International Criminal Court (ICC)
An international court set up in The Hague in 2002, to investigate *human rights violations committed by individuals in cases of genocide, war crimes, and crimes against humanity. Its remit is to act as a court of last resort, in cases where the national rule of law has become inoperative, which is why the ICC rejected most cases brought before it, including human rights violations following the *Iraq War. This reduced the initial opposition of the US, which feared that politically motivated charges could be brought against its nationals. Since its creation, the ICC has adjudicated human rights violations in *Darfur, Uganda and Congo. By 2007, the ICC was accepted by 104 countries. Although technically independent of the UN, the UN was crucial in its creation, and both organizations maintained close links.

(((∰))) SEE WEB LINKS
• The official website of the ICC.

International Labour Organization (ILO)
A specialized agency of the *UN since 1949, originally set up in 1919 as an agency of the *League of Nations to improve labour and living conditions throughout the world, by working towards an international code of labour law and practice. Its aim was to provide an international forum for labour demands and to recommend to governments constitutional means to answer these, through law and conciliation. The ILO became increasingly concerned with *human rights. One of its priorities was an effort to reduce child labour in less-developed countries, which affected an estimated 250 million children by 2000. It also provided technical assistance to developing nations. It was awarded the *Nobel Peace Prize in 1960.

(((∰))) SEE WEB LINKS
• The official website of the ILO.

International Monetary Fund, see IMF

Intifadah ('shaking off')
A violent protest against continued Israeli rule in the *Gaza Strip and the *West Bank, sparked off on 9 December 1987 by rumours of Israeli atrocities. Violence spread and erupted sporadically in the West Bank until 1994. According to *Rabin, by April 1994 the Intifadah had cost the lives of 2,156 Palestinians, with 18,967 injured, and of 219 Israelis, with 7,872 injured. Israeli impotence to end the violence despite heavy repression persuaded many to seek a negotiated settlement with the *PLO about Gaza and the West Bank, in the interest of peace. After the agreement on the autonomy of Gaza and

Jericho, the violence diminished, although *Hamas, a rival Palestinian organization, continued to incite violence against Israeli rule.

As *Arafat's *Palestinian National Authority proved unable to assert its full authority over the Palestinian areas, Arafat failed to convince the hesitant Israelis that concessions would bring peace. In turn, Israel's refusal to honour its own peace commitments after *Netanyahu's election in 1996 incited further Palestinian violence against Israel. A new Intifadah erupted on 27 September 2000, after *Sharon deliberately provoked Palestinian outrage by visiting the Temple Mount in Jerusalem. In the 'al-Aqsa' Intifadah, suicide bombers infiltrated Jewish civilian and military settlements, provoking an increasingly sharp reaction of the Israeli military. The second Intifadah never formally ended, though levels of violence declined in 2005. According to *Amnesty International, by 2006 the 'al Aqsa' Intifadah had cost the lives of some 4,000 Palestinians (mostly civilians) and 1,100 Israelis (of whom 700 were civilians).

Inuit (Canada)

A word used to designate the aboriginal people living in the Arctic regions of Canada. The Inuit speak six dialects of a common language, Inuktitut, and are divided into eight main tribal groups. Never exposed to the same degree of contact with Europeans experienced by more southern native peoples, the Inuit were more or less officially ignored until 1939, when a federal court ruled that they were a federal responsibility. Never subject to the Indian Act, they receive funding from the federal government for housing, education, and other basic programmes. Most of the Inuit converted to Christianity in the twentieth century.

After World War II, when the Canadian north was opened up to development and mineral exploitation, contact with non-aboriginal Canadians increased, and the traditional nomadic way of life became less common. Partly as a result of this increased contact some Inuit began to develop an artistic industry in soapstone carving and printmaking, which has brought greater economic self-sufficiency to many communities.

In the early 1970s a national organization, the Inuit Tapirisat of Canada, was founded to protect Inuit cultural and individual rights. The organization also includes in its mandate the negotiation of land claims and the protection of the Arctic environment. In 1999, much of the Northern Territories were handed over to Inuit home rule as *Nunavut.

In 2005, Inuits received either ownership or special land rights over vast areas in Labrador (Nunatsiavut), while in 2006 Inuits in Northern Quebec (Nunavik) received special rights over the land in the northern part of the province, including a share of the profits in future explorations.

(⊕) SEE WEB LINKS
- The official website of the Nunavut government.
- The official website of the Nunatsiavut government.

Invergordon mutiny (1931)

A mutiny of ratings (non-commissioned sailors) in the Royal Navy's Atlantic Fleet on Cromarty Firth, Scotland, led by Able Seaman Len Wincott, on 15 September 1931. It resulted from the *National Government's proposal for cuts in naval pay, in response to Britain's financial crisis: 7 per cent for admirals, 3.7 per cent for lieutenant-commanders, 13.6 per cent for unmarried able seamen. The cuts had been announced over the radio, before the sailors had been notified officially. When the cuts were slightly revised (with a limit of 10 per cent), the mutiny ended, and the ringleaders were subsequently discharged. It contributed to the financial crisis as foreign holders of sterling were alarmed by the prospect of the Royal Navy in mutiny. The *Gold Standard was suspended on 21 September, after the value of the pound had already fallen by over a quarter.

Ipperwash Lake, see LAND CLAIMS, NATIVE

Iqbal, Muhammad (b. 9 Nov. 1876, d. 21 Apr. 1938). Indian political philosopher

Born in Sialkot, he was educated at Cambridge and Munich, and was admitted to the Bar in 1908. He returned to India to practise law and was appointed a professor of philosophy. He became a leading poet in Urdu and Persian, and was an important force in the assumption of Muslim self-confidence, e.g. through his lectures collected in *The Reconstruction of Religious Thought in Islam* (1930). In his influential address to the *Muslim League at its conference in Allahabad, he advanced the idea of a separate Muslim homeland in north-west India, which was eventually realized after his death in the state of Pakistan. He attended the *Round Table Conferences of 1931 and 1932, and remained active in the Muslim League.

IRA (Irish Republican Army)

The origins of the IRA are to be found in the Irish Republican Brotherhood (popularly known as the Fenians), founded in Dublin and

New York in 1858. Fenian risings were repressed in 1867, but the Brotherhood took part in the *Easter Rising of 1916. In 1919, it was recognized by *Sinn Féin as the army of the Irish Republic, with recruits from the Irish Volunteers, to fight in the War of Independence. It was first commanded by Michael *Collins, with Sean McBride as Chief of Staff. After the signing of the December 1921 Anglo-Irish Treaty (which gave southern Ireland–the Irish Free State–virtual independence), the IRA split. Members fought on both sides during the Irish Civil War (1922–3), and were also active through terrorist acts in Britain. Many members who fought against the Free State were imprisoned, and the IRA was outlawed by the Irish government in two stages in 1931 and 1936. It was involved in bomb explosions in England in 1939, but during World War II hundreds of its members were interned without trial in Ireland and in the UK. It launched a new campaign against the security forces in Northern Ireland in 1956, but by 1962 the IRA appeared to have been defeated.

When Northern Ireland was plunged into disorder in 1968, the IRA once again rose to prominence. Initially it tried to protect Catholic homes from Loyalist attacks, though with so little success that the British army was called in. The IRA vigorously debated how it should respond to the campaign for civil rights, and in December 1969, the IRA Army Council voted to grant token recognition to the *Stormont, Dublin, and London parliaments. This angered hardliners in the IRA, who had advocated abstention from established institutions, and the use of physical force. This soon resulted in the **Provisional IRA** leaving the movement. It is this group that is now known as the IRA, also often called the 'Provos'. The remaining Official IRA called a cease-fire in 1972, and has been effectively inactive since. The Provisional IRA, however, embarked upon a terrorist campaign against the security forces, which continued, but for a brief period in 1972, until its cease-fire in 1994. This consisted of hunger-strikes, assassinations, and bombings in both Northern Ireland and Britain, including the assassination of *Mountbatten, and an attack on the British Cabinet in Brighton in 1984.

In what may have been a further split within its ranks, part of the Provisional IRA resumed its terrorist campaign on 9 February 1996, though the majority of the IRA kept a ceasefire from the *Good Friday Agreement. The IRA continued to be reluctant to give up its arms, and moved many of its operations overseas. According to a *CIA report published in 2002 during the *War on Terrorism, the IRA was an integral part of a worldwide terrorist network with links to Colombia, Cuba, and the Arabian peninsula. At the same time, these revelations put enormous pressure on the IRA and *Sinn Féin, its political arm, as it endangered funding from the USA. The IRA destroyed its weapons by 2005, formally declaring an end to its armed struggle on 28 July 2005.

Iran

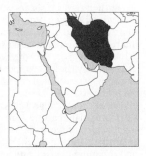

Overview A country whose history in the twentieth century was subject to three distinct factors. The first was its geopolitical position, as it bordered on the Russian Empire, with its continual quest for an ice-free port, to the north, and British India to the east. Its situation became even more precarious after World War I, when Mesopotamia (now *Iraq) became a British *League of Nations *Mandate. Second, matters were complicated by its substantial reserves in oil and gas. The third factor was the firm adherence of the vast majority of its population to *Shi'ite *Islam, a matter of overwhelming importance in uniting its ethnically heterogeneous population.

Early history (up to 1925) The first two (geopolitical and economic) factors dominated events in the first two decades of the century. Oil concessions were granted to British firms in 1901, which later became the Anglo-Persian Oil Company (later still BP). Growing informal control, especially by Britain, was formalized in the 1907 Russian convention. It divided the country into a northern section under Russian influence, a neutral part in the middle, and a southern area under British influence. This brought about violent protests from a traditionalist, Islamic society resentful of Western influence. A constitutional movement had developed in 1905 and managed to wrest a Constitution from the ailing Mozaffar al-Din Shah in 1906. This diverted some powers, including the handout of concessions to foreign companies, from the Shah. Despite the establishment of a parliament, however, there was little effective change in foreign influence. Foreign military presence was increased in 1911, and during World War I Iran was occupied by Russia and Britain in order to guard its oil reserves.

The Reza dynasty (1925–79) In 1921 a group of young officers led by Reza Khan assumed power, and in 1925 he deposed the last ruler of the *Qajar Dynasty, Ahmad Shah, and proclaimed himself Shah as Reza Shah *Pahlavi. He changed the name of the country from Persia to Iran (a derivative of Aryan, 'regal, noble') in 1925. This symbolized his general attempt to reform the country's traditionalist society, mainly in an effort to strengthen Iran's resistance against foreign intrusion. However, while this did create a more centralized, efficient state with a (marginally) more educated society, he achieved the worst of both worlds. He was distrusted by the foreign powers, and resisted at home by traditional communities whose values he attacked. His land reforms created even more landless peasants, while leading to the manipulated acquisition of land by large landowners, of whom he became the wealthiest. During World War II he insisted on remaining neutral, and was increasingly sympathetic to *Nazi Germany. This triggered another Allied occupation. He was forced to abdicate in favour of his son, Muhammad Reza *Pahlavi.

After the war, the well-organized armed forces suppressed separatist forces stationed in *Azerbaijan and Kazakhstan. Nevertheless, the Shah, who firmly supported the USA in the *Cold War, found it difficult to assert control, given the hostile anti-British sentiments among the population. In 1951 he was forced into exile by the popular revolutionary movement led by *Mussadeq. The latter nationalized the oil companies, but was unable to carry out further reforms, as he was overthrown in a royalist coup organized by the *CIA in 1953. Reza Pahlavi returned, and concluded the oil agreement of 1954, whereby the oil companies remained in state hands, but were managed, controlled, and exploited by a foreign consortium.

Continuous discontent and sporadic strikes (1956–61) led to the 'White Revolution' from 1960, a series of economic and social reforms. These included a land reform, carried out in three stages until 1971. In fact, these strengthened the landowners as an important pillar of the regime, by giving them generous compensation (to be paid by the peasants) and thus concentrating investment capital in their hands. Hence, despite fundamental reforms, the first large-scale demonstrations erupted in 1963. To maintain its power regardless of this growing unrest, the Shah's regime became increasingly brutal. The Shah also tried to remain in power through an astute foreign policy, gaining ever more help from the USA, while undercutting his opposition through a friendship treaty with the USSR. A reckless modernization campaign tried to destroy the social base of traditional *Islam. Instead, this policy created a host of inefficient small industries built overwhelmingly by foreign firms. In the mid-1970s, as over 50,000 tortured and maltreated political opponents of the regime languished in state prisons, the Shah's oppressive regime collapsed. In 1978–9 popular protest and general strikes reached such dimensions that they forced the Shah into exile.

Islamist rule (from 1979) A transitional government under S. Bakhtiar oversaw the triumphant return of the Islamic leader, *Ayatollah *Khomeini, from exile in Paris in February 1979. A new Constitution transformed the country into an Islamic republic which created effectively a theocracy in which the spiritual leadership had the final say. The oil industry was nationalized, and the Shah's institutions dissolved. Islamic law was reintroduced. In a popular act of defiance against the country that had enabled the Shah's dictatorship to endure for so long, crowds occupied the US embassy in Tehran, and thus precipitated the *Iran hostage crisis (1979–80). Consequent international isolation and internal turmoil were followed by the *Iran–Iraq War (1980–8), when Saddam *Hussein's forces tried to exploit Iran's weakness to gain some disputed territories. The war was fought with tremendous losses on both sides, but ultimately led to a stalemate, and in 1988 a ceasefire was agreed which maintained the status quo. While war caused tremendous damage to the economy, it nonetheless enabled the regime to strengthen its hold on Iranian society, under the conditions of a national emergency. For instance, the introduction of strict Islamic law led to thousands of executions per year, for crimes such as criticism of the government as well as ostensible 'Satanic' tendencies.

While economic, educational, and legal reforms towards Islam were comprehensive and relatively systematic, economic reforms embracing Islam were more apparent than real. For instance, banks were forbidden (by the Quran) to charge any interest rates, but took high commissions instead. Instead of undergoing any comprehensive reform, the economy deteriorated into chaos. In 1988 the pragmatist leadership faction under *Rafsanjani succeeded Khomeini, since when the country has undergone a careful moderation and opening up in its foreign and domestic policies. Nevertheless, the conservative religious leadership has remained extremely influential. Thus, it continued to support *Hamas and *Hezbollah as well as other *Islamic fundamentalist

organizations. In 1997 Sayed Mohammad
*Khatami was elected Prime Minster. He tried
to liberalize the economy and to promote free
speech, but was largely unsuccessful against
the continued power of the religious
leadership under Ayatollah Sayed Ali
*Kahmenei.

Contemporary politics (since 2005) In 2005,
Khatami was succeeded by *Ahmadi Nejad,
who launched a hostile rhetoric against Israel,
which he asserted ought to be 'wiped off the
map', and the USA. Months after his election
Iran resumed the enrichment of uranium,
which could be used for nuclear weapons.
This led to efforts by the three EU states of
Britain, Germany and France to persuade
Iran to abandon its policies. Assisted by the
USA, they led negotiations to convince
Iran to abandon its nuclear programme.
When this was unsuccessful in 2006, they
led an international effort to impose
*UN-sponsored sanctions on Iran. However,
China and Russia, which were both members
of the Security Council, were reluctant to
damage an important trading partner.
Stakes were raised in the rift between Iran
and the USA by the latter's accusation that
Iran was actively seeking to destabilize
public order in Iraq.

Iran hostage crisis (4 Nov. 1979–20 Jan.
1980)
Following the establishment of the Islamic
Republic of Iran under *Ayatollah
*Khomeini in 1979, public hostility against
the USA, which had heavily sponsored the
regime of Shah Reza *Pahlavi, formed an
important unifying force in the new state.
Against this background, supporters of the
revolution seized the US embassy in Tehran,
taking 66 US citizens hostage. All efforts of
President *Carter to free the hostages failed,
including economic measures and an abortive
helicopter rescue attempt. The crisis dragged
on through the American presidential
election, until Algeria successfully mediated
and the hostages were freed. It seriously
weakened Carter's bid for re-election.

Iran–Contra Affair
In 1985, elements within the US *National
Security Council centred around lieutenant
colonel **Oliver North** began to sell arms, via
Israel, to the Islamic republic of Iran. The arms
then went to Lebanese terrorists who, in return,
released some Western hostages held in Beirut
and Lebanon; the profits accruing to the USA
were channelled into the clandestine US effort to
support anti-Communist guerrillas in
Nicaragua, the Contras. This was all illegal, and

against declared *Reagan administration policy.
A Senate investigation began in 1986. It
uncovered the details of the affair but could not
conclusively prove the involvement of President
*Reagan or Vice-President *Bush. Reagan was
judged to be incompetent, not complicit.
Instead, leading members of the National
Security Council, most prominently Lieutenant
Colonel North and an associate, John Poindexter,
were found guilty of misleading *Congress.
Their convictions were later overturned on
technicalities. The issue dogged Bush from 1987
and revealed a willingness on the part of the
federal government comprehensively to
mislead the American public and government. It
also overshadowed much of Reagan's second
presidency, though compared to the *Lewinsky
Affair it did relatively little harm to his
reputation in the long run.

Iran–Iraq War (1980–8)
One of the longest wars of the century, and
the costliest ($350 billion) and bloodiest (over
500,000 dead and one million wounded) war
since World War II. It was fought over the
Shatt-al-Arab waterway, the confluence of the
Euphrates and Tigris rivers which forms Iraq's
only access to the Persian Gulf. Disputed
between Iran and Iraq since their existence, in
1975 the **Algiers Agreement** had given Iran
some 518 km^2 of land along the waterway in
return for Iran's cessation of support for
Kurdish rebels in Iraq.
   In 1980, the Iraqi leader, Saddam *Hussein,
took advantage of the political confusion after
the Iranian Revolution of 1979 and launched
an invasion into Iran. He demanded not only a
revision of the Iraq-Iran border, but also the
return of three islands in the Straits of
Hormuz seized by Iran in 1971, and the
granting of autonomy to minorities in Iran.
Superior Iraqi equipment gained some initial
successes in September 1980 around Abadan,
but Iran resisted strongly and in May 1982
counter-attacked, recovering the port of
Khorramshahr. The Iranian army even
advanced to occupy some Iraqi territory,
including the Magdnum and Fao islands in
1984 and 1986 respectively.
   The war developed into a war of attrition,
and eventually both countries, exhausted
from the long war, agreed to a cease-fire based
on *UN Resolution 598, which came into
effect on 20 August 1988. Two years later,
Hussein needed Iranian goodwill as he
prepared for the *Gulf War against Kuwait.
This prompted him to accept the Algiers
Agreement, order the release of all prisoners
of war, and command the withdrawal of all
Iraqi soldiers from Iranian territory. While no
country gained any territory, in some ways it

allowed both dictatorial regimes to establish themselves more firmly, by strengthening their respective armies, and by legitimizing the terror which they executed against internal opposition and national minorities.
KURDISTAN

Iraq

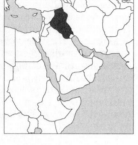

A country known in the ancient world as Mesopotamia, its cultural, ethnic, and religious tensions were reinforced by the discovery of oil and the competition for resources that went with it, and the intervention of foreign powers.

Contemporary history (up to the 1970s) A part of the *Ottoman Empire since 1638, Iraq became a British *League of Nations *Mandate in 1920, following the Ottomans' defeat in World War I. In an effort to create a viable state structure, the British installed the *Hashemite dynasty under *Faisal I to rule the country. With the help of his chief minister, *Nuri al-Said, he managed to establish a strong state, in which he was aided by his good relations with the British, who granted effective independence in 1932. Iraq tried to remain neutral during World War II, but after the abortive pro-German coup by *Rashid, under *Faisal II and *Abd al-Ilah it came under greater British control again.

In 1958 Faisal responded to the foundation of the *United Arab Republic by linking up with Jordan in the *Arab Federation. This broke up a few months later, as Faisal was deposed in a military coup and a republic proclaimed by the new leader, *Qassem. Qassem's attempts to deflect domestic attention away from current economic difficulties by attempting to occupy Kuwait was foiled by British and international guarantees for Kuwait, as well as the outbreak of a large-scale Kurdish rebellion in the north. In 1963 Qassem was deposed by a rival army faction.

After Iraq's failure in the *Six Day War, another coup brought to power the *Ba'ath Party in 1968. The new secular, nationalist regime sought to reform society, for example through the emancipation of women. The country's profits from oil revenues were used to build up a modern infrastructure, industry was diversified, and oil production was nationalized. This led to an economic boycott by most Western countries in 1972, and

induced the leadership under Ahmad Hasan Al Bakr to seek even closer cooperation with the USSR. Through his control of the Ba'ath Party, during the 1970s power shifted gradually to Saddam *Hussein.

Hussein's dictatorship (1979–2003) Hussein established a personal dictatorship, based on the loyalty of the elite revolutionary guards, the extensive secret police machinery, and the control of his own family over state, economy, and society. The repressive nature of Hussein's regime emphasized the fundamental problem of any Iraqi regime. Its economy, and hence his ability to maintain his position through extensive patronage, depended on the country's oil reserves, estimated to be the second largest in the world. However, most of these lay in rebellious *Kurdistan in the north, as well as in the territory inhabitated largely by the country's *Shi'ite minority in the southern wetlands. The increasing demands of both Kurds and Shi'ites for greater autonomy thus posed a fundamental challenge to the subsistence of the regime. The large Shi'ite minority (of around 40 per cent) posed an existential threat at the time of the Iranian Revolution in 1979, which established a Shi'ite theocracy there under *Ayatollah *Khomeini. To forestall a spillover into Iraq, and to satisfy Hussein's own thirst for greater power at a time of Iranian weakness, Iraqi forces attacked Iran, and precipitated the *Iran–Iraq War (1980–8). It ended in a stalemate between the two countries, though its effect on the morale of the decimated population, and the destroyed economy and infrastructure, was enormous.

Faced with a high foreign debt and rapid inflation, Iraq was especially hard-hit by a low world price for oil, caused by generous production quotas among other *OPEC countries. Hussein's occupation of Kuwait in 1990, which precipitated the *Gulf War, was thus an attempt to play to nationalist feelings which had always looked upon Kuwait as an Iraqi province. The occupation also presented an attempt, to gain control over the world's third-largest oil reserves, which would have given Iraq much power in the world market for oil. However, Hussein's attempted annexation failed, largely due to US resolve under *Bush.

Hussein's second defeat in 1991 was almost more catastrophic than the destruction caused by the Iran–Iraq War. He managed to hang on to power, but not without brutally repressing a rebellion of the Shi'ite population in the south, in which an estimated 300,000 Shi'ites were murdered. Hussein also killed thousands of rebellious Kurds, but in 1993 he was forced to accept Kurdish autonomy in the north. Throughout the 1990s, the *UN supervised a system of international sanctions. These appeared to be ineffective at limiting his power, and they increased the hardship for the population. The UN initiated an 'oil-for-food' programme, which allowed Iraq to export oil products for foodstuffs and medical supplies. Until 1998, the UN also destroyed large quantities of chemical and biological weapons amassed by Hussein. Following the *September 11 attacks, neoconservatives in the US administration led by George W. *Bush, *Wolfowitz and *Rumsfeld worked towards a policy of 'regime change', as Iraq became part of what it considered an 'Axis of Evil' (along with North Korea and Iran). On 20 March 2003, the US and the UK began the *Iraq War, and by 9 April they had toppled Hussein. After the war, the full scale of Hussein's *human rights atrocities were revealed, as a host of mass graves containing up to 15,000 bodies each were discovered.

Contemporary Iraq (2003–) UN Resolution 1483, passed in May 2003, authorized the US to control Iraq's process of democratization. Under overall US control, Iraq was divided into a British zone in the south, a larger northern section including Baghdad administered by the US, and a smaller central section run by a coalition of troops headed by Poland. The US administration in Iraq found it difficult to establish security for US troops and for the civilian population at large. Reconstruction was hampered because many US funds set aside for this were unaccounted for. Attempts to generate income for Iraqis through oil exports were sabotaged by constant attacks against pipelines, wells, and refineries. The US also found it difficult to encourage working administrative structures, as all of Saddam Hussein's supporters in the military and in public administration had been dismissed. Only in northern Iraq (*Kurdistan), where working administrative structures had been developed before 2003, did reconstruction become relatively successful. By contrast, from 2004 violence increased between the Shi'ite majority, and the Sunni minority, with attacks concentrated in the Sunni triangle around Baghdad.

In 2005, Sunni opposition to a new Constitution was overcome, which was accepted by over 78 per cent of the population. Late that year, Iraq's first democratic elections were held successfully, with 79.6 per cent casting their vote. The parliament, whose parties were divided along ethnic lines, found it difficult to negotiate a working government coalition that included representatives from all parties. In May 2006, a new government took office under the leadership of Nuri al-*Maliki. His government had considerable difficulty in creating order, as its own security forces relied

on US help to move against insurgents. Often, security forces were also reluctant to move against members of their own tribes.

Despite the fragile process of democratization, violence threatened to spiral out of control. In August 2006, the head of the US Command, George Casey, identified the outbreak of civil war as the greatest threat. A study group led by James Baker confirmed in December 2006 that Iraq was in danger of sliding into chaos. Ignoring the group's policy proposals, the US strengthened its military presence by 30,000 troops in an attempt to bring Baghdad and other centres under its control. This aim was challenged by the growing influence of Iran among violent Shi'ite groups.

Iraq War (20 Mar.–1 May 2003)
A war led by the US to effect regime change in Iraq and topple Saddam *Hussein.

The course of the war The US decision to go to war divided the international community, as a number of countries, led by France, Germany, and Russia, opposed military action on grounds of a lack of evidence that Hussein was a threat to the international order.

The US and the UK pressed ahead with the invasion of Iraq without a *UN resolution, supported by what they termed a 'Coalition of the Willing'. This included countries that could only provide minimal practical assistance, including Spain, Portugal, Poland, and Australia. The US-led force numbered 290,000 troops, including 45,000 British troops. Vastly superior equipment on the ground, satellite-guided missiles, and devastating weapons such as cluster bombs secured a rapid advance. The last important town was taken on 14 April, and on 1 May George W. *Bush declared an end to major combat operations. According to the *Project on Defense Alternatives*, up to 15,100 Iraqis had died up to that point. By contrast, 367 US troops had been killed.

Causes The US administration and the UK government had justified the war with allegations that there were strong links between *al-Qaeda terrorists and Hussein's regime. They also asserted that Hussein's regime had flouted *UN stipulations, in order to produce and store chemical and biological weapons of mass destruction. After the war, no evidence for either claim was found.

Consequences Following the war, Iraq was occupied by troops from the US and its allies, as they tried to oversee the reconstruction of economic, political, and administrative institutions. However, US troops became subject to frequent attacks, while also becoming embroiled in mounting violence between Shi'ite and Sunni groups. By 3 August 2007, over 3,648 US soldiers had died in action since the end of the war, with over 27,000 wounded. 163 British soldiers had died since 2003. Estimates for Iraqi civilian casualties differed widely. A pressure group (The 'Iraq Body Count') estimated that by early 2007, around 60,000 civilians had died as a result of the war and its aftermath. By contrast, the independent medical journal *The Lancet* estimated that the conflict had caused 100,000 excess civilian deaths by 2004. It estimated that by 2007, that number had increased to 650,000, with the likelihood of civilian deaths occurring being 65 times higher than before the invasion. Before the start of the war Bush had projected a total cost of $50 billion. By March 2007, the combined cost for the war and the subsequent occupation had risen to $500 billion. This necessitated drastic cuts in social spending, including *Medicare as well as the provision for war veterans.

Ireland, Northern, see NORTHERN IRELAND

Ireland, Republic of

The southern part of Ireland, whose society emerged deeply divided after a long struggle for independence and the civil war. Initially unable to reduce its independence on its large neighbour, the UK, Ireland experienced a dramatic economic boom as a member of the EU from the 1990s.

The Union (up to 1914) Together with *Northern Ireland, the territory came under British rule in the sixteenth century, and became an integral part of the UK with the Act of Union in 1801. Ireland subsequently sent 100 MPs to the House of Commons, and 32 members to the House of Lords (*parliament (UK)). Nevertheless, Ireland was treated more like a colony than like a component part of the UK, and throughout the nineteenth century there were popular demands for the recognition of Irish distinctiveness. From the third quarter of the nineteenth century, English politicians sought to alleviate Irish grievances through various *Land Acts, at a time when opinion in Ireland shifted increasingly towards demands for internal autonomy, Home Rule. The British *Liberal Party accepted the need for Home Rule in 1886, though the

unpopularity in England of Irish self-rule delayed the legislation until 1914. Meanwhile, in the last decade of the nineteenth century a distinctive national movement began to emerge. This led to a successful revival of Irish (Gaelic) culture in sports and cultural organizations, relatively unsuccessful attempts at reviving the Gaelic language, and a blossoming of a self-confident Irish literary movement, spearheaded by W. B. Yeats. Since then, (southern) Irish national identity and, since 1921, Irish nationhood has been marked by two central elements. The first of these has been the integrative element of the Roman *Catholic Church. Contrasting with the Protestant nature of the English establishment (*Anglican Communion), Catholic piety in one of Europe's most religiously observant societies has been the principal distinguishing factor of the southern Irish people, and a central underpinning of Irish *nationalism. This is why the Protestant minority has found it difficult to be accepted in a national community whose self-understanding is marked by Catholicism. The prevalence of Catholic culture is also a central reason why the Protestant majority of Northern Ireland has had no desire to become part of an Irish state dominated by Catholic nationalism.

The second major element underpinning Irish identity has been a highly ambivalent attitude towards the UK, before and after independence. Even after political independence, Ireland continued to remain heavily reliant on the British economy for its foreign trade, and thousands of Irish continued to emigrate to Britain in search of jobs. This had important cultural repercussions, as Liverpool, Manchester, and London remained a natural place for an Irish person to spend part of his or her life. At the same time, however, Irish nationalism was by its very nature anti-English, its return to an 'Irish' culture being a rejection of the strong English influence on Irish society. This explains why, even after independence, discussions about the nature of 'Irishness' and its relation to the UK remained the central issue in Irish politics. Irish politics is divided not along social or ideological lines, as in most other European, Latin American, or Australian countries. Instead, traditionally the defining difference between the two major Irish parties has been the more obstinate nationalism of the *Fianna Fáil, and the more pragmatic, conciliatory stance towards the British advocated by *Fine Gael.

The struggle for independence (1914–22) Although Home Rule was eventually granted in 1914, it was never enacted, owing to the outbreak of World War I. While large

Table 12. **Prime Ministers of the Republic of Ireland**

William T. *Cosgrave	1922–32	Jack *Lynch	1977–9
Eamonn *de Valera	1932–48	Charles *Haughey	1979–81
John A. *Costello	1948–51	Garrett *FitzGerald	1981–2
Eamonn *de Valera	1951–4	Charles *Haughey	1982
John A. *Costello	1954–7	Garrett *FitzGerald	1982–7
Eamonn *de Valera	1957–9	Charles *Haughey	1987–92
Sean *Lemass	1959–66	Albert *Reynolds	1992–4
Jack *Lynch	1966–73	John *Bruton	1994–7
Liam *Cosgrave	1973–7	Bertie *Ahern	1997–

Footnote: From 1922 to 1937, the head of the Irish Free State government was entitled 'President of the Executive Council'. Upon the establishment of the Republic of Ireland in December 1937, the title was changed to 'Taoiseach' in Irish Gaelic, and 'Prime Minister' in English.

numbers of Irish volunteered for service in the war, independence only came with the brutal British reaction to the *Easter Rising. This transformed its participants into martyrs, and thus became the catalyst for widespread demands for independence. Militant nationalist groups such as the Irish Citizen Army (est. 19 November 1913) and the Irish Volunteers (est. 25 November 1913) experienced a dramatic growth in membership, while the British incensed nationalist opinion further by repeated demands for conscription in the war. Individual attacks against British targets (mainly the army and government institutions) began.

In the *Coupon Elections of December 1918, the nationalist Sinn Féin received 73 out of 81 seats in southern Ireland. Its MPs refused to take up their seats in the British parliament, and on 21 January 1919 met in Dublin instead, setting up an alternative Irish chamber named the Dáil Éireann, with *de Valéra as its President. A War of Independence ensued, in which the regular British forces were supported by the *Black and Tans, against the nationalist forces of the Irish Republican Army, *IRA.

Civil war (1922–3) The War of Independence was ended with the Anglo-Irish Treaty of 6 December 1921, which came into effect on 6 December 1922. Southern Ireland received de facto independence, though foreign policy continued to be made in London, with the British monarch remaining head of state. Most contentiously, the treaty provided for the partition of Ireland, as six Ulster provinces remained part of the United Kingdom as Northern Ireland. These terms were bitterly opposed by the more radical nationalists led by de Valéra, but were accepted by the majority under the leadership of *Griffiths

and *Collins as the best possible deal. After a year of civil war, de Valéra finally gave in, and accepted the status quo, albeit with much reluctance.

Early statehood (1923–73) De Valéra founded a political party, the Fianna Fáil, which became the country's dominant political force in its dedication to rid Ireland of British influence and to bring about the unification of Ireland, on nationalist terms. The first President of the Executive Council (in effect, Prime Minister), *Cosgrave (1922–32) focused on healing the wounds of the civil war and establishing effective state institutions. In 1932 he was succeeded by de Valéra, who subsequently led Irish politics until 1959 (apart from brief interludes under *Costello, 1948–51, 1954–7) in the pursuit of real independence from the UK. He unleashed a six-year trade war with the UK in order to gain control over Irish ports, which he eventually won against the payment of £10 million in 1938. The real cost of this struggle was much worse, however, as British trade sanctions worsened the effects of the Great *Depression, causing even greater economic hardship.

Links to the UK were further severed when the Dáil passed a new national constitution on 14 June 1937 (to come into effect on 29 December), creating the state of Éire, with a President as head of state, and the title of President of the Executive Council changed to Taoiseach (Irish Gaelic, 'chief of the tribe'). The new constitution laid claim to legislate for the whole of Ireland, pending national unification. To emphasize its newfound sovereignty, Éire remained neutral during World War II, although it was friendly to the *Allies (Allied pilots who crashed in Éire were returned safely to Britain, Germans were imprisoned). After the war, the Republic of Ireland Act was passed on 21

December 1948, removing all references to the British *Commonwealth and Crown, establishing the state name, but retaining the Irish name Éire.

The Republic of Ireland was formally declared on 18 April 1949. Governments were now free to devote themselves to domestic politics, and throughout the 1950s tried to counter the economic problems and poverty that had developed with substantial capital investment. In the 1960s, under *Lemass there was considerable industrial development, while Irish society developed rapidly in other directions, for example substantial educational reforms which enabled the number of pupils in post-primary education to double within fifteen years from 1965.

As civil unrest ensued in Northern Ireland, Irish unification and the Republic's relationship with the UK returned to the forefront of the political agenda. The Sunningdale Agreement of 9 December 1973 provided for some cooperation on northern affairs between Britain and the Republic. The 1980s and 1990s saw increased cooperation between Irish and British heads of state on Northern Ireland issues, under *FitzGerald and *Reynolds, which looked promising in the wake of the IRA ceasefire of 30 August 1994, but increased tensions followed a resumption of IRA violence on 9 February 1996.

EEC/EU membership (since 1973) Ireland's entry into the EEC on 1 January 1973, negotiated by *Lynch, proved spectacularly successful. Direct transfer payments from Brussels improved Irish infrastructure, while Ireland's relatively important (but inefficient) agricultural sector profited from guaranteed subsidies as part of the *Common Agricultural Policy. In addition, successive Irish governments under the leadership of *Haughey and FitzGerald managed to attract considerable investment from foreign companies eager to exploit the advantages of a highly skilled, low-cost workforce and Ireland's access to European markets. This transformed Ireland into a successful economy by the early 1990s, with a low budget deficit, a low inflation rate, and a declining unemployment rate. It also made Ireland more independent from the British economy, with important cultural repercussions. Irish surplus labour was no longer limited to Britain, but could just as well operate on the European continent.

As Ireland became a more self-confidently European nation, and less reliant on its overwhelming neighbour, its national identity became more relaxed vis-à-vis the UK.

This in part made possible its more generous and constructive approach to a peaceful resolution to the violence in Northern Ireland, especially in its dialogue with the British government and the Ulster Protestant community. Finally, growing prosperity from the 1990s led to changing social and economic mobility, as Ireland developed into a country with net immigration. Prosperity also contributed to a degree of *secularization and the declining influence of the Catholic Church, though its influence remained strong. While divorce was legalized in 1994, *abortion continued to be illegal, and this was confirmed in two referendums in the mid-1990s and in 2002.

Contemporary politics (since 2002) Ireland continued to benefit from membership of the EU and its adoption of the *euro, becoming the EU's fastest growing economy in the late 1990s, with a GDP growth of 10.7 per cent in 2000. Following EU enlargement in 2004, Ireland was one of only three countries to allow unrestricted immigration of eastern European EU citizens. This led to an influx of 100,000 workers and created significant social and economic tension, but it did not lead to a growth in the unemployment rate, which remained the lowest in the EU. Based on the country's economic strength, the Prime Minister, Bertie *Ahern, was re-elected in 2007.

Irgun (Irgun Zvai Leumi, National Military Organization)
An underground *Zionist organization founded in 1931, supported largely by the non-socialist elements among the Jewish settlers in Palestine. Originally aimed at Palestinian Arabs, from 1939 onwards Irgun targeted British *Mandate forces as well. For much of World War II it declared a truce against the British forces, but it resumed its active terrorist campaign under its new leader, *Begin, in early 1944. Despite occasional cooperation, its methods were generally opposed by the *Haganah. Subsequently, its most spectacular action involved the bombing of the headquarters of the British army and the Palestinian administration in the **King David Hotel** in *Jerusalem on 22 July 1946, causing ninety-one casualties. It also carried out raids against Arabs, most notably on the town of Dir Yassin on 9 April 1948, when all 254 inhabitants were killed. It was incorporated into the Israeli army on 1 September 1948, despite strong resistance by its more radical members.

Irigoyen, Hipólito, see YRIGOYEN, HIPÓLITO

Iron Curtain

A term made famous by Winston *Churchill ('An Iron Curtain has descended across the Continent') in 1946 to describe the boundary between Communist Eastern Europe and the democracies of Western Europe.

Iron Guard (Garda de Fier)

A Romanian Fascist movement. Its name was used from 1930 for the *Fascist League of the Archangel Michael, founded in 1927 by Cornelieu Zelca Codreanu. With its traits of mysticism, *nationalism, *anti-Semitism, and romanticism, its aim was to restore the country to a new age of purity and harmony. It was supported by many farmers, as well as unemployed or otherwise disgruntled intellectuals. Despite some state suppression, it gained 17 per cent of the vote in the 1937 elections. It was too weak to assume power on its own, but in 1940, it became the only legal party under *Antonescu. It got out of control as its members attacked Jews (whose economic strength was vital to the country's economy) and held endless marches, many of which ended in violence. It was therefore abolished and disbanded after three days of heavy fighting. Its demise was fully supported by *Hitler, whose main concern at this time was to secure Romanian stability to ensure the oil supplies that were vital for his plans in World War II.

irredentism

Derived from the slogan 'Italia Irredenta' (Unredeemed Italy), it demanded the incorporation into the recently unified Italian state of all Italian-speaking areas which had remained under Austrian control after the 1866 Austro-Italian War, most notably *Trieste, the Istrian Peninsula, and the Trentino. It became an important issue not only for Austro-Italian relations up to and during World War I, but also for Italian *nationalism which was growing from 1900. The strength of irredentism contributed greatly to Italy's decision in 1915 to enter World War I on the side of the Allies. After the war, these irredentine lands were handed over to Italy (with the significant exception of *Fiume), including the predominantly German-speaking *South Tirol (Alto Adige).

LONDON, TREATY OF

Irwin Declaration, see HALIFAX, EDWARD FREDERICK LINDLEY WOOD

Isaacs, Sir Isaac Alfred (b. 6 Aug. 1855, d. 16 June 1948). Australian Governor-General 1931–6

Born in Melbourne as the son of a Jewish tailor, Isaacs became a barrister and received the prestigious appointment of Queen's Counsel in 1899. He served in the Legislative Assembly of the State of Victoria (1892–1901), and was a Protectionist member of the House of Representatives (1901–6), serving as Attorney-General from 1905 to 1906. Appointed to the high court in 1906, he interpreted law in favour of an extension of federal power against the individual states. He became Chief Justice in 1930. He was the first Jewish and the first Australian-born Governor-General of Australia.

Ishiwara Kanji (b. 18 Jan. 1889, d. 15 Aug. 1949). Japanese general

Ishiwara was regarded by many as a prophet and a genius for his writing on Japan's imperial mission in Asia. He played a key role in the planning of the Manchurian Incident of September 1931, involving the military takeover of north-eastern China. Before his posting to the Guandong Army, Ishiwara had established himself as a leading proponent of the idea that a war with the Western powers was inevitable. Influenced greatly by writers such as Nanbu Jirô, Ishiwara warned of an apocalyptic final war. In order to meet this challenge he recommended that Japan conquer east Asia so as to secure the natural resources of the region while, on the home front, he proposed that the institutions and society of Japan be remodelled. His plan, which became the Manchuria Five Year Development Plan in 1937, had the objective of increasing the economic production of the territory under Japan's control by the introduction of Japanese-managed capital-intensive industries in the region. Ishiwara's high standing within the imperial army was reflected in his appointment in 1935 as section chief of the operations division of the General Staff. Nevertheless, his increasing involvement in politics, especially his attempts to undermine the Ugaki Cabinet in January 1937, did lessen his reputation.

Despite his involvement in earlier Japanese aggression on the Asian continent, Ishiwara opposed the *Sino-Japanese War after the *Marco Polo Bridge Incident in 1937, mainly because he considered the Soviet Union to be Japan's major enemy. With the escalation of the war, Ishiwara was largely sidelined by army appointments which removed him from close command and he was forced from the service in 1941. Called as a witness at the *Tokyo Trials (1946–8), Ishiwara claimed his share of responsibility for the Manchurian Incident and expressed his amazement to the court that he was not standing in the dock with the accused. Ishiwara's brilliance and unorthodox behaviour attracted the admiration of many of his fellow officers while raising the suspicion of the military establishment.

Islam ('The way of peace')

A world religion which was spread by the Prophet Muhammad following a series of divine revelations beginning in 610. These were written down in the Quran and are regarded by **Muslims** as the words of Allah. The Quran founded a monotheistic belief in Allah as the creator of humanity, which in turn is endowed with the power to choose between good and evil. The five core duties of Islam are: (1) the belief in Allah and his Prophet Muhammad; (2) a pilgrimage to Mecca (the place of Muhammad's enlightenment and the religion's point of origin); (3) the giving of alms; (4) prayer (five times daily); (5) fasting in the month of Ramadan. The central documents of Islamic faith are the Quran (the word of God), the Sunna (the recorded actions of Muhammad), and the Shariah (the legal code). Islam spread rapidly in the first century after Muhammad's proclamations, but in the middle of the seventh century it split into *Sunni and *Shi'ite on the issue of the spiritual leadership in succession to Muhammad. The split has persisted throughout the twentieth century, and has made it extremely difficult for moves towards Arab unity (*Pan-Arabism) to be successful.

Islamic fundamentalism

Used in the English-speaking world mainly to describe Islamic revivalist movements which profess strict adherence to the Quran and Islamic law, the Shariah. It emerged in reaction to Islamic reform movements during the first half of the twentieth century, which were considered to be infused with Western culture, and to the strong political influence of Western countries on the Arab states. Islamic fundamentalists have had considerable political success from the 1970s. In 1979, a revolution brought the spiritual leader *Ayatollah *Khomeini to power in Iran. Arab dictators such as Saddam *Hussein and Muammar *Gaddafi have strengthened their positions by paying lip-service to the movement. In a number of countries such as the Sudan or Nigeria, concessions by the ruling elites to Islamic fundamentalism from the 1990s have greatly exacerbated tensions with moderate Muslims and Christian minorities. In many other Islamic states from Indonesia and Malaysia to Turkey, Algeria and Morocco, it has fed growing opposition movements. The strength of Islamic fundamentalists has derived from the appeal of certainty and justice to the poor and destitute, and from a religious network that could sustain itself beyond formal political organizations. Despite fundamentalism's pervasiveness, it has been a highly diverse movement whose precise nature has reflected the particular conditions of each country. Common to all movements, however, has been a call for more traditional gender roles, traditional dress, and the introduction of Islamic law as superior to a secular legal code.

isolationism (USA)

A persistent factor in US politics, the origins of which go back to Presidents Washington and Monroe. Isolationists advocate the avoidance of all alliances or participation in world affairs outside the American hemisphere, especially on a permanent or binding basis. They foiled Woodrow *Wilson in his attempt to take the USA into the *League of Nations, and during the 1930s isolationism was responsible for the *Neutrality Acts. Since US entry into World War II isolationism has been much less prominent, but by no means irrelevant. It has advocated political and military withdrawal from overseas bases and the establishment of a 'fortress America', protected by military systems such as the *SDI. The 1990s have seen a revival of isolationism in opposition to efforts to integrate the USA into the world economy, such as *NAFTA or the Asia-Pacific Economic Cooperation agreements. This was reinforced by the fall of *Communism and the lack of a clear threat to the US. Populists, particularly on the right, have asserted a form of isolationism as an alternative to international US involvement (and leadership). Although in evidence from the 1990s, it remained below the surface in response to *September 11, as under the neo-conservative leadership of George W. *Bush the US greatly increased its military involvement overseas, not least through the *Iraq War.

AMERICA FIRST COMMITTEE

Israel

A state on the Mediterranean whose right of existence has been persistently challenged by its neighbours. In turn, Israel has striven to consolidate its

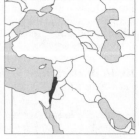

Table 13. **Prime Ministers of Israel**

David *Ben-Gurion	1948–53	Shimon *Peres	1984–6
M. Sharett	1954–5	Yitzhak *Shamir	1986–92
David *Ben-Gurion	1955–63	Yitzhak *Rabin	1992–5
Levi *Eshkol	1963–9	Shimon *Peres	1995–6
Golda *Meir	1969–74	Benjamin *Netanyahu	1996–9
Yitzhak *Rabin	1974–7	Ehud *Barak	1999–2001
Menachem *Begin	1977–83	Ariel *Sharon	2001–6
Yitzhak *Shamir	1983–4	Ehud *Olmert	2006–

demographic, geographic, and economic position in the area, especially vis-à-vis the Palestinian population.

Origins (up to 1947) The idea of a return of Jews to *Palestine, whence they had been scattered throughout Europe and Asia from 70 AD, had been current in some form or another throughout the centuries of their diaspora. It was revived in the late nineteenth century as modern *Zionism, as Jews were persecuted in *pogroms in eastern Europe, and discriminated against through *anti-Semitism in western Europe, most notably in France after *Dreyfus, as well as in Germany and *Austria-Hungary. The idea was propagated most successfully by *Herzl, who argued that peaceful and harmonious coexistence between Jews and Gentiles had proved to be impossible, and that Jews could only be free from persecution and discrimination in their own state.

In response, a number of Jews began to emigrate to Palestine to press for Jewish claims there, while the World Zionist Organization (WZO) was set up in 1897 in order to convince world opinion and political leaders of the necessity of a Jewish state in Palestine. In 1917 the WZO persuaded the British government to set up a *Jewish Legion which helped rid Palestine of *Ottoman Turkish rule. Led by *Weizmann, the WZO achieved a major diplomatic success with the *Balfour Declaration, which for the first time accepted the legitimacy of a Jewish state in Palestine.

When this failed to materialize after World War I, the WZO encouraged further Jewish emigration into Palestine, and won from the local British authorities important concessions relative to self-rule through the *Jewish Agency. Initially, the Jewish settlers coexisted peacefully and harmoniously with the indigenous, partly nomadic Arab population. However, as both Arabs and Jews saw their hopes for early independence dashed, an increasing sense of Arab *nationalism emerged, particularly as the Jewish influx continued. Sporadic attacks against Jewish

settlements occurred from 1920, in response to which the Jews created their own defence organizations, the *Haganah and, later, *Irgun Zvai Leumi. Meanwhile, the Jews created their own administrative and political structures, most notably through the *Histadrut and *Mapai movements. Tensions between Arabs, Jews, and the British authorities mounted in the period 1940–8, when almost 100,000 new settlers arrived (illegally) in Palestine.

Independence (1947) Ultimately, Britain was unable to resolve its contradictory promise of independence for Jews and Arabs, and in 1947 returned its *Mandate to the *UN, which recommended a partition of the country between Jews and Arabs. On the basis of this plan, *Ben-Gurion declared Israel's independence on 14 May 1948. The following day, the country was attacked by an Arab coalition consisting of the armies of Egypt, Transjordan, Syria, Lebanon, and Iraq. In its War of Independence, the young state managed to defend itself, and even to extend its borders.

Culture Once established, the country faced the major challenge of creating a homogeneous society out of population groups which had come from different parts of the globe, many of whom did not even speak the new official language, Hebrew. The social and cultural elite consisted of the Ashkenazi Jews, who were of European origin, though this masked fundamental cultural and religious differences between, for example, an eastern European Jewish proletariat and an assimilated bourgeoisie from the capitals of western Europe. A second group consisted of the much more traditional Sephardic Jews from northern Africa (particularly Morocco) and the eastern Near East (especially Iraq). Finally, a third group consisted of the non-Jewish Arab population who lived there. These made up a significant part of the rural population of Israel, and they were the least prosperous: their average income was 66 per cent of the average for Ashkenazis, and 80 per cent for the Sephardic Jews. The problems of integration continued because immigration reached new heights in the 1990s (over 6 per cent per annum, 1991–4).

Economy The main economic challenge for the new state was to create an agriculture and economy that would feed the population and provide it with the wherewithal to defend the country against military attacks. Strong socialist convictions among *Labour leaders such as Ben-Gurion and *Meir, as well as the need to provide occupations and housing for immigrants, added to the strong role of the state in the economy. This was only relaxed from 1977. Together with a subsequent policy of economic liberalization, and a reduction of military spending from over 25 per cent of GDP in the 1970s to 16 per cent by 1986, this resulted in considerable economic growth in the decade 1984–94, when GDP rose by 59 per cent, exports by 88 per cent, and private consumption by 92 per cent. Economic prosperity, generational change, and the influence of Western values resulted in an increasingly secular culture. Its challenge to the overwhelming social and cultural power of the orthodox Jewish rabbis became one of the country's main controversial domestic issues of the 1990s.

Security Domestic developments, however, were only one part of Israel's development in the five decades since its foundation. Perhaps no other country in the world was faced with such sustained hostility from its neighbours. Therefore, its foreign policy was marked by its efforts to secure its territorial integrity against the surrounding countries of the Arab League, whose 22 members all refused to make peace with Israel. Israel participated in the *Suez Crisis, though an even graver threat came in 1967, when in the *Six Day War it freed itself from the tightening grip of the armies of Egypt, Syria, and Jordan. The war resulted in the occupation of the *Gaza Strip, the *West Bank, East *Jerusalem, and the *Golan Heights. Possession of these territories was crucial to its safety requirements, but heightened the problem of the Palestinian minority, which had grown by almost a million people as a result of the annexations. The country was caught unawares in the 1973 *Yom Kippur War, in which, even though it repelled the Egyptian army, its reputation for military invincibility was shattered. Nevertheless, it convinced the pragmatic *Sadat that his Egyptian territory could not be reclaimed militarily, and led to the *Camp David Agreements of 1978.

Since the problem of Israel's Palestinian population had not been resolved, no other Arab country followed Egypt's peace treaty. In an attempt to stamp out the *PLO, under *Begin Israel attacked the Lebanon in 1982, and advanced to *Beirut. It managed to expel the PLO to Tunisia, but its occupation of southern Lebanon created a new, more radical Arab force, the *Hezbollah. Hezbollah's attacks caused increasing losses in the army, whose occupation of enemy territory triggered widespread criticism, not only internationally but also, for the first time, at home. Under *Peres, Israel withdrew from most of the Lebanon in 1985, but from 1987 Israel was challenged internally through violent Palestinian actions in the *Intifadah.

Prime Minister *Rabin eventually recognized that Israel's security could only be guaranteed in the long run through a recognition of the Palestinians' claims. On 4 May 1994, Israel recognized the PLO as the representative of the Palestinian people, and agreed to the establishment of the first areas of Palestinian self-government in Gaza and Jericho in preparation for an eventual sovereign Palestinian state. Peace treaties with other Arab countries followed, while the murder of Rabin convinced the majority of Israelis that increased efforts should be made to make peace with Israel's last major enemy, Syria. However, just before Israel's parliamentary elections in 1996, a series of suicide bombs organized by *Hamas caused renewed hostility towards the Palestinians, and led to the election of *Netanyahu.

Palestinian conflict Netanyahu refused to comply with the *Gaza–Jericho Agreement. Rather than supporting the continued withdrawal of Israeli troops from the West Bank, he agreed to the construction of new settlements for Israeli immigrants there. In 1997 he ordered the construction of settlements for 30,000 new Jewish settlers in East Jerusalem. Some progress was made in 1998, when *Arafat and Netanyahu signed the *Wye Agreement. Opposition by Israeli settlers and immigrants' representatives to the Wye Agreement, however, weakened Netanyahu's position and caused a suspension of the agreement's implementation.

New elections in 1999 produced a clear mandate for *Barak, who resumed negotiations with Arafat, but his readiness to make concessions to the Palestinians eroded his popular support, especially as this did not lead to a reduction in violence. His willingness to negotiate about the status of Jerusalem in late 2000 proved the final straw to many voters, who in 2001 elected the right-wing advocate of the settlers' interests, Ariel *Sharon. Sharon formed a coalition of 'national unity', but proved unable to quell

the new *Intifadah, which he had done so
much to bring about. Instead, the violence
deteriorated, leading to the military reoccupation of all Palestinian territories from
March 2002. Frequent military raids followed,
including the bombing of Arafat's compound,
and an incursion into a Palestinian refugee
camp in Jenin.

Sharon accepted the *Road Map for Peace.
However, convinced that a deal with the
Palestinian leadership and a realization of
international peace plans were unrealistic, he
began to pursue a unilateral resolution of
Israel's territorial disputes. Convinced that
Israel could not control the Gaza Strip, where
1.3 million Palestinians faced 7,500 Jewish
settlers, he announced in early 2004 that
Israel was going to withdraw completely from
the area. At the same time, Sharon continued
to promote the construction of Jewish
settlements on the West Bank, while
accelerating the construction of the wall
dividing the territories claimed by Israel from
the rest of the West Bank. The withdrawal of
Israeli settlers and troops from Gaza was
completed in August 2005, though not
without splitting the *Likud party, which
followed Netanyahu in opposing the
withdrawal. Sharon founded his own party,
*Kadima, which attracted leading members of
Likud and the Labour party, and called early
elections. Sharon suffered a severe stroke, so
that his deputy, *Olmert, led Kadima to
victory in the 2006 elections.

Contemporary politics (since 2006) In July
2006, two Israeli soldiers were abducted by
Hezbollah. Olmert responded with
military force, attacking Hezbollah bases in
southern Lebanon. In the conflict, Hezbollah
continued to strike northern Israel with
rockets, while the Israeli army
was ultimately forced to invade southern
Lebanon. After a month of fighting, the
UN brokered a cease-fire, leading to the
establishment of a 15,000-strong UN
peacekeeping force in southern Lebanon.
Olmert's excessive response, and his
underestimation of Hezbollah's strength,
made the civilian Prime Minister and his
Cabinet deeply unpopular.

Italian Campaign (World War II; 1943–5)
After victory in North Africa *Montgomery
and *Patton prepared to invade Italy. Forces to
land on Sicily set out from Malta in July 1943,
and by the end of the month both the island's
principal cities, Palermo and Catania, were
captured. On the mainland, German forces
moved down through northern Italy and took
over Rome's airfields. *Kesselring withdrew

his troops from Sicily and British and US forces
crossed to Reggio on the mainland.

As a result of the Allied advances, the
*Fascist Grand Council deposed *Mussolini on
25 July 1943, who was imprisoned the
following day. Despite assurances by
*Badoglio's new government to Germany that
it would continue to fight on the German side,
Italy agreed an armistice with the Allies on 3
September 1943. The Germans responded by
disarming all Italian troops in the area which
they occupied, while the King and his
government escaped into Allied protection. On
12 September the Germans liberated Mussolini
to place him at the head of the newly created
Italian Social Republic (of *Salò).

The 5th US Army landed at Salerno and
advanced towards Naples, and a third landing
established further bridgeheads in the
southern ports of Taranto and Brindisi. On 13
October 1943 the Italian government officially
declared war on Germany. By December 1943,
the Allies had advanced to a line just south of
Monte Cassino, where the German troops had
taken a stand on the mountain which was the
site of the ancient monastry of St Benedict.
The Allies bypassed it by landing 50,000 men
at Anzio, south of Rome, on 22 January 1944.
Fierce fighting again took place around the
bridgehead, and lasted until May. Monte
Cassino was heavily bombed and was finally
captured by Polish troops on 18 May. The
main advance was now resumed. Rome fell on
4 June, followed by Florence, after bitter
fighting, in August.

The Germans consolidated in the Po Valley,
along the so-called Gothic line, and fought a
hard battle through the autumn and winter
months of 1944. In April 1945 the Allies
launched their final attacks. Milan fell to them
on 29 April, and on 2 May the whole German
army group serving in northern Italy and
southern Austria surrendered.

Italian Social Republic, see SALÒ,
REPUBLIC OF

Italo-Ethiopian War, see ABYSSINIAN WAR

Italy
Long a highly
fragmented
country, even
after unification
in 1861 Italy
remained
characterized by
fundamental
regional tension
between the
north and the
south.

Liberal Italy (up to 1922) Northern Italy
experienced industrialization from the 1890s
onwards, allowing it to develop into one of
Europe's weathiest areas within a century.
With their diverse industrial production,
commercial activity, and financial
transactions, northern cities proved fertile
ground for the socialist and Communist
parties, though they also became strongholds
of the early *Fascist movement. By contrast,
southern Italy has, until recently, been
dominated by a sharecropping system that
kept the majority of the population employed
as landless labourers by a tiny number of large
landowners. Consequently, the south has
harboured *anarcho-syndicalism and, given
the continued importance of the Roman
*Catholic Church, political Catholicism after
1919. To assert central control over these
entrenched social and economic hierarchies,
the Italian government encouraged the spread
of the *Mafia, which had become the source
of authority in the whole of Sicily by 1900, and
which has since spread northwards. To the
resentment of the north, central government
sought to alleviate the lack of industry and
commerce in the south through enlarging the
administrative apparatus, making it costly
and cumbersome, but providing employment
particularly for southerners.

Another central element in Italian politics
until the conclusion of the *Lateran Treaties
in 1929, and one which has surfaced
periodically since, has been the relationship
between the secular Italian state and the
Roman Catholic Church. After the unification
of Italy, in which the Pope lost all the territory
which he governed, the *Vatican forbade all
Roman Catholics to participate in the new
liberal, secular state. The Vatican's stance
became increasingly challenged by the rise of
*anticlerical socialist candidates. In 1918 the
Church abandoned its resistance to political
participation by Roman Catholics, which led
to the foundation of the *Popular Party in
1919.

At the beginning of the twentieth century
Italy was dominated by *Giolitti, who tried to
modernize the state and respond to the social
problems of urbanization and
industrialization by social and electoral
reform on the one hand and *nationalism
(conquest of Libya in 1911-12) on the other.
Against the inclinations of Giolitti, the
*Socialist Party, and a sizeable minority of
public opinion, Italy entered World War I in
1915 on the side of the Allies with the
*irredentist aims of acquiring the Trentino
and *South Tirol (Alto Adige), as well as the
Istrian Peninsula. In the Treaty of *St Germain
it achieved most of these aims, with the
significant exception of the Istrian port of

*Fiume. After the war, the continued
growth of the *Socialist Party, the
foundation of a *Communist Party, the
emergence of an anti-socialist Christian
Popular Party, and the rise of a Fascist
movement created great domestic
instability. Political polarization hindered the
effective solution of postwar problems such
as the need for economic change and
demobilization. The fragmentation and
mutual hostility of the parties furthermore
prevented the formation of an anti-Fascist
*popular front and thus enabled
*Mussolini to come to power in his *March
on Rome in 1922.

Fascist Italy (1922–45) Mussolini's rule of
Fascist Italy can be divided into four periods.
1. From 1922 to 1925 Mussolini ruled in
cooperation with the old elites, in a
government that included many non-Fascists.
Many steps had already been taken, however,
to secure the predominance of the Fascist
movement in the state.
2. In the wake of the *Matteotti Crisis of
1925, Mussolini gave in to the radical Fascist
demands of men such as *Farinacci to establish
a *totalitarian state in which the movement
would control all areas of public life. In this
second phase, power was concentrated in
*Mussolini's hands, as all other parties were
abolished, the judiciary infiltrated, and
popular organizations such as the *Balilla
and the *Dopolavoro were created at the
expense of independent *trade unions,
clubs, and societies.
3. The decisive phase of Mussolini's regime
began around 1935-6, when Mussolini, who
had hitherto taken a relatively moderate and
independent international stance, defied the
international community through the
*Abyssinian War and embarked on a fateful
rapprochement with *Nazi Germany.
Increasingly influenced by the apparent
successes of *Hitler, Mussolini came to
emulate Nazism, most significantly through
imitating the *Nuremberg Laws by
introducing his own (albeit much milder)
*anti-Semitic laws in 1938. Dazzled by
Hitler's military successes in the first months
of World War II, Mussolini joined on his side
in 1940, though a series of military disasters
(de facto defeat in Greece and North Africa
1940-1) showed that the Italian army was
badly prepared and that Italy's economy was
wholly dependent on imported raw materials.
4. The fourth phase of Mussolini's rule was
inaugurated by a meeting of the *Fascist
Grand Council on 24-5 July 1943, which
deposed Mussolini and called upon General
*Badoglio to form a new government.
Following Badoglio's armistice on 3

September 1943 most of Italy passed into German occupation, while German parachuters liberated Mussolini from imprisonment and sent him to the north, where he headed a Fascist puppet state, the Republic of *Salò. During the time of the occupation, the Italian population suffered greatly as a result of fierce fighting between the Germans and the Allies, widespread partisan resistance (up to 250,000 Italians were active in the resistance, organized mostly by the *CLN), and German terror. Furthermore, out of a Jewish population of 40,000–50,000 in all of Italy, around 8,000 Jews were deported to German *concentration camps.

The Republic of Italy (since 1946) Italy became a republic following the abdication of King *Victor Emmanuel in 1946. However, the foundations of modern Italy were laid during the period of post-Fascist government 1943–5, largely through the establishment of a stable *Christian Democratic Party (Democrazia Christiana, DC), the restraint of the Communist Party under *Togliatti's leadership, and cooperation between the different parties, which gained Allied respect and confidence. The key to postwar Italy lay subsequently with the DC, which took part in every government until the party's dissolution in 1993, and whose leader and Prime Minister, *De Gasperi (1945–53), established a regime which pursued relatively liberal economic policies while emphasizing social welfare. In foreign policy, Italy became firmly established in the Western sphere following the receipt of *Marshall Aid, the pursuit of *European integration, and participation in *NATO.

The postwar development of Italy has been highly ambiguous. On the one hand, it became a modern, prosperous state which managed to overcome challenges such as that of widespread terrorism (especially by the *Red Brigades) during the 1970s. At the same time, it appeared that regions within the country had become more integrated, for example through the abolition of sharecropping in the south, or the development of a popular Christian Democratic Party with relatively strong support throughout the country. On the other hand, many of these achievements were very fragile and bought at considerable cost. Italy's economy was stifled by Europe's highest strike rate 1970–90, with 1,042 working days lost per 1,000 workers each year. Furthermore, the need to develop social

cohesion and the bridging of the north/south divide through social welfare payments have made Italy one of the world's most indebted economies. The victory over the Red Brigades hid the fact that the Mafia continued to spread unabated until the 1980s, and ultimately discredited the whole political system through a multitude of corruption scandals (*Tangentopoli). Finally, the disparity within the factions of the Christian Democratic Party, as well as the other smaller parties, which resulted from, and contributed to, the lack of strong leadership, prevented many badly needed administrative and institutional reforms.

Contemporary politics (since the 1990s) These deficiencies resulted in a fundamental crisis and a collapse of the political establishment in 1992–3. An alliance of newly formed right-wing movements, including the neo-Fascist National Alliance, led by *Berlusconi, gained a majority in the 1994 national elections. The Christian Democrat successor parties dwindled to a total of 10 per cent of the parliamentary seats, while the Socialist Party achieved barely 2 per cent of the vote. At the same time, doubts remained about the true ability of the system to reform itself.With 26 parties represented in parliament instead of eleven (1992), parliamentary representation became even more fragmented. To provide a more effective response to Berlusconi's 'House of Liberty' coalition, the main parties on the left formed the centre-left *Olive Tree coalition under Romano *Prodi, which won the 1996 elections. The stability of his government was achieved at the cost of an inability to introduce a crucial but divisive reform of the pension system. Prodi resigned in 1998, and was succeeded by Massimo D'Alema, who in turn handed over to Guiliano Amato in 2000. The coalition's disunity contrasted sharply with the slick, organized campaign by Berlusconi, who duly won the 2001 general elections. Berlusconi's government became the longest-serving government in Italy's postwar history, but it achieved this stability at the expense of delaying reforms yet further. Berlusconi took the unpopular step of sending troops to Iraq following the *Iraq War, while in domestic politics the economy stagnated and public debt rose.

Berlusconi narrowly lost the 2006 elections to Prodi's Olive Tree coalition, which returned to government with a one-vote majority in the Senate. Prodi announced a withdrawal of Italian troops from Iraq, initiated a law to recognize same-sex unions against the opposition of the Catholic Church, and began a closer Italian engagement in the EU.

Ivory Coast

Despite its ethnic diversity, the west African state has appeared as a beacon of political stability in the post-colonial era.

Contemporary history (up to 1995) Officially declared a French colony in 1893, it became a territory of *French West Africa in 1910, though it was not completely pacified until 1913. The territory became self-governing in 1956, joined the *French Community in 1958, and achieved full independence on 7 August 1960. Under *Houphouët-Boigny, it had some of Africa's highest growth rates in the 1970s through attracting considerable foreign investment. However, this was managed through allowing foreign companies to export most of their profits, so that most of the population benefited relatively little from this economic expansion. In addition, its agricultural exports were suffering from deforestation, which reduced the size of its forests by 80 per cent in the twentieth century. The decline of world market prices for its main exports, coffee and cocoa, from 1979 and again from 1986 led to a dramatic decline in income (decline in export revenue 1986–9: 50 per cent). The effect of this was compounded by a reduction of state services and employment, which triggered large-scale unrest. Houphouët-Boigny was thus forced to agree to some degree of democratization, which did not prevent him from manipulating the 1990 elections. He died of cancer, and was succeeded by Henri Konan Bédié as interim President.

Contemporary politics (since 1995) New presidential elections were not held until October 1995. Boycotted by the opposition parties, they resulted in an easy win for Konan Bédié, whose ruling Democracy Party of the Ivory Coast (Partie Démocratique du Côte Ivoire, PDCI) also won the parliamentary elections later in the year. An ever more desolate economic situation in one of the world's poorest countries led to growing popular protests. Crucially, the government became unable to pay the military. In 1999, army chief Robert Guéï led a successful coup, which was supported by large parts of the PDCI. Under strong pressure from the *UN, the *World Bank, and the *IMF, elections were held in 2000, which were won by the Front Populaire Ivoirien (FPI, Ivorian Popular Front). The new President, Laurent Gbagbo, derived his support mainly from the Christian south, whereas his opponent, Alassane Outtara, had derived his support from Muslims living in the north.

Owing to political and economic discrimination, Muslims in the north were incited to take up arms against the government in the south. A civil war ensued in 2002, which was not brought under control until 2005, when both sides agreed to a fragile cease-fire. A transitional government of national unity was established, though Gbagbo's continued presence in office continued to be opposed by the rebels.

Iwo Jima, Battle of (World War II)
(19 Feb.–17 Mar. 1945)

The tiny volcanic island of Iwo Jima lies some 750 miles (1,200 km) south of Tokyo in the Bonin archipelago, and was a major air base for the Japanese in World War II. In a bitter fight, the USA took the island in order to gain a base for an eventual landing on mainland Japan. The marines suffered over 20,000 casualties, including 5,000 killed. The island then served as an important base for US bombing raids on Japan.

J

Jackson, Jesse Louis (b. 8 Oct. 1941). US civil rights leader

He was born in Greenville, South Carolina, and studied at the University of Illinois and the Chicago Theological Seminary. He rose through the Southern Christian Leadership Conference to become an aide to Martin Luther *King, and stood near King when the latter was shot. After King's death, he began to try to expand the *civil rights movement to focus on the economic inequalities in American life for people of all races. He adopted a tone as sensitive to class as to colour, and tried to build up a 'rainbow coalition' of all minorities to overcome the traditional White, male power structure in the USA.

One of the most prominent and influential African Americans in the USA by 1980, Jackson was the first serious African-American contender for the Presidency when he ran for the Democratic nomination in the 1984 *primary elections. In 1988 he came closer to winning the nomination of a major party than any Black man before or since, with the possible exception of Colin *Powell in 1996. Under President *Clinton, he served on repeated humanitarian missions, securing, for example, the return of three US soldiers in Yugoslavia in 1999. In 2001, his image was tarnished by revelations that he was the father of an illegitimate child, as well as of financial irregularities in some of his organizations. Nevertheless, he continued to be one of the most prominent and popular African–American leaders.

Jamaica

Colonial rule (up to 1962) Under British sovereignty from 1655, Jamaica became the centre for the supply of sugar and rum for the *British Empire. It served as the hub of the Caribbean slave trade until the abolition of slavery in 1833. In subsequent decades, its economy attracted investment by large-scale US-owned banana plantations. A British Crown Colony from 1866, representative government was gradually introduced from 1884. The Great *Depression triggered considerable unrest and racial tension, which ultimately led to the foundation in 1938 of the People's National Party (PNP) by Norman *Manley, modelled on the British *Labour Party. In response, the conservative Bustamante Industrial Trade Union was created in 1938, from which the right-wing Jamaica Labour Party (JLP) emerged in 1943, created and led by *Bustamante. The JLP won the first elections on a universal suffrage in 1944, and narrowly won the 1949 elections, but lost the subsequent elections (1955, 1959) to the PNP. In 1958, Jamaica joined the Federation of the *West Indies, though Bustamante's successful campaign for Jamaican independence from the federation contributed towards its breakup in 1962.

Independence (from 1962) Jamaica became independent on 6 August 1962, in the week when a general election returned Bustamante to power. In 1972, power returned to the PNP under Michael *Manley. From 1974, he pursued a moderate socialist economic programme. With the aim of fostering individual and national self-reliance, social policies were introduced. The foreign-controlled bauxite mining companies were partly nationalized to give the state majority control. While popular domestically (the PNP won the 1976 elections with a record 56.4 per cent of the vote), these costly policies alienated international investors and led to a drastic capital flight from Jamaica. On the brink of bankruptcy, Manley refused to accept *IMF funds which would have forced him to make cuts in social spending. In the late 1970s, then, Jamaica drifted into economic and social chaos. Helped by massive US aid, the JLP under Edward Seaga won the 1980 elections, introducing drastic economic reform and restoring close relations with the USA. After a brief economic boom, however, the country was hit by a severe recession in 1982, and was devastated by Hurricane Gilbert in 1988. Both of these factors compounded the effects of the IMF-imposed austerity policies, and led to the defeat of the JLP in the 1989 general elections.

Contemporary politics (since 1989) To general surprise, once returned to power, Manley continued his predecessor's economic policies. Manley was succeeded by Percival J. Patterson (PNP) in 1992. In 1994, the banking system collapsed. The state took up much of the bill, at the cost of growing foreign public debts which amounted to over 140 per cent of GNP in 2000. In addition, Jamaica was suffering from increasing street violence and a malfunctioning criminal justice system. According to *Amnesty International, Jamaica also had the highest per capita incidence of murders committed by the police in 2001. In 2006, Patterson was succeeded by Portia Simpson Miller (PNP), who vowed to fight government corruption and to reduce the high rate of crime, especially of crimes committed against women.

Jameson raid (South Africa), see RHODES, CECIL JOHN

Janata Morcha, see BHARATIYA JANATA PARTY (BJP)

Japan

To some extent Japan's position, first as a paragon of modernity in Asia at the beginning of the century, then as regional bully, and, after 1945, as a model of industrial development, has been determined by the country's desire to seek a secure place in a rapidly shifting world. While the collective sense of insecurity no longer verges on feelings of alarm or national hysteria, the Japan of today still occasionally reflects upon its vulnerability even though it is proclaimed as an economic superpower.

Meiji era (1866–1912) In 1902, only half a century since Japan had been a largely feudal country in the most part isolated from the outside world, its government succeeded in cementing an alliance on equal terms with Great Britain. Victory in the *Russo-Japanese War (1904–5) confirmed Japan's position as Asia's only modern power. The territorial concessions in southern Manchuria which she was able to win from Russia, Britain, France, and the USA allowed her to obtain colonial possessions on the continent and to begin to pursue her ambitions there with some confidence. Korea was formally annexed in 1910 and the development of the South Manchurian Railway Company ensured Japan's growing involvement in the region.

Also at this time emerged the first worrying signs of flaws within Japan's constitutional system. Because the architects of its modern governmental structures had understood that existing institutions and public opinion would not keep pace with Japan's rapid social and economic change, they had designed a system of government in the late nineteenth century in which power was exercised by the small clique of oligarchs who ruled Japan. Accordingly, power was not concentrated in the formal structures and branches of the state, which instead owed responsibility to the 'transcendental' authority of the Emperor, through whom Japan was governed.

The Taishô era (1912–26) With the death of the Meiji Emperor in (1912) and the inevitable demise of the politicians who had led the modernization of the country, a vacuum was created within the political system which competing groups sought to fill. Already by the turn of the century, the importance of the Imperial Diet and its control over the national budget was such that Japan's rulers were forced to establish their

Table 14. **Japanese Prime Ministers since 1945**

Shidehara Kijuro	1945–6	Suzuki Zenko	1980–2
*Yoshida Shigeru	1946–7	*Nakasone Yasuhiro	1982–7
*Katayama Tetsu	1947–8	*Takeshita Noboru	1987–9
Ashida Hitoshi	1948	Uno Sosuke	1989
*Yoshida Shigeru	1948–54	Kaifu Toshiki	1989–91
*Hatoyama Ichirô	1954–6	Miyazawa Kiishi	1991–3
Ishibashi Tanzan	1956–7	Hosokaya Morihiro	1993–4
*Kishi Nobusuke	1957–60	*Murayama Tomiichi	1994–6
*Ikeda Hayato	1960–4	*Hashimoto Ryûtarô	1996–8
*Satô Eisaku	1964–72	*Obuchi Keizo	1998–2000
*Tanaka Kakuei	1972–4	Mori Yoshiro	2000–1
*Miki Takeo	1974–6	*Koizumi Junichiro	2001–6
*Fukuda Takeo	1976–8	*Abe Shinzo	2006–
Ôhira Masayoshi	1978–80		

own political party, the *Seiyûkai, in order to bring the legislature under their control. The coming catastrophe was foreshadowed by the political crisis of late 1912, in which the army boycotted its Cabinet post in a disagreement over policy, with the threat of governmental paralysis.

Nevertheless, the years that followed were relatively prosperous and peaceful, particularly while World War I occupied the European powers and left their markets in Asia open to Japanese competition. At the end of the war, economic uncertainty brought social unrest. In response, one form of party government was achieved in the 1920s, beginning with *Hara Takashi's Cabinets (1918–22), although international and domestic pressures ensured that democratic practice had only the most tenuous of footholds during the Taishô era. During these years there was a blossoming of intellectual and artistic life, as well as a more vigorous and popular political scene known as 'Taishô democracy'.

Japanese expansionism (1926–37) At the same time, nearly a decade of slow economic growth was capped by the international economic collapse of 1929. Years of deflation in agricultural prices, and the destruction of the market in traded commodities such as silk, imposed severe hardship, especially on Japan's rural population. Moreover, an unprecedented number of banking collapses put the financial system under strain. The economic crisis combined with political controversy. Abroad, Japan was forced to accept an inferior position for her navy in the Pacific at the *Washington Conference, which was confirmed and extended a decade later by the London Naval Treaty (1930). To many in the Japanese military, at a time when the security of Japanese resources and personnel in her overseas possessions was paramount, these crucial interests seemed to be sacrificed to Western diplomatic sophistry.

To such groups, politicians appeared to put the interests of their *zaibatsu sponsors above those of the Japanese people. The rash of political assassinations and intrigues during these years had little in common except that the conspiracies involving young political officers, gangsters, and idealistic youths made common cause with the interests of the rural poor and viewed the political class as their natural enemy. Far from the control of Tokyo, Japan's military adventurers took over Manchuria in an aggressive action (*Manchukuo), and the international opprobrium that followed encouraged Japan to leave the *League of Nations in March 1933. Late the following year, Japan also withdrew

from the Washington Naval Arms Limitation Treaty, deepening confrontation with the USA.

At home, the febrile political climate of the 1930s climaxed in 1936 with the so-called '26 February Incident', in which young officers attempted to assassinate the entire Cabinet and seize control of the government. The incident and its suppression allowed a hardline grouping including *Ishiwara Kanji and *Tôjô Hideki to consolidate a power base within the military high command. It was these individuals who, with support from business interests, the mass media, and the bureaucracy, pursued their policies for preparation for a total war with the West and the aggressive expansion of the Japanese presence in Asia.

World War II When Japan chose to attack the USA at *Pearl Harbor in December 1941 it was already involved in the *Sino-Japanese War. The decision to take on the colonial powers of Asia, was, therefore, a military gamble, the risks of which were well understood from the beginning. Initially, however, the gamble seemed to pay off, as the Japanese armed forces outmanoeuvred and outfought their opponents in campaigns which brought victories in *Hong Kong, *Singapore, *Malaya, *Burma, and the Philippines. But with Japanese control extending across most of the Pacific, the USA and the *British Empire were able slowly to push back Japan's armed forces in some of the most determined fighting of *World War II. With Okinawa already under the control of the Allies by the spring of 1945 and Manchuria lost to the *Red Army in a matter of days, the USA dropped atomic devices on *Nagasaki and *Hiroshima, bringing the conflict to a close by the unconditional ceasefire of Japan on 15 August 1945, with unconditional surrender formally coming into effect on 2 September 1945.

US occupation (1945–52) The arrival of Japan's American conquerors coincided with a widespread feeling of revulsion against the leaders who had allowed Japan to embark on its self-destructive spiral of war. Although the precise meaning of this foreign occupation has become a matter of debate since, it is certain that many of the reforms and innovations of this period had a positive and profound impact. Although the Allies had intended a punitive mission to demilitarize Japan and punish those it viewed as responsible (*Tokyo Trials), the American military administration, officially known as the Supreme Command of the Allied Powers (*SCAP) was also highly reformist in character. Economic, political, and social rights and freedoms were introduced and guaranteed by a new Constitution. Moreover, a health and welfare system and massive land reform sought to address social injustice and poverty.

Postwar recovery (1952–1990s) With the occupiers gone in the early 1950s, Japan's conservative establishment set about revising those reforms which they did not care for. The legislation of more centralized controls over the police and education systems by the governments of *Hatoyama Ichirô and *Kishi Nobusuke, however, provoked mass popular protests on the streets of Tokyo and in the Diet. The late 1950s were a fevered time, and for many opposition leaders the use of police against protesting crowds and in the Diet, as well as the return of political assassinations, evoked dark memories of the 1930s. In the workplace, during the same period, Japanese business leaders sought to counter the militant unions that dominated key industries, such as in automobile manufacturing and electronics, by establishing secondary unions which were much more conciliatory towards the management.

Japan's factories were also at the centre of the economic and social transformation of Japan during the 1960s. For those employed in Japan's larger enterprises in particular, new practices emerged which lessened the differences between workers and involved them more closely in the manufacturing process. Staffed with flexible and increasingly better-educated staff, Japanese businesses recorded unprecedented high economic growth from the 1950s until the early 1970s. This industrial expansion brought with it new wealth to salaried workers, who began to experience the joys and drawbacks of a mass consumer society for the first time. Underlining Japan's status as a leading economic power, in the *Japan–United States Security Treaty Prime Minister *Satô Eisaku was able to negotiate the return of a nuclear-free Okinawa to Japanese sovereignty at this time (Okinawa was officially handed over on 15 May 1972).

The story of Japan's economic miracle has been so remarkable as to be overwhelming in most historical accounts, but there was a darker side. A combination of the relatively rapid expansion of heavy and chemical industries, along with urban growth far in excess of demographic changes and a boom in mass consumer markets, especially cars, wrecked the quality of the environment. Under these circumstances, pollution became an issue of such enormity that opposition became a burgeoning political movement. The energy crisis of the 1970s (*oil price shocks) imposed inflationary pressures on

Japan, as it did on the rest of the industrialized world. For the Japanese, 1974 was the first year since 1945 that economic growth had been negative. Also during this period Japan suffered a sharp revaluation of its currency against the dollar, and the shock of having one of the main planks of its foreign policy undermined when President Nixon announced the surprise rapprochement of the USA with China. In characteristic style, the government of *Tanaka Kakuei responded by negotiating its own diplomatic settlement with the mainland Chinese.

Despite the second energy crisis and worldwide recession of the early 1980s, Japanese industry showed a remarkable ability to absorb the increased costs of raw materials. By the middle of the decade, a new confidence was evident in the country's prosperity and place in the world. At the Group of Five Plaza Accords in September 1985 it was decided to strengthen the yen against the dollar, in an attempt to resolve the trade imbalances caused by the success of Japanese export industries. This, in combination with structural reforms of the Japanese economy, which had the objective of transforming industrial demand from being export-led to being domestically driven, had the result of producing unprecedented asset inflation.

Contemporary politics (since 1990s) The bubble economy, as it came to be known, finally burst in the early 1990s, causing a slump in Japan's property values and wiping out more than half of the Tokyo stock exchange's share value. While much of Japan's economy remained relatively stagnant during the mid-1990s, economic depression commenced in 1997, the first year of negative growth since 1974. This was triggered by the government's deflationary policies, and led to the collapse of a number of prominent banks and companies which had come to rely on cheap credit for survival. Domestic demand was depressed, which in turn caused, and was affected by, relatively high rates of unemployment. The consequent deflation increased the real size of public and private debt still further. Economic decline also reflected an inability of the political establishment, led by the LDP, to respond effectively. Instead, the LDP was concerned with its own corruption scandals and the continued survival of its entrenched elites, while the *Socialist Party and the *Communist Party suffered from the challenges of political powerlessness and ideological renewal. This led to a reformation of the party system, and the formation of the New *Kômeitô and the *Democratic Party.

The LDP was revived by the long premiership of *Koizumi, who led the party to a spectacular election victory in 2005. By this time, Japan had managed to return to economic growth, stimulated in part by Koizumi's economic reforms of privatization and the consolidation of public debt. Under Koizumi, Japan also began to transform its pacifist foreign policy. Japanese troops supported Allied troops in Iraq following the *Iraq War. Owing to the nuclear threat emanating from North Korea, parliament also voted for a change in the Constitution, which forbade active military engagement overseas. In 2006, Koizumi was succeeded by Shinzo *Abe.

Japan, Constitution of (3 May 1947)

Japan's fundamental law, also known as the '**Peace Constitution**', was imposed on a reluctant domestic political establishment by the American occupation authorities after World War II. Despite such beginnings, it proved to be a remarkably durable institution which came to enjoy widespread support in Japan. It replaced the Meiji Constitution and instituted fundamental changes in the state and gave new rights to the people. These included the transfer of sovereignty from the Emperor to the people (preamble and Article 1), the concentration of executive power in the Prime Minister and his Cabinet (Articles 65, 66, 72–4), and the supremacy of the lower house of the legislature (Articles 67–71). It extensively guarantees *human rights including economic, social, and religious freedoms. Article 9 of the constitution is perhaps the most famous and contentious, committing Japan to the renunciation of war and belligerency and renouncing the use of force to settle international disputes.

Japan–United States Security Treaty (1951, 1960)

The Japan-US Security Treaty of September 1951 and subsequent agreements have provided the basis of Japanese foreign and defence policies since the war. The pact was signed in 1951 at the same time as the *San Francisco Peace Treaty which concluded the peace with the *Allies except the USSR and China. The first security treaty was widely viewed in Japan and elsewhere as unequal and many opposition forces within Japan argued that it was unacceptable. Under the terms of the treaty and its accompanying agreements, US forces stationed in Japan had no obligation to protect Japan, while the Japanese government had no control over the deployment of those forces inside or outside

its territory. During the 1950s when the misdeeds of US servicemen were the subject of media attention and public outcry, US personnel also enjoyed extraterritoriality.

The 1960 treaty did much to rectify this imbalance, requiring US forces to defend Japan while removing the possibility that they would interfere with domestic affairs. US service personnel also became subject to Japanese law. Despite these improved conditions, the treaty was ratified by the Diet amid scenes of massive popular protest. Since that time, the security relationship with the USA has attracted less controversy, although the case of US servicemen raping a Japanese teenager in Okinawa in 1995 reignited mass opposition to the presence of foreign military bases there.

Jarrow March (UK)

Sometimes known as the Jarrow Crusade, this was one of the most well-known episodes in the history of protest in Britain. It was a march from Jarrow, in the north-east of England, to London, in October 1936. The town of Jarrow had been devastated by unemployment as a result of the closure of Palmer's Shipyard on the River Tyne, and the town council organized a march of two hundred men to highlight the plight of local people. The march took twenty-six days, and ended with the local *Labour MP, Ellen Wilkinson, presenting a petition to parliament on 4 November. This called for government aid in alleviating the poverty caused by unemployment. The Prime Minister, Stanley *Baldwin, had refused to receive the marchers, although a small number of them did form part of a subsequent deputation to meet the Minister of Labour. The march gained much public sympathy, but the government did not provide the assistance which had been called for.

Jaruzelski, Wojciech Witold (b. 6 July 1923). Prime Minister of Poland 1981–5; First Secretary of the Polish Communist Party 1981–9; President 1989–90

Born in Kurów, he fought in World War II and thereafter stayed in the Polish army. He joined the Communist Party in 1947, and by 1956 had advanced to become Poland's youngest general. Jaruzelski became Chief of Staff in 1965, and served as Minister of Defence, 1968–83.

Jaruzelski was appointed Prime Minister as a hardliner who could deal with the growing *Solidarność movement. He suppressed the latter by force and imprisoned many of its leaders. When it became evident that popular discontent was too strong to be ignored forever, he entered into talks with Solidarność and thus ensured a peaceful transition to democracy. It is still not clear whether he declared martial law in December 1981 out of a genuine desire to suppress the movement, or to forestall an imminent invasion by the Soviet army whose repression would have been worse. After years of deliberation, on 13 February 1996 a parliamentary committee recommended that he should not face prosecution for declaring martial law. However, in 2001 he was charged for his role in the violent suppression of workers' unrests in 1970, in which forty-four workers were killed.

Jaurès, Jean (b. 3 Sept. 1859, d. 31 July 1914). French socialist

A student of the École Normale Supérieure, he became a professor of philosophy in Toulouse before becoming a member of the Chamber of Deputies, first as a moderate Republican 1885, and then as a Socialist from 1893. In 1904, he founded the Socialist newpaper *L'Humanité*. One of the greatest orators of his day, he became one of the chief architects of a single *Socialist Party, the SFIO, in 1905. In the increasingly tense international climate before World War I, his major concern was the quest for peace, which earned him the enmity of ultra-nationalists, one of whom assassinated him.

Jawara, Sir Alhaji Dawda Kairaba (b. 16 May 1924). Prime Minister of the Gambia 1962–70; President 1970–94

Born in Barajally, he qualified as a veterinary surgeon at Glasgow University. He returned to Gambia in 1954 and, as a member of Gambia's small educated elite, co-founded the People's Progressive Party in 1959. He won the 1962 elections and became Prime Minister. He led the country to independence in 1965, and established a republic in 1970. He remained popular, though he failed to diversify the country's economy, which remained heavily reliant on its export of peanuts. Partly as protection against further military coups (those of 1980 and 1981 were quelled with the help of the Senegalese army), he advocated union with Senegal, which came about in 1982. However, the differences between the two countries proved too great, and the union was dissolved in 1989. He was deposed in a military coup in 1994. He went into exile in Senegal, returning to Gambia in 2002.

Jayawardene, Junius Richard (b. 17 Sept. 1906, d. 1 Nov. 1996). Prime Minister of Sri Lanka 1977–8; President 1978–89

Born in Colombo, he became politically active during the 1940s, and joined *Senanayake's United National Party (UNP) upon its foundation in 1946. In the following governments of Senanayake and his son respectively, he served as Minister of Finance (1947–53), Agriculture (1953–6), and as Minister of State (1965–70). He became chairman of the parliamentary party in 1970, and became leader of the UNP after the death of the younger Senanayake in 1973. He guided the UNP to a landslide electoral victory, and stabilized its power through winning a further victory in 1982, and an extension of his term in office to six years through a referendum. In 1978, he changed the Constitution towards a presidential system, and the electoral system to proportional representation, to give greater weight to the country's troubled ethnic minorities. He was firmly committed to the West, and reversed most of Sirimavo *Bandaranaike's socialist policies. However, he was unable to prevent *Tamil unrest from developing into civil war in 1983, nor could he stop Indian interference through occupation of the Tamil areas in 1987.

Jedwabne Massacre (10 July 1941)

An anti-Semitic massacre formerly thought to have been committed by the *Nazi occupation force in Jedwabne, a Polish town of about 2,500 inhabitants about 100 km (60 miles) north-east of Warsaw. In 2001 a Polish historian, Jan Thomasz Gross, claimed that the atrocity was committed, in fact, by Poles of their own free will. In a book entitled *Neighbours: The Destruction of the Jewish Community in Jedwabne*, he showed that its 1,600 Jews were ordered by the Polish mayor to gather on the market square. They were butchered by the townspeople and subsequently incinerated. The massacre was by no means unusual in German-occupied eastern Europe in World War II. However, the revelations were notable for the debate they caused in Poland. The controversy raised difficult and painful questions about Polish *anti-Semitism before and during World War II, and it brought to the surface a discussion about the complicity of many Poles in many of the crimes committed by the Germans. On its 60th anniversary, the Polish President, *Kwasniewski, and the Polish Catholic Church publicly apologized for the massacre.

Jehovah's Witnesses

A worldwide community of around six million people which lives in the expectation of an imminent end to the world, after which only its own members, the 'elect of Jehova', will remain during a thousand-year reign of peace. Founded in the USA in 1872 as the 'International Bible Students' by Charles Taze

Russell (b. 1852, d. 1916), they oppose all organized religions as institutions of Satan and refuse obedience to the civil authority of any country, which leads them to pacifism. As a result, during World War II they were discriminated against in many countries, such as New Zealand and Australia, and persecuted in *Nazi Germany, where many of their members died in *concentration camps.

(⊕) SEE WEB LINKS

• The official website of Jehovah's Witnesses.

Jellicoe, John Rushworth, 1st Earl Jellicoe (b. 5 Dec. 1859, d. 20 Nov. 1935). British admiral

Born in Southampton, and educated at nearby private schools, he joined the Royal Navy in 1872. He was made a captain in 1897, and served in east Asia. In 1901, he entered the Admiralty as an inspector of ships, and served at sea again, before becoming a Rear-Admiral in 1907. In 1908, as Controller at the Admiralty, Jellicoe was involved in discussions over the new dreadnought class of ships. In 1910 he was made Commander of the Atlantic Fleet, and in 1911, he became second-in-command of the Home Fleet. From 1912, he was Second Sea Lord at the Admiralty, and just before the outbreak of World War I, he was made Commander-in-Chief of the Grand Fleet. In June 1916, the Royal Navy fought the Battle of *Jutland; it suffered heavier casualties than the Germans, and Jellicoe was criticized for excessive caution. At the end of 1916, he became First Sea Lord, being succeeded by *Beatty as Commander-in-Chief. In the face of the U-boat campaign against British commerce, he implemented the convoy system. However, *Lloyd George thought him unimaginative, and he was dismissed in December 1917. He served as Governor-General of New Zealand from 1920 to 1927.
LUSITANIA

Jenkins, Roy Harris, Baron Jenkins of Hillhead (b. 11 Nov. 1920, d. 5 Jan 2003). British Chancellor of the Exchequer 1967–70

Born in Pontypool, Monmouthshire, he was educated at Abersychan County School and Oxford. During World War II he worked as a code-breaker. In 1948, Jenkins became a *Labour MP in the Southwark by-election. He became an effective Minister of Aviation (1964–5), though his reputation was made as one of the most successful Home Secretaries (1965–7) and Chancellors of the Exchequer since World War II. In the former position, he instituted a string of liberal reforms, notably the legalization of *abortion and homosexuality. As Chancellor, his budgets

eliminated a large balance-of-payments deficit, though the austerity which so effectively reduced consumption did little to endear his government to large sections of the electorate. As Foreign Secretary in the last *Wilson government (1974–6), Jenkins was a committed advocate of British membership of the European Economic Community (*European integration).

Jenkins became President of the *European Commission in 1976, having lost to *Callaghan in the election for the Labour leadership. In this position, he was, together with *Schmidt and *Giscard d'Estaing, instrumental in the introduction of the *ERM. Alarmed by Labour's drift to the left, he re-entered British politics and co-founded the *Social Democratic Party (SDP) in 1981. He was its leader until 1983, when he was replaced by David Owen. He gained a sensational by-election victory for the SDP in 1982 at Glasgow Hillhead, a seat he lost in 1987. He was elected Chancellor of Oxford University in 1987, and was raised to the peerage in 1988. He wrote a number of biographies which, despite the absence of new or controversial insights, enjoyed considerable popularity, including *Asquith* (1964), *Truman* (1986), *Baldwin* (1987), *Gladstone* (1995), and *Churchill* (2002).

Jerusalem

A city that derives its unique importance from being a holy site for three world religions. For Christians, it is the site of the cruxifixion of Jesus Christ. But since the Middle Ages Christians have laid no territorial claims over the city, and instead were content to ensure access to their holy sites. After Mecca and Medina, its Al-Aqsa Mosque is the third most important holy site for *Islam. Since it was made the capital of King David's kingdom around 1,000 BC, Jerusalem has been at the epicentre of Jewish cultural, social, and religious consciousness.

Due to Jewish immigration, a majority of its growing population was Jewish from c.1875. The *UN intended it to be an international city in 1947, in order to ensure free access for all three religions. After the Israeli war of independence (1948–9), its larger, western half came under Israeli control, while the eastern half, which included the holiest site for the Jews, the Wailing Wall, came under Jordanian control. The eastern half was occupied by Israel together with the *West Bank during the Six Day War of 1967. Since then, the future of the city has been the most contentious issue in negotiations for peace between Israel and the Palestinians. Significantly, it was left out of the negotiations that led to the *Oslo and *Gaza-Jericho Agreements, and failure to reach an agreement on Jerusalem in January 2001 led to the final breakdown of the *Wye Agreements. In the meantime, throughout the 1990s, successive Israeli governments promoted the building of new Jewish settlements in Palestinian areas, a move which sparked off a new *Intifadah in 2000. By 2006, the city had a total population of 725,000, one-third of whom were Palestinian. As a result of the construction of settlements, one-third of the Jewish population lived in East Jerusalem.

Jewish Agency

An organization established by Britain to comply with its *League of Nations *Mandate, to represent the Jewish community in *Palestine. It was formally constituted in 1929, although it had in fact been operating since 1920. Half of its members came from Palestine, while the other half came from outside, nominated by the World *Zionist Organization. It became responsible not only for establishing kibbutzim settlements, but also for Jewish immigration, investment, and economic and cultural development. It also represented Jewish interests internationally, at the League of Nations and then at the *UN. Furthermore, it provided its leaders, such as *Ben-Gurion and *Eshkol, with administrative and diplomatic experience that proved invaluable when they took over the government of the new state of Israel in 1948. After the foundation of Israel the Jewish Agency ceased to exercise its administrative and domestic political functions, but continued to act as an international body for the global Jewish community which would assist Israel, for example, in matters of finance and immigration.

(⊕) SEE WEB LINKS

• The official website of the Jewish Agency.

Jewish Brigade (World War II)

Formed in 1944, despite strong reservations by the British, who feared an escalation of Jewish-Arab tensions in *Palestine. It numbered some 5,000 men and saw service in Egypt, north Italy, and the *North-West Europe campaign. Its members helped to smuggle out from Europe many survivors of the *concentration camps and the *Holocaust. It was officially disbanded in 1946, though some of its operations were taken over by the *Haganah.

Jewish Legion

A number of military units formed in 1917 to help the British liberate *Palestine from the rule of the *Ottoman Empire. One battalion was recruited in England, another in the USA, and others in Egypt and Palestine, joining General Allenby (b. 1861, d. 1936) as he advanced into Ottoman Turkey. After the war, many of its members such as *Ben-Gurion and *Eshkol proceeded to form the *Haganah.

Jews, see JUDAISM; ZIONISM; ANTI-SEMITISM; POGROMS

Jiang Qing (Chiang Ch'ing) (b. 1914, d. 14 May 1991). Wife of Mao Zedong

Born at Chucheng (Shantung province), she became an actress in Shanghai, where she was rumoured to have had a string of affairs with *Guomindang officials. In 1937 she fled from the Japanese to Communist-controlled *Yan'an, where she became a drama teacher. Here she met Mao Zedong and married him (1939), though the condition was imposed upon her by the party leadership to stay out of politics for thirty years. She almost kept this promise, but launched herself into political activity in 1963, when she urged a reform of the Beijing Opera along revolutionary lines. She propagated a return to popular art forms in opera and ballet, which should be filled with socialist values. Her influence increased dramatically during the *Cultural Revolution, which she used to settle old scores with former opponents and those who knew about her past activities in Shanghai. She joined the *Politburo in 1969, and consolidated her power by forming the *Gang of Four. However, upon *Mao's death, *Hua Guofeng moved swiftly to remove her from office. She was arrested and, in a show trial in 1981, sentenced to death, though this was commuted to life imprisonment. She committed suicide by hanging herself.

Jiang Zemin (b. 17 Aug. 1926). President of the People's Republic of China 1993–2002

Early career Born at Yangszhou (Jiangsu), he joined the Chinese *Communist Party (CCP) in 1946 and studied electrical engineering at Jiaotong University. He became a trainee at a motor vehicle plant in Moscow in 1955, and returned in 1956 to become director of a motor vehicle plant in China. He joined the Ministry of Machine-Building Industries (1962–70), but was purged in the *Cultural Revolution. As a protégé of *Deng Xiaoping, he began a steep rise after the death of *Mao Zedong in 1976. By 1985, he was Minister for Electronic Industries. In 1988, he became mayor and local CCP leader of China's biggest commercial centre, Shanghai. In this office he was relatively colourless. However, in the wake of the *Tiananmen Square massacre his apparent lack of political ambition made him acceptable to the different factions of the party. He became a compromise candidate for the post of General Secretary of the CCP, to which he was elected on 24 June 1989.

In power Jiang became concerned with concentrating as much power as possible in his own hands, in anticipation of the ageing Deng's inevitable decline. In November 1989, he became chairman of the Central Military Commission of the CCP. On 27 March 1993, he was elected President. Until his death, Deng remained the ultimate source of appeal and authority, but during the 1990s Jiang occupied the three most powerful positions in the country, and in this sense became China's most powerful leader since Mao Zedong. His encouragement of economic competition and planned liberalization of the country's economy led to substantial growth rates throughout the 1990s. His policies led to a discrepancy between a bloated, inefficient publicly-owned economy and thriving private enterprises. This in turn increased frictions within urban society, and between town and countryside. Jiang presided over the repatriation of *Hong Kong and *Macao, and successfully guided China into membership of the *WTO in 2001. In 2002, Jiang was succeeded as President and as leader of the CCP by *Hu Jintao. Jiang passed on his last important office, the chairmanship of the Central Military Commission, to Hu in 2004.

Jiangxi Soviet Republic (1931–4)

A Communist state proclaimed on 7 November 1931 after the 1927 breakdown of the Communist-*Guomindang alliance in China. In an area equivalent to one-sixth of China's territory, the Communists initiated an agrarian revolution, developing Jiangxi as a model for the rest of China. After the fifth encirclement campaign of the *National Revolutionary Army of the Guomindang, however, the *soviet collapsed, forcing the Communists to escape in the *Long March.

Jim Crow, see SEGREGATION

Jinnah, Muhammad Ali (25 Dec. 1876?, d. 11 Sept. 1948). Governor-General of Pakistan 1947–8

Early career Born in Karachi into a prosperous merchant family, he was educated in Bombay and England, where he was called to the Bar in 1895. He returned to Karachi in 1895, and established a law practice in Bombay in 1897. A fervent supporter of greater Indian self-government, he joined the Indian National *Congress (INC), which he

represented as part of a delegation making its case in London in 1905. Only gradually did he become specifically concerned about the Muslim minority in the country, and its desire for equal political and social rights, in preference to independence. He joined the *Muslim League in 1913, distanced himself increasingly from the INC, which under *Gandhi's leadership adopted a more distinctively Hindu identity, and he became more confrontational towards the British. Taken aback by the growing turbulence of Indian politics, he sought to retire to London in 1931, but by that time his intellect and personality had already made such an impact that Muslim leaders urged his return.

Leadership of the Muslim League He arrived back in India in 1935, and focused his energies on helping to create an independent India, but with maximum guarantees for its Muslim population. However, his programme failed to generate large Muslim support: in the 1937 elections, his Muslim League only managed to secure 109 out of the 482 separate seats reserved for Muslims. In particular, he was opposed by regional Muslim leaders who jealously guarded the privileges and status granted them by the British. Eventually, he found an electrifying slogan in the promise to create separate Muslim homelands in India. On the basis of this programme, he polled 75 per cent of the Muslim vote in the 1945–6 provincial elections. Jinnah still hoped to use his strong mandate to increase his bargaining power with *Nehru, to ensure extensive Muslim rights in a united India. Once this failed, with the breakdown of the *Cabinet Mission Plan, he accepted a separate Muslim state, to consist of the four Muslim-majority provinces in the west (later known as West Pakistan), and the Muslim-dominated East Bengal (later known as East Pakistan, independent since 1971 as Bangladesh). By the time of his appointment as Governor-General on 14 August 1947, he was already weakened by tuberculosis, from which he died a year later. The single greatest driving force behind the formation of Pakistan, his death before the establishment of its constitutional, political, and administrative structures struck a severe blow to the new state.

Jodl, Alfred (b. 10 May 1890, d. 16 Oct. 1946). Military adviser to Hitler

One of *Hitler's closest associates and an assistant to W. *Keitel since 1939, he was convicted of war crimes at the *Nuremberg Trials and executed.

Joffre, Joseph Jacques Césaire

(b. 12 Jan. 1852, d. 3 Jan. 1931). French marshal

As Chief of the General Staff since 1911, he managed to halt the German advance on Paris in September 1914, which frustrated German hopes for a quick victory. Hence, his position became almost unassailable, but as Commander-in-Chief from December 1915, he was responsible for the failure of the Battle of the *Somme, and for the war of attrition in *Verdun and across the Western Front. In December 1916 he was made marshal and thus effectively kicked upstairs by Prime Minister *Briand in a move to restore political control over the course of the war. He became President of the Allied War Council in 1917, and from 1918 he held various positions at the Ministry of War.

John XXIII (Angelo Giuseppe Roncalli)

(b. 25 Nov. 1881, d. 3 June 1963). Pope 1958–63

Ordained in 1904, he was an army chaplain during World War I and entered the papal diplomatic service in 1925 as the apostolic delegate to Bulgaria. After serving as apostolic delegate to Greece and Turkey from 1935 and as papal nuncio in liberated France from 1944, in 1953 he became a cardinal and Patriarch of Venice. Under his papacy the Roman *Catholic Church became less centralized. It became more aware of its worldwide importance. He started dialogue with other Christian denominations, which led for the first time to official Catholic participation in the *ecumenical movement. Most importantly, he called the Second *Vatican Council which he opened on 11 October 1962. The Church thus started to react to the social, political, and spiritual challenges of a world marked by increasing ideological and material divisions, as expressed in his *encyclicals for world peace (*Pacem in Terris*, 1963) and social harmony (*Mater et Magistra*, 1961).

John Paul I (Albino Luciani)

(b. 17 Oct. 1912, d. 28 Sept. 1978). Pope 1978

The Patriarch of Venice since 1969, he was made a cardinal in 1973. The election of the 'smiling Pope' raised many hopes for a reformist and liberal papacy, which were dashed by his sudden death only thirty-three days after his election.

John Paul II (Karol Wojtyla)

(b. 18 May 1920). Pope 1978–2005

Following his studies in philology and a brief career as an actor, he began studying theology at the illegal Polish theological seminary in

Kraków in 1942, and then continued his degree in Rome. Ordained to the priesthood in 1946, he became a professor at the Catholic University of Lublin. A suffragan bishop in 1958, he became archbishop (in 1964) and then cardinal (in 1967) of Kraków. On 16 October 1978, he was the first ever Pole, and the first non-Italian since 1523, to be elected Pope. He became known as the 'travelling Pope', energetically travelling round the globe in recognition of the worldwide role of the Roman *Catholic Church.

A conservative on doctrinal matters, John Paul II reaffirmed the Roman Catholic commitment to a male, celibate priesthood, total opposition to artificial contraception and *abortion, and the affirmation of Catholic practices such as the veneration of saints (especially the Virgin Mary). He also strengthened the conservatism of the Church through the appointment of conservative cardinals, and expanded the college of cardinals. He promoted organizations such as *Opus Dei, and opposed doctrinally more radical movements such as *liberation theology. John Paul II was progressive on political and social matters, e.g. through his pacifist condemnation of the *Gulf War and his *encyclical *Solicitudo Rei Socialis* (1988), which emphasized the social responsibilities of the Church. In 104 trips abroad, he built on his predecessors' progress towards recognizing the global dimension of the Church and the growing importance of Latin America, Africa, and Asia within it. Moreover, his visits to his native Poland in 1979, 1983, and 1987 gave a crucial stimulus to the anti-Communist opposition, the *Solidarność movement, which ultimately culminated in the downfall of *Communism in Poland and throughout Eastern Europe. In the last years of his life he suffered from Parkinson's disease, and from the late effects of an attempt on his life in 1981.

Johnson, Lyndon Baines

(b. 27 Aug. 1908, d. 22 Jan. 1973). 36th US President, 1963–9

Early career Born in Stonewall, Texas, into a moderately wealthy family, Johnson trained at a local teachers' college, and briefly taught in state schools in 1930 before entering politics as a legislative assistant to Richard Kleberg, a *Democrat member of *Congress. He became a strong supporter of Franklin D. *Roosevelt, who appointed him director of the Texan National Youth Administration in 1935. Johnson was elected to Congress in a special election in 1937, but narrowly lost the race for a Senate seat in 1941.

After war service in the navy Johnson narrowly beat ex-Texas Governor Coke Stevenson in 1948 for a seat in the Senate. He was later to be dogged by allegations that party bosses in Texas had rigged his election, and earned the sobriquet 'Landslide Lyndon' as a result. Johnson quickly rose to the leadership of the Democrats in the Senate (in 1953) and began to hone his soon-to-be legendary qualities of legislative ability and personal persuasion. He began a long association with civil rights by helping to push the 1957 *Civil Rights Act through *Congress and identifying himself strongly with it (though this was partly to hide his previous opposition to civil rights). Johnson's politics were always affected by his strong presidential aspirations, which were set back when *Kennedy defeated him, Stuart Symington, and Hubert *Humphrey for the Democrat presidential nomination in 1960.

Presidency Johnson became the vice-presidential nominee, though he considered Kennedy a privileged, rich, and inexperienced playboy. Once elected, his enormous energy led to great frustration in an office which neither he nor Kennedy rated very highly. His few bright spots came through his chairing of the President's Council on Civil Rights and the National Space Council.

Upon Kennedy's assassination he became President, persuading Congress to pass a number of controversial acts of the Kennedy administration, notably the Civil Rights Act of 1964. He also inaugurated his own War on Poverty, winning the 1964 election by a landslide. A Democratic majority in Congress bestowed much success on his subsequent legislative energy to realize his vision of the *Great Society. The legislative achievement, however, contrasted with growing urban and ethnic riots, the radicalization of Black politics, and inflation.

Most problematic for Johnson was his unswerving support for the escalation of the *Vietnam War. This alienated conservatives as well as his natural allies, the liberal middle classes and students. Resentment on the part of Kennedy supporters against Johnson resulted in bitter sniping, which exploded into open warfare when Robert *Kennedy entered the 1968 presidential race in a direct challenge to Johnson. Johnson withdrew from the Democratic primaries and sought a negotiated peace with North Vietnam, which was undermined by the *Republican campaign staff of Richard *Nixon. Effectively, Johnson—a man of towering ambition, compassion, and ego—was hounded from office, but not without an unparalleled legacy of anti-poverty and welfare legislation which

was the direct personal product of his Presidency. He died of a heart attack.

Johnson-Sirleaf, Ellen (b. 29 Oct 1938). President of Liberia, 2006–
Born in Monrovia, she studied economics at Harvard and became State Secretary in the Finance Ministry under President Tolbert in 1972. She served Samuel Doe as Finance Minister, but became his critic. She was imprisoned for a sentence of 10 years, but managed to escape to the USA. There she became the Director of the Africa programme of the UN Development Programme. She returned to Liberia in 1997, but lost the elections to Charles Taylor. In 2003 she joined the transitional government, and in 2006 was elected Africa's first female President. She fought against corruption ferociously, with unorthodox means. She fired all employees of the Finance Ministry, and called an international committee of experts to supervise the proper use of government and international funds.

Jordan, Hashemite Kingdom of

A heterogeneous Arab state with no oil reserves and few mineral resources of its own, Jordan has emerged as one of the most stable states in the region, thanks not least to the skills of its ruling dynasty.

Foreign rule Under the sovereignty of the *Ottoman Empire from 1518, the territory was liberated by the *Arab Revolt of 1916. It came under British control as a *League of Nations *Mandate, as part of a wider area covering *Palestine and Iraq. In 1921 the British turned Jordan into a separate Mandate under the *Hashemite *Abdullah ibn Hussein. With considerable British help, the latter created political and administrative state institutions, such as the *Arab Legion. In 1948, the country became independent as Transjordan.

First years of independence (1948–53) Its gains during the first Arab–Israeli War of 1948–9 proved to be a hollow victory, and became a fundamental burden for the next four decades. For after annexation of East *Jerusalem and the *West Bank, the original Transjordanian population of 400,000 suddenly found itself outnumbered by over

800,000 Palestinians, half of whom were refugees from areas that were now Israel. This put a tremendous strain on the economy, and challenged the domestic stability of the country through ethnic tensions between the Jordanians and the Palestinians. The newly acquired territories and Transjordan were united in 1950 as the Hashemite Kingdom of Jordan. Domestic tensions reached a peak in 1951, when Abdullah was assassinated by a Palestinian. He was succeeded briefly by his son, Talal, and then his grandson, *Hussein ibn Talal, who subsequently exerted firm control over the country's politics, buttressed by the loyality of his armed forces. In the 1950s the country's existence was fundamentally threatened by the *pan-Arabism of its neighbours, Egypt and Syria.

Hussein II (1952–99) Jordan lost its burdensome West Bank and East Jerusalem in the disastrous *Six Day War with Israel, though this brought its Palestinian problems to a head. Not only did Jordan lose important agricultural and industrial areas in the West Bank, but it now had to cope with an influx of one million Palestinian refugees, while Palestinian guerrillas such as the *PLO were using Jordan as their base for attacks on Israel. These attacks put Jordan's sovereignty at risk from further external military confrontation, while the number of Palestinians in arms, and the formation of a virtual Palestinian rival government, became an internal threat to the Jordanian authorities. Consequently, the PLO was expelled, though this was not achieved without a bloody civil war in 1970–1. For this, Jordan became ostracized in the Arab world until 1974, when it accepted the decision of all other Arab states to recognize the PLO as the sole representative of the Palestinian people, even though this questioned Jordan's own claim to the West Bank. After the outbreak of the *Intifadah, which demonstrated the allegiance of the Palestinians under Israeli occupation to the PLO, Jordan finally renounced its claims to its former territory in 1988 and entered a harmonious relationship with the PLO.

Jordan remained neutral during the *Gulf War, during which it experienced a sharp economic downturn and a large influx of Palestinian and other refugees from Iraq and Kuwait. In 1993, the first multi-party elections since 1956 resulted in a clear victory for the loyalists against the *Islamic fundamentalists. This strengthened further the authority of the King, under whom Jordan became, after Egypt, the second Arab state to sign a peace agreement with Israel

after the latter's recognition of the PLO on 26 October 1994.

Contemporary politics (since 1999) In 1999, Hussein was succeeded by his son, *Abdullah II, who spent the first years of his reign stabilizing his grip on power. He continued his father's ambivalent attitude towards the Palestinians, which encouraged their claims against Israel in order to deny them rights in Jordan. The *Iraq War provided a new economic and socio-cultural challenge. Jordan had profited greatly from illicit trade with Iraq in return for cheap oil, at a time when Saddam *Hussein's country faced a UN trade embargo. This source of revenue fell away after the fall of Hussein, while Jordan became subject to large-scale immigration of Iraqis as well as of terrorist groups evading capture by US forces. Moreover, the proliferation of terrorist groups in Iraq spilled over into neighbouring Jordan, as a number of terrorist attacks hit Jordan in 2005.

Jospin, Lionel (b. 12 July 1937). Prime Minister of France, 1997–2002
Born in Meudon, he graduated from the elite universities Institut d'Études Politiques and the École Nationale d'Administration (ENA). He joined the *Socialist Party in 1971, just after taking up a professorship in economics at Paris University IX. The party's expert on foreign policy, Jospin became party leader in 1981, *Mitterrand became President. From 1988 to 1992 Jospin served as Minister of Education, but in 1993 he lost his seat in the National Assembly and returned to university teaching. He returned to lead the Socialist Party in the 2005 presidential elections, when he came a close second to *Chirac. Jospin led his party to a triumphant election victory in 1997, and subsequently presided over a period of high economic growth and low inflation. His government also introduced a number of social welfare reforms and relaxed the country's relatively stringent immigration policies. In a sweeping tax reform in 2001, he provided marked relief especially for lower incomes and an overall reduction in the tax burden. From 2000, however, his government's performance was less assured, which manifested itself in a series of ministerial resignations owing to a number of scandals. Ironically, his unassuming nature became an electoral liability against the populist *Chirac, who managed to define the election campaign on issues like law and order. Jospin's centrism failed to unite the left behind him, so that in a political earthquake he missed the second round of the

presidential elections, coming third behind
Chirac and *Le Pen.

Joyce, William ('Lord Haw-Haw') (b. 24
Apr. 1906, d. 3 Jan. 1946). British traitor

Born in Brooklyn, New York, his family moved
to Ireland in 1909, and then to Britain in 1922,
where he was educated at Birkbeck College,
London. He joined the British Union of Fascists
(BUF) in 1933, and became deputy to *Mosley.
He left the BUF in 1937, forming the British
National Socialist League, which was more
pro-Nazi than the BUF. He fled to Germany in
August 1939 to escape arrest, and began to
work for the Ministry of Propaganda,
broadcasting on its English-language radio
station. He gained the nickname 'Lord
Haw-Haw', which was originally bestowed
on another broadcaster on the station.
Joyce was captured by the British army
in April 1945, and was hung in 1946
having been found guilty of treason. The
case was controversial: he was an American
citizen, but it was argued that he owed
allegiance to Britain since he also held a
British passport.

Juan Carlos I (b. 5 Jan. 1938). King of Spain
1975–

Born in Rome, he was the grandson of King
*Alfonso XIII, who had left Spain without
abdicating on 14 April 1931. In 1947, *Franco
defined Spain as a monarchy without
determining the monarch. At Franco's
instigation, he went to Spain in 1948 to finish
his studies and receive military training.
While he disagreed with Franco, he was
concerned to reconcile Spaniards still divided
by the *Spanish Civil War. In 1961 Franco
officially designated him to occupy the throne
after his death. As King, he was committed to
national reconciliation, the country's regional
diversity, and a complete democratization. He
chose a Prime Minister, *Suárez, who would
carry out his programme, so that direct,
universal elections could be held by 1977. He
supported Spain's constitutional definition as
a country of autonomous regions, and
promoted a special autonomy status for
Catalonia. A military coup of 1981, in which
the rebels seized the parliament, came to
nought, not least because of the King's
determination. As the democracy became
more firmly entrenched under *González
during the 1980s, he took a less active role in
politics, focusing on his ceremonial and
representative functions instead. More than
any other person, he ensured a peaceful
transition from the divisive, authoritarian
Franco years to a stable, Western democracy.

Judaism

One of the world's major religions, its
estimated world population of around fifteen
million is centred in the USA (5.7 million),
Israel (4 million), and the Soviet Union (1.5
million). Its beliefs are enshrined in the
Hebrew Scriptures (the Torah) and in its oral
traditions (the Mishnah and the Talmud).
Following centuries of persecution, during the
nineteenth century Jews were emancipated in
most countries. This presented Jews at least in
Europe with a new challenge, i.e. to what
extent it was possible or desirable to assimilate
to their respective (Christian) societies without
losing their identity and their religion. A
variety of responses to this challenge have led
to a number of divisions within Judaism,
which persist to the present day. The Reform
Movement sought to reconcile Judaism with
contemporary society, e.g. by allowing the
language of the country to be used in the
synagogue. Orthodox Judaism was a reaction
to these liberal reformists, seeking to reject
secular culture and to preserve ancient
practices; it included supporters of Hasidism,
an austere, mystical group which stressed the
development of a personal spiritual life and
attacked every manifestation of modernity.
Between these emerged Conservative
Judaism, whose 'positive historicism' aimed to
harmonize Jewish tradition with modern
knowledge. Finally, since the 1920s,
Reconstructionists have sought to reduce the
need for assimilation through emphasizing
the cultural value of Judaism as part of
civilization. The foundation of Israel in 1948
has presented Judaism there with problems of
a different nature, mainly about its role in the
new secular state.
   ZIONISM; ANTI-SEMITISM; POGROMS

Juin, Alphonse Pierre (b. 16 Dec. 1888, d.
27 Jan. 1967). French general

Born in Algeria, as Commander of the 1st
French Army he was captured by the Germans
in 1940, but released upon his decision to
*collaborate with the enemy in 1941. He
became military commander in Morocco, but
following the Allied invasion of neighbouring
Tunisia he changed sides and fought for de
*Gaulle. The resident-general of Morocco
from 1947 to 1951, he served as supreme
commander of the French army 1951–4, and
of the *NATO forces in central Western
Europe 1953–6. In the last years of his life he
was fiercely critical of de Gaulle's policy
towards Algeria.

July Plot (20 July 1944)

An assassination attempt against *Hitler. It
was planned by conservative army officers

and bureaucrats who had become increasingly disillusioned with Hitler's arbitrary rule. They wanted to put an end to the *Nazi regime; they felt certain this could avoid unconditional surrender and allow the conclusion of a 'just' peace with the Allies. They also hoped for a return to the rule of law, even if this did not necessarily entail a return to democracy. The plot was carried out by **Claus Count Schenk von Stauffenberg** (b. 1907, d. 1944), a young officer who had witnessed a mass execution of women and children by the *SS. He was the only one to have direct access to Hitler in his headquarters in East Prussia. Unfortunately, he was not able to prepare enough explosives before he carried them hidden in a briefcase to a conference attended by Hitler. He left the briefcase next to Hitler, but an attendant at the meeting unwittingly put the briefcase under the heavy oak table. This protected Hitler from the explosion, so that he received only a few minor wounds. The immediate culprits, including Stauffenberg, were executed that same night, while by the end of the year 5,200 people who were linked to the resistance group, or who were considered to be opposed to the regime, were sentenced to death and executed.

RESISTANCE, GERMANY

Jumayyil, Amin (b. 1942). President of Lebanon 1982–8

He was born in Beirut into a *Maronite Christian family; his father, Pierre Jumayyil (b. 1905, d. 1984), was one of Lebanon's most prominent politicians. This inspired him to his own involvement, and he entered parliament in 1970. More moderate and conciliatory than his father, he became President on the assassination of his brother, Bashir. From the start, he was caught in the dilemma that he needed to secure the withdrawal of Israel's occupying forces in order to gain support at home, but that, if successful, he would be hopelessly exposed to the Syrian-supported *Druze and Muslim militias. He secured a controversial agreement with Israel in 1983 and, after the Israeli withdrawal from most of Lebanon, had little effective control over the country. In the hope of achieving peace, he effectively recognized Syria's influence. However, fighting dragged on as he refused to relinquish the inbuilt Maronite majority in parliament. After leaving office, Jumayyil went into exile in Paris, but he returned to Lebanon in 2000.

Juppé, Alain Marie (b. 15 Aug. 1945). Prime Minister of France 1995–7

Born at Mont de Marsan, he graduated from the elite colleges École Normale Supérieure and the École Nationale d'Administration. In 1976, he became a protégé of *Chirac, working as his speech writer. After Chirac's election as Mayor of Paris in 1978 he became his economic and financial director, and from 1986 Juppé served as Deputy in the National Assembly. Chirac appointed Juppé secretary-general of the *Gaullists (RPR) in 1988, in which capacity he made a significant contribution to the party's victory in the 1993 elections. As Minister of Foreign Affairs (1993–5) he was the most outspoken and enthusiastic ally of Chirac's bid for the presidency, and was appointed Prime Minister after the latter's victory. Juppé struggled hard to realize the President's contradictory election promises of a reduction in unemployment, increased social spending, and a reduction of state spending. He was more a technocrat than a communicator, and his attempted public spending reforms in late 1995 caused the biggest popular protests in French society since 1968. The 1997 elections, called early by Chirac in the expectation of a clear victory for the right, became a disaster for Juppé, whose RPR was routed. A trusted aide to Chirac, he served as first president of the *UMP. Briefly made minister for the enviroment by *Sarkozy, he had to resign after failing to regain his seat in the 2007 parliamentary elections.

Jutland, Battle of (31 May–1 June 1916) The only major sea battle in World War I. It began with fighting between Royal Navy squadrons of battle-cruisers under *Beatty and a German squadron under Rear Admiral von Hipper. Beatty then sailed to join the main British North Sea fleet of some 150 vessels under *Jellicoe. At 6 pm they engaged the German High Seas fleet of 99 vessels under Vice-Admiral Scheer. Firing was at long range, approximately 14 km. The German fleet headed for home under the cover of night, but met the British fleet in the early hours of the morning. Technically, it was a draw, as the British lost fourteen ships, including three battle-cruisers, with 6,100 casualties, while the Germans lost eleven ships, including one battleship and one battle-cruiser, with 2,550 casualties. Despite the British numerical superiority, the German fleet had inflicted greater damage on the British and escaped. However, in the long run, the German Admiralty refused to risk another naval confrontation, enabling the British to retain control over the North Sea.

K

Kabila, Joseph (b. 4 June 1971). President of the Democratic Republic of Congo, 2001–
Born at Hewa Bora II, the oldest son of Laurent *Kabila was educated in Tanzania and at Beijing University. He returned to Congo with his father in 1997, becoming head of the military in 2000. Upon his father's murder, he assumed the presidency. Committed to bringing stability to his country, he negotiated a cease-fire to end one of Africa's bloodiest civil wars in 2002. He was confirmed in elections in 2006 that were monitored by international observers, and regarded to be remarkably fair. Nevertheless, Kabila struggled to appease his major opponent, Jean-Pierre Bemba, and to assert his government's authority in the eastern part of Congo.

Kabila, Laurent-Désiré (b. 1 Jan 1958 d. 16 Jan 2001). President of the Democratic Republic of Congo, 1997–2001
Born in Moba, Shaba province, he went to France to study philosophy. He returned to Congo in 1960, but after the military coup of 1961 became a leading figure of the underground movement. He opposed the *Mobutu regime from the beginning, but was unsuccessful at rallying sufficient resources in finance and manpower to succeed. In 1996, finally, he founded a broad coalition movement named the Alliance for the Liberation of Congo-Zaïre. His forces were increasingly successful against the ailing Mobutu, and in 1997 he took the capital, Kinshasa. He proclaimed himself President on 29 May 1997. Hopes that Kabila would create democratic rule and end the corruption of his predecessors, however, were soon dashed, as he amassed more and more powers. His consequent failure to integrate different groups into his government led to the continuation of the civil war. He was murdered by a bodyguard, and succeeded by his son, Joseph *Kabila.

Kádár, János (b. 26 May 1912, d. 6 July 1989). Hungarian dictator 1956–89
Early career Born an illegitimate child as János Czermanek in *Fiume, he joined the illegal Hungarian Communist Party in 1932 and advanced to become its First Secretary in 1943. He was imprisoned by the *Gestapo in 1944. After the war, he became the Deputy Chief of Police in 1945. He succeeded *Rajk as Minister of the Interior in 1948, and subsequently instigated a series of show trials beginning with that of Rajk himself. He was arrested himself in 1951, but released and rehabilitated in 1954. Kádár became General Secretary of the Communist Party in October 1956 and joined *Nagy's government as Minister of State.

In power A few weeks later, when it became clear that *Warsaw Pact troops were about to put an end to the *Hungarian Revolution, Kádár escaped to the Soviet forces. He signed a public request for Soviet intervention, which brought down Nagy and elevated him to the leadership of the Communist government. To secure his position, he instigated a repressive regime which led to the execution, with or without trial, of hundreds of alleged opponents, supporters of Nagy. He also had Nagy tried and executed in secret in 1958. In 1963, he eased his iron grip as the country had been brought to submission, and in 1968 he created a New Economic Policy. This created greater economic freedom, as some small-scale private economic activity was allowed. In part through the generous provision of Western loans, in the 1970s and 1980s the country became relatively prosperous by comparison with its *Comecon neighbours. However, the dominant state sector remained moribund, as available funds were used to subsidize consumption rather than modernize industry. The increasingly desperate state of the Hungarian economy led to his replacement as General Secretary of the Communist Party in May 1988, whereupon he was given the ceremonial title of president of the party.

Kadima (Israel)
A centre-right party founded by Ariel *Sharon in 2005. Sharon created the party after *Likud failed to support his plans for imposing a unilateral peace settlement on Palestine. Neither the details of Sharon's plans, nor other parts of the party's programme, had been worked out when Sharon suffered a severe stroke on 4 January 2006. Led by Ehud *Olmert thereafter, the party emerged as the strongest party from the 2006 elections, gaining 26 seats. It entered a coalition with *Labour, but lost in popularity owing to Olmert's handling of the war against *Hezbollah in 2006. This forced Olmert to

extend the coalition to encompass the ultra-nationalist Yisrale Beitenu party, weakening Kadima's distinctiveness yet further, Olmert's unpopularity persisted, however, so that the party continued to suffer from a lack of sense of direction and leadership.

KADU (Kenyan African Democratic Union), see KENYA

Kaganovich, Lazar Moisevich (b. 22 Nov. 1893, d. 25 July 1991). Soviet politician
Born in Kabany (near Kiev) into a poor Jewish family, he joined the *Bolsheviks in 1911. He fought in World War I, and after the *Russian Revolution in October 1917 Kaganovich helped to spread Bolshevism in *Belarus. He went to Petrograd (formerly St Petersburg) as a member of the Constituent Assembly, and acted as a political commissar of the *Red Army during the *Russian Civil War. His subsequent career was largely based on his participation in *Stalin's terror and the *Great Purge. In 1925, he became head of the Ukrainian Communist Party, and in 1928 became a Secretary of the Soviet Communist Party's Central Committee. As head of the agricultural section of the party (1929–34), he ruthlessly carried out *Stalin's collectivization policies. He was also First Secretary of the Moscow Party Committee (i.e. Mayor of Moscow), 1930–5. He became responsible for transport (1935), heavy industry (1937), the fuel industry (1939), and the oil industry (1940).

Kaganovich used the general uncertainties of the Great Purge, in which he allowed the execution even of his brother, to push through his targets mercilessly, eliminating all who stood in his way. During World War II, he extended the terror to the military, when he was responsible for the army's prosecution system. He returned as Chairman of the Ukrainian Party in 1947, though by this time he was already eclipsed by his erstwhile underling, Khrushchev. The latter outmanoeuvred him after Stalin's death, and compromised him greatly with his anti-Stalinist campaigns of 1956. He joined *Molotov and *Malenkov in the 'anti-party group' which attempted to oust Khrushchev in 1957. When this failed, he was made a manager at a cement factory in Sverdlovsk.

Kagawa Toyohiko (b. 10 July 1888, d. 23 Apr. 1960). Japanese Christian missionary
An early life filled with tragedy would seem to have been a great influence on Kagawa's later career. As a child, Kagawa lost both his parents and home. At middle school he was baptized a Christian, and went on to study

theology at Meiji University. Despite suffering from tuberculosis, Kagawa decided to devote his life to being a missionary in Kobe's slums. Kagawa's social work included involvement in labour and tenant disputes throughout Japan. His outspoken behaviour and links with the USA prompted the suspicions of the authorities who arrested him, although he was released shortly afterwards at the request of a prominent member of the government in 1926. After the war, Kagawa participated in the formation of the Japan *Socialist Party and he remained a prominent figure within the party. Kagawa also produced a number of books during his career, including the novel *Before the Dawn* (*Shisen o koete*) in 1924, which proved to be a best-seller.

Kaiser Wilhelm II, see WILHELM II

Kalinin, Mikhail Ivanovich (b. 19 Nov. 1875, d. 3 June 1946). Head of state of the Soviet Union 1919–46
Born in Verkhniaia Troitsa (near Tver, whose name was changed to Kalinin until 1990 in his honour), he became an active revolutionary after joining the Social Democratic (Workers') Party in 1898. He joined its *Bolshevik faction in 1903. He joined the *Russian Revolutions of 1905 and 1917, and became Mayor of Petrograd (St Petersburg). In 1919 Kalinin acted as Chairman of the Central Executive Committee and *de facto* head of state, a function that became official upon the foundation of the USSR in 1922. Subsequently, he was remarkable less for his actions, than for his unique ability as an old comrade of *Lenin to escape the *Great Purge and die a natural death, remaining in his (albeit ceremonial) high office throughout. He achieved this through a peculiar combination of adaptability, cunning, and blandness.

Kamenev, Lev Borisovich (22 July 1883, d. 25 Aug. 1936). Soviet politician
Born Lev Borisovich Rosenfeld in Moscow, he was forced to abandon his law degree at Moscow University in 1902 owing to his political activities. He went to Paris, where he became a friend of *Lenin, and married *Trotsky's sister. He returned to Russia in 1903, working for the *Bolsheviks until 1908, when he became joint editor of the party newspaper, *Proletaryi* (The Proletarian) in Switzerland. Back in Russia in 1914, he became a member of the *Duma in 1914 as well as editor of *Pravda*, but was arrested in 1915. He returned to Petrograd after the *Russian Revolution of February 1917, and became chairman of the Second Congress of

*Soviets in 1917. In 1918–26 he served as chairman of the Moscow Soviet (i.e. Mayor of Moscow). In the politically tempestuous 1920s, he lacked the political judgement which alone could have saved him (or any other of Lenin's former associates) from *Stalin's wrath. Thus, he first supported *Zinoviev and Stalin against Trotsky, but then sided with his brother-in-law against Stalin, taking sides with the 'Left Opposition' within the party. In 1935 he was arrested and sentenced to five years' imprisonment. Then, he was retried in the first of Stalin's show trials which marked the beginning of the *Great Purge. He was sentenced to death and shot, while Stalin's vindictiveness ensured the 'disappearance' of his entire family. He was rehabilitated in 1988.

Kampuchea, see CAMBODIA

KANU (Kenyan African National Union), see KENYA

Kapp Putsch (13–17 Mar. 1920)
After the German government disbanded further army and *Freikorps units to comply with the Treaty of *Versailles, one of the units affected marched on Berlin and declared its leader, Wolfgang Kapp (b. 1858, d. 1922), Chancellor. The government, forced to flee to Dresden and then Stuttgart, called a general strike which forced the insurrectionists to give up. The Kapp Putsch revealed the refusal of the army to defend the new German democracy against a coup from the military right, a fundamental source of weakness of the Weimar Republic throughout its existence.

Karadzic, Radovan (b. 19 June 1945). Bosnian Serb leader 1991–6
One of the main aggressors in the *Bosnian Civil War (1992–5), he was born at Petnica (Montenegro), and moved to *Sarajevo in 1960. He studied medicine and became a psychiatrist. The breakup of Yugoslavia propelled him into politics. Despite his Montenegrine heritage, he became accepted as leader of the Serb minority in *Bosnia through his fiery and radical rhetoric. He founded the Serbian Democratic Party in 1990, and on 24 October 1991 became President of the self-proclaimed Serb Republic of Bosnia-Hercegovina. With his capital in Banja Luka, a suburb of Sarajevo, throughout the civil war he claimed most of Sarajevo, as well as around 70 per cent of Bosnian territory, for his state. Supported by his patron, the Serbian President *Milošević, his forces made significant advances into Bosnian

territory. He was accused of war crimes before an international tribunal for the atrocities committed by his soldiers. Once the USA became involved in the search for a peace settlement his luck began to turn, as Bosnians and Croats agreed to unite in their fight against the Serbs. Forced by Milošević to give in, he reluctantly agreed to the *Dayton Agreement. In 1996 he bowed to international (and Serbian) pressure and resigned from office. He was indicted at the International Criminal Tribunal for the Former Yugoslavia in The Hague, but remained a fugitive from justice.

Karamanlis, Konstantinos (b. 8 Mar. 1907, d. 23 Apr. 1998). Prime Minister of Greece 1955–63, 1974–80; President 1980–5
Born near Serres, Macedonia, he qualified and practised as a lawyer until serving in parliament in 1935–6 for the Populist Party. He re-entered parliament in 1946, and subsequently contributed greatly to Greek reconstruction after World War II. Karamanlis joined the Greek Rally Party in 1951 and, after a successful period as Minister for Public Works, he succeeded Alexandros Papagos as Prime Minister. In 1955, he also founded the Greek Radical Union Party. His attempt to achieve domestic stability through US aid and membership of the EEC (*European integration) failed. In 1967, the election victory of his opponent, Georgios *Papandreou, precipitated the *Greek colonels' coup. He went into exile in Paris, but returned in 1974 to supervise the country's transition to democracy. He founded the New Democracy Party, which became the major right-wing force in Greek politics. He now successfully engineered Greek membership of the EEC and, as President, was a respected elder statesman with a soothing influence in the heated atmosphere of Greek politics, especially under the premiership of Andreas *Papandreou.

Károlyi of Nagykárolyi, Mihály Count (b. 4 Mar. 1875, d. 19 Mar. 1955). Prime Minister of Hungary 1918–19
Born in Budapest, he entered parliament in 1905. Of liberal views, he favoured a less pro-German policy for the *Austro-Hungarian Empire and equal rights for all nations within it. As leader of the Independence Party from 1913, on 31 October 1918 he became Prime Minister, and thereafter President of Hungary. He tried hard, but not very successfully, to cope with the problems of demobilization and economic collapse that followed the end of the war. When these problems were compounded by the loss of what Hungarians regarded as

their historic heartland, *Transylvania, the national outrage was such that he was deposed by Béla *Kun on 21 March 1919. He went into exile, but returned to become Hungarian ambassador to Paris (1947–9), where he sought and gained renewed exile.

Karzai, Hamid (b. 24 Dec 1957). President of Afghanistan, 2004–
Born in Kandahar, he studied political science in India before returning to Afghanistan in 1983, where he engaged in the struggle against Soviet occupation. Following the collapse of Soviet occupation, Karzai supported the *Taliban until 1996, when he joined the opposition. Of an influential Afghan family, Karzai was selected at an international conference of exiled Afghan leaders in 2002 as Chairman of the Afghan Transitional Administration. In 2004, he became President of Afghanistan's first elected government. Karzai relied very much on local leaders across the country for the implementation of policies. Much liked abroad, he was able to secure massive international reconstruction aid for the country, though much of this was spent ineffectively. The slow pace of progress undermined his authority, as did the Taliban revival in the south.

Kasavubu, Joseph (b. ?1910, d. 24 Mar. 1969). President of the Democratic Republic of Congo (later Zaïre) 1960–5
Born near Tshela, he became a teacher and then a civil servant. In the early 1950s, he became active in undercover nationalist associations to free the Congo of Belgians. In 1955 he became president of the Alliance des Bakongo, a cultural association of his Bakongo people, and subsequently turned it into a powerful political organization. On independence he became head of state. He formed a coalition with the Mouvement National Congolais (National Congolese Movement) of *Lumumba, whom he ousted early in 1961. In 1965 he himself was deposed by General *Mobutu in a bloodless military coup. He retired to live on a farm.

Kashmir

An Indian princely state which has been claimed by India and Pakistan since independence in 1947, and was the subject of two *Indo-Pakistan Wars. Initially, its Hindu Maharaja, Sir Hari Singh, had hoped to lead it to independence. Faced with insurgent Muslim border tribesmen, however, he declared his accession to India and called for military aid from the Indian army. Since the majority of the population was Muslim, Pakistan challenged the Maharaja's decision. After sporadic fighting, the first Indo-Pakistan War was ended in 1949, when a UN commission established a demarcation line allocating Azad Kashmir to Pakistan and the remainder of the state to India. The Maharaja abdicated in 1951 in favour of his son, but the state assembly declared the state a republic, and in January 1957 it was formally integrated within the Union of India as the state of Jammu and Kashmir. In the *Indo-Chinese War of 1962, substantial areas in the north-east were conceded to China. Renewed fighting in 1965 ended again in deadlock.

Kashmir continued to be claimed in its entirety by both India and Pakistan. Throughout the 1980s there were continued riots and protests to demand greater autonomy, as Jammu and Kashmir was subject to direct rule from the Union government in New Delhi. These uprisings, which claimed around 20,000 lives between 1990 and 1996, led to a promise of autonomy status by India's newly elected United Front government in 1996. From 1997, India and Pakistan took up negotiations again, but these yielded little results. India refused foreign help in settling the conflict, while Pakistan continued to support Muslim guerrilla forces operating in the Indian part. After the *September 11 attacks, Pakistan's position became more difficult. Its support for the US against the *Taliban limited Pakistan's leader, General *Musharraf, in his ability to aggravate *Islamic fundamentalist opinion yet further and rein in the secret service and radical Islamic factions in Kashmir. This brought India and Pakistan to the brink of a further military confrontation, as over a million soldiers faced each other in May 2002. A war between the two nuclear powers, however, presented a huge risk not only to international security but also to the *War on Terrorism, in which Pakistan was a crucial ally of the US.

Kassem, Abdul Karim, see QASSEM, ABDUL KARIM

Katayama Tetsu (b. 28 July 1887, d. 30 May 1978). First Socialist Prime Minister of Japan 1947–8
A graduate from Tokyo University's Faculty of Law, Katayama participated in the foundation of the Socialist People's Party in December 1926. He became its first Secretary-General, and in 1930 he was elected to the Diet. Although Katayama went on to take part in the formation of the Socialist Masses Party two years later, he was forced from the party with other leaders in 1940, because he abstained in a Diet vote to expel a member of

the assembly who had voiced criticisms of the army's conduct in China. After the war Katayama became secretary-general in the new Japan *Socialist Party which he helped to organize. In 1946 he was elected party chairman and in the following year he became Japan's first Prime Minister under the *Japanese constitution in an alliance with the Democratic Party and the People's Cooperative Party. While this coalition government was short-lived, it succeeded in overseeing the dissolution of the *zaibatsu (financial conglomerates), the institution of Japan's modern civil service system, and the introduction of an unemployment insurance system. Nevertheless, his premiership was later dismissed by his opponents and by members of his own party, for its failure to establish a foothold for his party in government for much of the postwar period. With *Nishio Suehiro, he later formed the DSP (1959), leaving that party in 1964.

Katô Takaaki ('Komei') (b. 3 Jan. 1860, d. 28 Jan. 1926). Prime Minister of Japan 1924–5

Katô's early career was with the Mitsubishi *zaibatsu, which always gave him its full support. In 1887 he entered public life and spent time in the Ministry of Finance and the Ministry of Foreign Affairs. During an earlier period as a student in England and later on diplomatic duties in London, Katô had developed a close affinity with Great Britain and was an advocate of an Anglo-Japanese alliance. As Foreign Minister (1913–15) he resigned following the presentation to China of the *Twenty-One Demands. He became president of the Kenseikai (predecessor to the *Minseitô) and was leader of the opposition until 1924, when his party came to power. During his two years as Prime Minister Katô introduced universal male suffrage, reduced the size and influence of the army, and lessened the power of the House of Peers. At the same time, however, he sponsored repressive legislation such as the *Peace Preservation Law and introduced military training into high school. Despite this, Katô's government is remembered as a high point in the democratic interlude that Japan experienced between the wars.

Katrina, Hurricane (29 August 2005)

A hurricane which devastated much of New Orleans, and led to the largest US domestic relief effort in history. New Orleans lies mostly below sea level, and is protected from the sea by a series of dams. Owing to decades of chronic under-investment, the dams could only withstand a hurricane up to force three— Hurricane Katrina hit the city at between force four and force five. The dams burst, flooding 80 per cent of the city. Over 75,000 citizens, who had ignored earlier warnings to leave New Orleans, fled to the higher-lying areas of the city, with many finding refuge in the Superdome. There they stayed for days without evacuation or outside help, amidst a breakdown of public order. Military convoys with relief did not arrive until 2 September, with large-scale evacuation beginning on 3 September. At local, state and federal level, aid and evacuation programmes only became effective three days later. In Louisiana, 1079 people died, while in neighbouring Mississippi, 231 died.

The mismanagement of the relief effort, and the apparent insensitivity of the President (who did not visit the area for days), led to a dramatic decline in Bush's popularity. It also raised accusations of racial prejudice, with campaigners for *civil rights asserting that relief would have been more forthcoming had the victims not been overwhelmingly poor and Black, but rich and White. *Congress approved a reconstruction budget of $200 billion, but much of the money's effectiveness in subsequent years was undermined by corruption.

Katyn Massacre

During their occupation of the eastern half of Poland in accordance with the *Hitler–Stalin Pact in 1939, the Soviet army imprisoned around 14,000 officers of the Polish armed forces, among them many conscripts including intellectuals and artists. These were secretly, but systematically, shot by officers of the Soviet *NKVD/*KGB, on *Stalin's orders. Traces of this act were only discovered in April 1943, when the mass grave of around 4,500 of them was discovered in the Katyn Forest (near Smolensk). The *Red Cross subsequently verified that they had been shot by Soviet soldiers, and the Polish government-in-exile demanded an explanation from the USSR. *Stalin denied any involvement, and used the accusations to break off relations with the Polish government-in-exile. Even though the Soviet version of events constituted the official doctrine adopted by the Polish Communist government, the event soured relations between the two countries for decades. Only in 1991 did the new Russian government under *Yeltsin admit that Stalin had, indeed, ordered the execution.

Kaunda, Kenneth David (b. 28 Apr. 1924). President of Zambia 1964–91

Born at Lubwe, he became a teacher and a minister in the Presbyterian *Church of

Scotland. Politically active from the early 1950s, he advanced to become president of the Zambian National Congress in 1958, and of the United National Independence Party (UNIP) in 1960. He won the elections of 1962, and became Zambia's first President upon independence. A strong critic of Western *capitalism, he created a socialist state, and became one of the world's leading opponents of *Smith's Rhodesian regime, as well as of *apartheid in South Africa. This raised his international profile and, as one of Africa's most respected elder statesmen, he was president of the OAU (*African Union), 1983–8. Despite his own outspokenness, he did not tolerate criticism at home, however, and suppressed two revolts in 1986 and 1990. As a result of the country's economic difficulties, discontent became such that he allowed multi-party elections in 1991, which he lost to *Chiluba. He remained an influential voice in public affairs, and was a hostile critic of Chiluba.

Kautsky, Karl (b. 16 Oct. 1854, d. 17 Oct. 1938). Marxist thinker

Born in Prague, he joined the Austrian Social Democrats while a student in Vienna. He lived with Engels in London (1885–90), after whose death he became the main interpreter of *Marxism. Together with Eduard *Bernstein he later wrote the Erfurt Programme of 1891, which committed the German *Social Democratic Party to Marxism, though he came to criticize Bernstein's revisionism and his undoctrinaire pragmatism. He vehemently opposed *Lenin's development of *Marxism-Leninism in Russia. From Germany, he moved back to Vienna in 1924, from where he emigrated to Amsterdam following the *Anschluss.

Kazakhstan

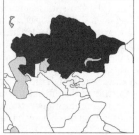

A vast central Asian state rich in mineral resources, the country has been stable since independence in 1991, but at the cost of democracy.

The territory came under the sovereignty of the Russian Empire from 1731. It joined the Soviet Union as an integral part of the Russian Socialist Soviet Republic in 1922. In 1925 it received greater autonomy as an Autonomous Soviet Socialist Republic, and in 1936 it became a distinct member of the Union. During

*Stalin's reign, it was used as a dumping ground for deported population groups from other parts of the USSR. Thus, it became home to a substantial minority of Ukrainians (5.2 per cent), Germans (4.1 per cent), and Crimean Tartars (2 per cent). It became independent upon the collapse of the Soviet Union in December 1991, and it sought to establish a close union with the central Asian republics of Uzbekistan and Kyrgyzstan, as well as to foster good relations with Russia.

Despite Kazakhstan's great wealth in mineral resources, and because of the government's reluctance to introduce tough market reforms, during the mid-1990s the economy suffered from high inflation (over 2,200 per cent in 1994) and a rapid decline in industrial production. This had formidable political repercussions, as the populist President, Narsultan Nasabayev (elected 1991, 1995), used the economic crisis to extend his presidential powers and rule over a parliament reluctant to impose economic reforms. His presidential powers were further extended in a constitutional amendment 1999, whereupon in a rigged election he was re-elected with over 80 per cent of the popular vote. In following years, the freedom of the press and freedom of speech were further curtailed. The economy experienced a substantial boom from 2000, growing at around 10 per cent per year, with a pipeline completed in 2005 transporting Kazakh oil direct to China. In 2006, the leader of the opposition was murdered by men linked to the Kazakh secret service.

Keating, Paul John (b. 18 Jan. 1944). Prime Minister of Australia 1991–6

Born in Bankstown (Sydney), Keating joined the Australian *Labor Party (ALP) in 1959, becoming President of the New South Wales (NSW) ALP Youth Council in 1966. In 1968, he became an officer for the Federated Municipal and Shire Council Employees' Union, and in 1969 was elected to the House of Representatives. Serving briefly as Minister for Northern Australia under *Whitlam in 1975, he became chairman of the pivotal New South Wales branch of the ALP in 1979. As treasurer under *Hawke, he became his principal lieutenant, overseeing the economic boom of the mid-1980s and ensuring the maintenance of good labour relations through his close contacts with the trade unions.

Keating was unsuccessful in his challenge to Hawke for the party leadership in June 1991, and resigned. However, as Labor looked destined to lose the next elections, in December 1991 Keating managed to replace Hawke as Labor leader and Prime Minister.

Against all predictions, he managed to win the 1993 elections. He continued his predecessor's careful economic policies which maintained a stable inflation rate, but was more prepared to accommodate the grievances of *Aborigines and Torres Strait Islanders in the face of opposition by the individual states. He effectively sought to increase his personal popularity through appealing to Australian nationalist sentiment, leading moves to abolish the monarchy (which was still shared with the UK) and spearheading (and fuelling) national outrage against the resumption of French nuclear testing in the Pacific. He failed to address more immediate problems such as the high unemployment rate and the strength of the *trade-union grip on the economy. After losing the 1996 elections to *Howard, Keating resigned from political life and took up a number of visiting professorships.

Keitel, Wilhelm (b. 22 Sept. 1882, d. 16 Oct. 1946). Military adviser to Hitler
From 1938 to 1945 he was Chief of the Supreme Command of the Armed Forces, and he became infamous not only for his arrogance, but also for his complete subjection to Hitler's whims. In 1940, he led the German-French armistice negotiations, and on 8 May 1945 Keitel signed the unconditional surrender of the German armed forces. He was sentenced to death at the *Nuremberg Trials.

Kekkonen, Urho Kaleva (b. 3 Sept. 1900, d. 31 Aug. 1986). President of Finland 1956–81
Born in Pielavesi, he studied law at Helsinki University and in 1936 entered the Eduskunta (parliament) for the Agrarian Party. He was Minister of Justice (1936–7), Minister of the Interior (1937–9), and four times Prime Minister in the period 1950–6. As President, he maintained a careful balance between good relationships with the West, and particularly with his Scandinavian neighbours, on the one hand, and the Soviet Union on the other. His efforts to reduce the polarization caused by the *Cold War were crowned with success at the *Helsinki Conference (1973–5). Owing to his domestic popularity, his tenure was extended by special legislation, but he was forced to resign in 1981 because of ill health.

Kellogg–Briand Pact (Pact of Paris)
(27 Aug. 1928)
An agreement suggested by *Briand and developed further by the US Secretary of State Frank Kellogg (b. 1856, d. 1937). It strove to guarantee a lasting international peace through the condemnation of war and the institution of a court of arbitration for the settlement of all international disputes. It was signed by fifteen states and subsequently adopted by forty-five further nations, including the Soviet Union. However, the absence of any sanctions that could be imposed on violators of the agreement rendered it virtually useless, and exposed the fundamental weakness of the existing international system.
LEAGUE OF NATIONS

Kemal Mustafa, see ATATÜRK

Kennedy, Edward Moore ('Teddy')
(b. 22 Feb. 1932). US Senator 1962–
Born at Boston, Massachusetts, like his brothers John and Robert he studied at Harvard, as well as the International Law School at The Hague and the University of Virginia. During the 1950s he served on his brothers' campaign staffs and learnt the rules of political organization before succeeding his brother as *Democratic Senator for his home state. In 1969, he became the Democratic whip in the Senate. Shortly thereafter, his presidential aspirations were effectively destroyed by his involvement in a car accident at **Chappaquidick**, in which his passenger, Mary Jo Kopeckne, was drowned, raising serious (and recurrent) questions about his moral values (he reported the incident only the following day). His subsequent challenge to Jimmy *Carter, the incumbent President, for the Democrat nomination in the 1980 *primary elections was unsuccessful. Nevertheless, he remained one of the most influential members of the Senate and a liberal standard-bearer. He became a crucial mediator in the *Northern Ireland peace process under President *Clinton. Under George W. *Bush, Kennedy was one of the most senior Senators leading the opposition to the President's taxation and social policies.

Kennedy, John ('Jack') Fitzgerald ('JFK') (b. 29 May 1917, d. 22 Nov. 1963). 35th US President 1961–3

Early career (up to 1952) Born in Brookline, Massachusetts, of Irish Catholic descent. John Kennedy (later known as JFK) was the second male child of **Joseph ('Joe') Patrick Kennedy**, an extremely wealthy banker whose money had been built up on the stock market, in the cinema industry, and the bootleg liquor industry at the time of *prohibition. Joe Kennedy had presidential ambitions himself, and was prominent in the *New Deal era. He was, however, compromised by his *appeasement tendencies towards the *Nazis whilst ambassador to London between 1938 and 1941. John F. Kennedy had been born with a deformed spine and an adrenal deficiency, which were complicated in later life by severe injuries sustained in World War II, when the navy boat of which he had command was sunk by the Japanese. Following the collapse of his own presidential hopes, his father's fierce political ambition was transferred to his first-born son, Joe Kennedy, but following Joe's death in World War II, John assumed the burden.

Senator (1952–60) John was elected to *Congress as a *Democrat with the help of his father's money and newspaper contacts in 1946. He was held in low regard by his colleagues in the House of Representatives, where he was seen as a playboy. In 1952 he was elected to the US Senate after a masterful campaign organized by his father and brother, Robert *Kennedy. Hospitalization whilst undergoing a corrective operation on his spine caused him to miss the vote censuring Senator *McCarthy, though many suspected that the strongly anti-Communist Kennedy may have wanted to avoid the vote anyway. He narrowly missed the 1956 nomination for Vice-President after delivering a stirring speech to the Democratic convention of that year, but following his re-election to the Senate in 1958, he decided to run for President in 1960.

Presidency (1961–3) In one of the closest elections in US history, Kennedy won 49.9 per cent of the popular vote, defeating Vice-President Richard Nixon by 0.3 per cent, after a campaign again organized by his brother Robert. The younger generation was drawn to his self-effacing wit, grace, dynamism, and youth, and he skilfully exploited his image as a young father, and representative of the junior officers of World War II. In his first year, he was mainly occupied by the *Cold War. He proposed a 'Peace Corps', and an *Apollo programme to place a man in space and then upon the moon by 1969.

The disastrous incursion of US-trained, *CIA-sponsored Cuban exiles into the *Bay of Pigs in Cuba in 1961 (to which Kennedy refused to lend direct US military support) earned him the lasting and ferocious enmity of a majority of Cuban Americans. His, difficult summit meeting with *Khrushchev in Vienna encouraged the Soviet leader to believe that Kennedy was lightweight. This perception culminated in the *Cuban Missile Crisis of October 1962, which proved a turning point of his fortunes in foreign policy. In early 1963 he signed an atmospheric nuclear test ban Treaty (*disarmament), while in a later speech at Washington University he called for global awareness of the need for states to respect common resources and to understand each other. In the summer of that year he delivered a rousing speech in front of the *Berlin Wall.

At home the *civil rights movement and the prospect of a re-election campaign in 1964 caused him to become more activist in the support of minority groups and to emphasize his liberal credentials. He began to prepare health insurance and welfare proposals, and talked of an anti-poverty programme. He was also responsible for the deepening involvement of US troops in Vietnam. His assassination in Dallas, Texas, has aroused deep controversy and doubts in the report of the commission headed by Chief Justice *Warren, which concluded that a lone assassin, Lee Harvey Oswald, was responsible.

Kennedy's bills to raise the minimum wage, to promote public works, to modify urban renewal programmes, and to cut taxes were all passed in the face of an often hostile Congress, and his legislative record compares reasonably well with that of the *Truman Administration. However, his Presidency is remembered in the popular mind for its style, not substance—for its youthful sophistication, its spirit of adventure, and its tragic end.

Kennedy, Joseph Patrick, see KENNEDY, JOHN FITZGERALD

Kennedy, Robert Francis (b. 20 Nov. 1925, d. 6 June 1968). US politician
Born at Brookline, Massachusetts, he studied at Harvard and the University of Virginia Law School, where he obtained an LL B in 1951. He entered politics as a campaign manager for his older brother, John F. *Kennedy, and then became a congressional legal counsel. When John became President in 1961, he was appointed Attorney-General, from which position he launched a fierce attack on organized crime and took steps to address the problem of racial discrimination. However, he was unable to curtail effectively the power of the *FBI and its director, *Hoover. Though his relations with President *Johnson were difficult because of a long-standing personal feud, he continued to serve as Attorney-General after John Kennedy's assassination until 1964, when he won election to the US Senate from New York. There, he developed a reputation as a compassionate liberal in matters of social and welfare policy, and as an opponent of Johnson's policies in Vietnam. He finally condemned the war in south-east Asia and declared his candidacy for President in March 1968, following the *Tet offensive. In a tumultuous campaign, he won a series of primary elections culminating in his victory

in California, where he was assassinated a few minutes after learning of his success.

Kenya

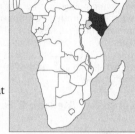

A culturally heterogeneous country whose economy has suffered from decades of mismanagement and graft.

Colonial domination

(up to 1963) An east African country which came under British influence in 1888, and was declared a Protectorate in 1895. The construction of a railway to Lake Victoria, which connected Nairobi to the coast, heralded the penetration of British influence into the country's interior. In 1920 it became a British Crown Colony. The good farmland was steadily taken up by White farmers and reserved for their exclusive use (albeit with African labour), while reserves on poorer soil were created for African peasants. This treatment of the various Kenyan peoples, the most populous of which were the Kikuyus, sparked off increasing resistance and led to the establishment of the Kikuyu Central Association (KCA) in 1924, under the leadership of *Kenyatta. It demanded restoration of, or compensation for, expropriated land, the expansion of education, and the removal of commercial restrictions on Africans in Kenya.

After the KCA was banned in 1940, the more broadly based Kenya African Union (KAU) was formed in 1944. In addition, a militant guerrilla movement began to emerge. Impatient with the KAU's moderation, its attacks on European settlers led to the violent *Mau Mau rebellion, 1952–9. As Kenya became all but ungovernable, the British were ready to discuss independence. This climate led in 1960 to the formation of the centralist **KANU (Kenyan African National Union)**, whose support came from the largest peoples (Kikuyu, Luo, and Kamba), and **KADU (Kenyan African Democratic Union)** under arap *Moi, which represented the smaller ethnic groups in demanding a decentralized state with strong regional autonomy.

KANU dominance (1961–2002)

The elections of 1961 were won by KANU, led by Kenyatta after his release from prison. He negotiated the country's independence on 12 December 1963. The political stability of the country was furthered by the dissolution of

KADU, many of whose members joined KANU, which developed into the country's single party. As a consequence, dissent was internalized, which allowed Kenyatta to maintain his regime with minimal repression. He established a market-oriented economy, but carried out land reforms and led a programme of 'Africanization', whereby important foreign-owned businesses were nationalized. The country became largely self-sufficient for food, while its industries remained relatively developed.

Kenyatta was succeeded by the former KADU leader, arap Moi, who claimed to continue Kenyatta's policies, while at the same time introducing a wide campaign to eliminate the alleged corruption of the Kenyatta years.

As the economy began to decline, owing to falling prices for its exports (e.g. coffee and tea) in 1982, his rule became increasingly authoritarian, in order to overcome growing popular unrest. In 1991, international aid was suspended in order to persuade arap Moi to introduce badly needed economic austerity measures, and to establish a multi-party democracy. As a result, the currency was devalued by 25 per cent and public expenditure reduced.

A general election was held in 1992, which was won by arap Moi, while his KANU party gained 112 out of 200 seats. However, ethnic tensions continued, and led to over 2,000 deaths and 250,000 refugees between 1992 and 1995. *Amnesty International concluded in 1995 that, despite the country's apparent democratization, oppositional leaders faced more harassment or persecution than ever before. Popular discontent rose after a three-year drought dramatically increased widespread poverty. Foreign attention was directed towards Kenya in 1998, when terrorists directed by *Bin Laden attacked the US embassy. Arap Moi's half-hearted attempts to respond to international pressure led by the *IMF and the *World Bank to introduce anti-corruption measures produced few results. A different response to the domestic and international pressure was attempted in 2001, when four members of the opposition (National Development Party) joined the government.

Contemporary politics (since 2002) In 2002, Mwai Kibaki of the National Rainbow Coalition won the elections with an absolute majority, triggering the first handover of government to the opposition in Kenya's history. As corruption continued, however, Kibaki became deeply unpopular. In 2006, three of his ministers had to resign owing to a range of corruption allegations, which also affected arap Moi's sons. In 2005, Kibaki lost a referendum for a new Constitution that would have increased his power. The political turmoil rendered the government unable to deal with Kenya's economic problems, notably the drought affecting the north of the country from 2000 to 2007.

Kenyatta, Jomo (b. 10 Oct. 1891, d. 22 Aug. 1978). Prime Minister of Kenya 1963–4; President 1964–78

Born in Gatandu and a member of the Kikuyu people. Politically active since the early 1920s, he became general secretary of the Kikuyu Central Association (*Kenya) in 1924, and in 1929 went to London to press the Association's demands for greater African equality. During his time in England, he developed his political ideas. In 1945 he founded the Pan-African Federation with *Nkrumah, whereupon the two became role models not only for their own respective countries, but for all Black African leaders. He returned to Kenya in 1946, but was arrested in 1952 for his alleged leadership of the *Mau Mau rebellion. After the KANU (Kenyan African National Union) won the 1961 elections in preparation for independence, he was released on 14 August 1961, and became KANU president. He became Prime Minister in 1963, and remained in this position after independence. On 12 December 1964, he became his country's first President. Against the left wing of the party, he established a pro-Western economic policy and successfully attracted investment into the country. Through his immense status, integrity, pragmatism, and popularity, he was able to keep Kenya's forty or so different peoples united.

Kérékou, Mathieu Ahmed (b. 2 Sept. 1933). President of Benin 1972–91, 1996–2006

Born in the provincial capital of Natitingou (western Benin), he enlisted in the French colonial army and became an officer in the armed forces of the newly independent state in 1961. In a decade of political instability and military coups he became vice-president of the military revolutionary council and took part in the overthrow of President Soglo in 1967. He only became politically active in 1972, however, when in a coup he declared himself President, Prime Minister, and Defence Minister all in one. His power was rubber-stamped by a Revolutionary People's Council in 1980, 1984, and 1989. In 1987 he took the first steps toward democratization by resigning as chief of the military. He gave way to popular protest and allowed presidential elections in 1991. Following his defeat he

became one of the few leaders of a Black African state to resign voluntarily, only to win a narrow election victory in 1996. Subsequently, he pursued a moderate economic policy, but he was unable to reduce his country's economic reliance on France on the one hand, and Nigeria on the other. He was re-elected in 2001, but did not run again in 2006 because of the constitutional age limit of 70 for presidential candidates.

Kerensky, Aleksandr Fedorovich (b. 4 May 1881, d. 11 June 1970). Prime Minister of Russia 1917

Born in *Lenin's home town of Simbirsk, he grew up there and in Tashkent, and obtained a law degree from St Petersburg University in 1904. Kerensky was elected to the fourth *Duma in 1912. A moderate socialist, he enjoyed the support of the *Mensheviks, though he never joined the party. After the *Russian Revolution in February 1917, he boosted his own position as deputy leader of the two rival political bodies, the *Duma and the Petrograd (formerly St Petersburg) *Soviet. He joined the provisional government as Minister of Justice and then Minister of Defence. He was also Prime Minister from 21 July 1917, and took personal command of the armed forces in August 1917. He staked his authority on a renewed military offensive against the Germans. The offensive failed and plunged the country into even greater military and economic chaos. With his authority eroding, he refused to acquiesce to the *Bolsheviks' more radical demands of land reforms and the transfer of political power to the soviets. All this contributed to his loss of popular support, and left him with no defence when Lenin launched the October Revolution. He went underground, and emigrated in 1918.

Kerr, Sir John, see WHITLAM, EDWARD GOUGH

Keynes, John Maynard, Baron Keynes of Tilton (b. 5 June 1883, d. 21 Apr. 1946). British economist

Born in Cambridge, and educated there and before that at Eton. He worked in the India Office (1906–8), and then returned to teach economics at Cambridge. During World War I, he worked at the Treasury, which he represented at the *Paris Peace Conference. Keynes was highly critical of the conference's results, though. In his book *The Economic Consequences of the Peace* (1919), Keynes criticized the stifling *reparations which were bound to cripple Germany and make it a continued focus of instability. He continued to advise the government on economic policy, although he was a strong critic of *Churchill's return to the *Gold Standard in 1925 at the prewar parity. He was an active Liberal in the 1920s, when he began to articulate his view that government spending on public works could push the depressed economy back into equilibrium.

Keynes challenged the orthodox creed concerning the ability of the market to correct itself, most comprehensively in *The General Theory of Employment, Interest and Money* (1936), which became the origin of *Keynesianism. His ideas failed to make an impact on government policy in the 1930s. In 1940, however, he once again became a government economic adviser, and in 1945 he headed a delegation to the USA which secured a large loan for Britain. His advocacy of government intervention to ensure full employment influenced the *Beveridge Report, and was influential at the *Bretton Woods Conference of 1944, which led to the establishment of the *International Monetary Fund, and the *World Bank. Until the 1970s his arguments underpinned the economic policy of governments in the postwar years, both in Britain and in western and northern Europe.

Keynesianism

An economic theory developed by *Keynes which holds that imperfections in the economy can be corrected through government policy. For example, if there is a recession, there is excess supply of goods over demand. The government can stimulate demand e.g. through welfare payments or employment schemes. As individuals thus receive higher incomes, their demand will increase. To finance these schemes, the government will have to raise more debts, which pushes up interest rates. This reduces supply because it becomes more expensive for producers to expand through loans. In this way, a government can increase demand and reduce supply until an equilibrium is re-established.

Keynes's ideas formed the basis of economic policy in most industrialized nations after World War II, but fell out of fashion owing to the inability of Keynesian demand management to cope with the economic recession of the 1970s, when rising inflation coincided with rising unemployment. During the late 1970s and the 1980s, it was replaced as the dominant economic theory by *monetarism. Concerns raised by the progress of *globalization, however, have raised awareness about the potential costs of unbridled monetarism. In response,

economists have re-shaped Keynes's ideas into neo-Keynesianism, which developed into a popular economic theory during the 1990s.

KGB (**K**omitet **G**osudarstvennoi **B**ezopasnosti, Committee for State Security)
The name for the Soviet Security Service since 1954, which included the operations of the *NKVD. It was to secure *Communist rule, supervise and eliminate all internal opposition, protect the state borders, and control the state administration and bureaucracy. In addition, it conducted foreign intelligence (i.e. spy) missions, and worked actively to maintain Soviet hegemony in the *Warsaw Pact states of Eastern Europe. Its effectiveness was greatly improved under the alert *Andropov, who introduced new techniques such as the use of psychology against dissidents. During the 1980s, it had over one million official employees, plus an even greater number of informers. As part of *Gorbachev's reforms of *glasnost and *perestroika, its operations against dissidents were wound down in 1990. Because of its involvement in the 1991 *August coup, its old structures were dissolved. It was completely reorganized, and succeeded by a much smaller Russian security service.
STASI

Khalkin Gol, Frontier Battle of (1939)

A conflict that ensued when Soviet troops under General *Zhukov intervened on behalf of Mongolian troops against the Japanese army which was advancing from Manchuria. The resulting Soviet victory ensured that the Japanese were eager to avoid another military confrontation with the Soviet Union, and led to the Soviet–Japanese neutrality pact of 1941.

Khama, Sir Seretse (b. 1 July 1921, d. 13 July 1980). President of Botswana 1966–80

Kama was educated in South Africa and Britain, where he trained as a lawyer. Following his marriage to an Englishwoman he was prevented by the colonial authorities from returning to Bechuanaland to succeed to his chiefdom. Renouncing his right to succession, he returned in 1956, and in 1962 founded the Bechuanaland (later Botswana) Democratic Party. After its success in the first elections of 1965, he became Prime Minister, and in 1966 became President upon independence. His main achievement was the establishment of one of the most stable democracies in Africa. He also fostered careful opposition to the racially oppressive regimes in Rhodesia and South Africa, despite his country's economic dependence on the two countries.

Khamenei, Ayatollah Sayed Ali

(b. 1940), President of Iran, 1981–9; religious leader of Iran, 1989–

Born in Mashad, he was a student of Ayatollah *Khomeini and became active in the opposition movement against Shah Reza *Pahlavi. Following the Iranian revolution, he became member of the revolutionary council and from 1981–7 served as President of the Central Committee of the Islamic Republic Party. President of Iran from 1981, Khamenei succeeded Khomeini as Iran's supreme religious leader. As such, the conservative Khamenei had boundless authority to guard the country's Islamic constitution. In this capacity, he was engaged in constant personal and political conflict with the country's secular elected leader, *Khatami. He enjoyed a more harmonious relationship with Kathami's successor, *Ahmadi Nejad, from 2005.

Khan, Abdul Ghaffar, see RED SHIRTS

Khatami, Zayed Mohammed (b. Oct 1943). President of Iran, 1997–2005

Born in Ardakan, he studied Islam under *Khomeini in Qom, and philosophy in Isfahan. In 1978 he became the director of the Centre for Islam, Hamburg (Germany). Following the Islamic revolution in 1979 he returned to Iran, and became a Member of Parliament. The (relatively) liberal intellectual was Minister for Culture in 1981, but had to resign, and became director of the Tehran national library. He surprised observers when he ran for the Presidency in 1997 and was elected to succeed *Rafsanjani. He tried to liberalize the country, but met entrenched opposition from the Islamic political and religious establishment, notably from Ayatollah *Khamenei. Following his re-election with 77 per cent of the vote in 2001, he continued his policy of normalizing foreign relations with other Arab countries and the states of the EU. Despite his popularity, however, he was unable to overcome civil rights abuses by the police and the army, nor was he able to overcome the conservative Islamic zeal of the judiciary.

Khilafat movement

An Indian Muslim movement aroused in 1919 by the harsh treatment of the *Ottoman Empire after World War I, and specifically by the treatment of the Ottoman Sultan, who was also the Caliph (khilafa) of *Islam. It was led by two brothers, Muhammad Ali (b. 1878, d. 1931), and Shaukat Ali (b. 1873, d. 1938). Its grievances were integrated into *Gandhi's non-cooperation movement by the Indian National *Congress (1920–2), which marked a high point of Indian *nationalism, and of Muslim–Hindu cooperation. It declined after *Atatürk's abolition of the caliphate in 1924.

Khmer Rouge (Red Khmer)

A term used to describe Communist groups in Cambodia led by *Pol Pot, the Khmer being the dominant ethnic group of Cambodia. They originated from the foundation of the Communist Party of Cambodia in 1960, of which Pol Pot became general secretary in 1963. He soon began to organize peasant rebellions against the rule of *Sihanouk, and from 1968 his Revolutionary Army of Kampuchea fought in a civil war against the government forces. Supported and sustained by the North Vietnamese Communists, the Khmer Rouge became involved in the *Vietnam War, and were subject to US attacks. They received a decisive boost with the fall of *Saigon in 1975, and assumed power soon afterwards.

The ideology of the Khmer Rouge was based neither on Maoism nor on *Marxism-Leninism. Instead, they had two fundamental goals. First, they aspired to institutionalize an assumed superiority of the Khmer people over the country. Second, they aimed to exert total control over Cambodia and its peoples. To this end, over 200,000 non-Khmer Cambodians were butchered, while an economy subjected to total state control collapsed. The Khmer Rouge regime was defeated in 1979, when Vietnamese troops invaded Cambodia and installed a new Communist regime. Pol Pot fled to the countryside, from where his Khmer Rouge continued to wage a guerrilla war against successive Cambodian governments. They were increasingly isolated as the Cambodian government became more stable and assertive. Their numbers dwindled after many troops accepted an amnesty in 1995, and in 1999 the last Khmer Rouge surrendered.

Khomeini, Ruholla (b. 24 Sept. 1902, d. 3 June 1989). Iranian revolutionary leader

Early career Born in Khomein into a family of scholars, he became a student of Islam with one of the most important Islamic theologians at the time, Ayatollah Haieri, with whom he moved to Qom. He soon attracted a following through his charismatic speeches, and in 1952 gained the high honour of becoming an Ijtihad. Critical of Shah Reza *Pahlavi's secular regime since the 1940s, he was arrested for his protests against the 'White Revolution', which was partly designed to reduce the influence of Islam in Iranian society. He was exiled in 1964. He became one of the leaders of the Iranian exile movement in Iraq, which he was forced to leave in 1978, following an improvement in Iran-Iraq relations. By now the accepted religious leader of his people, the *Ayatollah advocated the establishment of an Islamic theocracy in response to the Shah's 'alien' Western regime. Church and state should not only be indistinguishable, but the former should be superior to the latter.

In power On 1 February 1979 he returned to Iran after the fall of the Shah and guided his country's revolutionary social, legal, and political development until his death. He supervised the enactment of an Islamic constitution, and used the *Iran–Iraq War, which he proclaimed to be a 'holy war', to strengthen his own spiritual and political authority. In practical politics, he heeded a deep mistrust of politicians, and thus maintained his power by playing off parliament against the government. The longevity of the Iran–Iraq War led him to accept a cease-fire with Saddam *Hussein, but only with extreme reluctance ('I have drunk poison'). His death led to the outbreak of a power struggle between moderates and radicals within the regime, which was ultimately won by *Rafsanjani. Khomeini inspired *Islamic fundamentalist leaders beyond Iran, as he confounded predictions of a seemingly inevitable advance of *globalization and 'modernization' at the expense of Islamic religion and culture.

Khrushchev, Nikita Sergeevich (b. 5 Apr. 1894, d. 11 Sept. 1971). First Secretary of the Communist Party of the Soviet Union 1953–64

Early career (up to 1957) Born in Kalinovka near Kursk close to the Ukraine, where he moved with his family in 1909. He became active for the *Bolsheviks in the local mining community, and in 1918 joined the party. He fought in the *Russian Civil War, from which he returned in 1922 to become deputy manager of the mines in his local area of Yuzovka. He soon attracted the attention of the first secretary of the Ukrainian Communist Party, *Kaganovich, who came to rely on Khrushchev's energy and reliability without feeling threatened, because of Khrushchev's lack of formal education. Khrushchev followed Kaganovich to Moscow, where he became a student and continued his political career. With Kaganovich as first secretary, he became second secretary of the Moscow Communist Party in 1933 and was responsible for the building of its underground transport system, as well as other large urban projects.

Khrushchev succeeded Kaganovich in 1935, but returned to the Ukraine to become first secretary of the Central Committee in the Ukraine (1938–47). He survived *Stalin's *Great Purge partly because he actively supported it, and also because he had found favour with Stalin as a good friend of Stalin's deceased wife. During the war, he served in the *Red Army and took part in many major battles, e.g. at *Stalingrad. In late 1943 he devoted himself to the reconstruction and the Stalinization of the liberated Ukraine. In 1949, he once again became head of the Moscow Communist Party, while he was also a secretary of the Central Committee of the Communist Party of the Soviet Union (CPSU).

Succession to Stalin (1953–7) At the time of Stalin's death, he was the most junior member of the ruling group, which included *Malenkov, *Molotov, *Beria, and *Kaganovich. By October 1953, however, he had advanced to second-in-command behind Molotov, as first secretary of the Central Committee of the CPSU. He then managed to remove Beria and Malenkov from office, and strengthen his position through his shrewd and famous denunciation of excesses of *Stalinism at the XXth Party Congress on 25 February 1956. This gave him popularity at home and abroad, while compromising his rivals, who had been much more involved in Stalin's purges than himself. His power was finally secured in June 1957, when the '**anti-party** group' of Malenkov, Kaganovich, Molotov, and Shepilov gained a majority in the *Politburo for his dismissal. With the help of *Zhukov and the *KGB, he was able to insist on the decision's ratification by the plenary session of the Central Committee, which duly met and overturned the Politburo's decision.

In power (1957–64) Khrushchev was now free to get rid of his opponents, adding the dismissal of Zhukov for good measure. However, his erratic and contradictory policies soon eroded his authority. Abroad, any credit he had won for his anti-Stalinism and the signing of the Nuclear Test-Ban Treaty of 1963 (*disarmament) was eroded by his crushing of the *Hungarian Revolution and the *Cuban Missile Crisis. At home, his reform of the regional party structure alienated his support there, while his cut in army salaries and his ostensible preference for nuclear over conventional armaments caused the hostility of the army. His vicious campaign against religion leading to large-scale church closures did little to enhance his popularity. His ill-judged attempt to revive his standing through another wave of anti-Stalinism lost him even the support of the security forces

(KGB), many of whose officers had been executors of Stalin's orders. Finally, his welcome diversion of resources from heavy industry to food and consumer goods was accompanied by his ambitious and over-the-top promotion of agricultural pet projects like the unsuitable cultivation of maize. In October 1964, his colleagues in the Politburo had had enough and removed him from office while he was away on holiday. He devoted the last years of his life to vindicating himself in two volumes of memoirs.

Khudai Khidmatgar, see RED SHIRTS

kibbutz ('group')
A cooperative venture in Israel, usually agricultural, but sometimes industrial. It is owned collectively by its members, rather than by constituent families, whose children are educated collectively. Kibbutzim were first introduced in 1909 in an effort to combine *socialism and *Zionism. As tension developed with Arabs, they took on responsibility for their own defence. They became an important pillar of the Israeli economy, but during the 1980s they began to face problems of recruitment. In addition, many kibbutzim became less radical, as previous ideals such as the common rearing of children became more controversial.

Kiesinger, Kurt Georg (b. 6 Apr. 1904, d. 9 Mar. 1988). Chancellor of West Germany 1966–9
Despite controversy surrounding his membership of the *Nazi Party and his work first as a lawyer and then for the broadcasting service of the German Foreign Office during World War II, he had an active political career in West Germany. He served as an MP for the *CDU in 1949–58, and 1969–80. He was Minister President of the state of Baden-Württemberg (1958–66), before succeeding *Erhard as Chancellor to head a coalition with the *SPD. Encouraged by his Foreign Minister, W. *Brandt, he attempted a careful softening of West Germany's attitude to the *German question, and successfully overcame the country's economic crisis. However, he was criticized for his heavy-handed and inflexible response to the student protests which developed during his period in office. The CDU lost the 1969 elections when the SPD gained sufficient strength to form a government with the *Liberal Party. Kiesinger resigned as party leader in 1971.

Kim Dae Jung (b. 1924). President of South Korea, 1998–2003
Born in Kwangju, South Cholla province, he studied at the Universities of Konguk, Korea,

and Kyunghee. A newspaper editor, he was elected a member of the National Assembly in 1960 for the opposition Democratic Party, whose spokesman he became in 1963. When this developed into the New Democratic Party (1967), he became its leading member, narrowly losing the presidential elections of 1971. On an extended visit to the USA and Japan, he was abducted by the Korean secret service and brought back to Korea. He was arrested periodically, and in 1980 he was sentenced to death for this alleged organization of the *Kwangju uprising. Owing to international protests, this was commuted to life imprisonment, and in 1982 he was allowed to leave for the USA. He returned in 1985 to become co-chairman of the Council for Promotion of Democracy, together with *Kim Young Sam. He stood against the latter in the 1987 presidential elections to represent his Party of Peace and Democracy, but lost to *Roh Tae Woo. He merged his party into the new Democratic Party, in which he maintained a high profile. In 1998, he was finally elected President. Kim oversaw the recovery of South Korea's economy. He is best remembered for his 'sunshine' policy, which aimed at improving relations with North Korea. Direct talks with *Kim Jong Il were held in 2000. Kim Dae Jung was awarded the *Nobel Peace Prize in 2000.

Kim Il Sung (b. 15 Apr. 1912, d. 8 July 1994). Premier of the Democratic People's Republic of Korea (North Korea) 1948–72; President 1972–94
Early career Born of peasant stock near Pyongyang with the name Kim Song-ju. He formed a local *Marxist Young Communists' League in 1927, and was expelled from school for his political activities in 1929. He joined the Communist Party in 1931. He emigrated to Manchuria (*Manchukuo) in 1932, where he became a leader of the North-East Anti-Japanese United Army, under the direction of the Chinese *Communist Party. In 1941, Japanese military advances forced him to leave for the Soviet Union, where he fought with the *Red Army.
   Together with the Soviet army, in which he had risen to the rank of major, Kim led his partisan Korean People's Revolutionary Army into Korea in the dying days of World War II, after the Soviet declaration of war against Japan on 8 August 1945. A consistent advocate of a united Korea, he nevertheless lost little time in consolidating his own power base in the Soviet-occupied northern half of Korea. He established a North Korean Interim People's Committee, which set about instituting radical land reform, expropriating

landowners and nationalizing industry. At the same time the North Korean Workers' Party was formed, with Kim as chairman.

In power Kim was declared Premier upon North Korean independence on 9 September 1948, which also marked the withdrawal of Soviet troops. However, this did not end his aspirations for Korean unity. As Commander-in-Chief of the Korean People's Army, now reinforced by Korean units returning from the *Chinese Civil War, he launched an invasion of South Korea in 1950, thus precipitating the *Korean War. He succeeded in using the war's disadvantageous outcome to clamp down on his internal enemies. In addition, he encouraged his own personality cult among his people, acquiring the status of a demi-god over the decades. So complete was his control that from the 1970s he tried to ensure a dynastic succession after his death through his son, *Kim Jong Il, the latter's shortcomings notwithstanding. Kim Il Sung continued to pay lip-service to the ideal of Korean reunification, and even authorized talks between the two countries in the late 1980s. His death caused unparalleled mass hysteria among his people. Having embodied the regime and the country's political system during his long lifetime, he remained a crucial reference point for the country's *raison d'être*, in separation from South Korea, after his death.

Kim Jong Il (b. 16 Feb. 1942). Leader of North Korea 1994–

Born in Chabarovsk in the USSR while his father, *Kim Il Sung, was active in the *Red Army. He attended school in China, studied economics at the University of Pyongyang (1960–3), and became active within the Communist Party of North Korea, rising rapidly within its ranks. As Secretary (chairman) of Organization and *Propaganda from 1973, he became the designated successor to his father as leader of the country. A member of the *Politburo from 1974, he was appointed chairman of the Defence Committee in 1990, and became Supreme Commander of the armed forces in December 1991. After his father's death, however, he maintained his position with some difficulty at first. His leadership of the Communist Party was only confirmed in 1996, and could only be secured by the retention of the monstrous personality cult of his father. Moreover, Kim Jong Il secured his position by pouring almost all the country's scarce resources into the army, even at the cost of exacerbating widespread famine. Although information about him is difficult to come by,

Kim has the reputation of living a luxurious lifestyle and having a taste for expensive imported liquor.

Kim Young Sam (b. 20 Dec. 1927). President of the Republic of Korea (South Korea) 1993–8

Born near Pusan, he graduated in sociology from the Seoul National University in 1951. He became a secretary to Syngman *Rhee, but left the ruling Liberal Party in 1954, in protest against Rhee's dictatorial style. Together with *Kim Dae Jung, he subsequently emerged as one of the country's foremost oppositional leaders, becoming Chairman of the New Democratic Party. He was put under house arrest after the *Kwanju massacre in 1980, and later became co-chairman of the Council for Promotion of Democracy with Kim Dae Jung. His candidacy in the 1987 presidential elections against Kim Dae Jung split the opposition and allowed the government candidate, *Roh Tae Woo, to win. He consented to the merger of his Reunification Democratic Party (established in 1987) with the ruling Democratic Justice Party and the New Democratic Republican Party to form the Democratic Liberal Party under Roh Tae Woo in 1990. He was elected head of the party in 1992, winning the presidential elections of 18 December 1992.

South Korea's first civilian President in 32 years, he continued his predecessors' careful political reforms, while clamping down on popular protests with similar ferocity. Kim asserted civilian control over the military, and allowed the prosecution of his predecessors on allegations of corruption. He was barred by the Constitution from running for a second term, but his reputation was also shaken by the onset of the Asian economic crisis in 1997.

King David Hotel, see IRGUN

King, Revd Martin Luther, Jr. (b. 15 Jan. 1929, d. 4 Apr. 1968). US civil rights leader
Born in Atlanta, Georgia, the son of a Baptist minister, he graduated from Morehouse College, Atlanta, and went on to take a Ph.D. in systematic theology at Boston University. In his studies he was much influenced by the thinking of *Gandhi and Reinhold Niebuhr. In 1954 he was appointed pastor of the Dexter Avenue Baptist Church in Montgomery and at once became involved in the local campaigns of the *civil rights movement. He became leader of the bus protest which began in Montgomery on 1 December 1955 and which lasted over a year, during which time his home was bombed. King founded the

Southern Christian Leadership Conference and, operating from Atlanta from 1960, he became a national leader for civil rights. Imprisoned in Birmingham along with hundreds of others for taking part in a protest march, he wrote his famous 'Letter from Birmingham Jail', in which he justified his exposure of civil rights issues.

King was released in time for the *March on Washington of 28 August 1963, when the inspirational orator spoke from the Lincoln Memorial ('I have a dream') to a crowd of over 200,000. Public support after *Kennedy's assassination, and a rising tide of national sympathy for King's cause, enabled President *Johnson to achieve passage of the *Civil Rights Act of 1964. King was awarded a *Nobel Peace Prize in 1964, and continued to campaign in the south, leading a march on Selma, Alabama, in 1965. Here, blocked by state troopers, he knelt in prayer and withdrew, to the chagrin of his more militant *Black Power movement colleagues, who were becoming alienated from King's integrationist message. In 1966 he moved north to tackle racism in Chicago, where he met the opposition of the powerful Mayor Daley. By 1967 he was campaigning against the *Vietnam War and planning a Poor People's March on Washington. He was shot dead in Memphis, where he had come to support a sanitation workers' strike. To commemorate his ideals and his life, in 1986 the US *Congress voted the third Monday of January as Martin Luther King Day.

King, Rodney G., see RACE RIOTS, LOS ANGELES

King, William Lyon Mackenzie, see MACKENZIE KING, WILLIAM LYON

Kinnock, Neil Gordon (b. 28 Mar. 1942). British Labour leader 1983–92

Born in Tredegar, Monmouthshire, into a working-class family. He attended University College, Cardiff, where he was President of the Students' Union. He then worked for the Workers' Educational Association, and in 1970 was elected to parliament for the *Labour Party to represent Bedwellty. From the left wing of the party, he opposed British membership of the EEC (*European integration), and supported the *CND. After the party's defeat in 1979, he became its spokesman on education, and, after a further defeat in 1983, he became leader of the party.

Kinnock started an arduous process of reforming the party and shifting it to the right. Seeking to reclaim some of the middle ground from *Thatcher, he ended Labour's commitments to unilateralism and withdrawal from the European Community, along with its advocacy of nationalization as a major economic strategy. This culminated in a full-scale policy review after a further defeat in 1987. Despite the fact that he was one of the best platform orators of his generation, he often had difficulties performing well in parliament, such as during the Westland Debate in 1986. This, combined with the fact that he had moved away from some of his earlier convictions, gave him an image of unreliability and weakness. He resigned the leadership after defeat in the 1992 elections, and, ironically in the light of his earlier beliefs, became one of the British representatives on the *European Commission. In this position, he was responsible for reforming the bureaucratic apparatus of the Commission, though he failed at making the Commission more transparent to public perception.

Kiribati

A Pacific state of islands in east *Micronesia, consisting of some 33 islands, including **Ocean Island (Banaba)**, with its now exhausted phosphate deposits, and **Kiritimati (Christmas Island)**, scene of the British hydrogen bomb test of 1957. In 1892 the islands, together with the Ellice Islands, became a British Protectorate as the **Gilbert Islands**. In 1916 they were renamed the Crown Colony of the Gilbert and Ellice Islands. The islands were occupied by Japan in 1942, when the whole population of Ocean Island was deported. They were liberated by US marines in 1943 after fierce fighting. In 1974 the Polynesian Ellice Islanders voted to secede, becoming the independent state of *Tuvalu on 1 October 1975. On 12 July 1979 the remaining islands of the colony gained independence as Kiribati, which chose to remain a member of the *Commonwealth. On 1 October 1994 Teburoro Tito became President, and he was re-elected in 1998. In 2003, Anote Tong became President. Under his rule, Kiribati took up relations with Taiwan, whereupon China dismantled a satellite tracking station it had constructed in Kiribati. The economy has been overwhelmingly reliant on the export of copra (dried coconut flesh which is used to make coconut oil). Additional

revenue came from the sale of fishing rights and the development of tourism.

Kirk, Norman Eric (b. 6 Jan. 1923, d. 31 Aug. 1974). Prime Minister of New Zealand 1972–4

Born in Waimate (Canterbury) as the son of a cabinet-maker, he worked on the New Zealand railways, joined the *Labour Party, and took part in local government, becoming Mayor of Kaiapoi (1953–7). He was elected to the House of Representatives in 1957, and in 1965 successfully challenged A. H. Nordmeyer to the leadership of the parliamentary party. He became leader of the Labour Party the following year and, after two defeats, led it to a landslide victory in December 1972. He lifted wage and price controls, which triggered inflation. The encouragement of immigration, which led to an influx of 100,000 people (1973–5) led to large demands for state social spending on schools and social-security payouts. At the same time, state income was constrained through promises not to increase charges for state services such as the railways and the post office. This resulted in serious economic dislocations, which were aggravated further by the world recession which set in with the 1973 *oil-price shock. Kirk won strong applause for his condemnation of French nuclear tests in its Pacific territory of Mururoa, but became very unpopular when he banned the New Zealand rugby team from going to South Africa in opposition to *apartheid. In foreign policy, he changed the course of previous governments by withdrawing from the *Vietnam War and from *SEATO, as well as recognizing the People's Republic of China. He died after a brief illness, and was succeeded by Wallace Rowling, who was defeated in the 1975 election.

Kirov, Sergei Mironovich (b. 27 Mar. 1886, d. 1 Dec. 1934). Russian Communist revolutionary

Born in Urzhum in the Vyatka province, he moved to St Petersburg, where he became an effective *Bolshevik organizer in the *Russian Revolutions of 1905 and 1917. He took part in the *Russian Civil War, and was an important influence in the Bolshevik victory in the northern Caucasus. He became leader of the *Communist Party in Azerbaijan. He helped to create the Transcaucasian Soviet Federated Socialist republic in 1922, one of the first four republics to form the USSR. He became a close ally in *Stalin's brutal quest for power against the Old Bolsheviks (former followers of Lenin),

and in 1926 was made head of the Communist Party in Leningrad and north-west Russia. His eloquence and authority soon aroused Stalin's distrust, and he was shot by a minor party official. His murder, which was possibly ordered by Stalin himself, resulted in the execution of hundreds of Leningrad citizens and the deportation of thousands more, and triggered the *Great Purge.

Kisch, Egon, see WHITE AUSTRALIA POLICY

Kishi Nobusuke (b. 13 Nov. 1896, d. 7 Aug. 1987). Prime Minister of Japan 1957–60

One of the more imposing individuals to occupy the premiership in postwar Japan, his government did much to heighten domestic tensions through its attempts to renegotiate the *Japan-United States Security Treaty. A graduate of Tokyo University, Kishi entered the civil service, and was responsible for industrial policy in *Manchukuo. In 1941 he joined the Cabinet of *Tôjô Hideki, but was increasingly opposed to his policies as the war continued. Imprisoned in 1945 on suspicion of being a war criminal, he was released without trial and pursued a career as a Diet politician in 1953. In *Hatoyama's newly formed *Liberal Democratic Party, Kishi provided essential fund-raising services as party secretary-general thanks to his unrivalled contacts with Japanese big business.

Kishi's attainment of the premiership was largely the result of the unexpected deaths of more senior politicians, Shigemitsu Mamoru and Ogata Taketora, which cleared the way for his appointment. His prime objective was the renegotiation of the Japan-US Security Treaty. The attention that was given to this issue, particularly in the latter stages of the premiership, resulted in a huge public demonstration of opposition in the streets of Tokyo and brawling in the Diet. Taking responsibility for the chaos that had surrounded the ratification of the treaty, Kishi resigned.

Kissinger, Henry Alfred (b. 27 May 1923). US Secretary of State 1973–7

Born in Fürth (Germany) of Jewish parents, he came to the USA in 1938 and studied at City College, New York. During World War II he served in the US Army in Europe and later with the US military government in Germany, before returning to complete his studies at Harvard, where he became Professor of Government in 1962. He became a government consultant, and in 1968 a campaign adviser for Richard *Nixon, who appointed him Special Adviser on National

Security and then head of the National Security Council (1969–75).

As Secretary of State originally appointed by Nixon he repudiated the *Dulles strategy of *brinkmanship, believing in the need for pragmatic and flexible responses motivated by national self-interest. He was ultimately responsible for the *CIA coup to remove *Allende in Chile, and Kissinger strongly supported the secret bombing offensive against the *Vietcong in Vietnam and Cambodia. Ironically, he received the *Nobel Peace Prize for his contribution to ending the *Vietnam War, as he negotiated the US withdrawal from Vietnam on the least disadvantageous terms possible.

Kissinger did much to reduce *Cold War tensions. He was largely responsible for the Strategic Arms Limitation Treaty, SALT (*disarmament) of 1972. In addition, he helped achieve a resolution of the *Indo-Pakistan War (1971), and the recognition of Communist China (1972). In 1973, he contributed to the resolution of the *Yom Kippur War and restored US diplomatic relations with Egypt. He managed to remain untainted by the *Watergate scandal, continuing in office under President *Ford. As head of an international consultancy agency, he continued to exert considerable influence on US affairs after leaving office.

Kitchener, Horatio Herbert, 1st Earl Kitchener of Khartoum and of Broome (b. 24 June 1850, d. 5 June 1916). British general; Secretary of State for War 1914–16

Born in Co. Kerry (Ireland), he was educated in Switzerland, and at the Royal Military Academy, Woolwich. He served in the French army during the Franco-Prussian War in 1870–1, and joined the Royal Engineers in 1871. Kitchener commanded the Anglo-Egyptian army which conquered the Sudan in 1898, and was, briefly, Governor-General there (1899). He led the British army in the *South African (Boer) War in 1900–2, when the ruthless efficiency with which he won the war was extended to the treatment of civilians, some of whom he put into *concentration camps. In 1902–9, he commanded the Indian army. He subsequently served in Egypt, and was appointed Secretary of State for War when World War I broke out. Unlike many of his colleagues, he believed the war would be long, and set about raising a massive volunteer army. He was increasingly blamed for set-backs in the British war effort, such as blunders over the supply of artillery shells, and delays

over evacuation of troops from *Gallipoli. His authority was eroded by the appointment of Sir William Robertson as the government's senior military adviser, in December 1915. He was drowned when his ship, on its way to Russia, hit a German mine and sank.

Klaus, Václav (b. 19 June 1941). Prime Minister of the Czech Lands 1992; Prime Minister of the Czech Republic 1993–98; President of the Czech Republic, 2003–

Born in Prague, he received a doctorate in economics in 1967 and joined the Academy of Science. Owing to his democratic views he was forced to resign in 1970, and to take employment in the state bank. During the *Velvet Revolution of 1989, he was the economic spokesman for the civil rights movement. He became Minister of Finance after the collapse of the Communist regime. In 1991, he became President of the Democratic Citizens' Party (ODS), which won the Czech general election of 1992. Klaus thus became Prime Minister of the Czech part of Czechoslovakia, which became independent on 1 January 1993. He carried out the most radical *monetarist economic reforms of any leader of a former *Comecon state. Between October 1991 and October 1994, more than six million Czechs were given shares in over 1,800 companies. In 1998, he was forced to resign owing to accusations of corruption involving political payments from privatized companies. He continued to be an influential figure in Czech politics as President of the House of Representatives. In 2003, Klaus benefited from the disunity of the governing coalition, and was elected President. Even though his duties were largely ceremonial, he occupied an important position in the political crisis of 2006–7, when no party was able to form a stable government following the elections of June 2006.

Kohl, Helmut (b. 3 Apr. 1930). Chancellor of West Germany 1982–98

Early career One of the co-founders of the *CDU youth organization in 1946, he joined the CDU in 1947, three years before he finished high school. After receiving his doctorate in history and politics, he worked in industry until he became an MP in the state legislature of the Rhineland Palatinate. He advanced to become its Minister President from 1969 to 1976. He became CDU Chairman in 1973, but despite large gains in the 1976 elections he narrowly missed the necessary absolute majority to form a government. Kohl remained party leader, and in 1982, the *Liberal Party (FDP) switched its support from the *SPD to the CDU, enabling Kohl to form a coalition government.

In office Kohl persisted as Chancellor through his complete control of the CDU and his opponents' constant underestimation of his political cunning and intellect. The latter was true, for instance, of F. J. *Strauss, whom Kohl outmanoeuvred. He continued the conciliatory politics towards East Germany (Ostpolitik) of his predecessors, while maintaining a good relationship with the USA throughout. Moreover, Kohl established an excellent relationship with the French President, *Mitterrand, which was the foundation for their efforts towards further *European integration. Kohl's greatest moment came in 1989/90, when he took the initiative and realized German unification with the utmost skill. In particular, he focused on securing an agreement with the USSR before its imminent disintegration, and on preventing a mass exodus from the collapsing East Germany into West Germany. As a result, against all predictions, the CDU won the first and last free elections in East Germany in March 1990.

On 3 October 1990 Kohl became the first freely elected Chancellor of a united Germany since the years of the Weimar Republic. If his authority in the 1980s was periodically challenged from within his own party, after unification he enjoyed enormous prestige. He remained committed to raising the standard of living in eastern Germany, and was a driving force behind the creation of the *euro. He lost the 1998 election to *Schröder, and in 1999 was forced to admit that he had accepted about $ 2m in illegal party donations.

Koivisto, Mauno (b. 25 Nov. 1923). Finnish President 1982–91
Born in Turku, the Social Democrat (from 1947) became a successful banker, which prepared him for the post of Minister of Finance (1966–7, and 1972). In this position, and as President of the Bank of Finland (1968–82), he advocated a tight monetary policy. He served as Prime Minister in 1968–70, and 1979–82. As interim President from 1981 and elected President from 1982, he continued *Kekkonen's policy of neutrality, and in 1983 renewed the Finnish-Soviet friendship treaty for a further twenty years. Re-elected in 1988, he resigned in 1991 amidst the country's worst economic crisis since World War II.

Koizumi, Junichiro (b. 8 Jan. 1942). Prime Minister of Japan, 2001–6

Early career Born in Yokosuka City in the Kanagawa Prefecture, he graduated from the faculty of economics at Keio University and entered politics. In 1972 he entered the House of Representatives for the *Liberal Democratic Party, and in 1979 became Vice-Minister of Finance. Koizumi became Deputy Secretary-General of the LDP, and in 1988 he entered the Cabinet as Minister of Health and Welfare. Koizumi came from the heart of the LDP's establishment, as his father and grandfather had been ministers of the LDP. However, he lost his bids for the LDP leadership in 1995 and 1998 due to his outspoken and unorthodox manner. This helped him in 2001,. when in a deep party crisis he was seen as sufficiently detached from the traditional party elite to revive the government. He became leader of the LDP and Prime Minister, and led his party to a surprise victory in the elections to the upper house that year.

In office Owing to much resistance within his own party, he was unable to realize many of his economic plans, though his consolidation of public spending did lead to a reduction in public debt. Koizumi's popularity fell in 2004, but it rebounded in 2005, when Koizumi led the LDP to its best election result in decades, as it obtained 296 out of 480 seats. Koizumi fought the election as a referendum on his proposal to privatize the country's vast post office. In foreign policy, Koizumi took the unpopular step of sending troops to Iraq following the *Iraq War. Constitutionally barred from direct action, the troops were there in a supporting role, and by the time the troops were recalled in 2006 not a single soldier had died. At the same time, Koizumi supported the revision of Japan's pacifist Constitution to allow Japanese troops to engage in military action overseas. Koizumi's term as leader of the LDP ended in 2006, and he did not stand again for re-election.

Kolchak, Aleksandr Vasilievich (b. 16 Nov. 1874, d. 7 Feb. 1920). Russian admiral
Born in St Petersburg, of Tartar descent, he joined the Russian Imperial Navy and rose steadily in rank. A commander in the unsuccessful *Russo-Japanese War (1904–5), he helped to reform the Russian navy. During World War I he commanded the Black Sea fleet. He opposed the *Bolshevik *Russian Revolution of 1917, and became War Minister in a counter-government set up at Omsk in western Siberia. On 18 November 1918 he proclaimed himself supreme ruler of Russia. With *Denikin he led the *White Russian forces, and at first managed to drive back his enemies from Siberia. His forces collapsed,

however, and he was handed over to his enemies by his allied Czechoslovak forces. He was shot by the *Red Army in Irkutsk in February 1920.

Kômeitô (Japan)

Early history (1960s–80s) Sometimes known in English as the **Clean Government Party**, it was a Japanese Buddhist political party. It was established in 1964, though its sponsor, the Sôkagakkai, a lay organization of the Nichiren shô Buddhist sect, had backed successful campaigns in elections to Japan's Upper House since 1956. During the late 1960s the Kômeitô experienced a large increase in its vote, which in House of Representatives elections rose from just under 2.5 million in the 1967 ballot to over five million in 1969. Despite this early promise, the exclusive nature of its main support group ensured that the limits of its growth were quickly reached. Early policies were vague, although the Kômeitô had some success championing quality-of-life issues, including pollution control and a road safety campaign. In 1970 the party suffered a public relations disaster when it emerged that the Kômeitô had been involved in efforts to suppress the publication of criticisms of the Sôkagakkai and its leader, Ikeda Daisaku, over a period of years.

In a situation of near parity between government and opposition during the 1970s, the Kômeitô enjoyed influence by promoting cooperation among the parties of opposition, although in the latter half of the decade it moved towards a close relationship with the ruling *Liberal Democratic Party (LDP). Because of its position in the political centre, and thanks to the close contact of its leaders with Japan's ruling establishment, the Kômeitô was able to alternate between the two camps during the 1980s.

Contemporary politics (since 1993) Following the political changes of 1993, most of the parliamentary party joined in the merger to form the New Frontier Party (Shinshintô) in late 1994. However, a proportion of Upper House members, as well as approximately 3,000 local Kômeitô politicians, remained in the old organization, which retained the established party machine including its newspaper and headquarters. The Shinshintô won more votes than the LDP in the 1995 elections to the House of Councillors, but after its failure to overtake the LDP in the 1996 elections to the lower chamber, the House of Representatives, it disbanded.

Many influential members created the New Peace Party, which in 1998 merged with Kômeitô members as **New Kômeitô**. The party continued to enjoy the electoral and financial support of the Sôkagakkai, which by 2000 claimed a membership of around eight million households. Although this limited its potential for growth, it became influential as Japan's third largest party, and between 1999 and 2005 it supported a three-party government coalition led by the LDP.

((🌐)) SEE WEB LINKS

• The official website of New Kômeitô.

Konaré, Alpha Oumar (b. 1946). President of Mali, 1992–2002

Educated in Mali and Warsaw, Poland, where he received a doctorate in history. He returned to Mali, and in 1978 became Minister of Youth, Culture, and Sports under Moussa Traoré. He resigned from Traoré's increasingly corrupt government in 1980, and in 1992 he was elected President under the new Constitution. He won high domestic and international praise for stabilizing the country's political and economic system, and for creating a relatively vibrant public sphere. He was barred by the Constitution from running a third time for office.

Konev, Ivan Stepanovich (b. 28 Dec. 1897 d. 21 May 73). Soviet Marshal

Born in the Kirov area, he became a conscript in World War I and in 1918 joined both the *Bolsheviks and the *Red Army. He fought successfully in the *Russian Civil War, and continued his rise through the military ranks thereafter. He escaped *Stalin's purges of the Red Army, and commanded several army groups in World War II. In 1945 his 1st Ukrainian Army Group advanced through Poland and Silesia and played a major part in the capture of Berlin. After the war he became Commander-in-Chief of Soviet land forces (1946–50). After a temporary halt in his career ordered by the jealous Stalin, he became Commander-in-Chief of *Warsaw Pact forces (1955–60). He spent a year as Soviet army commander in East Germany (1961–2), and then retired.

Konfrontasi, see CONFRONTATION

Konoe Fumimaro (b. 12 Oct. 1891, d. 16 Dec. 1945). Prime Minister of Japan 1937–9, 1940–1

He entered politics as a member of the House of Peers in 1916. A member of the aristocracy, Konoe gave his support to the popular party governments of the 1920s, while emphasizing the important part played in Japan's Constitution by the peerage. Konoe opposed European colonialism in Asia, advocating more strident Japanese leadership in the region. With the support of the political establishment, he was appointed President of the upper chamber in 1933. During the 1930s, he was at the centre of Japan's political life, and formed his first government in 1937. As Prime Minister during the *Sino-Japanese War after the *Marco Polo Bridge Incident (7 July 1937), his government was the last that had any realistic opportunity to check the escalation of Japanese military aggression. After the war Konoe was to emphasize his role in bringing about Japan's acceptance of the Allies' peace terms, and his reluctance to involve his country in a war with the USA and Great Britain. Nevertheless, his Cabinets presided over the initiation of the war in China and the signing of the tripartite pact (*Axis). Moreover the influence which he retained within the ruling establishment until 1945 also carried some responsibility for the war. Konoe committed suicide on hearing of the occupation's (*SCAP) intention to try him.

Korea

A country whose history in the twentieth century was subject to intervention from its powerful neighbours, China, Russia/Soviet Union, and Japan.

Japanese rule (1905–45) To avoid any confrontation, Korea chose to isolate itself during the nineteenth century, though towards the end of that period it came under increasing pressure from the *imperialist powers of Britain, Japan, and the USA to open its borders to missionary and commercial activity. Following the Japanese victory in the Sino-Japanese War of 1894–5, Korea became subject to growing Japanese infuence. Japanese domination was confirmed by its victory in the *Russo-Japanese War (1904–5). Korea became a Japanese protectorate in 1905, and a colony in 1910. Japanese exploitation and the absence of political or even *human rights for Koreans triggered the growth of a variety of independence movements. Declarations of independence were made by students and other movements in 1918–19, while the March First Movement for national independence, which was brutally repressed, nevertheless resulted in the first large-scale mobilization of the masses.

In April 1919 a provisional government (in exile) was formed in Shanghai (China), under the leadership of Syngman *Rhee. From 1934, Communist-inspired and Soviet-supported partisans under *Kim Il Sung began a guerrilla campaign against Japanese occupation. In response, Japanese rule became more repressive, with a new policy to crush Korean culture and traditions: in the late 1930s, the use of the Korean language was forbidden, while clothing had to be Japanese. During World War II, almost a million Koreans were deported as virtual slave labour for Japanese firms, while others were forced to fight in the Japanese armed forces.

Division (1943–48) The *Cairo Conference between the USA, Britain, and China in 1943 established Korean independence as an Allied goal consequent on the defeat of Japan in World War II. On 8 August 1945 the Soviet Union attacked Japan, with the *Red Army quickly moving into northern Korea. This forced the USA to agree to joint occupation of the country in preparation for independence, with the territory north of the 38th Parallel under Soviet control, and the southern half under US administration. The USA, USSR, and UK signed the Moscow Agreement on 27 December 1945, which outlined a framework for the joint administration of the country and the creation of an independent state. However, this was never carried out.

Because of the developing *Cold War, the Soviet and US administrations became mutually hostile, each trying to establish a system of government after its own image. While the Communists in the north under their leader, Kim Il Sung, carried out a popular land reform in 1946, in early 1948 the USA (under the auspices of the *UN) sponsored elections for a national assembly. These elections were nationwide in theory, but only allowed to take place in the southern half of the country in practice. Thus, on 15 August 1948 the Republic of Korea (South *Korea) was proclaimed, with Syngman Rhee as President. In turn, the Democratic People's Republic of Korea (North *Korea) was created on 9 September 1948, under the leadership of Kim Il Sung. As each country claimed sovereignty over the whole of Korea, the relationship between the two countries deteriorated rapidly. Within a year, the USSR and the USA withdrew their forces from North and South Korea respectively, leaving behind a well-organized Communist army hardened by years of partisan warfare in the North, and a rather more incoherent army, founded as the Korean Constabulary, in the South.

Korean internal relations (since 1948) Kim Il Sung finally received permission from *Stalin to attack and invade South Korea in spring 1950. The *Korean War devastated the country, through tremendous loss of life and other human cost, as well as economic devastation, including the destruction of 85 per cent of Korea's industrial capacity.

Subsequently, the countries were separated by a demarcation line, which was extended by a 2 km (1.5 mile) demilitarized zone on either side. The border was hermetically sealed, with all lines of communication cut, thus making contact between separated relatives or friends impossible.

In subsequent decades, negotiations about possible reunification failed, while the relationship between the two halves was extremely tense, owing to the idiosyncratic leadership style of Kim Il Sung on the one hand and the fragile nature of the South Korean polity on the other. As the latter became more stable, tentative talks were held in the late 1980s in which the subject of reunification was discussed. However, reunification remained an impossibility during the lifetime of Kim Il Sung. His death in 1994, as well as the collapse of the Soviet Union, reopened questions about the viability of the North Korean regime. Ironically, from 1995 this increased rather than reduced tensions, as the North Korean government became even more bellicose in an effort to hide its own weaknesses. Manifestations of North Korea's aggressiveness did not diminish. *Kim Dae-Jong's commitment to reconciliation was frequently frustrated, not least by *Kim Jong Il's decision, in late 2002, to resume North Korea's nuclear energy programme.

Korea, North

The northern part of the Korean peninsula has, after pursuing a policy of total self-reliance for five decades, become the world's most isolated country.

Kim Il Sung's rule (1945–94) The northern half of *Korea was established as a Communist country under *Kim Il Sung on 9 September 1948. With help from the occupying Soviet *Red Army, popular social and economic reforms had already been introduced by this time, including the nationalization of Japanese property, expropriation of large landholding estates, a land reform, and social reforms. This gave the Communist regime considerable popular support, especially among peasants and industrial workers. It had also led to the emigration of many skilled and propertied people to the US-controlled South, depriving the country of important knowhow. After

encouraging a series of unsuccessful Communist insurrections in South *Korea, Kim decided to attack it, thus precipitating the *Korean War. The failure to achieve a victory, despite the heaviest of losses and devastations, led to a deep crisis within the North Korean Communist Party. Kim's position became even more difficult as a result of *Stalin's death in 1953, and *Khrushchev's subsequent attack on *Stalinism (together with its implied personality cult) at the 20th Soviet *Communist Party Congress in 1956.

Kim prevailed, with a departure from his policy of 'learning from the Soviet Union', and a new emphasis on self-reliance. The next two decades were marked by substantial economic growth, with rapid industrialization and the good use of its wealth in mineral resources, making the country economically relatively successful by Communist standards. Nevertheless, growth stagnated from the late 1970s, partly as a result of the *oil price shock, and partly because of its inability to access technological advances in the world market such as computers (in marked contrast to its South Korean neighbour). Rejecting the example of Communist China, Kim refused to open the country to foreign investment, or even to encourage private enterprise at a time when state and party had reached the limit of their ability to mobilize society. During the 1980s, stability was maintained increasingly by an overwhelming personality cult around the ageing Kim and by the military, which in the early 1980s contained almost 800,000 soldiers (over 4 per cent of the total population).

Kim Jong Il's rule (1994–) Kim Il Sung's death in 1994 resulted in a struggle for his succession. While it appeared that his son, *Kim Jong Il, had succeeded him, this was not officially confirmed until 1996. In a desperate attempt to overcome the country's economic problems, which resulted in food shortages and even famine, the country had to swallow its pride and accept the gift of rice imports from South Korea. Despite this, unofficial estimates suggested that as many as two million may have died of famine in the late 1990s. Meanwhile, Kim Jong Il continued to put vast financial resources into arms development, and in 1999 the North Koreans successfully fired a medium-range missile into the Pacific Ocean.

As part of the new *War on Terrorism, North Korea was assigned by the US President George W. *Bush to an 'axis of evil', together with Iraq and Iran. This was of little use in establishing a dialogue between the two countries. Under pressure from its major ally,

China, North Korea opened itself to outside countries, taking up diplomatic relations with Italy, Canada, and other Western industrial nations. Owing to a series of bad harvests, North Korea accepted shipments of food between 2002 and 2005, and it continued to encourage controlled aid projects thereafter. North Korea resumed its nuclear programme, successfully testing a nuclear device in 2006. Following renewed international efforts North Korea accepted, in 2007, to halt its nuclear programme, in return for supplies of oil, grain, and hard currency.

Korea, South

The southern half of the Korean peninsula has emerged as a stable and economically prosperous democracy since the 1980s.

The First Republic (1948–60) The **Republic of Korea** was created on 15 August 1948, in the southern half of the peninsula of *Korea. Its early politics were shaped by the constant perceived need to defend the country against the aggressive Communist regime of *Kim Il Sung in North *Korea. In the first years of its existence under President Syngman *Rhee, it was sustained by crucial US military, political, and economic support, enabling it to overcome successive Communist insurrections supported by North Korea. US troops had left the country by 29 June 1949, but returned little more than a year later, upon the outbreak of the *Korean War (1950–3).

South Korea remained dependent on US economic aid to help it overcome human and economic devastation, and to cope with around 1.5 million refugees from the North. A backward country in desperate need of social and political cohesion, it was ruled autocratically by Rhee, who used his country's vulnerability to *Communism as a justification for the limitation of political freedom. In 1960, his blatant fraud in the presidential elections caused a student uprising, which forced him to resign.

The Park era (1961–79) Despite the passing of a new Constitution in the Second Republic (August 1960), political freedom was still limited, again under the pretext of restricting Communism and other hostile political movements. This led to further political demonstrations, and ultimately to the May Military Revolution of 1961. Its leader, General *Park, restored some (though by no means all) political liberties, and proclaimed the Third Republic on 17 December 1963. Park increased his authority in the constitutional changes of 1972, making his power unlimited.

From 1961 until his assassination in 1979, Park used his powers to effect the country's fundamental economic transformation. Given the country's dearth of mineral resources, economic change was created through an export-oriented industrialization, whereby South Korea imported raw materials to focus on value-added finished goods. This depended crucially on the channelling of resources from consumption to investment, and the maintenance of Korea's central advantage, its cheap labour force. The implementation of these policies arguably required an authoritarian approach, especially as the economic benefits of most of them were not evident at the time: most investment came from abroad, where most profits flowed, while wages had to be kept at a low level.

Democratization (1980s) During the 1980s the country's economy developed to the visible advantage of the population, which in turn enabled some political liberalization. Park was succeeded by Choi Kyu Ha, who a few months later was succeeded by General Chun Doo Hwan. During the 1980s, the country was able to make use of its cheap and by now well-educated labour force, as well as the acquisition of knowhow and capital by some domestic companies, in order to benefit from the boom in technological and computer industries. This generated not only greater prosperity but also greater self-confidence, which had hitherto been over-reliant on an ideological superiority over its Communist rival, North Korea. Chun stayed in office until 1987, when the regime's customary authoritarianism became untenable in the face of rising student demonstrations, and growing international pressure pending the 1988 Olympic Games in the capital, Seoul.

The Sixth Republic (since 1988) A sixth new Constitution was passed on 12 October 1987, with *Roh Tae Woo as Chun's successor. Roh gained considerable popularity through supervising a process of political liberalization and an anti-corruption campaign directed against his own party. Following the first free parliamentary elections of 1988, Roh also managed to broaden his political base through the creation of the Democratic Liberal Party (DLP) in 1990. In contast, his opposition continued to be fragmented.

Roh was succeeded in February 1993 by *Kim Young Sam. The election of this former opponent to the regime, to become the country's first civilian President in over three decades, was a further indication of the country's gradual political transformation. Similarly, the conviction in August 1996 of Roh Tae Woo and Chun Doo Hwan on charges of corruption and masterminding the 1979 coup was an attempt to come to terms with Korea's illiberal past. In 1998, *Kim Dae Jung was elected President, but his term of office coincided with a deep economic recession in the region. He relaxed some of the country's restrictive business laws to enable foreign direct investment. This enabled major South Korean companies to escape outright bankruptcy, even if a number of conglomerates such as Daewoo were split up, with parts bought by foreign companies (in this case General Motors). Under Kim's leadership, many political prisoners accused of maintaining illegal links to the North were released in a number of amnesties. Contrary to his intentions, Kim Dae Jung was frustrated in his attempts to bring about a lasting improvement in relations with the North. Relations cooled from 2002, as North Korea resumed research on nuclear technology.

Contemporary politics (since 2003) In perhaps the greatest test to South Korea's democracy, Kim's successor from 2003, *Roh Moo-hyun, was impeached by parliament in 2004. This triggered massive popular protests, whereupon the Constitutional Court refused to confirm parliament's verdict. Subsequent parliamentary elections returned a majority for the President's Uri party, with Kim Dae Jung's Millennium Democratic Party reduced to nine seats. South Korea's political system continued to be in turmoil thereafter, as many prominent politicians of the major traditional parties were embroiled in corruption scandals. These involved payments of millions of dollars from Korea's large conglomerates such as Hyundai and Daewoo.

Korean War (1950–3)

Outbreak The first direct military conflict of the *Cold War. Encouraged by the fragile political climate in South *Korea and the poor state of its army on the one hand, and by Soviet military and economic assistance on the other, the North *Korean leader, *Kim Il Sung, ordered his forces to invade South Korea on 25 June 1950. Over 100,000 well-prepared troops crossed the demarcation line along the 38th Parallel to face around 60,000 South Korean soldiers, and advanced quickly to take the South Korean capital, Seoul, on 28 June.

The course of the war Whipped up by its military commander in Japan, *MacArthur,

the USA quickly responded to what it saw as a forceful extension of the Soviet sphere of influence: having just been forced to accept the victory of *Communism in mainland China, *Truman refused to accept the further spread of Communism. US forces stationed in Japan were dispatched to arrive on 1 July, while the *UN, at a time when it was boycotted by the Soviet Union, condemned the act of aggression and agreed to host the defence of South Korea. Thus, while the bulk of troops and technology came from the USA, with MacArthur (Ridgway from 1951) being appointed Supreme Commander, sixteen other UN members participated, including Australia, Canada, New Zealand, and the UK.

The UN forces established the Pusan perimeter in the south-east corner of the country. From there, they started the reconquest of South Korea on 15 September, through a number of seaborne landings around the peninsula, and took Seoul on 26 September. By 20 October, they had reached the Chinese border, occupying most of North Korea. At this stage, Chinese Communist troops came to the aid of the beleaguered North Korean forces. Over one million soldiers poured into the country, and pushed back the UN forces until Seoul was recaptured by the North on 4 January 1951. It was finally liberated on 15 March 1951 and, after an unsuccessful Chinese offensive in April, the war developed into a stalemate.

Outcomes After protracted negotiations involving the position of the future demarcation line and the exchange of prisoners of war, an armistice was signed on 27 July 1953, after *Stalin's death had enabled a slight relaxation of the Cold War. A new demarcation line came into effect, which led to territorial gains for South Korea, though the North gained some fertile lands in the west. The demarcation line was engulfed in a demilitarized zone for 2 km (1.5 miles) on either side, policed by the UN. The war cost the lives of around 35,000 UN troops (33,000 of whom were from the USA), while there were an estimated 900,000 Chinese casualties (killed or wounded). Around 600,000 South Koreans (military and civilian) died, with over 100,000 people being butchered during the occupations of Seoul alone. Over 700,000 North Koreans died, and over 1.5 million fled to the South.

Kosice Attack (26 June 1941)

Even though Hungary had joined in the German attack on Yugoslavia in *World War II, Hungary saw no reason to join in *Hitler's attack on the USSR on 22 June 1941. This changed when three unmarked aircraft attacked the towns of Kosice and Munkács. The aeroplanes were sent there to provoke the Hungarians into war, which is, in fact, what happened. The Hungarian government assumed the aeroplanes were from the Soviet Union and, following this ostensibly unprovoked attack, duly declared war on 27 June 1941.

Kosovo

A disputed territory claimed by *Serbia and Albania, which both nationalities regard as central to their cultural identity: It was the birthplace of the first independent Serbian state, and the location where Serbia was beaten into submission by the *Ottoman Empire in 1389. At the same time, it was the site where the Albanian hero Skaderberg held back the armies of the Ottoman Empire in the fifteenth century. Kosovo was occupied by Serbia before World War I, after which the Albanian majority was discriminated against and repressed. Repression of Albanians increased after World War II, when the Serb-dominated secret police became much more effective. Kosovo's prospects improved with the dismissal of the hardline Minister of the Interior, Alexandar-Markko Rankovic, and in 1974 its distinctiveness was recognized in the new constitution, which gave it autonomous status.

Civil war (1990s) Soon after *Tito's death, the Albanian population staged a series of public protests against continued discrimination. The region was one of the poorest in the country, while the few spoils that existed usually went to Serbs. This injustice had become all the more glaring owing to shifts in the relative sizes of the populations. The Serbian minority had decreased from around 30 per cent in 1946 to 10 per cent in the late 1980s, as a result of higher Albanian birth rates and Serbian emigration to Serbia. After renewed demonstrations in 1989, the little autonomy that had remained since 1981 was taken away, and Kosovo was fully integrated into Serbia.

Unofficial elections were held in 1992, which Serbia refused to recognize. These were won by the Democratic League of Kosovo under *Rugova. Tensions increased further during the *Bosnian Civil War, as Serbs who fled from Croat-and Muslim-controlled areas were resettled in Kosovo, in a blatant attempt to strengthen Kosovo's ties to Serbia. New elections organized by the Albanian population in 1998 led to the acclamation of Rugova as Albanian President, but when he was sworn in by the Albanian parliament, it was dissolved by Serb police. In protest, the 'Kosovo Liberation Army' (UČK) took up armed resistance against the Serbs. In return, the

Serb army and police units moved in. However, they not only fought the UČK, but also carried out programmes of ethnic cleansing, as whole villages were butchered and buried in mass graves. As the situation escalated and reports of *human rights violations surfaced, the US sprang into action.

Where the EU with its economic boycotts had been unsuccessful in bringing about change, *NATO started a campaign against Serbia after its leader, *Milošević, had refused to compromise. Between 24 March and 10 June 1999, a campaign of air strikes was conducted by NATO, and principally the US forces within it. Although there were a number of civilian casualties, targets were military, political (government offices), infrastructural (notably bridges over the Danube), and economic (affecting power supplies). Ultimately, the Serbs agreed to withdraw their forces.

Autonomy (since 1999) Sanctioned by the *UN, the peace-keeping mission KFOR was set up. This was composed of British, German, French, Italian, and US forces which each occupied a different sectors of Kosovo. Under these conditions, Albanians were encouraged to set up limited political institutions, and in 2000, the province's first elections at a local level were won by Ibraim Rugova's party, the moderate Kosovan Democratic League, with an overwhelming majority. Rugova (b. 1944, d. 2006) was also President of an interim administration, but this had only limited powers, as KFOR continued to hold the monopoly of power, with a particular mandate to prevent violence between the Albanian majority and the Serb minority in Kosovo.

Following Rugova's death his former aide, Fatmir Sejdiu became President, with Amin Ceku of the UČK being appointed Prime Minister, in a bid to preserve Albanian unity. This became crucial for the impending negotiations about the status of Kosovo. In 2007, Martti Ahtisaari of the UN proposed a plan that would keep Kosovo under international supervision, but which would grant Kosovo most of the powers of an independent state, including the right to conclude international treaties and join international organizations. The plan was cautiously welcomed by the Kosovan leadership, but bitterly rejected by Serbia under the leadership of *Koštunica.

Koštunica, Vojislav (b. 24 Mar. 1944). President of Yugoslavia, 2000–3, Serbian Prime Minister 2004–
Born in Belgrade, he graduated with a doctorate in jurisprudence, and in 1970 he

became a lecturer at the University of Belgrade. Four years later, he lost his position in the purges of 1974, and became an editor of political literature. He gained a seat in Yugoslavia's first multi-party elections in 1990 on a nationalist ticket. In 1992 he founded the ultra-nationalist Serbian Democratic Party, whose president he became. On this platform, he became head of a coalition of opposition parties in the 2000 presidential elections that accused *Milošević of selling out his country following the Kosovo War. When it became apparent that these elections had been manipulated, he put himself at the head of a popular movement that spread quickly and forced Milošević to resign.

As President of Yugoslavia, he had only limited authority over the parliaments of Serbia and Montenegro. Koštunica did oversee the peaceful relinquishing of power by Milošević's Socialist Party. He was concerned to prevent the breakup of Yugoslavia, and was often at odds with Serbia's democratically elected Prime Minister, *Djindjić, about the need to accommodate the demands of the United States and the EU.

In 2004, he led a coalition of liberal and moderate nationalist parties as Serbian Prime Minister. He was unable to prevent the breakaway of Montenegro as an independent state in 2006, but he was determined not to allow *Kosovo independence following the UN report on Kosovo's status in 2007. In early 2007, his party lost votes in the general election, and came behind its coalition partner, the pro-Western and pro-EU Democratic Party of Boris Tadic. He formed an uneasy coalition with the Democratic Party, which allowed him to remain in office.

Kreisau Circle (Kreisauer Kreis), see MOLTKE, HELMUTH JAMES COUNT VON

Kreisky, Bruno (b. 22 Jan. 1911, d. 29 July 1990). Chancellor of Austria 1970–83
Born in Vienna into a wealthy Jewish family, he studied at Vienna and obtained a doctorate in jurisprudence. He was imprisoned twice (1935-7, 1938) for his political activities on behalf of the Social Democrats. After the *Anschluss, he escaped to Sweden, where he became an official for the Austrian legation after the war (1946-51). After his return he worked in the President's Office (1951-3) and became Secretary of State in the Chancellery (1953-9), where he played an important part in negotiating the *Austrian State Treaty which gave Austria full sovereignty. A strong advocate of neutrality, he was Foreign Secretary (1959-66). He became president of the Social Democratic

Party, and in 1970 formed a minority government, though from 1971-83 he governed with an absolute majority. His understanding of neutrality did not preclude committed international involvement. His Jewish origins notwithstanding, he was very critical of Israel's policies towards the Palestinians, and became the first Western leader to recognize the *PLO in 1980. He was immensely popular at home thanks to his charisma and his ambitious social policies. He used the country's neutrality to entertain good and unproblematic relations with Austria's Communist neighbours, and was deeply committed to the problems of the less developed countries in Africa and Asia.

Kristallnacht ('night of broken glass') (9 Nov. 1938)
A *pogrom by *Nazi activists and *SA members against Jews. *Goebbels had made a speech in which he used the murder of a member of the German embassy in Paris by a Jew as a pretext to incite a 'spontaneous uprising'. In consequent lootings, over 7,000 Jewish shops and almost all synagogues were destroyed by the Nazi mob. At least ninety-one Jews died, and around 30,000 Jews were sent to *concentration camps at least for a while. Jews were also ordered to pay a 'compensation' of one billion marks. The pogrom backfired, in that few ordinary Germans took part, and most were appalled by the lawlessness of the act. Nevertheless, few could or would do anything to protest against the treatment of Jews.

Krupp
The largest arms manufacturer in Europe from the second half of the nineteenth century to 1945. Alfred Krupp (b. 1812, d. 1887) transformed the indebted steel works which he inherited into Europe's largest steel enterprise and the world's largest arms producer. The company continued to flourish under his son Friedrich Alfred (b. 1854, d. 1902) until it passed on to his daughter, who married Gustav Krupp von Bohlen (b. 1869, d. 1950) in 1906, who in turn became its effective head. Gustav constantly lobbied political parties and pressure groups during the Empire to support an aggressive foreign policy which would increase his sales. Forced by the *Versailles Treaty to manufacture tractors instead of tanks, he staunchly supported *Hitler, whose accession to power allowed him to make arms again. After World War II, Gustav was too frail to stand trial at *Nuremberg. Instead, his son was sentenced to twelve years' imprisonment as a major war criminal for maltreating foreign labour and

for using forced labour at *Auschwitz, though he was released early in 1951. The firm was restructured, but continued to operate successfully until it passed out of family control in 1968.

Ku Klux Klan (USA)

A US terrorist organization with a complex system of secret and ceremonial hierarchy established in the defeated states of the south in 1866. It had the aim of intimidating African Americans and preventing them from exercising their legal rights as US citizens to vote, hold property, run for office, or enjoy equal access to economic opportunity. Following the publication of the definitive book by D. W. Griffiths, *Birth of a Nation* (1915), the Klan re-emerged in altered forms while displaying its distinctive symbols—burning crosses, white robes, and hoods. Klan violence and murder spread across the entire country in the 1920s, when it boasted four million members. At that time, the Klan took as its target not just African Americans but also Roman *Catholics, Jews, foreigners, and various modes of behaviour which it considered immoral (especially relating to sex). After a long period of infighting and decline, it was energized by its opposition to the *civil rights movement in the 1960s. Since then, groups displaying Klan symbols have persisted, albeit isolated culturally and geographically.

Kubitschek (de Oliveira), Juscelino

(b. 12 Sept. 1902, d. 22 Aug. 1976). President of Brazil 1956–61

A medical doctor, he became a Deputy in the Federal Chamber in 1934. He was Governor of the state of Minas Gerais 1950–4, and became President as leader of the nationalist right-wing Social Democratic Party. The first Brazilian President from the business community, during his period of office industrial production rose by 80 per cent, and the economy grew by 7 per cent per annum. The mood of progress was epitomized by the new capital city of Brasilia, which was constructed under his leadership, transforming an area of wasteland in 1956 into a symbol of modernity in 1961. However, these advances were achieved at the price of immense foreign debt and soaring inflation. The worsening financial situation was compounded by corruption and mismanagement. These factors led to the surprise defeat of Kubitschek at the 1960 elections. Renominated for President in 1964, he was forced into exile by a military junta. He returned to Brazil in 1967 to become a banker.

kulak

The Russian term originally applied to moneylenders, merchants, and anyone who was acquisitive. It then came to apply specifically to wealthy peasants who, as a result of *Stolypin's agrarian reforms, acquired relatively large farms and were financially able to employ labour. A new section in the rural community had thus emerged which was marked by efficiency in cultivation and management, as well as wealth. The redistribution of landholdings in the agrarian reforms of 1917–18 reduced their numbers considerably, so that it is doubtful whether in following years they continued to form a distinctive social group. By contrast, during the 1920s, for *Stalin, a kulak was a wealthy peasant with property in the original sense and, effectively, any other peasant who resisted (or was charged with resisting) Communist policies. These groups were thus one of his central 'bourgeois' enemies. From 1928, he destroyed these kulaks through expropriation (collectivization), mass deportations of around six million people to less fertile lands (often Siberia), and executions.

Kun, Béla (b. 20 Feb. 1886, d. 1941).
Hungarian Communist dictator 1919

Born in Cehu Silvaniei, he graduated as a lawyer from Kolozsvar before World War I. As prisoner of war (1916–18) in Russia he became a Communist. He returned to Hungary to build up a Communist Party which gained increasing support as it promised all things to all people in a country suffering from severe economic and national dislocation.

Kun replaced *Károlyi in March 1919 on a wave of nationalist outrage at the Romanian occupation of Transylvania. This proved part of his eventual downfall: as he exhausted Hungarian troops in an effort to regain territory occupied by the Czechs and Romanians, he was unable to accept any peace which involved a compromise on formerly Hungarian territory. Domestically, he managed to offend virtually all sections of the society in his reforming zeal: the Roman *Catholic Church and the agrarian population through his destruction of traditional customs (e.g. the transformation of churches into cinemas, nationalization without redistribution of land), as well as urban workers and the bourgeoisie, through inflation and continued war. His regime collapsed on 2 August 1919 below the weight of the Nationalist Army under *Horthy, and the Romanians, who entered Budapest on 4 August 1919.

Kun's regime had allowed the co-ordination of the nationalist right, which then controlled the country for twenty-five years. The Jewish descent of Kun and many other leaders of his regime also added fuel to the already growing *anti-Semitism of the country. Kun himself fled first to Vienna and then to Moscow, where he became the President of *Comintern. In 1938 he became a victim of *Stalin's *Great Purge, and was sent to a labour camp, where he died.

Kuomintang (KMT), see GUOMINDANG

Kurdistan

Overview A state for the Kurdish nation which has not yet been established. The Kurds inhabit the border region of Turkey (around eleven million people, or 20 per cent of the population), Iran (around four million people, or 8 per cent of the population), and Iraq (2.5 million people, 15 per cent). In addition, there are smaller Kurdish minorities in Syria (800,000 people, 8 per cent of the population) and Georgia (400,000 people, 8 per cent of the population). As elsewhere in the *Ottoman Empire, *nationalism and a (vague) sense of common identity emerged in the late nineteenth century. The establishment of an independent Kurdistan was determined by the Treaty of *Sèvres. However, this never materialized, as Mustafa Kemal's (*Atatürk) victorious military campaigns forced the abrogation of the treaty by the Treaty of *Lausanne. In addition, Britain was interested in the Kurdish oilfields of Mosul, which it incorporated into its *League of Nations *Mandate in Iraq.

Iraq On account of the rich oilfields of Iraqi Kurdistan, it is here that Kurdish demands for independence have been most forceful and, for that same reason, it is here that these have been most brutally repressed. The first intermittent revolt (1924–32) was triggered by the incorporation of the northern areas around Mosul and Kirkuk into the administrative structure of Iraq. A further prolonged, armed struggle (1958–74), which peaked with the 1962 rebellion, was caused by the 1958 revolution in Iraq and the challenge by the new government to Kurdish rights. It was ended by promises for a limited autonomy, but fighting broke out in 1975, after the deportation of the Kurdish leader Mustafa Bazarni. The Kurds in Iraq sought to profit from the *Iran–Iraq War, when, supplied by Iran, they made considerable territorial gains against the Iraqi army. Ultimately, they were defeated, mainly through extensive use of gas warfare by the forces of Saddam *Hussein. Lacking any

protection after the end of the war, Kurdish leaders were brutally imprisoned, tortured, and killed. Renewed Kurdish resistance during the *Gulf War was again brutally repressed.

After its defeat in the war, however, Iraq had to accept the *UN's declaration of northern Iraq as a Kurdish 'safe haven', so that any Iraqi troops north of the 36th Parallel would be attacked by *Nato aircraft stationed in Turkey. For the first time, the area thus gained effective autonomy (challenged by Iraq) that was outside the purview of Iraqi troops. Elections could thus be held in 1992 for a parliament, in which the Kurdish Patriotic Union (KPU) and the Kurdish Democratic Party (KDP) each gained fifty out of 115 seats. The presidential elections of that year were narrowly won by Dzalal Tabani of the KPU, though neither of the elections were recognized by Iraq. Following the *Iraq War, the Kurdish part of Iraq achieved great levels of autonomy, which were enshrined in the 2005 Constitution. In 2006, a regional coalition government formed, in which the KDP and the KPU tried to overcome their differences. In contrast to central and southern Iraq, the Kurdish part of Iraq remained relatively peaceful.

Turkey In Turkey resentment against economic underdevelopment and Turkish unwillingness to recognize Kurdish distinctiveness led to the formation in 1984 of the Kurdistan Workers' Party (PKK). Declared illegal by the state, it committed numerous terrorist attacks, which claimed around 6,000 lives in the first ten years. The Turkish government was thus forced to recognize Kurdish cultural distinctiveness, but this did not lead to any political autonomy. The brutality of the PKK found its equal in that of the Turkish authorities. Hundreds of Kurdish activists were tortured and maltreated in Turkish prisons each year. Even after 1999, when the PKK's leader, Abdullah Öcalan, was imprisoned and sentenced to death, the brutality against Kurds continued.

In 2002 much of this pressure eased as Kurds were the main beneficiaries from sweeping new laws introduced under pressure from the EU. These established the right to the maintenance of Kurdish culture, and gave Kurds some protection against arbitrary imprisonment. Nevertheless, tensions between Kurds and Turks continued, with the PKK continuing to carry out attacks throughout Turkey. In 2005, a terrorist attack against a Kurdish bookstore increased tensions yet further, as the population caught the culprits, who were members of the Turkish secret service. In response to mounting Kurdish unrest, the Prime

Minister, *Erdogan, reversed the liberalization of recent years by introducing tough anti-terrorism laws in 2006 to deal with Kurdish insurgents.

Kursk, Battle of (5–15 July 1943)

Kursk had been liberated by the *Red Army on 8 February 1943, following victory at *Stalingrad during *World War II. In June *Hitler ordered the elimination of this Soviet salient, with its important rail junction, in Operation Citadel, through a pincer movement from north and south. Under Field Marshal Walter Model, he concentrated 2,700 tanks and assault guns, supported by 1,000 aircraft. The German plan had been anticipated by *Zhukov, who sent even greater numbers to defend the salient, and mined substantial areas. In the attack, many of the larger German tanks became stuck in the mud and hundreds were immobilized by mines. Backed by superior numbers of guns, tanks, and aircraft, Zhukov counter-attacked and forced the Germans to retreat. The Germans lost 70,000 men, 1,500 tanks, and most of their aircraft. The Soviet victory in this largest tank battle in history ensured that the German army was never again able to mount an offensive on the Eastern Front.

Kut, Siege of (7 Dec. 1915–29 Apr. 1916)

Kut al-Amara was a fortified town in *Mesopotamia (later Iraq). In the course of *World War I, it was captured by British and Indian troops under General Townshend on 28 September 1915. They continued their advance towards Baghdad, but were defeated at Ctesiphon (22–5 November 1915) and retreated to Kut. It fell after a four-and-a-half month siege by troops from the *Ottoman Empire, despite attempts of relief forces to break through. Ten thousand prisoners of war were marched across the desert, two-thirds dying on the way. Altogether, some 23,000 troops of the relieving forces were also lost. The defeat was a severe blow to the British campaign in Mesopotamia. Kut al-Amara was recaptured in February 1917.

Kuwait

Contemporary history An autonomous emirate since the eighteenth century, it recognized the suzerainty of the *Ottoman Empire in 1829, and came under British protection in 1899, becoming

officially a British Protectorate in 1913. From its foundation, Iraq has always claimed Kuwait as its own territory, but was forced to accept Kuwait's separate existence twice, upon its foundation in 1922, and in 1963. Oil production began in 1946, which transformed it into one of the world's wealthiest countries, with some of the world's largest oil reserves. By the 1980s, 60 per cent of its population consisted of foreign nationals, of whom one-third came from *Palestine, with most of the other immigrants coming from other Muslim countries. The ruling al-Sabah dynasty became the world's wealthiest family, while some of the wealth was also shared between Kuwait's nationals, through the absence of taxation, and a free medical and health system. Economic wealth and liberalism contrasted with religious traditionalism among the Islamic population, and political illiberalism. The Emir ruled independently of parliament (dissolved 1986–92), while political opponents were incarcerated.

Contemporary history (since 1990) On 2 August 1990, Kuwait was invaded by the Iraqi army led by S. *Hussein, who sought to integrate Kuwait as Iraq's nineteenth province. Most Kuwaitis left the country, though the annexation was welcomed by the disadvantaged Palestinian minority, which explains *Arafat's support for Iraq. Under the initiative of US President *Bush, a multinational force gathered in Saudi Arabia, and liberated Kuwait in the *Gulf War.

Liberation from *Hussein's dictatorship did not immediately translate into the advent of democracy. Though forced to concede parliamentary elections in 1992, which resulted in an unusually strong role for parliament in the Middle East, the ruling al-Sabah dynasty under Sheikh Jaber al-Ahmed al-Jaber al-Sabah remained firmly beyond the influence of parliament. In an economy heavily reliant on foreign labour that made up the majority of the resident population, the war had exacerbated social tensions. Thus, Palestinian and Egyptian workers, many of whom had sided with the Iraqi occupation forces, were discriminated against further. The government also moved to establish its control over the migrant Bedouin population. A further legacy of the war was long-term environmental damage, caused by the ignition of 600 oil wells, and the destruction of Kuwait's desalination plants. Towards the end of the 1990s the economy benefited greatly from an increase in the price of oil, but Kuwait's international situation continued to be fragile owing to border disputes with Iraq.

In 2003, Kuwait became an important country from which US and British ground forces launched the *Iraq War. In 2005, Sheikh Jaber successfully introduced full political rights for women, a move that had been defeated by parliament in 1999. Jaber died in 2006, and he was eventually succeeded by Sheikh Sabah al-Ahmed al-Jaber al-Sabah.

Kwangju Uprising (18–27 May 1980)
A student demonstration in Kwangju (South Cholla Province, South Korea), in protest against the imposition of martial law, and the arrest of several opposition leaders, including *Kim Dae Jung. In response to brutal police action, demonstrators attacked government, police, and military institutions, only to be silenced by an elite force of paratroopers. An estimated 2,000 people died as a result of government brutality. After the political liberalization of the 1980s, it became the most potent symbol for government brutality, while the prosecution of those responsible, especially former presidents Chun and *Roh, became one of the most contentious domestic political issues of the 1990s, and an important indicator of the seriousness of the state's commitment to political reform.

Kwasniewski, Aleksander (14 Nov. 1954). President of Poland, 1995–2005
Born in Bialogard, he studied transport economics at Gdansk University. He joined the ruling Communist Party in 1976, and became a leading member of the party's student league. He continued to move up the party's ranks, and in 1985 he entered the government as Minister for Youth Affairs. From 1988 to 1989 he was a member of the Round Table in which the government negotiated with the opposition and ultimately relinquished its power. In 1990 he became head of the reformed Communists, now renamed the Social Democratic Party. For the 1995 presidential elections, he headed a coalition of left-wing parties and narrowly won against Lech *Walęsa. Despite his Communist past, the reformist, youthful leader did much to reconcile the country's new political elites with former Communist circles and a more conservative agricultural population. In 2000 he was re-elected in the first round, with 53.9 per cent of the vote.

Kyoto Protocol
An international agreement signed in Kyoto in 1997. The Protocol represented the most comprehensive international commitment to reduce the emission of greenhouse gases, notably carbon dioxide, methane, and nitrous oxide. Sponsored by the *UN Framework Convention on Climate Change, the Protocol also envisaged the reduction of three industrial gases: hydrofluorocarbons, perfluorocarbons and sulphur hexafluoride. The Protocol envisaged a combined reduction of these gases by at least 5 per cent for each signatory by 2012, though the actual amount varied. The EU and other European states committed themselves to a reduction of 8 per cent, the US to a 7 per cent reduction, and states such as Canada, New Zealand and Japan to a reduction in emissions of 6 per cent. The Protocol was formally effective from 2005, when the required minimum of 55 states, representing 55 per cent of greenhouse emissions, had ratified the agreement.

The Kyoto Protocol to reduce *climate change faced three major challenges. Under the *Bush presidency, the USA, the world's largest polluter which alone accounted for 25 per cent of worldwide emissions, failed to ratify the Protocol. Moreover, the Protocol's period of validity coincided with a worldwide economic boom, so that in many countries such as Canada and Spain, energy-saving measures were greatly outweighed by increased economic production (and pollution). Finally, the fact that it took eight years for the treaty to be ratified increased the 'prisoner's dilemma': for as long as it remained unclear that other states would go ahead, individual governments had a disincentive to promote policies in accordance with the Protocol. As a result, it became likely that the Protocol's targets would be missed, despite considerable efforts by some governments.

At the same time, it became clear that there was little alternative to pursuing further international cooperation on reducing greenhouse gas emissions. Evidence on the link between greenhouse gas emissions and **global warming** became incontrovertible, while the pace of global warming accelerated to unprecedented levels during the 1990s and the first years of the twenty-first century. In 2006, a report commissioned by the British government, written by the respected economist Sir Nicholas Stern, warned against the consequences of ignoring the problem. From an economist's perspective, the Stern report argued that the costs of future environmental catastrophes caused by uninterrupted global warming at the present rate could reduce world GDP by 20 per cent. Owing to these factors, the UN launched a successor conference on climate change in Nairobi in 2006, to deliberate new emission targets after 2012.

((⊕)) SEE WEB LINKS

• The official website of the UN Framework Convention on Climate Change.

Kyrgyzstan

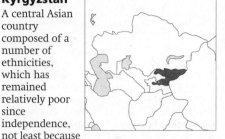

A central Asian country composed of a number of ethnicities, which has remained relatively poor since independence, not least because of corrupt political leadership.

Early history (up to 1991) Part of the Russian Empire since 1864, its population participated in the central Asian uprising against the Tsar in 1916. After the 1917 *Russian Revolutions it formed part of the Turkestan Soviet Republic in 1918. It became an autonomous territory in 1924, and formally joined the USSR as an Autonomous Socialist Soviet Republic in 1926. In 1936, it became a full member of the Union of Socialist Soviet Republics.

*Stalinist land reforms settled most of its half-nomadic population, though as a result of its geographical inaccessibility, poor soil, and relative lack of mineral resources, it remained one of the poorest areas of the Soviet Union. For 24 years the country was run like a private fiefdom by the local Communist leader, Turdakan Usulbayev, until he was ousted in 1985 as part of the anti-corruption campaigns begun by *Andropov and accelerated by *Gorbachev. Usulbayev was replaced by the conservative Absamt Massalyev, though even toward the late 1980s, politics were conducted more against a background of continuing traditional tribal divisions than a sense of national awakening. Attempts to further a national consciousness included, for example, the declaration of Kyrgizian as the only official language in 1989. The growth of this uncertain *nationalism backfired in June 1990, when a wave of xenophobia led to a massacre of the country's (relatively well-off) Uzbek minority. In response, Massalyev was forced to retire, and the head of the Academy of Science, Askar Akayev, was elected President.

After independence (1991) Akayev's election proved to be a decisive turning point, whereafter Kyrgyzstan (independent since 15 December 1990) developed differently from its central Asian neighbours, *Kazakhstan, *Turkmenistan, and *Uzbekistan. With perhaps the most energetic programme of economic and political reform of all the *CIS states, Akayev attracted unusually large foreign investment. After a period of dramatic economic decline, by 1995 the annual rate of inflation was relatively low for a former Soviet republic (34 per cent). Also, in marked contrast to his colleagues in the other central Asian republics, who extended their periods in office through referendums, he was confirmed in office in a free election (1996), gaining over 70 per cent of the vote against his opponent Massalyev, who gained 20 per cent. Akayev became more authoritarian in the late 1990s, imprisoning political opponents and manipulating elections. In 2000, he was thus confirmed in office with almost three-quarters of the popular vote. Like many of its neighbouring republics, its politics in the late 1990s became destabilized by Muslim rebel groups, which used some of the area's difficult mountain terrain to wage a nationalist campaign based on *Islamic values.

Contemporary politics (since 2005) Akayev rigged the elections of 2005 to ensure a further parliamentary majority, which triggered a revolution and forced him to flee the country. The new President, Kurmanbek Bakiyev, moved to ensure his own power base, leading to repeated confrontations with opposition groups inside and outside parliament.

La Guardia, Fiorello Henry (b. 11 Dec. 1882, d. 20 Sept. 1947). Mayor of New York 1933–45

Born in New York City of Italian-Jewish extraction, he qualified in law from New York University in 1910 and began public life as a lawyer. He was Deputy Attorney-General of New York (1915–17), and a *Republican member of *Congress (1916–19, 1923–33). Elected Mayor of New York in 1933, La Guardia worked closely with F. D. *Roosevelt, despite his Republican party convictions, to generate urban policy during the Great *Depression. Between 1941 and 1942 he also worked in Roosevelt's administration as Director of the US Office of Civilian Defense. He was an immensely popular defender of the public against vested interests and developed the city's infrastructure. He was also popular for his integrity and his resistance to organized crime. In a radio show of 1945 he offended so many special-interest groups that he was taken off the air. After retirement, he became Director of the *UN Relief and Rehabilitation Administration from April to December 1946.

Labor Party, Australian (ALP)

Early history (up to 1991) Australia's oldest political party emerged in 1891 as the Political Labor League out of a number of labour groups formed in the second half of the nineteenth century. The political Labor movement gained a vital stimulus from the general strike wave of the 1890s, which galvanized local Labor groups into action to achieve Labor representation in the state parliaments. Labor formed a national parliamentary party after the first federal elections in 1901.While always trying to extend its appeal to farming, professional, and middle-class interests, the ALP has relied on the support of working-class constituencies, with much of its active support coming from the relatively poor and disadvantaged Catholic community. Prominent Catholics in the ALP included *Scullin, *Curtin, *Chifley, *Lyons, *Lang, and *Keating. Its effective organization at grass-roots and parliamentary level gave the party considerable weight in the various state parliaments early on, and led to the modernization of other parties.

Labor formed its first governments at state level in Western Australia (1904–5) and Southern Australia (1905–9). Success at the federal level followed, with the ALP forming its first national governments under *Watson in 1904, and then under *Fisher (1908–9, 1910–13, 1914–15). While these governments established the ALP's credentials as a party that could be entrusted with power, they were relatively weak, since for the most part they were minority governments and faced a hostile Senate. The party was fundamentally split over the issue of compulsory military service overseas for Australia's effort in World War I. Despite its advocacy by prominent ALP leaders, the feeling against conscription among the rank and file was such that in 1916 a motion was passed expelling from the party all those who were in favour of conscription.

The subsequent breakaway of the *National Labor Party fundamentally weakened the ALP, which lost the subsequent elections to the *Nationalist Party led by its erstwhile leader, *Hughes. It remained out of office until 1929, only to be divided again by Scullin's handling of the Great *Depression, which was opposed by senior ALP members like Lang and Lyons. Benefiting from the internal divisions and the organizational weakness of the *United Australia Party, the ALP regained office under Curtin in 1941 and, as the party who led the country successfully through the war, remained in office under Chifley until 1949. The ALP increased federal powers against the individual states, and introduced some notable social reforms, such as the national housing policy, whereby 200,000 new homes were built for those with low incomes (1945–9).

The decline of class (since 1949) Deeply affected by the *Cold War, the ALP was fundamentally divided over its stance on *Communism. Many members criticized *Evatt's successful intervention against the outlawing of the Communist Party, and his controversial handling of the *Petrov Affair. Encouraged by *Mannix and the Catholic Social Movement, a fiercely anti-Communist group broke away in 1955 to form the *Democratic Labor Party in 1957. It was only under the able and charismatic leadership of *Whitlam that the party finally managed to resume power, though its over-ambitious legislative programme and (once again) a hostile Senate brought about his downfall in 1975.

The ALP's longest spell in power under *Hawke and Keating (1983–96) was based on a successful shift of Labor appeal to the political middle ground. They reduced inflation, introduced harmonious industrial relations, and liberalized the financial markets. Their populist and nationalist rhetoric also displayed a remarkable receptiveness to public opinion. This broadened the ALP's support so that at times it commanded a majority even in the Senate. Labour lost the 1996 elections to the *Liberal Party under *Howard, whose successful policies of economic liberalization made it difficult for the ALP to regain the political initiative.

The economic success of Howard's policies eroded further the ALP's electoral base among the working classes. Weakened further by the erosion of faith-based milieus and the decline of the Roman Catholic vote, the ALP lost political direction. Unable to find a response to Howard's stern (and popular) immigration policies, the ALP was not even able to capitalize on the unpopularity of Austalia's military contribution to the *Iraq War. In 2004, its representation in the House of Representatives declined further, from 65 to 60 (out of 150) seats. In opposition, Labor's difficulties manifested themselves in the quick succession of leaders. In December 2006, the party leadership changed a fourth time since 2001, though under Kevin *Rudd the ALP recovered in the polls.

((())) SEE WEB LINKS

- The official website of the Australian Labor Party.

labor unions, see TRADE UNIONS

Labour Party, Ireland

Founded by James Connolly and James Larkin in 1912, it is the oldest party in Ireland, and the only one which predates independence. Broadly nationalist, its most significant contribution has been as a coalition-maker, with *Fine Gael (in 1948-51, 1954-7, 1973-7, 1981-2, and 1982-7), and most recently with *Fianna Fáil (1994-7). Although the party has been grounded in standard European socialist ideals, and retains the general support of the trade unions in Ireland, the pecularities of Irish politics and society have forced the party to abandon or delay such hopes as nationalization of industry. In the 1980s and 1990s it fashioned itself as the party for progressives and youth in Ireland, headed by Dick Spring, who as Deputy Prime Minister (1982-7) and Minister for Foreign Affairs (1993-97), brought the party more closely into debates about the future of *Northern Ireland, and relations with Britain. In 1990, the party achieved perhaps its biggest triumph yet, when its candidate, Mary

*Robinson, was elected President. However, it suffered a heavy election defeat in the 1997 elections, when its representation in the Dáil Éireann was halved. In the 2002 elections, it was unsuccessful in benefiting from the weakness of Fine Gael, whose decline benefited other smaller parties, notably *Sinn Féin. In 2006, the party vowed not to support a new Fianna Fáil government after the upcoming 2007 elections, thus tying its destiny to the fortunes to Fine Gael. This backfired, however, resulting in increased support for Fine Gael, but a decline in votes for Labour. The party leaders have been: James Larkin (1912-14); James Connolly (1914-16); Thomas Johnson (1916-27); T. J. O'Connell (1927-32); William Norton (1932-60); Brendan Corish (1960-77); Frank Cluskey (1977-81); Michael O'Leary (1981-2); Dick Spring (1982-97), and Ruairi Quinn (1997-2002), and Pat Rabbitte (2002-).

((())) SEE WEB LINKS

- The official website of the Irish Labour Party.

Labour Party, Israel

Israel's major progressive party on the left, created in 1968 from the merger of the *Mapai Party with two smaller socialist parties. It combined *Zionism with *socialism, through the encouragement of Jewish immigration, social welfare policies, and the separation of the Jewish religion from a secular state. Labour also promoted negotiation with other Arab states to achieve a lasting peace settlement, even at the expense of surrendering the occupied *West Bank and *Gaza Strip. As the Mapai successor, Labour was at first considered the natural party of government, and was led by *Meir and *Rabin. However, the establishment of a strong and relatively cohesive conservative opposition in the form of the *Likud bloc, and allegations of corruption which forced Rabin to resign in 1977, ultimately led to its election defeat in 1977, when *Begin became the country's first non-socialist Prime Minister.

Weakened by internal leadership divisions between *Rabin and *Peres, which lasted for more than two decades (1974-95), the party failed to challenge effectively the popular Begin or his successor, *Shamir. Labour was also hit by Israel's demographic change, as its natural clientele, Jewish immigrants from central and eastern Europe, declined relative to other immigrants from Africa and the Middle East. Under the leadership of Peres, the Labour Party did participate in government (1984-90). From 1986, however, it governed as a junior partner of Likud, whose hardline policies against the Palestinians it was forced to tolerate. Unable to lead the party to a decisive victory, Peres was replaced (again) by Rabin in 1992. The Labour Party won 44 seats in the 1992 general elections against 32 for Likud, whereupon under the leadership of Rabin and a tireless Peres the party realized a major change in Israeli diplomacy, negotiating the *Oslo Accords which led to the recognition of the *PLO. As the transition towards Palestinian self-rule proceeded smoothly, support for Labour grew to new heights.

The party's popularity collapsed in February 1996, when a number of suicide bombs organized by *Hezbollah triggered calls for a tougher line against the Palestinians, and an election victory for Likud under *Netanyahu. Netanyahu became very unpopular during his term in office. In response, the Labour Party barred the veteran Peres from running for the direct elections to the Prime Ministership, as it was fearful that Peres would squander a near-certain victory. Instead, it backed Ehud *Barak, who responded to popular concerns about security. Barak was elected with a decisive majority, but in the parliamentary elections Labour's strength was further eroded: in conjunction with two smaller parties, the once dominant party only had 26 out of 120 seats. Barak never had sufficient parliamentary backing in his dealings with an increasingly radical and militant Palestinian leadership, and he lost early presidential elections in 2001 to *Sharon. The latter formed a grand coalition, with Peres representing the Labour Party as its most prominent member. As coalition partner with *Olmert's *Kadima, its leader, Amir *Peretz, became Defence Minister. He was partly blamed for Israel's failure to overcome *Hezbollah in 2006, and in 2007 Barat returned to lead the party.

Labour Party, New Zealand

Early history The nascent labour movement was at first tied to the *Liberal Party, whose leader, *Seddon, consciously sought to court its support through the introduction of legislation on social reforms, such as the introduction of pensions, women's suffrage, and industrial tribunals. Even under Seddon, however, representatives of labour became dissatisfied, as they felt that the Liberals were half-hearted about pursuing their interests. In 1906 some of them broke away to form their own political parties, and after several attempts at establishing a coherent party organization, the Labour Party was founded in 1916. It quickly gained the support of the urban working classes, thus depriving the Liberals of vital support. Helped by urbanization and the growing electoral weight of towns relative to the countryside, the weak organization of the *Reform and *United Parties, and by those parties' inability

to cope with the Great *Depression, Labour won the 1935 general election.

The politics of the welfare state In contrast to its sister parties in the UK and Australia, the first Labour government in New Zealand, under *Savage, commanded a comfortable majority in parliament. This enabled Savage to lay the foundations of the *welfare state, through the introduction of unemployment benefits, universal health care, and universal access to education. Labour continued to govern after the death of Savage, when *Fraser led the party through World War II. Weakened by internal divisions, and associated with tight wartime control and economic shortages, it lost power to the revived *National Party in 1949. Re-elected with a majority of one under *Nash in 1957, Labour was unable to hold onto power in the 1960 elections owing to its harsh and unpopular budgetary measures.

After several successive defeats, Labour took over government under the ebullient *Kirk in 1972. His generous fiscal and monetary policies compounded the effects of the worldwide economic depression which set in in 1973. Led by the rather colourless Wallace E. ('Bill') Rowling since 1974, it was routed in the 1975 elections. After twice failing to beat *Muldoon's National Party, Rowling was replaced by the more populist and charismatic *Lange, who duly won the 1984 elections.

Post-welfarist policies (from 1984) Buttressing his popularity through his anti-nuclear policies, Lange also benefited from a general economic upswing in the 1980s, which was complemented by the liberal, deregulatory policies of his Minister of Finance, Roger Douglas. While this was in some ways a prelude to *Bolger's reforms of the 1990s, Labour shied away from the anti-welfare implications of these policies. After a bitter row, Douglas was dismissed from the Cabinet for his 'extremism', though pressure from the party for his reinstatement led to Lange's resignation, just before the elections, in 1989. His rather stale successor, Geoffrey Palmer, failed to inspire the electorate, and was replaced after two months by Mike Moore, who had less than two months to change the mood of the electorate. Despite his best efforts, the party lost the 1990 elections to the National Party and was reduced to its smallest parliamentary size since 1931.

Contemporary politics (since 1999) Labour was unable to offer any convincing opposition to Bolger's ambitious legislation that followed, and in the following elections Labour was again defeated by the National Party. Led by Helen *Clark from 1993, the party was not able to return to power until 1999, when its parliamentary representation increased from 37 to 49 seats. Clark reversed some of her predecessor's post-welfarist policies by increasing taxation for the better off, and raising public spending for the provision of public health care and pensions. On the back of a thriving economy, Labour extended its parliamentary strength to 52 in 2002, and remained the largest parliamentary party with 50 seats in 2005. Clark ruled with a minority government, relying on shifting support for particular measures among the smaller parties. Under Clark's government New Zealand continued its economic boom, which had begun in the Bolger era, reducing unemployment to close to its 'natural' rate, at 3.8 per cent in 2006.

(⊕) SEE WEB LINKS

• The official website of New Zealand's Labour Party.

Labour Party, UK

Beginnings On 27 February 1900, the Labour Representation Committee was formed in a conference at Memorial Hall, Farringdon Street, London. It was a federation of socialist societies, such as the *Independent Labour Party, the *Fabian Society, and *trade unions. Initially it had only two MPs, but in 1906, partly as the result of an electoral pact with the *Liberal Party, it gained 30 seats, and became the Labour Party. Its first leader was Keir *Hardie, who was succeeded by Arthur Henderson (1908–10) and George Barnes (1910–11). The prewar high point of support for the Labour Party at a general election was 7.6 per cent in January 1910, and it was concerned to shore up its support in seats won. The party split in 1914, when its leader (since 1911), *MacDonald, resigned in opposition to World War I, whilst some of its prominent members, such as Henderson (leader again in 1914–17), supported the war effort.

The major party in opposition (1918–45) The party emerged from the war less badly damaged than its progressive rival, the *Liberal Party, and won 63 seats in the 1918 *Coupon Election. It became the official opposition, under William *Adamson (leader, 1917–21), *Clynes (1921–2), and again *MacDonald (1922–31). This growth in support, to 22.2 per cent, was mainly the result of the influx of working-class voters into the electorate, newly enfranchised by the 1918 Representation of the People Act. Labour also benefited from the collapse of the Liberal vote. During the interwar years, Labour adopted a distinctive political position,

through endorsing Sidney *Webb's 1918 party constitution, and developing a range of policy commitments. These included a national minimum wage, democratic control of industry, and reform of national finance. The party was also internationalist.

By 1920 its membership had grown to over four million (largely thanks to its affiliation to the trade union movement). It was a major force in municipal politics, and formed its first governments under MacDonald in 1924 and 1929–31. On both of these occasions, however, its efforts at reform were hampered by not having a majority in parliament, which prevented the implementation of a distinctly socialist programme. The financial crisis of August 1931 split the party. In defiance of his party, MacDonald and some of his supporters formed a *National Government with the help of Liberals and the *Conservative Party.

Labour's representation in parliament dwindled in the 1931 elections, when it was briefly led by Arthur Henderson. Subsequently, the party advocated increasingly doctrinaire socialist policies under George *Lansbury (1932–5) in the early 1930s. However, in 1940 the party joined *Churchill's wartime coalition, when *Attlee, *Bevin, and *Morrison all became central to government decision-making. Towards the late 1930s, the party's fortunes had begun to recover at the grass roots, while its support of the *Beveridge Report convinced a majority that, while the Conservatives were winning the war, Labour would win the peace.

The welfare state (1945–79) Buttressed by a landslide victory in the 1945 election, Attlee and his ministers implemented a substantial programme of nationalization, whilst developing the many welfare reforms begun during the war. The party's main achievement was *Bevan's establishment of the *National Health Service in 1948. Exhausted by its reforms, the party lost office in 1951. Labour was led by the reformist Hugh *Gaitskell (1955–63), who tried in vain to alter Clause IV of the party's constitution, which committed it to nationalization. Riven by internal disputes, the party did not return to power until 1964, when under Harold *Wilson it enacted a wide range of social and educational policies.

Labour lost office in 1970 owing to its inability to cope with the economy, but regained office 1974–9, first under *Wilson, and then under *Callaghan. This time it faced even worse economic problems, which were compounded by the *oil price shock of 1973. Despite significant policy shifts, whereby the party moved away from the *Keynesian policies which had been the hallmark of post-1945 economic management, it was unable to control inflation, largely because of its failure to impose restraint upon the trade unions. Strikes by the latter during the 1978–9 'Winter of Discontent', and failed referendums on the devolution of Scotland and Wales, left the party in disarray, and it was routed in the 1979 elections.

Thatcherism (1979–97) Labour began its long spell of opposition, first to *Thatcher and then to *Major, under the leadership of *Foot, who moved the party further to the left, endorsing the withdrawal from the EEC, increased nationalization, and unilateral nuclear disarmament (*CND). This led to a split in 1981, when some senior members on the right of the party left to form the *Social Democratic Party. The latter was never strong enough to gain a large parliamentary presence, but its split of the progressive vote was probably Labour's single biggest electoral handicap during the 1980s.

After a further disastrous election defeat in 1983, Foot was replaced by Neil *Kinnock, who from 1983 to 1992 moved the party back into the centre ground of politics, abandoning the commitments of the early 1980s, and developing the party's commitment to market forces. Labour still lost the 1987 and 1992 elections, largely because Kinnock's earlier support of the party's pre-1983 policies gave credence to the Conservative warning that Labour had changed in rhetoric but not in substance.

Contemporary politics (since 1997) Under John *Smith, the party began a process of internal transformation, with Smith sharply reducing the power of the trade unions in leadership elections. Smith was succeeded by Tony *Blair, who continued to reform the party by abolishing Clause IV, succeeding where Gaitskell had failed. Branding the party as 'New Labour', Blair completed the move to the centre ground by emphasizing the party's commitment to low taxation, law and order, and individual choice.

Labour was elected with two landslide majorities, in 1997 and 2001. It benefited from the continued weakness of the opposition and its ability to keep the political middle ground. This came at a price, as traditional core voters, disappointed by the relative lack of investment in public services, turned their backs on the party in local elections. Also, the over-reliance of the party leadership on focus groups, and its top-down approach to policy formulation, tarnished a party that had thrived on its image of probity and morality in the early years of Blair's leadership. In the first elections to the Scottish parliament, Labour won, though the use of proportional representation instead of

the first-past-the-post system denied it an absolute majority. The central party machine tried to interfere in the elections to the Welsh National Assembly, but it was ultimately forced to accept the Welsh choice for the First Minister, Rhodri Morgan (b. 1939). In both parliaments, Labour entered a coalition with the *Liberal Democrats.

From 2001, the party increased public spending on infrastructure and the *National Health Service. Little noticed by the electorate were a range of distributional policies such as increased support for pensioners, and a remarkably successful attempt to tackle the problem of homelessness. The party's greatest asset in these years also proved its central weakness. Much of the party's success derived from the partnership of Blair and his Chancellor of the Exchequer, Gordon *Brown. Whereas the former successfully appealed to non-traditional Labour voters, the latter commanded the loyalty of the party faithful. However, the tensions between the two increased, the longer Blair stayed in office. In 2007, Brown succeeded Blair as party leader. Under his leadership, Labour recovered in the polls, halting the surge which the Conservatives had enjoyed since 2005.

(⊕) SEE WEB LINKS

• The official website of the UK's Labour Party.

Lacoste, Robert (b. 5 July 1898, d. 18 Mar. 1989). Governor-General of Algeria 1956–8
A former member of the *Résistance, as Governor-General he gained a reputation for toughness, being held responsible for the official use of a host of ruthless measures (such as torture) against members of the *Front de Libération Nationale. He served as Senator for the Dordogne, 1971–80.

Lagos Escobar, Ricardo (b. 2 Mar. 1938). President of Chile, 2000–6
Born in Santiago, he studied law and economics, and taught as a professor at the University of Chile. An adviser to *Allende, he went into exile in 1973, and returned in 1978 to teach at the university. One of *Pinochet's most prominent critics, he co-founded the Partido por la Democracia (Party for Democracy, PPD) in 1987. He became Minister for Education in 1990, but in 1993 lost the presidential elections to *Frei. He continued to serve in the government of the Concertación Democrácia (the centre-left Democratic Alliance), and in 2000 succeeded Frei with the support of the Christian Democrats.

Lahore Resolution, see PAKISTAN

Land Acts (Ireland)

Legislation under the British and Irish governments since 1860 which addressed landlord-tenant relationships and landholding questions. The effective expropriation of Irish Catholics by Protestant landlords of English descent had been one of the central Irish grievances in the nineteenth century. Successive British governments therefore hoped that Irish protests against British rule would subside if the worst inequalities of ownership were remedied. The nineteenth-century Land Acts (1860, 1870, 1881, 1882, 1885, 1887, 1888, 1891, 1896) largely failed to remove landlord-tenant tension, or redress what many Irish peasants saw as the injustice of the landowning system in Ireland. This was mainly because parliament in Westminster was careful not to legislate too heavily against the landowning Anglo-Irish elite, which retained considerable influence in the English establishment.

The elites' perspective changed in the early twentieth century when, in response to an increasingly militant Irish nationalism, many English or Anglo-Irish landlords wanted to sell their lands and leave the country. The 1903 Land Act (Wyndham Act) encouraged landlords to sell large sections of their holding by offering them a 12 per cent bonus above the sale price. It was opposed by Irish nationalists such as Michael Davitt and John Dillon, but it transferred more holdings to the tenantry than any previous Land Act had done. The 1907 Evicted Tenants Act reinstated 735 tenants. The 1909 Land Act consolidated the financing of the Wyndham Act, and introduced compulsory purchase (requiring the landlord to sell if the majority of the tenants desired it).

After independence, the 1923 Land Act (Hogan Act) reduced rents, made compulsory the sale and purchase of all land remaining unsettled, and forgave all arrears up to 1920. The 1927 Land Law Act dealt with arrears after 1920. The 1933 Land Act eliminated all arrears before 1930, empowered the Land Commission to acquire land for those who had none, and abolished fixity of tenure. These measures of state-aided sale and purchase of land eventually abolished the old landlord system and greatly increased occupier ownership. At the same time, it made Irish agriculture extremely inefficient, as in a country that was plagued by relatively poor soil, plots were created of a size that were too small even for subsistence.

land claims (Australia)

The claims for land rights and compensation for land expropriation made by *Aborigines and Torres Straits Islanders, whose presence on Australian soil goes back over 40,000 years, against the majority of Australians descended from immigrants who entered the country after White settlement in 1788, taking away land inhabited by its original population. Reserves were established for Aborigines and Torres Straits Islanders in areas then considered worthless. Land claims emerged as a central issue in the 1960s, as mining companies started to exploit the mineral resources of the Aboriginal reservations without consultation or compensation. It coincided with, and reinforced, a general growth in Aboriginal self-consciousness. As individual states were slow to respond to their claims, Aborigines and Torres Straits Islanders lobbied the federal parliament, often with spectacular actions, such as the establishment in 1972 of a tent embassy for six months on the lawns of Parliament House in Canberra.

In 1975, an Aboriginal Land Fund Commission to buy land for Aborigines was formed, and in 1976, the federal parliament granted the Aborigines some land rights in the *Northern Territory. In the landmark *Mabo* v. *Queensland* ruling (1992), the Australian High Court for the first time accepted native rights to the land prior to British settlement. In 1994, the Prime Minister, *Keating, decided to address some of the grievances of Aborigines and Torres Strait Islanders. From 1 January 1994, they were able to claim government land totalling 5–10 per cent of the country's surface. However, this excluded lands already under cultivation, and did not affect the mining industry which only had to return land upon request after exploiting the land's mineral resources. Following his 1998 election victory, John *Howard announced that he would seek to institute a final settlement in time for the Australian centenary 2001. However, he refused to issue a blanket apology for the wrongs committed to the Aboriginal population by the immigrants. The issue of land claims continued to be unresolved.

WAITANGI TRIBUNAL

land claims, native (Canada)

Claims by the *native peoples of Canada for the repossession of lands and self-government. These demands have been based on their rights as the original inhabitants of Canada, and on treaty obligations undertaken by the Canadian government from the 1870s to the 1920s. As a result of immigration, *Canadian Indians or *Inuit were often expelled from their original lands, while promises for land titles in compensation were not fulfilled. It became the central demand for the native peoples, and while after World War II they received much government assistance in maintaining their culture, improving education, and setting up businesses, the land claims remained conspicuously unresolved. Several attempts to address the issue in the 1960s failed.

The creation of government-sponsored native peoples' pressure groups created a much stronger and more effective negotiating partner for the government. Claims were made for lands equal to half the area of Canada. Settlement of the claims was complicated by the different, often mutually exclusive demands of the different peoples, overlapping claims, and different and often contrary goals of local, provincial, and federal governments. The slow pace of progress on the matter has led to growing violence, as some native peoples took the law into their hands and offered armed resistance to the government. In 1990, the army was used to break the armed resistance of hundreds of Mohawk Indians in **Oka** (near Montreal) to defend what they defined as their land against commercial development. This was followed by other stand-offs, the most notable of which were those at **Ipperwash** and **Gustavson Lake**.

Of the several hundred claims made or in the process of being made, the first few land claims were granted in the late 1980s, starting with the James Bay and Northern Quebec Agreement of 1985 and leading to the settlement of the largest land claim to date, the creation of *Nunavut. While Inuits were granted further territories for self-rule in Northern Quebec, Labrador, and the Northern Territories, the government was less successful at responding to the manifold land claims of Canadian Indians. Under the brief Prime Ministership of Paul *Martin, the concerns of native peoples were given unusual priority by the federal government. Martin's successor, Stephen *Harper, was much less responsive to native land claims.

WAITANGI TRIBUNAL

Lang, John Thomas (b. 21 Dec. 1876, d. 27 Sept. 1975). Premier of New South Wales (Australia) 1925–7, 1930–2
Born in Sydney, the land agent and auctioneer was secretary of his local branch of the Australian *Labor Party (ALP) from 1903 and became a member of the legislative assembly of New South Wales in 1913. Rising to prominence after the ALP split in 1916 over compulsory military service overseas, he became treasurer (1920–2, 1925–7, 1930–2) and party leader (1923). As premier, he introduced widows' pensions, increased workers' compensation and re-established the forty-four-hour working week. At the same time, the aloof, pugnacious, and abrasive Lang remained a controversial figure, even within his own party. He lost the 1927 elections, but

returned to power in 1930. He responded to the Great *Depression with the Lang Plan, which was to suspend interest payments on overseas loans in order to reduce public expenditure. This was contrary to the action of all other state premiers, and of the federal government, led by an ALP ministry under *Scullin. He thus split the Labor Party in New South Wales, where he managed to impose his own authority on the state party machine, until it was integrated into the federal ALP in 1936. He was expelled from the ALP in 1943 for his criticism of *Curtin, and in 1944 founded the new Lang Labor Party. He was elected to the House of Representatives in 1946, but lost his seat in 1949.

Lange, David Russell (b. 4 Aug. 1942, d. 13 Aug. 2005). Prime Minister of New Zealand 1984–9
A graduate of the University of Auckland, he was called to the Bar in 1966. Elected to the House of Representatives for the *Labour Party in 1977, he became its deputy leader in 1979, and its leader in 1983. In addition to his office as Prime Minister, he was in charge of foreign affairs (1984–7) and education (1987–9). In foreign policy, he received worldwide attention through his tough implementation of Labour's non-nuclear policy. He thus banned nuclear vessels from entering New Zealand ports. Since this applied mostly to US warships, this aggravated US President *Reagan, who duly declared the *ANZUS inoperative (1985), in effect cancelling US military protection in the event of war (1986). Lange also (unsuccessfully) demanded firm French government action after French secret service agents sank *Greenpeace's vessel, the *Rainbow Warrior*, while it was at anchor in Auckland harbour.

Within New Zealand, he is probably best remembered for the economic policies of his Minister of Finance, Roger Douglas. Faced with the economic difficulties caused by the worldwide recession, his government pursued a relatively centrist economic policy, which stimulated demand through cutting taxes. He also shifted the tax burden from direct income tax to indirect taxation through the introduction of a goods and service tax. This ensured considerable support for his government, especially from centrist voters. Lange also privatized industries, and allowed the laying off of miners in unprofitable state-owned mines. Ever-mindful of his more radical labour constituency, he created a Ministry for Women, and introduced a Bill of Rights. He resigned in August 1989 after a quarrel with Douglas. He was succeeded by Geoffrey Palmer, and retired from the House of Representatives in 1996.

Lansbury, George (b. 22 Feb. 1859, d. 7 May 1940). British Labour leader 1931–5

Born near Lowestoft, Suffolk, Lansbury emigrated to Australia in 1884, but had an unsuccessful time there, and returned a year later. He immediately started a campaign against what he saw as misleading propaganda about the potentials of life as an emigrant. After initial work for the *Liberal Party he joined the *Labour Party. Together with Beatrice *Webb, he wrote the 1909 Minority Report of the Royal Commission of the Poor Laws, which became instrumental in the eventual abolition of the Victorian Poor Law system.

Lansbury was elected to parliament for Bow and Bromley in 1910, but resigned in 1912 over the harsh treatment of the *suffragettes. He did not return to parliament until 1922, though he achieved new prominence as a defiant Mayor of Poplar (1919–20). In this post, he chose to be imprisoned rather than to reduce unemployment relief benefits. He was in the Cabinet as First Commissioner of Works from 1929 to 1931. When *MacDonald formed the *National Government, he refused to join. Following Labour's electoral disaster of 1931, he was, with *Attlee, one of only two former Cabinet Ministers left on the Labour benches, and he was elected as leader of the Labour Party. When the Labour conference called for sanctions against Italy after the *Abyssinian War he resigned, to be succeeded by Clement Attlee. He was a lifelong pacifist and Christian socialist.

Laos

One of Asia's poorest countries, Laos has historically been characterized by a high degree of reliance on the politics and economy of its large neighbours, Thailand and Vietnam.

Colonial rule (1887–1954) A country dominated by Siamese (Thai) and also Vietnamese influence during the nineteenth century, it came under growing French influence in 1887, and was formally declared a French protectorate in 1893, as part of French *Indochina. This was originally a small part of today's Laos, but the French gradually acquired adjoining territories from the Chinese and the Thai, so that it reached its present borders by 1917. The French did little

to develop the country's poor soil and scarce mineral resources. Ruling formally through the monarchy (King Sisavang Vong, r. 1904–59), established in the holy city of Luang Prabang, they did create an administrative unit and a legal code, and provided a basic education system for the country's social elite. In this way, the French destroyed many indigenous traditions. At the same time, by developing the country's administrative and political distinctiveness they did much to encourage the otherwise weakly developed consciousness of a national identity in a landlocked country marked by ethnic, linguistic, cultural, and geographical heterogeneity.

In 1940, with the rest of Indochina, the French authorities in Laos followed the *Vichy government, and thus opened the country to Japanese military control. In 1941 the Japanese forced the cession of western Laos (acquired in 1907) back to Thai control, though this was reversed after World War II. France reclaimed the country in 1946 under King Sisavang Vong, and granted it autonomy within the *French Union in 1949. However, France failed to re-establish full control. The French-supported monarchy was opposed by the nationalist movement of Prince *Souvanna Phouma, which fought for a neutral Laos free of foreign interference. Apart from the colonial forces on the one hand, and the neutralist forces on the other, a third and final force were the *Vietminh-backed Communist forces under Prince *Souphanouvong, soon known as the *Pathet Lao.

Communist consolidation (1954–75) The royalist forces were fundamentally weakened by the withdrawal of French forces after the *Geneva Agreements of 1954. Despite its formal independence from that time, the country continued to be bitterly divided and engaged in civil war between the royalist forces established in the east, Souvanna Phouma's neutralist forces in the the north, and the Pathet Lao in the west. The latter became closely involved in the *Vietnam War, providing crucial supply lines to the *Vietcong in return for military support from North Vietnam. This enabled the Pathet Lao to advance gradually against the neutralist forces, bringing most of the north under its control. Meanwhile, the country suffered heavily from its involvement in the Vietnam War, as US bombing campaigns destroyed virtually all the infrastructure that remained after decades of civil war. As the Vietnam War came to an end, a ceasefire was agreed in Laos in 1973. A coalition government under Souvanna Phouma emerged in 1974, in which the representatives of the former warring factions had theoretical parity, but which the Pathet Lao dominated in practice.

In 1975 this fragile balance between the different forces was shattered in the face of Vietnamese Communist strength following the fall of *Saigon. King Savang Vattana (r. 1959–75) abdicated on 2 December 1975, and the coalition government resigned. The Communist-controlled People's Congress now proclaimed the Democratic People's Republic of Laos. The Communist government was under strong Vietnamese influence, despite initial efforts by the new Communist President, Souphanouvong, to create an independent role for his country. Vietnamese 'protection' forces had entered Laos to maintain order, while the poor and ravaged country was in desperate need of Vietnamese economic aid.

Communist rule (since 1975) Devoid of any industry, and lacking arable land, Laos remained heavily reliant on the import of food and manufactured goods, which led to the acquisition of substantial foreign debt. Meanwhile, it benefited from the illegal cultivation of opium, which became one of its most important exports. In 1986 Souphanouvong was replaced by Phumi Vongvichit as President. He introduced a programme of careful political and economic liberalization, while continuing to insist on the Communist monopoly of power. For the 1989 parliamentary elections, one-third of the parliamentary seats were granted to the opposition parties, while foreign investment was welcomed. In 1991 Nouhak Phoumsavan became President and introduced a new Constitution, which once again confirmed the Communists' monopoly of power. Thereafter, all hopes of political reform were dashed through the 1990s, although Laos was able to overcome some of its international isolation by joining *ASEAN in 1997.

Contemporary politics (since 1997) A moderate encouragement of private enterprise led to striking economic growth averaging about 7 per cent in the decade before the Asian economic crisis struck. Owing to its economic reliance on Thailand, it was particularly hit by the Thai crisis of 1997, and in the following two years the national currency, the Kip, lost nine-tenths of its value. The crisis accelerated the discrepancy between the economy of the capital, Viangchan (Vientiane), and the countryside which suffered from poor communications and infrastructure. Outside the capital, the average wage was less than $1 per day. In 2006, the eighth party congress of the Lao People's Revolutionary (Communist) Party passed its sixth five-year plan, in which it

aimed to stimulate economic growth through careful privatization and economic planning.

Largo Caballero, Francisco (b. 15 Oct. 1869, d. 23 Mar. 1946). Prime Minister of the Spanish Republic 1936–7
Born in Madrid, he was forced to leave school and work at the age of 7, eventually becoming a plasterer. Owing to his experience of social injustice, he became active in the *trade union movement, and soon rose within the ranks of the Unión General de Trabajadores (UGT, General Workers' Union) and the *Socialist Workers' Party, the PSOE. After organizing the 1917 general strike he was imprisoned, which made him a national hero and secured his election to parliament, the Cortes, in 1918. Increasingly on the pragmatic wing of the party, he became Secretary-General of the UGT, and Vice-President of the PSOE in 1918.

After *Primo de Rivera's abdication he joined the provisional Republican government, and in 1931 Largo became Minister of Labour. The radicalization of workers and the threat that they might defect to groupings further to the left pushed him to more radical positions in the mid-1930s. In addition, he was embittered and radicalized by right-wing hostility to his labour reforms in the countryside. He was imprisoned for his hostility to the Republic for most of 1935. At first, he opposed a coalition with the Republicans, and thus prevented the creation of a stable government coalition in 1936. In response to the outbreak of the *Civil War, he became Prime Minister himself at the head of a *Popular Front government. He was unable to resist the growing domination of his Cabinet by the *Communist Party, which was responsible for his resignation on 13 May 1937. After the Civil War he went to France, but was imprisoned, first by the *Vichy regime, and then by the *Gestapo, which sent him to the Sachsenhausen *concentration camp. He died in Paris.

Lateran Treaties (11 Feb. 1929)
Agreements between *Mussolini and Pope Pius IX which settled the dispute between the secular Italian state and the papacy. This conflict had been raging since the territories governed by the Pope had been integrated into a unified Italy (1860–70). The treaties re-established a miniscule papal state comprising 0.44 km^2 (0.17 sq. miles), *Vatican City. In return, the Roman *Catholic Church gave up its opposition to the Italian state. An additional treaty affirmed Roman Catholicism as the state religion, while in a financial treaty Italy agreed to pay the Pope 1.75 billion lire in compensation for loss of papal territory

because of Italian reunification. The treaties were revised by the Concordat of 1984, in which the Italian state realized the separation of church and state.

Latin American Integration Association (LAIA)

The **Latin American Free Trade Association (LAFTA)** had been formed in 1960 by the Treaty of Montevideo in an attempt to liberalize and harmonize trade between its eleven member states. This took insufficient account of the vast differences in economic development between the various members. For this reason, the LAFTA gave way to the LAIA on 12 August 1980. The LAIA promoted bilateral trade liberalization between individual member states, and established general tariff reductions in different bands, in an attempt to promote the economic development among its poorer members, notably Bolivia, Ecuador, and Paraguay. With twelve members, the LAIA is the largest regional integration group of Latin America, though it remained relatively ineffective owing to the disparity of its members.

ANDEAN GROUP; OAS; MERCOSUR

 SEE WEB LINKS

• The official website of the LAIA.

Lattre de Tassigny, Jean de (b. 2 Feb. 1889, d. 11 Jan. 1952). French general

A commander for the *Vichy government in Tunisia, he was arrested in 1942 for pro-Allies sympathies. He escaped in 1943 and became commander of the 1st *Free French Army in Algeria, with which he landed in southern France in 1944 and advanced into Austria in 1945. On 8 May 1945 he was the French representative when Germany's surrender was signed. In 1948, he took charge of the *Western European Union forces, and from 1950 he was Commander-in-Chief of the French forces in *Indochina. He was created marshal of France posthumously.

Latvia

An area colonized by the Teutonic Order of Knights in the thirteenth century. A German merchant and landowning elite emerged whose domination lasted until the early twentieth century. Under Polish rule since the

sixteenth century, and part of Russia since the late eighteenth century, there emerged a national, 'Latvian' consciousness only during the second half of the nineteenth century, with the development of a Latvian bourgeoisie and landowning elite.

Initial statehood (1918–39) In 1918 a Latvian Communist government proclaimed independence and called on the *Red Army for help. Against this, with German help a Latvian nationalist government was formed and declared an independent republic on 18 November 1918, under the leadership of Karlis Ulmanis as Prime Minister. The nationalists gradually managed to gain control over the country, and in 1920 Soviet Russia accepted Latvian independence. Though the powerful German landowning elite was expropriated, the country was otherwise notable for its protection of cultural rights for its Russian, Jewish, German, and Polish minorities. Latvia's remarkable stability was challenged by the rise of *Fascist groups in the wake of the Great *Depression. To forestall their further advance, in May 1934 Ulmanis took dictatorial powers himself, and subsequently tried to balance the interests of the country's varied cultural and economic groups without a parliament.

Soviet occupation (1939–90) The country was occupied by the Red Army in October 1939, and integrated into the USSR as a Soviet Republic in 1940. As a result, in World War II many Latvians supported the Germans, who occupied the country between 1941 and 1944. Thereafter, it was again occupied by the USSR. To weaken the Latvians' national identity, in 1945 *Stalin ordered the deportation of around 100,000 Latvians to central Asia and Siberia, and their exchange with an equal number of non-Latvians. In response to *Gorbachev's reformist policies of *glasnost, voices for independence re-emerged in 1986. The regional Communist Party was increasingly supportive of independence, and on 5 May 1990 the country was declared independent again, to the irritation of the Soviet Union.

Post-Soviet independence (from 1991) While the Constitution of 1918 was reintroduced, the character of the state had changed markedly. Since the Latvian proportion in the total population was only 54 per cent (as opposed to 75 per cent in 1918), Latvians felt threatened in their still fragile state, and thus refused to allow Russians the minority rights which Latvians themselves had been denied under Soviet rule. The economy suffered a severe crisis, as inflation reached almost 1,000 per cent in 1992. By 2000 inflation had been brought under control, but economic growth had recovered more slowly, and foreign indebtedness remained high. In 1999 inhabitants of Russian descent were given the right to citizenship, although in the subsequent year the Russian minority complained at a law to protect the Latvian language, which prescribed the use of Latvian in official matters. Despite early fears that the Latvian economy was unable to meet the *Copenhagen Criteria, Latvia succeeded in joining the EU and *NATO in 2004. Even after EU entry, Latvian concerns to increase the use of Latvian in schools and public affairs triggered sharp criticism from Russia.

ESTONIA; LITHUANIA

Laurier, Sir Wilfrid (b. 20 Nov. 1841, d. 17 Feb. 1919). Prime Minister of Canada 1896–1911

Early career Born at St-Lin (Canada East), he obtained a law degree from McGill University in 1864, and eventually settled in Arthabaska (Quebec), where he edited a newspaper. A Liberal member of the Quebec legislature from 1871, he soon dropped his early opposition to Canadian unity, and was elected to the national parliament in 1874. There he became the leader of the Quebec section of his party, and in 1877 he became Minister of Inland Revenue. In 1885 he led abortive protests against the execution of the *Métis leader Louis Riel (b. 1844, d. 1885), which particularly excited French Canadian opinion and led many Quebec Conservatives to swing their allegiance to his *Liberal Party. As Liberal leader from 1887, he gradually built up a national and cohesive party, whose defeat in the 1891 elections was due to his advocacy of favourable terms of trade with the USA. Despite his subsequent reputation for being pro-US and anti-British, he won the next elections and began a period in office characterized by his pragmatic ability for making compromises whenever necessary, and exercising authority wherever possible.

In office Laurier was Canada's first French-Canadian Prime Minister, holding the longest unbroken tenure of office. A firm believer in Canada's eventual independence, he resisted British attempts to create closer links within the Empire. He strongly promoted Canadian nationhood through the creation of two new provinces, Alberta and Saskatchewan, in 1905, Laurier promoted closer national integration through the building of a second transcontinental railway beginning in 1903. In the last years of government he gradually lost support. Laurier affronted Catholics by his refusal to grant them separate schools in the new provinces. His plans to create a Canadian navy to support the British were insufficient for supporters of the *British Empire, and too

much for the French Canadians in Quebec. Finally, his attempt to revive plans for more liberal trade with the USA encountered further hostility from supporters of the Empire, and revived that most persistent of Canadian nightmares, that of US encroachment.

Laurier lost the 1911 elections to *Borden, but continued as a vigilant leader of the opposition. He strongly supported Canada's participation in World War I. At the same time, he recognized the hostility of the French Canadians towards conscription for overseas service, and in 1916 proposed a compromise through holding a referendum. His proposals were rejected, and he was unable to stop a split within his party, when many Liberals joined the *Union government. He died before he could fully rebuild a united Liberal Party.

Lausanne, Treaty of (24 July 1923) A settlement which replaced the earlier Treaty of *Sèvres, after the success of Mustafa Kemal (*Atatürk) in the Graeco-Turkish War (1921–2). Greece had to surrender Smyrna (Izmir) and eastern Thrace, including Adrianople (Edirne). *Kurdistan lost its autonomy, while Turkey's reconquest of *Armenia was confirmed. In return for these gains, Turkey accepted that *Palestine and Syria were to be mandated to Britain and France. Italy was confirmed in the Dodecanese and Britain in Cyprus. The Aegean islands except Imbros and Tenedos remained under Greek sovereignty. The *Dardanelles remained demilitarized and open to shipping, as supervised by a *League of Nations Commission. This final settlement of the Turkish-Greek border resulted in a large refugee crisis, as over one million Greeks were forced to leave Turkey (mainly from Smyrna), while some 350,000 Turks were forced to leave Greece. It has remained the basis of Graeco-Turkish tensions ever since.

Laval, Pierre (b. 26 June 1883, d. 15 Oct. 1945). Prime Minister of France 1931–2, 1935–6; French dictator 1940, 1942–5

A student of law, he became an advocate of the working classes and joined the *Socialist Party in 1903. He became a parliamentary Deputy in 1914, but was increasingly at odds with his party owing to his opposition to the war. He was defeated at the polls in 1919, left the Socialists in 1920, but returned to the Chamber of Deputies as an independent in 1924, again representing the Parisian working-class district of Aubervilliers. After entering the Senate in 1927 he continued gradually to shift to the right, so that in his first period as Prime Minister he tried unsuccessfully to cope with an economic crisis through a rigid policy of deflation. In his second period in office, the *Saarland voted to return to Germany. He responded to national security concerns by concluding the French–Soviet Pact of 1935. Laval had to resign over his apparent condonation of *Mussolini's conquests in the *Abyssinian War.

Following the German invasion of France in 1940, Laval was instrumental in convincing the National Assembly to give Marshal *Pétain full powers to revise the constitution of the Third Republic. He fully supported Pétain's desire to *collaborate with Germany, and on 22 June 1942 announced his hope that Germany would win the war. He hoped to turn France into Germany's 'favourite province', and thus to avoid direct German rule as had happened in Poland, though this hope was betrayed in late 1942 when *Vichy France was occupied by German troops. Laval had been dismissed as Pétain's Chief Minister in December 1940 owing to personality clashes with the marshal, but he had to be reinstated at German insistence in 1942. In 1945 he fled to Spain, but was handed over to Austria. The American occupying forces turned him over to France, where he was executed after a short trial.

Law, Andrew Bonar (b. 16 Sept. 1858, d. 30 Oct. 1923). British Prime Minister 1922–3

Born at Kingston (New Brunswick, Canada), he was educated in Glasgow from 1870, and entered business in 1874, first in iron manufacturing, and then banking. He was elected to parliament for the *Conservative Party for Glasgow Blackfriars in 1900. He soon developed a reputation as a speaker, and was Parliamentary Secretary to the Board of Trade (1902–5). A diligent, ambitious, but solitary figure without major personal enemies, he became the surprise Conservative leader as a compromise candidate in 1911. Uniting the party in bellicose opposition, he was prominent in his support for *Carson and the mounting militancy in *Northern Ireland over Liberal proposals for Irish autonomy (Home Rule). In *Asquith's wartime coalition, he was Colonial Secretary. He was influential in *Lloyd George's replacement of Asquith, and became his Chancellor of the Exchequer, and a member of the War Cabinet. He was Lord Privy Seal in 1919–21, but then resigned, owing to ill health and a general weariness of office. He once again became Conservative leader in 1922, when he effectively toppled Lloyd George. He led the party through a successful general election, but weakened by cancer he resigned in May 1923.

Lawrence, Thomas Edward, 'Lawrence of Arabia' (b. 16 Aug. 1888, d. 19 May 1935). British soldier and author

Born in Tremadoc (Caernarfonshire), he was educated in Oxford. He developed a strong interest in archaeology as a child, and in 1911 went to work on the British Museum's excavation at Carchemish in northern Syria. He joined the British Military Intelligence Department in Cairo in January 1915. There, he took part in Henry McMahon's negotiations with Sherif *Hussein ibn Ali, aimed at securing Arab support for the war against Turkey. As British adviser to the Arab forces, he took an active part in the *Arab Revolt, but was captured and tortured before escaping. He assisted in the capture of Damascus in October 1918. By now deeply committed to the principle of Arab self-rule and resentful of imperialist domination of the Middle East, he failed to secure Arab self-government for Syria and Iraq at the *Paris Peace Conference of 1919. Nevertheless, as *Churchill's adviser on Arab affairs (1921–2) he was able to push for the granting of a considerable degree of self-rule for Mesopotamia (now Iraq) and Transjordan (now most of Jordan). Apart from brief service in the Tank Corps (1923–5), he served in the RAF (1922–3, 1925–35). His autobiographical account of the Arab Revolt, *Seven Pillars of Wisdom* (1926), became a contemporary classic, though less for his account of the plight of Arabs, than for his personal heroism in battle.

Lawson, Nigel, Baron Lawson of Blaby (b. 11 Mar. 1932). British Chancellor of the Exchequer 1983–9

Born in London, he was educated at Westminster School and Oxford. He worked as a City journalist, before entering parliament for the *Conservative Party for Blaby in 1974. As Financial Secretary to the Treasury (1979–81), he developed the Medium Term Financial Strategy (MTFS), which aimed to reduce the growth of money supply to a given target over a period of five years. He was Secretary of State for Energy (1981–3), and as Chancellor of the Exchequer (1983–9) he made his mark through tax-cutting budgets. For some years, the economy boomed. However, his decision to ease monetary policy after the 1987 stock-market crash (*Black Monday) resulted in high inflation and interest rates. Together with a collapse in the housing market, which had been overheated by generous tax incentives, this resulted in a particularly deep recession from 1989. His sentiments in favour of *European integration led to an inevitable clash with Prime Minister *Thatcher, and caused his resignation in 1989. He was made a peer in 1992.

Le Duan (b. 7 Apr. 1907, d. 10 July 1986). First Secretary of the Central Committee of the Vietnamese Communist Party 1960–76; General Secretary 1976–86

Born in the Quang Tri Province (central Vietnam), he joined *Ho Chi Minh's Revolutionary Youth League in 1928 and was a founding member of the *Indochinese Communist Party in 1930. A member of its Central Committee since 1939, he was imprisoned (1940–5) and then organized the party's activities in southern Vietnam. Le Duan returned to Hanoi in 1957 as the leading party figure second only to Ho Chi Minh himself. As the latter's health declined during the 1960s, he became the party's most influential figure and *de facto* leader of North Vietnam. With great diplomatic skill he ensured both Soviet and Chinese support in the *Vietnam War, as well as internal party unity in favour of aggressive policies towards South Vietnam. Having won the war in 1975, he tried to transform Vietnam into a major regional Communist power. This led to a futile but long-standing conflict with China, which escalated into sporadic violence. Instead of consolidating his own country, riven by decades of war, he actively intervened in neighbouring Laos and Cambodia. He dominated in state and party until his death.

Le Duc Tho (b. 14 Oct. 1911, d. 13 Oct. 1990). Vietnamese politician
Born Phan Dinh Khai into a learned gentry family in the Nam Ha Province, he joined the *Indochina Communist Party upon its foundation in 1930. He was briefly imprisoned by the French, but then escaped to China. He helped found the *Vietminh in 1941, and after World War II lived as a party representative in South Vietnam. He joined the party leadership (*Politburo) in 1955 in charge of the party's Organization Department. He became the chief negotiator for the North Vietnamese during the *Vietnam War. In 1968, he failed to achieve a halt to the US bomber offensives against North Vietnam. However, he was in a much stronger bargaining position as the war proceeded, so that at the *Paris Peace Accords of 1973, he was able to achieve a cease-fire. For this, he and his US counterpart *Kissinger formed perhaps the oddest couple ever to be offered the *Nobel Peace Prize. While Kissinger accepted, he refused. He remained a member of the Politburo of the Republic of Vietnam until his resignation in late 1986.

Le Pen, Jean-Marie (b. 20 June 1928). French politician
Born in Trinité-sur-Mer into a family of humble origin, he did not attend one of the French elite schools, but studied political sciences and jurisprudence at Paris University. He was elected to the National Assembly for the far-right Poujadist party in 1956, but in 1972 he created his own movement, the *Front National. He was marginalized by the political establishment, but in the 1980s Le Pen became increasingly popular as an orator. He sought to benefit from the division of the right (between the *Gaullists and the *UDF), whose pre-eminence was challenged in that decade by *Mitterrand's *Socialist Party. Nevertheless, the Gaullist leader, *Chirac, refused any political cooperation with Le Pen, and the two men subsequently became intense personal rivals. This rivalry came to a head in the 2002 presidential elections. Le Pen confounded all opinion polls by coming second in the presidential elections, as a result of which he entered the run-off elections against *Chirac. The great survivor of French politics, the impulsive and charismatic Le Pen was the first populist right-wing leader in post-war Europe to attract significant and persistent popularity.

League of Nations
An international organization of originally 45 members founded at the *Paris Peace Conference on 24 April 1919 to enable collective security, arbitration of international disputes, and *disarmament. It was inspired by the failure of the Hague Peace Conferences of 1899 and 1907 and President *Wilson's *Fourteen Points. From the start, the League was fundamentally weakened by the refusal of any isolationist *Congress to ratify the USA's entry. Germany was admitted in 1926, the Soviet Union in 1934. It supervised the administration of *Mandates, as well as the city of *Danzig and the *Saarland. It helped decisively in the settlement of refugees from Russia and Turkey during the 1920s, and it arbitrated successfully in territorial disputes between the USSR and Poland (1921), and Italy and Greece (1923).

The League of Nations proved unable to prevent aggression between its member states, notably the Japanese invasion of Manchuria (*Manchukuo), the Italian invasion of Abyssinia (*Abyssinian War, 1935–6), and Hitler's occupation of Czechoslovakia (1939). During the second half of the 1930s it became all but redundant, as Japan and Germany left in 1933, and Italy in 1937. The USSR was expelled in 1939 following its invasion of Finland in the *Winter War. In 1946 the League handed over its remaining functions to the UN.

Lebanon

An ethnically homogeneous country which for centuries has suffered from divisions and enmity between its various religious groups.

Before independence (1918–43) A part of the *Ottoman Empire since 1516, it came under French control in 1918, and was declared a French *League of Nations *Mandate on 1 September 1920. This Mandate entailed a large increase in the country's territory to its present size, which brought the number of Muslims to near parity with that of the *Maronite Christians who dominated the country's political and economic establishment. Its constitution of 1926, which shaped its political system for the rest of the century, was based on that of the French Third Republic. Political representation was awarded by religious group, to each according to its size. In the Chamber of Deputies, Maronite Christians were to be represented relative to Muslims at a ratio of six to five. The main offices of state were also reserved for different religions and sects, so that the President was to be a Maronite Christian, the Prime Minister a *Sunni Muslim, the Speaker a *Shi'ite Muslim.

National compromise (1943–1960s)

Released into independence in 1943, the new state still had an extremely underdeveloped sense of nationhood. By this time the Maronites, who had benefited considerably from French administration, looked to Western culture, while Muslims felt more Syrian than Lebanese. Upon independence, it was agreed that the current political system should be maintained, while each group should refrain from extremism, i.e. the Maronites accepted that Lebanon was an Arab country, while Muslims turned their attention away from other Arab states. In the next decades this compromise was challenged by four basic factors, two of them internal, two of them external.

First, demographic change eroded the Maronites' popular majority, since they had lower birth rates and higher emigration rates than their Muslim counterparts. Thus, by 1986, around 41 per cent of the population were Shi'ite Muslims, 27 per cent Sunni Muslims, 7 per cent *Druze, and only 16 per cent Maronite Christian. To growing Muslim resentment, the political system did not adjust to these shifting balances in the relative size of the religious groups. Secondly, the divisions among the sects were intensified by economic differences. The Christians formed not only the political but also the economic elite, especially in Beirut, whereas the Shi'ite Muslims formed the majority of the poorest sections of the population. Economic progress after 1945 increased these differences, and thus heightened general resentment against the Christian population.

Thirdly, Muslim Arab consciousness was intensified by the growth of *pan-Arabism, fostered by *Nasser in particular. Fourthly, perhaps the most crucial factor was the influx of refugees from *Palestine since 1947 and the establishment of Israel. The problem was compounded by the arrival of refugees after the *Six Day War. In Palestinian refugee camps, authority was exercised by the *PLO, which became a state within a state against whom the Lebanese authorities were powerless, as the PLO was supported by the Muslim part of the population. Following the PLO's expulsion from Jordan by *Hussein, the Lebanon became the headquarters of the PLO, which used the country as a base for military raids on Israel.

Civil war (1975–89) Consequently, during the 1970s and 1980s the country was riven by two separate but mutually reinforcing conflicts. After bitter fighting erupted briefly in 1973, civil war broke out in 1975, mainly between Muslim private militias supported by Syria, and Maronite Christian groups supported by Israel. In a conflict in which allegiances often turned, Syria invaded most of Lebanon and Beirut in 1976 and came to the aid of the Christian Maronites. Syria expelled the Palestinians to the south, and thus *Arafat's control over them increased. From 1978, Israel occupied a 'security zone' in southern Lebanon, in order to make cross-border attacks more difficult. In 1982 the Israeli army launched a full-scale invasion, which led to a siege of Beirut. The Syrians were expelled from most of the country, and the PLO was forced to withdraw its headquarters to Tunisia. It turned out to be a hollow victory for Israel, however, since its military actions temporarily defeated the PLO but provoked the foundation of much more radical Islamic groups such as *Hezbollah. Ultimately, heavy losses forced Israel in 1984 to withdraw to its security zone in southern Lebanon. Civil war continued unabated but, in the absence of a common enemy, rival factions became more and more fragmented, and turned on one another.

Contemporary politics (from 1990s) The remaining members of the last elected Chamber of Deputies before the outbreak of the civil war in 1975 signed a Charter for

National Reconciliation at *Taif in 1989, which envisaged constitutional reform. Given the state of anarchy and chaos that prevailed, it was unenforceable, however. As international (and particularly US) attention focused on Iraq in the buildup to the *Gulf War, in 1990 Syria quietly reoccupied Lebanon, securing a fragile peace by enforcing the Taif Accord. The country became practically a protectorate of Syria, whose 40,000 troops ensured that the Lebanese government could do little without Syrian consent. Syrian occupation also gave an added twist to the Middle East peace process, since Israel became even more reluctant to give up its six-mile security zone in southern Lebanon while Syrian forces remained in the rest of the country. For at least as long as the Israeli occupation of the southern Lebanese border continued, however, it was unlikely that Lebanon would find a lasting peace. The new political order of the early 1990s was confirmed in the elections of August/September 1996, which resulted in an overwhelming victory for the parties backing the pro-Syrian government, even in areas with a large Christian population.

Lebanon was governed between 1992 and 1998 by Rafik al-*Hariri, who returned to power after the elections of 2000. In that year, the last Israeli troops withdrew from the Lebanon and the militias which Israel had supported disbanded. This led to a developing and highly divisive public debate about the continued presence of Syrian troops. Al-Hariri was killed in 2005, reputedly at the orders of the Syrian secret service. This led to widespread protests about the country's Syrian domination. Yielding to international pressure, Syria withdrew its troops and intelligence services within months, before parliamentary elections at the end of May 2005.

The withdrawal of Syrian troops changed the balance of power between the factions. In particular, *Hezbollah, which continued to receive arms from Syria, became increasingly vocal in its demands for power. The organization's popularity was increased following Israel's attack on Hezbollah in Lebanon in 2006. Thereafter, Lebanese politics entered a stalemate, with no faction possessing sufficient authority to overcome the damage caused by the war.

Lebensraum ('living space')

A central aspect of *Hitler's racist ideology. Picking up on earlier German colonial fantasies of eastern Europe, Hitler argued that the superior 'Aryan' (German) race needed more space in which to live and prosper, and so should conquer the seemingly 'inferior' Slav people in order to create additional living space to the east.

SOCIAL DARWINISM; WORLD WAR II

Lee Kuan Yew (b. 16 Sept. 1923). Prime Minister of Singapore 1959–90

Born into a wealthy Singaporean Chinese family, he studied at Cambridge and qualified as a lawyer, being called to the English Bar in 1950. On returning to Singapore, he became a spokesman for the Chinese community as well as becoming involved in labour and *trade-union concerns. In 1954 he formed the People's Action Party, a democratic, socialist organization, which under his leadership has dominated Singaporean politics ever since. He took part in negotiations in London for self-government and in 1959 formed his first government, with a policy of greater industrialization. He led Singapore as a component state of the newly formed Federation of Malaysia in 1963, but in 1965 he reluctantly accepted Singapore's independence. At first a committed socialist, he gradually, but then wholeheartedly, accepted *capitalism, transforming his country into one of the world's most successful economies. At the same time, the state remained authoritarian and strongly interventionist, so that his leadership was never seriously challenged. He stepped down voluntarily to go into retirement. In 2004, his oldest son, Lee Hsien Loong, became Premier.

Lee Teng-hui (b. 15 Jan. 1923). President of Taiwan (Republic of China) 1988–2000

Born in Taipei, he studied at Kyoto University (Japan) during World War II, finished his degree at the National Taiwan University in 1948, and obtained a doctorate in agricultural economics from Cornell University (USA). A member of the *Guomindang, he became a university teacher before being appointed Minister of State in 1972. He became Mayor of Taipei in 1978, and Governor of Taiwan Province in 1981. In 1984, *Chiang Ching-kuo appointed him Vice-President and his designated successor. Against fierce opposition from a number of hardline members within the Guomindang, he was the first ethnic Taiwanese to be elected to the presidency. He continued his predecessor's reforms of political liberalization. On the all-important question of relations with mainland China, he steered a difficult course, assisting the country in its transition to become an internationally recognized, self-confident state, while also authorizing a dialogue with *Deng's Communist government about possible reunification, and increasing trade between the two countries.

He was confirmed in office by parliament in 1990, and in 1996 he won the country's first popular presidential elections. He resigned the chairmanship of the KMT when the party lost the elections for his successor in 2000.

Lega Nord (Northern League, Italy)

An alliance of northern Italian regional parties. Against the background of Italy's regional disparity in social and economic terms, its appeal is based on northern resentment against the redistribution of welfare and taxation from the prosperous north to the poor south. On 15 September 1996, the president of the Lega Nord, Umberto Bossi, proclaimed the 'Republic of Padania', with the aim of creating a rival state in Italy north of the River Po, complete with a separate government and administration. Although this was only supported by a minority, Bossi hoped to attract more support as the government failed to resolve its financial crisis on account of the insolvent south. A junior partner to *Forza Italia in the House of Liberties coalition, the Lega Nord joined *Berlusconi's government (2001–6).

Lemass, Sean (b. 15 July 1899, d. 11 May 1971). Prime Minister (Taoiseach) of the Irish Republic 1959–66

Born in Ballybrack, Co. Dublin, he joined the Irish Volunteers (militant nationalists) at age 15. He fought in the 1916 *Easter Rising, and on the anti-treaty side in the Irish Civil War (1922–3). He was captured by the Free State forces and imprisoned from December 1922 to December 1923. He was a founding member of *Fianna Fáil, and helped build its organization at the grass roots. He entered Dáil Éireann (the Irish parliament) in 1925 for Dublin city and remained its member until his retirement in 1969. He became Minister for Industry and Commerce in *de Valéra's governments (1932–48, 1951–4, 1957–9).

After succeeding de Valéra as Taoiseach, Lemass spent most of his premiership building up industry. He used tariffs, 'tax holidays' for foreign companies settling in Ireland, and the establishment of new government-commerce cooperative bodies to promote native industry. The economy improved significantly in the early 1960s, and Lemass laid the plans for Ireland's entry in the European Economic Community (which eventually bore fruit in 1973). His other major accomplishment was his meeting in 1965 with the Prime Minister of *Northern Ireland, *O'Neill, and his instigation of a more pragmatic attitude towards the north. Upon his retirement, he was succeeded by Jack *Lynch.

Lend-Lease Act (Mar. 1941)

An Act passed by the US *Congress allowing President *Roosevelt to lend or lease equipment and supplies to any foreign state whose defence was considered vital to the security of the USA. Some 60 per cent of the shipments went to Britain and its Dominions as a loan, in return for British-owned military and naval bases leased to the USA and for the accommodation of US troops, especially after the US entry into war in December 1941. About 20 per cent went to the Soviet Union. Altogether 38 nations received lend-lease aid. President *Truman ended lend-lease at the end of the war in September 1945.

Lenin, Vladimir Ilich (b. 22 Apr. 1870, d. 21 Jan. 1924). Founder of the USSR

Early career (up to 1903) Born Vladimir Ilich Ulyanov in Simbirsk (later Ulyanovsk), he was inspired by the execution of his eldest brother in 1887 for an assassination attempt on Tsar Alexander III to become engaged in revolutionary underground movements. He was expelled from Kazan University for his part in student demonstrations later that year, but in 1891 graduated with top marks as an external law student from St Petersburg University. After working as a lawyer in Kazan for two years, he went to St Petersburg in 1893, and became active in *Marxist circles. He formed important contacts with exiled Marxists in Switzerland during a tour there in 1895, but was arrested later that year and sent to exile in Siberia. There, he married Nadezhda Konstantinova Krupskaya (b. 1869, d. 1939), who subsequently exerted a considerable intellectual influence over him.

His time in Siberia allowed him to finish his first major publication, *The Development of Capitalism in Russia* (1899), which was a critique of the current populist Narodniki movement. After his release in 1900 he emigrated to central Europe, and founded the social democratic newspaper *Iskra* (The Spark). In his numerous newspaper articles, and his important treatise *What is to be Done?* (1902), he outlined his revolutionary ideas. Borrowing in large measure from *Kautsky, he developed the concept of an elite party, which would have to assume the leadership of the proletariat in the fight for *socialism and *Communism. These views led to a split within the Russian Social Democratic Workers' Party in 1903, whereupon he assumed the leadership of the more radical faction (*Bolsheviks) against the more moderate *Mensheviks.

Between the Russian Revolutions (1905–17) After a brief (but ineffective) presence in Russia during the 1905 *Russian Revolution, he returned to central Europe, where he collected funds, organized the separation of Bolsheviks and Mensheviks, and continued his writings, the most important of which during this period was *Materialism and Empirocriticism* (1909). At the outbreak of World War I, he was imprisoned by the Austrian police, but was soon sent to exile in Switzerland. In *Imperialism, the Highest Stage of Capitalism* (1916), he blamed *imperialism for World War I. In contrast to *Marx, he argued that socialist revolution would occur first in the least, rather than most, developed capitalist society. Having almost given up hope of such a revolution occurring in Russia, he was surprised by the outbreak of the *Russian Revolution in February 1917.

Due to his urgings for the ending of the war to consolidate the revolution, the Germans organized his return to Russia, where he arrived in April 1917. At first, demands in his 'April Theses' for an end to the war, the transfer of land to the peasants, and the transfer of power to the *Soviets went unheeded. Accused of complicity in the coup attempt of July 1917, he even had to go into hiding in Finland. There, he wrote *State and Revolution* (1917) in which he developed his notion of the proletarian dictatorship and justified the use of terror. The breakdown of the Russian war effort, and the rapid deterioration of the economy worked in his favour, and on 25–6 October 1917 (7–8 November according to the Gregorian Calendar) he persuaded his lieutenants, led by *Trotsky, to carry out the Bolshevik Revolution.

Leader of Russia (1917–23) Lenin became the Chairman of the Council of People's Commissars, effectively the Premier of the new Soviet government. He immediately put into practice his idea of a small, elite leadership by creating the *Politburo. This enabled him to impose upon a reluctant Bolshevik leadership the acceptance of the humiliating Peace of *Brest-Litovsk. Thereafter, the *Russian Civil War ensued, which he successfully directed from Petrograd (formerly St Petersburg) while his aides like Trotsky, Zinoviev, and *Stalin organized the *Red Army at the grass roots. His able leadership, and the terror executed by the loyal *Cheka bands enabled him to stay in power after the devastating Civil War, and the disastrous *Russo-Polish War. Despite his many writings, he was a pragmatist more than an ideologue, and calmed a lot of discontent through the *New Economic Policy, which soon restored production to prewar levels. In 1922, he suffered two strokes. Paralysed in speech and movement throughout most of 1923, he

was unable to stop the rise of Stalin who succeeded him.

Leningrad, Siege of (1941–4)

Following the *Barbarossa Campaign in *World War II, the German army had hoped to capture Leningrad. Owing to slow progress in the Baltic area, German and Finnish forces did not surround the city until September. Resistance was so fierce that the German High Command abandoned efforts to storm the garrison, relying instead on a blockade, which in the end lasted nearly 900 days. Few preparations had been made and, as evacuation of the population had been ruled out by *Stalin, there may have been over one million civilian deaths during the siege, caused by starvation, cold, and disease, as well as by enemy action. Over 100,000 bombs were dropped on the city, and up to 200,000 shells were fired at it. Soviet counter-attacks began early in 1943, but it took nearly another year for the siege to be completely lifted (27 January 1944).

Leo Frank trial, see FRANK TRIAL

Leopold III (b. 3 Nov. 1901, d. 25 Sept. 1983). King of the Belgians 1934–51

He was educated at Eton and at Ghent University. Following the German invasion in World War II he took command of the army, which was hopelessly outnumbered, and on 28 May 1940 he ordered a cease-fire, even though the Prime Minister ordered the Belgians to continue their resistance. He was resident at Laeken Castle until June 1944, when he was imprisoned by the Germans. After his liberation in 1945 he went into exile in Switzerland while a commission investigated his conduct during the war. It found no fault in his actions, and in 1950 a small majority voted for his return in a referendum. However, there were serious riots and Belgium was near civil war. He was finally persuaded to abdicate in favour of his son Baudouin I (b. 1930, d. 1993), who managed to unite his country and strengthen the monarchy.

Lesotho

A mountainous, landlocked country entirely surrounded by South Africa, with which its history has been closely enmeshed.

Contemporary history (up to 1995) Lesotho became the British colony of Basutoland in 1884 and was granted independence on 4 October 1966, under King Moshoeshoe II (b. 1938, d. 1996). The first government was formed by the conservative and pro-South African Basutoland National Party (BNP), which had won the first elections in 1965. The BNP's leader, Lebua Jonathan, severely curtailed the King's powers. Following its strong showing in the 1970 elections, Jonathan outlawed the rival socialist Basutoland Congress Party (BCP), suspended the constitution, and brutally suppressed all opposition. He was deposed with South African help in 1986, when a coalition of the military, royalists, and educated elites took over the government. The construction of the world's largest reservoir from 1986 to provide drinking water for Johannesburg has given a significant boost to the country's economy, but has deepened Lesotho's dependence on South Africa. A further military coup occurred in 1991, but South African pressure led to a general election in 1993, which was won by the BCP. One of the world's poorest countries, it relied heavily on a migrant labour force working in South Africa (almost 40 per cent of the working male population), whose earnings made up over half of national income.

Contemporary politics (since 1995) Political instability led to another army coup in 1995. In 1996, Letsie III became King. In fair but controversial elections held in 1998, the new Lesotho Congress for Democracy (LCD) under Bethuel Pakalitha Mosisili took 79 of 80 seats under an election system that favoured stronger parties. Army and popular revolts followed, and were brutally suppressed with the help of troops from South Africa and Botswana. The government subsequently tried to revive the economy through a large-scale programme of privatization. To stabilize the political system, it changed the electoral laws. In addition to the 80 seats determined by the first-past-the-post system, 40 seats were now determined by proportional representation. In 2002 Mosisili was elected to a second term, as the LCD gained 77 of the directly elected seats. The strongest challenger was the BNP, which obtained 21 of the seats awarded through proportional representation. Mosisili was re-elected in 2007, when the LCD took 61 seats. He emphasized the fight against *AIDS as a top priority, as Lesotho had one of the world's highest HIV infection rates, with around 25 per cent of the adult population being HIV positive in 2006, according to UNAIDS.

Lévesque, René (b. 24 Aug. 1922, d. 1 Nov. 1987). Premier of Quebec 1976–85
Born in Campbellton (New Brunswick), after service as a war correspondent during World War II Lévesque joined Radio Canada International and became one of *Quebec's best-known commentators. In 1960 he was elected to the provincial legislature for the *Liberal Party. He held various ministries and was reponsible, for example, for the nationalization of Hydro-Quebec. Disillusioned with the Liberal position on constitutional issues, he founded the *Parti Québécois (PQ) in 1968. He won the 1976 provincial elections and made French the only official language of Quebec. However, he failed to gain popular approval in a 1980 referendum on greater autonomy for the province, losing to a campaign led by *Trudeau and *Chrétien. He also failed to gain sympathy for Quebec's concerns for greater autonomy at the 1981–2 constitutional negotiations (*Canadian Constitution, Patriation of). His popularity waned as he introduced large public-sector spending cuts. He resigned to resume his career in journalism.
    QUIET REVOLUTION

Lewinsky Affair (USA)
An affair between Bill *Clinton and a White House intern, Monica Lewinsky, that emerged as part of the *Whitewater investigations. In January 1998, the independent council on the Whitewater investigation, Kenneth Starr, received congressional authority to investigate against Ms Lewinsky on the allegation that she had lied about having an affair with Clinton under oath. As the media reported on the scandal, Clinton publicly stated that he had not had an affair, and it was not until August that Clinton testified before a grand jury, admitting that he had an 'inappropriate' relationship with Ms Lewinsky. Clinton's earlier statement started the second impeachment trial in US history against a sitting President (the first was against Andrew Johnson in 1868). The House of Representatives voted to impeach the President on two out of four articles of impeachment, but the Senate rejected one of these and split evenly on the second, thus acquitting the President. In a settlement agreed on the day before he left office, Clinton admitted giving false testimony, paid a $25,000 fine and agreed to the suspension of his law licence. The trial marked the high point of the acrimony between Democrats and Republicans in *Congress during the Clinton Presidency, and made it difficult for Clinton to pursue any far-reaching domestic political reform.

Lewis, John Llewellyn (b. 12 Feb. 1880, d. 11 June 1969). President of the United Mine Workers of America (UMWA) 1920–60.
A son of Welsh miner immigrants born in Lucas, Iowa, he began work as a miner aged 17. In 1901 he began his active work for the United Mineworkers of America (UMWA), becoming acting president in 1919 and president in 1920. A leading member of the *AFL (American Federation of Labor), he successfully organized unskilled, mass-production workers into *trade unions. This resulted in a clash with AFL policy in 1935, and in 1936 all such unions, including his miners, were expelled from the AFL; they formed the Congress of Industrial Organizations (CIO), with Lewis as president. During the next four years he led a number of militant and bitter CIO strikes in such industries as steel, automobiles, tyres, and electrical products. In 1940, in protest against *Roosevelt's third-term nomination, he resigned his presidency from the CIO. From this organization he withdrew the miners, whose president he remained, in 1942. A strong personality, he would challenge any authority in the interests of his members. Although more moderate in later years, in 1947 he defied the *Taft-Hartley Act (1947) out of principle by refusing to declare the fact that he was not a Communist on oath.

Leyte Gulf, Battle of (Oct. 1944)
In the campaign to recover the Philippines from Japanese occupation during *World War II, US forces under General *MacArthur landed on the island of Leyte on 20 October 1944. On 23 October Japanese naval forces converged, to attack US transports. In a series of scattered engagements forty Japanese ships were sunk, forty-six were damaged, and 405 planes destroyed. US losses consisted of one light carrier, two escort carriers, and three destroyers. Following this major US victory, the Japanese fleet withdrew from Philippine waters.

Li Dazhao (Li Ta-chao) (b. 6 Oct. 1888, d. 28 Apr. 1927). Chinese Communist leader
Born of a peasant family, Li gained entrance to Tientsin University and later studied in Japan. He returned to China in 1916 and became professor of history and librarian of Beijing University, where he employed young *Mao Zedong as his assistant. From 1917 he was lecturing on *Marxism, and the *May Fourth Movement stimulated him into merging his study groups into the infant Chinese *Communist Party (1921). One of the leading intellectuals supporting the Communists at the time, he worked for good relations with

the *Guomindang. This cooperation deteriorated from 1926 and, after the occupation of Peking by warlord Chang Tso-lin, he fled to the Soviet Embassy, to no avail; he was captured and hanged.

Li Peng (b. Oct. 1928). Prime Minister of China 1987–1998
Born in Chengdu as the son of an official of the Chinese *Communist Party (CCP). When his father was executed by the *Guomindang, he was adopted by *Zhou Enlai. He joined the CCP in 1945. From 1948 to 1955, he studied at the Institute for Energy Sciences in Moscow. Upon his return, he became a chief engineer at electricity works in north-east China, and in 1966 became responsible for the energy supply in Beijing. He survived the *Cultural Revolution with his reputation relatively unharmed, and in 1981 became Minister for Electricity Supply. He joined the Central Committee of the CCP in 1982, and in 1985 became a member of the *Politburo. Largely on account of his technical and industrial knowhow, he succeeded the reformist Prime Minister Zhao Ziyang. He supported *Deng Xiaoping in the *Tiananmen Square Massacre, and emphasized the party's conservative *Maoist ideology in its attempts under *Jiang Zemin to adapt to economic reform. After serving as Prime Minister he remained powerful as the Chairman of the Standing Committee of the National People's Congress until 2003.

Liaquat Ali Khan (b. 1 Oct. 1895, d. 16 Oct. 1951). Prime Minister of Pakistan 1947–51
Born in Karnal (Punjab), he studied at Aligarh, Allahabad, and Oxford, and was admitted to the English Bar in 1922. He returned, and became active in politics almost immediately. He joined the *Muslim League and became a member of the Legislative Council of the United Provinces (1926–40). Especially during his time as secretary of the All-India Muslim League (1936–47), and then as chairperson of the Muslim League Central Parliamentary Board from 1945, he was *Jinnah's right-hand man. Appointed Finance Minister in *Nehru's interim government, he became Prime Minister upon Pakistan's independence in 1947. After Jinnah's death in 1948, he was the dominant figure in the first years of the country. He managed only with difficulty to keep abreast of the factional rivalries within the country's various Muslim groups. In foreign policy, he made peace with India, but found it hard to gain credence for his claim that Pakistan was a nation of equal weight in international affairs. By 1951, he began to lose favour (and control) even among his own

supporters. He was assassinated while addressing a public rally in Rawalpindi.

Liberal Democratic Party (LDP) (Japan)

Foundation Japan's most established party of government was formed in 1955 as a congeries of centre and conservative groupings with the encouragement of business interests. In many respects, anxiety concerning the electoral potential of the newly united *Socialist Party rather than any other common purpose created Japan's conservative consensus, but despite such beginnings the LDP was able to remain Japan's party in power for most of the postwar period.

One important consequence of the circumstances surrounding its birth has been that the LDP has resembled more an alliance of factions than a disciplined political party. Indeed, factionalism became a distinctive feature of the party. Except for a brief period in the 1990s, this was reinforced by the convention that the party president also served as Prime Minister. Because the parliamentary party had a decisive role in the election for the party presidency, the recruitment of faction members from among the LDP's membership in the Diet, and the provision of adequate supplies of money to ensure their loyalty, became an increasing preoccupation for party leaders. At the same time, the range of factions allowed the LDP to accommodate a broad range of constituencies of support and political ideologies.

Political hegemony (1955–93) Opposing wings within the party have disagreed on even the most fundamental issues. This explains its confused policies, for example towards the *Japanese constitution, which it first attempted to rewrite, during the 1950s and early 1960s, and then accepted as it was, despite continuing calls for reform from senior party members. While pursuing perhaps its most important policy goals of industrialization and high economic growth between 1955 and 1970, the LDP also managed to cast itself as an ally of farmers and small businessmen. In foreign affairs during the 1960s, one group within the party promoted calls for the recognition of Communist China, while party policy supported the nationalist regime in Taiwan.

No doubt such amorphousness gave the LDP flexibility during its period of continuous rule (1955–93). By virtue of the length of that rule, it has become well ensconced in its relationships with the bureaucracy and big business. While the label of 'Japan Incorporated' is too superficial, the linkages of this 'iron triangle' (party, business, and bureaucracy) have nevertheless been intimate. Seven of the fifteen men who occupied the premiership between 1955 and 1993 had a background in the bureaucracy. While the civil service provided much of the LDP's talent, business provided the financial resources necessary for success in Japanese elections. The expense entailed in winning an election to the Diet involved the LDP and its leaders in a number of highly publicized scandals such as the Black Mist, *Lockheed, and Recruit affairs in the 1960s, 1970s, and 1980s, respectively, while the party has rarely been free of less spectacular embarrassments.

For all the party's successes, there were periods where the LDP was vulnerable at the polls. Most ironically, between 1955 and 1976, when the party could claim credit for record levels of economic growth, its absolute share of the vote declined from 42 per cent in 1960 to 30 per cent in 1976. Indeed in every House of Representatives election between 1972 and 1983, more of the electorate voted for its opponents than voted for the government. Despite having only a wafer-thin majority after the 1976 Lower House election, the LDP government survived, thanks largely to the over-representation of the rural vote. The LDP recovered some of its former electoral position in the mid-1980s during an economic upturn and under the popular premiership of *Nakasone Yasuhiro. Even so, the party's confidence was undermined with its first ever loss of a majority in the House of Councillors in 1989.

Political renewal (1993–) Fittingly, the LDP's period of uninterrupted rule was brought to an end by its own hands, when Ozawa Ichirô led his faction out of the LDP and helped pass a vote of no confidence in June 1993. One year later, the LDP found itself back in power, although this time its government relied on an improbable, but durable coalition with its old rival the Japanese *Socialist Party (JSP). Throughout the late 1990s, the LDP was unsuccessful at dealing with the country's economic crisis which challenged Japan's economic model at its foundations. Led by *Obuchi, it continued in power in a coalition, from 1998, with the Liberal Party and, from 1999, with New *Kômeitô.

However, the party leadership continued to be entangled in a series of corruption scandals, which came to a head in the short government of Yoshiro Mori (2000–2001), who became Japan's most unpopular Prime Minister since 1945. The LDP's fortunes were revived when the LDP chose the relative outsider, *Koizumi, as its party leader. Under Koizumi, the economy revived, with the party appearing to be less out of touch with the electorate.

In 2005, the LDP was returned to the House of Representatives with an unprecedented majority. Koizumi was succeeded as party leader by Shinzo *Abe in 2006, who also became Prime Minister.

(((()))) SEE WEB LINKS

• The official website of the LDP.

Liberal Democrats (UK)

The popular short name for the Social and Liberal Democrats. It was formed by the merger of the *Liberal Party and the *Social Democratic Party in 1988, when it came under the leadership of Paddy Ashdown (b. 1941). Its life began badly, as it gained only 5 per cent of the vote in the European elections in 1989; but, after consistently achieving higher ratings in local elections, and in parliamentary by-elections, the party recovered to gain 18 per cent in the 1992 general election. The party is often seen as a centre party because of its commitment to a mixed economy. However, it was also committed to more radical policies such as constitutional reform, a federal Europe, and environmental protection. The party has been led by Charles Kennedy (1999–2006) and Menzies ('Ming') Campbell (from 2006), and by 2006 it was represented by 63 MPs in the House of Commons. This constituted the party's largest parliamentary representation since the Liberal Party formed its last government in the interwar years. However, much of this success had been achieved at a time of significant weakness in the Conservative Party, which made the Liberal Democrats highly vulnerable to the revival of the *Conservatives under *Cameron's leadership from 2005.

Liberal Party, Australia

Early history (up to 1949) The first Liberal Party emerged at national level from a fusion of anti-Labor parties (mainly Protectionists and Free Traders) under *Deakin in 1909. After brief spell in government it merged with the National *Labor Party to form the *Nationalist Party in 1917. The Liberal name was revived for the new party that emerged from a fusion of most of the *United Australia Party (UAP) and other groups to form Australia's largest and most successful conservative party. It was chosen for its associations with former prominent leaders with a social conscience, such as Deakin, *Isaacs, and *Barton. Much better organized than the UAP, the Liberal Party fashioned itself into a voice of the urban middle classes. It was ideologically more flexible than its predecessor, and was thus able to become an active proponent of limited government

while at the same time enacting major welfare legislation to benefit the working and the middle classes of society (such as health and university education).

Since 1949 Benefiting from the postwar mood of opportunity within Australian society, the Liberal Party won the 1949 election under the leadership of *Menzies, who remained Prime Minister until 1966. In coalition with the Country Party (*National Party), it continued to benefit from the weakness and the divisions within the Australian *Labor Party and remained in office until the *Whitlam government of 1972. Its ferocious opposition to the latter ensured that it regained office under *Fraser in 1975. However, defeated by *Hawke in 1983, the Liberal Party began an unprecedented period of opposition, which continued under the prime ministership of *Keating.

As the Australian *Labor Party took the political middle ground, and following the departure of its experienced leadership, it developed a right-wing policy and rhetoric modelled on that of *Thatcher and *Reagan. Led by John *Howard, it won the 1996 election with a landslide majority, gaining an absolute majority of seats (76 out of 148), and it formed its usual coalition with the National Party. From 1999, the party was faced with a resurgent Labor Party at the political left-of-centre, as well as the growth of the *One Nation Party on the far right. In response, Howard adopted a more nationalist, anti-immigration platform. In this way, the Liberal Party maintained its appeal to the middle classes, overcoming the challenges from the political right and left, with the success of its economic policies leaving the rival Labor Party struggling to find a response. In the 2004 elections, the Liberal Party increased its share of seats in the House of Representatives from 68 to 74 (out of 150). For the first time in several decades, it also obtained control of the Senate, increasing further its dominance in contemporary Australian politics. Committed to individual freedom and reducing government intervention to its core functions, the Liberal Party has nevertheless presided over a significant increase in government activity. In response to the terrorist threat before and after *September 11, the party presided over the introduction of significant government powers of surveillance, while markedly expanding Australia's military, security and diplomatic commitment abroad.

(((()))) SEE WEB LINKS

• The official website of the Australian Liberal Party.

Liberal Party, Austria

Traditionally, the Freiheitliche Partei Österreichs (FPÖ) could count on the support of 5–10 per cent of the voting population. However, under the leadership of Jörg Haider from 1986, the FPÖ moved to the far right, seeking to incite and exploit popular hostility towards the country's immigrants and resentment of the political system. Subsequently, the FPÖ went from strength to strength, capturing over 22 per cent in the 1994 national elections, and over 30 per cent in many state elections. In 1999 it became the second strongest party in the parliamentary elections by a margin of 415 votes, when it obtained 26.9 per cent of the popular vote. Its appeal had been strengthened by the perceived ossification of traditional Social Democratic and Christian Democratic elites, which were seen as distributing the spoils of power between themselves (*Proporz*). The FPÖ successfully presented itself as a party of the common person, and caused an international uproar when it joined the Christian Democrats in a government coalition. However, participation in government made it more difficult to conduct populist campaigns against the establishment, despite Haider's best efforts. The FPÖ declined sharply in the 2002 elections, though it continued in government, and in 2005 it split, with a disgruntled Haider creating a new organization on the far right, the BZÖ (Bündnis Zukunft Österreich, League for Austria's Future). In the 2006 elections both parties entered parliament, still commanding a combined vote of 15 per cent.

(⊕) SEE WEB LINKS

- The official website of the FPÖ.
- The official website of the BZÖ.

Liberal Party, Canada

Origins Emerging from the earlier Reformers with the creation of the Canadian Confederation (1867), its initial support was based on a coalition between Ontario Nonconformists and Quebec *anticlericals. Following the example of the British *Liberal Party under Gladstone, it demanded equal treatment of all denominations and the end of state interference in religious matters. The Liberals were anti-imperialists and hence tended to be more critical of the Canadian relationship with Britain than their *Conservative rivals. This greater commitment to Canadian *nationalism conflicted and oscillated with their preference for free trade, whose effect was to reduce Canadian independence from

the already dominant US market even further. This programme proved too narrow and divisive to create and sustain national support, so until 1896 the party was in government only once (1874–8).

History (1896–1993) Under the pragmatic leadership of *Laurier, the party built up a strong presence at the grass roots. It created a broad coalition of interests, toning down its most radical demands. For example, through de-emphasizing its anticlericalism the party was able to win the support of most voters in Quebec, a support which remained crucial for its success in becoming the principal party of government of the twentieth century. It was Laurier's return to one of the divisive issues of the Liberal programme, the liberalization of trade with the USA, that brought down the government in 1911. During World War I, the party almost split when Laurier's carefully constructed union between English- and French-speaking support broke down over the issue of compulsory military service overseas. In 1917, some left the party to join *Borden in a Unionist government.

Party strength and unity were restored during the leadership of *Mackenzie King, whose understanding, manipulation, and control of the political system ensured that he became Canada's longest-serving Prime Minister (1921–6, 1926–30, 1935–48). He created a rhetoric of change without legislating change. He articulated specific political concerns while actually blurring them in practice. He also maintained the ideological high ground while being a conciliatory pragmatist. He thus managed to keep the national support of mutually conflicting interests, such as western free traders and eastern protectionists, employers and employees.

This great coalition of interests gradually began to show signs of strain under Mackenzie King's successor, *St Laurent. The party lost its electoral base in the western provinces, until it was led back to power by *Pearson in 1963. He was succeeded by the more flamboyant *Trudeau, who served as Prime Minister from 1968 to 1979, and again from 1980 to 1984. Despite his best efforts to accommodate Quebec nationalists, for which he was much criticized, the vital Liberal support in that province began to erode at the hands of the *Parti Québécois under *Lévesque. Trudeau's charismatic but autocratic leadership style produced deep divisions, and after his departure the party struggled to become an effective alternative to *Mulroney's Progressive Conservative government from 1984.

Contemporary politics (since 1993) Headed by *Chrétien, the Liberals returned to power with a large majority in 1993, and continued to win an absolute majority of seats in 1997 and 2000. Their political predominance was largely due to the regionalization of its opposition, which turned the Liberal Party into Canada's only popular national party. After much equivocation, Chrétien made way for his former Finance Minister, Paul *Martin, as party leader and Prime Minister in 2003. Martin faced a new challenge from a revived opposition, as the Progressive Conservatives with their strongholds in eastern Canada, and the Canadian Alliance with its bases in the west merged to form a single, national Conservative party. Martin's period in office was dogged by a corruption scandal in which the Liberal Party was discovered to have been enriched by federal funds originally allocated to the federalist camp in the Quebec referendum in 1995. While responsibility for these scandals rested primarily with his predecessor, Martin compounded the situation by needlessly calling an election in 2004. The Liberals lost their absolute majority, making Martin's second administration dependent on the fragile support of other parties, notably the *New Democratic Party. Martin lost the 2006 elections after running a poor campaign, and was ultimately succeeded by Stéphane Dion as party leader.

((@)) SEE WEB LINKS

• The official website of the Canadian Liberal Party.

Liberal Party, Germany
Even though the heyday of German *liberalism dates back to 1866–78, the German liberal parties combined (the left-liberal Freisinnige Volkspartei and the right-liberal Nationalliberale Partei) achieved their highest-ever number of votes during the German Empire in 1912. Following the Empire's collapse in 1918, attempts to unite the liberal wings failed. Consequently, the divide between the left-liberal, republican Deutsche Demokratische Partei (DDP) and the right-liberal, initially monarchist, Deutsche Volkspartei (DVP) continued. Under *Stresemann the DVP soon came to accept the Weimar Republic. Indeed, as a result of their close involvement with the new state and its constitution, the DVP and DDP were blamed for the failures of the Republic. This led to the collapse of the Liberal vote from 1928 onwards. Indeed, disaffected Liberals flocked to support *Hitler in droves. In 1945, a Liberal Democratic Party was founded in Eastern Germany, but soon after its foundation it was increasingly controlled by, and subservient to, the Communist regime.

In West Germany, the **FDP (Freie Demokratische Partei, Free Democratic Party)** was founded in 1948, which subsequently attracted 5–10 per cent of the popular vote. However, until the advent of the *Green Party during the 1980s, the FDP's influence was disproportionate to its size. One of three parties in parliament during the 1960s and 1970s, no majority could be formed without it apart from a grand coalition of *CDU and *SPD. As a result, the FDP formed the junior partner in government 1949–59, 1961–6, and between 1969 and 1998. Its influence has been particularly strong in the area of foreign policy, which was determined by Walter Scheel (1968–74), Hans-Dietrich *Genscher (1974–92), and Klaus Kinkel (1992–8), and their commitment to solving the *German Question through 'Ostpolitik'. Following Genscher's departure, the party was at pains to develop a new and distinctive programme. In government until 1998, it spent the subsequent years in opposition to rejuvenate its leadership and its public profile.

((@)) SEE WEB LINKS

• The official website of the FDP.

Liberal Party, New Zealand
The Liberal Party emerged from 1890, representing those candidates who advocated a progressive (graduated) land and income tax instead of the current flat tax rate on property, and who opposed the unrestricted sale (rather than lease) of Crown (state) lands to settlers. The National Liberal Association was founded in 1890, and the party received support from many pre-existing interest groups, such as the trades and labour councils. Candidates who supported its two key demands achieved a majority in the 1890 elections, helped by a redistribution of seats and the introduction of universal malehood suffrage.

The party was initially led by Ballance, but it was under *Sedden's leadership from 1893 that it became a recognizable political party, dominating New Zealand politics until 1912. To strengthen the authority of the leadership against the grass roots, Sedden transformed the party organization and renamed it the Liberal and Labour Federation in 1899. Modelling his party organization on Joseph *Chamberlain's Birmingham party machinery set up in 1880, it was the first party to channel popular 'mass' politics. By removing authority from the rank and file to the leadership, however, the leaders soon lost touch with supporters on the ground.

Despite *Seddon's best intentions to represent the growing labour movement, his party organization, which was in the hands of members from farming and the middle classes, was increasingly seen as unresponsive to the interests of labour. This encouraged the desertion of many labour leaders, who eventually formed the *Labour Party in 1916. The Labour Party posed an existential threat to the Liberals (led by *Ward from 1906), who had put so much emphasis on courting the working and labouring classes through social reform. Increasingly sandwiched between Labour and the conservative *Reform Party, they were unable to govern without the support of Labour from 1919. In 1925 it campaigned as the 'National Party', and in 1927, the ailing party reformed itself as the **United Party,** which was led by *Ward and then by *Forbes. It won the 1928 election through exploiting current dissatisfaction with the Reform Party government under *Coates, but formed an ineffective government in coalition with Labour. In response to the Great *Depression, it formed a coalition with the Reform Party, with which it contested the 1935 general election as the 'National Political Federation'. In 1936, the two parties formally merged as the *National Party.

Liberal Party, UK

The Liberal Party emerged in the mid-nineteenth century when Liberals combined with Whigs and Radicals to dominate government for much of the next sixty years. Its 1905–15 government implemented an extensive pro-gramme of social legislation, which formed the basis of the British *welfare state. The party was divided in World War I, first in 1914 over whether or not to fight, and more importantly in 1916 over conscription, when many Liberals argued that it was wrong for a democracy to compel people to fight. The introduction of conscription under a Liberal-led government led to a crucial decline in (mostly pacifist) Nonconformist support, which had formed the backbone of the party's electoral support before the war.

Interwar years (1918–39) In addition to the collapse of the Liberals' moral world-view, in the years after the war their economic credo was increasingly difficult to maintain, as a return to Free Trade from wartime controls proved illusory and even unpopular given the current economic difficulties. Furthermore, the party was challenged by an increasingly coherent and well-organized Labour Party, and by a *Conservative Party which managed to attract much support from previously staunchly Liberal sections of the population. By the 1920s the party had effectively become ideologically redundant. Finally, the Liberals'

fortunes were shattered by a series of divisions, beginning with the *Coupon Election of 1918, in which they were divided between official Liberals led by *Asquith, and those Liberals led by *Lloyd George who were elected with Conservative backing.

The support of the divided Liberals thus declined markedly during the 1920s, most notably between the 1923 and 1924 general elections, when the number of Liberal seats in the Commons was reduced from 159 to 40. The party formally reunited under Lloyd George in 1926, but he never again enjoyed unqualified support from the rank and file. As a result, his efforts at ideological innovation, most notably the adoption of *Keynesianism in the 'Yellow Book' of 1929, led to a slight electoral gain that year, but failed to translate into renewal at grass roots, or long term electoral recovery.

A further split occurred in 1930–1, when Lloyd George wanted to support the minority Labour government under *MacDonald, whilst John *Simon favoured the Conservatives in their response to the Great *Depression. Despite the objections of Lloyd George, who was ill at the time, in August 1931, the deputy leader, Herbert *Samuel, led the party into a coalition with the Conservatives in the *National Government. Samuel replaced Lloyd George as leader in November 1931. Samuel resigned following the O'Hara agreements, though some so-called Liberal Nationals, led by John *Simon, continued to support the government. By 1945, the Liberal Nationals had become virtually indistinguishable from the conservatives. The Liberal tradition was therefore continued by those led by Samuel, who was succeeded by Archibald *Sinclair in 1935. The Liberals also supported Churchill's wartime coalition.

Further decline (from 1939) After World War II, the party's support declined even further under Clement Davies's leadership (1945–56), with six seats following the 1951 and 1955 elections. The Liberals did, however, maintain some support in Scotland, Wales, and the south-west of England. Joseph *Grimond became leader in 1956, and although he did not gain any more seats in 1959, the party made a recovery in the 1960s. However, despite winning 18 per cent of the votes in 1964 and 16 per cent in 1966, the 'first-past-the-post' electoral system meant that it gained only nine seats in 1964, and twelve in 1966. Under Jeremy Thorpe, the party refused Edward *Heath's offer of a coalition in 1974, but between 1977 and 1978, under David Steel's leadership, it supported *Callaghan's Labour government in the 'Lib-Lab Pact'. In

1981, the Liberals formed an Alliance with the *Social Democratic Party, and the two parties merged in 1988 to form the Social and *Liberal Democrats.

liberalism

An ideology that emphasizes the individual and his or her rights to liberty, the origins of which go back to the seventeenth century and the writings of John Locke. Liberalism became a central political, economic, and social movement in the industrializing countries during the nineteenth century. Its central tenets have been the freedoms of conscience, speech, and opinion. It has striven for parliamentary, constitutional government and an independent judiciary. In the tradition of Adam Smith's *Wealth of Nations* (1776), Liberals have warned against undue state intervention in the economy, the behaviour of which the state should influence only indirectly, through education and encouraging self-help. Perhaps the most crucial problem for liberals has been to define the point at which the state needs to regulate the rights of individuals so that they do not infringe upon each other. From the beginning of the century, liberals have generally moved towards a greater acceptance of the state, recognizing for example its ability to provide a minimum of social welfare as a necessary prerequisite to enable the poor and disadvantaged to realize their full potential. A central paradox of liberalism emerged during the second half of the twentieth century, when in most countries, organized liberal parties declined just as many of their fundamental tenets became generally accepted and realized.

Libération, see RÉSISTANCE, LA

liberation theology

A movement within the Roman *Catholic Church in Latin America. It was made possible by the greater room for regional diversity following the Second *Vatican Council (1962–5), and emerged from the Conference of Latin American Bishops in Medellín, Colombia, in 1968. The conference denounced *capitalism and *Communism as equally opposed to human dignity, and blamed the rich and powerful for the misery of the hungry and the poor. In order to liberate the poor, it called for the establishment of local *comunidades de base*, Christian communities of around fifteen people each, self-help groups in religious as well as secular, economic matters. The movement spread rapidly, and predictably met with fierce opposition from the elites. Hence, one of the movement's leading

proponents, Archbishop Oscar Romero, was murdered in El Salvador in 1980. Liberation theology, was opposed by the Vatican under *John Paul II and Cardinal Ratzinger (*Benedict XVI) through fear of the politicization of the Church. In 1985, the Vatican withdrew its teaching licence from the leading liberation theologian, the Brazilian Leonardo Boff, because of his support for armed struggle as a last resort.

Liberia

The oldest independent republic in Africa (1847) has been marked by fundamental poverty and social inequality.

Early history (up to 1970s) Liberia owes its origin to the American Colonization Society, which resettled African slaves from the USA. The resettled slaves and their descendants formed only a small minority of the total population, but controlled the country's politics and economy. Its currency was linked to the US dollar, while its economy remained heavily reliant on US support. In the 1920s the Firestone Rubber Company planted huge areas of rubber trees and provided a permanent and stable market. President *Tubman (1944–71) introduced a number of liberal, 'open door' policies designed to encourage foreign investment. These were successful in producing economic growth, though they did little to alleviate the poverty of the population, as profits went either abroad or to the Afro-American Liberian elite. In the 1970s, therefore, more than 60 per cent of national income was earned by an elite amounting to around 5 per cent of the population. During that decade, discontent about political and economic repression began to mount, which Tubman's successor, W. R. Tolbert, found increasingly difficult to overcome. Protest was organized around the trade unions, and became articulated through two political parties, the Progressive Alliance of Liberia (PAL) and the Movement for Justice in Africa (MoJA).

Political and civic unrest (1980s–90s) After the Easter rebellion of 1980, the traditional elite was overthrown and many of its members executed, as a group of junior military officers led by Samuel K. Doe came to power. However, the new regime did little to change the country's economic direction. It benefited from rising US aid as much as the old regime had done, and it too was soon faced with opposition, which it brutally suppressed. In consequence, the Libyan-supported National Patriotic Front of Liberia led by Charles Taylor began a guerrilla campaign on 24 December 1989. While *Reagan had wholeheartedly supported Doe's regime, *Bush was more sceptical and withdrew US aid in early 1990. Doe was murdered in autumn 1990, whereupon the country sank into anarchy. The country's various ethnic groups no longer fought the Afro-American elite, but each other instead. More than two-thirds of the entire population had been displaced by the war by 1996, as refugees either within the country or in Guinea and the Ivory Coast. A peace deal was brokered in 1996, and in 1997 Charles Taylor, who during the civil war had been the most powerful warlord in the countryside, became President. He struggled to establish his power, however, because he became entangled in the civil war in neighbouring Guinea, and because Liberia in return faced incursion by rebels from the neighbouring country. Taylor also remained controversial because of his involvement in the illegal diamond trade, and his disregard for human and political rights.

Contemporary politics (since 2003) Taylor resigned in 2003 and went into exile in Nigeria, from where he continued to try to influence Liberian affairs. A transitional government united the major factions until elections in 2006 led to the victory of Ellen *Johnson-Sirleaf. She instituted a *truth and reconciliation commission to help the country to deal with its past, and successfully requested the extradition of Taylor to the *International Criminal Court in The Hague. Johnson-Sirleaf tried to fight endemic corruption amongst government agencies, and to restore basic amenities to the war-torn population.

Libya

Formally a poor country in the southern Mediterranean, Libya's fortunes were transformed by the discovery of vast oil reserves in 1959, which enabled it to become the world's fourth largest oil producer.

Early history (up to 1969) With a predominantly Arab population, its component areas of Tripolitania, Cyrenaica, and Fezzan constituted part of the *Ottoman Empire from 1551 until 1911, when they were conquered by Italy. At first effective Italian control was largely confined to the coastal regions. The three provinces were united in 1934, and in 1939 Libya became an Italian province. After fierce fighting there in the *North African campaigns during World War II, the country was placed under British military rule in January 1943. Italy renounced all claims in 1947 and the country was declared independent by a *UN resolution in 1951.

The federal state was ruled by the Emir of Cyrenaica, Muhammad Idris al-Sanussi, who was proclaimed King Idris I. Despite political independence, it remained heavily reliant on British and US help for its survival, as it had no industry, no agricultural sector, and few known mineral resources. In return for their aid, both Britain and the USA were granted concessions for military bases.

Sudden wealth after the discovery of oil in 1959 caused serious tensions in the traditional, Muslim society, which were fuelled by the King's decision to 'modernize' the state. Political centralization through the abolition of the federal system and the enfranchisement of women alienated much of the Muslim population, and thus facilitated a military coup on 1 September 1969, which deposed the King and brought *Gaddafi to power.

Gaddafi's rule (since 1969) In a country that had been dominated by foreign powers for centuries, Gaddafi's appeal to an anti-capitalist and anti-Communist Arab *nationalism which emphasized Libya's Muslim heritage found a great response among the population. This encouraged him to support *Islamic fundamentalism as well as terrorist organizations which were fighting pro-Western Arab regimes, such as those in the Lebanon, Egypt, and Chad. During the 1980s, this was bound to cause ferocious tension with the USA led by *Reagan, and culminated in the US bombing raid on Tripoli in April 1986. In domestic affairs, Gaddafi brought foreign-owned companies into state control, established free universal health care, introduced a minimum wage, guaranteed a right to work, and provided a comprehensive education system. His creation of 'people's power', however, whereby power was exercised from the bottom up, through a multitude of local committees, could not hide the fact that he remained in total control of his country.

His unsuccessful military intervention in Chad during the 1980s (he claimed the north of the country with its suspected uranium reserves) and increasing foreign political isolation produced a change in Gaddafi's policies. He withdrew his forces from Chad, reallowed private ownership, stopped his support for terrorist activities, and even handed over evidence of his previous support of the *IRA to the British government. At the same time, his attempts at gaining international respectability remained ambiguous, as he continued, for example, to build the developing world's third largest chemical weapons factories. During the *Gulf War, he even condemned Saddam *Hussein's invasion of Kuwait.

Gaddafi's growing moderation resulted in opposition from radical Islamic groups, to which Gaddafi responded by imprisoning 2,000 militant Muslims in 1994. However, his policy changes failed to impress the USA and the UK, who persuaded the *UN to pass international sanctions against the country in 1992. This was caused by Gaddafi's refusal to extradite two Libyans suspected of bombing an aircraft which exploded over Lockerbie, Scotland, objecting to the ambiguity of British and US evidence. The economic blockade caused considerable shortages in the Libyan economy, though its main export, oil, was unaffected.

Contemporary politics (since 2001) Eventually, Gaddafi agreed to a compromise whereby the two suspects were extradited to the Netherlands, where they were tried under Scottish law, which resulted in one conviction in 2001. As a consequence, Libya gradually overcame its international isolation. In 2003, the US and the UK formally welcomed Libya back into the international community as it agreed to give up its weapons of mass destruction. Foreign companies returned to Libya, with the EU and the USA particularly eager to resume business with the former pariah state.

Lidice, see HEYDRICH, REINHARD

Lie, Trygve Halvdan (b. 16 July 1896, d. 30 Dec. 1968). UN Secretary-General 1946–53
A successful barrister born in Grorud (near Oslo), he joined the Norwegian Labour Party (later the Social Democrats) in 1919. He became its legal adviser and was elected to the Storting (parliament). He was Minister of Justice (1935–9), Minister of Supplies (1939–40), and Foreign Minister (1941–6), serving in the exiled Norwegian government in London, 1941–5. Owing to his internationalist convictions he was elected *UN Secretary-General in 1946, and again in 1950. Within weeks of presenting a twenty-year peace plan to the UN, he was faced with one of the organization's biggest challenges after World War II, the North Korean invasion of South

Korea. He responded by organizing UN assistance for South Korea, leading to the *Korean War. As a result, the USSR refused him its support, so that he resigned in 1953. He returned to Norwegian politics as Minister of Industry (1963–4) and as Minister of Commerce (1964–5).

Liebknecht, Karl (b. 13 Aug. 1871, d. 15 Jan. 1919). German Communist
A lawyer, he joined the *SPD in 1900. He served as a member of the Prussian Chamber of Deputies in 1908, and in the German parliament in 1912, where he was the sole MP to reject the taking of loans to finance the war on 4 December 1914. Because of his opposition to the war he was expelled from the party and imprisoned 1916–18. Together with Rosa *Luxemburg he founded the *Spartakist group and the *Communist Party on 1 January 1919. He was murdered in a Spartakist rising which he led.

Liechten-stein
A tiny duchy between Austria and Switzerland founded in 1719, it achieved independence on 6 August 1806. In the nineteenth century, its

economy was integrated into that of *Austria-Hungary. When that state collapsed in 1918, it began a process of reorientation towards Switzerland. A new Constitution was passed in 1921, and it entered a customs, economic, and currency union with Switzerland in 1923. Ruled by Duke Francis Joseph II (r. 1938–89), after World War II it developed into one of the world's most prosperous countries, becoming a low-tax zone for international corporations and banks; in the early 1990s, with around 30,000 inhabitants, it was home to around 40,000 holdings and corporations. Under the progressive Duke Hans-Adam II (r. 1989–), the population voted, in marked contrast to Switzerland, for an end to the country's economic isolation and entry into the European Economic Area, which came into effect on 1 May 1995. From 1995, Hans-Adam became involved in a bitter controversy with parliament and the judiciary. At issue was a proposed constitutional reform, and the future political role of the Duke. In 2001, a compromise was finally being worked out. From an international point of view, the country's lax banking laws were much more serious, as evidence mounted from 2000 that it had become a safe haven for money laundering and tax evasion. As a result of pressure, the country took steps to prevent the incidence of money laundering, though it continued to be a relatively safe haven for foreign accounts.

Likud ('Union'), Israel

An alliance of a number of right-wing parties which was established in 1973, and grew into a cohesive movement by 1977. Led then by *Begin, its victory in that year produced a major sea-change in Israeli politics, which had hitherto been dominated by *Mapai and its successor, the *Labour Party.

Political domination (1980s and 1990s) Likud was opposed to the trade union (*Histadrut) influence in the economy, though it did continue Labour's promotion of Jewish immigration. It pursued a hardline policy towards its Arab neighbours and the Palestinians, hoping to legitimize the eventual annexation of the *West Bank and *Gaza Strip through encouraging the creation of Jewish settlements there. Nevertheless, Begin concluded the *Camp David Accords which resulted in peace with Egypt, though this was perhaps as much a testimony to US pressure and *Carter's diplomacy as a demonstration of Begin's will to accommodate his Arab neighbours. This was shown in 1982, when Israel invaded the Lebanon in an abortive effort to wipe out the *PLO. Under the conservative *Shamir, Likud continued to govern until 1992 (except for 1984–6), though from 1981 with very fragile majorities. In opposition, it fiercely resisted the *Oslo Accords and the recognition of the *PLO. The general atmosphere of hatred which this helped to create against the Labour Party, and its leaders *Peres and *Rabin in particular, was held partly responsible for the assassination of Rabin by a militant Israeli.

Division (after 2005) *Hezbollah bomb attacks allowed Likud's new leader, *Netanyahu, to present it as the party of security, so that it was returned to power in the 1996 elections. Likud lost the elections of 1999, but in 2000 its leader, Ariel *Sharon, incited a renewal of the Palestinian *Intifadah. Amidst the growing violence between Israelis and Palestinians, Sharon became regarded as a guarantor of security, and he was elected Prime Minister in 2001. Despite his hardline stance against the Palestinians, however, Sharon continually feared being undermined by the even more right-wing Netanyahu, who continued to exert considerable influence over sections of the party. Faced with growing resistance within the party to his plans that Israel withdraw from Gaza, Sharon and other leading party members left Likud in 2005 to create a new party, *Kadima. Netanyahu returned to the leadership of Likud, but the party did poorly in the 2006 elections, as it was pushed into joint third place, behind Kadima and Labour.

Lin Baio (Lin Piao) (b. 1907, d. 13 Sept. 1971). Minister of Defence of China 1959–71

Born at Huanggang, he joined the Socialist Youth League when at school and in 1925 enrolled at the Whampoa Military Academy, where he graduated with high honours before joining *Chiang Kai-shek's *Northern Expedition in July 1926. On the split between the *Guomindang and the Communists in 1927, he joined the Chinese Communist Party and became one of the military commanders of the *Jiangxi Soviet. He commanded the 1st Army Corps in the *Long March to *Yan'an, where at 28 he became head of the Red Army Academy. In 1937, during the *Sino-Japanese War, he scored a morale-boosting victory at the battle of P'inghsing Pass. He was injured in 1939, and went to Moscow for medical treatment (until 1942). During the *Chinese Civil War his capture of Manchuria from the Nationalists was achieved through patient wooing of the peasantry. Lin built up an army of a million men, allowing him to capture Mukden (now Shenyang) in October 1948, and to move on to take Beijing in January 1949. A loyal supporter of *Mao Zedong, he was created a marshal (1955). As Minister of Defence and commander of the army, his support for Mao in the *Cultural Revolution was crucial. He used the upheaval to his own advantage by insisting that he receive constitutional guarantees for his succession, and using the purges to remove his opponents and increase his control over the army. Growing ever more fearful of his power, Mao blocked his attempt to become Chairman of the Republic in 1970. After an ostensible coup attempt against Mao failed, he was killed in an air crash in September 1971 while fleeing to the Soviet Union.

Lin Piao, see LIN BAIO

Lithuania

A Baltic country whose history has been closely enmeshed with that of its large neighbours, Russia and Poland.

Early history (up to 1918) Lithuania was tied to Poland for four centuries, during which time a Polish landowning elite emerged, while the towns were dominated by Jewish mercantile groups. After the territory was annexed by Russia in 1795, a nationalist movement began to emerge during the late nineteenth century which was directed against social and economic domination by the Poles, and the political domination of the Russians. After the *Russian Revolution of 1905 it received its own parliament. In 1915, it was occupied by German troops and encouraged towards independence, which was proclaimed in 1918.

Independence (1918–40) After the German defeat, Lithuania was sandwiched between Soviet Russia which challenged its independent existence, only accepting it in 1920, and Pilsudski's Poland which desired a revival of the union between the countries under Polish leadership. When that failed, Poland annexed substantial parts of middle Lithuania, including its capital, Vilnius. In return, Lithuanian troops occupied the German-speaking area around the Baltic town of Memel (Klaipéda). Subsequently, there was social unrest as large estates were expropriated, and many illiterate Lithuanian peasants moved into the cities to find that they were socially and economically disadvantaged compared with the urban elites, many of whom were Jewish. These problems were compounded by a weak parliamentary system, as proportional representation reproduced social divisions and created unstable multi-party coalition governments. An army coup brought to power Antanas Smetona, who gradually built up a *Fascist state.

Soviet occupation (1940–89) Under the terms of the *Hitler–Stalin Pact of 1939, Lithuania was occupied by the *Red Army on 14 June 1940, and was integrated into the USSR as a Soviet Republic on 3 August 1940. It was occupied by German troops in 1941, until the Red Army returned in 1944. In marked contrast to the other Baltic States (Latvia and Estonia), the absence of any major industries, ports, or minerals made the country much less important for the USSR. Hence, no efforts were made to tie it closer to the USSR through forcibly exchanging part of the Lithuanian population with non-Lithuanians. As a result, it retained a relatively homogeneous population, over 80 per cent of whom were Lithuanian.

Post-Soviet Independence (since 1989) After *Gorbachev's reformist policies of *glasnost*, it was the first and most vociferous of the Baltic States to demand its

independence. After violent clashes, this was recognized by *Russia under Yeltsin in 1991. Its economy, which was much weaker than that of its Baltic neighbours, had considerable difficulty in adapting to a *capitalist economic system. A brief period of recovery in the mid-1990s was halted in 1998, as Lithuania's economy was adversely affected by the economic downturn in neighbouring Russia. Meanwhile, the country's democracy continued to be characterized by a quick succession of prime ministers, and a rapidly-shifting political landscape. To overcome this fragmentation in part, the former Communist and Socialist parties merged in 2001. They became the largest parliamentary party under the newly elected Prime Minister, Algirdas M. Brazauskas. In 2004, President Rolandas Paksas was impeached on charges of corruption, passing on state secrets, and abuse of power. The ensuing elections were won by reform-oriented former President Valdas Adamkus. Despite continuing problems of corruption, Lithuania's economy grew markedly from 2001 to 2006, between over 6 and 8 per cent each year.

Little Entente (1920–38)

An alliance between Czechoslovakia, Romania, and Yugoslavia that emerged from a series of bilateral agreements made from 1920, and was formalized in 1929. It sought to protect the *status quo* in central Europe as established through the Treaties of *St Germain and *Trianon. In February 1933, a permanent council was established, and military consultations began soon afterwards. However, in concentrating on possible Hungarian and Austrian expansionism it failed to take into account the implications of the rise of *Nazism. Hence it proved completely unable to respond to the German invasion of the *Sudetenland or the *Munich Agreement of 1938.

Litvinov, Maxim Maximovich (b. 17 July 1876, d. 31 Dec. 1951). Soviet Foreign Commissar 1930–9

Born Max Wallach of a Jewish family in Belostok (Russian Poland), he joined the Russian Social Democratic (Workers') Party on its foundation in 1898. A firm supporter of *Lenin, he was soon imprisoned, but escaped in 1902 and then acted abroad as an arms agent for the 1905 *Russian Revolution. He returned to Russia but was deported and went to France and then London. After the *Russian Revolution of October 1917 he was appointed the first

*Bolshevik representative in London, from where he was deported in 1918. He then worked in the Soviet Foreign Office and from 1926 was virtually in control of Soviet foreign policy, although not appointed Foreign Commissar until 1930. He brought the USSR into the *League of Nations and, through his rhetorical emphasis on *disarmament and anti-*Fascism, played some part in portraying a more acceptable face of a country ravaged by *Stalin's terror and the *Great Purge. A strong advocate of collective security against the *Axis Powers, he was replaced by *Molotov before the signing of the *Hitler–Stalin Pact. He served as Soviet ambassador to the USA between 1941 and 1943.

Liu Shaoqi (Liu Shao-chi) (b. 24 Nov. 1898, d. 12 Nov. 1969). President of the People's Republic of China 1959–66

Born of a wealthy peasant family near Changsha (Hunan province), he attended the same school as *Mao Zedong who was five years his elder. In 1920 he went to Shanghai, where he joined the Socialist Youth League (1921). In late 1921 he went to study in the Soviet Union, and joined the Chinese *Communist Party (CCP). He returned in 1922 and became a Communist *trade-union organizer in Hunan, Guangzhou (Canton), and Shanghai respectively, before becoming a member of the Central Committee of the CCP in 1927. In 1932, he arrived in *Jianxi, where he resumed his friendship with Mao. He took part in the *Long March, and gradually rose to become the party's chief organizer, and an important theoretician. He disagreed with, but tolerated, the development of a cult around 'Chairman Mao'. An austere, hard-working, and incorruptible man, he published his views on *How to be a Good Communist* for the first time in 1939. Second in the political hierarchy only to Mao from 1945, his efficiency as party organizer stemmed from his good working relations with almost all leaders of importance. The pragmatic Liu became President after the failure of the disastrous *Great Leap Forward, when Mao Zedong was forced to 'retire' from this office. He stabilized the economy and society in the early 1960s, gaining increasing stature and authority in the process. He was thus the most immediate target of a threatened Mao in the *Cultural Revolution. He was imprisoned on 17 October 1969, and, after being forbidden medical assistance, he died from an illness. He was rehabilitated posthumously in 1980.

Lloyd George, David, 1st Earl Lloyd-George of Dwyfor (b. 17 Jan. 1863, d. 26 Mar. 1945). British Prime Minister 1916–22

Early career (up to 1916) Born in Manchester of Welsh parents, he was brought up in Wales after the early death of his father. Following his qualification as a solicitor in 1884 he worked in Porthmadog, where he became active in local politics for the *Liberal Party. He was successful in law, and was elected as Liberal MP for Caernarfon Boroughs in 1890. A fiery orator, he rose to national prominence in 1899, over his virulent opposition to the *South African (Boer) War at a time when many Liberals were embarrassed by their hostility to the war. In 1905, *Campbell-Bannerman appointed him President of the Board of Trade. He rapidly established a reputation for competence and energy, and in 1908 he followed *Asquith as Chancellor of the Exchequer.

Here he gained a crucial reputation for leadership, inventiveness, and success in difficult circumstances. His 1909 People's Budget introduced old-age pensions, with increasing demands for government expenditure being met by progressive direct taxation. He branded the resulting opposition by the Conservative House of Lords as an illegitimate attack of privilege against people, paving the way for the 1911 *Parliament Act, which reduced the powers of the Lords. He was also responsible for the National Insurance Act of 1911, which instituted a scheme of insurance against ill health.

Prime Minister (1916–22) Originally at the Treasury at the outbreak of World War I, his energy was required at the Ministry of Munitions, where he went in May 1915. He ended the shell shortage on the Western Front, and his vigorous pursuit of war made him the obvious choice to take over from Asquith as Prime Minister. His War Cabinet was highly efficient, and Britain's recovery from near-defeat is often attributed to his leadership. However, he failed to translate his enormous personal prestige at the end of the war into the badly needed invigoration of the ailing Liberal Party, which he split by his decision to continue working with his wartime *Conservative coalition partners.

Having won the *Coupon Election, he led the British delegation to the *Paris Peace Conference of 1919, where he was a moderating influence on French demands for German *reparations. Even more urgent was the need to find a response to Irish demands for independence. This was mostly granted in 1921 when southern Ireland gained effective independence as a Dominion, while *Northern Ireland remained a part of the United Kingdom. Unfortunately, Lloyd George was increasingly perceived to be failing on his election promise of 1918 to build the 'land fit for heroes' that soldiers returning from the war had hoped for, and the Conservatives became increasingly disillusioned with his leadership. They disliked his personal style and increasingly failed to see why this Liberal should be so indispensable to the Conservative Party, which had a large majority in the House of Commons. Despite the loyalty of most Conservative Ministers, the party forced his resignation as Prime Minister.

In opposition (from 1922) Deeply divided between the followers of Lloyd George and Asquith, the Liberals were unable to avoid being overtaken by the *Labour Party as the second party in British politics. Following Asquith's retirement, Lloyd George became leader of a united party once again in 1926, but even his energy and inventiveness, which he displayed in 1929 through the adoption of a new political programme partly inspired by *Keynes, was unable to regain the initiative for the Liberal Party. He opposed the Liberal Party's support of the *National Government's decision to call an election in 1931, and after this led a small group of Independent Liberals in the Commons. Despite his sympathy with some of Germany's grievances arising out of *Versailles, he opposed the *Munich Agreement, and supported British entry into the war in 1939. He refused office in *Churchill's coalition, as the latter wanted to make the offer conditional on Neville *Chamberlain's agreement.

Locarno, Treaties of (1925)

A series of international agreements discussed in October 1925, and signed in December, which greatly stabilized Europe. In the main agreement, Germany recognized its frontier with France and Belgium as specified in the Treaty of *Versailles, along with the demilitarized status of the Rhineland. This treaty was guaranteed by the UK and Italy. Meanwhile, Germany agreed with Poland and Czechoslovakia that, although it did not regard its borders with them as settled, it would not seek to revise them by force. France also signed treaties of mutual guarantee with Poland and Czechoslovakia. In return for its pledges, Germany was admitted to the *League of Nations as a permanent member of its council. The main figures at the Locarno Conference were Austen *Chamberlain, Gustav *Stresemann, and Aristide *Briand,

the latter two receiving the *Nobel Peace Prize in recognition of the treaty in 1926.

Lockheed Scandal

By 1971 the US Lockheed Aircraft Corporation was in severe financial trouble and it embarked on a policy of allocating $24 million as bribe money to win foreign orders. In February 1976 revelations to a US Senate subcommittee led to official action in Japan, the Netherlands, and Italy. In Japan payments had allegedly been made to ex-Prime Minister *Tanaka Kakuei who received 500 million yen to ensure that All Nippon Airways bought Lockheed aircraft. Tanaka was eventually sentenced to four years' imprisonment in 1983, but remained an influential figure in Japanese politics. More importantly, the scandal highlighted a general occurrence of corruption in Japanese political circles. In the Netherlands the husband of Queen Juliana, Prince Bernhard, Inspector-General of the Armed Forces, was discredited for having received $1.1 million, while in Italy two former defence ministers were named as having purchased Lockheed aircraft for the Italian air force against the taking of bribes.

Lomé Convention (28 Feb. 1975)

A trade agreement between the EEC (*European integration) and 64 countries in the Caribbean, the Pacific, and Africa, all former colonies of the EEC member states, signed in the Togolese capital of Lomé. It waived the tariffs for goods entering the EEC from these countries, and provided for substantial economic and development aid. It was succeeded by a number of revised treaties, culminating in Lomé IV, which was signed by 70 states on 15 December 1989. For ten years this provided for 99.5 per cent of the signatory states' exports into the EC to be free of tariffs, and for a development grant of 12 billion ECU (around $16.5 billion) for 1990–5. For the second five-year period under Lomé IV, the EC paid almost 15 billion ECU in aid. Lomé provided substantial aid to the signatory states, and gave their exports substantial advantages. However, there is little evidence that Lomé encouraged the economies of the signatory states to become more efficient. In 2000, the Lomé agreements were replaced by the *Cotounou agreements.

Lon Nol (b. 13 Nov. 1913, d. 17 Nov. 1985). President of the Khmer Republic (Cambodia) 1972–5

Born in Prey Veng district as the grandson of a provincial Governor, he was educated in Saigon and joined the civil service, himself rising to the rank of provincial Governor by

1945. An ally of *Sihanouk, he was Minister of Defence (1955–66), when he supervised a number of campaigns against Communist guerrillas. As Prime Minister (1966–7), he suppressed a peasant revolt in Samalut. Again Prime Minister from 1969, he opposed Sihanouk's policy of neutrality and in 1970 led a coup which deposed him. He established close ties with US and South Vietnamese forces in Saigon, allowing them to operate in Cambodia. On 10 March 1972 he took full power as President of the Khmer Republic, but by 1974 his inept leadership had reduced his control to Pnomh Penh and Battambang. After the fall of *Saigon, he was flown out by US helicopters in April 1975. He went into exile in Hawaii.

London Bombings (7 July 2005)

Four terrorist attacks in London which were carried out on behalf of *al-Qaeda. At around 9 am three bombs exploded on three different underground trains at rush hour. A separate bomb went off on a London bus. Over 700 people were injured in the blasts, 52 were killed, and several thousands were psychologically affected. Two weeks later, further bombs were planted, but failed to detonate.

London, Treaty of (26 Apr. 1915)

A secret treaty between Russia, Britain, and France on the one side, and Italy on the other. In an effort to induce Italy to enter *World War I within a month, the other powers confirmed Italian possessions of Libya and the Dodecanese, and promised Italian possession of Italia Irredenta, i.e. *South Tirol, Trentino, Istria, Gorizia, Gradisca, and *Trieste. It would also gain stretches along the Dalmatian coast, and Turkish areas in Asia Minor. Italy did enter the war on 24 May, but the opening of a southern front failed to change the balance of the war decisively. After the *Russian Revolutions of 1917, the *Bolsheviks refuted all treaties concluded by the previous Tsarist regime. The Treaty of London stood in flagrant violation of US President *Wilson's plans for a postwar order, and thus received little regard at the *Paris Peace Conference, where Italy was awarded much, though not all, of Italia Irredenta. Italian outrage against the violation of the treaty gave a stimulus to populist, *irredentist groups such as those led by *D'Annuncio and *Mussolini.

FIUME

Long, Huey Pierce (b. 30 Aug. 1893, d. 10 Sept. 1935). US Senator 1931–5

Born in Winn Parish, Louisiana, of moderate background, he early established himself as a successful lawyer, although he never graduated from his law studies at Oklahoma University and Tulane. He then entered state politics, building himself a strong and ruthless political machine, and rising through various political offices in Louisiana to become Governor (1928–32) and then Senator from 1931. He held both offices simultaneously until he succeeded in preventing his lieutenant governor, Paul Cyr, from following him as Governor.

Long used ruthless and corrupt methods to modernize his state and shore up his power base against the entrenched 'Bourbon' oligarchy that had been so influential. Known as 'Kingfish', he persuaded the state legislature to pass a series of welfare measures, especially for education. His programme of construction of roads, bridges, and public buildings was largely carried out by private contractors, against the vested interests of the public utility companies as well as the oil companies. Despite initial support, Long quickly turned against Franklin D. *Roosevelt, seeing the *New Deal as a watered-down version to his more radical 'Share our wealth' programme for the redistribution of income. Long's charismatic, if radical, appeal came close to dividing the *Democratic Party, but he was assassinated before he could run for the Presidency in 1936.

Long March (Oct. 1934 – Oct. 1935)

A march begun on 19 October 1934 by some 100,000 Communist Red Army soldiers from the *Jianxi Soviet, in a successful effort to break out of *Chiang Kai-shek's army's suffocating fifth encirclement. After a series of military set-backs, the military leadership passed to *Mao Zedong on 8 January 1935. While the 4th Army broke away from his leadership to march to Sichuan in the south, Mao shifted the emphasis of a revolution to the countryside, and decided to lead his men to the little-populated northern area of Shaanxi. Despite constant harassment and attack by *Guomindang forces, and difficult terrain along the way, he arrived with around 6,000 men in *Yan'an, having covered around 6,000 miles (9,600 km) in the year. He was later joined by other groups, including remnants of the severely reduced 4th Army, so that, in all, around 30,000 survived the epic journey.

López Mateos Adolfo (b. 26 May 1910, d. 22 Sept. 1969). President of Mexico 1958–64

A graduate in law, he became a university lecturer and entered politics in 1946. He became secretary-general of Mexico's major party, the Institutional Revolutionary Party (*PRI), and was a successful Minister of Labour under President Cortines (1952–8). Despite his pro-labour reputation, as President he broke the militant railworkers' strike of 1959, but afterwards he introduced a general profit-sharing plan for Mexican workers. He carried out a land reform whose extent was second only to that of *Cárdenas, as 30 million acres (around 12.1 million hectares) of land were redistributed to landless peasants. A low rate of inflation and a stable exchange rate were maintained, which attracted foreign investment. In foreign affairs, he finally settled a long-running border dispute south of El Paso with the USA, and maintained a foreign policy of conscious independence from the USA, refusing to break diplomatic relations with *Castro's Cuba.

López Portillo y Pacheco, José (b. 16 June 1920, d. 17 Feb. 2004). President of Mexico 1976–82

A professor of jurisprudence, he was an adviser to President *Echeverría. Upon his own election he struggled to stabilize the country's economy, despite the discovery of vast new oil reserves and the current high oil prices. In consequence, petroleum earnings increased from $500 million in 1976 to $13 billion in 1981. He squandered much of this wealth, and his government became prone to corruption. Mexico became over-reliant on oil exports, as became clear after 1981 when the decline in oil prices plunged the country into a deep economic crisis, which was made worse by an increase in foreign public debt to $57 billion by 1982. Given the economic hardships suffered by many Mexicans, he sought to defuse tension through political reform. To relax slightly the ruling Institutional Revolutionary Party's (*PRI) iron grip on power, he guaranteed the opposition a quarter of the seats in an enlarged Chamber of Deputies.

Lords, House of (UK), see PARLIAMENT (UK)

Lorraine, see ALSACE-LORRAINE

Los Angeles race riots, see RACE RIOTS, LOS ANGELES

Ludendorff, Erich (b. 9 Apr. 1865, d. 20 Dec. 1937). German general

A member of the German army's General Staff from 1908, he acquired a mythical reputation in World War I following his conquest of Liège and his victory at *Tannenberg in 1914. Until 1916, he effectively ran the German campaign on the Eastern Front. Together with *Hindenburg, he directed the German war effort (1916–18) and organized a total mobilization of the country's resources for the war. At the same time, he disregarded the German parliament's peace resolution of 1917, as well as any attempt at political reform. From September 1918 he pressed for an armistice. He left the army the following month. Ludendorff subsequently propagated the 'stab-in-the-back' myth, according to which the military was about to win the war in 1918 when the politicians stabbed the generals in the back and surrendered to the Allies. In 1923, he took part in the *Hitler Putsch.

Lugard, Frederick Dealtry, Baron Lugard of Abinger (b. 22 Jan. 1858, d. 11 Apr. 1945). British colonial administrator

Born in Madras, India, he was educated at Rossall School and the Royal Military College, Sandhurst. He gained an army commission in 1878, and having served in various countries, he joined the British East Africa Company in 1889. He persuaded the British government to make Uganda a protectorate in 1894, and then moved to Nigeria to work for the Royal Niger Company. There, in 1898, he raised the West African Frontier Force, which prevented French and German expansion in the area, and defeated the *Fulani. He then established the Northern Nigerian protectorate. Lugard was Hong Kong's Governor (1907–12), but returned to Nigeria in 1912, serving as its governor in 1914–19, having created a single colony from the northern and southern protectorates. Always commanding only a tiny military force of Europeans, his system of *indirect rule depended on negotiations with and use of existing traditional power structures. Though this approach was by no means original, his writings on the subject ensured that this system became almost universally adopted throughout the *British Empire by 1940. Between 1922 and 1936, he was a senior member of the *League of Nations Permanent *Mandates Commission.

Lula (Luiz Ignácio Lula da Silva) (b. 27 Oct 1945). President of Brazil, 2002–

Born into a poor family in the state of Pernambuco, he received little formal education before eventually becoming a worker in the automobile industry. He became a trade union leader, and in 1980 was instrumental in founding the Workers' Party (Partido dos Trabalhadores). Elected to Congress in 1986, he stood unsuccessfully for President three times before winning the elections of 2002 and 2006. He assured investors of Brazil's commitment to paying its debts, with his left-wing populism being more evident in the foreign policy arena. He sought to reduce the USA's influence over the continent by strengthening regional alliances such as *Mercosur, while also forming close relations with other emerging left-wing populist regimes in Venezuela, Bolivia and Ecuador.

Lumumba, Patrice Emergy (b. 2 July 1925, d. 17 July 1961). Prime Minister of the Democratic Republic of Congo 1960

Born in central Congo, he worked in the Belgian colonial administration as a postal clerk. Perhaps the first openly to demand independence on 28 December 1958, he founded the influential Mouvement National Congolais (National Congolese Movement) to bring together radical nationalists. He was briefly imprisoned before participating at the Brussels Conference (January 1960) on the independence of Belgian Congo. Upon independence he became Prime Minister and Minister of Defence. During the *Congo Crisis, his rival, President *Kasavubu, dismissed him and shortly afterwards he was put under arrest by Colonel *Mobutu. He escaped but was recaptured and murdered. His country's leading proponent of *pan-Africanism, he is regarded as a national hero and martyr by many in Congo.

Lusitania

A British transatlantic liner which was torpedoed on 7 May 1915 off the Irish coast, without warning, by a German submarine, with the loss of 1,198 lives. The sinking, which took 128 US lives, created intense indignation throughout the USA, which until then had overwhelmingly supported President *Wilson's policy of neutrality. Wilson sent a strong note of protest, but Germany refused to accept responsibility, claiming that the ship had been carrying war materials, and no reparations settlement was reached. However, the strength of the reaction caused the Germans to back down and stop their **submarine warfare**, as they were left in no doubt that further torpedoing of shipping would lead to US entry into the war. Two years later, when Germany had come effectively under a military government, submarine warfare was resumed in a desperate measure to try to starve the British into submission. The German leadership remembered the *Lusitania* incident, but argued (mistakenly) that Britain would surrender before the impact of the US entry into the war could have any major effect.

Luthuli, Albert John (b. 1898, d. 21 July 1967). President-General of the ANC 1952–67

Born in Bulawayo (Southern Rhodesia, now Zimbabwe), he studied at Adams College and stayed there to train teachers. He became

Secretary of the African Teachers' Association in 1928, but left in 1936, when he was elected chief of his people in Groutville (Natal). His effort to revive the economic fortunes of his own and other Black people directed his attention to the *ANC, which he joined in 1945. President of the Natal branch of the ANC from 1950, the government withdrew him from his chieftainship in 1952, whereupon he was elected president-general of the ANC. A committed Christian, he managed to extend the ANC's membership while maintaining the principle of non-violence. His willingness to cooperate with Whites (particularly from the *Communist Party), Indians, and Coloureds led to conflict with the ANC's more radical members, who broke away under *Sobukwe to form the *PAC. In 1961, he became the first African to receive the *Nobel Peace Prize, the money from which he used to buy farms for political exiles in Swaziland.

Luxembourg

A small country between France, Germany, and Belgium, Luxembourg has enjoyed disproportionate influnce as a founding member of the EU.

Independent since 1815, Luxembourg was divided between its larger, northern part, which became part of Belgium, and its southern part, which remained a Grand Duchy in 1915. Officially recognized as a neutral state since 1867, the Grand Duchy was nevertheless occupied by German troops during World Wars I and II. In 1948, it joined a customs union with the Netherlands and Belgium which became the *Benelux Customs Union in 1960. It also became an enthusiastic member of the European Community, and of all projects promoting further *European integration. This resulted partly from its geographical position at the heart of Europe, and partly from the direct benefit which it derived as one of the three main administrative centres of the European Union, as the seat of the *European Court of Justice and the Secretariat of the *European Parliament. Luxembourg also benefited from the large-scale presence of banking, and of a modern steel industry.

In 2000 Luxembourg had the world's highest per capita GDP. From 1984, it was governed by a coalition of the Christian Social

People's Party and the Social Workers' Party, led by Jacques Santer (b. 1937). In 1995, the latter was succeeded by Jean-Claude Juncker, who from 1999 led a coalition with the Democratic (Liberal) Party. In 2000, Archduke Jean (b. 1921) abdicated in favour of his eldest son, Henri. Two Prime Ministers, Gasthon Torn and Jacques Santer, served as President of the *European Commission, while Jean-Claude Juncker became a favourite for the post in 2005, though he declined.

Luxemburg, Rosa (b. 5 Mar. 1870, d. 15 Jan. 1919). Co-founder of the German Communist Party

Born in Russian Poland, she acquired German citizenship and entered the German *SPD (Social Democratic Party) in 1898. From 1907 to 1914 she taught at the Socialist Party school in Berlin. She was hostile to *Bernstein's revisionism, urging instead a revolution through the instrument of the general strike. At the same time, against *Lenin she insisted on a more democratic variety of *Communism. With K. *Liebknecht she opposed World War I and founded the *Spartakist Group to that end in 1916. She was murdered by members of the *Freikorps when she led a rising of Spartakist workers in the streets of Berlin.

Lyautey, Louis Hubert-Gonzalve (b. 17 Nov. 1854, d. 21 Mar. 1934). French marshal

Born in Nancy, Lyautey graduated from the French Military Academy of Saint-Cyr in 1873 and spent most of his professional life in the French colonial service. He became Resident-General of Morocco in 1912, but was recalled to Paris as Minister of War in 1916. Put off by the turbulence of parliamentary politics, Lyautey returned to Morocco in 1917 and served there until retirement in 1925. A paternalistic, but extremely successful, Governor, he carried out major infrastructural improvements, irrigation and engineering projects, and the introduction of modern farming methods. He respected inherent traditions and Islamic culture, as well as the role of the Sultan. Lyautey was widely respected in France, but his enlightened views were not shared by his successors in the colonial administration.
FRENCH EMPIRE

Lynch, John ('Jack') (b. 15 Aug. 1917, d. 20 Oct. 1999). Prime Minister (Taoiseach) of the Irish Republic 1966–73, 1977–9

Born in Cork, and educated at University College Cork, and King's Inns Dublin, Lynch gained his first fame as a sportsman. In the 1940s he captured five All-Ireland medals for hurling and one for Gaelic football. He was elected to Dáil Éireann (the Irish parliament) for Cork City in 1948, and served in a number of ministerial posts (including Education 1957–9, Industry and Commerce 1959–65, and Finance 1965–6) before succeeding *Lemass as leader of the *Fianna Fáil party in 1966, and being elected Taoiseach. His first government struggled with its reaction to the eruption of violence in *Northern Ireland which began in 1969. He famously announced that the government of the Republic would not 'stand by' while Catholics in Northern Ireland were harassed by Protestant paramilitaries. After questions of scandal involving connections between some of his ministers (e.g. *Haughey) and the Provisional *IRA, Lynch dismissed them and stated that peace and justice in Northern Ireland must come through consent. His government tried to reduce militant nationalist activity in the Republic. He was defeated in the 1973 elections by Liam *Cosgrave, but won in 1977 with a large majority. Internal party divisions led to his resignation in December 1979, when he was succeeded by Haughey.

Lyons, Joseph Aloysius (b. 15 Sept. 1879, d. 7 Apr. 1939). Prime Minister of Australia 1932–9

Early career Educated in his native Stanley (Tasmania), he became a teacher until he was elected to the Tasmanian state parliament in 1909. Lyons served as Tasmanian Treasurer and Minister for Education from 1914, and was elected leader of the state *Labor Party in 1916 because of his opposition to the introduction of compulsory military service. As premier of Tasmania (1923–8), he became noted for his successful reform of the state's financial structure. In 1929, he was elected to the federal parliament, where as Postmaster-General he became a senior member of *Scullin's Cabinet. As acting Treasurer (1930–1), Lyons was heavily criticized by his colleagues and the parliamentary caucus for his orthodox financial policies, though he became well-respected for his principled policies outside Labor.

In office Agonized by the opposition from his own party, he left Labor and started to cultivate citizens' groups, thus creating grass-roots support for a new movement, the *United Australia Party (UAP). He led the UAP to a landslide victory in December 1931, and won convincing victories in 1934 and 1937. His orthodox policies brought considerable financial and political stability during the years of the Great *Depression. The financial difficulties of these years precluded him from undertaking any striking reform initiatives, for which he was often criticized. The main achievement underpinning his long tenure lay in his tireless organization and motivation of the loosely structured and relatively short-lived UAP. During the last months of his life he was increasingly criticized for his seemingly hands-off style of government, but he remained in office until his death.

M

Maastricht, Treaty of (1992)

Officially known as the **Treaty of the European Union (TEU)**, it formally established the European Union (EU). It added to the European Community, which came to be recognized as the first pillar, the Common Foreign and Security Policy (CSFP) as the second pillar, and cooperation on Justice and Home Affairs (JHA) as the third pillar of the EU. This complex pillar structure was adopted because ministers wanted to cooperate on the sensitive policy areas of defence and immigration while keeping it away from the ever-growing influence of the *European Commission and the *European Court of Justice.

The TEU established the principle of subsidiarity, an ill-defined concept according to which the community institutions should only act if matters could not be better dealt with at a lower, national or regional level. The TEU also established a European citizenship. Effective through the national citizenship of each member state, it guaranteed mutual consular protection in third countries, and the right to vote (and be elected) in the local and European elections of any EU country of residence. Most importantly, perhaps, the TEU adopted a three-stage plan for the creation of European Monetary Union (EMU), and the adoption of the *euro in 1999. The TEU fundamentally changed the nature of the European Community. It failed, however, to reform its institutions and streamline them to reflect the Community's growing importance. Maastricht also failed to prepare the EU for its next great challenge, the integration of the applicant states of central, eastern, and southern Europe. To respond to these problems, the treaty provided for a further *intergovernmental conference to be held, to prepare for the Treaty of *Amsterdam.

Macao (Macau)

A small peninsula off southern China opposite *Hong Kong. With the neighbouring islands of Taipa and Coloane, Macao became a Portuguese

settlement in 1557. In 1582, Portugal signed a 500-year lease over the territory. In 1887, Portugal established a permanent claim over the area, but following the overthrow of the military regime in Portugal in 1974, it reverted to its status as Chinese Territory under Portuguese Administration. Following agreement about the return of Hong Kong to Chinese rule in 1984, Macao's return to Chinese administration under similar conditions became inevitable. In 1987, the Chinese and Portuguese governments agreed that Macao would return to Chinese administration on 20 December 1999 as a Special Administrative Region, in which *capitalism would be maintained. Transition to Chinese rule was never as problematic as for neighbouring Hong Kong; Macao's territory was much smaller (less than one-tenth in size) and much poorer (less than half the per capita income). Under Chinese rule, it obtained a relatively high degree of self-government. It received its own Constitution, and was governed by a Chief Executive and a legislative council. Since 1999, it has been governed by Edmund H. W. Ho as Chief Executive, who developed the area's prosperous gambling industry.

MacArthur, Douglas (b. 26 Jan. 1880, d. 5 Apr. 1964). US general

Born in Little Rock, Arkansas, he was commissioned into the US army at the Military Academy in West Point in 1903. He served first in Tokyo and in Mexico, distinguishing himself as a divisional commander in France in World War I. By 1930 he had reached the rank of general, and became Chief of Staff of the US Army until 1935. Sent to the Philippines to build up a Filipino defence force, he stayed on there until 1941, even after retiring in 1937. He was then recalled by President F. D. *Roosevelt to lead the defence against the Japanese attack. After leaving the Philippines to the Japanese in early 1942, in March 1942 he became Commander of Allied Forces in the South-West Pacific to lead the subsequent Allied counterattack in the Pacific. In pursuit of this goal he developed the strategy of 'island hopping' through which he bypassed heavily fortified Japanese-occupied islands to take control of the less well-defended ones. As commander of all US army forces in the

Pacific, he received the Japanese surrender on board the USS *Missouri* on 2 September 1945.

As commander of the *SCAP (Supreme Command of the Allied Powers) MacArthur was the effective Governor of occupied Japan, taking an active role in many reforms, including the drafting of the new *Japanese constitution. As Commander of *UN troops in the *Korean War, he oversaw a dramatically successful landing at Inchon in September 1950 and pushed North Korean troops back to the Chinese border. MacArthur was forced to retreat when the Chinese entered the war. In 1951 he resumed the offensive, but tension arose between him and President *Truman, who feared his demagogic popularity. Truman was also concerned that MacArthur was prepared to risk a full-scale atomic war. In a public and humiliating rebuke, he was dismissed in 1951. He failed to obtain the *Republican nomination for the presidential election of 1952, which was won by his fellow general, Dwight *Eisenhower.

McCain–Feingold Bill (2002), see
Congress of the United States

McCarran Act (USA, 1951)
US internal security legislation. Passed over President *Truman's veto, it required the registration of all Communist organizations and individuals, prohibited the employment of Communists in defence work, and denied entry to the USA to anyone who had belonged to a Communist or *Fascist organization. It arose out of the fear, stimulated by *McCarthyism and the *FBI, of a Communist conspiracy against the USA. In 1965 the *Supreme Court ruled that an individual could refuse to admit being a Communist by claiming the constitutional privilege enshrined in the Fifth Amendment against self-incrimination.

McCarran–Walter Act (USA, 1952)
A codification of US immigration law. Passed over President *Truman's veto, it maintained the basic 1924 quota system, with an annual quota total of 154,658 persons, but with some significant changes. At a time when *McCarthyism gripped the country, it gave the Attorney-General powers to refuse admission to any 'subversive' and to deport any member of a 'Communist or Communist-front' organization. Immigration quotas for eastern and south-eastern Europe were reduced. On the more positive side, the Act provided for selective immigration on the basis of skills. And, in a measure that was of more symbolic than practical significance at the time, it granted an annual quota total of 2,000 persons

per annum from eight previously banned Pacific nations, with Japan being allocated 185.

McCarthy, Joseph Raymond ('Joe')
(b. 14 Nov. 1908, d. 2 May 1957). US Senator 1947–57

Born in Grand Chute in rural Wisconsin, he was a farm worker and store-keeper until he went on to obtain a high school degree within one year (1929), gaining an LL B from Marquette University in 1935. He built up a successful law practice, entered politics, and was then elected to the US Senate in 1946, after a distinguished record of war service. He launched a campaign alleging that there was a large-scale Communist plot to infiltrate the government at the highest level. In February 1950 he announced that he had evidence of 57 'card-carrying Communists' in the State Department and some 205 'sympathizers'. Despite the conclusions of a Senate investigating committee under Millard Tydings that such charges were fraudulent, McCarthy continued to make repeated attacks on the administration, the military, and public figures.

McCarthy's demagogic methods of anti-intellectualism and social envy had an early popular appeal. In the wake of the Communist takeover in China, many people were very receptive to his warnings about the Red Menace, which appeared to be confirmed by the events such as the *Alger Hiss and *Rosenberg trials. McCarthy's baseless and inflammatory anti-Communist 'witch hunt' gripped the USA (1950–4). In 1953, as chair of the Senate Permanent Subcommittee on Investigations, McCarthy conducted a series of televised hearings, where his vicious questioning and unsubstantiated accusations destroyed the reputations of many of his victims. He was not censured by the Senate for his conduct until 1954, after a ferocious attack on the army. After the 1954 election, with the *Democrats again in control of *Congress, his influence rapidly declined.

McClung, Nellie Letitia (neé Mooney) (b. 20 Oct. 1873, d. 1 Sept. 1951).
Canadian suffragist

Born at Chatsworth (Ontario), she was a schoolteacher until her marriage in 1896. She became active in the woman's Christian Temperance Union, and in 1908 published her best-selling novel, *Sowing Seeds in Danny*. In 1911, McClung moved to Winnipeg, where she became active in the women's rights movement, continuing her activities upon moving to Edmonton. As a campaigner for women's suffrage and greater social equality for women, she spoke widely throughout

Canada, the USA, and Britain. Her speeches have been collected in *In Times Like These* (1915). She entered the Alberta Legislative Assembly as a member of the *Liberal Party (1921-6). In 1929, she was instrumental in the successful campaign to allow women to sit in the Canadian Senate. She moved to Vancouver Island in 1933, where she wrote part of her autobiography, *Clearing in the West: My Own Story* (1935), as well as short stories. She became a member of the Canadian Authors Association and sat on the first board of governors of the Canadian Broadcasting Corporation. McClung has often been criticized for her attachment to traditional notions of the family and her conservatism on issues such as temperance. However, it was perhaps precisely these values which formed the basis of her appeal, as they gave her a common language with her audiences, convincing them that women's rights would not lead to radical social and political transformations.

MacDonald, (James) Ramsay (b. 12 Oct. 1866, d. 9 Nov. 1937). British Prime Minister 1924, 1929–35

Early career (up to 1924) Born in Lossiemouth (Morayshire), he was educated at a village school in Drainie. He left home in 1885 to go to Bristol and then London, where he did a number of clerical jobs. While working as a journalist he joined the *Independent Labour Party in Southampton in 1894. With Keir *Hardie, he was at the heart of the creation of the Labour Representation Committee in 1900, whose secretary he became. As such, he concluded an electoral pact with the *Liberal Party, which enabled him and almost thirty other Labour members to be elected to parliament in 1906. He was elected leader of the parliamentary *Labour Party in 1911, but when war broke out in 1914, his pacifism, and criticism of the government's prewar diplomacy, meant that he was unable to support the Labour Party's desire to cooperate fully in the war effort. Increasingly marginalized after his resignation as party leader, he lost his seat in 1918. He was not re-elected until 1922, when his previous skilful leadership in parliament ensured his immediate re-election to lead the party.

In office (from 1924) In the 1923 election Labour became the second largest party in a hung parliament, and in January 1924 his consistent efforts at moderation and good relations with Liberals paid off when the latter supported him to become the first Labour Prime Minister. Owing to its weak parliamentary position, Labour achieved little in its short term of office (January to November 1924), but he demonstrated that it was a responsible party of government. Back in opposition, he was criticized in his own ranks for not giving stronger support to the 1926 *General Strike. Nevertheless, he led the party to victory in 1929, when it became the strongest party in parliament, though it still did not possess an overall majority. However, he became unable to find a coherent response to the Great *Depression, as he was paralysed by the conflicting demands of the Bank of England, which demanded cuts in public spending, and of his own party, which refused to contemplate cuts that would increase individual economic hardship still further.

In response, he formed a *National Government that was based on *Conservative and *Liberal support. Unsurprisingly, he was expelled and vilified as a traitor by the Labour Party, and replaced by George *Lansbury. His weak position, which gave the Conservative leader *Baldwin an increasingly important role in the government, was compounded by his deteriorating health. In foreign affairs, he hoped to develop collective security through the *League of Nations and, like many others, he did not see *Nazi Germany as a particular threat to Britain. Following his resignation, he remained an isolated member of the Cabinet until 1937. While his decision to rule with the help of the Conservatives undoubtedly played a major part in the weakness of the Labour Party during the 1930s, his earlier leadership and his moderation was an equally important contributor to the party's advance as the accepted second party of British politics, ahead of the Liberals.

Macedonia, Former Yugoslav Republic of

A landlocked Balkan country which has recently achieved remarkable political stability in the face of domestic and regional tension.

Early history Macedonia had been part of the *Ottoman Empire since 1317. A *nationalist movement, IMRO (Internal Macedonian Revolutionary Organization), was founded in 1893. After the first *Balkan Wars (1912-13), Macedonia was partitioned mostly between *Serbia and Greece, with a small part being retained by Bulgaria. Thus occupied by *Central Powers (Bulgaria) and Allied Powers (Serbia, then Greece), it was the scene of fierce fighting during *World War I. An Allied force landed at Salonika in October 1915 and, in September 1918 under General *Franchet d'Esperey, advanced against Bulgaria.

After the war the Treaty of *Neuilly confirmed northern Macedonia as part of Serbia, while southern Macedonia and Salonika remained Greek. In the following years, a large population movement transformed the ethnic composition of the population. Most notably, after the Treaty of *Lausanne around 350,000 Muslims living in Macedonia were expelled to Turkey, and replaced by 550,000 Greeks from Asia Minor. Despite continued activism by IMRO terrorists from Bulgaria between the wars, hopes for Macedonian independence remained unfulfilled. After World War II, northern Macedonia became a republic within the Yugoslav federation.

Independence (from 1993) After the breakup of Yugoslavia in 1991, it declared its independence in 1993 with the provisional title of the Former Yugoslav Republic of Macedonia **(FYROM)**. This created an extremely tense relationship with the Greek government, since FYROM developed rival claims for ethnicity and statehood. This rivalry was epitomized in a dispute about the state's name, as Greece objected to the use of Macedonia, whose historical heritage it claimed. The two countries eventually recognized each other in 1995, and the Greek economic blockade against the Republic was lifted.

The ethnic make up of the Republic continued to change, as Albanian refugees poured in from *Kosovo and Albania, increasing the size of the (discriminated against) Albanian minority to 25 per cent. Tensions were increased through the worsening economic situation, which escalated as a result of international sanctions and then war against its main trading partner, Yugoslavia. As the situation in Kosovo escalated and war erupted in 1999, Macedonia became an important stronghold for the moderate Kosovan opposition, but also for the rebel Albanian force, the UČK (Kosovo Liberation Army). Emboldened by the recognition of Albanian rights in Kosovo from 1999, the Albanian minority in Macedonia became more assertive. Following violent clashes between the Macedonian police force and Albanian rebels, *NATO followed the plea of the Macedonian government and increased its presence there. A civil war was narrowly avoided in 2001 when parliament agreed concessions granting linguistic and limited political autonomy to the Albanian minority. In return, UČK rebels agreed to give up their arms to NATO troops.

Contemporary politics (since 2004) In 2004, the government redrew regional boundaries and granted greater local powers as a further concession to the Albanian minority. In that year, the Social Democrat Branco Crvenovski became President, but in 2006 his party lost the parliamentary elections against Nikola Gruevski, who formed a coalition with Albanian parliamentary representatives. Both leaders pursued pro-EU and pro-Western policies. In 2006, *NATO announced that it intended to admit FYROM in 2008, and in December 2005 it became an official candidate for membership of the EU.

Macedonian Front (World War I), see SALONIKA CAMPAIGN

Machel, Samora Moises (b. 29 Sept. 1933, d. 19 Oct. 1986). President of the Republic of Mozambique 1975–86
Born in Xilembene (Gaza Province), he trained as a hospital nurse. In 1963, Machel went to Tanzania to join *FRELIMO (Frente de Libertaçao de Moçambique). In 1964, he was made a commander, and in 1966 he became a member of its central committee. He resigned his supreme leadership over the revolutionary forces when he became president of FRELIMO in 1969. In this position he led the struggle for independence, and became President when that was achieved on 25 June 1975. He was a politician of strong principles, providing refuge for the resistance movements against the White racist regimes in South Africa and Zimbabwe, *ANC and *ZANU, even though this threatened his regime as South Africa supported the hostile guerrilla movement, *RENAMO. Despite the difficulties caused by permanent civil war and economic hardships, his personal popularity never faltered. He died in an air crash over South Africa, and was succeeded by *Chissano. In 1998, his widow, Graca, married Nelson *Mandela.

Mackenzie King, William Lyon (b. 17 Dec. 1874, d. 22 July 1950). Prime Minister of Canada 1921–6, 1926–30, 1935–48

Early career Grandson of the anti-establishment rebel William Lyon Mackenzie (b. 1795, d. 1861), he was born at Berlin (Kitchener, Ontario) and studied at the Universities of Toronto, Chicago, and Harvard, graduating in economics. Canada's first Deputy Minister of Labour in 1900, he was elected to the House of Commons as a *Liberal in 1908, and in 1909 became Minister of

Labour under *Laurier. He failed to be re-elected in 1911 and 1917, during which time he became a forceful advocate of government intervention in industrial relations, as a mediator between employers and *trade unions. He remained active within the *Liberal Party, and in 1919 became party leader. He narrowly won the 1921 elections and reduced tariffs to gain the support of the *Progressive Party. When he lost the latter's support in 1926 the Conservative *Meighen formed a brief government, but Mackenzie King won the ensuing general elections of 1926, thanks to the return of Progressive support.

In office Mackenzie King introduced old-age pensions, and in international affairs insisted on Canadian autonomy from the UK, which led to the redefinition of its Dominion status in 1926. His failure to address adequately the Great *Depression led to his defeat at the 1930 elections. His effective opposition to *Bennett ensured his victory in 1935, though apart from the negotiation of a series of trade agreements his response to Canada's economic problems was not very coherent. Originally a supporter of *appeasement, he backed Canada's entry into World War II, promising (mainly to appease French Canadians) that there would be no compulsory military service overseas. He gained an increased majority in the 1940 elections, and proceeded to switch the economy to war production, mainly through vastly increasing state intervention. To nurture the promise of a better society after the war, he introduced unemployment insurance in 1940, and outlined proposals for a health insurance scheme. As war went on he was plagued by the controversial issue of conscription, introducing it for compulsory military service at home in 1940. In a referendum in 1942, a majority of Canadians supported the introduction of conscription for overseas service, relieving Mackenzie King of his original promise. However, the majority of French Canadians in Quebec voted against the measure, so that conscripts were not sent to Europe until 1944, this time with little opposition.

After the war, Mackenzie King showed little interest in realizing promises of a new social order, preferring minimal government intervention in economics and society. His curiously unimpressive legislative record stands in some contrast to the fact that he was Canada's longest-serving Prime Minister. However, his political longevity was due precisely to the fact that, in times of intense uncertainty and dislocation, he was the least divisive leader. He preferred rhetoric to potentially controversial action, legislating only when it became unavoidable.

McKinley, William (b. 29 Jan. 1843, d. 14 Sept. 1901). 25th US President 1897–1901

Early career Born at Niles, Ohio, he became a lawyer and, after service as a major in the US Civil War (1861–5), he entered *Congress as a Representative for his home state in 1876. He became an influential figure, and in 1890 his goal of a protective duty in certain imports was realized by the McKinley Tariff. He was defeated in 1890, and the following year was elected Governor of his home state.

Presidency McKinley ran for President on a commitment to the *Gold Standard as the basis of the American dollar's value. In 1898 he successfully led the country into war with Spain, in support of Cuban rebels demanding independence. In the ensuing Treaty of Paris Spain not only gave up Cuba but sold the Philippines, several Pacific territories (including *Guam), and *Puerto Rico to the USA for $20 million. While Cuba had gained independence, he forced the Cubans to accept the Platt Amendment, which gave the US an effective right to intervene in Cuban affairs at will. At the same time, the US annexed what was then the Kingdom of Hawaii (which became a state in 1959). On the basis of these victories, he was easily re-elected in 1900. Shortly thereafter, he was shot dead in Buffalo, New York State, and was succeeded by Theodore *Roosevelt, the Vice-President. McKinley has been described as the first 'modern' President of the US. He raised record finances for his first campaign, set up a war command in the White House equipped with the latest technologies, and was extremely conscious of the power of public opinion. He redefined US commitment in the Pacific, Asia, and the Caribbean.

McMahon Line

A boundary line dividing Tibet and India drawn by the British Secretary of State, Sir Henry McMahon (b. 1862, d. 1949) at the Simla Conference of 1913–14 along the highest mountain peaks in the area. The Chinese, who were not consulted, claimed over 50,000 square miles of land south of the line, and never ratified the treaty. After the reassertion of control by China over Tibet in 1950, boundary disputes arose between India and China culminating in the *Indo-Chinese War of 1962. Following the Indian defeat, a final settlement was still pending at the beginning of the twenty-first century.

Macmillan, (Maurice) Harold, 1st Earl of Stockton (b. 10 Feb. 1894, d. 29 Dec. 1986). British Prime Minister 1957–63

Early career Born in London, into the Macmillan publishing family, he was educated at Eton and Oxford. After service in World War I (in which he was wounded three times), he went into publishing. Soon active in politics, he was elected to parliament for the *Conservative Party in 1924. Throughout his career, he was haunted by the loss of life incurred in the war, and the suffering of the ordinary soldier. It was partly this, and the terrible poverty of his constituency of Stockton-on-Tees, that saw him placed firmly on the progressive wing of the Conservative Party. He lost his seat in 1929, but was re-elected in 1931. In the 1930s, he was highly critical of *appeasement and government economic policies. He was influenced by the work of *Keynes, and his belief that it was necessary for the state to cooperate with capital to create a mixed economy, in which the failures of *capitalism, such as high unemployment, could be remedied.

Macmillan gained his first experience of government under *Churchill, becoming Under-Secretary of State for the Colonies in 1942, and then Minister of State in North Africa with Cabinet rank. In this post, he was responsible for British policy in the Mediterranean until the end of the war, much of which involved working with his French and American counterparts. He lost his seat in the 1945 general election, but returned in a by-election later in the year as MP for Bromley. As Housing Minister (1951–4), he was enormously successful in organizing the largest local authority building programme ever seen in Britain. He became Minister of Defence in 1954, and then *Eden's Foreign Secretary in 1955. After finding that Eden liked to keep a firm control of foreign affairs, he was happy to become Chancellor of the Exchequer later that year.

Prime Minister Following the *Suez Crisis, Macmillan replaced Eden as Prime Minister. He proved to be extraordinarily adept at reviving the party's fortunes, through being attuned to the wishes of the potential Conservative constituency. Subsequently much criticized for his refusal to reduce public expenditure in 1958, this nevertheless contributed to an overwhelming election victory in 1959, despite the party's unpopularity when he took over. His famous proclamation to the South African parliament in 1960 that the days of colonialism were over as the 'winds of change' were blowing through Africa (see *Verwoerd) was an equally pragmatic acceptance that Britain could no longer afford to keep its colonies against their will. He had an extremely close relationship with US President *Kennedy, and was at the heart of the negotiations resulting in the July

1963 *Nuclear Test-Ban Treaty between the USA, the USSR, and Britain.

Macmillan never enjoyed full control over his party. His domestic position became particularly difficult after the 1963 *Profumo Affair. He resigned in October 1963 (officially on the grounds of ill health), and subsequently devoted much of his time to his duties as Chancellor of Oxford University, to which office he had been elected in 1960. From 1984 he was a prominent member of the House of Lords, and an outspoken critic of *Thatcherism.

McNamara, Robert Strange (b. 9 June 1916). US Secretary of Defense 1961–8
Born in San Francisco, California, he graduated from the University of California in 1937 and during World War II taught at the Harvard Business School. He joined the Ford Motor Company and rose rapidly to become its President. He resigned soon afterwards to join the administration of John F. *Kennedy, despite his *Republican sympathies. Repudiating the *Dulles concept of *brinkmanship, he advocated pragmatism and flexibility as a means to combat world *Communism. He successfully gained control over Pentagon spending, axing obsolete weapons and applying strict cost-accounting methods.

When McNamara visited Vietnam (1962, 1964, and 1966), he sought to boost the US-backed Saigon government against the *National Liberation Front. While supporting the early bombing offensive against North Vietnam in 1965, he came to repudiate full-scale military involvement and resigned from the *Johnson administration in February 1968. He was appointed President of the *World Bank, where his main concern was to ease the burden of debt repayment incurred by developing countries, many of whose economies were devastated by high oil prices in the 1970s. In his 1995 memoirs (*In Retrospect: The Tragedy and Lessons of Vietnam*), he expressed deep regret about the *Vietnam War, and his role in it.

Madagascar
An African island state in the Indian Ocean, it suffered from brutal colonial rule, subsequent political instability, and the lack of mineral resources.

French rule (1885–1960) Madagascar became a French protectorate in 1885, and a colony in 1896. Subsequent uprisings were brutally and successfully repressed (1899–1902, 1915, 1929). From 1940, the French authorities there gave allegiance to the *Vichy government. Madagascar was occupied by British and American troops in 1942, and handed over to de *Gaulle's *Free French forces in 1943. Some limited self-government was granted in 1946, when the island became an Overseas Territory of the French Republic. This failed to overcome the opposition to French rule, which organized itself as the Mouvement Démocratique de Rénovation Malgache (MDRM, Democratic Movement for Malagasy Renewal). The 1947 uprisings coordinated by the MDRM were suppressed by the French military, at the cost of over 80,000 lives. The island was finally granted autonomy within the *French Community in 1958, and became independent as the Malagasy Republic (Madagascar since 1975) on 26 June 1960.

Independence (since 1960) Madagascar was led as a socialist republic by Philibert Tsiranana (b. 1910?, d. 1978) until 1972, when he was replaced by a military regime amidst a series of popular disturbances. Sporadic outbreaks of violence continued throughout the 1970s and 1980s, in protest against the socialist one-party state backed by the military. However, increasing poverty and reliance on foreign (particularly French) aid forced the regime to grant political concessions and reform the economy. This led to the establishment of a new Constitution in 1992, and free elections on 17 February 1993. These were won by the leader of the opposition, Albert Zafy, with almost two-thirds of the vote in the second ballot. The 1997 elections were won by Didier Ratsiraka of the Association pour la Renaissance de Madagascar (AREMA), which renounced its earlier socialist programmes and gained 63 out of 150 seats in parliament. It struggled to cope with the devastating economic and humanitarian effects of the floods in 2000, which destroyed much of Madagascar's agricultural exports.

Contemporary politics (since 2002) Benefiting from popular discontent, Marc Ravalomanana won the presidency by a narrow margin, which was confirmed by the High Constitutional Court in May 2002. Ravalomanana encouraged the development of tourism, in order to diversify an economy over-reliant on the exports of its main staple, vanilla. He introduced a range of free-market reforms, and in 2006 he was re-elected. As a result of his efforts, Madagascar qualified for debt relief under the *HIPC initiative, though most of its population continued to live below the poverty line.

Madero, Francisco Indalecio (b. 30 Oct. 1873, d. 22 Feb. 1913). Mexican President 1911–13
Born in Parras Coahuila of a wealthy and influential family, he studied in Paris and at the University of California. Upon his return to Mexico he applied his economic skills to the family business, and soon became a leading spokesman not just for economic, but also for political liberalization. This put him into confrontation with the ruling Porfirio *Díaz, against whom he decided to stand in the 1910 election. Madero was gaoled during the election, which he lost. He called for an armed insurrection, which found a wide response. It sparked off the 1911 Mexican Revolution, which led to the overthrow of Díaz, and Madero's victory at the ensuing elections. He was unable, however, to contain the activities of the rebel movements (e.g. of *Zapata) which the Revolution had unleashed, and in 1913 he was killed by his own military chief of staff, Victoriano Huerta.

Madrid Bombings (11 Mar. 2004)
A number of bombs were planted by terrorists linked to *al-Qaeda on suburban trains, which detonated at rush hour. One hundred and ninety-one people died and almost two thousand were injured. Fearful that the bombings would be linked to his unpopular decision to support the USA in the *Iraq War, the Spanish Prime Minister, *Aznar, tried to link the attack to the *Basque terrorist organization, ETA. This manoeuvre was sharply criticized by civil rights organizations as well as the Spanish opposition, led by *Zapatero. The three days between the attacks and the general elections on 14 March saw the *Popular Party's lead diminish, with Zapatero's *Socialist Workers' Party securing a resounding victory at the polls.

Mafeking, Siege of, see BADEN-POWELL, ROBERT STEPHENSON SMYTH

Mafia, the
A clandestine network based on family ties and criminal bonds such as bribery. It emerged in Sicily during the eighteenth century in response to foreign rule, neglect, weak government authorities, and the persistence of feudalism. Its success was based on the network's infiltration of police, administration, and justice, which transformed it into the *de facto* source of authority and power. Its cohesion has been

based not so much on strong organization as on the development of a particular subculture marked by certain types of behavioural codes, such as *omertà* ('silence') and *vendetta* ('revenge'). The persistence and the rapid expansion of the Mafia in liberal Italy after unification (1860–1922) was implicitly encouraged by the central Italian state in order to weaken the old southern landed elites over which the state found it difficult to exercise control. In this sense, the Mafia became Rome's agents in Sicily and other parts of the extreme south, while the central government did little to stop its illegal activities.

Despite the anti-Mafia rhetoric of Fascist Italy, the Mafia was not so much overcome, but rather integrated into the structures of the *Fascist movement. Hence the Mafia re-emerged after World War II and resumed its compromise with the Italian state for some decades, acting as an intermediary between central government and the southern Italian locality in politics, economy, and society. However, its spread to the central government bureaucracy in Rome and even into northern Italy heightened public concern and brought it to the top of the political agenda of the 1980s. The central state's inability to cope with the problem, and the sheer extent of the Mafia's involvement with the political and administrative establishment was one of the central reasons for the collapse of the Italian political system 1992–3 (*Tangentopoli). According to official estimates published in 2000, the Mafia controlled around 15 per cent of Italy's economy.

Towards the end of the nineteenth century large-scale emigration from southern Italy had transported the Mafia to the USA. There, Mafia activity reached its peak in the 1930s during the Prohibition period, when it controlled the illegal trade in alcohol in its centres of New York and Chicago. It had extensive links into federal and state legislature, while enjoying the effective protection of the *FBI under J. Edgar *Hoover, who refused to recognize its existence. Despite subsequent attempts to strike against the Mafia, the American authorities were unable to overcome it and the Mafia continued to be at the heart of organized crime. In addition, the Mafia and other Mafia-type organizations have stepped in to fill the power vacuum left by the collapse of the Soviet Union in 1991, and of Communist state authority in other former Eastern Bloc countries. Their control of parts of the economy has been a significant hindrance to economic reform in these countries.

Maginot Line

A series of defensive fortifications in France built 1929–32 at the instigation of the then Minister of War, André Maginot (b. 1877, d. 1932), to secure the eastern border of France against a potential attack from Germany. Partly as a result of Belgian protests, it was not extended northwards to secure France's border with Belgium. Henceforth, French strategic planning was based on the assumption of the Line's impenetrability, and on the assumed impossibility of being attacked through the wooded Ardennes mountains in southern Belgium. Following the German *Blitzkrieg through the Netherlands and Belgium, therefore, France threw its military might at the plains of northern Belgium, where it expected the thrust of the German offensive. In fact, the Germans attacked through the Ardennes mountains, outflanking both the French army and the Maginot Line, which was virtually intact when France surrendered on 22 June 1940.

Mahathir Bin Mohamad, Dato Seri

(b. 20 Dec. 1925). Prime Minister of Malaysia 1981–2003

Born in Alor Star, he studied medicine and opened a practice. A member of *UMNO, he became a Member of Parliament in 1964 until its suspension in 1969. He was expelled from the party because of his outspoken hostility to *Abdul Rahman Putra's policy of compromise between the Malay, Chinese, and Indian groups of the population, advocating the predominence of the Malays instead. Readmitted as a sign of UMNO's reversal from Abdul Rahman Putra's ideals, he became Minister of Education in 1974, and Deputy Prime Minister in 1976. Prime Minister since 1981, the populist nationalist was again confirmed in office on 25 April 1995, when his national front coalition dominated by UMNO received a record two-thirds majority. He escaped political responsibility for his relative failure to respond to the 1997 Asian economic crisis by nationalist attacks against foreign capital. He won the 1999 elections with a renewed two-thirds majorty. Despite the setback of 1997, Mahathir is credited with overseeing Malaysia's transformation into a successful economy based on manufacturing and information technology.

Mahdism (Sudan)

A religious and political movement inspired by Muhammad Ahmad al-Mahdi (b. 1848, d. 1885), a man of great religious zeal and personal asceticism. In 1881, he proclaimed his divine mission to free Sudan from its Ottoman/Egyptian rulers, as a prelude to establishing a pure Islamic state. He came to control most of northern Sudan, and, after a ten-month siege of Khartoum, defeated the British General Gordon (b. 1833, d. 1885) and took possession of the capital. Gordon's perceived 'martyrdom' against the non-Christian ('pagan') Mahdi caused such commotion in Britain that its government was compelled to send a large military force to defeat his forces and establish British control over the Sudan.

Mahdism has remained an influential force in Sudan throughout the twentieth century. In the colonial days, it served as a focal point for Sudanese *nationalism against British/Egyptian rule, and after independence it played an often pivotal role in Sudanese politics. It provided the basis for the Umma Party, and the focus of opposition against the *Nimieri regime. Its leader, Sadiq al-Mahdi (b. 1936), a descendant of Muhammad Ahmad, was Prime Minister twice (1966–7 and 1986–9).

Mahoré, see MAYOTTE

Major, Sir John (b. 29 Mar. 1943). British Prime Minister 1990–7

Early career Born in London of humble origins (which he later often emphasized), he held a variety of jobs, including as an accountant. He served as a member of Lambeth Borough Council for the *Conservative Party in 1968–71. Elected to parliament for Huntingdonshire (Huntingdon from 1983) in 1979, he advanced quickly through the junior government ranks to become Minister of State for Social Security (1986–7), and Chief Secretary to the Treasury (1987–9). He was briefly Foreign Secretary in 1989, and was then Chancellor of the Exchequer until 1990, during which time, with Douglas Hurd, he secured Britain's entry to the *ERM.

In office In November 1990, he succeeded Margaret *Thatcher as Prime Minister, defeating Michael Heseltine and Dougles Hurd in the Conservative leadership election. Considered able and competent, but dull and unimaginative, his rapid political advance and subsequent success was possible precisely because few suspected it, while most thought he was the least divisive leader after Thatcher's traumatic demise. He ended the unpopular *poll tax and signed the *Maastricht Treaty. To general surprise, he was re-elected in 1992.

In many respects, Major took *Thatcherism to areas where even she was reluctant, such as the privatization of the railways and the attempted privatization of the Post Office. On the whole, however, his government was conspicuously lacking in major political innovations. Major never recovered from

'Black Wednesday' in 1992, when the Pound Sterling was forced to leave the ERM. This destroyed the Conservatives' reputation for economic management, which had been their unassailable advantage over the *Labour Party before. His problems were compounded by the advent of the energetic and resourceful Tony *Blair as leader of the Labour Party, and by perceptions of government 'sleaze', as highlighted in the Scott Report (1996), despite widespread acceptance of his personal integrity. Most of all, he was weakened by the divisions within his party over Britain's stance towards the EU.

Makarios III (b. 13 Aug. 1913, d. 3 Aug. 1977). Archbishop of Cyprus 1950–77; President of Cyprus 1960–77

Born Mihail Christodoulou Mouskos in Paphos on Cyprus. The son of a peasant, he became a novice monk, but after studying in Athens and in the USA, he decided to become a priest. He was ordained in 1946 and became a bishop in 1948. As Archbishop of the *Orthodox Church of Cyprus, he was the leading figure to propagate Enosis (union with Greece). He cooperated with *EOKA in its desire to rid the island of its British occupation, so that he was deported to the Seychelles in 1956. As leader of the Greek Cypriot community, he accepted the British offer of independence within the *Commonwealth, instead of union with Greece. For this he was opposed by his former allies, EOKA, during his presidency. EOKA staged a coup against him, in conjunction with the *Greek colonels. He was forced into exile, but when the coup failed owing to the Turkish invasion of parts of the island, he returned to hold office until his death.

Malan, Daniël François (b. 22 May 1874, d. 7 Feb. 1959). Prime Minister of South Africa 1948–54

Born in Allesverloren (near Riebeek West), he obtained a doctorate in divinity from the University of Utrecht (the Netherlands) in 1905, whereupon he returned to South Africa to become a minister for the Dutch Reformed Church. He subsequently engaged in the struggle for the official recognition of Afrikaans as a written language. As a supporter of *Hertzog, he was appointed editor of the *National Party (NP) newspaper *De Burger* in Cape Town (1915–23), and entered parliament for the NP in 1919. He was made Minister of Internal Affairs, of Education, and of Public Health in 1924, and became a champion of *Afrikaner identity through his bills granting the Afrikaans language official status and his skilful

negotiations to adopt a new flag. He opposed
the NP's fusion with *Smuts's South African
Party in 1934, founding the Gesuiwerde
Nasionale Party (Purified National Party)
instead. He became leader of a reunited NP in
1940. Despite subsequent competition from
the right, he managed to unite Afrikaner
*nationalism behind the NP, which enabled
him to win the elections of 1948.

Malan's attempt to incorporate South-West
Africa (*Namibia) into South Africa failed due
to the resistance of the UK and the *UN.
However, he successfully strengthened the
system of *apartheid through the 1950
Population Registration Act, requiring
everyone over 16 to be registered as White,
Coloured, Black, or Asiatic, and to be issued
with separate identity cards. Marriage
between Whites and non-Whites was
outlawed, and people of mixed race
(Coloureds) were denied the vote.

Malawi

A territory in
central Africa
which, upon
independence,
was subject to
authoritarian
and inefficient
rule before
making a
transition to a
fragile
democracy.

Colonial rule (up to 1966) Part of the
*British Empire as the Central African
Protectorate from 1891 (Nyasaland from 1907),
it was to be used primarily as a labour
resource for the mines and plantations of
South Africa and Rhodesia. In 1953 it became
part of the *Central African Federation,
together with Rhodesia (now Zambia and
Zimbabwe). In protest against the rule of the
White Rhodesian minority, a resistance
movement formed in the late 1950s under
*Banda, who co-founded the Malawi Congress
Party (MCP) in 1959. The party won the first
parliamentary elections of 1961, so that upon
independence on 6 July 1964 Banda became
Prime Minister under the British Crown.
Malawi became a republic within the
*Commonwealth of Nations in 1966.

The Banda era (1964–94) Banda's rule was
corrupt and ruthless in the suppression of
opposition. In 1967 he became the first and
only African head of state to recognize the
*apartheid regime in South Africa, visiting
the country in 1971. In return for

development aid, he allowed the South
African-supported *RENAMO forces to
conduct their operations in the civil war of
Mozambique from Malawi territory. However,
this backfired, as access was cut off to the
Mozambique ports, which had handled 90 per
cent of the land-locked country's exports.
Moreover, its insufficient resources were
overburdened by the arrival of 750,000
refugees from Mozambique (1975–92). Even
though economic growth rates remained
relatively impressive, the gains were almost
eliminated by the country's rapid population
growth, at over 3 per cent per year one of the
highest in Africa.

Democratization (since 1994) Increasing
foreign pressure through the withdrawal of
foreign aid forced Banda to agree to multi-
party elections in 1994, in which his MCP won
only 55 of the 177 parliamentary seats. He was
succeeded as President by Bakili Muluzi
(b. 1943) of the United Democratic Front, who
tried to counter the corruption of the Banda
regime, while seeking to overcome the effects
of the failed harvests of 1992 and 1994. Muluzi
was confirmed in office in 1999, albeit under
the suspicion of electoral fraud. He dismissed
his government after a few months owing
to allegations of corruption.

**Contemporary politics (since
2004)** Constitutionally barred from re-
election, Muluzi retired in 2004, with his
chosen successor, Bingu wa Mutharika, being
elected President. The president started a
high-profile anti-corruption campaign, in the
course of which much of the country's elite,
including Muluzi and the serving Vice-
President, Cassim Chilumpha, were accused
of embezzling millions of dollars. In the
course of this struggle, Mutharika left the
United Democratic Front and founded his own
party, the Democratic Progress Party. This
deprived him of support in parliament, so that
Mutharika faced the threat of impeachment.
While Malawi's elites were occupied with an
existential power struggle, the country faced a
severe drought in 2005 and 2006. Owing to
malnutrition and the prevalence of HIV
infections, life expectancy at birth was just 41
years for men and 42 for women (2006).

Malaya, see MALAYSIA

Malayan campaign (Dec. 1941–Feb. 1942)
Through an agreement with the French
*Vichy government the Japanese had
established military bases in *Indochina as
early as July 1941. At the same time they made
an agreement with *Phibunsongkhram for

free passage of troops through Thailand, which had been a Japanese ally since 1939. Thus on 8 December 1941 Japanese forces crossed into northern Malaya without hindrance, while their aircraft bombed *Singapore. Kuala Lumpur fell on 11 January and British, Indian, and Australian troops withdrew to Singapore, where they surrendered in February 1942.

During the remainder of *World War II, a guerrilla resistance force conducted sabotage, operating behind enemy lines. This was the Malayan People's Anti-Japanese Army (MPAJA), rapidly recruited and trained for jungle warfare by the British and consisting largely of Chinese, most of whom were Communists. After the successful completion of the *Burma campaigns, Allied troops were preparing to invade Malaya when Japan surrendered.

Malaysia

An ethnically diverse country whose autocratic governments have kept the tensions between the population groups under control.

Colonial rule (up to 1957) First colonized by the British in the late eighteenth century, a Federation of Malay States was created in 1895, consisting of Perak, Selangor, Negri Sembilan, and Pahang. In the following years British control was extended to the rest of the states of the Malay peninsula, which became known as the Unfederated Malay States (Kedah, Perlis, Kelantan, and Trengganu, as well as Johor). Finally, a third set of arrangements existed for the Straits Settlements, which were ruled by a Governor in Singapore.

Under British rule, Malaya became the world's leading producer of tin, its mines attracting substantial Chinese immigration, and of rubber, its plantations attracting Indian immigrants. The areas of tin mining and rubber production drew in substantial capital, and became relatively urbanized, leaving the native Malay population, which was traditionally engaged in subsistence farming in the countryside, in an economic backwater. The subsequent tensions between a significant Chinese minority with substantial economic power but few real political rights and a Malay majority in control of the political system, but suffering from economic

disadvantages, became the main theme of Malayan (and Malaysian) twentieth-century history.

These difficulties were heightened under Japanese occupation during World War II, when most Malays cooperated with the Japanese, against Chinese and Indian resistance. In response, after 1945 the British tried to introduce the Malayan Union plan, which aimed at the equality of Malays, Chinese, and Indians. This provoked strong resistance from the Malay population, articulated through *UMNO. The British were thus forced to alter their plans. They created, instead the Federation of Malaya in 1948, which assured Malayan dominance in politics and administration. It excluded Singapore, whose Chinese majority was able to hang onto British rule.

The Federation was immediately threatened by 'the Emergency', a Communist insurrection supported largely by the Chinese community. To stop Chinese support for the movement, over 500,000 Chinese were displaced and put into enclosed villages where their movements could be controlled. The rebellion was effectively quashed by the mid-1950s, partly owing to the increasingly successful cooperation of *Abdul Rahman Putra with the Chinese and Indian communities.

Independence (since 1957) Upon independence on 31 August 1957, the Federation of Malaya joined with Singapore, *Sarawak, and *Sabah to form the Federation of Malaysia on 16 September 1963. Its territorial integrity was immediately threatened by Indonesia in the abortive *Confrontation (*Konfrontasi*). Owing to increased demands from the Chinese community in Singapore, the city was effectively expelled from the Federation in 1965. However, ethnic tensions erupted again in 1969, and proved a watershed in Malaysian history. Abdul Rahman Putra's policies of compromise were abandoned. Henceforward, the Malayan predominance in government, state, and society was further underlined. The government actively encouraged a redistribution of wealth from the Chinese to the Malay community through positive discrimination.

Under Dato Seri *Mahathir Bin Mohamad, Malaysia achieved the second-highest growth rate of any Asian economy in the 1980s (after Singapore), through capitalist government planning. Underlying tensions between the different ethnic groups were compounded by an increasing government commitment to *Islamic fundamentalism. With this stance, however, Mahathir was unable to stop the rise of the Pan Islamic Party (Parti Islam Sa-Malaysia), which in 1999 became one of the largest opposition parties. The growth of the opposition movements was curtailed, however, by Mahathir's increasingly autocratic rule.

Contemporary politics (since 2000) In 2000 the main opposition leader, Anwar Ibrahim, was sentenced to fifteen years' imprisonment. Mahathir's hostility to *globalization and foreign interference was fuelled by the Asian economic crisis which set in in 1997. His reluctance to introduce necessary structural economic reforms meant that Malaysia was relatively slow to overcome its effects, but by 2003 robust economic growth at over 5 per cent per annum had returned. In 2003, Mahathir was succeeded by Abdullah Badawi, who won the 2004 elections by a landslide majority, and relaxed the authoritarian nature of the government.

Malcolm X (b. 19 May 1925, d. 21 Feb. 1965). US civil rights leader
Born Malcolm Little in Omaha, Nebraska, he later took the name Al Hajj Malik Shabazz, but was always known as Malcolm X. When he was a boy, his home was burnt down by the *Ku Klux Klan. His father, a Baptist preacher, died under mysterious circumstances. Later he moved to Boston, where he worked as a waiter and spent seven years in prison for burglary. Here he was converted to *Islam. He became a follower in 1952 of the ascetic Elijah Muhammad, founder of the *Nation of Islam (NoI). Muhammad sent him to become a minister in Harlem (New York).

As a brilliant speaker he became known nationally for his part in the *Black Power wing of the *civil rights movement. At first a strong advocate of Black separatism, he was prepared to condone violence as a means of self-defence. In 1964 he quarrelled with Muhammad and left the Black Muslims. After a pilgrimage to Mecca, he modified his views on separatism. He became an advocate of world brotherhood and formed the Organization of Afro-American Unity. Hostility developed between his followers and the NoI, one of whose adherents shot him at a rally. His *Autobiography* (1965) remained a best seller, its ideology of self-help and pride appealing especially to African–American young people.

Maldives, Republic of
A state comprising around 2,000 islands, lying on the equator, south-east of India. The Maldives came under British control in 1887

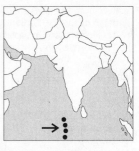

and were governed from Ceylon (now Sri Lanka). After the latter gained independence the islands were granted autonomy (26 July 1956), and on 26 July 1965 the Maldives became independent. The republic was governed almost as a personal fiefdom by A. I. Nasir until 1978. He was succeeded by Maumoon Abdul Gayoom, who was again confirmed in office in 1993 and 1999. He overcame the third coup attempt against him in November 1988, with the help of Indian troops. Under his government, public life in the Islamic state was liberalized, though freedom of expression and of political association continued to be curtailed. He promoted the growth of tourism as the country's main source of foreign income in the 1980s, and welcomed foreign aid programmes. However, only 74 islands were developed for tourism. This limited severely the contact between most of the population and the visitors, and concentrated the cultural, economic and environmental effects of tourism. Overall, Gayoom's authoritarian and elitist government did generate economic growth, an improved standard of living, and an increased average life expectancy, which rose from 47 years (1983) to over 65 in 2000.

Malenkov, Georgy Maksimilianovich (b. 8 Jan. 1902, d. 23 Jan. 1988). Chairman of the Soviet Council of Ministers 1953–5
Born in Orenburg, he joined the *Red Army in 1919 and fought in the *Russian Civil War in Turkistan. He joined the *Bolsheviks in 1920 and became a close associate of *Stalin. He rose through the party ranks and was deeply involved in the *Great Purge (1934–8). During World War II he served on the Defence Council. In 1946, Malenkov became a member of the *Politburo and a deputy Prime Minister. Generally considered the most likely of Stalin's successors, on Stalin's death in 1953 he became Chairman of the Council of Ministers (i.e. Prime Minister). Though he quickly tried to distance himself from his erstwhile mentor through pronouncing more liberal views, he was effectively outmanoeuvred by *Khrushchev's de-Stalinization campaign, which served to highlight his involvement in Stalin's terror. After a failed attempt to oust Khrushchev he was expelled from the party Central Committee in 1957, and was sent to

recover from the stress of Moscow politics as manager of the Ust'Kamenogorsk hydroelectric plant in eastern Kazakhstan. He died in Moscow.

Mali

A land–locked country in western Africa whose cultural origins go back to the fourth century, it emerged from dictatorship in 1991 to develop into a stable democracy.

Contemporary history (up to 1991) The territory was penetrated by the French towards the end of the nineteenth century, until it was made a French colony in 1880. Known as French Soudan from 1920, it received autonomy as a member of the *French Community. Following the collapse of a two-month political union with Senegal, Mali became independent on 22 September 1960.

Mali developed into a one-party state under Modibo Keita (b. 1915, d. 1977), whose socialist policies plunged the country into an economic crisis and made him unpopular. He tried to secure his position through imprisoning his opponents and purging the state machinery of potential rivals, which triggered a military coup against him on 19 November 1968. His successor, Moussa Traoré (b. 1936), failed to revive or restructure the economy, which continued to depend on large-scale foreign aid. Most significantly, he was reluctant to reduce an overblown public sector which consumed 60 per cent of all state expenditure, for fear of alienating the urban elites. He was confirmed in office in a number of rigged elections. In in the late 1980s his position became increasingly fragile, as he was forced to introduce unpopular economic austerity measures by the *IMF.

Contemporary politics (since 1991) Traoré was deposed on 25 March 1991, and a transitional government headed by General Amadou Toumani Touré devised a new Constitution in 1992. The Alliance pour la Démocratie au Mali–Parti Africain pour la Solidarité et la Justice (Alliance for Mali Democracy–African Party for Solidarity and Justice) won the ensuing elections. Its leader, Alpha Oumar *Konaré, introduced a series of measures to liberalize the economy. This yielded some moderate economic growth, but more importantly it qualified the country for

debt relief under the *HIPC scheme by almost $900 million in 2000. The 2002 elections, held under allegations of electoral irregularities, were won by Amadou Toumani Touré, who had brought democracy to Mali. In response to demands from the northern Touareg nomads, Touré promised measures to address their poverty and protect their distinctive culture.

Maliki, Nuri al- (b. 1 Jul. 1950). Prime Minister of Iraq, 2005–

Born in Hindija as a Shi'ite, he joined the opposition against Saddam *Hussein and escaped the death sentence by fleeing into exile in Syria. Al-Maliki continued to be active in encouraging opposition to Hussein, and in 2003 he returned as deputy leader of the Dawa party. Since the Dawa party had emerged as the strongest party in the 2005 elections, he became Prime Minster since the party leader, al-Djafaari, proved unacceptable to the Kurdish and Sunni parties. Al-Maliki proved to be hostile to reconciliation with Saddam Hussein and his supporters, and promoted Hussein's speedy execution after his death sentence had been confirmed by the Supreme Court. He was critical of the US at times, but continued to be entirely reliant on its army for his ability to govern.

Malta

An island state, Malta consists of two main islands (Malta and Gozo). It has occupied a historical importance disproportionate to its small size, due to its strategic position at the heart of the Mediterranean.

The islands were annexed to the British Crown in 1814. A legislative assembly was established in 1921 but there were spasmodic riots against colonialism throughout the 1920s; in 1933 the constitution was suspended. The islands were severely bombed during World War II, especially during the Great Siege of 1941–2. In all, around 14,000 tons of bombs destroyed some 35,000 buildings. George VI awarded the islands the UK's highest civilian honour, the George Cross, in 1942.

After the war Britain was reluctant to allow independence owing to the island's usefulness as a 'stationary aircraft carrier'. However, increasing resistance to British rule, which sometimes erupted into violent outbursts, eventually led to independence in

1964, with Giorgio Borg Olivier (b. 1911, d. 1980) as Prime Minister (1962–71). Olivier was succeeded by Dominic Mintoff (b. 1916), leader of the Labour Party, who dominated Maltese politics until his retirement in 1984. He negotiated an agreement with *NATO, which could continue to use naval bases, even after the withdrawal of all British land forces in 1979.

In 1987, the Labour Party lost the parliamentary elections to the Nationalist Party. Led by Edward ('Eddie') Fenech-Adami, who became Prime Minister, it sought to reduce the country's diplomatic and economic isolation. Malta applied for membership of the European Community in 1990. The application was withdrawn in 1996, however, when the Labour Party returned to power. Malta re-applied in 1998, after Fenech-Adami returned to power. Negotiations with the European Union started in the same year, and Malta entered the EU in 2004. As part of the EU, its proximity to Africa transformed it into a frontline state in the EU's efforts to deal with illegal African immigrants, as hundreds made their way to the tiny state every year.

Malvinas, Islas, see FALKLANDS WAR

Manchukuo

The Japanese puppet state in north-eastern China, established on 9 March 1932 and dissolved at the end of World War II. The *Guandong Army's invasion of Manchuria paved the way for Japan's attempts to establish a military hegemony in east Asia, while the development of a thoroughly integrated and advanced economy in the region came to be seen as germane to Japan's postwar economic growth. Under the leadership of *Ishiwara Kanji, Manchuria was occupied by military conquest in a series of actions which came to be known as the Manchurian Incident, beginning in September 1931. After further aggressive expansion, the state of Manchukuo was to occupy, at its fullest extent, the territories of Manchuria as well as parts of inner Mongolia in an area that covered an estimated 1.4 million km2 (550,000 sq. miles) and a population of thirty million. The Japanese military established China's last Emperor, *Pu Yi, as the puppet ruler, but the Guandong Army retained control over the state beyond even the influence of Tokyo. Manchukuo experienced a new form of Japanese colonial regime which chose to invest Japanese capital in the development of heavy industries and communications. From a Japanese point of view, the policy was such a success that operations in Manchuria produced, for example, 30 per cent of the Empire's pig iron by 1937.

Mandate

A form of trusteeship under which the former German colonies and the non-Turkish areas of the *Ottoman Empire were administered mainly by Britain, France, and South Africa, under the auspices of the *League of Nations after World War I. They comprised three categories: 'A-Mandates' (Iraq, Lebanon, *Palestine, Transjordan, Syria) were to be prepared for certain independence through self-government. 'B-Mandates' (Cameroon, Togo, Tanganyika, Ruanda-Urundi) were deemed unfit for impending independence and were to be governed effectively as colonies. 'C-Mandates' (South-West Africa and Germany's former Pacific territories) were to be governed as an integral part of the administering country. As a result, Papua New Guinea achieved independence only in 1975, and Namibia (formerly South-West Africa) in 1990. In practice, territories governed as Mandates were scarcely treated differently from colonies. In principle, however, the 'A-Mandates' created an important precedent for colonial states, as they established the expectation of *decolonization and of international scrutiny of colonial rule.

TRUST TERRITORIES

Mandela, Nelson Rolihlahla (b. 18 July 1918). President of South Africa 1994–9

Resistance (up to 1990) Son of a paramount chief of the Thembu (Xhosa) people near Umtata, he studied at Fort Hare University, where together with his close friend *Tambo he became one of the leaders of the *ANC Youth League. In 1952, they opened the country's first Black law practice. In 1953, he was banned for his ANC activities, which restricted his movements and put him under police surveillance. In 1956, he was accused of treason in a protracted trial which he successfully used as a platform for his opposition to *apartheid, and was eventually acquitted in 1961.

In the wake of the *Sharpeville Massacre Mandela decided that it was pointless to pursue non-violent means against a government that did not follow the rule of law. He led the formation of the ANC's armed wing, Umkhonto we Sizwe (Spear of the Nation), which proceeded to carry out acts of sabotage against the regime under his direction as Commander-in-Chief. For these activities he was arrested in 1962 and sentenced in 1964 to life imprisonment, which he spent first in detention at Robben Island, and then at Pollsmoor prison, both near Cape Town. During his imprisonment, he became the most powerful symbol of ANC resistance, partly because every Black leader from *Buthelezi to *Tutu demanded his release, and partly because his determined wife, Winnie *Mandela, continued to court and attract international media attention.

Mandela demanded unconditional release from gaol, rejecting the government's offer of February 1985 to free him if he renounced all forms of violence. The government used this to depict Mandela as a violent terrorist to the right-wing governments of the UK under *Thatcher, and the USA under *Reagan. At the same time, the increasingly isolated government remained at an impasse as it became clear that no solution to the country's political and economic problems could be found as long as the single most respected Black leader was imprisoned.

Democratic leadership (from 1990)
Mandela was released unconditionally under the pragmatic *De Klerk on 11 February 1990. Elected vice-president (2 March 1990) and then president (5 July 1990) of the ANC, he renounced violence after a second meeting with De Klerk, and thus opened the way for negotiations about the end of apartheid. After a series of tough negotiations he convinced De Klerk of the necessity of achieving a full democracy, without the maintenance of special minority privileges for Whites. Together with De Klerk he received the *Nobel Peace Prize in 1993, and on 10 November 1993 a provisional Constitution was passed which for the first time guaranteed equal rights to all South Africans.

Following the ANC victory in the 1994 elections, he became the country's first Black President on 10 May 1994. Since then, his attempt to bring about reconciliation between his country's different peoples and races has been made especially difficult through the hostility particularly of Buthelezi, ever-fearful of losing too much of his own support to Mandela. More than any other person, Mandela's integrity, enthusiasm, and charm have been instrumental in the astonishingly peaceful transition from a repressive apartheid regime to the more peaceful self-proclaimed 'rainbow nation'. The world's most admired elder statesman, he was succeeded by Thabo *Mbeki, but continued to be active in promoting peace and reconciliation in other African countries. In 2000, with Bill *Clinton he was instrumental in bringing stability to Rwanda and Burundi by brokering a peace deal at Arusha.

Mandela, Winnifred ('Winnie') (b. 1934). South African political activist
Born Winnifred Nomzamo in Bizana (Transkei), she became a social worker and joined the *ANC in 1958, when she also married Nelson *Mandela. She was imprisoned several times before her movements were strictly limited ('banned') by the government (1976–85), a restriction which she sought to defy as often as possible. Flamboyant and outspoken, her use of the international media to act as her husband's voice while he was in prison was instrumental in preserving the image of his imprisonment as the single most potent symbol of *apartheid injustice. Through this, she became a radical ANC leader in her own right. She surrounded herself with a personal bodyguard called the Mandela United Football Club, which in 1989 abducted four youths, killing one of them. She became implicated in this incident, and was found guilty on four charges of kidnapping.

Winnie was temporarily reunited with her husband after his release from prison in February 1990, but they separated in April 1992. As a result of the trial and the separation, she lost her support from the ANC, and had to resign as head of its welfare department. Owing to her considerable following among radical sections of the ANC youth, she was included in the Government of National Unity as Deputy Minister for Culture, Science, and Technology, but was dismissed on 27 March 1995 due to her confrontational rhetoric against the government. She was divorced from Nelson Mandela on 19 March 1996. In 1998, the *Truth and Reconciliation Committee found her guilty of complicity in murders committed by her Football Club, and for serious *human rights violations. In 2003, she was sentenced to five years' imprisonment on charges of multiple fraud.

Mandelson, Peter, see MORRISON, HERBERT STANLEY

Manhattan Project
The codename for the development of the atomic bomb during World War II. Warned by *Einstein and other scientists about German research into nuclear fission, the USA set up a large research establishment at Oak Ridge, Tennessee, in August 1942, where scientists from Canada, the USA, and Britain, together with refugee scientists from Italy, Germany, and Austria, worked. These included the Italian Enrico Fermi, who had discovered the atomic chain reaction in 1934, and J. Robert Oppenheimer, who became the project's director. Within the scientific community, the project became legendary for the informality, collegiality, and innovation among its members. An atomic bomb was developed in a surprisingly short time, but the extent of its

destructiveness was unknown until it was actually tested over New Mexico, on 17 July 1945. President *Truman ordered the dropping of one of these bombs on both *Hiroshima and *Nagasaki, which produced a rapid end to World War II.

NUCLEAR BOMB

Manley, Michael Norman ('Joshua')
(b. 10 Dec. 1924, d. 6 Mar. 1997). Prime Minister of Jamaica 1972–80, 1989–92

Son of Norman *Manley, he was born in St Andrew, and studied in Jamaica and at the London School of Economics. He worked for the *BBC (1950–1) before returning to Jamaica to become a *trade-union organizer. He became a senator (1962–7) before being elected into the Lower Chamber for the People's National Party (PNP). He succeeded his father as leader of the PNP in 1969, becoming Prime Minister in 1972. His socialist policies led the country into a deep crisis, which lost him the 1980 elections. He remained leader of his party, and returned it to victory in 1989, this time accepting the need for economic austerity. He retired due to ill health.

Manley, Norman Washington
(4 July 1893, d. 2 Sept. 1969). Leader of Jamaica 1955–62

Educated at Jamaica College, his studies in Oxford as a *Rhodes Scholar were interrupted by his service in World War I. He was called to the Bar in 1922, and was recognized as one of the foremost lawyers of his generation through his appointment as a KC (King's Counsel) in 1932. In Jamaica, in 1938 he founded the People's National Party (PNP). In the same year he successfully defended *Bustamante on charges of sedition. After winning the 1955 elections he was Chief Minister of Jamaica (1955–9), and Premier (1959–62). Despite his enthusiastic support of the Federation of the *West Indies, his decision not to become its Prime Minister despite his personal standing was a fundamental blow to its prestige. He became leader of the opposition in 1962, and in February 1969 retired in favour of his son, Michael *Manley.

Mannerheim, Carl Gustav Emil, Baron von
(b. 4 June 1867, d. 27 Jan. 1951). President of Finland 1944–6

Born in Villnäs, he was commissioned into the Russian Army in 1889, and served with distinction in the *Russo-Japanese War (1904–5) and in World War I. In response to *Lenin's Communist takeover in Russia in 1917 he used the Russian weakness to lead the fight for Finnish independence. A conservative nationalist, he suppressed the occupation of Helsinki by Finnish Communists. He continued to lead Finnish troops in the *Russian Civil War until 1921, when the beleaguered Soviet government finally recognized Finnish independence. As head of the Finnish Defence Council (1931–9) he erected a line of defensive fortifications, the Mannerheim Line, across the Karelian isthmus, within 30 km of Leningrad. He led the Finnish army in the *Winter War and during World War II, but was forced on both instances to accept defeat by the superior Soviet forces. As President, he concluded an armistice with the Soviet Union, and declared war on Germany in March 1945. He retired due to ill health.

Manning, Preston
(b. 10 June 1942). Canadian politician

Born at Edmonton (Alberta), the son of the former leader of the *Social Credit Party, Ernest C. Manning, Preston graduated from the University of Alberta and became a management consultant. In 1987 he was chosen to lead the *Reform Party at its founding congress. He organized a brilliant election campaign in 1993, when he and 51 other party members were elected to the House of Commons. In 1997, 60 members were elected, and he became the official leader of the opposition. He worked hard to unite the conservative parties into a single movement that could prove an effective challenge to the *Liberal Party, creating the *Canadian Alliance in the process. His bid for the leadership of the new party was unsuccessful, however, and in 2002 he resigned his seat and retired from politics.

Mannix, Daniel
(b. 4 Mar. 1864, d. 6 Nov. 1963). Archbishop of Melbourne 1917–63

Born in Co. Cork (Ireland), he attended St Patrick's seminary at Maynooth, where he became professor of moral theology (1895) and president (1903). Appointed coadjutor Archbishop of Melbourne in 1913, he soon became the best-known and most controversial clergyman in Australia, mainly because of his political involvement. He vociferously opposed *Hughes's conscription campaigns during World War I and supported Irish independence. He sought to enhance Catholic influence through the Australian *Labor Party (ALP). In 1957 he broke with the ALP and supported the *Democratic Labor Party, accusing the former of *Communism.

Mao Tse-tung, see MAO ZEDONG

Mao Zedong (Mao Tse-tung) (b. 26 Dec. 1893, d. 9 Sept. 1976)

Early career Born in Shaoshan (Hunan) into a wealthy peasant family, in 1910 he ran away from home in order to continue his school education. Mao became a student activist in Changsha (Hunan), and founded the New People's Study Society. After graduation, he left for Beijing (1918) and took employment at the Beijing University Library, where he became close to its director, *Li Dazhao. One of the founding members of the Chinese *Communist Party (CCP) in Shanghai (July 1921), he returned to the capital of his home province, Changsha, to organize the party there. In 1923, he was elected to the party's Central Committee. His further rise through the party hierarchy was blocked by his fundamental disagreement with *Marxism-Leninism and *Stalinism. Mao was convinced, that in China the revolution would emanate from its overwhelming mass of peasants, rather than its small urban proletariat (*Maoism). He was involved in the unsuccessful Autumn Harvest Uprising, and led its survivors to Jianxi province. With other leaders, including, *Zhu De, he formed the *Jianxi Soviet, but Mao's unorthodox views condemned him very much to the sidelines within the leadership.

Mao became the effective leader of the Communist Party only after the destruction of the Soviet, and the near-collapse of the *Long March, on 8 January 1935. He led the remaining forces, against all the odds, to *Yan'an. There, over the next decade, he established another *Soviet, strengthened his leadership over the party, and committed it to his ideal of a peasant revolution, which he developed further in a number of writings. In 1939, he married his third wife, *Jiang Qing. During the *Sino-Japanese War, he patiently built up his influence throughout northern China, which proved essential in the following *Chinese Civil War (1945–9). In that war, the discipline he had drilled into his troops, the popularity of his land reforms in areas under his control, and the corruption and disunity within the ranks of the opposing *National Revolutionary Army led to his victory, enabling him to proclaim the People's Republic of China on 1 October 1949.

In power (from 1949) Mao carried out economic reforms such as the collectivization of agriculture and the nationalization of industry with considerable skill. At the same time, his leadership was extremely erratic, keeping the majority of the population in uncertainty and insecurity. His abortive *Hundred Flowers campaign (1956–7) was followed by a wave of repression, while his ill-judged *Great Leap Forward was an unmitigated economic disaster. In its wake, he was forced to withdraw from his official positions within the party (1958), but this only exacerbated his ideological hostility to the pragmatic requirements of day-to-day government.

Mao unleashed the ill-defined *Cultural Revolution, successfully reasserting his control over the party and his status as demigod within the country at large, despite the human and economic cost which this involved. By the time of his death, the regime had become corrupt and subject to bitter infighting between the *Gang of Four and the rest of the party leadership. Undoubtedly he was a figure of unique historical significance in world history, and of unrivalled importance for twentieth-century China. The rapid demise of the Gang of Four after his death, and the assumption of power of *Deng Xiaoping, enabled a more sombre assessment of his personality, both of his outstanding qualities at the head of a revolutionary movement, and his disastrous and costly policies once in power.

Maoism

An ideology derived from the adaptation of *Communism and *Marxism to Chinese conditions by *Mao Zedong. The social base of Maoism was the peasantry, and he rejected Soviet attempts to force the creation of a proletariat in an industrially backward country. Communism could be realized primarily through a change in popular attitudes rather than changes in the class structure. In other words, Mao emphasized the importance of the human will, stressing the role of discipline in the attainment of revolution and Communism, rather than structural factors. Hence, Communism could only be created by a process of mutual education between the leaders and the led. The former would be made aware of popular concerns, and the latter would learn how Communism could solve their problems. In contrast to *Marx and *Lenin, Maoism assumed a continuing class struggle even when Communism had been achieved, so that it was necessary for each generation to gain revolutionary experience. Finally, against Soviet practice, Maoism favoured decentralization in order to further local initiative, which the Communist planners on a central level had to respond to.

CULTURAL REVOLUTION; GREAT LEAP FORWARD; MARXISM-LENINISM

Maori

The original population of New Zealand, whose relationship with the European settlers coming into the country was first defined in the Treaty of *Waitangi of 1840. At that time, there were around 100,000 Maoris living in New Zealand.

Adaptation to Pakhea influence (from 1900) By 1896 that figure had reached an all-time low of 43,113, mainly through disease. However, their immune systems gradually adjusted to European viruses. In addition, a generation of new leaders emerged in 1900, gathered together in the *Young Maori Movement. They were graduates from Te Aute College, and believed that, since pakeha (White) culture was there to stay, it was necessary for Maoris to adapt to that culture and society as much as possible. Prominent Young Maori leaders such as *Buck, *Pomare, and *Ngata gained considerable influence in the New Zealand government, which became increasingly concerned with Maori affairs. As a result, living conditions (e.g. housing) and sanitation were considerably improved, and this facilitated a growth of the Maori population.

At the same time, Maori life remained more influenced by traditional tribalism than by White culture. Community life, which was still largely restricted to the countryside, remained influenced not so much by its MPs as by tribal leaders, deriving their authority from custom and genealogy. In this way *Te Puea, who was born into a Waikato paramount family, affected Maori life much more than any leader of the Young Maori Movement.

Maori renewal (from 1918) In 1918 the *Ratana movement began, a spiritual movement of Maori renewal which in the 1920s became increasingly preoccupied with politics. It replaced the Young Maori Movement as the political representation of the Maori tribes during the 1930s. It increased its political effectiveness through entering an alliance with the *Labour Party, which was in office 1935–49. Especially under *Fraser (1940–9), attitudes began to shift, from encouraging Maoris to apply themselves to pakeha culture to supporting the development of an 'independent, self-reliant and satisfied Maori race working side by side with the pakeha and with equal incentives, advantages, and rewards for efforts in all walks of life' (Fraser, 1949).

Just as this became accepted (and it took some time for this view to be adopted by the *National Party, which was in power 1949–57, 1960–72), it became clear that this ideal was far removed from reality. Mass Maori participation in World War II had created unprecedented interaction between Maoris and pakehas, while after the war many Maoris moved to urban areas, where they were exposed to White culture more than ever before (in 1926, 9 per cent of Maoris lived in towns, in 1951 19 per cent, in 1954 24 per cent, and in 1990 over 75 per cent). It became clear that they were effectively discriminated against in employment, income, and housing.

Assertion of rights (from the 1950s) Participation in the war had also increased Maori self-confidence and assertiveness. This was further encouraged by a decline in tribal identities (mainly because of urbanization), which led to a more united, Maori identity. Maori interest groups formed, such as the influential Maori Women's Welfare League (est. 1951), and regional educational conferences were held in the early 1960s to raise Maori political consciousness. The 1962 Maori Welfare Act established local Maori committees to raise Maori concerns in towns and districts, and these were summarized in the New Zealand Maori Council, which subsequently came to articulate Maori demands nationwide. In 1971, Maoris decided to boycott the Treaty of Waitangi Day celebrations (the national holiday), with the Council citing fourteen major Acts that were a direct violation of the Treaty of Waitangi. In response, the new Labour government (1972–5) established the Treaty of Waitangi Act, which established the *Waitangi Tribunal in 1976. This could only decide on violations against the Treaty of Waitangi committed after 1976, but the Treaty of Waitangi Amendment Act 1985 made grievances that could be addressed by the court retrospective to 1840.

Contemporary issues (from 1990s) While the Waitangi Tribunal attempted to address many Maori grievances, as they were among the country's lowest income groups, they were especially hard-hit by the reversal in social policy during the 1980s, and particularly under *Bolger's governments from 1990. As a result, Maori protests reached new heights in the 1990s. The annual Treaty of Waitangi celebrations of 6 February were cancelled in 1995 because of Maori protests, and were permanently cancelled later in the year. Reluctantly, the government bowed to Maori pressure, so that later in 1995 it returned land for the first time to the largest Maori group of the Tainui, as well as paying a compensation of NZ$170 million. In that year the Prime Minister, as well as the Queen, publicly apologized for the wrongs committed against Maoris. In 1998 the Waitangi Tribunal ordered the government to transfer land back to Maoris, but a final land settlement was still not achieved. Moreover, substantial and disproportionate government spending on social and cultural programmes was only partially successful at reducing a disproportionately high unemployment rate. Constituting about 10 per cent of the New Zealand population in 2001, Maoris were a significant force in the country's closely-fought elections, with fifteen Maori MPs guaranteed by the electoral system introduced in 1996. Nevertheless, Maoris themselves appeared too divided to create a united political movement, with the Maori Party, founded in 2004, obtaining only two seats in the 2005 elections.

(⊕) SEE WEB LINKS

• An unofficial website containing further information on Maori culture.

Mapai (Mifleget Poalei Eretz Yisrael, Israel Workers' Party)

Founded in 1930 as the merger of two socialist parties, the Ahdut Haavoda and Hapoel Hatzair. It aimed at the establishment of a Jewish state in *Palestine. This would be an agricultural and industrial society in which social justice and equality would be realized. Closely linked to the *Histadrut, it quickly became the official representative of the Jewish community in Palestine, commanding the majority both in the self-governing national council, and in the *Jewish Agency. As such, it provided many of Israel's leaders up to and after independence, most notably *Ben-Zvi, *Ben-Gurion, *Eshkol, and *Meir.

From 1948, Mapai became the most important political party in Israel, continuously providing the Prime Minister. It was weakened in 1963 by the defection of Ben-Gurion in protest against the party establishment's protection of Pinhas Lavon, who was forced to resign over misuse of power only to become secretary-general of the party. Ben-Gurion founded the Rafi party in 1965, which only gained ten seats in the elections of that year. However, Rafi attracted prominent members of the Labour movement, such as Teddy Kollek, mayor of *Jerusalem (1965–93), *Dayan, and *Peres. Meanwhile, Mapai joined forces with a smaller socialist movement, Ahdut Haavoda-Poalei Zion (est. 1946) to form the Alignment in 1965. Its subsequent government was joined in 1967 by Dayan, in order to overcome the challenge of the *Six Day War. In 1968, this led to the eventual unification of most of Rafi with the Alignment to form the *Labour Party.

Maquis, see RÉSISTANCE LA

Maralinga, see WOOMERA ROCKET RANGE

March on Rome (27–9 Oct. 1922)

The events that led to *Mussolini's seizure of power. On 27 October the *Fascist movement mobilized, and attempted to cut off all lines of communication to the capital in order to prepare for a march on Rome to seize power in a coup. Since they were no match for the regular Italian army, it was rather the threat of civil war in a country already torn apart by political factionalism which persuaded the government elites to accommodate the Fascists when they learnt of these plans. Since Mussolini declined to accept a subordinate part in a new government, on 28 October he was eventually offered the premiership.

Mussolini's *blackshirt supporters were able to realize their march on Rome on 29 October not as a prelude to, but as a celebration of, their success. Therefore, Mussolini's seizure of power was founded not upon his own position of strength, but on the unwillingness of the political, economic, and social establishment to resist him, and on their hope that he might put an end to the perceived socialist threat.

HITLER PUTSCH

March on Washington (USA)

In 1941, President *Roosevelt signed an equal employment order designed to strike at racial discrimination in federal employment and forestall a march by 100,000 African Americans on the American capital which had been organized by civil rights leaders. The lesson of the potential symbolic power of a march became clear in the summer of 1963, when 250,000 people gathered in Washington to protest at the lack of equal *civil rights for African Americans, listening to speeches and prayers culminating in the 'I have a dream' speech of Dr Martin Luther *King. There have been several marches since, the biggest of which took place in 1995, under the leadership of Louis Farrakhan and the *Nation of Islam. It managed to assemble possibly up to a million African–American men peacefully under the banner of a Million Man March for moral renewal and Black pride.

RANDOLPH, ASA PHILIP

Marchais, Georges (b. 7 June 1929, d. 1 Nov. 1997). French Communist leader 1972–95

A member of the French *Communist Party since 1947, he became a member of the party leadership in 1959. From 1961 to 1970, he was responsible for party organization, and between 1970 and 1972 he served as deputy general secretary of the party. Marchais steered the party towards *Euro-communism. He advocated a unity bloc on the left between the Communists and the *Socialist Party, but became disillusioned by its lack of influence in the *Mauroy government. Marchais was unable to halt the party's decline, and was succeeded by Robert Hue.

Marco Polo Bridge Incident (7 July 1937)

When Japanese troops held manœuvres on the outskirts of Beijing, they requested from the local Chinese military authority permission to search for a missing soldier in the town of Wanping. The garrison of the *National Revolutionary Army refused entry, and a shot was fired. Fighting ensued, and the Japanese entered the city on 8 July. There is little evidence that the incident was an intended provocation, particularly since, under the command of *Ishiwara, the Japanese were relatively careful not to engage in a full-scale war. However, *Chiang Kai-shek responded to this local provocation by ordering army reinforcements against the Japanese. It thus marked the beginning of the *Sino-Japanese War.

Marcos, Ferdinand Edralin (b. 11 Sept. 1917, d. 28 Sept. 1989). President of the Philippines 1965–86

Born in Sarrat (Ilocos Norte) of a well-connected family, Marcos graduated from the University of the Philippines Law School and became a highly successful intelligence officer for the US army during World War II. A supporter of President *Roxas, he was a member of the House of Representatives for the Liberal Party (1949–59), and of the Senate (1959–65), whose leader he became in 1963. Supported by the Nationalist Party, Marcos was elected President in 1965, and in 1969 he became the first Philippine President to be re-elected, largely on account of his agricultural and educational reforms.

Marcos's early popularity waned when he used increasing force against his opponents. He declared martial law in 1972, in a coup that dissolved all political institutions and suspended *human rights. His reactionary policies triggered resistance by the Communist 'New People's Army', as well as the Muslim Moro National Liberation Front. Economic decline forced him to abandon martial law in 1981 and to open up the political system. His regime was badly shaken by the assassination of the opposition leader, B. *Aquino. In desperate need of legitimacy, Marcos called elections in November 1985, but he was outsmarted by Corazón *Aquino, who claimed victory on 9 February 1986. The military, led by General Fidel *Ramoz, refused

its continued support. Marcos fled to exile in Hawaii on 25 February 1986, where he died.

Marne, Battles of the (5–11 Sept. 1914, 15–20 July 1918)

Two crucial battles at the start and end of *World War I. In 1914, the Germans hoped to realize the *Schlieffen Plan through rapidly conquering France. Having overrun neutral Belgium, they advanced to within 25 km of Paris. They crossed the River Marne on 6 September 1914 in an attempt to outflank a French counter-attack by *Joffre. Eventually, they were forced to retreat, and moved north to the River Aisne where they dug in, setting the pattern of trench warfare for the next four years.

On 21 March 1918 the Germans launched a strong offensive north of the Somme. This failed to break the Allied line and did not reach its objective of Amiens. On 15 July, however, *Ludendorff renewed the attack further east. His troops crossed the Marne east of Château-Thierry and again Paris was threatened; but on 17 July Marshal *Foch ordered his counter-attack, successfully using tanks. Thus the last German offensive of the war was repelled and all German hopes for victory dissolved in the subsequent Allied attack.

Maronites

An Eastern Christian Church founded in the fifth century by a monk called Maron, who created a monotheistic Christian church. The Maronites established communion with the Roman *Catholic Church in the eighteenth century, but preserved most of their rights, including a Patriarch as their head, and their own liturgy. Upon the formation of Greater Lebanon in 1920, Maronites, who formed the largest single community of around 30 per cent of the population, were guaranteed the presidency and leadership over the army. After World War II, their relative influence declined as a result of the departure of the French, the rise of *pan-Arabism, and demographic changes in favour of the non-Christian communities. This made their entrenched commercial and political leadership untenable, and ultimately led to civil war in 1958, and 1975–89.

Marshall, George Catlett (b. 31 Dec. 1880, d. 17 Oct. 1959). US Army Chief of Staff 1939–45; US Secretary of State 1947–9; US Secretary of Defense 1950–1

Born in Uniontown, Pennsylvania, of a long-established Virginian family, he graduated at the Virginia Military Institute in 1901 and had a distinguished record in World War I with the US 1st Army on the Western Front. Rising rapidly in rank between the wars, he was appointed as Chief of Staff on 1 September 1939 to an army of some 200,000. When he left office in 1945 the army he commanded had risen to its greatest strength ever, at eight million. He attended all the major wartime conferences and was a strong advocate of an Allied landing on the Normandy coast, which eventually happened on *D-Day. In November 1945 he was asked by President *Truman to attempt to mediate in the renewed *Chinese Civil War, but had to report that US aid to the *Guomindang was being dissipated by wholesale corruption and that he had failed to achieve a pacification.

As Secretary of State he initiated massive aid to Greece and Turkey, and announced the European Recovery Program, which became known as the *Marshall Plan. He helped to create *NATO and supported the firm line taken by the Western powers over the Soviet blockade of West *Berlin. Ill health obliged him to resign in 1949, but he returned to office in 1950 when war in Korea broke out. He remained a distinguished government consultant throughout the 1950s. Marshall and *Rabin are the only generals ever to have received a *Nobel Peace Prize.

Marshall Islands, see MICRONESIA

Marshall, John Thurgood (b. 2 July 1908, d. 24 Jan. 1993). US Supreme Court Justice 1967–91
Born in Baltimore, Maryland, the great-grandson of a slave, he was a brilliant student, having graduated second in his class at Howard University. This followed his rejection from the University of Maryland on racial grounds. As the chief lawyer of the *NAACP from 1939, he argued its case in *Brown v. Topeka. President *Kennedy appointed him to the Court of Appeals for the Second Circuit in New York in 1961, and he became solicitor-general under Lyndon *Johnson. Johnson appointed him as the first African–American US Supreme Court Justice. He was a liberal judge, chiefly concerned with the active protection of the poor through the Constitution.

Marshall Plan (European Recovery Program) (1947–52)
A programme of economic assistance for war-torn Europe announced by US Secretary of State George *Marshall on 5 June 1947, which sought to lessen the *Communist appeal for the impoverished Western European countries through investment in their economic recovery. Aid comprised technical assistance, foodstuffs, industrial and raw

materials, and credits. Until the end of the plan in 1952 the USA provided a total of $13.2 billion, of which the UK and its dependencies received $3.2 billion, France $2.7 billion, Italy $1.5 billion, and Germany $1.4 billion.

The plan was extremely successful at forging Western Europe together behind US leadership, as the Soviet Union forbade its satellite states in Eastern Europe to accept the aid. It also made some contribution towards structural improvements for the recipient nations' economies, though the extent of this is unclear. Total industrial production in the recipient countries had increased to 35 per cent above its prewar levels by 1952. Most of that increase, however, occurred after 1950 as a result of the economic boom generated by the *Korean War. It failed to promote *European integration along the lines originally envisaged by the USA, so that it fell to its disappointed administrators such as *Monnet to promote closer cooperation independent of the plan.

OECD

Martin, Paul (b.28 Aug. 1938). Canadian Prime Minister 2003–6
Born in Windsor (Ontario), he is the son of a long-serving Cabinet minister who lost three successive leadership contests for the *Liberal Party. Paul Martin Jr. entered the House of Commons for the Liberals in 1988, and was not quite senior enough to beat *Chrétien in the 1990 leadership contest. He served as Minister of Finance from 1993, but resigned in 2002 in order to be free to contest Chrétien's leadership. To Chrétien's misgivings, Martin obtained the endorsement of the party rank and file. In office, he urged closer co-operation with the US. He was, arguably, the Prime Minister the most sympathetic to the concerns of *native peoples, making the settlement of *land claims and the provision of educational and health care facilities a major government priority.

Soon after taking up office, Martin called an election to receive popular approval. However, his government became increasingly embroiled in corruption allegations related to the Liberal Party under Chrétien's leadership. He lost his absolute majority against an invigorated *Conservative opposition, and relied on the support of the *New Democratic Party. To stave off criticism Martin appointed an independent commission, which confirmed many of the corruption charges brought against the Liberals. After losing a no-confidence vote and running an inept campaign, he lost the 2006 elections to the Conservatives led by Stephen *Harper.

Martinique

A Caribbean island under French sovereignty since 1635. In 1946, it became a French Overseas Department. In 1974 it was granted regional status, and in 1983 it received greater autonomy over its local police and taxation. An integral part of France, it was represented in Paris by four Deputies in the National Assembly, and two Senators. Support for its independence remained slight, as French transfer payments and economic links were chiefly responsible for the island's relative prosperity. As part of France it is part of the European Union, with the *euro as legal tender.

Martov, Julius (b. 24 Nov. 1873, d. 4 Apr. 1923). Russian revolutionary

Born Yuliy Osipovich Tsederbaum in Constantinople, he joined the Russian Social Democrats as a young man. He met *Lenin in 1895 and, like him, spent three years in exile (1897–1900). He then left Russia and published with Lenin the first Russian Socialist newspaper, *Iskra* (The Spark). Martov split with Lenin in 1903, mainly over the extent to which the party should be controlled by a small elite cadre. He became the most prominent *Menshevik leader and, after the first *Russian Revolution of 1917, advocated a coalition of all socialist groups, again in opposition to Lenin. After the October Revolution he became the official leader of the Menshevik Party, and from 1920 he continued his resistance from Berlin.

Marxism

The first consistent theory of *Communism, developed by Karl Marx (b. 1818, d. 1883) with his associate Friedrich Engels (b. 1820, d. 1895). The basis of their ideas was a belief in the materialist dialectic, according to which nature develops in constant circles, and matter is transformed from one state to the other (e.g. from water to steam, back to water). This imbued Marx and Engels with a fundamental belief in historical progress. History developed from an original, 'communist' state, distinguished by common ownership. Societies became marked, first, by feudalism, in which control was exercised through the nobility. After a revolution (such as the French Revolution 1789) power was exercised through property (*capitalism).

Ultimately, the repressed would rise again and establish the original, Communist state characterized by common ownership of production and full economic and social equality. Communism was thus seen as 'inevitable', the original and final stage of history.

In Marx's main work, *Das Kapital*, he argued that in the industrialized, capitalist society, which he observed in England, the main objective of the owners of production was to maximize their profits. Increasing mechanization would lead to an alienation of the workplace as traditional skills were replaced by machines. The owners of capital would also pay workers as little as possible, so that workers could not even maintain a minimal standard of living. This created a homogeneous proletarian class, defined as not owning the means of production, which became impoverished and alienated until its members had 'nothing to lose but their chains'. At this point, there would be an inevitable revolution as the proletariat would rise to introduce a non-exploitative, Communist society.

Marx's analysis of industrial society was innovative and brilliant, yet it contained substantial flaws. Among the most important was that his definition of class, as the basic distinction between those who owned the means of production and those who did not, was too crude. Furthermore, the idea that all members of a social 'class' increasingly develop a common culture and identity beyond very narrow and clearly defined concerns has been consistently disproved in the course of the nineteenth and twentieth centuries. Finally, Marx's conception of history was fundamentally flawed, as Communism never gained any ground in England or the USA, the most industrialized countries at the time.

MAOISM; TROTSKYISM; GRAMSCI

Marxism-Leninism

An interpretation of *Communism in which *Lenin sought to adapt the central tenets of *Marxism to the experience of Russia, an economically backward agrarian state. The emergence of *imperialism was considered to be a central, unforeseeable factor which had occurred since the development of Marxism. This enabled the propertied classes in industrially advanced countries to expand production and to spread the economic benefits to those workers who were prepared to accept the current economic system. This group of workers formed a so-called 'labour aristocracy', a process which prevented class unity. Left to itself, the proletariat would never rise up against the existing order. Hence Lenin emphasized the importance of the need for party elites and of 'professional revolutionaries', who would prepare and carry out the revolution and then create a Communist consciousness among the workers.

Masaryk, Jan (b. 14 Sept. 1886, d. 10 Mar. 1948). Czechoslovak Foreign Minister 1940–8
Born in Prague, the son of Tómas *Masaryk, he was educated in Prague and Vienna and served for a while in the *Austro-Hungarian army. In 1907 he emigrated to the USA, but returned to Prague in 1918 and became a personal assistant to *Benes. As ambassador to Britain (1925–38), he resigned in protest at his country's betrayal by the *Munich Agreement. In 1940, he became Foreign Minister of the Czechoslovak government-in-exile, a post which he continued to hold in the government after liberation. Much to his disappointment, he was unable to prevent the Soviet veto of Czechoslovak acceptance of *Marshall Aid. At the request of President Benes he remained in his post after the Communist coup of February 1948, but his death in mysterious circumstances three weeks later signalled the end of the old, liberal order of interwar Czechoslovakia, of which he, and particularly his father, had been such important symbols.

Masaryk, Tómas Garrigue (b. 7 Mar. 1850, d. 14 Sept. 1937). President of Czechoslovakia 1918–35
Born in Hodonín, the son of a coachman on a Habsburg estate had a brilliant career at school, which enabled him to attend the universities of Leipzig and Vienna. In 1882, he became professor of philosophy at Prague University, a post he held until 1914. In this position, he developed a theory of 'critical realism', a mixture of German idealism and western European positivism, to call for pragmatic policies of social action. He argued strongly against the creation of myths so prevalent in Czech *nationalism at the time; but also criticized Austrian and Hungarian *imperialism that claimed the Czech lands as part of *Austria-Hungary. He served on the Austrian imperial council in 1891–3 as a member of the Young Czech movement, and again in 1907–14 as the representative of the Realist Party, which he had founded. His ability to unite Czechs and Slovak was demonstrated by his leading role in the creation of a common Czech and Slovaks national council in 1915. He helped organize a Czechoslovak legion in Russia to fight against Austria-Hungary in 1917, and promoted unity among Czech and Slovak emigrant associations in the USA. He had thus become a pivotal figure in the events leading to Czechoslovakia's independence as a unitary state. As President, the open-minded intellectual epitomized the sophistication, liberal individualism, toleration, cosmopolitanism, concern for justice, and modernity of the country's political elite, and of the self-image of the state as a whole. He retired owing to old age.

Masire, 'Quett' Ketumile Joni (b. 23 July 1925). President of Botswana 1980–98
Born in Kanye, in the southern part of what was then the British Crown Colony of Bechuanaland, he was trained as a teacher in South Africa and returned eventually to become a journalist and the editor of the *African Echo*. Together with *Khama he co-founded the Bechuanaland (later Botswana) Democratic Party (BDP) in 1962 and became its general secretary. Deputy President dating from Botswana's independence in 1966, he held several ministries (e.g. for finance and planning) until he succeeded Khama as President. He opposed the *apartheid regime and granted asylum to many *ANC activists, but otherwise pragmatically sought good working relations with South Africa. His attempts to reduce his country's economic dependence on South Africa were counteracted by the droughts of the 1980s and early 1990s.

Massey, Charles Vincent (b. 20 Feb. 1887, d. 30 Dec. 1967). Governor-General of Canada 1952–9
The first Canadian-born Governor-General, he was educated at Oxford before returning to his native Toronto to teach at the University. After serving in World War I he became president of the family firm of Massey-Harris. In 1926 he was appointed first Canadian minister to the USA, before serving with distinction as Canadian high commissioner in London (1935–46). After the war he was chairman of an influential Royal Commission on the Arts and Sciences in Canada, whose recommendations resulted in the creation of the Canada Council to promote the arts. His close links with the UK eased the transition to appointing Governor-Generals who were Canadian-rather than British-born.

Massey, William Ferguson (b. 26 Mar. 1856, d. 10 May 1925). Prime Minister of New Zealand 1912–25
Early career Born in Limavady, Ulster (Ireland), he emigrated to New Zealand with his family in 1870 and settled at Tamaki. He

leased a farm at Mangere in 1877, became active in the local masonic lodge, and in 1890 became president of the Mangere Farmers' Club. Massey became president of the Auckland district of the National Association, and in 1894 entered parliament. He became prominent in parliamentary opposition to *Sedden's government, and was a champion of farming interests. He became leader of the conservative opposition in 1903, which in 1909 emerged as the *Reform Party. He worked hard at party organization, and created the first disciplined parliamentary party in New Zealand politics. These organizational efforts, his propagation of farming interests through demanding the private purchase (freehold) of state (Crown) lands, as well as his graphic warnings about the threats of an advancing *Labour Party, resulted in his narrow victory in the 1911 elections.

In office *Ward's *Liberal Party was able to hang on to government until 6 July 1912, when Massey became Prime Minister. His government forcefully suppressed a militant dockers' and coalminers' strike in 1912–13, one of the most bitter industrial disputes in New Zealand history. He was a committed supporter of the *British Empire thoughout World War I, though from 1915 the Ulster Protestant was forced to form a national government in coalition with the Catholic Ward, whom he disliked intensely. He emerged from the 1919 elections for the first time with a convincing majority, though he spent most of his time trying to stave off a decline in the prosperity which the farming community had enjoyed during the war. However, the political balance started to shift to the cities with the growth of urbanization, and he only just won the 1922 elections. His marginal majority in parliament made his last administration over-reliant on the particular concerns of individual MPs. He died in office.

Mata Hari (Margareta Gertruida MacLeod) (b. 7 Aug. 1876, d. 15 Oct. 1917). German spy

Of Dutch origin, the nightclub dancer worked in Paris from 1903, where she had countless affairs with French officers and government officials. In 1917, she was arrested and charged with passing on secrets to the Germans, and was subsequently convicted and hanged.

Matteotti Crisis

Giacomo Matteotti (b. 1885, d. 1924), the secretary of the newly formed Socialist Unity Party (Partito Socialista Unitario, PSU) and protégé of *Turati, was an outspoken opponent of *Fascism. In a parliamentary speech on 30 May 1924 he exposed and denounced Fascist foul play in the recent parliamentary elections and demanded that they be annulled. On 10 June, he was abducted and murdered by members of the *Fascist movement, and it soon emerged that several Fascist leaders, including *Mussolini himself, were implicated in the murder. There resulted a public outcry which extended even into Fascist ranks. Most of Italy's non-Fascist parliamentarians reacted with the *Aventine Secession, which gave them moral high ground but rendered them unable to influence political developments in the capital. Mussolini was thus able to use the fraternization of the anti-Fascist parties to outlaw them all and strengthen his own position.

Mau Mau (1952–9)

A militant guerrilla movement which had begun to develop in Kenya in the late 1940s. It insisted that an end to discrimination by Whites and greater African equality could only be achieved through violent struggle. Violence spread after the introduction of a state of emergency in October 1952. In a desperate attempt to quell the rebellion, the British colonial authorities established special detention centres and used suspect methods of interrogation (effectively torture). In 1958 at Hola Camp, from a group of eighty-eight hard-core detainees, eleven died and many more were seriously injured during interrogation. Political protest in Britain resulted in the decision (1959) to call a constitutional conference, resulting in Kenyan independence. Official casualties by 1957 were 95 Europeans and 1,920 Africans killed by Mau Mau guerrillas, and 11,503 Kikuyu people killed by the colonial forces. The origins of the term are not known; it may be related to the Kenya rift-valley Mau Escarpment.

Mauretania

A western African republic characterized since colonial times by ethnic tensions, between a well-educated Black minority and an underprivileged majority of Moors (a Muslim people of north-west Africa).

Contemporary history (1900–1980s)

Mauretania came under French influence after 1900. It became part of *French West Africa in 1920, though heavy Arab resistance to French colonial rule was not suppressed until 1934. A French Overseas Territory since 1946, it received autonomy within the *French Community in 1958, and was granted independence on 28 November 1960.

Mauretania was governed by the Parti du Peuple Mauritanien (PPM, Mauretanian People's Party) under President Mokhtar Ould Daddah (b. 1924, d. 2003). In 1976 Mauretania occupied the southern half of Western Sahara, with Morocco occupying the north. However, its limited resources were overstretched by the costs of the occupation, during which the size of its army increased tenfold. Its fragile economy ground to a halt, weakened further by attacks from the West Saharan guerrilla movement, POLISARIO. Mauretanian forces were compelled to withdraw from Western Sahara in 1979, though their retreat was also partly precipitated by a military coup which had deposed Daddah in 1978.

The Taya era (1984–2005) After a period of political instability, power passed to Maaonya Ould Sid'Ahmed Taya (b. 1945) in 1984. He managed to stabilize the political system, but failed to reduce the ethnic tensions between the Black minority and the Moors. Sporadic violence erupted, and in 1990 a group of Black Mauretanians staged an abortive coup against the government. As many as 100,000 Black Mauretanians (5 per cent of the population) fled into neighbouring Senegal that year. The President introduced a constitution in 1991 and elections in 1992. These were boycotted by the opposition parties, and Maaonya Ould Sid'Ahmed Taya was confirmed as President. During the 1990s Mauretania's relations to its neighbours, especially Senegal, worsened, and in 1999 the government announced its intention to withdraw from *ECOWAS.

Contemporary politics (since 2005) In 2005, Taya was deposed in a coup led by the head of the secret service, Ely Ould Mohammed Vall. Vall devised a number of constitutional changes, including the limitation of the President's terms of office, and promised elections within two years. Vall affirmed his country's friendship with the USA and Israel, though his key challenge consisted in reducing poverty in one of Africa's poorest countries.

Mauritius

A state of islands off the coast of eastern Africa, Mauritius has been characterized by a remarkably stable democracy, despite ethnic heterogeneity.

Contemporary history (up to 1995)

Consisting of the islands of Mauritius and Rodriguez, the state was named after Prince Maurice of Nassau by the Dutch who controlled the island (1598–1710). It came under French sovereignty in 1715, when African slaves were imported to work on sugar plantations, and was part of the *British Empire from 1810. After the abolition of slavery in 1833, labour for the plantations was imported from India. The population of Mauritius became ethnically and religiously heterogeneous, with 69 per cent of Indian and 27 per cent of African descent. A minority of Whites, largely descendants of French planters, formed the country's commercial and political elite. Mauritius became independent on 12 March 1968, as a member of the *Commonwealth. Ethnic tensions led to a series of riots in 1972, and triggered the introduction of a state of emergency.

In 1982 the Mauritian Labour Party (MLP) and the Mauritian Militant Movement (MMM) failed in their attempt to establish a *Marxist state. Anerood Jugnauth (b. 1930) proceeded to found the Mauritian Socialist Movement, which emerged as the strongest party after the 1983 elections. As Prime Minister, Jugnauth presided over an economic boom in which salaries increased by an annual average of 8.8 per cent over the next ten years. Unemployment vanished, and average annual income per head increased from $1,240 to $3,060 in 1994. The country profited particularly from the international economic blockade against the *apartheid regime in South Africa. Foreign investors came to Mauritius instead of South Africa, while many South African businesses came to Mauritius to escape the international ban. However, prosperity led to a relative decline in productivity, so that the high average wages became untenable in the long run.

Contemporary politics (since 1995)

Growing economic difficulties led to Jugnauth's defeat in the elections of 27 December 1995, when under the leadership of

Navin Rangoolam his rivals, the MMM and the MLP, won all of the parliamentary seats with 65.2 per cent of the popular vote. Jugnauth was re-elected in 2000, whereupon he embarked upon a campaign to overcome corruption in politics and public administration. Jugnauth became President in 2003, and in 2005 the Mauritian Labour Party was returned to power, with Rangoolam becoming Prime Minister. Rangoolam was elected at a time of impending crisis, as suger cane farmers, whose sugar constituted around 25 per cent of the EU's imports, lost their preferential access to EU markets at inflated prices, following a *WTO ruling in 2005.

Mauroy, Pierre (b. 5 July 1928). Prime Minister of France 1981–4
Lord Mayor of Lille and Deputy in the National Assembly since 1973, he belonged to the militant wing of the *Socialist Party. As the Prime Minister appointed to carry out the policies of newly elected President *Mitterrand, he abolished the death penalty, state control of the media, and restrictions on local radio transmissions. More importantly, to overcome the current economic recession, Mauroy introduced an expansionist social and economic programme, with vastly increased social benefit payments and the creation of some of 140,000 new jobs. Through the law of 13 February 1982, he also nationalized a number of key industries and banks. Owing to the spiralling costs of his policies, Mauroy had to backtrack and announce his first spending cuts within months. In 1983 health service charges were raised. In a vain attempt to stop the decline of the currency and a capital flight as investors and private individuals took their funds out of France, drastic foreign exchange controls of 2,000 francs per annum were introduced. Due to his government's rising unpopularity, he was replaced by Laurent Fabius. In 1992 he became a Senator.

Maurras, Charles (b. 20 Apr. 1868, d. 16 Nov. 1952). French ultra right-wing intellectual
A co-founder of the monarchist and chauvinist *Action Française, which he supported through numerous *anti-Semitic and *anticlerical writings. He backed the *Vichy government and was sentenced to lifelong imprisonment in 1945, but was released in the year of his death.

May Fourth movement (1919)
A wave of debate and argument triggered by a student demonstration in Beijing on 4 May 1919. Students were outraged by the terms of the *Versailles Treaty, whereby German territory in the Shandong peninsula,

and concessions which the Chinese had to make to the Germans, were passed on to the Japanese. In the following months hundreds of similar student demonstrations were held across the country. A lively intellectual debate ensued which was carried to a relatively popular level by a large number of magazines and newspapers. This re-evaluation of traditional Chinese culture in light of Western thought led to the widespread acceptance of the 'new culture', using some Western ideas to strengthen Chinese culture itself. This stimulated the growth of popular education and led to improvements in the emancipation of *women as traditions such as the binding of feet went rapidly out of fashion. The debate so generated formed a background to the emergence of the *Guomindang, and the formation of the Chinese *Communist Party (1921).

Mayotte

Geographically part of the *Comoros Islands, it voted twice (1974, 1976) against independence from French colonial rule and integration into the state of the Comoros. Its population has sought to lobby the French government for a change in its status from 'collective territory' to an overseas department, which would give its inhabitants French citizenship and full political rights as an integral part of France. After the second referendum, France considerably raised its investment in the island: owing to French aid and transfer payments, in 2000 Mayotte's GDP of $3,000 exceeded that of the unstable Comoros Islands more than fivefold. In 2000, France granted Mayotte the status of 'collectivité départementale', which entailed more political rights while stopping short of endowing Mayotte with the status of an overseas department.

Mbeki, Thabo Mvuyelwa (b. 18 June 1942). Vice-President of South Africa 1994–8, President 1999–

Early career Son of a former *ANC president, he joined the ANC Youth League in 1956. Also a member of the *Communist Party, Mbeki advanced quickly through the ANC's ranks. He went to Britain to study economics at the University of Sussex (1963–6), and then worked for the ANC offices in London

(1967–70). He left to receive military training in the Soviet Union before going to work at the ANC headquarters in Lusaka (Zambia). Becoming a close adviser to ANC President Oliver *Tambo, he was ANC spokesperson on foreign affairs, while simultaneously developing contacts with leading figures in White South African society and its business world. ANC chairperson since 1993, the pragmatic moderate was chosen for the pivotal post of first Vice-President to *Mandela.

In office With responsibility for the day-to-day running of the government, Mbeki was thus groomed as Mandela's successor. As President, Mbeki was successful in preventing ethnic violence which had developed in other post-colonial states with a substantial White majority. Under his leadership, South Africa's political influence on the continent continued to grow. Moreover, Mbeki presided over substantial economic growth while pursuing rigorous policies of positive discrimination in administration and business in favour of the previously disadvantaged Black majority. These policies, however, led to large-scale corruption, as appointments in economy and administration were often made not on grounds of ability. Mbeki also faced tremendous criticism over his refusal to respond to the growing *AIDS crisis in the country, as South Africa became one of the world's most affected countries. It was not until 2003 that Mbeki's government approved the distribution of anti-AIDS drugs through the national health system. Finally, Mbeki faced great criticism over his refusal to condemn *Mugabe's brutal regime in Zimbabwe, presumably because he was unwilling to judge a former hero of the anti-colonial struggle. The lack of sanctions from South Africa, on whose economy Zimbabwe depended, allowed the corrupt Zimbabwean leader to continue his corrupt rule. Recognizing that he had thus far been unsuccessful in reducing rampant crime, Mbeki announced sweeping measures to increase pubic security in 2007.

Medicare (Canada)
A system of comprehensive and universal health care which formed in many respects the apogee of the Canadian *welfare state. It was pioneered by the province of Saskatchewan, where the government of the *Cooperative Commonwealth Federation established a universal hospital insurance plan in 1945. This had been adopted in all other provinces by 1961. In that year,

Saskatchewan began to introduce a medical care insurance to provide universal access to doctors. *Pearson strongly supported the national adoption of the plan and in 1966 introduced the Medical Care Act, whereby the federal government subsidized the provincial provision of health care, on the condition that it included universal coverage.

Medicare (USA)
A health care scheme introduced to Congress by President *Johnson in July 1965 as one of a series of reforms for his *Great Society. Funded by compulsory health insurance, it meets a very high proportion of the cost of medical treatment and hospital care for persons aged 65 or over. The scheme also includes Medicaid for sick people with absolutely no personal resources. The American Medical Association (AMA) had staunchly opposed any more general provision as 'socialized medicine', having successfully resisted any medicare scheme from its first proposal by President Truman in 1947. As the proportion of the population over 65 grew steadily, the system became increasingly strained as the expenditure had to be met in spite of a growing budget deficit. Reform of Medicare formed a major theme of President *Clinton's 1992 election campaign. After some delay he entrusted his wife, Hillary *Clinton, with the passage of a health care bill. However, diverse opposition in *Congress, as well as fierce hostility by the pharmaceutical lobby and, once again, the AMA, led to the failure of health care reform in 1994. Although expenditure for Medicare and Medicaid continued to soar, the system was put on a more stable basis by the growth of income generated by the economic boom during the Clinton presidency.

MEDICARE (CANADA); NATIONAL HEALTH SERVICE (UK)

Médici, Emílio Garrastazú (b. 4 Dec. 1906, d. 9 Oct. 1985). Brazilian dictator 1969–74
An officer in the Brazilian army, he became the commander of the military academy in 1964. In that year he participated in the military coup which ended eighteen years of civilian government. He subsequently became a pivotal figure in the military dictatorship as director of the military intelligence services, and in 1969 became President himself. During most of his rule, which was marked by political repression and *human rights violations, Brazil enjoyed its own economic miracle of further industrialization and rapid economic growth. Yet, this accelerated Brazil's reliance on primary imports such as

oil, and increased its vulnerability to the 1973 *oil-price shock.

Meech Lake Accord (April 1987)

An abortive Canadian constitutional settlement, arising out of *Quebec's opposition to the patriation of the *Canadian Constitution in 1982. To satisfy Quebec's demands for recognition of more rights, Prime Minister *Mulroney and the premiers of all Canadian provinces met at Meech Lake (Quebec) to agree on a compromise. Quebec was recognized as having a 'distinct' society, while all of Canada was recognized as a bilingual country. Provincial competences were to be increased in aspects of immigration, constitutional rights, and federal spending programmes. The accord was fiercely criticized by some of the weaker provinces, who benefited from a strong Federal state, as well as by *Canadian Indians, whose plea for national constitutional recognition would have been hampered by the agreement. It broke down on 1 July 1990, after the provinces of Newfoundland and Manitoba had failed to ratify it within the necessary three-year period.

Meighen, Arthur (b. 16 June 1874, d. 5 Aug. 1960). Prime Minister of Canada 1920–1, 1926

Born at Anderson (Ontario), he graduated from the University of Toronto and opened a law practice in Manitoba. He entered the House of Commons as a *Conservative in 1908, and became solicitor-general under *Borden (1913–17). As Minister of the Interior (1917–20) he was responsible for some of the most important legislation of World War I, such as the creation and nationalization of Canadian National Railways and the introduction of compulsory military service overseas. His suppression of the general strike in *Winnipeg (1919) earned him the lasting hostility of the labour movement. Nevertheless, he became leader of the Conservative Party and Prime Minister in 1920. He lost the 1921 general elections owing to the rise of the Progressive Party, though the Conservatives recovered sufficiently to become the largest party in 1925. Following the collapse of *Mackenzie King's government in 1926, Meighen formed a minority government which lasted three months. Defeated in the ensuing elections, he retired as party leader. In 1932 he entered the Senate, and in 1941 was recalled to lead the Conservatives. He failed to enter the House of Commons in a by-election in 1942, however, and withdrew from politics.

Meir, Golda (b. 3 May 1898, d. 8 Dec. 1978). Prime Minister of Israel 1969–74

Born Golda Mabovitch in Kiev, Russia, she emigrated with her parents to Milwaukee (USA) in 1907. She married Morris Mayerson, and they changed their surname to Meir when they settled in *Palestine in 1921 to live and work on a *kibbutz. A strong socialist, she quickly emerged as a prominent member of the *Mapai Party during the 1930s. She also became head of the political department of the trade-union organization, *Histadrut, in 1934. A leading figure in the political department of the *Jewish Agency, she was involved in secret negotiations leading to the foundation of Israel, and was appointed Israel's first ambassador to the Soviet Union. Back in Israel, she was Minister of Labour (1949–56), where she helped in the integration of hundreds of thousands of immigrants into Israeli society. She was Foreign Minister (1956–66) until she became secretary-general of the Mapai Party, and was instrumental in the merger to form the *Labour Party in 1967. She succeeded *Eshkol as Prime Minister of a coalition government, though she found it difficult to work with the forceful *Dayan. She was heavily criticized for her policies at the time of the *Yom Kippur War, for which Israel had been unprepared. She resigned in March 1974.

Mellon, Andrew William (b. 24 Mar. 1855, d. 26 Aug. 1937). US Secretary of the Treasury 1921–32

Born in Pittsburgh, Pennsylvania, the son of a wealthy banker, he studied at the West University of Pennsylvania (now the University of Pittsburgh), joined his father's bank, and by 1920 was one of the richest men in the USA. Appointed by President *Harding in 1921, he served under his two *Republican successors, Presidents *Coolidge and *Hoover. He presided over the boom of the 1920s, convinced that government was an extension of big business, to be run on business lines. His tax cuts purposely helped investments of the rich, which he felt would bring employment and other benefits to the less well-off. After the *Wall Street Crash, he had no response to the Great *Depression other than government retrenchment. He donated his considerable art collection, together with funds, to establish the US National Gallery of Art (1937) in Washington.

Menderes, Adnan (b. 1899, d. 17 Sept. 1961). Prime Minister of Turkey 1950–60

Born in Aydin (Izmir), he practised as a lawyer until 1932, when he became a representative for the Republican People's Party in the Grand

National Council. There, he became a cautious critic of President Kemal (*Atatürk). On 7 December 1945, he co-founded the Democratic Party, which won the elections of 1950. He brought Turkey into *NATO and, amidst great controversy, accepted the independence of *Cyprus in 1959. He pushed hard for economic and bureaucratic reform. Many of these policies offended entrenched interests, while a severe economic crisis lost him the support of parliament and the people. Menderes continued to govern regardless, harassing the opposition. He was deposed by the army, sentenced to death for violating the constitution, and executed.

Mendès-France, Pierre (b. 11 Jan. 1907, d. 18 Oct. 1982). Prime Minister of France 1954–5

He entered the Chamber as the youngest Deputy for the *Radical Party in 1932 and remained in that position until the French collapse in 1940. He managed to join de *Gaulle in 1941, and became his Minister for the Economy in 1944, but resigned when his more progressive ideas for an economic recovery were rejected in 1945. He was governor of the *IMF 1947–58. Interested in principles and ideas rather than in holding office for its own sake, his career suffered from the structural weakness of the Chamber of Deputies of the Fourth Republic, whose unstable majorities favoured people of compromise rather than vision. However, as an outspoken opponent of the French *Indochina War, he became Prime Minister after the military débâcle at *Dien Bien Phu. Within thirty days of his taking office, France pulled out of *Indochina after signing the *Geneva Agreements. He granted self-government to Tunisia, and encouraged social and economic reforms in Algeria to meet the growing unrest there. He obtained special powers to tackle current economic problems, and managed to check inflation. By contrast, his drive to reduce alcoholism by inducing the French to substitute milk for wine proved misguided. His dynamic and effective, but increasingly controversial, government lasted seven months. Apart from a brief spell in government in 1956, he remained a respected critic of subsequent governments, and opposed both de *Gaulle's return in 1958, and *Gaullist policies thereafter. He retired from political life in 1973.

Menem, Carlos Saúl (b. 2 July 1935). President of Argentina 1989–99

Son of Syrian immigrants, he took a doctorate in law. He was *Peronist Governor of La Rioja province during the 1980s, and on 14 May 1989 he became the first leader of the opposition to win a democratic election in over 60 years. To placate the armed forces and stabilize the country's fragile political system, he proclaimed an amnesty in October 1989 and December 1990 for soldiers who had participated in illegal activities and human rights abuses during and after military rule. After stringent economic measures he led the country to economic recovery, so that the annual inflation rate declined from 4,923 per cent in 1989 to 7 per cent in 1993. In 1994 he successfully introduced a new constitution, which allowed his re-election, but also weakened the power of the President against parliament. He was re-elected in 1995. He stabilized the economy, but unemployment remained high at over 15 per cent, while his ministries continued to be plagued by corruption scandals.

Mensheviks ('the minority')

The term for the faction of the Russian Social Democratic Workers' Party which derived its name from the 1903 party congress, when it lost a vote to the *Bolsheviks ('the majority') over the editorial composition of the board of the party newspaper, *Iskra* (Spark). While Mensheviks generally enjoyed more support than the Bolsheviks, this vacillated over time, and they never managed to obtain a true mass base. The movement's greater moderation compared to Bolshevism resulted from the fact that in some ways it was actually more orthodox in *Marxist terms, in that it advocated the cementing of the bourgeois revolution before a proletarian revolution could take place. The Mensheviks never gained control of the *Duma, and after the *Russian Revolution of February 1917 they only shared control of the major *Soviets (e.g in Petrograd and Moscow) with the Socialist Revolutionaries. Their participation in the coalition provisional governments, various party splits, and in particular their support of the increasingly unpopular *Kerensky, led to a crucial decline in their popular support in the months before *Lenin's October Revolution of 1917. After Lenin had acquired power, Mensheviks were persecuted almost immediately, although the party was not formally outlawed until 1922.

Menzies, Sir Robert Gordon (b. 20 Dec. 1894, d. 15 May 1978). Prime Minister of Australia 1939–41, 1949–66

Early career Australia's longest serving Prime Minister was born in Jeparit (Victoria). He graduated in law from Melbourne University, and became a successful barrister (from 1918), receiving the prestigious appointment of a King's Council in 1929. He became a member of the state parliament of Victoria as a member of the *Nationalist Party and of the *United Australia Party (UAP, from 1931), and was attorney-general and solicitor-general for the state (1932–4). Menzies moved to national politics in 1934 and was elected to the federal parliament. Upon his election, he was immediately appointed Attorney-General, while becoming deputy leader of the UAP in 1935. Increasingly frustrated by *Lyons's style of leadership and his grip on power, Menzies resigned from Cabinet on 14 March 1939. He became Prime Minister four weeks later after Lyons's sudden death.

In office Unlike his predecessor, Menzies did not command universal support among the party's rank-and-file. Squabbling within the Cabinet and with his coalition partner, the Country Party (*National Party), led to his defeat at the 1941 elections, against the energetic *Curtin. After briefly losing the leadership of his party he regained it in 1943, and proceeded to form a new party in 1944 designed to be more avowedly a representative of the middle classes, the *Liberal Party. He led the Liberals to victory in 1949, and subsequently commanded the political centre-stage. His leadership role was enhanced by his fierce anti-*Communism which served him well during the height of the *Cold War. His pro-Britishness did not prevent him from furthering closer military ties with the USA, subscribing to its *domino theory and committing Australian troops to the *Korean War and the *Vietnam War. His credentials in domestic politics were heightened by the postwar economic boom which enabled him to enact many of the welfare proposals of the previous *Labor governments. At the same time, despite his commitment to ensuring a fair share of the boom for everyone, he was firm in his commitment to a capitalist free market. Meanwhile, his political longevity was underwritten by renewed splits in the *Labor Party from 1955. He vastly extended the involvement of the federal state in university education. After his retirement from politics, Menzies served as Chancellor of the University of Melbourne, 1967–72.

Mercosur (Mercado Común del Cono Sur, Common Market for the Southern Part of America)

An economic free trade area consisting of Argentina, Brazil, Paraguay, and Uruguay. Created in 1990, in the first years of its existence trade between its members rose from $3.7 billion in 1991 to $15.6 billion in 1995. On 1 January 1995, 85 per cent of the tariffs on trade between member states were lifted, whereupon the volume of trade within Mercosur jumped by 25 per cent in that year alone. Mercosur developed close ties with ANDEAN, and in 2006, it was joined by Venezuela.

(⊕) SEE WEB LINKS

- The official website of Mercosur.

Merkel, Angela (b. 17 July 1954). German Chancellor, 2005–

Early career Born in Templin (East Germany), the pastor's daughter studied physics and became a scientist at the Academy of Sciences. During the revolution in 1989, Merkel entered politics, becoming a member of the *CDU in 1990. A member of the last East German parliament, she became the spokesperson of the first and last freely elected leader of the GDR, Lothar de Maizère. In this capacity, she attracted the attention of Helmut *Kohl. Following German unification in 1990, she retained her seat in parliament, advancing into the party leadership as 'Kohl's girl' in 1991. Merkel served as a minister under Kohl from 1991 to the end of his government in 1998. Following the revelation of corruption practices under Kohl in 1999, the CDU was in a period of shock. She was one of the first to openly call for a break with Kohl. She had thus distanced herself sufficiently from him to be elected head of the party in 2000. A Protestant woman from the east, she struggled to establish her authority in a party dominated by alpha males. She persisted and, like her mentor, benefited from her opponents' constant underestimation of her cunning and her ability to learn from her mistakes.

In office In 2005, Merkel succeeded her rival, *Schröder, despite poor election results. She was well suited to leading a grand coalition with the *SPD, because the large majority of the combined parties made her relatively independent of her own party. Merkel presided over an economic resurgence, while at EU level she became noted for her constructive leadership. Under her leadership when Germany held the EU presidency in 2007, the EU agreed to reduce carbon emissions by 20 per cent by 2020, beyond the stipulations of the *Kyoto Protocol. She also pushed the other EU governments to agree to reform the European *Constitution and revitalize the process of *European integration.

Mers el-Kebir (3 July 1940)
Mers el-Kebir was a French naval base in the Gulf of Oran (Algeria), finally evacuated by

the French in 1968. In *World War II, shortly after the French surrender to the Germans in 1940, a British fleet arrived with orders to prevent the French fleet falling into German or Italian hands. When the French refused to scuttle their own ships or transfer them to British bases in the West Indies, the British bombarded the base, damaging three large battleships and killing over 1,000 French seamen. In retaliation the French bombed Gibraltar. The event caused deep resentment in France, leading many to support the *Vichy government, while hindering de *Gaulle's efforts at rallying French resistance at the side of the English.

Mesopotamia campaign (1914–18)
A campaign by British troops in Mesopotamia (now known as Iraq) against the *Ottoman Empire during *World War I. The British intended to protect the extensive British interests in Persia (now Iran), particularly control over Iranian oilfields. Furthermore, the British and Indian troops hoped to divert Ottoman forces from other battlegrounds closer to Europe, through advancing into the heart of the Ottoman Empire itself via the Rivers Tigris and Euphrates. However, the Allied forces were stopped at *Kut al-Amara, where most of the fighting of the campaign took place. Command of the operations passed from Delhi to London in 1916, but it was not until February 1917 that General Sir Frederick Maude recaptured Kut, thus clearing the way for the capture of Baghdad (11 March 1917). By the end of World War I, the British had conquered most of Mesopotamia up to the town of Mosul. As a result, after the war the area became a British *League of Nations *Mandate.

FAISAL I

Metaxas, Ioannis (b. 12 Apr. 1871, d. 29 Jan. 1941). Greek dictator 1936–41
Born on the island of Ithaca, he was commissioned into the Greek army in 1870. As army Chief of Staff since 1913, he supported the King's policy of neutrality in World War I, and was exiled when Greece did enter the war in 1915. Metaxas returned in 1920 and, after leading an unsuccessful coup, was exiled again 1923–4. Despite his monarchist leanings, he recognized the Greek Republic in 1924 and became active in politics, holding several ministerial posts from 1928. In April 1936, he became Prime Minister upon the restoration of the monarchy, and on 4 August 1936 he was given dictatorial powers. Metaxas was appointed head of the government for life in 1938. Corruption was reduced and social services

developed, while the armed services were made more efficient. In 1940 he led the Greek victory against the Italian invaders in World War II. He died just before the German occupation of Greece.

Methodist Church
After the death of John Wesley in 1791 it rapidly became a distinct Church separate from the established Church of England, gaining particular support in Wales. Many splinter groups formed during the nineteenth century, including the Methodist New Connexion, the Primitive Methodist Church, and the Bible Christians in Britain. In 1907, the Methodist New Connexion, the Bible Christians, and the United Methodist Free Churches formed the United Methodist Church, which itself reunited with the original, Wesleyan Methodist Church in 1932. Since then, the main Methodist body outside the Methodist Church in Great Britain has consisted of the Calvinistic Methodists in Wales. In the USA, two main Methodist churches had developed, one in the north and one in the south, which had split over the issue of slavery during the Civil War (1861–5). They were joined in 1868 by the Evangelical United Brethren to form the United Methodist Church. The American Methodist Conference has an episcopal structure with 'bishops' functioning as superintendants, whereas its British counterpart has a more presbyterian structure, i.e. with a leadership of elders all of equal rank. In 2007, there were around seventy million members of Methodist and related United Churches worldwide. These are linked through the World Methodist Council, founded in 1881.

(⊕) SEE WEB LINKS

• The official website of the United Methodist Church (USA).

METI (Japan), see MINISTRY OF INTERNA-TIONAL TRADE AND INDUSTRY

Métis
An umbrella term used in Canada to describe and define the people of mixed European and Indian descent. The Métis, especially in Manitoba, had established themselves by the early nineteenth century as buffalo hunters and provisioners to the North West Company. With the disappearance of the great buffalo herds, however, they were left with no means of providing for themselves. When a promised land grant of nearly 1.5 million acres was lost to predominantly European settlement after 1870, the Métis became increasingly agitated. Two unsuccessful rebellions led by Louis Riel

(b. 22 Oct. 1844, d. 16 Nov. 1885) left the Métis dispersed and with little political influence. Their population and their morale reached an all-time low just after 1900 until they began to organize and articulate their demands in the 1930s. A. H. de Tremaudan's *History of the Métis Nation in Western Canada* appeared in 1936, while the lobbying of newly created provincial interest groups led to the creation of the first provincial public inquiry into their concerns in Alberta (1934–6). Their concerns received greater attention from the 1960s onwards, as they lobbied for further cultural recognition and realization of *land claims in conjunction with the other native peoples, the *Canadian Indians and the *Inuit. In 1982, the Métis were recognized as a distinct aboriginal people in the *Canadian Constitution. Since then, the Métis have been formally represented by the Métis National Council which demanded the settlement of land claims, the recognition of Métis culture, and particular support for urban Métis.

NUNAVUT; LAND CLAIMS, NATIVE (CANADA)

(( )) SEE WEB LINKS

• The official website of the Métis National Council.

Mexico

Latin America's second largest country by population and its largest economy, Mexico has persistently sought to assert its autonomy vis-à-vis its northern neighbour, the USA, on whom it has relied economically. Despite its large oil exports, remittances from Mexicans living in the US have become Mexico's largest source of income.

The Díaz dictatorship (1876–1911) Gaining independence from Spain in 1821, Mexico did not achieve stability until the liberal dictatorship of *Díaz, whose policies led to a dramatic economic transformation. Foreign investment was attracted through generous concessions, while foreign trade increased ninefold, 1877–1907. Modest industrialization occurred and a considerable railway network was established, while the country's economic credentials were underlined by a federal budget surplus (1895–1911). In contrast, Díaz's social policies failed to take account of the strains created in Mexican society by economic change, which mainly benefited the wealthy and increased the gap between rich and poor. In addition, the new emphasis on mining and agricultural exports meant that production for the domestic market could barely keep up with demand created by a growing population.

The Mexican revolution and its aftermath (1911–17) The social tension thus created found an outlet when Francisco I *Madero, himself a member of the elite otherwise benefiting from Díaz's rule, challenged the dictator as he organized his re-election in 1910. An armed rebellion ensued which spread almost nationwide. Díaz resigned in 1911 and was succeeded by Madero, who was unable to contain the rebellion which he had unleashed. In the south-western state of Morelos he was opposed by *Zapata and his movement of landless peasants, who had become dispossessed in the process of economic rationalization encouraged by the Díaz regime. In the northern state of Chihuahua, *Villa led a well-equipped private army of unemployed workers and small cattle ranchers against the government from 1913. Finally, a resistance movement sprang up in the state of Coahuila, led by its Governor, *Carranza, who in 1913 claimed the Presidency for himself.

Madero was murdered by his military chief of staff, Victoriano Huerta (b. 1854, d. 1916), whose resignation in 1914 left a vacuum which was eventually filled by Carranza. Carranza defeated Villa in 1915, and oversaw the writing of a new constitution in 1917, a progressive document with socialist overtones (e.g. with regard to land redistribution and labour rights). The constitution has remained the underpinning of Mexican politics ever since.

Social transformation (1917–76) Following the death of Zapata in 1919, of Villa in 1923, and of *Obregón in 1928, it became possible for President *Calles to reinforce the political system through the creation of the National Revolutionary Party (*PRI) in 1929, which aimed at uniting the remaining forces that had been engaged in the revolution.

Calles continued to be the predominant influence within Mexican politics until the Presidency of Lázaro *Cárdenas (1934–40). Cárdenas tried to realize the radical implications of the Constitution by the distribution of 44 million acres (17.8 million hectares) to over 800,000 people, largely through communally owned farms (*ejidos*). He also reorganized the PNR into the Mexican Revolutionary Party (MRP), aiming to represent all sections of society in separate wings of the same party. Finally, in 1938 he expropriated the foreign-owned oil companies (giving compensation) and created Petróleos

Mexicanos (PEMEX), a source of national pride ever since. Mexico joined the *Allies in World War II and was the only Latin American country, together with Brazil, to send combat units to the front. Its most important contribution to the war, however, lay in its provision of a workforce of some 300,000 labourers to work in the USA. This institutionalized and recognized a tradition of Mexican emigration to the USA as an important hard-currency earner for the Mexican economy, and an equally important supply of cheap and flexible labour for the US market.

Under President *Alemán (1946–52), the MRP was finally reorganized into the PRI. The other hallmark of Alemán's presidency was the ambitious public works programme which aimed at creating a modern infrastructure. In the following decades, Mexico extended its model economic reputation through a relatively stringent anti-inflationary policy, which yielded significant economic growth at a yearly average of 6 per cent well into the 1970s. Paradoxically, social tensions increased, since this growth accentuated glaring social inequalities. Of all families, the wealthiest 10 per cent increased their share of total income from 35.7 per cent in 1958 to 39.2 per cent in 1970, while the share of national income of the poorest 10 per cent declined from 2.3 to 1.4 per cent. To reverse this trend, President Luis Echeverría (1970–6) aimed to raise the living standards of the poor, e.g. through state-maintained price controls of basic foodstuffs. This resulted in inflation, while the country's growing balance-of-trade deficit led to a flight of capital and a withdrawal of foreign investment that could only be met through excessive borrowing.

The oil economy (from the 1970s)

Echeverría's successor, *López Portillo (1976–82), hoped to revive the economy through the exploitation of the vast oilfields discovered in 1976. In fact, his administration squandered the income generated from Mexico's oil exploration, so that the structural imbalances of the economy were increased to breaking point. The decline of the price of oil after 1981 severely damaged projected hard-currency earnings, and increased foreign borrowing requirements yet further. By now one of the largest debtors in the world, Mexico was unable to meet its obligations in 1982, and was then, as on subsequent occasions (e.g. 1995), saved by a US-backed rescue loan. After negotiations with Mexico's creditors, President Miguel De la Madrid (1982–8) agreed to economic liberalization and the privatization of state-owned companies. In 1994, this culminated in the controversial establishment of *NAFTA, a free trade agreement with Canada and the USA which threatened the traditional state policy of supporting domestic small-scale industries and farmers.

To retain domestic stability despite the economic hardships of the 1980s (made worse by the disastrous earthquake of 1985 which killed over 20,000 people around Mexico City), Presidents De la Madrid and Carlos Salinas de Gortari (1988–94) began a careful process of political pluralization. They relaxed the ruling PRI's absolute grip on power, which resulted in the loss of several state elections in 1992 (despite accusations of electoral fraud). In 1993 Salinas carried out a constitutional reform to democratize the electoral system. These measures, however, were unable to reduce social and political tensions. On 23 March 1994 the PRI's presidential candidate, Luis Donaldo Colosio, was assassinated. (His campaign manager, Ernesto Zedillo Ponce de León, was subsequently elected.) In addition, in 1994 the *Chiapas Rebellion broke out, caused partly by fears about the effect of NAFTA on the Mexican Indian economy and culture. Domestic political instability contributed to a renewed economic crisis and a capital flight, which forced President *Clinton to realize further US credits and a credit guarantee worth $20 billion, in order to prevent a collapse of the Mexican economy and thus of NAFTA itself.

Contemporary politics (since 1997)

Although the economy recovered slowly, the 1997 elections resulted in a defeat for the government. For the first time in the PRI's history, its opponents formed the majority in the lower house, the Chamber of Deputies. In 1998 and 1999, a number of corruption and drugs scandals involving public officials and some of the country's leading banks further eroded public confidence. Leading members of the PRI were accused of links with drugs cartels, including the former chief of the police, Radolfo León Aragón, and the former Attorney-General, Mario Ruiz Massieu. The 2000 presidential elections were won by Vincente *Fox, the first President who did not come from the PRI or its predecessors since 1917. Fox was unable to realize his ambitious tax reforms designed to stimulate the economy and reduce poverty, since he did not command a majority in the Senate or the Chamber of Deputies. Fox's aims at combating corruption were also slow to materialize, since he lacked much necessary support from the traditional political elites. Fox was more successful at reorienting foreign policy towards a closer relationship with the USA. Fox pursued an active foreign policy on the world stage, seeking greater influence in Latin America and beyond. Under Fox, the economy stabilized from the economic crisis of the mid-1990s. His liberal economic policies were continued by Felipe *Calderón, who stepped up the struggle against domestic drug cartels.

MI5 and MI6

Neither title is now in official use, but both are popularly used to describe the British military intelligence services. The Security Service Bureau was established in 1909 to tackle counter-intelligence and threats to security in British territory, and was renamed MI5 in 1916. MI6 (the Secret Intelligence), was established in 1921, as the successor to the wartime MI11c, dealing with security outside Britain. During World War II, MI6 coordinated Britain's cooperation with resistance movements in Europe. However, its operations subsequently suffered from revelations that some of its agents were in fact working as double agents for the Soviet Union. The most notable disclosures related to Kim Philby, Guy Burgess, Donald Maclean, and Anthony Blunt, who had been recruited in the 1930s whilst they were students at Cambridge. In the mid-1980s, it was alleged that MI5 had sought to destabilize the Labour governments of 1974–9, but it does not appear that any disciplinary action was taken. Despite increased openness in the early 1990s, during which time the identity of some senior officers was revealed, attempts to make MI5 and MI6 publicly accountable have been largely unsuccessful.

(( )) SEE WEB LINKS

- The official website of the British security services.
- The official website of the British secret intelligence services.

Micronesia

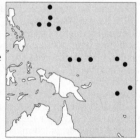

The regional name for the widely spread tiny islands of the north Pacific, numbering some 2,100. Except for US-controlled *Guam, they came under German control in 1885, but during World War I they passed to Japanese administration, which was confirmed as a *League of Nations *Mandate after the war. In World War II, Japanese control over the area was extended through the invasion of Guam, which enabled them to block the US advance to liberate the Philippines until 1944. After the war, Micronesia came under the control of the USA, which has administered it as a *UN *trust territory, with the exception of Guam.

From 1946 (until 1963), Micronesia was the scene of extended nuclear testing. The USA exploded 66 atmospheric test weapons on **Bikini** and **Enewetak Islands**. The test of 1 March 1954 not only made Bikini permanently uninhabitable but has resulted in extensive cancer cases and deformities among the population of the neighbouring island of **Rongelap**. From the 1970s, four separate island states emerged. The **Northern Mariana Islands**, the **Federated States of Micronesia**, and the **Republic of the Marshall Islands** negotiated separate autonomy statutes in 1979. While the USA remained responsible for their defence, they received full independence on 3 November 1986, which was recognized by the UN on 22 December 1990. The republics continued to rely heavily on US transfers, paid predominantly for the use of military bases. In 2003, Micronesia and Marshall Islands signed an agreement with the USA whereby the two states would receive $3.5 billion for twenty years. The island state of **Palau (Belau)** gained independence on 30 September 1994, but retained an association with the USA whereby the latter remained responsible for defence and foreign policy. In 1998 a nuclear claims tribunal was created to determine compensation from the US for victims of the tests and their descendents.

Midway Island, Battle of (4 June 1942)
The USA had a naval/air base on this tiny island 1,500 miles west of Hawaii, which the Japanese, under *Yamamoto, planned to seize by an amphibious operation in order to resume the offensive against the US begun in *Pearl Harbor. US intelligence learnt of the plan and a US naval force attacked, despite having an inferior fleet. The battle was fought by carriers 250 miles apart and by US land planes from the base. Four Japanese carriers, each with a complement of planes and some 1,500 men on board, were sunk, together with three transports carrying 6,000 men. One US carrier was lost. The battle was decisive in *World War II, shifting the naval balance in the Pacific towards the USA.
    CORAL SEA, BATTLE OF THE

Miki Takeo (b. 17 Mar. 1907, d. 14 Nov. 1988). Prime Minister of Japan 1974–6
Miki enjoyed a lifelong reputation as a politician with high moral standards, and as such has often appeared an unlikely member of Japan's ruling party. Miki's prewar political

pedigree was unorthodox. He had studied in the USA, returning to Japan to stand for election to the lower house of the Diet in 1937. At this time Miki developed a reputation as an independent politician, organizing opinion against war with the USA. Despite his failure to obtain the support of the authorities for his candidature in the 1942 Diet elections, he was re-elected. In 1946 Miki was involved with the establishment of the Cooperative Democratic Party which in a variety of guises represented a moderately conservative political outlook. He also participated in the formation of the *Liberal Democratic Party (LDP) in 1955 and held high Cabinet and party office from that time onwards. Miki was always identified with the wing of the LDP closest to the opposition parties and as a result, there was often speculation that he might lead his followers out of the party during periods when it appeared ideologically extreme or corrupt. After resigning from *Tanaka Kakuei's Cabinet in 1974 in protest against the premier's style of money politics, Miki chose to accept his party's offer to become Tanaka's successor. When Miki allowed the investigation of Tanaka to go too far, however, several factions united against him and he was forced to resign, and take responsibility for the LDP's poor performance in the 1976 House of Representatives elections.

Mikoyan, Anastas Ivanovich (b. 25 Nov. 1895, d. 21 Oct. 1978). President of the Presidium of the Supreme Soviet 1964–5

The supreme survivor of Soviet politics was born in Sanain (*Armenia), where he was educated at a seminary. After the *Russian Revolution of February 1917, he joined the *Bolsheviks, and rose quickly within the ranks of the regional Caucasian party hierarchy. He became a full member of the Central Committee of the Communist Party in 1923, was a candidate (i.e. non-voting) member of the *Politburo from 1926 and full member from 1935 until his retirement in 1966. In this position he held several governmental posts, serving as Deputy Chairman of the Council of People's Commissars (Council of Ministers from 1946) until 1964, when he became the formal head of the Soviet Union. His career was closely linked to his fellow Caucasian, *Stalin, even more so as he survived (and participated in) the *Great Purge and other acts of terror. It was a testimony to his political survival skills that he retained his position despite *Khrushchev's anti-Stalinist campaigns.

Milizia Volontaria per la Sicurezza Nazionale, see MVSN

Milner, Alfred, 1st Viscount Milner of St James's and of Cape Town (b. 23 Mar. 1854, d. 13 May 1925). British statesman

Born at Giessen (Germany) and educated at Tübingen, London (King's College), and Oxford. He was first a lawyer, then a journalist, and was private secretary to G. J. Goschen, Unionist Chancellor of the Exchequer. His growing interest in finance, and his belief in British *imperialism, saw him appointed to the Egyptian Finance Ministry (1889–92). He was then chairman of the Board of Inland Revenue, and at the request of Joseph *Chamberlain, he became high commissioner for South Africa in 1897. There, he advocated a hardline policy in order to secure British interests against assertive *Afrikaners, if necessary through war. However, he also made plans to reform and reorganize the country, in conjunction with his 'Kindergarten' of young imperialists, such as Geoffrey Dawson and Lionel Curtis. He left South Africa in 1905, and was active in the House of Lords. In World War I he helped in the Ministry of War Supply, and became a member of the War Cabinet (1916–18), later Secretary of State for War (1918–19) and for the Colonies (1919–21). His strong belief in Britain's imperial mission was a constant feature of his career, yet he was flexible enough to negotiate the basis of the 1922 settlement with Egyptian nationalists. This was not immediately accepted by *Lloyd George, and Milner resigned in 1921.

Milošević, Slobodan (b. 29 Aug. 1941, d. 11 Mar 2006). President of Serbia 1989–92; President of Yugoslavia 1992–2000

Born at Pozarevac (Serbia) of Montenegrin parents, he studied law at Belgrade University and in 1959 joined the League of Communists of Yugoslavia. He became chairman of the university committee on ideology before graduating in 1964. He was an economic and legal adviser to the Belgrade Communist Party, while working in industry, where in 1978 he was made President of Beobanka, the United Bank of Belgrade. Milošević became a full-time party worker as leader of the Belgrade party in 1984 and General Secretary of the Serbian Communist Party in 1987. He ended the autonomy of *Kosovo and integrated it into Serbia.

In 1989 Milošević became President of Serbia. Re-elected in 1992 as the President of 'rump' Yugoslavia (composed of *Serbia and *Montenegro) on a nationalist platform, he effectively accepted the breakup of the old Yugoslav state and the independence of *Slovenia and *Croatia. At the same time, he insisted on Serbian regional leadership, and for years supported the Bosnian Serbs in the *Bosnian Civil War, until this policy became too costly for the Serbian economy in the face of international sanctions.

In 1997 Milošević lost his absolute majority in the Serbian parliament, as the ultra-nationalist Radical Party surged ahead and became the second largest parliamentary party. This extremist opposition encouraged Milošević to pursue his nationalist agenda, which included the sanctioning of ethnic cleansing against Albanians in Kosovo. Milošević refused to compromise and recognize the Albanian majority's right to self-determination there, calculating wrongly that the US and the EU would continue to procrastinate on the matter.

In March 1999 *NATO started military action in Kosovo, which forced the Serbian police and armed forces to leave Kosovo. Milošević clung on to power, but after flagrantly manipulating the vote in the 2000 presidential elections, he was forced from power by a series of mass demonstrations. He was put under house arrest, and on 28 August 2001 he was extradited by the Serbian authorities to the *UN International Criminal Tribunal for the Former Yugoslavia in The Hague. Perhaps feeling that his conviction was inevitable, Milošević, who defended himself without recognizing the Court's authority, used his trial, which commenced in 2002, to embarrass his accusers and justify himself. He died from a heart attack while in custody.

Ministry of International Trade and Industry (MITI) (Japan)

A Japanese ministry created in 1949 through a merger of the Trade Agency and the Ministry of Commerce and Industry, which, along with the Ministry of Finance, is considered to have been an important catalyst for Japan's postwar economic development. During the early postwar period, it marshalled scarce foreign exchange, resources, and technology in its attempts to foster the industrial success stories of the period in shipbuilding, steel, and chemicals. At the same time, MITI was responsible for the establishment of home-grown oil, biotechnology, and aerospace industries, although these have proved to be less internationally competitive so far. Although its achievements may be qualified, the ministry's decision to create in Japan a value-added, highly industrialized economy appears to have been the correct one. Today, MITI's agencies and bureaus include organizations which oversee national resources, small and medium industry, industrial policy, international trade, the environment, and consumer protection.

MITI's influence in the business and political worlds is legendary. On retirement at around 50, officials from the ministry often find jobs as executives in the flagships of Japanese industry in a practice known as *amakudari* or 'descending from heaven'. Other old boys from MITI have had political careers; among them *Kishi Nobusuke and Shiina Estusaburo who enjoyed considerable influence within the *Liberal Democratic Party because their civil service experience gave them great fund-raising capacity. In 2001, it was reorganized as the **Ministry of Economy, Trade and Industry (METI)**.

Minseitô (Constitutional Democratic Association) (Japan)

Also known as Rikken Minseitô, it was founded in 1927 and became Japan's second major party of the prewar period, formed by conservative groups opposed to the *Seiyûkai. The Minseitô's early history was marked by electoral success in the 1928 Lower House elections, the first to operate under universal male suffrage. The following year the party formed a government under the premiership of *Hamaguchi Osachi although the polices of this administration in a period of domestic and international uncertainty proved to be highly unpopular. Like its rival, the Minseitô relied heavily on the financial support of business, especially the Mitsubishi *zaibatsu whose interests it continued to represent. Also like the Seiyûkai, the party was rarely free from factionalism, especially between Nagai Ryûtarô, a prominent party member and advocate of the new order in Asia, and Machida Chûji, the Minseitô party president in the late 1930s. Machida sought to protect the interests of business from the calls for economic rationalization as Japan's war plans developed. Although the party was eventually to participate in the *Imperial Rule Assistance Association it showed more reluctance than most in this.

Miranda v. Arizona (USA)

A 1966 US *Supreme Court decision under Chief Justice *Warren. In 1963 Ernesto Miranda was convicted in Arizona for rape on the basis of a confession given in police custody. The court ruled that Miranda had not been properly warned that any statement which he made could be used against him, that he had the right to remain silent, and that he had the right to consult a lawyer. In consequence, his confession was ruled inadmissible and his conviction overturned. In a second trial, evidence by Mrs Miranda against her husband resulted in another guilty verdict. Parolled in 1972, he died in a bar fight four years later. US police forces have incorporated a 'Miranda' warning in arrests since the decision, in the face of protests from legislators, anti-crime campaigners, and Presidents such as *Nixon and *Reagan.

Mitterrand, François (b. 26 Oct. 1916, d. 8 Jan. 1996). President of France 1981–95

Early career Born in the south-western town of Charnac (Charente) and raised by devout Roman Catholic parents, he studied law at Paris University. In the Battle of France, he became a prisoner of war in 1940. Mitterrand escaped from the Germans on his third attempt and joined the *Résistance movement, of which he became a prominent member, receiving the Croix de Guerre for his bravery in 1946. However, for cover he worked as a civil servant for the *Vichy government and even accepted its distinctions. The extent of his cooperation in this capacity led to intense public discussion during the last years of his presidency.

After the war, Mitterrand emerged as the leading socialist spokesman and served in eleven governments during the Fourth Republic, e.g. as Minister of the Interior under *Mendès-France in 1954. Even though he supported de *Gaulle's policies on Algeria, he opposed his introduction of the Fifth Republic and the institution of a strong presidency. This did not prevent him, however, from standing against de Gaulle in the 1965 presidential elections as the candidate of the left, when he managed to force him into the second round. In 1971, he became the undisputed leader of the left when he engineered the launch of the Parti Socialiste (*Socialist Party), and in 1972 he strengthened the left even further when he masterminded the creation of the Union de la Gauche (Union of the Left). He narrowly lost to *Giscard d'Estaing in the 1974 presidential elections, and suffered another set-back when the *Communist Party left the Union in 1976.

Presidency In 1981, he managed to defy his reputation as the 'eternal loser' when he won the presidential elections at his third attempt. The innovative socialist policies of his first Prime Minister, *Mauroy, became deeply unpopular as they plunged the country into a severe economic crisis. His successor, the technocrat Laurent Fabius, attempted to correct this in time for the 1986 parliamentary elections through stringent neo-liberal economic policies. This failed to revive the fortunes of the Socialist Party sufficiently, so that Mitterrand had no alternative but to appoint his political arch-

rival, the *Gaullist leader *Chirac, as Prime Minister. During the subsequent *cohabitation between the two men Mitterrand insisted on conducting Foreign and Defence policy, while Chirac had a relatively free hand in pursuing domestic policies.

In the presidential elections of 1988, the voters preferred the steady hand of Mitterrand to the apparently overambitious Chirac. He appointed Michel Rocard as his new Prime Minister, who lowered taxation and reduced the budget deficit. In foreign policy, Mitterrand continued to be the central driving force towards further *European integration, together with his friend, the German Chancellor Helmut *Kohl. High popularity ratings during the *Gulf War proved to be his swansong, however. He was greatly weakened by his ill-judged appointment of Edith *Cresson as Prime Minister (1991–2), and the fateful end of her successor, Pierre Bérégovoy (1992–3), who committed suicide on 1 May 1993 amidst allegations of corruption. Moreover, a general desire for change triggered by the unprecedented longevity of his tenure, and his increasing inability to govern owing to prostate cancer, made him unpopular during his last years in office.

Mobutu Sese Seko, Joseph-Désiré (b. 14 Oct. 1930, d. 7 Sept. 1997). President of Zaïre 1965–97

Born in Lisala, he served in the Belgian colonial armed forces (1948–56), and became a journalist. Upon independence, *Lumumba appointed the outspoken advocate for independence army chief of staff on 8 July 1960. Mobutu remained a decisive power behind the scenes until he took over government himself in 1965, replacing *Kasavubu. He formed a unitary party, the Mouvement Populaire de la Révolution (Popular Revolutionary Movement) in 1966, and established an authoritarian government. He used the economy and the administration largely to buttress his own power, and to give spoils to his supporters. Mobutu was elected unopposed in 1970, 1977, and 1984. His mismanagement of the economy and his corruption exacerbated the poverty of the population, which was thus unable to benefit from the country's wealth in mineral resources. Opposition to Mobutu grew steadily, and in 1996 an armed rebellion led by *Kabila gained momentum. He was forced into exile months before his death.

Mohammed VI (b. 21 August 1963), King of Morocco, 1999–

Born in Rabat, he went to the Royal College before obtaining a degree in political

science and law at the University of Rabat. He
went to Europe and served for a few months at
the *European Commission in Brussels. In
1984 he was officially proclaimed the heir to
his father, *Hassan II, and in 1985 he was put
in charge of coordinating the Moroccan armed
forces. In 1994, he was awarded the rank of
general in the army. Mohammed VI has been
more liberal than his father. In 2004, he
instituted a *truth and reconciliation
commission to unearth the human rights
violations committed during his father's
reign. At the same time, Mohammed
remained insistent on keeping Morocco's
stake in Western Sahara.

Moi, Daniel Toroitich arap (b. 2 Sept.
1924). President of Kenya 1978–2002

Born in Kurieng'wo Village, Baringo district,
he became a teacher in 1945, but resigned in
order to represent his native district in the
colony's legislative council from 1957, as one
of its first eight African elected members. He
became chair of the Kenyan African
Democratic Union (KADU) in 1960, and was
made Minister for Local Government in the
coalition government of 1963. He joined
*KANU after the dissolution of his party
(1964), and became Minister for Home Affairs
until 1978. Vice-President from 1967, he
succeeded *Kenyatta as President on 22
August 1978. He announced a purge of the
allegedly corrupt Kenyan bureaucracy and
imposed a stern regime. Discontented with
the lack of political rights, government
corruption, and economic hardship, the
country became increasingly restive during
the 1980s, erupting into violent ethnic
confrontations in 1992. Although technically
a democracy, the introduction of greater
political freedoms were 'postponed'
throughout the 1990s as popular discontent
was aggravated by economic decline.
Constitutionally barred from running again
for the presidency, he retired in 2002.

Moldova

One of Europe's
poorest
countries, its
geographic
position and
ethnic
heterogeneity
have led to
political and
economic
instability.

**Contemporary history (up to
1991)** Moldova is inhabited by a majority

(65 per cent) of Moldovans (of Romanian
ethnicity), with a substantial minority of
Ukrainians and Russians (13 per cent each of
the total population) in the east, and of
Gagauzy (3.5 per cent of the total population)
in the south. It became an Autonomous
Socialist Soviet Republic within the USSR in
1924, and reached its present territory in
1940, when *Stalin added to it Romanian
areas of northern *Bukovina and Bessarabia,
in line with the *Hitler–Stalin Pact. It was
occupied by Romanian troops (1941–4), but
was officially recognized in its entirety as part
of the USSR in 1947. Moldova declared its
independence from the moribund Soviet
Union days after the *August coup, on 27
August 1991.

After independence (1991) When the
Moldovan People's Front, which advocated
reunion with Romania, won the 1992
parliamentary elections with 40 per cent of
the vote, tensions emerged within the
country's national minorities. The Gagauzian
minority declared its opposition to Romanian
rule and its desire for greater autonomy,
which was granted on 23 December 1994,
·mainly because its small size posed no threat
to Moldova's territorial integrity.

Matters were more complicated with regard
to its Ukrainian and Russian minorities, which
lived mostly on the 10-mile wide and 100-mile
long stretch on the left bank of the River
Dnestr. They declared this the sovereign
Republic of Dnestr (also known as
Transdnestr) on 2 September 1990. This was
not recognized by Moldova, and led to
ongoing confrontations with neighbouring
Ukraine, as well as Russia, which continued to
have some 5,000 troops stationed in the
Dnestr area. Throughout the 1990s, politics
were extremely unstable, with frequent
changes of government. This led to an
inability to introduce economic reforms, with
Russia refusing to import Moldovan goods,
including wine.

Contemporary politics (since 2000) Political
and economic crisis came to a head in 2000,
when parliament was unable to find the
necessary majority to elect a President. In
response, the outgoing President dissolved
parliament. The ensuing elections produced a
victory for the pro-Russian communists under
Vladimir Voronin, who obtained a
constitutional majority in parliament.
Voronin moved to promote the rights of the
Russian minority and establish special
political ties with Russia. However, Russia was
uninterested in political compromise, and
relations worsened in 2006, when the Russian
energy supplier, Gazprom, doubled prices for

natural gas. Voronin subsequently pursued closer European integration, even though the EU made clear in 2006 that it did not intend to include new members beyond existing candidate member states in the near future. Owing to his pro-Western policies, Voronin was re-elected in 2005, with the help of the anti-Communist opposition.

Mollet, Guy (b. 31 Dec. 1905, d. 3 Oct. 1975). Prime Minister of France 1956–7

Son of a textile worker, he joined the *Socialist Party in 1923 and became a teacher in Arras. He became a *Résistance* leader in World War II, which he survived despite repeated interrogations by the German *Gestapo. In 1944 he became the government representative in liberated northern France and Mayor of Arras. Elected to the Chamber of Deputies in 1945, he served as leader of his party (1946–69). He joined a number of governments and headed the longest-lived coalition government in the history of the Fourth Republic, which lasted sixteen months. During this time, despite his desire to bring peace to Algeria, the unrest there escalated, while he also allowed himself to become involved in the *Suez Crisis.

Molotov, Vyacheslav Mikhailovich (b. 9 Mar. 1890, d. 8 Nov. 1986). Soviet Commissar (Minister) of Foreign Affairs 1936–9, 1953–6

Born V. M. Skryabin at Kukarkan (near Kazan), he joined the *Bolsheviks in 1906, and was thereafter exiled several times for his revolutionary activities. In 1912, he adopted the apt name Molotov ('The Hammer'). At the time of the first *Russian Revolution of 1917, he was one of the most prominent Bolsheviks present in Petrograd (formerly St Petersburg). After the October Revolution he carried out several duties in the provinces as a trusted aide to *Lenin. After *Stalin's accession to power, however, he became his right-hand man, collaborating closely with him to organize the *Great Purge and other terror campaigns, which even affected his own Jewish wife. Utterly loyal to Stalin, Molotov was Secretary to the Central Committee of the party (1921–30), and Chairman of the Council of People's Commissars (i.e. Prime Minister), 1930–41. As Commissar (Minister from 1946) of Foreign Affairs, he signed the *Hitler–Stalin Pact and, towards the end of World War II, served as close adviser to Stalin at the *Yalta and *Potsdam Conferences. Having fallen out of favour in *Stalin's last years, he was unable to wrest the party leadership from *Khrushchev, whose anti-*Stalinism campaign compromised him

greatly. After he had taken part in an unsuccessful coup against Khrushchev in 1957, Khrushchev gleefully made him ambassador to Mongolia (1957–60). He served as the Soviet representative at the *International Atomic Energy Agency until 1962.

Moltke, Helmuth James Count von (b. 11 Mar. 1907, d. 23 Jan. 1945). German resistance leader

The great-nephew of the famous Prussian General Helmuth Count von Moltke (b. 26 Oct. 1800, d. 24 Apr. 1891), he served as a legal expert in international law at the Supreme Command of the Armed Forces. He founded the **Kreisauer Kreis** (Kreisau Circle), a resistance group which met at his Kreisau estate and which looked forward to a moral and political regeneration after Hitler on the basis of Christian-conservative principles. It was discovered in January 1944, when Moltke was imprisoned and sentenced to death in the wake of the *July Plot.

Monaco

One of the world's smallest states of 1.95 km^2 (less than a square mile), the principality has been ruled by the Grimaldi family since 1454. It entered a customs union with France in 1865, which was complemented by a currency union in 1922. It obtained its first constitution under Prince Albert I (r. 1889–1922) in 1911. In 1918 an agreement was concluded with France whereby Monaco would become a French protectorate in the event of the Grimaldi family producing no successors. During World War II, it was occupied by Italy in 1941, and by Germany in 1943. From 1949 it was ruled by Prince Rainier III (b. 1923), who succeeded his grandfather, Louis II. His marriage to the actress Grace Kelly (renamed Princess Gracia Patricia) in 1956 attracted the attention of the world's tabloid newspapers and journals, and epitomized Monaco's position as a focal point for the international jet set. Following his death in 2005, Monaco was ruled by his son, Prince Albert II (b. 1958). Despite a democratization in the constitutional amendment of 1962, the Prince continued to wield considerable legislative powers. The Minister of State is responsible to the Prince, not to the National Council elected by general

suffrage. At the same time, the French state has exerted a crucial influence over the government and administration of the principality. Thus, the Prince selects the Minister of State from a list of three candidates presented by France.

Monash, Sir John (b. 27 June 1865, d. 8 Oct. 1931). Australian general

Born in Melbourne as the first-born son of Jewish immigrants, he graduated in engineering and law after a patchy university career, and took up a commission in the army in 1887. During World War I he served with some distinction at *Gallipoli. Promoted to major-general, he commanded the 3rd Division of the Australian Imperial Forces on the Western Front 1916–18. As lieutenant-general and corps commander from 1 June 1918 Monash was prominent in halting the German final offensive in July. With his troops he also took a leading part in the last *Allied counter-offensive in August 1918. After the war Monash organized the harmonious repatriation of 160,000 Australian soldiers. His reputation in the 1920s as perhaps the greatest living Australian reflected upon Australia's Jewish community as a whole, as it helped make *anti-Semitism publicly unacceptable. He was Vice-Chancellor of Melbourne University (1923–31), and Victoria's second university is named after him.

monetarism

An economic theory which is opposed to *Keynesian demand management. It holds that increases in the money supply always lead to inflation but never affect the level of employment. Increases in the money supply, for instance through higher welfare payments, might lead to excess demand, but this can only be met by higher prices, for which workers will seek compensation through higher wages. Because the price of labour per unit has increased, employers will not seek to increase output, so that the level of employment remains unaltered even though inflation (and excess demand) has occurred. Monetarism denies, therefore, that the state can interfere in the real workings of the economy in the long run.

Crucially, monetarism assumes that the market is perfect. Any disequilibrium or economic crisis that occurs is the result of constraints imposed on the market from outside. Social benefits distort the market, for instance, if they raise the price of labour beyond its natural market rate. In a monetarist economy, all the government can do is to hold the money supply constant using the interest rate, and to eliminate market constraints. Then, assuming that all individuals have perfect information, the market will be in perfect equilibrium with no inflation and only a small, 'natural' rate of unemployment. By contrast, Keynesians argue that it is precisely because individuals do not always have perfect information about the economic consequences of their actions that distortions in the market occur.

Monetarism was developed by Milton Friedman and his colleagues at the University of Chicago starting in the 1950s. It came to prominence during the 1970s, when Keynesian methods of regulating the economy seemed unable to overcome the unprecedented price and unemployment levels caused by the *oil price shocks of 1973 and 1979. Since then, most governments have accepted the control of inflation as a central economic objective, though they have been reluctant to carry out the more radical implications of monetarism such as the dismantling of the *welfare state.

KEYNESIANISM; THATCHERISM

Mongolia

A sparsely populated, landlocked country in central Asia which has struggled to free itself from the influence of its overbearing neighbours, Russia and China.

Since the collapse of Ghengis Khan's Mongol Empire in the thirteenth century, Mongolia was effectively a Chinese fiefdom. During the Chinese Revolution of 1911 it declared its independence, and became a monarchy. Nevertheless, the country was occupied by the Chinese, and a revolutionary movement grew with pivotal help from the Russian *Communist Party. During the *Russian Civil War, this movement under Suhe Bator (b. 1893, d. 1923), with *Red Army contingents, defeated occupying forces from China, as well as *White Army units.

Soviet rule (1921–92) Practically independent from 11 July 1921, on 26 November 1924 an independent Mongolia was proclaimed, the first Communist People's Republic outside the Soviet Union. Subsequently it became dependent on the USSR, particularly in the face of Japanese expansion in *Manchukuo. In response, its leader, Choibalsan, strengthened the

Communist Party's hold over society, destroying the power of the Lamaist Church, and slaughtering thousands of monks (1937–9). During World War II Mongolia sided with the USSR, on whose side it remained in the era of Chinese–Soviet confrontation that developed in the 1960s. A member of *Comecon, its underdeveloped economy was so dependent upon the USSR, that by 1985 over 95 per cent of its imports came from its Soviet neighbour, and 80 per cent of exports came from there.

Mongolia suffered greatly from the collapse of the Soviet Union and Comecon, though the country's leadership reluctantly accepted the need for a transition to a market economy. In marked contrast to other Communist countries in this period of transition, however, the Communist Party remained unreformed, and in government.

Democratization (1990s) A new Constitution abolishing Mongolia's status as a People's Republic was proclaimed in 1992, with a guarantee of civil rights and a commitment towards a market economy. The following elections of 28 June 1992 were won by the Mongolian Revolutionary People's Party (MRRP), which with 57 per cent of the vote gained 70 out of 76 seats in the new unicameral legislature.

In the elections of 30 June 1996, the opposition Democratic Union Coalition won a surprising landslide victory with its campaign for a quicker pace for reforms, supported mainly by younger generations. With 48 seats in the new legislature, it ended the 75 years of Communist rule. Under the leadership of the National Democratic Party (NDP), the Coalition tried to introduce far-reaching and controversial reforms, such as the privatization of the national bank in 1998. Popular protest at the social consequences of the government's economic programme led to the resignation of a succession of Prime Ministers, and in the 2000 elections the MRRP won a resounding victory, with 72 seats.

Contemporary politics (since 2000) The new government moderated (but continued) the programme of economic reform, while contending with an array of problems including social inequality, poverty among the agricultural population, and the agricultural effects of successive harsh winters. A coalition between the MRRP and the NDP from 2004 until 2006 ended in acrimony, and following the defection of a number of MPs from the NDP, the MRRP formed a new government. Since the end of Communism, the economy has shown substantial growth helped by rich mineral resources, but the increase in overall income has concentrated on a small section of the population, wth the majority continuing to live in poverty.

Monnet, Jean (b. 9 Nov. 1888, d. 16 Mar. 1979). French economist
A largely self-educated economist from Cognac, he was a civil servant at the Ministry of Commerce (1915–19), a consultant economist to the *Versailles conference (1918–19), and Deputy General Secretary to the *League of Nations (1919–23). In World War II he worked in the British Supply Council in Washington. In 1943, he joined de *Gaulle in Algiers to co-found the French Committee of National Liberation in 1943. He was in charge of developing a plan for economic recovery in a liberated France. The Monnet Plan, in operation from 1947 to 1953, nationalized industries such as Renault and Air France, but otherwise directed the economy very much in cooperation with private industry. A close colleague of *Schuman, he worked out the economic details of the Schuman Plan, which gave birth to the *ECSC, whose first president he became (1952–5). For the rest of his life, he was a strong proponent of further *European integration.

Montagu-Chelmsford proposals, see DYARCHY

Montenegro
A small Balkan state whose mostly Christian Orthodox population have felt a strong affinity for Serbia until independence in 2006.

Contemporary history (until 1999) Part of the *Ottoman Empire since 1582, it became independent in 1878, and was declared a Kingdom in 1910. It joined its neighbour, *Serbia, in the *Balkan Wars (1912–13) and World War I. From 1918 it was part of the Kingdom of Serbs, Croats, and Slovenes, which in 1929 became Yugoslavia. During World War II it was an Italian protectorate (1941–4). Thereafter, it became a federal republic of Yugoslavia. Partly in reaction to Serbia's brutality against uprisings in *Kosovo, in 1989 and 1990 there were increasing demands to follow *Croatia, *Slovenia, and *Bosnia-Hercegovina into independence. In contrast to Croatia and Bosnia-Hercegovina, it was of comparatively small interest to the Serbs, who formed only 2 per cent of the population, with Macedonians constituting 67 per cent, and Albanians 20 per cent.

The free elections of December 1990 were won by the Communists (renamed Democratic

Party of Socialists in 1991), who favoured remaining in union with Serbia. This was confirmed in a referendum in March, whereupon Montenegro joined Serbia in the Federal Republic of Yugoslavia on 29 April 1992. As the poorest state of former Yugoslavia, it had much to gain from its alliance with the comparatively wealthy Serbia.

Contemporary politics (since 1999) The lure of a union with Serbia weakened as Yugoslavia's economy began to suffer from international economic sanctions imposed first during the *Bosnian Civil War and then before the *Kosovan War in 1999. Moreover, when Serbia was attacked and its economy destroyed during the Kosovan War, the Montenegrin government under Milo Djukanović sought to distance the province from Serbia. In 2000 it introduced a currency reform, whereby the *euro became sole legal tender. Complete independence continued to be controversial, however, as popular opinion for and against independence was evenly balanced. Following elections in late 2000, Djukanović was able to form a new government, but his separatist coalition failed to obtain an absolute majority of seats in parliament. In 2002, a new agreement was negotiated with Serbia which would provide de facto independence, and maintain a nominal link with Serbia. In a referendum in 2006, over 55 per cent of voters declared their desire for independence, which was delared on 4 June 2006.

Montgomery, Bernard Law, 1st Viscount Montgomery of Alamein

(b. 17 Nov. 1887, d. 23 Mar. 1976). British field marshal

Early career Born in London, but brought up in Tasmania until 1901, he attended St Paul's School (London), and the Royal Military College, Sandhurst. He joined the Royal Warwickshire Regiment in 1908, and served in India, before seeing action in Belgium and France during *World War I. He became a staff officer in the 1920s, and trained soldiers until he was posted to India and Palestine in the 1930s. At the beginning of *World War II, Montgomery commanded the II, V, and XII Corps in England at different times.

In command Montgomery rose to prominence when in August 1942, at Alan *Brooke's behest, he succeeded General Auchinleck as Commander of the 8th Army in the North African campaigns. Though his predecessor had already halted the German advance, his success at the second Battle of *Alamein provided a much-needed boost for British morale and transformed him into a popular hero. Following this, Montgomery was involved in *Allied planning for the attack on Sicily in June 1943, although subsequently the Italian campaign was subject to the control of the US military leadership, with whom he generally had an uneasy relationship. In 1944, he commanded the British armies in Normandy with mixed success, and his operation 'Goodwood', involving the use of British troops near Caen, was widely criticized.

Against *Eisenhower's insistence on a gradual advance via a broad front in France, he lobbied unsuccessfully for a concentrated, narrow push towards Berlin. Neglecting most advice he did manage to implement a scheme for an airborne assault on Arnhem (September 1944) to capture a bridgehead over the Rhine ahead of the Allied advance, which proved to be disastrous and resulted in heavy loss of life. He had more success commanding Allied troops against the German *Ardennes offensive of December 1944. He formally received the surrender of the German forces in northern Germany on 4 May 1945. After the war, he held a number of senior posts, and was Chief of the Imperial General Staff (1946–8). As Deputy Supreme Commander of *NATO (1951–8), he had an important role in the new organization's strategic planning. Despite his mixed military record, he was able to arouse intense personal loyalty from his troops, while his public image of invincibility at a time of war was, perhaps, at least as important as his achievements in themselves.

Montreux Convention (20 July 1936)

Following Turkish fears that Mussolini was seeking to use Italy's bases in the *Dodecanese to extend its colonies in Asia Minor, an international conference was held in Montreux. Turkey obtained revision of the *Lausanne Treaty, permitting fortification along the *Dardanelles and Bosporus and imposing new restrictions on the aggregate tonnage of warships passing through these two straits.

Montserrat

A Caribbean island which came under British sovereignty in 1632. Part of the colony of the Leeward Islands in 1871, it joined the short-lived Federation of the *West Indies (1958–62), thereafter becoming a United Kingdom Overseas

Dependency. It derives a major part of its income from the offshore financial sector, and a financial scandal in 1989 led to the revision of its Constitution in 1990. In addition to his supervision of defence, internal security, and external affairs, the British-appointed Governor took over the supervision of the financial sector. In return, the powers of the popularly elected Legislative Council were enhanced, and the island's right to self-determination acknowledged. In 1997 a volcano erupted on the island, destroying the capital, Plymouth, and much of the island's infrastructure. In response, over 50 per cent of the population were evacuated from the island. Over half of the island has been inaccessible since, with the destruction of the tourist industry rendering the islanders reliant on overseas aid.

Morgenthau Plan (Sept. 1944)

A plan drawn up by the US Secretary of the Treasury, Henry Morgenthau Jr (b. 1891, d. 1967) which envisaged a postwar Germany as an agricultural, deindustrialized country which would be divided into a northern and a southern half, with the Rhineland, the North Sea coast, and other important strategic or industrial areas coming under international control. After initial acceptance by *Roosevelt, it was quickly withdrawn as completely impractical, as such a Germany would continue to be reliant on foreign finance. The plan was used extensively by *Goebbels in his *Nazi *propaganda to strengthen German resolve towards the end of World War II.

Mormon Church

One of today's fastest-growing religions, founded in the US in 1830 by Joseph Smith (b. 1805, d. 1844), based on his discovery of golden plates which contained the text of the Book of Mormon, which Mormons use as Scripture in addition to the Bible. In 1846 Smith's successor, Brigham Young, led his followers on the Mormon trail westwards to Utah, of which he became the first territorial Governor. The state of Utah, which became a US State in 1896, has continued to be predominantly Mormon and the Mormon Church retains a crucial political, cultural, economic, and social influence there. A belief that all one's ancestors can be posthumously baptized into Mormonism has led to an unrivalled commitment to genealogy and the establishment of the world's largest genealogical library in Utah's state capital, Salt Lake City. At the same time, as a result of the Church's emphasis on missionary work, most notably in South America, the Mormon

Church has grown significantly outside the USA. Officially known as the Church of Jesus Christ of Latter-Day Saints, the Church is the fifth largest organized religion of the USA, and claims over twelve million members worldwide.

((⊕)) SEE WEB LINKS

• The home page of the Mormon Church.

Moro, Aldo (b. 23 Sept. 1916, d. 9 May 1978). Prime Minister of Italy 1963–8, 1974–6

Born in Puglia and raised as a devout and active Roman Catholic, he became president of the student chapter of the University of Bari, where he studied law. In 1939 he transferred to the University of Rome and became president of the National Catholic Universities' Student Federation. He then lectured in law at the University of Bari and, in 1945, was elected to the Constitutent Assembly as a member of the *Christian Democratic Party (DC). A parliamentary Deputy from 1948, he was Minister of Justice (1955–7), of Education (1957–9), and of Foreign Affairs (1969–72, 1973–4). The leading figure of the left wing of the DC, as the party's secretary-general (1959–64) he steered it towards the left and thus enabled it to cooperate with the Italian *Socialist Party from 1963 onwards. While he was Prime Minister, the first steps towards abolishing sharecropping were made in 1964, as the landless tenants were given cheap credit to enable them to become landowners in their own right. In response to socialist influence, in 1967 a five-year economic programme was established, though central planning instruments for its implementation were never used. On 16 March 1978, Moro was abducted by the *Red Brigades, and he was found shot eight weeks later.

Moroccan Crisis, First (1905)

In an effort to split the Anglo-French *Entente Cordiale concluded a year earlier, the German Chancellor *Bülow convinced Emperor *Wilhelm II to land at Tangier in order to demonstrate German support for Moroccan independence against the spread of French influence. Bülow had calculated that the risk of war would make Britain reluctant to support French claims against Germany. In the international crisis that ensued, the French foreign minister, Delcassé, had to resign. However, the French agreement to an international conference and its acceptance of Moroccan neutrality was a superficial victory for the Germans. The *Entente Cordiale was strengthened through British support for

France and the intensified impression of a German threat to their common interests.

Moroccan Crisis, Second (1911), see AGADIR

Morocco

A stable secular Arab monarchy, which has been subject to international criticism owing to its occupation of Western Sahara since 1975.

Colonial rule (1904–56) A north-west African state under French influence since the *Entente Cordiale (1904), it became an official French protectorate in 1912, while the northern Rif area came under Spanish control. Under the leadership of *Abd al-Krim, tribal forces conducted a campaign against first the Spanish, and then the French, occupation forces from 1920 until 1934. However, despite the emergence of the nationalist Istiqlas movement in the cities in the 1930s, urban support for independence was slow to take off, thanks largely to the administrative skills of the French Resident-General, Marshal *Lyautey. This changed after the defeat of France in World War II in 1940. The Istiqlas Party was formally constituted in 1944. The French refused to accept its claims to independence, however, and in 1953 the Sultan, Mohammed Ibn Yusuf, was deported to Madagascar for his ostensible support of it. The start of a guerrilla campaign in 1955 proved the last straw.

Independence (since 1956) The French granted independence on 18 February 1956, and the Spanish on 7 April 1956. Mohammed Ibn Yusuf returned, and became King Mohammed V of the Kingdom of Morocco. Backed by his patronage of the army, the bureaucracy, urban commercial classes, and agrarian upper and middle classes, Mohammed sought to promote industrialization and the exploitation of the country's rich mineral resources. This policy was continued by his son, *Hussein II. Poverty continued to be widespread, however, while the political dissatisfaction about the King's absolutist rule led to a series of unsuccessful coup attempts (1971, 1972) and terrorist attacks (1973). Despite military support from the USA, he was unable to pacify *Western Sahara after its occupation in 1976. The cost of

the subsequent war constituted a heavy burden on the country's economy, leading to a drastic increase in state debt, which reached $21.6 billion in 1989 (99.6 per cent of its GDP). This led to a series of unpopular economic stringency measures, and triggered further unrest. A general strike was called in December 1990. Political reforms culminated in a constitutional referendum (1995) to establish a bicameral legislature.

Contemporary politics (since 1999) Hussein II died in 1999, and was succeeded by his son, *Mohammed VI (b. 1963). Much more liberal and reform-oriented than his father, he instituted a political amnesty, and allowed opposition leaders to return to the country. The youthful King also dismissed his father's political entourage, led by Driss Basri, who had been his father's Minister for Domestic Affairs. His reformist policies, which included the granting of rights to women, were not universally popular, however, and triggered hostile opposition from the country's strong Islamist groups. Mohammed encouraged negotiations over the state of Western Sahara, though he continued to be reluctant to relinquish Moroccan control over the area. Mohammed worked closely with the USA and the EU, cooperating especially with Spain to control the flow of illegal immigrants into the EU.

Morris, William Richard, see NUFFIELD, 1ST VISCOUNT

Morrison, Herbert Stanley, Baron Morrison of Lambeth (b. 3 Jan. 1888, d. 6 Mar. 1965). British Labour politician
Born in Brixton, he left school at 14, and held a variety of jobs, ranging from shop assistant to telephone operator. The loss of sight in his right eye prevented him from serving in World War I, although he was in any case a staunch pacifist. Morrison became part-time secretary of the London *Labour Party in 1915, and Mayor of Hackney in 1920. He was elected to the London County Council (LCC) in 1922, and to parliament as MP for Hackney South in 1923. As *MacDonald's Minister for Transport (1929–31) he created the London Passenger Transport Board, but when he lost his seat in 1931, he became prominent in London politics. As leader of the LCC (1934–40) he worked tirelessly to improve the city's education and sanitary conditions, which led, for example, to the creation of a Green Belt around the capital. He regained Hackney South in 1935 but remained unacceptable for the leadership as sections of

the party continued to be suspicious of his domination and drive.

His energy was rewarded when he became Minister of Supply and then Home Secretary in *Churchill's wartime coalition government (1940–5). During this time, he drafted Labour's proposals for nationalization and the social services in the 1945 election manifesto. As Deputy Prime Minister to *Attlee (1945–51), and as leader of the House of Commons and Lord President of the Council, he coordinated Labour's domestic parliamentary legislation. Ever mindful of the electorate, from 1947 he advocated 'consolidation', whereby Labour would not extend its nationalization programme, which he recognized was becoming increasingly unpopular. His advice was ignored, however, and the party lost the 1951 elections, just after he had succeeded *Bevin to the foreign ministry. Despite his resounding defeat by *Gaitskell for the 1955 leadership, there is little doubt that he was a crucial force in British politics in general, and in the development and achievement of Labour's programme in particular. His grandson, **Peter Mandelson**, became an influential—and controversial—adviser to Tony *Blair, and served as *Northern Ireland Secretary (from 1999–2001) and EU Commissioner (from 2004).

Mosley, Sir Oswald Ernald (b. 16 Nov. 1896, d. 3 Dec. 1980). British Fascist

Born in London, and educated at Winchester and the Royal Military College, Sandhurst. He served in World War I in the Royal Flying Corps and the 16th Lancers. He left military service in 1916 and moved to the Ministry of Munitions and the Foreign Office. In 1918 he entered parliament for Harrow. He was elected as a *Conservative, but became disillusioned with the party, and in 1922 and 1923, was re-elected in Harrow as an Independent. In 1924, Mosley joined the *Labour Party, and stood for Birmingham Ladywood, where he nearly defeated Neville *Chamberlain. Elected in a by-election in 1926, he joined *MacDonald's second Labour government, and became Chancellor of the Duchy of Lancaster. He produced the 'Mosley Memorandum' (1930), which proposed that the Labour government should implement public works schemes in order to tackle unemployment. When this was rejected by the Cabinet, he resigned from office, formed the New Party, and lost his seat at the 1931 general election.

Following a visit to Italy in 1932, when he was impressed by the achievements of *Mussolini, Mosley formed the **British Union of Fascists (BUF)**. He criticized every aspect of

the British political system, focusing on the decadence of the ruling elite. The party lost its early (moderate) middle-class support following violent outbursts at a meeting at Olympia in June 1934. It became increasingly *anti-Semitic, as became apparent in 1936 when it organized a march through Jewish areas in the East End of London. After the resulting Battle of Cable Street (4 October 1936), the government passed the Public Order Act (1936), which banned the wearing of political uniforms, and gave the police increased powers with which to prevent such marches. As a *Nazi sympathizer he was imprisoned during 1940–3, and kept under house arrest for the remainder of the war. He wrote extensively after the war, and in 1948 he founded the Union Movement, which he led until 1966, campaigning for European unity. He failed to be re-elected to parliament.

Mossadeq, Muhammad (b. 1880, d. 5 Mar. 1967). Prime Minister of Iran 1951–3

A wealthy landowner, he joined the first government of Reza Shah *Pahlavi, but then withdrew from politics until 1942. He became a government official, and in 1951 was named Prime Minister. A convinced nationalist, he nationalized the oil industry and proposed the reduction of foreign influence in all other matters. This restored some of the pride lost over one century of foreign (mainly British and Russian) dominance. Because of Mossadeq's popularity, Muhammad Reza Shah *Pahlavi was unable to control him and was himself forced into exile in 1953. However, Mossadeq's programme of nationalization ran counter to US interests. In a *CIA-sponsored coup by the Iranian army (codenamed 'Ajax'), he was removed and sentenced to solitary confinement, while the Shah returned to his throne.

Mountbatten, Louis Francis Albert Victor Nicholas, Earl Mountbatten of Burma (b. 25 June 1900, d. 27 Aug. 1979). British admiral and statesman

Born in Windsor, the grandson of Queen Victoria and great-uncle of Prince *Charles. He served in the Royal Navy in World War I. In 1917, his family changed its name from Battenberg to Mountbatten, owing to wartime anti-German sentiments in Britain. In 1940–1, he commanded HMS *Kelly*, which was torpedoed in 1940, and sunk in the 1941 Battle of Crete. As Chief of Combined Operations from 1942, personally selected by *Churchill, he was involved in planning Allied landings in North Africa, Italy, and Normandy. The big boost to his career came in October 1943, when he became Supreme Allied

Commander in South-East Asia, where he was instrumental in revitalizing the organization and morale of the British and *Commonwealth forces. His forces were successful in the *Burma campaigns, but their combined operations to take Singapore and Malaya were made largely unnecessary by the fall of Japan in September 1945.

Progressive in politics as in battle, Mountbatten accepted the impossibility of returning to the prewar colonial *status quo* in Asia, and recognized the expediency of working with newly emerging political leaders. This commended him to the post of Viceroy of India (1947–8), where he was given a free hand to negotiate the colony's release into independence. His diplomatic skills, and good personal relationships with many of the leaders, led to the establishment of good Anglo-Indian relations despite the colonial past. He stayed briefly as Governor-General, but returned to the navy in 1948 where he rose to become First Sea Lord and Chief of Naval Staff (1955–9). As Chief of Defence Staff (1959–65), he supervised the merger of the service ministries into a single Ministry of Defence. In 1979, while on holiday in Ireland, he was assassinated by the *IRA.

Mouvement Républicain Populaire, see MRP

Movimento de Liberación Nacional, Uruguay, see TUPAMAROS

Mozambique

A southern African state which has undergone a remarkable transition from brutal colonial rule and subsequent civil war to a relatively stable democratic regime.

Portuguese rule (1508–1974) Under Portuguese influence since 1508, it was used to supply slaves to Brazilian plantations. In the late nineteenth century, its interior was occupied by the Portuguese, who came to institute one of Africa's harshest and most racist colonial regimes. The country's resources were ruthlessly exploited, while no efforts were undertaken to educate an indigenous elite. Inspired by the process of *decolonization that occurred from the late

1950s in the English and French colonies of Africa, a resistance movement, *FRELIMO, was formed in 1964. It became increasingly successful in its guerrilla warfare against the government, and by 1974 controlled more than one-fifth of the country.

Civil war (1974–94) After the fall of the Portuguese dictatorship in 1974, independence came suddenly, unexpectedly, and with little preparation on 25 June 1975. Under the leadership of *Machel, a Communist People's Republic was proclaimed. With little coordination, a programme of nationalization of private companies and of agrarian reforms was introduced, which proved disastrous for an economy already wounded by the complete withdrawal of Portuguese expertise, capital, and machinery. The country's woes were greatly increased through a rising guerrilla campaign by *RENAMO, which originated in an attempt by Ian *Smith's racist Rhodesian government to destabilize the Communist regime. It was after the fall of Smith's government, when RENAMO switched its allegiance to the South African *apartheid regime, that the guerrilla movement became a potent force. While still too weak to replace the government, RENAMO launched an attack of unprecedented destruction of property and human life, on a scale only exceeded in twentieth-century African history by the massacres in Rwanda (1994).

After his death in 1986, Machel was succeeded by the more pragmatic *Chissano. He improved relations with the USA, appealed for funds from the *IMF, and relaxed some of his predecessor's socialist policies. Most importantly, he tried to reach a compromise with the RENAMO rebels to end the civil war. This was greatly facilitated by the end of the *apartheid regime in South Africa, which deprived RENAMO of its vital support and made it eager to reach a compromise.

Contemporary politics (since 1994) Free elections were held on 27–9 October 1994 amidst fears that RENAMO might not accept a possible defeat. However, RENAMO appeared to accept the result (37.8 per cent of the popular vote against 44.3 per cent for FRELIMO), partly because neither force was able to wage an effective military campaign after the decommissioning of 90 per cent of their respective troops.

New elections in 1999 confirmed Chissano in office. These elections were confirmed as fair by international observers, but were contested by RENAMO. Chissano's political success was acknowledged in 2000, when Mozambique became one of the first countries to qualify for substantial debt relief under the *HIPC initiative. By contrast, a series of devastating floods in 2000 and 2001 caused damages of up to $2 billion and destroyed much of the economic growth achieved in the 1990s. Even more serious was the development of *AIDS. According to UNAIDS, in 2006 over 16 per cent of the population aged 15–45 years were HIV positive. In 2005, Chissano was succeeded by Armando Emilio Guebuza. A veteran of the independence struggle, Guebuza vowed to fight corruption, and sought to address the poverty affecting the majority of the population.

MRP (Mouvement Républicain Populaire, Popular Republican Movement)

A French Christian socialist party, co-founded by G. *Bidault in 1944, which occupied an important position as a centrist party in the Fourth Republic. Among its representatives was R. *Schuman, a leading advocate of the party's policies of *European integration. In 1958, it supported de *Gaulle's return to lead the country. Increasingly marginalized by the political system of the Fifth Republic, it dissolved in 1967, with some of its members joining the *Gaullists.

Mubarak, Mohamed Hosni (b. 4 May 1928). President of Egypt 1981–

Born in the Minufiyya provice, he graduated from the Cairo Air Force Academy in 1950. He advanced to become Chief of Staff (1969–71), though it was his immaculate leadership of the air force as Commander-in-Chief (1971–5) during the *Yom Kippur War of 1973 which earned him his promotion to the rank of air marshal in 1974. He was appointed Vice-President of Egypt in 1975, and assumed the presidency after *Sadat's assassination. He remained loyal to the peace with Israel agreed upon at *Camp David, despite his opposition to the Israeli invasion of Lebanon in 1982. His efforts to improve relations with other Arab countries led to Egypt's readmission into the *Arab League in 1989. Towards the late 1980s, he was increasingly challenged by the growth of *Islamic fundamentalism, so that in popular elections he had to resort to increasing corruption to maintain his power and to keep the movement away from positions of political influence. He found it difficult to prevent the popularity of the *Muslim Brotherhood. From the early 2000s, he prepared his son for his eventual succession.

Mugabe, Robert Gabriel (b. 21 Feb. 1925). Prime Minister of Zimbabwe 1980–7, President 1988–

Rise to power A Shona from the the Southern Rhodesian town of Kutama, he became a teacher and worked successively in Southern Rhodesia (Zimbabwe), Northern Rhodesia (Zambia), and Ghana before returning to Southern Rhodesia in 1960. In 1961 he co-founded the Zimbabwe African People's Union (ZAPU), whose deputy secretary-general he became. Imprisoned in 1962, he escaped to Tanganyika. Disillusioned by the dominance of *Nkomo's Matabele people within the moderate ZAPU, in 1963 he co-founded ZANU (Zimbabwe African National Union). This militant party came to appeal to the Shona majority in Southern Rhodesia. During renewed internment (1964–74) he was elected leader of ZANU, though he also used this time to obtain a doctorate in law. Following his release he went to Mozambique to oversee a vast increase in ZANU guerrilla activity from there, while at the same time forging an alliance with ZAPU to form the Patriotic Front (Zanu-PF).

Growing authoritarianism (from 1980) After the end of the civil war and the transition to democratic government he won a landslide victory in the parliamentary elections in 1980. Disputes with Nkomo led to the temporary breakup of the Patriotic Front in 1982, which was not re-established until 29 December 1987. Originally a man of integrity and vision, he won the trust of the White settlers and even of many of the rival Matabele tribe during the early years of his rule.

As the country grew poorer and his rule became more unpopular, he sought to maintain his power by increasingly autocratic and despotic means. He sought to placate an impoverished population by the forced expropriation of White farmers from 1999. Mugabe also persecuted opposition leaders, as well as critical journalists. In 2000 his attempt to extend his presidential powers through a change in the Constitution failed in a referendum. In the same year, Zanu-PF only barely won the parliamentary elections, obtaining 62 out of 120 seats. In response, Mugabe tightened his rule by increasing the harassment of the opposition, so that in 2006 Zanu-PF was returned with a majority of two-thirds of parliamentary seats. Mugabe amassed great personal wealth which he invested overseas, as his regime became increasingly corrupt.

mujahidin ('holy warriors')

A term used for a coalition of Islamic groups which formed in the early 1980s in response to the Soviet invasion of Afghanistan. Aided by generous arms supplies from the USA (via Pakistan), their guerrilla warfare led to a withdrawal of the Soviet armed forces by February 1989. In 1992 the Communist government was finally overcome, but shortly after the establishment of an Islamic state, on 6 May 1992, the fragile coalition fell apart. Alliances between the different factions of the *mujahidin* were changing constantly while the country was in a state of anarchy. Out of this chaos emerged the *Northern Alliance and the *Taliban, which, during the 1990s, managed to bring most of the country under its control.

Mujibur Rahman, Sheikh (b. 1920, d. 14 Aug. 1975); Prime Minister of Bangladesh 1972–5; President 1975

Born in East Bengal as the son of a landowner, he studied law at the Universities of Calcutta and Dacca. An active member of the Muslim Students' Federation since 1940, he became a founding member of the *Awami League in 1949. Owing to his skills as party organizer he became the League's chairperson for East Pakistan (now Bangladesh) in 1963, and led it to an overwhelming victory there in 1970, on a platform of greater autonomy from (West) Pakistan. The scale of the victory came to legitimize demands for independence, whereupon the Pakistani army intervened and he was imprisoned. Released by Zulfikar Ali *Bhutto in 1972, he became Prime Minister of Bangladesh. He nationalized a number of key industries, while promoting a political structure modelled on the British *parliament. He had poor administrative skills, however, which he sought to compensate for by assuming presidential powers. He dissolved the Awami League and formed the Baksal movement as the only legal political organization, though he was assassinated soon after by a group of discontented army officers.

Muldoon, Sir Robert (b. 21 Sept. 1921, d. 5 Aug. 1992). Prime Minister of New Zealand 1975–84

Born in Auckland, he made his early career in accountancy, becoming president of the Institute of Cost Accountants in 1956. In 1960 he entered politics as a member of the *National Party and was elected to the House of Representatives. Never received with enthusiasm, he commanded great respect and credibility, which were crucial assets given the economic crisis that had arisen from the *Kirk government. This ensured he gained the party leadership in 1974, and victory in

the 1975 general elections, when he became Prime Minister and Minister of Finance.

In office Muldoon's years in office were a difficult time for the New Zealand economy. Oil prices had risen steeply in 1973 and the traditional market in Britain for New Zealand farm and dairy produce was reduced by Britain's entry into the EEC. Muldoon tried to overcome these problems through state intervention, by introducing price controls and farm subsidies. His foreign policy reversed the anti-nuclear and anti-racist policies of his predecessors. In an attempt to revive *ANZUS, he welcomed US warships in New Zealand even if they carried nuclear warheads. Declaring that sport and politics should be kept separate, he revived the sporting links with South Africa which had been broken by Kirk, despite calls by the *ANC for a boycott.

Mulroney, Martin Brian (b. 20 Mar. 1939). Prime Minister of Canada 1984–93

Early career Born at Baie-Comeau (Quebec), he joined the Progressive *Conservative Party while attending St Francis Xavier University, and became a party worker before resuming his studies at Laval University. After graduating in law he joined a large Montreal law firm, where he specialized in labour relations while continuing his activities for the Conservatives. Although not a parliamentary representative, he became the most powerful man in the Quebec Conservative Party as a result of his fund-raising activities and his pivotal position in the party machine. He ran unsuccessfully for the federal Conservative Party leadership in 1976, and narrowly beat *Clark for the leadership on 11 June 1983, when he was also elected to the House of Commons. A man of considerable charm and charisma, he built on his experience as a party organizer to run a successful election campaign against the *Liberal Party under *Turner, in which his party gained an unprecedented election victory in 1984.

In office His efforts to achieve a final settlement of the Canadian constitutional problem and address the concerns of French-speaking Canadians resulted in the *Meech Lake Accord. Mulroney was a firm supporter of *NATO, and allowed the deployment of US nuclear missiles on Canadian soil. In the 1988 elections, he lost his two-thirds majority, but still won a comfortable victory, thus becoming the first Conservative Prime Minister to be confirmed in office this century. The victory enabled him to realize a second central policy goal, the liberalization of trade with the USA, which culminated in *NAFTA. While his popularity benefited from the economic boom of the 1980s, he became increasingly unpopular as unemployment rose and economic growth came to a halt in the early 1990s. He faced increasing pressure to resign, amidst predictions that the Conservatives would lose the forthcoming elections, and in 1993 he made way for Kim *Campbell.

Munich Agreement (29 Sept. 1938)
After the *Anschluss, *Hitler moved to incorporate the *Sudetenland and the Czech lands into German territory. The British Prime Minister Neville *Chamberlain flew to Hitler's residence in order to avert a military conflict. At their final meeting in Munich, at which an agreement was signed, *Mussolini and the French Prime Minister, E. *Daladier, were also present. Hitler was allowed to annex the Sudetenland, but not the entire Czech lands. War had been avoided, which led Chamberlain to proclaim 'Peace in our time' upon his return to Britain. The agreement reflected the general desire for *appeasement at the time, while giving Britain another eleven months in which to prepare for war. Yet it also gave Hitler more time for rearmament, and his concession not to invade the Czech lands became void when German troops marched into Prague on 15 March 1939. Despite the agreement being about the carve-up of Czechoslovakia, Czechoslovak representatives had no say in it. Nor did the Soviet Union, a demonstration of mistrust that encouraged *Stalin to conclude the *Hitler–Stalin Pact without regard for Britain or France.
TESCHEN

Munich Olympic killings (5 Sept. 1972)
During the 20th Olympic Games in Munich, Palestinian terrorists from the 'Black September' group attacked the quarters of the Israeli team in the Games village. Two Israelis were killed and nine taken hostage. In the effort to rescue them they were all killed, together with five terrorists. The remaining terrorists were flown to Libya and their release was later forced after the hijacking of a German aircraft.
PALESTINE

Muñoz Marín, Luis (b. 18 Feb. 1898, d. 30 Apr. 1980). Governor of Puerto Rico 1949–65
Born in San Juan, he attended Georgetown University (1912–16) and subsequently worked as secretary to the Puerto Rican

resident commissioner in Washington (1916–18). Upon his return to Puerto Rico he became involved in journalism, and became editor of his father's newspaper, *La democracia*. Elected to the Puerto Rican Senate in 1932, he founded the Partido Popular Democrático (PPD, Popular Democratic Party) in 1939. Originally a strong advocate of independence, Muñoz changed his position after the appointment of Rexford Tugwell as Governor of Puerto Rico in 1941, whom he supported in his efforts to realize a *New Deal programme for housing and economic development. When Puerto Rico gained the right to elect its own Governor, Muñoz won an overwhelming victory. He supported Puerto Rico's new constitutional status as a Commonwealth, secured in 1952, though he failed in his efforts to reduce the influence of US capital on the island.

Murayama Tomiichi (b. 3 Mar. 1924). Prime Minister of Japan 1994–6
Japan's first Socialist Prime Minister for forty-seven years, he was plucked from relative obscurity in late 1993 to lead the Japan *Socialist Party (JSP) after its crushing defeat in the July 1993 House of Representatives poll. His party career prior to his election as leader was not marked by any conspicuous achievement, although he was a veteran of local and national politics, representing constituencies in the Oita prefecture for most of the postwar era. Possibly because he was so outstandingly unoutstanding, Murayama was chosen as the candidate to lead an unlikely and difficult coalition government in 1994. His administration included long-time political opponents, the JSP and the *Liberal Democratic Party (LDP). In the event, Murayama proved to be a capable Prime Minister, not least in his defiance of widespread expectations that his coalition would collapse sooner. Aspects of Murayama's administration were dogged by criticism, such as the government's tardy response to the humanitarian emergency that resulted from the Kobe earthquake of 17 January 1995 and the financial crisis of the same year involving the collapse of housing loan corporations. Nevertheless there were some qualified successes in facing up to Japan's legacy from World War II. He also took a measure of credit for the resolution of other long-standing controversies such as the Minamata mercury poisoning case.

Murray, John Hubert Plunkett (b. 29 Dec. 1869, d. 27 Feb. 1940). Australian colonial administrator of Papua New Guinea 1908–40

Born in Sydney, he graduated from Oxford and was called to the Bar in 1886. A Crown prosecutor in Sydney from 1896, he became chief judicial officer of *New Guinea. As administrator he brought most of Papua New Guinea under Australian control. He was particularly notable, however, for his relatively liberal and enlightened treatment of the native population, often against the wishes of the White settlers. Murray died in office, leaving behind a remarkable reputation, among Papuans as well as in Australia and in other colonial regimes.

Museveni, Yoweri Kaguta (b. 1944).
President of Uganda 1986–
Born in Mpororo, Kigezi, he went to university in Dar es Salaam, Tanzania, where he became active in the *FRELIMO movement which had its headquarters there. He returned to Uganda in 1970 to work for *Obote, but left for Tanzania again after *Amin's coup in 1971. He was active in organizing resistance to Amin and took part in his overthrow in 1979. In the corrupt 1980 elections, his Uganda Patriotic Movement was heavily defeated, whereupon he organized a struggle of armed resistance against Obote. On 29 January 1986 his troops entered the capital, Kampala, and he became President. The civil war continued in parts of the country, which increased his dependence on the army, whose power he tried desperately to control. His attempt at politics by consensus, however, and his successful economic management which made Uganda one of the fastest-growing economies in Africa, strengthened his standing with the population. He was re-elected in 1996, 2001 and 2006, though the opposition accused him of intimidation, a charge confirmed by international observers. Nevertheless, because of the stability he brought to his country, Museveni continued to be endorsed by Western governments as a model African leader.

Musharraf, Pervez (b. 11 Aug. 1943).
Leader of Pakistan, 1999–
Early career Born in Delhi, he was educated at Forman Christian College, Lahore, before joining the Pakistan Military Academy in 1961. He visited the Royal College of Defence Studies in England, and in 1964 was commissioned to an artillery regiment as an officer. He rose through the army's ranks, and in 1993 became Director of the General Military Operations. He became a general in 1998 and became Chairman of the Joint Chiefs of Staff in 1999.

In office Musharraf overthrew the corrupt Prime Minister, *Nawaz Sharif, and governed the country as Chief Executive from 1999, and as President from 2001. Musharraf strove to liberalize and revitalize the economy, which had come close to collapse, and to improve relations with India. Following the *September 11 attacks, he instantly came to the side of the US and became a crucial ally in its *War on Terrorism. He thus came to fight the *Taliban regime in Afghanistan which he had previously supported. Musharraf also attempted to use the crisis to strengthen his control within the country, notably by reigning in his powerful secret service the ISI (Inter-Services Intelligence), although this proved difficult. The ISI had sponsored radical *Islamic fundamentalist groups in Afghanistan and *Kashmir. As the Taliban revived its campaign against NATO forces in Afghanistan from 2005, Musharraf was under growing international pressure to control Pakistan's borders better, and to close it to Afghan insurgents escaping NATO troops. Owing to the strength of Pakistan's more fundamentalist Muslims, Musharraf was hesitant to combat the Taliban resolutely. By 2007, this allowed the Taliban to mount its resurgence in Afghanistan from Pakistan's territory. Despite continued domestic and international tensions Musharraf proved remarkably resilient as a leader, providing his country with unusual stability.

Muslim Brotherhood
An *Islamic fundamentalist movement created by the pious Egyptian Muslim schoolteacher **Hasan al-Banna** (b. 1906, d. 1949) in 1928. Aiming to rejuvenate *Islam, it sought to impose Islamic law (Shariah) upon all social and political activity. Although it expanded to other Arab countries, most notably Syria, the Brotherhood's political influence was mostly confined to Egypt, where its membership grew to some one million during the 1940s. Because of its increasing militancy, which developed very much against Hasan's original ideas, it was banned in 1948. It survived as an underground terrorist organization, which was both strongly anti-Western and against involvement with the USSR. In 1948, one of its members killed the Egyptian Prime Minister, in response to which Hasan was assassinated by government agents. An alleged assassination attempt on President *Nasser in Egypt in 1954 led to the execution of some of its most prominent members and further wide-scale arrests. Although formally banned since then, independents have represented the Brotherhood in the Egyptian parliament. In the 2005 elections, its representation increased from 18 to 88 seats.

Muslim League

An Indian party founded on 30 December 1906 in Dacca, initially in order to campaign for separate Muslim representation at all levels of government. It claimed to represent the grievances and demands of the entire Indian Muslim community. Hence in the first decades, it pursued the dual aim of winning greater rights of self-government from the British, and of winning greater rights for Muslims within that system. To achieve the former aim, it cooperated frequently with the Indian National *Congress (INC), with which it allied itself in the Lucknow Pact of December 1916. Briefly eclipsed by the *Khilafat movement, it was largely ineffective during the 1920s, when it claimed little over 1,000 members throughout the subcontinent. In the 1930s, the Muslim League undertook a major revision of its goals and organization to enable it to appeal to the disparate Muslim community.

In 1930, *Iqbal addressed its annual conference (attended by only seventy-five members) to demand, for the first time, a separate Muslim state in the west. This stance became gradually accepted, particularly after the Muslim League's catastrophic showing in the 1937 elections, when it gained but 104 out of 489 Muslim seats. Under its leader, *Jinnah, the demand for separate Muslim homelands became an accepted policy of the League on 23 March 1940. This broadened the League's base, and by 1944, it could claim over two million members, which in the 1945–6 elections translated into 75 per cent of the Muslim vote. It thus had a popular mandate for the creation of a separate Muslim state, and was able to achieve the creation of Pakistan in 1947. Initially dominant in Pakistan politics, now that independence had been gained, and after the death of the commanding *Jinnah, it lacked an integrative force, so that it dissolved into various groups during the 1950s.

Muslims, see ISLAM

Mussolini, Benito (b. 29 July 1883, d. 28 Apr. 1945). Italian dictator 1922–45

Early career Born in Predappio as the son of a socialist and anticlerical blacksmith, he was largely self-educated and became a primary school teacher (1901) and journalist. He lived with Rachele Guidi, from his home town, from 1909 (civil marriage 1915, religious marriage 1925), and together they had five children. A radical member of the *Socialist Party since 1900, his political views were marked less by Marx than by Nietzsche, Pareto, and Sorel. He became provincial party secretary and a committed opponent of *Guiolitti's conquest of Libya. In 1912 he became chief editor of the party newspaper *Avanti!*, whose circulation he increased from 20,000 to 100,000 copies by 1914. Mussolini broke with the socialists over World War I, passionately supporting Italy's entry, and founded his own newspaper, *Il popolo d'Italia*, in favour of a national socialism. He served in the war 1915–17. On 23 March 1919 he founded the *Fascist movement, originally under the name Fasci di Combattimento, which he sought to develop into an anti-socialist and anti-capitalist mass movement.

In power Mussolini came to power in a semi-constitutional coup known as the *March on Rome (1922). Following the *Matteotti Crisis he was pushed by the radical Fascist wing to outlaw all opposition and establish *Fascism as the guiding principle in public and private life, e.g. through the establishment of the *balilla or the *dopolavoro. Despite the concentration of power in the hands of Il *Duce, Mussolini's power continued to be circumscribed by the elites with whose help he had attained it. The fact that he had to take into account the opinions of the monarch, *Victor Emanuel III, the Church, industrial elites, and parts of the administrative system meant that, unlike in *Nazi Germany, *concentration camps or other extreme forms of the persecution of minorities were never possible in Italy.

From the mid-1920s his *nationalism became more aggressive, with his emphasis on the 'mare nostrum' (our [Mediterranean] sea) which led, for example, to the pacification of Libya (1923–31) and its integration into the Italian state (1939) as well as the invasion of Albania (1939). In 1935–6, he also conducted the *Abyssinian War, to international outrage. From 1936 he established ever-closer ties with *Hitler's Germany. Hence, in 1940 he entered World War II even though the Italian army was too weak for the demands of a large-scale war, which most Italians came to oppose. As a result, Mussolini was deposed by the *Fascist Grand Council on 25 July 1943, and imprisoned the following day.

Demise (1943–5) After the Italian armistice with the Allies, Mussolini was liberated by German paratroopers and brought to German-controlled northern Italy, where he was placed at the head of the Italian Social Republic (Republic of *Salò). There, his room for manoeuvre was severely restricted by the Germans, on whose army and security apparatus (*SS, *SA) he depended. He also relied on his Italian collaborators, most of whom came from the radical wing of the Fascist movement. When the Republic of Salò collapsed, he attempted to escape to Switzerland, but was discovered by Italian partisans and shot (with his mistress, Clara Petacci) without trial the next day. His body was taken to Milan and hung in the Piazzale Loreto, together with those of *Starace, Petacci, and *Farinacci.

Mustafa Ismet, see INÖNÜ, ISMET

Mustafa Kemal, see ATATÜRK

Mutesa II, Sir Edward Frederick William Walugembe (b. 19 Nov. 1924, d. 21 Nov. 1969). Kabaka of Buganda 1939–66; President of Uganda 1962–6

He attended King's College, Budu, and succeeded his father as Kabaka of the Buganda people while still a minor. He became active in the affairs of state after completing his studies at Cambridge. Although at first unpopular because of his exuberant lifestyle, he became a national hero for standing up to the British and their plans for an eastern African federation. As his endorsement became necessary for political success, *Obote formed an alliance with him, whereupon he became Uganda's first President. He now occupied a dual role, as President of all Uganda, and as leader of the territory of the Buganda within it. His sympathies lay with his tribe, which enabled Obote to depose him and take up the presidency himself. He wrote his autobiography, *Desecration of my Kingdom* (1967), in exile in London. He died of alcohol poisoning.

Mutual and Balanced Force Reduction Talks (MBFR) (1973–89), see DISARMAMENT

Muzorewa, Abel Tendekayi (b. 14 Apr. 1925). Prime Minister of Zimbabwe-Rhodesia 1979

Born in Old Umtali, he was ordained in 1963, and in 1968 became a bishop in the United Methodist Church. In 1971, he founded the moderate African National Council (ANC), and in 1977–8 was one of the principal negotiators with Ian *Smith in discussions which led to Black majority rule. The ensuing elections of April 1979 resulted in a victory for the ANC and his appointment as the first Black Prime Minister of what was now known as Zimbabwe-Rhodesia. However, the elections had been boycotted by the main parties, *ZANU and ZAPU, who continued their

guerrilla warfare. Soon seen as Smith's puppet, he was also shunned by the international community, so that he had to concede renewed negotiations to include representatives of all Black groups. In the free elections of March 1980, his party won but three of the eighty seats, which led to his subsequent political marginalization.

MVSN (Milizia Volontaria per la Sicurezza Nazionale, Voluntary Militia for National Security) (Italy)

Created in January 1923 to establish a militia answerable to *Mussolini alone, it initially consisted mainly of former *Blackshirt recruits. The bulk of the MVSN consisted of unpaid volunteers (over 90 per cent of the 750,000-strong force), who welcomed it as a social organization providing state benefits such as free medical care in return for their commitment to the *Fascist movement. In addition, there was a special militia whose members worked in various government departments (railways, ports, telegraphs, etc.), whose purpose was to ensure the allegiance of their departments to the state.
SA; SS

Mwanawasa, Levy (b. 3 Sept. 1948). President of Zambia, 2002–

Born in Mufulira, he studied law and graduated from the University of Zambia in 1973. He became a distinguished lawyer, and was the first Zambian to be appointed advocate to the High Court of England and Wales. In 1989 he rose to prominence when he defended former Vice-President Christon Tembo and others charged with plotting to overthrow the government of *Kaunda. Mwanawasa joined the ruling Movement for a Multi-party Democracy (MMD), and in 1991 was chosen by *Chiluba to become his Vice-President. He resigned in 1994, however, because of a row with a fellow minister. To universal surprise, Chiluba chose him as candidate for the presidency in 2001, and he narrowly won the elections in the following year. Mwanawasa was considered a man of the utmost integrity, and he was untainted by the mistakes of his predecessor. In office, he benefited from an increase in market prices for copper, Zambia's main export, which generated economic growth. He was re-elected in 2006, a year in which he also suffered a mild stroke.

My Lai Massacre (16 Mar. 1968)
An atrocity of the *Vietnam War committed by a US unit commanded by Lieutenant William Calley. After losing substantial numbers of soldiers through *Vietcong guerrilla attacks,

Calley's unit arrived at the village of My Lai, where they encountered a defenceless village population. Most of the soldiers under Calley's command started to shoot the inhabitants, killing several hundred of them. The massacre came to light in 1970. After a four-month court martial Calley was sentenced to life imprisonment on 29 March 1971, but his superior officer, Captain E. Medina, was acquitted. Calley served a short portion of his sentence before he was pardoned by President *Nixon. It remains unclear how exceptional this incident was in the war. The massacre was seized on by the war's opponents to show that the war was morally debasing as well as militarily disastrous.

Myanmar (Burma)

An Asian country which has been ruled by a brutal military regime, and which remains relatively closed to the outside world.

Foreign rule (up to 1948) Annexed by Britain in the three Burmese Wars of 1824–6, 1851–2, and 1885, Burma became a colony in 1886 as part of British India. Colonial hostility to the dominant role of *Buddhism in society triggered the formation of nationalist opposition, beginning with the Young Men's Buddhist Association in 1906, followed by the General Council of Burmese Associations in 1920. This was complemented by student opposition, which began to form soon after the creation of the University of Rangoon (1920), culminating in the student strikes of 1920, 1936, and 1938. The growing nationalist movement was provided with an official platform in 1937, when the Government of Burma Act (1935) came into force and made Burma a separate colony which was governed by a bicameral legislature. Resistance continued and, following the 1938 oil workers' strike, led to the formation of the Communist Party of Burma (CPB, 1939).

Most of the nationalist movement was led by the People's Revolutionary Party (PRP). In 1942 it cooperated with the Japanese, who duly invaded the country. The disparate nationalist forces led by the PRP and the CPB soon became disenchanted with Japanese rule, and formed the Anti-Fascist People's Freedom League (AFPFL) in 1944. Under its leader, General *Aung San, it orchestrated an anti-Japanese uprising which greatly facilitated the return of British troops. Under Aung San's able leadership, independence was soon negotiated. The Union of Burma was declared on 4 January 1948, with *Nu Thakin U as Prime Minister.

Military rule (since 1962) Burma's parliamentary system proved very fragile, as the government was challenged by CPB rebels, as well as by guerrilla movements from various ethnic minorities. Nu Thakin U resigned in 1958 after a split within the AFPFL, asking the army commander, *Ne Win, to take over the government. Nu Thakin U won the ensuing 1960 elections, but was deposed in 1962 by a military coup led by Ne Win.

Ne Win set up a revolutionary council, and proclaimed a Burmese way to *socialism. As businesses were nationalized and agricultural prices fixed, he effectively expropriated the successful Chinese and Indian merchant classes, thus depriving the country of its main entrepreneurial drive. The country was isolated from any contact with the outside world, with the exception of China. The subsequent decline in foreign trade led to a crucial lack of hard currency, and this meant that by the 1980s over half of its meagre export revenues were needed to service its foreign debt. The military regime was formally ended with the proclamation of the Socialist Republic of the Union of Burma in 1974.

Nevertheless, Ne Win continued his despotic rule with the help of the Burma Socialist Party, which retained its monopoly on power. As the economy deteriorated, the military was forced to resort to increasing violence to maintain its power. The brutality of the regime led to the creation of around one million refugees, of which around 200,000 were crowded together in camps in neighbouring Thailand and India. Ne Win resigned in 1988.

The consequent pro-democracy protests were gathering momentum so quickly that a coup of 18 September 1988 restored military rule through the State Law and Order Restoration Council (SLORC). In a conciliatory gesture towards the non-Burmese ethnic groups, the government changed the country's name from Burma to Myanmar in 1989. While suppressing political opposition through imposing house arrest or imprisonment on leaders such as *Aung San Suu Kyi, the regime did allow multi-party elections in 1990. Despite its subjection to government harassment, Aung San Suu Kyi's National League for Democracy (NLD) won, gaining 392 of the 485 seats, with the military's own National Unity Party gaining but ten seats in the National Assembly. The military never allowed the NLD to take up power. The military government of Than Shwe (b. 1933), from 1992, tried to defuse some of the popular resistance against the government, for instance by releasing Aung San Suu Kyi from arrest.

Contemporary politics (since 2000) From 2000 Aung San Suu Kyi was put under house arrest again, and she remained in this state almost permanently. In 2004, Than Shwe imprisoned his Prime Minister, General Khin Nyunt, because he had advocated entering into a dialogue with the NLD. In 2005, the military government surprised observers by transferring the capital from Rangoon to the formerly provincial town of Pyinmana in the country's interior.

NAACP (National Association for the Advancement of Colored People)
(USA)

It emerged in 1908–9 out of a call for a conference on Lincoln's birthday in 1909, with the aim of establishing a fully integrated organization. The NAACP was led by a group of young African Americans headed by W. E. B. *Du Bois together with concerned liberal Whites. Its main activities before World War II consisted of fundraising to finance civil rights litigation and to improve public awareness of the iniquities of *segregation and the vital contribution of African Americans to US society. The NAACP campaigned for Black rights mainly on the basis of the Thirteenth and Fourteenth Amendments of the US Constitution. On this basis it achieved a great legal victory in the case of *Brown v. Board of Education of Topeka, when it argued successfully for the abolishment of segregation. In the 1960s it assumed a central role in the *civil rights movement and exerted an important influence on the *Civil Rights Acts. It has continued to press for *affirmative action in favour of Coloured people, but was adversely affected by the decline of the civil rights movement in the 1970s and 1980s and its own perennial problems of financial administration and infighting. With about 500,000 members in the years after 2000, it continued to struggle to find a role in a changed political and legal climate for civil rights. The problems of direction and organization were on display in 2007, when its president, Bruce Gordon, left after only 19 months in office.

SEE WEB LINKS

• The home page of the NAACP.

NAADC (North American Aerospace Defence Command), see NORAD

NAFTA (North American Free Trade Association)

In operation since 1 January 1994, it aims to create a free trade area between Canada, Mexico, and the USA through the elimination of trade barriers on most industrial goods, as well as the financial and service sectors by 2015. It has been far less ambitious than the European Union. It emerged from the 'Free Trade Area' between Canada and the USA, which had been effective from 1 January 1989 following an initiative of Brian *Mulroney. In the 1992 and 1996 US presidential elections, a rich vein of populist opposition to NAFTA was uncovered. This was mainly based on fears that NAFTA would serve to export US jobs to Mexico. According to Joseph E. Stiglitz, however, the US lost far more jobs to Asian economies with a cheap and well-educated workforce, such as China and India. And, despite the commitment to nominal free trade, barriers continued to effect Mexican exports, for instance in agricultural goods. Overall, the USA benefited disproportionately. Between 1994 and 2004 US income increased relative to that of Mexico by over 10 per cent. As a result, under George W. *Bush the US proposed to extend the treaty to Latin America and the Caribbean.

SEE WEB LINKS

• The home page of NAFTA.

Nagasaki

A Japanese port in Kiushu, with a population of around 230,000 in early 1945. At the end of *World War II, the second atomic bomb was dropped on the city by the USA, three days after *Hiroshima on 9 August 1945. Its hilly terrain provided some protection from the explosion and radiation, which nevertheless caused around 74,000 deaths. On the following day, Japan offered an unconditional cease-fire, which came into effect on 15 August. Japan's unconditional surrender became effective on 2 September 1945.

MANHATTAN PROJECT; NUCLEAR BOMB

Nagorno Karabakh, see ARMENIA; AZERBAIJAN

Nagy, Imre (b. 7 June 1896, d. 16 June 1958). Prime Minister of Hungary 1953–5, 1956

Born in *Kaposvár, he served in World War I until he became a Russian prisoner of war in 1916. He was converted to *Communism and became active in the *Russian Revolution of 1917 and the ensuing *Russian Civil War. After a few years in Hungary (1921–8) he returned to the Soviet Union to study agriculture. When Hungary was occupied by the *Red Army in late 1944, Nagy returned and became Minister for Agriculture (1945–6), and carried out a major land reform. He was briefly Minister of the Interior, but he turned out not to be ruthless enough for the post. He retired and was appointed to a chair at the Karl Marx University of Economics in Budapest.

As he was not implicated in *Rákosi's *Stalinist excesses, Nagy was able to replace him in 1953. He relaxed press censorship, slowed the rate of farm collectivization, and reduced investment in heavy industry in favour of the manufacture of consumer goods. In 1955, he suffered a mild stroke and was replaced by Rákosi. He had become too popular to be ignored, however, and became Prime Minister again after the *Hungarian Revolution had succeeded in toppling the hard-line Communist regime in October 1956. He abolished the Communist monopoly of power, and withdrew the country from the *Warsaw Pact. Hungary was invaded by troops of the *Warsaw Pact on 4 November and, despite guarantees of safe conduct, he was arrested by *KGB troops. He was returned to the Hungarian authorities in 1958. With six others, he was sentenced to death and executed. *Kádár had him buried face down in an unmarked grave. He was rehabilitated posthumously on the anniversary of his death in 1990.

Nahhas Pasha, Mustafa al- (b. 15 June 1879, d. 23 Aug. 1965). Premier of Egypt 1928, 1930, 1936–7, 1942–4, 1950–2

Born in Samanud, he became a lawyer and co-founded the *Wafd Party, becoming its leader upon the death of *Saghlul Sa'd in 1927. As Premier, he negotiated the Anglo-Egyptian treaty of 1936, in which the British recognized Egyptian autonomy while maintaining a military presence in the country. During the war, he initiated a number of social reforms, though he is best remembered for his part in the creation of the *Arab League in 1944. In his last period in office, he demanded that the British forces leave the country and hand over Sudan to Egyptian rule. His inability to control the popular nationalist passions he had thus aroused caused his own downfall, and led to *Neguib's and *Nasser's *coup d'état*.

Najib, Muhammad, see NEGUIB, MOHAMMED

Nakasone Yasuhiro (b. 27 May 1918). Prime Minister of Japan 1982–7

A civil servant in Japan's Home Ministry, he entered politics in 1947 when he was elected to the Diet. He established a controversial reputation for himself early by petitioning the American authorities to leave his country. He was also somewhat unconventional by the standards of his time, proposing, for example, that Emperor *Hirohito had a moral responsibility for the war and arguing for a more open imperial family. As a prominent politician, Nakasone first entered the Cabinet in 1959 and his career in government included many of its key posts. He succeeded Suzuki Zenko as Prime Minister and president of the *Liberal Democratic Party in October 1982, and held power until his resignation in 1987. During his premiership, Nakasone sought to project a new, more confident image of Japan overseas, whilst instituting reforms of the public sector at home. His style of leadership attracted considerable opposition within his own party, but the support of the Tanaka faction, as well as his popularity with the electorate, ensured his survival. His reputation as an opportunistic politician earned him the nickname of the 'weathervane' of Japanese politics. Nevertheless his ability to read the electorate, as well as his skill as a communicator, have made him one of Japan's outstanding postwar premiers.

Namibia

One of the last African countries to obtain independence, Namibia avoided the ethnic and economic dislocations of other post-colonial societies like Zimbabwe.

South African rule (up to 1990) Known as South-West Africa until 1968, Namibia became a German colony in 1884, but was conquered by South African troops under J. *Botha and *Smuts in 1915. After five years of military rule it became a *League of Nations *Mandate, whereupon South Africa started to integrate the country as a fifth province. In 1946 Smuts applied to the *UN for the right to annex the country, which was refused. Ignoring the UN's demands to administer it as a *trust territory in preparation for independence, *Malan gave White Namibians direct representation in the South African parliament in 1949. *Apartheid laws were introduced, and the country was fully integrated into the South African economy.

Legal battles over the next few decades in the *International Court of Justice on the legality of South Africa's continued administration of South-West Africa ended in 1966, when the UN withdrew the Mandate unilaterally. South Africa was forced to rethink its strategy of incorporation following Angolan independence in 1975, as its new government allowed the Namibian independence movement, SWAPO (South-West African People's Organization), to set up bases there. South Africa thus started to work for a compromise solution which would give Namibia a degree of independence while enabling it to retain maximum possible influence. Following multi-party talks (with SWAPO excluded), 1975–7, negotiations were entered with the UN. In the subsequent decade the South African government found a number of reasons to stall the UN and prolong its own rule over the country. However, an international arms embargo against South Africa, imposed because of its occupation of Namibia and its *apartheid regime, finally took its toll.

In 1987–8 it became clear that the South African army could not win against the well-equipped and increasingly superior Cuban and Communist forces in Angola which were backing SWAPO. South Africa accepted defeat, and on 21 March 1990 Namibia became the last African country to gain independence under the leadership of *Nujoma. Namibia's largest port, Walfisbay, which had been part of the Cape since 1878 and thus an integral part of South Africa, came under joint administration in 1992.

After independence (from 1990) During the 1990s the government tried to remove the educational disparities between Black and White. In 1994 it passed a law enabling it to expropriate the wealthy (White) farmers by providing compensation. However, this law to reduce the inequality of landownership was applied sparingly.

The expropriation of White landowners in Zimbabwe from 2000 increased public pressure on the government to act, as 50 per cent of the agricultural land continued to be owned by a minority of less than 5,000 farmers. Namibia also suffered from the civil war in neighbouring Angola, as UNITA rebel forces operated from Namibian soil. In 1999 the government withdrew its soldiers from the Congo, where they had engaged in the civil war for the promise of the country's diamond resources. Following a constitutional change, which allowed the President to run for a third term in office, Nujoma was re-elected in 1999, but did not stand again in the 2004 elections.

Contemporary politics (since 2004) Nujoma was succeeded by Hifikepunye Pohamba, who won the 2004 elections by a landslide. Under Pohamba, the first expropriation of White-owned farms began in 2005, with the consent of the former owners. Pohamba moved against corruption in state-owned businesses, and declared the fight against the widespread prevalence of *AIDS as his central priority. In 2006, UNAIDS estimated that around 20 per cent of the adult population was infected with the HIV virus.

Nanjing (Nanking), Rape of

After the outbreak of the *Sino-Japanese War following the *Marco Polo Bridge Incident, on 13 December 1937 around 150,000 Japanese soldiers took control of Nanjing, after weeks of encirclement. An almost unbelievable atrocity followed over the next few weeks. Organized massacres were accompanied by individual acts, when Japanese soldiers killed Chinese at random for their amusement. In all, perhaps as many as 400,000 people died in these killings, which were complemented by tens of thousands of incidents of rape. These atrocities had been encouraged by the Japanese military leadership, which received nothing but praise for the taking of Nanjing from Emperor *Hirohito and the Japanese establishment, even though there was ample news coverage of the killings. After the war, most of the military leaders responsible for the massacre were left unpunished.

Nansen, Fridtjof (b. 10 Oct. 1861, d. 13 May 1930). Norwegian explorer and politician

Born near Oslo, he led expeditions to cross Greenland (1888), while further expeditions pointed to important conclusions about the Arctic sea currents. In 1897, he was appointed professor for zoology and maritime research in Kristiania (Oslo). In 1905 he entered politics, supporting Norway's independence from Sweden. In 1906–8, he was a Norwegian legate to Britain. After World War I, he became high commissioner of the *League of Nations (1921–30). In this capacity, he was particularly concerned with relief work for refugees, and created the so-called Nansen passport, a travel document for international refugees. This was applied to refugees from Russia (1921–3), Armenia (1924), Turkey (1928), and the *Saarland (1935). In all, it is estimated that his work helped to feed and rehabilitate some ten million refugees. The refugee passport was continued after 1946 as the London Travel Document, and the 1951 Travel Document of the Geneva Refugee Convention. In 1922, he received the *Nobel Peace Prize.

Naoroji, Dadabhai (b. 4 Sept. 1825, d. 30 June 1917). Indian politician

Born in Bombay, he became professor of mathematics in 1854. Naoroji was an ardent social reformer, promoting women's education and criticizing the caste system. He went to London in 1855, and subsequently shuttled back and forth between the two countries. He was the first Indian to be appointed professor at the Elphinstone College (Bombay), and in 1856–66 was professor of Gujarati at University College, London. He worked tirelessly for better British understanding of India, founding the British India Society in 1865, over which he presided until 1907. He was a founding member of the Indian National *Congress, whose president he was in 1886, 1893, and 1906. He was also the first (Liberal) Member of *Parliament in Britain (1892–5), sitting for Finsbury, to represent the case of India at Westminster. To this end, he gave evidence to a variety of Royal Commissions, and was himself a member of the Welby Commission (Royal Commission on Indian Expenditure) from 1897. Known as the Grand Old Man of India, he was one of the outstanding Indian public figures from 1845 to his death. The most important outline of his views was published as *Poverty and Un-British Rule in India* (1901).

Narasimha Rao, (Pamulaparti Venkata) Narasimha (b. 28 June 1921). Prime Minister of India 1991–6

Early career Born in the Karimnagar district (Andhra Pradesh), he studied law and graduated with an LLB. He joined the Indian National *Congress in 1945, and distinguished himself through his loyalty to the *Nehru dynasty consisting of Nehru, Indira *Gandhi, and Rajiv *Gandhi respectively. A member of the state assembly of Andhra Pradesh (1955–77), he was Chief Minister of that state in 1971–3. After serving as general secretary to the Congress (I) (1974–7), he entered the lower chamber, the Lok Sabha, in 1977. After Indira Gandhi's re-election in 1980, he was Minister for External Affairs (1980–4). Under Rajiv Gandhi he served as Minister of Home Affairs (1984), for Defence (1985), for Human Resource and Health and Family Welfare (1986–8), and for External Affairs (1988–9). He retired from politics after the electoral defeat of 1989. As perhaps the party's best-known and least controversial figure, the colourless Rao came to lead the party on 20 June 1991 after Rajiv's assassination.

In office Following his party's election victory of 26 June 1991, Narasimha Rao surprised most observers by staying in office for a full term, despite the fragility of his government and the general unpopularity of his economic reforms. These included liberalization and a reduction in state subsidies, in order to reduce the country's large debt. This did yield considerable economic growth, averaging over 5 per cent per year, though it benefited mainly the more prosperous middle classes rather than India's poverty-stricken masses. Rao became increasingly embroiled in corruption scandals, for which he was brought to court after his election defeat to Deve Gowda in 1996. In 2000, he was sentenced to three years' imprisonment for bribing four Members of Parliament in 1993 to support him in a vote of no confidence, but the sentence was later overturned on appeal.

NASA (National Aeronautics and Space Administration) (USA)

Established in 1958 in the wake of the Soviet Sputnik space mission. NASA was generously funded throughout the 1960s, in order to realize President *Kennedy's aim of putting a man on the moon by 1969. In July of that year it achieved this through the *Apollo Program, going on to a number of unmanned space flights and to placing spy satellites, together with weather and communications satellites, into the earth's orbit. Its programme to develop a reusable space shuttle suffered a severe setback in January 1986 with the disaster of a Challenger shuttle explosion. Subsequent investigations revealed both malpractices and inefficiencies, with slack quality control. The resumed shuttle programme authorized by President *Reagan was to be devoted to scientific research, with the US Department of Defense remaining responsible for military research and development in outer space. In the 1980s and 1990s, NASA pioneered the exploration of space within and beyond the solar system, while it established a lead in the development of new generations of communication satellites.

((⊕)) SEE WEB LINKS

• The official web page of NASA.

Nash, Sir Walter (b. 1882, d. 4 June 1968). Prime Minister of New Zealand 1957–60

Born in Worcestershire (England), Nash worked as a clerk in Birmingham until he emigrated to New Zealand in 1909. A Christian Socialist, he joined the *Labour Party in 1916 and was a member of its executive (1919–60). He was first elected to Parliament in 1929 and became the leading spokesman for the moderate wing of the party. With Peter *Fraser he organized the party on a national basis and formulated policies which won the election of 1935, when he became Finance Minister (until 1949). In addition, he was Minister of Social Security in

1938, where he was responsible for legislation on child allowances and national health. Together with the social-reform legislation established by *Liberal and Labour governments since *Seddon, these measures confirmed New Zealand's position as one of the world's most comprehensive *welfare states. He became leader of the opposition in 1950 and led Labour to a narrow victory in 1957. As Prime Minister, he initiated comprehensive social welfare in his first year of office, but spent the last two years coping with a dramatic deterioriation in the terms of trade, caused by a flood in imports. The austerity measures which he introduced in response lost him the 1960 elections.

Nassau Agreement

In December 1962 UK Prime Minister *Macmillan and US President *Kennedy met at Nassau in the Bahamas for defence discussions. Kennedy agreed to arm British Polaris submarines, operating under *NATO command, with nuclear missiles. The agreement infuriated President de *Gaulle, who regarded it as evidence of Britain's continued orientation towards the USA, and that Britain was not genuinely interested in *European integration. Four weeks later he vetoed the first British application to join the EEC.

Nasser (Nasir), Gamal Abd al- (b. 15 Jan. 1918, d. 28 Sept. 1970). President of Egypt 1954–70

Early career Born in Alexandria, he was commissioned into the army in 1938 and became an instructor at the Cairo Military Academy. He developed plans with fellow officers to overthrow King *Farouk from 1945–6. With this aim in mind, he helped found the Free Officers movement, which quickly gained momentum during Egypt's hapless performance in the war against the newly created state of Israel (1948–9). He took a crucial part in the successful coup of 1952. Under his fellow officer *Neguib, he became Minister of the Interior and ordered a large-scale crackdown on his opponents.

In power After a bitter power-struggle, Nasser overcame Neguib and became President on 17 November 1954. His personal integrity led him to reduce government corruption, carry out land reforms, and introduce some social provisions. Shunned by the pro-Israeli USA, and opposed to the former colonial power, Britain, he bought arms from the USSR. Following the withdrawal of Western aid, he built the Aswan High Dam with Soviet help. His decision to nationalize the Suez Canal was highly popular at home, but sparked off the *Suez Crisis. A leader of *pan-Arabism, he founded the short-lived *United Arab Republic with Syria, and encouraged further attempts at Arab unity. For a while he was regarded as the patron and protector of socialist independence movements throughout Africa and Arabia, but the popularity of Nasserism began to fade. At home more extreme left-wing groups criticized him and forced him to take an increasingly hostile attitude to Israel. When the latter retaliated by launching the *Six Day War (1967) his air force was destroyed and his army left in disarray. For the next three years he sought to re-establish links with the USA and started to move towards an agreement with Israel. After his death he was succeeded by *Sadat.

Nation of Islam (USA)

An Islamic sect also known as the **Black Muslims**. It was founded in Detroit, Michigan, in 1930 by the enigmatic Wallace D. Fard. Fard's disciple, Elijah Poole, succeeded him as head of the organization under the name of Elijah Muhammad. Poole proclaimed that Fard was in fact the form in which Allah (God) entered North America. The movement rejected Christianity (Elijah had formerly been a *Baptist minister) in favour of Black pride in an African and Islamic identity. It proclaimed that White people were, by nature, evil, and that a Black God was the source of all life and power in the cosmos. It also promulgated the separation of the virtuous Black race from intrinsically evil Whites by means of territorial separation in North America or by emigration to Africa.

By the 1960s tensions were evident in the Black Muslim movement, exemplified by the struggle between *Malcolm X and **Louis Farrakhan**. Upon the death of Elijah Muhammad in 1975, Farrakhan led a schismatic group with the title Nation of Islam, which is the organization known by that name today. Farrakhan espoused a programme of self-discipline, racial separation, and traditional Black Muslim beliefs as the key to the resolution of crisis in the Black communities of America's inner cities. He had accumulated thousands of followers and supporters by the 1990s. His reputation amongst non-African Americans, by contrast, was undermined by his *anti-Semitism, close financial and ideological links to *Gaddafi, violent anti-White rhetoric, and views which some characterized as misogynist. In 1995 Farrakhan's Nation of Islam organized the Million Man *March on Washington, which attracted the greatest number of African-American marchers since 1963.

( ) **SEE WEB LINKS**

• The official home page of the Nation of Islam.

National American Woman Suffrage Association (USA)

Founded in 1890, this organization campaigned for women to be given the vote in all public elections at every level, though until 1916 it principally worked for women's suffrage in state and municipal elections. Its membership rose from around 17,000 in 1905 to two million in 1917. Led by Anna Howard Shaw and Carrie Chapman *Catt, in 1916 it began to campaign for a change to the US Constitution to ensure that women had the vote at every level. Ultimately, women's crucial role in World War I, when they filled many social and economic positions hitherto occupied by men, proved the catalyst for equal political rights. It was disbanded in triumph when political equality was achieved on the passage of the Nineteenth Constitutional Amendment in 1920.

National Front (France), see FRONT NATIONAL

National Government (UK)

The term used to describe Britain's coalition government of 1931–40. It was formed in August 1931, when a financial crisis split the Labour government, with nine ministers resigning rather than agreeing to cut unemployment benefits. To cope with the effects of the Great *Depression, it was formed on 24 August 1931 and was supported by all parties, except the majority of the *Labour Party. Led by *MacDonald, it increased taxes and reduced benefits and public-sector salaries. This faced some public opposition, with some naval ratings staging the *Invergordon Mutiny. This resulted in further financial panic, and sterling fell by 25 per cent. Britain then abandoned the *Gold Standard and proposed a policy of protectionism. In October, the members of the coalition agreed to fight an election together, and won a massive total of 554 seats (473 were *Conservative, thirteen Labour, 35 Liberal National, 33 *Liberal) against Labour's 52 seats. MacDonald formed a second National Government, which implemented protection with a 10 per cent general duty on imports in the March 1932 Import Duties Act, and then concluded the *Ottawa Agreements later in the same year.

Samuel's Liberals resigned over the Ottawa Agreements, and MacDonald was replaced as Prime Minister by *Baldwin in 1935. Baldwin won a general election in that year, and held office until 1937. He was replaced by Neville *Chamberlain, who was Prime Minister until 1940. By 1935, the government had become Conservative in all but name, even though MacDonald himself remained a member (as Lord President of the Council) until 1937.

National Government of the Republic of China (1928–37)

A government established in Nanjing, after the successful *Northern Expedition had brought the *Guomindang and the *National Revolutionary Army into control of substantial parts of China. Led by *Chiang Kai-shek, it did much to encourage improved education facilities, a better infrastructure, and more industries. Yet these policies benefited mainly the cities. One of Chiang's most conspicuous failures was his unwillingness to implement a thorough land reform, which would have greatly increased the acceptance of his government by the peasantry. As it was, the government remained unpopular among large sections of the population. It was further weakened by its inability to impose its authority upon many local leaders and warlords. Under Chiang's authoritarian rule, corruption became widespread. Perhaps even more important was the National Government's failure to extend its control to the rest of China. It took five concerted efforts to overcome the stronghold of the Chinese *Communist Party in the *Jianxi Soviet. Even then, the National Revolutionary Army was unable to prevent the successful completion of the *Long March.

Chiang's fixation with the Communists completely diverted his attention from the aggression of the Japanese, who took Manchuria in 1931 (*Manchukuo). Most Chinese disagreed with Chiang's view that it was necessary first to overcome the internal enemy to present a strong front to the foreign aggressor, which lost him further popular support. At *Xi'an, Chiang was finally forced by *Chang Hsüeh-liang to cooperate with the Communists. The National Government was followed by the *United Front. The significance of the National Government lies in the fact that Chiang failed to take the opportunity to present himself as a positive and capable alternative to his Communist rival, *Mao Zedong.

YAN'AN

National Health Service (NHS) (UK)

Origins The public health service established under the 1946 National Health Service Act. This act applied to England and Wales, with separate legislation being passed for Scotland and Northern Ireland. The legislation had been opposed by many medical practitioners, who feared that it would threaten their professional independence and private practice. However, the Minister of Health, Aneurin *Bevan, skilfully pushed the plans through parliament, making some concessions to doctors by allowing private practice to continue.

Contemporary history The Act took effect from July 1948, and established a comprehensive health service aimed at diagnosing and treating illness. The vast majority of hospitals, as well as general practitioners, joined the scheme, which was to be administered by regional health authorities. One of its main principles was that treatment should be free at the point of delivery. Therefore, the NHS was funded partly from national insurance, but mainly from taxation. This principle was modified in 1951, when Hugh *Gaitskell introduced prescription charges covering half the cost of adult spectacles and dentures. This caused *Bevan to resign from the Cabinet. Charges have been steadily increased, and their range extended.

In the 1960s a hospital building scheme was instituted, but rising costs have caused problems for all governments, as a result partly of the NHS being successful in prolonging expectation of life, and partly because of the increase in the number of treatments possible. In 1989–90 the NHS was reorganized by *Thatcher's government, which instituted a controversial internal market to increase efficiency through competition. During the governments of John *Major and the first *Blair government, public spending on the NHS increased only insignificantly in real terms, despite the greater costs of treating an ageing population. It became an important issue in the 2001 elections, and in 2002 Blair staked the future of his second government on improving the NHS. He announced an effective income tax rise (in the form of national insurance contributions) and pledged unprecedent increases in funding to bring public spending on health up to the EU average. Average net increases of spending by 7.5 per cent in real terms led to accusations of waste (as some of the money flowed into higher incomes for nurses and doctors), but the NHS did see a significant reduction in waiting lists.
      MEDICARE

National Insurance, see WELFARE STATE

National Labor Party, Australia
A short-lived political party formed on 14 November 1916 after the expulsion of *Hughes and his supporters from the

Australian *Labor Party over their support for conscription in World War I. It merged with the *Liberal Party to form the *Nationalist Party.

National Liberation Front (NLF)
A South Vietnamese resistance movement formed in December 1960 at a secret location, sponsored by the Communist Party of North Vietnam. Based upon the organizational and operational experience of the *Vietminh, its primary aim was the overthrow of *Ngo Dinh Diem, and beyond this the unification of all Vietnam under the banner of 'freedom and democracy' (effectively under Communist rule). It came to encompass millions of members at grass-roots level, absorbing Communists in the South. It developed a complex power structure linked with its Communist sponsors in Hanoi. Its members rapidly infiltrated all of society, including Saigon itself. A foreign relations committee established links with all Communist countries and several neutral ones, sending representatives to the *UN and in 1968 to the Paris Peace Conference (*Paris Peace Accords). It provided a generous pool for recruitment for its military wing, the Liberation Army, or *Vietcong. It was merged with its North Vietnamese counterpart, the Fatherland Front, upon unification in 1975.

National Organization for Women (NOW), see WOMEN'S MOVEMENT

National Party, New Zealand
Contemporary history (up to 1986) Established as New Zealand's main conservative party by a merger of the *United and *Reform Parties in 1936, it derived its support from rural areas and the wealthier suburbs. After World War II, it benefited from the *Labour Party's increasing association with wartime controls, industrial unrest, and economic austerity. Led by *Holland, it achieved a majority in 1949, but despite its greater emphasis on private enterprise, the party did not seek to undo *Muldoon's and *Fraser's welfare legislation. It lost power in 1957, but was able to exploit *Nash's inability to cope with the country's economic difficulties in 1960, when it returned to power under *Holyoake. He maintained the party's commitment to the USA through sending troops to the *Vietnam War. He lost the election to a revitalized *Labour Party under *Kirk, whose idiosyncratic economic policies and inability to cope with the worldwide recession brought the National Party to power again in 1975, under *Muldoon's leadership.

Once in office, Muldoon defied his party's traditional commitment to market principles and deregulation. He sought to overcome the country's difficulties through a series of interventionist policies, such as wage and price freezes, protectionism to safeguard agricultural incomes, and intervention in financial markets to ensure low interest rates. This caused a party split and led to the formation of the New Zealand Party (NZP) in 1983, which sought to revert to the National Party's previous policies. This split was an important factor in the party's defeat in the 1984 elections, as the NZP drew away much of its support, and gained almost 12 per cent of the popular vote. Muldoon resigned later that year, and the NZP reunited with the National Party as it shifted again to the right.

Contemporary politics (since 1986) Led by *Bolger from 1986, the National Party adopted Labour's popular anti-nuclear stance, and rejected Muldoon's interventionist policies by seeking to eclipse Labour's liberal economic policies. It won the 1990 elections, and immediately carried out a radical shake-up of the country's welfare system by creating the first 'post-welfarist' society. Welfare benefits were no longer universal, but were handed out only to the very poorest section of the population. Bolger oversaw a strong, export-led recovery, which contributed to a decline in unemployment and a reduction in public debt. Although many of Bolger's economic policies were highly controversial, he narrowly won the 1993 elections. Following the 1996 elections, the National Party governed in a coalition with the controversial New Zealand First Party. Six months after Jenny *Shipley succeeded Bolger as Prime Minister the coalition broke apart. From August 1998, Shipley headed a minority government.

Shipley lost the 1999 elections, and in 2001 was succeeded as party leader by Bill English (b. 1961). After a catastrophic election defeat in 2002, the party was led by Don Brash from 2003, a former governor of the Bank of New Zealand. Under Brash, the party recovered at the 2005 elections, when it gained 18 per cent. However, it narrowly missed a majority, as it obtained two fewer seats than Labour. Brash resigned in 2006, as leaked emails revealed not just details of his private life, but also showed that Brash was aware of illicit funding practices. Brash also incited controversy by remarks about Maoris which his opponents branded as racist. He was succeeded by John Key.

(⊕) SEE WEB LINKS

• The official website of the National Party (New Zealand).

National Party of Australia

Its roots date back to 1920, when a group of independent members representing farming interests in the House of Representatives, against a shifting social, economic, and political emphasis towards town and industry, combined to form the **Country Party**. It sought to advance rural concerns through pressing for improved rural infrastructure, greater financial assistance, and a policy of low tariffs and free trade. Under the able leadership of *Page, it became a junior partner in a coalition with the *Nationalist Party in 1923, and subsequently was indispensable to every conservative government at the national level (with the Nationalist Party 1923–9, *United Australia Party 1934–9, 1940–1, *Liberal Party 1949–72, 1975–83, 1996–).

The party's electoral base was in northern New South Wales and in Queensland, where its party leader, Sir Johannes Bjelke-Petersen (b. 1911), was Premier (1968–87). It was renamed and reformed as the National Party in 1982, in an attempt to broaden its base beyond the declining rural population. In the late 1980s it was harmed by allegations and convictions of corruption, though in 1996 it gained eighteen seats and returned to government. Its representation declined to twelve seats after the 2004 elections, however. Also known as the Nationals, the party continued to function as the junior partner in a governmental coalition under John *Howard, emphasizing its significance as the voice of Australians living beyond the metropolitan areas.

(⊕) SEE WEB LINKS

• The official website of the National Party (Australia).

National Party, South Africa

Origins and rise (up to 1949) A political party founded by *Hertzog in 1914 in reaction to the emphasis of the South African Party (SAP) of Louis *Botha and *Smuts on harmony between Imperial Britain and South Africa in order to forge the English-speaking and the Afrikaans-speaking Whites into one nation. By contrast, the National Party (NP) was an *Afrikaner party committed to promoting Afrikaner issues, such as the Afrikaans language and culture, and greater emancipation from the British Crown. On racial issues, its 'fundamental principle' was 'the supremacy of the European population in the spirit of Christian trusteeship, utterly rejecting any attempt to mix the races'.

The NP was a main focus of Afrikaner opposition to South Africa's participation in

World War I through the occupation of German South-West Africa (Namibia). Originally mainly a rural party, it increasingly gained the support of (White) urban workers, who never forgave Smuts for his suppression of the 1922 trade-union-sponsored Rand Revolt. Thus, in 1924 it was able to form the first government in coalition with the Labour Party. When, during the Great *Depression, Hertzog decided to form a coalition with Smuts and to merge the NP with the SAP in 1934, a minority led by *Malan in the Cape defied the move and formed the Gesuiwerde Nasionale Party (Purified National Party). In response to South Africa's entry into World War II, Hertzog and Malan briefly reunited to form the Herenigte Nasionale Party (Reunited National Party), but Hertzog soon broke away again to form the Afrikaner Party.

Political hegemony (1949–92) With the support of the latter, Malan won a surprise victory in the 1948 elections, despite having gained only 37.2 per cent of the vote, against 47.9 per cent for Smuts' United Party. The NP won all subsequent elections until 1994, mainly because its support remained linked to a sense of Afrikaner identity and an Afrikaner 'milieu'. This was also sustained by the conservative Dutch Reformed Church, by clubs and societies dedicated to the preservation of Afrikaner culture and domination, and by the Afrikaner press. The NP also obtained the support of an increasing number of English-speaking Whites, as the economic benefits of apartheid to all Whites became apparent. After the rule of *Vorster, when the party became more pragmatic about its *apartheid ideology, the NP became painfully aware of the threat of conservative breakaway movements. In 1969, some dissidents broke away to form the Herstigte Nasionale Party (Re-established National Party), while in 1982 the arch-conservative minister of the Dutch Reformed Church, Andries Treurnicht led another breakaway movement to form the *Conservative Party.

Decline (from 1992) In response to considerable gains made by these conservative groups after the NP's commitment to the end of apartheid, *de Klerk called a referendum for 17 March 1992, in which the NP's new course was approved by 68.7 per cent of the (White) votes cast. The NP gained 20.4 per cent of the vote in the 1994 elections, and managed to attract enough of the 'Coloured' (mixed-race) vote to become the largest party in the Province of the Western Cape. However, in subsequent years the NP tried to expand its potential electoral base toward the Black population, as a result of which it lost much of its core support amongst Whites. Renamed the New National Party (NNP), in the 1998 general elections it obtained only 6.9 per cent of the vote, so that its parliamentary representation declined from 82 to 28 seats. In 2000, it merged with the Democratic Party to form the *Democratic Alliance (DA). Following some disagreements, a number of party members broke away from the DA to reconstitute the NNP in 2001. It entered an alliance with the *ANC and obtained seven seats in 2004, and in 2005 it dissolved, joining the ANC.

National People's Congress (NCP)
Constitutionally the highest state organ of power in China. The first Congress was elected in 1954 in accordance with the constitution of that year. Thereafter, it met every year, and was newly elected every five years. Between its sessions, its business was run by a permanent committee. In theory, the government was responsible to the People's Congress, whose legislative powers were confirmed in the 1982 constitution. In line with other Communist assemblies, however, in practice it remained principally a body of affirmation, not of criticism.

National Revolutionary Army (NRA)
A Chinese army organized by *Sun Yat-sen. It became the military arm of the *Guomindang, though relations were always tense. Large contingents were provided by local *warlords, and the loyalty of these troops remained with their sponsors, rather than with the Guomindang. None the less, its Guomindang officers became the power base of *Chiang Kai-shek, who succeeded Sun as army leader in 1925. Once its reorganization, which had started in 1924 with the creation of the Whampoa Military Academy, was complete, the NRA set out on the *Northern Expedition, in the hope that it would be able to recruit further numbers along the way. Indeed, army strength increased from 150,000 in 1926 to 600,000 in early 1928, and to over two million in 1930. However, this was a source of weakness as well as strength, as its heterogeneity increased. Unlike the Communist Red Army, which was tied together by strict discipline and a common ideology, most of its individual contingents remained interested primarily in their own profit, so that the NRA was prone to corruption and graft, as well as lack of coordination. Thus, despite its superior strength (three million soldiers in 1946) it was unable to prevail in the *Chinese Civil War (1946–9).

National Security Council (USA)

An integral part of the national security architecture of the USA, the NSC was founded by the 1947 National Security Act which also established the *CIA and the US Department of Defense. It advises the President and his staff on all matters of concern to national security, foreign or domestic, and includes the President, his adviser on national security, the Secretaries of State and Defense, and the Vice-President, as well as the Chairperson of the Joint Chiefs. In practice, it is represented by the National Security Advisor to the President. It has a staff of over 1,000 people committed to research and analysis. It also has the capacity to send agents beyond the purview of the CIA. The Council played a key role in the *Cuban Missile Crisis and the *Iran–Contra Affair.

SEE WEB LINKS
- The home page of the National Security Council serving the US President.

National Socialism, see NAZI PARTY

nationalism

An idea which developed in the nineteenth century, whereby population groups are bound together through their territorial, cultural, and/or ethnic links. It emerged partly as a result of the economic, social, and political uncertainties of the modern, industrializing world. In addition, it was often used by a section of the population to mobilize popular support against a ruling class of different origin or religion, as happened in many nationalist movements in *Austria-Hungary, and in many colonial countries.

Two types of nationalism can be broadly identified. An organic, cultural nationalism emerged largely in eastern and central European states, where, among a scattered people, a nation came to define itself by a common ancestry, common religion, and/or a common language. A second type of nationalism developed where the nation became identified with the existing state, a sentiment manipulated very successfully by Bismarck to justify the Prussian-dominated German state after 1871.

Common to most nationalist movements is a belief in national greatness supported by a glorified, mythical past, in a liberating mission (particularly in wartime), and some kind of 'divine' mission of the nation. Nationalism need not be hostile to other nations, but it did contribute towards widespread support for World War I on all sides. The new European territorial order after 1918 tried for the first time to take account of national communities, but its collapse from 1933 showed how fragile and flawed this had been. After World War II, the concerns of national communities (such as Poles and Germans) were largely ignored and subjected to the geopolitical considerations of the two superpowers. Under Soviet rule, nationalist sentiments were encouraged only if they did not challenge the hegemony of *Communism and the state. The collapse of the Soviet Union resulted in the (often violent) eruption of nationalist fervour in all former Soviet republics, as well as in eastern European states such as Czechoslovakia, and Yugoslavia.

Since 1989, new types of identity have emerged that have superimposed themselves on thriving nationalist sentiments. *Globalization as well as growing international migration created a growth of regional identities as individuals needed to identify with smaller, more easily identifiable cultural structures. This growing regionalism was complemented by the acceleration of transnational identities. One manifestation of this was the creation of more stable transnational structures, such as the *WTO, as well as firmer structures within the EU such as the *euro. A more sinister manifestation was the growth of international terrorism, which led to the *September 11 attacks and the *War on Terrorism.

Nationalist Party, Australia

With the official title of Australian National Federation, it was a conservative party formed in February 1917 by a merger between the *National Labor Party and the *Liberal Party. Emphasizing its commitment to World War I, it won a landslide victory in 1917, with *Hughes as Prime Minister. From 1922, it depended on the parliamentary support of the Country Party (see *National Party), whose leader, *Page, demanded *Hughes's resignation because of his former prominence within the Australian *Labor Party. Subsequently, the Nationalist-Country coalition under *Bruce and Page governed until 1929, when it was heavily defeated at the polls. In an effort to create a more effective organization, the party was absorbed into the *United Australia Party in 1931.

native land claims, see LAND CLAIMS, NATIVE (CANADA)

native peoples (Canada)

A term which describes the descendants of the original (aboriginal) inhabitants of Canada,

*Canadian Indians, *Inuit, and *Métis. According to the 2001 census, 958,000 Canadians were Canadian Indians, 266,000 were Métis, and 51,000 were Inuit, out of a Canadian population of 31 million.

NATO

Foundation A defensive military alliance founded on 4 April 1949 which established military cooperation among its member states and obliged them to defend each individual member in case of a military attack. Its members were Belgium, Canada, Denmark, the Federal Republic of Germany (since 1955), France, Greece (since 1952, left in 1974, rejoined 1979), Iceland (which has no military forces), Italy, Luxemburg, the Netherlands, Norway, Portugal, Spain (since 1982), Turkey (since 1952), the UK, and the USA. Spain and France (from 1966) were not members of the integrated military commands, so that in case of attack their troops were not automatically under NATO high command.

Geopolitical transformation (since 1989) NATO was created in response to the *Cold War, to contain the military threat posed by the Soviet Union and its satellite Eastern European states. The collapse of the *Warsaw Pact forced NATO to redefine its role to allow an efficient potential response to the instabilities of the former Soviet Union, such as a streamlining of its military organization, and the creation of Allied Rapid Reaction Forces (ARRF) for immediate mobilization in areas of crisis. NATO also allowed its troops to be at the disposal of the *UN, which led to their first-ever deployment in combat in the *Bosnian Civil War.

To readdress its relationship with the former members of the Warsaw Pact, NATO formed the **Partnership for Peace** in 1994, an alliance which established military consultation and cooperation between the signatory states. The Partnership for Peace was joined by twenty states from the former area of the Warsaw Pact, as well as the previously neutral states of Sweden and Finland. It fell conspicuously short of a military guarantee of the integrity of its member states' borders, but held out a promise of their future full membership in NATO. In 2002, NATO agreed on the integration of Latvia, Lithuania, Estonia, Slovakia, Slovenia, Romania, and Bulgaria.

Contemporary politics (since 1999) A watershed was reached when NATO forces intervened in *Kosovo in 1999. This exposed the military weakness of the alliance, as the military and technological superiority of the United States over the other member states became glaringly obvious. This was confirmed in response to the *September 11 attacks. For the first time in its history, the common defence clause in the case of an attack (Art. 5) was invoked. The US, in response, preferred not to make use of this offer, and to use only its own sophisticated missile systems and specialist units in its action against the *Taliban.

However, NATO troops played a leading role in the pacification of Afghanistan after the defeat of the regime in 2002. Under UN mandate, NATO led the International Security Assistance Force (ISAF), which aimed to secure the country against growing *Taliban resistance.

(⊕) SEE WEB LINKS

• The official home page of NATO.

Nauru

The world's smallest republic, the Pacific island state of 21.3 km² lies west of Kiribati and south of Micronesia. It was part of the German Marshall Islands protectorate until World War I, after which it came under joint British, Australian, and New Zealand administration under a *League of Nations *Mandate. The three countries divided up amongst themselves the profits from the exploitation of one of the world's richest phosphate deposits. During World War II it was occupied by Japan (1942–5), but thereafter reverted to its joint administration, now as a *UN *trust territory. From 1951, local government was gradually introduced and profits from phosphate exploitation shared, until Nauru gained independence on 31 January 1968. In 1993, Australia agreed to pay $A107 million in compensation for environmental damage caused by its phosphate mines. The island faced an existential crisis from the early twenty-first century onwards, when its reserves of phosphates, which had accounted for almost 100 per cent of its exports, had become depleted. The government tried to stem imminent economic decline for the country's 10,000 citizens by attracting offshore bank deposits through the institution of liberal banking laws. Australia became strongly involved in Nauru's affairs, as experts from the Treasury were sent to help with the island's finances. Australia also set up a camp for refugees at Nauru, which provided further income for local islanders. A turbulent political period came to an end in 2004, when Ludwig Scotty became Prime Minister, commanding a majority of sixteen out of eighteen seats in parliament.

Nawaz Sharif, Mian Muhammad (b. 25 Dec. 1949). Prime Minister of Pakistan, 1990–93, 1997–9

Born in Lahore, he graduated from Government College in Lahore before obtaining a law degree from Punjab University. He entered politics in that province, and entered the Cabinet of Punjab state as Finance Minister in 1981. In 1985 he became Chief Minister of Punjab, and in 1990 Prime Minster. He was forced to resign in 1993 and was succeeded by Benazir *Bhutto, but in 1997 his Pakistan Muslim League won an overwhelming victory in the elections. He strengthened his position against his personal rival, President Farook Leghari, and promoted the introduction of Islamic law, the Shariah, in 1999. In that year he was deposed in a coup and imprisoned. In 2000 he was sentenced to two terms of life imprisonment and fourteen years of hard labour, but later that year he was allowed to emigrate to Saudi Arabia.

Naxalites (India)

A radical Indian Communist terrorist organization, named after the Naxalbari area in the Himalayan foothills of West Bengal, where it first began its violent campaigns in 1967. Under the leadership of Charu Mazumdar, its members had broken away from the *Communist Party of India (Marxist). In 1969, they officially formed the Communist Party of India (Marxist-Leninist). This CPI (M-L) first organized armed risings of landless agricultural labourers out to kill landowners and government officials, especially in eastern India. Later it developed into an urban guerrilla movement, especially in Calcutta. Its programme of strikes, riots, and murders reached a peak in 1971, but it declined after Mazumdar's capture and death in 1972. The CPI (M-L) split into several factions, some of which adopted a policy of participating in constitutional politics, although a number of splinter groups continued to enact sporadic violent campaigns.

Nazi Party (NSDAP/Nationalsozialistische Deutsche Arbeiterpartei)

A *Fascist party founded by Anton Drexler (b. 1884, d. 1942) as the German Workers'

Party on 5 January 1919, it was renamed the National Socialist German Workers' Party in 1920. The following year, *Hitler took over as party leader and subsequently led it according to the *Führerprinzip*, whereby all authority came from the *Führer (leader), so that the whole party was organized hierarchically, from top to bottom. In the same way, the party derived its ideology entirely from Hitler's speeches and his book *Mein Kampf*. Banned after the abortive *Hitler Putsch in 1923, the party was refounded in 1925. It was unable to make substantial gains in the following years during the relative stability of the *Stresemann era, but in the severe economic crisis which resulted in a total of 3.2 million unemployed by January 1930, many desperate Germans chose to ignore the negative aspects of the party and were drawn by its positive message of renewal and strength.

The success of the Nazi Party, as opposed to other radical right-wing groups with similar radical and *anti-Semitic ideas, was the result less of its ideology than of the outstanding quality of Hitler's mesmerizing oratory, and of *Goebbels's innovative *propaganda. Following the worsening of the crisis, which led to an increase in unemployment to six million by January 1932, the party more than doubled its vote to become the largest party in the elections of July and November 1932. When Hitler refused to take any other political office except the Chancellorship, many in the party rank and file who were looking for change became impatient. This tactic lost some votes in the elections on 6 November 1932, but thanks to President *Hindenburg's right-wing advisers it paid off when Hitler was finally appointed Chancellor on 30 January 1933.

By 5 July 1933 all other parties had been disbanded. Throughout the next twelve years increasing pressure was exercised to encourage Nazi membership, so that by 1945 more than eight million people had joined. Nevertheless, the party's true popularity has been a subject of intense historical controversy, as individual members' motives for joining were diverse and not always ideological. What is clear is that the Nazi party's support was always lower than, and often distinct from, the widespread adulation for Hitler himself. The party was dissolved and banned in 1945.

Ne Win (b. 14 May 1911, d. 5 Dec 2002). President of Burma (Myanmar) 1962–88

Born in the Paungdale Pyay district, Ne Win studied at the University of Rangoon for a while, before joining the nationalist movement Do Bama Asi Ayon. There, he met *Aung San, who made him Commander-in-Chief of his Burma National Army (1943–5). He retained this position in the newly created Burmese army (1949–72), leading its campaigns against rebellious ethnic guerrilla movements. Briefly called in to head a caretaker government as Prime Minister (1958–60), in 1962 he deposed *Nu Thakien U. He abolished the parliamentary system, and proclaimed the Socialist Republic of the Union of Burma. He went on to expel 300,000 foreigners (mainly Indian and Chinese), in a disastrous attempt to gain control over the Burmese economy. Constantly harassed by Karen guerrilla forces and widespread domestic opposition, his ruthlessness alone ensured the survival of his regime. His influence in Burma remained strong even after his retirement, but he was put under house arrest shortly before his death.

Negrín López, Juan (b. 1892, d. 12 Nov. 1956). Prime Minister of Spain 1937–9

Born on the Canary Islands, he studied in Germany (1914–17) and became professor of physiology at the University of Madrid. He became a moderate socialist parliamentary Deputy in 1931, but his impact remained relatively modest until he became Minister of Finance in *Largo Caballero's *Popular Front government. He increasingly resisted Largo Caballero's policies, and on 18 May 1937 took over the government himself. To reduce domestic opposition to the regime, he ended the attempt to bring about a social revolution, focusing on the resistance to *Franco in the *Spanish Civil War instead. Nevertheless, as his Republican forces were defeated by Franco, he came to rely increasingly on the Soviet Union. He inspired many with his anti-*Fascist passion, though this also closed him to the possibilities of a negotiated peace. He died in exile in Paris.

Neguib, Mohammed (b. 20 Feb. 1901, d. 29 Aug. 1984). President of Egypt 1952–4

Born in Khartoum, he joined the Egyptian army in 1921, gradually rising to the rank of brigade commander during the war against the newly created state of Israel (1948–9). A man of integrity and honesty, he was chosen as nominal leader of the 1952 coup in which King *Farouk was deposed. As premier and then President, his plans to establish a multi-party democracy enjoyed considerable popular support. However, his political rival, *Nasser, increased his hold on the army and deposed him in 1954, putting him under

house arrest. He was released by *Sadat in 1971.

Nehru, Jawaharlal (b. 14 Nov. 1889, d. 27 May 1964). Prime Minister of Union of India 1947–64

Early career Born in Allahabad as the son of Motilal *Nehru, he received a European education, and was educated in England at Harrow School and Cambridge. In 1912, he was called to the English Bar. Returning to India more as an English gentleman than an Indian nationalist, he was converted to political action in 1920 by the ascendant *Gandhi in response to the *Rowlett Bills and the *Amritsar Massacre. Soon prominent within the left wing of the Indian National *Congress (INC), he came to Gandhi's attention. They were considerably different in outlook and temperament: Nehru was short-tempered, aggressive, and as a ladies' man with supreme charm (as *Mountbatten's wife was to find out) he did not think much of Gandhi's idea of chastity. None the less, the two men came to respect each other, and by 1930, he was widely seen as Gandhi's trusted lieutenant and protégé. He was more keen than most within the party to support Britain in World War II, but backed the Quit India campaign called in 1940. He was (again) imprisoned in 1943–5, and on his release he eclipsed Gandhi in practical influence over the independence negotiations, 1946–7.

In office Having acquired the popular name of 'Pandit' (teacher), perhaps his greatest failing was his lack of appreciation of Muslim grievances. He did not recognize these after the defeat of the *Muslim League in the 1937 elections, and effectively scuppered any chance for a compromise with *Jinnah after the *Cabinet Mission Plan. Furthermore, after the partition of India his non-conciliatory attitude towards Pakistan in matters ranging from financial and commercial relations to *Kashmir created tremendous tensions between the two countries. On the other hand, in marked contrast to Pakistan, he did create a remarkably stable democracy, the largest in the world, despite the country's linguistic, cultural, ethnic, and administrative heterogeneity.

In economic matters, his achievements were mixed. He did not cling to Gandhi's ideals of communitarianism, but instead promoted industrial and agricultural development. Many of his plans failed, however, partly because of maladministration, and partly because the growth of the economy was eclipsed by that of the population. Understandably suspicious of colonialism, Nehru pioneered the principle of *non-alignment. This deprived the country of important US financial and technological aid given to other less developed countries, and forced the country to rely on its own underdeveloped resources. Nevertheless, he died a much-revered leader, with his reputation sufficing to create a political dynasty through his only daughter, Indira *Gandhi, his grandson, Rajiv, and Sonia *Gandhi.

Nehru, Motilal (b. 6 May 1861, d. 6 Feb. 1931). Indian nationalist

Born in Agra, he studied law and built up an enormously successful legal practice in Allahabad. Politically active since the imprisonment of Annie *Besant in 1917, he joined his son, Jawaharlal *Nehru, in *Gandhi's non-cooperation movement (1920–2). When the Indian National *Congress (INC) declined into inactivity during the 1920s, together with C. R. Das (b. 1870, d. 1925) he organized the *Swaraj Party in early 1923, which was recognized by the INC as its political wing in 1925. It gained a majority in the Central Legislative Assembly, as well as in some provincial assemblies, though despite his very able leadership, he found it difficult to exercise much influence upon the colonial administration. He devised the Nehru Report of 1928 and presided over the important INC Calcutta Congress of 1938, where Gandhi achieved a compromise in demanding Dominion status within one year, and independence if this was not granted. Nehru took part in Gandhi's *Salt March in 1930, when he was arrested. He was released shortly before his death.

Nepal

A mountainous country between India and China which has suffered from economic under-development owing to political instability and long civil war.

Contemporary history (until 2001)

Conquered by the Gurkhas from Rajputana (northern India) in 1769, it was successively ruled by a number of aristocratic families, of which the Rana family emerged as the most influential. Gurkha rule was recognized

by the British colonial government in neighbouring India in 1816, though the country effectively came under British influence. Many Gurkhas enlisted in the British army in India, which became the country's most important source of revenue during the nineteenth and early twentieth centuries. By 1846 the Rana family had secured its predominance, and ruled through a system of hereditary prime ministers.

Internal dissatisfaction with this archaic system of government grew until a coup led to the restoration of the monarchy, albeit a constitutional one, under King Tribhuyan (1951–5) and King Mahendra (1955–72). First parliamentary elections were held in 1959, and were won by the Nepali Congress Party. However, the King dissolved government in 1960, and in 1962 proclaimed a new Constitution. In the new system of *panchayat*, substantial powers were given to local government through elected village councils, while the King's own central powers were removed from democratic control. King Mahendra's policies were continued under his son, Birendra Bir Bikram Shah, who succeeded his father in 1972.

In the 1980s, popular opposition to the King began to mount, under the leadership of the outlawed Nepal Congress Party (NCP). After futile attempts to suppress the growing movement, he gave in to popular demands and in 1990 lifted the ban on political organizations and appointed the Congress leader, Krishna Prashad Bhattarai, to head an interim government.

The elections of 1991 were won by the NCP, which was soon accused of corruption and mismanagement. As a result, the oppositional United Marxist Left gained ground, won the 1994 elections, and formed a minority government. The government struggled to establish its authority over parliament and within the country at large. Its greatest challenge was the opposition of the rebel movement of the Communist Party of Nepal-Maoist (CPN-M), which engaged in a guerrilla war from 1996. By 2002 it controlled over 50 per cent of the territory, with all attempts at realizing a political solution having failed.

Contemporary politics (since 2001)

In 2001 disaster struck the royal family: Crown Prince Dipendra opened fire on his family, killing his father, nine other members of the royal family, and himself. In response, Birenda's brother, Prince Gyanendra, was proclaimed King. Gyanendra dismissed parliament in 2002, declaring authoritarian rule. This led to growing opposition, which the King suppressed with increasing ruthlessness. In 2005, the CPN-M rebels signalled their support for the opposition by declaring a temporary cease-fire. Following a general strike in April 2006 the King was left with no choice but to accept the reconstitution of parliament, which proceeded to wrest political and security powers away from the King. The new interim Prime Minister, Girija Prasad Koirala, enjoyed the tacit support of the CPN-M, which signalled a willingness to be integrated in the new political system. Promising an end to civil war, the CPN-M entered the transitional government in 2007.

Netanyahu, Benjamin (b. 21 Oct. 1949). Prime Minister of Israel 1996–99

Early career Born in Tel Aviv, he grew up in the USA and Israel, and studied at the Massachusetts Institute of Technology, where he obtained a degree in architecture and business administration. After working as a management consultant, he became an officer in an elite anti-terror unit of the Israel Defence Force (1967–72). He published a number of books on Israel's fight against terrorism, and in 1976 was appointed director of the Jonathan Institute against terrorism. In 1982 he became deputy head of Israel's Mission in the USA. As Israel's ambassador to the *UN (1984–8), his telegenic personality gave him an excellent working relationship with the US media, an important source of support for him among Jewish groups in the USA. He returned to Israel to become Deputy Foreign Minister (1988–91) and Deputy Minister in the Prime Minister's Office (1991–2). Still largely unknown, he took over as Chairman of the *Likud Party in 1993, when its popular support was at a low ebb against the popular *Rabin. His fierce opposition to the *Oslo Accords gave way to tepid tolerance. In the 1996 general elections, his charm and charisma overcame doubts about his lack of policy commitments.

In office and subsequent opposition As Prime Minister, he walked a tightrope between US pressure to continue negotiations with *Arafat's *PLO, and satisfying the right-wingers within his government who insisted on Jewish settlers' rights in the *West Bank. After his election, he hoped to stall the peace process and concentrate on economic growth instead. However, his refusal to comply with the *Gaza–Jericho Agreement put the progress in Israeli–Palestinian relations achieved under his predecessors open to serious doubts. Netanyahu refused to implement the final stages of the Oslo Accords, insisting instead that the amount of land to be vacated by Israel be reduced. He also refused to negotiate on the status of Jerusalem. In the three years of his

government, the number of Jewish settlers in the West Bank increased by 20 per cent, making an Israeli withdrawal yet more unlikely and difficult. Netanyahu's policies led to growing unrest in the Palestinian territories, and to a growing radicalization of many young Palestinians impatient for the prospect of independence. His inability to control the escalating violence between the army and the Palestinian population led to his election defeat against *Barak. He declined to challenge *Sharon as Likud's candidate in the 2001 elections, but continued to rally right-wing opposition against the Prime Minister.

Netanyahu became the most prominent critic of Sharon from within the party. He resigned from the Cabinet in 2005 in protest against Israel's withdrawal from Gaza. After Sharon left Likud to found *Kadima, he returned to the leadership of Likud. His party was greatly weakened by the defection of many prominent members to Kadima, so that it only gained twelve seats in the 2006 elections. However, in the course of the year Netanyahu came to be seen as more reliable on security than *Olmert, so that the poll ratings for Likud revived.

Netherlands, The

A country on the mouth of the River Rhine which over the centuries has thrived as a naval power, a colonial power, and as an entrepôt for the European continent.

'Pillarization' The Netherlands are often referred to as **Holland**, which in fact forms just one of the country's historic provinces. It has been traditionally marked by a high degree of diversity. In particular, it has generally consisted of almost equal proportions of Roman Catholics and Protestants, with a significant number of agnostics. The Protestants were split between various denominations, the most important of which was the Calvinist Dutch Reformed Church. This denominational pattern was overlain by strong regional differences (e.g. the Friesians in the north have preserved their own language), which were underlined by stark economic diversity. The sparsely populated north and west of the country remained agricultural. The eastern provinces of north and south Holland became major commercial and industrial centres, through trade with its large colonial empire. They also benefited from Rotterdam's position at the mouth of the Rhine, Europe's most important commercial internal waterway.

As a result of this diversity, Dutch society has displayed a unique blend of traditionalism and progressivism, through the ideal of 'pillarization' (*verzuiling*). According to this idea, each section of the population should be free to pursue its culture without interfering with another culture ('pillar') of Dutch society. In this way, certain Protestant or Catholic sections of society remained fiercely conservative, whereas those areas with a heterogeneous immigrant population and social groups less pronounced in their religious views became noted for their openness to new ideas. Their openness became predominant in the second half of the twentieth century, as immigrants from the colonies arrived in large numbers, and as the power of the churches waned in an affluent society. A liberal consensus was achieved in two ways. One was decentralization, which has allowed a large degree of self-government for the nine provinces. The other was a liberal consensus that each person was free to believe or do as he/she liked, provided it did not adversely affect other members of society. As a result of this, for instance, the country introduced the most liberal drugs laws in Europe, tolerated euthanasia by law from 1994, and lowered the age of consent to 12 in 1995.

The era of the World Wars (1900–45) By the beginning of the twentieth century, the power of the monarchy had been sufficiently weakened to allow parliamentary government. Political life was dominated by social issues, and by the conflict between liberals on the one hand and Catholics and Protestants on the other about the role of the Church in the state, as manifested in the battles about the role of the Church in education. Highly conscious of its vulnerability as a completely flat country dwarfed in size by its aggressive German neighbour, it successfully maintained neutrality in World War I.

After the war, a number of social and political reforms were introduced, such as universal male (1917) and female (1922) suffrage. However, the country did not escape World War II, and was invaded by Germany (10–14 May 1940). With the help of the Dutch *Fascist Nationaal-Socialistische Beweging (NSB, National Socialist Movement) under *Seiss-Inquart the German *SS organized the mass deportation of Jews and others to *Nazi *concentration camps. While the Dutch

government, headed by Queen *Wilhelmina I, encouraged resistance from outside, domestic resistance movements formed, even though their task was made particularly difficult by the scant protection and few hiding-places offered by the flat countryside.

Decolonization and EU membership (since 1945) The country emerged from the war greatly weakened, while the collective memory of German atrocities survived until the end of the twentieth century. The country was also weakened by the Japanese occupation of its colony of Dutch East India (see *Indonesia). It attempted to reassert military control over the islands (1945–9), but despite the use of enormous force it was unable to prevent the achievement of Indonesian independence, which severed a link that had underlain Dutch economic prosperity for over 300 years.

Subsequently, the postwar governments were dominated by the social democrat Partij van de Arbeid (PvdA, Party of Work) and the Katholieke Volkspartij (KVP, Catholic People's Party). The country abandoned its traditional course of neutrality and became one of the main forces for *European integration, as well as cooperation among the Low Countries, which culminated in the *Benelux union.

During the 1970s, the country was plagued by considerable social instability owing to resentment of immigration from Indonesia and the former colony of Surinam (over 200,000 people). A major political shift took place in 1973, when the confessional Protestant and Catholic parties (e.g. the KVP) united to form the non-denominational Christen-Democratisch Appel (Christian Democratic Appeal), which became the central party of government until 1994.

Nevertheless, the party system remained fragmented, in line with the country's continuing diversity, so that in 1994 fifteen parties were represented in parliament. In that year the PvdA formed a coalition government under Wim Kok, together with the two liberal parties, Democrats '66 and the People's Party for Freedom and Democracy (VVD). This new 'violet' coalition thereafter tried to adapt the generous *welfare state to the economic reality of the 1990s, through encouraging greater private individual social insurance. It also transformed the labour market by increasing its flexibility. In response, the Netherlands became one of Europe's model economies, as its unemployment rate declined from 7 per cent in 1995 to 2.5 per cent in 2001.

Contemporary politics (since 2002) Despite, and partly because of, the Netherlands' successful economic adaptation to *globalization, the country experienced a fundamental cultural crisis. This came to a head in spring 2002, when two events challenged its liberal, tolerant self-image. In response to a public inquiry into the failure of Dutch soldiers under *UN command to prevent a massacre of Bosnians in Srebrenica, Kok's whole government took responsibility and resigned. The incident had caused huge debates about public values, and the ways in which the affair had been covered up by the political establishment. The second challenge was the murder, nine days before the elections scheduled for 8 May, of Pim Fortuyn. Fortuyn had created a personal, right-wing movement which was hostile to foreigners and Muslims. His rise to about 20 per cent in national opinion polls challenged the traditional party system and its base of mutual tolerance. Even after his death, his movement became the second largest parliamentary party, and became a junior coalition partner with the other winners of the elections, the *Christian Democrats led by Jan Peter Balkenende. In 2004, permissive consensus was undermined further by the murder by a young Muslim of the liberal film-maker Theo van Gogh, who had attacked Islam's undermining of Dutch liberalism. In 2005, parliament banned the wearing of burkas in public, while Balkenende, who won the 2006 elections, pursued a more rigorous policy on immigration.

Netherlands Antilles

A group of Caribbean islands (including *Aruba until 1986), which came under Dutch authority in 1678. Political life began to emerge during the late 1930s, and after World War II demands for greater autonomy from the Netherlands began to grow. In 1954, they were granted full self-government in internal affairs, while being declared an integral part of the Kingdom of the Netherlands at the same time. The five constituent islands are represented in a common federal parliament, though each island remains autonomous in its own internal matters. In the late 1980s the constitutional set-up seemed extremely fragile, with the established political parties advocating a breakup of the Antilles. These proposals were popularly rejected in a referendum in October 1994, but moves for a breakup continued, especially in the larger islands of St Maarten and Curacao. The two islands were granted greater autonomy in 2006, with a breakup of the Netherlands Antilles envisaged for 2007.

Neues Forum (New Forum) (Germany)

The most important opposition movement against the rule of the *Communist Party in East Germany, founded on 9 September 1989. It was composed of a wide range of people, including *human rights activists, pastors, intellectuals, and artists. The Forum's intellectual and artistic bias led to its failure to appreciate the general desire among East Germans to give up their separate statehood in favour of German unification (and West German living standards). The Neues Forum quickly lost popular support and merged into the Bündnis '90, which in turn merged with the West German *Green Party in 1993.

Neuilly, Treaty of (27 Nov. 1919)

The peace treaty between the Allied powers and Bulgaria after World War I, negotiated at the *Paris Peace Conference and signed at Neuilly Castle in Paris. Bulgaria had to cede the rich wheat-growing area of southern *Dobrudja to Romania and western Thrace to Greece, thus losing direct access to the Mediterranean. Smaller areas were to go to Yugoslavia and *reparations were to be negotiated. Bulgaria's army was also to be limited to 20,000 men.

Neutrality Acts (USA)

A series of Acts passed at the height of *isolationism, amidst fears that the desire for profits from the arms industry might fuel direct or indirect participation in war. They followed a Senate Committee chaired by Gerald P. Nye in 1934, which revealed the high profits among arms manufacturers during World War I. The Acts, which passed through *Congress 1935–9, prohibited loans or credits to belligerents. They placed embargoes on direct or indirect shipments of arms or munitions, making no distinction between aggressor and victim nations. The Acts of 1935 and 1936 both affected US policy on the *Abyssinian (Ethiopian) War. Similarly, two Acts in 1937 limited the US response to the *Spanish and *Chinese civil wars. The Act of 1939 repealed arms embargoes and authorized 'cash and carry' exports to any belligerent power, but continued to forbid US ships to carry 'belligerent cargo'. During 1940 President *Roosevelt fought for repeal of the Acts on the grounds that they encouraged aggression by the *Axis Powers and endangered US security. They were replaced by the *Lend-Lease Act of March 1941.

New Caledonia (Nouvelle Calédonie)

One of the largest islands in Oceania, which is surrounded by a group of Melanesian islands, it lies some 750 miles east of Queensland, Australia. It was annexed by France in 1853 and became a penal colony to which over 30,000 prisoners were dispatched (1864–97). The native inhabitants (Kanaks) from here and from *Vanuatu were imported as virtual slave labour by Australia in the nineteenth century, but forcibly repatriated from 1906 as part of the *White Australia Policy. Military government gave way to a civilian administration in 1885, but in 1942–5 it was occupied by the USA and served as headquarters to the US armed forces in the South Pacific under Admiral *Halsey. In 1946, it became a French Overseas Territory with limited self-government, and thus an integral part of the administration of mainland France. As such, it has been represented in Paris since 1953 by one Senator, as well as two members in the Legislative Assembly. In the 1980s, there were sporadic violent outbursts by Kanaks demanding independence. Their demands were not shared by a majority of the population, which enjoyed considerable prosperity as a result of direct and indirect French state support. Its economy suffered from the Asian economic crisis from 1997, and the depressed prices for nickel, as it held 20 per cent of the world's nickel reserves. Politics remained polarized between (mostly Kanak) supporters for independence and their opponents. Some reconciliation was achieved by the Noumea Accord of 1998. It provided for an eventual vote on independence between 2014 and 2019, and instituted a distinctive New Caledonian citizenship.

New Deal (USA)

The First Hundred Days The term used to describe President F. D. *Roosevelt's programme to deal with the effects of the Great *Depression in 1933–9. There are at least two claimants for coining the term, Roosevelt's adviser Raymond Moley and speech-writer Samuel Rosenman. It was first used in the 1932 election. The First New Deal Program (1933–5) aimed to restore public confidence and to relieve the plight of some fourteen million unemployed. Immediate measures of the First Hundred Days included an Emergency Banking Act (March 1933), an Economy Act (March 1933), and the establishment of a Federal Emergency Relief Administration (March 1933). In June, the National Recovery Administration (NRA) was set up, dedicated to such industrial issues as child labour, working hours and practices, and collective bargaining. In May 1933 an Agricultural Adjustment Administration (AAA) was established, aiming to limit production of staple crops and to stabilize prices by a policy of federal subsidies. The legislation for this as well as for the NRA was invalidated by the *Supreme Court.

Public works legislation Immediate measures were complemented by a programme of public works legislation:

1. The Public Works Administration (PWA), with an endowment of $3.3 billion, became engaged in various public building projects such as schools, hospitals, roads, and bridges.

2. The Tennessee Valley Authority was created in May 1933. An independent corporation backed by federal funds, it built dams and hydroelectric installations in seven states. It also took over a project begun in 1916, the Muscle Shoals project in Alabama extracting nitrate, and in addition to providing cheap electricity engaged in reforestation to check soil erosion throughout the Tennessee River Basin.

3. A Civilian Conservation Corps (CCC) was established in November 1933. Between 1933 and 1941 it found work for some two million young men in reforestation and other projects.

4. A Civil Works Administration, established in February 1934, also gave work to millions on a variety of public works projects.

After the 'First Phase' (from 1935) In 1935, Roosevelt replaced earlier emergency relief measures with the largest public works programme ever undertaken, the Works Progress Administration. It provided poor relief through the provision of work on public projects. In its eight-year history it cost over $11 billion and employed a total of over eight million people. Other legislation during this second phase included the 1935 Social Security Act (a scheme of unemployment insurance, disability insurance, and old-age pensions), and the 1935 Wealth Tax Act, which increased income tax rates as well as taxation on profits.

The National Labor Relations Act of 1935 (also dubbed the Wagner Act, after its proponent, Senator R. F. Wagner) sought to harmonize labour relations by involving workers in decision-making processes at their workplace. In 1938, the Fair Labor Standards Act was passed, but *Congress significantly lowered its stipulations on a minimum wage.

Evaluation The New Deal represented some of the most interventionist, far-reaching, and stunning reforms of US government ever undertaken by an administration. However, it failed to end comprehensively US economic problems. By 1937, another recession had taken hold which Roosevelt sought to combat with pump-priming and government job creation. The New Deal greatly improved the power of workers and organized labour, and encouraged some minorities, e.g. through the *Indian Reorganization Act. Its record on *civil rights, however, was less positive, as Roosevelt did not want to expose his legislation to new fronts. In the end, it was defence production in the run-up to and during World War II which transformed the American economy and banished memories of the slump completely.

New Democratic Party (NDP, Canada)

North America's largest social democratic party emerged in 1961 out of a fusion between the *Co-operative Commonwealth Federation (CCF) and the Canadian Labour Congress. Under the leadership of Tommy Douglas (1961–71), David Lewis (1971–5), and Ed Broadbent (1975–89), the party steadily increased its share of the popular vote from 13.5 per cent in 1962 to almost 19 per cent in 1984. Owing to the electoral system, however, the party consistently failed to gain much more than 10 per cent of the seats in parliament.

The NDP reached a peak in 1990, when under Bob Rae (b. 2 Aug. 1948) it ousted the *Liberal Party from power in the most populous province of Ontario, while gaining victories in British Columbia and Saskatchewan in 1991. Rae's policies, such as rises in the minimum wage and better pensions, proved a disaster for the provinces' finances, and he was comprehensively beaten in the 1995 elections. Owing to Rae's notoriety, and to the success of the emerging *Reform Party in articulating the specific concerns of the traditional western heartland of NDP support, the NDP suffered a disastrous result in the 1993 national elections. The NDP recovered under the leadership of Jack Layton (b. 1950), supporting the Liberal minority government of Paul *Martin (2004–5). In the 2006 elections, it was returned with 29 seats, with the bulk of its representation elected in British Columbia and Ontario.

(⊕) SEE WEB LINKS

• The official website of the NDP.

New Economic Policy (NEP)

A policy introduced in the USSR in 1921 which proposed to end widespread peasant hostility to the regime and terminate the chaos of the Russian economy, weakened by the *Russian Civil War and *Lenin's new Communist regime with its arbitrary expropriations, confiscations of food stuffs, etc. A lighter and fairer food tax was introduced, while many economic controls were lifted in order to allow private initiative. It was an instant success, restoring agricultural and industrial production to its 1913 levels within five years. By the mid-1920s, the NEP had run into problems such as rising prices relative to income ('scissors effect') and unemployment. Much more important, however, was that the NEP ran completely counter to *Stalin's idea of creating a proletarian society free of 'bourgeois' enterprise (*Stalinism), so that the policy was reversed in 1928 with a dramatic programme of collectivization.

KULAK

New Freedom (USA)

The name given to the proposals associated with Woodrow *Wilson in the 1912 presidential campaign which became the legislative proposals of Wilson's first term. Opposed to Theodore *Roosevelt's *New Nationalism, Wilson's proposals included the dissolution of trusts in big business in order to reinvigorate small and medium-sized firms. They also postulated free trade, health and safety reform, and progressive taxation.

New Frontier Party (Japan), see KÔMEITÔ (JAPAN)

New Guard

Perhaps the most prominent of Australian right-wing paramilitary movements, formed by Colonel Eric Campbell (b. 1893, d. 1970) on 18 February 1931. Appealing to patriotism, the monarchy, and anti-*Communism, it drew its membership from those hit by the Great *Depression, and agitated by *Lang's populism. Based in Sydney but spreading throughout New South Wales, its membership peaked at 50,000. However, *Lang's dismissal in 1932 reduced the heat in the state's political atmosphere, precipating a decline of the movement, which disbanded in 1935.

New Guinea

The world's second largest island after Greenland, New Guinea is separated from Australia by the Torres Straits. In 1914 the western half formed part of the Dutch East Indies (since 1818), while the eastern half was divided between Britain and Germany in 1884. After 1920 the two eastern territories became a *League of Nations *Mandate of Australia. Under *Murray's enlightened government, relations with the native peoples were relatively harmonious, though they were excluded from the country's government and administration. It was the scene of some of the heaviest jungle warfare in World War II. The presence of over one million US and Australian troops during this time did perhaps more to disrupt the traditional way of life of the native peoples than seven decades of European rule. The western half of the island joined Indonesia as West Irian in 1963, while the eastern half gained independence as Papua New Guinea on 16 September 1975.

New Hebrides, see VANUATU

New Kômeitô, see KÔMEITÔ

New Liberal Club (NLC)

A Japanese conservative splinter party formed by a small group of Diet members (five from the Lower House, one from the Upper House) who left the *Liberal Democratic Party in mid-1976. They did so in protest against the corrupt practices of the ruling party which had been publicized by the *Lockheed Scandal. In the House of Representatives elections of the same year, the party managed to have eighteen members elected. NLC seats were overwhelmingly won in urban areas with the votes of an unaligned electorate. Successive electoral performances never matched the dramatic success of its early days, however, and the NLC found it impossible to become more than a micro-party. The party stressed a liberal agenda of New Conservatism, with an emphasis on individualism, freedom of expression, and the interests of urban Japan. Facing financial and organizational difficulties the party chose to enter into a coalition with the LDP after 1983 and the NLC was dissolved. Although short-lived, the NLC provided an interesting example of the appeal that conservative politics could have beyond its traditional heartland in the countryside.

New Liberalism (UK), see HOBHOUSE, LEONARD TRELAWNY; HOBSON, JOHN ATKINSON

New Nationalism (USA)

The programme of *Progressive political and economic reform proposals associated with the 1912 presidential candidacy of Theodore *Roosevelt. It comprised social reform through progressive taxation to reduce inequalities of wealth. He also proposed health and safety legislation aimed particularly at women and children, as well as accident insurance for workers. Roosevelt's programme also sought to promote the economy through enlightened reform, including low tariffs and trust regulation—but not abolition—for businesses.

New Zealand

An immigrant country with two large population groups, *Maori and Whites, New Zealand long maintained its close relationship with the UK, before developing into a prosperous country with remarkably harmonious race relations.

The Liberal era (1890s–1930s) The country was settled by the *Maori around 900 AD. White settlement began to grow when the country was declared a British colony on 21 May 1840, after the conclusion of the Treaty of *Waitangi. With poor mineral resources, its prospects as an independent, viable country were secured by the invention of refrigeration. This transformed it into an important exporter of agricultural products, which have remained the backbone of its economy, despite the growth of the manufacturing sector in recent decades.

Refrigeration led to the first sustained economic boom, beginning in 1890, which enabled *Seddon's *Liberal Party government to enact the first series of social reforms such as industrial arbitration and old-age pensions. In addition, by 1893 universal suffrage had been introduced, making New Zealand the first country with equal suffrage. Especially under *Ward, the Liberals gradually started to lose their support among the urban labouring classes, who became increasingly attracted by the labour movement. Exploiting this weakness, the *Reform Party came to power in 1912 under *Massey, who steered the country through World War I, though from 1915 in coalition with Ward. In both world wars, New Zealand was the only Dominion where the introduction of conscription caused

Table 15. **New Zealand Premiers (Prime Ministers after 1907)**

Richard J. *Seddon	1893–1906	Keith Jacka *Holyoake	1960–72
Joseph *Ward	1906–12	John Ross Marshall	1972
William Ferguson *Massey	1912–25	Norman *Kirk	1972–4
Joseph Gordon *Coates	1925–8	Wallace Rowling	1974–5
Joseph *Ward	1928–30	Robert *Muldoon	1975–84
George William *Forbes	1930–5	David *Lange	1984–9
Michael Joseph *Savage	1935–40	Geoffrey Palmer	1989–90
Peter *Fraser	1940–9	Mike Moore	1990
Sidney *Holland	1949–57	Jim *Bolger	1990–97
Keith Jacka *Holyoake	1957	Jenny *Shipley	1997–99
Walter *Nash	1957–60	Helen *Clark	1999–

relatively little internal debate. World War I brought a period of prosperity to the country, so that the economic difficulties of the 1920s and of the Great *Depression in the 1930s were all the harder.

The rise of Labour (1930s–40s) The interwar period, therefore, was one of fundamental social and political transition. The growing hardship, and the awkward and unsympathetic responses of the Reform and *United Party governments under *Forbes and *Coates, led to the first convincing victory of the *Labour Party in 1935. Led by *Savage, it created a *welfare state, which remained the basis of the New Zealand policy until the 1980s. In the interwar period, Maori grievances began to be addressed with some sympathy by the government. This was partly through the efforts of the *Young Maori Movement under *Ngata, *Buck, and *Pomare, and partly in appreciation of the considerable Maori war effort. During this period, New Zealand's international status changed. Having been declared a British Dominion in 1907, its actual independence was recognized by the Statute of *Westminster of 1931, despite the fact that it had not desired this result and its parliament did not ratify the statute until 1947.

National Party ascendancy (1950s–90s) *Fraser's austere wartime policies and his cautious economic approach after World War II caused dissent within Labour, and led to a victory by the *National Party under *Holland in 1949. This inaugurated the subsequent conservative trend in New Zealand politics. Labour's welfare state was not challenged, but was indeed expanded, while greater emphasis was put upon market forces in the economy. Labour briefly returned to power under *Nash in 1957, before *Holyoake continued the National Party's political domination in 1960. A short but significant interlude of Labour

Party government occurred in 1972, when *Kirk reversed many previous foreign policy decisions, through the withdrawal of troops from the *Vietnam War and a commitment to anti-nuclear policies.

A watershed for the country's economy occurred in 1973 with the UK's entry into the European Community (*European integration). Even though New Zealand continued to receive some preferential treatment in the UK market, tariffs were now raised against its products in what had always been its most important market. In 1945, 70 per cent of its exports had gone to Britain, and in 1973 the figure was still over 65 per cent. The diversification of trade after 1973 meant that in 1989 Japan had advanced to be New Zealand's biggest market for exports (18 per cent), while the UK was fourth, taking 7 per cent of the country's exports. None the less, the necessary adjustment was painful, and economic difficulties increased through the worldwide depression which began with the 1973 *oil price shock.

The post-welfare state (since the 1980s) In response to these difficulties, the roles of Labour and the National Party in the 1970s and 1980s appeared reversed: *Muldoon's National Party tried to overcome economic difficulties through state intervention, while *Lange's Labour government from 1984 introduced liberal market reforms as well as cuts to social welfare benefits. These transformations caused fundamental shifts in attitudes and in the nature of the country, apparent in the 1990s. New Zealand's change of attitude and commitment towards its historical link with Britain was epitomized by *Bolger's support for the abolition of the monarchy, which was still shared with Britain. Moreover, after 150 years there appeared to be a new, clear recognition of Maori rights, as both Bolger and the Queen apologized for the wrongs committed to them. Finally, convinced that New Zealand could no longer afford its comprehensive welfare state, Bolger introduced the world's first 'post-welfare' state, whereby comprehensive benefits were abolished, and state grants were given only to the very poorest sections of society. As a result, although the overall tax burden did not decline significantly, public deficit was substantially reduced, inflation almost vanished, and employment rose. At the same time the crime rate shot up, so that the role of the state, reduced in the provision of social welfare, increased in areas of crime prevention and punishment.

The 1996 elections manifested a fundamental shift, as they were the first held under a new system of mixed proportional representation. This ensured that smaller parties, which had secured up to a third of the vote, could now enter the House of Representatives. In diversifying parliamentary representation away from a two-party system, it made consensus politics and coalition building an inevitable staple of New Zealand politics. In 1996 Bolger continued to govern in a fragile coalition with the *New Zealand First Party. He was removed as National Party leader by *Shipley, who proved unsuccessful at pacifying her coalition partner or at reversing her party's slide in the opinion polls.

Contemporary politics (since 1999) Labour returned to power in 1999. Led by Helen *Clark, Labour entered a coalition with the *Alliance. The new government moved to restore some of the social benefits abandoned under the previous government. It also became more involved in the economy, through the establishment of a government people's bank as a subsidiary of New Zealand Post, and the re-nationalization of Air New Zealand following the post-*September 11 crisis in the airline industry. Clark was returned in the 2002 elections, but she continued to rely on the informal support of other left-leaning parties, notably the Greens and the United Future Party, while the National Party was badly affected by the growth of special-interest parties in New Zealand's fragmented party system. Clark was returned in 2005. Under her government, the crime rate was reduced, while the unemployment rate was the second lowest of all *OECD countries. In 2004, New Zealand acquired its own Supreme Court, whose functions had previously been exercised by the Privy Council in London. This was but one example of how New Zealand had emerged into a self-confident, distinctive and successful nation.

New Zealand First Party

A party created in 1993 by Winston Raymond Peters (b. 1941), after Peters had been expelled from the *National Party caucus in 1993. In 1996 the party gained seventeen seats and joined a coalition government with the National Party. However, it suffered from the government's unpopularity, and in 1998 it left the coalition. In 1999 it was returned with five seats. Advocating a tough line on immigration, the party surprised observers by gaining thirteen seats in the 2002 election. In 2005, it supported Helen *Clark without entering a formal coalition with the *Labour Party. In return, Peters was appointed Foreign Minister.

(⊕) SEE WEB LINKS

• The official website of New Zealand First.

Ngata, Sir Apirana Turupa (b. 3 July 1874, d. 14 July 1950). Maori politician

Born in Kawaka (Te Araroa), Ngata was educated at Te Aute college, and received a scholarship to study at Canterbury University College, graduating in political science in 1893. Having qualified as a lawyer in 1896, he was the first Maori university graduate from a New Zealand university, and one of the first New Zealanders to hold the degrees of BA and LLB. He had a great influence on the Kotahitanga movement and was one of the founders of the *Young Maori Movement, entering parliament in 1905 for the Eastern Maori electorate.

A powerful orator, he emerged as one of the outstanding Maoris of the twentieth century. He was Minister for Native Affairs (1928–34), in which post he worked closely with the Maori leader, *Te Puea Herangi. In 1931 he began to inaugurate his Maori Land Development Scheme, which greatly expanded Maori land under cultivation. He established the Maori Purposes Fund to finance school construction and was chairman of the Maori Board of Ethnological Research (1928–34). He was interested in the kinship between the Maoris and Polynesians, and as president of the Polynesian Society he published his two-volume book, *Nga Moeatea*, in 1929. In 1934 he was forced to resign from the government, after a Native Affairs Commission had found him guilty of misusing funds to help further Maori projects. He was chiefly responsible for Maori recruitment during World Wars I and II, but managed to prevent them from being conscripted.

Ngo Dinh Diem (b. 3 Jan. 1901, d. 2 Nov. 1963). President of South Vietnam 1955–63

Born in Hue into a family of mandarins (i.e. officials) in the Vietnamese imperial court, he graduated in law from the French University of Hanoi. He served as a provincial Governor (1919–32), and then became Minister of the Interior (1933). He rejected Emperor *Bao Dai's subservience to the French colonial authorities as excessive, however, and resigned in the same year. The devout Catholic withdrew from politics, but in 1945 was captured by forces of *Ho Chi Minh, who offered him a place in his government. He refused, and in 1947 founded the National Union Front instead, a non-violent, anti-Communist party, which was equally anti-French. This background made him an appealing candidate for political leadership with the USA, which took over as the leading foreign influence in Vietnam after the *Geneva Agreements.

In 1954 he was invited to become Prime Minister of South Vietnam, because of strong pressure from *Eisenhower. In October 1955, he deposed Bao Dai as President of the new Republic of (South) Vietnam, and had himself confirmed in a rigged election in 1956. Personally an austere man, his preferential treatment of Catholicism at the expense of Buddhism, and his failure to carry out a land reform, alienated many groups in Vietnamese society. He maintained order through a harsh, anti-Communist, repressive regime, with his brother head of the political police. Increasingly out of favour with the USA for his brutality, he was assassinated along with his brother, with tacit US approval. His assassination deprived South Vietnam of its last strong leader with the ability to maintain his authority, before the country slid into the *Vietnam War.

Nguyen Van Linh (b. 1 July 1915, d. 27 Apr. 1998). General Secretary of Vietnamese Communist Party 1986–92
Born Nguyen Van Cuc in Hanoi, he soon became active against the French colonial occupation, was imprisoned, and sent to the French penal colony at Con Dao Island (1930–6, 1941–5). A member of the *Indochinese Communist Party since 1936, he became its chief organizer in central and south Vietnam, first against the French, and then against the US-backed governments of *Ngo Dinh Diem and *Nguyen Van Thieu. After the end of the *Vietnam War he became head of the party in Ho Chi Minh City (Saigon), where he introduced a number of unorthodox, but relatively successful, economic policies. As party general secretary and *de facto* Vietnamese leader he introduced economic reforms while insisting upon the maintenance of the party's political monopoly.

Nguyen Van Thieu (b. 5 Apr. 1923, d. 29 Sept. 2001). President of South Vietnam 1967–75
Born in the Ninh Thuan province, of modest family origin, he joined the *Vietminh in 1945, but left after the return of the French to *Indochina in 1946. He enlisted in the military academy in Saigon and then served in the French colonial army (1949–54). From 1954 he was commander of the Vietnam National Military Academy in Saigon. He reluctantly took part in the military coup which overthrew President *Ngo Dinh Diem in 1963. He became head of state of the military government in 1965, and then President of South Vietnam from 1967 onwards. Despite massive US military and economic aid, his corrupt administration failed to win the fight against the *Vietcong and North Vietnamese forces. He struggled to continue the war after the *Paris Peace Accords of 1973 and was highly critical of the USA for what he considered desertion. As *Saigon fell in April 1975 he fled to Taiwan and then to Britain.

Nicaragua

The largest Central American country has, like its neighbours, been subject to persistent US influence throughout the twentieth century; this was exercised by co-opting the local oligarchy, the most prominent of which were the Somozas.

Early history (up to 1937) Nicaragua gained independence from Mexico in 1839 after the end of Spanish control in 1821. However, the whole country was not unified until the rule of the liberal dictator José Santos Zelaya (1893–1909). His independent policies attracted the hostility of the USA, which forced him to resign; to end the chaos which ensued, US marines occupied the country (1912–33). In the light of *Roosevelt's *Good Neighbor Policy, US forces withdrew in 1933, leaving the country under the charge of President J. B. Sacasa and the leader of the US-trained National Guard, Anastasio *Somoza Garcia. The liberal rebel leader, *Sandino, continued to oppose the new order, which he regarded as a puppet regime of the USA, but he was murdered on Somoza's orders.

The Somoza regime (1937–79) In 1937 Somoza toppled Sacasa and inaugurated a ruthless family dictatorship that lasted for 42 years, though some of the time the family installed puppet presidents to hide their real power. The Somoza dynasty was backed by the personal loyalty of the National Guard and by the USA in recognition of its rabid anti-Communism. During the dictatorship, overall economic performance improved, though the benefit of this accrued to some big plantation owners (not least the Somozas themselves) and loyal elites rather than the mass of the population, which suffered from government neglect of traditional farming. Anastasio Somoza was assassinated in 1956, and was succeeded by his oldest son, Luis. During the 1960s various guerrilla groups emerged in opposition to the regime, combining in 1961 to form the Sandinista National Liberation Front (Frente Sandinista de Liberación Nacional, FSLN). Following Luis's death in 1967, power passed to his brother, Anastasio Somoza Debayle. His regime became even more corrupt and ruthless, which offended many who had previously been willing to tolerate the dynasty for the sake of stability, including the USA under *Carter.

Sandinista rule (1979–90) In 1979 the Somoza regime collapsed and the Sandinistas took over. Initially helped by the USA as well as Cuba, they immediately proceeded to carry out land reform, vaccination programmes, and a determined drive against illiteracy. Fearing the emergence of a second Communist regime after Cuba, however, *Reagan stopped US aid to the government and gave it to the opposing **Contra** rebels instead, who were led in part by former leading officers under the Somoza regime. (To this official aid Reagan added illegal funds from the secret sale of arms to Iran, thus causing the *Iran–Contra affair.) While it was true that *human rights offences were committed in the Sandinistas' efforts to gain control over the state and society, these never approached the scale or the character of the human rights violations of the Somozas and other (US-backed) dictators (for example in neighbouring Guatemala or El Salvador).

As a result of Reagan's policies, Nicaragua became highly dependent on Cuban and Soviet aid. The civil war rendered the government's reform programmes impossible by ruining the economy, so that output declined by 8 per cent in 1988, with inflation being at 33,000 per cent. On the advice of ex-President Carter, the Sandinista President, Daniel *Ortega, accepted his surprise electoral defeat in 1990 against Violeta Barrios de *Chamorro, who headed a fragmented anti-government coalition

(Unión Nacional Opositora, UNO). This facilitated the cessation of US sanctions and the end of the civil war as part of the *Arias peace plan. Most Contras had laid down their arms by 27 June 1990, though a small band of Contra guerrillas held out until February 1994.

Democratization (since 1990) Nicaraguan politics remained inherently unstable with the continued predominance of the Sandinistas in the military and administration. In July 1995 the constitution was amended to strengthen the role of parliament. In that year the Sandino movement split into a *Marxist wing led by Ortega and a reformist breakaway party, led by Sergio Ramírez. The 1997 elections were won by Arnoldo Alemán Lacayo, whose anti-Sandinista Liberal Alliance won 42 seats against 37 seats for the Sandinistas. The government's main problem, however, was caused by the devastating effects of Hurricane Mitch in 1998, which rendered 20 per cent of the population homeless and set back Nicaragua's efforts to overcome the poverty caused by the civil war.

Contemporary politics (since 2001) The Liberal Alliance proved relatively unstable, and lost the 2001 parliamentary elections, though its candidate, Enrique Bolaños Geyer, won the 2002 presidential elections. Without a parliamentary majority, Geyer was bitterly opposed by the Sandinista leader, Ortega. Under Geyer, economic growth returned, but the mass of the population continued to live in abject poverty. In 2006, Ortega emerged victorious from the presidential elections, and he took up office in 2007. Ortega vowed to work closely with *Chávez, while co-operating with the USA in trade and other matters.

Nice, Treaty of (2000)

A follow-up treaty to *Maastricht and *Amsterdam. It extended *Qualified Majority Voting (QMV) in the *European Council in two-fifths of the articles that had required unanimity before. However, unanimity was maintained in the more important policy arenas such as immigration, social policy, and taxation. It did manage to reform some of the institutions of the European community. The size of the *European Commission was to be reduced from 2005, when each country would be able to nominate only one commissioner, up to a maximum of 27. The size of the *European Parliament was reduced and new allocations of seats made to old and potential new member states. Finally, the nature of QMV was amended to accommodate the larger countries of the EU. Just like its predecessors, the Treaty of Nice failed to resolve sufficiently some of the institutional problems posed by the expansion of the EU from fifteen to 27 member states by 2007. At German insistence the Treaty provided for a further *Intergovernmental Conference (IGC) in 2003, to consider the deliberations of the *Constitutional Convention. Given the subsequent difficulty of some member states in ratifying the Treaty establishing a *Constitution for Europe, the Treaty of Nice remained the basis for the EU's organization.

Nicholas II (b. 18 May 1868, d. 16 July 1918). Tsar of Russia 1894–1918

The son of Alexander III, he was determined to defend his autocratic rule despite the growth of an articulate, political opposition. His overambitious foreign policy led to a humiliating defeat in the *Russo-Japanese War of 1904–5, while the *Russian Revolution of 1905 forced him to concede a parliament (*Duma) and political freedoms. He withdrew many of these freedoms once his forces had gathered enough strength to quell the revolution in 1906. Despite the proven weakness of the Russian military, he entered World War I, and in 1915 even took personal control of the armies, leaving the day-to-day running of the government to his wife and her shady adviser, *Rasputin. Thus he had to accept responsibility for the latter's unpopularity and corruption, for the rapid decline of the economy, and the dreadful performance of his army. Nicholas had little alternative but to abdicate in March 1917. He was later imprisoned and in 1918 moved by the *Bolsheviks to Siberia. The fear of counter-revolutionary action during the *Civil War led to the murder of Nicholas and his family in Ekaterinburg.

Niger

A landlocked, arid republic in west Africa which was heavily reliant on uranium, which made up around 50 per cent of its export earnings.

Contemporary history (up to 2000) Niger was brought under French control between 1896 and 1900, and remained under military rule until most resistance was broken. A civilian-ruled colony was established in 1892. It became an autonomous republic within the *French

Community in 1958 and fully independent in 1960, with special arrangements with France covering finance, defence, technical development, and cultural affairs.

The one-party state that emerged after independence under the leadership of Hamani Diori became notable for its corruption, and did not survive drought and economic decline. It was toppled on 15 April 1974 in a *coup d'état*, which brought to power Seyni Kountche (b. 1931). He established authoritarian military rule and a socialist regime. Increasing resentment of the lack of economic progress forced him gradually to introduce civilian rule, which was confirmed by a referendum on a constitutional charter in 1987.

The first free parliamentary elections for twenty years took place in February 1993, and in the elections of 27 March 1993 the leader of the opposition, Mahamane Ousmane, was elected president. He was deposed in a military coup of 27 January 1996, led by Ibrahim Bara Mainassara. Mainassara became President, and was concerned to open up the army and connect it more closely to society. He was shot in 1999, and after a short interlude in which the military assumed political power, elections were held in which Mamadou Tandja obtained the Presidency. His party, the Mouvement National de la Société et Développement (MNSD, National Movement of Society and Development), became the strongest party in parliament, and proceeded to form a coalition government.

Contemporary politics (since 2000) One of the world's poorest countries, Niger had a GDP per head of $190 in 2000, with two-thirds of the population living below the poverty line. In 2002 Tandja's authority was challenged by an army mutiny demanding better conditions and pay, but order was restored after several days. Niger's economy failed to revive, owing to high government indebtedness and mismanagement. The government responded inadequately to a locust plague in 2004, which destroyed much of the crops and brought about large-scale famine. Between 2004 and 2006, international organizations fed over one million people owing to the government's inability to deal with the country's economic crisis. In 2006, the UN ranked Niger at the bottom of the world's countries in terms of 'human development', which took into account life expectancy, education, and economic performance.

Nigeria

Africa's most populous country, its history has been characterized by its ethnic and religious diversity: its 430 ethnic groups are dominated by four peoples, the mainly *Islamic Hausa and Fulbe in the north, and the predominantly Christian Yoruba and Ibo in the

south. Ethnic tension between these groups, fuelled by an unequal distribution of the country's wealth in oil, has underlined many of Nigeria's political, social and cultural tensions.

Independence (1960s) Under British rule since the 1880s, the Hausa and Fulbe were little interfered with under the principle of *indirect rule, while the Ibo came to form an educated elite in the south. Under the leadership of *Awolowo, *Azikiwe, *Balewa, and *Bello, Nigeria achieved independence on 1 October 1960, and became a federal state with a constitution based largely on the British political system. This soon became paralysed because of the country's ethnic divisions, and unrest erupted in 1966. After two successive military governments, the leadership passed to General *Gowon.

Military rule (since the 1960s) The repression during these years triggered civil war between 1967 and 1970, when the Ibo fought in vain for independence as the state of *Biafra. After this, Nigerian domestic politics were characterized by military rule and frequent coups, except for a brief period of democratization introduced by General *Obsanjano, (1978–83). This instability and unrest was created by the fact that only military rule could (and did) establish the predominance of the northern Hausa-Fulbe, while the southern tribes of the Yoruba and Ibo were not only more educated but also had the country's significant oil reserves on their lands. In 1992 General Ibrahim *Babangida introduced a system of controlled democracy, in which two parties were allowed to operate, both to be controlled by him. Nevertheless, he lost the presidential elections of 12 June 1993 to *Abiola (a Yoruba). Babangida annulled the elections and established an interim government under Adegunle Oladeinde Shonekan. Both were forced into exile by the military coup of 17 November 1993, which brought to power General *Abacha. Abacha imprisoned Abiola and instituted a harsh system of repression previously unexperienced even in Nigeria.

Economic and environmental crisis Despite Nigeria being one of the world's largest oil producers, the average annual income per head was one of the lowest in the world at $300 (1993). This was due to corruption and economic as well as political mismanagement, leading to neglect of the country's industry and agriculture. Neglect also caused an environmental disaster in the largely Ibo coastal lands. According to a 1996 report by D. Moffat and O. Linden at Stockholm University, the coastal areas were contaminated by an estimated 23 billion cubic metres of oil every year. Oil production in the area generated 35 million tons of carbon dioxide per year (1995), which made it the world's largest single contributor to *climate change. The political and economic hardship was made possible by the tolerance of the world community, which felt dependent on Nigerian oil, and the obsessively non-political and unenvironmental stance adopted by the oil companies there, of which Shell was the most important.

Contemporary politics (since 1998) Growing domestic protest, worsening economic mismanagement, increasingly blatant corruption, and international protests undermined the military regime. Following Abacha's death in 1998, an interim military government freed political prisoners, among them Obsanjano. He won the ensuing 1999 elections, but embezzlement by government, military, and public administration continued to make Nigeria one of the world's most corrupt countries. Obsanjano made some progress in reducing corruption, dismissing prominent members of the government and the ruling party (2004–5). The continuing poverty of the Yoruba and Ibo population, as well as the growing fundamentalism of the Muslim north, exacerbated the social, cultural, and economic conflicts that had characterized Nigeria for decades. Ethnic violence flared up in different parts of the country, with over 50,000 people killed between 2001 and 2004. A further source of instability came from the Niger Delta People's Volunteer Force, which sabotaged oil installations from the late 1990s, demanding a greater share of the profits for the region. In 2007, Umaru Yar'Adua was elected president in rigged elections. Obsanjano's favoured candidate, he vowed to fight corruption.

Night of the Long Knives, see SA

Nimieri, Jaafar al- (b. 1930?). President of Sudan 1971–85
He graduated from Khartoum Military College in 1952, and became a commanding officer

of the Sudanese army. He led the 1969 coup against *Azhari and became chairman of the revolutionary council as well as Prime Minister. Elected President by a plebiscite, he played a major part in establishing an end to the civil war. However, from 1977 he increasingly created a power base around *Islamic fundamentalism, and declared Islamic law to be state law in 1983. This was unacceptable to the Christian-dominated south, and triggered a resumption of the civil war. Increasingly ruthless and isolated because of the country's economic problems, he was deposed in 1985. He was forced to flee into exile, but was allowed to return in 1999.

Nimitz, Chester William (b. 23 Feb. 1885, d. 20 Feb. 1966). US admiral

Born in Feriksburg, Texas, he graduated from the US naval academy in 1905 and served with the Submarine Force of the Navy during World War I. After various surface ship commands and shore appointments, he took over command of the Pacific fleet in 1941, after *Pearl Harbor. From his headquarters there, he deployed his forces to win the Battles of *Midway and *Coral Sea, and subsequently supervised the moves in the *Pacific campaign which led to successful actions off Guadalcanal, the Gilbert Islands, the Marshalls, the Marianas, and in the *Leyte Gulf. To a large extent he was responsible for making the Pacific fleet, weakened by Pearl Harbor, the instrument of Japan's defeat, concentrating on submarine and aircraft attack. After the war he was briefly chief of US naval operations (1945-7).

Nishio Suehiro (b. 28 Mar. 1891, d. 3 Oct. 1981). Japanese politician

Without completing his high school education, Nishio spent his early life as a machinist in an ordnance plant. There he became involved in the Yûaikaigi union movement in 1919. During the 1920s, he took part in various labour disputes as a union activist. He also supported the formation of the Socialist People's Party with Matsuoka Komakichi and was elected to the Imperial Diet in 1928. He did not participate in the *Imperial Rule Assistance Association, and with his reputation largely intact he emerged after World War II to play a leading role in the Japan *Socialist Party (JSP). His considerable influence allowed him to obtain the post of Chief Cabinet Secretary in the JSP-dominated government of *Katayama Tetsu. At the height of his powers, Nishio was implicated in the Shôwa Denkô scandal and although he was ultimately cleared of all charges, the legal

proceedings surrounding this incident dragged on for a decade. Nishio, whose political philosophy stressed the predominance of the parliamentary party, was viewed with suspicion by many left-wing activists. In particular his support for a security alliance with the USA, his endorsement of the Nationalist regime in Taiwan, and his intimate links with big business, invited a series of denunciations by delegates at the 1959 JSP congress. As a result, Nishio chose to lead followers out of the JSP to form a second party which became known as the Democratic Socialist Party (DSP). He was chairman of the DSP until 1967, although he continued to play an important role as the DSP's elder statesman until his death.

Niue

A Polynesian island in the Pacific. It was annexed by New Zealand and administered as part of the Cook Islands in 1901. In 1904 it was granted a separate New Zealand resident commissioner. In 1974, a new Constitution transformed it into a self-governing Associated Territory, with New Zealand responsible for foreign affairs and defence. It is a member of the *Pacific Forum.

Nixon Doctrine (USA)

Announced by Richard *Nixon in June 1969, it asserted that the USA would disengage its troops from mainland Asia, even if this threatened domestic stability there. Nixon had been elected in 1968 on a platform which included a pledge to end the *Vietnam War in a 'peace with honor'. Part of his policy for bringing this about was the policy of 'Vietnamization'—the gradual withdrawal of US troops and the assumption of the burden of fighting in the war by troops of the Republic of South Vietnam.

Nixon, Richard Milhous (b. 9 Jan. 1913, d. 18 Apr. 1994). 37th US President 1969-74

Early career The only President ever to be forced to resign from office on threat of removal by the Senate. Born of *Quaker parents in Yorba Linda, California, he attended a Quaker school and studied law at Duke University. He served in the US navy in World War II. Nixon was elected to the House of Representatives in 1946, when he developed a highly effective if negative campaigning style and patriotic, anti-Communist rhetoric. Nixon became prominent as an anti-Communist campaigner and a leading Congressional prosecutor of *Alger Hiss. Nixon was elected to the Senate in 1950, aged 36. His slashing campaign against his liberal *Democratic opponent, Helen Gahagan Douglas (whom he nicknamed the 'Pink Lady') earned him the sobriquet 'Tricky Dicky', which he could never quite shake off.

He became *Eisenhower's running mate in 1952, but narrowly avoided removal as the vice-presidential candidate following revelations that he took large sums of private money to supplement his congressional salary. The speech in which he defended himself was noted for its innovative use of TV, then a new medium. He served as Vice-President until 1961, and worked hard at broadening his base within the Republican party to ensure more moderate support. In 1960 he lost a very close presidential race to John *Kennedy and returned to California, where he was defeated for the governorship in 1962. Declaring his retirement in a bitter speech, he moved to New York to practise law whilst continuing to travel the USA campaigning for Republican candidates and building up personal support.

Presidency Nixon re-emerged in 1968, following *Johnson's withdrawal from the race, to be elected President with a plurality of votes, against a deeply divided Democratic Party. In office, he issued a new price and incomes policy, devalued the dollar, and thus ended the *Bretton Woods system. He created the Environmental Protection Agency in 1970, and promoted *civil rights, albeit with less rigour than Johnson.

In trying to fulfil his pledge to obtain 'peace with honor', he widened the Vietnam War to force the North Vietnamese leadership into submission by saturation bombing in Cambodia and Laos. When this failed, he reluctantly agreed to end the war in 1973. He initiated a new round of *disarmament talks with the Soviet Union which led to the SALT I agreement. Similarly, he recognized the People's Republic of China and opened diplomatic relations with it. This did not mean that his anti-Communism had diminished, as he very successfully undermined the *Allende regime in Chile.

Nixon won a landslide victory in the 1972 presidential election. Revelations about his paranoid and possibly criminal behaviour consequent upon the *Watergate scandal forced him out of office. President *Ford subsequently gave him an unconditional pardon, but the Watergate scandal and his resignation had profoundly shaken the authority of government. Nixon's reputation recovered gradually during the 1980s, amidst a resurgence of Republicanism and a re-evaluation of his political achievements.

Nkomo, Joshua Mqabuko Nyongolo
(b. 17 June 1917, d. 1 July 1999). Vice-President of Zimbabwe 1990–99

Educated in South Africa where he joined the *ANC (African National Congress), he returned to Bulawayo in Southern Rhodesia and became secretary-general of the Rhodesian Railways African Employees' Association. He was president of the Rhodesian branch of the ANC from 1957 until it was banned in 1959. He then founded the National Democratic Party in 1960 and, when that was banned, the Zimbabwe African People's Union. He was detained twice, 1962–4 and 1964–74. On release he led ZAPU's guerrilla campaign from Zambia, and in 1976 joined an uneasy alliance with *Mugabe's *ZANU to form the Patriotic Front. In the 1980 elections leading up to independence, ZAPU's support remained confined to the minority Matabele people, while Mugabe's overwhelming Shona support gave him a clear majority. He became Minister of Home Affairs, but in 1982 he fell out with *Mugabe, with whom he was reconciled only in December 1987 when he accepted the post of Minister for Local Affairs and Development. He also became vice-president of ZANU-PF (Patriotic Front) into which his ZAPU had merged. As Vice President, his influence was relatively slight, but his presence was an important prop for Mugabe.

Nkrumah, Kwame Francis Nwia Kofi
(b. 21 Sept. 1909, d. 27 Apr. 1972). Prime Minister of the Gold Coast 1952–7; President of Ghana 1957–66

Born in Nkroful, he studied at Lincoln University and the University of Pennsylvania in the USA, and at the London School of Economics in the UK. In Britain, he became active in the West African Students' Union and met several Black African leaders campaigning for independence and a *pan-African movement. As a result, he was invited to return to lead the Gold Coast's first political party founded by *Danquah, the United Gold Coast Convention, in 1947. On 12 June 1949 he founded the more radical Convention People's Party (CPP), which called for passive resistance and strikes to force independence from British colonial rule. Despite his being imprisoned in 1950, the CCP won the 1951 elections to the Legislative Assembly, whereupon he was released and became Prime Minister. After the country achieved independence as Ghana, he established a one-party dictatorship, declared himself president for life in 1962, but was overthrown in 1966. As the first Black African to lead his country to independence from British colonial rule, he inspired a generation of Black African leaders. He actively encouraged other African independence movements through his visits abroad and his writings, which include *Towards Colonial Freedom* (1946), his autobiography *Ghana* (1953), and *Africa Must Unite* (1963).

NKVD (Soviet People's Commissariat for Internal Affairs)

A ministry in the USSR which included and reorganized all the security forces in 1934, including OGPU, *Cheka's successor organization. Its responsibilities included political surveillance, internal security, supervision of political trials, administration of *Gulags and other prison camps, and border security. Under *Yezhov, it was the main instrument for *Stalin's *Great Purge (1936–8), as well as for the general terror of the 1930s and 1940s. Under the leadership of *Beria, in 1946 it became part of the MVD (Ministry of Internal Affairs), which controlled all police forces in the Soviet republics. It was also linked to the MGB (Ministry of State Security), as a result of which it became active in the build-up of the police and security forces in satellite countries, as well as in the Communist purges there before Stalin's death. After Beria's demise the NKVD was placed under the *KGB.

Nobel Peace Prize

The world's most prestigious prize, awarded for the 'preservation of peace'. It goes back to the legacy of Alfred Nobel (b. 1833, d. 1896), who wanted to use his fortune, made by his invention of dynamite, for the good of humanity through the creation of a Nobel Foundation. This would use the interest accruing from his legacy to finance a prize for physics, chemistry, physiology/medicine, literature, and peace. While the first four prizes are awarded in Sweden, the Nobel Peace Prize is awarded on Nobel's birthday (10 December) in Oslo, by the King of Norway, the winner being chosen by a committee made up of five members of the Norwegian parliament.
See TABLE 16.

SEE WEB LINKS

• The official website of the Nobel Foundation.

non-alignment

A principle during the *Cold War among states anxious not to align themselves with either the USA or the USSR. Most prominent of these was India, but many countries of south-east Asia and Africa took part in the movement. Despite their best efforts to steer a middle course between the two superpowers, the impact of non-alignment was negligible owing to the economic, religious, and political disparity among its member states, which made a common stance difficult.
BANDUNG CONFERENCE

NORAD (North American Air Defense Command)

Established in September 1957 to integrate the defence systems of Canada and the USA against a possible Soviet military threat. It came to supervise a line of 50 tracking, warning, and control stations across the northern Arctic from Greenland to Alaska, as well as the Mid-Canada Line which existed 1954–65. In 1963 the first nuclear missiles were deployed amidst much controversy in Canada. In 1981 it changed its name to **North American Aerospace Defense Command (NAADC)**.

Noriega Morena, Manuel Antonio

(b. 1934). Dictator of Panama 1983–9

As leader of the army and hence effectively of Panama, he was unable to overcome the country's economic crisis and the resulting capital flight, causing an increasing foreign debt as well as a growing budget deficit. These problems were made dramatically worse by the US trade embargo enforced by the *Reagan administration in March 1988. This was imposed because, even though Noriega had frequently collaborated with the *CIA since the late 1960s, he had fallen into disfavour from the mid-1980s owing to his involvement in drugs trafficking into the USA. Refusing to step down even after his defeat at the polls, Noriega was captured on 4 January 1990, after US President *Bush had ordered his troops into Panama City. He was taken to Miami, where in 1992 he was sentenced to forty years' imprisonment.

Normandy campaign (June–Aug. 1944)

Despite the success of *D-Day (6 June 1944) during *World War II, it was not until 30 July that the Allied troops managed to cut through the German defensive lines in north-west Normandy and begin the liberation of France. Field Marshal Model, transferred from the Eastern Front to replace *Rommel after the *July Plot, was unable to stem *Patton's advance, which now swept across France, while *Montgomery moved up the English Channel. Paris was liberated within a month,

Table 16. **Winners of the Nobel Peace Prize**

Date	Winner	Country
1901	Henri Dunant (b. 1828, d. 1910)	Switzerland
	Frederic Passy (b. 1822, d. 1912)	France
1902	Elie Ducommun (b. 1833, d. 1906)	Switzerland
	Charles Albert Gobat (b. 1843, d. 1914)	Switzerland
1903	William Randal Cremer (b. 1838, d. 1908)	UK
1904	Institute for International Law	
1905	Bertha von Suttner (b. 1843, d. 1914)	Austria
1906	Theodore *Roosevelt (b. 1858, d. 1919)	USA
1907	Ernesto T. Moneta (b. 1833, d. 1918)	Italy
	Louis Renault (b. 1843, d. 1918)	France
1908	Klas P. Arnoldson (b. 1844, d. 1916)	Sweden
	Frederik Bajer (b. 1837, d. 1922)	Denmark
1909	Auguste M. France Beernaert (b. 1829, d. 1912)	Belgium
	Paul Baron D'Estournelles (b. 1852, d. 1924)	France
1910	International Permanent Secretariat for Peace, Bern	
1911	Tobias M. C. Asser (b. 1838, d. 1913)	Netherlands
	Alfred Hermann Fried (b. 1864, d. 1921)	Austria
1912	Elihu Root (b. 1845, d. 1937)	USA
1913	Henri La Fontaine (b. 1854, d. 1943)	Belgium
1914	—	
1915	—	
1916	—	
1917	International *Red Cross Committee	
1918	—	
1919	Woodrow *Wilson (b. 1856, d. 1924)	USA
1920	Leon Victor Bourgeois (b. 1851, d. 1925)	France
1921	Hjalmar Branting (b. 1860, d. 1925)	Sweden
	Christian Lange (b. 1869, d. 1938)	Norway
1922	Fridtjof *Nansen (b. 1861, d. 1930)	Norway
1923	—	
1924	—	
1925	Joseph Austen *Chamberlain (b. 1863, d. 1937)	UK
	Charles Gates *Dawes (b. 1865, d. 1951)	USA
1926	Aristide *Briand (b. 1862, d. 1932)	France
	Gustav *Stresemann (b. 1878, d. 1929)	Germany
1927	Ferdinand Buisson (b. 1841, d. 1932)	France
	Ludwig Quidde (b. 1858, d. 1941)	Germany
1928	—	
1929	Frank Billings *Kellogg (b. 1856, d. 1937)	USA
1930	Nathan Soederblom (b. 1866, d. 1931)	Sweden
1931	Jane *Addams (b. 1860, d. 1935)	USA
	Nicholas Murray Butler (b. 1862, d. 1947)	USA
1932	—	
1933	Norman Angell (b. 1874, d. 1967)	UK
1934	Arthur Henderson (b. 1863, d. 1935)	UK
1935	Carl von Ossietzky (b. 1889, d. 1938)	Germany
1936	Carlos Saavedra Lamas (b. 1878, d. 1959)	Argentina
1937	Edgar Algernon R. Cecil of Chelwood (b. 1864, d. 1958)	UK
1938	International Nansen Bureau for Refugees	
1939	—	

Table 16 (*Cont.*)

Date	Winner	Country
1940	—	
1941	—	
1942	—	
1943	—	
1944	International *Red Cross Committee	
1945	Cordell *Hull (b. 1871, d. 1955)	USA
1946	Emily G. Balch (b. 1867, d. 1961)	USA
	John R. Mott (b. 1865, d. 1955)	USA
1947	Society of Friends (*Quakers)	
1948	—	
1949	John Boyd Orr (b. 1880, d. 1971)	UK
1950	Ralph *Bunche (b. 1904, d. 1971)	USA
1951	Leon Jouhaux (b. 1879, d. 1954)	France
1952	Albert Schweitzer (b. 1875, d. 1965)	France
1953	George C. *Marshall (b. 1880, d. 1959)	USA
1954	*UN High Commission for Refugees	
1955		
1956	—	
1957	Lester Bowles *Pearson (b. 1897, d. 1972)	Canada
1958	Dominique Georges Pire (b. 1910, d. 1969)	Belgium
1959	Philip J. Noel-Baker (b. 1889, d. 1982)	UK
1960	Albert John *Luthuli (b. 1899, d. 1967)	South Africa
1961	Dag *Hammarskjöld (b. 1905, d. 1961)	Sweden
1962	Linus Pauling (b. 1901, d. 1994)	USA
1963	International *Red Cross Committee	
	League of Red Cross Organizations	
1964	Martin Luther *King (b. 1929, d. 1968)	USA
1965	UNICEF	
1966	—	
1967	—	
1968	René *Cassin (b. 1887, d. 1976)	France
1969	*International Labour Organization (ILO)	
1970	Norman Ernest Borlaug (b. 1914)	USA
1971	Willy *Brandt (b. 1913, d. 1992)	Germany
1972	—	
1973	Henry Alfred *Kissinger (b. 1923)	USA
	*Le Duc Tho (b. 1910, d. 1990)	Vietnam
1974	Sean MacBride (b. 1904, d. 1988)	Ireland
	*Satô Eisaku (b. 1901, d. 1975)	Japan
1975	Andrey Sakharov (b. 1921, d. 1989)	USSR
1976	Mairead Corrigan (b. 1944)	UK
	Betty Williams (b. 1943) (Peace People)	UK
1977	*Amnesty International	
1978	Menachem *Begin (b. 1913, d. 1992)	Israel
	Mohammad Anwar al-*Sadat (b. 1918, d. 1981)	Egypt
1979	Mother Teresa (b. 1910)	India
1980	Adolfo Peréz Esquivel (b. 1931)	Argentina
1981	*UN High Commission for Refugees	1982
	Alfonso Garcia Robles (b. 1911, d. 1991)	Mexico
	Alva Myrdal (b. 1902, d. 1986)	Sweden
1983	Lech *Walesa (b. 1943)	Poland
1984	Desmond *Tutu (b. *1931)	South Africa

Table 16 (*Cont.*)

Date	Winner	Country
1985	International Doctors for the Prevention of Nuclear War	
1986	Elie Wiesel (b. 1928)	USA
1987	Oscar *Arias Sánchez (b. 1941)	Costa Rica
1988	*UN Peacekeeping Forces	
1989	*Dalai Lama (b. 1935)	Tibet
1990	Mikhail *Gorbachev (b. 1931)	USSR
1991	*Aung San Suu Kyi (b. 1945)	Myanmar
1992	Rigoberta Menchu (b. 1959)	Guatemala
1993	Frederik Willem de *Klerk (b. 1936)	South Africa
	Nelson *Mandela (b. 1918)	South Africa
1994	Yitzhak *Rabin (b. 1922, d. 1996)	Israel
	Shimon *Peres (b. 1923)	Israel
	Yasir *Arafat (b. 1929)	Palestine
1995	Joseph Rotblat (b. 1909)	UK
	Pugwash Conferences on Science and World Affairs	Canada
1996	Carlos Felipe Ximénes Belo	East Timor
	José Ramos Horta	East Timor
1997	International Campaign for the Banning of Landmines	USA
	Jody Williams	USA
1998	John *Hume	Northern Ireland
	David *Trimble	Northern Ireland
1999	Médecins Sans Frontières	Belgium
2000	*Kim Dae-Jong	South Korea
2001	Kofi *Annan and *United Nations Organization	Ghana
2002	Jimmy *Carter	USA
2003	Shirin Ebadi	Iran
2004	Wangari Maathai	Kenya
2005	*International Atomic Energy Agency	UN
	Mohamed el-Baradei	Egypt
2006	Grameen Bank	Bangladesh
	Mohammad *Yunus	Bangladesh

and the *Free French forces under de *Gaulle were given the honour of entering Paris first, on 26 August. While southern France was liberated after the 'Dragoon' landings on 15 August 1944, the Allied armies swept across northern and eastern France, reaching Brussels on 3 September, by which time the Allies had suffered some 224,000 casualties.

NORTH-WEST EUROPE CAMPAIGN

North African campaigns (June 1940– May 1943)

Origins (1940–41) In June 1940, Italy entered *World War II on the side of *Nazi Germany, mainly to fulfill *Mussolini's dream of establishing Italy's predominance around the Mediterranean, regarded as the mare nostrum ('Our Sea'). In September 1940, Italian troops crossed from the Italian colony of Libya to Egypt, which was defended by some 36,000 *Commonwealth troops under *Wavell. The Italians advanced to Sidi Barrani, but were repelled in December, when Wavell counter-attacked with a reinforced army of tanks. He reclaimed Sidi Barrani, capturing some 120,000 prisoners, and went on to take *Tobruk, Benghazi, and all of Cyrenaica. Meanwhile, by January 1941, all of Italian East Africa had surrendered to British troops. As well as revealing the ineffectiveness of the Italian army, it also opened the way for Allied supplies and reinforcements to reach the Army of the Nile.

German entry (1941–43) In response to the Italians' desperate position, the Germans formed an Afrika Korps under *Rommel, which arrived in March 1941. It was at first relatively ineffective because of *Hitler's refusal to send the necessary reinforcements and supplies, owing to his focus on the *Barbarossa campaign. In January 1942, Rommel was finally in a position to advance, leading his forces towards Egypt. He was unable to reach Alexandria in the face of British resistance at *El Alamein. Rommel was also hindered by persistent difficulties in ensuring that vital supplies were transported across great distances in the desert.

In October, the reinforced 8th Army of 230,000 men and 1,230 tanks, now under *Montgomery, launched its attack. Vastly inferior in number, Rommel's troops were forced to withdraw towards Tunisia. Rommel's position was made virtually hopeless by the success of 'Operation Torch', an amphibious landing on 8 November 1942 of US and British troops under *Eisenhower near Casablanca on the Atlantic, and Oran and Algiers in the Mediterranean. The *Vichy French troops were defeated within days, so that Rommel's *Axis forces were squeezed by advancing Allies to the east and west. Rommel was recalled in March 1943, and elite units of the Afrika Korps were evacuated from Tunis to Sicily. North Africa was liberated from the Germans and Italians with the fall of Tunis on 7 May 1943, when some 250,000 prisoners were taken.

North American Aerospace Defense Command (NAADC), see NORAD

North American Free Trade Association, see NAFTA

North Atlantic Treaty Organization, see NATO

North, Oliver, see IRAN–CONTRA AFFAIR

Northern Alliance (Afghanistan)
A loose alliance of primarily Pashtun Islamic groups which took control of Kabul in 1992. It disintegrated in 1993, but the alliance was reformed in 1996 as its leaders retreated from the *Taliban offensive. It controlled less than 10 per cent of Afghan territory between 1999 and 2001. It received a further blow in early September when its leader, Ahmed Shah Masood, was killed. A few days later, the *September 11 attacks changed the position of the Northern Alliance. As the principal opposition army against the *Taliban in the *War on Terrorism, it became the principal ally of the USA. After weeks of sustained bombing of Taliban positions by US missiles and bombs, Taliban resistance collapsed, and on 13 November the Northern Alliance captured the Afghan capital, Kabul. Under US

pressure, the Northern Alliance agreed on a *UN-brokered deal, which on 5 December 2001 established Hamid Karzai as interim leader of Afghanistan. Nevertheless, Northern Alliance regional leaders remained powerful in the north of the country, outside the capital.

Northern Expedition (1926–8)
A military campaign in which *Chiang Kai-shek led his *National Revolutionary Army out of its base in Guangzhou (Canton) in an attempt to unify China, to destroy the power of the many local *warlords, and bring the country under unitary (i.e. his own) control. He set off with a *National Revolutionary Army of around 150,000 men, composed of loyal officers trained at his *Whampoa Military Academy, as well as more loosely organized units under warlords who recognized Chiang's authority. Initially, Chiang was supported also by Communist forces, as well as military and technical assistance from the Soviet Union. The campaign proved a major success, in that by 1927 Shanghai, the Yangatze Valley, and Nanjing (Nanking) had been taken, which enabled Chiang to set up a *National Government at Nanjing. However, this had been achieved through a split with the Chinese *Communist Party (CCP), from whom the *Guomindang had wrested control over Shanghai in a massacre. This fundamentally weakened Chiang, as his need to overcome the CCP deflected from his original intention to take control over the whole of China. Moreover, Chiang's military successes, which had been achieved with an army inflated to around 600,000 soldiers by early 1928, had been achieved with the compliance of many local warlords, many of whom supplied men and material for his campaign. In return, their allegiance to Chiang was often minimal. Despite Chiang's conquest of Beijing, therefore, his actual control over many areas was relatively weak.

Northern Ireland
The part of Ireland which remained in the UK following the partition under the Government of Ireland Act (1920). It is composed of the six north-eastern counties of Ireland: Antrim, Armagh, Down, Fermanagh, Londonderry, and Tyrone. It is often referred to as Ulster, although strictly speaking the historic province of Ulster also includes three other counties which are now in the Republic of Ireland. The province was formed as a result of pressure from Unionists led by Edward *Carson, who did not wish to be part of a united Ireland independent from the UK.

It was governed by a Prime Minister heading a parliament at *Stormont in which the predominantly Protestant population had a built-in majority. The Protestants controlled most of the jobs and housing, and discriminated against the Catholic minority (about one-third of the population), fearing that Catholics wished to undermine Northern Ireland's position as part of the UK.

Sectarian violence (1960s–80s) Moderate reforms were attempted by Prime Minister *O'Neill in the 1960s, but in 1968 violence erupted after a series of demonstrations calling for equal civil rights for all. Subsequently, paramilitary organizations, such as the Provisional *Irish Republican Army (IRA), the *Ulster Defence Association (UDA), and the *Ulster Volunteer Force (UVF), clashed. By the end of 1993, there had been 3,112 deaths as a result of political violence. The largest group to suffer was the civilian population: many of the 2,174 deaths in this group included suspected terrorists. The British army lost 443 personnel; it had been sent to Northern Ireland in 1969, initially to protect Catholics against Loyalist violence, but its presence became resented by the minority and it was thus a target for the IRA. One of the events which provoked hostility was **Bloody Sunday** (30 January 1972), when troops fired on a Catholic demonstration in Londonderry, killing several civilians. In March 1972, when the *Stormont government proved incapable of maintaining order, the British government suspended the Northern Irish Constitution, dissolved Stormont, and imposed direct rule from London.

Throughout the 1970s and early 1980s, the British government sought to establish assemblies in which the different groups in Northern Ireland would share power. However, one or more groups have always opposed each attempt, most notably in May 1974, when a strike by the Loyalist Ulster Workers' Council brought down the Northern Ireland Assembly. In the 1980s the British government sought closer cooperation in resolving the problem with the government of the Irish Republic. In 1985 this resulted in the Anglo-Irish Accord (Hillsborough Agreement), which gave the Republic a consultative role in Northern Ireland. This angered Unionists, but reassured the nationalist *Social Democratic and Labour Party (SDLP).

Towards peace (from 1993) On 15 December 1993 the British Prime Minister, John *Major, and the Irish Taoiseach, Albert *Reynolds, made the *Downing Street Declaration. This proclaimed the two governments' intention to promote reconciliation 'leading to a new political framework founded on consent'. They reaffirmed their opposition to political violence, and committed themselves to bringing all democratic groups together in talks. In response, on 31 August 1994 the IRA announced a 'complete cessation of military operations'. This was followed on 13 October 1994 by a loyalist ceasefire, and from then many British troops were withdrawn from Northern Ireland. The British government and the Unionists then made the surrender of all arms by paramilitary groups a precondition of all-party talks. This was rejected by *Adams.

On 9 February 1996, the IRA ceasefire was broken when it bombed Canary Wharf in the London Docklands. *Sinn Féin refused to condemn the incident, whereupon the British and Irish governments broke off direct negotiations. Nevertheless, elections for representatives at all-party negotiations were held on 30 May 1996. They signalled growing support for the more extremist parties, as the *Democratic Unionist Party gained 18.8 per cent and Sinn Féin 15.47 per cent. By contrast, the performance of the more moderate *Ulster Unionist Party (24.17 per cent) and the SDLP (21.4 per cent) was relatively disappointing.

It was not until the IRA finally declared a ceasefire on 9 Sept. 1997 that negotiations could resume, headed by *Clinton's envoy, George Mitchell. After an ultimatum presented by the British and Irish governments, the parties consented to the *Good Friday Agreement in 1998. Elections to the new Northern Irish Assembly were won by the Ulster Unionist Party with 28 seats, followed by the moderate Catholic SDLP with 24. The UUP's leader, David *Trimble, became First Minister, with the SDLP's Seamus Mallon as his deputy. The government was based on a broad coalition of Protestant and Catholic parties, including Sinn Féin but excluding the Democratic Unionists. While the administration of day-to-day matters proved surprisingly smooth, the issue of decommissioning of weapons held by the IRA and the reform of the Royal Ulster Constabulary continued to be extremely contentious. As the IRA refused to honour its original promise to decommission its arms within two years of the Good Friday Agreement, David Trimble resigned in summer 2001. This led to the suspension of the Northern Ireland Assembly. David Trimble briefly returned as First Minister, but he resigned again in October 2002 over the slow progress of Sinn Féin's decommissioning of weapons. Self-rule was suspended once more.

Contemporary politics (since 2003)

Elections on 26 November 2003 produced a further stalemate: the largest party was now Ian *Paisley's DUP, which refused any contact with the largest Catholic party, Sinn Féin. Paisley continued his resistance to working with Sinn Féin even after the IRA had destroyed all its weapons in 2005. In response to this move, the British army halved the number of remaining soldiers stationed in the province. In 2006, the political stalemate was ended through the *St Andrews Agreement, which provided for elections in 2007. These were won by the DUP and Sinn Féin, which entered a historic coalition under the unlikely leadership of Ian Paisley as First Minister.

Northern Mariana Islands, Commonwealth of, see MICRONESIA

Northern Territories

The Japanese term for the islands of Kunashiri, Etorofu, Shikotan, and Habomai to the north of Japan, which have been at the centre of a territorial dispute between Japan and the Soviet Union since 1945, when they were occupied by the USSR. Since that time the Soviet and Russian governments have argued that Japan's acceptance of the terms of the 1951 *San Francisco peace agreement (to which the USSR was not a signatory) settled the issue. Under the treaty, the Kuril Islands were defined as Soviet territory. Japan has since argued, with the backing of the USA, that the Territories are not part of the Kuril chain. The stakes remain high in this dispute, since the area occupied by these islands has rights to many natural resources, including some of the world's richest fishing grounds. While under *Putin Russia was prepared to enter into negotiations, no progress has been made from a Japanese point of view.

Northern Territory (Australia)

A part of South Australia until 1911, when its population was just over 3,000, it was transferred to the federal government and became the responsibility of the Ministry for External Affairs. A legislative council was established in 1947, which in 1974 became an elected body of nineteen members. Its status was redefined in 1978, when it received internal self-government headed by an administrator and a chief minister, while remaining dependent on the federal government for most of its income. Since 1976, around one-third of its area has been given as reserves to its numerically significant population of *Aborigines and Torres Straits Islanders.

LAND CLAIMS (AUSTRALIA)

North-West Europe campaign (Sept. 1944 – May 1945)

Following the *Normandy campaign, in *World War II, *Montgomery's forces captured Antwerp on 4 September and crossed the Albert Canal, though his controversial attempt to seize the lower Rhine by dropping the 1st Airborne Division at Arnhem ended in failure. Meanwhile, the US 1st Army captured Namur, and was the first to reach German soil, taking the city of Aachen on 21 October 1944. The US 3rd Army moved east and reached the Moselle. However, the Germans consolidated their forces and established strong defensive lines along the Rhine, from which they embarked on their *Ardennes offensive. Once that was defeated, Montgomery's forces pushed forward to the Rhine. In March, the Rhine was finally crossed at the town of Wesel, which had been completely flattened by air attacks. In the south, French forces moved up the upper Rhine towards Lake Constance. The US 7th Army pushed east towards Munich and the 3rd Army crossed the Rhine at Frankfurt, and swept through central Germany into Bohemia. On 11 April Montgomery reached the River Elbe. Following the capture of Berlin by the *Red Army and the suicide of *Hitler, Montgomery received the surrender of the German forces in north-west Europe on Lüneburg Heath on 4 May. Four days later, VE day, the war in Europe was declared at an end.

Norway

A northern European country which, even though it is not a member of the EU, has been distinguished by a disproportionate engagement in international affairs, most notably through international organizations like the *League of Nations and the UN.

Nationhood Despite centuries of foreign rule by Denmark and Sweden, Norway remained distinct from its Scandinavian neighbours, not least through its social, cultural, and religious diversity. Partly because of remote, foreign rule, and also because of its mountainous geography which made communication between its cut-off regions and valleys difficult, Norway had become relatively fragmented by the beginning of the twentieth century: linguistically, between Bokmaal (formerly referred to as Riksmal), the language formerly spoken and still written in the towns, and Nynorsk (Landsmal); religiously, between pietism in the north and west and other variants of Protestantism elsewhere; socially, as urban communities experienced some degrees of urbanization and social change, which their more isolated rural communities were spared. Politically, the country developed with close reference to Sweden. During its imposed union with Sweden (1814–1905), politics developed inversely from Sweden, enabling Norwegians to articulate their difference from their dominant neighbour. In contradistinction to Sweden, Norway became extremely progressive, adopting a constitution in 1814, establishing parliamentary rule in 1884, and introducing universal male suffrage in 1898 (extended to women in 1913). In 1905 it gained independence, with Prince Charles of Denmark elected King as *Haakon VII on 18 November 1905.

Social consensus (1905–40) Despite the differences within Norwegian society, at first politics remained stable, thanks to a 1906 electoral reform which allowed the Liberals to take 65 per cent of the parliamentary seats with 33 per cent of the popular vote. During World War I, together with its Scandinavian neighbours it remained neutral. After World War I, even the most arbitrary electoral boundaries could not guarantee a clear majority for any party. Encouraged by the economic difficulties of the 1920s, the party system began to fragment as political groups sought to represent the particular interests of their constituencies. The divisions within society came to the fore on the controversial issue of temperance, debates over which led to two referendums, three general elections, and four governments (1920–5). In this period the Labour Party became more radical, while a Communist Party was established in 1923.

It was only in the wake of the Great *Depression that a social, economic, and political consensus was found in 1935 by the Social Democrats, in imitation of their peers in Sweden (*Social Democratic Labour Party, Sweden). This involved an agreement between agricultural and urban workers, whereby the former would benefit from debt restructuring for farmers, rural tax relief, and agricultural import tariffs, while the latter would gain social welfare benefits and public works. Urban workers accepted higher food prices in return for benefits, which would be paid for through high taxation. The money in circulation shot up by over 25 per cent in 1936 alone, while subsidies in agriculture

increased fourfold, 1930–8. These policies were interrupted by World War II, in which Norway was invaded by Germany, partly for strategic reasons, and partly for its mineral deposits. The King and his government fled to London, and the country was administered with the help of *Quisling, who in reality was never more than a German pawn.

Welfare state expansion (1945–1990s) After the war, the Social Democratic consensus was resumed under Einar Gerhardsen, who dominated Norwegian politics until the 1960s (Prime Minister 1945–51, 1955–65). Social security was improved, *trade unions became an important pillar of the economic order, and agriculture remained heavily subsidized. In foreign policy, the government jettisoned its traditional commitment to neutrality and joined *NATO in 1949. It joined *EFTA in 1960, but despite its reluctance to join a more closely knit union, internal debates soon began about membership of the much stronger EEC (*European integration). In 1963 it failed in its bid for EEC membership, while in 1972 the successfully negotiated agreement for membership was voted down in a referendum. Social Democratic domination led to Labour governments, 1971–2 and 1973–81. During this period, conservative opposition became more united. After the Labour Party failed to overcome the economic recession induced by the 1979 *oil price shock, the conservative parties dominated government from 1981 to 1986. Their attempts to reduce government spending, which entailed a challenge to important aspects of the welfare state, returned the Labour Party under *Brundtland to its traditional dominance.

Brundtland also undertook necessary cuts in budget expenditure and social welfare, yet she reinforced other trends of social democracy. In particular, she took up the country's traditional commitment to international affairs going back to *Nansen, and Trygve *Lie. The Norwegian government continued to be one of the world's largest per capita donors in aid to less developed countries. Brundtland herself became a prominent world figure on women's rights, the environment, and the division of affluence between the developed and developing countries (north–south conflict).

Brundtland failed in a second attempt to persuade Norwegians to enter the European Community, which was rejected in another referendum in 1994. The main reason for this was the country's economic heterogeneity, particularly the coexistence of a large, wealthy oil-producing sector with a large agricultural and fisheries sector. The predominance of the former enabled the continuation of the social welfare state and effective subsidizing of the agricultural sector at a time when this was no longer possible even in Sweden. As a result, the majority of Norwegians preferred to hang on to their model of large-scale state intervention, which would have been under threat from the *Common Agricultural Policy of the European Union.

Contemporary politics (since 1997) In 1997, elections resulted in a defeat for the Labour Party, although they remained the country's largest party. The new Prime Minister, the conservative Kjell-Magne Bondevik, embarked on careful market-oriented reforms without fundamentally challenging Norway's economic and social model. His minority government relied on the support of the right-wing populist Progressive Party, led by Carl Hagen. The elections had manifested a deep popular unease among some sections of society against Norway's traditionally tolerant stance towards immigration.

Bondevik resigned in 2000 over disputes on environmental policies. Despite a continuing slide in the popularity of the Labour Party, confirmed in the local elections of that year, Jens Stoltenberg of Labour proceeded to form a new minority government. Bondevik returned to form another minority government in 2001, but in 2005 Stoltenberg was able to reverse Labour's decline and form a majority coalition with the Green Party. Stoltenberg reversed some of the tax reforms of his predecessor while maintaining the policy of putting oil revenue into a protected fund for the benefit of future generations.

Novotny, Antonín (b. 10 Dec. 1904, d. 28 Jan. 1975). First Secretary of the Communist Party of Czechoslovakia 1953–68
Born in Letnany (near Prague), he was trained as a locksmith and worked in an arms factory near Prague. In 1921 he joined the Communist Party and worked for it throughout the interwar years. As a result of his political activities, he was incarcerated in the Mauthausen *concentration camp (1941–5). After the war, he rose quickly within the ranks of the Communist Party owing to his friendship with *Gottwald, whom he succeeded as First Secretary, and de facto leader of the country. He also became State President in 1957. A hardline *Stalinist throughout his life, he was completely out of sympathy with *Khrushchev's reversals of Stalinist repression. Instead, he refused to condemn the repressive Communist policies during the late 1940s and early 1950s, which culminated in the *Slánski trial, and for

which he was partly responsible. His adherence to *Comecon policies of concentrating on heavy industry led to a severe economic recession (1961–3) and to student unrest. His complete ignorance of Slovakian concerns and distinctiveness cost him the support of the Slovakian Communist Party, which conspired to replace him with its leader, *Dubček, in early 1968.

NOW (National Organization for Women), see WOMEN'S MOVEMENT

NSDAP, see NAZI PARTY

Nu Thakin U (b. 25 May 1907, d. 14 Feb 1995). Prime Minister of Burma 1948–56, 1956–8, 1960–2
Born in Wakema, he studied at Rangoon University, where he was leader of the Rangoon University Students' Union (1935–6). A member of the nationalist Do Bama Asi Ayon, he was interned by the British in 1940. During the country's Japanese occupation (1942–5), together with *Aung San he joined the Japanese puppet regime under Ba Maw, as Minister of Foreign Affairs. He became vice-president of the Anti-Fascist People's Freedom League (AFPFL), and in July 1947, following Aung San's assassination, became president of the AFPFL and chief negotiator of the country's transition to independence. As such he became Burma's first Prime Minister.

During his years in office Nu Thakin U sought to build a neutral state. He also sought to provide a traditional, integrationist base for the heterogeneous state by elevating *Buddhism as state religion. This increased hostility from the non-Buddhist ethnic groups, particularly the Christian Karens. The existence of Communist guerrillas increased his reliance on the army even further, forcing him to ask the army leader, *Ne Win, to form a caretaker government in 1958. He was thus unable to resist the army coup of 1962, when he was imprisoned. Released in 1969, he organized armed resistance from Thailand, and retired in 1973. He returned to Burma following an amnesty in 1980. In 1988, he re-emerged on *Aung San Suu Kyi's side as the leader of the pro-democratic opposition movement.
MYANMAR

nuclear bomb
The first and only nuclear bomb to have been used in warfare was the **atomic bomb**, which was developed in the *Manhattan Project, and exploded over *Hiroshima and *Nagasaki on 6 and 9 August 1945 respectively. It worked through fission of

highly enriched uranium, though since then plutonium has also been used. It was the first weapon of mass destruction. Through their explosive power and heat they killed 150,000 people, while even more suffered from radiation subsequently. Immediately, the atomic bomb became a symbol, if not a fact, of superpower status, as the Soviet Union developed its bomb by 1949, the UK by 1952, France by 1960, and China by 1962. Since then, India and Pakistan, Israel, and North Korea have also achieved nuclear capability.

An even more powerful nuclear weapon was developed in the **hydrogen bomb**, based on destruction through nuclear fusion. It was acquired by the USA in 1952, the USSR in 1953, the UK (1957), China (1967), and France (1968). Finally, an even more potent weapon was created in the enhanced hydrogen bomb, developed by the USA in 1977, which used a beryl coating to vastly expand its radioactive power.

The nuclear bomb in its various forms shaped politics throughout the *Cold War era (1948–91). As the USA and USSR especially developed the ability to destroy the earth several times over, an all-out war became too costly to contemplate. Both countries came close to a nuclear war in the *Cuban missile crisis, but thereafter promoted nuclear *disarmament. The nuclear bomb shaped the political and social culture of postwar generations, articulated by organizations like *CND and Pugwash, as well as individuals like *Einstein and *Russell, as nuclear weapons became the epitome of the dangers of scientific research in particular, and 'modernity' in general.

nuclear missile defence, see SDI

Nuclear Non-Proliferation Treaty
(1 July 1968), see DISARMAMENT

nuclear tests (UK), see WOOMERA ROCKET RANGE

nuclear tests (USA), see MICRONESIA

Nujoma, Samuel ('Sam') Daniel (b. 12 Mar. 1929). President of Namibia 1990–2004
Born in Ongandjera of the most populous people of Namibia, the Ovambo. An early opponent of *apartheid and South African rule, he founded the socialist **South-West African People's Organization (SWAPO)** in 1959, which was carried largely by Ovambo support. Operating from Zambia and Angola (since 1975), its support from the Angolan government and Cuban troops guaranteed its survival against the South African army,

which at times penetrated deep into Angolan territory. Following a successful Cuban offensive against South African troops in early 1988, P. W. *Botha decided that South Africa could never win the guerrilla war, and accepted Namibian independence. In the parliamentary elections of 7–11 November 1989, SWAPO gained 57 per cent of the vote. Nujoma became President on Independence Day, 21 March 1990. In the presidential and parliamentary elections of 7–8 December 1994, he was confirmed in office with 72.7 per cent, which ensured a two-thirds majority for SWAPO, enabling it to change the Constitution. In the 1999 elections SWAPO even increased its majority, to 55 out of 72 seats. Nujoma was concerned to withstand pressure to expropriate white farmers, but struggled to maintain national unity as he was faced with public discontent in the outlying Caprivi region. In 2005, he made way for his successor, Hifik epunye Pohamba, also from SWAPO.

Nunavut
After years of negotiations to settle *Inuit *land claims, the Canadian government agreed in 1992 to transfer an area in the Northwest Territories called Nunavut ('Our Land') to the *native peoples living in the territories. It was to extend over an area of 2.2 million km^2 (850,000 sq. miles), with 350,000 km^2 (135,000 sq. miles) being directly transferred as their property. For the negation of further land claims, they were given a compensation of $580 million. The deal was confirmed by a referendum of the *native peoples in the Northwest Territories, with 8,334 in favour and 7,020 against the proposal. Nunavut received internal autonomy in 1999, though because of the difficulty of attracting business investment this far north, it continued to rely on federal funding. In 2006, talks began on transferring provincial powers to Nunavut, which would finally resolve all land claims in the area.

(((⊕))) SEE WEB LINKS

• The official website of the Nunavut government.

Nuremberg Laws (15 Sept. 1935)
Although Jews had been discriminated against from the outset of the *Third Reich in Germany, the laws which were announced at the annual Nuremberg mass rally of the *Nazi Party actually stripped them of their citizenship and severely limited their political and economic rights. The Laws were in fact proclaimed in a haste, and it took months for the ministerial

bureaucracies to work out how 'Jewishness' was to be defined in detail. As the Laws were designed to prevent mixed-'race' offspring, Jews were forbidden to marry Germans or people from similar extraction. As an insult with its implications of immorality, Jews were barred from employing women under the age of 45 in their households.

Nuremberg Trials (Germany)

Proceedings against some of the leading figures of the *Nazi regime held before a military tribunal composed of American, British, French, and Russian judges in the town where the annual mass rallies of the *Nazi Party had been held 1933–8. The four charges were conspiracy against peace, crimes against peace, violation of the law and customs of war, and crimes against humanity. In the first, most famous trial (20 November 1945–1 October 1946), twelve were sentenced to death, among them *Ribbentrop, *Keitel, *Jodl, *Streicher, *Bormann (in absentia), and *Göring (who committed suicide before the execution). Three were acquitted, while seven (including *Speer, *Hess, *Dönitz, and von *Schirach) received long prison sentences. Also accused were the Nazi organizations (the *SS, the Security Service, and the *Gestapo), which were declared criminal.

The main trial was followed up by twelve further trials of 177 people altogether, of whom twenty-four were sentenced to death, though only half of those executions were carried out. By 1966, all those convicted to a prison sentence had been released, with the notable exception of Hess. The trials raised substantial legal objections, as the charges, such as 'crimes against peace', were ill-defined. The trials set an important precedent for international law, not least by establishing the principle that individuals were not allowed to commit universal crimes against humanity even if such crimes were lawful in their states.

The trial and the interrogations conducted in its run-up revealed a singular unwillingness on the part of all the accused (with the notable exception of *Göring) to accept responsibility for their crimes. The trial revealed many details about Nazi atrocities, but its effect on the population was ambiguous. It allowed many Germans to project their culpability onto the accused. Once these had been convicted, it strengthened the popular mood to let bygones be bygones, and consider, that the necessary retribution had been done, so allowing the 'zero hour' of German history to commence.

TRUTH AND RECONCILIATION COMMITTEE

Nyerere, Julius Kambarage (b. Mar. 1922, d. 14 Oct. 1999). Prime Minister of Tanganyika 1961; President of Tanganyika and later Tanzania 1962–85

Early career Born in Butiama (Musoma) as the son of a chief of the Zanaki tribe, he became a teacher and in 1949 was the first African from Tanganyika to study in Britain, when he went to Edinburgh University. He returned to continue teaching, but in 1954 his political career took off when he became a member of the legislative council. In that year, he also became president of the TANU (Tanganyikan African National Union). Despite constant harassment by the British colonial authorities, he became his country's leading advocate of independence. He became the colony's Chief Minister in 1960, and Prime Minister upon the attainment of full self-government.

Presidency Following independence in 1962 Nyerere established a one-party state, in order to internalize possible dissent or tension within the country's ethnically heterogeneous population. In contrast to many African leaders, he had a very clear understanding that Western models of *Communism or *capitalism were not easily applicable to Africa, and that they had to be adapted to the local context. This was the origin of his *Arusha declaration, in which he adapted *socialism to focus on the ideal of the *Ujamaa. Ultimately Tanzania was unable to isolate itself from the capitalist-dominated world market. He accepted responsibility for the failure of his economic policies, and resigned in 1985 in favour of Ali Hassan Mwinyi (b. 1925). He remained an influential figure, able to unite the different groups of the country, regardless of region, ethnic origins, or religion. He died of leukaemia.

O

OAS (Organization of American States)

An international body consisting of most American and Caribbean states, founded on 30 April 1948 (with effect from 13 December 1951) to promote cooperation and consultation between its members. Cuba's membership was suspended in 1962. Canada did not join, but obtained observer status in 1972. The OAS suffered from ideological, structural, and economic differences between its diverse members. Thus, during the 1980s the USA opposed Argentina during the *Falklands War, and won little acclaim from other members for its invasion of Grenada and Panama. Through smaller-scale trade agreements such as *Mercosur and the ANDEAN pact, a number of Latin American members have striven to increase economic and political cooperation amongst themselves, in order to reduce the economic and political dominance of the USA. At the same time, from 1995 the OAS has striven to support the creation of a Free Trade Area of the Americas as an extension of *NAFTA. This aim, however, was severely challenged by other aims such as the common fight on drugs and international money laundering, which exposed the economies of the main drug-producing states, notably Colombia. Given the difficulty of establishing free trade across the entire continent, the USA came to prefer the conclusion of more regional agreements, such as the *Central American Free Trade Area.

LATIN AMERICAN INTEGRATION ASSOCIATION; CENTRAL AMERICAN COMMON MARKET; PAN-AMERICANISM

(⊕) SEE WEB LINKS

• The official website of the OAS.

Obama, Barrack (b. 4 Aug. 1961), US Senator 2005–

Born in Hawaii, he graduated from Columbia University, and became active in social work in Chicago. In 1991, he obtained a law degree from Harvard, where he had become the first African-American President of the *Harvard Law Review*. Obama moved back to Chicago, where he was elected to the Illinois Senate as a *Democrat in 1996. In 2004 the telegenic moderate became the first African American to be elected to the US Senate. The second African American after *Jesse Jackson to launch a serious bid for the presidency,

Obama collected more money in donations than any other candidate in the early months of the campaign. Obama campaigned on his opposition to the *Iraq War, and his ability to overcome the polarization between Democrats and *Republicans.

Obote, Apollo Milton (b. 1924, d. 18 Oct 2005). President of Uganda 1966–71, 1980–5

He was born in Lango as the son of a local chief. He was active in the movement for Kenyan independence, but returned in 1955 to join the Uganda National Congress, which he transformed into the Uganda People's Congress (UPC) from 1962. Upon Ugandan independence, he became Prime Minister, and in 1966 deposed *Mutesa II to assume the presidency. His government was plagued by scandals, and he became dependent upon the army under *Amin. With the latter, his increasingly repressive regime expelled 30,000 Kenyan workers in 1970. The Kenyans' departure precipitated an economic crisis, which further increased his unpopularity. He was deposed by Amin in 1971, and went into exile in Tanzania. After Amin's overthrow he was 'elected' President in a corrupt and violent election. Having abandoned his socialist policies, he was supported by the USA and the UK, despite reports of continuing *human rights violations under his regime. His repressions triggered off opposition by the National Resistance Army under *Museveni. Never a figure of much integrity or charisma, he was deposed in 1985 and retired to Zambia.

Obregón, Alvaro (b. 19 Feb. 1880, d. 19 July 1928). President of Mexico 1920–4

Son of a farm labourer, in 1912 he led a group of armed peasants to support President *Madero in his struggle against General Huerta. His military skills resulted in quick promotion in *Carranza's constitutional army. As its military leader he was responsible for the decisive defeat of *Villa's troops in 1915. Alarmed by Carranza's attempt to circumvent the new constitution's stipulation that a President must not be re-elected by nominating a puppet candidate, he overthrew Carranza and probably gave the order for his assassination. Elected President himself, he hesitated to institute land reform as promised by the Revolution, fearing that this would entail a decline in production. He contributed to the stability of the new political order by achieving US recognition of the new state. He also co-opted moderate labour unions at the expense of anarchists and Communists, and boosted the political system by ensuring the peaceful transfer of power at the end of his presidency, which occurred for the first time since 1880. He won the 1928 elections, but was murdered by a religious fanatic.

Obuchi, Keizo (b. 26 June 1937, d. 14 May 2000). Prime Minister of Japan 1998–2000
Born in Agadsuma, he inherited his father's constituency and entered the House of Representatives in 1963. He became a minister in the Post and Telecommunications Ministry, and became the Chairman of the House of Representatives' finance committee. An increasingly influential member of the *Liberal Democratic Party, he became the Minister for Foreign Affairs in 1997. He succeeded *Hashimoto as Prime Minister, and sought to overcome the country's recession by lowering taxation and increasing public spending. He created a coalition with the New *Kômeitô Party, in order to enable him to pass structural economic reforms. However, the coalition proved to be riven by conflicts, and on 3 April Obuchi suffered a stroke. He died the following month.

Ocean Island (Banaba), see KIRIBATI

O'Connor, Sandra Day (26 Mar. 1930). US Supreme Court Justice 1981–2006
Born at El Paso, Texas, she faced a great deal of sexual prejudice after graduating from Stanford Law School — at one point she was offered a job as a secretary in a law firm. Despite this, she rose through the Arizona legal system and *Republican establishment, in a remarkable career. A member of the Arizona Senate (1969–75), she became its first female majority leader (1973–4). In 1975, she returned to the law, and was appointed to the Arizona Court of Appeals in 1979. In 1981, she became the first female *Supreme Court Justice, appointed by *Reagan. On the court, she aligned herself initially with the conservative *Rehnquist, but began to move towards the middle ground. An advocate of state rights, during the 1990s she came to occupy the centre vote in a court also composed of four liberal and four conservative justices.

October Putsch (Sept.–Oct. 1993)
A stand-off between the popularly elected Russian President, *Yeltsin, and the Congress of People's Deputies, whose members had been selected out of a pool of Communist candidates. In September 1993, Yeltsin replaced his deputy and Communist opponent, Rutskoi, with the controversial ultra-reformist Gaidar. With the Supreme *Soviet and the Congress of People's Deputies in defiant mood, Yeltsin dissolved both chambers and announced elections for December for two reformed chambers (a *Duma and a Senate) and a new constitution. Yeltsin defended his illegal actions with his popular support, maintaining that the Congress and the Soviet were acting against the will of the people. The Soviet responded by deposing Yeltsin on account of corruption, and declaring Rutskoi President. Under the leadership of Rutskoi and Congress leader Ruslan Khasbulatov, the parliamentarians occupied the White House. However, most of the army stood behind Yeltsin, who had the White House surrounded and its energy supplies cut. On 4 November 1993 Russian elite units stormed the parliament, which cost the lives of 148 people. The leaders of the putsch were imprisoned, but released on 26 February 1994 as part of a general amnesty which also included the leaders of the *August coup (1991).

October War, see YOM KIPPUR WAR (1973)

Oder–Neisse Line
The current border between Germany and Poland, which was agreed at the *Yalta and *Potsdam conferences, when the German territories of Pomerania, *Silesia, and East *Prussia were placed under Polish administration pending a general peace treaty. As a result, Poland, which itself had lost large areas to the east of the *Curzon Line to the Soviet Union, Polonized these areas through the expulsion of virtually its entire German population. The areas were accepted as Polish territory in the Warsaw Treaty of 1970 (*German question), but the border was not formally recognized by the German Federal Republic until 1990.

OECD (Organization for Economic Co-operation and Development)
A consultative body established on 12 April 1960 to further economic and political consultation among the 25 leading industrial nations. It emerged from the Organization for European Economic Co-operation, set up on 16 April 1948, in order to coordinate the *Marshall Plan. With 30 members by 2007, it pursued the common aim of economic prosperity through cooperation and the promotion of world trade, and democratic and political stability in the face of *globalization.

(((●))) SEE WEB LINKS

• The official website of the OECD.

oil price shock (1973, 1979)

The trigger for two worldwide economic crises in the 1970s and early 1980s, caused by a sudden and drastic increase in the price of crude oil. In 1973 Arab states responded to US and general Western support for the *Yom Kippur War by a dramatic and unprecedented reduction in oil production. All oil exports to the USA and the Netherlands (Europe's central entrepôt for oil) were halted. This caused a quadrupling of the price of crude oil, to around $6 per barrel. It was the first time oil had been used as a political weapon, while the Arab oil-producing countries realized for the first time their global power.

The second oil price shock was caused by the Iranian Revolution in 1979. Prices for crude oil jumped to $23 per barrel, and reached a peak of $34 per barrel. The motives for this were less political. Instead, it was caused by nervousness and uncertainty about the stability of a major regional power among the oil-producing states in the Persian Gulf. In addition, defensiveness against *Khomeini's new aggressive *Islamic fundamentalist theocracy caused an unusual burst of Arab solidarity, enabling the realization of oil-producing quotas which reduced supply and increased prices.

Impact Both oil price shocks caused economic and social upheavals unprecedented since World War II. The high oil prices plunged the fledgling states of Africa and Latin America into deep economic crises. This usually led either to political coups or, as regimes tried to avoid public dissatisfaction, to large-scale borrowing and a sharp rise in Third World debt. Particularly for African countries, this problem of high debts was compounded by the fall of commodity prices in the 1980s, which made up most of their export earnings.

In Anglo-American and European societies, too, the oil price shocks caused the greatest economic dislocations since 1945. After more than two decades of more or less uninterrupted economic boom and full employment, these countries had lost their flexibility in the labour market. *Trade union movements refused to compensate for the increases in production costs by significant reductions in their real wages. This led to spiralling unemployment, though this effect was rather less marked in the USA and Canada. Ultimately, the oil price shocks were the catalysts for the demise of a *Keynesian welfarist perception of almost inevitable growth and prosperity. Subsequently, economic and social life was characterized by greater flexibility and insecurity.

Perhaps their most dramatic impact was on the Communist *Comecon countries. These experienced the economic crises with a time-lag, as prices for Romanian and Soviet oil, which were not immune from world price fluctuations, were fixed every five years. Even the oil-producing USSR and Romania were adversely affected by this development, since they too had to pay higher prices for high-quality goods and machinery made in Asia or the West with their limited funds of hard currency. Given the increasingly run-down nature of these command economies, the oil price shocks dealt a crucial blow to regimes running an already bankrupt economic system. The ideological *raison d'être* of these countries demanded the maintenance of full employment and at least constant living standards. It was the inability of these command economies to absorb the effects of the oil price shocks that formed the underpinning to the (economic) collapse of Eastern Europe and the Soviet Union in the late 1980s.

Ojukwu, Chukwuemeka Odumegwu (b. 4 Nov. 1933). Leader of Biafra 1967–70

Born in Zungeru, he studied at Oxford (1952–5) and then joined the Nigerian army. He had reached the rank of lieutenant-colonel by 1966. He became military Governor of his native Eastern Region after the coup of 15 January 1966, in which he did not participate. However, he refused to accept *Gowon's leadership after the second coup of 1966, accusing the new leadership of suppressing the Ibo people. He declared his territory independent, which led to the bloody *Biafran War (1967–70). Ojukwu's forces were defeated, however, and on 11 January 1970 he sought political asylum in the Ivory Coast. He returned after a pardon in 1982, though he was largely unsuccessful in his bid to resume a political career. Imprisoned after the 1983 coup, he was released in 1984 and retired.

Oka Incident, see LAND CLAIMS, NATIVE

Okinawa, see JAPAN–UNITED STATES SECURITY TREATY

Olive Tree (Italy)

A fragmented coalition of centre-left parties in Italy. Created in 1995, it became the major centre-left coalition, known as the Union, and formed a government in 1996–2001, and from 2006. Led into the 1996 election by *Prodi, it obtained a majority against *Berlusconi's *Forza Italia. However, with the responsibility of government its internal political differences were accentuated, especially when a number of cuts in public spending had to be enacted to prepare the country for entry into the *euro. Prodi was unable to keep the coalition united behind his policies, and in 1998 he was succeeded by Massimo D'Alema, the leader of the Democratic Socialists (*Communist Party, Italy). Two years later, D'Alema was in turn succeeded by the more popular Guiliano Amato.

The coalition lost the 2001 elections to Berlusconi's House of Liberties Alliance. It regrouped in 2006 under Prodi, and narrowly won the elections by 25,000 votes. With a narrow majority in both Houses of Parliament, the new Union government, which combined not just the three parties comprising the Olive Tree alliance, but seven other splinter parties, struggled to assemble the compromises necessary to realize essential social reform. In an effort to overcome the fragmentation of the centre-left, the two largest parties of the Union, the Christian-Democratic Margherita Alliance and the ex-Communist 'Refondazione' proposed to unite as the 'Democratic Party' in 2008.

Olmert, Ehud (b. 30 Sept 1945). Prime Minister of Israel, 2006–

Born in Binyamina, he studied psychology and then law, graduating from Hebrew University in 1973. A member of the Knesset since 1973, he made his name as Mayor of Jerusalem between 1993 and 2003. He ran the successful *Likud election campaign in 2003, whereupon *Sharon made him Vice Prime Minister. He followed Sharon into his *Kadima party, and became acting Prime Minister after Sharon suffered a severe stroke. He led Kadima to a resounding victory in the March 2006 elections, but his popularity waned owing to his handling of the war against *Hezbollah, as he had clearly misjudged the ability of the air force to overcome Hezbollah stations in southern Lebanon. With little military background except national service (part of which he completed at a newspaper), Olmert was also blamed for failing to stop rocket attacks on Israeli territory from Gaza. A public enquiry, the Winograd Commission, criticized him strongly for his lack of planning during the Lebanon war, and thus weakened his position further.

Oman

A country whose history in the nineteenth and twentieth centuries was characterized by a power struggle between the political

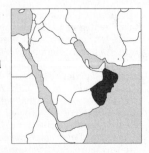

leadership of the Sultan, and the religious leadership of the Imam.

Oman was the most powerful Arab state in the nineteenth century, when its control stretched from eastern Africa to the Iranian coast. Its sultans were gradually forced to accept British sovereignty. A civil war (1913–20) was fought between the tribes of the hinterland supporting the Imam and those of the coast supporting the Sultan, which included the inhabitants of the capital, Muscat, many of whom were Indians. The war resulted in the clear division of power between the two authorities, though this did not prevent future conflict. A further uprising by the Imam and his supporters (1955-7) was suppressed with the support of British troops.

Oil was discovered and exported from the area during the 1960s, and presented further encouragement for oppositional groups. The People's Front for the Liberation of the Occupied Arabian Gulf started an uprising in 1965, in order to liberate the entire peninsula from British troops. With the help of troops from South *Yemen, it restricted its operations to Oman in 1974, when it was renamed the People's Front for the Liberation of Oman (PFLO). It was defeated in 1976 by Sultan Qaboos bin Said (b. 1940), who had deposed his father in 1970 with British support.

Qaboos bin Said introduced a number of economic and social reforms. Feeling under threat from the *Islamic fundamentalist revolution in Iran in 1979, he cooperated even more closely with the Westernized Arab states of Saudi Arabia and Egypt, as well as the USA itself. The USA was allowed in 1980 to set up military bases in the country, to provide strategic control over the Hormuz Strait. The Sultan continued with careful economic reforms, but was not prepared to accompany these with any democratic reforms that would have curtailed his autocratic power, save for the institution of a National Consultative Council in 1981, which consisted of 82 members. To satisfiy internal Muslim opposition, in 1996 Islamic law was introduced and constitutionally enshrined. In an attempt to diversify the economy, which was heavily reliant on the production of oil, Qaboos bin Said concluded a free trade agreement with the USA in 2006, and developed tourism.

One Nation, (Australia)

A right-wing party founded as the One Nation Party in 1997 by Pauline Hanson. In the 1998 general elections, it attracted 8.5 per cent of the national vote, but because of the electoral system obtained only one seat in the House of Representatives. In 2001, it caused a further upset in the state elections of Queensland, when it gained 9 per cent of the popular vote. The party's success forced its emotive anti-immigration concerns and its opposition to granting special *Aboriginal rights to the top of the political agenda, and forced a polarization of the debate. At the national general elections in December 2001, its popular support was halved as the *Liberal Party positioned itself further to the right. Pauline Hanson resigned from her functions within the party in 2002. In 2003, Hanson was found guilty of manipulating party membership lists, though the ruling was later overturned by the High Court. The party, which had renamed itself One Nation, continued its decline, losing its electoral base even in Queensland.

(((●))) **SEE WEB LINKS**

• The official website of One Nation.

O'Neill, Terence Marne, Lord O'Neill of the Maine (b. 10 Sept. 1914, d. 12 June 1990). Prime Minister of Northern Ireland 1963–9

Born in London, and educated at Eton, he served in World War II in the Irish Guards, achieving the rank of captain. He was elected to *Stormont in *Northern Ireland for the *Ulster Unionist Party in 1946, and became Minister of Finance in 1956, before succeeding Brookeborough (*Brooke) as Prime Minister. He was seen as a reformer who wished to remedy some of the grievances of the Catholic minority in Northern Ireland. He tried to develop economic relations with the Irish Republic, and met with the Irish Taoiseach (Prime Minister), Sean *Lemass, in 1965. However, his commitment to liberal reforms remained confined to rhetoric, rather than structural change. Still, even the language of accommodation proved controversial within his own ranks, which eventually forced him to resign in April 1969, to be succeeded by *Chichester-Clark.

OPEC (Organization of Petroleum Exporting Countries)

Founded in 1960, it consisted of the main Arabian oil-producing countries, as well as Indonesia, Nigeria, and Venezuela. OPEC aimed to counter the influence of the large oil companies and to gain greater control over the price of oil. Following the *Yom Kippur War of 1973, the cartel quadrupled the price of oil and banned all oil exports to the USA and the Netherlands, in protest against the pro-Israeli attitudes of its main customers in general, and of these two countries in particular. In 1979, it managed to raise the price of oil and thus cause another worldwide recession, but since then its ability to keep oil prices high has vanished due to conflicts among its member states, such as the *Iran–Iraq War and the *Gulf War. It surprised many observers with its success at pushing up the price of oil in 2000, but this did not lead to a major recession in the major Western capitalist economies.

OIL-PRICE SHOCK

(((●))) **SEE WEB LINKS**

• The official website of OPEC.

open door policy (USA)

A US policy towards China conceived in 1899 by Secretary of State Hays and President *McKinley. It was predicated upon free trade between all areas of China controlled by foreign states (the UK, France, Italy, Germany, Russia, and Japan). The policy sought to ensure access to the Chinese market for the US in light of the fact that the US did not own formal spheres of influence in China. At the same time, it defined the US economic and political interest in China.

IMPERIALISM; BOXER REBELLION

Orbán, Viktor (b. 31 May 1963). Prime Minister of Hungary, 1998–2002

Born in Székesfehérvar, he graduated in jurisprudence from Eotvos Lorand University. In 1989 he became a national figure by demanding the withdrawal of Soviet troops during the burial of Imre *Nagy. He co-founded the Young Democrats (FIDESZ), and as party leader from 1994 he set out to shift the party from the progressive centre to the capitalist right. On this basis, he won the 1998 elections. Orbán promoted Hungary's integration into *NATO and the *EU, and secured a large personal following through his youthful energy, charisma, and populist rhetoric. Surprisingly, he lost the 2002 elections, but remained a high-profile member of the opposition.

Organisation de l'Armée Secrète (OAS, Secret Army Organization)

A terrorist organization of diehard Algerian settlers of French descent, founded in 1961 when it became evident that the new French President, de *Gaulle, would not be opposed to Algerian independence as a means to end the *Algerian War of Independence. Led by *Salan and a group of French army officers, it staged an unsuccessful revolt in Algiers, as well as carrying out several bomb attacks in mainland France. Its greatest challenge to the new political order of the French Fifth Republic came with its abortive attempt to assassinate the President himself, whose car was machine-gunned in March 1962. Salan was captured in Algiers the following month, and after further arrests the OAS gradually disintegrated.

Organization for Economic Co-operation and Development, see OECD

Organization of American States, see OAS

Organization of Co-operation of the African and Malagasy States, see BRAZZAVILLE BLOC

Organization of Petroleum Exporting Countries, see OPEC

Orlando, Vittorio Emanuele (b. 19 May 1860, d. 1 Dec. 1952). Prime Minister of Italy 1917–19

Born in Palermo, he became an expert in public law and administration, and accepted professorships at Modena (1885), Messina (1886), Palermo (1889), and Rome (1901–31). He participated in various governments as Minister of Education (1903–5), of Justice (1907–9, 1915–16), and of the Interior (1916–17). On account of his good standing among those sections of the population which were opposed to Italy's participation in World War I (Catholics, socialists, and some liberals) he formed a government at the height of the disastrous Battle of *Caporetto.

Orlando led his country to victory in the war, but failed to realize Italian territorial claims at the *Paris Peace Conference, i.e. over the port of *Fiume. As a consequence he resigned in June 1919. In 1922 he tried twice to form a stable coalition government, but his failure to do so persuaded him to accept *Mussolini's coming to power following the *March on Rome. Disappointed by the growing radicalism of Italian *Fascism, he openly broke with the movement in 1925 and resigned from the Chamber of Deputies. To avoid swearing an oath of allegiance to the *Duce, he resigned his chair at the University of Rome in 1931. One of *Victor Emanuel III's advisers in the coup that ousted Mussolini after a meeting of the *Fascist Grand Council, he became President of the Chamber of Deputies in 1944 and in 1946 became a member of the Constituent Assembly. In 1948 he was made a senator for life.

Ortega Saavedra, Daniel (b. 11 Nov. 1945). President of Nicaragua 1985–90, 2007–
An active member since 1962 of the Sandinista National Liberation Front (FSLN), a guerrilla movement fighting against the

*Somoza regime, he joined its leadership in 1965 before being arrested in 1967. Released in 1974, he spent some time in Cuba before returning to coordinate the Sandinistas' victory of 1979. He led the Sandinista junta and was elected President in the 1984 elections, which were boycotted by several opposition parties. To general surprise, he lost the 1990 elections to his most prominent critic, *Chamorro. Nevertheless, he remained an influential figure in Nicaraguan politics and, as leader of the official Sandinista movement, he ran for the presidency in 1996 and 2001, but was defeated each time by the candidate of the centre-right Liberal Alliance.

In 2006, he was successful in his bid to win re-election. However, he vowed not to confront the USA and to encourage trade between the two countries. He did, however, also entertain good relations with *Chávez, who sought to enlist Ortega in his anti-USA alliance.

Orthodox Churches, Eastern

The ancient Christian Churches of the Middle East and eastern Europe. Each church is independent, but a special honour is accorded to the Ecumenical Patriarch of Constantinople. There is a sizeable Orthodox population in the USA, but the majority of the 150 million Orthodox members in the world live in the Soviet Union, Bulgaria, Romania, Serbia, and Greece. The Soviet and Eastern European Churches suffered considerable persecution under Communist regimes. In recent years there has been a *rapprochement* between the Orthodox Churches and the Roman *Catholic Church, following the lifting in 1965 of mutual excommunications imposed in 1054. Originally, the Catholic Church looked forward to a union with the Eastern Church on the condition that the latter accept the authority of the Pope, but since the Second Vatican Council (1962–5) this approach has been rejected in favour of *ecumenical dialogue.

Eastern Orthodoxy accepts the Nicene Creed and its worship is centred around an elaborate celebration of the eucharist. It accords great importance to mysticism, the veneration of icons, and the use of traditional languages such as Old Slavic. After 1989, the Eastern Orthodox Churches in the former *Soviet Union, Romania and Bulgaria were freed from state restrictions. In many instances, the Churches were now enlisted by the new regimes to help fashion new national identities. However, this did not lead to a general surge in the number of believers.

OSCE, see CONFERENCE ON SECURITY AND COOPERATION IN EUROPE

Oslo Accords (Aug.–Sept. 1993)

After months of secret negotiations sponsored by the Norwegian government, between representatives of the *PLO and Israel, this was the breakthrough in the quest for a comprehensive peace settlement which had eluded the Middle East for almost five decades. Israel now recognized the PLO as the legitimate representative of the Palestinian people, while the PLO recognized the sovereignty of Israel and renounced violence in the pursuit of a lasting peace. This was signed at a conference in Washington on 13 September 1993, which also determined a series of principles for Palestinian autonomy, whose details were to be negotiated. This became known as the *Gaza–Jericho Agreement.

On 24 September 1995 an agreement was signed between Israeli and PLO representatives at the Egyptian resort of Taba, which followed up the original Oslo Accords and is thus referred to as 'Oslo B'. It provided in detail for the withdrawal of Israeli troops from the *West Bank in different stages over six months, with the Palestinian police forces simultaneously extending their authority over the area. While a number of issues remained unresolved, such as the disputed status of the city of Hebron, it provided a crucial step towards Palestinian self-rule, which was complemented by the establishment of an elected *Palestinian National Authority. Although initially the agreement was scrupulously followed, the subsequent assassination of *Rabin and the election of the conservative *Netanyahu led to a standstill in its implementation. The *Wye Agreement attempted to salvage the Oslo accords, but its ultimate failure to prevent the growing confrontation between Israelis and Palestinians, and the Israeli invasion of the self-governed territories in 2002, rendered the Oslo Accords all but redundant.

Ostpolitik ('Eastern policy'), see GERMAN QUESTION

Ottawa Agreements (10 July–20 Aug. 1932)

A series of trade agreements between Britain and its Dominions, extended to its Crown Colonies in the following year. The British abandonment of the principle of free trade at the height of the *Great *Depression in 1931 paved the way for the establishment of a system of **Imperial Preference**, a concept originally championed by Joseph *Chamberlain from 1897. According to this, while tariffs were raised for imports from all countries outside the *British Empire, agricultural products from the Dominions were allowed to enter Britain free of duty. In return, the Dominions gave preferential treatment to manufactured goods imported from Britain. As a result, trade within the British Empire increased slightly. However, its global effect was negative as the British Empire reduced its trade with the rest of the world. Furthermore, even though the agreements may have strengthened imperial bonds, they failed to protect domestic farmers from foreign imports. With modifications, Imperial Preference was maintained after World War II, and provided a major stumbling block to British entry into the EEC (*European integration). When Britain did join in 1973, it had to abandon most of its preferential trade agreements, apart from the continued partial exemption of New Zealand dairy products from import duties.

DECOLONIZATION; PROTECTIONISM

Ottoman Empire

Early history An Islamic state founded in 1299, which at its peak in the sixteenth century covered the entire region between today's Hungary in the north, western Iran in the east, Saudi Arabia in the south, and Algiers in the west. Thereafter, it experienced a gradual territorial decline, largely owing to over-expansion. The Empire became increasingly difficult to defend as Western (European) arms and wealth became superior. In addition, the ruling elite became increasingly corrupt, and from the seventeenth century the intellectual and diplomatic prowess of the Sultans declined. These problems became more pronounced in the nineteenth century, when the growth of *nationalism created increasing resistance to its rule in the Balkans. It lost effective control over Bosnia, Montenegro, Bulgaria, and East Roumelia in 1878. It also lost authority over Tunisia (1881) and Egypt (1882). Indeed, towards the end of the century it was artificially propped up by the European powers in order to prevent Russian control of the strategically crucial *Dardanelles.

Despite attempts to Westernize the administration and the army, which led to the introduction of a Constitution in 1876, Sultan Abdülhamit II (r. 1876–1909) resisted as much as possible any limitation to his autocratic rule. This triggered revolts by the *Young Turks in 1908 and 1909, which led to the abdication of Abdülhamit II and the reintroduction of constitutional rule by Muhammad V. The revolts and the subsequent reforms came much too late, and in fact weakened the state further. In 1908, Bulgaria and East Roumelia were lost, and

Crete had become Greek. The Empire lost control of Libya to Italy, and after the two *Balkan Wars it had lost most of its European possessions by 1914.

Collapse Despite its unique track record of losing wars, the Ottoman Empire participated in World War I on the side of the *Central Powers, whereupon it also lost its Arab empire. The severe terms of the Treaty of *Sèvres, which determined the partition of the Turkish heartland of Anatolia, the creation of a separate state of *Armenia, and the loss of further territory to Greece, aroused intense Turkish nationalism. This was translated into a liberation movement under Kemal (*Atatürk), whose conquests were consolidated in the Treaty of *Lausanne. He then destroyed the twin pillars of the Ottoman Empire by abolishing the Sultan, and the unity between the state and the Muslim religion. On 29 October 1923, the Republic of Turkey was proclaimed in its stead.

MAP 2

P

Paasikivi, Juo Kusti (b. 27 Nov. 1870, d. 14 Dec. 1956). President of Finland 1946–56
Born in Tampere, he was a diplomat and, as Conservative Prime Minister from May to November 1917, guided the country to independence. He was subsequently the main proponent of cooperation and friendship with Russia and the Soviet Union, in contrast to *Mannerheim's confrontational stance. Whereas the ebullient Mannerheim led the country through the War of Independence (1917–20), the *Winter War of 1939–40, and the *Continuation War (1941–4), each time Paasikivi quietly led the negotiations for peace at the end. Ultimately, as Prime Minister (1944–6) and President, he was able to impress upon the country his view that Finland could never maintain its sovereignty if it continued to entertain hostile relations with the USSR. His dogged policy of neutrality formed the cornerstone of Finnish politics until 1991.

PAC (Pan Africanist Congress)
A militant South African political movement founded in 1959 by disgruntled members of the *ANC, who rejected that organization's multi-racial attitudes and its sympathies towards *Communism. The PAC aimed to create a greater sense of urgency in the campaign against *apartheid, and it identified the struggle against White rule with the simultaneous struggle for *decolonization elsewhere on the African continent. Led by *Sobukwe, it quickly organized mass protest against the pass laws which led to the *Sharpeville Massacre. Banned in 1960, its organization had been destroyed by South African police by 1965. At one time almost as strong as the ANC, the PAC's support rapidly declined after its legalization in 1990, so that it managed to attract only 1.2 per cent of the popular vote in the 1994 elections. This was the result of the poor leadership of Clarence Makwetu, the lack of external funding, and its misjudgement of the general mood amongst Blacks, which proved unsusceptible to its traditional radical slogan of 'one [White] settler, one bullet'. In the 1999 and 2004 general elections, it had only three seats in parliament.

(((●))) SEE WEB LINKS

• The home page of the PAC.

Pacific campaign (1941–5)

Japanese advances (1941–2) On 7 December 1941 the Japanese entered *World War II by attacking the US naval base of *Pearl Harbor in Hawaii. While the attack did not, as the Japanese had hoped, wipe out the entire US Pacific fleet, it took a surprised USA a few months to gather its forces in the area. During this time, Japan used its alliances with the *Vichy colonial government in *Indochina as well as with Thailand for a rapid advance into neighbouring Malaya, and *Singapore. In Burma (*Myanmar) as well as in the Dutch East Indies (*Indonesia), its advancing armies were welcomed by the respective independence movements as liberators from European colonialism. After their naval victory in the Battle of the Java Sea (27 February–1 March), the Japanese occupied the Dutch East Indies, and by April the Philippines and northern New Guinea were occupied.

Allied fightback (from 1942) As the enemy advanced precariously close to Australian New Guinea, which surrendered British and Commonwealth garrison at Singapore could no longer defend, US General *MacArthur organized a resolute stance against the Japanese. US success at the Battle of the *Coral Sea lifted the threat of a military invasion off Australia, while the subsequent Battle of *Midway Island shifted the balance of naval power decisively in favour of the USA. In August 1942 US marines landed on Guadalcanal and Tulagi in the *Solomon Islands, where fighting raged until February 1943. The remaining Solomon Islands were retaken during the year, while in November 1943 US marines captured *Kiribati.

Japanese defeat (1944–5) Having established control over the Pacific as such, MacArthur embarked upon the *Philippines campaign, and advanced north to various Pacific islands that could be used for an eventual invasion of Japan. The USA occupied New Guinea from 1943, and during 1944 US forces gradually moved back towards the Philippines. The Japanese were defeated at the Battle of the *Philippines Sea. In July 1944 the Mariana Islands were taken, from which bombing raids on Tokyo were launched. The Battle of *Leyte Gulf marked the effective end of

Japanese naval power, while on the mainland the *Burma campaign had reopened land communication with China. Manila fell in March 1945.

From April to June 1945 US forces gradually captured Okinawa, a chain of Japanese islands off the Japanese coast. This victory came at the cost of very high casualties on both sides (5,900 Japanese planes, as well as 1,900 kamikaze attacks; 763 US planes and 12,000 dead). Faced with US estimates that an invasion of mainland Japan would cost hundreds of thousands of *Allied lives, President *Truman ordered instead the dropping of the atomic bomb on *Hiroshima and *Nagasaki, after which Japan surrendered unconditionally on 2 September 1945.

Pacific Forum

An international organization formed as the **South Pacific Forum (SPC)** in 1971, largely on the initiative of New Zealand. It hosted a series of occasional meetings between the heads of governments of its member states, i.e. Australia, Cook Islands, Fiji, Kiribati, the Republic of the Marshall Islands, the Federated States of Micronesia, Nauru, New Zealand, Niue, Papua New Guinea, Solomon Islands, Tonga, Tuvalu, Vanuatu, and (Western) Samoa. In 1985 it concluded the Treaty of Raratonga, which declared the South Pacific a nuclear-free zone from December 1986. However, this was not recognized by the USA, France, or the UK. Palau joined in 1995, and *New Caledonia and French Polynesia were granted associate membership in 2006. In 2000, the SPC formally changed its name to the Pacific Forum.

(⊕) SEE WEB LINKS

- The official home page of the Pacific Islands Forum Secretariat.

Padlock Act (Canada)

Passed in 1937 as the Act Respecting Communistic Propaganda, it was a statute legislated in Quebec which empowered the provincial attorney-general to confiscate any literature and close any building used for the propaganda of *Communism or *Bolshevism. It was declared unconstitutional by the Canadian Supreme Court in 1957, as an infringement on federal jurisdiction.

Page, Sir Earle Christmas Grafton (b. 8 Aug. 1880, d. 20 Dec. 1961). Australian politician

Born at Grafton (New South Wales), he graduated from the University of Sydney and became a successful surgeon. After service in World War I, Grafton was elected to federal parliament with the endorsement of the

Farmers' and Settlers' Association, With ten other representatives of farming interests, he created the Federal Country Party (*National Party). Its leader from 1921, he became instrumental in the fall of *Hughes in 1923, forming a coalition with *Bruce as Deputy Prime Minister and Treasurer (until 1929). Page reorganized federal–state budget relations, so the federal government gained control over public borrowing. In opposition from 1931, he rejoined the Cabinet when *Lyons lost his absolute majority in 1934. This time he was very much a junior partner in the coalition, with much less responsibility and freedom of action than he had enjoyed under Bruce. He became caretaker Prime Minister for nineteen days upon the sudden death of Lyons in 1939, while the *United Australia Party chose a successor. A few months later he lost the leadership of his party, following a strong attack on the Prime Minister, *Menzies. He served as Australia's representative on the British War Cabinet (1941–2) and, back in Australia, was member of the Advisory War Council (1942–5). As Minister for Health (1949–56), his main achievement was the introduction of a national health scheme in 1953.

Pahlavi, Muhammad Reza Shah

(b. 26 Oct. 1919, d. 27 July 1980). Shah of Iran 1941–79

Born in Tehran, he succeeded his deposed father on 17 September 1941, and was subsequently anxious to avoid his predecessor's mistake of having been too reserved toward UK and US influence. Unfortunately, he ultimately went too far in this endeavour, when he came to rely predominantly on US aid against internal popular opposition to his secular reforms. Thus, he resisted the coup by *Mussadeq and, after a brief period in exile (1953), returned to speed up a programme of comprehensive social, economic, and cultural reform. Known as the 'White Revolution', his measures redistributed some land, and sought to diversify industry through a generally ill-conceived attempt at industrialization. These changes were designed less to bring about social peace, than to buttress the regime's corrupt allies in the military and among powerful landowners and other owners of capital. Hence, his reforms increased further domestic opposition, such as that led by *Ayatollah *Khomeini. Pahlavi murdered thousands of political opponents each year, while tens of thousands suffered imprisonment and torture. He was finally unable to contain the unrest that had built up against him for so long, and was forced to flee the country on 16 January 1979. He ultimately settled in Egypt, comforted by his enormous wealth, amassed at the expense of his own people and kept secure in foreign bank accounts.

Pahlavi, Reza Shah (b. 16 Mar. 1878, d. 26 July 1944). Shah of Iran 1925–41

Born in Alasht (Mazandaran), he became an officer of the Persian Cossack Brigade. He led the army coup of 21 February 1921 which overthrew the Qajar dynasty and established a military dictatorship under Ahmad Shah. Pahlavi served successively as Minister of War and Prime Minister, until he led another coup which deposed Ahmad and installed himself as Shah. Subsequently, he strove to rid Iran of all foreign influence, and to make efficient use of the country's increasingly important oil reserves. To this end, he reformed the bureaucracy and administration. He greatly improved the organization, training, and equipment of the army. Meanwhile, he assumed complete control over economic developments, using the state's growing resources to encourage the development of industries. Thus, the building of the Trans-Iranian Railway (1927–38) was achieved without foreign finance. His legal and educational reforms had the unfortunate side effect of alienating substantial sections of Iran's devout *Islamic *Shi'ite community. While his reforms did much to strengthen the country's politics and economy, they were unable to prevent Iran's occupation by Soviet and British forces during World War II, in response to his insistence on complete neutrality. He was obliged to abdicate in favour of his son, Muhammad Reza *Pahlavi, and died in exile in South Africa.

Paisley, Revd Ian Richard Kyle (b. 6 Apr. 1926). Northern Irish politician

Born in Armagh, he was ordained as a Presbyterian minister in 1946, and established the Free Presbyterian Church of Ulster in 1951. From the mid-1960s he was the most prominent Unionist opponent of concessions to Catholics, and of any weakening of *Northern Ireland's position in the UK. He was first imprisoned in 1968 for 'unlawful assembly', and in 1969 he led the Protestant Unionist Party, a breakaway from the *Ulster Unionist Party. In 1970 he was elected to both the *Stormont and Westminster parliaments, and in 1971 he founded the *Democratic Unionist Party (DUP). He represented the DUP in the Northern Ireland Assembly (1973–5), but consistently opposed power-sharing. In 1979 he was elected to the *European Parliament. He vociferously opposed any attempt to solve the problems of Northern Ireland through closer involvement, or even consultation, with 'Popish' (i.e. *Roman Catholic) southern Ireland. This was the basis for his opposition to the 1993 *Downing Street Declaration, as well as the *Good Friday Agreement of 1998. As Paisley led his DUP to electoral success, pressure on him to compromise grew. Following the *IRA's decommissioning of weapons in 2005, he gave up a lifetime commitment not to talk to *Sinn Féin. His acceptance of the *St Andrews Agreement and his triumph in the 2007 provincial elections prepared the way for Paisley to end his career as First Minister of Northern Ireland.

Pakhtunistan, see RED SHIRTS

Pakistan

A highly heterogeneous country which has suffered from the inability of central government to impose itself on its different regions and  tribes. Pakistan's instability was heightened by its development into a frontline state next to Afghanistan, first in the *Cold War and then in the *War on Terrorism.

Origins The country came under British control in the first half of the nineteenth century, as part of British India. Its name is derived from the Urdu word *pak* ('ritually pure'), and means 'Land of the Pure'. It is also an acronym for its most important component peoples: **P**unjabis, **A**fghans, **K**ashmirs, **S**ind, and the peoples of Balukhis**tan**. At the beginning of the twentieth century there were few moves towards independence, partly because those living in the north (*Punjab and *Kashmir) were great beneficiaries of the British *Raj, and occupied important posts in the administration and army of British India. It was among the more disadvantaged Muslim minority in north central India that a Muslim cultural and political identity began to form, largely through reformers such as Sir Sayyid Ahmad Khan and Muhammad *Iqbal, organizations such as the University of Aligarh (founded by Khan), and the *Muslim League.

Under its leader, *Jinnah, the Muslim League formulated demands for greater Muslim rights in a vast country in which Muslims accounted for around 25 per cent of the total population. This demand became all the more urgent with the increasing momentum of the Indian National *Congress (INC) under *Gandhi, which made self-government or even independence under a Hindu-dominated government all but inevitable during the 1930s. The weakness of the scattered Muslim community was demonstrated in the 1937 provincial elections, in which the Muslim League gained but 21 per cent of the seats reserved for Muslims. It had particular difficulties with its message of Muslim rights in areas with a Muslim majority, such as the Punjab or East Bengal. However, Jinnah's campaign soon gathered mass support.

Agitated by the INC's failure to include members of the Muslim League in provincial governments, an isolated Jinnah developed a more radical rhetoric. The Pakistan Resolution of 23 March 1940 (also known as the **Lahore Resolution**) warned that if conditions for Muslims, especially in areas with a Muslim minority, did not improve, Muslims would lay claim to separate states as their homelands. The idea of separate states caught on in those areas with a Muslim majority, i.e. in the western provinces, and in East Bengal. After *Nehru's awkward handling of the *Cabinet Mission Plan, independence for Pakistan as a separate state was hastily pursued by *Mountbatten, and was granted on 15 August 1947.

West Pakistan (1947–71) With Jinnah as first President, the new state consisted of the western Provinces of Baluchistan, Sind, Punjab, and North-West Frontier (subsequently known as West Pakistan). Separated by 1,000 miles of Indian territory was the eastern half of Bengal, which also belonged to the new state and became known as East Pakistan. The new state was confronted by a host of problems. The most immediate of these was extensive migration, as the division of British India into a Muslim and a Hindu state led to an exodus of around five million Hindus and *Sikhs out of Pakistan, and the immigration of around eight million Muslims into Pakistan. Moreover, Pakistan contested its borders, as it competed with India over control of Kashmir. This has led to strained relations with India throughout its existence, and the conduct of three *Indo-Pakistan Wars.

In addition to these strains, the new state also suffered from the tension between the majority of the population living in East Pakistan and the important posts in government, administration, and the military being dominated by officials from the wealthier and better-educated parts of the west. These problems were compounded by the complete lack of any tradition or history as a single, unitary state. While East Bengal was relatively homogeneous, the west consisted of regions with widely different economies and ethnicities, with different degrees of religious observance. Some of the tribes of the North-West Frontier, with their devout observance of *Islam and their history of autonomy in British colonial times, contrasted with the more secular elite of the Punjab, which had been well integrated into the British administration.

The problem of finding a compromise that would create a viable, integrated, constitutional entity bedevilled the country throughout its existence. The task became more difficult after the early death of Jinnah and then *Liaquat Ali Khan, so that Pakistan continued to be ruled by the *Government of India Act (1935) until 1956, when the first Constitution was passed. However, the new political settlement failed to stabilize the country sufficiently to prevent the 1958 army coup, led by *Ayub Khan.

Ayub Khan abolished the recently established democracy without much resistance, and devised a second constitution in 1962. His precipitation of a costly and unsuccessful war with India over Kashmir in 1965, and increasing economic difficulties, led to his resignation in 1969. Democratic elections were held in 1970, but when these were won by the *Awami League in East Pakistan, the West Pakistan political establishment led by *Yahya Khan refused to hand over power, and sent troops to secure control in East Pakistan instead. It caused a short but extremely violent civil war, and led, after Indian military intervention, to the independence of East Pakistan as Bangladesh in 1971.

Contemporary history (1970s–90s) Zulfikar *Bhutto became the new President in late 1971, and created a populist, socialist regime. His programme of nationalization, public works, and independence from US financial assistance failed to overcome the effects of the *oil price shock of 1973, leading Pakistan into an economic crisis instead. He was deposed in an army coup led by *Zia-ul-Haq in 1977. Zia-ul-Haq improved the country's relations with the USA after the Soviet invasion of neighbouring Afghanistan in 1979, when Pakistan came to host up to three million Afghan refugees, as well as bases for Afghan guerrillas. US military and civilian aid led to high economic growth throughout the 1980s.

In 1988, Zia died in a plane crash. His successor, Ishaq Khan, supervised the transition back to a democracy, with the elections won by the regal Benazir *Bhutto. She failed to establish control over the country, however, and was dismissed by Khan in 1990 on charges of corruption. She was re-elected in 1993, but once again struggled to maintain control in a country plagued by crime, the international drugs trade, and the growing assertiveness of some of its provinces (Sind and Baluchistan) and tribes (North-West Frontier).

Bhutto was dismissed by President Leghari on charges of corruption and mismanagement in 1996, and was ultimately succeeded by Muhammad *Nawaz Sharif in 1997. Sharif proceeded to strengthen his position by changing the constitution which limited the power of the Prime Minister. He also confronted the judiciary, which he sought to conciliate towards his policies. Finally, in 1999 he sought to introduce Islamic law throughout the country. This led to widespread demonstrations, while the deteriorating economic situation had already eroded Sharif's popular support. His order to the army to withdraw forces from *Kashmir and his dismissal of *Musharraf led to a successful army coup, headed by Musharraf himself.

Contemporary politics (since 1999)

Musharraf suspended the Constitution, moved to put Pakistan's political and judicial institutions under military control, and tried to stabilize the economy to placate international creditors. After establishing control, his regime became more liberal, but it was only after the *September 11 attacks that Musharraf's regime was welcomed in the international arena. His decisive support of the US *War on Terrorism brought great foreign policy benefits, and enabled him to gain badly needed international loans. His pro-US stance was criticized by many Islamic factions within Pakistan, to which Musharraf responded by adopting a moderate stance towards radical Islamist groups in *Kashmir. These were responsible for a terrorist attack on India's parliament in 2001, which brought both countries to the brink of another war. Tensions eventually declined, with Musharraf concerned to improve relations between the two countries.

Under Musharraf, the economy grew substantially, despite the economic and human cost of the 2005 earthquake, which killed around 75,000 people. The stability of Musharraf's rule was predicated on his ability to tolerate different tribal groups and Muslim factions as long as these did not challenge his authority. However, this was increasingly criticized by the US for fostering terrorism, as many *Taliban fighters found refuge, or were even recruited, in Pakistan. Radical Islamist activity proliferated. In 2007, the army violently ended the occupation by some violent groups of the Red Mosque, which lay close to the presidential palace.

Palestine

A disputed territory between the River Jordan and the Mediterranean.

Early history (before 1914) It was ruled by the Kings of Judah until the expulsion of the Jewish people after the unsuccessful Bar Kochba rising, 132–5 AD. Since then it has been populated by a majority of Arabs, though it remained a central reference point to the dispersed Jewish people as their homeland, Eretz Israel (Land of Israel). In the light of renewed *pogroms in eastern Europe, a first wave of Jewish immigration into Palestine began in 1882, and there was another wave in 1904–14. Though the second wave contained many intellectuals and people of middle-class origins, the 60,000 Jews who had immigrated in total by 1914 were driven less by a vision of a new state than by the hope of making a new living, free from persecution.

The growth of nationalism (1920s–40s) In 1918 the area, which had been under the authority of the *Ottoman Empire since 1517, came under British rule, formalized as a *League of Nations *Mandate in 1920. The *Balfour Declaration of 1917 had fostered the hope of a Jewish state in Palestine, which was given further impetus by a third wave of Jewish immigration (around 35,000 people), this time with explicitly *Zionist aims. At the same time, however, British encouragement of Arab *nationalism, partly through T. E. *Lawrence, also fostered an increasing sense of identity among Palestinian Arabs. They began to feel threatened, particularly by relatively sophisticated and well-organized Jewish quasi-state institutions, such as the *Histadrut or *Haganah. Arab attacks on Jewish settlers climaxed in 1929, when over 200 Jews were massacred in Hebron, and in 1936–9, during the Arab uprising. Tensions intensified partly because Jewish immigration continued, as 80,000 people arrived in 1924–31. In 1932–8, 200,000 Jews immigrated, fleeing from the rise of *anti-Semitism in Europe (particularly, though not exclusively, in Germany and Austria). The unspeakable suffering of Jews in *Nazi *concentration camps such as *Auschwitz changed world opinion, and made the creation of an Israeli state inevitable.

In Israel's shadow (1947–1980s) Palestinian Arabs, supported by Arabs elsewhere, refused to accept this, and in 1948–9 they rose against the new state of Israel, but to no avail. Western Palestine came under Jewish rule, the *Gaza Strip under Egyptian sovereignty, and eastern Palestine became Jordanian territory as the *West Bank. The latter territories came under Israeli administration after the *Six Day War in 1967; but perhaps the darkest days for Arabs in Palestine (Palestinians) came in 1970, when their leaders and many of their people were violently expelled from Jordan by fellow Arabs. They gradually recovered from this blow, and became increasingly self-confident as their leadership, especially the *PLO, grew in international stature. The Palestinians' most concerted effort to have their claim for their own state recognized came in the *Intifadah uprising, which finally convinced Israel that it could not defy Palestinian demands forever. In 1988, in response to Jordan's final renunciation of its claims to the West Bank, the PLO declared it the independent state of Palestine, and later that year finally recognized the state of Israel.

Contemporary politics (since 1990s) Israel refused to accept the legitimacy of the PLO until the *Oslo Accord and *Gaza–Jericho Agreement (1993). Under these agreements, a *Palestinian National Authority (PNA) was established, with *Arafat being elected its first President in 1996. This controlled most of the Gaza strip, as well as a number of disparate Palestinian communities in the West Bank. Following the election of *Netanyahu in 1996, it became increasingly clear that the Oslo Accord, with its promise of an eventual independent Palestinian state, had collapsed. Given this apparent failure of his policies, which was compounded by the dire economic situation of the population in the areas under PNA control, Arafat lost more and more popular support. Meanwhile, a growing number of Palestinian youths became radicalized and lent their support to the *Intifadah.

Meanwhile, throughout the 1990s Israel increased its stake in the Palestinian territories through its construction of Jewish settlements in areas under Israeli control. Jewish settlements were promoted from the 1980s, and doubled in number between 1993 and 2002. By then, 200,000 settlers lived in the West Bank and Gaza, and a further 120,000 resided in East Jerusalem. By 2006, this number had risen to over 250,000 in the West Bank, and 200,000 in East Jerusalem. To protect Israel from the further incursion of suicide attacks, in 2002 Israel began to construct a security wall between the border of Israel and Palestine. This was criticized by pro-Palestinian observers. It included some Palestinian territory on the Israeli side, and severely restricted the movement of Palestinians living along the wall. Paradoxically, the wall was also criticized by right-wing Israelis, as a de facto recognition of Palestinian separateness.

Palestine Liberation Organization, see PLO

Palestinian National Authority (PNA)

The government of the areas in the *Gaza Strip and the *West Bank handed over to Palestinian rule in response to the accords of *Oslo, *Gaza–Jericho, and *Wye. In 1996 *Arafat was elected its President, with over 80 per cent of the popular vote. It consisted of an assembly of 88 seats, of which al-*Fatah occupied 50 after the 1996 elections. It became a significant factor in the Palestinian economy, as it employed around 30,000 paramilitary police and as many civilian administrators. Nevertheless, it was accused of mismanagement, with an investigation concluding that leading members of al-Fatah had embezzled over $300 million before 1997. Its corruption added to the economic problems of the Palestinian territories, as Palestinians were no longer allowed to work in Israel. Mismanagement and growing powerlessness against Israel fuelled popular discontent and helped radicalize a disproportionately young population against the status quo. The PNA was also accused by *Amnesty International of *human rights violations, for instance for the illegal detainment of 500 prisoners on charges without trial of collaborating with Israel. It was also accused by Israel of secretly developing its police force into an army, in violation of its treaty obligations to Israel.

Contemporary politics Arafat was succeeded by *Abbas, but owing to years of mismanagement, al-Fatah lost the 2006 elections to *Hamas. Since Hamas refused to recognize Israel, the PNA was cut off from most of its funds, which came from abroad. This increased poverty even further, as the PNA was unable to pay many of its employees. In 2006, over 50 per cent of the Palestinian population lived below the poverty line, with over 25 per cent of the working population being unemployed. In 2007, Hamas asserted sole authority over *Gaza, whereupon Abbas reasserted his authority over the PNA, though its reach was subsequently limited to the *West Bank.

Palme, Olof Joachim (1927–86). Prime Minister of Sweden 1969–76, 1982–6

Early history Born in Stockholm into a wealthy family, he studied at Kenyon College, Ohio, and then read law at Stockholm University. As chairman of the National Union of Students (1952–3), he attracted the attention of the *Social Democratic Party hierarchy, and in 1953 he became personal secretary to *Erlander. Palme became a member of the Riksdag (parliament) in 1956, and quickly rose through his ministerial appointments, as Minister without Portfolio (1963–5), Minister of Transport (1965), and Minister of Education (1967), until he succeeded Erlander as Prime Minister.

In office As Sweden was already one of the most affluent societies in the world, he saw his main task as reducing the inequalities with which that affluence was shared. He introduced comprehensive education, women's emancipation legislation, and reforms in higher education. However, in a country already tired of high taxation and state intervention, his policies increased the regulatory role of the state even further.

From 1973, Palme had to rule with a minority government. Discontent at the way in which excessive taxation and state regulation appeared to stifle the economy was heightened in the wake of the 1973 *oil-price shock. Palme was unable to find answers to the economic crisis, and for the first time in Sweden's history, a right-wing coalition formed the government in 1976. Palme returned at the head of another minority government in 1982. As a firm adherent to Sweden's neutrality, Palme won international respect as a committed supporter of *decolonization and anti-*imperialism, of poorer countries in general, and of *disarmament. Thus, despite his holding the office of Prime Minister, he did not hesitate to participate in demonstrations against the *Vietnam War, to *Nixon's great irritation. He was murdered under mysterious circumstances; the assassin has never been found.

pan-Africanism
The idea of independence and unity for the African peoples, with an emphasis on the richness of African culture, and its equivalent worth to that of the European powers which were busy colonizing Africa. It was expressed through a series of Pan-African Conferences, the first of which was held in London in 1900. Principally under African-American/Caribbean leadership until 1945, under *Garvey and *Du Bois the movement also emphasized the roots of Blacks in the Americas, seeking to highlight their distinctive African cultural and ethnic heritage.

The sixth Pan-African Conference in Manchester in 1945 saw a fundamental shift, as leadership passed to a new generation of African nationalist leaders, most notably *Nkrumah and *Kenyatta. Ultimately, the movement failed in its ideal of African unity, as the borders established by the colonial powers proved surprisingly enduring. Furthermore, the differences and rivalries between the different tribes and peoples, encouraged by the colonial powers, were much larger than anticipated. Nevertheless, pan-Africanism had a large, if unquantifiable, impact. The writings and teachings of Nkrumah and Kenyatta became central to virtually every independence movement on the continent. In particular, the early independence granted to Nkrumah's Ghana gave an important stimulus to independence movements elsewhere in Africa. The idea of pan-Africanism became the basis for the foundation of the Organization of African Unity (*African Union).

Pan Africanist Congress, see PAC

Panama
A Central American country whose history has been conditioned by the Panama Canal, a seaway 50.7 miles (81.6 km) long dividing the country  and connecting the Atlantic and the Pacific Oceans.

Early statehood (up to 1968) Panama gained its independence from Colombia in 1903, when the canal's chief engineer, Philippe Bunau-Varilla, organized a separatist uprising which the Colombian troops were unable to overcome because of US intervention. On 3 November 1903 the USA immediately recognized the new country with the French citizen Buneau-Varilla as its official representative, with whom it concluded the **Hay–Buneau-Varilla Treaty** of 18 November 1903. The USA secured the right to complete the canal, whose construction had been interrupted by a financial panic in 1893, and received total autonomy in perpetuity over the canal and a ten-mile zone on either side. It was opened on 15 August 1914. Subsequently, life in the canal zone was marked by prosperity, in sharp contrast to that in Panama outside, which was characterized by political instability and poverty, with bananas becoming the main export goods. In 1936 the annual rent for the canal payable to Panama was increased, but public opinion became nevertheless increasingly hostile to the existence of the de facto US colony splitting the country.

In 1954 Panamanian rights over the canal were marginally extended and rent payments increased, and from 1960 the flag of Panama was raised for the first time in the canal zone, alongside that of the USA. However, the issue remained controversial and led to a brief breakdown in relations between the two countries in 1964. The re-election of the corrupt neo-Fascist Arnulfo Arias Madrid (b. 1901, d. 1988) as President in 1968 precipitated a constitutional crisis which was resolved by a coup led by the leader of the National Guard, Brigadier General Omar Torrijos Herrera (b. 1929, d. 1981).

Military rule (1968–89) Torrijos's rule provided the country for the first time with the stability necessary for economic prosperity. From the 1970s Panama developed into an international centre of finance and trade, facilitated by the presence of the canal, its good infrastructure, and the use of the US dollar as the de facto national currency. The Torrijos regime also provided the continuity necessary for negotiations with the USA. Finally, in 1977 a deal was struck with US President *Carter to hand over full sovereignty over the canal by the year 2000, with both countries guaranteeing the zone's neutrality.

Meanwhile, the 1972 Constitution gave Torrijos special powers and institutionalized his military regime. After his death in 1981, the state continued to be ruled by the military behind a façade of civilian Presidents whose function was to present an acceptable democratic face to international opinion (and creditors), and to provide scapegoats for unpopular measures at home. Power became concentrated in the hands of the military leader, General *Noriega. Despite his former work for the *CIA, he was increasingly opposed by the USA as evidence mounted about his involvement in the drugs trade. To force his resignation, the USA declared a trade embargo against Panama in 1988. In May 1989 Noriega annulled the presidential election of the oppositional Guillermo Endara (b. 1936) to declare himself President. To break Noriega's resistance, on 20 December 1989 President Bush dispatched more than 14,000 US troops to Panama. They captured Noriega on 4 January 1990 and took him to face trial in Miami, where he was subsequently sentenced to 40 years' imprisonment. In addition, they installed Endara as President. As a result of the US sanctions and invasion, GNP declined by 22 per cent between 1988 and early 1991, while the damage directly resulting from the invasion amounted to up to $2 billion.

Democratization (1990s) Endara proved unable to cope with these economic problems, so that popular support for his coalition plummeted from 73 per cent in 1989 to 17 per cent in 1991. As a result, on 9 May 1994 a former associate of Noriega, Ernesto Pérez Balladeres, was elected President. He instituted a number of liberal economic reforms, which provided for substantial economic growth, but which also contributed markedly to a growing disparity between rich and poor. His attempt to change the constitution so that he could run again for President failed in a referendum in 1998. The ensuing elections were won by Mireya Elisa Moscoso Rodríguez, the widow of former President Arias Madrid. She won against Martín Torrijos, son of Omar Torrijos, whose Nueva Nación obtained most seats in parliament. On 31 December 1999, US control over the Panama Canal was relinquished, and Panama regained control over its entire territory.

Contemporary politics (since 2004) In 2004, Martín Torrijos, the son of former President Omar Torrijos, was elected President. Although he came from the centre-left Democratic Revolution Party (PRD), Torrijos focused on reducing state spending and introducing social reforms, such as pension reform. This, however, did little to reduce the country's glaring social inequalities. According to the International Fund for Agricultural Development (IFAD), 39 per cent of the rural population and 86.6 per cent of the indigenous population lived in extreme poverty. In 2006, Panamanians agreed in a referendum to widen and deepen the Panama Canal, in order to enable larger container ships to use it.

pan-Americanism

The principle of cooperation between the republics of the hemisphere, which emerged in the 1890s, and was subsequently used by the USA mainly as an excuse to extend its hegemony over Latin America. After World War I, the USA replaced the UK as the dominant trading and financial power in Latin America. At the same time, it refused to acknowledge Latin American efforts, spearheaded by Argentina, to replace rising US military domination by a pan-American treaty in which every American country renounced the right to intervene directly into the affairs of another. The issue was a constant bone of contention throughout the period between the first and the sixth pan-American conferences (1889–1928).

The presence of US troops in sovereign countries became an increasing embarrassment to the USA as it sought to lead world opinion against Japanese military involvement outside its borders in Manchuria (*Manchukuo). In his inaugural address on 4 March 1933, *Roosevelt announced the *Good Neighbor Policy which committed the USA to respecting the integrity of other nations as it respected its own. US military forces withdrew from all Latin American countries, retaining, however, their bases in Cuba and the Panama Canal zone. In addition, the Platt Amendment of 1901 was abrogated in 1934 (*Cuba), and Haiti regained control over its own finances.

After World War II, the relationship between the American states was formalized in the *OAS (Organization of American States) and the Rio Treaty (*Inter-American Treaty of Reciprocal Assistance). However, the strongest military and economic American power by far, the USA has continued to dominate and influence the affairs of Latin American countries, e.g. through the establishment of ever-closer economic ties with individual countries, and through the support of American-trained indigenous political elites such as the *Somoza family in Nicaragua and General *Trujillo in Costa Rica.

pan-Arabism

A secular movement which strives for Arab unity based on the belief in a distinct Arabian language, history, and culture. Its origins go back to the *Ottoman Empire, but it emerged as a mass movement after World War I in opposition to the imposed colonial rule and the artificial creation of separate Arab territories through the British and French *Mandates in Arabia. Since the independence of the Arab states, and the failure of *Ba'athist efforts to achieve Arab unity, emphasis has shifted to Arabian solidarity and co-operation. This aim was furthered particularly by common opposition to the establishment of a Jewish state in *Palestine, which led to the creation of the **Arab League** on 22 March 1945. However, the concept of pan-Arabic cooperation became increasingly one of rhetoric rather than substance following Egypt's peace treaty with Israel in 1978, the *Iran–Iraq War, and the *Gulf War. It was further undermined by deep divisions between *Sunni and *Shi'ite Muslims.

NATIONALISM; ISLAMIC FUNDAMENTALISM

Pankhurst, Dame Christabel Harriette (b. 22 Sept. 1880, d. 13 Feb. 1958). British suffragette leader

Born in Manchester, she grew up in London. In 1903, with her mother, Emmeline *Pankhurst, she formed the Women's Social and Political Union (WSPU). She graduated from Manchester University in 1906, having campaigned vigorously for votes for women with Annie Kenney. She was imprisoned briefly in 1906, and the next year she became secretary of the WSPU. Her organization of a huge rally in June 1908 attracted over half a million supporters to Hyde Park in London, and she was again imprisoned later that year. In 1912–14 she directed the work of the WSPU from Paris, in order to avoid arrest again, but in World War I, like her mother, she devoted herself to recruiting for war service. Once female suffrage had been achieved in 1918, she opposed continuing the WSPU as a political organization and went to live in Canada and the USA.

Pankhurst (née Goulden), Emmeline (b. 4 July 1858, d. 14 June 1929). British suffragette leader

Born in Manchester, she joined the *Independent Labour Party in 1893. Frustrated by the organization's failure to promote the issue of women's suffrage, she and her daughter Christabel *Pankhurst founded the Women's Social and Political Union (WSPU) in 1903. As leading *suffragettes, they put pressure on the *Liberal government to grant votes for women. For her militant tactics she was frequently imprisoned, most famously in 1913, when she was sentenced to three years for arson. Released after a year (August 1914), she abandoned the suffrage campaign to encourage women to assist the war effort by joining the police and services, or by going into industry. She lived in Canada after the war, where she was involved in child welfare and the National Council for Combating Venereal Disease. She returned to England in 1926 and but for her death would have stood as *Conservative candidate for Whitechapel in 1929.

Papandreou, Andreas (b. 5 Feb. 1919, d. 23 June 1996). Prime Minister of Greece 1981–9, 1993–6

Early career Born in Chios as the son of Georgios *Papandreou, he studied at Athens University and received a doctorate from Harvard, after which he became professor of economics at the University of Minnesota in 1951, and at Berkeley in 1955. He returned to Greece in 1960, and became a deputy for his father's Centre Union Party, joining his government as Minister of the Presidency (1964–5). After the military coup of 1967 he was exiled to Sweden and then Canada. Papandreou founded the Panhellenic Resistance Movement in 1968, and headed the Panhellenic Socialist Movement (PASOK) after his return in 1974.

In office Papandreou was a maverick and populist Prime Minister with an anti-Western streak, who had a penchant for quarrels with his neighbours. This did not prevent him from obtaining large funds from the European Economic Community and the USA, using Greece's position as a frontline state against the Communist *Warsaw Pact during the *Cold War for all it was worth. Many of these funds were dissipated by corruption and for the maintenance of his own nepotist power structure: his son Georgios served as Education Minister, while his wife's cousin Georgios Liani was Sports Minister. Most importantly, his controversial wife, a former American nude model, was head of his private office and thus controlled all access to him. Ultimately, this proved too much even for his own party which he had controlled so tightly. As his health deteriorated and her power increased, Papandreou tried hard to have her accepted as his successor. The party rebelled and replaced him with Costas Simitis as Prime Minister and leader of PASOK on 18 January 1996.

Papandreou, Georgios (b. 13 Feb. 1888, d. 1 Nov. 1968). Prime Minister of Greece 1944, 1963, 1964–5
Born in Kalentzi, he graduated in law from the University of Athens, and studied in Germany. He became a lawyer and entered politics as a Liberal. An opponent of *Metaxas, he became a prominent politician and held several ministerial appointments (1923–35). In 1933, he founded the Democratic Party, which in 1935 became the Social Democratic Party. During World War II, he was active in the resistance movement until he was forced to flee, becoming active in the Greek government-in-exile.
  Papandreou returned to Greece in 1944 to head a brief government. He was always, however, unacceptable to the army, and although his new Centre Union Party had a wide following, he never held office for any length of time. He clashed with *Constantine II and resigned in 1965. It was to prevent a new electoral victory for his party in 1967 that the *Greek colonels seized power.

Papen, Franz von (b. 29 Oct. 1879, d. 2 May 1969). Chancellor of Germany 1 June–17 Nov. 1932
A monarchist on the right wing of the *Centre Party, he was a member of the Prussian state parliament 1920–8 and 1930–2. He succeeded *Brüning as Chancellor and

proceeded to lift the ban on *SA activities and call new elections, thus fulfilling the conditions which *Hitler had hinted at as necessary for him to support a right-wing government. The elections produced large gains for the *Nazi Party and the *Communist Party, and hence rendered parliamentary government impossible. Meanwhile, on 20 July 1932 von Papen deposed *Prussia's *SPD government by obtaining a presidential decree from *Hindenburg, thus destroying the most important remaining bastion of the SPD and of democratic government. When he demanded a presidential declaration of a state of emergency, the army refused to back him, and he had to resign. He became one of the principal motivators behind Hitler's appointment as Chancellor, though as his Vice-Chancellor he was unable to contain him. As ambassador to Austria (1936–8) he helped in the preparations for the *Anschluss, and then was sent as ambassador to Turkey. He was acquitted at the *Nuremberg Trials, but convicted in a separate trial in 1949 to eight years in a labour camp, which he never served owing to the time he had already spent in prison.

Papua
Formerly known as Irian Jaya (West Irian), it is the western half of an island also known as New Guinea, inhabited by over 200 tribes with as many languages, numbering a total of just over one million inhabitants. It was claimed by the Dutch from 1875, in response to fears that the Australians would take possession of the whole of the island. It remained relatively unexplored by the Dutch, who used it mainly as the site for a penal colony.
  Upon Indonesian independence in 1949, the Netherlands retained control over the territory because of Irian's tenuous links with Indonesia. This remained a contentious issue in relations between the Netherlands and Indonesia, which regarded continued Dutch presence in the area as an affront to its sovereignty. Under the nationalist 'Guilded Democracy' of President *Sukarno, Indonesian forces invaded the country (1961–2), whereupon the Dutch, under pressure from the *UN and the USA, conceded defeat.
  Since then Irian Jaya has been subject to extensive Indonesian immigration and cultivation programmes. Indonesian dominance of government posts, and cultural and linguistic infringements on its indigenous peoples, have produced widespread resentment, expressed in the formation of the guerrilla Free Papua Movement. The demand for independence grew during the 1990s, emboldened by the weakness of the Indonesian government, and the independence granted to East Timor.

However, Indonesia refused to grant independence. Instead, by 2001 it granted the province autonomy. Re-named Papua, its people were granted a greater share of revenues from its mineral resources, and were allowed to fly their own flag.

Papua New Guinea

Perhaps the world's most diverse country, its population of 5.7 million comprises over two hundred distinct Melanesian cultures, and over eight hundred local languages (representing around one-third of the world's indigenous languages).

Colonial rule (up to 1975) The eastern half of the island of *New Guinea. The area was divided between British and German administration in 1884, but British rule was transferred to Australia. Its Lieutenant-Governor, *Murray, embarked upon a relatively enlightened native policy, in marked contrast to the Germans in the north. In 1920 the territory was united as a *League of Nations *Mandate under Australian administration. World War II was an especially traumatic experience for the island, as 1.5 million Allied troops and 300,000 Japanese soldiers passed through an area previously accommodating fewer than 5,000 White settlers. While one-third of Papua New Guineans in the hinterlands remained completely untouched by these events, along the more accessible valleys and coast Papuans were deeply involved in the war effort, while many settlements and buildings were destroyed.

After the war, the territory came once again under Australian administration as a *UN *trust territory, but this time the Australians provided considerable grants to develop the education and health systems. In 1964 a House of Assembly was created, in which Papua New Guineans had political control for the first time in their history. Self-government was granted in 1973, and independence was achieved on 16 September 1975.

Independence (since 1975) Owing to the country's heterogeneity it was difficult for a functioning government with clear majorities to emerge. Papua New Guinea's economy continued to be dominated by Australian capital: Australian government grants still provided around 20 per cent of state income

in 1990. In 1989 a civil war erupted on the Island of Bougainville, as the Bougainville Revolutionary Army strove for independence. The war cost the lives of over 10,000 people, and was not resolved until 2001, when the island was granted far-reaching autonomy with a view to independence about ten years later.

Contemporary politics (since 2002) In 2002, Michel Somare, who had led the country into independence, was re-elected to head a multi-party coalition. Under *Howard, Australia provided help for the police force and the administration, but this was rescinded in 2005, when the constitutional court declared this unconstitutional. This did little to establish law and order in the towns and rural regions of the country. Papua New Guinea thus continued to suffer from an absence of administrative capacity, a lack of infrastructure, widespread poverty, and relative international isolation, with little change in sight.

Paraguay

A landlocked South American country whose political system has always been more or less authoritarian.

Contemporary history (until 1989) Paraguay took decades to recover from the disastrous war against Uruguay, Brazil, and Argentina (1865–70), in which it lost 90 per cent of its male population. In the 'constitutional phase' (1890–1936) political parties emerged, mainly the conservative Colorados and the Liberals (Azules). However, they were unable to form stable governments, and the governing elites maintained their power by rigging elections. The country was plunged into renewed economic turmoil by the victorious *Chaco War with Bolivia (1932–5), which exhausted Paraguay's fragile economy. Subsequently, the military extended its political control, though stability was only achieved with the 1954 coup of General *Stroessner.

Stroessner strengthened his grip on power through combining party and military leadership, so that he himself became leader of the Colorado Party. In 1967 he introduced a new constitution, but the changes were apparent rather than real. He provided a significant and much-needed boost to the economy when he agreed to the construction of the Itaipú hydroelectric project (1973–82), one of the largest civil engineering projects of the century, in conjunction with Brazil. From

1976 to 1981 the economy grew at an annual average of 10 per cent, one of the highest growth rates in the world. However, this also caused inflation, while the end of the Itaipú project led to economic stagnation. As a result, Paraguayan society became more dissatisfied, with the first unauthorized opposition rallies being held in 1984. Stroessner's efforts at tightening his rule were hindered by internal divisions within his *Colorado Party from 1987, between more reform-orientated traditionalists and hardline supporters.

On 3 February 1989 Stroessner was finally removed by the army's second-in-command, Andrés Rodríguez. Rodríguez was subsequently elected President (May 1989) and swiftly established freedom of the press and of party association. In 1993 the Colorado Party's candidate, Juan Carlos Wasmosy Monti (b. 1938), won the Presidential elections. Although declining somewhat, throughout the 1990s the Colorado Party's hold over the political system and its influence over the armed forces was still strong enough to prevent the stabilization of the political system. The 1998 presidential elections were overshadowed by the threatened candidacy of former General Linos César Oviedo Silva. The popular general was sentenced to imprisonment on account of corruption, and this allowed the official candidate, Raúl Cubas Grau, to win the elections. Cubas's pardon of Oviedo was declared void by the constitutional court, whereupon Cubas was impeached by parliament in 1999. In that year, the political system suffered a further setback through the murder of the Vice-President, Luís María Argaña.

Contemporary politics (since 1989) The new President, Luis Angel Gonzáles Macchi, tried to stabilize the government, but his attempts were eroded by Paraguay's virtual economic collapse. It was unable to meet its debt repayments, and was plagued by escalating rural poverty and growing inflation. At the same time, all attempts at economic reform faced great popular opposition, as the withdrawal of the state threatened to make services even more expensive.

Beneath the dominance of the Colorado Party, tensions continued among Paraguay's political elites. Oviedo was charged also with involvement with drugs cartels, while former President Cubas was charged with corruption. When Macchi left office in 2003, he was banned from leaving the country. He was sentenced to imprisonment for corruption in 2006. With an economy shackled by rampant corruption, the efforts of Macchi's successor, President Óscar Nicanor Duarte Frutos, to combat corruption and encourage the rule of law stimulated modest economic growth at between 2 and 3 per cent per year.

Paris, Pact of, see KELLOGG–BRIAND PACT

Paris Peace Accords (27 Jan. 1973)
A peace treaty negotiated chiefly between *Le Duc Theu and *Kissinger, signed by representatives of the Democratic Republic of Vietnam (North Vietnam), the Republic of Vietnam (South Vietnam), the Provisional Revolutionary Government of South Vietnam (PRG), and the USA. The accords were concluded after more than four years of negotiations, which were begun after the *Tet offensive in 1968 but frequently interrupted, e.g. by US bombing offensives. They provided for the withdrawal of US troops and thus an end to direct US military involvement. In return, democratic elections were to be held in South Vietnam, in order to end the rivalry between the official government of *Nguyen Van Thieu, and the Communist PRG. Nguyen Van Thieu rejected the treaty, however, and with US assistance continued to defy the *Vietcong and North Vietnam's People's Army. Peace was enforced only in a final offensive of the People's Army, which led to the collapse of Nguyen's regime on 30 April 1975.

Paris Peace Conference (1919–20)
Overview A congress attended by the participant powers of *World War I, which led to the imposition of five peace treaties on the defeated *Central Powers in the suburbs of *Versailles (Germany), *St Germain-en-Laye (Austria), *Trianon (Hungary), *Neuilly (Bulgaria), and *Sèvres (*Ottoman Empire). It was dominated, especially at the beginning, by *Clemenceau (France), *Lloyd George (UK), and *Wilson (USA), and to a lesser extent by *Orlando (Italy), who made up the Big Four. At the same time, the conference was an important step towards statehood for the British Dominions, which demanded, and received, representation independent of Britain.

Guiding principles The various treaties that emerged were extremely problematic and proved a tremendous burden for subsequent stability in Europe. This was essentially the result of incompatible, and self-contradictory, goals of the victorious powers.

1. Wilson aimed at a just peace and national self-determination based on the *Fourteen Principles. Even by itself, this proved to be an impossibility, notably in those areas without a single dominant national ethnicity, where historical claims were ambiguous, and in pockets where national communities lived in isolation, surrounded by other ethnicities. Nevertheless, new states were created in an effort to take account of nationality and initial frictions were, perhaps, inevitable.

2. Wilson's ideas for a 'just' peace clashed fundamentally with the French position, which was to punish Germany so severely that it could never start another war. The French succeeded in placing Germany's areas left of the River Rhine (*Ruhr District) under international (mainly French) control, while the *Saarland came under the authority of the *League of Nations—all this in blatant disregard of US aims.

3. British aims hovered somewhere between the French and the American positions. While Britain did manage to moderate the demands of the other two countries, notably France, its lack of alternative vision did little to enhance the conference's outcome.

Evaluation The conference thus produced the worst of all worlds, with nationalistic conflicts left unresolved and sometimes worsened. Even in Italy, a victorious power, it led to *irredentist resentment. The defeated countries (which were mostly barely consulted), harboured immense grievances which rendered their domestic and foreign politics hostile and aggressive. Finally, the *League of Nations, which had been created to settle unresolved conflicts and smooth out the problems of the peace settlement, was crucially weakened from the outset by the refusal of the world's most powerful nation, the USA, to enter, as a result of an *isolationist *Congress. The instabilities created by the various peace settlements have often been seen as a direct cause of World War II. While it is true that *Mussolini and *Hitler came to power partly through exploiting the resentment caused by the Paris Peace Conference, it would be wrong to conclude that its outcome made World War II inevitable. There was a period of considerable calm and normalization in the 1920s, while it was the economic crises immediately after the war (1918–23) and during the Great *Depression that made continental Europe so volatile and gave nationalist movements their potency.

Paris Peace Treaties (10 Feb. 1947)
From July 1946 until February 1947, delegates from twenty-one nations met in Paris to decide on peace terms for Germany's five allies in *World War II: Bulgaria, Hungary, Finland, Italy, and Romania. Italy was obliged to cede most of the Istrian peninsula, including *Fiume (Rijeka), and some Adriatic islands to Yugoslavia, and the Dodecanese to Greece; *Trieste became a free city, a status it retained until 1954. Italy also had to accept some minor frontier adjustments and renounce all claims in Africa. Romania regained *Transylvania, but ceded Bessarabia (*Moldova) and the northern *Bukovina to the Soviet Union. Bulgaria's sovereignty over south *Dobrudja, which it had regained from Romania in 1940, was confirmed. Hungary remained limited to its frontiers of the Treaty of *Trianon. Finally, Finland had to cede Petsamo to the Soviet Union. A peace treaty with Austria was not concluded until 1955, while bitter Allied disputes over the division of Germany during the *Cold War prevented the conclusion of a peace treaty with Germany until German reunification in 1990.

Park Chung Hee (b. 30 Sept. 1917, d. 26 Oct. 1979). President of the Republic of Korea 1963–79
Born in Sonsan into a poor family, he became a primary school teacher in 1937. In World War II, he went to Manchuria and received training at the *Manchukuo as well as the Japanese Military Academy. After the war, he went to South *Korea to enlist in the Korean Constabulary, which was soon transformed into the armed forces. As one of the army's senior members he led the 1961 May Military Revolution. He formed a military junta, and in 1963 had himself formally elected President. While maintaining a politically illiberal regime, he encouraged industrial development and educational reforms. In 1971–2, he changed the constitution to the Yushin (Revitalizing Reform) rule. This created a fully authoritarian government. He banned all anti-government activities, while many intellectuals were arrested and killed. He proclaimed martial law in 1972 and was then re-elected twice in 1972 and 1978. His government not only became increasingly authoritarian, but also increasingly corrupt. He was assassinated by the head of the South Korean Central Intelligence Agency.

parliament, UK
The legislative assembly of the *United Kingdom is divided into two houses, the Commons and the Lords, both of which sit in the Palace of Westminster. The Commons in particular served as a patron to the establishment of parliamentary systems throughout the world (even though in many post-colonial African countries they proved completely inappropriate and short-lived). For example, the parliamentary systems of Canada and New Zealand are based on the constitutional and procedural precedent established by the British parliament.

The most important part of parliament is the **House of Commons**. This is directly elected at general elections, and the leader of the party with a majority in the Commons is asked by the monarch to form a government. If no party has a majority, there may be a minority government, or a coalition, in which the Prime Minister is usually the leader of the largest party. Once Members of Parliament (MPs) have been elected to the Commons, the Prime Minister forms a Cabinet of Ministers. This formulates policy, presenting proposals to parliament which are read three times as bills, and debated. They will also be discussed in Standing or Select Committees, and then voted on. Bills may also be presented by individual members, although this rarely results in the passage of legislation.

Before receiving royal assent, bills must also be discussed by the **House of Lords**. The 1911 Parliament Act reduced the Lords' power to a suspensive veto of two years, and gave the House of Lords no authority over financial legislation. The veto was reduced to one year in 1949. Membership of the Lords was traditionally by the inheritance of a title. In 1958 the Life Peerages Act created non-hereditary peerages which would be granted to a person (male or female) for the term of their life. From 1963, women holding hereditary peerages were permitted to enter the Lords. Despite these reforms, the existence of a second chamber based on privilege and birthright was a unique anachronism for a democracy, and gave the *Conservative Party a huge inbuilt majority in the second chamber.

Fundamental reform was initiated by the *Labour Party under Tony *Blair. In 1999, hereditary peers were no longer eligible to sit in the House, but they were allowed to select 92 peers who would continue as representatives for a transitional period. These were now outweighed by 26 *Anglican bishops and over 500 appointed life peers whose party affiliation broadly represented national party strength. Ironically, as the House could now claim greater legitimacy in its composition, it became more assertive in its stance against a series of government bills. An all-elected chamber was high on the agenda in 2007, as Tony Blair pushed for a final reform before he was to leave office in the summer of that year.

(()) SEE WEB LINKS

• The official website of the Houses of Parliament.

Parti Québécois (PQ) (Canada)

A political party founded by *Lévesque in 1968 which united various separatist movements to form a coherent strategy for gaining the independence of the largely French-speaking province of Quebec from the rest of Canada. Since the majority of Quebeckers were against a severance of ties with Canada, the PQ developed the idea of 'sovereignty-association', a vague plan whereby Quebec would become a sovereign state, but would retain close links with Canada, including a common currency.

The PQ quickly gained popular support, allowing it to win the 1976 provincial elections in Quebec. In a 1980 referendum, however, 60 per cent voted against sovereignty. The party was subsequently weakened and divided about whether to pursue pragmatic government or continue to push for independence.

The PQ lost power to the *Liberal Party in 1984, regaining it only under the leadership of Jacques Parizeau (b. 1930) in 1994, one year after the *Bloc Québécois (BQ) had been successful in the provincial elections.

The PQ organized another referendum on the sovereignty of Quebec in 1995, which it narrowly lost. To increase popular support for sovereignty, Parizeau gave way to the more charismatic *Bouchard in early 1996. Under Bouchard's leadership, the PQ turned its attention increasingly to the province's economic problems. As Quebec was one of the net recipients of federal funds, fostering economic growth was considered crucial in furthering support for independence. The goal of economic recovery, however, has forced the PQ to take more conciliatory attitudes towards the province's pro-federalist Anglophone business community. Economic issues also pushed the question of independence into the background, causing a further decline in the PQ's popularity. This was not halted by Bouchard's more radical successor from 2001, Bernard Landry. In the 2003 provincial elections, the PQ gained only 45 out of 125 seats in the provincial assembly. From 2005, it was led by André Boisclair (b. 1966), who confirmed the PQ's commitment to another referendum on sovereignty. This was rejected in the 2007 elections, when the PQ was pushed into third place and lost the status of the official opposition.

(()) SEE WEB LINKS

• The home page of the Parti Québécois.

Parti Socialiste (PS), see SOCIALIST PARTY, FRANCE

Partido Social Obrero Español (PSOE), see SOCIALIST WORKERS' PARTY OF SPAIN

partisans

Members of organized, quasi-military resistance movements, who are not members of regular military units, but freely participate in violent campaigns against regular military units. The term is most frequently used to describe the Communist resistance movement under *Tito in Yugoslavia, though partisans were active throughout the Balkans. Partisan warfare was particularly suitable for this part of Europe on account of the rugged terrain, which posed great difficulties for the occupying Hungarian, German, and Italian armies.

Partito Comunista Italiano (PCI), see
COMMUNIST PARTY, ITALY

Partito Nazionale Fascista (PNF), see
FASCIST MOVEMENT, ITALY

Partito Popolare Italiano (PPI, Italian People's Party), see CHRISTIAN DEMO-
CRATIC PARTY, ITALY; POPULAR PARTY, ITALY

Partito Socialista Democratico Italiano (PSDI), see SOCIALIST PARTY, ITALY

Partito Socialista Unitario (PSU), see
SOCIALIST PARTY, ITALY

Partnership for Peace, see NATO

Pašić, Nikola (b. 1 Jan. 1845, d. 10 Dec. 1926). Prime Minister of the Kingdom of Serbs, Croats, and Slovenes 1921–4, 1924–6
Born in Zajecar in Serbia, he studied engineering in Belgrade and Zurich, where he became interested in politics. First elected to the Serbian parliament in 1878, he founded the Radical Party in 1881 and was exiled 1883–9 due to his opposition to the King, Milan I Obrenovic. He dominated Serbian politics from 1891, when he first became Prime Minister, until his death. Pašić pursued the policy of creating a Greater Serbia, to which end he led his country through the *Balkan Wars of 1912–13. In 1917 he skilfully negotiated the *Corfu Pact, which effectively provided for the creation of a Serb-dominated Kingdom of Serbs, Croats, and Slovenes (Yugoslavia from 1929) after the War. As Prime Minister of the new kingdom, he furthered Serbian predominance with considerable success, despite the domestic tensions which this caused.

Passchendaele, Battle of (31 July–10 Nov. 1917)
The third Battle of *Ypres, named after a village which became the furthest point of advance in this Allied offensive during *World War I. Despite the disastrous casualties suffered at the *Somme, General *Haig continued to believe that frontal assaults in superior numbers must succeed if sufficient troops were thrown at the enemy. Hence, he planned to seize the Passchendaele ridge and then sweep into Belgium. Constant shelling

and torrential rain reduced Flanders to a sea of mud, which made advance all but impossible. The ruined village of Passchendaele itself was only reached after several attacks on 9 November. By then, it was too late to continue the offensive further. For a most marginal territorial gain, the Allies had suffered some 300,000 casualties and had been exposed, for the first time, to the German use of mustard gas. Passchendaele itself was surrendered in the retreat before *Ludendorff's final offensive five months later. In Canadian and British popular memory, the battle became one of the major symbols of the futility and human cost of the war.

Patel, Sardar Vallabhbhai (b. 31 Oct. 1875, d. 15 Dec. 1950). Deputy Prime Minister of India 1947–50
A successful criminal lawyer born at Nadiad, he went to England (1910–13) to be admitted to the Bar. There, he was profoundly influenced by *Naoroji. Upon his return he became a successful lawyer in Allahabad, and in 1917 he became active in local politics. In that year, Patel became a loyal follower of *Gandhi, supporting him in all his major campaigns. Although less well known than Jawaharlal *Nehru, he gained a firm hold of the organization of the Indian National *Congress (INC). In the end, however, what counted more was Gandhi's favour, so that the more moderate and conciliatory Patel was reduced to playing second fiddle to Nehru.

As Home Minister from 1946 he was responsible for the most successful achievements of Nehru's administration. He transformed the INC from a popular movement into an organized political party. Of even greater achievement was his successful creation of a viable administrative and governmental structure for an independent India. Most significantly, he oversaw the transformation of the 562 princely states into twenty-six viable administrative units which formed an integral part of the Union of India.

Pathet Lao (Lao Nation / 'Land of the Lao')
A term originally used to describe the areas in Laos freed from French control in the First *Indochina War by the Communist guerrillas. It was then increasingly used more generally, as a descriptive term for the Communist movement in Laos. This emerged in 1950 with the formation of the Free Laos Front, which closely coordinated its campaigns in the Indochina War with the *Vietminh forces. After the *Geneva Agreements, it was transformed into the Lao Patriotic Front (1956), under the presidency of

Souphanouvong. Given its association with the Vietnamese Communist movement under *Ho Chi Minh, it was closely involved in the *Vietnam War, as a crucial *Vietcong supply route: the Ho Chi Minh Trail went through the territory controlled by the Pathet Lao. Meanwhile, in tandem with events in Vietnam, a cease-fire ending the civil war between the forces of *Souvanna Phouma and the Pathet Lao came into effect after the *Paris Peace Accords of 1973. Together with Souvanna Phouma it participated in the compromise government of 1974. After North Vietnam's takeover of South Vietnam and Cambodia in 1975, the Pathet Lao (now officially the Lao People's Revolutionary Party) gained military and thus political control over the entire country.

Patton, George Smith (b. 11 Nov. 1885, d. 21 Dec. 1945). US general
Born in California, he graduated from the US Military Academy in 1909 and joined the staff of General John *Pershing, with whom he fought in Mexico (1916) and France (1917). Between the wars he became an expert on tank warfare, and in World War II he commanded a corps in the *North African campaign and then the 7th Army in Sicily. He temporarily lost his command in 1943, after a publicized incident in which he hit a soldier suffering from battle fatigue. This was doubly unfortunate since his warfare was always concerned with making sure that he protected all of his men as much as humanly possible and the incident conveyed an apparent callousness that was not present. In 1944, Patton returned to lead the US 3rd Army at *D-Day and in the *Normandy campaign. He continued in a spectacular sweep through France, across the Rhine, and into Czechoslovakia. As military Governor of Bavaria, he was criticized and relieved of his command in October 1945 for his fervent anti-Communism which led to accusations of leniency toward *Nazis.

Paul VI (Giovanni Battista Montini) (b. 26 Sept. 1897, d. 6 Aug. 1978). Pope 1963–78
The son of a wealthy landowner, he was ordained in 1920 and went to the Gregorian University in Rome. In 1923 he joined the papal diplomatic corps. For the following thirty years he was active in the Secretariat of State, whose business he directed from 1944 onwards. He became Archbishop of Milan in 1954, and was widely tipped to become Pope in 1958, though eventually *John XXIII was elected. However, John XXIII made him a cardinal in the same year and promoted him wherever possible, giving him an important role at the Second *Vatican Council in 1962.

As pope, he continued his predecessor's drive for the liberalization of the church, e.g. convening a second session of the Vatican Council within three weeks of his election. He also continued to develop the *ecumenical movement, and in 1965 the hostility between the Roman *Catholic Church and the *Eastern Orthodox Churches was formally lifted.

Some of the most sweeping changes of his papacy were to be introduced after the end of the Second Vatican Council in 1965. In 1970–1, the order of services was restructured, and it became common to celebrate mass in the vernacular instead of Latin. Paul VI was also the first Pope to travel outside Europe, a gesture through which he recognized the growing importance of Africa, Asia, and Latin America to Roman Catholicism. He was conservative on moral issues, particularly in his opposition to birth control, as expressed through the *encyclical *Humanae Vitae* (1968).

Paul, Alice (b. 11 Jan. 1885, d. 9 July 1977). US women's rights activist
Born at Moorestown, New Jersey, she became a founder of the 1916 US National Woman's Party and campaigned for women to be granted the vote at all levels of government. A militant *suffragist, she energized the movement through her hunger strikes and her fiery rhetoric. After political equality in 1920 had been achieved through the Nineteenth Amendment to the Constitution, she developed a feminist programme which included a campaign for equality of rights between men and women to be enshrined in the US Constitution. She also proposed a world political party to argue for the rights of women across the globe, and European agitation for equal rights. The latter was not well received in Britain and France, and found little resonance in other European states plagued by domestic economic and political instability in the 1930s. She lived to experience the explosion of feminism in the 1960s and 1970s before she died at Moorestown.

Paulus, Friedrich (b. 23 Sept. 1890, d. 1 Feb. 1957). German field marshal
In January 1942 he became commander of the 6th Army, with which he took the city of *Stalingrad in November 1942. He was encircled by the *Red Army, however, and following *Hitler's orders he refused to break out or capitulate for as long as possible. Nevertheless, owing to heavy losses he surrendered on 31 January 1943 and became a Soviet prisoner of war until 1953. He spent the last years of his life in East Germany.

Pavelić, Ante (b. 14 July 1889, d. 28 Dec. 1959). Croatian Fascist leader

Born in Bradina (Bosnia), he trained and practised as a lawyer in Zagreb, entering local politics in 1920. Elected to parliament in 1927, he criticized the increasing centralization of government and its dominance by Serbs under *Alexander I. He fled to Italy in 1929 when Alexander I assumed dictatorial powers. Here he became leader of the *Ustase terrorist movement, and organized Alexander's murder in 1934. As head of the *Fascist Independent State of Croatia (1941–5) he was responsible for brutal atrocities against both Jews and Orthodox Serbs. He went into hiding in 1945 and then escaped to Argentina, where he founded an Ustase government-in-exile. He died in Madrid.

Paz Estenssoro, Victor (b. 2 Oct. 1907, d. 7 June 2001). President of Bolivia 1952–6, 1960–4, 1985–9

Born in Tarija and educated at the University of Mayor de San Andrés, he worked in finance and banking in the 1930s before becoming a university professor of economic history and government economic adviser. In 1941 he co-founded the National Revolutionary Movement (Movimiento Nacionalista Revolucionario, MNR), which was initially nationalist but became increasingly left wing. He served as Minister of Finance in the populist Villarroel government (1943–6) while transforming the MRN into the anti-establishment voice of the disadvantaged and dissatisfied. In exile in Argentina following the military coup of 1946, he returned in 1952 to head a new government which revolutionized Bolivian politics and society. The suffrage was granted to the indigenous majority, who also gained grants of arable land on the central plateau, and the tin mines were nationalized. He was succeeded by his Vice-President in 1956, but was re-elected twice before an army coup forced him again into exile. He returned from Peru in 1971, but was forced to leave the country again (this time to Paraguay) in 1974. Following the reintroduction of democracy, he failed to be elected President in 1980 but succeeded in 1985. In his final term of office, the erstwhile radical instigated a draconian programme of economic liberalization and privatization which stabilized the country's economy and, implicitly, its democracy.

PCF (Parti Communiste Français), see COMMUNIST PARTY, FRANCE

PCI (Partito Comunista Italiano), see COMMUNIST PARTY, ITALY

PDS, see COMMUNIST PARTY, GERMANY

PDS (Partito Democratico della Sinistra), see COMMUNIST PARTY, ITALY

Peace Constitution, Japan, see JAPAN, CONSTITUTION OF

Peace Preservation Law (Japan)

One of the most significant instruments of intellectual and political repression in prewar Japan. Enacted in 1925 to coincide with the introduction of universal male suffrage, it made illegal associations which had as their aim the alteration of Japan's imperial system and the system of private property. The law was used with great success to clamp down on left-wing and radical groups in Japan. After 1945 it was revoked as part of the US occupation's (*SCAP) attempts to dismantle the structures that had given rise to Japanese militarism.

Pearl Harbor

A major US naval base on the island of Oahu in Hawaii. A surprise attack by Japanese carrier-borne aircraft on 7 December 1941, delivered without a prior declaration of war, brought the USA into *World War II. A total of 188 US aircraft were destroyed, eight battleships and eleven other navy vessels were sunk or damaged. The attack was a strategic failure, however, because the crucial element of the US Pacific fleet, its aircraft carriers, were out of the harbour on that day.

Pearse, Patrick Henry (b. 10 Nov. 1879, d. 3 May 1916). Irish revolutionary

Born in Dublin, and educated at private school and the Royal University of Ireland, Pearse's early career was as an educationalist and lecturer, particularly in Irish Gaelic. He had joined the Gaelic League in 1895, soon edited its newspaper, and founded a bilingual school (Scoil Éanna in Ranelagh). His early career convinced him that Irish nationhood could only be attained after the Irish language and traditional Irish culture were revived. He was originally a constitutional nationalist, supporting the Home Rule demands of John *Redmond, but soon became convinced that Britain would not pass Home Rule over Ulster Unionist objections. In 1913 he joined the Irish Republican Brotherhood, and was elected to the Provisional Committee of the Irish Volunteers (of which he was a founder member in November 1913). His famous oration over the grave of Irish patriot Jeremiah O'Donovan Rossa in 1915, with its final words 'Ireland unfree shall never be at peace', became a mantra for fiery nationalists. He led the ill-conceived and unsuccessful *Easter Rising of 1916, which led to his imprisonment. He was court-martialled, condemned to death, and executed in Kilmainham gaol (Dublin). In addition to his political and military activities, he considered his work for the Irish language central to his life, and wrote stories, essays, and poetry in Irish and English.

Pearson, Lester Bowles ('Mike') (b. 23 Apr. 1897, d. 27 Dec. 1972). Prime Minister of Canada 1963–8

Born at Newtonbrook (Ontario), he served in World War I before studying at the Universities of Toronto and Oxford. After Oxford, he returned to Toronto University to teach history, and began working for the Department of External Affairs. He became first secretary in the Canadian high commission in London in 1935, and in 1942 was sent to Washington as second-in-command of the Canadian legation. As Canadian ambassador to the USA from 1945, he attended the founding conference of the *UN, in which he continued to take a strong interest. Recalled by *Mackenzie King to become Deputy Minister of External Affairs in 1946, he left the civil service to become a *Liberal MP in the House of Commons in 1948. Following his election, he was appointed Minister for External Affairs, and subsequently formulated Canada's foreign-policy principles that were to be in place for the rest of the century: a commitment to *NATO allied to a strong commitment to the UN as the best mechanism for international peace.

Pearson was president of the UN General Assembly in 1952, and in 1956 found a relatively face-saving way out of the *Suez Crisis for British and French troops, through their temporary replacement by a **UN peacekeeping** force. He was rewarded for this accomplishment with the 1957 *Nobel Peace Prize. From then on, involvement in international peacekeeping came to be regarded by Canadians as an important part of their identity. Pearson became Liberal Party leader in 1958, and in 1963 he was Prime Minister with a minority government, failing again in 1965 to produce a majority. Nevertheless, he further expanded the *welfare state, introducing for instance a national pension plan and a universal healthcare system. The least political of Canada's Prime Ministers, he retired in 1968 and was succeeded by *Trudeau.

Peng Dehuai (P'eng Te-huai) (b. 1898, d. 29 Nov. 1974). Chinese general

One of the most important Chinese generals. He enlisted in the Hunan provincial army in 1916 and, during the *Northern Expedition, was a regimental commander in the *National Revolutionary Army. A brigade commander by 1928, he joined the Chinese *Communist Party and became commander of the 5th Red Army. He joined forces with *Mao Zedong and *Zhu De, and became deputy commander of their 4th Red Army. He played a pivotal role in the defence of the *Jianxi Soviet, and in the success of the *Long March, in which his unswerving support for Mao was crucial in Mao's assumption of power. He had an important role in the Chinese *Civil War, and in 1950–4 commanded the Chinese forces (Chinese People's Volunteers) in the *Korean War. He was in total control of the army as Minister of National Defence from 1954, but criticized the disastrous *Great Leap Forward, for which he was dismissed from office. His support within the leadership ensured his continued presence in the *Politburo, though he was the first victim of the *Cultural Revolution, which started with defamations against him. He was imprisoned and put into solitary confinement until his death. He was rehabilitated posthumously under *Deng Xiaoping, and became a symbol for Mao's authoritarian nature.

Pentagon Papers (USA)

In spring 1971, psychiatrist Daniel Ellsberg and journalist Antony Russo stole a classified 1967 study of the origins of the *Vietnam War and a secret 1965 study of the Gulf of *Tonkin incident from the Department of Defense. They then passed the so-called 'Pentagon Papers' to the *New York Times* and the *Washington Post*. The papers revealed intimate details about the secretive and often duplicitous workings of various administrations under *Eisenhower, *Kennedy, and *Johnson. The *Nixon administration obtained a temporary restraint on publication, on grounds of national security, which was overturned by the *Supreme Court. The newspapers then published selected documents which stimulated the already intense opposition to the war. Federal officials also obtained fifteen indictments, including charges of conspiracy, theft, and espionage, against Ellsberg and Russo. The charges were dropped in 1973 after it was revealed that government evidence had been obtained by illegal means.

Peres, Shimon (b. 16 Aug. 1923). Prime Minster of Israel 1977, 1984–6, 1995–6

Early career Born Shimon Peresky at Vishneva, Poland, he arrived in *Palestine in 1934. He became active in the *kibbutz movement as well as the *Haganah. As Haganah's director of manpower from 1947, he was instrumental in the (often illegal) manufacture and purchase of arms by the Haganah and then the Israeli army. He continued in this activity during his studies in New York and at Harvard, and while acting as Director-General of the Defence Ministry. In addition to enabling Israel's armed forces to withstand any attack with modern weaponry, he also laid the foundations of a domestic defence industry, for example through the creation of aircraft factories. He continued in his office after his election to parliament (Knesset) in 1959.

Peres resigned from the government in 1965 to join *Ben-Gurion's new Rafi party as Secretary-General. A member of the *Labour Party from 1968, he held various ministries from 1969. After *Meir's retirement in 1974, he narrowly lost the leadership to *Rabin and became Rabin's Minister of Defence, despite their usual disagreements and controversies. Peres and Rabin shared an unusual combination of mutual dislike, bitter rivalry, and respect, which marked not only their relationship but also the fate of the Labour Party from the 1970s until Rabin's death.

Political leadership (1977–99) Peres challenged Rabin for the leadership in 1977, once again unsuccessfully, but succeeded him when Rabin was forced to retire later in the same year. Unfortunately, his organizational skills, integrity, and vision were disproportionate to his political instincts. In 1977 he became the first socialist Prime Minister to lose an election, and in 1981 he lost to *Begin a second time. He won an unconvincing victory in 1984, which compelled him to share power with the *Likud Bloc. He conducted the army's withdrawal from most of the Lebanon and presided over some economic austerity measures. Peres again failed to win the 1988 elections and was forced to support Shamir as Finance Minister. He rebelled against the government in 1990, and Shamir formed a government without him. He became leader of the opposition. Never having won convincingly against Likud, he was replaced by his old rival, Rabin, in 1992.

Rabin duly won the elections of the same year and formed a Labour government, with Peres as his foreign minister. Having opposed Likud's confrontational policies towards the Palestinians throughout the 1980s, Peres became the driving force behind a series of talks which culminated in the *Oslo Accords of 1993, designed to become the foundation stone of a lasting peace settlement in the Middle East. To achieve this, he persevered against mistrust of the *PLO, and the reluctant scepticism of Rabin. He continued to be the main driving force in Israel towards a comprehensive peace settlement, for which he was awarded the *Nobel Peace Prize in 1994, together with Rabin and *Arafat. After Rabin's assassination in 1995 he became Prime Minister again. Despite initial support for his peace initiatives in the wake of Rabin's murder, he lost the 1996 elections to *Netanyahu after a series of devastating suicide bombs by *Hamas.

Contemporary activity (since 1999) In the 1999 prime ministerial elections, Peres had to withdraw from his intention to run in favour of his party rival, *Barak. In return, he was the Labour Party's candidate in the 2000 presidential elections, which once again he lost against expectations. After the failure of Barak, he was invited to become Foreign Minister in *Sharon's government. Despite his personal respect for Sharon, in 2002 he led the Labour Party into opposition in protest against Sharon's hardline policies. Peres and the Labour Party re-joined Sharon's government in 2005, to secure the Israeli withdrawal from Gaza. Peres joined Sharon's *Kadima party, and served under *Olmert as Vice-Premier, intending to stand again for election as President in 2007.

perestroika ('restructuring')
Together with *glasnost, the central pillar of Mikhail *Gorbachev's efforts to reform Soviet economy and society. In appreciation of the poor state of the Soviet Union's economy, which was centrally planned by appointees of the *Communist Party, Gorbachev wanted to increase the efficiency of the economy and, implicitly, of the party. Gorbachev's aim was thus to reform the Communist Party to enable promotion by merit and intelligence as well as the traditional commitment to party ideology. Through perestroika, more party officials in important posts were replaced then at any time since the days of Stalin's *Great Purge. This increased Gorbachev's power initially, but it also brought to the fore many who were even more reformist, such as the Mayor of Moscow, Boris *Yeltsin. At the same time, perestroika caused considerable resentment among the more conservative elements within the party, which led to the *August coup of 1991. It failed because Gorbachev sought to correct the problems in state and society caused by the Communist Party through the party itself. Caught between bitter conservatives and impatient progressives, Gorbachev lost more and more political support, so that he became the ultimate victim of perestroika.

Pérez de Cuéllar, Javier (b. 19 Jan. 1920). UN Secretary-General 1982–91

Born in Lima (Peru), he studied law and entered the Peruvian diplomatic service. He served in France, the UK, Brazil, and the Soviet Union, and in 1971 became Peru's ambassador to the *UN. In 1979 he was appointed UN Under-Secretary for Political Affairs and in 1981 Secretary-General to succeed Kurt *Waldheim. He was unable to resolve peacefully the dispute which led to the *Falklands War in 1982, but was more successful in his mediation of the *Iran-Iraq War in 1988, and the resolution of the war in Namibia (1988). In 1995, he ran unsuccessfully against *Fujimori in the presidential elections. On 28 November 2000, he became the caretaker Prime Minister and Foreign Minister of Peru, to oversee Peru's transition from the Fujimori dictatorship to a democratically-elected government. Following elections in spring 2001, he withdrew from political life in July 2001.

Perkins, Frances (b. 10 Apr. 1882, d. 14 May 1965). US Secretary of Labor 1933–45

Born at Boston, Massachusetts, she graduated from Mount Holyoke College, and took a graduate degree at Columbia. She took up social work, working in New York City from 1910 until 1929. Like many progressives of her generation, she was deeply affected by the New York Clothing Co. Triangle Factory fire on 25 March 1911, whereupon she campaigned for better health and safety legislation. She caught the attention of Franklin D. *Roosevelt, who as Governor appointed her state industrial commissioner (1929–32). During the *New Deal, against bitter business and political opposition, she became Roosevelt's Secretary of Labor, the first woman Cabinet member in the USA. She served in this position throughout Roosevelt's Presidency. Perkins played an active role in minimum wage and maximum hours legislation, and helped to draft the Fair Labor Standards Act (1938). More than anyone else, she was responsible for the 1935 Social Security Act, having chaired the committee which drafted it. This became a milestone in American government, giving it a role in the provision of social security.

Perón, Evita (Maria Eva de Duarte) (b. 7 May 1919, d. 26 July 1952). Argentinian legend

A radio and television actress before she became the second wife of Juan *Perón in 1945, her political instincts formed the foundation of her husband's political success until her death from cancer. Snubbed by the establishment, she built up a large popular following through her support for the poor and for women's rights. Through her husband, she achieved female suffrage in 1947. After her death she became idolized, and her myth became a powerful link uniting the disparate strands of *Peronism.

Perón, Isabel (María Estrela Martínez Cartas) (b. 5 Feb. 1931). President of Argentina 1974–6

The third wife of Juan *Perón, she met him when she was a nightclub dancer in Panama in 1955. After his 1973 election victory, Perón made her Vice-President, so that upon his death in 1974 she became Latin America's first woman President. Unlike Evita *Perón she was insecure and indecisive. In 1975 the economy went out of control and social unrest grew, so that a military coup became only a question of time. She resigned officially as head of the Perónist movement from her exile in Madrid in 1985.

Perón, Juan (Domingo) (b. 8 Oct. 1895, d. 1 July 1974). President of Argentina 1946–55, 1973–4

A colonel in the Argentinian army, he took part in the 1943 military coup which ousted Ramón Castillo (b. 1873, d. 1944) from the presidency. He became Secretary of Labour in the new regime, a position which he used with his politically astute wife Evita *Perón to gain popular support among old labouring groups, new urban residents, and recent migrants from the countryside. This coalition ensured his victory in the presidential elections of 1946. He immediately used the postwar economic boom to improve the living standards of the workers and labourers at the expense of large landowners. He nationalized the foreign-controlled railways, the docks, and the largest telephone company, and by 1947 he had paid off Argentina's entire foreign debt. From 1949 the economy performed badly. After his triumphant election victory of 1951, when he was re-elected with 67 per cent of the vote, his popularity waned rapidly. In 1952 his popular wife, Evita, died of cancer. In 1955 he tried to improve his standing through fuelling general hostility against the Roman *Catholic Church, which led to mass demonstrations and the burning down of several cathedrals on the one hand, and to Perón's excommunication on the other. Since the Perónist government appeared to be increasingly out of control, the military ordered him to leave the country or risk civil war, so in 1955 he fled to Paraguay and then on to Spain. Following years of political unrest, social strife, and economic instability, Perón was seen as a last chance to save his country from ruin when he was re-elected in

1973 with 62 per cent of the vote. The ensuing economic recovery and social stability were short-lived because of the economic crisis triggered by the *oil-price shock. After his death he was succeeded by his third wife, Isabel *Perón.

Peronism

An ill-defined Argentinian political ideology, also known as *justicialismo*, which espouses Juan *Perón's policies of social justice, economic *nationalism, and international *non-alignment. It remained strong within Argentina after Perón's departure in 1955, largely among the trade unions, which cherished the memory of the early years of his presidency. In May 1989, the Peronist *Menem was elected President, but his economic programme, including the privatization of state-owned industries to foreign buyers, betrayed many Peronist principles. Indeed, Menem managed to redefine Peronism as a movement of compromise. It shed its traditional image of a party composed of rowdy trade unionists and led by shady Mafia-type characters, and moved to attract the political centre ground. Under Eduardo Duhalde, the Peronists lost the 1999 presidential elections, but he became President amidst a deep economic and political crisis in December 2001. Duhalde was succeeded by Néstor Kirchner in 2003, under whom the Peronist Justice Party continued to defend its overwhelming majority in parliament.

Pershing, John Joseph (b. 13 Sept. 1860, d. 15 July 1948). US army Chief of Staff 1921–4

Born in Montana, he graduated from West Point in 1886 and served in the later Indian wars, gaining the nickname 'Black Jack' for the strict discipline and training he imposed on the men under his command. He served in the Spanish–American War (1898) and in the Philippines. In 1914 he became commander of the 8th Cavalry Brigade, and led a US expedition into Mexico in 1916. In May 1917 he was appointed commander of the American expeditionary forces in France. His talent for organization was largely responsible for the moulding of hastily trained US troops into an army of well-integrated combat units. He strongly resisted pressure from the British and French to integrate the American forces into their armies. His assault in September 1918 of the Saint-Mihiel salient marked the beginning of the Allied advance to victory in World War I. He became army Chief of Staff from 1921–4, before retiring to head the American Battle Monuments Commission.

Peru

A South American country which has benefited from rich deposits of mineral resources, notably gold, oil, zinc, copper, and silver.

Autocratic rule (up to 1980) An independent republic since 1821, for more than a century power was concentrated in the hands of a small elite consisting of about 40 families. Especially under the leadership of President Leguía (1908–12, 1919–30), the economy underwent significant economic expansion with the help of US capital, through improving the infrastructure, as well as attracting US conglomerates such as Standard Oil. This resulted in the emergence of a middle class which challenged the elite's maintenance of power through dictatorial governments (1919–39) and demanded a share in the body politic. In addition, there was mounting popular dissatisfaction among the indigenous population about the complete failure of the government to improve their situation. In response, *Haya de la Torre founded the American Popular Revolutionary Alliance (*APRA) in 1924, which subsequently gained a significant following among the middle and working classes.

After a democratic interlude under Prado (1939–45) and Bustamante (1945–8), in which the economy thrived owing to the demand generated by World War II, autocratic rule was re-established by General Odría (1948–56), under whom American investment flourished. After the army prevented Haya de la Torre from accepting his election to the presidency in 1962, Fernando Belaúnde Terry (b. 1912) was elected President. Like his predecessor, Pedro Beltrán (1956–62), he failed to address the country's social problems adequately, despite a moderate land reform in 1964 and the introduction of Indian community projects. He also encouraged the exploration of the Amazonian rainforest, which led to the subsequent exploitation of significant oilfields. Reformist-oriented military rule (1968–75) introduced a more radical land reform in 1969, and nationalized many foreign-owned companies, notably the oil industry.

Democratization (1980s and 1990s) Belaúnde emerged victorious from the first elections held with universal suffrage on 18 May 1980. He introduced a series of unpopular economic austerity measures to cope with the country's increasing debt burden. This resulted in his defeat in the 1985 elections, after which Alán García Pérez became the first president from the APRA. His confused policies proved disastrous, as the economy suffered an annual decline of 4.2 per cent per capita (1985–90). Living standards declined to the level of the 1960s, as 60 per cent of the total workforce was unemployed or underemployed.

This led to the surprise victory in June 1990 of Alberto *Fujimori. He introduced stringent economic reforms, and changed the constitution after leading a coup against the old political system in April 1992. He was also spectacularly successful at fighting the *Sendero Luminoso guerrilla movement, which had been plaguing the country since the 1980s. In addition, Fujimori tried to stem the influence of the drug barons, who turned Peru into the world's second largest cocaine producer (after Colombia). His economic reforms stopped the country's economic decline, though 80 per cent of all Peruvians were still living in absolute poverty in 1995.

Much of Fujimori's success was achieved through his iron grip on power, based on his support from the corrupt secret service. Leading members of the opposition were prosecuted, and freedom of speech was curtailed. Against opposition from the constitutional court, Fujimori stood for a third period in office. He won the ensuing elections in 2000, albeit through evident vote-rigging. Shortly after the election, some of the criminal activities of the secret service leadership and its links to the Colombian drugs cartels came to light, whereupon Fujimori fled to Japan.

Contemporary politics (since 2001) An interim government under former *UN Secretary-General *Pérez de Cuellar prepared new elections in 2001. These were won by the leader of the opposition, Alejandro Toledo Manrique. He tried to stabilize the country's fledgling political institutions and establish civilian control over the armed forces. Toledo also aimed at improving the economic conditions for the majority of the population living in poverty, though many of his policies of economic stabilization (such as the privatization of public utilities) proved to be deeply unpopular. Toledo presided over a sustained economic growth, although he proved less adept at politics. In his term of office, he worked with five different Prime Ministers. Against a left-populist candidate backed by *Chávez, Alán García Pérez won his second term in office in 2005. García was committed to tight fiscal spending, though this did not address the plight of 49 per cent of the population who lived below the poverty line.

Pétain, (Henri) Philippe (b. 24 Apr. 1856, d. 23 July 1951). French marshal and Nazi collaborator

Born in the Pas-de-Calais region and educated at a Dominican college, he graduated from the Military Academy of Saint-Cyr and was commissioned into the infantry in 1878. He was promoted to colonel in 1912, and rose rapidly during World War I, becoming general in 1915 and the commander of the 2nd Army. Pétain became a national hero as the defender of *Verdun (1916–17), and became Commander-in-Chief of the French army in May 1917. He fought successfully against *Abd al-Krim, and served as inspector-general of the army (1922–31). He was Minister of Defence in 1934 and subsequently retired, but in 1939 he was appointed ambassador to Spain. He was recalled to serve as Deputy to Prime Minister *Reynaud in May 1940, and became the last Prime Minister of the Third Republic on 17 June 1940 following Reynaud's refusal to sue for peace against the Germans.

Pétain concluded an armistice with the Germans which left him in control of two-fifths of French territory, which he proceeded to govern from the spa town of *Vichy. On 10 July 1940, the National Assembly transferred to him all executive and legislative powers. Initially, he hoped to gain concessions from Germany in return for his *collaboration, such as the return of French prisoners of war. He was also eager to secure for France a special place in the German world order which he believed to be the inevitable consequence of the war. As Germany became increasingly defensive against the Allies, he hoped that France would take a pivotal role in negotiating a compromise peace. He was forced by the Germans to retreat across the Rhine to Sigmaringen in 1944, and surrendered to the French authorities in April 1945. He was sentenced to death, though the sentence was commuted to life imprisonment.

The role of Pétain in the *Vichy regime has been very controversial. He was the octogenarian leader who gave the government its credibility, but there is general agreement that some of his deputies, notably *Laval, were the main culprits of Vichy. At the same time, rather than being an unpolitical patriot who stepped in to save his country, he had been dallying with shady right-wing figures for years in order to win political power. Through giving credence to the regime, he was greatly responsible, amongst others, for his government's persecution of Jews and the sending of French citizens to forced labour in Germany.

Petrov Affair (Australia)

On 3 April 1954 a Soviet diplomat in Australia, Vladimir Petrov, asked for political asylum, subsequently making allegations of widespread Communist activities in official Australian circles. Exploiting the incident for all it was worth, *Menzies hinted at possible involvement by leaders of the Australian *Labor Party (ALP) and hastily set up a Royal Commission just before the general election. Accusations against Labor were fuelled by the action of ALP leader *Evatt, who served as defence council for some of the accused members of his staff. Ultimately, none of the allegations were substantiated, and it was revealed that no information had been passed to the Soviet Union since 1949. The affair facilitated *Menzies's win at the 1954 elections, split Labor through the creation of the *Democratic Labor Party, and led to the cessation of diplomatic relations with the USSR (1954–9).

Phibunsongkhram, Luang (b. 14 July 1897, d. 12 June 1964). Prime Minister of Thailand 1938–44, 1948–57

From a farming family, he graduated from the Military Academy in 1915, and left the Army General Staff College in 1924. After receiving training in France, he took part in the 1932 Revolution. He rapidly advanced in the army to become Minister of Defence, in which post he strongly influenced the moderate Premier Phya Bahol, whom he ousted in 1938. His government was autocratic, militarist, and nationalist. He signed a friendship treaty with Japan in 1941, though the country's isolation, its dependence on Japan, and his ruthless suppression of the anti-*Fascist Free Thai Movement, aroused opposition to such an extent that he was forced to resign in 1944. He returned to power after a renewed coup, this time using the *Cold War to emerge on a wave of anti-Communist feeling. He joined *SEATO, which made its headquarters in Bangkok, and received strong support from the USA. Following three unsuccessful coups against him in 1948, 1949, and 1951, he was ousted in a putsch in 1957. He went to Japan, where in 1960 he became a Buddhist monk.

Philippines

A southern Asian country consisting of 7,017 islands characterized by fundamental geographical, ethnic, cultural, and linguistic diversity, with a population

divided by the use of 87 different indigenous languages and dialects.

Colonial rule (up to 1946) A Spanish colony since 1565, Spanish neglect and refusal to grant political rights led to an increasing number of peasant uprisings against colonial rule until the revolution of 1896–8, which led to the proclamation of the first Republic by *Aguinaldo on 1 November 1897. Against the background of the Spanish–American War of 1898, Aguinaldo accepted the help of the USA against the Spanish, with American assurances of independence. However, after the Peace Treaty of Paris (10 December 1898), the country was claimed by the USA, which had purchased it from Spain for $20 million. The USA overcame the various movements opposing its colonial rule by 1902. In subsequent years the country was integrated into the world economy, with the introduction of new crops for export to the USA (sugar cane, coconut, etc.). New plantations and adaptation to these new crops led to a fundamental structural change within the economy, which continued to bedevil the country throughout the rest of the century. Property became more concentrated in the hands of a few owners of capital, while even more farmers became landless tenants.

As political parties began to form, the National Party under *Quezón became the most important. He was instrumental in working for eventual independence. In particular, he negotiated the 1916 Jones Act, which developed the political system further through the creation of a senate. The Act also created a greater sphere for self-government, envisaging independence 'as soon as a stable government can be established'. This was followed by the Tydings–McDuffie Act (1934), which created a political system closely modelled on that of the USA. The status of the Philippines changed officially from a colony to an interim 'Commonwealth', which was to obtain full independence after a ten-year transitional period. This timetable was disrupted by the Japanese invasion of December 1941, which lasted until liberation by *MacArthur in the *Philippines campaign (October 1944–July 1945).

The Philippines became an independent republic and were assisted by US financial aid, but only on the condition of the controversial Bell Trade Act (1946). This established free trade between the USA and the Philippines, guaranteed parity between the national currency (the peso) and the US dollar, and imposed a severe limitation on Philippine sovereignty by granting the USA 99-year leases on military bases throughout the country. Moreover, US companies and citizens were given equal economic rights in the Philippines, which guaranteed de facto US control over the economy.

Authoritarian rule (1946–86) Subsequently, Filipino politics was characterized by the imbalance between a tiny, wealthy, and influential landowning elite on the one hand and a large propertyless majority, a situation that led to extensive corruption in politics and administration. Government suppression of the *Hukbalahup movement healed few wounds, as the harsh treatment of the left-wing guerrilla movement, who had led the domestic anti-Japanese movement during the war, contrasted sharply with the lenient attitude taken towards collaborators with the Japanese.

President D. Macapagal (1961–5) was the first to attempt to halt the country's decline into bankruptcy and ungovernability, but in 1965 he was succeeded by *Marcos. Extremely popular at first, Marcos ruled on a nationalist platform, obtaining some reduction of US influence in the country. He also led a populist campaign to reduce corruption. He was re-elected in 1969, when it soon became apparent that he had solved none of the country's more fundamental problems. In 1969 the Muslim Moro movement started an armed rebellion on Mindanao island. Soon afterwards the Communists, excluded from the political system since the destruction of the Hukbalahup movement, launched a guerrilla movement of their own, the New People's Army. Endangered also by growing discontent caused by economic decline, Marcos proclaimed martial law on 23 September 1972, dissolved the political institutions, and imprisoned prominent opposition leaders such as Benigno *Aquino.

Over the next decade Marcos maintained power through army support. Through an extensive system of patronage Marcos rewarded his supporters with government contracts, state lands, and access to important posts. However, with the deterioration of the economy, Marcos was unable to pay for the spoils he had to distribute to remain in office. Pressure from the *IMF and the *World Bank forced him to introduce unpopular austerity measures and political liberalization, though he still ordered the assassination of Aquino in 1983. This incident catapulted the opposition into more open and defiant resistance. Marcos hoped to surprise the fragmented opposition by calling an early election for February 1986.

Democratization (since 1986) The opposition was united by Aquino's widow,

Corazón, who claimed victory after widespread government vote-rigging. Defied by important sections of the army, Marcos was forced to flee to the USA. Corazón *Aquino did manage to restore greater peace to the islands, but failed to pacify the Moro rebels. She was unsuccessful in her attempt to carry out a large-scale land reform, largely because, having been supported by a plethora of parties for her election without actually leading one, she lacked her own popular base. Nevertheless, she did manage to get the USA to close its last military base in 1991, while she also supervised the proclamation of a new constitution on 2 February 1987.

Aquino was succeeded by *Ramos in 1992, who introduced a programme of economic liberalization in order to overcome the economic stagnation of the early 1990s. He continued his predecessor's efforts at bringing peace to the country, and in September 1996 signed a peace deal with the Moro National Liberation Front. This granted autonomy to fourteen provinces on the island of Mindanao, with a view to ending a civil war that had claimed 120,000 lives. However, the agreement was not accepted by a number of splinter groups led by the Moro Island Liberation Front and the Abu Sayyaf rebels, which continued to demand independence for the entire island through a violent campaign including bombing, extortion, and kidnapping. The government's ability to deal with these challenges was undermined by its own weaknesses, however.

Contemporary politics (since 1998) Ramos was succeeded by Joseph Ejercito Estrada, a former actor and Vice-President. Estrada began a military offensive against separatist rebels on Mindanao, and promoted the liberalization of the economy. As corruption allegations against him became all but proven, a popular movement supported by former presidents Corazón Aquino and Ramos forced Estrada to leave office. He was succeeded by his Vice-President, Macapagal Arroyo of the Christian Democrats. Since she had not been elected, Arroyo was eligible to stand in the 2004 elections, which she won. However, subsequent allegations of corruption and electoral fraud led to widespread demands for her resignation, which she resisted. These political turbulences notwithstanding, the economy grew consistently after 2000. However, almost 50 per cent of the population continued to live below the poverty line, while the economy remained reliant on remittances from Filipinos abroad, which amounted to $15 billion in 2006.

Philippines campaign (Oct. 1944–July 1945)

Towards the end of *World War II, after the Battles of the *Philippines Sea and *Leyte Gulf, General *MacArthur proceeded to liberate the Philippines from the Japanese. US forces landed north of Manila on 9 January 1945, and three weeks later further forces landed in the Batangas province and advanced north. The two armies surrounded Manila, which was entered on 4 February. Aided by local resistance forces, the city quickly capitulated, and by July MacArthur could announce that all the Philippine islands were liberated, although detached groups of Japanese, in accordance with their instructions to fight to the last man, were still at large when the war ended.

Philippines Sea, Battle of (19–21 June 1944)

A naval battle in *World War II fought off Palau (*Micronesia). As US marines landed (15 June) and fought their way across the island, a naval battle between US and Japanese fleets under Admirals Raymond Spruance and Jisaburo Ozawa developed. Altogether, the Japanese lost 476 planes and three aircraft carriers, while US losses amounted to 130 aircraft. US victory and capture of Palau paved the way for the reoccupation of the Philippines.

Phoney War (Sept. 1939–Apr. 1940)

The lull in military campaigns at the beginning of *World War II, between the German occupation of Poland in September 1939 and the attack on Denmark and Norway in April 1940, which was almost immediately followed by the German attack on France. This pause was caused by British and French military inability to attack Germany outright. Further German attacks were similarly delayed by the need to wait for armaments, bad weather, and the reluctance of the army leadership to conduct a rapid military campaign.

Pilsudski, Joseph Klemens (b. 5 Dec. 1867, d. 12 May 1935). Polish leader 1926–35

Born near Vilna (Russian Poland), he studied at the University of Kharkov. He became a leading agitator for the Polish Socialist Party from 1893, though the fight for Polish independence against Russian occupation became his central concern. In 1887 Pilsudski was exiled to Siberia, where he remained until 1892. He returned to Poland and founded an underground newspaper which agitated for Polish independence. When war broke out in 1914 he raised a force of Polish volunteers to join the Austro-Hungarians on the Russian front. German refusal to guarantee the ultimate independence of Poland after the

*Russian Revolution in February 1917 led him to withdraw his support for Germany, whereupon he was interned (1917–18). When the new Republic of Poland was proclaimed, he became head of state (1918–22) and army Chief of Staff (1918–23). In the *Russo-Polish War, he successfully exploited the *Russian Civil War to extend Poland's eastern border. He withdrew from politics in 1922, but in 1926 carried out an army coup, dissolved parliament, and appointed his own protégés such as *Beck to important political positions. He himself remained as Minister of War and general inspector of the armed forces until his death. His regime failed to modernize the Polish army, or its economy. Furthermore, his ingrained hostility to Russia blinded him and his followers to the growing threat of *Nazi Germany.

Pinochet Ugarte, Augusto (b. 25 Nov. 1915, d. 11 Dec. 2006). Chilean dictator, 1973–90

A professional soldier who had graduated from the Santiago Military Academy in 1936, he rose to become Commander-in-Chief of Chile's armed forces in September 1973. Eighteen days after his appointment he masterminded a military coup in which President *Allende was deposed and killed. Pinochet became President of the Council of Chile (a junta of military officers) and imposed harsh military rule, imprisoning over 100,000 people during the first three years of his rule alone. Many of these were tortured, and thousands disappeared. In 1974 he was proclaimed President of Chile. He pursued liberal economic policies, which reduced unemployment and inflation, but also depressed real wages. As a result, his free-market policies provided some long-term economic stability, but at considerable social cost, notably the growth of social inequality. In 1978 he organized a plebiscite in which his policies were approved by 75 per cent. A new Constitution in 1980, again endorsed by a plebiscite, gave him authority to be sworn in for another eight years as President.

During the 1980s international pressure against his regime grew, most crucially from the USA, with whose help (via the *CIA) he had come to power in the first place. In addition, the deterioration of the economy since the 1982 financial crash weakened his authority domestically, so that in 1988 he called another referendum. He lost the gamble, however, as 55 per cent voted against his stay in power. He accepted the verdict and stood down in 1990. On a visit to England for medical treatment in 1998, he was arrested and put under house arrest for sixteen months. In 2000 Pinochet was stripped of his immunity, and until his death he was involved in constant legal battles about his responsibility for the crimes committed while he was in power.

Pius XII (Eugenio Pacelli) (b. 2 Mar. 1876, d. 9 Oct. 1958). Pope 1939–58

Educated at the Gregorian University in Rome, he was ordained priest in 1899 and entered the papal diplomatic corps at the Secretariat of State in 1901. The Pope's representative (nuncio) in Munich in 1917, he became the papal nuncio to Germany 1920–30. During this time, he concluded an agreement between the Roman *Catholic Church and the state of Bavaria in 1924, and with *Prussia in 1929. In 1930, he was appointed papal Secretary of State and created cardinal. He was responsible for a concordat between the Catholic Church and *Nazi Germany in 1933, though subsequently he was reluctant to protest openly against Nazi violations of the agreement. During World War II, he remained strictly neutral, though he was particularly concerned to relieve distress, especially among prisoners. None the less, he became heavily criticized for his refusal to defend the Jews against persecution. His willingness to come to an agreement with *Hitler contrasted with his refusal of any compromise with the Communist governments of postwar Europe. He is also remembered for establishing the Assumption of the Virgin Mary as an infallible doctrine of the Roman Catholic Church (*Munificentissimus Deus*, 1 November 1950), on the basis of Church tradition rather than scriptural evidence.

Plaid Cymru (Party for Wales)

A Welsh nationalist party which was formed in 1925 to promote a cultural and linguistic revival, and to call for 'home rule' (autonomy) for *Wales. It consistently fought elections from 1929, but support for it only grew significantly in the 1960s. In July 1966, its chairman, Gwynfor Evans, won the Carmarthen by-election. Despite gaining 11.5 per cent of the Welsh vote in 1970, the party did not win any seats in a general election until February 1974, when it won Caernarfon and Merioneth. It won two or three seats at every election from then on, until 1992, when it won four seats. It staged a spectacular success in the first elections to the Welsh Assembly in 1999, when it took a number of safe Labour seats as loyal Labour supporters remained at home to protest against government policies. Normally the principal party of opposition, Plaid entered a surprise coalition with Labour following the 2007 elections.

(∰) **SEE WEB LINKS**

• The official website of Plaid Cymru.

Platt Amendment, see CUBA

Plessey v. *Ferguson* (USA, 1896)

The case produced the ruling by the *Supreme Court that racial segregation was legal and constitutional if there was equal provision of separate facilities for Black and White. It rested on the question of whether the state of Louisiana's law requiring separate car facilities for Whites and Blacks violated the Thirteenth and Fourteenth Amendments of the Constitution. The Court ruled by an eight to one decision that racial distinction in itself did not constitute discrimination. Although the ruling was widely, and on the whole rightly, seen as upholding racial discrimination, the *NAACP amongst others used the decision to undermine the substance of segregation, since most segregated facilities were demonstrably unequal. Beginning with the, *Brown case, the NAACP challenged segregation itself in the courts.

PLO (Palestine Liberation Organization)

Early history (to 1980s) The PLO was founded in 1964, largely on Egyptian initiative, as a movement to unite various Palestine Arab groups opposed to Israeli presence in *Palestine, most importantly al-*Fatah (the Palestine National Liberation Movement), the Marxist Popular Front for the Liberation of Palestine, and the Democratic Front for the Liberation of Palestine. Its charter called for a democratic and secular Palestinian state and for the elimination of Israel. After the *Six Day War, when the *West Bank became occupied by Israel, the PLO became dominated by al-*Fatah, which proceeded to organize guerrilla raids by commandos (*fedayeen*) from Jordan against Israel. Chaired by *Arafat, the PLO's assertive claim to represent the Palestinian people (which formed the majority of the population of Jordan) became a fundamental challenge to the authority of King *Hussein. Hussein expelled the PLO from Jordan after a series of bloody battles in 1970–1.

Thereafter the PLO was based in Lebanon. With Syrian backing it achieved a major diplomatic triumph in 1974, when it was recognized by all Arab states (including a reluctant Jordan) as the sole representative of the Palestinian people. The growing strength of the PLO prompted Israel to take action against Palestinian refugee camps in 1981 and to invade Lebanon in 1982, forcing the PLO to move its headquarters to Tunisia. Frustration about the continued failure to bring about a quick resolution to the demands for a Palestinian state led to several splits and challenges to the leadership of Arafat, who came to rely increasingly on diplomacy rather than violence. Hence, the PLO was outsmarted by more radical organizations such as *Hezbollah and *Hamas, which instigated the *Intifadah.

Contemporary politics (from 1990s) The actions of its militant competitors, however, convinced Israel to accept the PLO as the most moderate of the popular Palestinian groups. It negotiated successfully for Palestinian autonomy through the *Oslo Accord and the *Gaza–Jericho Agreement. In the first elections for the *Palestinian National Authority (PNA, which included the *Gaza Strip and the *West Bank) in 1996, the PLO won an overwhelming victory. Arafat was elected President with 88.1 per cent of the vote, and the PLO gained a large majority in the Palestinian Council. More important than the actual majority (Arafat faced but one opponent) was the high voter turnout, which indicated its support against admonishments from radical opponents for voters to stay at home. Subsequently, the movement which had been defined by its opposition found it hard to adjust to a positive, constructive role. It failed to build a civilian and legal infrastructure in the areas under its control, and it was accused by international donors of the misuse and squandering of financial aid to Palestine. As poverty within the Palestinian areas worsened, popular pressure on the PLO grew, which was compounded by the breakdown of the *Wye Agreement. Although Israeli attacks on the Palestinian territories in 2002 helped to restore some of its popularity, the military intervention also destroyed much of the PLO's governing and security infrastructure. Following Arafat's death in 2004, the PLO was led by Mahmoud *Abbas, who struggled to assert his authority on the PLO in the way of his predecessor. The PLO lost the elections to the PNA in 2006 to Hamas. As its armed followers were not prepared to accept the loss of power, this resulted in a state of near civil war, until the PLO reached a power-sharing agreement with Hamas in 2007.

pogrom

A term originally used for officially initiated *anti-Semitic popular attacks against Jews in Russia from 1881. With many rioters being brought in by train, the assaults were carried out by well-organized groups of hooligans who looted Jewish properties and murdered entire Jewish communities. After a temporary pause, pogroms reached a new peak in 1903, again encouraged by officials eager to please the anti-Semitic Tsar Nicholas II. A further outbreak of pogroms by lawless bands occurred during the *Russian Revolution of 1905. As sporadic pogroms became the norm, Jews endured harassment, were banned from trading on Sundays, and were denied the possession of agricultural property in their principal area of settlement, Pale. Many Jews responded by large-scale emigration to *Palestine, western Europe, and especially the USA, which received 750,000 Russian Jews (1900–10). More generally, the term has been used to describe organized massacres of Jews throughout the twentieth century, especially in the *Nazi *concentration camps during the *Holocaust.

Poincaré, Raymond (b. 20 Aug. 1860, d. 15 Oct. 1934). President of France 1913–20; Prime Minister 1912–13, 1922–4, 1926–9

A member of the Chamber of Deputies 1887–1903, he was a Senator 1903–13, and 1920–9. Though not wanting war in order to regain the *Alsace and his native Lorraine from Germany, as Prime Minister and then as President he strove to improve France's military and international position in case war did break out. To some extent, he succeeded in carving out a more political role for the president whose constitutional role was that of a mere figurehead, thanks to the turbulence of World War I and his skill at political manoeuvre. Nevertheless, he failed to make any significant impact on the actual running of the war, and had little influence on the policies of *Clemenceau during or after the war. Back in the Senate, Poincaré provoked *Briand's resignation and succeeded him as Prime Minister. He maintained and even accelerated his country's hardline stance towards Germany, and in early 1923 ordered the French occupation of the *Ruhr. However, this policy backfired, since the crisis cost the already debt-stricken French state dearly, while it brought financial ruin to Germany. As a result, he was forced to settle for a less stringent policy on German *reparation payments after all. Following a severe economic crisis, Poincaré once again became Prime Minister in 1926. Through the introduction of some austerity measures he managed to stabilize the franc and balance the budget. This time, he cooperated with *Briand, allowing him to continue in his more accommodating policy towards Germany. His government enjoyed relative stability, but he had to resign in 1929 owing to ill health.

Pol Pot (b. 19 May 1928, d. 15 Apr. 1998). Prime Minister of Kampuchea (Cambodia) 1975–9

Born Saloth Sar of a prosperous and well-connected peasant family in Kompong

Thom province, he studied in Pnomh Penh and Kompong Cham, and became a member of *Ho Chi Minh's Indochinese Communist Party and in 1949 went to study electrical technology in Paris. On his return in 1953, he briefly fought against the French in the *Indochina War. He became a member of the central committee of the newly founded Communist Party of Kampuchea in 1960, and was appointed its secretary in 1963. He went north to organize guerrilla resistance against *Sihanouk's regime, and led his *Khmer Rouge forces in the civil war against *Lon Nol's regime. Once he came to power (which was officially kept secret until 1976), his relationship with Vietnam, which had supported his guerrilla campaign, soon soured because Pol Pot asserted his own independence and authority. With unimaginable brutality, he set out to create a truly Communist society and to break all resistance. During the almost four years of his government, around one million people died in his reign of terror, as a result of assassination, imprisonment, or hunger caused by a collapsed economy. He was deposed in January 1979 after the Vietnamese invasion, whereupon he withdrew to fight a guerrilla campaign from the countryside.

Poland

A country in central Europe which developed a strong sense of cultural nationhood in the absence of statehood between the eighteenth and twentieth centuries, at a time when Poland was a victim of its aggressive European neighbours.

Foreign rule (up to 1918) Poland lost its independence in the three Polish partitions (1772, 1793, 1795), when it was carved up between Russia, *Prussia, and *Austria-Hungary. To fight these powers, many Poles signed up to fight for Napoleon, who established a Grand Duchy of Warsaw in 1807; but after the Vienna Congress much of its territory was governed as the kingdom of Poland in personal union with the Emperor (Tsar) of Russia. Several uprisings (1830–1, 1846, 1863) were brutally repressed, though increasing attempts to 'Russianize' or 'Germanize' the Poles in the respective occupied areas strengthened the nationalist movement towards the end of the nineteenth

century. When World War I broke out, most Poles joined *Pilsudski to fight with Austria-Hungary against Russia, in order to secure the independence of the kingdom. The Treaty of *Versailles, which was based on *Wilson's principle of national self-determination, finally recognized the independent Poland which had been proclaimed in 1918.

Interwar Poland (1918–39) Even though Poland was to be an independent state from now on, for most of the century this independence was at best incomplete. From 1918, it took another five years until all the borders of a state which had been out of existence for so long were fully determined. Most significantly, in the *Russo-Polish War Poland extended its borders to the east to include large areas of Belorussia (now *Belarus) and the *Ukraine. Poland was engaged in a series of border disputes with Czechoslovakia over *Teschen, and with Lithuania, whose territory around Vilnius it had acquired in 1920 and incorporated in 1922.

Given the resentments its acquisitions of formerly German territories had created in Germany, by 1924 Poland had thus managed to offend all of its neighbours bar Romania. As problematic was the need to integrate the new national minorities, which now composed over 30 per cent of the population, and to harmonize communication and cultural structures in a country which had doubled in size, 1918–24. This task was made particularly difficult through the relatively backward state of Poland's agriculture, which employed almost 70 per cent of the working population. The state thus lacked the tax revenue to enable it to encourage a programme of economic consolidation. Finally, state-building was made all but impossible through the weakness of state institutions, which had been modelled on the French Third Republic. Governments changed frequently, thanks to a fragmented parliament in which parties represented particular national, social, or cultural interests.

In 1926 Pilsudski carried out a coup and established a dictatorship. He distributed power among his associates such as *Beck and *Smigly-Rydz, but the lack of a popular base made it even more difficult to carry out reforms, even if they had been attempted. Given the growing threat presented by the Soviet Union and Germany, Poland was unable to rally support from its hostile central European neighbours to present a common front against *Hitler and *Stalin.

World War II In September 1939 the unreformed Polish army was unable to prevent the country's invasion by Germany and the USSR which inaugurated *World

War II in Europe. The German occupying forces, which ruled over all of Poland from 1941, inflicted unimaginable terror on the Polish people, as hundreds of thousands of Poles were shot, and almost its entire Jewish population of three and a half million people was systematically murdered in the *concentration camps of *Auschwitz and elsewhere. Perhaps as many non-Jewish Poles lost their lives in the war. Together with the total destruction of its industries and cities, the war left deep scars on Polish society. No treatment of Poles by any power could remotely compare to the atrocities committed by the Germans. At the same time, Russian occupation of Poland during the nineteenth century, the *Hitler–Stalin Pact of 1939, subsequent atrocities such as the *Katyn Massacre, and the appalling idleness of the *Red Army during the *Warsaw Rising made it difficult for most to see the advance of Soviet troops in 1944 as a 'liberation'.

Communist rule (1944–89) After the war, the country was subject to Soviet control. By 1947 the hegemony of the Communist Party was established under *Bierut, who proceeded to introduce *Stalinist policies. Perhaps the most important figure in Communist Poland, however, was *Gomulka, who ruled the country from 1956 to 1970. He appreciated that *Marxism-Leninism needed to be adapted to the specific conditions of Poland. In particular, he came to a *modus vivendi* with Cardinal *Wyszinski, whose toleration was crucial as the Roman *Catholic Church had traditionally been a bearer of Polish national identity, and still played an important role in the lives of most people. Gomulka also appeased the majority of Poles still living in the countryside by continuing to allow private ownership there.

Polish society thus achieved considerable degrees of freedom unmatched by its neighbours in East Germany, the USSR, or Czechoslovakia after 1968. Despite the failings and inefficiency of the planned economy, the country was industrialized and urbanized, while there were significant improvements in literacy levels and life expectancy. Unfortunately, the rapid expansion of heavy industry, and the concurrent urbanization, could only be achieved at the permanent expense of the production of consumer goods. Thus the standard of living remained low as there were few luxury items to buy, which caused discontent to mount against a political and economic system few Poles had actually chosen.

The replacement of Gomulka with *Gierek (1970) offered a temporary reprieve through increases in economic production of up to 10

per cent per year, though again little was done to produce more consumer goods. These growth rates were largely achieved through foreign, hard-currency loans, and did not indicate a general improvement in economic competitiveness. In the absence of lasting improvements to the standard of living, Polish society continued to be extremely volatile in its response to increases in the price of basic foodstuffs, which had become a regular trigger for popular discontent by the 1970s.

This was no different in 1980, when unannounced increases in the price of bread and meat caused demonstrations of such a scale as to take the Communist leadership by surprise and cause the dismissal of Gierek. A group of leaders around *Wałęsa managed to channel the disparate protests into the demand for the legalization of an independent *trade union, *Solidarność. Once this had been allowed, protesters used Solidarność as a vehicle for political opposition. Under pressure from his hardline Communist neighbours, *Jaruzelski declared martial law in late 1981 and banned trade union activity.

The Communist government proved unable to suppress the political opposition, for three reasons.

1. Solidarność had established such a strong footing among the Polish people that it was able to develop a flourishing underground movement.

2. The visits of the Polish Pope, *John Paul II, in 1979, 1983, and 1987, were a crucial outlet for public hostility to the regime. They also demonstrated the continued importance of the Church (which had aligned itself with the Solidarność movement at the grass roots), as it was able to reach areas beyond the purview of the Communist state.

3. The ascendancy of *Gorbachev in the Soviet Union: in particular, Gorbachev made it clear that the USSR would no longer intervene to shore up a Communist system against the will of its people.

Democratization (1990s) Jaruzelski was thus forced to enter into negotiations with the opposition led by Solidarność, which led to the election in 1989 of Poland's first non-Communist Prime Minister since 1945, Thadeusz Mazowiecki (b. 1927). The capitalist transformation of the moribund Polish economy resulted in an economic roller-coaster ride. Industrial production declined by 24 per cent, while inflation shot up to almost 600 per cent in 1990. By 1994 industrial production had grown again by 13 per cent, while inflation had been reduced to less than 50 per cent. Nevertheless, the tremendous levels of hardship endured by much of the population during this period sharply reduced the popularity of the Solidarność movement, which was further weakened by numerous internal divisions.

In 1990, Wałęsa managed to be elected President, but in the 1991 parliamentary elections Solidarność won but 5 per cent of the vote, less than 2 per cent more than the Polish Party of the Friends of Beer. By contrast, the reformed Communists, under the banner of the Federation of the Democratic Left (SLD), and the Agrarian Party (PSL) went from strength to strength. They formed a coalition government after winning the 1993 parliamentary elections, while Wałęsa was humiliated when he lost the 1995 presidential elections to a former Communist minister, Aleksander *Kwasniewski.

The parliamentary elections of 1997 resulted in a victory for the 'Electoral Action Solidarity', led by Jerzy Buzek. With its parliamentary allies it passed a law whereby all candidates for political office had to be investigated for their links to the Polish secret service under the former Communist regimes. This helped destabilize the government, as a number of prominent members had to resign when their secret connections to the former dictatorship were revealed. An administrative reform reduced the centralization of the political system by creating a more federative structure of sixteen administrative districts. Meanwhile, Poland continued in its efforts to prepare for membership of the EU, through often painful institutional, social, and legal reform. In 1999 the health system was reformed. Economic growth was relatively stable at over 4 per cent per year, but much of this was distributed very unevenly. Poland's structural imbalances, especially its overblown agricultural sector, continued, while a dramatic budget deficit and the state's continued public indebtedness led to highly unpopular spending cuts. Buzek's Electoral Action Solidarity became very unpopular, and scraped into parliament with 5.6 per cent of the popular vote in 2001.

Contemporary politics (since 2001) The 2001 elections saw a return of the SLD, whose leader, Leszek Miller, became Prime Minister. Under Miller, the government continued to carry out unpopular structural reforms in preparation for EU accession, which materialized in 2004. At this historic point, Miller had become extremely unpopular, so that he resigned. In 2005, parliamentary and presidential elections saw victory for the Law and Justice Party, led by twins. Lech Kaczynski became President, with Jaroslaw Kaczynski becoming Prime Minister, in 2006. The Kaczynski brothers had been elected on a populist platform, and in office they pursued a militant policy of promoting Polish interests in the EU. They were criticized for forming an alliance with an anti-Semitic Peasant Party, while frequent criticisms of Germany have led to a cooling of relations with its western neighbour.

Politburo

The highest policy-making committee of Communist Parties, modelled on the organizational structures of the Soviet Union. There, a Politburo was founded after the *Russian Revolution of February 1917 to realize *Lenin's organizational ideas for an elite cadre of leaders to guide the revolution. Once *Communism had been established, the Politburo continued in its function as the highest executive organ of the Communist Party and the state. Its real workings changed over time. Under *Stalin, its members were increasingly subject to the dictator's will. *Khrushchev successfully invoked its theoretical responsibility to the Party Central Committee to overrule its decision in 1957 to topple him. Under *Brezhnev, *Andropov, and *Chernenko, it became more the collective body it had originally been designed to be. It was abolished under *Gorbachev. As the model for the governments of all the Communist Eastern Bloc countries, the institution of the Politburo was largely abandoned with the collapse of Communism (1988–9).

Poll Tax (Community Charge) (UK)

A flat rate of local taxation, which replaced the local taxation based on rates, measured on the value of the property. Rates had never been popular, as single people living in big houses had to pay the same as large families in similar properties, regardless of income. In addition, by the 1980s, most people were either exempt from paying rates because of their low income, or the rates were assisted by the social services. As a result, a minority of the population actually footed the bill for local expenditure, which, according to the *Conservative Party under Margaret *Thatcher, made local government unaccountable to the majority of the population, and wasteful.

In 1990, rates were replaced by a poll tax, which was a flat rate for every individual, based on the principle that everybody benefited from the same local services (street lighting, rubbish collection, etc.). Since virtually everyone had to pay, it would also put pressure on local government to keep local spending (and hence the poll tax) low. However, the tax proved deeply unpopular.

It was seen as unjust, since everyone had to pay the same rate, regardless of income. More crucial was that, since the majority had been exempt from, or assisted with, local taxation before, far more people were worse off after the introduction of the tax. So unpopular was the tax that it looked as though it would lose Thatcher the next elections. Consequently she was replaced by John *Major, who duly abolished it as soon as possible (1991). In *Scotland, where the tax was introduced a year earlier (1989) than in the rest of Britain, it epitomized the failure of a government dominated by English interests to take into account Scottish opinion. This fuelled further popular demands for devolution.

Pomare, Sir Maui Wiremu Pita Naera
(b. 13 Jan. 1876, d. 27 June 1930). New Zealand politician

A Maori born in Pahou Pa (near New Plymouth), he attended Te Aute College, where he joined the Seventh-day Adventist Church. He studied medicine at the Church's college in Michigan (USA), and graduated from there in 1899. On his return, in 1900 he became a government health officer in a *Maori district, where he worked for improved sanitation and the registration of births and deaths. An MP for the *Young Maori Party from 1911, he became Minister without Portfolio under *Massey in 1912, and Minister of the Cook Islands (1916), where he instituted a number of economic, legal, and educational reforms. As Minister of Health (1923) he reorganized care for the mentally ill and for lepers, and in 1926 he became Minister of Internal Affairs. Most of all he is remembered for his policies towards the Maori population, whose number had declined to their lowest level of 40,000 when he began his work in 1900, and which thereafter began to rise steadily, thanks in part to his sanitary, legal, and economic reforms.

Pompidou, Georges Jean Raymond
(b. 5 July 1911, d. 2 Apr. 1974). President of France 1969–74

A graduate of the prestigious École Normale Supérieure, he became de *Gaulle's adviser on economics and education in 1944. Pompidou held a number of government posts until 1954, and became director of the Rothschild bank. Throughout, he stayed close to de Gaulle, for whom he was the principal negotiator of the *Évian Agreements. He was little-known when de Gaulle appointed him his Prime Minister in 1962. De Gaulle, who was mainly concerned about foreign policy and desired to appear above all parties, left the day-to-day running of the government to him, which he managed with considerable success. He also built up a party machine to enable the survival of *Gaullism after de Gaulle's inevitable retirement. Presumably because of his rising stature, de Gaulle dismissed him in 1968 in the wake of the *student revolts, but by then Pompidou's position was strong enough to become the natural Gaullist contender for the presidency after de Gaulle's resignation in 1969. As President, perhaps his biggest achievement was to ensure that the Fifth Republic, and indeed *Gaullism, could survive without de Gaulle. In fact, as President he guarded his power and influence even more jealously than his predecessor. He maintained much of de Gaulle's foreign policy, but was much more favourably disposed towards the UK, and much less enthusiastic about his predecessor's closeness towards West Germany. As a result, he no longer objected to the enlargement of the EEC (*European integration). In domestic policies his presidency coincided with a period of considerable economic prosperity.

Poona Pact, see GANDHI, M. K.; AMBEDKAR, BHIMRAO

Popular Front (PF)
A governing coalition of parties which was formed during the 1930s, including the Communist party. This was facilitated by a new directive of the world Communist movement, the International, which now encouraged its members to abandon previous policies of non-cooperation in favour of building a common front against *Fascism. Although open to all pro-democratic parties, the PF was supported principally by left-wing parties. PF governments were intrinsically unstable due to the heterogeneity of their members, and because some of their members, notably the Communists and the socialists, competed for the same electorate.

In **Spain**, it was the election of a Popular Front government by a narrow margin in February 1936 which increased the divisions with conservatives and contributed to the outbreak of the *Spanish Civil War. Despite chronic disunity among its members about the nature and extent of the reforms to be undertaken, the Popular Front proceeded to transform the economy along collectivist lines, while adminstrative power was given to workers' and peasants' councils. The PF was defeated by General *Franco in early 1939.

In **France**, a Popular Front government was led by L. *Blum from 1936. Its social reforms included the introduction of a 40-hour working week, paid holidays, and collective bargaining. However, the PF was unable to overcome the financial difficulties caused by its social programme, which was accompanied by a sharp increase in military expenditure.

Blum had to resign when the *Communist Party, which had refused to join the Popular Front but upheld its majority in the Chamber of Deputies, rejected Blum's policy of non-intervention in the Spanish Civil War. There followed a number of short-lived governments supported by the same coalition, but the PF finally broke up in the wake of the *Munich Agreement.

In **Chile**, a PF government, which was directed not so much against Fascism as against the military, was established in 1936. The Radicals dominated the coalition: hence their more moderate policies of furthering state involvement in economics received priority over welfare reform. Alarmed by the steady rise in Communist support, however, and influenced by the *Cold War, the Radicals switched sides to end the Popular Front and cooperate with the right to outlaw and persecute the Communists in 1948.

Popular Party (Partido Popular)
(Spain)

Spain's major centre-right party. Founded in 1989, it was created from a number of parties that emerged from conservative and centre-right groups of the late *Franco era. The most important of these had been the Popular Alliance, itself an amalgamation in 1977 of conservative parties that included the Democratic Reformation movement of Manuel Fraga Iribane. Whereas throughout the 1980s the Popular Alliance had been eclipsed by the *Socialists under *Gonzalez, under the patient leadership of *Aznar from 1990 the PP embraced more centrist social, cultural and economic policies. In this way, the PP reconciled many of the dictatorship's adherents who remained sceptical under Gonzalez toward the democratic political system. In 1996, Aznar was able to form a coalition government, and in the 2000 elections the PP gained an absolute majority of seats in parliament. Aznar did not seek a third term and was succeeded as party leader by Manuel Rajoy Brey. After the party's shock defeat in the 2004 elections, which followed the *Madrid Bombings, the party became directionless. It took time to adjust to its role in opposition, while it also tried to keep up with the pace of *Zapatero's policies.

Popular Party (Partito Popolare Italiano, PPI) (Italy)

A political party with Roman *Catholic support, it emerged once the Pope rescinded the ban on Italian Catholics participating fully in the secular Italian state. Founded by the Sicilian priest **Luigi Sturzo** (b. 1871, d. 1959) on 18 January 1919, the party stood for decentralization, constitutional reform including women's suffrage and proportional representation, corporatism, and social legislation. In the 1919 parliamentary elections, it won 100 out of 508 seats. Despite its relative strength, the party was unable to resist the rise of the *Fascist movement. It suffered from its own disunity (some members on the right actually supported *Mussolini), as well as from its ideological aversion to *socialism, which made it impossible for it to unite with the *Socialist and *Communist Parties to form a *Popular Front. In addition, a Vatican eager to come to an accommodation with *Mussolini (*Lateran Treaties) exerted pressure on the PPI not to be too hostile towards the Fascists. In July 1923 Sturzo was forced to resign and go into exile (October 1924).

Under *De Gasperi, the party continued its independent stance against the Fascists and took part in the *Aventine Secession. The party was outlawed in 1926, but many of its leaders became active in the foundation of the *Christian Democratic Party (DC) in 1943, although the new party was rejected by Sturzo himself.

The name Partito Popolare Italiano was also used by a successor party to the Christian Democrats from 1994. It was part of the centre-left Union governments aligned to the *Olive Tree alliance in 1996–2001, and from 2006.

Portsmouth, Treaty of (5 Sept. 1905)

A peace treaty which ended the *Russo-Japanese War, signed in Portsmouth, New Hampshire (USA). Japan gained the southern half of Sakhalin island. More importantly, Korea was confirmed to be under Japanese influence, and was later declared a colony (1910). Finally, Japan gained control of previously Russian territory in Manchuria as well as the South Manchuria Railway. These provisions provided Japan with a stepping-stone towards expansion on the Chinese mainland, and especially into Manchuria.

Portugal

Portugal was the last European country to transform its economy and politics in the light of *decoloniz-ation, since when its  membership of the European Community and the EU has enabled its economy to grow at a remarkable pace.

Early history Since the fifteenth century, Portuguese wealth was predominantly based on its extensive colonial empire. Over-reliance on its Empire precluded a large number of social, economic, and political reforms, and plunged the country into a deep crisis after the loss of its most important colony, Brazil, in 1822. In the wake of this disaster, the state was too weak to carry out potentially divisive social reforms, while economic change was hindered by the shortage of mineral resources which would enable industrial revolution to occur. The strong military, political, and social elite proceeded, therefore, to compensate for the loss of Brazil by doing what it did best, that is, extending the Empire elsewhere, principally in Africa. This increased the role of the military and reduced the power of the state, already shaken by political conflict, even further through impoverishing it. To reverse the trend of the state's increasing disintegration, in 1907, the Prime Minister, João Fernando Pinto Franco (b. 1855, d. 1929), established a dictatorship. However, his attempt to maintain the power of the monarchy was rendered futile when King Charles I (b. 1863) and his heir were assassinated on 1 February 1908.

Under the new king, the youthful Emanuel II (b. 1889, d. 1932), matters slid into further chaos, and on 4 October 1910 a republic was declared. Despite desperate attempts at social and economic reform, the new regime failed to bring any order into the state finances. The separation of the Roman *Catholic Church and the state (20 April 1911) and further harsh *anticlerical laws were intended to liberate society and integrate it into the republic, but had the opposite effect of alienating even more people from a fragile political order. Portugal's participation in World War I from 1916 wrought even greater havoc upon the state's finances. As a result, the First Republic became western Europe's most unstable political system in the twentieth century, with eight presidents, twenty insurrections, and 44 governments between 1911 and 1926.

Estado Novo (1930s–1974) Having lost all credibility and most popular support, the First Republic was easily replaced by a military coup on 28 May 1926. Unfortunately, the military possessed no magic formula for Portugal's problems either. Its leader, *Carmona, was ultimately forced to rely on the civilian *Salazar, who restored the state's finances, and thus laid the foundations of the longest surviving dictatorship in Europe, the *Estado Novo. Salazar's fiscal conservatism in fact hindered Portugal's development into an industrial, technological nation. Its economy remained heavily reliant on agriculture, so that by 1993, 65 per cent of the population still lived in the countryside. This made it difficult for the country to finance and fight its increasingly bitter colonial wars. These had erupted in response to Salazar's attempt to bind the colonies to metropolitan Portugal through administrative integration, instead of following the general trend of *decolonization evident elsewhere in Africa. By the time of his death in 1968, over 200,000 troops were engaged in a seemingly endless battle to defend the colonies. Most crucially, the bitter colonial wars alienated the military, and led to the coup of 1974.

European integration (from 1974) The new regime pushed through a rapid and over-hasty programme of decolonization, nationalized about 60 per cent of the economy, and carried out a major redistribution of land. A socialist constitution was drawn up by a constituent assembly, and over the next decade a stable two-party system crystallized under *Soárez and *Cavaco Silva. The two were anxious to integrate Portugal into the European Community (*European integration) and to encourage the development of high-technology industries. Cavaco Silva sought to further this aim with some success through a large-scale programme of privatization, and tight fiscal policies to reduce inflation.

Contemporary politics (since 1995) In 1995, Cavaco Silva lost the elections to a rejuvenated Socialist Party under António Guterres. The Socialists continued many of Cavaco's economic policies, and presided over continuing growth as Portugal reaped the harvest of EU membership as well as EU regional transfers. In 1999, Portugal fulfilled the criteria for joining the European single currency, the *euro. As the Socialist government became entangled in a number of corruption scandals, Guterres was forced to resign in 2001. Elections in 2002 led to the return of the centre-right Social Democratic Party (PSD) under José Manuel *Barroso. Barroso's departure in 2004 led the party into disarray, and in 2005 the Socialists returned to power, under José Socrates. The economy continued to grow, but, like his predecessors, Socrates struggled to overcome an excessive budget deficit.

Potsdam Conference (17 July–2 Aug. 1945)

A congress held by the victorious Allies in *World War II at the former Hohenzollern palace in Potsdam outside Berlin. After *Tehran and *Yalta, this was the last war conference of the 'Big Three', and was convened to decide on a new postwar order, now that war in Europe had come to an end. The Soviet Union was led by the experienced and hard-edged *Stalin, while the USA was represented by its new President, *Truman. Nine days into the conference, on 28 July 1945, the veteran *Churchill was replaced by the inexperienced *Attlee as the UK's representative. Polish authority over German lands east of the *Oder-Neisse Line, with which Stalin had compensated the Poles for lands east of the *Curzon Line which he had taken away from them, was accepted, albeit under US and British protest. At the same time, the expulsion of Germans from all non-German territories (Poland, Czechoslovakia, and Hungary) was accepted and legalized.

With regard to Germany itself, measures were to be taken to extinguish *Nazism, and to prepare the German people for democratic government, so that Germany could never again pose a threat to its neighbours. In particular, this meant complete German disarmament, destruction of war industries, dissolution of militarist or *Fascist organizations, the lifting of Nazi laws, punishment of war criminals, and the removal of Nazi sympathizers from public or privileged office. More positively, there was to be decentralization, re-establishment of local self-government, establishment of democratic parties, and a renewal of the legal and educational system. Germany's economic unity was to be preserved, though this was undermined by the decision that each power could take *reparations from its own occupied territories. These results were confirmed by France on 7 August 1945. With regard to subsequent developments, Stalin has generally been considered the winner of the conference, as he managed to legalize his control over almost half of German territory. However, while the inexperience of Truman and Attlee did not help, it has often been overlooked that the USSR had not only created a *fait accompli* by liberating most of these areas, but that, together with Poland, it had suffered the greatest destruction and loss of life of any country in the war.

POTSDAM DECLARATION

Potsdam Declaration (26 July 1945)

An ultimatum of the Allied governments to Japan, with which Britain and the USA were still at war, drawn up at the *Potsdam Conference. Britain and the USA demanded unconditional Japanese surrender. Japan was to be stripped of its empire, and occupied until a peaceful polity had been established. Failure of the Japanese to comply would result in complete destruction. Finally, the Declaration left the position of the Emperor,

whom the Japanese revered as a demi-god, ambiguous. These demands increased the mood of defiance among the more radical military circles in Japan. At the same time, they undermined the moderate peace faction among policy-makers, which only asked for the preservation of the Emperor's status. As Japan failed to respond, President *Truman authorized the dropping of the atomic bomb on *Hiroshima and *Nagasaki, thus fulfilling his threat, and to bring a quick end to the war.

Powell, Colin Luther (b. 5 Apr. 1937). US Secretary of State, 2001–5

Early career Born to a Jamaican-American family in New York in 1937, Powell rose through the Reserve Officers' Training Corps and service in Vietnam to the top ranks of the US military by the early 1970s. Under the *Reagan administration, Powell's ability to command a briefing session with crisp and precise language gained him the position of presidential national security adviser. In 1989 he became the first American of African descent to serve as Chairperson of the Joint Chiefs of Staff, reflecting the status of the military as the most racially integrated organization in American society. He was Commander of US forces during the *Gulf War, demonstrating his sure touch with the media when he explained US policy towards Iraq. Given the memory of the *Vietnam War, Powell was insistent that US military action had to be accompanied by clear political and legal direction and possessed of overwhelming force.

In office After retirement he led a US delegation to Haiti with Jimmy *Carter and successfully convinced the dictators there to quit the country in the face of a US military invasion. Despite his popularity, he declined to run in the 1996 and 2000 presidential election campaigns, but in 2001 he was appointed Secretary of State. In this position, he exercised a moderating influence on a conservative administration. Given the low popularity of George W. *Bush abroad, Powell remained much respected among foreign governments and allies. Even so, his hands-off approach in the conflict between Israel and the Palestinians from 2001 was criticized. The administration tried to capitalize on Powell's reputation to win over sceptics to the *Iraq War. In 2003, it was Powell who was sent to the UN Security Council to present 'evidence' of Iraq's weapons of mass destruction, evidence that turned out to be spurious after the US invasion of Iraq. Inside the administration, Powell was fiercely hostile towards *Rumsfeld and the power he wielded in decisions that should have been made by the State Department.

Powell, (John) Enoch (b. 16 June 1912, d. 8 Feb 1998). British politician

Born in Birmingham, he was educated there and at Cambridge. In 1937 he became professor of Greek at Sydney University, Australia. In 1939, he enlisted in the Royal Warwickshire Regiment, but was soon involved in intelligence work, first in Egypt, then Cairo. After the war, he entered the research department of the *Conservative Party, and was subsequently elected to parliament for Wolverhampton South in 1950. He worked in the Ministry of Housing under *Eden, whom he ardently supported in the *Suez Crisis. As Financial Secretary to the Treasury under *Macmillan, he resigned in 1959 over government refusals to cut public expenditure. He was Minister of Health in 1960-3. During the *Heath government he gained a following through his populist and xenophobic attacks on immigration, his opposition to British membership of the EEC, and his concern for *Northern Ireland. He became an obstinate voice of Ulster as representative of the *Ulster Unionist Party (1974-87). One of the most inspiring and intelligent of British postwar politicians, his career was hindered by his inability to conform to the views of others, and by his preference for being critical, rather than constructive.

Prague Spring (Jan.–Aug. 1968)

After his election as First Secretary of the Communist Party in January 1968, the reformist *Dubček proceeded to transform the moribund party and the state system, in order to overcome the discontent and demonstrations created by two decades of economic mismanagement and repressive government. He proposed to end unfair trials, and released or pardoned all those unfairly convicted in political trials. Press censorship ceased in March, travel restrictions eased, and elections to posts within the Communist Party were to become secret. In some ways, he was remarkably successful. Despite enormous dissatisfaction in the country, the hegemony of the Communist Party remained generally uncontested. It is unclear, however, to what extent this would have remained the case in the long run. Most crucially, despite his care to cultivate good relations with Moscow, he completely underestimated the challenge his reforms presented to his neighbours. The Communist Parties of East Germany and Poland had their own problems of legitimacy. Their leadership understood clearly that reforms inspired by the Czech model could

well result in the collapse of their Communist systems. *Brezhnev refused to contemplate the danger of a collapse within the *Warsaw Pact. On 20 August 1968 Soviet troops, aided by units from East Germany, Poland, and other Warsaw Pact members entered the country without resistance from the Czechoslovak army or the population. The Prague Spring was over, and *Husák headed a new hardline regime which was to rule the country for another two decades.

Prasad, Rajendra (b. 3 Dec. 1884, d. 28 Feb. 1963). President of India 1950–62

Born in Saran into a wealthy Bihar family, he was educated in Calcutta and became a successful lawyer. Of the inner circle of M. K. *Gandhi's followers, which included Jawarhalal *Nehru and Sadar *Patel, he was the one whose ideals most closely resembled that of the Mahatma. He presided over the Indian National *Congress 1934, 1939, and 1947, and was Minister of Food and Agriculture in the interim government of 1946-7. A conciliatory figure whose authority derived from the application of Gandhian principles, he presided over the Constituent Assembly (1946-9). As the first President of the Republic of India, he was uncomfortable with Nehru's confrontational policies against Pakistan, as well as his promotion of industry.

PRI (Partido Revolucionario Institucional, Institutional Revolutionary Party) (Mexico)

Originally founded in 1929 as the National Revolutionary Party (Partido Nacional Revolucionário, PNR) by *Calles, it sought to consolidate within a single movement the new political establishment, consisting of military leaders, civilian officeholders, and co-opted labour leaders. It was reformed and renamed by *Cardenás in 1938 as the Mexican Revolutionary Party (Partido de la Revolución Mexicana, PRM). The aim of the new movement was to represent the concerns of society as a whole through organizing its most important social groups in four separate sectors: peasants, labour, the military, and the middle classes. Thus it created an outlet for the social concerns of these groups while enabling the party oligarchy to retain control over the competing sectors within the single movement.

Under *Alemán, the party was further reorganized and renamed as the PRI. Signifying the military's decline of importance within the Mexican state and Mexican society, it consisted of merely the peasant sector, the labour sector, and the 'popular' sector. Through this structure, the

PRI managed to articulate the contradictory concerns of different social groups, and to encourage them thus to articulate their support. The PRI had a near-complete monopoly of power through the 1970s. Because of the country's economic difficulties of the 1970s and 1980s, its support was eroded, and opposition parties managed to win state governorships for the first time in 1988. In the 1990s, the PRI tried to maintain power through promoting internal reform and greater transparency. In 1999, its candidate for the presidency was selected, for the first time, through primary elections. Despite this, its candidate, Francisco Labastida Ochoa, lost the 2000 Presidential elections to Vincente *Fox. It was the first time in the seventy-one years of the PRI's existence that the party did not present the President. It recovered in the 2003 parliamentary elections, but in 2006 it was pushed back into third place.

primary elections (USA)

Preliminary elections in the USA which select candidates within each party. National conventions began in 1832, nominating a party's candidate for President. At first, delegates were chosen by a closed 'caucus' system, that is, senior party members in the state chose the delegates behind closed doors. Beginning with Wisconsin in 1903, however, democratic primary elections steadily replaced caucus primaries. They are held by the state, and the results are legally binding on the delegates. Primary elections are also used for a wide range of local and state elections. In the south until the 1960s, the Democrats were so dominant that their primaries for various offices virtually ensured the election of candidates. There are both open and closed presidential primaries. In the former, any adult voter in a state may take part, regardless of her or his own party preference. In the latter, only those who are registered members of the party may vote.

The *Kennedy presidential campaign in 1960 was the first to use primaries as a way of circumventing party bosses and proving the electability of a candidate. In 1968 the New Hampshire primary revealed such discontent with President *Johnson that his ambitions for re-election were very seriously compromised. In that year, Richard *Nixon used the *Republican primaries to prove his popularity. Jimmy *Carter and Bill *Clinton respectively used Democrat primaries to introduce themselves from relative obscurity to the American people. By 1988, southern presidential primaries were being coordinated for one giant election ('Super Tuesday'). From then on, the trend towards shortening the primary season and grouping together state primary elections on one day continued, in order to reduce the political divisiveness and the growing cost of the primary elections.

Primo de Rivera y Orbaneja, Miguel

(b. 8 Jan. 1870, d. 16 Mar. 1930). Spanish dictator 1923–30

Born in Jerez de la Frontera, he graduated from the military academy of Toledo and was commissioned in 1889. Thanks to his family connections, quick mind, and courage, he became brigadier-general in 1911. His outspokenness in political matters forced his career into a temporary lull, but also won him increased standing within the army. In 1923, he instigated a military coup against the weak and discredited civilian regime, with the tacit support of the King, *Alfonso XIII. He consolidated his support through successfully ending the war in Morocco and defeating *Abd al-Krim. Extensive economic planning, e.g. through subsidies and public works, led to a temporary truce with the working-class movement and the moderate trade unions. Ultimately, however, his programmes of modernization of the economy and of the army lost him the support of the two pillars of his regime: the landowning elite and the military. He was thus compelled to resign weeks before his death in exile (Paris). The legacy of his rule was ambivalent. It enabled the creation of a republic through completely discrediting the monarchy, while also providing an inspiration to the *Falange, which was founded by his son Antonio.

Prodi, Romano (b. 9 Aug. 1939). President of Italy, 1996–8, 2006–

Born in Scandiano, he studied law and became a professor of economics at Bologna university, making his name as one of the founders of the Italian school of industrial economics. He served as minister for industry (1978–9), and in 1982–9 he acted as chairman of the state-owned Institute of Industrial Reconstruction. As an economic expert without party allegiance he was asked to lead the *Olive Tree Union into the 1996 elections, which he won. However, he struggled to keep the disparate coalition together, and ultimately lost the support of the left-wing over his economic reforms, so that he had to resign.

Following the resignation of the Santer Commission, Prodi was called to become president of the *European Commission (1999–2004). More a broker than a visionary, he failed to give the Commission a distinctive profile. Indeed, he presided over a divided Commission which failed to impact positively on the European *Constitutional Convention. Although a committed European, Prodi began to prepare to return to Italian politics in the last year of his office.

At the head of the centre-left Union led by the Olive Tree, Prodi succeeded in forming a broad coalition against *Berlusconi, which narrowly won the 2006 elections. Confounding predictions that he would find it impossible to keep the coalition together, he benefited from his coalition partners' reluctance to allow Berlusconi a return to power. Prodi was thus able to balance a diversity of interests, while in foreign policy he steered Italy towards a close engagement with the EU and the UN.

Profumo Affair

A British political scandal which suggested that national security might have been breached. The person at the centre of the affair was John Profumo, the Minister of War. In March 1963, he had told parliament that he had not had any 'improper' relationship with a call-girl, Christine Keeler. In June, it emerged that she had been his mistress, while having a similar relationship with Lieutenant-Commander Yevgeny Ivanov, an assistant naval attaché at the Soviet Embassy in London. In response to the public outcry that followed, Profumo resigned from parliament. The resulting inquiry by Lord Denning concluded that national security had not been compromised. However, the affair weakened Prime Minister *Macmillan, who was criticized for not having investigated Profumo fully, and it contributed to an atmosphere of sleaziness and decadence at the end of a long period of *Conservative government (1951–64).

Progressive Coalition, New Zealand,
see ALLIANCE, NEW ZEALAND

Progressive Party, Canada, see
CONSERVATIVE PARTY, CANADA

Progressive Party, South Africa

Established in 1959, when eleven out of fifty-three Members of Parliament for the *United Party (UP) broke away in disgust at the UP's objections to *Verwoerd's plans to grant more land to Black reserves. It adopted a liberal programme, demanding a Bill of Rights, a qualified (but not universal) franchise, and the abolition of racial discrimination. However,

from the 1961 elections until 1974 it was represented in parliament by just one MP, the outspoken **Helen Suzman** (b. 1917), while it was maintained financially by the head of the Anglo-American Corporation, Harry Oppenheimer. In 1974 it won six seats, and was strengthened by the addition of further breakaway groups from the UP, so that in 1977 it changed its name to the Progressive Federal Party. In 1977, it also became the largest party of opposition, and in 1978 it finally came to demand a universal franchise. In 1987, its position as official opposition was lost to the *Conservative Party, and in 1989 it dissolved and its members joined the new Democratic Party, which developed into the *Democratic Alliance.

Progressive Party, USA

The name adopted by a variety of differing political parties in the twentieth century. The first Progressive Party, nicknamed the 'Bull Moose' party, formed the basis of Theodore *Roosevelt's 1912 presidential campaign in which he polled 28 per cent of the popular vote. However, the Progressive Party was less a personal movement than a motley collection of activists with particular agendas drawn from across the political spectrum. The policies promoted by progressivism during the first three decades of the twentieth century comprised, in varying mixtures, conservationism, suffrage reform, prohibition of drugs and alcohol, health and safety legislation, progressive taxation, professional administration, economic controls, and corporate regulation. The Progressive Party thus built upon a contemporary faith in the perfectibility of society, rational methods of government, and the possibility of forming legislation based on universal, scientific truths and principles. It ran no candidates in the 1920 presidential elections, but in 1924 the Progressive Party and the American Federation of Labor (*AFL) joined forces to support Robert LaFollete for President, who garnered over 16 per cent of the vote. Increasingly absorbed into western *Republican and northern *Democrat groupings, it dissolved in 1925, though its influence continued into the *New Deal.

The unsuccessful presidential candidacy of Henry Wallace in 1948 as a self-styled 'Progressive' bore no ideological connection to the earlier Progressive Party. Instead, he absorbed the support of those who would have supported the Socialist Party, as well as the Communists for favouring closer relations with the Soviet Union. Since then, some fringe groups have attempted to appropriate the title 'progressive'.

Prohibition (USA)

This was a culmination of the US temperance movement, whose Anti-Saloon League had been founded in 1893. The movement had enjoyed growing popular support at the end of the nineteenth century, as it enjoyed popular support from many Protestant and other Churches, as well as the Progressive movement (*Progressive Party). Most states adopted restrictions on the sale of liquor, and in January 1919 Prohibition was adopted through the Eighteenth Amendment to the US Constitution. The Volstead Act, passed by *Congress in 1919 over President Wilson's veto, enacted that federal law enforcement was to prevent the manufacture, distribution, or sale (but not consumption) of liquor, wines, and beer. Moderates had only sought the banning of liquor sale and had expected each state to act unilaterally.

The Amendment came into force in January 1920 and, despite the securing of some 300,000 court convictions, drinking continued. Speakeasies (illegal bars) and bootlegging (illegal distilling of alcohol) flourished. The success of gangsters like Al Capone, who controlled the supply of alcohol, led to the spread of the *Mafia and the corruption of officials in the police and government. The issue had a large role to play in politics and some candidates forcefully represented anti-Prohibition, e.g. Al Smith. After the Wickersham Commission reported in 1931 that the prohibition laws were unenforceable and encouraged public disrespect for the law, the Eighteenth Amendment was repealed by the Twenty-first Amendment. A number of states and counties retained partial prohibition, but by 1966 no state-wide prohibition laws existed.

propaganda

A term derived from the *Congregatio de Propaganda Fide*, a commission of cardinals set up by Pope Gregory XV in 1622 with the purpose of spreading the Christian Gospel amongst the heathen. Propaganda gained its negative connotations during World War I, when it described the attempts by the belligerent nations to discredit their opponents and to promote their own national cause through inflammatory rhetoric, lies, and the invocation of popular prejudice. Subsequently, the development of a perfect propaganda machine by *Goebbels (the dissemination of rhetoric through popular radio broadcasts, the promotion of the cinema, and the staging of mass rallies) was a crucial factor in ensuring the success of *Hitler and the *Nazi Party before and after

1933. Propaganda has also been used by other movements. Proponents of *anti-Semitism across Europe have used it, as have dictatorships led by *Mussolini and *Franco. *Communist regimes too have sought to strengthen their emotional appeal, particularly when they were deficient in economic or political appeal.

protectionism

The attempt to protect domestic industry or agriculture from competition, by raising import tariffs which increase the price of foreign imports relative to domestically produced goods. There have been three central reasons for the introduction of protective tariffs. First, protection has been a way of raising government revenue. Second, throughout the twentieth century it has been used by populists as part of a wider, *nationalist rhetoric which extolled the virtues of the home country against supposed 'rivals' abroad. Third, it came to be seen as a genuinely useful policy in cases when domestic industry was nascent and would otherwise have been swamped by superior industrial goods from more developed countries abroad, or in times of economic difficulty. Thus, while these factors were usually effective in combination, in Europe the first and second motives caused several protectionist waves before World War I, while the third reason was the main factor behind the heavy protectionism after World War I.

Protectionism has suffered from two fundamental flaws. First, it makes economic sense for a country only if other countries do not retaliate by imposing protective tariffs themselves. In the 1930s, one of the fundamental causes of the Great *Depression was the existence of high protective tariffs in every country, which drastically reduced world trade. The second, even greater, problem is that protectionism is divisive by its very nature. Protection of domestic, more expensive goods works only through raising the price of cheaper, imported goods. This leads to higher prices, which is always resented by those consumers whose jobs are not safeguarded through protection. Hence, protectionism always involves a choice among policy-makers about which groups to favour at the expense of other groups, in marked contrast to free trade, where all groups are left subject to market forces.

The problems inherent in protectionism have led to its gradual decline after World War II. Through supranational trade organizations such as the European Economic Community or through global talks (*GATT,

*WTO), trade has been liberalized substantially around the world. This has not always been advantageous, particularly to the fledgling economies of Africa, which were being swamped by cheap imported goods. Nevertheless, the trend against protectionism continued through the creation of *NAFTA and the *Central American Free Trade Area (CAFTA), even if these trading blocs were unable to reduce fears that they left the weaker, developing economies exposed to the stronger ones.

EUROPEAN INTEGRATION; OTTAWA AGREEMENTS; ISOLATIONISM; TARIFF REFORM

Provisional IRA, see IRA

Prussia

The kingdom of Prussia, itself in existence since 1701, made up two-thirds of the German Empire founded in 1871, and three-fifths of its population. The King of Prussia was also the German Emperor and, but for six years, the Prussian Minister President was also the Imperial Chancellor. Quite apart from its constitutional prerogatives, therefore, Prussia occupied a pivotal position in the Empire, and its position relative to the other German states and to the country as a whole was a central constitutional question. During the Empire its state parliament, whose members were elected on a highly restrictive franchise, developed into a bulwark of conservatism, which frustrated any liberal or social democrat attempts at constitutional reform.

During the Weimar Republic, the political problem posed by Prussia was reversed. A universal franchise returned a majority for the Centre Party, the *SPD, and the *liberal parties combined. With its large working classes given an equal franchise, Prussia became a solid democratic stronghold, distinguishing itself from radical right-wing and left-wing states (e.g. Bavaria and Saxony respectively). The dismissal of the state government by von *Papen in 1932 therefore fundamentally weakened the Weimar Republic and heralded its end. It meant, for instance, that the police, a state matter in Germany, were no longer in democratic hands throughout most of Germany. Prussia was officially dissolved by the Allied Control Council of occupied Germany, on 25 February 1947.

PSOE (Partido Social Obrero Espa-ñol), see SOCIALIST WORKERS' PARTY OF SPAIN

Pu Yi (P'u-i) (b. 1906, d. 17 Oct. 1967).
Emperor of China 1908–12
Proclaimed Emperor Hsuan T'ung at the age of 2 by his great-aunt the Dowager Empress

Cixi, he was the last Emperor of China, and the last ruler of the Qing dynasty. He was forced to abdicate in 1912, though he was allowed to remain resident in the Forbidden City by the new Chinese Republic. Briefly restored by a warlord in 1917, he was forced to leave Beijing in 1924. In 1934, he accepted the Japanese offer to become Emperor of the Japanese puppet state of *Manchukuo. He was himself little more than a Japanese pawn, but served to give the state some legitimacy. He was captured by the Soviet *Red Army and handed over to the People's Republic of China, where he was re-educated until 1959. He spent the remaining years of his life as a common citizen, publishing his memoirs, *From Emperor to Citizen: The Autobiography of Aisin-Gioro Pu Yi* (2 vols., 1964–5).

Puerto Rico

A Caribbean island formerly under Spanish control, it came under US sovereignty during the Spanish–American War in 1898. Puerto Rico had its own senate and house of delegates. Public life became politicized during the 1930s, when demands for independence first emerged. In 1939 the Partido Popular Democrático (PPD, Popular Democratic Party) was founded by Luis *Muñoz Marín, and it won the elections in 1940. Muñoz introduced some social reforms, but was particularly notable for his success in diversifying the economy through the development of industrial enterprises. Following an abortive revolt against US rule in 1950, it received its current status in 1952 as a Commonwealth voluntarily associated with the USA. It has internal autonomy and rights similar to those of other US states, and its inhabitants have enjoyed US citizenship since 1917. However, its member in the US House of Representatives has no voting powers, and Puerto Ricans continue to be barred from voting in national elections, while being free from federal income taxation.

Muñoz retired in 1965, and from 1968 the PPD alternated in power with the breakaway Partido Nuevo Progresista (PNP, New Progressive Party). Even though the two parties were very similar in their domestic policies, they differed on Puerto Rico's relationship with the USA. The PNP favoured incorporation as the 51st state of the USA, while the PPD wished to continue the current constitutional settlement. The independence movement, once strong in the 1950s, declined during the 1960s as a result of the economic prosperity which the relationship with the USA yielded. By 1993, a non-binding referendum showed that there remained only a plurality of votes in favour of the current settlement (48.4 per cent), while 46.2 per cent voted to become an equal state within the USA, and 4.4 per cent favoured independence.

Throughout the 1990s domestic politics were dominated by the PNP, but the 2000 elections were won by Sila María Calderón of the PPD, which also won a majority of seats in the House of Representatives. Calderón was succeeded, in 2005, by Anibal Acevedo Vila (PPD), who was elected by a margin of 0.2 per cent.

Punjab

An area divided between Pakistan and India. It became a *Sikh kingdom in 1799, but was subjected to British rule after the Anglo-Sikh wars of 1846 and 1848. Towards the beginning of the twentieth century, Punjab was already experiencing considerable communal tensions between the Muslim majority comprising around 50 per cent of the population, the Hindus forming around 38 per cent of the population, and the Sikhs, who made up around 12 per cent of the population. These tensions were underlined by different cultural and linguistic identities. Matters were complicated by the fact that the different religious communities were riven by tensions within themselves.

As religious, economic, and cultural competition between the various groups intensified, sporadic unrest burst out into open rebellion (1913–15). This was suppressed by the British, with nationalism growing in the wake of the *Amritsar Massacre of 1919. Inter-communal tension continued, inevitably flared up with the partition of India into a Muslim and a Hindu state, in the process of which the Punjab was also formally divided in 1947. Millions of Muslims moved west to Pakistan, while millions of Hindus moved east to the Indian areas of the Punjab. In 1970, the Pakistan areas became a separate province, as Punjabis were increasingly influential in public life. In the Indian areas of Punjab, despite an administrative reform in 1966 whereby Punjab was divided into the Punjabi-speaking state of Punjab in the north, and the Hindi-speaking state of Haryana in the south, competition between Hindus and Sikhs demanding an

autonomous state continued. A militant Sikh movement developed, which in 1984 assassinated the Indian Prime Minister, Indira *Gandhi. The partition of Punjab has remained bitterly resented by both India and Pakistan, and was the main subject of the 1965 *Indo-Pakistan War. It was also the scene of heavy fighting in the 1971 Indo-Pakistan War. The government of the Province was normally controlled by the *Congress Party (INC), but between 1997 and 2002 it was governed by a Hindu-Sikh nationalist alliance led by the *Bharatyia Janata Party. In 2002, power reverted back to the INC.

Putin, Vladimir (b. 7 Oct 1952). President of Russia, 2000–

Early career Born in Leningrad, Putin studied law and in 1975 entered the foreign section of the *KGB. He rose through its ranks, but in 1992 he quit to become advisor to the Mayor of St. Petersburg. In 1996 he joined the staff of President *Yeltsin, who in 1998 appointed him Head of the Russian intelligence services. In 1999, Yeltsin appointed him Premier, and he succeeded him at the end of the year in a deal which granted the corrupt Yeltsin immunity from any future prosecution.

Presidency In 2000, he won the presidential elections in the first round, and in 2004 he was re-elected with a landslide majority. Despite having been a relative political outsider, he proved adept at not offending too many entrenched interests at once. In particular, he refrained from persecuting Russia's powerful oligarchs who had enriched themselves in the Yeltsin era, but ended their privileged access to government resources. He also expected political non-interference in return. Putin presided over a remarkable economic reversal, as high prices for Russia's oil and gas reserves provided for economic growth, allowing the state to sharply reduce its foreign debt.

On the basis of Russia's command of increasingly scarce mineral resources, Putin expanded Russian influence abroad, which had diminished sharply in the Yeltsin era. Through the Rusian energy company, Gazprom, he used the gas supply to Russia's neighbours to increase his influence in their domestic policies, such as in 2005, when Russia announced the doubling of energy prices a few months before elections in Ukraine. The growth of Russian influence cooled his relations with George W. *Bush, though Putin maintained good relations with the EU leaders.

In domestic affairs, Putin reduced freedom of speech by cracking down on private TV channels and newspapers critical of the government. Moreover, he was responsible for many *human rights violations committed by the Russian army inside *Chechnya. Human rights campaigners also held his government responsible for the murder of government critics such as Alexander Litvinenko. Putin's policies did bring political and economic stability to Russia, though economic growth sharply increased income inequalities among the population.

Q

Qaddafi, Muammar al-, see GADDAFI,
MUAMMAR AL-

Qassem, Abdul Karim (b. 1914, d. 9 Feb.
1963). Iraqi ruler 1958–63
Born in Baghdad as the son of a carpenter, he
joined the Iraqi army and rose to the rank of
brigadier. Strongly nationalist and anti-
British, Qasem led the Iraqi Revolution of 14
July 1958. He named himself Prime Minister
of the new Republic of Iraq, and was, in fact,
its dictator. His rule was erratic, and
increasingly reliant on the loyalty of the army.
This disintegrated when he lost his claim for
the incorporation of Kuwait because of British
intervention in 1961. A rebellion in
*Kurdistan in 1961 tied down many of his
loyal military units, and in 1963 a dissident
army group, supporting his more extreme
*Ba'ath rivals, seized power. He was shot in
the coup.

Qatar

A small state on
the Saudi
Arabian
peninsula, it has
become
politically and
culturally one of
the more liberal
states on the
Persian Gulf.
   An emirate
since 1766, in the early nineteenth century
it came under the sovereignty of the Emir of
Bahrain, since when the two countries have
had difficult relations. It gained independence
in 1868, though in 1872 it came under the
suzerainty of the *Ottoman Empire. Qatar
became a British protectorate in 1916,
remaining completely autonomous in its
internal affairs. In 1968 it joined the
Federation of Arab Emirates, but on
1 September 1971 it declared its own
independence. Ruled in authoritarian manner
by Sheikh Khalifa bin Hamad al-Thani, in 1986
it became engaged in a military conflict with
Bahrain over the Hawar islands, where
considerable oil and gas reserves are
suspected.
   On 27 June 1995, Sheikh Khalifa was
deposed by the Crown Prince, Sheikh Hamad
bin Kahlifa at-Tani, who was immediately
recognized by his neighbours and the USA. He
continued his predecessor's attempt to
diversify the country's industry, and to
substitute for the export of crude oil, of which
its reserves were declining, through exports of
gas, which it possessed in abundance. In 1996
a coup attempt led by a member of the royal
family failed, and in 2001 the perpetrators
were sentenced to death. In 2000, Qatar's
long-standing border disputes with Bahrain
and Saudi Arabia were settled, and in 2005 a
Constitution introduced some liberal reforms.
Qatar has become a pioneer in the export of
liquefied gas, beginning the construction of
the world's largest liquefied natural gas plant
in 2005.

Quakers (Society of Friends)

A religious body which believes in the
immediacy of divine revelation as mediated
through the 'inner light of Christ' in each
individual, thus rejecting all forms of dogma,
sacraments (as outward symbols), and paid
ministers. From its foundation in the middle
of the seventeenth century by George Fox,
Quakers have had a notable influence on
society through their belief in community
service and their passionate practice of
pacifism. In 1947 the Society of Friends
received the *Nobel Peace Prize for the social
work conducted by Quakers during the two
World Wars, and for their relief work in the
war-torn areas of Europe immediately after
*World War II. There are currently around
500,000 Quakers, half of whom live in the
USA, and 30,000 in the UK.

(((⊕))) **SEE WEB LINKS**

• The home page of the Society of Friends.

Qualified Majority Voting (QMV)

A voting procedure in the Council of Ministers
of the European Community and the
*European Council. This has provided a key
for determining a majority sufficient to pass
EU legislation for certain legislative acts. As
the growing size of the EC/EU made decisions
by unanimity impractical, QMV was seen as a
way to prevent large member states or
regional alliances dominating a minority.
Following the Treaty of *Nice, a complex
formula for QMV was operative, whereby
member states received different numbers of
votes according to their size, ranging from
fifteen for the largest states (Germany, the UK)
to three for the smallest (Malta since 2004).

For legislation to pass under QMV, all these votes were added up, and 74.6 per cent of the total and a majority of the number of member states were needed to pass. At the request of a member state, the population could be taken into account, whereby a measure needed the support of states that represented at least 62 per cent of the population. Although the majority of decisions by the council were subject to QMV, in practice around 90 per cent of the legislation for which QMV was required continued to be passed with unanimity.

Quebec

Colonized by the French as New France, it came under British control in 1763. In order to obtain the support of the French-speaking majority against the emerging USA, the British allowed its distinctive culture and education to continue. Ever since, its identity has been closely linked to the perceived threat to its culture from the USA to the south and from the English-speaking areas to the west.

Contemporary history (up to 1976) For almost a century after the creation of the Confederation of Canada in 1867, it chose to ally itself with Canada's English-speaking areas, since the USA was clearly the greater threat to its existence. An agricultural territory largely without industries before 1900, 500,000 of its population had emigrated to the USA (1850–1900) in search of employment. Initially a bastion of the *Conservative Party, it became a *Liberal stronghold from 1896/7, when *Laurier became Canada's first Prime Minister from Quebec. The province's crucial support for the Liberal Party beyond Laurier's period in office ensured that the federal government, which had been hitherto preoccupied with the development of Ontario and the new western provinces, began to invest more heavily in Quebec's infrastructural and economic development. This facilitated its industrialization from around 1900, which was triggered by demand in the US market. The Great *Depression caused further emigration to other parts of Canada and the USA, and focused increased attention on the province's relative backwardness compared with the rest of Canada. This led to the victory of the *Union Nationale party in 1936, which continued to govern the province until 1960, with one brief interruption (1939–44).

Economic progress during the 1940s and 1950s did not bring social or cultural change, and this led to the election victory of the Liberals in 1960, heralding the *Quiet Revolution. Industrial relations were regulated, education became a state matter, and industries came under provincial control.

The power of the provincial government was substantially enhanced, both within Quebec society, and against the federal government in Ottawa. It was soon recognized that this development would lead to a fundamental shift of Quebec's role within Canada. A hitherto backward and insulated society which had sought to preserve its culture against its principal threat, US cultural and economic domination, had attained economic and social maturity without threatening its identity.

The politics of separatism (since 1976) To a more self-confident and assertive Quebec, the principal threat to its cultural identity appeared to be no longer the USA, but an English-speaking Canadian majority seemingly refusing to recognize its distinctiveness. This was expressed most violently by the *Front de Libération du Québec, while Quebec's assertiveness also sustained the transformation of provincial politics, with the separatist *Parti Québécois (PQ) winning the 1976 provincial elections. Its referendum on the province's sovereignty failed, however, as most Québécois defined their distinctive identity within, rather than outside, a Canadian context. The move for further sovereignty gained ground during the 1980s, owing to the failure of the federal Constitution in 1982 (*Canadian Constitution, patriation of). The *Meech Lake Accord also failed to take sufficient account of the province's grievances. In a renewed referendum of 1995, the *Bloc Québécois narrowly lost. In reponse, separatism's most popular advocate, *Bouchard, became Premier in an attempt to address the province's economic problems and further boost the popularity of the PQ. However, the Province's economic backwardness relative to the rest of Canada and the potential costs of separation became a liability for the PQ. The Liberal Party won the 2003 provincial elections by gaining 76 out of 125 seats, and formed a government headed by Jean Charest (b. 1958). In the 2007 elections, the PQ only came a distant third, with the more moderate Action Démocratique becoming the official opposition. Charest continued to govern at the head of a minority government.

Quemoy

An island six miles off the coast of mainland China, which in 1949 the Nationalist forces had managed to defend against Communist encroachment. It became part of the Republic of China (Taiwan), which regarded it as a base for a future reconquest of mainland China, while using the island in the 1950s as a base for guerrilla raids against the People's Republic. Conversely, it was seen by *Mao as the epitome of provocation to the sovereignty of Communist China, and a symbol of his failure to extend his authority over all of China. Mao ordered an invasion twice in 1954 and 1958, each time to withdraw in the face of heavy US presence. It became protected by a US-Taiwanese alliance, and was heavily fortified. Nevertheless, in subsequent decades it became a primary focus for Communist Chinese sabre-rattling, with Communist China periodically conducting regular military manoeuvres nearby. The island was under direct military rule until 1992, when civilian government was restored. In 2000, direct shipping links were restored to mainland China.

Quezón y Molina, Manuel Luis (b. 19 Aug. 1878, d. 1 Aug. 1944). President of the Philippines 1935–42

Born in Baler on Luzon, he studied law and became an attorney in 1903. Originally an opponent of US control, Quezón was elected Governor in 1906, thanks to his charisma and active US help. He was elected to the Philippine Assembly in 1907, where he became the parliamentary leader of the largest party, the Nationalist Party. As resident commissioner for the Philippines in Washington (1909–16), he lobbied hard for Philippine independence, which resulted in the Jones Act of 1916, which extended Filipino autonomy. On his return Quezón joined the Senate and became its President. He continued to advocate independence, but was equally concerned about preparing his country for statehood through the creation of an efficient administration, and a viable economy. Elected President of the transitional Commonweath of the Philippines, his attempts at reform were hampered by the power of entrenched interests, and the growing dependence on the USA in the face of Japanese expansionism. Upon the Japanese invasion in 1942, he presided over a government-in-exile in Washington until his death.

Quiet Revolution (*Révolution Tranquille*) (Quebec)

A term which first appeared in Canada's main national newspaper, the *Globe and Mail*, to describe the changes in the Canadian province of *Quebec, introduced by the provincial *Liberal government of Jean Lesage, 1960–6. Succeeding a Conservative, traditionalist government with a rural base (*Union Nationale), Lesage tried to respond to the social changes brought about by the industrialization of Quebec. He ended the control of the Roman *Catholic Church over the education system through the creation of a modern system of state schools, revised the labour laws, and introduced legal equality for women. The Quiet Revolution interfered directly in the economy, most importantly through the nationalization of the electricity industry under *Lévesque, which had hitherto been largely controlled by capital from English-speaking Canadians. The Quiet Revolution heightened Quebec's self-confidence, increased the power of the provincial government which was dominated by French-speaking interests, and thus sparked off the growth of popular demands for sovereignty.

Quisling, Vidkun Abraham Lauritz Jonsson (b. 18 July 1887, d. 24 Oct. 1945) Prime Minister of Norway 1942–5

Born in Fyresdal, the son of a Lutheran pastor, he had a brilliant early career in the army and became a general staff officer by the age of 24. He entered politics in 1931 and was Minister of Defence (1931–2). He left the government, however, in order to found the *Fascist Nasjonal Samling Party in 1933. His aim was to combat *Communism, which he had encountered as a member of the Norwegian legation to the USSR and as part of *Nansen's team to help Russian refugees. After the outbreak of World War II, he visited *Hitler in December 1939, in order to encourage him to undertake the conquest of Norway. After the invasion of April 1940, as leader of the only permitted political party he collaborated fully with the Germans. In 1942 Quisling became Prime Minister of the puppet pro-German government. After Norway's liberation in 1945 he was arrested, charged with high treason, and executed. In English, 'quisling' has since come to denote *collaboration with the enemy.

Quit India campaign, see SATYAGRAHA

R

R101 disaster, see AIRSHIPS

Rabin, Yitzhak (b. 1 Mar. 1922, d. 4 Nov. 1995). Israeli general; Prime Minister 1974–7, 1992–5

Early career Born in *Jerusalem, the son of Russian immigrants, he joined the elite professionals of the Haganah Jewish defence force, the Palmah Brigade, and was its commander 1943–8. As army Chief of Operations (1959–64), he had a difficult relationship with the then Deputy Defence Minister, *Peres, with whose career his became inextricably linked. As army Chief of Staff since 1964, he led the military during the spectacularly successful *Six Day War in 1967. Israeli ambassador to Washington from 1968, he returned to Israel in 1973 and joined parliament for the *Labour Party. He became Minister for Employment under *Meir in March 1974. In the following month Rabin beat his political rival, *Peres, to become leader of the Labour Party after Meir's resignation.

During his first term as Prime Minister, Rabin was unable to reduce the corruption scandals that had plagued the party in the years before. Following the revelation, on the eve of the 1977 general elections, that his wife held an illegal foreign bank account, he was forced to resign. Shortly thereafter, the Labour Party had to concede power for the first time to *Begin's *Likud Bloc. He was succeeded as leader of the Labour Party by Peres, whom he continued to oppose within the party. As Minister of Defence (1984–90), he supervised the withdrawal of Israeli troops from the Lebanon, but was also responsible for the army's brutal attempts to suppress the *Intifadah uprising 'with might, power and beatings' from 1987. The Israeli inability to overcome the Intifadah convinced him that Israel could never rely on its army to preserve peace in the long run.

Second term (1992–95) Taking the party leadership from Peres again in 1992, he became Prime Minister on 13 July 1992, with Peres as his Foreign Secretary. Strongly encouraged by the latter, the erstwhile military hardliner began to work for regional peace. After recognizing the *PLO in the *Oslo Accords, he signed the *Gaza–Jericho Agreement, in which the first Palestinian areas were given autonomy status. This served as a prelude to further negotiations for Palestinian autonomy, while it also paved the way for a peace treaty with King *Hussein of Jordan on 26 October 1994. Together with Arafat and Peres, he was awarded the *Nobel Peace Prize on 10 December 1994. He was murdered by an Israeli extremist after addressing a peace rally of over 100,000 supporters. While always more cautious and reserved than his party rival, Peres, his credibility as the former leader of the Six Day War was vital in convincing many Israelis that their security would not be put at risk by a peace treaty with the PLO.

race riots, Los Angeles (USA)
The sporadic eruption of racial tension in a city which is home to the largest community of Mexican Americans, and one of the largest communities of African Americans. The most well-known of these were the **Watts riots**, in the slum areas of the Watts district which were mainly inhabited by African Americans, beginning on 11 August 1965, as a protest against long-standing social injustice. Some 34 people died and over 1,000 were injured during a week of riot, which was eventually quelled by the National Guard. The riots helped to create a White backlash against gains that were being made by African Americans as a result of the *civil rights movement. Since then, racial tension has persisted.

On 29 April 1992, the acquittal of four policemen for the beating of the African-American **Rodney G. King**, despite clear and well-publicized video evidence, led to renewed riots aimed at Asian and White shopkeepers and pedestrians. They were brought under control through the declaration of a state of emergency, and the calling in of army, police, and National Guard, by 2 May. In total, they led to 58 dead and 2,300 wounded, as well as property damages totalling $1 billion.

Radek, Karl (b. 1885, d. 1939?). Russian Communist
Born Karl Sobelsohn, he was an active Social Democrat in Germany and Poland in 1901, and became a *Bolshevik follower of *Lenin after meeting him and other Russian Communist leaders in 1904. He worked as a journalist for the German *Social Democrats from 1907, until he went to Russia to become

a member of the central committee of the Petrograd *Soviet in 1917. He subsequently became responsible for the development of the German *Communist Party and frequently travelled to Germany, where his *propaganda helped fuel the revolution of 1918. In 1924 he was released from his duty as a follower of *Trotsky. Expelled from the Soviet *Communist Party in 1927, he was readmitted in 1929, when he became active as a journalist. He was imprisoned in 1936 and sentenced to ten years' imprisonment early in the following year, which he did not survive.

Radhakrishnan, Sir Sarvapalli (b. 5 Sept. 1888, d. 16 Apr. 1975). President of India, 1962–7

Born in Tirutani into a brahmin family, he was educated in Madras and taught philosophy there, at Mysore and Calcutta, before teaching as professor of eastern religion and ethics at Oxford 1932–52. He wrote extensively on Hindu religious and philosophical thought, seeking to reinterpret it for modern times. He also served as India's first 'ambassador extraordinary' to the Soviet Union 1949–52 and then as Vice-President of India, before succeeding President *Prasad. Having made a lasting impression as a renowned and exceptional scholar, as President he is best remembered for guarding the peaceful transition of power after *Nehru's death.

Radical Party, France

A French political movement with a fundamental commitment to a republic which originated in quasi-mystical perceptions of the French Revolution (1789). After the creation of the Third Republic in 1870, the Radicals aimed at strengthening it as a strong, secular state. The perception of crisis which set in following the *Dreyfus Affair, and the ambiguous role played by some religious orders in it brought the place in France of the Roman *Catholic Church to the political agenda. This ushered in the party's golden age in 1899. Reconstituted as the Radical and Radical-Socialist Party in 1901, it won a tremendous victory in the 1902 elections on an *anticlerical campaign. In 1904, the separation of church and state was passed as law. Returned in even greater numbers by the 1906 elections, the party formed a government under G. *Clemenceau. However, with the clerical issue settled, Radicalism had little else to offer apart from maintaining the authority of the French state, and few of its proposed social reforms ever became law. The government fell in 1909, and though the party continued to dominate the

political scene until 1936, it was continuously hampered by a weak political programme and organization. Meanwhile, the party shifted further to the right, especially in opposition to the *Popular Front. As a member of the 'Third Force', it formed many postwar governments, together with the *MRP and the *Socialist Party. During the Fifth Republic, however, the party has become increasingly marginalized. It helped found the *UDF in 1978, a party with which it has been aligned since.

Radical (Union) Party (*Unión Civica Radical*, Radical Civic Union, UCR) (Argentina)

Argentina's main consistently democratic political party was founded in 1892. Radicals consisted of a coalition of groups which had failed to take part in Argentina's agricultural export boom, such as parts of the old nobility. These joined forces with groups which had done well but failed to attain corresponding political power, such as the newly prosperous middle classes and landowners of the upper Littoral. Following the introduction of universal male suffrage in 1912, the leader of the well-organized Radicals, *Yrigoyen, was elected President in 1916. They dominated the 1920s politically through control of both Houses of Congress and the presidency (under Yrigoyen and Marcelo T. de Alvear). In 1930, however, Yrigoyen was deposed by a military *coup d'état*.

Despite a long spell in opposition Radicals continued to form the largest party, but split in 1956 into the Intransigent Radicals strictly opposed to *Perón, and the Popular Radicals in favour of dialogue with *Peronism. The latter Radicals formed two democratic governments (1958–66), which were fundamentally weakened by disunity and the need for the mutually exclusive support of both Peronists and the military. The central voice of the middle classes, the Radicals formed the opposition to the governments of the military and the Peronists, and did not return to power until 1983 under *Alfonsín, who won the elections on a wave of disgust against a discredited military and a popular desire for a stable democracy. Nevertheless, Alfonsín could not prevent Peronism from becoming a popular force again, and in 1989 the Peronists returned to government. Under Ferdinand de la Rúa, the UCR returned to power in 1999. It turned out to be a pyrrhic victory, however, as the new government presided over a period of deep political and economic turbulence. De la Rúa resigned in December 2001, with power ultimately returning to the Peronists. The Radical Party continued as Argentina's major opposition party, but in 2005 it only held 40 seats compared to 141 seats occupied by the governing Peronist Justice Party.

Raffarin, Jean-Pierre (b. 3 Aug. 1948). Prime Minster of France, 2002–5

Raffarin became a successful marketing director before entering politics in 1976, serving as President of the regional council of Poitou-Charentes from 1988, and as member of the *European Parliament from 1989. A Senator from 1995, he entered the government of Alain *Juppé as Minister for Small Business and became party secretary of the *UDF. Following the election defeat for the conservative parties in 1997, he left his party and joined the small Liberal Democracy Party, whose Vice-President he became. Raffarin strongly argued for greater unity among right-wing parties, and thus joined the *UMP upon its foundation. In 2002, Raffarin became *Chirac's surprise appointment as Prime Minister. Raffarin was commended by his moderate political outlook and his provincial origins, after the presidential election had just demonstrated the popular aversion to the Parisian political establishment. At the 2002 elections he led the UMP to a resounding victory. However, his popularity declined because he was unable to find solutions to the long-term problems of mass unemployment and the social exclusion of the suburban poor. He resigned after the French rejected the government's advice to approve the Treaty establishing a European *Constitution in a referendum.

Rafsanjani, Hashemi Ali Akbar (b. 25 Aug. 1934). President of Iran 1989–97

Born in Rafsanjan, Kerman, he received religious instruction at Qom from the age of 14, and soon came under the spell of *Khomeini. On account of his lack of formal education, he obtained the title of Hojjat al-Islam, just below that of an *Ayatollah. He spent several periods in imprisonment during the regime of Shah Reza *Pahlavi (1963–4, 1967, 1972, 1975–7), and was one of the leading organizers of the Iranian Revolution of 1978–9 until Khomeini's return from exile. A founding member of the Islamic Republican Party and a member of the Revolutionary Council, he became Khomeini's deputy in the Supreme Defence Council. After a power struggle with the hardline faction of the Revolutionary Council around Khomenei, he came to succeed Khomeini himself. A moderate only by Iranian standards, he did pursue a pragmatic policy which focused on consolidation of the Islamic order, rather than further reforms based on the Qu'ran. For

instance, in 1994 privately owned banks were allowed to operate in Iran for the first time since the Revolution. Nevertheless, he continued to rule with the help of internal terror, while jealously guarding his 'Islamic credentials' in order not to be outmanoeuvred by hardliners within the theocracy.

Rainbow Warrior

Name of the ship belonging to the environmental organization *Greenpeace, which was blown up on 10 July 1985 in Auckland Harbour as it was preparing to set sail for *French Polynesia in order to protest against nuclear testing at the Mururoa Atoll. One photographer was killed in the incident. The revelation that the two culprits captured by the New Zealand police were agents of the French secret service forced the resignation of the head of the secret service and of the Minister of Defence, Charles Hernu, despite initial attempts at a cover-up. The French public were outraged at the tough prison sentences of ten years given to the agents, and proceeded to boycott New Zealand goods. The dispute was not resolved until the following year, when New Zealand handed over the agents in return for an official apology and French compensation payments.

Raj, British

A term derived from the Sanskrit word *raja* (king), it denotes the British Empire of India. Its beginnings date back to the foundation of the British East India Company in 1600, though the Raj was not formally established until the subcontinent had come under British control in its entirety in 1858, and Queen Victoria was proclaimed Empress of India in 1877. British control over the directly ruled territories (about three-fifths of the total area) was exercised by a Secretary of State in the British Cabinet and a Viceroy in India. The administration was staffed by the Indian Civil Service, which in later years was gradually opened to Indians, although Europeans and Indians remained socially separate. In addition there were in India some 700 princely states, bound by treaty to the Crown, in which the princes preserved control over domestic affairs. Supported by the *Indian army consisting of some 175,000 men (most of whom were Indian), the Raj could only exist in a country with 450 million people with popular cooperation. As this began to diminish with the campaigns of *Gandhi, the position of the Raj was steadily weakened from the 1920s, and it became increasingly clear that the status quo could not be maintained.

Rajagopalachariar, Chakravarti

(b. Dec. 1878, d. 25 Dec. 1972).
Governor-General of India 1948–50

Born in Thorapolli (Salem district), he was
admitted to the Bar in 1900 and became a
successful lawyer. He became a loyal follower
of *Gandhi, whose defiant campaigns of
non-cooperation he supported. Known as
'Rajaji', he was general secretary of the Indian
National *Congress (INC) 1921–2, and ran the
Congress disobedience campaigns in southern
India. He was chief minister of Madras
(1937–9), but resigned as part of Congress's
protest against the British declaration of war
against Germany on India's behalf. More than
*Nehru, he appreciated the *Muslim League's
demands for minority safeguards for Muslims,
and took part in the independence
negotiations. Chosen by Nehru as first and last
Governor-General of India before it became a
republic, he fell out with him during the
1950s and became one of the principal
founders of the oppositional Swatantra Party.

Rajk, Laszlo (b. 9 Mar. 1909, d. 15 Oct.

1949). Hungarian Communist leader

Born of a Jewish family and educated in
Budapest, he became a Communist while a
student. He joined the *International Brigades
to fight in the *Spanish Civil War, but became
a prisoner-of-war and returned to Budapest
only in 1941. He then became active as the
secretary of the illegal Communist Party until
he was captured by the Germans in 1944.
Released from a German *concentration
camp only in May 1945, he soon became
Minister of the Interior, in which capacity he
organized a terror campaign to facilitate the
Communist takeover of the state in 1948.
Shortly afterwards, he became one of the first
victims of *Stalin's purges, despite his
previous unstinting loyalty to the despot. Rajk
was moved to the Foreign Ministry and
replaced by *Kádár, and on 19 May 1949 the
show trials had been prepared sufficiently for
him to be arrested. He was persuaded to admit
to false charges, ostensibly for the good of
Communism. He was duly sentenced to
capital punishment, and executed. The lavish
funeral after his posthumous rehabilitation
on 6 October 1956 was attended by over
200,000 people, and marked one of the
triggers of the *Hungarian Revolution.
  SLÁNSKI TRIAL

Rákosi, Mátyás (b. 9 Mar. 1892, d. 5 Feb.

1971). Prime Minister of Hungary 1952–3

Born in Ada, Rákosi became a Communist and
was a commissar for *Kun's Communist
regime. After its collapse he fled to Moscow,
but he was sent back in 1924 to revitalize the

ailing Communist Party, which had been
forced underground by the regime of *Horthy
and *Bethlen. He was imprisoned in 1925 and
sentenced to life imprisonment in 1935. He
was sent to the USSR in 1940, however. As the
formerly leading Communists had mostly
died in the *Great Purge of *Stalin, Rákosi
became a leading figure in the Hungarian
Communist Party. After Hungary's liberation
from German occupation in December 1944,
he became Deputy Prime Minister, though as
General Secretary of the Communist Party he
exercised central political control. Rákosi thus
engineered the 1948 Communist takeover of
the state. As a devoted *Stalinist, he instituted
a repressive regime and orchestrated his own
purges, culminating in the show trial of *Rajk.
The brutality of his regime fell out of favour
with the USSR after *Stalin's death, and he
was forced to resign the leadership to *Nagy.
He returned to power in 1955, but memories
of his terror were so strong that he was forced
by the Soviet Union to return into exile there.

Rama IX, see BHUMIBOL, ADULYADEJ

Ramaphosa, Matamela Cyril (b. 17

Nov. 1952). South African trade unionist

Born in Johannesburg, the law student of the
University of the North became active in the
South African Students' Organization, the
Student Christian Movement, and the Black
People's Convention, before gradually moving
on to support the *ANC. He became legal
adviser to the Council of Unions of South
Africa, and in 1982 was appointed general
secretary of the National Union of
Mineworkers. Having co-founded the
Congress of South African Trade Unions
(COSATU) in 1985, he led a strike involving
over 200,000 miners in 1987. One of the most
influential and prominent supporters of the
ANC within South Africa during the 1980s, he
became its secretary-general in 1991. In 1994
he failed in his bid to become *Mandela's first
Vice-President against the former ANC
spokesperson in exile, *Mbeki. He left the
government in 1996, to take up the
directorship of various companies.

Ramos, Fidel Valdez ('Eddie') (b. 18

Mar. 1928). President of the Philippines 1992–8

Early career Born in Lingayen into one of the
country's most influential families, he
graduated from the US Military Academy at
West Point, and was then trained at Fort
Bragg. He participated in the *Korean and
*Vietnam Wars. Ramos became the chief of
the notorious Philippine Constabulary, which
was responsible for the terror that kept
*Marcos in power. However, in 1986, when

popular resistance to Marcos became almost overwhelming, he sided with Corazón *Aquino and was thus to a considerable extent responsible for the end of the Marcos regime. He was rewarded by Aquino by his appointment as Chief of General Staff (1986–8), and as Minister of Defence (1988–91).

In office Ramos was as important to the young democracy as he had been to the Marcos regime, strengthening Aquino's government against various coup attempts, as well as against the rebellious Communist New People's Army. With Aquino's blessing, he was elected President on 11 May 1992, but was faced by a hostile Congress, in which he did not command a majority. He sought to continue Aquino's efforts to stabilize the political system, most controversially by appeasing the military. On 2 Sept. 1996 he signed a peace treaty with Nur Misauri, the leader of the rebel Moro National Liberation Front. Although some rebel groups opposed the agreement, it provided the basis for a settlement of a brutal civil war raging since 1972. Ramos was barred by the constitution from standing for the presidency again, but remained an influential figure in the Philippines.

Randolph, Asa Philip (b. 15 Apr. 1889, d. 16 May 1979). US labour union organizer
Son of a Methodist minister, he was born in Crescent City, Florida, and in 1911 moved to Harlem, New York. In 1914 he co-founded the *Messenger*, an outspoken magazine with radical views on racial and economic issues. In 1925 he became the first President of the Brotherhood of Sleeping Car Porters. After a long campaign Randolph finally gained recognition for his predominantly Black union and a contract with the Pullman Company in 1937. As US involvement in World War II deepened, his threat to lead a *March on Washington contributed to the end of race restrictions on employment in the defence industries (June 1941). As President of the Non-Violent Civil Disobedience League against Military Segregation, his activities helped to persuade President *Truman to end segregation in the armed forces in 1948. In 1955 he helped to reunite the AFL with the CIO, becoming a Vice-President of the combined *AFL-CIO. In 1963, with Martin Luther *King, he helped to organize the *March on Washington, one of the largest civil rights demonstrations ever held.

Rankin, Jeanette (b. 11 June 1880, d. 18 May 1973). US women's rights and peace activist
Born in Montana, she became the first woman to be elected to *Congress as a Representative for Montana in 1916, at a time when nationwide universal female suffrage had not yet been introduced. Her pacifism in World War I ensured her defeat in the 1918 elections, but she came to be seen as a prophet of *isolationism. She returned to Congress in 1940, having maintained her prominence by a variety of means associated with pacifist and feminist groups throughout the 1930s. The only dissenter in the war vote in 1941, she lost her seat in 1942 and disappeared from public significance for the duration of World War II. She re-emerged as a vocal critic of the *Truman Doctrine and the *Cold War.

Rao, P. V. Narasimha, see NARASIMHA RAO, PAMULAPARTI VENKATA

Rapallo Treaty, see RATHENAU, WALTHER

Rashid Ali al-Gailani (1892–1965). Prime Minister of Iraq 1933, 1936–8, 1940–1
Born in Baghdad from a distinguished *Sunni family, he graduated from Baghdad Law School. In 1924, he became Minister of Justice, and in 1925–8 he served as Minister of the Interior. His nationalist sentiments made him strongly hostile to the Anglo-Iraqi Treaty of 1930 negotiated by *Faisal I, as he resented Britain's strong residual influence. He founded the nationalist National Brotherhood Party in 1931. His first period in office as Prime Minister lasted six months, though he remained as one of the pivotal figures in Iraqi politics. He was Minister of the Interior (1935–6), and in December 1938 became Chief of the Royal Cabinet. A group of increasingly powerful anti-British and pro-German colonels made him Premier. His subsequent denial of help to the British army, and his expulsion of the *Hashemite dynasty, led to the intervention by British forces, who deposed him and reinstated Faisal I. He fled to *Nazi Germany, and remained in exile in Saudi Arabia until 1958, when he returned to support *Qassem's revolutionary regime. He was soon linked with attempts to oust Qassem, for which he was sentenced to death. He was pardoned, and released from prison in 1961.

Rasputin, Grigori Yefimovich (b. 1864?, d. 30 Dec. 1916). Russian monk
Born in Prokoskoye in Siberia, the son of a peasant, he claimed mystical healing powers. He came to live at the Tsarist court in 1907. His beneficial treatment of the haemophiliac Crown Prince won him a disastrous hold over Tsarina Alexandra, an influence which increased when her husband *Nicholas II left the court to command the army in 1915. Rasputin and the Tsarina were thought to be lovers, and together they virtually ruled

Russia, dismissing all of the more liberal ministers. The resulting government inefficiency was responsible to a great degree for the failure to get adequate supplies to the Tsar and the army. Rasputin's drinking habits and sexual excesses discredited the court and in December 1916 he was murdered by a group of noblemen led by Prince Yusupov.

Rassemblement pour la République (RPR), see GAULLISM

Rastafarianism

A cult which spread from the West Indies to both the USA and the UK among young Blacks during the 1980s. It sees the (deposed) Emperor of Ethiopia, *Haile Selassie (born Ras Tafari Mekonnen), as symbolically the rightful protector of African civilization and the representative of the true message of the Gospels. It was a Black interpretation of Christianity, whereby Blacks were God's chosen people. Rastafarianism helped to give Black minority groups a degree of self-respect in an often hostile and essentially White culture.

Ratana, Tahupotiki Wiremu ('Bill')

(b. 25 Jan. 1873?, d. 18 Sept. 1939). Maori spriritual and political leader

A Maori Methodist farmer who in November 1918, when Maoris suffered from an influenza epidemic, had an apparition of God, telling him 'I have travelled around the world to find the people upon whom I can stand. I have come back to *Aotearoa to choose you, the Maori people...Cleanse yourself. ... Unite the Maori people.' During the 1920s, his message of Maori unity and God's choice of the Maori people provided an important boost to Maori confidence and self-belief. Encouraged by his healing powers, a community began around his house, Ratana Pa, and it developed into the Ratana Church, which by 1988 had 36,000 members.

From 1922, the **Ratana Movement** became preoccupied with politics, gradually displacing the *Young Maori Movement in its appeal. It won its first parliamentary seat in 1932, and in 1943, the party gained *Ngata's Eastern Maori seat, thus representing all four Maori constituencies. In 1935, it joined an alliance with the *Labour Party, which under *Muldoon and *Fraser passed significant legislation such as the introduction of the secret ballot for Maori electors, equal unemployment benefits, better housing opportunities, and improved health and educational provision. Yet its alliance with Labour deprived it of potential influence in the governments of the *National Party,

which was in power for most of the 1950s, 1960s, and 1970s. In the 1970s, the political influence of the movement declined, and in 1979 a group of younger Maori politicians, impatient with the Labour/Ratana alliance, founded a new party, Mana Motuhake.

Rathenau, Walther (b. 29 Sept. 1867, d. 24 June 1922). German Foreign Secretary 1922

In 1899 Rathenau joined the board of the electrical conglomerate AEG (Allgemeine Elektrizitäts-Gesellschaft), and became its chairman in 1915. He joined the left-*liberal DDP (Deutsche Demokratische Partei), which was one of the supporters of the Weimar Republic, in 1918. As a financial adviser to the government he became a representative in the negotiations for the *Versailles Treaty. He served as Minister for Reconstruction in 1921, after which he became increasingly involved in foreign policy. As Foreign Secretary from 1 February 1922 he concluded the **Rapallo Treaty** with Soviet Russia on 16 April 1922, whereby the two countries would resume diplomatic relations and renounce any claims for *reparations arising from World War I. The treaty was heavily criticized by Britain and France, but for Germany and Russia it was a first step out of diplomatic isolation. Owing to his Jewish origins, Rathenau was murdered by members of the same far-right Consul Organization which had previously killed M. *Erzberger.

Rawlings, Jerry John (b. 22 June 1947). Ruler of Ghana 1979–2001

Born in Accra, Rawlings attended Achimota College and Teshie Military College (1968). He then trained as a jet pilot but, shocked by corruption among senior military officers, he plotted with thirteen other young officers, and in May 1979 led an abortive coup to overthrow the military government. Released from prison after a further coup on 4 June 1979, he became chairman of the Armed Forces Revolutionary Council, which in effect controlled the country. In a widespread purge against corruption, several army officers, including the three former heads of state, were executed. After four months he handed over power to a civilian President, Hilla Limann. In December 1981 he re-established himself as chairman of the Provisional National Defence Council of Ghana. His original popularity, achieved by his stance against corruption, was eroded owing to his policies of economic liberalization and privatization, which caused widespread poverty and unemployment. This forced him to reintroduce a democratic constitution, and in a general election in 1993 he was confirmed

President. He was re-elected in 1996. Barred by the constitution from running for office for a third time, he retired in January 2001, becoming Ghana's first leader to hand over power peacefully.

RC (Rifondazione Comunista), see
COMMUNIST PARTY, ITALY

Reagan, Ronald Wilson (b. 6 Feb. 1911, d. 5 June 2004). 40th US President 1981–9

Early career Born the son of a shoe salesman in Tampico, Illinois, he graduated from Eureka College with a BA in 1932, progressing through careers as an Iowa radio sports announcer, a Hollywood movie actor, and a television announcer before being elected Governor of California in 1966. Initially a *Democrat, Reagan became a *Republican in 1962 but always drew support from conservatives in both parties. He enjoyed support from many workers disconcerted by the *civil rights movement, student activism, and the domestic unrest consequent upon the *Vietnam War. In 1968, Reagan was defeated in the *primary elections by *Nixon for the Republican presidential nomination, but not before laying claim to the sympathies of *Goldwater supporters who favoured a radical right-wing agenda. In 1976 he lost the nomination again, in an extremely close race with the incumbent President, Gerald *Ford.

Presidency Reagan won the Republican nomination in 1980, and defeated President *Carter in a landslide victory. Optimism and confidence characterized Reagan's political persona, and his effective rhetoric reassured a country unsettled by the tumults of the 1960s and 1970s and perceptions of American decline. He was most reassuring in his active, interventionist foreign policy. Reagan assumed a rigorous stance against the Soviet invasion of Afghanistan and the deployment of Soviet intermediate range missiles in Eastern Europe. In response, he embarked on a huge programme of military rearmament, which included the deployment of Pershing nuclear missiles in western Europe and culminated in the *SDI initiative.

Reagan was also highly concerned about the spread of Communism outside Europe, and especially in Central America. He funded the right-wing guerrillas fighting against the Nicaraguan government, ordered his troops to invade Grenada, and propped up the corrupt right-wing dictatorship in El Salvador against left-wing guerrillas. His intervention in the Lebanese civil war (1982) was unsuccessful and resulted in the loss of hundreds of American lives, though his

bombing of government targets in Libya did produce a more moderate policy on the part of *Gaddafi. Reagan's policies were not without risk, especially as the Soviet Union went through an uncertain period before 1985. Moreover, the Soviet Empire collapsed due to its long-term difficulties and self-contradictions. However, it is also clear that Reagan's acceleration of the arms race hastened the collapse of the Soviet economy.

At home, Reagan sought to stimulate the economy by introducing sweeping tax cuts which yielded disproportionate benefits to the wealthy. According to his version of 'trickle-down economics', this gave them an incentive to work harder, stimulate jobs, and thus benefit everyone. In the early years of his administration, this coincided with a period of high interest rates determined by the *Federal Reserve System. The decline of world commodity prices in the mid-1980s did ensure economic recovery, though overall Reagan's economic policies resulted in a dramatic increase in the national debt. Beyond economics, he secured the appointment of right-wing *Supreme Court Justices Sandra Day *O'Connor and Antonin Scalia, and appointed William H. *Rehnquist as Chief Justice.

Reagan's second term in office was marred by the *Iran–Contra affair. He managed to avoid implications by referring to his constantly failing memory, an assertion made credible by his unintellectual reputation. Indeed, this reputation in part accounted for his popularity, which allowed him to connect with many voters. His popularity also soared after he was shot by John Hinckley Jr, from which he took months to recover. Increasingly reliant on his advisers and on scripted appearances in public during his second term, he excelled at communicating with his audience in direct, clear, and passionate language. In 1994 it was announced that he was afflicted by a degenerative neural disorder, Alzheimer's disease, and he retired from public life.

Red Army (Russia/Soviet Union)
Formed and named by *Trotsky in 1917 in order to fight the *Russian Civil War, it consisted of many units of the old imperial army. To ensure loyalty to *Lenin's new Communist regime, political commissars or 'advisers' were attached to all units. The commissars' constant terror against individuals or groups deemed to be disloyal, the army's superior numbers, and Trotsky's organizational abilities ensured the Red Army's eventual superiority in the Civil War. After the Treaty of *Rapallo (1922) close

cooperation with Germany produced great advances in combat techniques and armament production. However, the army suffered a devastating blow during the *Great Purge, when most of its officers were killed. Low morale, incompetent leadership, and inability to adapt to harsh winter conditions accounted for its poor showing in the *Winter War with Finland. It learnt some important lessons from its difficulties there, but was none the less surprised and initially overwhelmed by the German attack in World War II. Old, 'imperialist' command structures were re-established, though the presence of the political commissars continued to have a demoralizing effect. It changed its name to the Soviet Army in 1946, when army, navy, and air force were placed under a single Ministry of the Armed Services, which was later reorganized as the Ministry of Defence.

Red Brigades

The most active of all Italian terrorist groups, they emerged from the Metropolitan Collective of Milan, founded by students and workers dissatisfied with the compromise policies of the *Communist Party. Their first terrorist campaigns date from the early 1970s, and throughout the decade they committed dozens of murders in an effort to undermine the Italian democratic state. Their efforts climaxed in the murder of *Moro in 1978, but since then their activities have gradually diminished, mainly as a result of better anti-terrorist methods employed by the police.
BAADER-MEINHOF GROUP

Red Chapel (Rote Kapelle), see
RESISTANCE, GERMANY

Red Cross, International

An international aid organization founded by the Swiss Henri Dunant in 1863, after he had witnessed the Battle of Solferino (1859). Its guidelines were laid down in the *Geneva Convention (1864), in which it committed itself to the impartial care of wounded in battle under the sign of the red cross against a white background, an inversion of the Swiss flag. Its mandate was extended in a number of further conventions. It helped in wars and afflictions throughout the century, on the basis of humanity, impartiality, neutrality, independence, voluntarism, unity, and universality. Its international headquarters remained in Geneva, where it co-ordinated the activities of 186 national Red Cross (or Red Crescent in Muslim countries) organizations. In 2007, it adopted a third symbol associated with neither Christianity nor Islam, the red crystal.

SEE WEB LINKS
• The official website of the International Committee of the Red Cross.

Red Guards (China)

A major instrument of the *Cultural Revolution, consisting of bands of students which followed *Mao Zedong's instruction to root out the enemies of the (permanent *Maoist) revolution. In 1966–7, hoards of marauding youths roamed through the streets, venting their frustrations against the establishment in party, bureaucracy, and education facilities. Teachers were attacked and denounced for being 'bourgeois', and even parents became subject to denunciation and public censure. They soon got out of control, and were overpowered by the military in 1967.

red scares (1919–20, USA)

A term relating to allegations about Communist subversion, following the *Bolshevik revolution in Russia in 1917. In February 1919 workers in Seattle staged a general strike, which the city Mayor declared was part of a *Bolshevik plot. There were a number of bomb outrages across the country—probably the work of anarchists— and further strikes and May Day demonstrations. The formation of the American Communist and Labor Party in August 1919 confirmed for many Americans that the country was in crisis. Two hundred and fifty Russian immigrants were shipped back to Russia, and J. Edgar *Hoover, a young member of the staff of Attorney-General Mitchell Palmer, reported that 'revolution was imminent'. Palmer authorized widespread raids, over 6,000 persons were arrested, and 556 of them deported. Public hysteria built up during early 1920, but subsided when 1 May passed off peacefully. One result of this first scare was the 1924 *immigration legislation.

Red Shirts

A movement of the Pakhtu people in the North-West Frontier province of British India. Correctly titled **Khudai Khidmatgar** (Servants of God), it was formed in 1929 by **Abdul Ghaffar Khan** (b. 1890, d. 1988), a Muslim follower of *Gandhi. It provided the main support for Khan's influence within the province until 1946, during which time it supported the *Congress Party rather than the *Muslim League. Despite his campaigns for a separate state of **Pakhtunistan**, Khan was forced to accept the state's absorption into Pakistan, which banned the movement.

Khan was arrested several times, and became a national opposition leader, mainly through the *Awami League.

Redmond, John Edward (b. 1 Sept. 1856, d. 6 Mar. 1918). Irish politician

Born in Ballytrent, Co. Wexford, he was educated at Trinity College Dublin. His father, an MP, secured him a position as clerk of the House of Commons, and he was called to the Irish Bar in 1886. Redmond became an MP for New Ross in 1881, and joined Charles Stewart Parnell's Irish Parliamentary Party. Redmond led the minority of the party which supported Parnell after his fall over the O'Shea divorce scandal, and was elected a Parnellite MP for Waterford in 1891 (the seat he held until his death in 1918). When the party reunited in 1900, Redmond became its leader. He pushed the Liberal government into introducing the third Home Rule bill for Ireland in 1912. Opposition to Home Rule from Ulster Unionists forced the *Asquith government to insist on partition, which Redmond reluctantly accepted only as a temporary solution. World War I delayed the enactment of Home Rule, and Redmond suggested that the Irish Volunteers be used for internal defence, not for foreign service. Asquith rejected this, and Redmond was persuaded to encourage Irish enlistment in the British army. This alienated him further from the militant nationalists, whose popularity increased dramatically at his expense after the *Easter Rising of 1916. He died before his Irish Parliamentary Party was virtually wiped out by *Sinn Féin at the 1918 *Coupon Elections.

Reform Party, Canada

A political party founded in Alberta in 1987 by Preston *Manning, who became its first leader. It was designed to give a voice to its particular constituency in the west of Canada, in favour of unrestricted capitalism and against special rights for the province of Quebec. In response to the failure of the *Meech Lake Accord in 1990, and to growing demands for separation or special rights in Quebec, it benefited from the weakness of the *Conservative Party and gained 52 seats in the 1993 general elections. In an effort to go beyond its political base in the western provinces, it reconstituted itself in 2000 to join the Canadian Alliance, which merged with the Progressive Conservative Party in 2003 to create the Conservative Party.

Reform Party, New Zealand

A conservative political grouping formed in 1909 from various political reform leagues organized at local level from 1905 onwards,

under the leadership of *Massey. It retained its loose organization, being principally opposed to the professionalization of politics which had emerged under *Seddon's *Liberal Party government, and which continued to develop with the *Labour Party in 1916. As a result, the party was little more than a vehicle to keep Massey in power. This became particularly problematic after his death, when the party could point to few distinctive policies of its own, except for its hostility to concessions to the labour movement, and its strong rural individualism. *Coates managed to revive the organization of the ailing party with some skill, but ultimately he was forced to concede a union with the United Party to form the *National Party in 1936.

Rehnquist, William Hubbs (b. 1 Oct. 1924). US Supreme Court Chief Justice 1986–2005

Born in Milwaukee, Wisconsin, he became a lawyer after distinguishing himself in the air force during World War II. He obtained BA, MA, and LLB degrees from Stanford and a Harvard MA. Rehnquist became a clerk to the *Supreme Court in 1952, a *Republican politician, and an assistant Attorney-General of the United States under the *Nixon administration in 1969. He was confirmed as a *Supreme Court Justice in 1971. Rehnquist dissented from the judgment in *Roe v. Wade, and became associated with efforts to remove *abortion rights from the federal sphere to the discretion of the states. Appalled by judicial activism, he advocated a classical, minimalist role for the court after the tumult of the 1960s. In 1986, he was appointed by Ronald *Reagan to replace Warren *Burger as Chief Justice. In this position, he presided over the court's shift to the right, culminating in its controversial role in ensuring the 2002 *Bush election victory.

Reichskristallnacht, see KRISTALLNACHT

Reichstag Fire (27 Feb. 1933)

Less than a month after *Hitler's appointment as Chancellor, the German parliamentary building, the Reichstag, burnt down. The balance of scholarly opinion is that the *Nazis were not involved in the planning or execution of this, and that the arsonist arrested at the scene of the crime, Marinus van der Lubbe, acted on his own. At first, the Nazi leadership was confused and uncertain how to react. Hitler then seized upon the opportunity to pass an Emergency Act on 28 February 1933, which allowed him to imprison *SPD and *Communist Party activists and MPs. Having seriously restricted his most important opponents, he called elections on a pretext of 'national emergency'. He failed, however, to get the absolute majority he desired, which necessitated the *Enabling Act.

Reid, Sir George Houstoun (b. 25 Feb. 1845, d. 13 Sept. 1918). Prime Minister of Australia 1904–5

The son of a Presbyterian minister from Scotland, he arrived in Australia in 1852. He became a lawyer in 1879, and entered the parliament of New South Wales (NSW) as a committed proponent of free trade (1880–4, 1885–1901). Reid became leader of the opposition in 1891, and was premier of NSW from 1894 to 1899, cautiously supporting a federation of Australian states. Elected to the federal government in 1901, he supported a defensive coalition against the growing *Labor Party. On this basis, in 1904 he formed a government in a coalition with protectionists. With a majority of only one seat, he was unable to enact any major legislation. He retired from parliament in 1908, and became Australia's first high commissioner in London (1910–16). He was elected unopposed to the British House of Commons in 1916.

Reith, John Charles Walsham, 1st Baron Reith of Stonehaven (b. 20 July 1889, d. 16 June 1971). Director-general of the *BBC 1927–38

Born in Stonehaven, Kincardine, he became a locomotive engineer after leaving school. He was wounded in World War I, and subsequently worked in private industry. Despite his lack of knowledge about broadcasting, in 1922 he became the general manager of the BBC, and in 1927 he was appointed its first director-general. Conscious of the power of broadcasting, he consistently sought to keep the BBC free from political interference, and to extend its national coverage. He also promoted programmes which had a broadly educational content, on subjects such as news, drama, classical music, and literature. In 1936, he inaugurated British television, but this closed during World War II. In January 1940, he became Minister of Information under Neville *Chamberlain, and a month later, he was elected to parliament for Southampton. Under *Churchill, he was briefly Minister of Transport until he became Minister of Works in October 1940. He did not have an easy relationship with Churchill, and was dismissed in 1942. The subsequent years were a disappointment to a man of his supreme drive

and vanity. He chaired the National Film Finance Corporation (1948–51) and the Colonial Development Corporation (1950–9), and was Lord High Commissioner of the *Church of Scotland (1967–8).

RENAMO (Resistencia Nacional Moçambicana, Mozambique National Resistance)

A right-wing resistance movement against the rule of *FRELIMO in Mozambique, established from 1975. It functioned originally with the help of the intelligence services of the Rhodesian *Smith government, which tried to destabilize the FRELIMO regime because of its support for *ZANU. Increasingly, it derived its main support from South Africa, which objected to FRELIMO's support for communism, the *ANC and the Namibian independence movement, SWAPO. Despite its vast inferiority in numbers to FRELIMO's forces, it continued extensive guerrilla attacks, exerting ferocious brutality on some of the civilian population. By 1989, it had destroyed three-quarters of the country's educational facilities, as well as countless hospitals. It is estimated that almost 50 per cent of all children in Mozambique in 1975–89 died directly or indirectly because of the war. RENAMO is estimated to have killed over one million civilians, while 20 per cent of the population became refugees.

The end of the South African *apartheid regime stopped its vital source of support, and forced RENAMO to negotiate a peaceful compromise with FRELIMO leader *Chissano. It participated in the multi-party elections of 1994, when it gained 112 out of 250 parliamentary seats. Its main electoral base was in central Mozambique, which had been the heartland of their military operations. Despite initial protests, it accepted the outcome of the elections. RENAMO boycotted parliament from 1999, when it suffered another narrow election defeat at the hads of FRELIMO. It stopped short, however, of reverting back to armed conflict, and it contested the elections of 2004.

reparations (Germany)

The payment by a country defeated in war to its victors in money, kind, or labour. The official rationale is to compensate the victors for the cost of the war, but in fact reparations have served to weaken the former enemy's economic potential, in order to deprive it of the foundation for speedy rearmament and retaliation. After the Franco-Prussian War (1870–1), France had to pay 5 billion francs in reparations to Germany.

When Germany was defeated in *World War I, it was ordered to pay 226 billion gold marks in 1921. This was subsequently reduced to 132 billion, payable in 37 years, plus a proportion of German export earnings (26 per cent). Following the financial collapse of 1923 and the political crisis after the French invasion of the Rhineland (*Ruhr District) in the same year, the payments were revised in the **Dawes Plan** (16 August 1924). Devised by the American banker Charles Dawes (b. 1865, d. 1951), who received the 1925 *Nobel Peace Prize for it, it restructured the reparation payments so that they were low for the first five years, to give German industry time to recover, before then rising again.

When it became clear that the German economy would be unable to meet the increased payments due after five years, the terms were revised by the **Young Plan** (21 August 1929). This substantially reduced the original reparation payments while granting Germany a loan of $300 million. A payment under the plan was made in 1930, but payments were suspended after the international financial crisis of 1931. In 1932, when the Weimar Republic had all but collapsed, the Lausanne Conference absolved Germany from further payments.

The reparation payments formed the central political issue during the Weimar Republic, not only because of their tremendous size, but also because they were legitimized by the war-guilt clause of the *Versailles Treaty. In this clause, Germany was given the sole responsibility for World War I, which Germans considered unacceptable. Every government of the Weimar Republic was judged on how it managed to reduce the payments, and successive governments wilfully escalated the country's economic crises in order to prove the impossibility of paying off the reparations.

After *World War II, the defeated *Axis Powers were obliged to make reparations payments once again. In the areas under Western control, reparations payments were relatively small, mainly because the desire to punish Germany and Austria soon gave way to the need to befriend these countries as allies in the developing *Cold War. Reparations were a much bigger liability for the areas under Soviet control. The USSR, which had suffered disproportionately great damages during the war, reasoned that it had greater need for reparations, while it maintained its influence in these regions through occupation. It is estimated that Eastern German reparations payments to the USSR (formally ended in 1954) exceeded those of Western Germany to the other Allies by 26 times.

Republican Party (USA)

Early history up to Eisenhower (1952) Also known as the **Grand Old Party (GOP)**. The present Republican Party was formed in 1854. Its early success was built upon a successful coalition among north-eastern evangelicals and north-western farmers. With Abraham Lincoln (b. 1809, d. 1865) it won its first presidential election in 1860, a result that triggered the US Civil War (1861–5). In 1869–1932 it lost only four presidential elections, two each to Grover Cleveland (b. 1837, d. 1908) and Woodrow *Wilson.

The party's traditional social base was eroded through the country's rapid industrial progress, which created a growing number of industrial workers in the cities. In its efforts to find a response to the increasing problems of an industrial and urban society without losing its agricultural base, it split when Theodore *Roosevelt formed his *Progressive Party and promised reform and regulation to deal with socio-economic problems.

After World War I the party's *isolationist policy and its focus on domestic economic expansion brought it back to power, in three successive Republican Presidencies under *Harding, *Coolidge, and H. J. *Hoover. The party was thus strongly identified with the unprecedented prosperity of the 1920s. It was also associated with the overheating of the economy and financial speculation which led to the *Wall Street Crash and the ensuing Great *Depression. With their ideas of economic and military non-interventionism Republicans had difficulty adapting to the turbulent 1930s. They were defeated by the *Democrats under F. D. *Roosevelt in four consecutive presidential elections. By the end of World War II the Republican Party had recovered somewhat, but it surprisingly lost a further presidential election to *Truman in 1948. It regained the White House only through the massive, non-partisan popularity of General *Eisenhower in 1952.

Eclipse (1960s) and revival (from the 1970s) Thereafter, while the GOP continued to have problems in gaining control of *Congress, in presidential politics it profited from a number of political, social, and economic shifts. Under the Democratic Presidencies of *Kennedy and Johnson (1961–9), *civil rights legislation and *desegregation undermined the strength and unity of Democratic support in the south, previously a backbone of Democratic support. This was further eroded through the Democrats' identification with the *Vietnam War. The Republicans also gained a strong base in the so-called 'Sunbelt' of the south-west. In addition, the GOP benefited greatly from the economic prosperity and growth in the west, where 'new' electronic and high-technology companies became concentrated. As a result the GOP was the dominant party in presidential politics in the 1970s, though *Nixon's *Watergate scandal and *Ford's rather lacklustre leadership led to the brief Democratic presidency of *Carter (1977–81).

Dominant in the 1980s once again, the GOP flourished under *Reagan, whose policies of huge military spending and tax cuts (at the cost of a record budget deficit) did much to consolidate the Republican electoral base, which was to a large extent dependent on defence spending and government contracts. This presented the GOP with a fundamental dilemma in the 1990s: as a budget deficit of $268.7 billion by 1991 called for an inevitable cut in government expenditure, this was bound to hit two of its major constituencies, those working for the military directly, and firms dependent on military contracts. Following George *Bush's decision to raise taxation (contrary to his earlier promises), the Republicans lost the 1992 presidential elections.

In the 1994 elections to *Congress, the Republicans led by Newt Gingrich managed to square the circle, by focusing demands for expenditure cuts on welfare payments, which affected primarily the Democratic constituency. However, by 1996 this had backfired and given President *Clinton his greatest boost for re-election, as he managed to portray Gingrich and his Republican challenger, Bob Dole, as cold-hearted and uncaring. For the 2000 presidential elections, George W. *Bush managed to reunite the GOP and reignite it through the chance of victory.

Contemporary politics (since 2001) Once in office, Bush abandoned his slogan of 'compassionate conservatism' by endorsing anti-environmental legislation, and by proposing a large tax cut which mainly benefited wealthy taxpayers. Bush also restored the bond between the GOP and its constituency in the military, through vast increases in military expenditure. Bush's immense personal popularity following *September 11 contributed greatly to the GOP's success in the 2002 mid-term elections, when it regained control of the Senate and increased its lead in the House of Representatives. This left the GOP free to enact Bush's more controversial policies on education and economics, and support his judicial nominees, John G. *Roberts and Samuel Anthony Alito Jr. Under Bush, the party energized its grass-roots base, particularly Christian conservatives and fundamentalists. This enabled the Bush team

to secure his re-election in 2004, despite the *Iraq War, largely on the basis of moral values. The unpopularity of the war, and a re-energized Democratic organization, resulted in the loss of *Congress in 2006, leaving the GOP *primary elections for the 2008 presidential race wide open.

⊕ SEE WEB LINKS

• The home page of the Republican Party.

resistance, Germany

Following *Hitler's accession to power, by 1939 over 150,000 members of the *Communist Party and the *SPD had been sent to *concentration camps, while around 40,000 had emigrated abroad. Subsequently, the scope for opposition to the *Nazi regime was very limited, in part because of the *SS and *Gestapo, but also because Hitler came to enjoy such overwhelming popular support. One oppositional group became known as **Red Chapel (Rote Kapelle)**; it consisted of diverse groups of socialists with members in several ministries which enabled them to pass military and other national secrets to the Soviet Union. However, they were discovered between summer 1941 and summer 1942, and over forty of their members were executed.

Although Hitler managed to placate much of the Church establishment, individual bishops and priests like Bishop von Galen and Dietrich Bonhoeffer also offered resistance. More often than not, however, resistance by individual, lesser-known priests was brutally persecuted. A different approach was taken by the **White Rose (Weisse Rose),** a group mainly of students from Munich which began to distribute pamphlets in the summer of 1942 urging Germans to rise against the regime. They were arrested in February 1943 and executed. Apart from individual acts of resistance, for example the hiding of about 4,000 Jews by other Germans, the one act of resistance which came close to having any lasting effect was the *July Plot of 1944, carried out with the support of more conservative groups.

resistance, Italy, see CNL; CNLAI

Résistance, La (France)

After 1940, individual groups began to form which were dedicated to the active sabotage of the German occupying forces in the north, and the *Vichy government in the south. In opposition to the right-wing *Pétain government, resistance groups such as the **Libération-Sud** and the more intellectual **Franc-Tireur** tended to be more overtly left-wing. The most important group was **Combat,** led by Captain Pierre Frenay, which was made up largely of professionals in Lyons and the south-east. In the north, organizations such as the trade-union-based **Libération-Nord** emerged, though the dominant force came to be the **Front National**, especially after the French *Communist Party had abandoned its official neutral stance in June 1941 following *Hitler's attack on the Soviet Union.

In early 1943, de *Gaulle's deputy, Jean Moulin, succeeded in co-ordinating the most important groups through the **Conseil National de la Résistance** (National Resistance Council). The effectiveness of the *Résistance* was enhanced further by its ability to recruit men who wanted to avoid the compulsory labour service of Frenchmen in Germany, introduced in February 1943. It was at that time that the **Maquis** became a potent force of the resistance movement. Named after the term from Corsican folklore, *prendre le maquis* ('taking to the bush'), it consisted of those people of the *Résistance* whose names were on German blacklists and who had to go into hiding. Hence, it existed mainly in the inaccessible terrains of the Alps and the mountainous Massif Central. There were considerable tensions between Communist and non-Communist sections of the Maquis, but both became active in the fight against the occupying forces following the Allied landings for *D-Day and in southern France in 1944. In all, up to 300,000 people (around 2 per cent of the population) participated in the *Résistance*. The significance of the *Résistance* lies not only in the heroic sacrifices of many of those who took part, but also in the sense of dignity which its actions bestowed upon the French nation both during and after World War II.

Restitution Agreement (10 Sept. 1952)

An agreement reached between West Germany and Israel in which the former paid survivors of the Holocaust living in Israel 3 billion marks in compensation. Similar agreements were reached with representatives of Jewish survivors outside Israel. On 29 June 1956, compensation was extended to all victims of the *Nazi regime. In contrast, East Germany refused to accept any responsibility for the atrocities of the *Third Reich.

Reuther, Walter Philip (b. 1 Sept. 1907, d. 9 May 1970). US labour union leader

Born in Wheeling, West Virginia, he left school at 16 to become an apprentice, but was dismissed for protesting against Sunday work. In 1926 he went to Detroit and became a foreman at the Ford Motor Company. Dismissed for trade union activity in 1932, he soon joined General Motors, where he helped found the United Automobile Workers' Union. As its president from 1946 until his death, he pioneered negotiations for guaranteed employment, wage increases tied to productivity, and welfare provisions for his members. A strong anti-Communist, in 1952–5 he was president of the Congress of Industrial Organizations, which had been tainted by Communist associations in the 1940s and 1950s, and fought strenuously to rid unions of corruption and racketeers. In 1955 he led the reunion between the CIO and *AFL. However, disagreement with George Meany, president of the AFL-CIO, led him to take the UAW out of the organization in 1969. Shortly before his death he formed a short-lived Alliance for Labor Action with the *Teamsters. A strong supporter of *civil rights, *cooperative organizations and the *Great Society, he fought for the right of organized labour to participate in industrial planning. In his belief that trade unions had to take stands on non-industrial policy issues, he became an important influence in the *Democratic Party. Reuther was also in the vanguard of attempts to link unions to business with productivity bonuses for workers and index-linked wage increases and pension benefits. He died in an aeroplane crash.

Reynaud, Paul (b. 15 Oct. 1878, d. 21 Sept. 1966). Prime Minister of France 1940

A wealthy lawyer, he was a parliamentary Deputy for the National Bloc (1919–24), the Democratic Alliance (1928–40), and the Independent *Radicals (1946–62). He held various ministries from 1930 onwards and distinguished himself especially as Minister of Finance (1938–40), when he engineered an economic recovery through undoing much of the social legislation of the *Popular Front government. He opposed *Daladier's policy of appeasement, and took over from him to become the last Prime Minister of the Third Republic in March 1940. In May he asked the President, Albert Lebrun, for the appointment of Marshal *Pétain as Deputy Prime Minister. After fleeing to Bordeaux he was forced to resign on 16 June 1940. He was imprisoned by the *Vichy government, tried at *Riom, and spent the last years of the war in German *concentration camps. In 1948 he was briefly Minister of Finance again, and in 1953–4 Deputy Prime Minister. In 1958 he chaired the constitutional committee which wrote the Constitution of the Fifth Republic. However, he became opposed to the presidential system, to de *Gaulle's policies on Europe, and the construction of the *nuclear bomb.

Reynolds, Albert (b. 3 Nov. 1932). Prime Minister (Taoiseach) of the Irish Republic 1992–4

Born in Rooskey, Co. Roscommon, he spent many years as a businessman. He was first elected to Dáil Éireann (the Irish parliament) in 1977 as the *Fianna Fáil member for Longford. He was Minister for Post and Telegraphs (1979–82), for Transport (1979–82), for Industry and Energy (1982), Industry and Commerce (1987–8), and Finance (1988–91). He replaced *Haughey as leader of the party in February 1992. His administration saw the passage of the *Maastricht Treaty Referendum in June 1992 and the signing of the *Downing Street Declaration in 1993. He led Fianna Fáil to an electoral victory in January 1993, and formed a coalition with *Labour. He continued in his involvement in the *Northern Ireland peace process, and his public acceptance of Gerry *Adams as a legitimate spokesperson of the Catholic community in Northern Ireland encouraged the *IRA to declare a ceasefire which began on 30 August 1994 (lasting until 9 February 1996). Labour pulled out of the coalition on 16 November 1994 in disagreement over a judicial appointment to the presidency of the high court. Reynolds resigned, and was succeeded by *Bruton.

Rhineland, see RUHR DISTRICT

Rhodes, Cecil John (b. 5 July 1853, d. 26 Mar. 1902). British imperialist

Early career Born in Bishop Stortford, Hertfordshire (UK), he went to South Africa to work on his brother's cotton farm in Natal in 1870. He returned to study at Oxford in 1873, from where he graduated in 1881, while he used his vacations in South Africa to dig in the diamond fields with increasing success. By 1880 he was able to found the De Beers Mining Company, which in 1888 expanded to become De Beers Consolidated Mining Company. At the same time, his growing familiarity with the prosperity and beauty of the *Afrikaner-dominated Transvaal made him one of the prime movers towards a Federation of South Africa under British sovereignty. Elected to the Cape legislature in 1880, he secured the annexation of Bechuanaland (now Botswana) to the British Crown in 1884–5. To secure control and mineral rights in Matabeleland (now Zimbabwe), his agents secured a treaty with the Ndebele King Lobengula.

The British South Africa Company On 13 July 1889 he founded the *British South Africa Company, which subsequently administered and colonized the territory named Southern Rhodesia in his honour in 1898. As Prime Minister of the Cape (1890–6), Rhodes carried out local government reforms and ended some forms of racial discrimination. However, he had to resign following his encouragement of the disastrous **Jameson Raid**, when his friend Leander Starr Jameson (b. 1838, d. 1917) unsuccessfully tried to trigger an uprising in the Transvaal to establish British sovereignty over it. This venture destroyed the coalition between Afrikaners and English-speakers upon which his support had rested, and destroyed his chances of renewed political leadership. He subsequently divided his time between the management of his affairs in Southern Rhodesia and the Cape. He supported the *South African War, hoping for subsequent reconciliation between English-speakers and Afrikaners once British sovereignty had been established in all South Africa. The trustees of his will, in which he bequeathed his vast fortune to further the imperialist cause, established the prestigious Rhodes Scholarships for scholars with outstanding intellectual and leadership qualities to study at Oxford for two years.

Rhodesia, see ZAMBIA; ZIMBABWE

Ribbentrop, Joachim von (b. 30 Apr. 1893, d. 16 Oct. 1946). Nazi Foreign Secretary 1938–45

He joined the *Nazi Party in 1932 and became a mediator between *Hitler and von *Papen later that year. After Hitler came to power he was increasingly involved in diplomatic missions, and achieved his first success with the conclusion of the German-British Naval Treaty of 1935. He was ambassador to the UK 1936–8. However, as Foreign Secretary his policies were increasingly directed against Britain, most notably through the *Hitler–Stalin Pact, which was a major diplomatic coup. He was found guilty at the *Nuremberg trials and executed.

Richthofen, Manfred Freiherr von (b. 2 May 1892, d. 21 Apr. 1918). German pilot

Also known as the 'Red Baron', he was Germany's most famous and successful fighter pilot during World War I. He was killed in action in north-western France, and H. *Göring took over the command of his squadron.

Rikken Seiyûkai, see SEIYÛKAI

Rio de Janeiro Treaty, see INTER-AMERICAN TREATY OF RECIPROCAL ASSISTANCE

Riom Trial (Feb.-Apr. 1942)

Trials held in the French town of Riom, in which prominent representatives of the Third

Republic, such as *Blum and *Daladier, were accused by the *Vichy government of causing the French defeat in 1940. The defendants turned the tables on their accusers, however, so that the trial had to be postponed indefinitely. Nevertheless, the accused remained in prison and were later deported to Germany.

Road Map for Peace (2002)

A peace plan proposed by George W. *Bush and supported by the Middle East peace quartet, consisting of the USA, Russia, the EU and the UN. The plan called for the phased introduction of a peaceful settlement between Israel and Palestine, beginning with an end to Palestinian attacks on Israel and the holding of Palestinian elections. The plan called for a cessation of Israeli settlement construction in the occupied lands, and a wide-ranging international settlement on borders, the question of refugees, and water resources. The plan was accepted by Israel and the Palestinian authorities. However, Israel continued to construct settlements undisturbed, while the Palestinian authorities were too weak and insufficiently willing to assert authority over Palestinian groups launching attacks on Israel. The plan was thus never seriously put into action, though it continued to be significant as a reference point for peace activists.

Roberts, John G. Jr (b. 27 Jan. 1955). US Supreme Court Chief Justice 2006–

Born in Buffalo, he graduated from Harvard Law School in 1979 and became a law clerk for *Rehnquist at the *Supreme Court. Roberts then joined the *Reagan administration as Special Assistant to the Attorney General, and in 1982 he became a member of the White House Counsel's Office. From 1986 he practised law in Washington DC, until in 2003 George W. *Bush appointed him to the US Court of Appeals for the District of Columbia Circuit. Roberts began his appointment as Chief Justice quietly, as the court avoided major devisive issues, for instance on abortion or *civil rights.

Robinson, Mary (b. 21 May 1944). President of the Irish Republic 1990–7

Born in Ballina, Co. Mayo, and educated at Trinity College Dublin (BA 1967, MA 1970, LLB 1967), King's Inns Dublin and Harvard University (LLM 1968), Robinson initially pursued a legal career, becoming a barrister in 1967, and Reid professor of constitutional and criminal law at Trinity College Dublin (1969–75), and lecturer in European community law (1975–90). She was a Senator

from 1969 to 1989. During the 1970s and 1980s, her legal career merged with interests in civil and social rights and greater European cooperation. In 1990 she was nominated by the *Labour Party for the presidency, for which she was elected against the establishment candidates nominated by *Fianna Fáil and *Fine Gael. This was widely interpreted as signalling a shift in Irish society against social, cultural, and economic conservatism, a shift which as President she tried to encourage further. In addition to encouraging social and civil reform, she attempted to raise the international profile of Ireland by increasing participation in many international forums. She declined to stand for re-election, and became *UN High Commissioner for *Human Rights.

Rockefeller family

One of the wealthiest and most influential families in twentieth-century America. John Davison Rockefeller (b. 1839, d. 1937) was born in New York, but moved to Cleveland, Ohio, where he built up an oil business which by 1882 controlled 95 per cent of the nation's oil-refining capacity, under a board of trustees with Rockefeller as president. This was the first inter-state trust, which stimulated antitrust legislation. A pious *Baptist, he became interested in educational philanthropy. America's first billionaire, he gave away altogether some $600 million in his lifetime.

His son John Davison Jr (b. 1874, d. 1960) continued his father's philanthropic interests, building up the Rockefeller Foundation and funding the Rockefeller Center in Manhattan. He donated the sites for the *UN Building and the Lincoln Center in New York City, together with the restoration of Colonial Williamsburg. His son Nelson Aldrich (b. 1908, d. 1979) was attracted to public life; he was elected for four consecutive terms as Governor of New York (1959–73), and also served as Vice-President to Gerald Ford 1974–7. His moderate conservatism made him a *bête noire* of the Republican right. Nevertheless, as Vice-President he associated himself with the idea of devolving power and money for social provision and law enforcement to the states, the so-called 'New Federalism' which later energized the right. Nelson's nephew, John Davison IV, was Governor of West Virginia (1976–84), serving that state as Senator from 1985.

Roe v. Wade (USA)

The case that federalized the right of a woman to seek and obtain an *abortion. Jane Roe (a pseudonym for Norma McCorvey, representing all pregnant women in a class action) had lost her job after becoming pregnant in 1969. She wished to end her pregnancy, but abortion was illegal in Texas except in cases of extreme danger to the mother. Two female attorneys were at that time seeking to overturn restrictions on the abortion laws, and recruited McCorvey to be a plaintiff. They attacked the abortion restrictions of Texas in the federal courts on the grounds that they undermined rights under the Fourteenth and Ninth amendments to the US Constitution (the due process and specific enumeration of powers clauses, the latter of which was taken to uphold a right to privacy). By 1971 the case had reached the *Supreme Court, after a circuit court decision declared the Texas law unconstitutional without overturning it. After two new justices filled the vacant positions on the court, the case was reheard in 1972. Forty-two supplementary organizations filed briefs in support of a woman's right to abortion. The decision overturned all state laws restricting a woman's right to an abortion in the first three months of pregnancy and eased restrictions on abortions performed within six months of conception.

Impact The judgment caused a storm of controversy which has continued to divide US society ever since, with religious and conservative groups condemning both the right to abortion and the court's decision, and liberal and feminist groups upholding both. In practice, the principle of the 'right to choose' established by *Roe* has been undermined by a series of political and legal decisions. Among the obstacles thus established are the Hyde Amendment banning federal *Medicaid funds from funding abortions for women on low incomes (in 2002, only nineteen states assisted low-income women with the costs for abortions). In 1992 the *Casey* v. *Planned Parenthood* ruling by the Supreme Court qualified the 'right to choose' by ruling that individual state restrictions on abortion were legal as long as they did not impose an 'undue' burden on women. The issue of abortion became one of the most acrimonious political and cultural issues of the 1980s and 1990s. It caused a fundamental and seemingly irreconcilable split in the *Republican Party while contributing to the hostility between conservatives and liberals, especially from the 1980s.

Roh, Moo-hyun (b. 1946). President of South Korea, 2003–
Born in Gimhae, he studied law and became a district court judge. He opened his own law firm, and became a human rights lawyer. He

entered parliament for *Kim Dae Jung's Millennium Democratic Party (MDP), and succeeded Kim as President. In his first months of office, Roh appeared as indecisive and inept. Following corruption charges against the main parties, the MDP split, with some of Roh's supporters founding a new party, Uri. With only a small parliamentary base, the President was powerless against a parliamentary motion to unseat him. This did not receive the required assent of the Constitutional Court, however. Following popular outrage against parliament's action, the Uri party was returned with an overall parliamentary majority in 2004.

Roh Tae Woo (b. 4 Dec. 1932). President of the Republic of Korea (South Korea) 1988–93
Born in Talsong, North Kyongsang province, he enlisted in the South Korean army, graduating from its military academy in 1955. He rose steadily within army ranks to become a general. In 1979, he assisted General Chun Doo Hwan in the December coup, becoming commander of the powerful secret service ('Defence Security Command') in 1980. He joined the newly founded Democratic Justice Party in 1981, retiring from the army in order to pursue a political career. He held various ministerial posts, and from 1983 supervised the organization of the 1988 Olympic Games. In 1987, he won the country's first direct presidential elections for sixteen years, succeeding Chun in the first peaceful transition of power since World War II. He surprised his people by introducing political reform, inaugurating the Sixth Republic in 1988. He also relaxed the country's foreign policy, opening dialogues with the Soviet Union, and even North *Korea. Nevertheless, student demonstrations continued unabated, in protest against *human rights violations and political and economic corruption, forcing him to retire. In 1996, he was sentenced to imprisonment for 22 years and 6 months on charges of corruption and for his pivotal role in the brutal suppression of the *Kwangju uprising of 1980, in which around eight thousand protesters were killed. He was pardoned by President-elect *Kim Dae Jung in late 1997.

Röhm Putsch, see SA

Rokossovsky, Konstantin Konstantinovich (b. 21 Dec. 1886, d. 3 Aug. 1968). Marshal of the Soviet Union (1944) and Poland (1949)
Born in Velikje Luki (near Warsaw), he was conscripted into the Russian imperial army in 1914. He joined the *Red Army in 1918, and the *Bolsheviks in 1919. As a professional

soldier he had reached the rank of lieutenant-general by 1938. During the *Great Purge, he was himself imprisoned for three years and was lucky to escape execution. He was reinstated in response to the German attack on the USSR in June 1941. He took a leading part in the defence of Moscow, as well as the decisive siege of *Stalingrad. Rokossovsky took part in the Battle of *Kursk and in August 1944 he won a major battle at Bobruisk in the Ukraine, utterly defeating the German Ninth Army. He then directed operations against East *Prussia and in Poland, where he ignored appeals for help from the *Warsaw Rising. After the war, he remained in Poland effectively as *Stalin's sentinel, acting as Minister of Defence (1945–56) and Deputy Prime Minister (1952–6) under President *Bierut. The presence of the person who had allowed the defeat of the Warsaw Rising caused tremendous popular resentment, which led to his removal to the Soviet Union in 1956. There, he became Deputy Minister of Defence 1956–62.

Romania

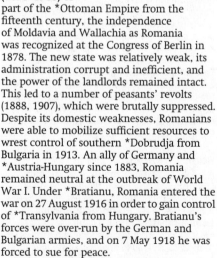

An eastern European state which benefited, during the twentieth century, from substantial oil reserves.

Independence
(1878–1918) A part of the *Ottoman Empire from the fifteenth century, the independence of Moldavia and Wallachia as Romania was recognized at the Congress of Berlin in 1878. The new state was relatively weak, its administration corrupt and inefficient, and the power of the landlords remained intact. This led to a number of peasants' revolts (1888, 1907), which were brutally suppressed. Despite its domestic weaknesses, Romanians were able to mobilize sufficient resources to wrest control of southern *Dobrudja from Bulgaria in 1913. An ally of Germany and *Austria-Hungary since 1883, Romania remained neutral at the outbreak of World War I. Under *Bratianu, Romania entered the war on 27 August 1916 in order to gain control of *Transylvania from Hungary. Bratianu's forces were over-run by the German and Bulgarian armies, and on 7 May 1918 he was forced to sue for peace.

Territorial transformations
(1918–44) Romania re-entered the war on 9 November 1918, so that it gained the status of a victorious ally. In the *Paris Peace Conference it received unusually generous treatment in an effort to strengthen the state against *Bolshevist Russia, mainly at the expense of the defeated Hungary. It gained control over Transylvania, Banat, northern *Bukovina, and Bessarabia, more than doubling the size of its territory. Romania's new minorities included substantial communities of Ukrainians, Bulgarians, gypsies, Germans, Hungarians, Tartars, Turks, and Jews. The permanent and peaceful integration of these groups was beyond the means of a weak and bankrupt state, even if this had been the intention of the ruling elites.

Romanian elites had little sympathy for these minorities, most of whom had been enemies in World War I. Strikingly, the Romanians of the new territories also more often than not remained distinct, feeling alienated from a state with different political and administrative customs. These tensions were exacerbated by the 1923 constitution, which created a central state where a decentralized one would have been much more appropriate. The state's credibility further declined as a result of poor economic management. In a series of contradictory policies, foreign investment was severely restricted, but industrialization encouraged. Agriculture was promoted, but tariffs on food exports levied.

By 1928 the liberals, who had been in government for eight years, were swept from power by a right-wing nationalist government under Iliu *Maniu (b. 1873, d. 1953). He wasted his overwhelming popularity, and thus a genuine opportunity to carry out reforms, through his own hesitations, and inter-party squabbles. The inability of the political establishment to find a coherent response to the economic slump of the Great *Depression furthered the growth of the right wing. Ultimately, the *Iron Guard was contained, but only through the application of increasingly dictatorial methods, first by King *Carol II and then also by *Antonescu.

The country's real weakness was displayed in 1940. Despite its close contacts with Nazi Germany, many of its territories were carved up between Germany and the Soviet Union under the terms of the *Hitler–Stalin Pact and the second *Vienna Award, including Bessarabia, northern Transylvania, and southern *Dobrudja. Neverthless, during World War II Romania gave Germany vital support as its major supplier of oil, and as a co-belligerent from 22 June 1941, following *Hitler's attack on the Soviet Union. It lost many of its troops in the Battle of *Stalingrad. In the face of imminent defeat, on 23 August 1944 Antonescu was deposed, and war was declared on Germany the following day, in an effort to mollify the advancing *Red Army.

Communism (1944–89) The Soviets installed a Communist regime under *Gheorghiu-Dej, which eliminated all opposition, forced King Michael I to abdicate on 30 December 1947, and proclaimed a Communist People's Republic. Private ownership was abolished, so that by 1960, 98 per cent of all firms and 80 per cent of farms had been nationalized. Gheorghiu-Dej established a ruthless regime with the help of the Soviet *NKVD-*KGB and, increasingly, his own security forces. Opposition leaders were harassed, imprisoned, or killed, and press censorship was established. Since the country had a long border with the Soviet Union, Gheorghiu-Dej ensured *Stalin's satisfaction with the regime, especially since Romania was still full of *Red Army troops.

The Soviet armed forces were withdrawn in 1958, however, in response to Romanian support in the suppression of the *Hungarian Revolution. This enabled the Communist leadership, headed by *Ceausescu after 1965, to gain a certain degree of independence from the Soviet Union. It was thus the first East European country outside the USSR to take up diplomatic relations with West Germany, and was the only *Warsaw Pact country not to break off relations with Israel after the *Six Day War in 1967. Romania's popularity in the West was further increased by the fact that it financed more and more of its misguided investment in heavy industry with help from the West, and became Eastern Europe's first member of the *IMF.

The dire condition of its economy was for a long time overshadowed by its wealth in oil. However, its reserves had largely dried up by the 1980s, which made it difficult to keep up repayments on loans. Romania was also hit by the *oil price shock of 1979, which affected *Comecon countries with some time-lag and caused a near-collapse of industry, while food rationing was introduced in 1982. To cope with the growing popular resentment that was inevitable in this state of affairs, harsh measures were introduced by the security forces, which were exacerbated by Ceausescu's increasing megalomania. For instance, in 1981, all private typewriters were ordered to be confiscated to prevent the writing of letters of complaint to foreign embassies.

Democratic transition (1989–2004) Even these measures could not prevent the collapse of the regime in December *1989, following the collapse of Communism in East Germany,

Poland, and Hungary. Ceausescu was arrested and executed on Christmas Day 1989. Important parts of the old political establishment retained control of the state, so that Romania's anti-Communist revolution was relatively ineffective compared to Czechoslovakia (*Velvet Revolution), East Germany, or Poland.

From 1990, *Iliescu stabilized the 'new' regime by minimizing the break with the Ceausescu regime. The bureaucracy and administration were largely unchanged, and discrimination against national minorities continued. The dreaded secret police continued in operation as the state security forces. In 1990 the government called the radical miners into Bucharest three times to brutally suppress student demonstrations. After 1992 some economic indicators improved, such as inflation, which came down from 2,600 per cent to less than 50 per cent in 2001. In 1996 Iliescu lost power to the centre-right led by Emil Constantinescu, but he regained it in 2000. Given Iliescu's continued closeness to the old elites, Romania moved away from its goal of qualifying for EU membership.

Contemporary politics (since 2004) In 2004, Traian Basescu was elected President, with the oppositional Democratic Alliance forming a majority coalition in parliament. This broke the power of the traditional elites, with the new government and President eager to fight corruption. A powerful anti-corruption directorate was set up, which brought up evidence of corruption against prominent politicians and businesspersons. Owing to Romania's rapidly improving record on fighting corruption, and improvements in creating new, transparent administrative structures, Romania was able to join the EU in 2007. The elites took their revenge for Basescu's reformism by successfully initiating impeachment procedures against the President. Since Basescu remained popular, however, he won a resounding victory in a referendum, which allowed him to continue his fight with the country's entrenched elites.

Rome, Treaty of (25 May 1957)
A treaty signed by Belgium, France, Italy, Luxembourg, the Netherlands, and West Germany, following the success of the *ECSC. It established the **European Economic Community (EEC)** from 1 January 1958, to create a common agricultural and industrial market as well as to achieve an increasing harmonization of the members' economies. The EEC remained separate from the ECSC. In addition to these two bodies, **EURATOM** was created, a body set up simultaneously with the

EEC by the six member states for common research into the peaceful use of nuclear power. The three bodies have been supported by a common *European Parliament, which initially had an advisory role. In addition, the treaty set up a *European Commission to control and initiate common legislation, and a *European Court of Justice to watch over breaches of Community law. Since 1966, a *Common Agricultural Policy (CAP) has been at the heart of the EEC, while a customs union has been established and barriers to trade have been progressively removed. Originally, the ECSC, EEC, and EURATOM were administered by separate institutions, but on 1 July 1967 these were merged to create a common administrative bureaucracy. The three organizations were subsequently summarized as the **European Community (EC)**.

Rommel, Erwin (b. 15 Nov. 1891, d. 14 Oct. 1944). German field marshal

Born at Heidenheim, he was educated at Tübingen and joined the army in 1910. In World War I, he was awarded the highest German military decoration for bravery, and quickly rose through the ranks. He remained an officer in the army after the war, and after 1933 he attracted the attention of Nazi Party leaders for his efficiency. By 1940 he held the rank of general and commanded a Panzer (tank) division in a brilliant assault through the Ardennes to the Channel. In 1941 he was sent to command the Afrika Korps, an elite tank formation which bore the brunt of the fighting in Libya, where he earned the respect of his opponent *Montgomery and the nickname 'Desert Fox'. In 1943–4, he commanded Army Group B in Italy. He was then entrusted with defence of the Channel coast in northern France against possible invasion, but proved unable to prevent the *D-Day landings. Heavily wounded in the *Normandy campaign on 17 July 1944, he was recalled to Germany. He supported the unsuccessful *July Plot against *Hitler, and hence was given the alternative of a public trial (ending with an inevitable conviction and the persecution of his family) or suicide (in which case his family would be spared). He chose the latter. His son became a notable Mayor of Stuttgart.

Rongelap Island, see MICRONESIA

Roosevelt, (Anna) Eleanor (b. 11 Oct. 1884, d. 7 Nov. 1962). UN diplomat

Born in New York City to a wealthy family, and niece of President Theodore *Roosevelt, she was educated in England, and in 1905 married her remote cousin Franklin D.

*Roosevelt. When the latter developed poliomyelitis in 1921, she helped him to overcome the disease and took on many public duties. A strong supporter of *New Deal policies, she helped to democratize the White House by her press conferences and her journalism. She built up her own political connections, and became a leading advocate of civil and women's rights. Actively and publicly involved in numerous social projects, from equal rights for minority groups to child welfare and slum clearance, her strong activism and influence during her husband's presidency aroused some criticism. She was also deeply admired by millions of Americans. A delegate to the *UN, she was appointed chairperson of the UN Commission on *Human Rights (1946–51). As such, she helped draft the Universal Declaration of Human Rights of 1948, and travelled the world tirelessly as a UN representative. She wrote a syndicated and influential column for over twenty years. She also helped found the liberal lobby group Americans for Democratic Action, which became very influential in the Democratic Party.

Roosevelt, Franklin Delano (b. 30 Jan. 1882, d. 12 Apr. 1945). 32nd US President 1933–45

Early career Born at Hyde Park, New York, to a wealthy family, he went to Harvard and Columbia Law School. He married Theodore *Roosevelt's niece, and a distant cousin of his, Eleanor *Roosevelt, in 1905. Elected for the New York Senate in 1910, he was appointed Assistant Secretary for the Navy by President *Wilson in 1913. Roosevelt was unsuccessful as the running mate of James M. Cox in the 1920 presidential elections. In 1921 he was stricken with poliomyelitis, and henceforth was mostly confined to a wheelchair. In the days before television, this did not seriously harm his political career, and he was elected Governor of New York as a reforming *Democrat in 1928.

Presidency He was elected President in 1932 on a promise to end the Great *Depression with wide-ranging government reform, and implemented this in his *New Deal programme, which gave work to millions of people and hope to the nation. While its economic effects remain controversial, the New Deal created the impression that his policies had overcome the economic crisis, and became the basis of his longevity in office. Roosevelt was quick to recognize the effectiveness of the new medium, radio. Through his regular 'fireside chats' he was the first President to become familiar to a majority of US citizens. In the 1936 presidential election he won a crushing victory, gaining every state except Maine and Vermont.

In his second term (1937–41), inherent weaknesses of the New Deal became more obvious, in particular many of his policies' shortsightedness and their expensive reliance on subsidies. Moreover, the opposition of the *Supreme Court to some of his policies caused Roosevelt's ire. Arguing that the law should not interfere with policies that had received an overwhelming popular mandate, he embarked upon an ill-advised, unsuccessful, and unpopular attempt to 'pack' the court with liberal justices. Roosevelt moved the Democratic Party towards an association with *liberalism, and a related affinity with the poor, the workers, and minorities that was to last for the rest of the century.

World War II (1939–45) In the last years of his second term, Roosevelt skilfully steered the USA away from policies favoured by *isolationists, who had succeeded in passing a series of *Neutrality Acts through *Congress. After the fall of France in 1940 he made the USA a powerful supporter of Britain's war effort, most importantly through the *Lend-Lease Act. Thus, in August 1940, by his Destroyer Transfer Agreement with Winston *Churchill, he exchanged 50 pre-1914 US destroyers for naval bases in the West Indies, Newfoundland, and British Guyana, thus providing Britain with much-needed convoy escorts.

In 1940 he ran for an unprecedented third term against the Republican Wendell Wilkie. He met much opposition from southern Democrats, but he benefited from the upswing in the US economy resulting from military expansion. A firm supporter of China in the *Sino-Japanese War, he denied Japan war supplies, a policy which helped to precipitate the latter's action on *Pearl Harbor in December 1941. The attack triggered the subsequent declarations of war from the *Axis Powers. The USA now found itself in alliance not only with Britain but also with the Soviet Union. Roosevelt extended the lend-lease agreement to the latter, but was subsequently criticized for being too trusting of *Stalin, particularly by conceding too much Soviet influence over postwar Europe. By contrast, his relationship with *Churchill was excellent, though he had to work hard to convince the British Prime Minister to embark on a cross-Channel attack, which eventually came to pass at *D-Day.

On the strength of his wartime leadership, he won a fourth term in office in 1944. However, his health soon deteriorated, so that he died two months after participating in his last major wartime conference at *Yalta. He was succeeded by *Truman. Perhaps the greatest US President of the twentieth century, he fundamentally changed the nature of US politics. In particular, he extended the role of the federal government and restored popular confidence in that government's leadership at times of existential domestic and international crisis. In the process, the USA became a major actor in global politics which continued to shape world history for the rest of the century and beyond.

Roosevelt, Theodore (b. 27 Oct. 1858, d. 6 Jan. 1919). 26th US President 1901–9

Early career Born in New York City, he graduated with a BA from Harvard in 1880. He entered the New York state legislature in 1881, and served as US Assistant Navy Secretary (1897–8). In 1898, he distinguished himself in the Spanish–American War as a commander of a volunteer force of 'rough riders'. He was Governor of New York State, 1899–1901. Vice-President under McKinley in 1901, he became the youngest US President upon the latter's assassination.

Presidency A *Republican, Roosevelt was also a key progressive reformer, whose blend of *nationalism and reformism led him to belligerent foreign policy rhetoric and active domestic regulation. He believed that the Presidency was a 'bully pulpit', by which he meant a platform from which to exhort the nation to great deeds. His administration's policies—nicknamed the 'square deal'—included selective attacks on trusts and monopolies in business. It supported conservation legislation, and created the federal system of food and drugs regulation. Abroad, he announced the *Roosevelt Corollary, promising that the USA would act as an international police power 'walking softly but carrying a big stick'. He also sent the expanded US navy on a world cruise to demonstrate US power, gained a lease on the *Panama Canal Zone, and in 1906 won the *Nobel Peace Prize for mediation in the *Russo-Japanese War of 1904–5.

After the Presidency In 1912 he ran against his successor, William Howard *Taft, as a *Progressive on a platform of *New Nationalism. Despite being shot during the campaign, which necessitated a short hospitalization, Roosevelt's 'Bull Moose' ticket gained what was to be the biggest third-party vote of the twentieth century in percentage terms (27.8 per cent). He thus split the opposition to the *Democrats so that

Woodrow *Wilson, their candidate, was elected President. Roosevelt lost the Republican nomination in 1916, but continued to criticize Wilson for what he perceived was his hesitancy to become engaged in World War I.

Roosevelt Corollary (USA, 1904)

Announced by Theodore *Roosevelt in his December 1904 message to *Congress, the policy asserted the 'international police power' of the United States. It would intervene in the affairs of any nation in the Western hemisphere whenever it deemed that 'chronic wrong-doing or impotence' made such intervention necessary. The policy represented a sweeping extension of the Monroe Doctrine (1823) by which the USA sought to prevent the interference of non-American powers within the western hemisphere on its own authority. It provided the basis for extensive US intervention in the internal affairs of most Latin American countries, and for turning especially the countries of Central America into informal US colonies for most of the century.

Rosenberg, Alfred (b. 12 Jan. 1893, d. 16 Oct. 1946). Chief Nazi ideologist

A refugee of German descent from Estonia, he joined the *Nazi Party in 1919 and became editor of the party newspaper, the *Völkischer Beobachter* in 1923. In his attempt to systematize a Nazi ideology, he published *Der Mythos des 20. Jahrhunderts* (The Myth of the Twentieth Century, 1930). In it he proposed, among other things, the creation of a new religion based on the superiority of the German race. He led the fight against the Churches, and contributed towards the cultural policies of the Nazis. In 1934 he was officially put in charge of supervising the ideological development of the Nazi Party, and from 1941 to 1945 he was Minister for the Occupied Eastern Territories, though his actual influence on developments in these areas was relatively modest. At the *Nuremberg Trials he was found guilty and executed.

Rosenberg, Julius (b. 12 May 1918, d. 19 June 1953) and Ethel (b. 28 Sept. 1915, d. 19 June 1953). Spies against the US

In September 1949, the USA became aware that the Soviet Union had developed nuclear technology years ahead of expectations and was thus capable of dropping atomic bombs. The following year Klaus Fuchs, a physicist involved in the development of the American atomic and hydrogen bombs, was arrested in England and confessed to having been part of a spy-ring. As a result, Henry Gold was arrested in the USA, and he identified Julius and Ethel Rosenberg, who worked on atomic weaponry and had admitted Communist sympathies, as spies. They were arrested, found guilty of conspiracy and treason in a sensational trial at the height of *McCarthy's anti-Communist campaigns, and sentenced to death. Many believed that their Jewish background helped to single them out from a number of spies uncovered at the time. They appealed to every court, including the *Supreme Court, and their executions were stayed several times; but finally, amid great controversy, they were electrocuted in June 1953. The memoirs of Soviet leader Nikita *Khrushchev, written after he had been deposed, appear to support the contention that the Rosenbergs had worked for the USSR between 1944 and 1945.

NUCLEAR BOMB; MANHATTAN PROJECT

Round Table Conferences

A series of conferences held in London to discuss a revision of India's constitution. It was based upon the 1929 Irwin Declaration, in which the Viceroy, Irwin (later known as *Halifax), declared that India's constitutional progress pointed to Dominion status. This reiterated a statement by the then Secretary of State for India, Montagu, made in 1917. However, awarding India Dominion status was controversial after the 1926 *Imperial Conference had defined it as a status of total domestic and external autonomy. Irwin hoped to respond to the growth of Indian *nationalism, but he was not able to prevent the second *satyagraha. Nevertheless, the first conference met in 1930, and consisted of Indian nationalist leaders, princes, and British and Indian government officials. However, it was relatively fruitless owing to the absence of *Gandhi, who had been imprisoned after the *Salt March.

Gandhi was able to attend the second conference, but since by now *Congress was committed to the goal of complete independence, the trip to London was useful to Gandhi more as a way to gain publicity and present his case directly to the English people. By the time of the third conference in 1932, the conciliatory Irwin had been replaced as Viceroy by the politically less able Willingdon. The disobedience campaign had been resumed, and Gandhi was back in prison. The conference failed in the attainment of Dominion status, or the creation of a lasting, conciliatory settlement. Nevertheless, it did provide the basis for the 1935 *Government of India Act. Moreover, its significance lay in its very existence, the novelty of the British government discussing its colonial affairs with representatives of those concerned. This became a blueprint for other *decolonization negotiations after World War II.

Rowell–Sirois Commission (Canada)

A Royal Commission set up by the Canadian government to investigate the evolution of the relationship between national government and the provinces since the creation of Canada in 1867. Named after its successive chairmen, it convened in 1937–40 and recommended a shift of taxation from provincial to national government, in order to reduce imbalances between the provinces: social welfare should become a national matter, while richer provinces should provide support for their poorer neighbours. The commission's report proved the framework for subsequent federal–provincial relations as many recommendations were gradually realized, culminating in the patriation of the *Canadian Constitution in 1982.

Rowlatt Act (1919)

Legislation introduced by the British colonial government in India. It was based upon the recommendation of a committee chaired by Mr Justice Rowlatt, which introduced emergency powers for the authorities similar to those used during World War I. The Act was considered a necessary prelude to ensure public calm for the introduction of the 1919 *Government of India Act. However, it aroused strong opposition throughout India, and directly led to the popular protests that triggered the *Amritsar Massacre. Thus, it virtually destroyed any positive impact the subsequent introduction of some self-government through *dyarchy might have had, and instead gave the nationalist movement a significant boost. It united *Congress behind M. K. *Gandhi's leadership, as well as his *satyagraha campaigns of civil disobedience.

Rowntree, (Benjamin) Seebohm

(b. 7 July 1871, d. 7 Oct. 1954). British industrialist and philanthropist

The son of the industrialist and philanthropist Joseph Rowntree, Seebohm was born in York, and educated there at Bootham School, and at Owens College, Manchester. He entered his family's chocolate firm in 1889, and as a director of Rowntree's, he introduced a number of innovations such as a works doctor, a five-day week, employee pension and profit-sharing schemes, and a works council. As director of the welfare department of the Ministry of Munitions in 1915–18, he encouraged the munitions factories to adopt many of these practices. He was also widely known for his investigation of the causes and consequences of poverty. His pioneering study of York, *Poverty: A Study of Town Life* (1901), illustrated the limits of customary voluntary solutions to poverty, and highlighted the necessity for government to take a greater role. In 1936, he carried out a further survey in York, which showed that poverty levels had decreased somewhat, but that it was still widespread, with 17.5 per cent of the population falling below a newly defined poverty threshold. The Rowntree reports triggered a host of similar studies in Britain and abroad, and became the basis of subsequent social legislation. He established the Rowntree Trust, which continued his surveys and research into poverty and unemployment.

SEE WEB LINKS

- The official website of the Joseph Rowntree Foundation.

Royal, Ségolène (b. 22 Sept. 1953). French presidential candidate, 2007

Born in Dakar (Senegal), she studied at the prestigious Sciences Po University as well as the École Normale d'Administration. She attracted the attention of *Mitterrand and worked in the presidential office from 1982. In 1988, she was elected into the National Assembly for the *Socialist Party, and in 1992 she was appointed Minister for the Environment. She held various offices in the government of *Jospin, but she never advanced to a major portfolio. Nevertheless, she steadily advanced in the opinion polls and in 2006 beat the pretenders of the party establishment to become the nation's first female candidate for the presidency.

Rudd, Kevin (b. 21 Sept 1957). Leader of the Australian Labor Party, 2006–

Born in Queensland, Rudd became a diplomat before becoming a consultant. The fluent Chinese speaker and committed Christian entered parliament as a member of the Australian *Labor Party (ALP) in 1998. Eight years later, Rudd put up a surprise challenge to the leadership of the ALP, which he won. Rudd advocated the signing of the *Kyoto Protocol, as well as the withdrawal of Australian troops from Iraq. He tried hard to reclaim the middle ground by charging the *Howard government with increasing the cost of education.

Rugova, Ibraim (b. 2 Dec. 1944, d. 22 Jan 2006). Albanian leader

Born in Cerce, he studied Albanian literature at the University of Priština, where he continued his studies up to postdoctoral level. In 1981 he was given a Chair at the Albanian Institute of the University of Priština, and in 1988 Rugova became the President of the Kosovan writers' association. In 1989 he co-founded the Kosovan Democratic League (KDL), which won the elections of 1992, even though these had not been recognized by the Serb authorities. Rugova now became President of a self-proclaimed Republic of *Kosovo, and propagated passive resistance against the oppression of the Serb police forces and army units. He was briefly imprisoned during the Kosovan War in 1999. He was greatly supported by the Allied powers, however, because of his relative moderation and his democratic credentials, in contrast to the leaders of the various Albanian rebel brigands. After the war, he became the head of a transitional governing council in a liberated Kosovo. In the municipal elections of 2000, the KDL was confirmed as the strongest political force in the province. The moderate nationalist, Rugova seemed poised to take his country into independence. However, he died from lung cancer, one year after being diagnosed with the disease.

Ruhr district

Together with parts of the neighbouring Rhineland, it has formed the industrial core of Germany owing to its rich coal deposits and its proximity to the Rhine which could be reached via the River Ruhr. As the home to the *Krupp works, it was also the home of Germany's military production, so that after World War I it was demilitarized, while most of the Rhineland was occupied by French troops. In 1923, when Germany was slightly behind in its *reparation payments, French troops occupied the Ruhr District in order to compensate France by using the mineral resources. In protest, the population engaged in a campaign of non-cooperation (11 January–26 September), but Germany's support for the passive resistance brought the country to financial ruin and thus had to be called off by *Stresemann. After World War II, an international Ruhr Commission (1949–53) was set up to oversee German production of coal and steel, but it became redundant with the foundation of the *ECSC (*European integration).

Rumsfeld, Donald H. (b. 9 Jul. 1932). US Secretary of Defense, 1975–7, 2001–6

Born in Chicago, Rumsfeld attended Princeton and joined the US navy in 1954. In 1957, he worked for *Congress and joined an investment bank, and in 1962 he was elected to the House of Representatives, where he met Gerald *Ford. In 1969, he joined Nixon's Cabinet, and in 1973 he became US ambassador to NATO in Brussels. Rumsfeld became Ford's Chief of Staff (1974–5) before becoming the youngest US Secretary of Defense. In 1977, Rumsfeld became a private businessman, though he continued to be an influential 'neo'-conservative, arguing that modern wars were won through superior technologies. Following the *Gulf War, Rumsfeld argued that Saddam *Hussein continued to be a threat to world peace, and that it was in the US national interest to remove him by force.

Appointed by George W. *Bush on *Cheney's advice, Rumsfeld's preparations for the *Iraq War were accelerated after *September 11, though a link between *al-Qaeda and Saddam Hussein was never found. Rumsfeld strongly believed that the US military needed strong political leadership. This underlay his fateful decision not to comply with the military's request after the war to put sufficient numbers of troops on the ground to secure the peace. Rumsfeld oversaw spiralling levels of violence in Iraq under US occupation, with US soldiers continuing to be exposed to hostile attacks. Following the 2006 Congressional elections, which generated a Republican defeat in both Houses largely owing to the unpopularity of the Iraq occupation, Rumsfeld resigned. With a sharp intellect, Rumsfeld became a highly divisive political figure, in part through his policies, and in part through his gift for straight-talking.

Rundstedt, Gerd von (b. 12 Dec. 1875, d. 24 Feb. 1953). German field marshal 1940–5

He was recalled from retirement in 1939 to lead the German attack on Poland and France. In 1941 he was dismissed after his failure to meet *Hitler's targets for the invasion of the Soviet Union, but he was reinstalled to command the German army in France. After *D-Day, he was dismissed again in July 1944, to be reinstated two months later to lead the *Ardennes offensive. He was finally discharged in March 1945.

Rusk, David Dean (b. 9 Feb. 1909, d. 20 Dec. 1994). US Secretary of State 1961–9

Born in Cherokee County, Georgia, he won a *Rhodes Scholarship to Oxford in 1931, and then taught political science at Mills College, California, until the outbreak of war. Whilst in Oxford, he developed a dislike of pacifists and isolationists. He enlisted in the army and served under General *Stilwell in China (1944–5). In 1946 he joined the US diplomatic service, and in 1950 became an Assistant Secretary of State concerned with the Far East, strongly backing the case for war in Korea. In 1961 President *Kennedy appointed him Secretary of State, an office he held for eight years, during all of which he consistently and dogmatically advocated a policy of US involvement in the *Vietnam War and opposition to Communist China. After leaving office he became a professor of international law.

Russell, Bertrand Arthur William, 3rd Earl (b. 18 May 1872, d. 2 Feb. 1970).
British mathematician, philosopher, and peace campaigner

Born at Trelleck (Wales), he was educated at home by private tutors, and at Cambridge, where he became a lecturer in 1895. In the next two decades, among a host of publications on politics, philosophy, and mathematics, perhaps his most important was the *Principia Mathematica* (3 vols., 1910–13). He was also active in radical politics, and in 1907 stood unsuccessfully for parliament as a *Liberal Party candidate supporting women's suffrage. When World War I broke out in 1914, he was involved in campaigns against the war, and was imprisoned for six months in 1918. This lost him his fellowship at Cambridge, but whilst in prison, he began writing *The Analysis of Mind* (1921).

Russell stood for parliament again in 1922–3, this time for the *Labour Party. Meanwhile, he continued to write on subjects including education, marriage, morality, and government. An erstwhile supporter of *appeasement, he came to support World War II, seeing *Nazism as a great danger to the values he held dear. He returned to teach at Cambridge when his fellowship was restored in 1945. He became widely known through his ability to communicate complicated ideas, which he did, for example, through his *A History of Western Philosophy* (1945), and his 1948–9 BBC *Reith lectures on 'Authority and the Individual'. The hydrogen bomb tests in 1954 (*nuclear bomb) led him to found the *CND movement and also Pugwash. He was imprisoned again in 1961 (for one week) for demonstrating outside parliament against nuclear weapons. In his final years, through the Bertrand Russell Peace Foundation, he rallied academic opposition to US policy in Vietnam.

(⊕) SEE WEB LINKS

- The home page of the Bertrand Russell Peace Foundation.

Russia

Extending significantly into Europe and Asia, Russia has been characterized by the political, economic and cultural ambivalence arising from its intermediary location between the two continents.

Before Communism (up to 1917) The world's largest country by area, it expanded from the fifteenth century to include the sparsely populated areas towards the east. From the seventeenth century, Russia included the more fertile and densely populated areas towards the south and west. By the beginning of the twentieth century, Russia comprised well over a hundred peoples, and was able to hold on to its peripheral areas (notably Poland and the Caucasian peoples) only with difficulty.

Ruled by Tsar *Nicholas II, it was engaged in rapid industrialization, though this still affected only the major towns. Nevertheless, industrialization did create a significant working population, as well as a burgeoning urban commercial middle class. It was still autocratically ruled by the Tsar, who refused to allow any political participation except in local government. The country's increasing backwardness relative to other countries was highlighted by humiliating defeat in the *Russo-Japanese War (1904–5). Economic hardship and the lack of civil liberties and political rights led to the *Russian Revolution of 1905. As the state gathered its forces, it was ultimately able to crush the rebellion. Despite some reform under *Stolypin, the government's failure to address the root causes of the 1905 Revolution, and the economic and military collapse of World War I, led to the *Russian Revolutions of 1917, which ultimately led to the establishment of a *Bolshevik government under *Lenin.

The Yeltsin era (1991–2000) Subsequently, Russia became a constituent part of the *Soviet Union, albeit the most important one by size, economic performance, and participation in the armed forces. Thus, while the end of the Soviet Union (USSR) was desired by several other Soviet republics, ultimately the USSR's peaceful breakup on 31 December 1991 could only come about because it was desired by Russia itself as the linchpin of the

USSR. Indeed, Russia succeeded to the USSR's permanent seat in the *UN Security Council, as well as in other diplomatic forums.

Under the leadership of *Yeltsin, drastic economic reforms led to further reductions in living standards, as inflation soared to 930 per cent in 1993, while GDP declined by a total of 15 per cent in 1994 alone. According to official estimates, almost one-third of the population lived below the poverty line. The economy was further burdened by a long and costly war in *Chechnya, which also turned out to be a humiliation for *Yeltsin and the Russian elite forces there. These factors naturally led to growing discontent with Yeltsin, and the rise of extremist opposition groups, particularly of right-wing *nationalist parties and reformed Communists. These attempted to depose the President in the *October Putsch of 1993, whereupon Yeltsin created vast presidential powers for himself in the 1993 constitution.

The new constitution sought to address the country's diversity through the creation of a complex web of altogether 89 administrative districts with differing degrees of autonomy: 21 limited republics with extensive legislative autonomy, ten autonomous districts (*Okrug*), one autonomous territory, six regions (*Krai*), 49 areas (*Oblasti*), and two cities with special status (Moscow and St Petersburg). At an economic level, Yeltsin's reluctance to confront entrenched economic elites led to the decline of the state's economic authority. The state became increasingly unable to collect its personal and corporate tax revenue, which in turn allowed too many inefficient businesses to survive.

The Putin era (2000–) The insolvency of the state produced a deep economic crisis in 1998, leading to a sharp reduction in national income in general, and state salaries and pensions in particular. After appointing and then firing a succession of Prime Ministers, Yeltsin handed over power to Vladimir *Putin, who became interim President in 2000 until he was confirmed in that office in general elections.

Under Putin, the economy recovered markedly, with growth rates of between 5 and 7 per cent per annum. Putin also increased financial discipline, so that the state began to be able to collect tax revenues. Russian growth rested on its abundance of mineral resources, whereas most sectors of the economy (including its energy companies) continued to be relatively inefficient, with foreign investment barred by protectionism (especially in the energy sector).

Under Putin, Russia became an increasingly influential force in world affairs. Putin was critical of the *Iraq War and the subsequent US occupation of Iraq. Russia also differed from US policy in its assessment of the threat emanating from Iran's nuclear policies, and maintained friendly relations with Iran. In domestic affairs, Putin embarked on a brutal policy of subjection in Chechnya. He also reversed some of his predecessor's policies by reducing the powers of Russia's component territories. At the same time, democracy was severely restricted. According to Amnesty International, in 2005 the government curtailed the activities of non-governmental *human rights organizations, while human rights activists were murdered or convicted on spurious charges.

Russian Civil War (1918–21)

The war that followed the *October Revolution, which had established the world's first Communist government under *Lenin. It was fought on several fronts, with considerable foreign intervention against the Communists.

1. In Siberia, an All Russian Government was formed at Omsk. Led by *Kolchak, its *White Armies, which were aided by a Czech legion made up of released prisoners of war, gained control over sectors of the Trans-Siberian railway and advanced westwards beyond the Urals.

2. In the south-east, they were comple-mented by troops of Cossacks.

3. In the south-west, White troops under *Denikin advanced north from the Ukraine and the Caucasus, with the help of British troops from Iraq which secured the Baku oilfields.

4. From the north, a multi-national force under General *Miller, made up of British, French, US, and Canadian troops, landed at Murmansk and occupied Archangel (1918–20).

5. The attack was complemented in the west by attacks from nationalities hitherto under Russian control, i.e. Finns, Estonians, Latvians, Lithuanians, and Poles. Ultimately, *Trotsky's *Red Army was unable to overcome this fifth element, so that the Communist government accepted the inde-pendence of these states, which in the case of Finland and Poland had acquired much-extended territories.

The Red Army was helped considerably when most of the Allied troops were withdrawn in 1919 following a refusal of the White Armies to agree to a negotiated peace. Finally, the Whites were weakened by poorer discipline and disunity amongst themselves. The resentment of peasants under their control at their refusal to carry out land reforms stood in sharp contrast to the peasant support of the Red Army, effectively galvanized through *Cheka terror. By 1921, virtually the entire country was under Communist control. The country lay economically and socially in ruins. At the same time, Lenin, who had always believed in the possibility and even the desirability of a civil war, was able to use this to his advantage to tighten his grip on the country.

Russian Revolution (1905)

A series of urban revolts, which triggered off extensive peasant unrest, a number of military mutinies, and discontent among non-Russian national groups.

Defeat in the *Russo-Japanese War had just demonstrated the weakness of the Tsarist state. The underlying cause for discontent in the urban areas was the discrepancy between rapid economic and social change due to industrialization on the one hand, and the continued denial of political rights in Tsarist Russia on the other. More immediately, the revolution itself was caused by the military's brutal response to a Sunday March by St Petersburg workers, who wanted to deliver a petition for better working conditions to the Tsar. Despite the moderation of the demands, many strikers were gunned down in what became known as Bloody Sunday (22 January 1905). Demonstrations followed in St Petersburg and other towns, and found a particular response in the non-Russian parts of the Empire. The Tsar himself was never really in danger, as he was still seen by most as a father figure who was unaware of the currupt and inefficient state administration below him, and of the conditions of his subjects. Nevertheless, he was forced to concede some political demands, in particular the establishment of a *Duma.

The government brutally cracked down on the demonstrators, and re-established control by the end of 1905. Ensuing peasant revolts were suppressed with equal brutality (1906–7), though *Stolypin's subsequent land reforms also did something to alleviate their grievances. The differences in the objectives and priorities of the various groups involved were a major reason for the essential failure of the revolution. Perhaps its most significant outcome was that among large sections of the population, the Tsar lost his image of the benevolent ruler, which was an important precondition for the 1917 *Russian Revolutions.

Russian Revolutions (1917)

From the end of the nineteenth century, rapid industrialization, urbanization, professionalization, the spread of literacy, as well as *Stolypin's land reforms of 1906, created rapid economic and social change. This was not accompanied by sufficient political, legal, or administrative reforms, despite the 1905 *Russian Revolution. The tensions inherent in Russian society were multiplied by the strains of World War I. As commander of the unsuccessful and demoralized imperial army, Tsar *Nicholas II, weakened by the unpopularity of his wife and her adviser, *Rasputin, lost any credibility.

The **February Revolution** was triggered on 8 March (23 February in the old Russian Calendar), when workers in the largest armaments works of Petrograd (formerly St Petersburg) went on strike against the worsening living conditions. They were joined immediately by soldiers and workers elsewhere. Nicholas II tried to dissolve the State *Duma, but, when this failed, he abdicated. Radical workers' councils (*Soviets) formed, first in Petrograd, and then across the country. They were dominated by workers, soldiers, radical intellectuals, and (outside Petrograd) peasants' representatives. Politically, they were dominated by Socialist Revolutionaries and Mensheviks, with the former generally composing the largest single group. Meanwhile, the *Duma managed to form a provisional government, at first with the blessing of the Petrograd Soviet. Against the wishes of the latter, however, the new government under Prince Lvov (b. 1861, d. 1925) continued the war, and suffered further humiliating defeats. Army desertions accelerated, and peasants began to expropriate the land, livestock, and other resources of local landlords in the summer of 1917. Against this background of chaos, *Kerensky took over the government in July 1917. However, he failed to introduce the radical measures needed to reverse the ongoing disintegration, most notably an end to the war and land reform as a visible sign of change from the Tsarist regime. The Soviets thus became radicalized further towards the direction of *Lenin, who promised peace, bread, and power to the Soviets.

The **October Revolution**, however, was not the direct result of this growing popular radicalization, nor of the growing Bolshevik support in the Petrograd and Moscow Soviets. On 7 November (25 October in the Russian Calendar) Lenin's aide, *Trotsky, carried out the world's first 'modern', successfully planned revolution, through ordering his Bolshevik forces to occupy crucial logistic and strategic points in Petrograd such as the telegraph and telephone offices, the railway stations, newspaper offices, and the offices of the government. With minimal force, the political order had been toppled, and the *Marxist-Leninist ideal of an elite-led revolution realized. The new order, however, was established within the population only gradually, through *Cheka terror and the *Russian Civil War.

Russo-Japanese War (1904–5)

A war caused by the conflicting *imperial ambitions of Japan and Russia in Manchuria. Although tensions developed over the years, the Japanese attack on the Russian Port Arthur (8–9 February 1904) came as a surprise. Largely as a result of military and naval disorganization, and the incompetence of most of its officers, the Russians suffered a series of military defeats, which forced them to sue for peace. In the Peace of Portsmouth (5 September 1905), Russia was forced to relinquish its interests in Manchuria. This first defeat of a European by an Asian power revealed to many the weakness and the corruptness of the Russian state.
MANCHUKUO

Russo-Polish War (1919–21)

Despite having only recently gained independence for the first time since the eighteenth century, Poland's nationalist president, *Pilsudski, refused to accept the *Curzon Line as its eastern border, and demanded instead the restoration of the eastern lands that were lost after the first Polish partition of 1772. Taking advantage of the chaos of the *Russian Civil War, Polish troops moved eastwards, deep into Ukrainian territory. The *Red Army's response was vigorous, however, and Pilsudski was thrown back to the outskirts of Warsaw. The Polish army regrouped and, with the help of *Weygand, Pilsudski achieved the 'miracle of the Vistula' and again advanced deep into Russian territory. In the Peace of Riga (18 March 1921), Poland gained a new eastern border around 200 km (120 miles) to the east of the Curzon Line.

Rwanda

A central African country with one of the highest population densities in the world, its history has been marked by the economic and political dominance of the Tutsi minority over the Hutu majority.

Foreign rule (up to 1964) A German colony in east Africa from 1899, it became a Belgian *League of Nations *Mandate in 1919 and a *UN *trust territory in 1946. The colonial authorities ruled through the power structures that had been in place since the sixteenth century, whereby the majority of the population from the Hutu (Bahutu) tribe (90 per cent of the population) were ruled by an aristocratic and landowning elite of the Tutsi tribe (9 per cent of the population). In 1959 a Hutu uprising, in which thousands of Tutsis were massacred and around 150,000 fled, signalled the end of the Tutsi monarchy. Elections in 1961 were won by the party of the Hutu Emancipation Movement, whose leader, G. Kayibanda, became the first President upon independence in 1962. Frequent attacks by Tutsi rebels from neighbouring Burundi resulted in the dissolution of the economic and currency union with that state in 1964.

History since independence (1964) In 1973, a bloodless coup brought General Juvénal Habyarimana (b. 1937, d. 1994) to power, a moderate Hutu who attempted to bring about a reconciliation between the Hutu and the Tutsi. This was made more difficult by the country's intense poverty and an increasing inability of the agricultural system to sustain a rapidly growing population. Growing competition for scarce resources, heightened by rival farming traditions (cattle farming by Tutsis, arable farming by Hutus), nurtured Hutu resentment against century-long Tutsi domination. This was fuelled by Tutsi memory of the 1959 massacres by Hutus.

In 1990 the Rwanda Patriotic Front (RPF) consisting of Tutsi rebels exiled in 1959 invaded the northern part of the country. A *UN-brokered peace settlement was achieved in 1993, whereupon Habyarimana also announced the democratization of the country. His death in a plane crash on 6 April 1994 sparked off a civil war which led to a genocide which in world history was perhaps only surpassed by the massacre of Jews in the *Holocaust during World War II. Within weeks, around 500,000 people were brutally murdered or killed in action, mostly by the Hutu army. The Tutsi RPF won control over the capital on 4 July 1994, and over most of the country within two weeks thereafter, when the RPF declared an end to its military activities. The fear of reprisals from the advancing RPF led to the flight of over three million (mostly Hutu) refugees into the neighbouring countries, out of a total population of 7.2 million. It is estimated that over 100,000 Hutus were killed by Tutsis, mostly belonging to the RPF.

Contemporary history (since 2000) A peace agreement was negotiated in Arusha, whereupon Tutsi and Hutu representatives created a transitional parliament with a power-sharing executive. In 2000 Paul Kagame became President, and in 2001 local elections were held for the first time after the war. Despite this gradual return to political stability, reconciliation was challenged by the fate of 120,000 prisoners accused of atrocities in the genocide. Moreover, even after the Arusha agreement Hutu militias used their bases in neighbouring Democratic Republic of Congo to attack army bases largely controlled by Tutsis. As a result, the Rwandan army became engaged in operations in neighbouring Congo, which drained the scarce public funds of one of the world's poorest countries. In 2000, the *IMF and *World Bank cancelled over 70 per cent of Rwanda's foreign debts. Kagame was re-elected in a landslide victory. In 2005, the government initiated an amnesty of around 36,000 prisoners who had been implicated in the genocide. At the same time, the major leaders inciting genocide were tried at an International Criminal Tribunal in Arusha. In 2006, Kagame carried out an administrative reform, in order to create ethnically more mixed administrative areas.

BURUNDI

Rydz-Smigly, Edward (b. 11 Mar. 1886, d. 12 Dec. 1941). Polish dictator 1935–9
Born in Brezezany, Galicia, he rose within the military as *Pilsudski's aide in the *Russo-Polish War (1919–21). He succeeded Pilsudski as general inspector of the armed forces, in which capacity he exerted considerable political influence. Most important, however, was his dismal failure to prepare the Polish army against possible attack from *Nazi Germany, due to his preoccupation with a potential confrontation with the Soviet *Red Army. His leadership during the war with Germany was at best uninspiring. He fled to Romania, but returned in 1941. He died in mysterious circumstances.

SA (*Sturmabteilung*)

Founded in Germany in 1920 to establish
order at the meetings of the *Nazi Party, the
SA was developed into a paramilitary
organization from 1921. Banned after the
*Hitler Putsch, it was re-established in 1925.
Its membership rose to over 700,000 in 1933,
so that its size, as well as the plans of its
leader, Ernst Röhm (b. 1887, d. 1934), to
incorporate the army into the SA and develop
an 'SA-state', became a threat to other
institutions, in particular the regular army.
Since Hitler needed the co-operation of the
army for his military plans, he ordered the
Röhm Putsch ('Night of the Long Knives') in
which Röhm and other SA leaders were
murdered on 30 June 1934. Hitler also used
the opportunity to get rid of other opponents,
such as his predecessor as Chancellor, K. von
Schleicher (b. 1882, d. 1934). To make his
actions more acceptable to public opinion,
Hitler persuaded President *Hindenburg to
legalize the murders retrospectively as an act
of national self-defence. The Putsch signalled
the rise of the *SS as the party élite, and it
secured the army's support for Hitler. As a
result, the political importance of the SA
declined against that of the *SS.

Sa'adist Party (Egypt)

An Egyptian political party, founded in 1937
as an offshoot of the *Wafd Party. Led by
Ahmad Mahir (b. 1885, d. 1945), its members
claimed that the Wafd had betrayed the
principles of its founder *Saghlul Sa'd. It was
part of the government in 1938–9, and led an
anti-Wafdist coalition, 1944–9. It represented
the upper and middle classes of Egyptian
society, but disappeared after the fall of the
monarchy.

Saarland

A German state on the border with France
and Luxembourg. After unsuccessful French
attempts at annexation in the *Versailles
Treaty, it was placed under the trusteeship of
the *League of Nations for fifteen years. In the
1935 plebiscite, 90 per cent voted to belong to
Germany. After World War II, it was
administered separately from West Germany,
and on 1 April 1948 it entered a customs union
with France, which also controlled its main
industry, the coal and steel works. The Saar
Statute negotiated between Germany and
France in 1954 aimed at a 'Europeanization' of

the Saarland, with its own representatives in
European institutions, but this was rejected
in a plebiscite on 23 October 1955. The
elections of 18 December 1955 produced a
majority for those parties who favoured a
return to Germany, and on 1 January 1957 the
Saarland was incorporated into Germany. This
accession of a federal state became a
constitutional precedent for the incorporation
of the five newly created East German states
into West Germany in 1990.

Sabah

Ruled as **British North Borneo** from 1881, it
was occupied by the Japanese in World War II.
Thereafter, it was united with Labuan in 1946,
and became a Crown Colony. Despite
Indonesian claims to the territory, it became a
state in the Federation of Malaysia in 1963,
when it adopted the name Sabah.

Sacco–Vanzetti Case (USA)

In 1921, Nicolà Sacco and Bartolomeo Vanzetti,
Italian immigrants and *anarchists, were
found guilty of the murder of the paymaster
and a guard of a shoe factory in Massachusetts,
and sentenced to death. Frequent and
irrelevant mention of their political beliefs and
circumstantial evidence formed the basis of the
state's case. The two were executed in August
1927. Widespread condemnation of, and
protest at, the nature of the trial and the result
(especially among writers and intellectuals)
occurred inside and outside the USA. It led
Massachusetts Governor Fuller to order a
review of the trial, which declared that the
verdict had been 'fair'. The conclusion
convinced few, and it was not until 1977 that
Governor Dukakis signed a special posthumous
'pardon' which overturned the verdict.

Sadat, Muhammad Anwar al- (b. 25
Dec. 1918, d. 6 Oct. 1981). President of Egypt
1970–81

Early career Born in Mit Abu al-Kum, he
graduated from the Cairo Military Academy in
1938, and in 1942 was imprisoned for plotting
to expel the British from Egypt with the help
of the Germans. He escaped, and after the war
joined the Free Officers movement which in
1952 deposed King *Farouk. As a close friend
and ally of president *Nasser he became
Vice-President in 1969, and was chosen to
succeeded him as President.

In power Sadat restored relations with more conservative Arab states such as Saudi Arabia. In an effort to improve relations with the USA, he expelled around 20,000 Soviet advisers. He gradually introduced market-oriented reforms and encouraged foreign investment, though this was not universally popular as it greatly increased domestic income inequalities. Owing to Israeli refusals to vacate the Sinai peninsula occupied by them since the *Six Day War (1967), he launched the *Yom Kippur War in October 1973.

Through the Yom Kippur War his position was strengthened sufficiently to enter peace negotiations with Israel. His desire for peace was derived from his pragmatism, since he realized that Egypt could not regain the Sinai by force, and was too poor to afford current high military expenditure. His extraordinary visit to *Jerusalem to address the Israeli parliament (*Knesset) in 1977 inaugurated a series of US-sponsored talks, culminating in the peace agreement at *Camp David in 1978. This attracted bitter hostility from the other Arab states and the *PLO, who withdrew diplomatic relations and financial support. He was shot by four assassins while reviewing a military parade. He had received the *Nobel Peace Prize in 1978.

Saghlul, Sa'd (b. 1860, d. 23 Aug. 1927).
Egyptian nationalist; Premier 1924
Born in Ibyana, he studied law in Cairo and Paris. As Education Minister (1906) he insisted on the use of Arabic in primary schools. He was Minister of Justice (1910–12), and in 1913 was elected to the legislative assembly, where he became leader of the opposition. After World War I, he led a delegation (wafd) to London to petition for an Egyptian delegation to the *Paris Peace Conference (1919) which would have meant the recognition of Egypt's sovereignty, but this was rejected. He was expelled until 1923, when he became leader of a nationalist movement called the *Wafd party. He won every subsequent election until his death, but was only briefly Premier, owing to the hostility of the British and of King *Fuad.

Sahara, see WESTERN SAHARA

Said, Nuri al- (b. 1888, d. 14 July 1958).
Prime Minister of Iraq 1930–2, 1938–40, 1941–7, 1949–52, 1953–7, 1958
Born near Baghdad of mixed Arab-*Kurdish descent, he enlisted in the army of the *Ottoman Empire. He defected in 1914 and fled to Egypt. When the *Arab Revolt broke out he became Chief of Staff to Emir Faisal.

When the latter became King *Faisal I of Iraq he was his chief adviser and virtual founder of the Iraqi army. Said was to form no less than fourteen governments as Prime Minister during the rest of his life. In 1942, he proposed a confederation of Middle Eastern territories (including a Jewish enclave in *Palestine), but this was frustrated by constant inter-Arab tensions and rivalries, and the Arab-Jewish hostilities in Palestine/Israel. The most important pillar of the *Hashemite dynasty in Iraq, he was Prime Minister of the short-lived *Arab Federation of Iraq and Jordan in 1958. He was captured and murdered in the coup of July 1958.

Saigon, fall of (30 Apr. 1975)
The occupation of the capital of the Republic of Vietnam (South Vietnam) by the northern Vietnamese People's Army, which marked the end of the *Vietnam War. Despite the end of direct US military involvement after the *Paris Peace Accords of 1973, the President of the Republic of Vietnam, *Nguyen Van Thieu, continued fighting the *Vietcong. In January 1975 the People's Army captured Phuoc Binh, eighty miles north of the city. Ban Me Thuot in the central highlands fell next, while further north Hue fell on 26 March and Da Nang, which had been the US naval base, on 29 March. Though Nguyen Van Thieu still had over a million men under arms, his forces collapsed in panic, with soldiers trying desperately to reach any port to escape. As the People's Army moved into Saigon, Nguyen Van Thieu resigned on 20 April. By 28 April Saigon's port had fallen, while US helicopters continued to carry away the last US personnel and as many Vietnamese refugees as could crowd into them. On 30 April North Vietnamese troops entered the city, which they renamed *Ho Chi Minh City.

St Andrews Agreement (13 Oct. 2006)
A peace agreement negotiated between the British and Irish governments as well as the major political representatives, including Martin McGuinness from *Sinn Féin, and Ian *Paisley from the *Democratic Unionist Party. The agreement aimed to resume the Northern Ireland peace process which had been stalled until 2005, when the *IRA completed the destruction of its weapons. It provided for a resumption of *Stormont and the construction of a government in which Paisley would, as First Minister, share power with Sinn Féin by 26 March 2007, following a referendum in Northern Ireland.

St Christopher (St Kitts) and Nevis

A federal state of two Caribbean islands, which came under British control in 1624. They were linked by the British in 1882 into one colony which also included Anguilla. (Anguilla declared its independence in 1967.) In 1932, the state's main political party, the Labour Party, was founded by Robert Bradshaw (b. 1916, d. 1978), who won every election from 1937 until his retirement in 1976. During this time, the state had been a member of the short-lived Federation of the *West Indies (1958–62). The Labour Party lost power in 1980, and subsequently tried to avert early independence because of what it regarded as the excessive constitutional guarantees awarded to Nevis. St Kitts and Nevis gained independence on 19 September 1983, as a constitutional monarchy within the *Commonwealth. Kennedy Alphonse Symmonds (b. 1936) of the centre-right People's Action Movement became the first Prime Minister after independence. It was not until 1995 that the Labour Party was able to regain power under its leader, Denzil Douglas. He was re-elected in 2000 and 2004, on the promise to address any constitutional imbalances felt by the people of the smaller Nevis.

St Germain, Treaty of (10 Sept. 1919)

The peace treaty signed in the Parisian suburb of St Germain-en-Laye between the Allied powers and Austria after *World War I, in the framework of the *Paris Peace Conferences. Austria was forced to accept the breakup of *Austria-Hungary, and the creation of the Kingdom of Serbs, Croats, and Slovenes (Yugoslavia from 1929) from its former provinces of Dalmatia, *Slovenia, and *Bosnia-Hercegovina, as well as the creation of *Czechoslovakia. In addition, Galicia returned to Poland, and *Bukovina was ceded to Romania. The Trentino and *South Tirol were ceded to Italy. Austria thus became a land-locked Alpine republic, reduced to entirely German-speaking areas (with the exception of a small Slavonic minority in Carinthia). Nevertheless, it was forbidden to carry the title of German Austria, nor was it allowed *Anschluss with Germany, as had been demanded by the majority of the population in a referendum in March 1919.

The Austrian army was limited in size to 30,000 men, with *reparations to be decided at a later stage. The Treaty was signed with the greatest reluctance by representatives of the newly created Austrian Republic. For Austria, association with the harsh terms of the Treaty became a great subsequent burden and source of instability.

TRIANON, TREATY OF; MAP 1

St Kitts and Nevis, see ST CHRISTOPHER AND NEVIS

St Laurent, Louis Stephen (b. 1 Feb. 1882, d. 25 July 1973). Prime Minister of Canada 1948–57

Born at Compton (Quebec), he studied law at Laval University and was appointed law professor there in 1914. A successful lawyer, he was president of the Canadian Bar Association (1930–2), and in 1937 became an adviser to the *Rowell–Sirois Commission. Despite his complete lack of political experience, *Mackenzie King made him Minister of Justice in December 1941, whereupon he was elected to parliament in 1942. The only minister from Quebec, he supported Mackenzie King's introduction of conscription for service overseas despite the fierce opposition of most of his home province. He became responsible for external affairs in 1946, and in 1948 succeeded Mackenzie King as leader of the *Liberal Party and Prime Minister. A grandfatherly figure with a sharp mind, he extended Mackenzie King's careful beginning of a *welfare state through broadening old-age pensions and introducing hospital insurance. He backed *Pearson's support for *NATO and the *UN, while he oversaw the integration of Newfoundland into Canada. Despite overwhelming election victories in 1949 and 1953, he appeared increasingly inactive, and was caught out by *Diefenbaker's well-organized *Conservative Party during the 1957 elections. He resigned as party leader in 1958 and withdrew from politics.

St Lucia

A Caribbean island which passed into British control in 1814. It joined the Federation of the *West Indies, upon whose collapse it reverted to

British colonial rule until 1967. It became a semi-independent state 'associated' with Britain until 1979, when it became an independent member of the *Commonwealth. From 1964, it was governed by John G. M. Compton, though despite his support for independence he lost the first post-independence elections in 1979. Nevertheless, the conservative and pro-Western politician resumed government in 1982, and was confirmed in office in elections in 1987 and 1992. In 1997 the centre-left St Lucia Labour Party (SLP) led by Kenny Antony came to power. In 2005, the veteran Compton came out of retirement to lead his United Workers Party to victory in the 2006 elections. Compton was faced with overseeing structural changes to the economy, as St Lucia was severely affected by the *WTO's ruling that EU preferences given to banana imports from St Lucia and other Caribbean islands were to be phased out.

St Vincent and the Grenadines

A group of Caribbean islands which became a British colony in 1763. It joined the Federation of the *West Indies (1958–62), and subsequently reverted to British colonial status. A semi-independent associated state of the United Kingdom from October 1969, it was granted full independence in 27 October 1979, as an independent member of the *Commonwealth. In 1984 James Fitzallen Mitchell of the New Democratic Party was elected Prime Minister. He won the subsequent elections of 1989 and 1994, despite opposition allegations of corruption and *human rights abuses. Mitchell resigned in 2000, and in the 2001 and 2005 elections the United Labour Party won a landslide election victory under Ralph Gonsalves. Gonsalves successfully helped diversify the economy and attract tourism, but the country continued to be heavily reliant on banana exports.

Salan, Raoul Albin Louis (b. 10 June 1899, d. 3 July 1984). French general

A graduate from the Military Academy of Saint-Cyr in 1919, he joined de *Gaulle's *Free French army in west Africa in 1943, when the defeat of the *Vichy government was certain. This earned him a reputation for duplicity, but he was nevertheless appointed the French military commander in *Indochina in 1945, though he was withdrawn in 1953 just before the battle of *Dien Bien Phu. In Indochina, he had developed very strong political views about the need for French colonies, thus his appointment in 1956 as military commander in Algeria was very controversial. Mistrusted by both the Algerians of European origin and by de Gaulle's followers, de Gaulle 'promoted' him to a desk job as Inspector General of Defence almost immediately upon his return to power in 1958. He was dismissed from military service in 1960. He went to Spain and founded the Algerian resistance movement, the *Organisation de l'Armée Secrète, which he led in their unsuccessful *coup d'état* in Algiers. Sentenced to death *in absentia*, he was captured in Algiers in 1962, but given life imprisonment. He was released in 1982 following a general amnesty by President *Mitterrand.

Salandra, Antonio (13 Aug. 1853, d. 9 Dec. 1931). Prime Minister of Italy 1914–16

Born in Troia, he obtained a law degree from the University of Naples in 1872. He took up a chair in administrative law in Rome in 1879, where he came to believe in the necessity of the rule of law and the authority of the state. He entered the Chamber of Deputies in 1886 as an opponent of *Giolitti. He was Minister of Agriculture (1899–1900), of Finance (1906), and of the Treasury (1909–10). As Prime Minister he initially favoured Italy's neutrality during World War I, but subsequently came to favour military intervention on the side of the Allies. Following a series of military disasters against the Austrian imperial army in 1916 he was forced to resign. He supported *Mussolini's rise to power, but retired from active political life in 1925.

Salazar, António de Oliveira (b. 8 Apr. 1889, d. 27 July 1970). Prime Minister of Portugal 1932–68

Early career Born in Vimieiro (Beira Alta), he studied at a Roman *Catholic school to prepare for the priesthood, but then decided to study economics instead. He became the star student of Coimbra University and gained a doctorate in finance and economics in 1918. His academic reputation earned him the offer to become Finance Minister, but he accepted the appointment to a professorship at his university instead. He accepted the renewed offer to become Finance Minister in 1926, only to resign a few days later when his demands for sweeping powers were rejected.

In power When *Carmona's military regime remained as incompetent in the management of the country's finances as its republican predecessors, he was finally offered the Finance Ministry with the authority he demanded. He managed to balance the hitherto chaotic budgets, a feat which gave him sufficient authority to become the dominant figure of the regime. This position was confirmed by his appointment as Prime Minister. He was responsible for establishing the *Estado Novo, whereby, according to the 1933 Constitution, Portugal became a *Fascist, *corporatist state devoid of political parties or other democratic institutions. Despite the economic and political difficulties arising from the *Spanish Civil War (1936–9) and World War II, he enjoyed considerable popularity, as he was seen as a guarantor of stability and prosperity. However, as he became older and increasingly stubborn he failed to see that economic change, political repression, and military defeats in the African colonies produced widespread dissatisfaction. He suffered a stroke in 1968, from which he did not recover. Salazar was succeeded by *Caetano, who was eventually overwhelmed by the pent-up tensions that had developed under Salazar.

Salisbury, Robert Arthur Talbot, 3rd Marquess of Gascoyne-Cecil (b. 3 Feb. 1830, d. 22 Aug. 1903). British Prime Minister 1885–6, 1886–92, 1895–1902

Born in Hatfield, and educated at Eton and Oxford. He was elected to parliament for the *Conservative Party to represent Stamford in 1853, and held his seat until becoming Marquess in 1868, when he entered the House of Lords (*parliament). He was Secretary of State for India (1874–6), and then Foreign Secretary (1878–80). He led the Conservative Party from 1885, and in 1886 formed an alliance with Joseph *Chamberlain and the Liberal Unionists, thus successfully exploiting Liberal divisions over Irish 'Home Rule' (autonomy). Further reasons for his longevity in office were a close grasp of the wishes of the Conservative electorate, whom he sought not to alienate through radical or excessively enterprising measures. Salisbury also displayed a firm control over the House of Lords. Both of the latter qualities were notably absent in his nephew and successor, *Balfour, which goes a long way to explaining the weakness of the Conservative Party in the decade after his resignation. In addition to being Prime Minister, he was also Foreign Secretary (except for 1886–7) until 1900, when he was succeeded by Henry Lansdowne.

Salò, Republic of (Italian Social Republic)

The northern Italian Fascist republic (1943–5) with its headquarters at Salò, on Lake Garda. It was governed by *Mussolini once he had been freed from imprisonment by the Germans. Utterly dependent on the German military and the extreme wings of the Fascist movement as his power base, Mussolini ruled with considerable brutality to compensate for absent popular support until the republic collapsed in April 1945.

Salonika campaign (World War I) (Oct. 1915–Nov. 1918)

After the failure of the *Gallipoli campaign in *World War I, Salonika became the base for an Allied **Macedonian Front** against Bulgaria. In fact there was little action until late in the war. In September 1918 a combined force of French, Serbs, British, Greeks, and Russians attacked, under the command of General *Franchet d'Esperey. They advanced so rapidly that they had reached the Danube and Constantinople by the time the war ended in November.

SALT (Strategic Arms Limitation Talks), see DISARMAMENT

Salt March (12 Mar.–6 Apr. 1930)

Perhaps M. K. *Gandhi's best-known act of civil disobedience, known as the second *satyagraha ('hold fast to the truth'). It expressed increasing frustration by *Congress at its own impotence and, specifically, the British refusal to grant Dominion status to India. Gandhi chose the hated salt tax as the object of his campaign. At the time, the Indian government maintained a monopoly over the manufacture of salt, an essential basic commodity which was thus heavily taxed. Those using their own salt, e.g. if they were living close to the sea, were subject to heavy punishment. The 61-year-old Mahatma started the 240–mile-long march from Sabarmati to the coastal town of Dandi together with seventy-eight of his followers. He was joined by thousands along the way, in a march that received vast international and national attention. Encouraging every Indian to defy the salt laws and provide for his/her own salt where possible, at his final destination he symbolically picked up a lump of salt. When the protesters marched on to a government salt depot, he was arrested, as were between 60,000 and 90,000 other Indians in subsequent months, as well as the entire Congress leadership. Gandhi was released and called off the campaign in March 1931. According to the **Gandhi–Irwin Pact**, Gandhi could participate in the second *Round Table Conference, and the production of salt was permitted for domestic consumption. Moreover, the Pact allowed peaceful picketing to support the campaign for Indian-made goods (*svadeshi*), while Congress dropped its demands for an inquiry into the arrests made during the campaign.

Salvation Army

An international organization for evangelical and social work. In 1865 William Booth (b. 1829, d. 1912) founded the fundamentalist Christian Revival Association to work for the destitute in the slums of London. Renamed the Salvation Army in 1878, it was run on quasi-military lines, with its members being awarded military ranks. One of Booth's sons, Ballington, spread the Army's work to the USA through the foundation of the **Volunteers of America** in 1896. His brother, William Bramwell, succeeded their father as General to head the Army, and extended its work into other European countries, as well as Asia. In 1929 Edward Higgins became General, and its work was again extended, mainly into Africa. The Army continued to thrive under the leadership of the founder's fourth daughter, Evangeline Booth, from 1935. By 1960 it was active in eighty-four countries, with some 800 day schools and over 1,750 other institutions including hospitals, clinics, and maternity homes, children's homes, and night shelters. In 2007, it claimed a membership of around 1.5 million in 111 countries, providing relief to ex-prisoners, the homeless, and the old.

((⊕)) SEE WEB LINKS

• The official website of the Salvation Army.

Samoa

A Pacific islands state which has become a remarkably stable democracy since independence. Known as Western Samoa until 1997, it consisted of a group of Polynesian islands in the central Pacific divided in 1900 between US and German colonial government. At the beginning of World War I, the western, German part was occupied by New Zealand troops. New Zealand administration, subsequently legitimized as a *League of Nations *Mandate, was considered by the Samoans as racist and insensitive to local customs, and was thus resisted in the so-called Mau protests until the more sensitive approach taken by the new New Zealand *Labour government after 1935. Samoa became a *UN *trust territory in 1946 and, after gradually acquiring more self-government, it became independent on 1 January 1962. Though it

retained a traditional system of government, as 47 out of 49 seats in the legislative assembly were reserved for clan chiefs, the first free elections were introduced in 1991. In 1998, Tofilau Eti Alesana, who had been Prime Minister since 1982, was succeeded by Sailele Malielegoai Tuila'epa. He continued to diversify the economy by promoting tourism and foreign direct investment. Despite corruption allegations, Tuila'epa was re-elected for a third term in office in 2006.

AMERICAN SAMOA

Samuel, Sir Herbert Louis, 1st Viscount Samuel of Mount Carmel and Toxteth (b. 6 Nov. 1870, d. 5 Feb. 1963).
British Liberal leader 1931–5

Born in Liverpool, and educated at Oxford. He was elected to parliament for the *Liberal Party to represent Cleveland in 1902, and entered the Cabinet in 1909 as Chancellor of the Duchy of Lancaster. He was Foreign Secretary under *Asquith in 1916, but refused to serve under *Lloyd George. He lost his seat in 1918, and was high commissioner of *Palestine in 1920–5. In 1925–6, he headed the Royal Commission on the coal industry. He returned to parliament in 1929 and, as Liberal leader, was Foreign Secretary in the *National Government in 1931–2. He resigned in protest against the protectionist *Ottawa Agreements, and lost his seat in 1935.

San Francisco Conference (15 Apr.–26 June 1945)

An international conference attended by representatives of the fifty countries that had declared war on Germany by 1 March 1945. It discussed and determined the aims and structure of the *United Nations Organization (UN). It also drafted the UN Charter, which was ratified at the first session of the UN General Assembly on 24 October 1945.

San Francisco, Peace Treaty of (8 Sept. 1951)

The peace treaty which followed Japan's unconditional surrender in World War II on 2 September 1945. It was signed by forty-eight countries that had been at war with Japan, though not by China and the Soviet Union. It restored Japan's full sovereignty, albeit with the continued presence of a number of US bases in the country. It brought the work of the Supreme Allied Command of the Pacific (*SACP) to an end, with the occupying US forces leaving the country by 28 April 1952.

JAPAN–UNITED STATES SECURITY TREATY

San Marino

The world's second smallest republic emerged from the area under control of the San Marino monastery south of the Italian town of Rimini.

Independent since 1263, it acquired its current borders in 1462 and received its republican Constitution in 1599. It formed a customs union with Italy in 1862, and has since been closely linked to the country through a series of friendship treaties. Nevertheless, it was able to retain neutrality in World War I, and was neutral in World War II until it was occupied by the Germans on 22 September 1944. From 1945 until 1957 politics were dominated by a socialist–Communist alliance, which was followed by a number of centrist coalitions which excluded the Communist Party. San Marino has two heads of state, called governing captains (*capitani reggenti*), who are elected by parliament for a period of six months. Although not a member of the European Union, it had a currency union with Italy, which meant that it joined the *euro in 1999.

Sandino, Augusto César (19 May 1895, d. 21 Feb. 1934). Nicaraguan resistance fighter

Son of a wealthy plantation owner, he joined the guerrilla movement in its fight against the US occupation of Nicaragua in 1926. After its end in 1933 he continued to oppose the new President Sacasa, as well as the National Guard under Anastasio *Somoza García, as too compliant with the USA. Sandino agreed to meet the new authorities to try and reach a peace agreement, whereupon Somoza ordered his abduction and execution upon his leaving the presidential palace. A martyr at the hands of Somoza, Sandino inspired those who subsequently fought against the Somoza regime, and who united in 1961 to form the 'Sandinistas', the **Frente Sandinista de Liberación Nacional** (Sandinista Movement of National Liberation).

Sanguinetti, Julio María (b. 6 Jan. 1936). President of Uruguay 1985–90, 1995–2000

Born in Montevideo, he studied law and joined parliament in 1958 for the progressive Colorado Party. He was Minister of Industry and Commerce (1969–71) and of Education and Culture (1971–2). After the liberalization of the political system in 1981 he became his party's General Secretary, and on 25 November 1984 was elected President (he took

office in 1985). The first democratic ruler for twelve years, he stabilized the political system but was unable to overcome the country's economic problems. Prevented from immediate re-election by the constitution, he was elected in 1995 with a majority of only 20,000 votes. Despite his close associations with his party, he promoted a coalition with the Colorado Party's traditional rivals, the more right-wing Blancos, in order to overcome the fragmentation of the policial system.

São Tomé and Príncipe

A small republic in the Gulf of Guinea consisting of an archipelago of islands. A Portuguese colony from 1521, it was transformed into a Portuguese overseas province in 1955. Following the armed guerrilla struggle for independence carried out by the Marxist Movimento de Libertação de São Tomé e Príncipe (MLSTP, Liberation Movement of Sao Tomé and Príncipe), it received independence on 12 July 1975. The MLSTP subsequently established a socialist one-party state with Angolan and Cuban help.

From 1988, however, it opened up the political system, and a multi-party democracy was introduced in 1990. Transformed into a social democratic movement, the MLSTP became the largest party, and in 1995 the political system proved stable enough to overcome a military coup (15–22 August 1995). In 2001, Fradique de Menezes of the opposition Democratic Movement of Forces for Change (MDFM) was elected in the first round. Despite the occurrence of a number of corruption scandals involving the government uncovered over a number of years, the *IMF and the *World Bank granted the country relief from over 80 per cent of its foreign debt. Menezes was challenged in an unsuccessful coup in 2003, and in 2006 he was re-elected, with his MDFM becoming the largest party in parliament. Menezes, a wealthy businessman, was committed to using growing revenue from off-shore oil deposits to improve infrastructure and general welfare.

Sarajevo

The capital of *Bosnia-Hercegovina, it became one of the principal centres of the

*Bosnian Civil War. For most of the war, it was almost totally surrounded by rebel forces of the Serb Republic of Bosnia-Hercegovina, whose government under *Karadzic operated from Pale, a Serb-controlled suburb of Sarajevo. The city survived the war thanks to intervention by the *UN, which organized food supplies in painstaking negotiations with the Bosnian Serbs. Its population was reduced from 415,000 in 1991 to an estimated 300,000 in 1995. The city was reunited as the capital of Bosnia-Hercegovina by the *Dayton Agreement.

Sarajevo, assassination in (1914)

The principal city of *Bosnia-Hercegovina which had been formally annexed by *Austria-Hungary in 1908. In protest against the Austrian encroachment in the Balkans, on 28 June 1914 the heir to the Austrian throne, Francis Ferdinand (b. 1863, d. 1914), and his wife, were assassinated by Gavrilo Princip of the Young Bosnia terrorist organization. He was assisted by the Black Hand terrorist organization from *Serbia. Austria-Hungary accused the Serbian government of complicity, of which it was in fact innocent, and imposed harsh demands in retaliation. Although Serbia met most of these, war followed on 28 July which immediately escalated into *World War I.

Sarawak

A territory on the island of Borneo, it was ceded by the Sultan of Brunei to a wealthy British adventurer, Sir James Brooke, in 1841, and remained in the Brooke family until Japanese occupation (1942–5). In 1946 it became a British Crown Colony. Despite Indonesian claims for the territory, which led to the *Confrontation (Konfrontasi), the majority of its population opted for entry into the Federation of Malaysia in 1963.

Sarekat Islam (SI, Islamic Association)

A political organization founded in the Dutch East Indies (later Indonesia) in 1912. It emerged from the Sarekat Dagang Islam (Islamic Traders Association) founded in 1909, in an attempt to resist growing Chinese competition in the batik trade. Led by Haji Umar Said Tjokroaminoto, it promoted the strength of indigenous trade through cooperatives, and increasingly challenged the Dutch colonial government. By 1919, it had acquired a mass following of nearly two million people. It was fundamentally weakened by effective police action by the colonial forces against its members. It was also criticized by many nationalist groups for its relative moderation. As important was the rift between the association's *Islamic and *Communist followings. It broke with the Indonesian *Communist Party (PKI) in 1921–2. Subsequently, the Communists developed a much more effective and organized opposition to the colonial government, causing support for the SI to decline.

Sarkozy, Nicolas (b. 28 Jan. 1955). French President 2007–

Born in Paris as the son of a French mother and a father who had immigrated from Hungary, he studied at Sciences Po university and became a lawyer. He entered local politics, served as a member of the *European Parliament, and in 1988 was elected to the National Assembly. Sarkozy's straight-talking, populist style and his political cunning threatened *Chirac, who sought to neutralize him by giving him the difficult portfolios of Interior Minister in 2002, and Finance Minister in 2004. Sarkozy's popularity increased further, however, not least through his tough stance on immigrants. Chirac was thus unable to stop him becoming president of the *UMP in 2004. Sarkozy subsequently resigned from ministerial office and concentrated on establishing control of the party, which acclaimed him as its presidential candidate with near unanimity.

In office Having been elected with a clear majority of the votes, Sarkozy's administration granted self-government to universities, rendered labour laws more flexible, and initiated public-sector reform. He minimized opposition to these policies by consulting with, and thus dividing, his opposition. Sarkozy conducted an assertive foreign policy, hoping to inspire the EU through his leadership.

Sarney Costa, José (b. 1930). Brazilian President 1985–90

Sarney entered politics as a federal deputy, becoming Governor of Maranhão (in 1965) and a member of the Senate. In 1985, when the military returned power to democratic government, he became the running-mate of Tancredo Neves, who was elected President. However, Neves died before taking office, so that ironically Sarney, a protégé of the military regime, became Brazil's first guarantor of democratic government after twenty-one years of military rule. Unable to tackle his country's crippling economic, financial, and social problems, he made them worse through his indecisiveness. Inflation soared from 227 per cent in 1985 to almost 1,500 per cent in 1990, while GDP per capita remained stationary overall. He was unable to renegotiate the country's enormous foreign debt, which was the highest in the developing world. Finally, he failed in his attempt to carry out a reform of labour representation to destroy its neo-corporatist structures and make the labour market more dynamic and flexible.

Sassou-Nguesso, Denis (b. 1943). President of the Republic of Congo, 1979–92, 1997–
An officer in the Congolese army, he participated in various coups in the 1960s and early 1970s. In 1979, he became President himself, but he lost power in Congo's first democratic elections in 1992. Sassou-Nguesso never accepted this result, and gathered a growing army around him which engaged in civil war. He recaptured power in 1997, and in 2002 he organized elections in such a way that his victory was a certain outcome. Sassou-Nguesso was able to benefit from Congo's significant offshore oil reserves, which allowed him to prop up his power, even if it did not diminish poverty in his country. In 2006, he became head of the *African Union for one year.

Satô Eisaku (b. 27 Mar. 1901, d. 3 June 1975). Prime Minister of Japan 1964–72
The brother of *Kishi Nobusuke, another famous postwar Prime Minister, although his period in power was to be much longer and less controversial. Satô was one of the so-called Yoshida school, a bureaucrat recruited by *Yoshida Shigeru into the political world. After a period in the railways ministry during the war, Satô entered the government as Chief Cabinet Secretary to Yoshida's second Cabinet in late 1948 despite the fact that he was not a member of the Diet. Elected to the Diet the following year, he established himself as a close member of Yoshida's inner circle, serving as Post and Telecommunications Minister and Minister of Construction. Though Yoshida was largely excluded from the new conservative order established after the formation of the *Liberal Democratic Party, Satô's career was only temporarily affected and thanks to his family connections he joined Kishi Nobusuke's Cabinet as Minister of Finance in 1958. He continued to serve in *Ikeda Hayato's administration and was his successor in 1964. His premiership, which survived for over seven and a half years, saw the peak years of Japan's economic growth. Aside from his guidance of economic policy, Satô's skilful handling of diplomacy allowed him to ensure the return of Okinawa from the USA. He also improved relations between Japan and South Korea. He was awarded the *Nobel Peace Prize in 1974.

satyagraha ('hold fast to the truth')
A tactic of civil disobedience, passive resistance, and non-cooperation developed by M. K. *Gandhi in South Africa (1907–14), where it enabled him to unite the disparate Asian community and force the South African government to repeal many of its discriminatory acts.

In India, Gandhi led three satyagraha campaigns, though in each case these were more about uniting nationalist opposition behind himself, than about forcing the British out of India, which remained a more long-term objective. His first satyagraha (1920–2) saw him become the uncontested leader of *Congress. It also marked a last period of nationalist cooperation between Congress and the *Muslim League. He hoped to restore this unity in the second satyagraha of 1930–4, when he embarked on his *Salt March. Though spectacularly successful in demonstrating his leadership of Congress and the volatility of British rule against united Indian resistance, this time Gandhi failed to unite the Muslims behind the campaign. Instead, the Muslim League responded with *Iqbal's demand for a separate Muslim homeland in the west.

Finally, the third satyagraha, also known as the **Quit India Campaign**, represented an attempt to maintain his authority over the radical wing of Congress led by *Bose, which demanded resistance against Britain because of its declaration of war on Germany on India's behalf in 1939.

Thus, while failing to keep the unity of the nationalist community, the satyagrahas did maintain the unity of the predominantly Hindu Congress. They were successful because of their focus on Gandhi's personality and leadership, and the existence of a liberal colonial government which, on the whole, did allow a free press, and which was constrained by the rule of law. This explains why the method was less successful in other contexts, e.g. in South Africa under *apartheid, where such tactics were rendered ineffective by the extent of state repression and the absence of an independent press.

Saudi Arabia
The world's largest oil producer with about one quarter of all known oil reserves, Saudi Arabia maintained remarkable political and cultural stability.

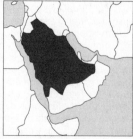

Early history (up to 1990) Part of the *Ottoman Empire since 1517, it was reclaimed by the Bedouin tribes rallied under the leadership of *Abd al-Aziz ibn Saud from 1902. In the Treaty of Jeddah (1927) he was recognized as King of the Hejaz, of the Nejd and its peoples, and of the Principality of Asir. In 1932 the country was proclaimed the Kingdom of Saudi Arabia. Until the discovery of oil it was a poor desert state whose only wealth came from the pilgrimages to the holy cities of Mecca and Medina. An oil concession was awarded to a US firm, Standard Oil of California, in 1933, and oil was first exported in 1938. In 1944 the oil company was reformed as the Arabia–American Oil Company (ARAMCO). Ibn Saud was succeeded by his son Saud (r. 1953–64), who was deposed by his brother *Faisal. The latter introduced Western administrative and economic reforms. Subsequently the country's vast oil revenues, which increased further after ARAMCO was fully nationalized in 1979, were used to establish an exemplary medical health care system, and an education system to reduce the country's dependence on foreign skilled labour. There were also attempts to increase domestic food production, which were hampered by the lack of water and the poor soil of most of the country. Faisal was murdered in 1975, and succeeded by his brothers Khalid (r. 1975–82), *Fahd (r. 1982–2005), and *Abdullah (r. since 2005).

Despite the introduction of Western *capitalism, traditional Islamic law (Shariah) remained the basis of the legal system. As the country's spiritual and secular leader, the King consulted tribal chiefs and other religious leaders on important matters, but was unfettered by political parties, a parliament, or even a Constitution. As a token concession to demands for greater political freedoms, a consultative assembly was set up in 1993. However, all of its members were appointed by the monarch, its meetings were held in secret, and it had no powers of decision.

Geopolitical significance For three reasons, the country enjoyed continued Western military and diplomatic support, as shown in the *Gulf War, when it was defended from a spread of Iraqi aggression. (1) Its brand of *Islam was traditional, but not politically radical. It was also deeply anti-Communist and thus opposed to the regimes of *Nasser and *Assad. (2) It was important to the West geopolitically as it served as a politically moderate counterweight to Iraq and Iran. During the *Cold War, it contained the largest US military base east of Germany and west of Japan. (3) With the world's largest known oil reserves, the country was of crucial importance as a 'swing producer': with the greatest financial and physical ability to vary supply, it was the best guarantor for low and stable oil prices.

Contemporary politics (since 1990) In the 1990s, the government attempted, with some success, to open up the economy to foreign investment and reduce its reliance on oil production. The economic transformations this entailed, however, led to a growth in Islamic nationalism. It created substantial support for a religiously based anti-Americanism, which at its extreme was exploited by—and helped support—Osama *Bin Laden and his terrorist activities. Although the Saudi government was at first sceptical vis-à-vis the US reaction against the *Taliban following the *September 11 attacks, it gave cautious assistance to the US in its *War against Terrorism. In particular, it hoped to exert a moderating influence in the Middle East, by attempting to promote peace between Israel and Palestine from 2001. King Abdullah introduced careful political reform, and in 2005 municipal elections were held for the first time. Abdullah continued the fight against corruption, but the government's major concern was the continued fight against terrorism, as bomb attacks against foreign nationals (and especially US citizens) continued.

Sauvé, Jeanne-Mathilde (née Benoît) (b. 26 Apr. 1922, d. 26 Jan. 1993). Canadian Governor-General 1984–90

Born at Prud'homme (Saskatchewan), she studied at the Universities of Ottawa and Paris and began a career in journalism, becoming a pronounced supporter of women's rights. She entered the House of Commons in 1972, and was the first female Cabinet member from Quebec, serving as Minister of Science and Technology, Minister of Environment (1974), and Minister of Communications (1975–9). During *Trudeau's last government she was Speaker of the House of Commons, transforming its administrative practices. The first woman to be appointed Governor-General, she was a passionate supporter of national unity.

Savage, Michael Joseph (b. 23 Mar. 1872, d. 27 Mar. 1940). Prime Minister of New Zealand 1935–40

Early career Born in Rothesay (Australia) of Irish immigrant parents, he became active in the Australian *Labor movement when he worked as a gold miner from 1900. Attracted in part by *Seddon's social legislation, he emigrated to New Zealand in 1907 and began work in a brewery. He became active in the trade union movement and in 1916 joined the *Labour Party upon its foundation. He became national secretary of the party in 1919, and won the elections to become a Member of Parliament later that year. He was deputy leader of his party from 1923, and leader from 1933, following the death of *Holland.

In office His pragmatic image, underlined by his straightforward character, led the party to a landslide victory in the 1935 elections. As Prime Minister, he also took over the portfolios of external affairs, native affairs, and broadcasting. With increasing expertise in public relations, he became a skilful manipulator of the media, and introduced radio broadcasts into parliament in 1936. He accepted the need for armaments, and firmly supported Britain at the outbreak of World War II. At home, in 1938 he created the *welfare state whose structures and principles persisted in New Zealand until the 1980s. It provided medical and hospital benefits, unemployment and sickness benefits, and improved provisions for orphans and the elderly. Education became free and universal, while the provision of low-cost loans enabled vast numbers to become homeowners. He was re-elected in 1938, but in 1939 became too ill to govern effectively. He died in office and was succeeded by *Fraser.

Saverne, see ZABERN AFFAIR

SCAP (Supreme Command of the Allied Powers)
The official name of the Allied (effectively US) command over Japan under General *MacArthur. Following *World War II, the SCAP accepted the Japanese cease-fire of 14 August 1945 and signed the instrument of surrender on board the battle-ship *Missouri* on 2 September. The SCAP then established itself in Tokyo and created a successful postwar order for Japan. At the heart of this was the drafting of the new, pacifist *Japanese constitution. It organized the *Tokyo Trials, but displayed tact in not persecuting Emperor *Hirohito, insisting only that he renounce his status as a deity.

The army of some 5.5 million soldiers was demobilized, and military installations destroyed. In addition to these political and military matters, social reform included a land reform through the redistribution of land from large to small landholders. The SCAP was also faced with the task of repatriating some three million homecoming troops, and another three million civilians from colonies

and occupied territories to Japan. As in Germany, the US administration became increasingly conciliatory towards the defeated power in the light of the *Cold War. This was particularly the case in Japan, whose importance to the USA became clear in the *Korean War. This led to the end of US occupation in 28 April 1952, after the Peace of *San Francisco, at a time when Japan had already resumed its position as Asia's wealthiest country.

Schacht, Hjalmar (b. 22 Jan. 1877, d. 3 June 1970). President of the German Central Bank 1924–30, 1933–9
In 1918 he co-founded the left-liberal DDP (Deutsche Demokratische Partei), but in the following years moved increasingly to the right until he supported *Hitler's appointment as Chancellor in 1933. Schact's skilful handling of the German economy after 1933 was an important contributor to Hitler's popularity and his ability to rearm Germany. He was Economics Minister (1934–7), but lost this post and the presidency of the national bank for opposing Hitler's and *Göring's more extreme autarky/rearmament schemes. Because of loose contacts with conservative *resistance circles he was imprisoned after the *July Plot. He was acquitted of war crimes at the *Nuremberg Trials.

Schengen Agreement (14 June 1985)
Signed in Schengen (Luxemburg), the treaty sought to abolish border controls of private and commercial traffic between the signatory states. A second Agreement (Schengen II), signed in 1990, enhanced the provisions for common policing through the creation of the Schengen Information System. Immigration controls to third countries were harmonized, and external border controls to third countries enhanced. Originally signed by a core of European Community member states, it was incorporated into the *EU by the Treaty of *Amsterdam. Its members consisted of the EU countries before the 2004 enlargement round, minus Great Britain and Northern Ireland. Although not members of the EU, Norway and Iceland were also members of the Schengen area. Upon enlargement in 2004 and 2007, the new eastern European member states were not automatically accepted as members, as these countries first had to adapt to the information systems and the rigid border controls which became a precondition for membership.

Schirach, Baldur von (b. 9 May 1907, d. 8 Aug. 1974). Nazi youth leader
President of the *Nazi student league (1928–32), he became the national youth

leader of the Nazis (1931–40), and of Germany in 1933. In this capacity he built up the *Hitler Youth into a national mass organization. From 1940 to 1945 he was the Nazi Governor (*Gauleiter*) of Vienna. At the *Nuremberg Trials, he was sentenced to twenty years' imprisonment.

Schlieffen Plan

The military plan developed in 1905 by the Chief of the General Staff, Alfred Graf von Schlieffen (b. 1833, d. 1913), in case Germany was involved in a two-front war against France and Russia. In such an event, German forces would first circumvent the French defence lines by attacking through Belgium and the Netherlands to secure a quick victory in the west, before taking on the Russians in the east. The plan had no regard for political considerations at all, so that when it was implemented at the start of *World War I, Belgium, despite its neutrality, was simply overrun, an act which finally spurred the British to join forces with their French allies and declare war on Germany. The plan also strengthened the Germans' desire to go to war as soon as possible, because they held that if war became inevitable, they would have to strike as quickly as possible to surprise the French.

MARNE, BATTLES OF THE

Schlüter, Poul Holmskov (b. 3 Apr. 1929). Danish Prime Minister 1982–93

Born in Tondern (northern Schleswig), he studied law at Aarhus and Copenhagen. A leading member of the youth movement of the Konservative Folkeparti (KF, Conservative People's Party), he joined the Folketinget (parliament) in 1964. In 1974, he became president of the KF, and in 1982 was the country's first conservative Prime Minister in the twentieth century. Schlüter was a vigorous proponent of *European integration and *NATO. However, his government had to accept seventeen defeats in parliament on foreign policy. His determination to restructure the Danish economy led him to accept a compromise whereby he was enabled to pursue many of his economic reforms, while the opposition determined much of foreign policy. Through a reform of the country's extensive social security system, he managed to reduce public debt and inflation, but failed to stop a rise of the unemployment rate to over 10 per cent in the early 1990s. He was forced to resign after it was revealed that his government had repatriated *Tamil refugees to Sri Lanka without ensuring their safe conduct there. In 1994, he gained a triumphant victory in the elections to the *European Parliament. He left parliament in

1998, but in 2002–3 he represented Denmark at the European *Constitutional Convention.

Schmidt, Helmut (b. 23 Dec. 1918). Chancellor of Germany 1974–82

Early career Born in Hamburg, he was a conscript and then an officer during World War II. Schmidt joined the *SPD in 1946, and as a student of politics (1946–9) he became the president of the socialist German student league (1946–7). He served as an MP 1953–62 and 1965–87. Schmidt achieved national prominence as Interior Senator of the city-state of Hamburg in 1962, when he coped successfully with a catastrophic flood in the city. At the national level, Schmidt served under *Brandt as Defence Secretary in 1969, and Finance Secretary in 1972.

In office Schmidt had to cope with the effects of two *oil-price shocks. Although the economy performed badly by German standards, the German economy fared much better than the economies of other industrialized nations. It was in this period that the strength of the national currency, the Deutsche Mark, was enshrined. In domestic politics, Schmidt was faced with the terrorist challenge of the *Baader-Meinhof Gang. On the international scene, his commitment to friendship with France and to *European integration led to the creation of the *European Monetary System, a forerunner of the *ERM. At a time when the *Cold War became more tense following the Soviet invasion of Afghanistan, Schmidt backed the controversial deployment of Pershing nuclear missiles in Europe. This response to the arrival of Soviet SS20 missiles in East Germany ultimately lost him the support of his own party. Always to the right of the SPD, his growing rift with his own party led to the defection of his coalition partner, the *Liberal Party (FDP). He did not survive a no-confidence motion by the *CDU, and Schmidt was succeeded by *Kohl as Chancellor in 1982. A highly articulate thinker who did not suffer fools gladly, Schmidt continued to be an influential elder statesman, not least through his position as co-editor of the German weekly newspaper, *Die Zeit*.

Schröder, Gerhard (b. 7 Apr. 1944). Chancellor of Germany, 1998–2005

Early career Born in Mossenberg, he completed an apprenticeship as a salesman while completing his high school exams at night school. Schröder studied law at Göttingen University, and from the age of 19 became active in politics. He joined the *SPD and in 1978 became head of its federal youth organization. Schröder became a member of the federal parliament in 1980, and in 1986 became Minister President in the state of Lower Saxony. A pragmatic politician without any discernible ideological commitments, his brash, undisguised hunger for power made him few friends in the federal SPD in the early 1990s. However, as one SPD leader after another faltered against Helmut *Kohl, he finally won the party's nomination for Chancellor in 1998.

In office Schröder led his party to victory in its second best result since 1949, and formed a coalition with the *Green Party, commanding a comfortable majority in the federal parliament. His majority in the second chamber of states, however, eroded within a year, and it was not until the retreat of the left-wing Lafontaine from government that his authority began to solidify. Schröder's domestic political position was further enhanced by a corruption scandal involving the *CDU. His government tried to establish itself firmly as a party of the centre ground, by introducing moderate pension reform and increasing social security benefits, and realizing a tax reform.

Even though Schröder failed to fulfil his promise and reduce unemployment, he won the 2002 elections on the promise to keep German troops out of any *Iraq War. As the German economy continued to lag behind other states, Schröder began to initiate some drastic reforms of the labour market. This divided the SPD, which lost control of most states, including its bastion of North-Rhine Westfalia in 2005. Always at his best when pushed into a corner, Schröder called new elections. Although the SPD lost, it confounded expectations of electoral meltdown owing to Schröder's impressive electoral performance. Schröder immediately retired from politics, to take up a number of lucrative positions, including at the Russian energy giant Gazprom, at the behest of his political friend, Vladimir *Putin.

Schumacher, Kurt (b. 13 Oct. 1895, d. 20 Aug. 1952). West German political leader
After volunteering for military service in World War I, in which he lost an arm, he became a member of the workers' and soldiers' council of Berlin following the 1918 revolution. He edited an *SPD party newspaper (1920–4), and co-founded the SPD paramilitary movement in 1924. An MP from 1930, he resolutely opposed the *Nazi regime and spent most of the time during the *Third Reich in *concentration camps (1933–43, 1944), from which his health never recovered. After the war, he became SPD leader in

Western Germany. In this position, he strongly disapproved of the forced merger of the SPD and the *Communist Party (KPD) in Soviet-occupied Eastern Germany. He narrowly lost the first national elections, and resolutely opposed Chancellor *Adenauer's policies of integration with the Western powers at the expense of speedy reunification.

Schuman, Robert (b. 29 June 1886, d. 4 Sept. 1963). Prime Minister of France 1947–8
Born in Luxembourg of a wealthy Lorraine family (*Alsace-Lorraine), he studied law in Strasbourg and the German city of Bonn. After World War I he entered French politics as a parliamentary Deputy for Metz and was chairman of the parliamentary finance commission for seventeen years. In September 1940 he was arrested and transported to Germany, but escaped in 1942 to join the *Résistance movement. A devout Catholic, he co-founded the Christian Democrat *MRP in 1944. A member of the Constituent Assemblies of 1945–6, he was a Deputy in the National Assembly 1946–62. Schuman was Minister of Finance in 1946 and 1947, before becoming Prime Minister in 1947, when he had to govern France in the face of Communist unrest.

Schuman is best remembered as Foreign Minister (1948–52), when his visionary policies sparked off reconciliation between France and Germany. Recognizing that France had limited resources to control a hostile West Germany, he proposed to Adenauer the pooling of economic resources as a way to build cooperation and friendship between the two countries. What became known as the Schuman Plan initiated a process that led to the creation of the *ECSC in 1952. Schuman served as the first President of the *European Parliament (1958–60). Schuman was bitterly opposed by some contemporary politicians, most notably de *Gaulle. Nevertheless, he is judged to have been one of the most influential politicians of the Fourth Republic. With *Monnet, he is remembered as the founding father of *European integration. The day of the release of the Schuman Plan (9 May 1950) is remembered annually as 'Europe Day' throughout the EU.

Schuschnigg, Kurt von (b. 14 Dec. 1897, d. 18 Sept. 1977). Chancellor of Austria 1934–8
Born in Riva del Garda, then part of the Austro-Hungarian Empire, he was educated in Innsbruck and became a lawyer. In 1927 he was elected to the Austrian parliament as a member of the *anti-Semitic Christian Social Party. He became Minister of Justice 1932 and Minister of Education 1933, in the *Dollfuss

government. He continued the latter's authoritarian regime at the head of the Popular Front, and thus prevented a return to democratic government. Despite his best efforts to maintain Austrian independence against growing *Nazi demands inside and outside Austria for *Anschluss, Austria's future had long become a matter beyond his control, subject to *Hitler's relations with *Mussolini. Once the latter gave up his resistance to German unification with Austria, it became a matter of time. In a desperate last effort to prevent the inevitable, he bowed to Hitler's demands to appoint *Seyss-Inquart into his Cabinet in February 1938. He tried to shore up his support through proposing a referendum on *Anschluss, which Hitler then used as a pretext to force his resignation on 11 March 1938. The following day, German troops marched into Austria. He was imprisoned throughout the war and after liberation in May 1945 became a professor of political science in the USA (1948–67).

Scopes Case (USA)

In March 1925 the Tennessee legislature had made it unlawful to teach any doctrine which denied the literal truth of the account of creation as presented in the King James version of the Bible. In July 1925 John T. Scopes, a biology teacher at Dayton High School, Tennessee, went on trial charged with violating state law by teaching Darwin's theory of evolution. In a case led by William J. Bryan for the prosecution, the justice ruled out any discussion of constitutionality. National interest in the trial was inspired by the journalism of H. L. Mencken, who portrayed it as a battle between science and superstition. The trial marked the beginning of an erosion of religious fundamentalism in public education and brought Bryan's reputation into question. Since Scopes was clearly guilty, he was convicted and fined $100. On appeal to the state Supreme Court the constitutionality of the state law was upheld, but Scopes was acquitted on the technicality that he had been fined 'excessively'. The law itself was not repealed until 1967.

Scotland

Linked with England since the 1707 Act of Union, Scotland maintained a separate established church (*Church of Scotland), its own legal system, and a distinctive education system which placed a high emphasis on university education and the teaching of science. It received its own Cabinet minister, Secretary for Scotland (Secretary of State from 1926) in 1885. In the twentieth century, demands for political independence emerged in the late 1920s, and led to the formation of the *Scottish National Party (SNP) in 1934. However, for much of the century, Scotland's wellbeing was tied closely to that of England. Its poor soil could sustain little agriculture, while its industries were largely export-orientated and thus depended on the *British Empire.

Demands for autonomy (from 1970s) These conditions changed dramatically in the 1970s, when the discovery and exploitation of vast offshore oil reserves led to a reassessment of Scotland's relationship with England among many in the population. The SNP's support dramatically increased in the early 1970s, and in 1973 the Kilbrandon Report recommended devolution through the creation of an elected Scottish Assembly. In 1978, *Callaghan's government passed the Scotland Act, providing for the holding of a referendum to approve its plans for the Assembly, which was to have legislative powers in areas such as education, health, and housing. The referendum would have to be approved by over 40 per cent of the electorate, and by a majority. In a referendum on 1 March 1979, 1,230,937 supported the assembly, with 1,153,502 against. This only represented 32.85 per cent of those eligible to vote, against 30.78 per cent, and devolution was defeated.

During the 1980s, support for devolution increased yet further, as the *Conservative Party under *Thatcher displayed little sympathy for, or understanding of, Scottish grievances. Neither her *poll tax nor her *monetarist policies, which were supported by a majority of the English population, were supported by a majority of Scots, which highlighted further the differences between the two countries.

Devolution (since 1997) In the 1990s the three major parties of Scotland, *Labour, the *Liberal Democrats and the SNP worked out plans for a Scottish Assembly, elected through a system of proportional representation. Following Labour's election victory at *Westminster in 1997, a Bill on Home Rule was passed in London. This was accepted in a Scottish referendum with an overwhelming majority. The new Scottish parliament obtained some tax raising powers as well as autonomy on matters such as public health. In the first elections of 1999, Labour gained 56 out of 129 seats, and formed a coalition with the Liberal Democrats. The new first minister, Donald Dewar, died after one year in office, and was succeeded by Henry McLeish. McLeish was forced to resign over the use of political funds in his constituency, so that in 2001 Jack McConnell became the third First Minister in three years.

Like his predecessors, McConnell governed in a coalition with the *Liberal Democrats. His government showed its distinctiveness vis-à-vis England when, in contrast to the rest of Great Britain, it rejected the introduction of university fees in Scotland, while also funding the *National Health Service at different levels. McConnell's Labour-led government suffered from the growing unpopularity of *Blair's government in London, so that his party lost the Scottish elections of 2007. For the first time, the SNP emerged as the strongest party, one seat ahead of Labour. The SNP's leader, Alex Salmond, became Scotland's First Minister at the head of a minority government.

Scottish National Party (SNP)

A Scottish political party which calls for *Scotland to become independent from the UK. The party was formed in 1934, after a merger of the National Party of Scotland (founded 1928), and the Scottish Party (1932). It won its first seat in parliament at the Motherwell by-election in April 1945. However, the seat was lost in the general election later in the year, and the SNP won no more seats until the 1967 Hamilton by-election. Subsequently, its support soared, as awareness of Scotland's distinctiveness increased. In 1970, it gained 11.4 per cent of the Scottish vote. This support nearly doubled in February 1974, to 21.9 per cent (winning seven seats), and in the second general election of the year, the party gained 30.4 per cent of the vote, and eleven seats. When devolution for *Scotland was not secured in 1979, the party's support fell to 17.3 per cent, and it won only two seats. Its low point was 11.8 per cent in 1983, but the party recovered to 21.5 per cent and three seats in 1992. It failed to overtake the *Labour Party as Scotland's biggest party, partly because the latter favoured more moderate devolution to outright independence. As a result, after Scottish devolution in 1999 it concentrated on more immediate policies, especially since it became the principal opposition party in the new Scottish parliament. In the 2007 elections, it obtained one seat more than Labour. This allowed its leader, Alex Salmond, to become First Minister. Given that he did not command a parliamentary majority, however, he was unable to pursue his demand for independence.

Scottsboro Case (USA)

In April 1931 nine Black youths were accused by two White girls of multiple rape on a train near Scottsboro, Alabama. They were found guilty and sentenced to death or long-term imprisonment. The sensational case highlighted race relations in Alabama and across the USA. In the initial trial, the two lawyers assigned to defend the nine accused had been given less than an hour to prepare their case, with one of them being drunk. After two interventions by the US *Supreme Court and a series of retrials by the state of Alabama, verdicts of not proven were reluctantly accepted by the state, which paroled all the boys. In 1946, fifteen years after their imprisonment, the last of the accused were released from prison.

Scouts, see BADEN-POWELL, ROBERT STEPHENSON SMYTH

Scullin, James Henry (b. 18 Sept. 1876, d. 28 Jan. 1953). Prime Minister of Australia 1929–31

Born in Trawalla (Victoria), he left school at 14, but continued his education at night school. He joined the Political Labor Council in 1903, and was elected to the federal parliament in 1910. Despite losing his seat in 1913, he became one of the leading opponents of compulsory military service overseas during World War I. Scullin was elected to the House of Representatives in 1922, and in 1927 became deputy leader of the *Labor Party, taking over the leadership in 1928. As the party's expert on economic policy he led attacks against the *Bruce-*Page government's economic measures.

In 1929 Scullin became Australia's first Roman Catholic and Australian-born Labor Prime Minister. He abandoned the *Gold Standard, but his tough deflationary policies to deal with the oncoming Great *Depression through a rigorous cut in state expenditure led to strong opposition from within his own party. He also alienated many supporters by reinstating his suspended treasurer, Edward G. Theodore (b. 1884, d. 1950) before he had been cleared of allegations of corruption. Scullin thus split the Labor Party, many followed *Lyons, leaving Labor for the *United Australia Party (UAP), while others followed *Lang and John A. Beasley (b. 1895, d. 1949) by advocating the downfall of Scullin's government and the establishment of a rival Labor organization. Partly because of declining health, and partly because of his inability to reunite the Labor Party, he resigned the party leadership in 1935. He retired from parliament in 1949.

SDI (Strategic Defense Initiative) (USA)

A US defence system intended to protect the USA from ICBMs (intercontinental ballistic missiles) by destroying them in space before they reached their target. Its development was started under *Reagan in 1983, when huge funds were spent on the development of the SDI despite criticism that it could never be infallible. While it worsened US–Soviet relations and inaugurated a new round in the arms race between the two countries, pressure from the programme contributed to the collapse of the Soviet Empire, whose military and financial resources were already overstretched. During the 1990s the unsuccessful programme was abandoned, but under President George W. *Bush the concept was revived by his controversial endorsement of the nuclear missile defence programme.

SDP, see SOCIAL DEMOCRATIC PARTY (UK)

SEAC (South East Asia Command)

The *Allied command system in the Far East during *World War II was created after reorganization in May 1943. Vice-Admiral Lord Louis *Mountbatten was appointed Supreme Commander of South-East Asia, with General *Stilwell as his deputy; the latter remained directly responsible to the US Joint Chiefs of Staff for his role in China. The idea was almost certainly that of *Churchill, who planned an early recovery of *Singapore by means of amphibious operations. The SEAC headquarters were first in New Delhi, but Mountbatten later moved them to Kandy (Sri Lanka). There were considerable tensions within SEAC, not only between Mountbatten and Stilwell, but also as to whether land-based operations in Burma were to precede the recapture of Singapore. Mountbatten would have preferred a direct assault on Singapore, but pressure from *Chiang Kai-shek resulted in the decision to recapture Burma first and reopen the Allied supply routes to China via the Burma Road. The *Burma campaign was thus revived, with Rangoon liberated by May 1945. SEAC's next task, to regain Singapore, was made redundant by Japan's surrender.

SEATO (South-East Asia Treaty Organization)

A defence alliance formed in 1955 specifically to withstand Soviet aggression in Asia, it was formed by Australia, New Zealand, the USA, Thailand, the Philippines, France, Pakistan, and the UK. However, the signatories refused to intervene collectively in the wars of *Vietnam, Laos, and Cambodia, and in 1975 the weak alliance was dissolved.

Second World War, see WORLD WAR II

secularization

A term used to describe a decline of the prestige and power of religious belief, practice, and institutions. During the earlier twentieth century it appeared to be an unstoppable process in Europe, owing to four factors: (1) industrialization and the failure of the Churches to recognize the spiritual needs of rapidly expanding new communities; (2) the partiality of a Church towards unpopular and repressive hierarchical structures, which happened, for instance, with the support given by the Roman *Catholic hierarchy to *Franco's authoritarian regime in Spain and the *Fascist *Vichy regime in France; (3) the experience of World War I, which was particularly disillusioning e.g. for pacifist Nonconformists in the UK; (4) the emergence of a new kind of critical theology. As churchgoing and traditional religious practice declined, there was an increased interest in other forms of mysticism and spirituality.

Of the traditional Christian denominations, the Roman Catholic Church was better able to withstand the process of secularization than most Protestant denominations. Its doctrinal conservatism provided emotional support at a time of economic and social uncertainty. Its structures, especially at the grass roots, were also successful in adapting to urbanization and the changing cultural needs of society. However, from the 1960s cultural pluralism made Catholic clubs and societies less attractive, while growing individualism and liberalism challenged doctrinaire conservatism. Catholic church attendance began to decline, especially in Europe, though in many developing countries it continued to prosper.

Among other (non-Christian) religions, secularization has manifested itself in the foundation of secular states in countries where one particular religion is socially and culturally predominant, such as in Egypt and Turkey. In recent years, secularization has been halted or even reversed in some instances by fundamentalist movements, which have been particularly successful in the case of *Islamic fundamentalism. Thus, the Iranian Revolution of 1979 managed to transform a secular state into a theocracy, while the majority of secular Arab states, such as Egypt or Turkey, have been put under threat by the growth of fundamentalist movements. Within Christianity, secularization has been particularly pronounced on the European continent. Elsewhere, Christianity has remained strong, even though there was some shift away from established religions to more independent evangelical denominations.

Security Council, see UNO

SED, see COMMUNIST PARTY, GERMANY

Seddon, Richard John (b. 22 June 1845, d. 9 July 1931). Premier of New Zealand 1893–1906

Early career Born in Lancashire (UK), he emigrated to Australia in 1863, where he found employment in mining and engineering, and arrived in New Zealand in 1866. He was attracted to the Waimea gold mines, where he used his experience to become prosperous. He became involved in local politics, and was elected the first mayor of the newly created borough of Kumara. Seddon became a radical Liberal member of the House of Representatives in 1879. As the representative of a mining constituency, he was one of the first to recognize the importance of the nascent labour movement, and advocated those measures which would improve the condition of the workforce or extend the franchise. He was primarily engaged in 'parochial' politics in the 1880s, but gradually realized that a strong state was best suited to improve conditions in outlying areas such as his constituency, the west coast. He entered the government in 1891 to become responsible for mines, defence, and public works, and his populist and crude style became a major asset. His popularity also increased owing to his tireless tours of the country.

In office He became Premier in 1893 and steered his party to victory in the general elections of that year. As Native Minister (1893–99), he pursued paternalistic policies, encouraging *Maori people to sell their land to the government. In 1896 he concentrated power into his own hands through taking over the portfolios of the Treasury and Labour. Incapable of delegating, he was also Minister of Public Works (1893–6), of Defence (1893–6, 1900–6), and Education (1903–6). Overall, he is remembered as laying the foundations of the *welfare state in New Zealand. His government passed the Industrial Conciliation and Arbitration Act in 1894, and he accepted the introduction of votes for women, despite his personal opposition. He passed the Old Age Pensions Act of 1898 against strong opposition, and introduced a pension scheme for teachers in 1905. He was also an imperialist, urging the administration of Fiji and the Samoan Islands, and annexing the *Cook Islands in 1901. He died in office in 1906, having led the *Liberal Party through five successive election victories.

Seeckt, Hans von (b. 22 Apr. 1866, d. 27 Dec. 1936). German general
A general staff officer during World War I, in 1920 he became the supreme commander of the German army which he developed into an elite force whose autonomy he refused to surrender to political control. The army maintained its power structures and its traditions from the days of the Empire, so that even *Hitler never managed to control it completely, as became clear in the *July Plot of 1944. Seeckt remained hostile to the Weimar Republic. While he was ready to use the army against insurrectionists from the left, his defence of the Republic against insurrectionists from the right in the *Kapp Putsch and the *Hitler Putsch remained ambivalent. He was relieved of his post in 1926 owing to personal animosities with President *Hindenburg, and became a right-wing Liberal MP (1930–2). In 1933 and 1934–5 he was military adviser to *Chiang Kai-shek in his attempt to defeat *Mao Zedong's *Long March in China.

segregation (USA)
A policy predicated upon the physical separation of racial groups and practised in the USA, particularly in the southern states, from the late nineteenth century until the 1970s. Opposition to segregation from the 1950s onward fuelled the *civil rights movement. The system of excluding members of one race from public facilities, institutions, or positions was informally in place from colonial times. The informal segregation persisted after the Civil War, but was placed on a legal footing in the late nineteenth century, most famously in the 1896 *Plessey v. Ferguson case. For the first half of the twentieth century, exclusion or second-class provision for African Americans and non-Whites was thus maintained in public transportation, education, entertainment, and religious and military organizations. This was known as the '**Jim Crow**' system, named after earlier caricature portrayals of Blacks. Whites and African Americans were leading separate lives outside (and usually inside) the workplace, where people of colour tended to hold subordinate positions when employed in White organizations.

African–American groups responded in protest in different ways. Marcus *Garvey and the *Black Consciousness movement sought to stimulate Black nationalism and pride, while other groups favoured integration and gradual change. The policy of the increasingly influential *NAACP was not to challenge segregation directly but to emphasize the inequality of separate provision. The *Supreme Court decision in *Brown v. Topeka struck directly at this perspective. Civil rights legislation and further court decisions followed, until all forms of legal segregation, including legislation relating to inter–racial marriage, were outlawed and given the morally repugnant status accorded to South African *apartheid. However, statistical evidence suggests that informal segregation, particularly in housing and education, persisted into the new millennium.

Seiyûkai (Constitutional Friends Association) (Japan)

Japan's pre-eminent prewar party, also known as **Rikken Seiyûkai**, founded in 1900. From its earliest days, the Seiyûkai dominated the Diet, controlling more than half the seats in the Lower House. In its origins, the party possessed firm ties with members of the oligarchy which had ruled Japan since the Meiji Restoration of 1868. Its founder and first president Itô Hirobumi (b. 1841, d. 1909) and Saionji Kinmochi (b. 1848, d. 1940) served as Prime Ministers, but they chose to continue along the lines of their predecessors by including few party men in their Cabinets.

During the presidency of *Hara Takashi, the Seiyûkai party machine was developed to its full potential. At the time, local patronage in the constituencies guaranteed impressive performance in elections even while the electorate itself was enlarged many times. Its electoral predominance coupled with the economic and social crisis of 1918 propelled the Seiyûkai into office under Hara's leadership. After Hara's assassination, the party became more disunited and suffered a severe electoral reverse in 1924. After that the Seiyûkai alternated with the *Minseitô as the party in power. Moreover, factionalism, which had been existent within the organization from its beginnings, increasingly manifested itself in open splits and defections, as some politicians preferred to join the government regardless of which party had formed it. In 1939, Japan's most important political party of the prewar period fragmented, overwhelmed by its chronic factionalism.

Senanayake, Don Stephen (b. 20 Oct. 1884, d. 22 Mar. 1952). Prime Minister of Ceylon (Sri Lanka) 1947–52

A devout Buddhist, he worked on his father's rubber plantation before entering politics. He was elected to the Ceylon Legislative Council in 1922 and became Vice-President of the State Council in 1936. In 1931 he was appointed Minister of Agriculture and Land, an office he held until 1947, during which time he encouraged the development of cooperative farms and of hydroelectric schemes. As leader of the United National Party he negotiated full independence from Britain in 1947, and the new Constitution for Ceylon (now Sri Lanka), of

which he became Prime Minister. He was firmly committed to a multi-ethnic Ceylon, though he was unable to allay the fears of the Tamil minority against discrimination by the Sinhalese. He was killed in a riding accident and was succeeded by his son Dudley Shelton Senanayake, who was Prime Minister 1952–4 and again 1965–70.

Sendero Luminoso (Shining Path) (Peru)

A Peruvian guerrilla movement founded in 1970 by Abimael Guzmán to follow the example of *Maoism in seeking to establish *Communism through a peasant-based (rather than proletarian) revolution. It only became active on the national scene in 1980, and initially focused its activities on the Ayacucho district, killing officials and peasants loyal to the government, as well as bombing government buildings. A guerilla war ensued, which was joined in 1983 by the socialist **Tupac Amaru** guerrilla force. An estimated 25,000 people died, with thousands disappearing. More than half of Peru came under martial law. The struggle was complicated by the increasingly powerful drug barons, who began to finance the Sendero Luminoso in return for its protection. While it retained much influence in the countryside, it was on the defensive after the election of *Fujimori in 1990. Guzmán was captured and imprisoned in 1992, while the number of activists declined from around 8,000 to an estimated 700 in 1995. Guzmán's successor, Ramírez Durand, was captured and imprisoned in 1999.

Senegal

The west African country had developed a relatively large educated elite under colonial rule, which allowed it to create a remarkably stable multi-

party democracy, a rarity on the African continent.

Contemporary history (up to 1980) Colonized by French tradesmen from 1659, it became the first French colony in Africa in 1854. A part of *French West Africa, it was made a French Overseas Territory in 1946, an autonomous republic in 1958, joined in a short-lived federation with Soudan (which then became Mali) in 1959, and became

independent in 1960, with *Senghor as the country's first President.

Senegal had developed a relatively rich and active political culture, dating back to the nineteenth century, when its towns had elected a deputy to the French Assembly in Paris (1848, and from 1876). As a result, Senegal was relatively stable politically upon independence. Senghor quickly established his domination in the political sphere, asserting himself against his rival, Mamadou Dia (b. 1911), in 1962. He created a single-party state gradually through the absorption or banning of other political parties (1966–74). Despite the absence of a multi-party democracy, however, there was considerable discussion within Senghor's own party, renamed the Parti Socialiste (PS, Socialist Party) in 1976. Senghor maintained good relations with France, and gradually introduced market-orientated measures to undo his earlier policies of nationalization and moderate state planning.

The Diouf era (1980–2000) Senghor and his more efficient successor, *Diouf, failed to change significantly the country's key economic problem, its over-reliance on its main crop, peanuts. In 1982, Senegal entered a confederation with Gambia, in which both countries retained their sovereignty but were committed to pursue common goals in economic, education, foreign, and defence policy. **Senegambia** fell apart in 1989, mainly because of mutual mistrust, and Gambian protests about Senegalese dominance.

In the 1990s Diouf continued his policies of political liberalization through involving some politicians of the opposition in his government, though the integration of the opposition also had the effect of cancelling out any major challenges to his own power. Despite impressive economic growth rates in the 1990s, Senegal's main problems continued to be the growing armed conflict in the region, notably the separatist movement in the southern part, the Casamance. Other problems included the difference between town and country expressed in the latter's appalling medical and educational provision, and a large number of unemployed in Dakar and other cities.

Contemporary politics (since 2000) In 2000, the opposition united in the second round of the presidential elections, whereupon Diouf lost to Abdoulaye Wade, an event that ended the Socialist Party's 40-year grip on power. Wade attempted to broker a peace agreement with the rebel Movement of the Democratic Forces of the Casamance, which was successful in 2004 even if the ensuing peace remained fragile. Wade

ruled with the help of a fragile coalition in parliament, which was subject to repeated disputes. In 2005, Wade won the *Houphouët-Boigny Prize sponsored by *Unesco, though his opponents accused him of manipulation in 2007, when he won a second term.

Senghor, Léopold-Sédar (b. 9 Oct. 1906, d. 20 Sept 2001). President of Senegal 1960–80

Early career Born in Joal, he gave up his study for the priesthood to attend the public secondary school in Dakar. He went to Paris in 1928 to study at the Lycée Louis le Grand, from which he graduated in 1931. Inspired by current French political, cultural, and social instability, he began to develop his vastly influential concept of *négritude*, which rejected the traditional belief in White superiority, criticized White concepts like *capitalism, and extolled the virtues of African culture.

As a naturalized French citizen Senghor was conscripted into the army in 1932, and thereafter worked as a teacher. He continued to publish tracts on politics and culture, as well as poetry. He fought in World War II, became a prisoner of war, and from 1942 worked in the *Résistance*. He became a Deputy in the French Constituent Assembly in 1946. He founded the Senegalese Democratic Bloc in 1947, advocating an endogenous African social and political structure based on traditional village communities. This extended his support to the Senegalese countryside, which enabled him to become President upon his country's independence.

In office Senghor abolished the rival office of Prime Minister from 1962 until 1970, when he filled the position with his capable lieutenant, Abdou *Diouf. He nationalized the country's major industries, and strengthened the system of cooperatives. He became a respected elder statesman of the African continent, though owing to economic problems his popularity declined during the 1970s. He became the first African leader upon independence to resign office voluntarily. A prolific poet, he was the first African to be admitted to the Académie Française in 1984.

September 11 (2001)
A term denoting four interrelated terrorist attacks on the United States on that date. They were organized by Osama *Bin Laden, and carried out by a total of nineteen hijackers who boarded four different planes. At 8.46 am, a hijacked Boeing 767 (American Airlines 11) crashed into the 94th floor of the North Tower of the World Trade Center in New York (WTC). Sixteen minutes later, a hijacked

Boeing 767 (United Airlines 175) crashed into the 78th floor of the WTC's South Tower. Whereas the WTC withstood the initial impact, the explosion and the debris this caused destroyed the building's fireproofing system, and the heat caused by the burning of 10,000 gallons of airplane fuel caused the steel support to heat up and collapse under the pressure of the building. At 9.59 am, the South Tower collapsed, and the North Tower collapsed twenty nine minutes later. Altogether, 2,830 people are believed to have died in the disaster.

In a third attack, American Airlines flight 77 was hijacked and directed towards the Pentagon, headquarters of the Department of Defense. The plane crashed into the building at 9.38 am, with 125 staff killed. A fourth plane, United Airlines flight 93 to San Francisco, crashed into a field in Somerset County, near Pittsburgh, at 10.06 am. It was presumably headed towards the White House when a number of passengers, who had heard about the WTC attacks by contacting the outside world on their cellphones, overwhelmed the hijackers in the cockpit, causing the plane to crash. All 265 passengers and crew members on the four planes died.

Immediately, the most damaging attack on US soil since 1812 caused pronouncements of solidarity by political leaders throughout the world. For the first time in the organization's history, *NATO invoked Article five of its founding treaty, stating that this attack on the US was treated as an attack on all NATO members. Within the first few weeks of the attack, the rumours about the culpability of Bin Laden hardened, and in a videotape released in October 2001 he all but admitted responsibility. The attacks triggered the ensuing *War on Terrorism led by the administration of George W. *Bush.

Serbia

A country which has dominated the history of the western Balkan region since the early twentieth century.

Early history (until 1992) After several uprisings, Serbia became autonomous within the *Ottoman Empire in 1830. It became an independent state after the Congress of Berlin in 1878, and was declared a kingdom in 1883. After the assassination of King Alexander I Obrenovic (1903), Peter I Karadordevic became King. Under his reign, parliamentary government was established, which came to be dominated by *Pasic, the leader of the Radical People's Party. As *Austria-Hungary advanced to annex neighbouring *Bosnia-Hercegovina in

1908, it came into increasing conflict with a self-confident Serbia, which did everything to block Austrian pretensions to Balkan predominance. Serbia emerged victorious and strengthened from the *Balkan Wars (1912–13), in which it almost doubled its territory. Growing tensions with an insecure but openly defiant Austria finally triggered the outbreak of World War I, after the assassination of Archduke Francis Ferdinand in *Sarajevo.

During the war, Serbia was occupied by Austrian troops, which forced the Serbian government and king to retreat to Corfu. There, it concluded the *Corfu Pact with representatives from Croatia and Slovenia, which became the basis after 1918 for the creation of the Kingdom of Serbs, Croats, and Slovenes under its regent *Alexander (king from 1921). In 1929, this became *Yugoslavia, though in practice the kingdom was dominated by Serbia, which developed into the most industrialized and politically influential part of *Yugoslavia. This did not change much after World War II, despite constitutional guarantees for the country's other constituent parts. After *Tito's death, its predominance became more openly challenged.

Milošević era (1992–2000) Slovenia, Croatia and Bosnia-Hercegovina had declared their independence by 1992, though under *Milošević, Serbia tried to prevent the break-up of Yugoslavia by force, supporting a civil war first in Slovenia, then Croatia, and finally (and most persistently) in Bosnia-Hercegovina. In 1995 Serbia reluctantly agreed to the *Dayton Agreement, in order to achieve a lifting of damaging international sanctions, and to consolidate Serb gains made in the *Bosnian Civil War.

Meanwhile, the Albanian-dominated province of Kosovo demanded a restoration and extension of its autonomy from 1992. These demands were repressed with increased brutality, which included, after 1996, targeted actions of ethnic cleansing carried out by Serbian army and police forces. Since Serbia refused to withdraw its forces from Kosovo, on 23 March 1999 NATO planes, led by the US air force, began an extensive bombing campaign. In over 35,000 sorties, government offices were destroyed and much of Serbia's economic infrastructure annihilated. After 73 days, Milošević succumbed and withdrew his forces from Kosovo. He consequently moved to secure his own power within Yugoslavia by attempting to change the constitution in his favour, and by reducing the influence of an increasingly distant Montenegro within the Yugoslav Federation.

Contemporary politics (since 2000) Against all expecations, the opposition managed to rally against the government on a nationalist platform led by *Koštunica. Milošević was swept from power by popular demonstrations in 2000. The subsequent years were spent rearranging the Yugoslav Federation into an even looser alliance to accommodate Montenegro. Under *Djindjić, the Serb government attempted to establish the rule of law against Belgrade's criminal underworld and *Milošević's still–powerfull allies. In 2003, these assassinated *Djindjić. In the absence of a charismatic successor, and owing to popular disillusionment with slow economic progress, the nationalist Serbian Radical Party won the elections of December 2003. More moderate forces rallied behind Koštunica, who became Prime Minister, with Boris *Tadic, leader of the pro-Western and pro-*European integration Democratic Party elected President in 2004.

Despite the concessions made to Montenegro, that territory declared its independence in 2006. While the breakup of this Union caused relatively little resistance, most Serbians continued to be resolutely opposed to the independence of Kosovo. The country became particularly divided over whether to respond to pressure to cooperate with the international Criminal Tribunal in The Hague and extradite former Serbian leaders for war crimes trials. Continued resistance to these demands slowed down economic reconstruction, as international aid and EU assistance were held back in response.

Sèvres, Treaty of (10 Aug. 1920)
A peace treaty after World War I, negotiated as part of the *Paris Peace Conferences and signed between the Allies and the *Ottoman Empire. Adrianople (Edirne), Eastern Thrace, and Smyrna (Izmir) were ceded to Greece. Rhodes and the Dodecanese Islands were passed on to Italy. A short-lived independent Republic of *Armenia was created, while *Kurdistan gained autonomy. The Ottoman Empire lost all of its Arab possessions: Syria became a French *League of Nations *Mandate, while Iraq, *Palestine, and Transjordan (*Jordan) became British Mandates. The Bosphorus and *Dardanelles were demilitarized and placed under international control, while the Ottoman army was restricted to a strength of 50,000 men. The treaty incensed Turkish nationalist opinion and united it around Mustafa Kemal (*Atatürk). It was never ratified by the Ottoman parliament. Kemal reclaimed Smyrna from Greece in a successful military campaign in 1922, which led to the treaty's

replacement by the Treaty of *Lausanne in 1923.

Seychelles

Under French sovereignty from 1743, the islands became part of the *British Empire in 1814. They were governed from Mauritius until they became a separate Crown Colony in 1903. In 1964, France-Albert René (b. 1935) founded the Seychelles People's United Party (SPUP) which demanded independence. It was opposed by the Seychelles Democratic Party (SDP), which was funded by the small, landowning (White) elite and demanded closer ties with the UK instead. The British granted universal suffrage in 1970, and autonomy in 1975. The islands became independent on 29 May 1976. René assumed power in a *coup* in 1977, and subsequently modelled his socialist policies on *Nyerere's example in Tanzania. The SPUP was reformed into the Seychelles People's Progressive Front (SPPF) in 1977. It promoted the development of tourism, which subsequently became the Seychelles' most important economic sector: in 1991, income from tourism was double that from all its other exports combined, making the Seychelles one of the most affluent states (per capita) in Africa. In the early 1990s René introduced some economic liberalization, as well as democratic reforms. René won the elections of 1993 and 1998. To persuade investors of the Republic's political stability despite a deep economic crisis, René called early elections in 2001, which he won amidst allegations of corruption from the opposition. René resigned in 2004, and was succeeded by his deputy, James Michel, who was confirmed in office by popular elections in 2006.

Seyss-Inquart, Arthur (b. 22 July 1892, d. 16 Oct. 1946). Austrian Nazi leader

Born into the German minority in Stannern (Moravia), he qualified and practised as a lawyer in Vienna. As an active member of various *Fascist movements he stood in close contact with the Austrian Nazi Party (National Socialists) from 1931, and joined the party in 1938. During the 1930s, he co-ordinated the activities of the Austrian *Fascists with the German *Nazi Party. In February 1938 he was imposed on *Schuschnigg as Minister of the

Interior. He became Chancellor after Schuschnigg's forced resignation on 11 March 1938, only to invite openly the already advancing German army into the country. He was made Governor of Austria by Hitler, and in 1939 Governor-General of Poland. As commissioner in the Netherlands (1940–5), he was responsible for the brutal Nazi regime there during the occupation, which led to thousands of summary executions, and the deportation to *concentration camps of hundreds of thousands of Jews and opponents of the regime. He was sentenced to death at the *Nuremberg Trials.

SFIO (Section Française de l'Internationale Ouvrière), see
SOCIALIST PARTY, FRANCE

Shamir, Yitzhak (b. 15 Oct. 1915). Prime Minister of Israel 1983–4, 1986–92

Born Yitzhak Yzernitzky in Rozhinay (Poland), he became a radical *Zionist while studying at Warsaw University. He emigrated to *Palestine in 1935, where he finished his degree at the Hebrew University in *Jerusalem. He joined the *Irgun in 1936, though in 1940 he attached himself to its more radical and militant breakaway group, the *Stern Gang. Captured twice by the British he escaped each time, finally finding political asylum in France before returning to the newly established state of Israel in 1948. After an initial unsuccessful attempt to enter parliament (the Knesset) in 1949, he became a businessman, a period interrupted by work for Israel's secret service (Mossad), 1955–65. Having left business, he began to work for *Begin's conservative Herut Party in 1970, and represented it in the Knesset from 1973.

Shamir's loyalty to Begin was severely tested, as he opposed the *Camp David Accords, which involved the withdrawal of Israeli troops and settlers from the Sinai peninsula. Nevertheless, as Foreign Minister from 1980 he supervised the implementation of the agreement, while supporting the formal annexation of the *Golan Heights in 1981. As Prime Minister, he was unable to achieve major legislation, as from 1984 he depended upon the fragile support of the *Labour Party. Nevertheless, he continued to encourage Jewish settlement in the *West Bank, while constantly frustrating efforts by the USA to find a compromise peace solution for the Middle East. He retired from political life in 1996.

Sharon, Ariel (b. 27 Feb. 1928). Prime Minister of Israel, 2001–6

Early career Born in Kfar Malal, he joined the *Haganah in 1942, and continued to serve in the military after the foundation of Israel. He graduated from Jerusalem Law School in 1962, and, following his service in the *Six Day War, he became commander of the army's southern command. Sharon resigned from active service after the *Yom Kippur War, and in 1973 entered parliament, the Knesset. He served as an adviser to Yitzhak *Rabin, and in 1977–81 he was appointed Minister for Agriculture under *Begin. As Minister of Defence from 1981, Sharon was responsible for Israel's invasion of the Lebanon, which aimed at destroying *Arafat's *PLO. Ironically, this action elevated Arafat's status, and a particular enmity between the two men emerged. He was Minister without Portfolio (1983–4) and Minister of Trade and Industry (1984–90), and from 1990 to 1992, as Minister of Construction, he oversaw a massive programme of Israeli construction to settle Jewish immigrants in the *West Bank. He entered *Netanyahu's government as Minister of National Infrastructure. As Foreign Minister from 1998, Sharon headed the negotiations with the Arafat's *Palestinian National Authority. Sharon led the *Likud opposition from 1999, and he bitterly opposed *Barak's peace negotiations with Arafat and the additional protocol to the *Wye Agreement that resulted from this.

In office Alleging that Barak was about to relinquish control of one of Judaism's holiest sites, the Temple Mount in Jerusalem, he staged a well-publicized visit on 27 September 2000. Since the Temple Mount contains some of the holiest sites for Muslims also, Palestinians considered this a spectacular provocation. In the following days, the *Intifadah broke out again. The renewed violence made the negotiation of a peace agreement impossible for any Israeli Prime Minister, and in a special election in 2001 Sharon was elected on his promise of toughness instead. The growing cycle of violence culminated in the occupation of Palestine by Israeli troops in March 2002. He also scored a victory against Arafat when the latter was forced to concede power to a Cabinet led by a Prime Minister. Sharon faced strong right-wing opposition to any conciliatory gestures in the pursuit of peace.

Having done much to avert a peace settlement with Palestinians, in his last eighteen months in office Sharon changed course. Convinced that no Palestinian leadership was likely to be strong enough to negotiate and ensure a peace settlement, he decided that Israel had to establish a resolution of its borders itself. He thus decided that Israel should pull out of Gaza unilaterally, and promised to impose a border on the West

Bank unilaterally. Having lost the support of his own party for these plans, Sharon founded a new party, *Kadima. Before he could lead it to new elections, he suffered a severe stroke, leaving him permanently in a comatose state.

Sharpeville Massacre (21 Mar. 1960)

A massacre caused by the police opening fire on demonstrators from the *PAC in the Black township of Sharpeville (near Vereeniging, Transvaal), in which sixty-nine people were killed and 186 injured. It came to symbolize the repressive nature of the White regime, triggering large-scale protests from the PAC and *ANC. At the same time, it allowed the White *apartheid regime to tighten its grip on the country through increased repression, declaring a state of emergency and outlawing both the PAC and the ANC. This almost destroyed Black nationalist opposition in the subsequent decade, while the 'stability' thus imposed heralded a period of unequalled economic growth.

Shastri, Lal Bahadur (b. 2 Oct. 1904, d. 11 Jan. 1966). Prime Minister of India 1964–6

Born in Moghalsarai, he joined *Gandhi's call for non-cooperation in his first *satyagraha in 1921, and dropped his studies. He resumed his degree afterwards, and graduated in 1926 with a first-class degree (Shastri), from which he took his name. Deeply impressed and influenced by Gandhi's ideals, he became a loyal follower, first of Gandhi, and then of *Nehru. He joined the latter's government and became one of Nehru's principal lieutenants, first as Minister for Railways (1951–6), and then in a variety of other functions, including Minister of Home Affairs. He was chosen as Nehru's successor owing to his conciliatory manner. Shastri was a remarkably skilful politician, and defended India well against attack in the second *Indo-Pakistan War of 1965. The war was formally ended in the *Tashkent Agreement of 10 January 1966; he died the following day, still in Tashkent, of a heart attack.

Shevardnadze, Eduard Amvrosievich (b. 25 Jan. 1928). President of Georgia 1992–2003

Early career Born in Mamati, he joined the *Communist Party in 1948 and became a leading member of the Communist Youth League, whose Georgian leader (first secretary) he became in 1957. He then worked in the Communist party machine and became Deputy Minister (1964–5), and then First Minister (1965–72) of the Georgian Ministry of Public Order. There, he worked assiduously to reduce the influence of the local *Mafia, and in 1972 took his case against the Mafia activities of his local party boss, V. P. Mzhavanadze, to *Brezhnev. He was appointed first secretary of the Communist Party of Georgia in Mzhavanadze's stead, and became the most reform-oriented leader of a Soviet republic, within the limits tolerated by Brezhnev. A candidate member of the *Politburo from 1978, he supported *Gorbachev, whom he had known since the 1960s, in his rise to power.

Soviet Foreign Minister (1985–90, 1991) His appointment to replace the grim and dreary Andrei Andreevich Gromyko (b. 1909, d. 1989) as Foreign Minister was the first indication of Gorbachev's earnest will to reform. His charm, efficiency, and imagination contributed greatly to the success of the country's more relaxed foreign policy and the establishment of a genuine working relationship with US Presidents *Reagan and *Bush. He resigned to general surprise on 20 December 1990, apparently in protest against Gorbachev's increasingly unpopular policies. In November 1991, he returned to his office after the *August *coup* against Gorbachev until the dissolution of the Soviet Union on 31 December 1991.

Shevardnadze became President of the newly founded Republic of Georgia on 10 March 1992, and subsequently used his energy again to fight against Mafia corruption, to end his country's civil war, and to prevent the breakaway of *Abkhazia. Although he was relatively unsuccessful in realizing any of these goals, he did manage to achieve some degree of economic and political stabilization. Russian soldiers began to withdraw from Georgian territory in 2000, and in 1999 he inaugurated an oil pipeline from Azerbaijan. As his popularity waned, Shevardnadze lacked the political strength to carry out domestic reform. After rigging the 2003 elections, he was deposed in the 'rose revolution'.

Shi'ite

The smaller of the two main branches of *Islam which is the Shi'at Ali (the Party of Ali), as it recognizes Ali's claim to succeed his cousin and father-in-law, the Prophet Muhammad, as the spiritual leader of Islam during the first civil war in the Islamic world (AD 656–61). In most of the Islamic world the *Sunnis are in a majority, but the Shi'ites comprise around 80 million adherents, or 13 per cent of all Muslims. They are predominant in Iran, Iraq, and the United Arab Emirates.

Shining Path, see SENDERO LUMINOSO

Shipley, Jenny (b. 4. Feb. 1952). Prime Minister of New Zealand, 1997–9

Born in Gore, she graduated from Christchurch Teachers College in 1971. She settled down near Ashburton (central Canterbury), and became active in politics for the *National Party. Shipley was elected as a Member of Parliament for her constituency in 1987. In 1990 she became Minister for Social Welfare and Women's Affairs, and in 1994 she became Minister for Health. As such, she was responsible for introducing a radical reform of the welfare system. This entailed a privatization of much of the health system, and a reduction in social security. She succeeded Jim *Bolger as Prime Minister in 1997. She continued her predecessor's coalition with the New Zealand First Party for half a year, but when the coalition broke apart in 1998 she headed a minority government. She retired as Leader of the Opposition in 2001.

Siam, see THAILAND

Sierra Leone

A poor west African state whose history suffered from the absence of clear political or tribal structures.

Contemporary history (up to 2000) Freetown in west Africa was set up by the British in 1788, as a refuge for escaped slaves (mainly from the Americas). Established as the first British Crown Colony in Africa in 1808, its hinterland was explored from 1890 and declared a British protectorate in 1896, though it was administered separately until 1951.

Sierra Leone gained independence on 27 April 1961, under Prime Minister Sir Milton Margai (b. 1895, d. 1964) of the Sierra Leone People's Party. The latter's domination was brought to an end by a military coup in 1967, and a further coup established the predominance of the All People's Congress (APC) under Siaka P. Stevens. He extended his power in a one-party state in 1978, and survived several coup attempts and domestic instabilities until his retirement in 1985. He was succeeded by Joseph S. Momoh (b. 1937, d. 2003), who formed a civilian government in the same year. Momoh was deposed on 30 April 1992 in a military coup by Valentine Strasser (b. 1965). This sparked off ethnic violence, which had been more or less under the surface since independence, leading to anarchy, civil war, and the displacement of one-third of the population.

As the rebels advanced, Strasser announced his readiness for reconciliation, which led to presidential elections in February and March 1996. These were won by Ahmed Tejan Kabbah of the Sierra Leone People's Party, but although they were generally considered fair, they failed to impress the guerrilla Revolutionary United Front (RUF) under Foday Sankoh, which continued its military operations. In April 1996 the civil war continued with renewed ferocity. Tejan Kabbah was deposed in a coup in 1997, but returned six months later in a deal with the rebels brokered by *ECOWAS. Fighting against the rebels continued, with the RUF gradually extending its hold over the diamond-rich interior. The civil war led to a humanitarian catastrophe, as over one million refugees were estimated to be uprooted within the country, with a further 500,000 refugees being put up in camps in neighbouring Guinea and Liberia.

Contemporary politics (since 2000) In 2000 a contingent of 800 elite British troops landed in Freetown to support the government, secure the capital and train government soldiers. This led to the first successes in the government's fight against the RUF, which in turn became more conciliatory. In 2002, a peace agreement was signed, with Tejan Kabbah winning the elections of that year. Starting from extremely low levels, the economy began to recover, though most of the benefits resulting from the country's diamond resources eluded the population. As the country attempted to recover from the brutal legacy of the civil war, a *Truth and Reconciliation Commission was set up.

(()) SEE WEB LINKS

- The official website of the Truth and Reconciliation Commission of Sierra Leone, which contains an account of its findings.

Sihanouk, Norodom (b. 31 Oct. 1922). King of Cambodia 1941–55, 1993–2004; President of Cambodia 1960–70, 1975–6, 1991–3

Born Prince Samdech Preah at Pnom Penh, he was placed on the throne in 1941 by the French Governor-General on the death of his grandfather. When the French returned after World War II he chose to cooperate with them despite nationalist opposition, in order to gain eventual independence. This was finally granted in 1953, in the context of the *Indochina War. He abdicated in favour of his father and became Prime Minister. Sihanouk built up his own political movement, and suppressed all other parties, which gave him control of Cambodian affairs until 1970. He steered a neutral course between the USA and the USSR, which became all the more difficult after the outbreak of the *Vietnam War.

In 1970 he was deposed in a US-backed coup by *Lon Nol. Sihanouk was offered asylum by *Zhou Enlai (Chou En-lai) in China, where he founded the National United Front of Cambodia. He returned in 1975 and became nominal head of state under *Pol Pot, but in 1976 was put under house arrest. He went into exile again after the Vietnamese invasion in 1979. In 1982 he became President of an exiled coalition government, in alliance with the *Khmer Rouge. He thus gradually managed to unite the opposition parties behind him, and be accepted by the *UN as the official representative of the country. In a remarkable comeback, he was able to return as interim President in 1991, after the Vietnamese withdrawal from the country. He was proclaimed King, albeit with largely ceremonial powers, in 1993, and retired eleven years later owing to ill-health.

Sikhism

A religion which emerged from a community gathered around the Guru Nanak (b. 1469, d. 1539). Nanak accepted the mission of the Prophet Muhammad, as an agent of the Hindu supreme being Brahman, the path to whom lies through many incarnations. Sikhism soon spread throughout *Punjab, and the fourth guru, Ram Das, established the holy city of *Amritsar. Subsequently, Sikhs were in conflict with Moghuls, Afghans, and other peoples and religions, which led to the particular development of humility and sincerity on the one hand, and the sword on the other, as the twin pillars of the religious community. Ironically, it was when the line of personal gurus became extinct with the death of the tenth guru, Gobind Singh, that the Sikhs achieved their greatest power, with the creation of an independent Sikh kingdom by Ranjit Singh in 1799.

Under British rule since 1849, in the late nineteenth and early twentieth centuries Sikh identity was strengthened through their distinct, preferential treatment by the British. In addition, the Sikh Sabha movement produced a revival in Sikh culture, language, and literature. In Sikhism, caste distinctions were formally abolished, making this a much less prominent feature than in *Hinduism. After independence, when the Sikh homeland, the Punjab, was partitioned between India and Pakistan, most Sikhs lived in India, where they formed over 50 per cent of the population in the state of Punjab.

Nevertheless, there continued a strong movement for independence, which operated in the line of the Sikh militant tradition of the sword. There are a total of about 20 million Sikhs worldwide.

AMRITSAR MASSACRE (1984)

Sikkim

An erstwhile Buddhist kingdom, it was subject to many aggresive encroachments by Buthan, Nepal, and, finally, China, so that Britain declared a protectorate over the small state in 1889. Ruled feudally by chogyals (kings), it transferred to an Indian protectorate after 1947, though it retained its own internal autonomy. India defended its northern border in the 1962 *Indo-Chinese War. Popular pressure for incorporation into India was finally successful, against the resistance of the chogyals, after a 1974 referendum. It was incorporated as the twenty-second state of the Indian Union on 16 May 1975.

Sikorski, Władysław (b. 20 May 1881, d. 4 July 1943). Polish general and statesman

Born in Tuszów Narodowy (Galicia), Sikorski studied engineering at the universities of Lvov and Kraców. In World War I he joined *Pilsudski in the fight against the Russians. He was interned by Germany which refused to recognize Polish independence (1917–18). In the *Russo-Polish War he commanded troops against the *Red Army at Vilnius and then Warsaw. He became Chief of the Polish General Staff (1921–2) and then Prime Minister (1922–3), and intermittently Minister of War until 1925. He opposed Pilsudski's regime, which gave him an army command only in 1928.

In the dying days of Polish resistance against the German invasion, Sikorski became Prime Minister and Minister of War, and thereafter escaped to London to head the Polish government-in-exile. He succeeded in maintaining a tolerable relationship with *Stalin until news of the *Katyn massacre, signing the Polish–Soviet agreement of 30 July 1941. His death in an aeroplane crash deprived the Polish government-in-exile of its legitimate leader who was able to maintain internal discipline, and who was recognized by the Allies. His death made all the easier the imposition after liberation of a Communist government under *Gierek.

Silesia

A prosperous area in central Europe, which from 1763 until 1918 was divided between Prussia, which controlled over 80 per cent of the territory, and Austria. After World War I, following a series of plebiscites, Upper Silesia (the coal and steel-producing area) went to Poland and most of Austrian Silesia to Czechoslovakia. Germany retained Lower Silesia. As part of the *Munich Agreement, the Czech areas of *Teschen were occupied by Poland in 1938. In 1945, almost all of Silesia was put under Polish administration. This led to the expulsion of over 1.5 million German Silesians 1945–6, and a further half million in the following years. West Germany formally recognized the area as Polish in 1990, as a prelude to German unification.

GERMAN QUESTION

Simitis, Costas (b. 23 June 1936). Prime Minister of Greece, 1996–2004

Born in Athens, he studied law at Marburg (Germany) and then at the London School of Economics. Back in Greece he joined the political resistance before being forced into exile. He held a number of university posts in Germany, before returning to Greece in 1974. He co-founded the pansocialist Hellenic movement (PASOK), and became a minister in 1981, succeeding Andreas *Papandreou in 1996. Under Simitis, relations with Turkey improved in unprecedented ways. Simitis introduced a series of economic reforms, as a result of which Greece confounded expectations by qualifying for adopting the *euro in 2002. The effects of economic growth were felt very unevenly, so that Simitis became quite unpopular. As a result, he resigned as PASOK leader in an attempt to enable his successor, George Papandreou, to do better in the forthcoming elections. His party lost, and he was succeeded as Prime Minister by Kostas Karamanlis.

Simon Commission (1927–30)

A commission established by *Baldwin to inquire into political conditions in British India. It consisted of seven members, and was chaired jointly by John *Simon and Clement *Attlee. It met a hostile reception in India, and was boycotted there because it had no Indian members. It recommended giving greater autonomy to Indian provincial governments, but maintaining a veto for the Viceroy. It also rejected parliamentary government for India as a whole. The report was discussed at the *Round Table Conferences, and it had some influence on the 1935 *Government of India Act.

Simon, John Allsebrook, 1st Viscount Simon of Stackpole Elidor

(b. 28 Feb. 1873, d. 11 Jan. 1954). British Foreign Secretary 1931–5

Born in Manchester, and educated at Fettes and Oxford. He was called to the Bar in 1899, and was elected to parliament for the *Liberal Party to represent Walthamstow in 1906. In 1910, he was appointed Solicitor-General, and in 1913 entered the Cabinet as Attorney-General. Despite his initial opposition to British participation in World War I, *Asquith made him Foreign Secretary (1915–16). However, he resigned in opposition to conscription. He then served with the Royal Flying Corps. He lost his seat in the 1918 *Coupon Election, but returned to parliament in 1922, representing Spen Valley. He served as chairman of a commission on India (1927–30), which issued the *Simon Report, advocating greater Indian participation in government.

As leader of the breakaway Liberal Nationals, he was Foreign Secretary in *MacDonald's *National Government in 1931. He supported disarmament and *appeasement, and felt unable to intervene rigorously during the Manchurian crisis of 1931 (*Manchukuo). Meanwhile, the *Ottawa Agreements further divided Simon's Liberal Nationals from the rest of the Liberals led by *Samuel, who left the government. Simon remained, as Home Secretary under Baldwin (1935–7), Chancellor of the Exchequer under N. *Chamberlain (1937–40), and Lord Chancellor in *Churchill's coalition (1940–5). By the end of his career, he and his Liberal National followers had become Conservatives in all but name.

Singapore

An island state on the tip of the Malay peninsula, it has become one of the world's most prosperous economies, embodying like no other the ideal of an Asian 'tiger economy'.

Foreign rule (up to 1965) Singapore was recognized as a British settlement in 1823, and became a British Crown Colony in 1867. As a gateway from India to eastern Asia and Australia, its commercial and military importance grew, so that it became home to the largest British naval base in Asia and Australia. The surrender of Singapore to the advancing Japanese in 1942, therefore, came as a great strategic and military blow for the British, whose ability to defend the *British Empire had been effectively destroyed. Liberated after the Japanese surrender on 3

September 1945, it became a separate colony and in 1959 achieved internal self-government, with *Lee Kuan Yew elected Chief Minister. For a small city-state surrounded by Malayan territory, integration seemed inevitable, and in 1963 it joined the newly created Federation of Malaysia. However, its Chinese majority soon rebelled against the discrimination against Chinese in Malaysia, where they were in a minority. By mutual consent, Singapore left the federation in 1965 and became an independent state, though it retained its strong commercial links with Malaysia.

Independence (from 1965) With the help of strong government interference, Singapore became one of the world's fastest-growing economies, with an annual average growth in GDP of over 6 per cent per head (1980–93). By 1995 the GDP per head had surpassed that of Britain and equalled that of Canada. The Prime Minister since 1990, Goh Chok Tong, maintained Lee Kuan Yew's policies, as he tried to cope with the problems of economic success, e.g. overcoming his country's labour shortage through the promotion of capital-intensive industries. At the same time, he tried to lure investment away from *Hong Kong as it approached Chinese rule in 1997. These economic policies proved relatively successful, as Singapore proved to some extent immune to the Asian economic crisis from 1997.

Contemporary politics (since 1997) The government continued to focus on investment in education, finance, and high technology. Singapore also keenly promoted regional integration through *ASEAN, in order to promote economic liberalization to benefit its own export-led economy. Goh Chok Tong was succeeded by his deputy, Lee Hsien Loong, who was the eldest son of Lee Kuan Yew. Goh continued to act as a senior advisor to Lee, thus cementing a small oligarchy's hold on power.

Singapore, fall of (World War II) (8–15 Feb. 1942)
The largest British army and naval base in Asia and Australia with around 80,000 British, Australian, and Indian troops under A. E. Percival (*Wavell) in 1941, Singapore was equipped with strong coastal defences. However, no fortifications had been built against attack from its Malayan hinterland, which was also under British control. After swiftly overrunning Malaya (*Malayan campaign), Japanese forces under General *Yamashita massed opposite the island of Singapore at the beginning of February 1942.

During the night of 7/8 February armoured landing craft crossed the Strait of Johore, followed by many swimming Japanese troops, surprising the garrison of Australian troops opposite. The defenders blew up the single causeway connecting Singapore with its hinterland and retreated. The causeway was quickly repaired by the Japanese who, supported by the superiority of their air force, moved on to the island. On 15 February, Percival surrendered. The fall of Singapore, long perceived as an invincible fortress of the *British Empire, symbolized more than any other event the real weakness of Britain's pretensions to defend and control her vast Empire. This provided an important stimulus to colonial independence movements after World War II, and foreshadowed the process of *decolonization after 1945.

Singh, Manmohan (b. 26 Sept 1932). Prime Minister of India, 2004–
Born in Punjab, he graduated from Cambridge with a first-class degree in Economics. He received his doctorate from Nuffield College, Oxford University, and joined the Delhi School of Economics. Singh served as economics adviser to the government in 1971, and thereafter held a number of high public offices, including governor of the Reserve Bank of India. As Finance Minister (1991–6), he introduced a number of market-oriented reforms that initiated a sustained period of economic stability and growth. These policies were largely maintained by *Vajpayee. When the Indian National *Congress returned to power in 2004, Sonia *Gandhi supported Singh's appointment as Prime Minister, not least to reassure international and national observers of the new government's commitment to financial probity. Although not the most charismatic politician, Singh's low-key manner has been successful at integrating a highly disparate governing coalition, which has included the *Communist Party (CPM), and committing it to his liberal economic policies.

Single European Act (1986)
The first substantial revision of the Treaty of *Rome, which added to the principle of the common market the four freedoms—of goods, persons, services and capital. Signed in 1986, the Act came into effect on 1 July 1987, and its goals were to be realized by 1 January 1993. In response to the extension of European Community concerns, decision-making was simplified: *Qualified Majority Voting was adopted on a range of issues affecting the internal market, so that unanimity was no longer required. The

*European Council was formally recognized as the most important intergovernmental body of the European Community. The *European Parliament also received greater powers. The Single European Act was unsuccessful in a number of immediate goals, especially as freedom of services in the capital market proved difficult to realize. However, its effects were far-reaching and immediate. The freedom of persons, for instance, allowed every individual to settle anywhere within the EC and enjoy virtually all the social, legal, and employment rights of the host nation. The SEA set in motion an accelerating process of *European integration. Negotiations about a single currency, which was in itself not a new idea, began in earnest in 1988, as a single currency was pushed by the *European Commission under *Delors as the logical corollary to a single market.

EUROPEAN INTEGRATION

Sinn Féin (Ireland)

Sinn Féin (Irish Gaelic: 'we ourselves') grew out of a nationalist movement articulated by Arthur *Griffith between 1905 and 1908. It was initially an intellectual movement calling for an independent Ireland under a dual monarchy along the model of *Austria-Hungary. In 1912 it opposed the Home Rule party of John *Redmond, and became gradually more politically active (although it took no direct part in the 1916 *Easter Rising). In the 1918 British *Coupon Elections it won 73 seats, as compared with 25 for the Irish Unionists, and used this success to claim a mandate for an independent Ireland. The Sinn Féin MPs refused to attend *parliament at Westminster, and set up a parliament in Dublin, the Dáil Éireann (the Irish parliament, not yet recognized as sovereign), in 1919. The party split over the treaty partition of Ireland (1921–2), with the anti-treaty wing fighting against the Irish Free State during the Civil War (1922–3). The party declined following this, with many of its members joining *de Valéra's *Fianna Fáil.

Sinn Féin revived in *Northern Ireland as Provisional Sinn Féin in January 1970, following the split within the Irish Republican Army (*IRA). As the IRA's political wing, it has called for British withdrawal from Northern Ireland, and the subsequent establishment of a united Ireland. It has contested elections on the basis that it will not take up seats in the UK parliament if elected. Its electoral support was relatively modest (around 10 per cent or less), but increased sharply following the *Downing Street Declaration. It gained 15.5 per cent in the elections of 30 May 1996 for delegates to all-party peace talks.

After a renewed ceasefire in 1997 it became instrumental in the *Good Friday Agreement. Under the leadership of Gerry *Adams, Sinn Féin was transformed from being seen as an extremist Catholic party and the political arm of the IRA to being the main Catholic Party of Northern Ireland by 2001. It became the only party with parliamentary representation at *Westminster, the Northern Ireland Assembly, and the Irish parliament, the Dáil Éireann. In the 2003 Northern Ireland elections, it obtained 23.5 per cent of the vote. As the central Roman Catholic political party, it became crucial to any political agreement. In 2006 it agreed with *Paisley's *Democratic Unionists the *St Andrews Agreement. This provided for elections in March 2007, in which it increased its representation in the Northern Ireland Assembly to 28. It was thus destined to enter a Northern Irish government with the *Democratic Unionist Party.

(⊕) SEE WEB LINKS

• The official website of Sinn Féin.

Sino-Japanese War (1937–45)

Although the Japanese had occupied Manchuria since 1931 and created the colony of *Manchukuo there, the attention of the *National Government under *Chiang Kai-shek had been diverted by its attempt to overcome the Chinese *Communist Party (CCP). Chiang was eventually forced by his own generals (led by *Chang Hsüeh-liang) at *Xi'an to declare a truce with the Communists and form a *United Front against the Japanese. The *Marco Polo Bridge Incident of 1937 provided the trigger for hostilities, leading to the rapid advance of the well-equipped *Guandong Army. Within six months, the Japanese had taken most of the Yangtze Valley, Guangzhou (Canton), and the capital of the National Government, *Nanjing (Nanking). Chiang recognized, however, that ultimately the Japanese lacked the numbers to conquer the whole of China, and by 1939 their advance had halted. Chiang's *National Republican Army engaged the Japanese in open warfare, while *Mao Zedong's Communist Red Army weakened the Japanese through guerrilla attacks. War was formally declared only after the Japanese attack on *Pearl Harbor. Thereafter, the Japanese were diverted in military operations throughout the *Pacific and south-eastern Asia, while Chiang received some US aid. The Japanese were eventually defeated in World War II.

The main significance of the war for China lay in the reversal of relative strength between Communist and Nationalist forces. While the

Communists grew in strength through peasant support, secured through effective administration and land reforms, the Nationalists' strength declined rapidly during the war through heavy losses incurred in frontal assaults against the Japanese. In this sense, it served as a prelude to the Communist victory in the *Chinese Civil War (1946–9).
YAN'AN

Sino-Soviet frontier dispute (1969)

The exact position of the border between north-east China and the Soviet Union had long been a matter of dispute. The disagreement turned into a military confrontation because of worsening ideological differences between the two countries after 1960, and the militant *nationalism which was part of the *Cultural Revolution. In March 1969 two battles were fought for possession of the small island of Zhen Bao (Damansky) in the Ussuri River. The Chinese ultimately retained control, and talks in September 1969 brought the crisis to an end. In 1977 there was a limited agreement on rules of navigation on the river, but tension continued along the frontier until 1989.

Six Day War (5–10 June 1967)

The immediate causes of the war were Egyptian pressure on the *UN Emergency Force in Sinai to withdraw from the Israeli frontier, and a build-up of Egyptian forces in Sinai during May 1967. At the same time Egypt launched a new naval blockade in the Gulf of Aqaba off the Israeli port of Eilat. Meanwhile, Israel was encircled as Jordan, Syria, and Egypt concluded a defence agreement, while Iraqi troops were stationed in Jordan, close to Israeli territory. Brilliant use of weaponry and paratroops brought Israeli troops to the Suez Canal within two days, encircling the Egyptian Sinai army. Following the shelling of Israeli targets by Syria and Jordan, the war widened. Eastern *Jerusalem was seized and the whole of the *West Bank was cleared of Jordanian troops. In the north (9–10 June) Israeli tanks occupied the *Golan Heights, captured Kuneitra, and advanced 30 miles into Syria. In pre-emptive air strikes the Egyptian air force was destroyed on the ground, while other airfields in Syria, Iraq, and Jordan were also bombed. Jordan accepted a UN cease-fire on 7 June, Egypt on 8 June, Syria on 9 June, and Israel on 10 June. The war was over.

Israel now occupied the whole of Sinai, including the *Gaza Strip, and Israeli troops remained established on the east bank of the Suez Canal until the *Yom Kippur War. In some respects, however, the Israeli victory had ambiguous consequences. In particular, Israeli occupation of the West Bank and the Gaza Strip transformed the problem of self-determination for the Palestinian people from one that concerned Arab countries and Israel alike to one of exclusively Israeli concern. Instead of dividing the Arab countries, the 'Palestinian problem' now united them against Israel (see *Palestine).

Slánski Trial (Nov. 1952)

Rudolf Slánski (b. 1901) was one of the earliest members of the Czechoslovak Communist Party. A ruthless ideologue, he was a committed and loyal supporter of *Stalin. He was general secretary of the party from 1944, and played an instrumental role in the establishment of the Communist state in 1948. After the *anti-Semitic purges of the late 1940s in the USSR, and also e.g. in Hungary under *Rákosi, Stalin put great pressure on *Gottwald to agree to a number of show trials to eradicate supposed Jewish and *Titoist influence from the Communist Party. Slánski was arrested on 23 November 1951 and, under torture, he admitted all the charges laid before him, including accusations of 'cosmopolitanism' (i.e. *Zionism). Together with ten fellow Jews, he was entenced to death on 26 November 1952, and hanged on 3 December. He was rehabilitated posthumously during the *Prague Spring in May 1968.

Slim, William Joseph, 1st Viscount

(b. 6 Aug. 1891, d. 14 Dec. 1970). British field marshal

Born in Bristol, and educated at King Edward's School (Birmingham). He worked for an engineering company before enlisting in the Royal Warwickshire Regiment at the outbreak of World War I. He served at *Gallipoli and was commissioned. Slim joined the Indian army in 1919, where he served until World War II. He commanded Indian troops in successful campaigns against *Vichy French forces in Syria in 1941. In the *Burma Campaigns he fought the Japanese forces which were approaching the Indian frontier. In October 1943, he took command of the newly formed 14th Army. He resisted Japan's Imphal offensive in March 1944, and after victory at Kohima, moved down the Irrawaddy River, subsequently recapturing Rangoon and most of Burma in 1944–5. A formidable character who could speak a variety of Indian languages, his crushing defeat of the Japanese ensured his reputation. He was later Chief of the Imperial General Staff (1948–52), and Governor-General of Australia (1953–60).

Slovakia

An independent republic in east central Europe, whose population, under the strain of economic transformation, has oscillated between populist nationalism and the politics of economic reform.

Before independence (up to 1993) Slovakia formed the eastern part of *Czechoslovakia from 1918, but many Slovaks soon felt disillusioned by a government composed of largely Czech elites which appeared to ignore their concerns. Slovakia experienced World War II very differently from the Czech lands, as it was governed by a *Nazi puppet government under *Tiso. Even though the Slovak revolt against the regime on 29 August 1944 was easily repressed by the Germans, it nevertheless provided an important boost for Slovak self-confidence. After the war, the Slovak self-image of heroic resistance soured relations with the Czechs, who had not undertaken a similar revolt. The Communist government tried to placate the Slovaks by transferring whole industries from the Czech lands to the agrarian Slovakia. Nevertheless, during the 1950s and 1960s, Slovak resentment was channelled through the Slovak Communist Party, which was increasingly resentful of the *Stalinism of *Gottwald and *Novotny, who were both Czech. A rebellion of the Slovak wing of the party resulted in the leadership of the Slovak *Dubček, and the reforms of the *Prague Spring.

Disappointment at the failure of the Prague Spring was barely muted by the fact that the hardline *Husák was also a Slovak. In the subsequent two decades Slovak distinctiveness received little official recognition. Slovak desires for greater autonomy resurfaced during and after the *Velvet Revolution of 1989, and ultimately led to independence on 1 January 1993.

Political transformation (1993–2006) Ethnically less homogeneous than the Czech Republic, the first years of independence were marked by sporadic hostility against the Hungarian minority (10 per cent of the population), while on 15 November 1995 Slovak was reaffirmed as the country's only official language. The first years of independence were characterized by the increasingly autocratic rule of Vladimir Mečiar, who tried to entrench his own rule and that of his Movement for a Democratic Slovakia (HZDS). This led to frequent confrontations with the President, Kováč, and caused mounting popular protests. Under Mečiar, economic growth and foreign investment slowed, with the lack of reform endangering Slovakia's entry into the EU.

The 1998 elections resulted in a landslide victory for the disparate opposition movement. Under the Prime Minister, Mikuláš Dzurinda, the economy developed with breathtaking speed into a model economy in Europe. Dzurinda strengthened political institutions, notably in local and regional government, guaranteed rights for ethnic minorities, and established an independent judiciary. As a result of these reforms, Slovakia was able to complete negotiations with the EU in time for accession in 2004. Benefiting from very low tax rates and low labour costs, GDP per capita increased by over 4 per cent after 2000.

Contemporary politics (since 2006) Economic development was uneven, however, with the imbalance between rich and poor growing. Discontent against Dzurinda's liberal policies grew. In the 2006 elections, the increase in the popular vote for Dzurinda's party was far outpaced by the populist socialist Smer Party. Its leader, Robert Fico, formed a coalition with the HZDS and became Prime Minister.

Slovenia

A small Alpine republic, Slovenia formed the wealthiest state of Yugoslavia, and became the most prosperous and politically stable central and eastern European country to join the EU in 2004.

Yugoslavia (1918–91) A part of Austria since 1282, it maintained its linguistic and cultural distinctiveness, which experienced a resurgence from the late nineteenth century. After World War I Slovenia became part of the Kingdom of Serbs, Croats, and Slovenes (Yugoslavia from 1929), though at the Treaty of *St Germain it failed to realize its claims for southern Carinthia, which remained part of Austria. Its relative wealth within Yugoslavia derived largely from its mineral resources, though Slovenia also developed an economy based on skilled labour, attracting much foreign investment.

During World War II, the north was annexed as part of Austria, while the south became part of Italy. After the war, it regained its territorial integrity, including the areas on the Istrian peninsula which had been lost to Italy since 1920. It became part of a Federal Yugoslavia in 1946, ruled by the Communist *Tito until 1980. In response to the collapse of *Communism in Eastern Europe and to growing Serbian *nationalism, a constitutional amendment was introduced in September 1989, in which it reserved the right to secede.

Contemporary history (since 1991) With *Croatia, Slovenia declared its independence on 25 June 1991. Like its southern neighbour, it was subject to military intervention by the Serb-dominated Yugoslav army, but the ensuing civil war ended swiftly. On 18 July 1991, its independence was effectively recognized by Yugoslavia (Serbia). The reason for the brevity of the war, in marked contrast to that of its neighbour Croatia as well as *Bosnia-Hercegovina, was its unusual ethnic homogeneity, with over 90 per cent Slovenes and only 2 per cent Serbians. It did not directly border on Serbia, which was in danger of overstretching its military resources, given its involvement in the conflicts in Croatia and Bosnia.

After a short period of economic adjustment to *capitalism, Slovenia developed a dynamic economy. From 1990, it was led by Milan Kučan, while the government consisted of a surprisingly stable five-party coalition led by the Liberal Democratic Party (LDP). The economy adapted to the conditions of a market economy so effectively that Slovenia became the wealthiest of the twelve applicants for membership of the European Union, and the first to adopt the *euro in 2007. The LDP had extended its power in 2000, but lost the 2004 elections to the centre-right Democratic Party, led by Janez Jansa. The government continued the liberal economic policies of its predecessor, announcing widespread privatizations.

Smallwood, Joseph Roberts ('Joey') (b. 24 Dec. 1900, d. 17 Dec. 1991). Premier of Newfoundland 1949–72
Born at Gambo (Newfoundland), Smallwood became a journalist and radio broadcaster, and ran a piggery at the air base in Gander during World War II. In 1946, he was elected to a convention called to advise the British government on the future status of the

colony. His tireless advocacy of confederation with Canada paid off when a second referendum on 22 July 1948 narrowly approved incorporation with Canada. Subsequently remembered as 'the last father of confederation', he became Premier of the interim government of Newfoundland on 1 April 1949, and was made leader of the provincial *Liberal Party. Despite some idiosyncratic economic policies, which included an abortive attempt at industrialization, he brought greater prosperity to the region as a result of successfully lobbying for generous federal spending. Faced with an increasingly critical public, he lost the leadership in 1972, and retired in 1977.

Smith, Ian Douglas (b. 8 Apr. 1919). Prime Minister of Rhodesia 1965–79
Born in Rhodesia, he served in the British Royal Air Force (1941–6). After his return to Rhodesia he joined the United Party and became a member of the South Rhodesian Legislative Assembly (1948–53). Upon the creation of the *Central African Federation he became chief whip of the United Federal Party (UFP) in the new federal parliament in 1953. He broke with the UFP in 1961 and proceeded to co-found the right-wing, segregationist, and racist Rhodesian Front (RF), as whose leader he was elected Prime Minister of Rhodesia. In an effort to preserve racial discrimination despite British hostility, he proclaimed the Unilateral Declaration of Independence in 1965, declaring Rhodesia a republic in 1970. International pressure, as well as increasingly successful guerrilla organizations led by *Mugabe and *Nkomo forced him to concede the principle of Black majority rule from the mid-1970s. However, his obstinate, although ultimately abortive, efforts to enshrine the predominant position of Whites in a new Constitution prolonged the civil war until 1979, when an agreement was reached with the Black opposition. Succeeded by *Muzorewa and then by Mugabe, he led White opposition in Zimbabwe immediately following independence in 1980, though he became increasingly marginalized as the Whites came to trust Mugabe.

Smith, John (b. 13 Sept. 1938, d. 12 May 1994). British Labour leader 1992–4
Born in Dalmally, Strathclyde, and educated at Dunoon Grammar School, and Glasgow University. He was called to the Scottish Bar in 1967, and was elected to parliament for the *Labour Party, to represent Lanarkshire North (1970–83) and Monklands East (1983–94). He held junior offices under Harold *Wilson

from 1975, and entered the Cabinet as Secretary of State for Trade and Industry (1978–9). In opposition, he held a number of portfolios, before becoming Neil *Kinnock's Shadow Chancellor in 1987. In this post, he excelled in parliamentary debate, although his shadow budget before the 1992 election did little to improve the party's prospects. He succeeded Kinnock in the leadership and continued his drive to reform the party towards the political centre ground, most critically through ending *trade-union power in leadership elections through the introduction of one member, one vote ballots. After his sudden death, he was succeeded by Tony *Blair, a radical modernizer devoid of trade-union links.

Smuts, Jan Christiaan (Christian)
(b. 24 May 1870, d. 11 Sept. 1950). Prime Minister of South Africa 1919–24, 1939–48

Early career Born in Bovenplaats (Cape Colony) and a childhood friend of *Malan, he was educated at Stellenbosch and studied at Cambridge University (1891–4) before returning to the Cape in 1895. Smuts moved to the Transvaal and was appointed state attorney (1898). He became a distinguished leader in the *South African War, agreeing with Louis *Botha in 1902 that it was better to accept an honourable peace while *Afrikaner forces were still relatively strong.

Throughout his life, he was committed to Botha's ideals of reconciliation between English- and Afrikaans-speaking Whites. In Botha's first Transvaal government of 1907, he became Colonial Secretary and Minister for Education. In 1908, he had a pivotal role in drawing up the Constitution of the Union of South Africa, becoming Minister of the Interior, Mines, and Defence in 1910, exchanging the first two portfolios for Finance in 1912. As Botha's deputy he supported the invasion of German South-West Africa (Namibia) during World War I, which he led as second-in-command.

In 1916, he accepted a British request for help in the struggling campaign in East Africa, and was appointed a lieutenant-general in the British army. He represented South Africa at the Imperial Conference of 1917, and was persuaded by *Lloyd George to stay in London and join the British War Cabinet. He set up the Royal Air Force as an independent service, became involved in British domestic politics (e.g. persuading Welsh miners not to go on strike), influenced strategic planning, and undertook countless diplomatic missions. He influenced the establishment of the *League of Nations, and took part in the *Paris Peace Conference.

Prime Minister 'Weary and sick of honours' bestowed upon him by the British, he retired to South Africa, only to be made Prime Minister on Botha's death a few days later (27 August 1919). His conciliatory attitude towards the Unionists who favoured close ties with Britain continued to anger the Afrikaners, while his suppression of the general strike in the gold mines of 1922 triggered the opposition of Labour. Meanwhile, his suppression of the millenarian Black peasant Israelite movement in Bulbek in 1921 showed his willingness to use force against the last remnants of rural Black resistance to colonialism. In opposition, he was hostile to *Hertzog's nationalist policies which he feared would alienate the English-speaking population. Under the influence of the Great *Depression, he became Minister of Justice and Deputy Prime Minister under *Hertzog in 1933.

While less of a segregationist than Hertzog, he accepted the 1936 racial laws (which formed the basis of the introduction of *apartheid in 1948), satisfied that he had secured a good compromise. He broke with Hertzog when the latter opposed South Africa's entry into World War II and was defeated in parliament. Despite continuing *Afrikaner opposition he committed troops to the British war effort. In 1945, he took part in the establishment of the *UN in *San Francisco, successfully drawing up a preamble to the charter enshrining fundamental *human rights. However, he was subsequently shaken by the UN's hostility to South Africa's racial policies and its desire to annex South-West Africa.

Accepting that an industrializing South Africa needed a skilled labour force, he improved the rights of Indians in Natal, invested in the education of Blacks, and relaxed the controls over Black urbanization. These measures were met with general hostility, however, and in 1948 he unexpectedly lost the elections to *Malan. The most internationally respected South African statesman before *De Klerk, at home his intellect became a burden as he failed to develop a 'common touch'. Smuts never fully appreciating the potential of Afrikaner *nationalism on the one hand, and African grievances against segregation on the other.

Snowden, Philip, Viscount Snowden of Ickornshaw
(b. 18 July 1864, d. 15 May 1937). British Chancellor of the Exchequer 1924, 1929–31

Born in Ickornshaw, Yorkshire, and educated in York. He worked as a school teacher, an insurance clerk, and for the Inland Revenue.

He joined the *Independent Labour Party in 1894, was its Chairman in 1903-6, and became an MP for Blackburn in 1906. He opposed British entry into World War I and lost his seat in 1918, though he was re-elected for Colne Valley in 1922. A crucial moderating influence upon the *Labour Party, he insisted that only moderate and gradual policies would ensure electoral success.

As the party's first Chancellor of the Exchequer under *MacDonald in 1924, Snowdon surprised many by proposing a tax-cutting budget. As Chancellor of the Exchequer again in 1929, he rejected schemes to tackle unemployment through public spending, and in 1931, he supported the proposal to cut unemployment benefits, which resulted in MacDonald forming the *National Government. He was, briefly, Chancellor of the Exchequer in this government, but went to the House of Lords as Lord Privy Seal in November 1931. The lifelong free trader resigned the following year, in opposition to the imposition of protection (*tariff reform) in the *Ottawa Agreements.

Soares, Mário Alberto Nobre Lopez
(b. 7 Dec. 1924). President of Portugal 1985-96

Born in Lisbon, Soares studied history, philosophy, and jurisprudence at the University of Lisbon. There, he became active in student politics in opposition to the *fascist *Estado Novo of *Salazar. As a lawyer, he defended many people against the government, and in 1961 edited the 'Programme for the Democratization of the Republic'. He was briefly deported to the Portuguese colony of São Tomé (1968-9) and, after he lost his campaign for a seat in the rigged 1969 elections, in which he was a leading critic of the government's policies, he left for France, where he resided until 1974. In 1973, in West Germany, he took part in the refounding of the Portuguese Socialist Party and became its general secretary. He returned to Portugal after the 1974 coup. His moderation and integrity had a crucial stabilizing effect on the fragile political system over the next decade. He became Foreign Secretary, then Minister without Portfolio, and in 1976-8 and 1983-5, he was Prime Minister. In that position, he promoted close relations with Spain (especially after the election of *González in 1982), and successfully sought entry into the European Community, which was finalized on 12 June 1985. He was elected President on 16 February 1986, and again on 13 January 1991, and was the first civilian to hold that office in six decades.

Sobukwe, Robert Mangaliso (Wonder) (b. 5 Dec. 1924, d. 26 Feb. 1978).
South African opposition leader.

Born in Graaf Reinet, Cape Province, Sobukwe went to the University of Fort Hare, where he joined the *ANC Youth League, whose secretary he became in 1949 on a radical platform. He became a university lecturer, and from 1957 he edited *The Africanist* newspaper. On 6 April 1959 he became the first leader of the newly established *PAC (Pan-Africanist Congress), believing that Blacks should liberate themselves to establish a democratic society. The charismatic leader proceeded to organize demonstrations which led to the *Sharpeville Massacre, whereupon the PAC was banned and he was sentenced to three years' imprisonment with hard labour. Just before his release was due in 1963, the government passed a law allowing his further detention (without trial) for incitement to violence. He used his time in prison to gain an external BSc degree in economics from the University of London. Released in 1969, his movements were restricted to Kimberley, where he qualified as a lawyer in 1975. He died of cancer.

Soccer War (July 1969)

A brief war between El Salvador and Honduras, which derived its name from the qualifying match between the two countries for the football World Cup, when tensions between the two countries came to a head. It was provoked by the migration from overpopulated El Salvador into Honduras of altogether half a million people, in the years since 1930, as well as El Salvador's commercial superiority over its neighbour. The war was soon stopped owing to international pressure. Its consequences were especially severe for El Salvador, whose underperforming economy was unable to reassimilate the over 100,000 migrants returning from Honduras.

Social Credit Party of Canada

A party founded in 1933 whose ideology was based on the theory of 'social credit' as advanced by the Alberta radio evangelist, William Aberhart (b. 1878, d. 1943). Adapting the 'social credit' ideas of the British engineer Clifford Douglas, he argued that the Great *Depression was caused by the failure of banks to print enough money. Hence, all that was needed was to print and supply more money to the consumers, as this would stimulate demand and revive production. The party gained prominence in the west, where it governed in Alberta (1935-71), and British Columbia (1952-75, 1975-91). However, while in government it implemented few of its ideals, instead pursuing free-market conservative policies to suit its western rural constituencies. As an essentially regional party it was relatively unsuccessful in gaining seats in the federal House of Commons, and its importance on a provincial and national level declined during the 1980s. Its role as a regional party of the west was taken up by the *Reform Party.

Social Credit Political League (New

Zealand), see DEMOCRATIC PARTY, NEW ZEALAND

social Darwinism

The (mis)application of Charles Darwin's theories of evolution to human society. In an attempt to find a biological (rather than economic) way to explain social inequalities and injustices, it held that human beings were created biologically unequal, and that social injustice was the natural consequence. Closely related to this idea was the concept of eugenics, a pseudo-scientific attempt to create a better society through social engineering, i.e. the control of human mating, and abortion of disabled unborn children.

After World War I, in many countries, and particularly in central Europe, the focus shifted to more aggressive inter-'racial' applications of social Darwinism. A host of right-wing groups combined the idea of the 'survival of the fittest' with their latent *anti-Semitism. Many developed a hierarchy with the nordic, 'Aryan' race at the top, Slavs near the lower end of the scale, and Jews at the bottom. What distinguished the *Nazis from the many other right-wing groups holding these ideas was that they were prepared to carry this idea to its extreme and terrible conclusion. The genocide of Jews in *concentration camps was thus mainly an attempt to ensure the 'strength' of the supposedly 'Aryan' German 'race'. After World War II, social Darwinism was accordingly discredited.

Social Democratic and Labour Party (SDLP), Northern Ireland

A moderate Catholic party founded on 21 August 1970 by former supporters of the Nationalist Party, the National Democratic Party, and the Republican Labour Party. Its first leader was Gerry *Fitt, who was replaced in 1979 by John *Hume. The party stands for equal civil rights for all people in Northern Ireland, and a fair distribution of the province's wealth. It supports the eventual unification of Northern Ireland with the Irish

Republic, but only if this receives the consent of the majority of people in Northern Ireland. The SDLP withdrew from *Stormont in 1971, and in the 1970s it supported initiatives promoting cross-border cooperation. In the 1980s, through its leader, John *Hume, it has sought to promote dialogue between all groups in Northern Ireland. From the 1970s to the 1990s, the SDLP received around 20 per cent of the vote in general elections. Ironically, in political terms it suffered from the peace process which it had been so instrumental in bringing about, for this legitimized *Sinn Féin and made it attractive to much of the SDLP's core constituency of moderate Catholics. In the 2001 British parliamentary elections, the SDLP was eclipsed for the first time by Sinn Féin as the most popular Catholic party in Northern Ireland. Led by Mark Durkan since 2001, the party's decline continued, as the SDLP obtained only 17 per cent of the vote at the 2003 provincial elections. In 2007 the SDLP obtained 16 seats in the Northern Ireland Assembly, on 15.2 per cent of the popular vote.

(⊕) SEE WEB LINKS

• The official home page of the SDLP.

Social Democratic Labour Party, Sweden

Early history Founded by August Palm (b. 1849, d. 1922) in 1889, its programme and organization were greatly influenced by the German Social Democratic Party (*SPD). At the same time, it was always ready to provide pragmatic support for the dominant Liberals on matters of political and social reform. The party's strength greatly increased with the foundation of the Swedish Conference of Trade Unions in 1898, which has subsequently been the party's major organizational backbone. Its leader since 1892, Hjalma Branting, was elected to the Riksdag (parliament) in 1898, and from 1902 its number of seats grew steadily to 64 out of 230 by 1917. In that year the party received a major boost from the introduction of universal suffrage through a Liberal–Social Democratic coalition. It was not until 1932, however, that it could finally establish itself as Sweden's dominant political party, since it was the only party to have developed a consistent response to the Great *Depression through *Keynesian demand management and taxation in order to finance public works.

In its subsequent period in government which lasted until 1976 (interrupted only briefly in 1936), it developed a model *welfare state that achieved great prosperity as well as a relatively equal income distribution. It was marked by generous benefit payments, a steep system of progressive income taxation, and close cooperation with the *trade unions in economic matters.

Contemporary history (since 1980s) Following the *oil price shocks of the 1970s, which hit the country, with its lack of energy resources, very hard, the party underwent a period of uncertainty as its model of the welfare state became untenable. It stopped being the natural party of government and was out of office 1976–81 and 1991–4, as its conservative opponents argued convincingly for a reform of the welfare system, and became better organized. In the 1998 general elections it obtained 36.5 per cent of the popular vote, its worst ever electoral performance since 1921. Under Goran Persson, the party formed a series of minority governments from 1996, but in 2006, a right-wing coalition gained a small majority in the Riksdag. The party's inability to generate a majority in the face of a fragmented party system was part of a wider European political phenomenon. The growing popularity of non-traditional parties made it difficult for established parties to attract cross-generational, cross-regional, and cross-class majorities.

Social Democratic Party (SDP) (UK)
A political party formed in March 1981 by four leading politicians (the 'Gang of Four') from the right of the *Labour Party: Roy *Jenkins, David Owen, Bill Rodgers, and Shirley Williams. It reflected their general concern that Labour had become too left-wing, and their specific opposition to Labour's support for withdrawal from Europe, and its endorsement of unilateral nuclear disarmament (*CND). It advocated policies associated with the centre ground of British politics, such as a mixed economy, but also argued for more radical measures such as Scottish devolution. The party began with fourteen MPs, but doubled this number before the 1983 general election, owing to by-election successes and defections. It soon formed an Alliance with the *Liberal Party, and made much headway in local politics. However, the first-past-the-post electoral system prevented the party from making a decisive breakthrough in parliament. After the 1987 general election, the Alliance split. The two parties of the Alliance merged in 1988 to form the *Liberal Democrats. However, three MPs soldiered on for a separate SDP, including Owen himself, though none stood for re-election in 1992.

Social Democratic Party, Italy, see SOCIALIST PARTY, ITALY

Social Democratic Party, Japan, see SOCIALIST PARTY, JAPAN

Social Democratic Party of Germany, see SPD

Social Democratic Party, Spain, see SOCIALIST WORKERS' PARTY OF SPAIN

social market economy, see CDU

socialism
A diffuse ideology that was developed in the early nineteenth century by pioneers like Robert Owen in Britain, and Saint-Simon and Louis Blanc in France, in response to the evils of *capitalism that became evident during the industrial revolution. Appalled by mass poverty and inequality of wealth, socialists argued for a more egalitarian social system. This would then transform society not just in material, but also in moral terms, as individualism and self-interest gave way to association, solidarity, and community. However, socialists differed widely about how this goal was to be achieved. While many emphasized voluntary action, most notably through the foundation and development of *cooperative movements, an increasing number of socialists became disillusioned with the gradualism of this approach, and emphasized direct political action instead.

It was at this point that cooperation between socialist and liberal parties ended, and socialist, or social democratic, parties were founded which aimed specifically at working-class votes. This occurred at varying times throughout Europe, starting with Germany in 1869, while in Britain this process only occurred after 1900. The need for socialists to distinguish themselves from *liberalism and other voluntarist ideologies to the right was complicated by the development of a 'scientific socialism' in *Marxist ideology. According to this, socialism was a transitional phase to a Communist society, in which all ownership was abolished. This was less of a problem in Anglo-Saxon countries, where *Communism never gained a mass following. In continental Europe, however, the distinction between socialists and Communists was often blurred in theory, though in practice their distinctions became more pronounced during and after World War I. During the war, socialist parties supported the state orders in which they operated, despite their theoretical commitments to internationalism and solidarity. As universal franchises were introduced in the first decades of the twentieth century, socialism became a dominant political idea, not just among socialist parties, but also among liberals, who accepted the need for social legislation in an attempt to halt their own demise. Similarly, as socialists gained their first experiences in government, they became more pragmatic, as the success of their programme now depended upon the cooperation of the middle and propertied classes (who remained in control of the bureaucratic machinery).

Socialism gained its widest appeal and realization in the years during and after the apocalyptic experience of World War II, which led to the widespread popular desire for a just society. Even where conservative governments remained in power, they were forced to adopt a series of social welfare reform measures, so that in most industrialized countries, the post-World War period saw the creation of a *welfare state. Socialism came under heavy attack after the 1973 *oil-price shock. Social welfare systems were criticized by *monetarists and conservatives as a hindrance to self-advancement. They were also under attack as the root cause of the failure of the European and Australian and New Zealand industrial societies to compete with new, capitalist Asian economies. Thus, socialists were under intense pressure to refashion themselves from the 1990s, and to harmonize their ideal for social justice and community with the maintenance of individual incentive and dynamism. Many socialists thus advocated pragmatic policies in the light of *globalization, advocating social reform only if this did not endanger domestic economic growth.

Socialist Party, France

Early history (up to 1969) Formed in 1905, the **SFIO (Section Française de l'Internationale Ouvrière**, French Section of the Socialist International) united the hitherto fragmented socialist groups. These included the *Marxists under J. *Guesde, the revolutionary socialists, and the pragmatic socialists whose outstanding figure was *Jaurès. The party had considerable success, gaining 104 seats in the Chamber of Deputies in 1914. However, the Marxist principle of non-participation in bourgeois government adopted from the followers of Guesde kept the SFIO out of government for 30 years. In 1920, the majority left to form the *Communist Party (PCF), but the SFIO soon recovered as the second largest parliamentary party. Under its leader, *Blum, an alliance was concluded in 1934 with

the PCF, which proceeded to win the 1935 general elections. The new *Popular Front government under Blum lasted only from 1936 to 1937, but the participating parties continued to support the following government until it split over the *Munich Agreement.

During World War II, many socialists took an active part in the French *Résistance. The party participated in several postwar governments in the Fourth Republic and supported de *Gaulle's return in 1958. Thereafter, however, it became increasingly marginalized in the political system, and in 1965 it regrouped with other parties of the left as the Social Democratic Federation of the Left.

Contemporary history (since 1969) In 1969, it transformed itself into the **Parti Socialiste** (PS, Socialist Party), which was led by *Mitterrand from 1971. During the 1970s, the fortunes of the PS improved steadily and in 1981 the PS finally gained an overall majority, with Mitterrand elected President. As his Prime Minister, Laurent Fabius, was unable to recover from the innovative but disastrous policies of *Mauroy, the PS lost its parliamentary majority in 1986 to the *UDF and the *Gaullists. It formed the government again in 1988, when Mitterrand appointed Michel Rocard his Prime Minister (1988–91). However, the party's fortunes plummeted, partly as a result of the inept leadership of *Cresson (1991–2), which her successor, Prime Minister Pierre Bérégovoy (1992–3) was unable to reverse. Reinforced by the increasing dissatisfaction with the long reign of Mitterrand himself, the PS was routed in the 1993 general elections, when its representation in the National Assembly shrank from 260 to 54 seats. This foreshadowed its defeat in the 1995 presidential elections, when *Jospin lost to *Chirac. The party appeared in a desperate situation, but under Jospin's leadership it rebounded in the 1997 parliamentary elections, gaining 241 seats. A period of *cohabitation ensued, involving a ruling coalition of five left-wing parties including the *Communist Party, but its policies turned out to be moderate so as not to endanger economic growth. This split the left, as more radical sections refused to unite for the 2002 presidential and parliamentary elections. Owing to these divisions, Jospin failed to enter the second round of the presidential elections. Jospin resigned, and a disunited Socialist Party obtained but 140 seats, and faced an overwhelming majority of the right-wing *UMP.

The party was divided in the 2005 referendum on the Treaty establishing a European *Constitution, but recovered under the leadership of François Hollande. His partner, Ségolne *Royal, was chosen by party members as the socialist candidate for the 2007 presidential elections. However, the Socialists were yet again defeated in the battle for the presidency. This led to demands that the party reconstitute itself as a more centrist social democratic party.

(⊕) SEE WEB LINKS

• The official website of the French Socialist Party.

Socialist Party, Italy (Partito Socialista Italiano, PSI)

Origins 1892–1918 Established by *Turati in 1892, its power base developed mostly in the industrializing northern Italy. During the first four decades, the party was fundamentally weakened by its own divisions between the 'maximalists', who demanded socialist revolution and confrontation with the current capitalist state, and pragmatists like Turati who favoured working within the parameters of the current state to help the plight of the working people. For most of the period before World War I, Turati was able to lead the party on a pragmatist course. The party found itself in opposition to the state in World War I, when it favoured strict Italian neutrality instead of participation.

The Fascist challenge (1918–45) After the war, the PSI became the largest party in government. However, it was paralysed by the focus of its parliamentary leaders on the lofty goal of revolution, rather than pragmatic action. Frustrated by the PSI's unproductiveness, some of its members seceded in 1921 to form the *Communist Party (PCI) under Amadeo Bordiga, *Gramsci, and *Togliatti. This did not strengthen the pragmatist wing, however, as in 1922 Turati was expelled from the party for his efforts to cooperate with the other parties against the *Fascist movement. Turati founded the Unitary Socialist Party (Partito Socialista Unitario, PSU), with *Matteotti as its secretary. Thus divided, the socialists were too weak to take on *Mussolini, as became clear when they challenged him by joining the *Aventine Secession, which ended with the party leaders' incarceration and expulsion. The two socialist parties reunited in Paris in 1930, and in 1934 the PSI agreed to cooperate with the PCI in a *popular front against Mussolini's Fascist dictatorship.

Postwar Italy (1945–1980s) The socialists took part in the Italian post-Fascist governments first through the *CLN and then as part of the first postwar coalitions. Given the growing ideological divisions in the *Cold War, in 1947 Prime Minister *De Gasperi

broke with the PSI and the PCI, and in the same year a number of socialists on the right seceded to form a **Social Democratic Party**, the **Partito Socialista Democratico Italiano (PSDI)**. Even though the PSDI never obtained much more than half of the number of votes cast for the PSI, it nevertheless acquired considerable influence through being one of the most permanent participants in coalition government. By contrast, the PSI used its time in opposition to move closer to the centre, away from the PCI. From 1959, when *Moro became secretary-general of the *Christian Democrats (DC), deliberations began about a possible return of the PSI to government. The PSI finally re-entered government in 1963 in a coalition led by Moro, and in 1966 the PSI and the PSDI reunited, only to split again in 1971. In the 1970s, the coalition fell apart while the PSI found itself in a deep crisis due to declining membership and bad results in the polls.

Dissolution (1980s–1994) The PSI's fortunes gradually improved under *Craxi's leadership, who in 1983 not only became Italy's first socialist Prime Minister, but also continued to lead Italy's longest single government to date (1983–6). Few embodied the corruption of the Italian political system more then Craxi, and the party was deeply involved in the corruption scandals that emerged in the late 1980s and early 1990s (*Tangentopoli). In the 1993 local elections, its support declined to 1.2 per cent in its former northern strongholds. In response to its deep unpopularity, at the 47th party congress in Rome on 13 November 1994 it was decided to dissolve the party.

Socialist Party, Japan (Japan Socialist Party, JSP)

Creation (1945–51) Japan's largest socialist party and Japan's main opposition party between 1955 and 1993. As it was formed by an alliance of Christian socialists, millenarian *Marxists, *trade union members, radicals, and liberals, it is not surprising that the factions of the JSP, like those of the *Liberal Democratic Party (LDP), have been a source of conflict throughout the organization's history. In the first years after its formation in 1945, the JSP was propelled into government as the largest partner in two ruling coalitions. However, the experience proved an unhappy one after government policy opened divisions within the party, while the involvement of leading members of the Cabinet in the Shôwa Denkô scandal did much to sully the new party's image.

Contemporary history (1951–1980s) The JSP divided between left and right socialist parties in 1951 over the issue of Japan's peace settlement with the USA, but reunited in 1955. In the intervening period, the strength of the left-wing faction grew thanks to unprecedented electoral success and it emerged stronger than the JSP's right wing. Despite the merger, factional rivalry continued to such a degree that left-wing activists were able to drive out Nishio Suehiro and 40 of his followers from among groups on the party's right in 1959. This defection had the effect of undermining the JSP's confidence in its own abilities to provide a viable challenge to the LDP for many years afterwards. Indeed, the strength of the party's organization and Diet (the House of Representatives) suffered chronic difficulties from this period. The JSP's lower house strength that had peaked in 1958 at 166, was 118 in 1972.

While the national party has rarely been free from crisis, local party organizations have had some spectacular successes. By the mid-1970s, as many as 137 local chief executives controlled a population of 40 million with the backing of Japan's opposition parties, including the JSP. Many of the JSP's problems have stemmed from its reliance on a combination of the trade union vote and rural constituencies. With a poor organization and few material spoils to compete for, the JSP demonstrated a tendency towards ideological disputes.

Contemporary politics (since 1990s) The JSP recorded a record low of 69 seats in the 1993 House of Representatives elections. Ironically, this disappointing performance brought the JSP into power at the head of a coalition government for the first time in nearly 50 years. The party continued in government until 1998, but its coalition with its erstwhile foe, the LDP (since 1994), was deeply divisive within its own ranks. In 1996 many members left to form the New Socialist Party. More consequential was the defection in that year of many members to form the *Democratic Party of Japan. In 1996 the party changed its name to the **Social Democratic Party**. As a result of haemorrhaging support in the late 1990s, the socialists became a marginal parliamentary force in the new millennium, when the party's representation declined from nineteen seats (2000) to six seats (2005).

Socialist Workers' Party of Spain (Partido Social Obrero Español, PSOE)

Early history (up to 1960s) Established on 2 May 1879, it experienced slow growth in a country that was still barely industrialized and urbanized. Where there was economic change,

notably in Catalonia, the workers had become mostly followers of *anarcho-syndicalism. In contrast to this movement, which also had substantial support among the peasants and landless labourers (most notably in Andalusia), the PSOE suffered badly because of its inability to penetrate the countryside. After 1900, the party moved from a doctrinaire insistence on revolution to the gradualist advocacy of piecemeal reforms, but this caused the separation of the Spanish *Communist Party (PCE) in 1920. Its freedom of action was severely limited under the dictatorship of *Primo de Rivera. However, in marked contrast to the Communists and anarchists, the PSOE tacitly cooperated with him through its affiliated Unión General de Trabajadores (UGT, General Workers' Union), which assisted in the reform of labour relations.

The PSOE was organizationally in a strong position at the end of Primo de Rivera's regime, which enabled it to move to lead the republican coalition which won the 1931 municipal elections. However, the PSOE's insistence that the republic was merely a transitional institution on the way to a socialist revolution, and its consequent half-hearted support for the new regime in which it participated, fundamentally weakened the republic throughout. This became particularly apparent under *Largo Caballero's leadership. During the *Spanish Civil War, it gave way increasingly to the Communist Party as the principal defender of the republic.

Contemporary history (from 1960s) During the *Franco regime the party was outlawed in Spain, though a clandestine party organization began to grow in the 1960s. Led by *González, it quickly reorganized after it was legalized again in 1975, and was transformed into a moderate, pro-*European integration, social democratic party. Benefiting from the popularity and credibility of its leader, it won the 1982 elections and remained in power until 1996. In opposition, the party was cast into the shadows by Aznar's success at stimulating economic growth. It was also weakened by a legacy of scandals involving former ministers, such as the involvement of government ministers in illegal acts of state terrorism against suspected *Basque terrorists. Under Joaquín Almunia Amman its share of the vote declined to 34 per cent in the 2000 general elections. Almunia resigned, handing over the party leadership to the young José Rodríguez *Zapatero.

Although it trailed in the polls until the *Madrid Bombings, the party won a surprise victory at the 2004 elections. Zapatero introduced cultural reforms such as the legalization of same-sex unions, and negotiated more autonomy for the provinces of Catalonia (which was subsequently recognized as a nation) and Valencia. The party's pacifism was recognized by a law passed in 2005, whereby military missions abroad subsequently needed parliamentary approval, as well as the consent of NATO, the EU or the country for which military aid was determined. These initiatives left the PP in disarray, so that in Zapatero's first years of government, the PSOE rode high in the polls.

Solana Madariaga, Javier (b. 14 July 1942). High Representative of the Common Foreign and Security Policy (CFSP) of the EU, 1999–

Born in Madrid, he studied physics and became a lecturer at the Complutense University in Madrid. Solana was appointed to a chair in solid–state physics in 1975, but in the 1977 elections he entered parliament as a member of the Spanish *Socialist Party. The Prime Minister, *Gonzalez, appointed him to the difficult post of Minister for Culture in 1982. He became Minister of Education and Science in 1988, and Foreign Minister in 1992. As *NATO General Secretary from 1995, he promoted the alliance's expansion to include Poland, Hungary, and the Czech Republic. He also coordinated NATO's response to the *Bosnian civil war. As the first public representative of the CFSP since 1999, Solana was initially limited in his effectiveness by having few powers of his own. However, as the representative of the EU's growing activism in foreign affairs, Solana enjoyed substantial informal power, overseeing, for example, the growing deployment of EU troops overseas.

Solidarność ('Solidarity') (Poland)

Under Communism (1980–9) In response to an unannounced increase in Polish food prices on 1 August 1980, strikes erupted at the Lenin shipyard in Gdansk. Under the charismatic leadership of *Wałęsa, they spread across Poland, as demands became less economic and more political, e.g. for independent *trade unions. The various strike committees met on 17 September 1980 to form the Solidarność trade-union movement, which was accepted by a state overwhelmed by the sheer scale of the protests on 10 November. In response, up to 80 per cent of the total Polish workforce registered with the union, which was also increasingly seen as a direct political challenge to the political hegemony of the Communist state. Gaining more and more concessions from a confused state, the union became increasingly radicalized. At the same time, the Polish government was faced with a growing threat from the hardline governments of *Brezhnev (USSR),

*Honecker (GDR), and *Husák (Czechoslovakia) to 'help' through military intervention akin to the *Prague Spring.

Possibly forestalling a military intervention, *Jaruselski declared martial law on 13 December 1981. Trade union activities were banned, and Solidarity leaders imprisoned. Naturally, this increased popular discontent even further, and meant that the government could not be shored up indefinitely, particularly as *Gorbachev's leadership from 1985 made it unlikely that the Soviet army would support the Polish government against a popular insurrection. The union was allowed again in 1988, when the government also started negotiations about a democratization of the political system. In the restricted elections of 1989, every candidate supported by the union won, so that Wałęsa's closest adviser, Mazowiecki, became Prime Minister.

After Communism (post-1989) After the collapse of Communism, the importance of Solidarność as a political force declined rapidly. This was caused by deep divisions within the leadership (not least caused by Wałęsa's own erratic personality), and disagreements about a reformist programme. As a sign of its waning influence, Wałęsa was elected President with difficulty in 1990, while in 1993 the movement itself failed to gain the 5 per cent necessary to enter the Sejm (parliament). It reformed itself in 1996, when it headed a new coalition comprising some further 40 interest groups. Under the name Electoral Action Solidarity, it won the 1997 elections and, under the leadership of Jerzy Buzek, formed a government with the liberal Freedom Union. Although the electoral pact had endeavoured to overcome the fragmentation of the party system, in government it suffered greatly from its internal rifts. These were heightened by frequent clashes with the President, *Kwasniewski, and the departure of the Freedom Union from the government. Its failure to integrate Catholic, agricultural labourers' votes, workers, and intellectuals became manifest in the 2001 elections, when it suffered a heavy defeat at the polls.

Solomon Islands

An archipelago of islands in the Pacific, which has seen strong tensions between two opposing islands, Guadalcanal and

Malaita. By 1914 Germany controlled some of the islands in the north-west. These passed to the *League of Nations *Mandate of Australia in 1920 and now form part of Papua New Guinea. The remaining islands were made a British protectorate in 1893. Occupied by Japan in 1942, they were the scene of very fierce fighting in World War II, particularly on Guadalcanal. From 1952 onwards, Britain steadily introduced a parliamentary system in the islands which had come under its authority, establishing a unicameral legislature under a Governor-General in 1960. These islands gained independence on 7 July 1978.

In 1998 bitter tensions erupted on the main island of Guadalcanal, between the Isatabu majority and the Malaitan minority from the neighbouring island. The Isatabu Freedom Movement launched violent attacks against Malaitans, whereupon a Malaitan Eagle Force responded by instigating a coup in 2000. Following an Australian-brokered peace deal, new elections were held in 2001, which led to the appoinment of Sir Allan Kemakeza as Prime Minister. However, he was unable to restore peace, so that the islands slipped back into anarchy. In 2003, Kemakeza asked for international aid, which was forthcoming with a UN peacekeeping force made up mainly of New Zealand and Australian troops. This force restored order, but this remained fragile: the appointment of Snyder Rini, an associate of Kemakeza, as Prime Minister caused widespread rioting. Rini resigned after eight days in office, with Manasseh Sogavare becoming the new Prime Minister.

Somalia

A country on the horn of Africa, recently characterized by extreme poverty and political instability.

Colonial rule

The strategically important territory on the horn of Africa was divided and governed by three colonial powers. France took control over French Somaliland (now *Djibouti) in 1884–5, Britain declared a protectorate in Jubaland in 1886, and Italy established a colony in 1889. In 1925, Britain ceded Jubaland, which had been administered from Kenya, to Italy. The growth of political life and of a sense of *nationalism began in the 1940s, at a time when Italian Somaliland was occupied by British troops (1941–9). In 1950 the southern part was restored to Italian administration, as a *UN *trust territory. In the run-up to independence, elections to a legislative assembly were held in the southern region in 1956, and in the British-controlled north in 1958. On 26 June 1960 the northern part became independent, and was unified with the southern region as the Somali Republic on 1 July 1960.

Communism Under President Shermarke, territorial claims in Ethiopia and Kenya led to regional tensions. He was assassinated in 1969, whereupon a military junta under Muhammad Siad Barre (b. 1919, d. 1995) proclaimed a socialist People's Republic. Military assistance from the USSR enabled the army to become one of the best-equipped in Africa. It tested its strength in a war with Ethiopia (1977–8) to press its claim for the territory of Ogaden, though the tables were turned when the USSR started to support Ethiopia instead. Nursing its wounds from military defeat, it improved its relations with its Arab neighbours and the USA, with which it began a programme of military cooperation in 1980. Under the Barre regime, the country underwent little economic improvement. It suffered from high military expenditure, which was compounded by guerrilla warfare against *Islamic fundamentalists in the north and the Patriotic Front in the south. Economic performance was not helped by Communist economic planning, whereby all land had been nationalized. When falling commodity prices for its exports in the 1980s led to further economic decline, Barre attempted to meet popular discontent through a process of democratization, but he was overthrown in 1991.

Anarchy (since 1991) As the civil war spread, various guerrilla groups mushroomed, establishing a multitude of individual fiefdoms. This pushed Somalia to the brink of a humanitarian catastrophe, in which, by 1992, 50,000 people had died, over one million had sought refuge abroad (mostly in Ethiopian and Kenyan camps), and 1.5 million faced starvation. Led by US President *Bush and *Boutros Ghali, the *UN intervened in an attempt to restore peace and order. Despite a large military presence, however, the UN-sanctioned troops were unable to appease the country. Demoralized by the hostility of the population and the growing casualties incurred by guerrilla attacks, the US and European troops ended their engagement in March 1994, while the 20,000 Asian and African troops were withdrawn by March 1995. Attempts to negotiate a peace settlement between the rival clans failed owing to their mutually contradictory aims.

On 15 June 1995 one of the strongest leaders, Muhammed Farah Aideed (b. 1930?, d. 1996), was elected 'President' by fifteen clan chiefs, though this was not recognized by Ali Mahdi Muhammad, who had officially succeeded Barre as President, nor by other leaders. Aideed and Muhammad were amongst a number of leaders who co-signed a peace agreement in 1997, but fighting continued. A transitional government was instituted in 2000, with Abdulkassim Salad Hassan as its president. However, the government struggled to control the area in and around the capital, much of which continued to be controlled by rival factions such as the United Somali Congress. In the southern part of the country, rival leaders joined in the Somali Reconciliation and Restoration Congress, which was supported by Ethiopia as a rival to the transitional government in Mogadishu.

In 2004, rival warlords agreed on an interim government under Abdullahi Yusuf Ahmed. His government was recognized by the UN, but it was weakened by subsequent internal dissent. In 2006, the Union of Islamic Courts (UIC) brought most of the country, including the largest city, Mogadishu, under its control. The UIC transformed Somalia into an Islamic state, but its iron grip also created remarkable stability. Ethiopian troops moved in to aid the interim government, whereupon resistance by the UIC collapsed in 2007.

Somme, Battle of the (1 July–18 Nov. 1916)

The bloodiest battle in history, orchestrated by General *Haig to relieve pressure on the embattled Allied positions at *Verdun during *World War I. Fighting extended over a 20 mile front, and the brunt of the offensive was borne by the British. A preliminary eight days' bombardment pounded 52,000 tonnes of ammunition onto the German positions. This loosened the soil to such an extent that heavy rainfall transformed the area into a sea of mud, in which countless soldiers drowned when the attack was ordered on 1 July. Contrary to Haig's calculations, the German positions were not weakened sufficiently by the initial bombardment, so that on the first day of the Allied attack, the British suffered 57,470 casualties, with over 19,000 dead. On that day, the Germans lost just 185 men. Instead of stopping the slaughter there and then, Haig continued the attack. After twenty weeks, around 10 km (6 miles) had been gained, while the Germans held on to the strategically important railway junction of Bapaume. Revisionists have argued that the battle was crucial in that it weakened the German troops,

while new forms of warfare were introduced during the battle, particularly tanks, though their success was limited by the difficult terrain. Nevertheless, this hardly justified the slaughter of one million men, 600,000 of whom were on the Allied side (400,000 British). This 'mule-like' stubbornness earned Haig the sorry reputation of a donkey leading heroes.

Somoza (1933–79). Nicaraguan dictatorship
Anastasio Somoza García (b. 1896, d. 1956) was the son of a wealthy coffee planter. Educated in the USA, he returned to US-occupied Nicaragua in 1926, where he became head of the US-trained National Guard in 1932. He became the most powerful man in Nicaragua after the withdrawal of the US troops in 1933, and proceeded to eliminate all opposition, e.g. through ordering the execution of *Sandino. In 1937 he removed President Sacasa (in power since 1933) to take over the office himself. He continued to rule as an unfailing ally of the USA, and with the support of both the National Guard and the landed elite, whom he endowed with wealth, influence, and money. He was shot on a visit to Panama, and even the personal doctor of *Eisenhower, sent over by the concerned US President himself, was unable to save him.

He was succeeded by his eldest son, **Luis Anastasio Somoza Debayle** (b. 1922, d. 1967), who carried out some half-hearted social reforms. Any interest in improving the social conditions of the population, however, was abandoned under his successor, his brother **Anastasio Somoza Debayle** (b. 1925, d. 1980). He was even more ruthless than his predecessors, and this eventually lost him the support, most crucially, of the USA. A year later, his regime collapsed. He was assassinated in exile in 1980.

Song Qingling (Soong Ch'ing-ling)
(b. 27 Jan. 1893, d. 29 May 1981). Chinese socialist
Born at Shanghai, she was educated at Wesleyan College for Women at Macon, Georgia. She became *Sun Yat-sen's secretary in 1913, and married him in that same year. As Sun's widow, she was able persistently to speak out with impunity against the *National Government and *Chiang's confrontational policies against the *Communist Party. She opposed her sister's marriage to Chiang, and broke with her brother, T. V. *Soong, over his support of what she considered a corrupt regime, which violated the spirit of her late husband. Although not a Communist until the very end of her life, she was a much-respected figure in the Communist People's Republic of China, of

which she was made Deputy Chairwoman (1959) and Honorary President (1981).

Soong Chi'ing-ling, see SONG QINGLING

Soong, Tse-ven Paul ('T.V.') (b. 4 Dec. 1894, d. 24 Apr. 1971). Chinese Minister of Finance 1928–33
Born in Shanghai, he graduated from Harvard before returning to China, where he became a pivotal supporter of *Chiang Kai-shek. He was responsible for the financial administration in the *National Government, introducing a finance reform, establishing the Central Bank of China in Guangzhou (Canton), and financing the *Northern Expedition. A supporter of cooperation with the *Communist Party against the Japanese, his financing skills were constantly outstripped by Chiang's need for increasing military spending. As Chiang's representative to the USA during World War II and as Prime Minister 1945-7, he secured many substantial loans from the USA, though much of that money went into his own pocket. He retired to the USA in 1949 as one of the richest people in the world.

Soudan, see MALI

Souphanouvong Tiao, Prince (b. 13 July 1909, d. 9 Jan 1995). President of the Laos People's Democratic Republic 1975–86
One of the nephews of King Sisavang Vong (r. 1904–59), he studied engineering in Paris and then worked as an engineer in Laos (1938–45). Upon the Japanese surrender in 1945, he agreed to become head of a Communist movement against the French colonial forces, with the strong support of *Ho Chi Minh's *Vietminh forces. Disunity with the leadership of other anti-French movements led him to create the *Pathet Lao, and to engage independently in the anti-colonial struggle. Following Laotian independence, agreed at the *Geneva Agreements of 1954, he joined the two short-lived coalition governments of his half-brother *Souvanna Phouma (1957, 1962), in an effort to resolve peacefully the differences between the various factions. After repeated arguments, he resumed the fight against Souvanna Phouma, with the help of the Vietnamese *Vietcong. He led the Pathet Lao into a coalition government in 1974, though without taking up a government post himself. It was the fall of *Saigon and Communist victory in the *Vietnam War that enabled him to take over government in 1975, and declare the People's Democratic Republic of Laos. He consolidated his power with Vietnamese help,

in return for which he found himself more dependent on Hanoi's counsel than he wished. He was forced to retire through ill health.

South Africa

Africa's wealthiest nation underwent a remarkable transition from being the country with the continent's most violent race-relations throughout much of the twentieth century, to a remarkable stability between its different ethnicities from the 1990s.

Origins (up to 1910) A country on the southern tip of Africa consisting of the former Cape Colony (under British control since 1806), the Natal Province (a British Crown Colony since 1856), the Orange Free State (OFS, independent since 1854), and the South African Republic (independent since 1852, from 1902 known as the Transvaal). Efforts by British administrators, particularly in the Cape, to annex the two independent *Afrikaner republics to create a British-led union were given a decisive stimulus with the discovery of gold in the Transvaal in 1886. In addition, the creation of British-controlled territories in the north (*Botswana) and north-east (*Zimbabwe) during the 1890s provided a strategic reason to link these landlocked areas to the Cape/Natal and thus to the sea.
   Despite heavy losses, the British managed to fulfil their aspirations through the *South African War (1899–1902), whereby the OFS and Transvaal became two British Crown Colonies. They received self-government in 1907, and in 1910 they joined with the Cape and Natal to form the Union of South Africa.

Between two World Wars (1910–49) With the general support of the White population, the new state maintained and extended laws of racial segregation which had already existed in the various provinces. Led by Presidents whose views on nationhood were formed by their experience of the South African War, until the early 1960s the main area of conflict among Whites was the question of national sovereignty. The Union's first Prime Ministers, J. *Botha and *Smuts, believed that unity between the English-

Table 17. **South African Prime Ministers (and Presidents since 1984)**

Louis *Botha	1910–19	Hendrik *Verwoerd	1958–66
Jan *Smuts	1919–24	Balthazar Johannes *Vorster	1966–78
James *Hertzog	1924–39	Pieter Willem *Botha	1978–89
Jan *Smuts	1939–48	Frederik Willem *de Klerk	1989–94
Daniel *Malan	1948–54	Nelson Rolihlahla *Mandela	1994–99
Johannes *Strijdom	1954–8	Thabo *Mbeki	1999–

speaking minority and the Afrikaner majority of Whites could best be established through gaining as much independence as possible while maintaining formal links with the *British Empire.

South Africa's entry into World War I against Germany as part of the British Empire, which led to the South African occupation of South-West Africa (*Namibia), proved to be a major divisive issue and even led to an abortive rebellion by Afrikaners. Afrikaner opposition to the war increased the fortunes of the *National Party (NP) founded in 1914, whose leader, *Hertzog, became Prime Minister in 1924. Hertzog joined with *Smuts to form the *United Party in 1934, in order to cope with the effects of the Great *Depression. Hertzog increased racial segregation, depriving people of mixed race ('Coloureds') of the franchise. Afrikaans was recognized as an official language in 1925, while South Africa's independence from Britain was increased.

Despite Hertzog's opposition, a parliamentary majority led by Smuts voted in 1939 to join Britain in World War II. Despite Smuts's importance in the establishment of the *UN in the closing stages of the war, South Africa became increasingly isolated there and in world opinion because of its continued occupation of South-West Africa, and its laws of racial discrimination and segregation.

Apartheid (1949–90) Those laws were intensified in 1948, when the victory of the NP under *Malan and the advent of *Verwoerd as Minister for Native Affairs (1950) marked the beginning of the system of *apartheid. This was an attempt to maximize White control in an industrializing, urbanizing economy which was increasingly dependent on Black labour. Its ultimate goal was to establish a 'White' South Africa, with those of other races forced to live in inadequate and overcrowded homelands (*bantustans). An elaborate system of racial discrimination was established, with Whites enjoying full political rights while Coloureds, Indians, and Blacks (Bantus) had progressively fewer rights. Protest campaigns by the *PAC, the *ANC, and the *Communist

Party (SACP) were severely repressed after the *Sharpeville Massacre of 1960.

Active resistance was all but crushed by 1965, and in the subsequent decade the 'stability' thus created caused an unparalleled economic boom, stimulated by the availability of cheap labour and foreign investment. Apartheid was challenged more successfully from 1976, when the *Soweto uprising became a symbol of the repression of the apartheid system. Its annual commemoration worldwide, the continued imprisonment of Nelson *Mandela, the prominence of Winnie *Mandela and *Tutu within South Africa, and the increasing effectiveness of the ANC led by *Tambo and *Mbeki from exile served to heighten international concern about apartheid. Concerned by South Africa's growing economic, cultural, and political isolation, its leaders, *Vorster and P. W. *Botha, tried to relax some of the more extreme aspects of the system while maintaining its substance. An international economic boycott proved an increasing burden on the economy, while South Africa became embroiled in costly wars in Angola and Mozambique.

South Africa withdrew from its military engagements abroad in the late 1980s, and ended the occupation of Namibia in 1990. Domestically, the political deadlock was broken by *de Klerk, who recognized that apartheid could no longer be maintained. He also appreciated the essential role of the hitherto stigmatized and banned ANC and its imprisoned leader, Nelson Mandela, whose singular popularity provided a quintessential point of contact for negotiations. Together with other political prisoners, Mandela was released in 1990, when the ANC, PAC, and SACP were also legalized again. Negotiations were delayed and threatened by intra-Black violence between the ANC and *Buthelezi's *Inkatha movement on the one hand and White right-wing opposition, as evidenced in the growth of the *Conservative Party, on the other.

Democratization (1990–9) The end of apartheid was officially proclaimed with the declaration of a provisional Constitution in 1993, coming into force on 27 April 1994. In the first multiracial elections of 1994, the ANC gained 62.6 per cent of the popular vote, the NP 20.4 per cent, and Inkatha 10.5 per cent. These parties proceeded to form a Coalition Government of National Unity, which ended its deliberations on a permanent Constitution in April 1996. Shortly afterwards, the NP left the coalition government, initiating a normalization of politics through the creation of a constitutional opposition in parliament. In 1999 Thabo Mbeki succeeded Mandela as President, and formed a coalition with Inkatha despite the ANC's increased representation in parliament, with almost two-thirds of the seats.

Attempts at cementing racial harmony in the post-apartheid era led to the creation of the *Truth and Reconciliation Commission, which was chaired by Tutu. Ethnic tensions were never far below the surface, however. From 2000, Mbeki struggled to pacify radical Blacks in townships who were attracted by *Mugabe's policies of forced expropriation of White farmers in neighbouring Zimbabwe. Attacks by Blacks against outlying White farms were often left unpunished by the security forces.

Contemporary politics (since 1999) Instead, the government tried to reduce unrest and dissatisfaction in the townships through large-scale provision of sanitation and electricity, though this was limited by its conflicting aim to keep public spending and inflation under control. After a period of economic difficulty, by 2000 inflation had been reduced to 5 per cent, with annual GDP growth exceeding 5 per cent. For the majority of the population, the supply of basic services (such as health and electricity) had been improved, but official unemployment persisted at over 30 per cent. Furthermore, throughout the 1990s capital investment was hindered by South Africa's crime rate, one of the highest in the world. As a result, a disproportionate and increasing amount of wealth was spent on personal and public security, in order to stem the emigration of wealthy Whites.

After 2000, South Africa's growth declined slightly, mainly owing to large-scale corruption and government intervention in the economy. In 2003, South Africa finally adopted official schemes to reduce the incidence of *AIDS. According to UNAIDS, by 2006 around 15 per cent of the adult population was infected with the HIV virus. Although the capital crime rate had declined since 1995, Mbeki announced a sharp increase in government spending on security in 2007, as the crime rate still remained one of the highest in the world.

South African Communist Party (SACP), see COMMUNIST PARTY, SOUTH AFRICA

South African War (1899–1902)
Also known as the **Boer War**, it was a colonial war in which the British tried to extend their rule from the Cape Colony and Natal to include the independent *Afrikaner republics of the Transvaal and the Orange Free State (OFS). It was caused less by strategic interests than by the discovery of vast gold mines, especially in the Transvaal, which had transformed the republic from a poor agricultural state into a major potential regional power overnight. As British intentions to annex the two republics became increasingly evident, the Afrikaners decided in favour of a pre-emptive strike in the hope of overwhelming the British garrisons in Natal and rousing the Afrikaners of the Cape into rebellion. After a series of heavy defeats, the British appointed Lord Roberts (b. 1832, d. 1914) as Commander-in-Chief, with Lord *Kitchener as his Chief of Staff. They inflicted a humiliating defeat on their opponents at Paardeburg on 27 February 1900, and proceeded to march towards Pretoria. They formally annexed the OFS in May and the Transvaal in September 1900.

In response, guerrilla warfare began under the military leadership of Louis *Botha and Christiaan de Wet (b. 1854, d. 1922), when Afrikaner commandos undertook raids against British garrisons and towns not only in the Transvaal and the OFS, but also through the Cape. The British responded by burning Afrikaner farms and destroying their cattle to deny them the means to continue the raids. After Kitchener had replaced Roberts as Commander-in-Chief in November 1900, a comprehensive network of blockhouses was created to restrict the Afrikaner commandos' freedom of movement. In addition, *concentration camps were erected to intern civilians believed to support, or be connected with, the enemy.

In 1902, Botha decided to sue for peace while the Afrikaner forces still possessed the strength to bargain an advantageous peace, so that on 31 May 1902 the Treaty of Vereeniging was concluded. It proved a Pyrrhic victory for the British, however. The war had exposed the weakness of the British army, which had needed a total of half a million soldiers to win over two small, ill-equipped armies. Furthermore, even after annexation British control over the reluctant OFS and the Transvaal, which had no liking for the *British Empire whatsoever, remained extremely weak. Finally, the memory of the war ensured the continued bitterness of many Afrikaners against the Empire, and the relationship with Britain remained the most divisive issue in White South African politics until 1961.

South East Asia Command, see SEAC

South-East Asia Treaty Organization, see SEATO

South Pacific Community

An international organization founded in 1947 as the South Pacific Commmission (SPC) by Australia, New Zealand, Britain, France, the Netherlands, and the USA, to coordinate programmes of economic development and social welfare for states of the South Pacific. The Netherlands withdrew in 1962, and Britain in 1996. In 1998, the SPC changed its name to the South Pacific Community. Sixty years after its foundation, it was composed of 26 members. Its aim was to promote cooperation amongst its members in the areas of fisheries, agriculture, health, community education, and socio-economic and statistical services.

(🌐) **SEE WEB LINKS**

• The home page of the South Pacific Community.

South Pacific Forum, see PACIFIC FORUM

South Tirol (Alto Adige)

An autonomous German-speaking region in northern Italy. Originally part of the Austrian province of Tirol, it was separated from eastern and northern Tirol, which remained Austrian, and acquired by Italy at the Treaty of *St Germain in 1919. The Italianization programmes introduced under *Mussolini in an attempt to destroy the region's distinctiveness heightened local hostility to the Italian state. After World War II, *De Gasperi promised regional autonomy, though the Italian government remained reluctant to fulfil this promise. The problem was not solved until 1992, when all the autonomy measures agreed between Italy and Austria in 1969 were finally realized, whereby the region gained considerable self-government in matters of social security, communications, and finance.

Southern Rhodesia, see ZIMBABWE

Souvanna Phouma, Prince (b. 7 Oct. 1901, d. 10 Jan. 1984). Prime Minister of Laos 1951–4, 1956–8, 1960, 1962–73

A nephew of King Sisavang Vong (r. 1904–59), and half-brother of *Souphanouvong, he studied as an engineer in Paris and Grenoble before returning to *Indochina in 1931. After the collapse of Japan in 1945 he served briefly in the provisional government, but when his uncle welcomed the return of the French in 1946, he joined the neutralist Free Laos (Lao Issara) movement, in opposition both to the French-supported monarchists, and the *Vietminh-aided Communist *Pathet Lao. As Prime Minister he managed to negotiate Laotian independence through the *Geneva Agreements, while failing to obtain a truce with the Pathet Lao led by Souphanouvong. He finally managed to form a coalition government with the Pathet Lao in 1957, though this broke up in 1958 owing to internal squabbles, and the withdrawal of US aid. Civil war resumed between his forces and the Pathet Lao until 1973, apart from a brief period in 1962–3, when he formed another coalition government. He tried desperately to maintain a semblance of neutrality for his country, despite the heavy involvement of the Pathet Lao in the *Vietnam War. He continued to strive for a reconciliation between all the warring factions in Laos. Following the *Paris Peace Accords, he agreed to a cease-fire and to a coalition government with the Pathet Lao under the leadership of Souphanouvong, though this did not come into effect until 1974. He was greatly weakened personally by a heart attack, and politically by the fall of *Saigon, which made a Communist takeover by the Vietnamese-sponsored Pathet Lao inevitable. He resigned, but remained on friendly terms with the new government of Souphanouvong.

soviet ('council')

A representative institution which gained prominence in Russian history during the 1905 *Russian Revolution, when it was formed first in St Petersburg and then elsewhere to coordinate strikes and revolutionary activities. Soviets were again formed throughout the country after the February 1917 *Russian Revolution, when the Petrograd (formerly St Petersburg) Soviet formed a rival centre of power to the nationally elected *Duma. They increasingly became strongholds for the *Bolsheviks, who used their control as the basis of the October 1917 *Russian Revolution, and their subsequent national takeover of power. Theoretically, they remained the fundamental unit of the state's organization, with the Supreme Soviet of the USSR acting as the nominal equivalent of a parliament. However, in practice Soviets were less representative institutions than mostly passive organs of the *Communist Party.

Soviet Union (Union of Socialist Soviet Republics, USSR)

Through the establishment of *Communism in 1917, which it subsequently sought to extend to all parts of the globe, no other country apart from the USA has exerted such a profound influence over the course of twentieth-century history.

Creation (1917–22) Soviet Russia emerged under the leadership of *Lenin out of the 1917 *Russian Revolution. It was the world's first and most powerful *Communist state, the ideology of which was based on *Marxism-Leninism. Despite the absence of a blueprint for his October Revolution or for how a Communist country could be achieved in practice, Lenin was quick to transform state, society, and the economy. Elections to the Constituent Assembly had made clear the limited popular support for the *Bolsheviks, and so Lenin proceeded to outlaw his political opposition in early 1918. The hegemony of the *Bolshevik Communist Party was realized through political commissars who ensured the loyalty of the *Red Army, the personal union between the highest offices of party and state, and the brutal terror of loyal *Cheka bands in the countryside.

The termination of World War I through the Treaty of *Brest-Litovsk created a short breathing space which was needed to enable the new regime to prevail in the *Russian Civil War. The war posed a great danger to the Communist leadership, and imposed severe hardships throughout the country. At the same time, Lenin had always considered the possibility of a civil war in response to a Communist revolution, and in some ways he welcomed it, because the war allowed him to take a firmer grip on the country. Landowners were expropriated almost immediately, while banks, commerce and industry were nationalized.

This rapid economic transformation compounded the enormous economic dislocations of the war, so that levels of industrial production in 1921 had been reduced to around 14 per cent of their 1913 levels. At the same time, government grain requisitioning not only deprived peasants of their produce, but also incriminated those who had refused to sell their grain to the government in the hope of better prices. These economic and social disturbances led to mass peasant uprisings and, more critical from Lenin's point of view, a rebellion of sailors at Kronstadt, who had previously been regarded as loyal and reliable. Lenin's response was the *New Economic Policy (NEP), which reversed many of the earlier drastic economic measures, and quickly restored production to 1913 levels. With the Communist Party now much more firmly in control over most of former Tsarist Russia, the USSR was founded on 30 December 1922, as a federal union of national republics. (However, these republics enjoyed only nominal autonomy within the USSR.)

Stalinism (1923–53) With Lenin's health deteriorating, the struggle for the succession began in earnest in 1923. It was a manifestation of the growing importance of the Communist Party relative to the state that the new party secretary, *Stalin, was able to claim power for himself, though *Trotsky (leader of the *Red Army) and *Zinoviev (leader of *Comintern) initially appeared as more likely successors to Lenin. Henceforward, the First (or General) Secretary of the Communist Party would always be the effective leader of the state (though rarely its titular head). Stalin had three principal aims throughout his rule (*Stalinism): to consolidate his own power, to advance Communism through the elimination of what he considered to be the bourgeoisie, and to extend Soviet power. He gradually outmanœuvred all his rivals within the top ranks of the party, while terror throughout the country brought his supporters to the local and regional power bases.

Once Stalin's power was sufficiently secure, he stopped the NEP and pushed for the advance of Communism in society and the economy. The first Five-Year Plan (1928–33) introduced large-scale investment in heavy industry, at the expense of agriculture and consumption. In the countryside *kulaks and other peasant proprietors were expropriated: by 1932, Stalin could claim to have collectivized 62 per cent of all farms, and by 1937 this figure had risen to over 90 per cent. The force and rapidity of these measures led to chaos and anarchy in vast parts of the country, with peasants enriching themselves at the expense of their neighbours, or destroying their cattle rather than let them come under the ownership of the state. A catastrophic famine ensued, in which almost eleven million people died. Thus, a socialist society and economy were achieved with some success, but only at extraordinary human cost.

To maintain his control over the state and party in these circumstances, Stalin extended his terror in the 1930s. After the murder of his last potential rival, *Kirov, in 1934, Stalin reorganized the security forces and, with the help of the new *NKVD, carried out the *Great Purge. This enabled him to re-establish control over the country with an iron grip. Stalin's third goal, the extension of

Table 18. **Leaders of the Soviet Union and Russia since 1917**

Soviet Union

COMMUNIST PARTY LEADERS:

Vladimir Ilyich *Lenin	1917–22
Joseph *Stalin	1922–53
Nikita *Khrushchev	1953–64
Leonid *Brezhnev	1964–82
Yuri *Andropov	1982–4
Konstantin *Chernenko	1984–5
Mikhail *Gorbachev	1985–91

Russia

PRESIDENTS:

Boris *Yeltsin	1991–2000
Vladimir *Putin	2000–

Soviet power, was mostly a product of the 1930s. The *Hitler–Stalin Pact gave him a perfect opportunity to reclaim lands lost from 1917, and to extend Soviet territory even further. The eastern half of Poland came under Soviet control, while parts of Finland were annexed after the *Winter War. In 1940, Estonia, Latvia, and Lithuania were annexed.

When Germany attacked the USSR on 22 June 1941, three factors facilitated the rapid German advance, for which the USSR paid so dearly. First, the Red Army had been significantly weakened by Stalin's purges, which had removed most of its experienced officers. Secondly, Stalin had assumed that *Hitler would not risk his vast possessions in Europe in an attack on the USSR, so that he was completely unprepared for the attack when it occurred. Thirdly, it took Stalin as the supreme war leader some time to adjust to the tactical and military requirements of the war. Once an able command structure under *Zhukov had been created and was allowed to function relatively freely, however, the Red Army was able to turn the tide at the battle of *Stalingrad and in the defence of Leningrad (formerly St Petersburg).

Like the Civil War twenty years earlier, World War II allowed the leadership to extend its power still further, as entire nationalities were uprooted and sent to Siberia and other remote areas, most notably the *Chechens and the Volga Germans.

With around twenty million dead, and its formerly German-occupied areas in ruins, the USSR had suffered the greatest civilian and military losses of all victorious powers in World War II. Stalin was therefore able to claim large territorial gains for the USSR, whereby the Baltic States, parts of East *Prussia, and substantial parts of Poland (as well as Sakhalin and the Kurile Islands in the east) were incorporated into the Soviet Union. In addition, Soviet troops occupied Eastern Europe and most of the Balkans, which Stalin now transformed into Soviet satellite states.

Under leaders mostly trained in Moscow and unswervingly loyal to Stalin, and with 'comradely' assistance from the NKVD, Communist systems were established in these countries that sought to mirror the political and social set-up of the USSR. Ironically, it was in these years, when his power both within and outside the USSR was at its peak, that Stalin suffered from increasing paranoia. He started to demote almost all his aides, and increased his terror yet again, directing it against Jews and other perceived enemies. Just before another wave of purges, he died.

Khrushchev's rule (1953–64) Stalin's death led to tremors throughout the Communist bloc, and precipitated an uprising in East Germany on 17 June 1953. Within the USSR, a collective leadership was soon established between *Khrushchev, *Malenkov, *Molotov, *Kaganovich, and *Bulganin. However, it was Khrushchev who quickly established his authority at the expense of the others. At the XXth Party Congress in 1956, Khrushchev laid bare some of the atrocities of the Stalinist regime, in order to accelerate a process of 'de-Stalinization', which involved the reversal of Stalin's policies, and the dismissal from office of many of Stalin's protégés.

Khrushchev tried hard to give agriculture a new impetus through a massive campaign to cultivate 'virgin lands' in Kazakhstan, with mixed results. His economic reforms included a greater emphasis on consumer goods, and a shift of priorities away from traditional industries, such as coal and steel, to modern industries (e.g. chemical industries). In foreign policy, Stalin introduced a policy of careful *détente* with the USA, while at the same time his policy to advance Soviet influence wherever possible resulted in the *Cuban Missile Crisis, which ultimately led to the brink of a nuclear war. Khrushchev's major problem was that, having denounced collective responsibility as well as autocratic Stalinism, he could never impose the harsh discipline on the state, party, and army that alone would have ensured his survival in the way that it had done for Stalin. This point was well understood by *Brezhnev, who succeeded Khrushchev upon his dismissal in 1964.

The Brezhnev era (1964–82) Brezhnev reintroduced collective responsibility within the *Politburo, so as to share the responsibilities of, and to maximize general allegiance towards, the leadership. Brezhnev was careful not to alienate important groups within the party, and the same was true for the economy, where he led *propaganda drives to improve efficiency, but never embarked on fundamental reform. Finally, he kept the military happy through promising to maintain the current levels of influence and allowing it to intervene in situations such as the *Prague Spring which posed a direct challenge to its hegemony.

In fact, the Brezhnev era, which continued in essence under his short-lived successors *Andropov and *Chernenko until 1985, managed to produce stagnation disguised as stability. As Western technology developed in leaps and bounds, an isolated Soviet economy suffered from lack of know-how. Funds were increasingly used to subsidize foodstuffs and other articles on a day-to-day level, so that industrial plants suffered from wear and tear and from underinvestment. Furthermore, the economy was squeezed by exorbitant military spending, and found it increasingly difficult to compete with *NATO (and specifically US) high-technology armament programmes such as *SDI. Meanwhile, the Soviet invasion of Afghanistan, begun in 1979, exposed serious shortcomings in the military, while popular unrest in Poland could be contained only with difficulty, and then only superficially.

Dissolution (1985–91) A new era began with the coming to power of *Gorbachev in 1985. Despite the stagnation of the Brezhnev years, Gorbachev's reforms of *glasnost and *perestroika, initiated from 1986, were by no means inevitable, as the new Soviet leader could well have tried to muddle through in the way of his predecessors. However, his policies soon developed a dynamic of their own, as reforms revealed further cracks that had been papered over, which necessitated further reforms, and so on. Perhaps the biggest strain that was exposed was the very composition of the USSR, whose constituent nationalities demanded increasing recognition of their own political and cultural rights. Ultimately, it became clear that the root problem of the Soviet Union was that of Communism itself. As Gorbachev's reforms produced some halfway-house between Communism and *capitalism, the economy fared even worse, and discredited moderate reforms even more. The initiative was soon taken by *Yeltsin, the increasingly popular head of the Russian Soviet Republic. By 1991, his authority eclipsed that of Gorbachev, especially after he saved the latter in the *August coup.

The collapse of central Soviet power was complete with the resignation of Gorbachev on 25 December 1991. On 31 December, the USSR broke up into its constituent republics which were now independent: *Armenia, *Azerbaijan, *Belarus, *Georgia, *Kazakhstan, *Kyrgyzstan, *Lithuania, *Moldova, *Russia, *Tajikistan, *Turkmenistan, *Ukraine, *Uzbekistan. Of its former Baltic republics, the independence of Lithuania had been recognized on 29 July 1991, while Estonia and Latvia had gained their independence on 21 August 1991.
MAP 5

Soweto (South Western Townships)
A sprawling Black residential area ('township') outside Johannesburg (South Africa), which came to epitomize the *apartheid regime. The township was created in response to a large influx of Black labour into Johannesburg after the discovery of gold in 1885, in order to keep the Blacks out of the White residential areas. Built on a layout allowing optimal levels of state control, miles of identical rows of makeshift houses were erected without running water, electricity, or proper roofs, in order to save money and discourage permanent residence. It soon became the largest conurbation in South Africa. Since it had no industries of its own, most of the adult population depended on a single railway line to commute daily into work. As a protest partly against these living conditions, and partly against the inadequate education system for Blacks, schoolchildren marched through the streets of Soweto on 16 June 1976, whereupon police opened fire on them. There followed a series of riots in townships throughout South Africa, though these were soon brought under control by police violence. As a symbol of apartheid repression the Soweto revolt was commemorated

annually by the *ANC, bringing the injustices of apartheid to international attention. Following the ANC's coming to power, the 16 June was declared a national holiday in 1995. A 2001 census put Soweto's population at just under 900,000, though estimates put the figure closer to two million inhabitants. Although poverty was still widespread, almost all households were connected to electricity.

Spaak, Paul-Henri (b. 25 Jan. 1899, d. 31 July 1972). Prime Minister of Belgium 1938–9, 1947–9 Born at Schaerbeek, he qualified as a lawyer in 1922 and practised law until entering parliament as a Socialist in 1932. He became Belgium's first Socialist Prime Minister in 1938. After the German invasion he moved to London, where he was Foreign Minister of the government-in-exile. Here he played a major role in the establishment of the *UN, and became the first President of its General Assembly. He was one of the architects of the *Benelux customs union and became president of the consultative assembly of the *Council of Europe (1949–51). Spaak played a major part in forcing the abdication of King *Leopold III. He was Foreign Minister 1954–7 and again 1961–6, and served as Secretary-General of *NATO 1957–61. As one of the first and foremost proponents of *European integration in politics as well as economics, Spaak was a key figure in the establishment of the *ECSC and the EEC.

Spain

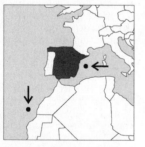

One of Europe's most powerful countries in the sixteenth century, Spain experienced traumatic decline until the early twentieth century. Plagued by the memory of a bitter civil war, the Franco era stifled cultural and political development until the introduction of a constitutional monarchy brought remarkable stability and prosperity.

Restoration of the monarchy (1876–1931) Nineteenth-century Spain was marked by an inability to overcome the diverse and often conflicting economic tensions arising from the loss of its vast colonial empire. These difficulties were reinforced by political and administrative tensions emerging from Napoleonic rule at the beginning of the century, and regional tensions caused by the distinctiveness of its regions, particularly in

the *Basque territory and Catalonia. In the second half of the nineteenth century, these regional differences became more marked owing to the rise of *nationalism, and economic change. The permanence of these conflicts was caused by, and in turn increased, chronic political instability, and by the civil wars of 1833–40 and 1872–6. The latter war restored the monarchy, which remained weak because of the early death of Alfonso XII (b. 1857, d. 1885) and the infancy of *Alfonso XIII. The tensions of the nineteenth century increased during the early twentieth. Illusions about world-power status were finally destroyed by defeat in the Spanish–American War of 1898. This resulted in the loss of the Philippines, Cuba, Puerto Rico, and *Guam. To compensate for this, Spain tried to conquer territory in Morocco. That war led to even greater instability, as northern Morocco was not secured for Spain until 1926, while the cost of the war was completely disproportionate to any meagre economic gain that possession of the colony might have entailed.

On the domestic front, economic change and industrialization, which was confined to a few regions, led to the growth of the *Socialist Party and its affiliated trade union, the General Workers' Union (UGT). This period also saw the growth of *anarcho-syndicalists, who had a large following among the landless labourers in the countryside, especially those living in a sharecropping system. Socialists and anarcho-syndicalists operated outside and against the political system, and not only preached revolution but tried to bring it about through general strikes (e.g. in 1917) and frequent bomb attacks. While it appeared that the prosperity arising from Spain's neutrality during World War I might result in greater acceptance of the regime, an economic crisis from 1917 furthered general unrest.

To forestall the ostensible breakup of the country, and frustrated by disastrous losses in the conquest of Morocco, the army staged a coup on 13 September 1923. Its leader, *Primo de Rivera, tried to bring about badly needed reforms through progressive social policies and an improvement of labour relations. His attempts were doomed, however, since he tried to carry them out mostly against the country's entrenched interests. Equally importantly, he lacked any political basis, so after losing the support of the army he had no option but to resign in 1930. The municipal elections of 1931 produced a narrow victory for the republican parties, and induced King Alfonso XIII to leave the country.

Second Republic (1931–9) The eminent moderate Republican *Alcalá Zamora became

President. The new Prime Minister, *Azaña, began an ambitious reform project to reduce the overwhelming influence of the Roman *Catholic Church, grant (successfully) autonomy to Catalonia, end all privilege by birth, and reform the military. In other words, the Republicans took on virtually all the established interests at the same time, and the more they failed in most of their endeavours, the more dogged they became. The 1933 elections produced a victory for the right-wing parties, which were subsequently opposed by incessant demonstrations and strikes.

In 1936 a left-wing *Popular Front won the elections, amidst continuing unrest. The general chaos precipitated a military coup attempt by the army under *Franco. This failed to take over the government in a decisive sweep, and had the paradoxical effect of creating even greater chaos, leading to anarchy within the Republic. The conflicts between the interests and groups that supported the Republic, however, were ultimately responsible for the defeat of the Second Republic in the bitter *Spanish Civil War of 1936–9.

The Franco dictatorship (1939–75) After the war, Franco established an authoritarian regime in which political parties were banned with the exception of the *Falange, while press censorship and the lack of a constitution added to Franco's control yet further. He was not interested in reconciling the two sides of the Civil War. Instead, he had thousands of his former enemies executed immediately after the war, and ensured the discrimination of his former opponents throughout the regime.

With the defeat of *Hitler's *Nazi dictatorship in Germany and *Mussolini's government in Italy, *Fascism turned into a liability. Franco progressively toned down the Fascist elements of his regime. Instead, he emphasized the role of the Roman Catholic Church, which was formalized through the 1953 Concordat with the *Vatican. The Law of the Principles of the National Movement (17 May 1958) recognized the role of the Roman Catholic Church, the monarchy, and society based on, and represented by, estates, as the three central pillars of the state (*corporatism). The conservatism of this state was greatly undermined, however, by the country's economic and industrial progress, which went hand in hand with increasing *secularization. Franco's hierarchical state was less and less based on social reality, and relied increasingly on his presence alone. This made it very difficult for his regime to survive him.

Democratization (1975–1990s) Franco was succeeded by *Juan Carlos, who became King upon Franco's death in 1975. To bring about rapid democratization, Juan Carlos appointed the energetic *Suárez as his Prime Minister, who devised legislation for the establishment of a democratic system, and won the ensuing elections in 1977. The young democracy was tested by a military coup on 23 February 1981, which failed thanks partly to the defiance of the King. In 1982 the election victory of the Socialist Party under *González inaugurated a period of social democratic rule which lasted until 1996. During this time, Spain was fully integrated into the international community through the confirmation of Spanish membership of *NATO after narrow approval at a plebiscite in 1986. It became a member of the EEC on 1 January 1986 and a pillar of further *European integration, after ending the blockade of *Gibraltar imposed by Franco in 1969.

International integration required and in part precipitated a structural transformation of the Spanish economy, as it attracted a significant amount of investment in modern technology and industry. The rewards were not immediately apparent, as Spain continued to be plagued by a long-term average unemployment rate of around 25 per cent until the early 1990s. Despite concerted efforts to reconcile regional autonomy with national integration, and to address the grievances of the Basque and Catalan peoples in particular, González was unable to reduce those regions' strivings for greater autonomy. He was also unable to contain the Basque terrorist organization ETA, which remained the most active European terrorist organization of the 1980s and 1990s. Evidence of government corruption and resentment at the loss of the González government's sparkle led to his defeat in the 1996 elections.

The elections, which brought to power the *Popular Party (PP) under the leadership of *Aznar, were widely considered to mark the coming of age of Spanish democracy. They established a national two-party system consisting of a moderate right-wing and a moderate left-wing party, which were complemented by a number of regional splinter parties. Aznar presided over a highly successful economy, which benefited from increased domestic demand and from export-led growth. As a result, Spain qualified for membership in the European Monetary Union, and adopted the *euro in 1999.

Contemporary politics (from c. 2000) In the 2000 elections the PP obtained an absolute majority. Aznar moved to secure the regional payments received by Spain from the EU in the context of the EU's eastern enlargement due 2004. In the face of public opinion, Aznar became a prominent backer of the US-led *Iraq War in 2003. In return for its support, Spain received US assistance in its fight against Basque terrorism.

Following the *Madrid Bombings, the 2004 elections produced a victory for the Socialist Party under *Zapatero. He continued to promote economic growth, so that by 2006, unemployment had declined to below 10 per cent. The government introduced a tax reform in 2005 and increased the retirement age, while constitutionally its most significant actions consisted of the granting of greater autonomy to Spain's regions, notably Catalonia.

Spanish Civil War (1936–9)

Outbreak (1936) The first 'modern' civil war in Europe, an all-out confrontation involving the extensive use of an air force, naval power, and mechanized armed units. It began on 18 July 1936 as an attempted army coup led by *Franco involving Spanish elite forces in Morocco, in order to topple the *anticlerical, anti-landowning *Popular Front government. By 21 July 1936, Franco was in control of Morocco, the Balearic Islands, the conservative and firmly Roman *Catholic Navarre, Old Castile, Leon, and the cities of Seville and Saragossa. The Republicans had remained in control of most of the territory, and were helped by the loyalty of the air force and the navy. This advantage was lessened through the help of the German *Luftwaffe* (air force). Most importantly, the Republicans were riven by disunity and lack of organization and coordination within and between their forces, often culminating in anarchy. By contrast, the Nationalists under Franco were united around his command. From September 1936, the new Republican leader, *Largo Caballero, improved the efficiency of the forces, and managed to halt Franco's advance on the outskirts of Madrid in November 1936.

Course of the war (1936–9) The failure to take Madrid led Franco to prepare for a long battle. He consolidated his popular base through the use of the *Falange, and began a series of military operations aimed at extending the territory under his control. By June 1937, the tide had shifted decisively in Franco's favour, as he had taken control of the *Basque country and the prosperous industrial regions of northern Spain. Subsequently, he no longer had to fight on two fronts.

Meanwhile, Largo Caballero had been replaced as Prime Minister by *Negrín in May 1937. Negrín's immense efforts at restructuring the Republican forces, and at reconciling previously hostile sections of the population to the regime through abandoning its programme of social and economic revolution, came too late. Tired and exhausted, the Republic crumbled in early 1939, with Franco declaring victory on 1 April 1939.

Outcome The war, which had cost the lives of over half a million people, furthered the polarization of Spanish society between urban workers, anticlerical socialists and Communists, and landless labourers on the one hand, and the army, landowning and propertied elites, and monarchist middle classes supported by the Roman Catholic Church on the other. These divisions were heightened by Franco's recriminations against his former enemies after the war, when tens of thousands of Republicans were executed.

Spartakists

A German revolutionary group founded by *Luxemburg and *Liebknecht in 1916 to unite those among the Social Democratic Party (*SPD) who opposed the war, named after the slave who led a revolt against the Roman Empire (71 BC). In 1917 it became affiliated to the Independent Socialist Party (USPD), and on 1 January 1919 it supported the newly created *Communist Party. Later that month, the Spartakists led a revolt in Berlin, which aimed at carrying further the German revolution of November 1918. The group was suppressed brutally by the *Freikorps, and it collapsed after the murder of both Liebknecht and Luxemburg.

SPD (Sozialdemokratische Partei Deutschlands, Social Democratic Party of Germany)

Early history (before 1933) Founded in 1869 as a political party committed to social upheaval, it was Germany's most popular party by 1890. Despite its goal of international *socialism, the increasingly pragmatic leadership under *Bernstein and others accepted the outbreak of World War I and supported it as a necessary evil. In 1917, those of its members who opposed the war founded the Independent Socialist Party (Unabhängige Sozialdemokratische Partei Deutschlands, USPD), which merged with the *Communist Party in 1920. After the collapse of the Empire in 1918, the SPD did more than any other party to establish a democracy instead of a socialist republic. The SPD remained the most popular party throughout most of the Weimar Republic, and provided its first President in *Ebert. It was the only party to vote against the *Enabling Law of 1933, but by then the SPD on its own was too weak to foil it. Subsequently, the SPD was banned and many members were persecuted, though some managed to escape abroad.

Contemporary history (after 1945) After World War II, in Eastern Germany the SPD was forced to merge with the Communist Party in 1946, a measure that eliminated an independent socialist party. In Western Germany, the SPD narrowly lost the 1949 election, and spent the following twenty years in opposition to the *CDU. In 1955 it transformed itself from a workers' party to one that aimed at representing all sections of the population. The first SPD government under *Brandt made a profound impact upon German society through its new approach to the *German question (Ostpolitik), its social policies, and its liberalization of German society. Under *Schmidt, the SPD continued in government until 1982, when the defection of the *Liberal Party (FDP) deprived the government of its majority at national level.

In 1990 it became the principal party to govern at the state level, which enabled it also to control the second chamber of the German parliament, the Bundesrat. Ironically, its prominence at the state level made it difficult for the central party to rein in the powerful party barons and present a unified front against the CDU. In 1998 one of the most outspoken state leaders, *Schröder, was selected to challenge *Kohl. The SPD won the general elections of that year, and formed a coalition with the *Green Party. Unlike the first SPD government headed by Brandt, the SPD's election victory was not accompanied by any major ideological shift. Instead, the SPD sought to occupy firmly the electoral centre ground, through moderate policies of fiscal, pension, and health service reform.In Schröder's second period of office, however, the party was internally split on Schröder's labour market reforms. The party had lost most state elections of the previous years, and in 2005 it narrowly lost the federal elections. The SPD continued in government in a grand coalition with the CDU.

((⊕)) SEE WEB LINKS
• The official website of the SPD.

Speer, Albert (b. 19 Mar. 1905, d. 1 Sept. 1981). German Minister of Armaments Production 1942–5
Originally of liberal inclination, he was, by his own account, mesmerized by one of *Hitler's speeches and joined the *Nazi Party in 1931. He became Hitler's architect and, owing to Hitler's passion for art and architecture, one of his closer associates, though he appears not to have been involved in the dictator's political decisions. He planned monumental buildings to satisfy Hitler's quest for grandeur, but in 1942 he became Minister for Armaments Production, and in 1943 he was made responsible for Germany's entire war production. In this capacity he achieved great success, as despite bombings and labour shortages production peaked in 1944.

After the war, Speer was sentenced to twenty years' imprisonment at the *Nuremberg Trials. He avoided the death penalty by his insistence that, as a 'technocrat', he did not know about the *Holocaust, and because he was one of the few Nazi leaders to show remorse at the horrors of the Nazi crimes that were revealed during the trial. More recently, however, it has been revealed that he must have known about the extermination of Jews in the *concentration camps (owing to his presence at the Wannsee Conference). There is also evidence that he was fully aware of the horrors which the forced labour encountered in the munitions factories for which he was responsible. He wrote one of the most important, compelling, and flawed personal accounts of the war in his *Erinnerungen* (*Inside the Third Reich*, 1969).

Spence, William Guthrie (b. 7 Aug. 1846, d. 13 Dec. 1926). Australian trade unionist
Born on the Scottish Orkney Islands, his family arrived at Geelong (Victoria) in 1852. A pivotal figure in the Australian *trade-union movement, he helped found a number of unions until he became secretary of the Amalgamated Miners' Association (1882) and of the Amalgamated Shearers' Union (1886). He was a moving force behind the formation of the Australian Workers' Union, which for a long time was the biggest single Australian trade union. He was its secretary (1894–8) and president (1898–1917). A strong advocate of using trade unionism to support the political *Labor movement, he became a member of the New South Wales Legislative Assembly in 1898. He entered the federal parliament in 1902, but had to transfer his allegiance to the *Nationalist Party because of his vote for compulsory military service overseas in 1916.

Sri Lanka
A south Asian island off the east coast of southern India, Sri Lanka experienced harmonious social and cultural development in

the first half of the twentieth century, followed by growing ethnic strife in the second.

British rule (up to 1948) A British colony from 1796, during the nineteenth century it was transformed into a plantations colony, whose economy was dominated by the cultivation of tea, coffee, and coconuts, at the expense of self-sufficiency in food production. These products were shipped to other parts of the *British Empire, creating an important indigenous commercial middle class. At the same time, the British imported *Tamils from southern India as cheap labour, a minority which remained at the bottom of the social and economic scale, even after independence.

In the early twentieth century the country was marked by a relatively harmonious transition to independence. A relatively advanced educational sector produced an articulate population which became increasingly organized, for example in trade unions in the cities and *Marxist groups in the countryside. Once the prosperous Tamil and Sinhalese communities demanded a greater political role, this was granted in 1931, following recommendations by the Donoughmore Commission. Only three years after Britain itself, Ceylon was granted universal, equal suffrage for parliamentary elections. During the 1930s and 1940s, politics was dominated by *Senanayake. He was responsible for innovative social policies which saw the irrigation of dry areas in order to promote the cultivation of foodstuffs. Other remarkable policies during this era included increased spending on education and food subsidies.

Early independence (1948–56) On 4 February 1948 Ceylon was released into independence, without any of the strife and tension which had just occurred in neighbouring India and Pakistan. Senanayake carried on with his inclusive policies, continuing his agricultural projects and insisting on the mediating role of the secular state between the Buddhist Sinhalese majority, which constituted around 75 per cent of the population, and the Tamil (largely Hindu, but also Christian) minority, which made up around 18 per cent of the population. His early death in 1952 was a tragic blow to the country, since his successor and son, D. S. Senanayake, was unable to keep the United National Party (UNP) united and inspire the population.

Ethnic conflict (from 1956) In 1956 he was outmanoeuvred by his rival, Solomon *Bandaranaike, whose election marked a watershed in Ceylonese politics. He pursued a more anti-Western policy but, more importantly, he had been elected on a platform of guarding the interests of the Buddhist and Sinhalese majority. Sinhalese replaced English as the official language, while he managed to offend both Hindu and Christian Tamils through his discrimination against them on educational matters. He was succeeded in 1960 by his wife, Sirimavo *Bandaranaike, who pursued more radical socialist policies. She lost the 1965 elections to Senanayake's UNP, but regained power in 1970. With the help of the Marxists and other left-wing groups, in 1972 she passed a new socialist constitution wherein the country's name was changed from Ceylon to Sri Lanka. By 1974 she had nationalized the last plantations. Private enterprise had been stifled in most other areas of the economy, too, so that she was completely unable to respond to the 1973 *oil price shock.

In 1977 Bandaranaike's government collapsed, and the UNP gained power under *Jayawardene. He revitalized the economy through privatization and liberalization, and passed a new constitution in 1978. He abolished his predecessor's discrimination against the Tamils, for example by introducing Tamil as an official language next to Sinhalese. Ironically, however, it was during his rule that the ethnic tension that had built up during the Bandaranaike years exploded into open warfare and civil war in 1983. Matters were complicated by Indian intervention (1987–9), though even after India's withdrawal it proved impossible to reach either a political solution to the problem or a military one, owing to the ragged state of the army.

Early elections in 1994 led to a surprise defeat for the UNP at the hands of the People's Alliance, a left-wing coalition headed by C. Bandaranaike Kumaratunga. The latter became the new head of state, with her mother, the veteran Sirimavo Bandaranaike, as Prime Minister. Kumaratunga pursued a policy of military confrontation to force the Tamil rebel force, the Liberation Tigers of Tamil Eelam (LTTE) into negotiations. The LTTE responded by starting a large-scale military offensive in 1999, which extended its control on the Jaffna peninsula without defeating the government there completely. In the military impasse that ensued, negotiations between the two sides made little progress. The LTTE rejected a constitutional revision suggested by Kumaratunga which suggested autonomy for Jaffna as part of a federal state structure.

Contemporary politics (since 1999) Kamaratunga won the 1999 presidential elections, but lost its absolute parliamentary majority in 2000. She opposed the concessions made by Prime Minister Ranil Wickramesinghe in his successful negotiations with the LTTW. In a coup she called new elections in 2004, which her People's Freeedom Alliance won. Mahinda Rajapakse became the new Prime Minister, and in 2005 he narrowly won the presidential elections against Wickramesinghe. Rajapakse believed in centralization and the maintenance of the unitary state, which fuelled Tamil opposition further. Sri Lanka has been badly affected by the *tsunami of 2004, which killed around 30,000 people. It received generous international aid, though the government refused to provide aid to the LTTE to reconstruct the areas under its control. Although both sides officially declared their respect for a 2002 ceasefire, sporadic violence mounted, leading to open military confronation from 2006.

SS (*Schutzstaffel*) (Germany)

Founded in 1925 as the internal police of the *SA and the *Nazi Party, the SS became an independent organization following the Röhm Putsch in 1934. Led by *Himmler, it developed an internal security service (the *Sicherheitsdienst*) under *Heydrich, which from 1936 was responsible for uncovering opposition within the German population. During World War II, SS task forces (*Einsatzgruppen*) roamed through occupied eastern Europe, rounding up villages and executing their Jewish residents. Hundreds of thousands of Jews were killed in this way.

In 1933, the Order of the Skull (*Totenkopfverbände*) was formed, which supervised the *concentration camps. In 1939, it formed the nucleus of the **Waffen-SS**, which recruited an increasing number of voluntary members as well as conscripts as it grew from 100,000 to 900,000 men. Many of these (particularly the conscripts) fought as regular troops, but a large number also committed atrocities, while some went to reinforce the concentration-camp guards. Given the administrative confusion in Nazi Germany, which was heightened to near-chaos in the eastern occupied territories, it was its simple command structure which made the SS so effective. Responsible only to Himmler and then to Hitler, the organization effectively stood above the law.

Stalin, Iosef Vissarioniovich

Dzhugashvili (b. 21 Dec. 1879, d. 5 Mar. 1953). Soviet dictator 1923–53

Early career Born I. V. Dzhugashvili, he was born in Gori, Georgia, and was educated at a Gori church school and the Orthodox seminary in Tbilisi, from which he was expelled for his revolutionary views in 1899. He became active in the revolutionary movement, and joined the *Bolshevik wing of the Social Democratic Party in 1903. Always a man more of practical bent than of theoretical discourse, he bolstered the regional party by leading several 'expropriations', which were in effect bank robberies of millions of roubles. He came to *Lenin's attention and was co-opted to the membership of the party's Central Committee in 1912. Stalin became involved in the publication of the party newspaper, *Pravda* (Truth), and in 1913 received *Bukharin's help in writing his first theoretical article on 'Marxism and the National Question'. He was again arrested in 1913 and sent to Siberia, from where he returned after the *Russian Revolution of February 1917.

Although at first sceptical of Lenin's violent opposition to the war and his non-conciliatory attitude towards the *Mensheviks, his efficiency and ability to work in the background without offending others gained him the appointment as People's Commissar (i.e. Minister) for Nationality Affairs. During the *Russian Civil War, he was also active as a political officer on the western front in the *Russo-Polish War. On 3 April 1922, Lenin appointed him General Secretary of the *Communist Party. Originally given an adminstrative appointment, he used his new position at the heart of the party to build up speedily a personal power base.

Stalinism and the Great Purge (1923–39) In the power struggles that ensued in the last year of Lenin's life, Stalin thus occupied a central position between what were then seen as the main protagonists, *Trotsky, *Zinoviev, and *Kamenev. By 1927, his position was secure, though he subsequently confirmed his power by removing all possible opposition not just within the party, but in the population at large. His rule was associated with brutal and arbitrary terror throughout, but it peaked at different times. In his fanatical view that the drive towards *Communism needed to be completed through the destruction of all private property and large-scale industrialization, he embarked on an ambitious Five-Year Plan in spring 1929 (covering the period October 1928 – September 1933).

Through the persecution of *kulaks and other peasant proprietors, he destroyed peasant communal agriculture and much of traditional peasant culture. Meanwhile, industrialization was achieved successfully, but only with the help of slave labour and the constant threat of forced labour camps. His drive to eliminate the bourgeoisie everywhere (*Stalinism) led to the large-scale expropriation, imprisonment, and execution of industrial managers, university teachers, soldiers, civil servants, and former political opponents in the *Great Purge. He sought to escape involvement in a major war through the *Hitler–Stalin Pact, which had the added benefit of adding Eastern Europe to his control. By early 1941, he had annexed Estonia, Latvia, Lithuania, eastern Poland, and parts of Romania.

World War II Calculating that *Hitler would be as content with his new possessions as he was, Stalin was completely taken by surprise by the German invasion of the Soviet Union in the *Barbarossa campaign beginning 22 June 1941. After providing uncharacteristically chaotic leadership in the first year of the war, whose effect was worsened by his execution of many able generals during the Great Purge, he became an able co-ordinator of the war effort. He used the war not only to further his own image as national hero and liberator, but also to weaken the *nationalism of the country's different peoples which, as a Georgian, he appreciated only too well. Thus, he forcibly resettled altogether millions of Crimean Tartars, *Chechens, and Volga Germans.

Late Stalinism (1945–53). After the war, he applied the methods of resettlement to the Baltic States of Estonia, Latvia, and Lithuania, when he 'exchanged' a large proportion of their ethnic population with a similar number of other Soviet nationalities. Having been victorious in World War II, he successfully manipulated the *Yalta and *Potsdam Conferences to extend his country's influence towards the states of Eastern Europe. With the exception of Yugoslavia, these had become effective satellite states by 1948, and in the next few years he strengthened his grip over them through encouraging purges, the method he knew best. Towards the end of his life, he became increasingly paranoid, anti-intellectual, and *anti-Semitic. A new purge known as the Doctor's Plot was planned but not carried out owing to his death from a cerebral haemorrhage. He was undoubtedly one of the most ruthless and brutal dictators of the twentieth century, second only to *Hitler. Nevertheless, the memory of suffering during World War II, and his role in defeating Hitler, turned him into a hero in the memory of many Russians.

Stalingrad, Battle of (Sept. 1942 – Jan. 1943) The decisive battle on the Eastern Front, and in many ways the turning point of *World War II, when Germany switched from offensive to defensive warfare. The German 6th Army under von *Paulus and the 4th Panzer (tank) Army under Ewald von Kleist led the summer offensive of 1942, extending the gains made in the *Barbarossa campaign to include *Kursk, Kharkov, all the *Crimea, and the Maikop oilfields. In September, they reached the key city of Stalingrad (now Volgograd) on the Volga in September. Stalingrad was a centre of communications and munitions production, and had, by virtue of its name, tremendous symbolic value to both Stalin and Hitler. Soviet resistance successfully prevented the river being crossed, though through prolonged house-to-house fighting, most of the city was taken by the Germans. However, a Soviet counter-attack in November saw six armies under Marshals *Zhukov, *Koniev, and *Rokossovsky advancing from north and south. They annihilated the Romanian forces that were fighting on Germany's side, and encircled the 6th Army. German efforts to relieve Paulus remained unsuccessful due to insufficient air- and manpower, while Paulus was unable to break out of the encirclement. Weakened by bitter cold and frost, and incessant *Red Army bombardments, on 31 January 1943 Paulus decided to surrender his troops. Paulus thus ignored *Hitler's explicit orders to fight to the last man, with the last troops surrendering on 2 February. The battle claimed 146,000 German and Romanian lives. Of 90,000 exhausted and malnourished prisoners of war, only 6,000 returned home after the war.

Stalinism

An adaptation of *Communism by *Stalin, whose practice was easier to discern than his theory. First and foremost, it entailed the ruthless maintenance of power through the cold-blooded elimination of oppositional leaders, groups, or entire sections of the population (such as the *kulaks). Secondly, it denoted the overwhelming importance of the state security machine, which almost became a state within a state. Thirdly, in the economic sphere, it led to a system which saw the nationalization of industry and the promotion of heavy industry, as well as the near-complete collectivization of agriculture. Moreover, it focused on industrialization, and the development of heavy industry in particular, at the expense of agriculture as well as consumer goods. Finally, in political terms it meant the overwhelming dominance of Communist Party hierarchy, and particularly the party leader, over state institutions.

These practical aspects of Stalinism had the main purpose of keeping the particular leadership in power. Furthermore, it was used in the 1920s and 1930s to establish a truly Communist society through the rooting out of all elements that were perceived as 'bourgeois', i.e. those with property, links with bourgeois countries, or simply those in positions of responsibility. Finally, from World War II its purpose was to ensure the spread of Communism through the creation of a close system of satellite states in Eastern Europe, whose societies and political structures were to match those of the USSR as closely as possible. Towards the end of Stalin's life, and especially after *Khrushchev's drive against Stalinism from 1956, it became mostly a derogatory term for excessive, paranoic violence.

Stambolisky, Alexandar (b. 1 Mar. 1879, d. 14 June 1923). Prime Minister of Bulgaria 1919–23

Born in Slavoviza, the son of a wealthy peasant family went to study agriculture in Germany. Upon his return he became head of the Bulgarian Agrarian National Union in 1908, gaining a seat in parliament. He was imprisoned in 1915, but in 1918 the powerful, populist leader was released in the hope that he might be able to contain growing army unrest. With the more traditional forces discredited, his party polled 31 per cent at the elections of August 1919, whereupon he became Prime Minister. He established effectively a one-party agrarian state which discriminated heavily against urban dwelling areas, e.g. through severe property restrictions. Despite his success in gaining relatively light terms of punishment at the *Paris Peace Conference, he was none the less opposed by many right-wing and military groups for allowing the reduction in the size of the army. They also opposed his efforts to improve relations with Yugoslavia, which had just taken control of *Macedonia, and with Communist Soviet Russia. On 9 June 1923 he was deposed in a right-wing coup. Five days later he was discovered in hiding, and brutally murdered, his severed head being sent to the capital, Sofia, in a cake tin.

Starace, Achille (b. 1889, d. 28 Apr. 1945). Italian Fascist

One of the earliest Italian Fascists, he led the *Fascist movement in Trentino. He was Secretary of the National Fascist Party 1931–9. During this time he managed to increase party membership to 2.6 million, though his efforts to tighten party organization to translate greater party membership into increased effectiveness were widely opposed. He became increasingly resented by the Fascist old guard, so that *Mussolini was eventually forced to withdraw his support. He was executed by Milanese partisans.

Stasi (*Staatssicherheitsdienst*, State Security Service)

The East German security service in operation since 1945/6 (though officially not founded until 1950). Its activities, whose vast extent was only revealed after its dissolution in 1990, contributed significantly to the survival of the Communist regime. In a country of seventeen million inhabitants, it had 91,000 full-time agents and up to 175,000 secret collaborators at any one time. In the surviving Stasi archives are files on six million people. Despite its effectiveness in internal surveillance and international spy operations, it was unable to prevent the revolution against the GDR's Communist system in 1989. To the contrary, by utilizing vast amounts of manpower and economic resources, the Stasi apparatus helped accelerate the GDR's economic collapse.

Stauffenberg, Claus Count Schenk von, see JULY PLOT

Stavisky Scandal (1934)

During 1933 Serge Stavisky, a naturalized Frenchman from Russia, floated forged bonds on the Paris Bourse (stock exchange). When the police finally came to arrest him on 8 January 1934, he committed suicide. Enquiries into the delay in prosecuting him found that he had been backed and protected by a number of parliamentary Deputies and Ministers of the Third Republic. An official of the Public Prosecutor's Office was found murdered, which added to the charge of cover-up. Amid the sense of economic and social crisis pervading at the time, *Action Française and other right-wing groups exploited the incident to the utmost by suggesting that it showed not just the incompetence, but also the corruptness of the current French political system. In a series of demonstrations, the most violent was on 6 February 1934, when fourteen people were killed and over 230 wounded. Prime Minister *Daladier, himself appointed to handle the crisis a few weeks earlier, resigned. It took a 'government of national unity', under the veteran President *Doumergue, to pacify the country again. For the right, the scandal became a potent example of the failure of the Republican political system. To the left, it signalled an imminent takeover by *Fascism, as had happened recently in Italy and

Germany. This fear was exaggerated, but nevertheless became the catalyst for the formation of the *Popular Front.

Stern Gang

Founded as the Lohamei Herut Yisrael (Fighters for the Freedom of Israel), it derived its popular name from its first leader, Stern (b. 1907, d. 1942). Dedicated to the expulsion of the British and the creation of a state of Israel, it broke away from *Irgun in protest against the latter's cease-fire against the British during World War II. After Stern was killed by the British in 1942, its leadership included *Shamir, among others. It operated in small groups, attacking British service personnel and organizing the assassination of government officials, as well as destroying installations. Its victims included Lord Moyne, the British Minister for the Middle East in Cairo (1944), and probably Count *Bernadotte, the *UN mediator in *Palestine (1948). It was suppressed after 1949, although some members joined the Israeli defence forces.

Stevenson, Adlai Ewing (b. 5 Feb. 1900, d. 14 July 1965). US politician

The grandson of Vice-President Adlai E. Stevenson (1893-7), he received his law degree from Northwestern University. After qualifying in 1926 he became a lawyer in Chicago, doing much work for the city administration. In 1934–40 he was also on the board of directors at Hull House (see *Addams). During World War II he held various government appointments and in 1948 he was elected Governor of Illinois with a landslide victory. His energetic administration attacked gambling and corruption and imposed greater efficiency on the bureaucracy. Chosen as the *Democrat candidate for the Presidency in the elections of 1952 and 1956, on both occasions he suffered heavy defeats against *Eisenhower. A highly intelligent liberal reformer and internationalist, his presidential campaigns were marked by brilliant and witty speeches. A chief US delegate at the *UN founding conference in 1945, President *Kennedy appointed him US ambassador to the UN (1961–5), with Cabinet rank. He died in office.

Stimson, Henry Lewis (b. 21 Sept. 1867, d. 20 Oct. 1950). US Secretary of State 1929–33; Secretary of War 1911–13, 1940–5

Born in New York City, he graduated from Yale and Harvard Law School, and was admitted to the New York Bar in 1891. He worked for President Theodore *Roosevelt and in 1911 was first appointed Secretary of

War. After serving in World War I he returned to his law practice until he was appointed Governor-General of the Philippines (1927–9), where he pursued a policy of conciliation. In 1929 President *Hoover appointed him Secretary of State. As such he formulated the 'Stimson Doctrine' in response to the Japanese invasion of Manchuria in 1931 (*Manchukuo). This contained: (1) a refusal to grant diplomatic recognition to actions which threatened the territorial integrity of the Republic of China; and (2) a refusal to recognize any territory or agreement obtained as a result of aggression, in violation of the *Kellogg–Briand Pact. He returned to his law practice in 1933.

Despite his staunch progressive *Republican convictions, he supported F. D. *Roosevelt's foreign policies, advocating aid for Britain and a resumption of conscription in 1939. This recommended him to Roosevelt, who appointed him Secretary of War. As such, he guided the recruitment and training of the US armed services for war. He supported the recommendation in 1945 to drop the atomic bomb, arguing that its use would save more lives than it cost.

Stolypin, Piotr Arkadievich (b. 14 Apr. 1862, d. 18 Sept. 1911). Prime Minister of Russia 1906–11

Born in the German city of Dresden, he joined the Russian bureaucracy and worked in the Ministry of Interior from 1884. In 1903, he became Governor of Saratov province, where he commended himself through his repression of the local peasant uprisings in the 1905 *Russian Revolution. He was called back to Moscow and became Prime Minister. The outstanding statesman of the last decade of the Tsarist era, he quelled the revolution and re-established government control in the cities as well as the countryside. In a further, deeply controversial move, he changed the electoral laws to produce a more conservative and docile *Duma in 1907. At the same time, his land reforms after 1906 undermined peasant communal land tenure through both the transfer of title into individual ownership and the consolidation of landholdings, thus creating the foundation of greater agricultural efficiency. He was assassinated by left-wing revolutionaries.

KULAK

Stormont (Northern Ireland)

The seat of the former government and parliament of *Northern Ireland. It is situated in a suburb of Belfast, and comprises the parliament buildings, Stormont Castle, and Stormont House. The government of

Northern Ireland was created by the Government of Ireland Act of 1920, as a subordinate body to Westminster, but with its own Cabinet and Prime Minister. The Protestant majority in the province ensured a permanent Protestant majority in Stormont, though this was enhanced through manipulation of constituency boundaries. It failed to prevent the breakdown of law and order in the late 1960s, and was suspended in March 1972. Under direct rule from Westminster, Stormont's former duties have been carried out by the Secretary of State for Northern Ireland, with administrative assistance from civil servants of the Northern Ireland Office. It was revived as the home to the Northern Ireland Assembly, which came into existence in 1998 following the *Good Friday Agreement. The Assembly was suspended from 2002, but was due to be revived in 2007, following the *St Andrews Agreement.

Strategic Arms Reduction Talks (START) (1982–92), see DISARMAMENT

Strategic Defense Initiative, see SDI

Strauss, Franz Josef (b. 6 Sept. 1915, d. 3 Oct. 1988). Bavarian Minister President 1978–88
One of the co-founders of the *CSU in 1946, he became its general secretary in 1949, deputy president in 1952, and president in 1961. A member of the federal parliament (1949–78), he became Secretary for Special Affairs in 1953, Secretary for Nuclear Issues in 1955, and Foreign Secretary in 1956, when he oversaw the rearmament of the West German army as part of *NATO begun in 1955. He resigned over allegations of lying to parliament in 1962, but he rejoined the government as Finance Secretary (1966–9). His briskness and his right-wing views were constant points of friction with the more centrist *CDU, and also cost him general popular support outside Bavaria. As a result, under his leadership in the 1980 elections against H. *Schmidt, the CDU/CSU sustained the worst defeat since the parties' creation. By contrast, his popularity in Bavaria, where he continued to win the state elections with record majorities, remained extremely high.

Streicher, Julius (b. 12 Feb. 1885, d. 16 Oct. 1946). Nazi propagandist
Born near Augsburg, he joined the *Nazi Party in 1922 and took an active part in the *Hitler Putsch of 1923. In 1928–40 he was the Nazi leader (*Gauleiter*) of Franconia, though his main contribution to Nazi rule lay in his fanatic, ferocious, and extremely vulgar *anti-Semitic propaganda. He was executed after the *Nuremberg Trials.

Stresemann, Gustav (b. 10 May 1878, d. 3 Oct. 1929) German Foreign Minister 1923–9; Chancellor of Germany 1923
Born in Berlin, he entered parliament for the National *Liberal Party (Nationalliberale Partei) in 1907, and in 1917 became leader of the party's parliamentary group. After 1918 he co-founded the German People's Party (Deutsche Volkspartei, DVP), and subsequently steered it towards an acceptance of and cooperation with the Weimar Republic, despite his personal monarchist tendencies. As Chancellor (August to November 1923) he contributed towards a stabilization of the currency following the hyperinflation earlier that year. Streseman also found the political courage to call for an end to civil disobedience in the *Ruhr District and the Rhineland following the French invasion. From 23 November until his death he served as Foreign Secretary, during which time he made a central contribution to the stabilization of the Republic through his policy of moderate revisionism, particularly through the establishment of better relations with France. In 1924, he achieved a revision of German *reparation payments through the Dawes Plan, and following the *Locarno Treaty of 1925 Germany was admitted to the *League of Nations in 1926. In that year he also received the *Nobel Peace Prize together with his French colleague *Briand.

Strijdom, Johannes Gerhardus (b. 14 July 1893, d. 24 Aug. 1958). Prime Minister of South Africa 1954–8
Born in Klipfontein (Cape Colony), he graduated from university at Stellenbosch and Pretoria, submitting the first ever application in Afrikaans to practise law in 1918. The republican nationalist became active for the *National Party (NP) in 1923 and was elected to parliament in 1929. He joined *Malan's opposition to *Hertzog's alliance with *Smuts in 1933, and, following the split of the NP in 1934, rebuilt the NP organization in the Transvaal. Minister of Lands and Irrigation from 1948, in 1954 the fiery orator became the first Prime Minister without direct memories of the *South African War. His most lasting policies concerned the strengthening of the government's freedom of manoeuvre on *apartheid, adding sympathizers to the number of Senators and high court judges so that any apartheid laws would be guaranteed a smooth passage. Under his Minister of Bantu Affairs, *Verwoerd,

mixed-race trade unions were abolished, racial segregation in universities was encouraged, and people of mixed race ('Coloureds') were disenfranchised. He died in office, having just secured the NP's biggest election victory to date.

Stroessner, Alfredo (b. 3 Nov. 1912, d. 16 Aug 2006). Dictator of Paraguay 1954–89
Born in Encarnación of German descent, the longest-serving Latin American dictator joined the military and became its supreme commander in 1953. He led a coup in 1954 and assumed the presidency, which was subsequently confirmed in nine successive rigged elections. Under his authoritarian leadership, social inequalities increased, so that in 1981, around 1 per cent of the population possessed about 80 per cent of the land. A growing economic crisis which accelerated in 1985 increased political repression, and growing opposition from his own supporters led to his eventual removal in a military coup on 3 February 1989. In 2002, a Paraguayan judge issued an international arrest warrant against Stroessner, who lived in exile in Brazil.

student revolt, France (May 1968)
During the 1960s an educational crisis developed following the explosion in student numbers in previous decades without a corresponding transformation of the university system. Agitated (as students elsewhere) by the *Vietnam War and political stagnation at home, students of Paris University first took to the streets at Nanterre in March 1968, in response to the arrest of a Nanterre student for his participation in bombings of US targets. After further protests the campus at Nanterre was closed on 3 May. To cope with the spread of the unrest, classes were suspended at the Sorbonne while the police brutally suppressed student demonstrations. Across the country, there were demands by workers for participation in the demonstrations, though only in Nantes was a central strike committee actually formed which became the *de facto* city government for a week. Professionals moved against their antiquated organizations, and artists complained about state participation in (and censorship of) the arts.

On 29 May, de *Gaulle left the country, but he returned on 30 May and broadcast a defiant message which proved a decisive turning point. He dissolved the National Assembly and called new elections, in which the *Gaullists won an overwhelming majority. Mollified by significant pay increases, the workers withdrew their support, and the students became increasingly marginalized. Since the revolt was not supported by the one French revolutionary party, the *Communist Party, it is doubtful whether the May events ever had the potential to escalate into a revolution. Moreover, student revolts in other countries such as Germany and Mexico appeared similarly threatening when they occurred, but all were ultimately contained; yet the sense of fundamental crisis generated by them was real enough.

Sturmabteilung, see SA

Sturzo, Don Luigi, see POPULAR PARTY, ITALY

Suárez González, Adolfo (b. 25 Sept. 1932). Prime Minister of Spain 1976–81
Born in Cebreros (Avila), he received a doctorate degree in law from the University of Madrid, and rose quickly in the bureaucracy of the *Franco regime to become director-general of radio and television (1965–8, 1969–73). As director of the *Falange National Movement from 1975, he prevented its opposition to the post-Franco reforms. *Juan Carlos appointed him Prime Minister in 1976 to oversee the establishment of a democratic government. In close cooperation with the King, Suárez effected this with the Law of Political Reform of 18 November 1976. With his party, the Democratic Union Centre (DUC), he won the ensuing elections of 1977. However, his popularity declined owing to the economic crisis consequent upon the 1979 world recession. The stability of the political system was seriously challenged by continued terrorist attacks by the *Basque ETA. He resigned in 1981, weeks before the attempted coup of that year. Having lost the support of his own party, he founded the Democratic Centre and Social Party, which gained but two seats in 1982. Nevertheless these elections were won by *González, and successfully completed the first stage of Spain's democratic transition, to which he had been a crucial contributor. He retired from politics in 1991.

submarine warfare, German, see LUSITANIA

Sudan
Africa's largest country by area; the discovery of oil has led to bloody civil and religious conflict.

Early history Under Ottoman/ Egyptian rule

since 1821, the territory became an Anglo-Egyptian 'condominium', under British sovereignty and Egyptian administration. It was governed by *indirect rule, whereby the influential positions were given to Muslims from northern Sudan. Inspired by Egyptian independence, which inevitably raised questions about the future administration of Sudan, two nationalist movements emerged. The Umma Party (*Mahdism) stood for immediate independence. By contrast, the National Unionist Party under al-*Azhari's leadership favoured constitutional links with Egypt. The latter won the 1953 elections and led the party to independence on 1 January 1956.

Independence was the catalyst for a bloody civil war, which became the central issue of Sudanese politics. Its essence was the rebellion by the southern minority (around one-third of the total population), which was largely Christian, against the rule of the central government, which was dominated by groups from the Muslim north. The army coup of 1958 led to a brief military government under *Abboud until 1964, when unstable civilian rule was resumed with *Azhari as head of state. In 1969 Azhari was himself replaced by *Nimieri, who gained control in a military coup.

Nimieri managed to bring about an end to the civil war following negotiations in the Ethiopian capital of Addis Ababa in 1972, whereby he guaranteed the south enhanced autonomy on religious and cultural matters. He introduced disastrous economic policies which took up vast foreign investment with the aim of achieving a fivefold increase in food production. This aim had to be abandoned owing to the lack of careful planning, the lack of an infrastructural base, and unsuitable climatic and agricultural conditions. Faced by a growing economic crisis, Nimieri sought to enlist the support of the growing *Islamic fundamentalist movement through openly pursuing Islamic policies. An administrative reform took away the autonomy of the southern region, and in 1983 he declared the supremacy of Islamic law.

Civil war (1980s–1990s) This triggered renewed civil war. Nimieri was overthrown in a military coup in 1985, and in 1986 civilian rule was restored under al-Mahdi. The new government was too weak, however, to reverse Nimieri's Islamic policies, which were supported by many powerful groups in the north, as well as the army. An army coup of 20 July 1989 brought to power a group of Islamic officers, which resumed the establishment of Islamic codes and practices in Sudanese

politics and society. In 1993 the military junta appointed Omar Hassan al-Beshir as President in 1993.

Meanwhile, the civil war escalated, as the SSIA (Southern Sudan Independence Army), which demanded independence for the south, split from the SPLA (Sudan People's Liberation Army), which focused on greater autonomy within Sudan, in 1991. The government remained determined to crush the SPLA, since the south was rich in mineral resources. In June 1995 the SPLA and the SSIA came to an agreement with the Muslim opposition of the north, led by the Umma Party and the UNP. They agreed to coordinate their activities in a National Democratic Front. This agreement was undermined by al-Beshir, who made generous political concessions to the Umma Party and northern opposition groups. Some parties were allowed to operate, and Nimieri was allowed to return and resume his political activities. In the process of these domestic political shifts, the governing party, the National Congress, split in 1999 as its Secretary, Hassan al-Turabi, led an unsuccessful attempt to curb al-Bashir's powers. Nevertheless, in the 2000 general elections (not held in the rebellious south), al-Bashir was elected with 85 per cent of the popular vote.

Contemporary politics (since 2002) As al-Bashir shored up his powers further, the civil war continued to rage in the south, encouraged by rising oil exploration which increased the stakes both for the government and for the secessionists. It was estimated that between 1983 and 2000 the war claimed almost two million casualties, and created over four million refugees. Under great pressure from the USA, both sides agreed to a surprise peace deal in 2002, whereby Islamic law would not be applied to the south and a referendum for independence would be held there. Both sides agreed to share oil (and non-oil) revenues equally, while an agreement of 2005 finalized power-sharing arrangements, as well as considerable autonomy for the south.

With a fragile peace established between north and south, a civil war erupted in the western province of *Darfur, which led to genocide as Sudanese troops tried to suppress and kill the native population. International efforts at intervention were hampered by Sudan's refusal to co-operate, and by China's compliance. China was a major customer of Sudanese oil, and prevented UN security council resolutions against Sudan.

Sudetenland

A term in use particularly after 1938 for the north-west frontier region of the Czech lands

(Bohemia) which had become an area of German settlement over the course of centuries. In response to the rise of *nationalism among both its German and Czech population, mutual antagonism had grown since the late nineteenth century, whipped up by the spread of cultural and linguistic associations. In 1919, it became part of *Czechoslovakia under the terms of the *Paris Peace Conference. This incited vociferous German protests, and led to sporadic violence between Germans and Czechs. In the June 1919 local elections, over 90 per cent of the German vote went to German ethnic parties. Many among the German-speaking population were mollified by the new country's liberal treatment of national minorities, and the relative financial prosperity of the new state, in marked contrast with the economic and political helter-skelter of Weimar Germany or Austria. However, the effects of the Great *Depression, which hit its industries particularly hard, and the growth of the German *Nazi movement, both encouraged a revival of German *nationalism. In May 1935, the *Fascist Sudeten German Party (SdP) led by Konrad *Henlein gained 63 per cent of the Sudeten German vote. The SdP subsequently exaggerated its demands so as to make them unacceptable to the Czech population, and this provided the background for *Hitler's annexation of the area and the *Munich Agreement.

After Germany's defeat in 1945, Czechoslovakia took possession of the area again. On 21 June 1945, the new government issued the **Beneš Decrees**, according to which all Sudeten Germans were expropriated as collaborators. This document, whose implication of the collective guilt of all Sudeten Germans was never accepted by the latter, formed a crucial pillar of Czech identity. It surfaced to the political agenda in 2001, when it was used by the Czech Prime Minister, Milos Zeman, to whip up nationalist fervour ahead of the 2002 general elections. In return, the Benes decrees were similarly invoked for populist purposes by Jörg *Haider of Austria.

Suez Crisis (July–Nov. 1956)

Following the Anglo-American refusal to finance the Aswan Dam in southern Egypt, the Egyptian President, *Nasser, nationalized the Suez Canal on 26 July 1956 to provide much-needed investment capital. In response, Britain and France wished to overthrow the President, partly because most of the shares in the canal had been owned in these countries. Britain and France were also alarmed by Nasser's Arab *nationalism, the nature of which was hostile to the continuing colonial presence of the two powers in the African and Arab world. To provide a pretext for military intervention, Israel agreed to begin military hostilities by invading the Sinai peninsula from 29 October, and on 5 November British and French forces began to land in Port Said and occupy the Suez Canal, ostensibly to ensure the safety of the canal's traffic.

Large sections of the British and French public were opposed to the invasion and, more crucially, the occupation was greeted with international hostility led by the USA. Faced with a plummeting national currency which the USA refused to support, Britain and France agreed to a cease-fire on 6 November, and withdrew their troops over the following month. The crisis confirmed the loss of British and French superpower status, as they proved unable to act on the international scene without US support. In Britain, it led to the resignation of Anthony *Eden two months later, while in France it accelerated the collapse of the Fourth Republic. Instead of humiliating Nasser, the crisis increased his appeal in the Arab world as the one who had successfully overcome an assault of Britain, France, and Israel.

PAN-ARABISM

suffragettes

American and British women campaigning for the right of women to vote. In Britain, the suffragettes from the Women's Social and Political Union led by Emmeline and Christabel *Pankhurst advocated civil disobedience to further their cause, as opposed to the suffragists from the law-abiding National Union of Women's Suffrage Societies. After several government attempts to introduce limited female suffrage, the suffragettes became more violent, in 1912 resorting to arson, for example. In 1913, the suffragette Emily Davison threw herself under the King's horse at the Derby and was killed. By contrast, the National American Woman Suffrage Association under the leadership of Anna Howard Shaw (1847–1919) and Carrie Chapman *Catt, which had emerged in 1890 from the fusion of the American Suffrage Association and the National Association for Woman Suffrage founded two decades earlier, refused to engage in such violent methods. Nevertheless, in both the USA and Britain it was only partly the suffragettes' efforts, and partly the women's vital contribution to World War I, which persuaded the government to grant female suffrage. British female suffrage was granted to women over 30 in 1918, and extended to women over 21 in 1928. In the USA, women were enfranchised through the 19th amendment to the constitution, adopted in January 1918 and coming into force on 28 August 1920.

WOMEN, EMANCIPATION OF

Suharto, Hadji Mohamad (b. 8 June 1921). President of Indonesia 1968–98
Born on the island of Java, he trained as a bank clerk and joined the Dutch colonial army in 1940, but after the Japanese invasion he became a policeman. In 1945 he joined the republican forces in central Java to fight the Dutch. After independence, he rose within the ranks of the Indonesian army to become commander of the forces which occupied West *Irian in 1962. In 1965, he was responsible for defeating the *Communist coup. In its aftermath, he purged the government and administration of Communists and other possible opponents of the state, and dismantled *Sukarno's power. In 1967 he became Acting President himself, and in 1968 he formally succeeded Sukarno.

Suharto headed a nepotist and corrupt regime, which remained ruthlessly anti-Communist. This earned him assistance from the USA, despite the brutality of the government, not only in occupied areas like *East *Timor but in Indonesia itself, where, according to *Amnesty International, hundreds of thousands of opponents of the regime had been killed. Despite a modest relaxation of repression during the 1990s, he failed to create a popular base, relying on military support instead. Ultimately, Suharto lost the support of the military, and was forced to resign. Suharto continued to have powerful supporters in the political and administrative elites, however, so that investigations into his corrupt regime proved slow to yield results. In 2006, the government dropped corruption charges because of Suharto's ill health.

Sukarno, Achmad (b. 6 June 1901, d. 21 June 1970). President of Indonesia 1949–68
Born in Surabaya, Sukarno studied engineering in Bandung, where he became involved in the foundation of the Partai Nasionalis Indonesia (PNI) in 1927. Imprisoned by the Dutch colonial authorities (1929–31), he was exiled to Sumatra in 1933. He returned to Jakarta following the Japanese invasion, supporting the Japanese war effort in return for Japanese acceptance of his leadership among the nationalist community.

By the end of World War II Sukarno had acquired a unique position of authority among the Indonesian peoples, enabling him to declare Indonesian independence on 17 August 1945. He became President on 18

August, and subsequently united the heterogeneous resistance forces against the Dutch who were eager to reclaim their erstwhile colony. He was officially confirmed President upon independence in 1949. Increasingly dissatisfied with democracy, he introduced a system of Guided Democracy. With the consent of the army, he became Prime Minister in 1959, and subsequently sought to consolidate support for his authoritarian government through *nationalism, e.g. the acquisition of West *Irian and the *Confrontation with Malaysia. He declared himself President for life in 1963. He was greatly weakened by his ambiguous role in the unsuccessful Communist putsch of 1965, which led the army to replace him with its leader, General *Suharto.

Sukarnoputri, Megawati (b. 23 Jan. 1947), President of Indonesia, 2001–4
Born at Yogyakarta, she is the daughter of Indondesia's first president, Achmad *Sukarno. As such, she was part of the political establishment, and became leader of the Indonesian Democratic Party. However, in 1996 she lost *Suharto's support and had to resign. She created the rival Indonesia Democratic Party–Struggle (PDI–P), which in the 1998 elections received over 30 per cent of the vote and became the strongest parliamentary party. Parliament only made her Vice-President, however. The Muslim parties in particular supported her rival for the Presidency, Bacharuddin Habibie. When Habibie became tainted by corruption allegations and was faced with growing popular unrest, he resigned and Sukarnoputri succeeded him. She was faced with the difficult task of stabilizing Indonesia's fragile political system while trying to overcome its economic instability. Her popularity declined as she appeared to be indecisive, and unable to put a halt to the endemic corruption in the government and bureaucracy. She lost the country's first presidential elections in 2004 to S. B. *Yudhoyono

Sun Yat-sen (Sun Yixian) (b. 12 Nov. 1866, d. 12 Mar. 1925). President of the Republic of China 1911–12, 1917–18, 1921–5
Born into a peasant family in southern China (Guandong province), fifteen miles from *Macao, he joined his brother in Hawaii, where he was educated. He graduated from the Hong Kong College of Medicine in 1892. Appalled by the corruption and the weakness of China which led to its disastrous performance in the Sino-Japanese War of 1894–5, he plotted an uprising in Guangzhou (Canton), but was discovered and fled to Japan.

There, he founded the Revolutionary Alliance in 1905, based on the Three Principles of the People: nationalism, democracy, people's livelihood. From exile, he organized a number of unsuccessful uprisings in 1907 and 1908, but in 1911 he was able to return to China after the successful *Wuchang Revolution.

Although he was elected President of the Republic of China in Nanjing (Nanking), he resigned almost immediately to make way for *Yuan Shikai. The two men were soon at odds, which forced Sun into exile once again. In 1914, he married *Song Qingling. He returned to China after Yuan's death in 1916. He struggled hard to reunite and develop the revolutionary movement and establish his authority over the various warlords on whose support he depended. After forming a series of short-lived governments, in 1921 he set up a National Government in Guangzhou (Canton), but again he lacked the support necessary to widen his base. At last, he changed tactics. With help from *Comintern, he reorganized the *Guomindang, and extended his Three Principles by the Three Policies: alliances with the *Communist Party, the Soviet Union, and the workers and peasants. He set up the pivotal Whampoa Military Academy under *Chiang Kai-shek, which trained the future leaders of the Nationalist movement. In 1924, he was elected president for life of the Guomindang. Though success came to Sun only in the last two years of his life, this sufficed to make him be remembered as the 'Father' of the Chinese Republic. His significance also came from his posthumous importance, when his legacy was fashioned in opposite directions to legitimize both Communists and Nationalists.

Sunni

The majority tradition of *Islam, comprising around 72 per cent of all Muslims, and distinguished from *Shi'ite Islam in recognizing successors to the Prophet Muhammad (caliphs) without insisting that these had to be his descendants. Together with the Shi'ites, they believe that the word of Allah (God) was delivered through the Prophet and laid down in the Quran, and in the accounts of Muhammad's life (Sunnah). United by the doctrines in these texts, which describe the nature of God and define Islam as a monotheistic religion, there are four different Sunni schools which seek to define the rather more ambiguous matter of the relationship between Allah and the individual person. The most rigid of these, the Hanbali school, demands strict adherence to the letter of the Quran and allows only limited interpretation. It is predominant in

Saudi Arabia. The Shafii school allows interpretation of the Quran according to a given methodological framework, and predominates in Indonesia, the Arabian coastline, and southern India. The Maliki school tolerates a limited interpretation of the Quran through reason and comparison with modern life. It prevails in most Muslim-dominated African states. Finally, the Hanafi school is the one most firmly rooted in rational thought. It allows the use of secular and customary law, which has made it adaptable to the more secular and heterogeneous states where Islam predominated, such as the *Ottoman Empire or its successor state, Turkey.

Supreme Court (USA)

The highest court in the USA, established by Article 3 of the US Constitution. Its members are appointed by the President, with the advice and consent of the Senate. Early in its history, under the guidance of Chief Justice John Marshall (1801–35), it established its right to judge whether bills passed by *Congress or by state legislatures conform to the provisions of the constitution, with power to declare them unconstitutional if they do not. During the early nineteenth century it also established itself as the highest Court of Appeal.

Early history (up to 2000) The decisions of the court have played a central role in the history of the USA, not only balancing the relationships between executive and legislature, and between states and the federal government, but also contributing to the evolution of social, economic, and legal policies. The commerce clause of the constitution has enabled it powerfully to influence the economy by invalidation of any state legislation deemed likely to burden interstate commerce 'unduly'. Moreover, its interpretation of the Fourteenth Amendment of the constitution has enabled racial discrimination steadily to be eliminated. Justices hold office 'during good behavior', that is, they are not forced to retire as long as they can perform their duties. In 1937 a major confrontation between F. D. *Roosevelt and the court erupted, as Roosevelt sought to appoint more liberal justices to counterbalance its conservative composition of old conservative justices, and to expand the court from nine to fifteen members. He was defeated in this endeavour, though since then justices have been entitled to retire at 70.

Even though the Justices are, on the whole, appointed by the President along political lines, this has not always been mirrored in the court's decisions. The main reason for this was that a commitment to legal principles, such as a commitment to states' rights or the upholding of strict constitutionalism, mirrored a left-right political agenda only imperfectly. Nevertheless, after a series of new appointments by Ronald *Reagan, George *Bush, and George W. *Bush, the Supreme Court did assume a more right-wing position.

Contemporary history (since 2000) With Chief Justice *Rehnquist presiding, the Court made one of its most controversial rulings by determining the *Bush election victory in **Bush v. Gore** (December 2000). In particular, it ruled that the Florida Supreme Court's decision to extend the time limits for the recount of votes was unconstitutional. The 5:4 decision reflected the court's political composition. It constituted a rare direct intervention in the political process, and in the electoral organization of a state. The ruling was particularly problematic as the Court had a direct interest in this issue because of the President's decisive influence on the composition of the Court. At the same time, the Court's growing conservatism did not prevent it from asserting its rights against the executive, notably when it ruled in 2004 that detainees in Guantanamo Bay did have access to US Courts to challenge their detention.

(⊕) SEE WEB LINKS

• The home page of the Supreme Court.

Surinam

A country north of Brazil characterized by a fragile social and cultural balance between three distinctive ethnic groups.

Colonial rule (up to 1975)
Surinam became a Dutch colony as Dutch Guyana in 1667. During the nineteenth century it consisted largely of sugar plantations. After the abolition of slavery, the plantations' demand for labour was filled by the organized immigration of mainly Hindu but also Muslim Indians (until 1918), and subsequently by Muslims from the Dutch East Indies (today's Indonesia). The colony received some limited self-government in 1867, but the German occupation of the Netherlands during World War II interrupted ties with the Netherlands and increased demands for independence.

Universal suffrage was granted in 1949, whereupon three major parties formed, representing the three major

ethnic communities: Creole, Indian, and Indonesian. In 1954 Surinam received full autonomy as an equal part of the kingdom of the Netherlands. Politics came to be dominated by the Creole National Party of Surinam (Nationale Partij Suriname), which ruled in conjunction with the United Hindu Party (Verenigde Hindoostaanse Partij).

Contemporary history and politics (from 1975) Independence in 1975 was accompanied by a Dutch assistance programme worth $1.5 billion, though in the long run the country's economy was significantly weakened by the emigration of a total of 140,000 Surinamese to the Netherlands.

The army commander, Desi Bouterse, staged a military coup in 1980, and formally assumed power in 1982. This led to the suspension of Dutch aid, which, together with the social unrest triggered off by political repression and economic decline, forced the military to agree to elections in 1988. Bouterse remained in charge of the army and staged another coup in 1990. His party lost the 1991 elections, which gave a majority to the Front for Democracy and Development (FDD), a new party which sought to appeal across ethnic lines. In 1993 its leader, President Ronald R. Venetiaan, managed to subordinate the military to civilian leadership. Although it continued to be the largest party, the FDD lost the 1996 elections to the National Democratic Party, which formed a coalition government under Jules Wijdenbosch as President. Under Wijedenbosch, however, the economy deteriorated further, and in 2000 he was forced to succumb to domestic pressure and call early elections. These were won by the FDD, with Venetiaan returning to the presidency. The economy stabilized, and Venetiaan was re-elected in 2005.

sustainable growth, see BRUNDTLAND, GRO HARLEM

Suzman, Helen, see PROGRESSIVE PARTY, SOUTH AFRICA

Svoboda, Ludvík (b. 15 Nov. 1895, d. 20 Sept. 1979). President of Czechoslovakia 1968–75
Born in Hroznatín (Moravia), he served in the *Austro-Hungarian army during World War I, and remained in the new Czechoslovak army in 1919. A Communist since the 1930s, in 1939 he escaped German occupation by

going to the Soviet Union, where he took over command of the Czech Army Group which in 1945 liberated Prague. He became Minister of Defence in the new government, but fell victim to the *Stalinist purges of 1950, when he was dismissed, expelled from the party, and imprisoned. After *Stalin's death he was released, and soon became commander of a military academy. He retired in 1959, but was later appointed by *Dubček to succeed *Novotny as President. Initially opposed to the *Warsaw Pact invasion of 1968, he quickly adapted himself to *Husák's new hardline regime.

SWAPO (South-West African People's Organization), see NUJOMA, SAMUEL DANIEL

Swaziland

The landlocked country bordering on South Africa and Mozambique has remained one of the last vestiges of absolute monarchical power.
Swaziland was declared a British protectorate in 1903 to protect it from further *Afrikaner encroachments from the Transvaal, though by that time virtually all the country's mineral and property rights (over 60 per cent of the land) had already passed into the hands of White capital. It remained under British sovereignty until 1968, when it gained independence under King Sobhuza II (b. 1921, d. 1982). He concentrated all important political powers in the monarchy, so that opposition parties were banned in 1973, and parliament permanently dissolved in 1977. The power vacuum created by Sobhuza's death led to a period of instability until the crowning of Prince Makhosetive (b. 1968) as King Mswati III in April 1986. He managed to impose some authority on the National Council torn apart by warring factions and personal feuds, and on 26 September 1993 allowed elections (though parties were still banned). Meanwhile, the country remained one of glaring inequalities, as almost all of the fertile or mineral-rich land remained in the hands of foreign (mostly South African) capital administered by a tiny White minority. The vast majority of Black Swazis continued to suffer from malnourishment, under-education, and inadequate sanitary conditions. Despite growing international criticism, Mswati III

continued to resist a surrender of his absolute powers. A new Constitution in force from 2006 enshrined the King's absolute powers and banned political parties. Mswati was slow to respond to the country's *AIDS epidemic. Swaziland had the world's highest infection rate, with one-third of the adult population infected by the HIV virus in 2006 (according to UNAIDS). This meant that life expectancy was reduced to 39 years for women, and 36 years for men.

Sweden

A Scandinavian country which in the twentieth century has become best known as a model of a social democratic *welfare state, in which *capitalism was severely curtailed through state intervention.

The rise of social democracy In the sixteenth and seventeenth centuries, Sweden was one of Europe's most powerful countries. Its political and economic power declined thereafter, and in 1905, Sweden was forced to concede the independence of Norway, which it had ruled before. A relatively poor state in the nineteenth century, it began to prosper towards the end of the century as it became a large exporter of wood pulp, while its reserves of iron ore led to the expansion of industry. The growth of an industrialized, urbanized society was reflected in the establishment of the *Social Democratic Labour Party in 1889. This combined with the Liberals to press for social and political reform, against a conservative political establishment dominated by the interests of agriculture, and of the monarchy and aristocracy. It became the last independent Scandinavian country to adopt universal suffrage, introduced by a Liberal/ Social Democratic coalition in 1917.

The welfare state (from the 1930s) After a period of instability in the 1920s, which the country shared with the rest of Europe, the Great *Depression triggered a social consensus and political stability that stood in marked contrast to the political instabilities of the rest of Europe, and which has been the hallmark of Swedish politics ever since. The Social Democratic government under Per Albin Hansson (Prime Minister 1932–6, 1936–46) engaged on a period of social reform which created a lasting alliance between agriculture and industrial workers in the cities. Agricultural debts were restructured and import tariffs raised. In return for more expensive food, urban workers received social welfare benefits and public works in periods of depression. Taxes were raised to pay for public works, which would reduce unemployment and stimulate demand. Large businesses supported this agreement in return for industrial peace and the maintenance of private property. There is no evidence that this application of *Keynesian demand management actually helped Sweden overcome the effects of the Great Depression. However, the coincidence of the onset of the new policies with the economic upturn caused by the improvement in the world economy convinced most that the new consensus was, indeed, the source of economic betterment. This led to a long era of Social Democratic government.

World War II (1939–45) During *World War II, Sweden was the only Scandinavian country able to maintain the neutrality which its neighbours, Norway and Denmark, had also declared. This was partly because Sweden was strategically less important, while Norway also had crucial reserves of ore. Sweden therefore did not need to be occupied by the Germans, as long as the Swedes continued to allow *Nazi Germany to transport its troops into Norway, and the iron ore out of Norway. A rare neutral country with access to world markets, Sweden also conducted much trade with Germany. Its exports of ball bearings were crucial to the German armaments industry, though in fairness they were also supplied to the Allies. At the same time, the country remained extremely vulnerable, sandwiched as it was between Germans occupying Norway and Denmark on the one hand and a Finland invaded by Russians in the *Continuation War on the other. Sweden also acted as an important haven for refugees from continental Europe, Finland, and Scandinavia, not least for Social Democrats such as *Brandt.

Contemporary history (1945–96) After the war, the Social Democratic Prime Ministers *Erlander and *Palme continued the construction of the welfare state interrupted by the war. *Trade unions were strengthened, workers' benefits improved (sick pay, statutory holiday leave), pensions raised, and taxation increased so that Swedes came to suffer one of the world's highest rates of taxation, while enjoying one of the world's highest living standards. Full employment became the central economic priority. This system, which became so central to Sweden's *raison d'être*, was challenged by the series of world depressions that set in with the 1973 and 1979 *oil price shocks. Initially, the state tried the easy alternative, stimulating exports through a devaluation of the currency. As this increased inflation further and led to even greater wage demands, it became clear that structural reforms were needed, particularly a reduction of the role of the state and a decline in trade union influence.

Since 1976 there has been an alternation of governments, each trying unsuccessfully to reduce welfare payments, limit public sector pay rises, and reduce trade union power. One successful approach to Sweden's problems led to its entry into the European Union in 1995, which had been approved by a referendum in 1994. This provided further impetus for structural reforms under the governments of *Bildt and Ingvar G. Carlsson (1986–92, 1994–6), notably the liberalization of the agricultural sector, and efforts towards public deficit reduction.

Contemporary politics (since 1996) In March 1996 Carlsson was succeeded by Goran Persson, another representative of the right wing of the Social Democratic Labour Party. Persson's party lost in the 1998 elections, but he continued to form a minority government with the support of the Communists and environmentalists. Persson continued with his reforms, and in 2000 the Lutheran Church was disestablished. Spurred by the reforms of the 1990s, Sweden has enjoyed continued economic growth and prosperity. Persson's government became rocked by scandal, as a public enquiry accused it of gross mismanagement in response to the *tsunami, which cost the lives of over 500 holiday-making Swedes. In 2006, the elections were won by an alliance of centre-right parties led by Frederik Reinfeldt, who became the new Prime minister.

Switzerland

An Alpine state which, despite internal cultural, religious and linguistic heterogeneity, has been able to establish neutrality

(and its own identity) against its powerful neighbours (France, *Austria-Hungary, Italy, and Germany).

Structure Switzerland consists of twenty cantons, six semi-cantons, and one federal city, its capital, Bern. Its unique structure is based on the Constitution of 12 September 1848, and the amended federal Constitution of 29 May 1874. It is governed by an executive federal council composed of seven life members, and two legislative bodies, one proportionately representing the Swiss people and one representing the cantons and semi-cantons. The cantons have retained extensive autonomy, and are responsible for education, the police, construction, and public health. Each canton also has its distinctive legal system. The Swiss Constitution has received particular attention owing to its unique elements of direct democracy. Since the middle of the nineteenth century, cantonal matters were increasingly decided by plebiscite, while any constitutional change had to be approved in a referendum by a simple majority of votes cast, as well as by a majority of cantons.

Neutrality Switzerland derived its original importance as a major European crossroads between northern, southern, and western Europe. This attracted considerable commerce, and ultimately led to a rise of the banking sector from the late nineteenth century. Its geographical location also stimulated the growth of an extensive railway network, which triggered industrial change and innovation towards the beginning of the twentieth century. Defined since the Congress of Vienna (1814) as a country of 'permanent neutrality', it refrained from entering *World War I. After the war it joined the *League of Nations, but refused to take part in any action that could compromise its neutrality.

Polarization between the social democratic movement on the one hand and the established liberal and conservative parties of the bourgeoisie on the other reached a climax in late 1918. A general strike was called in November, while at the same time the introduction of proportional representation robbed the liberals of their parliamentary majority, and led to the growing parliamentary strength of the Social Democrats. These differences were overcome in response to the rise of *Hitler in Germany, and his increasingly aggressive foreign policy. During *World War II, the country remained again a neutral island in war-torn Europe. While the Swiss undoubtedly had to be careful not to aggravate Hitler, it is also the case that the government was more ready than

necessary to restrict the entry of Jews eager to flee the *Nazi *concentration camps. Moreover, during the 1990s it emerged that Swiss banks had been instrumental in helping the Nazi regime to obtain finances, while selling gold in international markets obtained from the bodies of the victims of the *holocaust.

Contemporary history (1945–2002) After World War II, it continued its dogged policy of neutrality. Switzerland's desire for stability was further reflected in the political consensus prevalent in the country since 1960. Despite a plethora of active political parties, the major political parties, the Liberal Democratic Party, the Christian Democratic People's Party, the Social Democratic Party, and the Swiss People's Party, have been able to monopolize the seats in the national executive council by a ratio of 2:2:2:1. Political stability and international insularity also led to socio-political stagnation in certain areas. In 1971 Switzerland became the last European state (with the exception of the Vatican City and Andorra) to introduce the female franchise nationwide; the last canton, Appenzell Inner Rhodes, was forced to allow women to vote by the federal court in 1990.

Switzerland's unique stability in the twentieth century has been a major contributor to its development as perhaps the world's wealthiest nation. In particular, its banks achieved a reputation for stability and secrecy amongst international investors, enabling the banks to achieve a turnover in 1990 of almost 1,000 billion Swiss francs (around £550 billion, or $900 billion), a figure surpassing that of its GNP by a factor of three. Switzerland's emphasis on its neutrality even in a post-Cold War world became more difficult to justify after neighbouring Austria gave up its neutrality and became a member of the European Union in 1995.

Contemporary politics (since 2002) Switzerland's economy continued to grow through the 1990s (by over 3 per cent in 2000), but the bankruptcy in 2002 of the national carrier, Swissair, served as a reminder of the risks inherent in the Swiss economic model. Meanwhile, the popularity of the right-wing populist Christian Blocher also served to undermine the Swiss model of tranquility and consensus. In 2002, Switzerland voted to become a full member of the *UN. In 2003, Blocher's Swiss People's Party won the elections and became the largest party, and obtained a second seat in the national executive council, at the expense of the Christian Democrats, whose representation was reduced to one seat.

Sykes–Picot Agreement (May 1916)

A secret agreement negotiated between British and French diplomats in the Middle East, Sir Mark Sykes and Georges Picot. Following the defeat of the *Ottoman Empire in *World War I, France was to be pre-eminent in Syria (including Lebanon), southern Anatolia, and northern Mesopotamia (Mosul). Britain would establish protectorates in southern Mesopotamia (Baghdad and Basra), the Persian Gulf, Arabia and the Hejaz, *Palestine, and the Jordan Valley. Thus Egypt would be linked with the British Indian Empire. Russia was to have a free hand in *Armenia and northern *Kurdistan. A copy of the agreement was published by the *Bolsheviks after the *Russian Revolution. This caused international dismay and Arab anger, as it was the promise of British support for Arab independence which had incited the *Arab Revolt against the Ottoman Empire in 1916. The Sykes–Picot Agreement formed the basis of the *League of Nations settlement for the Middle East in 1920.

LONDON, TREATY OF

syndicalism

A labour movement originating in France and influenced by *anarchism. Syndicalists believed in the inevitability of class warfare and the need for workers to take direct action themselves. Thus, rather than socialist parties, the central agents for the workers were held to be the *syndicats*, the trade unions, whose ultimate weapon was the general strike. Syndicalism was very influential in France in the first decades of this century, as well as in Spain (until the end of the Republic) and Italy, where many of its adherents became attracted by *Fascism.

Syngman Rhee (b. 26 Apr. 1875, d. 19 July 1965). President of the Republic of Korea (South Korea) 1948–60

Born Yi Sung-man in P'yongsan (Hawanghae Province), he became a nationalist activist while still a student, joining the Independence Club on its formation in 1896. After imprisonment for an alleged attempt to overthrow the monarchy (1898–1904) he studied in the USA to gain a doctorate degree in political science at Princeton. Briefly in Korea 1910–12, he was expelled by the Japanese colonial authorities, and then founded a Korean nationalist society in the USA. In 1919, he was named *in absentia* Premier (then President) of the Provisional Government of Korea in Shanghai, a body set up by nationalist opponents of the Japanese colonial regime. This position, as well as his connections with the USA, predestined him to lead US-occupied South *Korea to statehood, becoming its first President.

Never relinquishing his claim to represent all of Korea, Syngman was bitterly opposed to the end of the *Korean War and the USA's *de facto* acceptance of the country's division. After 1953 attention shifted from the threat of Communism to his own attempts to erode the constitution in order to extend his powers. He suppressed all forms of popular protest, until this became impossible in the wake of the fraudulent 1960 presidential elections. He resigned and went into exile in Hawaii, where he died.

Syria

A heterogeneous Arab country whose economy has suffered from inefficient over-centralization, and whose political development has been closely entangled with that of its neighbours, Israel, Lebanon, and Iraq.

Early history (up to 1970) A part of the *Ottoman Empire from 1517, during World War I it was occupied by British troops, with active Arab help. Immediately after the Arab leader, Faisal (*Faisal I), was rewarded for his support by being made King of Syria, he had to give up his throne, as the Treaty of *Sèvres transformed it into a French *League of Nations *Mandate. French rule was relatively unpopular, leading to a number of uprisings. In World War II, its French colonial administration followed the *Vichy government, so that in July 1941 British and *Free French forces occupied the country. De *Gaulle declared Syria's independence for 28 September 1944, though effective autonomy was not achieved until the complete withdrawal of British and French forces on 17 April 1946.

From 1948, its nationalist governments were staunchly opposed to the creation of the state of Israel, and took part in all Arab–Israeli military confrontations. After losing the *Six Day War of 1967, Syria lost the *Golan Heights to Israel. As a result of the strong appeal of *pan-Arabism in the country, Syria joined with *Nasser's Egypt to form the *United Arab Republic in 1958. This was dissolved in 1961 after a military coup. In 1963, another coup brought to power the *Ba'ath Party. From 1966, its ideological Marxist wing dominated the government, though it was not until 1970–1 that politics were finally stabilized, under the pragmatist wing of the party led by Hafez al-*Assad.

Hafez Assad's rule (1971–2000) Assad's rule lacked a popular base throughout, and was founded instead on the loyalty of the army. He was fortunate in that the discovery of oil in 1966 increased the country's economic well-being, and provided him with the wherewithal for extensive patronage. In foreign policy, he used Syria's geopolitical position between the sensitive countries of Turkey, Iraq, the Lebanon, and Israel, to extract extensive aid from the USSR. Despite his extensive support for extremist Arab terrorist organizations in the USA, he never incurred US wrath openly, as the Americans hoped for Syrian recognition of Israel.

In the 1980s Syria became increasingly involved in Lebanon, where its military intervened directly in 1982, against Israeli forces. As a result of the support of the majority of the (Muslim) Lebanese population, Syria's presence there proved more enduring than that of Israel. During the 1990s, Syria exerted decisive influence on Lebanese affairs. Owing to its long-standing hostility to Iraq, it supported Iran in the *Iran–Iraq War, and even sent 20,000 troops to fight alongside US troops in the *Gulf War. By 1996 it had become the last Arab power to refuse to accept the *Oslo Accord, demanding the return of the Golan Heights as the *sine qua non* for a peace agreement with Israel.

Following the USSR's collapse in 1991, Assad successfully opened his country to Western *capitalist influences. Nevertheless, his position remained challenged by economic problems, as the general standard of living was depressed by his enormous military spending, which consumed around 50 per cent of state expenditure. Assad's control over the country remained firm, however, and just before his death in 2000 he managed to ensure the succession of his son, Bashar, to the Presidency.

Contemporary politics (since 2000) As President, Bashar al-*Assad widened a campaign he had been spearheading as Vice-President to fight corruption, which had the consequence of removing many potential opponents. Bashar Assad was less rigorous against political opponents, although he refused to contemplate genuine democratization. At an economic level, however, he did initiate liberalization and the promotion of private initiative, as many cities were plagued by up to 50 per cent unemployment. Following the *Iraq War, he faced US pressure to clamp down on fundamentalist terrorists in Iraq seeking refuge in his country. Assad complied with growing international pressure to withdraw Syrian troops from Lebanon in 2005. However, Syria remained influential in Lebanon through providing support for *Hezbollah. In opposition to the US policy in Iraq, Syria formed stronger ties with Iran, through stronger political contacts, and by welcoming Iranian capital investment.

T

Taff Vale judgment (1902)

A judgment by the House of Lords which made the Amalgamated Society of Railway Servants liable to pay damages for losses incurred during a strike with which it had been involved. In 1901, this case was first brought to the High Court by the Taff Vale Railway Company, which won it. The society won an appeal, but the Lords' decision overturned this in 1902. It had the effect of making all unions liable to pay out of their funds for financial losses caused by a strike. Before this decision, it had been generally held that unions were not liable for losses. The judgment was a significant catalyst in the formation of a political working-class movement, as many of the unions subsequently enrolled in the Labour Representation Committee (*Labour Party) in order to fight the judgment. When the *Liberal Party replaced the *Conservatives in government, it immediately passed the Trade Disputes Act (1906) which reversed the judgment.

Taft, William Howard (b. 15 Sept. 1857, d. 8 Mar. 1930). 27th US President 1909–13

Early career Born in Cincinnati, Ohio, into a wealthy local family, he was a gifted lawyer who became US Solicitor-General in the Harrison administration, a federal justice, High Commissioner of the Philippines, and Secretary of War. His reputation as a safe pair of hands led Theodore *Roosevelt to nominate him as his successor, and Taft was elected President for the *Republicans in 1908 with 51.6 per cent of the popular vote.

Presidency The dynamic Roosevelt came to regret his support for the highly cautious, conservative Taft, who conceived of himself as an administrator, and believed in a strictly restricted interpretation of the presidency. When he called a special session of *Congress to lower tariffs, he failed to engage in political persuasion or coalition-building, and tariffs ended up being raised to an all-time high. He abandoned the Roosevelt policy of governmental regulation of trusts in favor of regulation by specific lawsuit. Further disillusionment for Republican progressives came when Taft supported his Secretary of the Interior, Richard Ballinger, over the environmental campaigner Gifford Pinchot in the matter of the development of Alaskan land for the exploitation of oil. In the election of 1912 the radical and *Progressive elements in his party broke away to support Theodore Roosevelt and Taft was left to come third in an election which Woodrow Wilson won with a plurality of votes. After 1912 he retired to the law, and was appointed Chief Justice of the United States by Warren *Harding, in which capacity he presided very competently as a strict constitutionalist.

Taft–Hartley Act (USA)

Passed by *Congress in June 1947, over the veto of President *Truman. Named after its sponsors, Senator Robert Taft and Representative Fred Hartley, it banned the closed shop in US labour unions and the secondary boycott. It allowed employers to sue *trade unions for breach of contract and for damages inflicted on them through strikes. The President was empowered to order a 60-day 'cooling-off period' before strike action could be taken. Also, union leaders were forced to take oaths stating that they were not Communists. Finally, unions were required to register themselves and to file financial reports with the Department of Labor. Despite protests from the unions, the Act has remained relatively unchanged.

Taif Accord (1989)

A peace settlement concluded in the Saudi Arabian port of Taif, when sixty-two of the seventy-three surviving members of the 1972 parliament met to negotiate a new Lebanese Constitution to end thirteen years of civil war. Under heavy pressure from Lebanon's effective guardian, Syria, the meeting was called after Amin *Jumayyil ended his term of office as Lebanese President without a successor. Parliament would in future be composed of 50 Christians and 50 Muslims (previously 55:45). While the President would continue to be chosen from the *Maronite community, the Prime Minister would be a *Sunni Muslim, while the Speaker of parliament would be a *Shi'ite Muslim. It had many critics among the Muslims, as Christians were still highly over-represented, since their proportion of the total population had declined from just over 50 per cent in the 1940s to 35 per cent in the late 1980s.

Taiwan (Republic of China)

An island 100 miles off the Chinese coast, which is effectively sovereign, but which formally still adheres to the concept of being part of China, along with the People's Republic.

Japanese rule (1895–1945) Taiwan became Japan's first colony following its victory in the Sino-Japanese War (1894–5). Japanese became the official language, while Chinese customs were repressed. The Japanese ended the factionalism and infighting between the various *warlords and criminal groups that had dominated the island for so long. After centuries of neglect by the Chinese imperial government in Peking, the island prospered after land reform and the introduction of education, as well as economic measures such as the expansion of railways and the introduction of electricity. During World War II, most islanders supported its colonial power. The island served as Japan's unsinkable 'aircraft carrier', from which the invasion of the Philippines was launched.

The Guomindang era (1945–1980s) After World War II, Taiwan reverted to the rule of the Nationalist Chinese government led by *Chiang Kai-shek. The new Governors from mainland China treated the island with disdain, while their corrupt and arbitrary government led to widespread rioting in 1947. Nevertheless, after Chiang's defeat in the *Chinese Civil War, in 1949 the island became his last refuge. Together with over one million people he arrived in Taiwan to use it as a last bastion of the Nationalist Republic of China, while mainland China became the Communist People's Republic of China. In subsequent years, the country's politics were dominated by two central issues: the heterogeneity of its population and relations with the People's Republic, over which the small island continued to claim sovereignty.

After 1949, the island was composed of three major population groups: a small aboriginal population of Malaysian-Polynesian origin; the Taiwanese majority of over 80 per cent of the total population, which had arrived on the island from the fourteenth to the seventeenth centuries; and the Nationalists from mainland China, who arrived around 1949 and made up around

15 per cent of the population. The latter group was extremely heterogeneous in itself, an amalgam of mostly *Guomindang (KMT) officials and their families from different parts of China, united not by culture or tradition but by politics. It was this group which controlled the country's government and administration, as well as the economy, through its command of the only legal party, the Guomindang under Chiang's leadership.

Throughout its existence after 1949, Taiwan's political and economic development was closely affected by the Communist People's Republic of China on the mainland. In the first decade, Chiang was determined to prepare for the reconquest of the mainland sooner rather than later, via bases on the islands of *Quemoy and Matsu. However, *Mao's government proved to be more stable than Chiang had anticipated. In 1959, the USA made clear its refusal to support an offensive war against China. As a result, Chiang shifted his attention to domestic political growth. He promoted Taiwan's development into a prosperous, well-organized exporter of high technology, again as a positive contrast to the Chinese mainland, which was ridden with economic problems. This development continued with even greater speed under his son, *Chiang Ching-kuo, who recognized the growing tension between economic liberalization on the one hand and political illiberalism on the other. Diplomatically, Taiwan became increasingly isolated from 1972, when the UN recognized the Communist People's Republic as the sole representative of China. Taiwan's position was weakened further in 1979, when the USA took up direct diplomatic relations with the People's Republic, even if it continued to guarantee the island's security against attack.

Democratization (1980s–90s) As a way of increasing domestic stability, and to emphasize Taiwan's distinctiveness from mainland China, Chiang Ching-kuo carefully relaxed the Guomindang's monopoly of political power, with competitive national elections being introduced in 1980 and 1983. More importantly, he appointed a Taiwanese, *Lee Teng-hui, as his Vice-President and successor. Under Lee, a two-party system emerged, with the oppositional Democratic Progressive Party (DPP) winning a sensational victory in the local elections of 2 December 1994. In the early 1990s a number of constitutional amendments were passed, all of which effectively challenged mainland China's claim of sovereignty over the island. Not the least of these was the conduct of direct, democratic presidential elections in

1996, which Lee won despite angry interference from Communist China.

Contemporary politics (since 2000) A political shift occurred in 2000, when the DPP broke the KMT's monopoly of power and won the presidential elections. However, the new President, Chen Shui-bian, was blocked by the KMT's majority in parliament. The political establishment struggled to accommodate the precedent of a President and a parliamentary majority each pursuing contrasting political agendas. The KMT and the DPP were both weakened by internal conflicts. Following the integration of *Hong Kong into mainland China in 1997, the Chinese government put pressure on Taiwan as the one Chinese territory beyond its control. In 2005, a law passed in mainland China, determining that any Taiwanese attempt to renounce Chinese unity would trigger military measures, caused mass demonstations in Taiwan. Chen was re-elected with a wafer-thin majority in 2004, but continued to be hampered by a hostile parliamentary majority, as well as by corruption allegations. While unsuccessful in formalizing Taiwan's claim for independence, Chen successfully pursued an incremental policy of developing a Taiwanese separate identity, through the use of Taiwanese dialect, the removal of statues dedicated to Chiang Kai-sheck, and populist rhetoric against mainland China.

Tajikistan

A heterogeneous central Asian country whose political stability since 1918 has only been possible under autocratic regimes.

Early history (up to 1991) Under the sovereignty of the Russian Empire since 1868, after the 1917 *Russian Revolutions it became part of the Turkestan Socialist Soviet Republic in 1918. As an Autonomous Soviet Republic within *Uzbekistan from 1924, it joined the Soviet Union in 1925. In 1929 it became a full Soviet Republic, and a separate component of the USSR. Until the 1950s, the country was essentially ruled directly from Moscow. This led to relatively weak central control over the mountainous and inaccessible territory, and in many areas collectivization was never successfully introduced during *Stalin's rule. By the same token, the country's economic development, standard of living, and rate of education (especially for women) remained extremely low.

Contemporary history (since 1991) Throughout Soviet rule, politics was dominated by tribal rivalries. This became even more marked with the country's independence following the collapse of the Soviet Union after the *August coup of 1991. Superimposed on these tribal frictions were ethnic rivalries, especially with the large minority (24 per cent) of Uzbeks, as well as the educated Russian elite (7.6 per cent). Among many Tajiks, *Islam was a key unifying factor, so that politics became dominated by the struggle between an Islamic opposition on the one hand and the former Communist leadership on the other. This tension erupted into civil war, which spilt over into neighbouring Afghanistan, where Tajiks formed the second largest ethnic group.

The country's formerly desolate economy plunged even further into chaos. It declined throughout the 1990s, with rampant inflation and high rates of unemployment. Despite this, the former Communist leadership under Imomali Rachmanov (since 1994) managed to remain in power, through widespread use of torture and executions, and with the help of a *CIS 'peace contingent', containing around 25,000, mainly Russian, soldiers. A peace agreement between the warring factions was signed in 1997, and a constitutional amendment accepted in 1999. Two parliamentary chambers were created, and the President's term of office was extended to seven years. Rachmanov was re-elected in 1999, amidst allegations of electoral fraud and the continued curtailment of the political opposition. In 2001 economic and social stability was boosted when the *War on Terrorism broke out in neighbouring Afghanistan, as it brought substantial capital inflows from the USA and other donors concerned to stabilize the region. In the years before his controversial re-election in 2006, Rachmanov cracked down on the opposition, with the opposition leader, Mahmadruzi Iskandarov, sentenced to 23 years imprisonment in 2005.

Takeshita Noboru (b. 26 Feb. 1924, d. 19 June 2000). Prime Minister of Japan 1987–9 Although a less controversial figure than many of his contemporaries, Takeshita's achievements have been substantial by comparison with any other Japanese political leader of recent times. The son of a sake maker, Takeshita spent his early adulthood in the Imperial Army Air Corps. After 1945, he taught in a middle school before entering local politics in 1951 in Shimane Prefecture. From this platform he launched his campaign for election to the Lower House in 1958. In a long political career, Takeshita managed to acquire experience in many of the most important Cabinet posts including Chief Cabinet Secretary and Minister of Construction. As Minister of Finance in the *Nakasone government, he designed the consumption tax which he was later to introduce as Prime Minister. This enabled a fundamental reform of the Japanese revenue system, despite widespread and virulent opposition. His remarkable political skill was based on his expertise in fund-raising, his adeptness as a party boss, and his ability as a consummate parliamentarian. He resigned from office because he was implicated in the Recruit scandal, but retained considerable influence within the *Liberal Democratic Party.

Taliban

A radical Islamic group of militias in Afghanistan formed by former Afghan refugees in Pakistan in 1994. By 1996 they controlled most of Afghanistan, including the capital, Kabul. Acting on their radical interpretation of the Quran, the freedom of movement and the education of girls and women were extremely restricted, and female employment became very limited. Intellectuals were imprisoned or killed, and all aspects of 'modern' culture (cinemas, radios, etc.) were banned. Hundreds of thousands were killed during their rule on account of their tribal affiliation, religion, or opinions. In 1999 alone an estimated 100,000 people, mostly Tajiks, were driven from their homes. Much of the leadership of this fragmented movement was provided by Osama *Bin Laden and his al-Qaeda network. As a result, the Taliban became complicit in the *September 11 attacks, and were swept from power in the ensuing *War on Terrorism, when US military support allowed the Afghan opposition to regain power.

After the establishment of international control under *Karzai in Afghanistan, Taliban fighters fled to the barely accessible areas in the remote part of Afghanistan and Pakistan. There they regrouped, and from 2005 they began to retake control of some of the south. In 2006, they announced a major spring offensive against *NATO forces for 2007.

Tambo, Oliver Reginald (b. 27 Oct. 1917, d. 24 Apr. 1993). President-general of the ANC 1977–90

Born in Bizana (Cape Province), he became a close friend of *Mandela while studying at Fort Hare University. Together they were founding members of the *ANC Youth League in 1944. They opened the first Black law practice in the country (1952), and he became secretary-general of the ANC (1954–8). He left for Lusaka (Zambia) just before the ANC's ban in 1960, and set up its headquarters there. He was acting president-general for the imprisoned Mandela (1967–77) before becoming president-general himself. He suffered a severe stroke in 1989, but was able to return to South Africa in 1991.

Tamils

A large ethnic minority in Sri Lanka consisting of Sri Lankan Tamils (12.6 per cent of the population) and Indian Tamils (5.5 per cent). The former group arrived from southern India centuries ago, and settled predominantly in the north and east of the country. They became involved in agriculture, although many moved into the cities (especially Jaffna) and became professionals or engaged in commerce. By contrast, the Indian Tamils were brought in by the British colonial regime in the nineteenth century, to work on the tea plantations. The latter group did not mix either with the Sri Lankan Tamils or with the island's predominant Sinhalese population.

Both Tamil groups began to cooperate gradually from the 1950s, when Tamils considered themselves threatened by Sinhalese discrimination under the various *Bandaranaike governments. Their fears were aggravated by the introduction of Sinhalese as the official language, the promotion of Sinhalese in official government jobs, and official disregard for Tamil educational institutions. This led to growing violence between the Tamil and the Sinhalese communities, and resulted in the formation of the Liberation Tigers of Tamil Eelam (Tamil Tigers), a guerrilla group that plunged the country into civil war in 1983. Peace was restored briefly by Indian troops (1987–9). However, the Tamil Tiger leadership was increasingly radicalized, and continued with its intermittent attacks. In a civil war that claimed over 60,000 deaths by 2000, the Tamil Tigers launched their most successful offensive in 1999, when they encircled 25,000 Sri Lankan troops on the Jaffna peninsula. The Tamil Tigers were unable to force their surrender, however. A military stalemate ensued, and led to the conclusion of a peace agreement in Geneva in 2002.

The government's architect of the peace deal, Ranil Wickramesinghe, was defeated in the 2003 elections, which produced a majority for the United People's Freedom Alliance. This opposed making more concessions to the Tamil Minority. Growing discrimination led to renewed fighting, with the LTTE initiating a number of bomb attacks, and facing open attacks by the Sri Lankan military.

Tanaka Giichi (b. 22 June 1864, d. 29 Sept. 1929). Prime Minister of Japan 1927–9

A career soldier whose reputation within the military was established on the basis of his knowledge of Russia and the Russian military. A participant in the *Russo-Japanese War of 1904–5, Tanaka promoted reforms in army training and was a key figure in the foundation of the Military Reservists Association. In 1925, he became the president of the *Seiyûkai and was invited to form a government in 1927, in a bid to bring order to a banking crisis and remedy a weak China policy. The Tanaka Cabinet was responsible for large-scale crackdowns on left-wing groups. He was forced to step down over the failure of his China policy, especially after Emperor *Hirohito made known his displeasure at the government's inability to rein in the *Guandong Army.

Tanaka Kakuei (b. 4 May 1918, d. 16 Dec. 1993). Prime Minister of Japan 1972–4

Tanaka Kakuei, the 'bulldozer-computer' of postwar Japanese politics, achieved remarkable political success in a society where educational credentials are prized, despite the fact that he left school at the age of 15. From these beginnings Tanaka qualified as an architect and returned from Korea after the war as a rich man. Ironically, for a politician famed for his ability to win elections, his first attempt at entering the Diet (House of Representatives) in 1946 failed. Nevertheless, he succeeded in being returned for his constituency in Niigata Prefecture the following year. His career was briefly interrupted by a bribery scandal soon after, although he survived this to establish his reputation as a skilled operator within the legislature. In 1957 he took his first Cabinet post as Minister of Posts and Telecommunications, after which his ministerial career flourished.

In 1972 Tanaka became Japan's youngest postwar Prime Minister to date, but he had to resign in December 1974, as the economy faltered and he was facing allegations of illegal political practices. In 1976 Tanaka was at the centre of further accusations over his role in the *Lockheed Scandal and these ultimately culminated in a criminal conviction in 1983, which effectively ensured that he would not hold governmental office again. Nevertheless, thanks to a lengthy legal appeal procedure, Tanaka remained a powerful force within the ruling *Liberal Democratic Party (LDP) until the mid-1980s. During this period he

controlled the government through his faction, which he had built into the most powerful organization within the LDP. In many ways the epitome of a Japanese dynamic postwar politician, he facilitated the normalization of relations with Communist China. He is also remembered for his ambitious but ultimately flawed plans to reorganize the Japanese economy.

Tanganyika, see TANZANIA

Tangentopoli ('Bribe city')

A large-scale criminal investigation in the early 1990s against widespread corruption and bribery in Italian administrative, political, and business circles. This included the examination of the links between the *Mafia and over 400 Members of Parliament, as well as the bringing of charges against 160 individuals about payment of bribes to the state electricity company, ENEL, in May 1995.

On 30 October 1993 the President of the electronic conglomerate Olivetti, Carlo de Benedetti, was imprisoned after admitting the payment of 11 billion lire ($7 million) to political parties in return for state contracts. A host of government ministers from the 1980s were convicted of accepting illegal payments either for themselves or their political parties, the most prominent being ex-Prime Minister *Craxi, who was sentenced in 1994 (*in absentia*) to eight-and-a-half and five-and-a-half years' imprisonment on two counts of corruption, with over 40 charges still pending. Furthermore, Paolo Berlusconi, the brother of Prime Minister *Berlusconi who had been elected on a promise to fight corruption, was sentenced on 22 December 1994 to seven months' imprisonment on charges of bribery as manager of his brother's holding company, Fininvest.

Connected with these efforts to purge the Italian establishment were intensified efforts in the campaign against the *Mafia. In 1993 around 22,000 people were under investigation for links with the organization. On 27 August 1994 one of the most sought-after mafiosi, Lorenzo Tinnirello, was arrested and charged with 119 murders. In addition, there were investigations against a number of prominent politicians, such as the former Minister of Defence, Salvo Ando, and the former chairman of the Sicilian *Christian Democrats, Calogero Mannino. The most prominent case revolved around ex-Prime Minister *Andreotti, who was accused of being a member and protector of the Mafia for fourteen years. The charges against Andreotti, who more than any other politician represented the political system during the late 1970s and 1980s, epitomized the moral bankruptcy of the established parties and directly contributed to their collapse in 1993–4. At the same time, it proved difficult to find a new political leadership which had sufficient experience of politics to be successful, but which had not taken part in the corruption of the 1980s and early 1990s. In 1999 the problems facing the prosecution were epitomized by Andreotti's acquittal, and the re-election of Berlusconi as Prime Minister in 2001.

Tannenberg, Battle of (World War I; 23–31 Aug. 1914)

According to the *Schlieffen Plan, Germans were concentrating their military efforts on the Western Front. When the 1st and 2nd Russian Armies, under Generals Rennenkampf and Samsonov respectively, attacked sooner than expected in the east, the inferior German forces initially had to withdraw. According to a plan drawn up by Colonel Max Hoffmann and executed by Generals *Hindenburg and *Ludendorff, the Germans first encircled the 2nd Army near Tannenberg. The Germans had intercepted Russian wireless signals. They also trusted (correctly) that Rennenkampf would do little to relieve his arch-rival Samsonov. A few days later, the German army also fought successfully against the 1st Army near the Masurian lakes. Despite their numerical inferiority, the Germans had relatively few casualties and took 137,000 prisoners of war.

The battle ended the threat of a Russian invasion, but at a time when German advances to the west were disappointing, its psychological effects were even more important. It transformed Ludendorff and especially Hindenburg into mythical figures, and their position was so strong that they became virtual dictators of Germany 1916–18. Especially in the late stages of World War II, the image of Tannenberg was often invoked in *Nazi *propaganda to encourage a belief in ultimate victory even if the enemy was already on German soil.

Tanzania

An east African country with few mineral resources, Tanzania has enjoyed remarkable political stability since independence.

Foreign rule A German colony from 1891 (German East Africa), the colonial forces were defeated by the British under *Smuts in 1916. After the war, Britain came to administer it as a *League of Nations *Mandate, when it became known as Tanganyika. It was governed under the principle of *indirect rule, which invested considerable autonomy in the village and tribal chiefs. The British were relatively restrained in their colonial administration, as they focused their attention on the adjacent colony of Kenya, which they could rule without reference to the League of Nations, as well as on the colony of *Zanzibar. It became a *UN *trust territory after World War II. In 1952, *Nyerere founded TANU (Tanganyika African National Union), through which he managed to unite the country's ethnically mixed population around the demand for Britain to honour its obligation to the UN and release the country to independence.

African socialism Independence was achieved on 9 December 1961 with relatively few complications, compared for example, to Kenya (*Mau Mau) or Zimbabwe (Rhodesia). In 1964 it was united with Zanzibar under the name of Tanzania, though the two parts retained considerable autonomy with separate parliaments and administrative systems. In 1972 TANU merged with Zanzibar's major African Party, the ASP (Afro Shirazi Party), to form a new unity party, the Chama Cha Mainduzi (CCM, Party of the Revolution).

Tanzania became a model for an African way to *socialism based on indigenous cultures. The *Arusha Declaration of 1967 inaugurated a policy whereby the village became the administrative and economic unit, as large businesses became nationalized and subject to state planning. The aim of this policy was to achieve economic self-sufficiency, and to reduce income inequalities. However, the policy stifled private initiative, partly through lack of incentives, and partly through an overblown bureaucracy which tried to coordinate the vast network of villages and state-owned companies. In 1979 Nyerere declared war on Uganda, which led to the overthrow of the dictator *Amin.

Contemporary politics (from 1985) By the 1980s it had become apparent that Nyerere's socialist policies had failed to increase production. Under his successor, Ali Hassan Mwinyi (b. 1925), the economy was liberalized. This led to much unemployment (up to 40 per cent in 1994) and poverty, which was compounded by the fall in world market prices for its main export commodities, coffee and cotton. In an attempt to stave off popular unrest, Mwinyi introduced a multi-party state in 1992, while the 1995 presidential elections were won by the government's candidate, Benjamin Mkapa, with 62 per cent of the votes, protests by the opposition notwithstanding. Even though Mkapa's policies led to economic stabilization and growth from the late 1990s, unemployment was not significantly reduced, and one-fifth of the population continued to live in absolute poverty. Mkapa was re-elected in 2000, and presided over substantial economic growth as well as the drastic reduction in foreign debt under the *HIPC initiative. In 2005, Jakaya Kikwete, of the CCM, was elected President.

Tardieu, André (b. 22 Sept. 1876, d. 15 Sept. 1945). Prime Minister of France 1929–30, 1932

A *Radical member of the Chamber of Deputies 1914–24 and from 1926, he was a close ally of *Clemenceau, whose tough policies during World War I and at the *Versailles Treaty he actively supported. Minister for Public Works 1926–8 and Minister of the Interior 1928–30, he held several other ministries until 1934. Though a virulent anti-Communist, he also alienated many Radicals through his policies of 'national retooling', which encompassed proposals for social reform and the modernization of industry and agriculture. He lacked the necessary parliamentary support to implement most of his proposals. He left the Radicals in 1932 to co-found the Centre Républicain, which he represented in the Chamber until 1936.

tariff reform (UK)

An issue which was at the heart of British politics for over a century until the 1930s. In 1846, the repeal of the Corn Laws (a tariff on imported grain) enshrined the doctrine of free trade (ideally the absence of import duties) as the linchpin of British politics.

Free trade came under sustained pressure from 1900, owing to the imposition of import duties by Britain's main industrializing trading partners. In 1903, Joseph *Chamberlain proposed a *protectionist scheme of 'Imperial Preference'. Accordingly, Britain would only impose duties on foodstuffs imported from outside the *British Empire, while in return Britain's colonies and Dominions would exempt British industrial goods from import duties. The scheme was designed to strengthen the Empire through increasing the trade flow of primary goods to Britain, and industrial machinery from Britain.

Chamberlain hoped that the Empire would prove an effective emotional motive to mobilize support. However, the tariff divided Britain between those who benefited from it and those who did not. It was unpopular with industrial workers, as it would lead to an increase in the price of basic foodstuffs, while a large proportion of British businesses, which concentrated on trade with the Americas, would have suffered. As a result, Chamberlain's campaign divided the *Conservative Party, and gave the ardently pro-free-trade *Liberal Party a crucial boost which enabled it to win the 1906 elections.

The issue of fair trade re-emerged in 1923, when *Baldwin unsuccessfully fought an election primarily on this issue. The emotional appeal of free trade diminished only as a consequence of the Great *Depression, when Britain simply had to respond to the protective tariffs raised worldwide. Tariffs were adopted by *MacDonald's *National Government under the *Ottawa Agreement of 1932. Imperial Preference ended with Britain's entry into the European Economic Community (*European integration) in 1973.

Taruc, Luis (b. 21 June 1913, d. 4 May 2005). Filipino resistance leader

The son of sharecropping peasants in Luzon, he was educated at Manila University and in the 1930s took up the cause of landless peasants, who were particularly affected by the Great *Depression. In 1935 he joined the Socialist Party and the Philippines Anti-Fascist Front. In 1942 he formed the *Hukbalahap on Luzon, and became its commander-in-chief. By 1945 his forces had almost total control of the rural areas of the island, and welcomed the return of the US liberation forces against the Japanese. In 1946, he was elected to the House of Representatives. When denied his seat, he returned to his guerrilla activities at the head of a People's Liberation Army. He finally surrendered in 1954, and was imprisoned until 1968.

Tashkent Agreement (4–10 Jan. 1966)

An agreement signed in the Soviet city of Tashkent by the Indian Prime Minister, Lal Bahadur *Shastri, and the President of Pakistan, *Ayub Khan, to end the second *Indo-Pakistan War over *Kashmir. Both countries agreed not only to withdraw their troops from each other's territory and repatriate their prisoners of war, but also to start normalizing their diplomatic relationship. Unfortunately, the proposed beginning of friendly Indo-Pakistan relations was made more difficult by the death of

Shastri only hours after signing the agreement. The agreement did little to mollify the deep hostility between the two countries since their independence in 1947, and was unable to prevent the outbreak of renewed hostilities in 1970.

Tawney, Richard Henry (b. 30 Nov. 1880, d. 16 Jan. 1962). British economic historian and social critic

Born in Calcutta, he was educated at Rugby and Oxford. He was a social worker and investigator at *Toynbee Hall, and then, in 1908, became engaged in adult education as the first tutorial teacher for the Worker's Education Association (WEA). He served in the Manchester Regiment in World War I, and was almost fatally wounded in the Battle of the *Somme. In 1919, he began to teach for the London School of Economics, where he was professor of economic history in 1931–49. His academic writing centred on sixteenth- and seventeenth-century economics, his most famous work being *Religion and the Rise of Capitalism* (1926). He was active in the *Labour Party, failing four times to be elected to Parliament. However, his work *Secondary Education for All* (1922) was the basis of Labour's education policy, and was central in the writing of its 1928 policy statement *Labour and the Nation*. He also had much influence on social thought through *The Acquisitive Society* (1920), which argued that material acquisitiveness was morally wrong, and *Equality* (1929), which criticized 'the religion of inequality' dominating England based on class privilege. He exerted much influence over the social thought of the Labour Party and on the *Anglican Church, and made a significant impact on the history of adult education.

Te Puea Herangi (b. 1884, d. 12 Oct. 1952). Maori leader

Born in Whatiwhatihoe as the granddaughter of the second Maori King, Tawhiao (b. 1825?, d. 1894), she first gained prominence by leading a campaign against the conscription of Maori in World War I. In 1921, she became prominent through her leadership in improving her community of Ngaruawahia. With *Ngata she encouraged her people, the Waikato, to restore and preserve their traditional culture. Through community projects, she hoped to raise their awareness of their own identity, while she realized their economic independence through the development of previously idle Maori lands. Hoping to combine a revived Maori culture with social progress, she accepted elements of the White (Pakeha) culture, such as education

and health programmes, if they could be accommodated into Maori customs and institutions. One of the most influential women in New Zealand history, she was the first Maori woman to receive national attention and recognition. She was awarded a CBE.

Teamsters' Union (USA)

Formed in 1903, its full title is International Brotherhood of Teamsters, Chauffeurs, Warehousemen and Helpers in America. In the late 1950s its president, David Beck, was indicted for having links with criminals, whereupon the *trade (labor) union was expelled from the *AFL-CIO. Congress then passed the Landrum–Griffin Act, which gave the secretary of labor considerable powers over the finances of unions. Beck's successor, *Hoffa, was found guilty of trying to influence a federal jury while on trial for misusing union funds in 1964. Thereafter, the union sought to recover its reputation by cooperating closely with such responsible union leaders as Walter *Reuther of the United Automobile Workers. Led by Hoffa's son, James P. Hoffa, since 1999, and counting 1.4 million members in 2007, the union has maintained great bargaining power within the USA, not least owing to its ability to paralyse interstate commerce.

(⊕) SEE WEB LINKS

• The official website of the Teamsters' Union.

Teapot Dome Scandal (USA)

When Warren G. *Harding was elected US President in 1920, he brought into his administration many of his friends, who became known as the 'Ohio gang'. Harding transferred the management of the US navy's oil reserves at Teapot Dome, Wyoming, from the navy to the Interior Department under his old friend Albert B. Fall. Fall allowed the secret exploration of oil reserves at Wyoming by the Mammoth Oil Company, and of other reserves at Elk Hills, California, by the Pan-American Petroleum and Transportation Company. Harding, who was not personally involved, died before the full extent of scandal and the involvement of Fall was exposed by Senator Thomas J. Walsh during 1922–4. Fall was found guilty of accepting a $400,000 bribe and imprisoned in 1929.

Tehran Conference (28 Nov.–1 Dec. 1943)

An inter-Allied conference between *Churchill, *Roosevelt, and, for the first time, *Stalin, in the Iranian capital of Tehran. Stalin's demand for a second front in France in the summer of 1944 was coordinated with plans for a Soviet summer offensive in 1944. The three leaders discussed the establishment of the *UN after the war, and Stalin pressed for a future Soviet sphere of influence in the Baltic States and Eastern Europe. Finally, Stalin indicated Soviet willingness to join the war against Japan once Germany had been defeated.

CAIRO CONFERENCE; YALTA CONFERENCE; POTSDAM CONFERENCE

Teleki, Pál Count (b. 1 Nov. 1879, d. 3 Apr. 1941). Prime Minister of Hungary 1920–1, 1939–41

Born in Budapest, Teleki had a distinguished career as a geographer at the university before being elected to the Hungarian parliament in 1909. He attended the Paris *Peace Conference and became Prime Minister (1920–1), passing a series of *anti-Semitic laws in response to the previous *Kun regime. He returned to academic life, but in February 1939 *Horthy reappointed him Prime Minister. He managed to disband some of the country's more extreme *Fascist groups, but allowed anti-Semitic laws to stand. He believed that the only way to regain territory lost by Hungary at the Treaty of *Trianon was to negotiate through *Hitler. In this he was successful, via the two *Vienna Awards. He tried desperately to keep Hungary out of World War II, but the attraction of joining forces with the apparently unstoppable Hitler made the pressure to join the war at Germany's side irresistible. Feeling bound to a treaty of friendship with Yugoslavia, he committed suicide rather than give in to the pressure from *Horthy, his Cabinet, and the army to allow the Germans to attack Yugoslavia through Hungarian territory.

Temple, Right Revd William (b. 15 Oct. 1881, d. 26 Oct. 1944). Archbishop of Canterbury 1942–4

Born in Westgate, Durham, he was educated at Rugby and Oxford. He taught philosophy at Oxford, before being ordained an *Anglican priest in 1909. He was a headmaster, and then Bishop of Manchester (1921–8) and Archbishop of York (1928–42), before becoming Archbishop of Canterbury in 1942. He was an outstanding theologian and, inspired by his friend *Tawney, became a leading advocate of the Anglican Church's responsibility to speak out on social issues. This led to frequent clashes with the government, though it also enlisted his support for the *Beveridge Report and, most crucially, for *Butler's 1944 Education Act. His concern for social issues was also demonstrated in his concern for adult education, as president of the Workers' Education Association (1908–24). His preoccupation with *ecumenism was influential in the creation of the World Council of Churches.

Templer, Sir Gerald (b. 11 Sept. 1898, d. 25 Oct. 1979). British field marshal

Born in Colchester, he was educated at Wellington College and the Royal Military College, Sandhurst. He served with the Irish Fusiliers in France from 1917, and after *World War I in Persia, *Palestine, Iraq, and Egypt. In *World War II, he served in France in 1940, and from 1943 he held commands in North Africa and Italy. He was commander-in-chief and high commissioner in Malaya (1952–4), where his military efficiency ensured victory against the Communist guerrillas rising against British colonial rule, though he also saw the necessity of Malayan independence. He was chief of the Imperial General Staff (1955–8).

Teng Hsaio-P'ing, see DENG XIAOPING

Teschen Dispute

A small area surrounding the city of Teschen, ruled by the Austrian Habsburgs from the eighteenth century until World War I. It became highly industrialized in the later nineteenth century. Conflicting claims by Czechoslovakia and Poland led to violent clashes in 1919, which were arbitrated by the *League of Nations in 1920. Accordingly, the area was divided so that the northern half, which included half the city as Cieszyn, went to Poland, while the southern half, with its rich coalfields, went to Czechoslovakia (Tesin). The issue soured the relations between the two countries for twenty years. In 1938, Poland became an often-overlooked beneficiary of the *Munich Agreement, whereby Germany invaded the *Sudetenland, while the Poles annexed the Czech part of Teschen. In 1945 the Soviet Union decreed that the 1920–38 compromise be restored.

Tet offensive (29 Jan. – 25 Feb. 1968). An assault launched in the *Vietnam War by *Vietcong guerrillas and North Vietnamese army units, timed to coincide with the first day of the Tet holiday (the lunar New Year). Under the command of *Vo Nguyen Giap attacks were mounted against Saigon, Hue, some ninety towns, and hundreds of villages. There were heavy casualties on both sides and the main attacks were successfully repulsed by US troops. Although technically a defeat for the North Vietnamese forces, the extent of the offensive, despite the might of over 500,000

US troops, shocked US public opinion and convinced the *Johnson administration of the need to end US involvement. Talks were begun in Paris in 1968, which were only concluded five years later with the *Paris Peace Accords of 1973.

Thailand

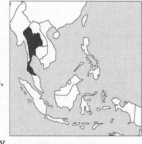

A country in south-east Asia, which, compared to its neighbours (Myanmar, Laos, Cambodia and Vietnam) has enjoyed remarkable political stability and economic prosperity, thanks to the strength of the monarchy and the military.

Absolute rule (until 1932) Formerly known as Siam, it was the only country in south-east Asia that escaped colonial rule, as a result of its geopolitical situation between the French and the British colonial empires. This enabled King Chulalongkorn (r. 1868–1910) to play off the British against the French, though he was forced to concede around one-third of the country's possessions to these powers (Laos and Cambodia in the east, and Burma in the west).

Chulalongkorn Westernized the country, through abolishing slavery and introducing extensive judicial, tax, and educational reforms. These were continued under King Vajiravudh (r. 1910–25), who introduced compulsory schooling in 1922. Ironically, the monarchy's reforms served to undermine its own power in the long run. Partly in response to the hardships caused by the Great *Depression, but partly also because of the establishment of an educated middle class, King Prajadhipok (r. 1925–35) was forced to relinquish the absolute power of the monarchy in the 1932 revolution.

The Phibunsongkhram era (1938–57) A period of brief parliamentary government followed, though during the rule of King Ananda Mahidol (r. 1935–46), *Phibunsongkhram led a coup in 1938 which established the predominance of the military in the country's political sphere. In an attempt to consolidate his support around *nationalism, he renamed the country Thailand, after its ethnic majority, the Thais, in 1939. He then used the outbreak of World War II in Europe to reclaim some of the country's territories lost to the British and French, gaining these with the help of the Japanese in 1940–1. In return he allowed the Japanese to occupy his country (1941–4) as a springboard for its military operations against *Singapore and India. Thailand formally declared war on Britain and the USA in 1942.

In consequence, a resistance movement began to form against Phibunsongkhram, while wartime shortages and Allied bombing campaigns increased opposition on a popular level. Phibunsongkhram was thus forced to resign in 1944. A series of weak democratic governments followed, which were at great pains to repudiate the country's former links with Japan, surrendering all areas which Thailand had brought under its control during its alliance with Japan. The reign of King *Bhumibol Adulyadej started with a military coup by Phibunsongkhram, who restored stability on a strongly anti-Communist platform. This yielded considerable returns not only in domestic support but also in US aid, which was paid annually from 1950.

Economic growth (from the 1950s) Phibunsongkhram was toppled in a bloodless coup in 1957, whereupon Sarit Thanarat suspended the constitution, outlawed political activity, and declared martial law. In 1963 he was succeeded by Thanom Kittikachorn, who continued the military dictatorship except for the period of 1968–71, which was marked by a return to constitutional rule. Throughout this period of undemocratic rule, the country's economic and social development continued uninterrupted. The governments were always strongly pro-Western, allowing the USA to use its bases there for air raids in the *Vietnam War. They were also staunchly *capitalist, while gradually expanding medical and educational provisions (e.g. in 1960 compulsory education was extended from four to seven years). A brief democratic period (1973–6) was followed by renewed military rule, which gained some stability only under General Prem Tinsulanonda, who was Prime Minister 1980–8. During this period the country achieved spectacular rates of economic growth averaging around 10 per cent per year. In 1991, the army, fearful for its diminishing political power, led a coup against Tinsulanonda's democratically elected successor, General Chatchai Choonhavan.

After nationwide demonstrations, which led to the intervention of King Bhumibol Adulyadej, the army's chosen Prime Minister, General Suchinda, was forced to resign. A new civilian coalition under Chuan Leekpai (Democratic Party) carried out an extensive, if at times controversial, land reform. More importantly, on 4 January 1995 it passed fundamental changes to the Constitution designed to strengthen Thailand's democracy. The voting age was lowered from 21 to 18, the equal status of men and women was enshrined in the Constitution, the Prime Minister had to be a member of the elected lower House of Representatives, while the power of the Senate, consisting mostly of army officers, was greatly reduced. The success of this reform remained questionable, however, after the 1995 election produced a parliamentary majority for the pro-military parties led by the Chart Thai, many of whose members were accused of having links with organized crime.

Contemporary politics (since 1997) Thailand became one of the epicentres of the Asian economic crisis which commenced in 1997. This was caused by structural imbalances created by cheap credit, speculation, and the lack of economic supervision. The popular discontent this caused was defused through the completion of the constitutional reform in 1997. This democratized the political system, and led to a transformation of the Thai party system. The elections of 2001 were won by a newly founded party, the Thai Rak Thai ('Thais love Thais') led by the populist magnate Thaksin Shinawatra. Despite several corruption allegations against him, his movement capitalized on its promises for radical economic reform to obtain 248 out of 500 seats. In 2004, Thailand suffered from the *tsunami, in which over 5,000 people died.

Thaksin's popularity subsided rapidly after his triumphal re-election in 2005. It emerged that his clan derived economic benefits from his political position, while he sold his telephone company to a foreign company in 2006, days after changing a law making this possible. This sparked countrywide protests, with Thaksin ultimately calling new elections in which no parties other than his own were permitted. After a strongly worded intervention by King Bhumibol, the elections were eventually annulled, and in September 2006, the army under Surayud Chulanont staged a coup, promising a return to democracy by late 2007.

Thälmann, Ernst (b. 16 Apr. 1886, d. 18 Aug. 1944). German Communist leader
An unskilled worker from Hamburg, he joined the *SPD in 1903, co-founded the Independent Socialist Party (USPD) in 1917, and the *Communist Party (KPD) in 1920. A member of the Hamburg parliament (1919–33), Thälmann became KPD leader in 1921. He received around 1.9 million votes in the presidential elections of 1925, and around five million in 1932. Under the *Nazis, he was imprisoned in solitary confinement for eleven

years before he was executed at the Buchenwald *concentration camp.

Thant, U (b. 22 Jan. 1909, d. 25 Nov. 1974). UN Secretary-General 1961–71
Born at Pantanaw, he graduated from Rangoon University and became a schoolteacher (1928), and was later headmaster (1931–47). In 1948 he joined the Burmese Civil Service, serving at the Ministry of Information (1948–53). He then became secretary to the Prime Minister, *Nu Thakin U, in 1954, and in 1957 became Burma's permanent representative to the *UN. His achievements as UN Secretary-General included assistance in the resolution of a number of crises at the height of the *Cold War, most notably the *Cuban Missile Crisis and the *Vietnam War. He also worked toward the admission of the Communist People's Republic of China to full membership of the UN Security Council (1971). He was involved in the formation of a UN peacekeeping force in Cyprus 1964, and the negotiations for an armistice to end the *Six Day War.

Thatcher (née Roberts), Margaret Hilda, Baroness Thatcher of Kesteven in the County of Lincolnshire (b. 13 Oct. 1925). British Prime Minister 1979–90

Early career Born in Grantham (Lincolnshire), she was educated at Kesteven and Grantham Girls School, and at Oxford, where she studied chemistry. She was then a research chemist, and stood unsuccessfully for parliament as *Conservative candidate for Dartford in 1950 and 1951. She married Denis Thatcher, a wealthy businessman, in 1951, and having studied law, was called to the Bar in 1954. In 1959, she was elected to parliament for Finchley and, in 1961, became Parliamentary Secretary to the Ministry of Pensions and National Insurance. After taking a prominent role in opposition (1964–70), she served under *Heath as Secretary of State for Education.

By late 1974, when Heath had lost his third election, she was still relatively unknown. In the leadership contest of 1975 she was the only serious challenger to Heath and, after a surprising success in the first ballot, gathered so much momentum as to achieve an overall majority in the second. The manner of her election meant that she had to be careful in her first years of opposition to conciliate many leading figures in the party who had been her seniors before 1975. However, her increasing conviction that Britain needed a radical policy overhaul to establish free and private enterprise liberated from government and *trade-union interference struck a chord during the strike waves of 1978-9, which became known in popular memory as the 'winter of discontent'.

Economic policies Thatcher won the 1979 elections through her uncompromising twin message that the *Labour Party was the party of government intervention, and that it had become a hostage to *trade union power. In office, she broke with postwar Conservative policy to realize economic policies of *monetarism. The effects of the prevalent world depression caused by the 1979 *oil price shock were exacerbated through drastic reductions in state spending, and a policy of high interest rates to reduce inflation, the new number one target of economic policy.

The record of her economic achievements was mixed. She did drastically reduce inflation, as well as public debt. During the 1980s, economic fortunes improved, and unemployment recovered from its high levels of 1979-81. However, inflation decreased not only in Britain, but in all industrialized countries, and Britain's inflation rate remained among the highest in Western Europe. It is also unclear to what extent the economic recovery of the 1980s was the result of her policies, and to what extent it was the consequence of a decline in commodity prices which affected all other countries as well. At any rate, her claim to have improved long-term British economic prospects was belied by the recession which set in in 1989, which caused a sharp decline in house prices, and which underpinned her eventual fall from power.

Thatcher lost little time in pursuing her second major preoccupation, the reduction of trade-union power. She exploited the unions' inevitable weakness during the 1979-82 depression to pass legislation making trade unions more democratic in their decision-making, and more responsive to their members' wishes. Her battle against the trade unions climaxed in 1984-5, when she stood firm and eventually overcame the eleven-month-long miners' strike. It was a decisive victory over the trade-union movement and its hitherto excessive power, albeit achieved at an enormous social cost. Furthermore, it is arguable that, in line with the rest of the world, trade-union power and membership declined more owing to the difficult economic circumstances of high unemployment and job insecurity during the 1980s and 1990s, than in response to any of her anti-union legislation.

Foreign policy The initial unpopularity of her government was reversed as the 'iron lady' reclaimed the Falkland Islands from Argentine occupation in the *Falklands War of 1982. In consequence, she won the 1983 elections with a record majority. In foreign policy, her close relationship with US Presidents *Reagan and *Bush gave her enormous clout, which ensured that her reputation abroad eventually exceeded her rather more controversial image in Britain. Again, her record is mixed. Her pragmatic and pioneering insight in 1984 that *Gorbachev was a man one 'could do business with' stood in sharp contrast to her great reluctance to accept the inevitability of German reunification after the fall of the *Berlin Wall on 9 November 1989. Her undoubted hostility to *European integration was also compromised by her eventual acquiescence to the signing of the *Single European Act in 1986.

Political success Her longevity despite the ambiguous success of her policies stemmed from three basic factors. First, she created a rhetoric in which her strong leadership was portrayed as successful, while the Labour Party would continue to be wedded to *socialism and trade unionism regardless of its party reforms under *Kinnock.

Second, she was extraordinarily fortunate in the foundation of the *Social Democratic Party in 1981, which throughout the 1980s split the opposition between two almost equal camps: thus she was able to gain record parliamentary majorities despite gaining less than 45 per cent of the popular vote.

Third, she had a shrewd appreciation of the needs of the Conservative political constituency and ways to expand it. For example, the Housing Act of 1980 gave council tenants the right to buy their houses or flats, and about half a million properties were sold between 1979 and 1983. As new homeowners, these people had effectively received a social promotion, and were now keen to underline their new status as 'middle class' by switching their allegiance from Labour to Conservative. Her programme of large-scale privatization had a similar effect of strengthening her middle-class constituency, through their purchase of cheap shares, which also increased government revenue. But perhaps the best example in this respect is her policy of taxation. Although the total tax burden increased during her time in power, direct taxation fell, which enhanced her tax-cutting image among her middle-and upper-income constituency. The consequent increase in indirect taxation hit the poorest sections of society particularly hard, but these would have been unlikely to vote Conservative anyway.

Fall from power Despite her record victories at three successive elections, by 1989 she had increasingly lost her political touch, notably by failing to appreciate the unpopularity of the *poll tax. It seemed unlikely that she could win another victory against a rejuvenated Labour Party, and her obstinate opposition to the European Community was increasingly at odds with her senior Cabinet colleagues. Challenged by the charismatic Michael Heseltine, himself an earlier casualty of her iron control over the Cabinet, she narrowly failed to win a sufficient majority in the first round of the 1990 leadership elections and resigned (perhaps a little rashly), taking into account the not altogether selfless advice of her senior Cabinet colleagues such as John *Major. Adored by the rank-and-file in the Conservative Party, her frequent political criticism of her successor and her increasingly hostile stance on the EU compounded the difficulties of the Conservatives in the 1990s to find consistent policies.

Thatcherism

A term describing the ideology of Margaret *Thatcher, which formed the basis of the British *Conservative governments under her and *Major from 1979. It combined a number of features, none of which was innovative in itself. It was based on *monetarism and a belief in reducing the power and actions of the state in economy and society, and promoting the private sector wherever possible. This economic *liberalism stood in curious contrast to Thatcher's moral conservatism, in which the state was accorded a bigger role to uphold what was seen as the moral fabric of society, against the encroachments of liberal permissiveness. It appreciated the European Community as an economic tariff-free zone but, with a rhetoric bordering on the xenophobic, fiercely opposed further *European integration in the cultural and, above all, political sphere. The influence of Thatcherism could be seen in the government of the *Labour Party, which under Tony *Blair and Gordon *Brown accepted her monetarist policies of low inflation and low personal taxation.

Third International, see COMINTERN

Third Reich ('Third Empire')

A term used by *Nazi *propaganda to identify Nazi Germany as the final (and inevitable) stage in a historical process, from the loose federation of German territories in the Holy Roman Empire (until 1806), to the Second German Empire created by Bismarck 1866/71, which collapsed in 1918. Notwithstanding the aspiration that it would last for a thousand years, the Third Reich lasted from 1933 to 1945.

Thomas, Clarence (b. 23 June 1948). US Supreme Court Justice 1991–

The youngest ever Justice of the *Supreme Court and the second African-American Justice. A conservative, Thomas studied at Holy Cross College and Yale, and rose through legal practice and then academic law to become George *Bush's Supreme Court nominee in 1991. He was subjected to a furious assault from womens' groups and liberals after a fellow law professor, Anita Hill made allegations of sexual harassment against him, but he dismissed the allegations as 'high-tech lynching'. The controversy over his nomination raised serious questions about the Senate's power to advise and consent. Conflating as it did issues of race and workplace sexual conduct, and demonstrating the insensitivity of the fourteen-strong all-male Senate Committee, the issue caught the imagination of media and public, leading to a surge in membership for the National Organization for Women in 1992. As Supreme Court Justice, Thomas has tended to be more activist than his colleagues in striking down Congressional legislation.

Thorez, Maurice (b. 28 Apr. 1900, d. 11 July 1964). French Communist politician

Born the illegitimate son of a grocer, he became a full-time official of the French *Communist Party in 1920. A talented bureaucrat rather than a charismatic leader, he rose quickly to join the party's executive committee (*Politburo) in 1925. As the party's general secretary from 1930 until his death, he kept the party on a *Stalinist path faithful to the directives from Moscow. He was a member of the Chamber of Deputies from 1932 to 1939 and, following the *Stavinsky scandal, he supported the *Popular Front against the rise of *Fascism. He spent the years 1939–45 in the Soviet Union, and became a member of the Constituent Assemblies (1945–6) upon his return to France. A member of the National Assembly until his death, he was a Minister without Portfolio (1945–6), and Deputy Prime Minister (1946–7), but then the other parties began to shun the Communist Party as a result of the onset of the *Cold War.

Three Mile Island (USA)

The name of a nuclear power station on an island in the River Susquehanna, Pennsylvania. In March 1979 a series of human errors and instrumental failures resulted in the overloading of the reactor core of the plant, releasing radioactive gases and pushing the core temperature over the 5,000 degrees Fahrenheit mark. The accident resulted in the temporary closure of all nuclear power stations of a similar design, a moratorium on the licensing of new reactors, and a new public awareness of the potential dangers of nuclear power. The accident significantly stalled the development of nuclear power in the USA.

CHERNOBYL

Tiananmen Square

The world's largest square in the centre of Beijing. It has frequently been the centre of demonstrations in China. On 5 April 1976 around 100,000 people met to mourn the death of *Zhou Enlai, and implicitly to demonstrate against the erratic rule of *Mao Zedong. The crowd was put down by the police, while the incident was used by the *Gang of Four to demote Zhou's protégé, *Deng Xiaoping. In 1978, as soon as he had re-emerged as China's most powerful person, Deng reversed the official 'counter-revolutionary' label attached to the demonstration.

Similarly, the death of *Hu Yaobang sparked off demonstrations on Tiananmen Square, which students, teachers, and *human rights activists began to occupy from 22 April 1989 while boycotting lectures at Beijing University. The demonstration took place against a background of reform in other Communist countries such as the Soviet Union and Poland. A month later, the number of demonstrators had swelled to over one million people. On 30 May, art students erected the Goddess of Democracy, a 10 metre (30 foot) high statue loosely modelled on the American Statue of Liberty. Martial law was imposed on 20 May, and 300,000 troops advanced into Beijing. It put the occupation to a bloody end on 3–4 June, killing every person in sight. Eleven students who had joined hands to protect the Goddess of Democracy were mown down, together with up to 3,000 other people. Up to 10,000 were wounded, and countless arrests made. While the massacre incensed world opinion and damaged China's reputation for years, the demonstration enabled the conservative hardliners within the party to reassert themselves. They regained their influence over *Deng Xiaoping, while the reformist party secretary, Chao Tzu-yang was dismissed from office.

Tibet (Xizang)

A mountainous country which in the fifteenth century came under the influence of the Buddhist Lama sect. From the sixteenth century, the Lamaist monks under their leader, the *Dalai Lama, obtained the secular rule over the country, whereafter a unique monastic theocracy developed. Thanks to its spiritual power, the monks ruled for centuries, often without an army. By the early twentieth century, however, Lamaist rule had become comparatively inefficient, so that Tibet became subject to foreign influence, as Britain (1906) and Russia (1907) recognized it as a Chinese sphere of influence. With the fall of the Qing dynasty in 1911, it was completely independent again until 1950, when troops of the Communist People's Republic of China marched in. It was annexed in 1951, though formally it remained autonomous.

In 1959, the fourteenth Dalai Lama gave up his futile attempts at cooperation and, together with 100,000 followers, left for exile in India. From then on, China sought to integrate the country through a settlement programme for Chinese people. China outlawed the Tibetan language and culture, and arrested or otherwise silenced Tibetan or Lamaist leaders. Aggression peaked in the early years of the *Cultural Revolution in the late 1960s, when foreign vistors were banned from entering Tibet, and in the late 1980s, around the *Tiananmen Square demonstrations, when *Hu Jintao introduced martial law. By 2002, China's economic investment had brought significant prosperity to Lhasa, whose Chinese immigrants now made up the majority of the population. Chinese commitment to the development of the capital was confirmed by plans to develop a 'Special Economic Zone'. Modernization threatened the destruction of indigenous Tibetan culture. For this reason, the connection of Lhasa to the Chinese railway network in 2005 was criticized by exiled Tibetans as promoting further the exposure of Tibetans to goods, people, and values from China.

Tigray, see TIGRÉ

Tigré

A formerly independent territory which came under Ethiopian suzerainty in 1894. It was occupied by the Italians in 1935 and was administered as part of *Eritrea. It was liberated by the British, who exercised control until 1952, when it reverted to Ethiopian suzerainty. In subsequent decades, the Ethopian leadership was determined to quell every desire for greater autonomy, which gave rise to the Tigré People's Liberation Front (TPLF). By early 1990, the TPLF controlled most of the territory. Together with the Eritrean liberation forces, the TPLF advanced into

Ethiopia and its capital, Addis Ababa, in 1991. It deposed the Communist leadership and established a new government under the Tigréan leader, Meles Zenawi.

Tilak, Bal Gangadhar (b. 23 July 1856, d. 1 Aug. 1920). Hindu scholar and politician

Born in Ratnagiri into an orthodox Chitpavan brahmin familiy, he studied at Poona and obtained a law degree in 1879. Known as Lokamanya ('revered by the people'), he was imprisoned 1897–9 for alleged sedition in his weekly Marathi-language newspaper *Kesari* (Lion). At first the radical nationalist was without much influence in the inner circle of the moderate Indian National *Congress. However, the nationalist movement was radicalized by the partition of *Bengal in 1905, and in 1907 he formed his own movement to demand Indian self-rule. He was imprisoned in 1908, and upon his release in 1914 he formed the Indian Home Rule League, together with Annie *Besant. He re-entered the Congress movement in 1915, and in 1919 approved of the *Government of India Act, urging cooperation with the British.

Timor Leste (East Timor)

Emerging out of a bitterly-fought war of independence in 2002, the world's newest democracy has been struggling to achieve political and economic stability.

Foreign domination (up to 2002) Facing Australia's north coast, Timor Leste was a Portuguese colony from the fifteenth century. It was invaded on 7 December 1975 by Indonesian troops, who had planned to bring the territory and its 650,000 inhabitants under control within three weeks. Instead, one of the longest and bloodiest guerrilla wars in history developed. In order to withdraw food supplies to the rebels, the Indonesian occupiers systematically destroyed fields, forced the evacuation of entire villages, and organized internment in camps for half of the population, many of whom died of disease and malnutrition. Unsurprisingly, a considerable influx of Indonesian investment in infrastructure and education failed to pacify the country, partly as a result of repeated massacres and *human rights

violations against the predominantly Christian population.

East Timorese protests against Indonesian occupation never ceased, and following *Suharto's fall, the Indonesian government signalled that it was willing to enter negotiations about the future of East Timor. It released José *Gusamão from prison and agreed to hold a referendum in 1999, when 75 per cent of East Timorese voted in favour of independence. In response, Indonesia stepped up its campaign of intimidation and suppression, by encouraging loyal militias to commit atrocities against the population. This, combined with the plight of more than 200,000 refugees, brought more decisive action on behalf of the *UN. It sent peacekeeping troops, under the aegis of Australia, into East Timor to wrest control from Indonesia. During the 25 years of Indonesian occupation, about one-fifth of its one million inhabitants died of enforced hunger or violence committed by Indonesian troops. In August 2001, over 90 per cent of the electorate participated in the first elections to the constituent assembly, to prepare the country for independence in May 2002, with Gusmão as president.

Contemporary politics (since 2002) The government continued to rely heavily on Australian military and security help. In 2006, a mutiny in the small army ignited widespread looting and popular protest, which the authorities were barely able to control. Gusmão called on Australian help, and dismissed his Prime Minister, as well as those ministers responsible for the army and the police. To stabilize the country, he appointed José Ramos-Horta as Prime Minister. Ramos-Horta, a former Nobel Peace Prize winner, proved a popular choice, and in 2007 he was elected to succeed Gusmão as President.

Tiritakene, Sir Eruera Tihema (b. 5 Jan. 1895, d. 11 Jan. 1967). Maori politician

Born in Kaiapoi (Canterbury), Tiritakene served in World War I, and in 1920 was attracted by the *Ratana movement, becoming a minister in the Ratana Church in 1939. In 1932, he was the first Ratana candidate to win a seat in the House of Representatives when he won a by-election for the Southern Maori electorate. He pressed for an end to long-standing *Maori grievances, e.g. demanding equality in the workplace. As a result of the alliance between Ratana and the *Labour Party, he was Labour's chief policy adviser on Maori affairs, 1935–58. As chairman of the Maori War Effort Organization 1939–45 he was a member of the

War Cabinet. In 1957–60, he was associate minister for Maori affairs.

Tirol, see SOUTH TIROL (ALTO ADIGE)

Tirpitz, Alfred von (b. 18 Mar. 1849, d. 6 Mar. 1930). German Secretary of State in the Imperial Navy Office 1897–1916

Born in Küstrin, he entered the navy, where he was responsible for the development of the torpedo from 1877. He advanced to naval chief officer in 1892. As Secretary of State, through the careful manipulation of popular support on the one hand, and Emperor *Wilhelm's enthusiasm on the other, he was able to increase the German navy vastly in size. This raised serious concerns in other European nations, especially the United Kingdom, and led to the arms race which culminated in *World War I. During that war, his navy remained largely inactive apart from the indecisive Battle of *Jutland. He resigned in 1916 in protest against the (temporary) scaling down of the use of U-boats after the sinking of the *Lusitania. In 1917 he helped found the patriotic German Fatherland Party (Deutsche Vaterlandspartei). He was an MP for the far-right DNVP (Deutsch-nationale Volkspartei, German-National People's Party) 1924–8.

Tiso, Jozef (b. 18 Oct. 1887, d. 18 Apr. 1947). President of the Slovak Republic 1939–45

Born in Vel'ká Bytca, he was ordained a *Roman Catholic priest in 1910. After World War I he became interested in politics. He became an influential figure in the Slovak People's Party, which demanded Slovak autonomy within *Czechoslovakia. He was briefly Minister of Health in a coalition government 1927–9. Tiso became leader of his party in 1938 and, under German pressure, proclaimed *Slovakia an independent republic on 14 March 1939, with himself as President. He established a 'Christian Socialist' state and gave considerable prominence to the Roman *Catholic Church. At the same time, he refused to become a *Nazi puppet and, due to its unpopularity, suspended the deportation of Jews to Nazi *concentration camps. Thus, although he was a collaborator, it is arguable that Slovakia would have fared worse under direct occupation. He was arrested in hiding in May 1945, and hanged for high treason.

Tito, Josip (b. 25 May 1892, d. 4 May 1980). Prime Minister of Yugoslavia 1945–53; President 1953–80

Born Josip Broz in the Croatian town of Kumrovec near the Slovenian border, into a family of mixed Croatian and Slovenian ancestry. He fought in World War I in the *Austro-Hungarian army, but was captured by the Russian army in 1915. As a prisoner of war he joined the *Bolsheviks and, from 1917, he served in *Trotsky's *Red Army against the *White Russians in the *Russian Civil War. He returned home to a newly independent Kingdom of Croats, Slovenes, and Serbs, and became a pivotal figure in the Croatian Communist Party organization. He went underground and changed his name to 'Tito' when the Communist Party was outlawed in 1922. Imprisoned for six years for his illegal party activities, he was expelled in 1934 and went to Moscow, where he was recruited by *Comintern. Tito was made general secretary of the Communist Party of Yugoslavia in 1937, and returned that year to rebuild the party.

After the German invasion in 1941, Tito formed the Partisan Army of National Liberation, which came to lead a highly successful guerrilla war against the occupying forces. His forces soon also turned against the rival guerrilla organization, the *Chetniks. He emerged victorious from the war and, although bound by the *Allies to form a government of national unity, immediately established his predominance. He expelled his opponents, and gave the cold shoulder to *Stalin. The break with the USSR in 1948 enhanced his domestic appeal. As the first and most powerful Communist to break with the Soviet Union, he became a self-confident proponent of *non-alignment, with great prestige in the West. As a Slovenian-Croat leader of a country dominated by Serbs, he understood the country's ethnic dynamics like few other leaders, which was the principal reason for the relative stability enjoyed by the Yugoslav state until his death. The fragility and superficiality of this stability, however, emerged soon after his death, when his country collapsed in a bitter civil war.

Tobruk, Siege of (Apr. 1941–June 1942)
When General *Wavell's army countered Italian attacks in the *North African campaign, during *World War II, he captured Tobruk in January 1941, taking some 25,000 prisoners of war. In response to the Italian defeats in the campaign, the Germans formed the Afrika Korps under *Rommel, which arrived in Libya in March 1941. This changed the balance of forces in the desert radically, as British forces were simultaneously siphoned off to aid Greek resistance against the *Axis Powers. The British withdrew east, and in April a largely Australian garrison was left to defend Tobruk, which was subjected to an

eight-month siege and bombardment. In November 1941, after being reinforced by sea, the garrison broke out, capturing Rezegh and linking up with the 8th Army troops of General *Auchinleck. In June 1942, however, Rommel counter-attacked and after heavy defeats the British again withdrew, leaving a garrison of two divisions, mostly South African and Australian, in Tobruk. They were subjected to a massive onslaught by German and Italian troops and on 20 June capitulated: 23,000 prisoners and vast quantities of stores were lost. Tobruk was recaptured on 13 November by the troops of General *Montgomery. The incident confirmed Australian suspicions that Britain used the troops of her Dominions lightly and without due consultation.

DIEPPE RAID

Togliatti, Palmiro (b. 26 Mar. 1893, d. 21 Aug. 1964). Italian Communist

Early political activity (before 1945) Born in Genoa, Togliatti grew up in Sardinia and in 1911 received a scholarship to the University of Turin. In 1917, he joined *Gramsci and others in setting up the weekly Turinese newspaper *L'ordine nuovo*, and together they took part in the foundation of the Italian *Communist Party (PCI) in 1921. He supported *Gramsci's quest for the leadership of the party, achieved in 1926, and became leader of the party himself after Gramsci's arrest later that year. In the following years, Togliatti became an ardent supporter of left-wing cooperation against *Fascism. During the *Spanish Civil War, in which he fought 1937-9, he developed the view that revolutions did not have to lead to *Marxism and a proletarian dictatorship, as long as they were led by the working classes and resulted in an improvement of their conditions. He went to the USSR in May 1940 and delivered a series of radio broadcasts to Italy, 1941-3.

Postwar Italy (from 1944) He returned to Italy on 27 March 1944. To the surprise of many, he urged for unity against *Fascism rather than for Communist revolution in the first instance. The moderation of the leader of the PCI, by far the largest and most important political movement at the time, was vital in convincing the Allies of the stability and reliability of a post-Fascist Italy. Furthermore, he made a crucial contribution to the viability of Italy's postwar political system as he enabled the growth of other nascent parties, such as the *Christian Democrats (DC). In the quest for national unity he participated in the governments 1944-7.

Ultimately, his party had to pay dearly for his moderation and his willingness to share power. In 1947, the PCI was expelled from the government by Prime Minister *De Gasperi, whose personal anti-Communism was amplified by the *Cold War. Disillusioned with Soviet Communism due to *Khrushchev's anti-Stalinism and the Soviet invasion of Hungary in 1956, Togliatti urged a specifically Italian road to Communism. This new *Eurocommunism, accepted by the Italian Communist Party in 1956, was content to operate within a democratic framework, independent of Soviet influence, and rejected the spread of Communism through force.

Togo

One of the world's poorest countries, in west Africa, its economic recovery has been hindered by the decline of economic aid from the EU and other international donors in response to its poor *human rights record.

Foreign rule (up to 1960) A German colony in west Africa from 1884, it became a *League of Nations *Mandate after World War I, when it was divided between a smaller western part, which was administered by the British from Ghana, and an eastern part administered by France. It became a *UN *trust territory after World War II, and in 1956 western Togo was officially incorporated into Ghana after a referendum. The eastern part received autonomy within the *French Union in 1956, and became independent as the Republic of Togo in 1960.

The Eyadéma era (1967-2005) Domestic tensions in a society polarized between poor groups in the north and relatively prosperous, powerful, and educated groups in the south, as well as external frictions with Ghana, led to two military coups in 1963 and 1967, when the army under Gnassingbé Etienne Eyadéma (b. 1937) intervened to restore order. As President, Eyadéma carried out infrastructual investment and educational reforms. In 1974 the price for its main export, phosphates, increased fivefold, whereupon he nationalized its production. However, he squandered the extra income on prestige buildings and industries that did not reflect the country's economic realities, instead of modernizing, for example, the agricultural sector.

When the world price of phosphates fell, the country plunged into massive debts, which could only be overcome through drastic austerity measures. During the 1980s, therefore, Eyadéma's rhetoric of African *nationalism failed to maintain popular support, and he was forced to concede a certain degree of liberalization. Electoral manipulation ensured his political survival in presidential elections. However, in the 1994 parliamentary elections, his Rassemblement du Peuple Togolais (RPT) lost to the opposition. Subsequently, he was forced to contend with Edem Kodjo of the Union Togolaise pour la Démocratie (UTD) as Prime Minister. In protest against yet another rigged election victory for Eyadéma in 1998, the UTD and other oppositional groups boycotted the 1999 parliamentary elections, which were duly won by Eyadéma's RPT. In the following years, the government tried to split the opposition by making ostensible concessions, while persecuting and murdering those who persisted in their opposition. Meanwhile, the people continued to suffer from a bankrupt economy, and a near-defunct education system.

Contemporary politics (since 2005) Upon Eyadéma's death in 2005 his son, Faure Gnassingbé, took over as president. His rule was fiercely opposed by Gilchrist Olympio, the son of Togo's first President and leader of the Union des Forces du Changement (Union of the Forces for Change, UFC). This led to violent unrest, until Olympio and Gnassingbé agreed to settle their differences peacefully, A new government of national unity was installed in 2005, preparing the country for elections in 2007.

Tôjô Hideki (b. 30 Dec. 1884, d. 23 Dec. 1948). Prime Minister of Japan 1941–4
In his early career, Tôjô demonstrated outstanding qualities as an army officer, graduating top of his class at staff college in 1915. Afterwards he held various staff appointments, until being posted to the *Guandong Army, where he combined forces with the bureaucrat *Kishi Nobusuke and Aikawa Yoshitsuke the industrialist to form the Manchuria faction. He was Chief of Staff of the Guandong Army 1937–8, before becoming Vice-Minister of War (1938–9), and then Minister of War (1940–4). As leader of the 'Control Faction' within the Imperial Army, he helped promote the continuing armed engagement of Japanese forces in China. He accelerated the preparations for conflict with the USA, while other leaders sought its de-escalation, and then advocated Japan's unrestrained prosecution of the war. He was a

supporter of the alliance with the *Axis Powers and worked to ensure cooperation with *Vichy France to secure Japanese bases in *Indochina, from which Japan's *Malayan campaigns were to be launched after Japan's entry into World War II. His political intrigues in October 1941 contributed to the fall of Prime Minister *Konoe Fuminaro's government. As Konoe's successor he gave the orders that launched the attack on *Pearl Harbor. During 1942 he gradually took increased powers in the government, including responsibility for the military procurement ministry. He also became Chief of the General Staff. Once the course of the war turned decisively against Japan in 1944, Tôjô's position was undermined, and his Cabinet resigned in July. After the war he was found guilty at the *Tokyo Trials and hanged.

Tokyo Trials (May 1946–Nov. 1948)
After *World War II, 28 Japanese military, diplomatic, and political leaders were brought before an international tribunal to be judged by the *Allies and nations affected by the war with Japan. The accused were charged with conspiracy to commit aggression, and conventional war crimes. Seven, including *Hirota Kôki and *Tôjô Hideki, were sentenced to death. Sixteen received life imprisonment, two others were given shorter terms, and the remaining three did not complete the trial through death or illness. Scholarly opinion since has drawn attention to the dubious legal and procedural basis for these trials.

NUREMBERG TRIALS; ISHIWARA KANJI

Tonga
A Pacific island kingdom consisting of some 170 small Polynesian islands, which has been governed with remarkable stability. British involvement in  its internal affairs began in 1890, and was increased by two treaties (1901 and 1905), which declared Tonga a British protectorate. Nevertheless, the government and administration remained stable and independent of British control, as they had already been Westernized during the long reign of King George Tupou I (r. 1845–93), who introduced a constitution (which is still intact) in 1875. Under the popular Queen Salote Tupou III (r. 1918–65), the education system was improved, as was the provision of health

services. Further health and economic reforms were introduced by her scholarly son, King Taufa'ahau Tupou IV. He ascended to the throne in 1965, and achieved independence from Britain on 5 June 1970. Aristocratic privilege was ensured by an inbuilt majority in parliament. As the country had never been formally colonized, it had one of the world's most homogeneous ethnic populations. Since 1999 a number of biotechnology companies have collected data on the genetic pool of the 100,000 islanders, in return for which Tonga is to receive some of the profit of any medication developed as a result. King Taufa'ahau Tupou IV died in 2006, and was succeeded by his son, King Tupuot'a Tupou V. He announced a series of political reforms, including the reduction of the number of parliamentary seats reserved for the nobility.

Tonkin Gulf Resolution (7 Aug. 1964)
A resolution of the US *Congress approving 'retaliatory' air raids on North Vietnamese targets and giving President *Johnson authority to 'take all necessary steps including the use of armed forces' to help members of *SEATO to 'defend their freedom'. It was passed in response to alleged attacks on 2 and 4 August by North Vietnamese patrol boats against the US destroyer *Maddox* in the Gulf of Tonkin. Subsequent investigation revealed that the intelligence information on which it was based was inaccurate, and may have been contrived by elements within the US government. Nevertheless, it constitued effectively a blank cheque for Johnson's policies in Vietnam, and triggered the start of active US military involvement in the *Vietnam War through retaliatory bombing raids of North Vietnamese cities. Reaction against this mistake by Congress led to the *War Powers Act of 1973.

totalitarianism
A term often used as an antonym to pluralism to describe a state in which politics, society, and economy are all subject to the control of an elite or a party. There are three common features of totalitarian states. The first is a particular, often revolutionary, *Weltanschauung* (world-view) which pervades public life and legitimizes the state. The second is a fusion of the polity and the economy, so that the state controls the economy to varying degrees of inefficiency. The third is the suppression or control of institutions which would otherwise make up a civil society, such as clubs, societies, and the media. However, the precise meaning of the term is elusive, as its use has undergone substantial change over the years. Initially

used to describe Italian *Fascism from 1923, it was appropriated by opponents to describe the *Third Reich and *Stalinism. From the beginning of the *Cold War it was increasingly used to describe Communist regimes in the Soviet Union and elsewhere. There have been serious doubts about the usefulness of the term. For example, it is doubtful if it could be used legitimately to describe the Soviet Union without discriminating between its leaders such as *Stalin and *Brezhnev. It was also unclear that *Stalin's Soviet Union, *Hitler's Germany, and *Mussolini's Italy had enough in common to be summarized usefully by one term.

Touré, Ahmed Sékou (b. 9 Jan. 1922, d. 26 Mar. 1984). President of Guinea 1958–84
Born in Faranah, he briefly attended a teacher's college before being expelled in 1937. He subsequently became active in the trade-union movement, and in 1946 helped found the Rassemblement Démocratique Africain (RDA), together with *Houphouët-Boigny and other African leaders. As secretary-general of the Guinean branch of the RDA, he became vice-president of the government council of Guinea. Touré found himself at odds with the RDA over membership of the *French Community. In a referendum of 28 September 1958, the majority of the population followed his leadership and rejected links with France, whereupon he became Guinea's first President. With the support of the USSR, he established an authoritarian one-party state often described as the 'Tropical Gulag'. The political system did not survive his death and was replaced by a military dictatorship.

Toynbee Hall (UK)
The most prominent of a number of university settlements engaged in social work in London's poor East End. It was founded in 1884 by Samuel and Henrietta Barnett, and named after the Oxford philosopher, Arnold Toynbee. Its primary purpose was to bring intellectuals from universities into contact with working-class poverty, to help and educate both the poor and the intellectuals. The list of students involved there reads almost like a dictionary of British social reform (e.g. *Beveridge, *Attlee, *Keynes, *Tawney), and testifies to its enormous influence. Most students left convinced that voluntary solutions to social problems were insufficient, and that more direct state intervention was required to fight the problems of poverty, unemployment, and inadequate sanitary provision. Their writings

became crucial for the renewal of the *Liberal Party's programme ('New Liberalism') after 1900, and the social views of the nascent Labour movement (*Labour Party).

ADDAMS, JANE LAURA

trade unions

Collective organizations of workers/ employees which aim at promoting the welfare of their members, especially through securing higher wages and shorter working hours. As a rule, they developed in industrializing nations first among skilled workers, who were in relatively short supply and thus had greater bargaining power. Hence, the first workers to organize unions in Britain were engineers (1850), and in Germany printers (1866) and cigarworkers (1865). Unions of unskilled labour, whose members could easily be made redundant if they went on strike, only became successful and increased in strength after 1900 as unions improved their organization and their political influence. This could be accomplished either directly (the *CGT in France) or indirectly through *socialist parties (the *Labour Party in Britain and Australia, the *SPD in Germany). Among the different types of trade unions were the free trade unions (e.g. in Britain, the USA, Australia, and Canada), Communist trade unions (which emerged from the turn of the century in Russia, Czechoslovakia, France, Austria, Spain, and Poland), *syndicalist trade unions, and Christian trade unions (e.g. in Belgium, the Netherlands, and Germany).

In most countries, trade unions experienced a dramatic decline in membership after the economic recession of the 1970s. In Europe, northern countries have generally been more unionized than southern ones: in 1990, in Denmark 80 per cent of the workforce belonged to a trade union, in Belgium 75 per cent, Republic of Ireland 44 per cent, the UK 43 per cent, Germany 42 per cent, Italy 40 per cent, Portugal 30 per cent, Greece 18 per cent, Spain 10 per cent, and France 10 per cent. By contrast, the less unionized countries in the European south have had a much higher annual strike rate. In 1994, for example, there were 1,268 official strikes in Spain with 4.8 million participating workers. In France, the unionized workers were heavily concentrated in the public sector, so that strikes against government reforms tended to be extremely effective: protests against *Juppé's social reforms in December 1995, for example, brought the entire country to a standstill for weeks.

The reason for this paradox is that countries with a traditionally strong degree of unionization tend to have developed and sophisticated mechanisms for wage bargaining, which avoid strikes altogether. Similarly, countries with very weak trade unions have also seen a low strike rate, since workers are insufficiently organized for industrial action. By contrast, in countries where trade unions are sufficiently strong to organize workers, but where they do not enjoy a near-monopoly over wage bargaining, large-scale strikes occur most frequently. In those systems, trade unions feel more compelled to go on strike to impress their membership, and they are unable to control industrial action by non-unionized workers. With their relatively rigid craft-based membership structures, trade unions worldwide have been challenged by the advent of *globalization from the 1980s. Frequent job changes have led to a loss of traditional worker identities, often forcing an abandonment of trade-union affiliation.

TUC; AFL-CIO; INDUSTRIAL WORKERS OF THE WORLD; OIL-PRICE SHOCK

trade unions, Canada, see CANADIAN LABOUR CONGRESS; CONFÉDÉRATION DES SYNDICATS NATIONAUX

Transkei, see BANTUSTAN

Transylvania

A fertile plateau area of the Carpathian mountains, rich in mineral deposits. With its original Romanian population (since the tenth century) it came under Magyar (Hungarian) rule in the early eleventh century, whereupon it was colonized by Magyars, Szekelers, and Germans. It became an autonomous part of the *Ottoman Empire in 1541, but in 1683 reverted to the rule of the Austrian Emperor, as part of Hungary. There were sporadic tensions relating to discrimination against the Romanian majority of the population, which intensified in the late nineteenth century in response to Hungarian attempts to impose Magyar culture on the entire population (magyarization). It became part of Romania in 1918, though most of its area was briefly returned to Hungary in response to the second *Vienna Award, 1940 (until 1947).

For most of the twentieth century, therefore, incorporation into the relatively backward Romania was a constant source of resentment among the Hungarian, Szekeler, and German minorities. Particularly under *Ceausescu, they were discriminated against, as the state tried hard to destroy their cultural identities. Even after the fall of Ceausescu, the policies of discrimination continued. From 1995, school examinations could only be taken in Romanian, while the curriculum was changed to avoid the teaching of the history of the country's minorities. As a result of the EU membership of Hungary (2004) and Romania (2007), minority rights were recognized, which was expected to lead to an improvement in communal relations.

Trenchard, Hugh Montague, 1st Viscount Trenchard of Wolfeton (b. 3 Feb. 1873, d. 10 Feb. 1956). Founder of the Royal Air Force

Born in Taunton, Somerset, he served in the army in the *South African (Boer) War, and, after service in Nigeria, joined the Royal Flying Corps (RFC) in 1913. From 1915, he commanded the RFC on the Western Front, and towards the end of the war, developed the use of aeroplanes as bombers. The RFC had been part of the army, but in April 1918 he saw it created into a separate *Royal Air Force (RAF)*. As Chief of Air Staff (1919–29), he developed the RAF as a flexible, cost-effective alternative to the army, as a way of policing the Empire. In 1927 he became the first air marshal. Later, as commissioner of police (1932–5), he reorganized the Metropolitan Police Force, establishing a college and a forensic laboratory at Hendon.

Treurnicht, Andries Petrus, see CONSERVATIVE PARTY, SOUTH AFRICA

Trianon, Treaty of (4 June 1920)

The peace treaty imposed upon Hungary by the victorious *Allies after *World War I, as part of the *Paris Peace Conference. Hungary had to accept the breakup of *Austria-Hungary. It was forced to cede Slovakia and Ruthenia to *Czechoslovakia, *Croatia to the new Kingdom of Serbs, Croats, and Slovenes (Yugoslavia from 1929), and *Transylvania to Romania. Hungary thus lost two-thirds of its prewar territory, and three-fifths of its pre-war population. The terms of the treaty caused so much resentment as to destabilize Hungarian politics for the following decade and cause it to side with *Nazi Germany in World War II, after it had regained much of its lost territory in the *Vienna Awards of 1938 and 1940.

Trieste

The only major port of *Austria-Hungary, it had been part of Austrian territory almost continuously since 1382. It was claimed by Italy and became a central focus for *irredentism. After World War I it became Italian following the Treaty of *St Germain. After World War II it was claimed by both Italy

and Yugoslavia. Although the Allies had promised to return the city to Italy, they did not want to upset Yugoslavia, whose independent stance against the USSR they sought to encourage. Its future was resolved in London on 5 October 1954, when Italy obtained the city and the area to the north, while the area to the south became Yugoslav territory. In the Treaty of Osimo (1975), Yugoslavia compensated Italians for their properties which lay in the Yugoslav-administered parts. In 1994, the validity of this treaty was denied by the Italian right-wing populist Prime Minister, *Berlusconi, since he argued that one of its signatories, Yugoslavia, had ceased to exist. He demanded the return of Italian property from Yugoslavia's successor state in the area, *Slovenia, and for over a year blocked *Slovenia's association treaty with the European Union.

Trimble, David (b. 15 Oct. 1944). First Minister of Northern Ireland 1998–2001, 2002

Born in Belfast as a Protestant, he studied law and became an academic at the Queen's University, Belfast. A member of the Orange Order, he joined the *Ulster Unionist Party and became one its most outspoken, uncompromising members. As such, he led the march of the Orange Order through Dumcree in 1995, as a way of expressing Protestant loyalty towards the United Kingdom against the *Downing Street Declaration. As leader of the UUP from 1995, he came to accept the need for compromise with *Sinn Féin. His erstwhile hardline credentials allowed him to carry the majority of his party along in supporting the *Good Friday Agreement, which in 1998 created the Northern Ireland Assembly. For his decisive leadership in the peace process, he was awarded the *Nobel Peace Prize together with John *Hume.

Trimble became First Minister in a Cabinet that included Sinn Féin and the *Social and Democratic Labour Party. He twice risked his office to force the *IRA to honour its promise to decommission its weapons. In 2000, the Good Friday Agreement was suspended to forestall Trimble's resignation, and in 2001 he did resign over the issue. In each case, his political gamble paid off, and the IRA did respond by putting more of its weapons beyond use. Unease within his party against his willingness to negotiate with Sinn Féin continued. This greatly weakened his leadership position after his party was beaten by the more radical *Democratic Unionist Party in the Northern Ireland Assembly elections of 2003. Trimble lost his seat in the

UK parliament at the 2005 elections, and moved to the House of Lords instead.

Trinidad and Tobago

A Caribbean island state off the Venezuelan coast comprising the islands of Trinidad and Tobago. They became British colonies in 1797 and 1627 respectively, forming an administrative unit from 1888. This joined the Federation of the *West Indies in 1958, but demanded and gained full independence on 31 August 1962. It became a republic with an executive President in 1976. From 1956 to 1981, Trinidad and Tobago was governed by *Williams of the social democratic People's National Movement. The party lost power in 1986, only to regain it under Patrick Manning in 1991. Manning benefited from disillusionment with the governing National Alliance for Reconstruction, and the insecurity caused by an attempted coup by the *Islamic fundamentalist Jamaat al Muslimeen (Black Muslim Group). Under Basdeo Panday, the United National Congress returned to power in 1995, and held on to it with an extended, absolute parliamentary majority after the 2000 elections. New elections followed in 2001 and 2002, with Patrick Manning returning to power from 2001. Jamaat al Muslimeen continued to sponsor a number of terrorist attacks, with general violence increasing in 2004 and 2005. While the government struggled to control violence and crime, it was successful at presiding over a growing economy, as Trinidad and Tobago benefited from high world prices for its major exports, oil and gas.

Triple Alliance

A defensive military alliance between Germany, Italy, and Austria, initially concluded in 1882 by Bismarck to offset a possible alliance between France and Russia. It was renewed for the last time in 1912, and formed the basis of the fateful German assurance in the summer of 1914 that it would support Austria in the event of a military conflict with Serbia, following the assassination of Archduke Francis Ferdinand in *Sarajevo. To intense German irritation, Italy remained neutral in the first nine months of *World War I and eventually turned against its former partners to fight on the *Allied side in 1915, following the Treaty of *London.

TRIPLE ENTENTE

Triple Entente

In 1907, the *Entente Cordiale between Britain and France was supplemented by a series of agreements between Britain and Russia, which itself was a military ally of France. The Triple Entente, though only an informal alliance, confirmed German paranoia about an 'encirclement' by these great powers, and thus helped to increase its tendency towards aggressive behaviour which ultimately led to *World War I. Ironically, it was only after the outbreak of hostilities in August 1914 that the Triple Entente was transformed into a military alliance.

Trotsky, Leon (b. 7 Nov. 1879, d. 21 Aug. 1940). Soviet Communist leader

Born Lev Bronstein of Ukrainian Jewish parentage, he became a Social Democrat as a student. He founded the South Russian Workers' Council in 1897, was arrested (1898), and exiled to Siberia (1899). He fled abroad (1902), and returned briefly to become a *Menshevik leader in the St Petersburg Soviet during the 1905 *Russian Revolution, before being imprisoned and going abroad again in 1907. In May 1917 he returned to Russia, became a *Bolshevik, and was a pivotal figure in the 1917 *Russian Revolution. As the new Minister ('People's Commissar') for External Affairs he concluded the treaty of *Brest-Litovsk, and as Defence Minister from March 1918 he was largely responsible for the *Red Army's eventual success in the *Russian Civil War. In his preoccupation with defence he failed to nurture sufficient internal party support for himself and his views, so that after *Lenin's death it was *Stalin who received Communist support. He was dismissed from the government in 1925, expelled from the Communist Party in 1927, and exiled in 1929. He was murdered by a Stalinist agent in Mexico.

Trotskyism

The adaptation of *Communism by *Trotsky, which he formulated mostly during his years in exile, notably in his *Transitional Programme* (*The Death Agony of Capitalism and the Tasks of the Fourth International*) of 1938. He was a fierce critic of *Stalinism, noting that in the Soviet Union power had gone not to the proletariat, but to the bureaucracy. Trotsky criticized *Stalin's confinement of the Communist revolution to the Soviet Union, and insisted that there should be 'permanent revolution' sweeping from country to country which would establish *Marxism on a global scale. Disregarding Trotsky's original ideals, however, the term was most commonly used in a derogatory manner by Communists in the Soviet Union and former Eastern Bloc countries to describe any Communist ideals or practices which deviated from current official orthodoxy.

Trucial States, see UNITED ARAB EMIRATES

Trudeau, Pierre Elliott (b. 18 Oct. 1919, d. 28 Sept. 2000). Prime Minister of Canada 1968–79, 1980–4

Early career Born in Montreal (Quebec), he was educated at the Universities of Montreal and Harvard, and at the London School of Economics. On his return to Canada, he became a strong *trade union supporter in the 1949 asbestos strike, which launched him as a social and political critic. A law professor at the University of Montreal, he welcomed the *Quiet Revolution, though he firmly rejected the conclusion of many of his contemporaries that this should lead to Quebec's sovereignty. Instead, he advocated acknowledgement of *Quebec's *nationalism within Canadian society. He entered parliament in 1965, and was soon appointed Parliamentary Secretary to *Pearson, before becoming Minister of Justice in 1967. In his brief period of office he liberalized laws on abortion and homosexuality, and became known as a strong supporter of federal rights against the particularist demands of Quebec.

In office In 1968, Trudeau became leader of the *Liberal Party, and Canada's second-longest serving, and perhaps most controversial, Prime Minister. In 1970, the Quebec Cabinet Minister Pierre Laporte was abducted (and later killed) by the terrorist *Front de Libération du Québec (Quebec Liberation Front). In response, Trudeau invoked the *War Measures Act, with its controversial limits on personal freedoms. In an attempt to satisfy Quebec nationalism, he made French the second official language throughout Canada. This fuelled resentment within the western provinces, which began to feel that their concerns were being ignored because of the government's constant preoccupation with Quebec. From 1973, he tried to cope with Canada's economic difficulties caused by the world recession, but in 1976 his attention was again drawn by Quebec, when the separatist *Parti Québécois took over the provincial government there.

He narrowly lost the 1979 elections and resigned as Liberal leader.

Only three weeks later *Clark's budget was defeated and a new election called, which Trudeau won. His successful intervention in the 1980 Quebec referendum on sovereignty galvanized him into trying to solve Canada's (and thus Quebec's) constitutional status once and for all. He ended all the remaining judicial and legal prerogatives over Canadian affairs resting in London, and proclaimed a Charter of Rights and Freedoms. After protracted negotiations with the provincial governments, the Consitution Act was passed on 17 April 1982 (see *Canadian Constitution, Patriation of). However, the act was not ratified by Quebec, and thus served more to underline than solve the country's constitutional problems.

Trudeau's economic policies failed to cope with high inflation and unemployment. In foreign policy, the advent of *Reagan and *Thatcher as the dominant Western leaders on the international scene pushed him into a role of irksome opposition, advocating a north-south dialogue between industrialized and developing countries, as well as the reduction of nuclear arms. Increasingly unpopular in Canada from 1981, he resigned on 30 June 1984 to make way for *Turner. He retired from active politics, though he spoke in opposition to the *Meech Lake Accord.

Trujillo y Molina, Rafael Leonidas (b. 24 Oct 1891, d. 30 May 1961). President of the Dominican Republic 1931–61

The creator of the most comprehensive and ruthless dictatorship in Latin America, he had already made a fortune as a local commander of the armed forces by monopolizing the supply of his soldiers with food, clothes and other provisions. As Commander-in-Chief from 1927, Trujillo took part in the *coup* to overthrow President Vásquez and eliminated all other opposition to become President himself. He immediately began to establish legal monopolies, involving his own firms, on essential supplies such as meat, salt, and rice. He came to control virtually every aspect of the economy, his business interests covering tobacco, insurances, banks, fruit exports, and even prostitution. In addition, every public employee was forced to pay a levy of 10 per cent of their earnings to his party, whose finances he controlled. He thus established complete and direct control over the lives of virtually every individual in the Republic, which he complemented by the ruthless quashing of all opposition. In contrast to most other Latin American dictators, Trujillo managed to stay in power through the Great

*Depression of the 1930s. He also withstood the general democratizing tendencies in Latin America after World War II. As he amassed an ever-greater fortune, his collaborators became jealous and disgruntled. His erstwhile protégés organized his assassination, whereupon his businesses were nationalized.

Truman Doctrine (USA)

One of the key US policies during the *Cold War. In February 1947, the British government announced that it could no longer afford to support Greece and Turkey against Communist insurgents. Believing in the policy of *containment of what was perceived to be an expansive and *totalitarian Communist Bloc, President *Truman called for the USA to step into the breach and reverse its traditional policy of non-involvement in European affairs. On 14 March 1947 Truman specifically called for aid to Greece and Turkey. He pledged that the USA would 'support free peoples who are resisting attempted subjugation by armed minorities or by outside pressures'. $400 million in military and economic aid were sent and used, primarily in defence against the Communist rebels which in Greece were largely supported not by *Stalin, but by *Tito.

Truman, Harry S. (b. 8 May 1884, d. 26 Dec. 1972). 33rd US President 1945–53

Early career Born at Lamar, Missouri, his parents could never decide whether the S in his name stood for the name of his paternal or maternal grandfather, and so it remained just an initial. From working on the farm, he fought in World War I, and then opened a haberdashery store, which effectively bankrupted him. He studied law at night school in Kansas City (1923–5), and then built up a law practice. At this time, he also entered local politics as a *Democrat. He became a presiding justice at Jackson County Court and then Senator for Missouri in 1935, backed by a notoriously corrupt party machine run by Tom Pendergast. It was typical of Truman's loyalty to his friends that he attracted adverse criticism in his later political life by refusing to abandon Pendergast.

In the Senate he quickly gained a reputation for scrupulous integrity, and was made chairman of a Special Commission Investigating National Defense. In this capacity, he uncovered considerable graft, waste, and inefficiency in the federal administration of President *Roosevelt. Ironically, this brought him to Roosevelt's attention and he was selected to run as Vice-President in 1944.

First term Having met the President only twice, he himself became President on Roosevelt's death after 82 days in office and with little experience of government. At home he aimed to develop his predecessor's *New Deal policies, though many of his efforts were foiled by opposition from Southern Democrats allied with *Republicans in *Congress.

His lack of political experience did little to ease his problems in foreign policy. At the *Potsdam Conference, he was unable to prevent *Stalin from extending Soviet influence over Eastern Europe. Nevertheless, he was perhaps much more sombre about Stalin than his predecessor. He authorized the dropping of the atomic bomb over *Hiroshima and *Nagasaki to end the war in Japan without further loss of US troops, insisting on unconditional Japanese surrender. In September 1945 he decided to confront the Soviet Union by ending *lend-lease. He accepted the division of Europe through the *Iron Curtain from 1947, after the Soviet refusal of *Marshall Aid, and his announcement of the *Truman Doctrine.

Second term In 1948 Truman won the presidential election against the Republican Thomas E. Dewey, contrary to the prediction of the polls, the commentators, the journalists, and many fellow politicians. In his State of the Union message in January 1949 he put forward his Point Four and *Fair Deal programs. Although *Congress allowed little of the latter to pass into law, he did manage to achieve his 1949 Housing Act, which provided for low-cost housing on a considerable scale. By his executive authority he had already ended, in July 1948, racial segregation in the armed forces, and in schools financed by the federal government.

In foreign policy, Truman continued to secure western Europe from Soviet encroachment through the creation of the first peacetime military pact in which the USA was involved, *NATO. In his efforts to contain Communism, however, his support of *Chiang Kai-shek proved futile, since he was unable to prevent the victory of *Mao's Chinese *Communist Party in the *Chinese Civil War. Although it is difficult to see how Truman could have changed this outcome, it proved a major setback to American confidence in its ability to prevent the spread of *Communism. Truman took US troops into the *Korean War, insisting that this be under *UN auspices. In 1951 he dismissed General *MacArthur for insubordination and publicly advocating all-out war with Communist China. This demanded courage, since MacArthur was very popular and the anti-Communists were approaching the full tide of their strength. He did not run for re-election in 1952, although he remained active in politics long after his retirement, as his reputation grew as one of the strongest and most successful Presidents, especially in foreign policy.

Trust Territories of the United Nations

Former *Mandates which had still not become self-governing by the time the *League of Nations was officially dissolved in 1946. The *UN placed them into the administration of particular member states, with the objective of preparing them for independence. Thus, they were essentially like Mandates, except that there was much stricter control by the UN, and greater pressure on the administering countries to release the territories into independence as soon as possible. The only administering country to defy this pressure was South Africa, whose trust territory only gained independence as Namibia in 1990. In 1994, Palau became the last Trust Territory to achieve independence, although its state finances continued to be heavily reliant on the US, which maintained a naval base there. With its mission accomplished, the UN's Trusteeship Council, which had formally supervised the economic and political progress of the territories, suspended its activities in November 1994.

Truth and Reconciliation Commission (TRC)

A committee that met from 1996 to 1998 in an attempt to find a way of dealing with past atrocities committed under *apartheid. Chaired by Archibishop *Tutu, it investigated many of the over 100,000 known *human rights violations committed by all sides in South Africa, from the *Sharpeville Massacre until the end of the apartheid system in 1993. In a novel procedure, those who had committed crimes were to reveal their actions in full detail. Counselling was provided for victims and their families, as well as for the families of the culprits. Amnesty could be granted to those who had committed crimes for a political party, and who had presented full and frank testimony. In this way, amnesty was granted to most of those who had committed crimes and shown remorse, but a number of high-profile cases, involving former Defence Minister Malan or the murderers of Steven *Biko, were handed over to the criminal courts.

The Commission's final report was criticized by almost all groups in South African society: victims demanded punishment for the guilty, the *ANC complained that it, too, had been criticized for human rights violations, while many Whites complained that the ANC and other Black resistance groups had not been indicted extensively enough. Nevertheless, the Commission was born out of the recognition that in other former dictatorships, attempts at dealing with the past had failed. The TRC presented a pioneering attempt to establish an account of the truth, publicize it, and promote an acknowledgement of the human suffering caused by past wrongs. Although most transitional governments to democracy did not engage in such a comprehensive attempt in dealing with the divisive past, the TRC has served as a model elsewhere. In June 2001 a TRC was established in Peru, in order to uncover the *human rights violations of the 1980s and especially the *Fujimori period of the 1990s. Further TRCs, adapted to local circumstances, were established in countries like Timor Leste, Sierra Leone, Liberia, Chile and Guatemala.

((⊕)) SEE WEB LINKS

- The home page of the South African TRC.
- The official website detailing the activities of the TRC in Sierra Leone.
- The official website of the Liberian TRC.
- The official website of the TRC in Timor Leste.

tsunami (tidal wave)

An oceanic tidal wave caused by sudden shifts on the ocean's floor, most commonly through earthquakes. The most devastating tsunami was caused by an earthquake off the coast of Sumatra (Indonesia) on 26 December 2004. This pushed the ocean upwards, causing a tidal wave several metres high, which spread so quickly that it reached the coast of Sri Lanka, several thousand miles away, in less than two hours. The tsunami killed an estimated 300,000 people in coastal areas from Indonesia and Thailand in the east, to India, the Maldives and the east African coast in the west. Over one million people lost their homes. The international catastrophe, which affected domestic communities and tourists from all over the world, triggered massive international relief efforts, with donor countries and private organizations pledging over $6.5 billion for reconstruction.

TUC (Trades Union Congress) (UK)

An organization of *trade unions founded in 1868, initially as a central parliament of labour, through an annual assembly. From 1871, a permanent parliamentary committee represented the interests of trade unions to the government and individual MPs. In 1919, Ernest *Bevin proposed that a general council should replace the committee, and develop the industrial side of the TUC, as opposed to its political work. The council was established in 1921, with the aim of coordinating the activities of its component trade unions, for example through making the strike of one union more effective by threatening supportive action from other unions. The TUC was closely involved in the 1926 *General Strike, after which its relationship with the government was cautiously conciliatory. However, its role increased in World War II, when it was involved in industrial planning and management.

Until 1979, TUC leaders were often involved in discussions with Labour and Conservative governments. However, it lost much prestige and public support following strikes in the late 1960s and 1970s. Legislation by the *Thatcher governments weakened trade unions in the economic sphere, while the reforms of the *Labour Party under *Kinnock, *Smith, and *Blair reduced the TUC's political influence on the party. By 2006 its total membership had declined to around 6.5 million, though this number had been stabilized since the mid-1990s. The TUC's public figurehead is its general secretary. Since this became a full-time post, the holders of the office have been Fred Bramley (1923–5), Walter Citrine (1925–46), Vincent Tewson (1946–60), George Woodcock (1960–9), Vic Feather (1970–3), Len Murray (1973–84), Norman Willis (1984–93), John Monks (1993–2003), , and Brendan Barber (2003–).

TAFF VALE JUDGMENT

((∰)) SEE WEB LINKS

• The home page of the TUC.

Tudjman, Franjo (b. 14 May 1922, d. 10 Dec 1999). Croatian President 1990–99

Born at Veliko Trgovisce, he became a conscript soldier in the army of the *Fascist Independent State of Croatia in 1941. He escaped and joined *Tito's *partisan army in the fight against the *Ustase movement. After World War II he became active in the Ministry of Defence and the General Staff, and in the 1950s became the country's youngest general. He studied history at Zagreb in 1961, and in 1963 was appointed professor there in order to work on the history of the Croatian labour movement. He became involved in the underground Croatian nationalist movement, for which he was expelled from party and office in 1967. He spent several years in prison

for 'counter-revolutionary activities' (1971, 1981–4).

In 1989 Tudjman was a founding member of the Croatian Democratic Alliance. Its organization spread rapidly throughout Croatia, enabling the CDA to gain an absolute majority in the 1990 elections. He pushed for Croatia's rapid independence, through the passing of a new Constitution on 21 December 1990, and his country's exit from Yugoslavia on 26 June 1991. Tudjman united his country through ethnic *nationalism which did not stop short of *human rights violations against the Serb minorities in Croatia. At the same time, his control of the media and his harassment of the opposition stifled internal political debate, while the economy was stifled through the country's international isolation and the corruption inherent in the domestic economy. He died in office.

Tunisia

A north African country of relative economic prosperity, its political stability in the face of growing Islamic fundamentalism has been based on *human rights violations and the curtailment of political freedoms.

Foreign rule (up to 1956) A part of the *Ottoman Empire from 1574, it became a French protectorate in 1881. After World War I, nationalist opposition among the French-educated Tunisian intellectual elite emerged to demand greater involvement of Tunisians in their own affairs. From its establishment in 1934, the Neo-Destour Party (Parti Socialiste Destourien) led by *Bourguiba became the main opponent to French colonial rule, though under his leadership the party advocated piecemeal, rather than revolutionary, change of government. In World War II, Tunisia was liberated from German occupation by *Free French and Anglo-US forces at the end of the *North African campaigns in 1943, whereupon French colonists sought to reimpose control. A decade of growing unrest followed before France offered autonomy (1954) and a customs union.

Independence (from 1956) Bourguiba became Prime Minister upon independence, President in 1957, and in the (enforced) absence of political opposition he was re-elected until he became President for life in 1975. State control over society, economy, and education was in some ways quite successful, as education became universal and women were given greater equality and independence. However, combined with the lack of political freedom, this led to the emergence of an *Islamic fundamentalist movement which threatened the very existence of the secular state. This slowed down the efforts of Bourguiba's successor, *Ben Ali, to introduce a process of political liberalization. Nevertheless, the Constitution was revised in 1988 and 1994, so that oppositional groups could attain token representation in the National Assembly (34 reserved out of 182 seats). Ben Ali was only able to contain growing fundamentalist opposition with the imprisonment of political opponents. He also tried to shore up his personal support by advocating his own brand of nationalism, which sought to overcome the French cultural influence that continued to exist beyond the twentieth century. In 2002, the Constitution was amended to allow Ben Ali to run for two further terms in office.

Tupac Amaru, see TUPAMAROS; SENDERO LUMINOSO

Tupamaros (Movimento de Liberación Nacional) (Uruguay)

A socialist urban guerrilla organization named after the eighteenth-century Inca revolutionary against Spanish rule, **Tupac Amaru**, founded by Rául Sendic in 1963. It sought to overthrow an increasingly repressive state through bombings, kidnappings, and assassinations, and thus became a model for other socialist guerrilla forces in Latin America. They were suppressed by the military in the 1970s, however, and in 1985 agreed to form a legitimate political party.

Turati, Filippo (b. 25 Nov. 1857, d. 29 Mar. 1932). Italian Socialist

Born in Como, he studied at the University of Bologna and in 1883 published *Il delitto e la questione sociale*, in which he argued for a causal link between crime and social deprivation. In 1889 he co-founded the Milanese Socialist Association, and in 1892 founded the Italian *Socialist Party, which was committed to fight social injustice through gradual, democratic means. He was able to impress the party with his pragmatic course until 1900, but thereafter his position was significantly weakened by constant inter-party struggles about whether to cooperate

with or confront the government. He was against Italian entry into World War I, and found himself in a minority within his own party afterwards when he opposed the ideal of a *Communist revolution. Expelled from the party for his anti-Fascist efforts, he founded the Partito Socialista Unitario (Socialist Unity Party), of which his close political ally, *Matteotti, became secretary. Following Mussolini's establishment of a Fascist dictatorship in response to Matteotti's murder, Turati fled to Paris, where he remained active in his fight against *Fascism and contributed to the reunion of the two socialist parties in 1930.

Turkey

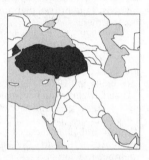

The successor state to the *Ottoman Empire, founded by Mustafa Kemal (*Atatürk) on 29 October 1923. The new state rested on six pillars: (1) republicanism, whereby the power of the Sultan was abolished; (2) *nationalism, though this tended to be less aggressive against other countries than against the country's own minorities, particularly the Kurds in the Turkish areas of *Kurdistan; (3) populism, which in the absence of a multi-party democracy was intended to gather popular support for the regime; (4) statism, whereby the state was the most important instrument of change, and became heavily involved in economics and society; (5) secularism, which reduced the power of *Islam to purely religious functions, with the state regulating religious institutions and freeing education from Islamic influence; (6) reformism, which emphasized the introduction of new, often Western, methods in state, society, and army.

Contemporary history Under the rule of Atatürk and *Inönü, both of whom were backed not only by popular support but also (perhaps more importantly) by the army, these aims were achieved to a considerable degree; though in view of later events, it is doubtful whether Islamic cultural and popular customs were truly rooted out. In World War II, the country remained neutral until it formally declared war on Germany and Japan in January 1945, which was a precondition for membership of the *UN.

In 1945, Inönü relaxed the authoritarian control of his ruling Republican People's Party (RPP) to allow the formation of other parties. A right-wing Democrat Party (DP), which was opposed to the interventionist policies of the RPP, was formed in 1946, and duly won the elections of 1950. Under *Bayar and *Menderes, Turkey became an important member of *NATO in 1952, owing to its geopolitical significance as the organization's easternmost member. Turkey offered NATO the additional advantage of being able to control the movement of the Soviet Black Sea Fleet through the Bosporus at Istanbul. Furthermore, it became the alliance's outpost in Asia Minor. In domestic politics, Menderes liberalized the economy, though in some ways this backfired towards the end of the decade when it led to a period of economic crisis. At the same time, he relaxed controls on Islamic activity in society and culture, which resulted in fierce opposition by the RPP and other opposition leaders.

After his loss of parliamentary support, Menderes continued to rule in an authoritarian manner, until he was toppled by the army. The army thus emerged as the most important upholder and guarantor of Atatürk's state, a role which it subsequently maintained. The RPP under Inönü returned to power with a series of coalition governments in 1961, but in 1965 the elections were clearly won by the DP's successor party, the Justice Party (JP), under *Demirel. In the 1960s, politics became increasingly polarized, through the growth of *Islamic fundamentalism on the one hand and *Marxism on the other, both of which opposed the values of the capitalist West. As the JP government also frequently clashed with the administrative machine still dominated by the RPP, a second military coup of 1971 suspended the 1961 Constitution and curtailed political rights once again.

Democratization (from 1973) In 1973, political life was resumed. Under the leadership of *Ecevit, in the dispute with Greece over the status of *Cyprus, Turkey ended negotiations in 1974 by creating a *fait accompli*, when the Turkish army occupied the island's north-eastern part. Internally, during the 1970s there was little scope for decisive action as the decade was dominated by a series of minority governments. This prevented thorough economic and social reforms, which alone could have prevented the growth of Islamic fundamentalists in state and society. A renewed army coup in 1980 and the suspension of democratic life until 1987 merely gave further cause for popular

resentment. Martial law was imposed for five years (1980–5), during which period arbitrary arrests and torture in prisons became much more widespread. It was in this period that the militant Kurdish Workers' Party (PKK) emerged (1984), demanding independence for Kurdistan. Its violent attacks against Turkish property and soldiers led to an ever-increasing spiral of violence between the PKK and the Turkish state.

Democratic life was resumed in 1987, with the right-wing successor party to the JP, the True Path Party (DYP), coming to power in 1991. It tried to address the two central challenges to the Turkish state in the early 1990s: (1) the economic stagnation of Turkey; and (2) the rise of the Islamic fundamentalist Welfare Party on the one hand and the violence of the PKK on the other. These two central economic and political challenges were mutually reinforcing, as around 20 per cent of the average annual budget was spent on the fight against the PKK.

As the governments of Demirel and Tansu Ciller (b. 1946) reduced public expenditure, this created yet more fertile ground for the opposition, particularly the Islamic Welfare Party. Muslim feelings were further encouraged, albeit unwittingly, by Turkey's post-*Cold War foreign policy, whereby it attempted to become the leading Turk nation, sharing a common Islamic identity with the other countries inhabited predominantly by Turk peoples (Azerbaijan, Kazakhstan, Kyrgyzstan, Turkmenistan, and Turkistan). In the elections of 24 December 1995, the Welfare Party under Necmettin Erbakan (b. 1926) thus became the biggest party, with 21.3 per cent of the vote. After months of negotiations, it formed a coalition with the DYP, despite the fact that the government of an Islamic party posed a fundamental threat to the Turkish state, whose secularism had been its *raison d'être* since its creation in 1923.

Contemporary politics (since 1998) In contrast to earlier interventions, the military left the confrontation with the Welfare Party to the judicial system. For offences against the secular constitution, the constitutional court banned the party in 1998. Its successor, the Party of Virtue, was banned in 2000. A more moderate Islamic party emerged, the Justice and Development Party (AKP) under Tayyip *Erdogan. While the veteran Ecevit had resumed office in 1999, he was defeated at the 2002 elections by the AKP, with Erdogan becoming Prime Minister in 2003.

After passing a wide range of *human rights measures including a ban on torture and greater civic rights for those who criticized the state, Turkey was formally allowed to begin EU membership negotiations in 2005. Thereafter, Turkey's line towards the EU hardened, as the state reversed some of its liberalization measures in its fight against the PKK's demands for independence for *Kurdistan. Following his inability to name the next President owing to the opposition of the republican establishment, Erdogan called new elections in 2007. In these, the AKP increased its share of the popular vote to 47 per cent.

Turkish Republic of Northern Cyprus, see CYPRUS

Turkmenistan

A country whose national identity was fostered and shaped when it formed part of the Soviet Union, Turkmenistan remained one of the poorest countries of central Asia despite a wealth in mineral resources.

Early history (up to 1991) Turkmenistan came under the sovereignty of the Russian Empire in the 1880s. An uprising against the Tsarist regime in 1916 was followed by bitter fighting in the *Russian Civil War, so that a Communist regime was not established until 1920. It became part of the Turkestan Soviet Socialist Autonomous Republic in 1921, and a separate Soviet Republic in 1924, formally joining the USSR in 1925.

In response to *Stalin's policy of the collectivization of agriculture, the majority of the country's nomadic tribes became settled. Despite the existence of considerable mineral resources, it acquired little industry. Its population was the poorest educated in the Soviet Union, and productivity was extremely low even by Soviet standards. The population's misery was compounded by the party leadership's corruption. Thus, to maintain even a minimal standard of living, the Soviet Union subsidized the state budget by two-thirds. This, and the existence of only a small educated elite which was mostly Russian, led to very hesitant calls for independence when the Soviet Union collapsed. In early 1991, more than 90 per cent of the entire electorate voted to retain a union with Russia.

Contemporary history (since 1991) Once independence had become inevitable after the *August coup, close links with Russia were nevertheless maintained, as the latter financed, for example, its armed forces. Its politics remained deeply corrupt, as President Saparmurad Niyazov, who was already strengthened by the absence of any political opposition, attempted to bolster his reputation even further by emphasizing his position as 'God's representative' in Turkmenistan. Elections, too, continued to follow the traditional Soviet pattern: in the 1995 general elections, all 49 official (ex-Communist) candidates endorsed by Niyazov won without opposition, with an average of 99 per cent of the popular vote.

Contemporary history (since 1999) In 1999, parliament passed a constitutional amendment declaring Niyazov President for life. In the general elections of that year, Niyazov's Democratic Party of Turkmenistan once again won every parliamentary seat. Niyazov continued to foster his own personality cult, sending a satellite into space that contained his writings, entitled 'Ruhname', to save them for posterity. Owing to his corruption and the absence of foreign investment resulting from this, Turkmenistan's rich mineral reserves continued to be under-exploited. The state verged on bankruptcy, so that in 2006 Niyazov abolished most pensions. Niyazov died in late 2006, but his Democratic Party maintained its iron grip on power. In 2007, Kurbanguly Berdymukhamedov, Niyazov's former dentist, was elected President in a rigged election.

Turks and Caicos Islands

A group of some fifty Caribbean islands incorporated into the Bahamas in 1799, and ruled as a Jamaican dependency, 1859–1959. When the Federation of the *West Indies collapsed because of Jamaican independence, it became a British Overseas Territory in 1962. A self-governing territory in domestic affairs since then, constitutional government was temporarily suspended (1986–8) by Britain as the government was charged with corruption.

Turner, John Napier (b. 7 June 1929).
Prime Minister of Canada 1984

Born in Richmond (UK), his family left for
Canada in 1932. After studying at the
Universities of British Columbia, Oxford, and
Paris, he became a lawyer in Quebec in 1954
and was elected to the Canadian House of
Commons in 1962 for the *Liberal Party. In
1968, he lost in a leadership bid to *Trudeau,
who subsequently appointed him Minister of
Justice (1968–72) and of Finance (1972–5). In
September 1975 he resigned to general
surprise and withdrew from politics, but ran
for the Liberal leadership in 1984, successfully
beating *Chrétien on 16 June. He was
appointed Prime Minister on 30 June 1984,
and immediately called a general election, in
which his party was reduced to forty
parliamentary seats by *Mulroney. He
continued his political career as a relatively
ineffective leader of a divided party until
1990.

Tutu, Right Revd Desmond Mpilo (b. 7
Oct. 1931). Archbishop of Cape Town 1986–96

Born in the Transvaal of mixed Xhosa and
Tswana descent, he was ordained an
*Anglican priest in 1961. He went to Britain
for further studies in 1962, receiving a
Master's degree in theology from King's
College, London (1966). On his return, he
became a lecturer in the seminaries in the
Cape and then in Lesotho. He left for Britain
again to become Associate Director of the
World Council of Churches (1972–5). His
subsequent appointment as Dean of
Johannesburg in 1975 was so offensive to
many White Anglicans in South Africa that he
was removed, becoming Bishop of Lesotho
(1976). As secretary-general to the South
African Council of Churches (1978–85) he
used his position to become the most
outspoken opponent of the *apartheid regime
during the 1980s. He was confirmed in this
role through the award of the *Nobel Peace
Prize in 1984.

He became Bishop of Johannesburg in 1985,
and in 1986 he became the first Black to be
elected to the highest Anglican see in the
country, the Archbishopric of Cape Town.
Always demanding the release of Nelson
*Mandela, he effortlessly changed his role
from arch-critic to arch-conscience of the
nation after Mandela's release in 1990, with
no fear of occasionally criticizing even
Mandela himself. Second to Mandela, Tutu
was perhaps the only South African to enjoy
the near-universal confidence of all sections of
the population. As a result, he was chosen to

chair the *Truth and Reconciliation
Commission (TRC). Following the publication
of the controversial TRC report, he continued
to be an outspoken advocate of peace and
justice.

Tuvalu

A Pacific state of
nine Polynesian
islands,
formerly called
the **Ellice
Islands**, which is
acutely
threatened by
the projected
rise of sea levels
owing to global
warming. Made a British protectorate in 1892,
it was incorporated into the British Crown
Colony of the Gilbert and Ellice Islands in
1916. This was never popular, owing to the
cultural differences between the islanders of
both territories. Ellice Islanders were
outnumbered seven to one, so that their
islands became the neglected part of the
territory. When Britain moved towards
granting independence to the islands, the
Ellice Islands lobbied hard, and ultimately
successfully, to become a separate entity.
They were granted self-government apart
from the Gilbert Islands (*Kiribati) in 1975,
and received independence as Tuvalu on
1 October 1978. Tuvalu's economy was reliant
on subsistence farming, with its only export
income deriving from copra and the sale of
fishing licences. From 1998 Tuvalu
experienced a cash windfall of several million
dollars per year by selling its internet suffix
(.tv) to a company which sold it on to media
and other corporations. Tuvalu was admitted
to the UN in 2000. In 2002, it filed a lawsuit
against the USA and Australia for their failure
to sign the *Kyoto Protocol.

Twenty-One Demands (Jan. 1915)

A Japanese ultimatum to China, announced
after Japan entered World War I on the
*Allied side and occupied the German base of
Qingdao. Delivered at a time when the other
foreign powers were preoccupied with the
war in Europe, the demands would have
imposed virtual protectorate status on China.
The most strident ones, which included the
imposition of Japanese advisers throughout
Chinese government, were later retracted.
The threat of military force left the Chinese
President, *Yuan Shikai, little choice but to
concede the remaining articles. These

included the extension of Japanese leases and rights in Manchuria, the takeover of the German concessions in Shandong, an increase of Japanese interests in Chinese mining concerns, and an embargo on future territorial concessions to any other power.

The demands, once accepted, allowed the Japanese to consolidate their power in China, although this episode also had the effect of provoking deep resentment against the Japanese within the country and among Japan's allies.

U

U Nu, see NU THAKIN U

U Thant, see THANT, U

U-2 Incident
On 1 May 1960 a US high-altitude Lockheed U-2 spy plane was shot down by Soviet forces over Soviet territory, and its pilot Gary Powers taken prisoner. It worsened already tense relations between the USSR and the USA at a time when the *Cold War was at its peak. The USA has been careful to assert that no subsequent flights over the USSR took place. Powers was exchanged for a Soviet spy in February 1962.
    EISENHOWER, DWIGHT DAVID

UDF (Union pour la Démocratie Française, Union for French Democracy)
A French political party founded in 1978 by *Giscard d'Estaing. In 1966 he had set up the FNRI (Fédération Nationale des Républicains Indépendants, Independent Republican Party) out of the small rump of members of the CNI (Centre Nationale des Indépendants, National Centre of Independents) who had supported de *Gaulle's Algerian policy in 1962. The FNRI was boosted by Giscard's election to the presidency in 1974. The President formed the UDF to create a broad non-*Gaullist centre-right party out of the FNRI and other smaller parties, such as the *Radicals. Thereafter, the UDF regularly gained around 20 per cent fewer seats than the Gaullists, with whom it held government 1978-81, 1986-8, and 1993-7. Often referred to as Giscardistes, the party subscribed to the ideas of individual liberalism and social reform outlined by its founder and leader in his book *Démocratie française* (1976). In 1996, Giscard d'Estaing was succeeded as party leader by the former Minister of Defence (1993-5), François Léotard. The UDF experienced a deep crisis in 1997-8, when in the general elections it lost half of its seats in the National Assembly, while Léotard was formally charged with money laundering. The party split, and, led by François Bayrou, it suffered an even worse fate in 2002, when it was eclipsed by the *UMP and gained but 29 seats. Formerly a movement created for the advancement of Giscard d'Estaing, it was at pains to establish a new popular agenda. In 2007 it split yet further, after Bayrou's good showing in the presidential elections encouraged him to form a new political movement, the **Democratic Movement**.

● The official website of the UDF.

UDI (Unilateral Declaration of Independence), see ZIMBABWE

Uganda
A landlocked country in east Africa, marked by poverty and ethnic tension.

Contemporary history (up to 1986) Uganda became a British protectorate in 1894. The colonial authorities ruled through pre-existing power structures, however, which did little to reduce the rivalry between the 40 different ethnic groups. After 1900, many Indians settled there and began to dominate the business community, even though they had originally been brought into the country to work on the railway line from Lake Victoria to the Indian Ocean.

Upon independence on 9 October 1962, *Mutesa II, who was the leader of the country's largest ethnic group (the Buganda), became President, though real power was exerted by Prime Minister *Obote. Uganda experienced a series of crises which were caused by ethnic conflicts and increasing army brutality. Obote tried to emulate *Nyerere's *Arusha Declaration in Tanzania and introduce an adapted version of *socialism, but this was contested by the business community, and opposed by Britain and the USA. Obote was replaced by *Amin, who led a corrupt and oppressive regime. Economic progress was sacrificed to finance the army, while his nationalist Africanization policies, especially the expulsion of the Indian community, proved economic suicide. His ill-judged attack on Tanzania led to the collapse of his army in 1979, and, after a tumultuous transition period, Obote returned to power.

Again Obote failed to integrate his country's mutually hostile groups, who were further antagonized by his regime through his austere economic policy under the guidance of the *IMF. He was deposed on 27 July 1985, and the virtual anarchy that followed was ended by *Museveni's accession to power.

Contemporary politics (since 1986)

Museveni only gradually restored stability as Uganda's economic troubles worsened. During the 1980s the price of coffee, which made up over 90 per cent of its exports, tumbled. Nevertheless, Museveni's rule provided Uganda with one of the highest economic growth rates in Africa. In 1994 elections to a constitutional assembly were held, which was made up of a multitude of groups and factions. It decided (22 June 1995) not to introduce a multi-party democracy. As a result, political parties remained inactive. This stance was implicitly endorsed on 9 May 1996, when Museveni was confirmed in office in a general election by an overwhelming majority across tribal groups.

Through his economic reforms, Museveni had developed into something of a darling of the *World Bank, and other organs of the international community. Despite the high military expenditure involved in Uganda's participation in the civil war in neighbouring Congo, Uganda became the first country to qualify for the *HIPC Initiative in 2000. Museveni also attracted interest through his success in combating HIV/*AIDS infections.

Through investing in sex education, the availability of condoms, and antiretroviral therapy, the number of women in antenatal clinics infected with AIDS, which had risen from 11 per cent (1985) to 31 per cent (1990), had declined to 8.3 per cent in 2002 (according to UNAIDS).

Ujamaa (Tanzania)

A Swahili term for brotherhood, it describes the cooperative village units set up in Tanzania following the *Arusha declaration. As a result, the number of Ujamaas increased from 180 (comprising 58,000 people) in 1968 to around 7,000 (comprising over twelve million people) ten years later.

Ukraine

A country which formed part of the Russian Empire from the seventeenth and eighteenth centuries, and which during the nineteenth century was

subject to intensive campaigns to replace its culture and language with those of Russia.

Early history (1917–91) Nevertheless, independence was declared with the encouragement of the German occupying forces in January 1918, after the collapse of Tsarist Russia in the *Russian Revolutions of 1917. Reoccupied by the *Red Army during the *Russian Civil War, the Ukraine became a founding member of the USSR as the Ukrainian Socialist Soviet Republic (1922). As the USSR's most fertile agricultural state, the Ukraine was particularly hard-hit by *Stalin's economic policies and his neglect of agriculture, so that it bore the brunt of the ensuing famine of the late 1920s and early 1930s with around seven million people dead. Following the *Hitler–Stalin pact, Volhynia and Galicia were taken from Poland and incorporated into the USSR, with around one million people deported to the eastern USSR. Following the German invasion in the *Barbarossa campaign, Ukraine fared even worse. Estimates put the number of Jews killed or deported at over 500,000, while over two million Ukrainians were deported as slave labour. Meanwhile, around 25,000 villages and hundreds of towns were devastated from the war, and destroyed by the retreating armies. In total, around six million civilians are likely to have died from 1941 to 1944.

Ukraine's borders were expanded in 1945, as northern Bukovina and Transcarpathia were added to its territory. Economic production soon revived, but at enormous human cost as resources were concentrated on production rather than consumption. Aided by *Khrushchev and *Kaganovich, Stalin ordered the blanket deportation of 300,000 Ukrainians as punishment for alleged collaboration with the Germans. In 1954 *Crimea was added to its territory.

Ukraine benefited from Khrushchev's rule. He promoted investment in agriculture, though it was industry which showed the most remarkable growth rates in this period. A limited decentralization of power encouraged local elites. This gave rise to expressions of local assertiveness, which from 1959 were met with a renewed policy of Russification, notably through the privileging of the Russian language. He also allowed controlled expressions of Ukrainian national identity, as long as these were not directed against the USSR. *Brezhnev allowed a remarkable flowering of Ukrainian culture from the mid-1960s, though from the early 1970s the Soviet authorities again reversed this policy to try and contain the growth of separatist tendencies which this led to. In the 1970s and 1980s, the Ukrainian economy

declined owing to the stagnation of the
Brezhnev era, with declining productivity
levels in agriculture and industry. In 1986, the
nuclear catastrophe at *Chernobyl caused 54
deaths and demonstrated the inability of the
Ukrainian Communist party to deal with a
catastrophe of such proportions.

Post-independence (1991) *Gorbachev's
reformist policies caused a resurgence of
Ukrainian *nationalism, so that in the wake
of the *August coup the President of the
Ukrainian parliament, Leonid Kravchuk,
proclaimed Ukrainian independence (24
August 1991). Kravchuk was elected President
in December 1991. The following years were
characterized by rifts with Russia, in which the
Ukraine jealously guarded its own
independence against its overbearing
neighbour. This was complicated, however, by
Crimean demands for union with Russia. The
government proceeded relatively cautiously
towards privatization, but was unable to
prevent the extensive economic dislocation
that followed the breakup of the USSR and its
other traditional markets in *Comecon. The
resulting popular frustrations resulted in the
election in 1994 of a parliament composed
largely of former Communists. In the same
year, Kravchuk lost the presidential elections
to Leonid Kutchma.

Kutchma tried to introduce reforms such as
the liberalization of prices as well as
privatization, but many of his reforms were
vetoed by parliament. Moreover, Kutchma was
unable to establish the institutional authority
of government. The system of taxation had
virtually broken down by 1998. The state was
unable to pay its salaries and pensions,
and was brought to the verge of bankruptcy
(1998–2001). Kutchma successfully introduced
a constitutional referendum in 2000 which
increased his powers against the obstinate
parliament. However, the weak state
continued to be unable to assert its authority
and prevent a series of political murders and
popular protests fuelled by a decade of
economic decline.

**Contemporary politics (since
2004)** Economic dislocation fuelled cultural
division, as Kutchma's authority relied
increasingly on support from the Russian-
dominated east of the country. By contrast,
the western parts of the Ukraine suffered
disproportionately from economic decline,
and demanded more market-oriented reforms
and closer cooperation with the EU. Led by
Viktor *Yushchenko, the western-oriented
opposition led the Orange Revolution, which
toppled Kutchma's heir apparent, Viktor
Yanukovych. Once in power the opposition
movement broke apart, with Yushchenko
falling out with his outspoken Prime Minister,

Yulia Tymoshenko. In 2006, Yushchenko
appointed his erstwhile rival, Yanukovych, as
Prime Minister, against protests from his
former allies in the Orange revolution. As
Yanukovych persistently tried to undermine
the powers of the President, Yushchenko
dissolved parliament in 2007, and called for
new elections. These prepared the ground for
a renewed electoral confrontation between
reformist and conservative forces.

Ulbricht, Walter (b. 30 June 1893, d. 1 Aug.
1973). East German leader 1949–71
Born in Leipzig, he was a joiner and became a
member of the *SPD in 1912. Ulbricht joined
the *Communist Party (KPD) upon its
foundation in 1919, becoming part of its
leadership in 1923. After a brief period in
Soviet Russia he served as a member of the
parliament of Saxony (1926–8), and in 1928
was elected to the national parliament. He
remained there until the *Nazi ban on the KPD
following the *Reichstag Fire of 1933.

Ulbricht emigrated first to France and then to
the Soviet Union, where he was groomed for
the role he was to take up after the war when he
returned to Soviet-occupied Eastern Germany
at the head of the 'Ulbricht Group' to reform
the KPD. In 1946, he became one of the moving
spirits behind a unification of the SPD and the
KPD. Even though the first East German
President was Wilhelm Piek, and the first Prime
Minister was Otto Grotewohl, the real power in
the new East Germany lay with Ulbricht, owing
to his connections with the Soviet Union. He
became the Communist Party leader in 1950,
replaced Piek in 1960 in the office of President
of the State Council, and became Chairman of
the Defence Council in the same year.

Under Ulbricht, the Communist Party
gained a very strong hold over the East
German state and society, a fact which
contributed significantly to the stability of
East Germany relative to its Eastern European
neighbours until the mid-1980s. Ulbricht was
bolstered by the success of the *Berlin Wall,
which had stopped the haemorrhage of
skilled labour to West Germany. During his
last years in office, he tried to steer a slightly
more independent course from that of the
Soviet Union. His self-confident assertion that
the GDR had advanced into a 'model' of
socialism challenged the USSR, while his
economic policies became increasingly
erratic. With the consent of the Soviet Union,
he was replaced by *Honecker.

Ulster Defence Association (UDA)
(Northern Ireland)
The UDA is the largest Loyalist paramilitary
group in *Northern Ireland. It was established
in 1971, as an umbrella for a number of
smaller 'defence associations', which sought

to defend Protestant areas against the *IRA. One of its component parts, the Ulster Freedom Fighters, carried out a consistent terrorist campaign against nationalist and republican targets, resulting in the UDA being banned in 1992. It was led by Johnny 'Mad Dog' Adair, who was one of the most controversial beneficiaries of the *Good Friday Agreement and its amnesty terms for 'political' prisoners.

Ulster Unionist Party (UUP) (Northern Ireland)

The term '**Unionist**' became prominent in British politics in 1886 when Lord Hartington and Joseph *Chamberlain formed the Liberal Unionists and allied with the *Conservative Party. They were committed to maintaining the union of Ireland with the rest of the United Kingdom. As the issue remained at the centre of British politics, Conservatives and Liberal Unionists became known simply as 'Unionists'. When Ireland was partitioned in 1921, Conservatives in *Northern Ireland became known as the Ulster Unionist Party, and later the Official Unionist Party. This party formed the government at *Stormont from 1921 until 1972, but it was subject to much internal tension from the 1960s, which resulted in Ian *Paisley forming the *Democratic Unionist Party (DUP) in 1971. The party was deeply divided over *Faulkner's support for power-sharing, and he was replaced as leader in 1974 by Harry West. It faced opposition from a variety of other (mainly more hardline) Unionist groups in the 1970s, when it maintained its support for majority rule. James Molyneaux became party leader in 1979, and together with Ian *Paisley he vigorously opposed the 1985 Anglo-Irish Agreement.

In 1991 the UUP entered inter-party talks, and it did not oppose the 1993 *Downing Street Declaration. David *Trimble replaced Molyneaux as party leader in 1995. In general elections in the early 1990s, the UUP won around 35 per cent of the vote in Northern Ireland, and about ten seats in the British parliament. However, its share of the vote dropped to 24.17 per cent in the elections of delegates to all-party peace talks in Northern Ireland (30 May 1996), with much support shifting to the more radical DUP. After the UUP received 21.3 per cent of the popular vote and 24 out of 108 seats in the Northern Ireland Assembly in 1998, Trimble became Northern Ireland's First Minister. The party continued to lose ground amongst its Protestant core over its perceived inability to deal with the IRA's equivocation in keeping the terms of the *Good Friday Agreement. In 2005, it was humiliated in the British general election, when Trimble lost his seat to the DUP, with the UUP gaining only one seat compared to the DUP's nine. In the 2007 Northern Ireland elections it lost further ground, gaining only 18 seats.

((⊕)) SEE WEB LINKS

• The official website of the UUP.

Ulster Volunteer Force (UVF) (Northern Ireland)

A Protestant paramilitary group in *Northern Ireland. It was formed in 1912 to prevent more autonomy for Ireland from Great Britain (Home Rule), as the Protestant majority in the North feared they would suffer from being ruled by the Catholic majority in southern Ireland. Armed to the teeth and led, amongst others, by Edward *Carson, it was prepared to use force and achieve its goals through civil war, with the thinly disguised encouragement of the *Conservative Party led by Bonar *Law. A clash with the southern Irish nationalists was averted by World War I. Many of its members joined the 36th (Ulster) Division, which suffered heavy casualties on the *Somme in 1916. After the war the UVF cooperated with the *Black and Tans, until the Anglo-Irish Treaty of December 1921. The UVF was revived in 1966, in opposition to *O'Neill's reforms. It was declared illegal in that year.

UMP (Union pour la Majorité Présidentielle, Union for the Presidential Democracy)

A centre-right political movement in France, founded by Jacques *Chirac following his victory in the Presidential elections of 2002. Its avowed aim was to end the period of *cohabitation and create a parliamentary majority for Chirac's policies. It was composed mostly of members of the *Gaulllist RPR and a number of smaller parties, as well as some adherents of the *UDF. The party was led by Chirac loyalist *Juppé, and gained 355 out of 577 seats in the National Assembly and an absolute majority in the French Senate in the 2002 parliamentary elections. However, its subsequent Prime Ministers, *Raffarin (2002–5) and Dominic de Villepin (2005–) became increasingly unpopular, leading to a decline of authority of Chirac himself. In 2004, the party elected Chirac's rival, *Sarkozy, as its president. Sarkozy skilfully constructed his own power base within the party. This gave him a united platform from which to launch his successful bid for the presidency in 2007.

UNESCO (United Nations Educational, Scientific, and Cultural Organization)

A specialized agency of the *UN, formed in November 1946 to further the extension and improvement of education worldwide, especially in less developed countries. It established two centres, one in Mexico and one in Egypt, to train teachers for basic education among the least-developed nations. It also had centres in Montevideo, Cairo, New Delhi, Nairobi, and Jakarta, for research into the general improvement of worldwide living conditions, with special emphasis on peace, *human rights, and youth needs. In 1984 its directorate under Amadou Mahtar M'Bow was accused by the USA of an overtly political and left-wing approach to its educational and cultural activities, so that in 1985–6 the USA, UK, and Singapore withdrew support and funding (amounting to 30 per cent of its total budget). Through internal restructuring it regained the trust of its member states. At the end of the millennium it focused particularly on education, as it aimed to combat illiteracy in the small states of Micronesia and the Caribbean, and in Africa. In this way, UNESCO also became involved in the restructuring of Afghanistan after the fall of the *Taliban. It was composed of 191 member states in 2007, with six associate members.

(((∰))) SEE WEB LINKS

• The home page of UNESCO.

Union Nationale (Canada)

A political party in *Quebec formed in 1935 by Conservative leaders to break the hold of the *Liberal Party on the province. Like the *Cooperative Commonwealth Foundation and the *Social Credit Party, it emerged as a response to the Great *Depression, to achieve social justice by state intervention if necessary, inspired in this instance by the support of the Roman *Catholic Church. Led by **Maurice Duplessis** (b. 1890, d. 1959), it won the 1936 provincial elections, and with one brief intermission (1939–44) held power until 1960. The province experienced considerable economic progress during that time, but the party refrained from divisive social and educational reforms, continuing instead to rely on the Roman *Catholic Church for the maintenance of its education and health systems. This system broke down shortly after Duplessis's death, when it was superseded by the *Quiet Revolution introduced by the Liberals in 1960. The party regained power with an unconvincing majority (1966–70), and thereafter disintegrated, giving way to the separatist *Parti Québécois as the political voice of French-speaking Quebec.

Unionists, see ULSTER UNIONIST PARTY

United Arab Emirates

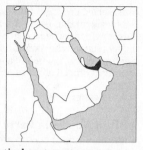

One of the most prosperous and liberal countries of the Arabian peninsula.

Contemporary history (up to 2004) An independent federation of relatively autonomous states founded in 1971, consisting of the emirates **Abu Dhabi**, Dubai, Sharjah, Ajman, Umm al-Quaiwain, Fujairah, and Ras al-Khaimah (joined 1972). Before this, they had been known as the **Trucial States**, a term which derived from the perpetual truce which their rulers concluded with Britain to abstain from piracy in 1853. Under British military protection since 1893, a federal agreement was concluded in 1968 which originally included the emirates of Bahrain and Qatar, but these eventually decided not to join. Upon independence in 1971, the federation was governed by the Emir of Abu Dhabi, Sheikh Zayed bin Sultan al-Nahayan (b. 1918, d. 2004), as President of the Supreme Council. As the world's eighth largest oil producer, the UAE advanced to become one of the wealthiest countries in the world during the 1970s and 1980s. As a result, its social structure has been dominated by the tension between the continued conservative tribalism of its native population and the majority of its population, which were immigrants. One of the leading advocates of an anti-Iraq coalition in the *Gulf War, its relations with Iran were equally poor. In 1992 Iran occupied the island of Abu Musa, which both countries had administered in cooperation until then. By contrast, the United Arab Emirates agreed peacefully to settle a border dispute with neighbouring Qatar in 1999.

Contemporary politics (from 2004) In 2004, Sheikh Zayed was succeeded by his son, Sheikh Khalifa bin Zayed. He continued the liberal policies of his father, granting more rights to foreign workers. He also continued the policy of economic diversification. Dubai advanced into a major luxury tourist destination, while companies such as Emirates airlines and Dubai ports acquired global importance.

United Arab Republic (UAR)

A short-lived political union between Egypt and Syria, proclaimed on 1 February 1958, at the height of *pan-Arab sentiment. *Nasser was elected President three weeks later. It was soon evident that the UAR was dominated by Egypt, which caused Syria to secede in 1961. Egypt retained the name and flag until 2 September 1971, when *Sadat changed his country's official name to Arab Republic of Egypt.

ARAB FEDERATION

United Australia Party

Australia's largest conservative party, it was founded in 1931 when some members of the Australian *Labor Party (ALP) left out of opposition to the *Scullin government, and joined the *Nationalist Party under *Hughes. Led by the former ALP member *Lyons, it won an absolute majority in the 1931 elections, and from 1934 governed with the Country Party (*National Party). Lyons's most important quality was his ability to keep the different sections of the loosely organized party together and galvanize their support during the elections. His successor, *Menzies, was unable to keep the party united and resigned in 1941. Regaining the leadership in 1943, he reorganized the UAP to found a more cohesive, better-organized *Liberal Party.

United Front (China)

The second coalition between the *Guomindang (KMT) and the Chinese *Communist Party (CCP) as well as other nationalist groups (1937–45). After an earlier period of cooperation had broken down in 1927, *Chiang Kai-shek had formed the *National Government, one of whose most important goals had been the destruction of the Communists. Now, following the *Xi'an Incident the two foes joined forces in order to focus on the common foreign enemy, the Japanese. The CCP pledged to cooperate fully in the *Sino-Japanese War, and sent delegates led by *Mao Zedong to a newly formed People's Political Council. However, the alliance was extremely fragile, as both sides continued to mistrust each other deeply, for good reasons. Mao summed up the Communist goal during the United Front as: '70 per cent expansion, 20 per cent dealing with the Guomindang, and 10 per cent resisting Japan'. Indeed, most of the open warfare was borne by the KMT's *National Revolutionary Army, while Mao's policy of internal reform and expansion of Communist control proved extremely successful. The United Front effectively broke down in 1943, when communication between the two partners all but stopped. It ended officially with the Japanese surrender in World War II in 1945. By this time, the Communists had strengthened sufficiently to renew the fight with their former enemies in the *Chinese Civil War, this time successfully.

YAN'AN

United Kingdom

(of Great Britain and Northern Ireland)

The UK has experienced the period since 1900 as one of decline, fundamental transformation, and remarkable recovery. At the beginning of the twentieth century, together with the USA it was the world's major power. Its *British Empire reached dimensions unparalleled before or since. Alone among the European participants of World Wars I and II, it survived these existential conflicts not only victorious but also unoccupied. And yet, 80 years later, its economy had declined to occupy a middling rank among Western industrialized nations, with its GDP per head below the average for the European Community. It had long ceased to be a world power, and retained sovereignty over only a few isolated small island colonies. By 2006, Britain's economy had revived, growing steadily since the 1990s to become one of Europe's most dynamic and prosperous economies.

Challenges to the Empire (1900–14) The first signs that all was not well with the UK, its Empire and its relative levels of prosperity and power came during the *South African (Boer) War (1899–1902). The fact that it took so long to defeat a cobbled-together army of farmers led to much soul-searching, and triggered *Haldane's badly needed army reforms. The fact that vast numbers of city dwellers were unfit even to join the war gave rise to renewed concerns about the physical health and conditions of the poorer classes. This led to the success of *Baden-Powell's Scout and Guide movements, and increased interest in social research conducted, for example, by *Rowntree and the *Fabian Society. Ultimately, it led to the acceptance of the need for some social reform, as advocated by *Tawney, *Hobson, and *Hobhouse.

Following the defeat of *Balfour's *Conservative Party over Joseph *Chamberlain's campaign for *tariff reform, the *Liberal Party gained a majority in the 1906 elections under *Campbell-Bannerman. It was not until his succession by *Asquith (1908), with the inexhaustible

Table 19. **Prime Ministers of the United Kingdom since 1895**

Marquess of *Salisbury	1895–1902	Clement *Attlee	1945–51
Arthur James *Balfour	1902–5	Winston *Churchill	1951–5
Henry *Campbell-Bannerman	1905–8	Anthony *Eden	1955–7
Herbert *Asquith	1908–16	Harold *Macmillan	1957–63
David *Lloyd George	1916–22	Alec *Douglas-Home	1963–4
Andrew *Bonar Law	1922–3	Harold *Wilson	1964–70
Stanley *Baldwin	1923–4	Edward *Heath	1970–4
Ramsay *MacDonald	1924	Harold *Wilson	1974–6
Stanley *Baldwin	1924–9	James *Callaghan	1976–9
Ramsay *Macdonald	1929–35	Margaret *Thatcher	1979–90
Stanley *Baldwin	1935–7	John *Major	1990–97
Neville *Chamberlain	1937–40	Tony *Blair	1997–2007
Winston *Churchill	1940–5	Gordon *Brown	2007–

*Lloyd George as Chancellor of the Exchequer, that a serious programme of social legislation was enacted. Old-age pensions and unemployment insurance were introduced. An unprecedented revolt by the House of Lords against the 1909 budget also led to a major consitutional reform in 1911, when the veto of the Lords was no longer absolute, but restricted to two years (*parliament).

World War I (1914–18) Participation in World War I proved a traumatic experience for the UK, which had declared war on Germany on behalf of the entire British Empire on 4 September 1914. Disastrous losses at the *Somme and *Passchendaele under *Haig, and at *Gallipoli, led to rapid disillusionment and frustration. In 1916 Lloyd George replaced Asquith to provide more charismatic leadership. Ironically, even though the UK emerged from the war greatly weakened economically and financially, the British Empire reached its greatest dimensions, as former colonies of the German and *Ottoman Empires were added as *League of Nations *Mandates. This extension of power was more superficial than real, as the Dominions of Australia, New Zealand, South Africa, Newfoundland, and Canada received ever-greater autonomy, culminating in the Statute of *Westminster (1931), which gave them de facto independence. More crucially, in 1921 a compromise was found whereby southern Ireland received autonomy and Dominion status, while *Northern Ireland was given Home Rule, but as an integral part of the UK.

The inter-war years (1918–39) Like other European countries, British politics and society experienced deep ruptures after World War I, though in contrast to its large European neighbours, the British political system proved stable enough to accommodate these changes. The war had crippled public finances. It had been funded largely through

government borrowing, which led to increased taxation, high interest rates, and currency instabilities in the interwar period. To overcome the financial consequences of the war, British ministers pursued the policy of *appeasement, hoping to escape another war through trying to avoid the arms race that had precipitated World War I. In domestic politics, the interwar period was marked by the decline of the Liberal Party and the gradual rise of the *Labour Party. As the progressive vote was weakened and split by this process of transition, politics became dominated by the Conservative Party. The Conservatives benefited from their alliance with Lloyd George at the *Coupon Elections of 1918, and then formed a government on their own under Bonar *Law. Labour formed its first minority government under *MacDonald in January 1924, but was replaced by *Baldwin's Conservatives, 1924–9.

The economy suffered under the misguided reintroduction of the *Gold Standard in 1925, while the defeat of the *General Strike in 1926 displayed the social and economic weakness of the labour movement in British society, despite its growing political strength through the Labour Party. The *Arcos raid displayed the general volatility of the interwar period, though compared to its bigger European neighbours (France, Italy, Spain, Germany), interwar Britain proved a beacon of stability. In 1929, MacDonald formed Labour's second minority government.

Most of MacDonald's ministers were reluctant to respond to the Great *Depression in the way prescribed by the current economic orthodoxy. MacDonald formed a *National Government that rested on the support of Conservatives, Liberals, and a few of his Labour supporters, but it was opposed by the majority of his own Labour Party. He was at the head of an increasingly

Conservative-dominated national government until 1935. The Gold Standard was finally abandoned, as was free trade, when tariffs and Imperial Preference were adopted in the *Ottawa Agreements of 1932. After a brief period of government under Baldwin (1935–7), Neville *Chamberlain tried to avert another war through signing the *Munich Agreement (1938), though this failed to prevent the German occupation of the Czech lands.

World War II (1939–45) Chamberlain was forced to declare war on Germany on 3 September 1939, after *Hitler's invasion of Poland (*World War II). After Germany's invasion of Norway in April 1940, the discredited Chamberlain was replaced by the ebullient *Churchill. Between the summer of 1940 and 1941, Britain remained the only major country holding out successfully against Hitler. This success, and the fact that Britain was the only European belligerent never invaded by the German army, had a deep impact on the British perception of distinctiveness and difference from the rest of Europe.

Alarmed at the retreat at *Dunkirk and the Battle of *Britain, the British underwent a fundamental sea-change in social and political attitudes in the first years of the war. This was best expressed in the widely received *Beveridge report of 1943, and found an outlet in the victory of the Labour Party under *Attlee in 1945 in the greatest recorded electoral swing in British politics. Aided by a diverse group of able ministers (*Bevin, *Bevan, *Morrison, and others), the government nationalized industries such as mining, electricity, and the railways, and created a social *welfare state, most notably through the foundation of the *National Health Service. A state that would provide for its citizens 'from the cradle to the grave' became the accepted norm of government in the following decades, until 1979 and even beyond. Although the wartime experience set Britain apart from the European continent, the social legacy of the war was remarkably comparable to other West European states.

The welfare state (1950s–1979) The introduction of the welfare state was largely accepted by the Conservative governments (1951–64), which were led successively by Churchill, *Eden, *Macmillan, and *Douglas-Home. This period marked effectively the end of the British Empire through the decolonization of most of Africa, while the disastrous *Suez Crisis of 1956 brought home the message that had been unavoidable since the fall of *Singapore in 1942: Britain was no longer a world power, and was able to pursue her global interests only with the consent (and support) of the USA. A youthful *Wilson led the Labour Party to victory in 1964, and remained in power until 1970, but neither he nor his successor, *Heath (1970–4), were able to deal with the burgeoning *trade union movement, which stifled any attempt to deal with the economic problems of inflation and a balance-of-payments deficit. Wilson returned to power in 1974 and gave way to *Callaghan in 1976, but neither found an effective response to worsening global economic conditions caused by the *oil price shock of 1973.

Whereas Britain had emerged from World War II as Europe's strongest economy, by the 1970s it had been overtaken by other economies such as Germany and France. In part, this was the result of a natural process, as other countries began to catch up with the economic losses caused by the war. Britain also banked on economic development in its colonies and Dominions, even though the growth rate in most of these was well below that experienced on the European continent. Britain had misjudged the determination of continental European states to proceed with *European integration without the UK, creating the European Economic Community (EEC) in 1958. While Britain *decolonized most of its overseas territories in the 1960s, it filed two unsuccessful applications to join the EEC. Its third application was successful, and it joined what had developed into the EC in 1973. This inaugurated the start of an uneasy relationship with the European integration project. Whereas membership proved to be extremely beneficial in economic terms, Britain subsequently resisted all attempts at further political integration.

The policies of Thatcherism (1979–97) Upon coming to power in 1979, *Thatcher abandoned *Keynesian demand management and changed the political battleground, away from the postwar consensus on comprehensive welfare policies to a new focus on the market. With the Labour Party in disarray under *Foot's leadership and the breakaway of the *Social Democratic Party, Thatcher became the longest-serving (and first woman) UK Prime Minister in the twentieth century. She reduced the power of the state through privatization and cuts in social services and made the reduction of inflation, rather than of unemployment, the primary economic target. This was unpopular at first, but the *Falklands War restored her popularity and enabled her to win the 1983 election.

Thatcher was responsible for a sea-change in social and cultural attitudes, but in the short run her major economic impact was that it halted economic decline relative to other European economies. Ultimately, her resistance to *European integration and her autocratic government style (as displayed by her insistence on the *poll tax) led to her replacement by *Major, who continued to pursue her basic policies, albeit in a rather more sober and lacklustre style. Major was weakened by a tiny parliamentary majority which made him beholden to the warring factions within his own parliamentary party. His most lasting achievement was the beginning of the *Northern Ireland peace process. This gained him few votes in domestic politics, where his weak, grey, and indecisive image contrasted with a dynamic, disciplined Labour party led by Tony *Blair.

Contemporary politics (since 1997) Blair won the 1997 elections, and embarked upon an ambitious project of constitutional reform which saw the granting of Home Rule to Scotland and Wales from 1999. Under Gordon *Brown, indirect taxes were raised and income tax was lowered slightly. The economic growth rekindled during the Major years continued, and contrasted sharply with the sluggish performance of other economies such as Germany or the US. In 2000–1 an outbreak of the infectious foot-and-mouth disease devastated large parts of the countryside, as almost four million animals were slaughtered. Although the government was criticized for not responding quickly enough, the general election, which occurred as the epidemic subsided, returned another huge Labour majority (413 of 659 parliamentary seats). Facing increasing criticism at the near-collapse of the country's rail infrastructure in 2000, and the poor state of the National Health Service, Blair's new government embarked on a quest to improve public services without abandoning his pro-business policies.

Following the *September 11 attacks, the UK became Europe's most committed supporter of George W. *Bush's foreign policy. Britain was the only country to assist the US-led *Iraq War with significant forces of its own. The divisions which this invasion caused within Europe increased pressure for a more coherent foreign policy within the EU. The UK was at the forefront of such aspirations, and this led to the adoption, at the 2003 *Intergovernmental Conference, of the European Security Strategy. The UK was thus pursuing the difficult strategy of both being influential within the EU, and maintaining its 'special relationship' with the US.

Blair was the first Labour Prime Minister to be elected to a third consecutive term in office, in 2005, albeit with a reduced majority.

This made Blair more dependent on the parliamentary Labour Party, and it increased the difficulty of passing his more controversial reforms, such as an overhaul of the public sector. In 2005, the Conservative Party elected its fifth leader since losing power in 1997, David Cameron. He re-energized the party by increasing its appeal to centrist voters. As Prime Minister from 2007, Brown introduced constitutional reform, promising a more transparent government.

ENGLAND; WALES; SCOTLAND; NORTHERN IRELAND;

United Malays National Organization (UMNO)

A Malaysian political party formed in 1946 by Dato Omn bin Jaafar (b. 1895, d. 1962), then Prime Minister of Johore, in response to British attempts to form the Union of *Malaya. Its chief aim was to fight for national independence, while protecting the interests of the indigenous Malay population. Since independence in 1957, UMNO has been the dominant party in Malaysia, the continuous rise of *Islamic fundamentalism forcing it to emphasize increasingly its Islamic ideals. Despite various frictions within the party, its rule has remained virtually unchallenged, largely through the creation of the National Front, a coalition in which most opposition parties came under its patronage.

ABDUL RAHMAN PUTRA

United Nations Organization, see UNO

United Party, see LIBERAL PARTY, NEW ZEALAND

United Party, South Africa

Founded as a response to the Great *Depression in 1934 as the United South African National Party, it was a fusion between *Smuts's South African Party, and most of *Hertzog's *National Party (NP). It split in 1939 when Hertzog left in opposition to South Africa's entry into World War II. Nevertheless, its surprise defeat in the 1948 elections was less due to its internal weaknesses than to the country's electoral geography. Despite its considerable majority in terms of votes cast, it failed to win a majority of seats because its support was concentrated in urban areas. The death of its deputy leader, Jan Hofmeyr (b. 1894, d. 1948), and its leader, Smuts, dealt the party a heavy blow from which it never really recovered. Despite polling a majority of votes over the NP until 1961, it lost its direction. It became as racist as the NP in a misguided attempt to woo NP voters, which led to the breakaway of its liberal-minded members to form the *Progressive Party in 1959. Further defections occurred until the party was dissolved in 1977.

United States of America (USA, or US)

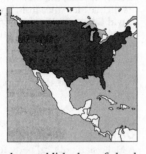

Overview A confederacy developed after the 1776 Declaration of Independence, asserted in the 1783 Articles of Confederation, and re-established as a federal republic by the Constitution of the United States in 1787. The nineteenth century was characterized by the establishment of the territorial integrity of the USA as it exists today. By 1912 all 48 states of the continuous landmass of the USA had been created (Hawaii and Alaska were added in 1959), whereas the Civil War had created a lasting framework for the evolution of federal–state relations. From an international perspective, perhaps the most striking feature of US history in the twentieth and beginning of the twenty-first centuries was the country's economic, cultural, military, and geopolitical growth. So far had US hegemony advanced that historians and political scientists debated whether the US was bound to decline just as other empires had collapsed, from the Greek and Roman Empires in antiquity to the *British Empire and the Soviet Union in the twentieth century. Others argued that the US had built up an unstoppable comparative advantage over any other nation that would see its international dominance not less but more pronounced.

From a domestic perspective, the twentieth century was distinguished by the increasing diversity of the US population. A growing number of immigrants after 1900 came from non-Western and non-Northern European backgrounds, while the post-World War II period has seen large groups of immigrants especially from Latin America as well as Asia. The cultural diversification was paralleled by a growing awareness of the injustice and discrimination suffered by Blacks and African Americans even after the abolition of slavery during the Civil War. Before the beginning of the twentieth century, the *Supreme Court decision of *Plessey* v. *Ferguson* confirmed the discrimination inherent in US society, while marking the beginning of a growing opposition to the status quo expressed in the judgment. Especially since 1945, domestic history has been characterized by the attempt to create a stable harmony between an integrative and inclusive civic and constitutional patriotism on the one hand and the recognition of distinctive individual identities on the other.

The growing tension between an increasing geopolitical assertiveness and the growing heterogeneity of US society has been mediated by a number of fundamental political changes at an institutional level. Public life has been transformed through the relative decline of party bosses and elites, the growth of communication, the importance of the media, and the introduction of direct popular elections of senators in the Seventeenth Constitutional Amendment (1913). The nature of the electorate has also changed dramatically, by the doubling of the electorate through the introduction of women's suffrage, and through the large-scale removal of discrimination against minorities.

1900–33 The potential power of the US, and many of its implications, were apparent at the start of the twentieth century. By 1900 the USA had overtaken the UK as the world's leading

Table 20. **Presidents of the United States of America since 1897**

William *McKinley	1897–1901	John F. *Kennedy	1961–3
Theodore *Roosevelt	1901–9	Lyndon B. *Johnson	1963–9
William Howard *Taft	1909–13	Richard M. *Nixon	1969–74
Woodrow *Wilson	1913–21	Gerald R. *Ford	1974–7
Warren Gamaliel *Harding	1921–3	James Earl *Carter	1977–81
Calvin *Coolidge	1923–9	Ronald *Reagan	1981–9
Herbert C. *Hoover	1929–33	George *Bush	1989–93
Franklin Delano *Roosevelt	1933–45	Bill *Clinton	1993–2001
Harry S *Truman	1945–53	George W. *Bush	2001–
Dwight D. *Eisenhower	1953–61		

industrial nation, producing around 30 per cent of the world's manufactured goods. Within 40 years industrial production had risen more than sixfold in value. The dramatic shift in the economic position of the USA led to a reassessment of its geopolitical role. Under President *McKinley the USA extended, in 1898, its sovereignty to the Philippines, *Guam, Hawaii, and *Puerto Rico. It controlled Cuba even after its nominal independence from 1902, and gained sovereignty over the Panama Canal in 1903. While the extension of US control in Latin America and the Pacific followed commercial interests, McKinley and his supporters also felt that US involvement abroad appropriately reflected the country's importance in the world. However, this position challenged a tradition of maintaining the structure of minimalist government which had endured for over a century. Divisions over the country's foreign-policy role, and the appropriate response to its economic transformations, split the *Republican Party under Theodore *Roosevelt and *Taft, and led to a surge in support for the *Progressive Party. Progressivism became more important as a political movement than *socialism ever did. Socialism never became as important as in the industrial societies of Europe, Australia, and New Zealand, as divisions in the labour force were less of class than of national origin. The development of class-consciousness was also hindered by the high degree of social mobility and physical migration in America. Progressivism, by contrast, was so successful because it reflected an optimism about the application of rational modes of government. This optimism was relatively unshaken by World War I, which was considered to be a crisis of government in far-away Europe.

In 1917 the *Wilson administration reluctantly took the USA into World War I. Neutrality had been observed not just because of the US reluctance concerning large-scale involvement in a crisis of the 'old world'. Entry on the side of the Allies was divisive, and was opposed by Americans of German and Irish origin. Ultimately, US neutrality allowed the British to sustain their naval blockade against the Germans. When the Germans sought to break through this by submarine warfare, this risked American lives. After the sinking of the *Lusitania, the US intervened decisively in the war. The war left the US as the greatest creditor in the world. The US had also assumed a moral leadership role through the declaration of the *Fourteen Points. Abroad, this resulted in the creation of the *League of Nations at the *Paris Peace Conference. At home, this caused a tremendous political backlash. The Senate

refused to ratify US entry into the League of Nations, and a return to *isolationism (disguised under the slogan of 'normalcy') was endorsed by Wilson's successors to the Presidency.

The non-interventionist *Republican Presidents *Harding, *Coolidge, and H. J. *Hoover oversaw an unprecedented boom in the American economy. Techniques of industrial mass production, also known as Fordism, created mass consumption, even though very unevenly. Apart from their economic effects, items such as the motor car and radio revolutionized communications and popular culture. The boom of the 1920s had rested on unstable economic foundations, which were exposed by the *Wall Street Crash and the ensuing Great *Depression

1933–51 In the greatest economic slump of US history, unemployment, which was at four million in 1930, rose by more than 300 per cent to affect a quarter of the working population by 1932. With Republicans struggling to find an appropriate response to the crisis, the *Democrats under Franklin D. *Roosevelt constructed a political coalition built upon the interventionist economics and social rhetoric of the *New Deal. The government was interventionist, and involved with matters of education, social security, and welfare from which it had previously been excluded. The New Deal fundamentally altered Americans' expectations of government and created a lasting framework for a continuous, contentious debate about the nature of government intervention in society and the economy.

The New Deal created lasting monuments to state intervention through the construction of highways and dams. It also alleviated economic hardships. However, it did not bring about a lasting economic revival. Prosperity returned with the all-out mobilization of the economy for military production from the late 1930s and early 1940s. In 1941 America entered World War II, fully committed to liberal internationalism. The USA developed a vast defence industry which lifted the economy into unprecedented levels of production and prosperity and generated a political rhetoric geared against *totalitarianism. It was during this conflict that an American self-conception began to dominate which emphasized its mission to bring the values and liberties enshrined in the US Constitution to the rest of the world. This endeavour was manifested in the creation of the *UN in the *San Francisco Conference, and in the *Bretton Woods Conference. It was also apparent, however, in the *Cold War, where this sense of mission was underlined by US national self-interest. As the expansion of *Communism became apparent in occupied postwar *Berlin and the *Chinese Civil War, President *Truman convinced *Congress to maintain a US global commitment and ensure the survival of freedom. The US also moved in defence of *capitalism, evident, for instance, in the *Marshall Plan. For wartime prosperity and production could only be maintained and extended if the US engaged with the rest of the world. If in the immediate postwar years the US economy relied on its exports, from the 1960s onwards it came to rely additionally on its capital imports.

1951–80 From the 1950s, the USA's continued engagement in the Cold War led to self-doubt concerning its own international role. Meanwhile, US society was fundamentally transformed in this period. Attitudes towards minorities were transformed from the 1950s. The *Supreme Court's judicial activism under *Warren, accompanied by the fervour and idealism of the *civil rights movement, pushed America towards greater integration of its society. These legal changes were underlined by the political changes that began under John F. *Kennedy, but which found their full expression in *Johnson's *Great Society programme of 1964. The federal government now supervised the advancement of equal opportunities. It also extended the purview of the federal government in culture and social legislation.

Although during the 1960s the legal and political establishment did much to achieve racial equality, these efforts were undermined by social and economic inequalities in inner-city areas. The domestic activism of the Johnson years was undermined by the polarization of society owing to the *Vietnam War. It was also challenged by the growing assertiveness of particular minority groups such as the *American Indian Movement or the *Black Power movement. Further social transformations related to the women's liberation movement, following the development of new contraceptive technologies in the 1950s and the pill in the 1960s. The social and cultural changes of this period profoundly altered society by disrupting traditional patterns of domestic life and language. This caused a fundamental sense of crisis, which was underlined by growing unease about the Vietnam War.

The late 1960s were not just a period of dislocation, and they did not affect everyone equally. The first landing on the Moon through the *Apollo programme provided welcome relief, and in the long run the contestation of conflict made US society stronger, not weaker. However, to many contemporaries the *Watergate scandal deepened a sense of crisis which now had affected perhaps the most cherished of all institutions, the Presidency. Even capitalism and the economic hegemony of an economy reliant on fossil fuels was exposed to existential challenge through the *oil price shocks. After the brief presidency of *Ford, President *Carter's ambition to stimulate economic growth and give his country a new sense of purpose failed. The *Iran hostage crisis appeared to confirm the powerlessness of the US on a world stage.

1980–2001 At a time when many considered the decline of US hegemony to be in evidence, the reassuring Ronald *Reagan was elected 40th President of the USA. Through lowering taxation, allowing the *Federal Reserve System to pursue a policy of low inflation, and engaging in record military spending levels, Reagan revived the US economy. He was no more successful at intervening in Latin American or Middle Eastern domestic conflicts than his predecessors. However, successful military intervention in Grenada, as well as the pursuit of a clear-cut, simple, and confrontational rhetoric of good and evil against the Soviet Union, restored US confidence.

Reagan's military spending accelerated Soviet desperation in the arms race, but it was his successor, George *Bush, who presided over the end of the *Cold War. Bush tried to stabilize the Soviet Union by helping defeat the *August coup, while he encouraged German unification after the fall of the *Berlin Wall. Bush's greatest success was his pursuit of the *Gulf War, which he fought at the head of an unprecedented international coalition. In domestic politics, however, the moderate Bush lost the support of conservatives and the evangelical right inside the Republican Party. Badly damaged by the end of the economic boom of the Reagan era, he lost out to Bill *Clinton.

The first Democrat President to be elected for two consecutive terms since Roosevelt, Clinton presided over an unprecedented economic boom fuelled by technological innovation and stock market speculation. Facing increasing resistance by a hostile Congress since 1996, Clinton became increasingly active in foreign politics. He failed to define an international role for the US in a post-Cold War world, but he did make US patronage in conflict resolution indispensable. Following the most controversial election in over a century, Clinton was succeeded by George W. *Bush as President.

At the beginning of the twenty-first century, the US continued to be the world's most powerful military power. At the same time, its geopolitical pre-eminence faced two new challenges. First, China's booming exports provided the country with the world's largest reserve of the US currency, at over $800 billion in 2007. The stability of the currency was thus crucially dependent on the Chinese. In foreign policy, too, China became increasingly assertive, for instance by rivalling the US in providing foreign aid to African countries. Second, with energy resources becoming increasingly scarce and costly, the US, as the country consuming one-quarter of the world's energy, became vulnerable to its relative lack of mineral resources. The US reliance on crude oil reshaped the balance of power, as oil-rich countries like Venezuela or Russia found their geopolitical power enhanced, at the expense of the US.

Since 2001 In economic policy, the Bush administration tried to stimulate a flagging economy through a series of controversial tax cuts spread over ten years, amounting to $1.35 trillion (2001) and $350 billion (2003). The administration's economic policies aimed at reducing the economic involvement of the federal government, a rationale pursued by earlier Republican administrations. By contrast, the *September 11 attacks fundamentally redefined much of US foreign and domestic policy. By declaring *War on Terrorism, Bush created a foreign and domestic political agenda aimed at punishment and prevention. 'Preventing' acts of terrorism before they had been committed proved contentious, as evidenced by the Patriot Act (2001), which dramatically curtailed civil rights. Under its provisions, over 1,000 individuals, mostly Muslims, were imprisoned without trial (and proof) as 'enemy combatants'.

In foreign policy, Bush abandoned his predecessors' policies of bolstering the *UN as arbiter of international affairs, by taking the War on Terror wherever US interests required. US-led forces invaded Afghanistan to defeat the *Taliban (2002), and Iraq (2003) to topple Saddam *Hussein. These turned out to be pyrrhic victories, as it became clear that the US had been woefully unprepared for its biggest task of national reconstruction since World War II. Owing to the Bush administration's failure to rally sufficient international support before the war, the US faced the military and economic cost of rebuilding Iraq largely on its own. Based on figures obtained from Congress, the *New York Times* estimated in 2007 that the Bush administration spent around $200 billion per year on Iraq. The war drained US military reserves to such an extent that it

became increasingly difficult for the US to provide a credible policy against Iraq's more dangerous neighbour, Iran, which was developing nuclear weapons. These difficulties exposed growing rifts within the Bush administration over how to deal with the rogue states of Iran and North Korea.

In domestic policy, the Bush administration was successful at appointing its nominees to the Supreme Court, including John G. *Roberts as Chief Justice. However, the administration was severely constrained by the 2006 mid-term elections, which produced a Democrat majority in both Houses of Congress, and by the Supreme Court, which declared a string of measures in the War on Terrorism (such as covert phone tappings) unconstitutional. The President's authority eroded as even senior Republicans began to question his policies in Iraq. In no mood to compromise, Bush struggled to fend off Congressional demands for greater oversight over his administration.

United States Virgin Islands, see
VIRGIN ISLANDS OF THE UNITED STATES

UNO (United Nations Organization, or UN)

Overview After the failure of the *League of Nations to prevent the crises of the 1930s which culminated in World War II, the major *Allied countries (the USSR, China, the UK, and the USA) agreed in Moscow (October 1943) to create a new, improved international peacekeeping organization after the war. Following further negotiations at *Dumbarton Oaks and *Yalta, the charter of the UN was discussed and drafted in *San Francisco in spring 1945, and signed by 51 nations on 26 June 1945. Its administration is headed by a Secretary-General, a post which has been filled by *Lie (1946–52), *Hammarskjöld (1953–61), U *Thant (1961–71), *Waldheim (1972–81), *Pérez de Cuéllar (1982–91), *Boutros Ghali (1992–6), *Annan (1997–2006), and *Ban (since 2007). In contrast to the League, its membership included the major world powers (though the People's Republic of China was not admitted until 1971).

Security Council The UN is guided by a strong executive, the **Security Council**, which consists of five permanent members (USSR/Russia, China (Taiwan until 1971, then the People's Republic), France, the UK, the USA), each of whom has a right to veto any decision which the Council may take. The Council also consists of ten temporary members which are elected for two years. As a result of the right of veto, the Council was relatively ineffective during the *Cold War,

Table 21. **Secretaries-General of the United Nations Organization**

Trygve *Lie	1946–52	Javier *Pérez de Cuéllar	1982–91
Dag *Hammarskjöld	1953–61	Boutros *Boutros Ghali	1992–97
U *Thant	1961–71	Kofi *Annan	1997–2006
Kurt *Waldheim	1972–81	*Ban Ki-Moon	2007–

when unanimity was difficult to establish between the USA and the USSR. For example, the UN could only intervene in the *Korean War because of a temporary Soviet boycott of the Council which made it impossible for the USSR to exercise the veto. The Security Council has come under growing criticism because its composition of permanent members has failed to reflect the shifts in the global balance of power since 1945. The exclusion from the Council of India, Brazil or Japan was increasingly difficult to justify if the Council was to claim legitimacy. Reform proposals were made after 2001, but they failed owing to the reluctance of the existing permanent Security Council members to share their exclusive powers.

General Assembly There ia also a General Assembly consisting of all 192 member states (2006), each of which has one vote. It can debate any issue which concerns the UN charter. Resolutions need a simple majority except for constitutional matters, which need a two-thirds majority. Its resolutions on international security are binding, but not its 'recommendations' to individual states, for example its hostility against *apartheid in South Africa. Owing to the process of *decolonization, the Assembly's character has changed substantially not only in size but also in quality. A disproportionate number of the new states that have been admitted since 1945 are less developed countries in Africa and Asia, so that the relative influence of the industrialized countries in the Assembly has diminished. The diversity of the Assembly has been its greatest asset in terms of legitimacy, but its heterogeneity has also prevented effective and rapid action.

Other organizations Other principal organs are the *Economic and Social Council, which investigates issues such as population growth, human rights, drugs, and women's rights, and the *International Court of Justice. There are also a host of specialized agencies (e.g. *UNESCO, *IMF, *WHO) which are autonomous relative to the UN, but which have the same goal of international peace and justice.

International peacekeeping Despite its original aim, the UN was never able to develop an armed force of its own, so that in its military interventions it has always relied on

troops supplied by individual member states. This has reduced its scope for independent action, so that its greatest successes have been in the arbitration and supervision of peace agreements, such as in the Middle East from 1947, *Kashmir (1948/9), *Cyprus (since 1964), and the *Iran–Iraq War (1980–8).

The record of the UN's larger-scale military interventions has been rather mixed, as these depended mostly on the political will of the countries who supplied the military forces and finance. Hence, its successes in the *Korean War (1950–3), the *Gulf War (1990–1), and Haiti (1994–5) were founded on US military strength. By the same token, such missions have often destroyed the UN's impartial reputation and this, together with an ultimate lack of military resolve, was the main reason for the UN's failures in Somalia (1992–4) and the *Bosnian Civil War. At the same time, the UN's failures have usually reflected insufficient resolve by its member states, as was apparent in the genocides of Rwanda and Sudan (*Darfur, 2004–).

Hopes for a more effective UN following the end of the Cold War have been dashed, largely because the collapse of the Soviet Union fundamentally diminished the rivalry between the superpowers and their willingness to accept neutral, multilateral intervention. This eroded the resolve of the USA and other countries to give financial and military support to UN activities, at a time when the UN was engaged in more missions than ever before. Under the leadership of Kofi Annan, however, the UN's reputation recovered somewhat. Annan was able to point to some genuine successes beyond peace keeping, notably in assisting the establishment of civilian institutions which in the case of Timor Leste enabled that territory to proclaim independence in 2002. In 2001, Annan and the UN were jointly awarded the *Nobel Peace Prize.

The UN continued to be criticized for its cumbersome bureaucracy. Annan achieved only partial reforms, with his successor, *Ban, poised to focus on internal reform while pursuing a less activist external role for the UN.

( ) SEE WEB LINKS

• The home page of the UN.

Upper Volta, see BURKINA FASO

Uruguay

A small country in Latin America which—in contrast to its larger neighbours— has been characterized by relative economic and social stability.

The welfare state (c. 1903–1950s) Uruguay gained independence in 1828 as a compromise between Argentinian and Brazilian claims over the territory. A model of democratic and economic stability in the early twentieth century, its political life was dominated by the Colorado Party, representing commercial interests, and the Blancos, representing landowners. The Colorado President José Batlle y Ordóñez (1903–7, 1911–15) laid the foundations for Latin America's first *welfare state. As a result, wide-ranging social legislation was introduced, including the eight-hour working day, minimum wages for farm labourers, and pensions. In addition, public works reduced unemployment and created a good infrastructure, while public monopolies were established out of nationalized, previously foreign-owned companies.

At Batlle y Ordóñez's instigation, the social harmony thus created was institutionalized in a constitutional revision of 1919, whereby the President ruled in conjunction with a National Council of Administration which contained a guaranteed minority from opposition parties. These advances were made possible by Uruguay's economic prosperity, deriving principally from flourishing agricultural exports. The weakness of this over-reliance on exports was exposed by the Great *Depression during the 1930s, when European and US markets tried to close off their domestic economies. President Gabriel Terra took on special powers to rule as a virtual dictator in 1933, while his elected successor from 1938, General Alfredo Baldomir, restored full democracy in 1942, albeit with some hesitation. Meanwhile, the country industrialized relatively successfully to make it less dependent on world trade. Many were given work in an expanded state administration, which reduced social tension and attracted employees' support for the state.

Economic and political crisis (1960s–1980s) After an export boom stimulated by the *Korean War in the early 1950s, the economy entered a long period of decline. This was accelerated by social expenditure which the country could no longer afford, and a bloated state administration which took up 35 per cent of all state spending. In the late 1960s social unrest emerged, which was exacerbated by the activities of the *Tupamaros. Following his election in 1971, President Bordaberry gradually assumed dictatorial powers, with the consent of the military and leading elites. Parliament was dissolved in 1973, and civilian institutions were placed under military control. The economy was radically transformed, through (1) liberalization (reduction of import tariffs), (2) privatization, (3) promotion of domestic industry, and (4) promotion of foreign investment. However, living standards continued to fall, while the regime's brutal suppression of opponents made the dictatorship increasingly untenable.

Democratization (1980s–2004) A new constitution to prepare for a return to democracy was rejected in a plebiscite in November 1980, so that new elections were not held until 1984. They were won by *Sanguinetti, who returned to the Presidency in 1995 after the defeat of the Blancos under Luis Alberto Lacalle de Herrera (President 1990–5). While foreign debts and inflation remained high, the most important priorities remained a reduction in the number of state employees (20 per cent of the total workforce) and pension reform, as the number of pensioners amounted to half of the total active working population. Throughout the 1990s the economy grew steadily at an average of 3–4 per cent each year, though inflation declined only gradually.

From the late 1990s, Uruguay's economy was badly affected by the economic difficulties of neighbouring Brazil, and the economic collapse of its other neighbour, Argentina, in 2001. In the first three months of 2002, the economy contracted by 10 per cent. In July 2002 the country's banks were in a state of near-collapse until they were rescued by a $1.5 billion loan from the *IMF. This was largely a response to the political stabilization of recent years. From 1995 to 2000 the erstwhile political enemies, the Blancos and Colorados, formed a governmental coalition, and in 2000 they agreed on a common presidential candidate, Jorge Battle Ibáñez (b. 1927). He consolidated the budget and reduced Uruguay's indebtedness. However, this sparked off mass protests, because it increased the number of citizens living below the poverty line.

Contemporary politics (since 2004) The 2004 parliamentary elections produced a political earthquake, as they were won by the left populist Encuentro Progressista/Frente Amplio under Tabaré Vázquez Rosas, who was also elected President in the first round. Vázquez launched an emergency programme to help the poor, restored economic relations with Cuba, and launched a *Truth and Reconciliation Committee to investigate *human rights violations in the 1970s and 1980s.

USA (US), see UNITED STATES OF AMERICA

Ustase (Yugoslavia)

A paramilitary organization founded in 1929 in response to the discriminatory rule by King *Alexander I, in order to assert the rights of the Croatian people in a Serb-dominated state. In 1934, together with Macedonian terrorists it was successful in organizing Alexander's assassination. Led by Ante *Pavelic, it welcomed the *Nazi occupation of Yugoslavia, and collaborated fully with this. It established 'The Independent State of Croatia', to which the Serbian minority in Croatia was forced to assimilate, e.g. through conversion to Catholicism. Moreover, thousands of Serbs were raped and murdered. When the Ustase regime collapsed after German withdrawal, it was now the turn of the Communists (popularly associated with Serbia, even though they were led by *Tito) to commit mass killings of Ustase members and those suspected of cooperation. The Ustase terror was one of the reasons for the bitter tension between Croats and Serbs in general, and for the Serbian Croat minority living in Croatia in particular, whose popular memory of the atrocities survived well into the 1990s.

Uzbekistan

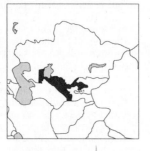

The most populous of the central Asian republics, Uzbekistan has been marked by rampant economic and political corruption benefiting a small elite.

Foreign rule (up to 1991) Geographically and historically at the heart of central Asia, its Uzbek people, who are also the most numerous of central Asian peoples, have tended to consider themselves the leading nation of the area, much to the annoyance of their neighbours. Uzbekistan came under the sovereignty of the Russian Empire in the 1860s and 1870s. It was transformed into a Soviet Republic in 1924, and became formally part of the Soviet Union in 1925. In 1944 the country was forced to accommodate 160,000 Mekhetian Turks expelled by *Stalin from

*Georgia. From the Stalinist era onwards, the country's economy was concentrated on the production of cotton, and until the 1980s it accounted for over two-thirds of the total Soviet cotton production. A further characteristic of the later Soviet era was the endemic corruption of the local party hierarchy.

Under the leadership of the self-styled 'Father of the Nation', Sharav Rashidov (1959–83), production figures of cotton were manipulated to such an extent that in 1978–83 alone around 4.5 million tons of cotton went 'missing'. The full extent of the network of corruption and bribery, which extended to *Brezhnev's son-in-law in Moscow, was only unravelled gradually from the *Andropov years after 1983. Rashidov was found guilty posthumously, while the former Minister of Cotton was sentenced to death. However, the dismissal of most of the party hierarchy and their replacement mostly with Russians led to a nationalist backlash, as Uzbeks felt that foreign rulers were being imposed upon them.

Since independence in 1991 The collapse of the Soviet Union, and external independence on 31 August 1991, led to an extensive search for a unifying cultural identity for a heterogeneous people. While Islam was used as one unifying factor, another was periodic xenophobia, which led to massacres of Mekhetian Turks in 1989. In other ways, some continuity was maintained through the autocratic rule of President Islam A. Karimov (from 1991). The former Communist leader banned virtually all political opposition, and was thus—not surprisingly—re-elected in 1995 and 2000. Karimov's foreign policy focused on greater regional cooperation with his neighbouring republics of Kazakhstan, Kyrgyzstan and Tajikistan, as well as cooperation with Turkey. Meanwhile, his relatively slow programme of economic reform led to a stagnant economy in the 1990s, offering little prospect for the poverty-stricken Uzbeks, over 80 per cent of whom lived below the poverty line.

In 2005, unrest spread in the eastern city of Andijan, which was brutally suppressed. This led to further *human rights violations against the political opposition, whose members were not just imprisoned, but often also tortured. Foreign correspondents left the country in 2005 and 2006 because of safety concerns, while growing foreign criticism led Karimov to expel all Western troops who had used Uzbekistan as a base for their operations in Afghanistan. The corruption and brutality of Karimov's regime not only led to a withdrawal of foreign aid, it also meant that the majority of the population continued to be excluded from the benefits emerging from Uzbekistan's mineral resources.

V2, see BRAUN, WERNHER VON

Vajpayee, Shri Atal Bihari (b. 24 Dec. 1924). Prime Minister of India, 1996, 1998–2004

Early career Born in Gwalior, Madhya Pradesh, he graduated in political science. In 1951 he co-founded the Bharatiya Jana Sangh, and in 1957 he entered the Lok Sabha (parliament). In 1977 he became a founding member of the Janata Party. In 1980 this became the Hindu nationalist *Bharatiya Janata Party (BJP), which opposed the secularism of the dominant *Congress Party. In the 1980s the BJP benefited from the growing weakness of Congress, as well as the increasing religious nationalism through which many Indians came to express their national identity. Vajpayee was Foreign Minister (1977–9), and after the 1996 elections he was asked to form the government as leader of the strongest party. As Prime Minister he was unable to gather sufficient parliamentary support, however, and he was forced to resign after two weeks.

In office The BJP emerged from the 1998 elections with a slightly increased majority, and proceeded to form a minority government under his leadership. His period in office has been marked by a surprising stability, and he was confirmed in office following early elections in 1999. His relationship with neighbouring Pakistan has been marked by repeated military posturing which oscillated with a willingness to negotiate over contentious issues, notably *Kashmir. He was also faced with autonomist unrest in other areas of the country, notably in *Assam and *West Bengal. Encouraged by strong economic growth, he called elections six months early, in 2004, but he suffered a surprise defeat at the hands of Sonia *Gandhi. Although still influential in the party, he gradually withdrew from the leading positions within his party.

Vanuatu

A Pacific state consisting of 82 islands in Melanesia, formerly called the New Hebrides. From the 1860s until the introduction of the *White Australia Policy in 1906, a total of 35,000 islanders were recruited to work on Queensland sugar plantations, where they were introduced to Western civilization. An Anglo-French joint administration was established in 1906, and governed the territory until independence on 3 July 1980.

Vanuatu remained an extremely heterodox country, owing to the existence of 110 different languages and dialects, and an education system divided between French and English schools. In 2000 it emerged that the Prime Minister, Barak Sope of the Melanesian Progressive Party, had benefited from illegal payments from an Asian businessman in return for the award of government contracts. This led to a successful vote of no confidence, which brought to power Edward Natapei, of the Vanuaaku Pari. Natapei lost his majority in 2004 and was replaced by Serge Vohor. After Vohor tried to take up diplomatic relations with Taiwan without consulting his Cabinet, he was forced to resign. He was replaced by Ham Lini.

Vargas, Getúlio (Dornelles) (b. 19 Apr. 1883, d. 24 Aug. 1954). Brazilian Provisional President 1930–4; President 1934–45, 1950–4

Born in the state of Rio Grande do Sul, he practised law before entering state politics in 1908. Elected to the Federal Congress in 1922, he became Minister of Finance in 1926, and returned to his home state to become Governor in 1928. Following a split between the various state oligarchies about how best to respond to the Great *Depression, Vargas was installed as the new provisional President by the military in the coup which ended the First Republic. At first he decided to let the military carry out social and economic reform. Their failure culminated in the secession of the largest state, São Paolo, from the Federation of Brazil. The crisis enhanced Vargas's own role as mediator, and through generous concessions, such as a promise to return to constitutional government and the introduction of female suffrage, he restored federal unity. He was elected President in 1934.

In an emerging age of mass politicization, Vargas continued to exploit the fears and divisions of the elite. After two unsuccessful political coups by the popular left and right wings respectively, both of which he helped to provoke, he frightened the elites into abolishing the new constitution and establishing a dictatorship in 1937–8. His subsequent government until 1945 became known as the Estado Nôvo (New State, after *Salazar's regime in Portugal). He proceeded to rule the country as a benevolent dictator relying on the advice of a number of experts. He modernized the country through centralization, the diversification of agricultural production, and improvements in transport and communication. Vargas also promoted technical education, the implementation of a new labour code, the national ownership of mineral resources and key industries, and the of the expansion of industry. The ultimate pragmatist, he joined World War II on the *Allies' side, fully realizing that under the impact of war, he would soon have to share his power both with the population and the military.

From 1943 he began to encourage participation in state-run *trade unions, and in 1945 he built up a political machine with the foundation of two parties (conservative and labour) designed to appeal to different social groups. This enabled him to win the 1945 elections, but he was removed from office by a military suspicious that he would use this opportunity to begin another long reign. In contrast to his previous ability to be all things to all people, in his second period of office from 1950 he lost his political touch and managed to offend even his loyal supporters. Unable to manage the economy, he tried to quench oppositional activities and in 1954 his guard became involved in an assassination attempt on an opposition journalist. Faced with widespread demands for his resignation, he committed suicide.

Vatican City

A sovereign Roman Catholic bishopric established by the *Lateran Treaties. Its titular head is the Pope as Bishop of Rome, though it is governed in practice by a Cardinal as state secretary. It comprises the area around St Peter's basilica in Rome, a number of churches in Rome, and the papal summer residence in Castel Gandolfo. Although Vatican City is not a member of the European Union, it is tied to Italy in a Customs and Currency Union, and since 1999 its currency has been the *euro.

(()) SEE WEB LINKS

• The official website of the Papacy and the government of Vatican City.

Vatican Council, Second (1962–5)

A conference of all Roman Catholic bishops worldwide called to conclude the disciplinary reforms discussed at the First Vatican Council

(1869–70), and to bring the Church up to date in all matters of teaching and organization, with the ultimate goal of Christian unity. It was convened by Pope *John XXIII and met in four sessions, three of them held under his successor, *Paul VI. Together, it issued sixteen conciliar statements: two on the church, two on priests, and one each on the liturgy, divine revelation, religious life, the laity, the episcopate, missionary work, education, ecumenism, non-Christians, the Eastern Churches, religious freedom, and social communication. Most importantly, they established the *ecumenical dialogue with other Christian denominations, reduced the overbearing weight of the papacy within the Church, and re-emphasized the Church's commitment to peace and social justice.

Velasco Ibarra, José Maria (b. 19 Mar. 1893, d. 30 Mar. 1979). President of Ecuador 1934–5, 1944–7, 1952–6, 1960–1, 1968–72

Born in Quito and educated as a lawyer, he dominated Ecuadorian politics for fifty years. His success was based on his charisma and his populism, which enabled him as a Conservative to appeal to the liberal bourgeoisie, as well as to the petty bourgeoisie and the popular masses, who appreciated the extensive public works he realized. However, he remained at heart a representative of the conservative oligarchy, so that he failed to carry out any meaningful social reforms, attempting to repress left-wing protests against deteriorating living conditions.

Velvet Revolution (1989)

A term used to describe the relatively peaceful transfer of power in Czechoslovakia from the Communist Party to the civil rights movement, which the state had unsuccessfully tried to fight for over a decade. The collapse of *Communism in Poland and Hungary, and the growing popular protests in Eastern Germany, triggered demonstrations against the Czechoslovak regime in Prague and Brno from August to October 1989. Initially, these were repressed, but the state security forces became powerless against the ever-growing number of demonstrators. Leading *human rights activists from *Charter '77 created the Civic Forum on 18 November 1989, in order to coordinate and organize the opposition, and to engage in negotiations with the government. It called a general strike on 27 November, which showed that the old government completely lacked any popular basis. The Communist government collapsed, with the party's political monopoly being withdrawn on

29 November. On 10 December a new government consisting mostly of non-Communists was formed. Subsequently, the two most consistent and respected critics of the Communist regime of the previous two decades were elevated into office: on 28 December *Dubček was elected Speaker of parliament, and on 29 December Havel succeeded *Husák as President. The Velvet Revolution was complete, and was confirmed by the free elections of 8–9 June 1990, in which the Revolution's leaders were endorsed.

Venda, see BANTUSTAN

Venezuela

A South American country whose modern history has been shaped by its wealth in mineral resources.

Early history
Independent since 1830, it plunged into chaos following a bloody civil war (1861–8), and order was not restored until the dictatorship of General Cipriano Castro (1899–1908). He was succeeded by his Vice-President, General Juan Vincente Gómez (b. 1864, d. 1935), whose authoritarian regime lasted until his death. Gómez centralized the power structures at the expense of local elites, encouraged oil exploration from 1917, and established a relatively sound system of public finance. His regime was followed by two increasingly liberal military regimes under General López Contreras (1935–49) and General Isaias Medina Angarita (1940–5). In 1941, Venezuela's first popular political movement, Democratic Action (Acción Democrática, AD), was created. Four years later, the AD managed to take over power with support of the military. In 1948, however, democratization was halted by a military coup led by General M. Pérez Jiménez (b. 1914, d. 2001). He remained in office until 1958, when he was deposed by a coalition of army and civilian forces, which led to the Presidency of the civilian *Betancourt.

Democratic politics (1961–98) The new Constitution of 1961 established what would prove for decades to be one of the most stable democracies of Latin America. An amnesty of 1969 integrated the socialist rebels, while power alternated between the social-democratic AD and the Christian Democrats

(Partido Social-Cristiano, COPEI). The political system was strengthened by the high oil prices of the 1970s, which were of particular benefit to the country with the world's fifth largest proven oil reserves. This led to over-reliance on oil and under-investment in agriculture and other areas, which caused a deep recession with the decline of oil prices during the 1980s.

Government efforts to overcome recession proved insufficient, even though its measures reduced agricultural imports from 74 per cent of domestic consumption (1983) to 20 per cent (1988). In 1989, annual debt servicing amounted to 45 per cent of total export earnings alone. Real wages declined by 38 per cent, 1983–8. In response to its failure to pay its debts, President Carlos Andrés Pérez (1989–93) introduced stringent austerity measures. Amidst growing violence, Hugo *Chávez Frías unsuccessfully staged a coup in 1992. After Pérez's impeachment for corruption in 1993, the former President Rafael Caldera Rodriguez (1969–74, 1994–9) was elected with the support of eighteen parties. Under Rodriguez, poverty increased largely due to the decline of the price of oil on the world markets, which amounted to around 80 per cent of Venezuela's export earnings in 1997.

Contemporary history (since 1998) The demise of traditional politics was sealed in 1998, with the election to the Presidency of *Chávez Fríaz. Chávez declared a fight against corruption in the Venezuelan institutions, and vowed to help the country's poor. He declared the existing constitution bankrupt, and pressured the existing parliament, in which he did not command a majority, into granting him emergency powers. Using popular referendums as an instrument to bypass established institutions, he created a constitutional assembly, in which his supporters commanded an overwhelming majority.

A new Constitution was drawn up and adopted in 1999. It shored up the powers of the President, widened the power of the military, and strengthened the parameters for state intervention in the economy. This coup against the political establishment was accompanied by the destruction of the trade union movement, the limitation of freedom of speech, and the curtailment of the independence of the judiciary. These tumultuous events led to a dramatic decline in foreign direct investment. Despite the recovery of the oil price since 1998, the economy continued to deteriorate, with 80 per cent of the population living in poverty by 2002. Many of the disaffected middle classes supported a coup against Chávez in 2002, but the disorganization and divisions among its leaders, and the dictator's continued support among the urban poor, underpinned his survival.

Having transformed Venezuela's political system, Chávez embarked on social and economic transformation. In 2005, he announced the expropriation of land from large landowners who were not deemed to use it optimally. A year after his re-election to a third term in office in 2006, Chávez announced his intention to stay in office until 2021.

Verdun, Battle of (21 Feb.–16 Dec. 1916) A battle of attrition in *World War I. It was based on a plan of General von Falkenhayn, Chief of the German General Staff, to concentrate the whole weight of his resources against the French fortified city of Verdun. He hoped to bind all French forces to this area, and eventually overcome his opponent through sheer numbers and determination, regardless of the human cost. After the heaviest artillery bombardment to date, and with exceptionally heavy casualties, he captured the forts of Douaumont and Vaux. Nevertheless, under the inspiring leadership of Generals Nivelle and *Pétain, Verdun itself did not fall. Relieved to some extent by the Battle of the *Somme, the French regained their positions through counter-attacks on 24 October and 15 December 1916. While the successful resistance proved to be crucial for French morale, it was another example of the massive human cost of trench warfare in World War I, as around 400,000 Allied and 350,000 German troops lost their lives over a few square miles of land.

Versailles, Treaty of (28 June 1919) The peace treaty between the Allies and Germany after World War I. It formed the centrepiece of the *Paris Peace Conferences. It consisted of 440 Articles in fifteen parts.

Territorial provisions The second and third parts determined its territorial cessions. Moresnet and *Eupen-Malmédy were transferred to Belgium, *Alsace-Lorraine to France, much of upper *Silesia to *Czechoslovakia and (mainly) Poland, western *Prussia and parts of Pomerania to Poland, Memel (Klaipéda) to Allied control (ultimately to *Lithuania), and northern Schleswig to Denmark. These territorial losses were, very loosely, based on the nationality ideal of the *Fourteen Points, whereby regions with national majorities should be united with their mother countries. For strategic reasons, despite their overwhelmingly German population, *Danzig (Gdansk) became a Free City, and the *Saarland was placed under *League of Nations control for fifteen years.

War guilt Germany lost its colonies in part four of the treaty, while part five contained restrictions of its army to 100,000 professional soldiers, and outlawed heavy artillery and possession of an air force. Perhaps most gallingly for the Germans, in Article 231 they had to accept full responsibility for the outbreak of the war. On this basis, Germany was to make *reparations payments, the full extent of which was to be determined later. To ensure that payments would be forthcoming, all territories west of the Rhine (most notably the *Ruhr Valley) were occupied by Allied (mainly French) forces. Altogether, Germany lost 13 per cent of its territory, which had produced 75 per cent of Germany's output in iron ore, 30 per cent of steel, and 28 per cent of coal.

Impact The terms were deeply controversial at the negotiating table and later in public debate, and were criticized in J. M. *Keynes, *The Economic Consequences of the Peace* (1919). Significantly, the US Senate failed to ratify the treaty, so that a separate peace was concluded between the USA and Germany in 1921.

The terms of Versailles were much milder than those demanded by France. Paradoxically, they were both too weak and too strong. They gave Germany an overwhelming sense of resentment, making demands for a revision of the Versailles Treaty the dominant and destabilizing theme of German domestic politics until the rise of *Hitler. At the same time, in marked contrast to Hungary and Austria, the peace treaty left Germany with sufficient potential in time to re-emerge as a significant great power. Germany thus retained the wherewithal to make the treaty's revision a distinct possibility, if necessary by force.

TRIANON, TREATY OF; ST GERMAIN, TREATY OF

Verwoerd, Hendrik Frensch (b. 8 Sept. 1901, d. 6 Sept. 1966). Prime Minister of South Africa 1958–66

Early career Born in Amsterdam (the Netherlands), his family migrated to South Africa in 1903. He studied at Stellenbosch, then in Germany (1925–8), and was appointed professor upon his return to Stellenbosch. His interest in social work led him to become one of the main proponents of (White) social welfare in South Africa. In 1936, he went to the Transvaal to help rebuild the *National Party (NP) organization which had all but collapsed after the 1934 split. He came to work closely with *Strijdom, whose republican convictions he shared. He was defeated in elections to parliament in 1948, but in July became a member of the Senate. A fanatical proponent of *apartheid, who was considered a 'man of vision' on racial segregation by many *Afrikaners, he became Minister for Native Affairs in 1950.

In office In spite of considerable Black opposition, he 'solved' the question of the Black influx to the industrial centres by promoting residential segregation. Other efforts included a law discouraging mixed-race attendance at church services (1957), the creation of Black homelands (*bantustan) such as Transkei, and an Education Act for Blacks (1953). As Prime Minister, he continued to promote segregation, promoting self-government for Black homelands and residential, educational, and political segregation of people of mixed race ('Coloureds'). On 3 February 1960, he responded to *Macmillan's speech to the South African parliament ('The wind of change is blowing through this continent') by stubbornly protesting South Africa's destiny as a 'true White state in Africa'. On 9 April 1960 he miraculously escaped an assassination attempt, and used the subsequent emotions to call a referendum, in which a majority approved his plan for a republic, which he established in 1961. Given the passionate opposition of most *Commonwealth members to apartheid, he withdrew the Republic's application for continued membership in 1961. He was assassinated in parliament.

Vichy Regime (France, 1940–4)

After hostilities broke out between France and Germany in *World War II and German troops advanced in the *Blitzkrieg, *Pétain became the last Prime Minister of the Third Republic on 17 June 1940. He obtained an armistice five days later, which left him in control of two-fifths of French territory in southern France, which he governed from the spa resort of Vichy. Trusting in Pétain as the saviour of France at its darkest hour, and encouraged by the threats of *Laval, the Chamber of Deputies effectively voted itself out of existence. On 10 July 1940, it transferred all powers to Pétain and his new 'État Français'.

Pétain made full use of his dictatorial powers, as he considered the previous republican system, rather than the army, to have been the root cause of France's defeat. With his full support, and under the effective guidance of Laval, the old republican motto 'liberty, equality, and fraternity' was replaced by 'family, country, and work'. In contrast to the Republic's *anticlericalism, the Roman *Catholic Church was given a special role to guide moral regeneration.

In common with other *Fascist regimes, the emphasis on a new national community

included hostility to those who were deemed to be outside, in this case Jews, Protestants, Freemasons, and Republicans. Vichy's *anti-Semitism was the culmination of the anti-Semitism which had been holding together various factions of the French right since the *Dreyfus Affair and beyond. This prepared the ground for active *collaboration in rounding up a quarter of the country's Jewish population (around 76,000) for the *Nazi *concentration camps, in order to win favours from the Germans. Under Pétain's Chief Ministers, Laval (1940, 1942–4) and *Darlan (1940–2), the state became more and more accommodating to the Germans, creating a niche for itself in the new German world order. However, the Vichy regime received few concessions in return.

In November 1942, after the US landing in Morocco to participate in the *North African campaigns, German troops entered the state to secure it against possible invasions from the Mediterranean, which restricted Pétain's and Laval's freedom of action even further. In 1944 the state effectively ceased to exist as the retreating Germans forced Pétain to set up a government-in-exile of the Vichy state in the south German town of Sigmaringen.

Victor Emanuel III (b. 11 Nov. 1869, d. 28 Dec. 1947). King of Italy 1900–46

A figurehead in theory, his position was enhanced by the instability and the frequency of Italian governments before 1922. In 1915, he supported the controversial decision for Italy to enter World War I. In 1922, he refused to heed *Facta's advice to stop *Mussolini through the declaration of martial law, appointing him Prime Minister instead. He continued to support Mussolini even after the *Matteotti Crisis, out of fear of a socialist government. He was against Italian participation in World War II, so that in 1943 he was ready to accept the request of the *Fascist Grand Council to depose Mussolini. As most anti-Fascist parties in the *CLN were opposed to the monarchy, he found himself forced to delegate his royal powers to his son, Umberto, though he did not abdicate until just before the referendum on 2 June 1946, which abolished the monarchy.

Vieira, João Bernardo 'Nino' (b. 1939?). Prime Minister of Guinea-Bissau 1978–80; President 1980–1999, 2005–

Born in Bissau, he became an electrician and joined *Cabral's Partido Africano da Independência da Guiné e de Cabo Verde (PAIGC, African Party for the Independence of Guinea and Cape Verde). He received military training in China and, in the guerrilla war leading up to independence, becoming leader of the southern front in 1964. From 1970 he was in command of all military operations. After independence he became Commander-in-Chief of the armed forces, and in 1978 became Prime Minister. In 1980 he took over the leadership after ousting L. Cabral, and in 1984 established civilian rule, with the PAIGC as the only party allowed. He introduced a series of liberal reforms, but his highly authoritarian rule was only slightly relaxed when he allowed free elections in 1994. He faced a military revolt in 1998, and in a year-long civil war increasingly lost ground to the rebels. In 1999 he conceded defeat and went into exile in Portugal. Although constitutionally barred from re-election, he returned in 2005 and won the elections against the official candidate of the PAIGC.

Vienna Awards (1938, 1940)

Two revisions of the Treaty of *Trianon in Hungary's favour, mediated by the German and Italian Foreign Ministers, *Ciano and *Ribbentrop, in an attempt to draw Hungary closer to the *Axis Powers at a time of growing European tension. The first Vienna Award of 2 November 1938 returned to Hungary the region of Felvidék in southern Slovakia, which had a Magyar-speaking population. By the second Vienna Award of 30 August 1940, Hungary gained some two-thirds of the long-disputed *Transylvania from Romania. Hungary was obliged to return the territorial gains made in both agreements in the *Paris Peace Treaties of 10 February 1947.

Vietcong (Vietnam)

A term used for the military arm of the *National Liberation Front (NLF), or National Front for the Liberation of South Vietnam, founded in 1960. In the early days its activities were restricted to terrorist and increasingly guerrilla warfare, which were organized from its headquarters in Laos. By 1963, when *Ngo Dinh Diem was murdered, the NLF had gained control over the majority of the 2,500 villages in the south. Increasingly the Vietcong became engaged in more formal confrontations with the South Vietnamese army; with the Americanization of the war from 1964, it became militarily more closely allied with General *Giap's forces in the North, from whom its supplies came along the Ho Chi Minh route.

Vietminh

It was formed in 1941 as the League for the Independence of Vietnam by *Ho Chi Minh and other Vietnamese Communist leaders such as *Vo Nguyen Giap in southern China.

Aided by the USA and its Allies, it started its guerrilla activities against the Japanese occupying forces in Vietnam in 1943. It liberated much of North Vietnam and entered Hanoi in August 1945. The Vietminh managed to gather considerable grass-roots support (including nationalists, socialists, Catholics) against a common enemy. However, it came under the increasing control of the Vietnamese (Communist) Workers' Party from 1945. After the *Geneva Agreements (1954), its support continued to grow in South Vietnam. It thus became the model and predecessor for the *National Liberation Front, as well as its military wing, the *Vietcong.

Vietnam

Indochina's most populous and powerful state struggled to overcome the effect of foreign rule until 1975, but it was not until the 1990s that it managed to overcome the legacies of its civil war and its aggression against its neighbours. Since then, Vietnam's economy has grown at up to 10 per cent per annum.

Colonial rule (until 1945) It came under French influence in 1862, when a French naval attack forced the Vietnamese Emperor to concede the southern part of the country, Cochin-China, to colonial control. The French also gained access to the entire country for Catholic missionary activity. Two decades later, France acquired the remaining Vietnamese territory, the historic provinces of Annam and Tonkin (1884). In 1887, France united these territories with Cochin-China and Cambodia to form the Indochinese Union. Laos became part of *Indochina in 1893. Under colonial rule, an infrastructure was developed, while an elite was educated according to French cultural and educational standards. French customs were introduced with mixed success, while the alphabet was Latinized. As a concession to national pride, the Emperor remained, but was subdued as a puppet of the colonial authorities.

A disparate anti-colonial movement began to form during the 1920s, with the Communists, many of whom had been influenced by the *Communist Parties of France and the Soviet Union, emerging as the most effective and cohesive movement. Under instruction from the *Comintern in Moscow,

*Ho Chi Minh founded the Revolutionary Youth League of Vietnam in 1925, from which emerged the Indochinese Communist Party, established in Hong Kong, in 1930. The party only became a dominant force, however, during World War II, when from 1943 the *Vietminh forces, became the central resistance force against Japanese occupation.

By the time the Japanese left in August 1945, the Vietminh coalition was in control of most of the country, enabling Ho Chi Minh to declare an independent Democratic Republic of Vietnam on 2 September 1945. However, the French soon returned and re-established control over the slightly more Francophile Cochin-China in the south. French efforts to reassert control over the rest of Vietnam led to the *Indochina War (1946–54), in which they failed to overcome the popular forces of Ho Chi Minh's armies. In the *Geneva Agreements of 1954, the country was separated into two 'regroupment zones' along the 17th Parallel. This was not intended to become a political border, as elections were to be held in both parts in preparation for reunification in 1956. However, the southern part was now controlled by the resolute anti-Communist, *Ngo Dinh Diem. This meant that two mutually antagonistic political systems and ideologies competed with each other.

South Vietnam (1949–1960s) South Vietnam, which from 1949 was officially called the Associated State of Vietnam, was established as a member of the *French Union, under the Presidency of *Bao Dai. Given its subservience to the French, which was greatly exacerbated due to the Indochina War, the state never gained widespread acceptance at the grass roots. In 1954, after the Geneva Agreements, it was officially renamed the Republic of Vietnam, under the leadership of Ngo Dinh Diem. He established a dictatorship which managed to instil some discipline into a government and administration otherwise riven with conflict and factionalism. This did little to endear him to the majority of the population, particularly as he never carried out the land reform that he had promised. Around 2 per cent of the population continued to control around 45 per cent of the cultivated land. He was weakened considerably by the continued growth of the Communist movement in his own country, and the active attempt by the Communist north to undermine his government with the foundation of the *National Liberation Front and the *Vietcong from 1960. These tensions erupted into the *Vietnam War, which the South lost despite heavy US involvement.

North Vietnam (1945–75) North Vietnam (Democratic Republic of Vietnam) was ruled by the Indochinese Communist Party (Vietnamese Workers' Party from 1951) since its creation in 1946. Despite its authoritarian leadership structures, it managed to gain the support of the majority of the population. The party was seen as the liberator from foreign rule, as the organizer of a land reform (from 1955) which ended drastic inequalities in land ownership, and as the organization of the revered 'Uncle Ho' (Chi Minh). Moreover, the party was able to consolidate its position in state and society through the active economic and military support of the Soviet Union and, from 1949, Communist China. Ultimately, it was the party's widespread popular support that ensured success in the Indochina War, and later in the Vietnam War. Despite their military superiority the French and then the US troops were unable to identify the enemy, as Communist fighters were shielded by the civilian population. In addition, to most Vietnamese these wars became wars of liberation in their own country. As a result, the Vietnamese were prepared to suffer much higher casualties than the French or the USA, whose interest in the war was never clear-cut, and at best indirect. Thus, North Vietnam emerged victorious in the war, though not without heavy losses, including around 700,000 civilian casualties and the destruction of 45 per cent of the towns, 75 per cent of industrial capacity, and 25 per cent of agricultural production. The USA withdrew after the *Paris Peace Accords of 1973, while South Vietnam struggled on until the fall of *Saigon on 30 April 1975. Thereafter Vietnam was finally reunited, under Communist leadership.

United Vietnam (since 1975) The Socialist Republic of Vietnam was proclaimed on 7 July 1976. The hardline leadership of *Le Duan failed to integrate the two halves, with their different economic, social, religious, and cultural traditions. He encouraged instead the emigration of around one million of the wealthy and skilled population of the south (many of whom were of Chinese origin) as the epitome of *capitalism. The integration of the country was also fundamentally hampered by Le Duan's foreign ambitions, which aimed at making Vietnam a major regional power in competition with China. Thus, the country's rich resources were squandered on further warfare. Its unusual alliance with both China and the Soviet Union gave way to intense rivalry with the former and intense dependence on the latter. Vietnam's forces invaded Kampuchea (Cambodia) (1978–9) and installed a puppet regime there. Vietnam's continued abrasiveness towards China led to a brief but fierce military conflict, in which China engaged in a punitive invasion of its border territories in February 1979.

As a result of persisent warfare, the economy collapsed in the late 1970s, and was given little space to recover in subsequent years. After Le Duan's death in 1986, the reformist wing of the Communist Party gained control over party and state with the accession of *Nguyen Van Linh. He withdrew the Vietnamese army from Cambodia in 1989, and created a climate for restored relations with China, culminating in a non-aggression pact in 1993. Economic growth was actively encouraged, with a law allowing joint ventures with foreign companies being passed in 1988.

In 1992 the new Constitution declared a transition to a market economy as the official aim of the state, while the control of the party was slightly diminished through the separation of office between party leader and head of state. The latter office was filled in that year by General Le Duc Anh, who normalized relations with the USA. The two countries took up diplomatic relations on 5 August 1995. During the presidency of Trân Duc Luong (1997–2001), Bill *Clinton in 2000 became the first US President to visit Vietnam.

Contemporary history (since 1997) Vietnam was less affected by the Asian economic crisis that set in in 1997 than many of its neighbours, not least because its economy had been less exposed to cheap credit. According to the UN Development Programme, Vietnam has been spectacularly successful at reducing the number of people living below the poverty line, from 58 per cent in 1993, to 29 per cent in 2003. With the election of the reformist Nong Duc Manh as general secretary in 2001, the Communist Party confirmed its commitment to market liberalization. At the same time, it improved its relations with China and Russia, in an effort to promote its financial and security concerns. Nong Duc Manh was reappointed in 2006, with Nguyen Minh Triet succeeding Trân Duc Luong to the presidency. In 2007, Vietnam became the 150th member of the *WTO.

Vietnam War (1964–75)

Origins The *Geneva Agreements, which ended the first *Indochina War in 1954, failed to create a united Vietnam. Instead of reunification, which had been planned for 1956, the north continued to be governed by the Communist government of *Ho Chi Minh, who received support from the USSR and China, while the south was ruled by the

violently anti-Communist *Ngo Dinh Diem, with increasing US support. In 1959, the Communist government formally decided to undermine Ngo's government, through strengthening the *Vietminh agents there, and through the creation of the *National Liberation Front in 1960. Under the influence of the *domino theory, the USA feared the spread of *Communism throughout Asia at a time when the *Cold War was at its peak. In response to growing Communist guerrilla activities in South Vietnam, the *Kennedy administration decided to send more US troops as military advisers. Numbering around 2,000 by the time he took office in January 1961, Kennedy increased their presence to over 16,000 in 1963.

The course of the war (1963–9) North Vietnamese strategists led by *Vo Nguyen Giap mistakenly assumed that growing attacks against the south would weaken US resolve to assist the government of Ngo Dinh Diem and his successor, *Nguyen Van Thieu. Instead, after the *Tonkin Gulf Resolution of 1964, President *Johnson authorized direct US involvement in the confrontation, which now escalated into a full-scale war. During the height of the war (1965–8), US troops involved rose from 125,000 to around 550,000 in 1967. These troops were complemented by a South Vietnamese army, with similar numbers, and smaller contingents from South Korea, Thailand, Australia, New Zealand, and the Philippines.

Aided by vastly superior technology, particularly in the air, the USA was able to achieve military superiority over the North Vietnamese forces, numbering around 200,000 (including South Vietnamese guerrilla forces), by 1968. Given the *Vietcong's support among the population, which allowed it to escape and hide easily, the USA never managed to control the countryside. Continued attacks against military bases or troops inflicted heavy casualties. The *Tet offensive fuelled even further popular opposition to US involvement in the war. In fact, the sight of thousands of bodybags containing dead soldiers aroused such opposition to the war that *Johnson started negotiations for a peace settlement in 1968. Despite a unique legislative record in domestic politics, Johnson was unable to win even the *primary elections because of his identification with the war.

'Peace with honour' (since 1969) *Nixon was duly elected on a platform of 'peace with honour'. In practice, this led to the resumption of large-scale US bombings, the spraying of napalm gas and 'agent orange' against Vietcong bases in the Mekong delta, and military offensives on the ground. The USA also focused on training the South Vietnamese army in order to make it more self-reliant. Eventually, the USA gratefully accepted the *Paris Peace Accords and disengaged from the war in 1973. The war continued until the fall of *Saigon in 1975, when the last US military advisers left the country. The war had a fundamental effect on US society, as a hitherto confident superpower was defeated by a small, underdeveloped Communist country. The US was also traumatized by the memory of over 50,000 dead, and the brutality of a war that left hundreds of thousands physically or mentally injured.

Villa, Francisco 'Pancho' (b. 5 June 1878, d. 20 July 1923). Mexican revolutionary
A latter-day Robin Hood of the Mexican Revolution, his original name was Doroteo Arango. Together with *Zapata he joined *Madero in his resistance against *Díaz, whom they defeated in 1911. Following Madero's assassination in 1913, however, he soon broke with the moderate leader of the 'constitutional' army, *Carranza, and returned north to establish a stronghold in the state of Chihuahua. There, he expropriated the landowners and used their revenues to equip his army, with which he returned in 1914 to join Zapata in the occupation of Mexico City. He ceased to be a threat to the national government when his troops were decisively defeated in 1915 by those of Carranza, which were led by General *Obregón. In 1916, his attack on the US town of Columbus, New Mexico, provoked a US -military intervention under General *Pershing. He retired in 1920, and was assassinated in 1923.

Vimy Ridge, Battle of (9–14 Apr. 1917)
A ridge, lying north-east of Arras in France. It had been occupied by the Germans at the beginning of *World War I (1914) and had long resisted French attacks. On 9 April, Canadian troops under Lieutenant-General Julian Byng, launched a massive artillery barrage and then attacked with four divisions. They took 'Hill 145' and then gained the long ridge itself, capturing 4,000 German prisoners. In holding the ridge for the next few days, casualties mounted, reaching one in ten of the 100,000 Canadian troops involved. It became a key defensive position against the German offensive on Arras and Amiens in March 1918.

Virgin Islands of the United States
The larger part of the Caribbean Virgin Island group consisting of some 60 islands, they were under Danish sovereignty until they were bought by the USA in 1916 for $25,000,000.

Their residents became US citizens in 1927, and a civilian administration took over from the US navy in 1931. Defined by a 1936 Organic Act as an 'unincorporated territory' of the USA, their inhabitants have consistently opposed greater independence for fear of economic decline. In 1972 they were granted a Deputy in the US House of Representatives, albeit without the right to vote. Their economy has continued to be heavily reliant on the United States and its dependent territories.
BRITISH VIRGIN ISLANDS

Vittorio Veneto, Battle of (World War I) (24 Oct. – 3 Nov. 1918)
The town of Vittorio Veneto in north-eastern Italy is named after Victor Emanuel II, in whose reign Venetia had been gained from Austria. Following the humiliating Italian defeat at *Caporetto during the summer of 1918 the *Austro-Hungarian armies were gradually forced to retreat from their gains. Finally in October, Italian forces under General Diaz, supported by a British force under Lord Cavan, broke the enemy line by separating the Austrians in the mountains from those on the plains. It was a decisive victory, resulting in 30,000 killed on the Austrian side, and 427,000 taken prisoner. It resulted in the immediate Austrian request for an armistice on 3 November.

Vo Nguyen Giap (b. 1912). Vietnamese general
Born in An Xa (Quang Binh Province, central Vietnam) and educated at Hue and the French University of Hanoi, he joined the Revolutionary Party of Young Vietnam (Tan Viet) in 1926 while still a student. Arrested upon joining the Indochinese Communist Party in 1930, he gained parole in 1932 and took a doctorate in economics in 1937. He became a history teacher until he was re-arrested in 1939. He managed to escape to China, though his wife died in prison and his sister was executed. With *Ho Chi Minh he co-founded the forerunner of the *Vietminh in March 1941, and returned to Vietnam to organize the resistance movement against Japanese occupation. He became commander of the Armed Propaganda Brigade, a forerunner of the Vietnamese Liberation Army.
Vo Nguyen Giap became the chief military leader of the Vietminh forces both during the *Indochina War, and in the *Vietnam War. As such, he successfully developed the strategy of clandestine guerrilla warfare against a technically superior enemy. As Minister of Defence of the Democratic Republic of Vietnam and Commander-in-Chief of its

armed forces, he was responsible for the battle of *Dien Bienh Phu and the *Tet Offensive of 1968. He was Minister of Defence and Deputy Prime Minister of the Socialist Republic of Vietnam from 1976 until he was dropped from the party's leadership (*Politburo) in 1982.

Vojvodina

A part of *Austria-Hungary from 1699, this territory half the size of the Netherlands became the home of twenty-four national groups. In the Treaty of *St Germain, most of its area became part of *Serbia, though a small part came to be part of Romania. Occupied by German and Hungarian troops in World War II, it became part of Serbia again in 1945, though with autonomous status from 1946. Following demonstrations against Serbia, its autonomy was lifted in 1990, so that it became an integral part of Serbia again, ruled directly from Belgrade. While Serbians just formed the majority of the population (55 per cent), their proportion increased, to the protests of the other nationalities, during the *Bosnian Civil War and the military conflict with Croatia (1992–5), when tens of thousands of Krajina Serbs, who had fled from Croatian rule, were settled there.

Vorster, Balthazar Johannes (b. 13 Dec. 1915, d. 10 Sept. 1983). Prime Minister of South Africa 1966–78; President 1978–9

Early career Born in Jamestown, he studied at Stellenbosch, where he attended *Verwoerd's lectures on sociology. Active for the *National Party (NP) from the 1930s, he became a lawyer and moved to Port Elizabeth, where he became a leading party member and an activist for *Afrikaner *nationalism. A committed republican, he was interned for seventeen months for his opposition to the war effort, 1942–3. He moved to Brakpan (Transvaal), but was not elected to parliament until 1953, when he was also admitted to the Johannesburg Bar. As Deputy Minister of Education, Arts, and Science from 1958, he handled Verwoerd's controversial extension of the University Education Act, which provided for racial segregation at university level. As Minister of Justice from 1961, he commended himself through his toughness in dealing with the unrest caused by the *ANC, *PAC, and the outlawed *Communist Party in the wake of the *Sharpeville Massacre. Leading activists were placed under house arrest, and the Criminal Procedure Act allowed the detention of any person without trial for 180 days.

In office Vorster was the first South African Prime Minister (apart from *Smuts in 1945–8) to allow a relaxation of *apartheid, however moderate, through the discouragement of 'petty apartheid'. In consequence, he allowed sports competitions between teams of different races, and eventually also allowed mixed-race teams. Gradually, a small number of restaurants and other public amenities for other races opened up in White areas. However, as the *Soweto riots of 1976 showed, his attempts to improve race relations failed owing to his unwillingness to change the essence of apartheid, racial segregation. He sought to overcome the country's increasing isolation through improving relations with its African neighbours and the *UN in general, e.g. by accepting the international status of South-West Africa (Namibia). The South African military intervention in Angola from 1975 foiled any international sympathy South Africa might have gained from this. Ill health forced him to retire in 1978 and accept the ceremonial post of President. He was forced to resign from the presidency after eight months in office owing to his former involvement in alleged irregularities in the Department of Information.

Voting Rights Act, see CIVIL RIGHTS ACTS

Vyshinsky, Andrei Yanuarievich (b. 10 Dec. 1883, d. 22 Nov. 1954). Soviet state prosecutor 1935–9

Born in Odessa of Polish descent, he joined the *Mensheviks in 1903 and became a student of law at Kiev University. He joined the *Red Army in the *Russian Civil War, and the *Bolshevik Party in 1920. He became professor of law at Moscow University, whose Rector he became in 1925. In subsequent years he became a noted prosecutor in political trials against *Stalin's opponents. In 1935–9, he was state prosecutor of the USSR, in which capacity he was chief agent of Stalin's *Great Purge. He held that a prisoner's guilt was absolute once a confession had been made, regardless of the conditions in which the confession was obtained. He was *Molotov's Deputy People's Commissar (later Minister) of Foreign Affairs (1940–9), and advanced to become Foreign Minister in Stalin's last years (1949–53), but was demoted under *Khrushchev to become Soviet representative at the *UN (1953–4).

Wafd (al-Wafd al-Misri) (Egypt)

Egypt's main nationalist party was founded in 1923 by *Saghlul Sa'd, after he had led an unsuccessful delegation (wafd) to demand independence from the *British Empire after World War I. It won an overwhelming election victory in the 1923 elections for the Chamber of Deputies, though it was consistently opposed by King *Fuad, who at first refused to appoint a Wafdist government. However, the party continued to thrive with overwhelming electoral support. Tight parliamentary organization under its leader from 1927, al-*Nahhas, increased its strength further. It finally came to power briefly in 1929, but was soon affected by divisions over its response to the Great *Depression. Although primarily opposed to British rule, it spent most of its energy on its incessant feuds with the King, even to the point of contradicting its principles in 1941, when it returned to government with the help of the British. In power, the party was weakened by corruption, and thus unable to respond to Egypt's growing domestic political instability. It was dismissed from power in 1952, six months before King *Farouk was deposed by *Nasser.

Waffen-SS, see SS

Wahabism

An *Islamic movement which developed during the eighteenth century in central Arabia, providing a rigorous, puritanical interpretation of *Sunni teaching. During the nineteenth century Wahabis were persecuted by the Ottoman Turks, which made them very receptive to the uprising of *Abd al-Aziz ibn Saud against the Ottoman Empire. Ibn Saud broke with them in 1929, however, fighting against them to assert his authority. Nevertheless, a large number of Wahabis continue to live in Saudi Arabia, while Wahabi *mujahidin have been fierce participants in the Afghan Civil War since 1979.

Waitangi, Treaty of (6 Feb. 1840)

A document which defined the relationship between the *Maori and European settlers, and which enabled the British colonization of New Zealand. It was drawn up rather hastily, owing to pressure from the settlers who wanted to develop the land and increase immigration to develop a self-sustaining British colony. As a result, there were many inconsistencies between various versions, including the Maori and English versions, whose different interpretations have been at the heart of the disputes between Maoris and other New Zealanders ever since. The treaty contained three articles.

1. Maori chiefs agreed to accept the sovereignty (in the Maori text: 'governorship') of the English Queen.

2. In return, Maoris were guaranteed the full possession of (in the Maori text: 'chieftainship over') their lands. The Queen would have 'exclusive rights of pre-emption' over lands Maoris wished to sell.

3. Maoris were to have the same rights as British subjects (even though British subjects were not subject to a pre-emption clause).

Despite the refusal of a few chiefs to sign, the British representative, William Hobson, proclaimed sovereignty over all of New Zealand on 21 May 1840. During the second half of the twentieth century, there were growing debates about the legality of the treaty, and to what extent White rule over New Zealand was established through cession, proclamation, or occupation.

WAITANGI TRIBUNAL

Waitangi Tribunal (New Zealand)

A court established in 1976, to which all violations of *Maori rights as defined by the Treaty of *Waitangi were referred. However, it could only decide on violations of the treaty committed after the establishment of the tribunal in 1976. Maori protests continued until the tribunal became vastly more effective in 1985, when it was given power to judge retrospectively on all Maori land claims since the original treaty of 1840. It gave the Maoris a powerful instrument of redress, and enabled them to be heard successfully in their claims for rights of landownership, as well as for fishing rights. Indeed, their success in reversing government legislation in the past, or amending government legislation in the present, became an embarrassment to the government among its White (Pakeha) constituency.

In 1990 the government felt compelled to reassert its 'right to govern' as established by the Treaty of Waitangi, which was ultimately paramount over any Maori land claim. Nevertheless, Maori pressure continued, so that on 22 May 1995 the government for the first time returned land to the largest Maori group of the Tainui, as well as paying compensation of NZ$170 million. The tribunal is composed equally of Maori and Pakeha staff, and promotes conciliation and negotiation. Its first concern is to establish the historical circumstances of the claim. It will issue a recommendation only if the two parties fail to reach agreement on a claim. The Waitangi Tribunal has gone to great lengths to be accepted by both Maori and Pakeha communities, but insufficient government funding has diminished its effectiveness.

LAND CLAIMS (AUSTRALIA); LAND CLAIMS (NATIVE), CANADA

Waldheim, Kurt (b. 21 Dec. 1918). President of Austria 1986–91

Born near Vienna, he attended the university there before and after World War II, in which he served as a young staff officer on the Eastern Front. There, he was involved in military activities resulting in the deportation of Jews and the shooting of Yugoslav partisans. He entered the Austrian foreign service from university and was Foreign Minister (1968–70), before being elected successor to U *Thant at the *UN. His period in office (1972–81) was at a time when the Security Council was regularly deadlocked, so that his efforts at international conciliation seldom succeeded, for example over the *Iran hostage crisis, over Namibia, and in the Middle East.

After Waldheim announced his candidacy for the Austrian Presidency, his wartime record was severely criticized by the World Jewish Congress, since when the precise nature of his involvement in the *Nazi atrocities, and his responsibility for them, has aroused heated discussion. Particularly his refusal to admit his complicity in the murder of Yugoslav *partisans as an officer of the German army, in the face of photographic evidence, caused an international outcry. He stuck to his candidacy, however, and was elected with a clear majority. Despite his diplomatic status, he suffered several humiliations and was barred as a war criminal from visiting the USA. He refrained from standing for a second period in office. The Waldheim affair was a major landmark in the way Austrians considered their past. The legitimacy of postwar Austria had been founded on the idea that it had been Hitler's 'first victim' when it was 'conquered' in the *Anschluss. Henceforth this became harder to sustain, as the enthusiasm with which many Austrians had supported *Hitler and his *anti-Semitism became subject to international scrutiny.

Wales

Early history (up to 1914) A constituent part of the *United Kingdom, which has been under English rule since the thirteenth century, and linked to England since the Acts of Union of 1536 and 1542. A cultural revival in the eighteenth century was reinforced by the spread of Nonconformity, which became an integral part of Welsh identity. Consequently, at the beginning of the twentieth century, the position of the (minority) *Anglican Church as the established Church of Wales became an important political issue, until a disestablishment bill was passed in 1914. Its implementation was delayed by the outbreak of World War I, so that the Church of Wales was not disestablished until 31 March 1920. Many of the funds released by this went towards the establishment of the University of Wales and other institutions.

Contemporary history (1920–97) Over-reliant on Wales's position as the world's leading exporter of coal, its economy experienced a sharp decline after World War I. This led to steady emigration to mining areas in England, and to further afield, predominantly to the USA and parts of the *Commonwealth. This period also experienced a sharp decline in the Welsh language, which virtually ceased to be spoken as a first language in the industrial south. After World War II, the British government in Westminster made further concessions to Welsh distinctiveness. A National Council for Wales was established (1949), and a Minister for Welsh Affairs has been appointed since 1951 (as Secretary of State since 1964).

Among parts of the population (especially in the predominantly Welsh-speaking north-west), demands for greater political autonomy grew, expressing themselves in their most radical form in terrorist attacks against English-owned property. The growth of nationalist sentiment expressed itself in the revival of the Welsh language, and in increased support for *Plaid Cymru, which won its first seat in parliament in 1966. However, in a referendum on 1 March 1979, a Welsh Assembly and greater autonomy were rejected by 956,330, with 243,048 in favour. Concern with the Welsh cultural identity continued, and led to the creation of a Welsh-language television channel in 1982.

Contemporary politics (since 1997) Support for autonomy only grew slowly, because the cultural and social differences between north and south Wales stood in the way of united demands for Home Rule. Owing to the influence of its Scottish membership, the

British *Labour Party became committed to devolution during the 1990s. Following its election victory in 1997, Labour offered Wales a limited form of autonomy, with a Welsh Assembly without taxraising powers. A referendum in 1997 approved this with a narrow majority of 50.3 per cent. In 1999, the first Welsh Assembly was elected, with the Labour Party becoming the strongest party, and Plaid Cymru coming second. Labour formed a minority administration under its First Minister, Alun Michael. Michael never enjoyed the full support of his party, however, and he was replaced in 2000 with Rhodri Morgan, who entered a coalition with the *Liberal Democrats. The new administration continued to be challenged by the country's north-south divide. It was committed to improving the weak infrastructure between north and south, and to assisting the deprived areas in much of rural Wales. At the same time, the south benefited hugely from Cardiff's new capital status, with many public sector jobs and private investment developing in the area. In 2007, Morgan lost the elections, though Labour remained the strongest party in the assembly.

Wałęsa, Lech (b. 19 Sept. 1943). President of Poland 1990–5

Trade union leader Born in Popovo, he became an electrician and worked at the Lenin shipyard in Gdansk (*Danzig). He became the leader of the *Solidarność (Solidarity) movement in September 1980, and was imprisoned following the imposition of martial law on 13 December 1981. Released in November 1982, he remained the symbol of popular opposition to Communist rule, and in 1983 received the *Nobel Peace Prize. The Communist Party was finally forced to legalize the outlawed Solidarność in 1989, whose membership grew rapidly to become ten million strong. Increasing quarrels with his erstwhile protégé, Tadeusz Mazoviecki (b. 1927), who was elected Prime Minister on 24 August 1989, split the movement when Wałęsa decided to stand for the presidency against him.

Presidency The first freely elected President of Poland for fifty years, in his controversial term of office he sought to strengthen the presidency at the expense of parliament and thus personally brought down at least two of the six Prime Ministers who served under him. A devout Catholic, he also aimed to safeguard the role of the Roman *Catholic Church in state and society. Uneducated and inarticulate (by his own admission), his recovery from an approval rate of just 5 per cent in 1994 was not sufficient to ensure his re-election against the ex-Communist *Kwasniewski in 1995. He stood again in

2000, but performed dismally in the polls. He was described by his former ally, A. Michnik, thus: 'His power lies in his ability to destroy. His tragedy lies in his inability to build.' He was responsible more than any other person for the collapse of Polish Communism. As President he encouraged economic liberalization and market reforms, though he failed to bring stability to Poland's young democracy.

Wall Street Crash (Black Thursday)
(24 Oct. 1929)

In the USA, the introduction of new technologies of production, such as the assembly line, and the return of war loans led to an overall increase in the standard of living, as well as a dramatic increase in the inequality of income distribution. A relatively small proportion of the population could afford new items of consumer culture, which resulted in unsustainable overproduction and overconfidence in the economy. This led to careless investments and an exaggeration of share values, and the resulting speculative 'bubble' was fuelled by a policy of low interest rates pursued by the *Federal Reserve System.

The bubble burst on Black Thursday, when panic gripped investors who rushed to sell their shares. The value of industrial shares halved in only two months, though the slide continued until July 1932, when their value was around 15 per cent of their peak in 1929. This triggered the Great *Depression, in which US unemployment rose from 1.5 million in 1929 to over twelve million (around 25 per cent) in July 1932. The effects of the crash spread very quickly throughout the world. The rest of the world was heavily dependent on the USA, which produced over 40 per cent of all industrial goods. Moreover, US investors sought to make up for the capital shortage through the immediate withdrawal of US investments and loans abroad. The resulting financial and economic collapse was felt deeply throughout Europe and around the world. It dramatically accelerated a worldwide economic slump that contributed materially to the advent of *Nazism and *Fascism in much of Europe during the 1930s.

Wallace, George Corley (b. 25 Aug. 1919, d. 13 Sept 1998). Governor of Alabama 1963–7, 1971–9, 1983–7

Born in Clio into a farming family, he graduated from the University of Alabama Law School (1942) and, after military service, became a state attorney. In 1947 he was elected an Alabama State Congressman and then a District Justice (1953–8). When first elected Governor of Alabama in 1962 he resisted the desegregation of state schools and universities.

In his 1963 inaugural speech, he famously declared that he stood for 'segregation now, segregation tomorrow, segregation forever'. Unable to run for a second consecutive period in office, he was succeeded in the Governor's office by his wife, Lurleen. He stood in the presidential campaign of 1968 as leader of the newly established American Independent Party. His main support was in the south, and he polled over ten million votes. In 1972 he sought the *Democratic Party's presidential nomination, but his campaign ended when an assassination attempt left him paralysed. He stood again unsuccessfully in 1976, by which time he was becoming reconciled to civil rights for African Americans. For the 1982 election as Governor he publicly recanted his opposition to desegregation, polled a substantial number of Black votes, and was re-elected. He retired from politics in 1987 through ill health.

Wallenberg, Raoul (b. 1912, d. 17 July 1947?). Swedish diplomat

Born into a family of financiers, he graduated from the University of Michigan in 1935, and established a Swedish export business together with K. Lauer, a Hungarian Jew. Given the nature of the business, he often travelled to German-occupied Europe. In 1944, after the Nazi occupation of Hungary, he took action to try and save the Jewish population there from near-certain death in the *Nazi *concentration camps. Through the Swedish legation at Budapest, he designed a special passport and set up 30 'e' houses whose residents were covered by diplomatic immunity. Through his contacts, bribery, and his sheer personality he managed to persuade the Germans to leave the houses untouched. Directly or indirectly, he thus saved the lives of over 30,000 Jews. When Soviet troops occupied Hungary, he was taken to their army headquarters, and disappeared. His whereabouts have attracted continued speculation. In May 1996 it emerged that, while in Budapest, he had also been supplying US intelligence through the Swedish embassy about the state of the Hungarian resistance movement. Consequently, he had been arrested by the USSR as a US spy, which both the USA and Sweden had denied in embarrassment. He became an honorary citizen of the USA, Canada, and Israel *in absentia*, and a tree in Jerusalem's 'avenue of the righteous' commemorates his courage and sacrifice for the Jewish people. In 2001, a Swedish–Russian team of historians accepted that he was most probably shot by the *NKVD.

Wallis-et-Futuna

A group of Pacific islands between *Tuvalu, *American Samoa, and *Fiji. Under French colonial rule since 1842, it became an Overseas Territory with limited rights of self-government in 1961. Since then, it has sent one representative to the French

National Assembly, and one to the Senate, while internal matters have been largely settled by its indigenous kings.

Wannsee Conference, see CONCENTRATION CAMPS

War Measures Act (Canada)

A statute of 1914 which allowed the federal government to govern by decree whenever it was faced with 'war, invasion or insurrection, real or apprehended', thus severely curtailing civil liberties. It was enforced during both World Wars, and to a limited degree during the *Korean War. More controversially, it was invoked by *Trudeau in 1970, in response to kidnappings by the *Front de Libération du Québec.

War on Terrorism

Origins The response by the administration of George W. *Bush on the attacks of *September 11. Immediately after the attacks, Bush declared that this constituted an act of war. Recognizing the international background of the attackers, however, the war was not directed specifically against one particular country. Instead, the war was to be waged against any country harbouring terrorists. It was on this basis that Afghanistan became the first nation to be targeted by the US. The US supported the *Northern Alliance troops by pounding the ruling *Taliban regime which harboured the *al-Qaeda network with bombs. Once the Taliban were destroyed, the US sent elite troops to pursue al-Qaeda fighters in the mountains and caves of the Afghan interior, though by winter 2002 al-Qaeda's leader, Osama *Bin Laden, had not been captured.

The War on Terrorism allowed the huge mobilization of US resources that previous campaigns had been unable to muster. It lent itself to language that captured the moral high ground, though this could backfire, for instance in Bush's ill-judged reference to a 'crusade' against an 'axis of evil', with its connotations of religious warfare. The War on Terrorism also allowed the US to define its aims flexibly and adjust them pragmatically to the current military and political situation.

Problems The War on Terrorism contained a number of serious problems. (1) Since terrorism was by its nature without established, visible structures, it was impossible to define. This meant that the war aims were elusive, and that the war could in theory be carried on forever. (2) From the start, Bush struggled to define where the War on Terrorism would go after Afghanistan. In early 2002, the Bush administration extended the rhetorical War on Terrorism to Saddam *Hussein of Iraq, but this proved very divisive amongst America's allies. (3) As shown by the examples of Uzbekistan, Kazakhstan, and Tadjikistan, the War on Terrorism relied on assistance from dictatorial regimes whose values were themselves not far removed from the aims of terrorists. (4) The War on Terrorism relied on Afghan anti-Taliban war lords. These maintained their power through money generated from harvesting opium. This rendered the US virtually powerless to prevent the harvesting of a bumper crop of opium in 2002. (5) The War on Terrorism elevated captured al-Qaeda fighters at least potentially to prisoner-of-war status, which the US sought to deny.

Despite these problems, President Bush remained hugely popular throughout his first term in office. In his second term beginning in 2005, this popularity waned. This process began with Hurricane *Katrina, but was underlain by his inability to pacify Iraq following the *Iraq War. Bush also struggled to keep detained terrorist suspects in *Guantanamo Bay away from the reach of the *Supreme Court, while covert *CIA missions to detain terrorist suspects in Europe and fly them to Guantanamo generated a hostile response from the *European Parliament in 2006.

War Powers Act (USA, 1973)
A US law designed to constrain the President in his war-making powers independent of *Congress. It followed upon public outcry after the Gulf of *Tonkin incident, and the subsequent actions of US Presidents. Enacted over the veto of President *Nixon, it provides that Congress should be informed within 48 hours of any overseas military activity. Congress should endorse any military action overseas by the USA within 60 days, after which it may order withdrawal without the option of a presidential veto.

Ward, Sir Joseph George (b. 26 Apr. 1856, d. 8 July 1930). Premier (Prime Minister from 1907) of New Zealand 1906–12, 1928–30

Early career Born in Melbourne, his family arrived in New Zealand in 1860. He became a successful grain merchant and entered local politics, becoming Mayor of Campbelltown (1881–5, 1896–7). He entered parliament in 1887, and because of his administrative skills he soon entered government as Postmaster-General (1891–6). As Colonial Treasurer (1893–6), he advocated public works and financial assistance to farmers through cheap loans. He retired from political life in 1897 because of the collapse of his business, but he was immediately re-elected and in 1899 he became Colonial Secretary (Internal Affairs) and Minister of Trade and Customs, and in 1900 Minister of Railways. He continued to push for improved communications throughout the *British Empire, and in 1901 realized the universal penny postage in New Zealand. He was instrumental in the creation of the world's first government department of public health, of which he became a minister in 1901. He was also responsible for the creation of public-sector pensions in 1902.

In office Ward succeeded *Seddon in 1906 as Prime Minister, becoming also Minister of Defence, as well as retaining the office of Postmaster-General. He continued Seddon's policies of social reform, creating a sickness and old-age insurance fund in 1910, drawing up a workers' dwelling Act, and providing for widows' pensions. He raised the country's financial contribution to the British navy in the developing European arms race, and introduced compulsory military training for young men in 1910. However, in the 1911 elections the resurgence of the opposition and *Massey's organization of farming interests ended the long predominance of his *Liberal Party, and he resigned in 1912 to become leader of the opposition. In the national government during World War I, he became Deputy Prime Minister and Finance Minister, proving particularly adept at raising and repaying loans to finance the war. He lost his seat in the 1919 elections, but returned to parliament in 1925, and in 1928 became leader of the United Party, which had emerged from the Liberals. He became Prime Minister again, with the support of the *Labour Party. He tried in vain to alleviate the sufferings caused by the Great *Depression through active state intervention, and resigned owing to ill health on 15 May 1930.

warlords
A term used to describe the leaders of personal armies throughout China. They dominated China from the collapse of central government after *Yuan Shikai's death in

1916, until the establishment of the *National Government through *Chiang Kai-shek's *Northern Expedition. Warlords usually had control over an area commensurate with their military strength, which enabled them to collect taxes and control other resources, such as manpower or food production. Most of them were either defeated in the Northern Expedition, or they accepted Chiang's leadership; as Chiang was dependent upon their support, they retained considerable authority in their own localities.

Warren, Earl (b. 19 Mar. 1891, d. 19 July 1974). Chief Justice of the US Supreme Court 1953–69

One of the most liberal Chief Justices, who presided over the *Supreme Court's refashioning of US civil rights in the 1960s. Born in Los Angeles as the son of a Californian railroad worker, he obtained a BA from the University of California in 1912, gained his JD in 1914, and was also awarded an LL D in that year. He became Attorney-General of California (1938) and then Governor in 1943 (until 1952). In 1948 Thomas E. Dewey chose him to serve as his Republican vice-presidential candidate. In 1953 *Eisenhower appointed him Chief Justice in the expectation that he would be a moderate conservative influence on the court. In fact, he presided over the decisions which outlawed *segregation, increased the *civil rights of defendants (*Miranda* v. *Arizona*), curtailed the powers of federal investigators, and reformed the criminal system with the application of the Fourteenth Amendment 'due process' clause of the Constitution. Under his direction, the court also established a right to privacy in *Griswold* v. *Connecticut* (1965). Warren's court used the First, Third, Fifth, Sixth, and Fourteenth Constitutional Amendments to alter the political and social landscape of America. He also chaired the Warren Commission, which investigated the murder of John F. *Kennedy.

Warsaw Ghetto

Although by no means unique in the German-occupied eastern territories during *World War II, this was the largest and best-known of all the Jewish ghettos during this period, and remains a terrible symbol of the unspeakable atrocities committed against the Jewish population. After the entry into Warsaw of the forces of *Nazi Germany in September 1939, the Germans quickly sealed off the Jewish quarters. Hunger, filth, and squalor reigned, and the ghetto almost burst at the seams, as altogether 400,000 Jews from all over occupied Poland were sent there. Matters deteriorated sharply after the Wannsee

Conference of 1941 (see *concentration camps). An increasing number of Jews were transported from the ghetto straight into the gas chambers of the *Nazi extermination camps. By July 1942, up to 12,000 Jews per day were sent to die in the gas chambers of the Treblinka concentration camp. The attempt by the *SS to deport the remaining inhabitants and dissolve the ghetto on 19 April 1943 led to the desperate resistance of a force of about 1,100 badly armed Jews. This was squashed by 16 May 1943. 12,000 Jews were killed during the fighting itself, mostly through German arson attacks and executions. After the uprising, 7,000 Jews were gassed in extermination camps, while 30,000 were shot there. In all, over 300,000 Jews of the ghetto were murdered.

Warsaw Pact

A military alliance founded on 14 May 1955 with the 'Warsaw Treaty of Friendship, Cooperation, and Mutual Assistance'. It was formally a response to the entry of West Germany (Federal Republic of Germany) into *NATO. It had a dual function, as the chief military rival to NATO, and as the most effective way to ensure the control of the Soviet Union over the countries of Eastern Europe. Its commander was always a Soviet general, while further bilateral treaties allowed the deployment of Soviet troops in each of the member states. Under Soviet leadership, forces of the Warsaw Pact crushed the *Hungarian Revolution of 1956. Once again in 1968 it intervened to crush the *Prague Spring, while intervention loomed large in Poland just before the introduction of martial law in 1981 (*Solidarność). Its original members consisted of the USSR, Albania, Bulgaria, the GDR (East Germany), Poland, Romania, Czechoslovakia, and Hungary. Albania halted active membership in 1961, and left the Pact in 1968. The Warsaw Pact was dissolved on 1 April 1991, at a time when *Communism had collapsed in Eastern Europe, and the USSR was about to implode.

Warsaw Rising (1 Aug.–2 Oct. 1944)

In *World War II, as the *Red Army advanced into Poland in the summer of 1944, Soviet contacts in Warsaw encouraged the underground Home Army to stage an uprising. This was supported by the exiled Polish government in London, which wanted to liberate the city with Polish resources in order to strengthen its own bargaining position against the Soviet Union. Resistance troops led by General Tadeusz Komorowski gained control of the city against a weak German garrison. However, heavy German air raids lasting sixty-three days, followed by a strong German counter-attack, finally overcame the uprising. In retaliation, *Hitler ordered the total destruction of what was left of the city.

The *Red Army, which had already advanced as far as the city's Praga suburb, refused to come to the aid of the Poles, and halted its advance. It was happy to see the destruction of the Polish resistance movement, which had formed the nucleus of the support for the Polish government-in-exile. This greatly facilitated the imposition of a Communist puppet government after liberation, on 1 January 1945.

Washington Conference (Nov. 1921 – Feb. 1922)

A conference attended by Belgium, Britain, China, France, Italy, Japan, the Netherlands, Portugal, and the USA, aiming to reduce tensions in the Far East and to discuss naval disarmament. The main results were an agreement between the UK, France, Japan, and China to recognize each other's existing Pacific territories. Furthermore, the powers undertook to guarantee China's independence and territorial integrity, while the Japanese promised to return the region around Kiaochow. Finally, a naval convention was signed in which the nine powers agreed not to build capital ships (warships over 10,000 tons, with guns larger than 8–inch) for ten years. For that period, a ratio for capital ships of 5.25:5.25: 3.15:1.75:1.75 between the UK, the USA, Japan, France, and Italy was agreed, while the USA and UK agreed not to strengthen the fortifications of their naval bases between and including Singapore and Hawaii.

Watergate Scandal (USA)

In 1972 five employees of a *Republican Party organization with strong links to the presidential aides of Richard Nixon were arrested for breaking into the headquarters of the *Democratic Party's national committee in the Watergate complex in Washington, DC. They intended to wiretap the phone conversations of the committee. It was soon discovered that their actions formed part of a campaign to help President *Nixon to win the 1972 election.

The White House denied all knowledge of the incident, but after intensive investigations, initially led by journalists of the *Washington Post* (Carl Bernstein and Bob Woodward), it became apparent that several of the President's staff had been involved in illegal activities and in an attempt to cover up the whole operation. A number of White House officials and aides were prosecuted and convicted on criminal charges. An independent inquiry appointed in

1973 discovered the practice of secret tape recordings of all White House conversations. Nixon refused to release the relevant tapes, citing 'executive privilege' as a reason. On 24 July 1974, the *Supreme Court ordered the release of these tapes. These revealed the President's close involvement in the original crime and its subsequent cover-up. Just before the Senate was to vote in favour of impeachment, Nixon resigned on 9 August 1974.

Although he had not yet been indicted, he was pardoned for any federal offences he might have committed by his successor, President *Ford. However, the pardon did not apply to members of his staff, some of whom were later tried and imprisoned. Coming at the end of the disastrous *Vietnam War, the crisis of the executive aggravated a deep sense of public insecurity which Ford and *Carter were unable to alleviate.

Watson, John Christian (b. 9 Apr. 1867, d. 18 Nov. 1941). Prime Minister of Australia 1904

Born in Valparaiso (Chile), he arrived in Sydney in 1886, became active in the Trades and Labour Council (TLC) from 1890, becoming a representative for Labor in the New South Wales Legislative Assembly in 1894. He took part in adapting the Labor movement for the advent of an Australian federation, and in 1901 became the leader of the federal parliamentary party. He was the first Prime Minister from the Australian *Labor Party, though the brevity of his minority government (four months) prevented him from enacting any major legislation. In 1916, he was expelled from Labor for his support for conscription and he subsequently backed *Hughes and the *Nationalist Party.

Wavell, Archibald Percival, Earl Wavell of Cyrenaica (b. 5 May 1883, d. 24 May 1950). British field marshal, Viceroy of India 1943–7

Born in Colchester, he was educated at Winchester and the Royal Military College, Sandhurst. He gained a commission in the army in 1901, and served in the *South African (Boer) War, in India, and (in World War I) in France and *Palestine. He trained troops in the 1920s and 1930s, and in 1937 returned to Palestine to command the British troops there. In July 1939, he became commander-in-chief in the Middle East, and from 1940 was successful against Italian troops, notably at the Battle of Sidi Barrani. Wavell was forced to retreat in 1941, when troops had to be diverted to Greece.

Disagreements with *Churchill and others over priorities in the Middle East and North Africa led to his dismissal in June 1941. He commanded the British and *Commonwealth troops at the fall of *Singapore, but continued to command the British forces in India, first as commander-in-chief and then, from 1943, as Viceroy. In preparation for independence, he displayed unexpected skill and astuteness in his attempt to create a coalition representing diverse Indian groups. However, he was replaced by *Mountbatten in March 1947. He wrote extensively on military issues, and edited a popular volume of poetry, *Other Men's Flowers* (1944).

Webb, Sidney James, 1st Baron Passfield (b. 13 July 1859, d. 13 Oct. 1947), and **Beatrice, neé Potter** (b. 22 Jan. 1858, d. 30 Apr. 1943). British social reformers
Sidney Webb joined the *Fabian Society in 1885 and developed many of its ideas on *socialism, while Beatrice began her research on the British *cooperative movement. They married in 1892, and soon engaged in full-time social research. In 1894, they co-founded the London School of Economics, together with Robert *Haldane, in order to promote research into social policy. Their own research bore considerable fruits, most notably *The History of Trade Unionism*, and *English Local Government*, a work whose quality was paralleled by its size (11 vols., 1903–29). In 1913 they established a further platform for their views, through the creation of the journal *New Statesman*. Beatrice was a member of the Royal Commission on the Poor Law (1905–9), where together with *Landsbury she was largely responsible for the minority report which recommended a breakup of the existing Poor Law, to be replaced by separate agencies to cope with different social problems, such as unemployment, old age, etc. This solution became gradually established over the next decades. Sidney served on the London County Council 1892–1910. He drafted the Labour policy on domestic affairs in 1918 (*Labour and the New Social Order*), and was elected an MP in 1922. He became President of the Board of Trade in 1924, and Colonial Secretary in the year he was raised to the peerage, 1929.

Weimar Republic, see GERMANY

Weizmann, Chaim (b. 27 Nov. 1874, d. 9 Nov. 1952). President of Israel 1948–52
Born in Motol in Russian Poland, he received a doctorate degree at the University of Freiburg, and from 1904 lectured at the University of Manchester. He became a leading *Zionist

figure in England and lobbied successfully to bring about the *Balfour Declaration. Chairman of the Zionist Commission to *Palestine in 1918, he was the president of the World Zionist Organization (1920–31, 1935–46). In 1929 he succeeded in obtaining from Britain recognition of the *Jewish Agency, in which he played a major part. He supported the establishment of the Hebrew University in *Jerusalem and other cultural institutions that were prerequisites for statehood. He was an effective and influential lobbyist for the international recognition of a state of Israel after World War II, gaining the sympathy of the *UN as well as of the USA under *Truman. The importance of his role in the establishment of an Israeli state was reflected in his election as the country's first head of state.

Welensky, Sir Roy (b. 20 Jan. 1907, d. 6 Dec. 1991). Prime Minister of the Central African Federation 1955–63
Born in the slum-quarter of Salisbury (Southern Rhodesia, now Zimbabwe) of Lithuanian refugees, he worked as a railway official in Northern Rhodesia, became leader of the Railway Workers' Trade Union in 1933, and a member of the Northern Rhodesian parliament in 1938. In 1941 he helped to form the Labour Party of Northern Rhodesia. Claiming to be 50 per cent Jewish, 50 per cent *Afrikaner, and 100 per cent British, he was a major proponent of the creation of the *Central African Federation which he hoped would strengthen the British presence in the area. To this end, he founded the Federal Party and entered the Federation's first parliament in 1953. Succeeding *Huggins as Prime Minister, he was unable to increase the White-ruled Federation's popularity among the Black majority of the population, particularly in Nyasaland (Malawi) and Northern Rhodesia (Zambia). He supported White rule in Southern Rhodesia, but opposed *Smith's Unilateral Declaration of Independence (*Zimbabwe) which followed the breakup of the Federation. His attempt to build up an opposition to Smith through founding the *New Rhodesia Party in 1964 failed, and so he retired to a farm near his home town of Salisbury (Harare).

welfare state

Origins (from 1883) A state that is concerned about the welfare of its citizens, in addition to its traditional purview of internal security, defence, and foreign policy. After initial legislation in industrializing countries which specified minimal working conditions, the first state to accept a responsibility for social welfare through a redistribution of wealth was Germany, through its social insurance legislation (pensions, accident insurance, and health insurance) of 1883–8. However, German social insurance remained extremely limited until World War I so that New Zealand has often been described as the world's first welfare state, on account of the extensive labour and insurance legislation in place there by 1903. In the UK, the 'New' Liberal government laid the foundations of a welfare state, most notably through the introduction of unemployment insurance in 1911. After World War I, the most significant departure was F. D. *Roosevelt's *New Deal from 1933, in which the federal government financed extensive public works schemes.

Expansion (from the 1930s) Whereas in Sweden and Denmark welfare policies became part of an emerging social and political consensus during the 1930s, in most industrialized countries, it was World War II which brought about a fundamental shift in attitudes towards a welfare state. This was particularly the case in most European states, where social policy helped generate consensus and cohesion among groups deeply affected by the suffering and divisions of war. In the UK, the 1942 *Beveridge Report became the basis of a new welfare state which would provide for its citizens 'from the cradle to the grave'. A commitment to full employment and universal secondary education was made in 1944, while a comprehensive system of national insurance (to provide for pensions, unemployment benefit, etc.) and a *National Health Service were established in 1946. Such measures, as well as the nationalization of industries engaged in transport and the exploitation of mineral resources, were taken by most Western European countries. The Scandinavian countries' welfare provisions, pioneered by the Swedish *Social Democratic Labour Party in the 1930s, became particularly famous for their scope and quality.

When *Keynesianism, its underlying economic rationale, was first challenged in the 1970s, the economic implications of the welfare state began also to be reassessed. Permanently rising unemployment levels, declining economic growth, and a declining birth-rate after the 1960s (and a subsequently ageing population) made the social welfare provision of the early 1970s unsustainable. New Zealand was one of the few countries to have scaled down its social welfare so dramatically that it was possible to speak of a 'post-welfare state' after 1991, but some of these policies were reversed with the return of the *Labour government in 1999. In all industrialized countries, however, the welfare

state was continually reformed from the 1980s in the face of *globalization. This usually entailed a reduction of state expenditure, a cut in welfare costs for employers, and increased inducements for individual economic incentive. At the same time, the popularity of the welfare state made it difficult for any government to abolish it altogether.

Weltpolitik ('world policy')

A term used to describe Germany's aggressive and expansive foreign policy through the acquisition of colonies and the building of a navy from 1884 to 1918. The aim of this policy had been ostensibly to placate the demands from heavy industry for a greater navy and to generate national pride among dissatisfied working classes. However, there is little evidence that it was successful, particularly in the latter aim.

West Bank

An area of *Palestine west of the River Jordan, allocated by a *UN Partition Plan of 1947 as a separate Arab state alongside an independent state of Israel. It was occupied by Jordan in 1948, and formally annexed in 1949, although only Britain and Pakistan recognized this. Some tension existed between Palestinian Arabs of the area and the Jordanian government, which they regarded as autocratic.

Following the Arab–Israeli *Six Day War of 1967 the whole area was occupied by Israel. *PLO forces, operating from Jordan until 1971 and later from Lebanon, mounted continuous guerrilla attacks. At the same time Israeli occupation became more aggressive, with increasing numbers of Jewish settlers expropriating Arab land from the 1980s. Thousands of Arab refugees fled to Lebanon and Jordan, and some were forcibly evicted. From December 1987 onwards Israeli troops used ever harsher methods to suppress the Palestinian protest of *Intifadah. This began on the *Gaza Strip but quickly spread to the West Bank, with stone-throwing Arab youths being beaten and shot in increasing numbers. During the second Intifadah, which began in 2000, the West Bank became the source of many attacks against Israel, both because of its long border with Israel and because of the large number of new Jewish settlements within its territory. In response, Israel began constructing a controversial wall along its border with the West Bank. Unimpressed by the criticism of the International Court of Justice in 2004, Israel had completed over half of the 420-mile (670 km) long wall, which was 8 m high, by 2006.

West Indies, Federation of the
(1958–62)

An attempt to create a self-governing federal state consisting of the ten British colonies of the West Indies. Under the assumption that each of these islands or group of islands was too small to become independent on its own, plans and campaigns for the creation of a federation emerged in the 1920s and were discussed with greater urgency after World War II. After eleven years of extensive negotiations, the Federation finally came into being. It consisted of the larger colonies of Trinidad and Tobago and Jamaica, as well as the colonies of Antigua and Barbuda, Barbados, Dominica, Grenada, Montserrat, St Christopher (Kitts), Nevis, Anguilla, St Lucia, and St Vincent and the Grenadines. Led by the former Prime Minister of Barbados, *Adams, the Federation enjoyed considerable support amongst popular and intellectual circles. However, it was wrecked by the ambitions of the oppositional movements in Trinidad and Tobago and Jamaica, which successfully sought to increase their own popularity through appeals to patriotism. The two island states were released into independence in 1962, which wrecked the Federation. The other eight territories resumed closer ties with Britain as semi-colonial 'associated states'. All of them (except Anguilla and Montserrat) gained full independence by 1980.

Western Sahara Africa's last remaining colony.

Partition (1975–9) Under Spanish sovereignty since 1884, a treaty of partition between Spain, Mauretania, and Morocco was signed in 1975. Accordingly, Spain withdrew its troops by March 1976, when the country was divided up into a northern half occupied by Morocco and a southern half administered by Mauretania. The Moroccan part was particularly rich in mineral resources (especially phosphate), some of whose proceeds were given to Mauretania. Increasing popular resentment boosted the guerrilla movement **POLISARIO** (Frente Popular de Liberación de Seguía el-Hamra y Río de Oro, **Po**pular Front for the **Li**beration of **Sa**guira Hamra and **Ri**o de **O**ro), which had originally been formed to fight against the Spanish. On 28 February 1976, POLISARIO unilaterally proclaimed the **Sahara Arab Democratic Republic** (SADR). By 1979, its guerrilla operations in Mauretania had weakened that country's military and economy to such an extent that the two sides concluded a peace agreement on 5 August 1979.

Moroccan rule (since 1970s) In response, Morocco immediately occupied the southern part of the country. Over 100,000 US-equipped Moroccan troops were confronted by about 20,000 POLISARIO guerrillas, operating from and largely equipped by Algeria. The SADR was admitted into the OAU (*African Union), whereupon Morocco withdrew. Exhausted by massive military expenditure, Morocco signed a truce with POLISARIO in 1991, but successfully caused the periodical postponement of a referendum on its independence first due in 1992. At issue was the registration of voters, as Morocco insisted on the admission of over 100,000 Moroccans who had immigrated under the sponsorship of the Moroccan government. The deadlock in the negotiations between POLISARIO and Morocco appeared to be broken with the appointment of former US Secretary of State James Baker as mediator. An agreement was reached to hold the referendum in 2000, but this was postponed as Morocco made new demands for voter registration. Initial hopes that the more liberal King *Mohammed VI would moderate Moroccan demands were thus disappointed. POLISARIO's government-in-exile had its seat in Algeria, and was recognized by over 60 states worldwide.

Westminster, see PARLIAMENT (UK)

Westminster, Statute of (11 Dec. 1931)

A British Act of Parliament which redefined the relationship between Britain and her self-governing Dominions (Canada, New Zealand, Australia, South Africa, Eire, and Newfoundland), granting them effective sovereignty in accordance with the *Imperial Conferences of 1926 and 1930. The foundation of the present *Commonwealth of Nations, it defined the relationship as 'Autonomous communities within the British Empire, equal in status, … united by a common allegiance to the Crown and freely associated as members of the British Commonwealth of Nations'. The Statute was subsequently ratified in all parliaments of the Dominions.

WEU (Western European Union)

A military alliance to effect collective security for its member states which emerged from the Treaties of *Dunkirk (1947) and *Brussels (1948). It was founded in 1954 (effective from 6 May 1955) in conjunction with the admission of West Germany into NATO, as an added forum of security and cooperation in the face of German rearmament. Throughout, its existence has been overshadowed by *NATO and through it American military involvement in Europe. Its members are Belgium, Germany, France, Greece (since 1994), the UK,

Italy, Luxemburg, the Netherlands, Spain (since 1989), and Portugal (since 1989). Since the fall of the *Berlin Wall in 1989, there have been efforts to make the WEU more effective, notably by transforming it into the military arm of the EU. Since a number of the WEU's members were not part of the EU, this was not possible. However, the WEU did transfer its crisis management capacities to the defence operations of the EU in 2001. The WEU is still nominally distinctive, but in practice has become inextricably linked to the foreign policy actions of the EU.

⊕ SEE WEB LINKS

• The official website of the WEU.

Weygand, Maxime (b. 21 Jan. 1867, d. 18 Jan. 1965). French general

Born in Brussels, he was commissioned into the French army in 1888. Weygand was Chief of Staff to General *Foch in World War I, and in 1920 was sent to aid the Poles in their ultimately successful defence against the advancing Red Army. In 1923–4 he served as high commissioner of Syria and the Lebanon. A member of the war council 1924–9, he became Chief of the French General Staff 1930–5, when he completed the subjection of Morocco.

In May 1940 Weygand was called from retirement to command the French army. Unable to stem the German advance, he pressed for capitulation, effectively overruling Prime Minister *Reynaud. He was Minister of Defence for the *Vichy government from June to September 1940, and was then sent to North Africa as Marshal *Pétain's emissary. Dismissed in 1941 as a result of German pressure, he was arrested and interned in Germany, 1942–5. He was cleared of the charge of *collaboration in 1948. He became a critic of all policies of *decolonization relating to territories which he considered an integral part of France, notably Algeria.

FRENCH EMPIRE; ALGERIAN WAR OF INDEPENDENCE

White Army

An umbrella term for the various counter-revolutionary armies that fought the *Bolshevik *Red Army in the *Russian Civil War. The name 'Whites' has been used to describe those loyal to a monarchy, ever since the French Revolution (1789), when monarchist forces adopted the white flag of the Bourbon dynasty as their symbol.

White Australia Policy

A policy established when responsibility for immigration passed to the newly created federal government of Australia in 1901.

Building on established anti-Chinese immigration restrictions, the aim was to maintain racial harmony, and to keep out Asians who might be willing to work at much lower wages. As a result, immigration was restricted to White immigrants from Europe, preferably from the British Isles. To enforce this, a **dictation test** for would-be immigrants was introduced in 1901 which could be in any European language (any 'prescribed' language after 1905). It was also used to keep out 'undesirable' Europeans, such as the celebrated case of **Egon Kisch,** a Czechoslovak Communist who was given a test in Scottish Gaelic (1934). As a result, by 1941, Australia was sparsely populated, while 97 per cent of the population could trace back their origins to the British Isles. Subsequently, *Calwell and *Chifley encouraged immigration from eastern and southern Europe. During the 1950s, as Australia focused more on its proximity to Asia, this racist policy became untenable. The controversial dictation tests were replaced by entry permits in 1958, and during the 1960s the system was completely dismantled.

White Rose (Weisse Rose), see
RESISTANCE, GERMANY

Whitewater (USA)

The name of a $200,000 housing development near the Whitewater rapids in Arkansas. The venture involved investments by Bill and Hillary *Clinton, amongst others, and its failure occurred during the first years of Clinton's time as Governor of Arkansas. An investigation set up in 1993 set out to discover whether there had been any conflict of interest. Especially under independent counsel Kenneth Starr, the investigation broadened to investigate any suspicion of wrongdoing by the Clintons, leading to the discovery of Clinton's affair with Monica *Lewinsky in 1998. After ten years, the $65 million investigation failed to find any evidence to connect the Clintons with acts of fraud committed by their business partners. The investigation, spanning both the terms of Clinton's office, defined the embittered partisanship that marked Clinton's Presidency, with a Conservative *Congress being bitterly opposed to the President on ideological, moral, and personal grounds.

Whitlam, (Edward) Gough (b. 11 July 1916). Prime Minister of Australia 1972–5

Early career Born at Kew (Victoria), he graduated in arts and law from the University of Sydney, served in the Royal Australian Air Force during World War II, and became a barrister in 1947, receiving the prestigious appointment of Queen's Counsel in 1962. He joined the Australian *Labor Party (ALP) in 1945, and entered the House of Representatives in 1952. As deputy leader (from 1960) and leader (from 1967) he was instrumental in healing the divisions which had characterized the party since the *Petrov Affair.

Prime Minister The first Labor Prime Minister since 1949, he set out to improve relations with Asian countries, taking up diplomatic links with the People's Republic of China. He also withdrew Australian troops from the *Vietnam War. His government abandoned conscription, abolished university fees, and introduced universal healthcare (Medibank). However, he was hampered by an economic crisis caused by the 1973 *oil-price shock, while his legislation faced constant hostility from the *Liberal-Country Party majority in the Senate. The Country Party (*National Party) forced him to call a new election in 1974, which he won. When the Senate refused to pass his budget in October 1975, the Governor-General, **Sir John Kerr** (b. 1914, d. 1991) took the unprecedented step of intervening to dismiss Whitlam and appoint *Fraser as leader of a minority government. New elections were called on December 1975, in which Whitlam's Labor Party was defeated. He resigned after Labor's defeat in the 1977 elections, and served as ambassador to *UNESCO (1983–8). Whitlam's dismissal by Kerr was legal, as it followed the letter of the law, but it violated its spirit. It raised questions about Australia's constitutional system founded on the royal prerogative, and led to growing calls for the abolition of the monarchy.

Wilhelm II (b. 27 Jan. 1859, d. 4 June 1941). German Emperor (Kaiser) 1888–1918
Upon his accession to the throne the young, self-confident monarch soon clashed with his Chancellor, Otto von Bismarck (b. 1815, d. 1898), whom he dismissed in 1890 to increase his own political influence. In an effort to end the increasing political polarization of German society, he proclaimed the conciliatory 'New Course' in 1890, but when this failed to stop the rise of *socialism, he ordered his Chancellor to reintroduce measures to persecute the *SPD through the Revolutions (Subversions) Bill, (*Umsturzvorlage*, 1894–5) and the Penitentiaries Bill (*Zuchthausvorlage*, 1899), measures which failed to get the necessary parliamentary support.

Subsequently Wilhelm's influence waned, and his political statements, such as those made in the *Daily Telegraph Affair, became increasingly incoherent as well as controversial. He was an enthusiastic supporter of *Tirpitz's plans for naval expansion, and he fully approved of his Chancellor *Bethmann Hollweg's handling of the events following from the assassination of the Archduke Francis Ferdinand in *Sarajevo. Although his precise influence on the outbreak of the war is subject to dispute, he did not have a decisive say, though his opinion contributed to a bellicose atmosphere in the German leadership. During the war he moved into the background. When the military began to collapse and workers' councils at home started to rise against the system, his generals led by *Hindenburg refused to support him. Wihelm abdicated on 10 November 1918 and fled to Doorn in the Netherlands, where he died.

Wilhelmina (b. 31 Aug. 1880, d. 28 Nov. 1962). Queen of the Netherlands 1890–1948
The only daughter of King William III, she contributed greatly to the strengthening of the monarchy through accepting the growth of parliamentary power. When her country was invaded (1940–5), she and her ministers maintained a government-in-exile in London. Through frequent radio talks she became a symbol of resistance for the Dutch people. She returned in 1945, but abdicated in 1948 in favour of her daughter Juliana.

Wilkins, Roy (b. 18 Feb. 1901, d. 18 Sept. 1981). US civil rights leader
The grandson of a slave, he was born at St Louis, Missouri. He graduated from the University of Minnesota and then worked as a journalist on the *Kansas City Call*, a newspaper for the Black community. In 1931 he joined the *NAACP (National Association for the Advancement of Colored People), editing its journal *Crisis* (1934–49). Appointed chief executive of NAACP in 1955, he consistently advocated the policy of legal redress in order to gain civil rights. Deeply committed to non-violence, in August 1963 he was one of the organizers of the *March on Washington with Martin Luther *King and A. Philip *Randolph. In 1968 he served on the US delegation to the International Conference on Human Rights. In his later years at the NAACP he came under increasing pressure from more militant Blacks to move away from his non-violent integrationism. He retired in 1977, remaining a director emeritus of NAACP.

William II, see WILHELM II

Williams, Eric Eustace (b. 25 Sept. 1911, d. 29 Mar. 1981). Chief Minister of Trinidad and

Tobago 1956–9; Premier 1959–62; Prime Minister 1962–81

Educated in Trinidad and Oxford, he was appointed associate professor at Howard University, USA, in 1939. Returning to Trinidad, he founded the People's National Movement (PNM) in 1955, at the head of which he won every subsequent general election. As a moderate socialist, he emphasized the need for education and social welfare. He attracted foreign capital through tax incentives, which benefited the exploration of the country's considerable oil reserves.

Wilson, (James) Harold, Baron Wilson of Rievaulx (b. 11 Mar. 1916, d. 24 May 1995). British Prime Minister 1964–70, 1974–6

Early career Born in Huddersfield (Yorkshire), he studied at Oxford University. He taught economics there before World War II, and then went to work as a civil servant in the economics section of the War Cabinet secretariat. Originally a Liberal, he drifted towards the *Labour Party in the late 1930s. In 1945, he was elected to parliament for Ormskirk. He was President of the Board of Trade from 1947 until February 1951, when he resigned, in support of *Bevan, over *Gaitskell's imposition of health prescription charges. As this associated him with the left of the party, he was subsequently at pains to advocate the interests of party unity. This enabled him to become Gaitskell's Shadow Chancellor in 1956. As Labour leader after Gaitskell's death in 1963, Wilson set about creating the image of a modern, dynamic party, keen on utilizing what he called 'the white heat of the technological revolution' to boost Britain's prosperity.

First terms in office Wilson won the 1964 elections against a tired and worn-out *Conservative Party under *Douglas-Home, though in the end only by a surprisingly narrow margin. In 1966, he increased his majority to almost 100. His 1964–70 governments faced enormous economic difficulties, including a balance-of-payments deficit and a sterling crisis, the latter leading to devaluation of the pound in 1967. He failed to implement a successful prices-and-incomes strategy, while his attempts to limit *trade-union power floundered in the face of strong union opposition. The late 1960s were a time of increased racial tension in Britain, which the government tried to deal with by restricting immigration under the 1968 *Immigration Act, and by passing anti-discrimination

legislation in the form of Race Relations Acts in 1965 and 1968. The 1964–70 governments also developed comprehensive education, expanded higher education, ended the death penalty, and liberalized laws on sexual relations, divorce, and *abortion. The age of majority was reduced to 18. In foreign and *Commonwealth affairs, the decision was made to withdraw British military forces from east of Suez (1968), though Wilson's government failed to find a solution to Ian *Smith's Rhodesian Unilateral Declaration of Independence (*Zimbabwe).

Final term in office Labour's defeat in the 1970 general election was a shock to many, including Wilson, but he returned to office with a slender majority in 1974. His government inherited a massive balance-of-payments deficit from *Heath, five times worse than that of 1964. In a renewed effort to deal with inflation, he was again unsuccessful in dealing with the *TUC in a 'social contract'. In 1975, he confirmed British membership of the European Community after a referendum, which he had held in order to avoid Labour having to reach a decision on the issue over which it was deeply divided. Wilson announced his retirement on his sixtieth birthday, handing over to James *Callaghan.

Wilson had led Labour to victory in three general elections, more than any other Labour leader before. His longevity at the head of the party derived from the fact that he was never closely associated with any one wing of the party, which enabled him to enlist the support of all sections. At the same time, he was seen as an intellectual and divorced from the rank and file of the party, which partly explains his inability to deal with the trade unions.

Wilson, Thomas Woodrow (b. 28 Dec. 1856, d. 3 Feb. 1924). 28th US President 1913–21

Early career Born at Staunton, Virginia, the son of a stern Presbyterian minister, he enrolled at Princeton University in 1875, received a doctorate from Johns Hopkins University, and returned to Princeton in 1890 as Professor of Jurisprudence. In 1902 he was appointed president of the university, where he was responsible for a number of major changes in its educational and social organization. In 1910 he resigned to run as a reform-minded Governor of New Jersey, and was elected. In his short tenure in this position he instituted a number of important reforms, and in 1912 he benefited from the divisions within the *Republican Party to be elected President.

Presidency Based on his idea of the *New Freedom, Wilson sought to stimulate competition by reducing the power of corporate trusts, promote equal opportunity, and check corruption. He encouraged trade through a reduction in tariffs, making up for the lost revenue through the introduction of a low income tax. Wilson also reformed the banking system, which led to the Federal Reserve Act of 1913. A compromise between demands for greater regulation and *Democrat fears at the power of Wall Street, the measure established the *Federal Reserve System. This consisted of twelve Federal Reserve Banks in different parts of the country, which were owned by their member banks and linked by a Federal Reserve Board. In foreign policy, Wilson was soon faced with the outbreak of World War I.

At first, Wilson concentrated on conserving US neutrality. Gradually, however, he came to the view that the USA should support Britain and France against Germany, which he considered a threat to democracy and humanity. The German policy of unrestricted submarine warfare from February 1917 led to the declaration of war in April (*Lusitania; *Zimmermann Note).

Fourteen Points From then on he worked to realize his vision, proposed in the *Fourteen Points, of a peaceful and democratic postwar world. However, he failed to take fully into account the persistence of European nationalism and the strength of a feeling of retribution after World War I. As a result, the ensuing *Versailles Treaty fell far short of his ambitions. Wilson's Presbyterian background and respect for legal traditions made him favour an international peacekeeping forum. He won the *Nobel Peace Prize for the creation of the *League of Nations. However, Wilson faced a tough and ultimately unsuccessful battle to have US membership in the League ratified, as *Congress feared a permanent US involvement overseas. Wilson suffered a severe stroke during his campaign for ratification in September 1919. He never fully recovered, and for the last year of his presidency the second Mrs Wilson, a lady of powerful personality, largely directed such business as could not be avoided or postponed.

Windsor, House of

The official name adopted by the British royal family in 1917. During World War I, anti-German feeling in Britain was so strong that *George V felt that the German title, Saxe-Coburg-Gotha, should be removed from his family name. The German name was derived from the marriage of Queen Victoria (herself from the House of Hanover) to Prince Albert of Saxe-Coburg-Gotha in 1840. Windsor was an acceptable alternative as Windsor Castle in Berkshire was a long-standing home of the royal family.

Wingate, Orde Charles (b. 26 Feb. 1903, d. 24 Mar. 1944). British major-general
Born in Naini Tal, India, and educated at Charterhouse and the Royal Military Academy, Woolwich. He was commissioned in 1922, and then served in the Sudan and *Palestine. In the 1930s, he gained experience of guerrilla warfare, through his training of Jewish irregular forces, operating in *Palestine against Arabs who were resisting Jewish immigration. In 1941, he put this into practice by organizing Somalis and Ethiopians to fight against the Italian occupiers in Abyssinia, in order to restore Emperor Haile *Selassie as ruler. Called by *Wavell, he went to India in 1942, and created and led the Chindits. This Burmese guerrilla force had mixed success fighting behind Japanese lines. A great military innovator, he tread a line between genius and instability that was difficult to determine. Wingate died in an air crash in 1944, before he could fully develop his plans.

Winnipeg General Strike (15 May–25 June 1919).
Canada's best-known general strike was caused by the breakdown of industrial negotiations in Winnipeg's building and metal trades, in an atmosphere of general social unrest and economic uncertainty. The central issue consisted of the employees' demands for collective bargaining. A general strike was called, which was supported almost unanimously, including by public-sector employees. Sympathetic strike action in other cities was also triggered off. The employers and the local elite reacted by accusing the strikers of revolutionary intent. Worried by the potential impact of the strike in other cities, the government intervened. Federal employees were threatened with dismissal, the Immigration Act (*immigration legislation) was altered to allow deportations of strike leaders. Moreover, the legal definition of sedition was extended. On 21 June, a confrontation with the police resulted in thirty injured strikers, and one dead. Of its imprisoned leaders, *Woodsworth became Canada's first socialist MP in the House of Commons (1921), while in 1920 four other socialists were elected to the Manitoba legislature while still in prison. The defeat of the strike struck a heavy blow against the Canadian labour movement. It took over thirty years before the main goals of the strike, union

recognition and collective bargaining, were realized by Canadian workers.

Winter War (30 Nov. 1939–12 Mar. 1940) Following the Finnish government's refusal to grant Soviet demands for naval bases and a frontier revision, the *Red Army attacked on three fronts. Led by General *Mannerheim, the Finns' superior skill in manœuvring on frozen lakes, across the Gulf of Finland, and in the forests, on skis, kept the Soviet forces at bay. After fifteen weeks of fierce fighting, however, Soviet troops breached the defensive Mannerheim Line. On 12 March 1940 Finland was forced to accept peace on *Stalin's terms, ceding its eastern territories and the port of Viipuri (Vyborg), altogether 10 per cent of its territory.

women, emancipation of

Overview The achievement of complete (a) economic, (b) social, (c) political and (d) religious equality of women with men, an aspiration whose realization in the course of the twentieth century has been gradual, varied and incomplete. Perhaps the most crucial agent of women's emancipation has been the process of industrialization. In agricultural, pre-industrial societies women are generally regarded as responsible for the preparation of food and the bearing of children with very few possibilities for an independent life outside the family. In industrializing countries women are increasingly compelled to join the industrial labour force out of sheer economic necessity. As the demand for labour increases with new areas of employment developing, women are more and more able to find employment in the service sector. They are able to join the 'lower' professions (primary school teaching and nursing) and 'lower' white-collar clerical and administrative positions. As the process of industrialization matures with an increase of the service sector relative to the industrial sector (which is disproportionately dominated by male labour), the economic opportunities for women increase accordingly.

As the economic status and independence of women rises, women become less dependent on marriage and on a husband to provide for them, which leads to a corresponding increase in their social independence. As a consequence, there occur social changes such as a decline in the birth-rate in industrialized countries and changes in marriage patterns, i.e marriage at later ages and higher divorce rates. This leads to the eventual introduction of the political equality of women to reflect their greater social and economic independence.

Apart from the interdependent (a) economic, (b) social, and (c) political factors promoting the equality of women, emancipation is inversely affected by (d) the strength of traditional religious sentiment in any society, which tends to emphasize the pre-industrial image of the family and the importance of the woman as the bearer of children. These four factors are the most important elements that account for the differences in the position of women in different countries. In many African countries with few or no industries the role of women is still confined to the home in relative dependence on her husband, a situation exacerbated in some countries by the strong hold of conservative Christian, Hindu, and Muslim movements. By contrast, emancipation is relatively advanced (though by no means complete) in industrialized countries, even though this has not been an automatic process.

Contemporary history Especially in the USA and the UK, women's political rights were brought into general political consciousness by the *suffragettes. In fact, the two World Wars created conditions most favourable to social, political, and economic change in favour of women. As men were fighting on the front, women had to take up occupations hitherto dominated by men. Political emancipation was also accelerated in countries that experienced revolutions which emphasized their own universal popularity among both men and women, as happened in Soviet Russia after 1917, Eastern Europe and Communist China after 1945, Germany (1918/19), and in countries such as Turkey (1922/23). Among democratic countries, the first countries to introduce women's suffrage were New Zealand (1893) and Australia (1902), both immigrant countries with mobile societies where traditional family values were less pronounced. In the USA, women were enfranchised in 1920. In Europe, the political, social, and economic role of women changed more gradually. Women were enfranchised in the UK in 1918 and, on an equal level with men, in 1928. Switzerland was the last European country to give women the vote in 1971. Legal equality was not established in most Western democracies until the 1960s and 1970s, e.g. the facilitation and fairer treatment of women in divorce.

By contrast, in countries where religion retains a strong social and political influence, women have retained an inferior social, political, and economic role. This applies to countries influenced by conservative tendencies within *Sunni *Islam (Iran, Saudi Arabia). Even in societies that espoused the equality of women as a central principle,

attitudes among men towards emancipation were slow to change. A study conducted in 1994 on social behaviour in eastern Germany explored how the attitudes of men had changed in a country where women had been completely emancipated legally, politically, and economically for forty years. It found that male perspectives had changed relatively little, so that women, in addition to their new status in full-time employment, were expected to perform the traditional female role of housekeeper and preparer of food.
GOLDSTEIN, VIDA JANE MARY

Women's movement (feminism)

After the achievements of the 'first wave' of twentieth-century feminism—suffrage—the 'second wave' emerged from women's participation in the civil rights struggle of the 1960s and the new left. What separated this from earlier movements was the strategic insight that the 'personal is political'. In France, the writer Simone de *Beauvoir was highly influential. In the USA, Betty *Friedan's *The Feminine Mystique* (1963) played a key role in unleashing a critique of the constraints of 'Mom-and-Apple-Pie' America. Friedan helped to found the **National Organization for Women (NOW),** a movement 'toward true equality for all women in America, and toward a fully equal partnership of the sexes' (Statement of Purpose, 1966). NOW worked to achieve an end to sexual discrimination in employment and to promote other issues, such as reproductive rights (legalization of *abortion) and paid maternity leave. Despite the movement's considerable support, and some successes, the income gap between men and women actually widened during the 1970s. An equal rights amendment passed by Congress in 1972 was never added to the constitution, being ratified by only thirty-five states, three less than the minimum required.

From the 1970s, various women's movements have shifted their attention to issues outside traditional politics: the fight against prostitution, pornography, and the exploitation of women's bodies, either publicly (e.g. in advertising) or privately (e.g. date rape). Feminism has also focused on changing social and cultural attitudes to women, particularly through the medium of language (i.e. by trying to make language gender-neutral). This latter attempt, in particular, has been resisted by the charge of 'political correctness' in the context of an emerging predominance of conservative values in Western society. However, feminism continues, enriched by an increasing diversity of voices, as demonstrated by the UN 1995 Conference on Women at Beijing.

women's suffrage, see SUFFRAGETTES

Woodsworth, James Shaver (b. 29 July 1874, d. 21 Mar. 1942). Canadian politician Known as the 'social conscience of Canada', he was born at Etobicoke (Ontario) and was ordained a Methodist minister in 1896. During his ministry among immigrant slum dwellers in Winnipeg he became politicized, supporting *trade unions and leaving the Church in 1918 in protest against its support for World War I. Briefly imprisoned for his support of the *Winnipeg general strike in 1919, he was elected to the House of Commons in 1921. In 1926, he managed to use his support for *Mackenzie King to secure the introduction of old-age pensions, which formed the basis of the Canadian *welfare state. In 1933, he was chosen to lead the new *Cooperative Commonwealth Federation. A lifelong pacifist, he was the only parliamentarian to record his opposition to Canada's entry into World War II.

Woomera rocket range

A weapons-testing zone including areas of South and Western Australia, established in 1946. It includes the sites of Emu and Maralinga, which were used for British nuclear tests from 1953 until 1963, with a minimum of precautions. A Royal Commission found in 1985 that some sites were still contaminated, and that some *Aborigines had been severely affected by radiation. In December 1994, the Australian government agreed to pay A$13.5 million in compensation.
NUCLEAR BOMB

World Bank

A specialized agency of the *UN, it was established as the International Bank for Reconstruction and Development (IBRD) at the *Bretton Woods conference (1944), and came into operation in 1946. Its aim has been to encourage economic growth particularly of its poorer members. It derived its funds from member countries, and borrowed from the world money markets. After a series of reconstructional loans to help members after World War II, from 1949 it concentrated on development loans, particularly to less-developed countries. Today, the World Bank group comprises five autonomous branches:-
(1) The IBRD (founded 1945 to provide loans and development assistance to poorer and middle-income nations; 184 members in 2007); (2) The International Finance Corporation (founded in 1956 to assist the private sector in developing countries; 1794 members in 2007); (3) The International Development Association (established 1960 to

provide interest-free loans to governments in the poorest countries; 165 members in 2007; (4) The Multilateral Investment Guarantee Agency (established in 1988 to assist developing countries in attracting foreign investment; 154 members in 2007); (5) The International Centre for Settlement of Investment Disputes (established 1966 to assist in the conciliation of investment disputes between governments and foreign investors; 143 members by 2007).

Under President James D. Wolfensohn (1995–2005), the World Bank tried to become more transparent and effective. It endeavoured to meet mounting criticism by enhanced cooperation with non-governmental organizations and by trying to follow development projects more closely in the affected member states. Despite these marked improvements, the World Bank continued to face political pressure from two fronts: the concerns for effeciency by its largest donors, notably the US *Congress, and public criticism against its ostensible subservience to capitalism even in countries where this may not be appropriate. From 2005, the Bank was directed by Paul Wolfowitz, a trusted former aide of George W. *Bush. Wolfowitz was unable to secure sufficient support within the institution, and was forced to resign in 2007.

IMF

(⊕) SEE WEB LINKS

- The official website of the World Bank.
- The official website of the International Finance Corporation.
- The official website of the Multilateral Investment Guarantee Agency.

World Health Organization (WHO)

A specialized agency of the *UN, founded on 7 April 1948, with its headquarters in Geneva. In its mission to promote general worldwide health, it created health services in less-developed countries, organized campaigns against epidemic diseases (e.g. smallpox, *AIDS, tuberculosis), implemented international quarantine and sanitation rules, funded research programmes and the collection and collation of statistics, and sponsored the training of medical specialists. By 2007, it had 193 member states.

(⊕) SEE WEB LINKS

- The home page of the WHO.

World Trade Organization, see WTO

World War I (the Great War) (1914–18)

Background The first war which involved total military mobilization on a global scale,

after earlier global confrontations had only led to brief and strictly limited military battles outside Europe. This in itself was the result of vast improvements in communications, which allowed the speedy deployment of troops via railways and ships (to colonial Empires). German unification in 1871 had transformed the traditional European balance of power, which rested on the assumption of a weak and fragmented Germany in the heart of Europe. When Germany began to assert its nationhood through militarism and a self-conscious foreign policy, it became an enthusiastic, if belated, participant in *imperialist conquests for colonies. Since Britain, Russia, and France had already created vast colonial Empires, German aspirations for the few remaining unclaimed territories in Africa, Asia, and Oceania heightened tensions and suspicions among the traditional powers of a more general nature. In the effort to claim its 'place in the sun', Germany pursued an ambitious programme of naval expansion. The ensuing arms race threatened Britain in particular, which aimed at having a bigger navy than its two closest rivals put together, in order to be able to defend the worldwide trading system upon which its economy and Empire rested more than any other country. As a result, international alliances were formed that left Germany increasingly isolated, e.g. the Anglo-French *Entente (1904), and the *Anglo-Russian entente of 1907 (*Triple Entente).

Causes Tensions between Germany and Britain erupted first during the *South African War, when Germans supported the *Afrikaners, and the *Daily Telegraph Affair. A number of international crises heightened the tensions, notably in Morocco (*Algeciras and *Agadir) and *Zabern (Saverne). Last but not least, Europe was destabilized by the fragile multi-ethnic state of *Austria-Hungary. Paralysed by its own bankruptcy and the forces of *nationalism, its aggressive claims over *Bosnia-Hercegovina and *Serbia ultimately produced the immediate cause of the war. After the assassination in *Sarajevo, by Serbian nationalists, of the heir to the Austrian throne Archduke Francis Ferdinand, Austria declared war on Serbia on 28 July 1914.

The conflict spread beyond the Balkans through German assistance to Austria, specifically the German declaration of war against Russia (1 August) and France (3 August). Again, Germany's aggressive stance was the result of a sense of weakness, whereby it did not have the resources to compete for long in the arms race which it had helped to precipitate. Given the international tensions, which had increased since 1900, the German political and military leadership believed that war was inevitable. Thus, the Germans were keen to strike before a relative decline of their military power could take place, and in the hope of dividing the *Triple Entente.

True to the *Schlieffen Plan, Germany attacked France through Belgium on 3 August 1914. In this way, German troops avoided the fortifications along the Franco-German border, though this also infringed upon a neutral country. It was this violation of Belgian neutrality that finally convinced the British government that it, too, was vitally threatened by a German regime that did not respect the rule of international law. On 4 September, therefore, Britain declared war on Germany, in her own name, and that of the *British Empire and her Dominions.

Amongst the Dominions, Canada, Newfoundland, Australia, and New Zealand readily ratified the British move, as they crucially depended upon the free-trading system which Britain tried so hard to protect against German expansionism. Only in South Africa did the entry into the war cause considerable political tension. With the memory of the recent *South African War, there were strong residual anti-British and pro-German feelings amongst the vociferous *Afrikaners. Perhaps more controversial than entry into the war itself was the issue of conscription, which became important from around 1916. It caused relatively little controversy in New Zealand, but split the British *Liberal Party. It was passed only after acrimonious political battles in Canada in 1917. It was rejected in two referendums in Australia, and was never introduced in Ireland (even though this was not a Dominion) or South Africa.

The course of the war The *Central Powers of Germany and Austria-Hungary were joined by the *Ottoman Empire (1914) and Bulgaria (1915). They faced the Allied Powers consisting of *Serbia, Russia, France, Belgium, Luxemburg, the British Empire, Japan (1914), Italy (1915), Romania (1916), Portugal (1916), and Greece (1917). The USA entered the war as an Associate Power of the *Allies on 6 April 1917, after the resumption of German submarine warfare (*Lusitania). Despite the importance of the naval arms race in the outbreak of the war, only one important naval battle took place (at *Jutland, 1916). Instead, fighting took place predominantly (1) on the Western Front (west of Germany); (2) the Eastern Front (east of Germany); (3) in northern Italy; (4) in the Balkans; (5) on the

fringes of the Ottoman Empire; (6) in the colonies.

1. The **Western Front** was opened by a rapid German advance which avoided the fortifications at the Franco-German border by invading through Belgium and Luxembourg. The advance was brought to a halt just outside Paris, at the first Battle of the *Marne. The Germans retreated slightly, and stabilized their positions around an arch stretching from *Ypres in northern Belgium to Soisson (halfway between the Franco-Belgian border and Paris) and Verdun. From late 1914, the conflict developed into a war of attrition. In battles at *Passchendaele, *Verdun, and the *Somme, large-scale offensives achieved little strategic gain, yet resulted in previously unimaginable slaughter. Hundreds of thousands of men were lost as each side sought to pummel the other to exhaustion. Another dimension to the horror was added in 1916, when the Germans introduced chemical warfare.

Despite a final German offensive at the *Marne in 1918, this attritional war was eventually lost by the Germans, mainly as a result of two factors. First, the introduction of mechanized warfare by the Allies, especially the use of tanks, made a crucial difference in the Allies' favour. Secondly, in a war which caused such dramatic losses, the Allies' resources of manpower and equipment were greater. The entry of the USA into the war in 1917 added to this imbalance. In summer 1918, most of France was regained from German occupation, with the Germans suffering a heavy defeat resulting from *Foch's use of tanks at the battle of Amiens (8 August).

2. On the **Eastern Front** as the Germans tried in vain to overcome France before Russia mobilized her troops, immediately after the outbreak of the war the Russian army tried to press its advantage and advanced into exposed German territory. Under *Hindenburg and *Ludendorff, the Russians were beaten in the battles of *Tannenberg and the Masurian Lakes (5–15 September 1914), though they remained in parts of *Prussia until 1915. After an Austro-Hungarian offensive in the spring and summer of 1915, the Russian advance collapsed, with most of Poland falling into German and Austrian hands. In September 1915, Tsar *Nicholas II took personal command of his troops. In summer 1916 a Russian counter-offensive produced victories, but heavy casualties eroded Russian morale. The Russian war effort was thrown into confusion by the *Russian Revolutions of 1917, which the German and Austro-Hungarian armies turned to their advantage in a summer offensive, when they reclaimed the *Bukovina and almost all of Galicia. Russian troops were at the point of collapse. After a further German offensive the new *Bolshevik leaders under *Lenin and *Trotsky were left with no alternative but to accept the harsh peace treaty of *Brest-Litovsk imposed upon them.

3. Italy's entry into the war in 1915 opened up a new military front, but did not bring about the collapse of the *Central Powers that had been anticipated by Britain and France (Treaty of *London). In eleven battles at the Isonzo River (1915–17), the Italians failed to break through *Austro-Hungarian lines. In fact the Italian army suffered twice as many casualties (725,000) as their opponents. The twelfth battle of the Isonzo, known as the Battle of *Caporetto, produced a victory for the Austrian army, but the Austrian advance was halted and its troops were finally overcome at the battle of *Vittorio Veneto.

4. In the **Balkans**, the Central Powers overcame Serbia, taking Belgrade in October 1915. Allying themselves with the Ottoman Empire and Bulgaria, they overcame Romania in 1916, but failed to take Greece.

5. The **Ottoman Empire** proved to be more resilient militarily than had been anticipated. At *Gallipoli, the troops from Australia, New Zealand, and Britain incurred heavy losses, but failed to make headway against the Turks. Meanwhile, British advances in the *Mesopotamian campaign were halted with the defeat at *Kut al-Amara in 1915. Nevertheless, in 1917 the Empire was in retreat. The *Arab Revolt (1916) had freed most of the Arabian penninsula, and the British had successfully taken Baghdad in 1917. In 1918, the country collapsed, with the Russians advancing deep into Armenia, the British taking *Kurdistan and, *Palestine, and the French taking Lebanon and Syria.

6. The German **colonies** were protected by relatively few troops, so that Togo, German Oceania, German New Guinea, and its Chinese territory in Qingdao had all surrendered by November 1914. On 9 July 1915, German South-West Africa (now Namibia) surrendered to South African troops under Louis *Botha and *Smuts, while Cameroon surrendered on 18 February 1916. Of all the colonies, only German East Africa (Tanganyika) held out until the end of the war, surrendering on 14 November 1918, three days after Germany itself.

End of the war Although there were virtually no foreign troops on their respective territories in autumn 1918 Austria-Hungary disintegrated, while Germany's collapse was only staved off by its military surrender.

Bulgaria signed an armistice on 30 September, the Ottoman Empire on 30 October, Austria-Hungary on 3 November, and the German Empire on 11 November. This was followed by the *Paris Peace Conference, in which peace terms were dictated to the defeated countries. The Central Powers lost the war due to inferior numbers and equipment on the battlefield. Especially with the entry of the USA and the defeat of Russia in 1917/18, the war developed as a confrontation between, mainly, parliamentary democracies on the one hand, and autocratic regimes on the other. For instance, in Austria-Hungary, parliament had been suspended for the first three years of the war, while Germany had become a virtual military dictatorship 1916–18. Ultimately, the war proved that democratic systems were much better able to raise resources than authoritarian ones in which large parts of the population would have had no stake and for which they will not allow themselves to be mobilized fully.

Consequences Apart from the immeasurable economic damage, the cost of the war was a severe blow especially to the British Empire, which bore almost 30 per cent of the total cost (Germany bore 20 per cent, France 15 per cent, and the USA 14 per cent). It was the human cost, however, which had such tremendous effects on the minds and culture of generations to come. This cultural effect was at least as prominent among Europeans as among the non-European belligerents in the Dominions whose sufferings were, perhaps, disproportionately high in relation to their population or their interest in the war. With a population of under eight million people, Canada contributed a total of over 600,000 men, of whom 60,000 were killed. New Zealand sent over 100,000 people out of a population of around one million people, 16,781 of whom were killed. Of around five million Australians, 330,000 fought in Europe, of whom almost 60,000 died. In total, around sixty-five million soldiers participated in the war. Of these, around twenty-one million were wounded. It resulted in almost ten million dead (including around one million missing), among them 1.8 million Germans, 1.7 million from the Russian Empire, 1.4 million French, 1.2 million from Austria-Hungary, 950,000 from the British Empire, 460,000 from Italy, and 115,000 from the USA. Relative to the size of the population, the biggest losses were suffered by Serbia, whose number of dead represented almost 6 per cent of the population, followed by France (3.4 per cent), Romania (3.3 per cent), and Germany (3 per cent).

World War II (1 Sept. 1939 – 2 Sept. 1945)
The world's biggest military confrontation,
which started with the German invasion of
Poland, and was extended into a global war by
the Japanese attack on *Pearl Harbor.

Causes While by the late 1930s most of
continental Europe was governed by
authoritarian regimes, *Hitler's *Nazi regime
outstripped all others in aggressiveness,
efficiency, and the resources which it could
mobilize. The ideological foundation of the
regime, as outlined in Hitler's book, *Mein
Kampf* (1925, 1926), was the *Social Darwinian
idea that Germans were in the forefront of the
superior 'Aryan' race. 'Roman Peoples'
(French, Italians, Spanish, etc.) were
considered inferior, while the Slavic Peoples
(Poles, Russians, etc.) were penultimate in
Hitler's racial ranking, destined at best to be
servants to the 'Aryans'. Most terrifyingly, he
considered the Jews to be the most inferior
race of all, whose presence posed 'a problem'
as long as they existed alongside Aryans.
These mad, prejudiced, *anti-Semitic, and
wholly unscientific ideas formed the basis of
Nazi aggression and propaganda. They were
the source of his hostility to the *Versailles
Treaty, which through the 'war guilt clause'
had humiliated the 'Aryan' race, through the
*reparations had stifled German
development, and through the territorial
losses had deprived 'Aryans' of vital 'living
space'.

Once he was firmly in power, Hitler set
about revising the Versailles Treaty to
establish German predominance with
accelerating speed. After a successful vote by
the *Saarland to accede to Germany (acquired
through legal means on 13 January 1935), he
broke the Versailles Treaty by introducing
conscription on 16 March 1935. He introduced
the racist *Nuremberg Laws on 15 September
1935, and on 7 March 1936 ordered the
military occupation of the demilitarized
Rhineland (see also *Ruhr District). On 12
March 1938, German troops marched into
Austria to instigate *Anschluss. On 1 October
1938, Hitler ordered the occupation of the
*Sudetenland. As his foreign policy became
more aggressive, so did his racial policy,
leading to the *Kristallnacht of 9 November
1938. The invasion of the Czech lands
(Bohemia and Moravia (on 15 March 1939) was
the first act of aggression which clearly went
beyond a revision of the Versailles Treaty. By
now, other powers such as Britain and France
had woken up to the possibility of a war, so
that on 31 March 1939, Britain assured Poland
of its help in the event of a German attack,
with France later doing the same. Yet Hitler
was unimpressed. Having taken the other

territories with such ease, he attacked Poland
on 1 September 1939, after gaining support
from the Soviet Union in the *Hitler-Stalin
Pact, and the confirmation of the *Fascist
German–Italian *Axis with the 'Pact of Steel'
on 22 May 1939.

War in Europe, 1939–1941 After *Blitzkrieg
tactics fully exploited the German technical
and military dominance over the inefficient
and ill-equipped Polish army, Poland was
occupied by 28 September 1939 and,
according to the Hitler–Stalin Pact, divided
between Germany and the USSR. After a brief
*phoney war, neutral Denmark was attacked
and occupied on 9 April 1940, while the
invasion of Norway lasted from 9 April to 10
June 1940. German success in the Norway
campaign, only days before the British had
planned to land there, provoked a political
crisis in Britain, and led to the replacement of
Neville *Chamberlain with the defiant
*Churchill.

On 10 May 1940, the German army began its
western campaign. As in World War I,
Germany disregarded the neutrality of
Belgium and Luxembourg, and this time also
of the Netherlands. German forces cut
through to the Channel, separating the Low
Countries from France, and encircled the
*British Expeditionary Force, as well as many
French and some Belgian troops, at *Dunkirk.
France surrendered on 22 June 1940.
Northern and western France (including
Paris), as well as Belgium, the Netherlands,
and Luxembourg, remained occupied, while
in the south of France a puppet government
under *Pétain was established in *Vichy. This
left only Britain undefeated, and Hitler was at
the peak of his success.

Throughout the following year, Germany
failed to establish air superiority over the
British Royal Air Force in the Battle of
*Britain. As a result, in October 1941 Hitler
had to postpone his plans for an invasion of
Britain, Operation 'Sea Lion'. In 1941, the war
spread significantly. Italy, which had joined
the war on 10 June 1940, aimed at establishing
its hegemony in the Mediterranean, thus
taking the war to North Africa and the
Balkans. This proved to be a great liability to
Hitler, who was forced to join the *North
African campaign as well as the costly
occupation of the Balkans to prevent the
defeat of the ill-prepared Italian forces.

By 22 June 1941, Hitler no longer allowed
himself to be distracted by the ongoing
campaigns in the south or against Britain.
Instead, he embarked on the *Barbarossa
campaign, taking the war to the Soviet Union.
This was the absolute conclusion to his
dreams: the ultimate gain of 'living space' for

'Aryans', and the subjection of all Slav peoples as slaves. He complemented this ultimate goal with the final stage in his *anti-Semitic policies, agreed at the Wannsee Conference: the extermination of Jews in *concentration camps. By the end of 1941, then, German territorial control was at its peak, with the German army stretched to the limit by a 2,200 mile (3,500 km) long front in the USSR, *partisan warfare in the Balkans, and an ongoing campaign in North Africa.

Despite its initial reluctance to get involved in the war, by 1941, the USA had become a major player, even before its official entry. Through the *Lend-Lease Act and the *Atlantic Charter, it was ideologically committed to the defeat of Hitler. The US supported this with extensive, and crucial, arms supplies to Britain and, from 1941, the USSR. The USA was thus emotionally and militarily ready when Hitler declared war on it on 11 December 1941, four days after *Pearl Harbor. US troops poured into the UK in preparation for a landing in France, postponed after the *Dieppe Raid until 1944, and they hastened *Rommel's demise in Africa through the 'Operation Torch' landings in Morocco.

By the summer of 1943, the war had turned decisively in the Allies' favour: Germany and Italy had been expelled from North Africa, while the Allies landed in Italy on 10 July 1943. Meanwhile, in the main battleground of the war, *Zhukov's *Red Army had won the decisive battles of *Stalingrad and *Kursk. German troops subsequently fought in rearguard actions, their position becoming more desperate as Italy changed sides after the fall of *Mussolini, and joined the war on the side of the Allies (13 October 1943). After the *D-Day landings had opened up a new front in the west, at a time when the *Red Army had regained virtually all of the Soviet Union from German occupation, Germany collapsed. Once they had overcome the German defensive positions in Normandy on 30 July 1944, it took the US and British forces around two months to liberate France in the *Normandy and *North-West Europe campaigns.

Apart from the German troops being demoralized, overstretched, and exhausted, they were further weakened by Hitler's personal direction of the campaigns, as his high-risk strategies and his orders never to retreat depleted army numbers more rapidly. More importantly, apart from racial objectives, which the *SS as well as the army carried out with brutal efficiency, especially in Eastern Europe, there was no political plan for the government of these territories, or the role they should play in the war effort. Indeed,

German atrocities dramatically increased popular hostility and resistance, and thus eased the task of the liberating armies.

From May 1944, the strategic bombing of Germany entered a new stage, destroying not only war production, but also supply routes and oil refineries. After a number of last, desperate measures such as the V1 and V2 bombs developed by *Braun and the *Ardennes offensive, the Allies proceeded to occupy Germany. Berlin fell on 2 May 1945, two days after Hitler had committed suicide. *Montgomery accepted the capitulation of Germany's forces in the north and west on 4 May, and on 7 May, *Eisenhower accepted the German surrender, signed by *Jodl, in Rheims. The act was repeated on 8 May at Berlin, in the presence of representatives of the Soviet Union, and became effective on 9 May 1945.

War in Asia/Pacific Japan's motives for entering World War II resembled very much those of Germany in World War I. A new, powerful nation had emerged whose self-confidence and self-understanding led to an aggressive foreign policy. This upset the geopolitical balance of power and was thus diametrically opposed to the concerns of its neighbours in particular, and to the traditional European and US interests in the area in general. Japan had benefited from the European and American preoccupation with Europe in World War I by extending its influence in China (*Twenty-One Demands).

In consequence, during the 1920s, over 90 per cent of new foreign investments in China were from Japan, and 25 per cent of Japanese exports went to China. Against a background of worldwide *appeasement, in the *Washington Conference Japan accepted a limitation on its naval programme, for which it was richly rewarded with US trade: in the 1920s, 40 per cent of Japanese exports went there, while it imported virtually all of its oil and manufactured goods from there. The general prosperity confirmed those forces arguing for peaceful economic and political development, and inaugurated the relatively democratic Taishô period.

Japan's vulnerability as a country virtually devoid of mineral resources, and with a small agricultural sector, became clear during the Great *Depression. The USA increased tariffs for Japanese imports, while a new era of Sino-American friendship led to the displacement of Japan as China's major trading partner. Since economic prosperity and foreign policy were seen as two sides of the same coin, these difficulties strengthened the military hardliners, whose prestige was enhanced when in 1931 Manchuria was occupied with very little resistance, and the puppet state of

*Manchukuo was established. By 1936, the Taishô system had been dismantled, and replaced by a military dictatorship. The new drive for militarism gave the economy its much needed boost, as the value of industrial production rose sixfold between 1930 and 1941. In that period, the four *zaibatsu conglomerates tripled their total assets.

This kept the momentum for military expansion going, and in 1937, after the *Marco Polo Bridge Incident, the *Sino-Japanese War broke out. The USA, traditionally well-disposed towards China, finally decided to limit Japanese aggression, and on 26 July 1939, *Roosevelt gave six months' warning of trade sanctions. Japan responded by trying to increase its economic self-sufficiency, through further conquest. Taking advantage of the occupation of France, Japanese troops established airbases in northern *Indochina as well as Thailand. It also started to import oil from the Dutch East Indies. The USA retaliated with further trade restrictions, so Japan faced the real threat of being cut off from vital oil imports.

Under such circumstances, Japan's oil reserves would have lasted for less than two years, whereupon Japan would have been forced to give in. Instead, its military leadership chose confrontation, calculating that in 1941 its naval forces in the Pacific were almost at parity with those of the UK and the USA, while increasing US armaments would soon shift this balance in favour of the latter. Japan also took advantage of Hitler's recent attack on the Soviet Union, whose attention was now diverted away from Asia. On 7 December 1941 Japan attacked the USA as a pre-emptive strike in a war that its leaders regarded as inevitable, in order to prevent an equally unavoidable deterioration of the current balance of power away from itself.

Japan's entry into the war extended World War II to Asia and the USA, and threatened, for the only time in their history, the states of Australia and New Zealand. Through its bases in Indochina and Thailand, Japan embarked upon a *Malayan campaign to reach the British 'bastion' of *Singapore, which fell in February 1942. Helped by local anti-colonial movements, Japan occupied Burma as well as Dutch East India (*Indonesia), whose oil production was crucial to the Japanese war effort. Within six months of Pearl Harbor, Japanese influence was at its peak, as it also occupied one-third of China.

However, Japan never fully established dominance against the US navy. In May 1942, Japan's efforts to occupy Australian New Guinea were foiled by the US victory at the Battle of the *Coral Sea, while the Battle of the

*Midway Islands checked Japanese expansion eastwards, and confirmed US naval superiority. In preparation for an assault on the Philippines, and ultimately on Japan itself, during 1943, the *Pacific campaign was largely focused on the painstaking conquest of the Japanese-controlled Micronesian islands. After success in the Battles of *Leyte Gulf and the *Philippines Sea, the US forces under *MacArthur began with the reconquest of the Philippines. Meanwhile, *Mountbatten's *Burma campaign liberated Burma and destroyed three Japanese armies. After successfully taking the Japanese island of *Iwo Jima, the USA began a bombing campaign against Japanese cities, in preparation for an invasion. Encouraged by victory in Europe, and the successful development of the atomic bomb, the Allies under the leadership of the USA issued the *Potsdam Declaration on 26 July 1945, demanding unconditional Japanese surrender. As this was not forthcoming, and in order to save US lives and cut short the gruesome war, *Truman authorized the dropping of the atomic bomb on *Hiroshima and *Nagasaki. Japan immediately ended hostilities, effective from 15 August, and formally surrendered unconditionally on 2 September 1945. Five months after the end of hostilities in Europe, World War II had come to an end.

Consequences The war caused destruction and murder of unparalleled proportions. Of around 110 million participating soldiers, an estimated twenty-seven million were killed. Of these, around half came from the Soviet Union, 6.4 million were Chinese, four million German, 1.2 million Japanese. Great Britain lost 326,000 soldiers, the USA 259,000, Canada 42,000, Australia 27,000, and New Zealand 11,625. Between twenty and thirty million civilians died, including around six million Jews who were murdered in the concentration camps. Through air raids, deportations, mass atrocities, etc., around seven million people were killed in the Soviet Union, around six million in China, 4.2 million in Poland, and 3.8 million in Germany. In total, the Soviet Union lost twenty million people (one-sixth of its total population), China around twelve million, Poland six million (one-sixth of the total population), Germany seven million, Japan two million, Yugoslavia 1.7 million (one-sixth of the total population). France lost 600,000 people (1 in 64), the UK 400,000 (1 in 126), and the USA 300,000 (1 in 716). Relatively unburdened with civilian losses, Australia lost around 1 in 266 people, Canada 1 in 274, and New Zealand 1 in 146.

Apart from the actual horrors of the war, two geopolitical consequences stand out. In south-east Asia, World War II marked the beginning of the end of European *imperialism and colonialism. The Philippines became a sovereign state in 1946. Indonesia gained its independence in 1949, after a bitter struggle with the Dutch colonial forces. *Ho Chi Minh's *Vietminh resisted the return of the French to Indochina, which became independent after the *Indochina War in the *Geneva Agreements of 1954. In China, the War turned the tide decisively towards *Mao's *Chinese Communist Party, against *Chiang Kai-shek's *Guomintang.

The second, and most fundamental, shift concerned the relative decline of European power on the world stage. The ensuing *Cold War was determined by two power blocs dominated by the new superpowers, the USA and the USSR. The war had demonstrated their singular geopolitical importance, as they had contributed the lion's share to the Allied victory: the US materially, the USSR in human cost.

Wrangel, Piotr Nikolaevich Baron (b. 15 Aug. 1878, d. 25 Apr. 1928). Russian general

Born in St Petersburg, he joined a cavalry regiment as a private in 1901, and by 1910 had graduated from the Academy of the General Staff. He commanded a cavalry corps during World War I, but following the 1917 *Russian (October) Revolution he joined the counter-revolutionary forces. In the ensuing *Russian Civil War, Wrangel became commander of the Caucasian army, with which he advanced deep into Russian territory. He was dismissed after a quarrel with *Denikin, whereupon he left for Constantinople. He returned after Denikin's defeat and took command of the rump forces of the *White Army in the *Crimea, trying to galvanize popular support through land reform. Despite early successes he was defeated by the *Red Army, whereupon he organized the evacuation of over 150,000 soldiers and civilians across the Black Sea to Turkey. He died in Belgium.

WTO (World Trade Organization)

The successor to *GATT, founded by the Marrakesh Agreement of 1994 and effective from 1 January 1995. Its aim has been to promote economic liberalization, mutuality, and preferred trade rules for all member states. Its highest decision-making organ is a ministerial conference of all member states which meets every two years. Beyond this, it acts as an arbiter in international trade disputes between member states. At the same time, its commitment to economic *globalization has made it the target of mass demonstrations. This reflected widespread concern that unbridled economic liberalization would help the economy of the strong against the weak member states, and that globalization destroyed cultural diversity.

The WTO has acted as arbiter in trade disputes between members, and it directed negotiations for a world-wide reduction in tariffs. In 2000, an agreement was launched at Doha and subsequently negotiated between member states. By 2007, what became known as the 'Doha round' had still not been concluded, chiefly because of the reluctance of the wealthier states, notably the US and, to a lesser exent the EU, to reduce agricultural subsidies. In 2007, Vietnam became the 150th member of the WTO.

Wuchang Revolution (10 Oct. 1911–1 Jan. 1912)

An uprising in China by the revolutionary movement which had been gathering momentum for over a decade. Its outbreak was triggered by the accidental explosion in the city of Wuchang of a bomb in the revolutionary headquarters on 9 October. With the revolutionary leaders *Sun Yat-sen and Huan Hsing absent, the revolutionaries (around 2,000) decided to strike on 10 October, taking control of the city within hours. This was followed by the rapid secession of cities and provinces from the authority of the Qing dynasty, and by 4 December, Shanghai and Nanjing (Nanking) had fallen into control of the revolutionary movement, which by this time controlled over two-thirds of China. Sun Yat-sen was elected President on 29 December 1911. The declaration of the Republic of China on 1 January 1912 effectively ended the revolution. The victory over the Manchu Qing dynasty was complete when *Yuan Shikai persuaded the child emperor, *Pu Yi, to abdicate.

Wye Agreement (October 1998)

Concluded in Wye Plantation near Washington D.C., and mediated by President *Clinton, it aimed to revive the peace process between Palestinians and Israelis following the collapse of the *Oslo and *Gaza-Jericho Agreements. Israel committed itself to withdrawing from 13 per cent of the West Bank territory within 90 days, and to transfer a further 14 per cent of the land under joint Israeli–Palestinian control to sole control of the *Palestinian National Authority. The Palestinians also received a transit corridor that connected its territories in the Gaza strip and the West Bank. In return, the *PLO agreed to change its charter which called for the abolition of the state of Israel. However, tensions between Palestinians and the Israeli army continued, so that the Israelis refused to implement most aspects of the agreement. An additional protocol negotiated between *Arafat and *Barak came into force in 1999. The Israeli army withdrew from further territory, and the transit corridor was opened in 2000. However, even under Barak the agreement was not implemented in full, as violence between Palestinians and Israelis escalated. In March 2002 much of the West Bank was re-occupied by the Israeli army, nullifying all the painful peace accords reached in the 1990s.

Wyszynski, Stefan (b. 3 Aug. 1901, d. 28 May 1981). Primate of Poland 1948–81

Born in Zuzela, he studied at the Roman Catholic University of Lublin, before becoming a teacher at a seminary, where he was noted for his social catholicism and his progressiveness. During World War II he went underground, and in 1945 was appointed Bishop of Lublin. In 1948, he became Bishop of Warsaw, and in 1953 was made a cardinal. An outspoken critic of government repression, he was arrested and confined to a monastery, 1951–6. Then, he reached an understanding of coexistence with *Gomulka. The Roman *Catholic Church subsequently refrained from criticism in matters not of direct concern, and was in return given the freedom to minister to the spiritual needs of its flock. Even though the Church thus became careful not to call for open opposition to the government, its very presence as a social and cultural force that allowed refuge from the Communist state machinery became the greatest challenge to the state, which in the 1980s it proved unable to overcome.

X

Xi'an Incident (12–25 Dec. 1936)

After nine years, *Chiang Kai-shek's policy of fighting the Chinese *Communist Party (CCP) before turning against the foreign aggressor, Japan, had come under increasing criticism within his own ranks, especially in the northern armies which had lost Manchuria to the Japanese in 1931 (*Manchukuo). In early 1936, their leader, *Chang Hsüeh-liang, entered secret negotiations with the *Communist Party about a common front against the Japanese. When Chiang Kai-shek came to Chang's headquarters in Xi'an, the capital of Shaanxi Province, in order to discuss his latest strategic plan for a battle against the Communists, Chang put him under house arrest. After being held for thirteen days, Chiang finally agreed to Chang's eight demands, mainly an end to civil war, and a *United Front with the Communists against the Japanese. Chang accompanied Chiang back to Nanjing, whereupon it was Chang's turn to be detained and this lasted for as long as Chiang was alive (though from 1949 he was under house arrest).

SINO-JAPANESE WAR

Yahya Khan, Agha Mohammed (b. 4 Feb. 1917, d. 8 Aug. 1980). President of Pakistan 1969–71

Born in Peshawar, he was educated at Punjab University and the Indian Military Academy, whereupon he served in the Indian army on the North-West Frontier, in the Middle East, and in Italy. He returned to create the Pakistan Staff College in 1947. A protégé of *Ayub Kahn, he assisted in the 1958 coup, commanded the Pakistan army in the 1965 war with India, and in 1966 he became Commander-in-Chief of the Pakistan army. In 1969 he used his mentor's unpopularity to replace him as President. In response to growing protests in East Pakistan, he reversed his predecessor's 1962 constitution and offered elections with an equal vote in both parts of Pakistan. This backfired, however, and led to an overall majority for the East Pakistan *Awami League, and ultimately for independence for East Pakistan as Bangladesh, after a bloody civil war. This made his position untenable, and forced him to resign in favour of Zulfikar Ali *Bhutto.

Yalta Conference (4–11 Feb. 1945)
A meeting between the *Allied leaders *Stalin, *Churchill, and the ailing *Roosevelt in the *Crimea. With their armies already on German territory, the final stages of strategy for *World War II were discussed, as well as the proposed occupation of Germany. The new border between the Soviet Union and Poland along the *Curzon Line was agreed. For its resulting territorial losses, Poland was to be granted territorial gains in the west; although Stalin mentioned the *Oder-Neisse Line as a new border between Poland and Germany, this was left undecided pending the follow-up conference (eventually held at *Potsdam). Germany and Austria were each divided into four postwar occupation zones, as France was accepted as a fourth main Allied power. Finally, Stalin promised Soviet entry into the war with Japan around three months after German capitulation. The results represented a far cry from the drastic *Morgenthau plan proposed only months earlier. Also, the conference was notable for the continued atmosphere of goodwill and harmony, despite the availability of secret reports in the USA and Britain about the aggressive and sometimes brutal activities of the Soviet military governments in its occupied areas.

Yamamoto Isoruku (b. 4 Apr. 1884, d. 18 Apr. 1943). Japanese admiral
Educated at the Japanese Naval College, he was wounded in the *Russo-Japanese War (1904–5), after which he went on to naval staff college. He served as a naval attaché in Washington, and in the 1930s was responsible for developing the Japanese Navy Air Corps. As Vice-Minister for the Navy he spoke against the *Axis agreement with Germany and Italy, but was nevertheless appointed Commander-in-Chief of a combined squadron in 1939. Yamamoto always opposed Japan's participation in a conflict with the USA, but once the decision had been taken to go to war he devised the raid on *Pearl Harbor and directed the Battle of the Java Sea. He suffered defeat, however, in the Battles of the *Coral Sea and *Midway Island. In April 1943, US intelligence identified his movements and his plane was destroyed over the Solomon Islands.

Yamashita Tomoyuki (b. 8 Nov. 1885, d. 23 Feb. 1946). Japanese general
Born near Tokyo, as a young officer he served in the *Russo-Japanese War and in World War I. He attended staff officers' college (1926) and then held a series of staff appointments. He was one of the young army officers involved in the 26 February Incident (1936) although he is believed to have opposed the coup itself while having some sympathy for its objectives. He was perceived as a close rival of *Tôjô Hideki, and for that reason he may have been kept away from Tokyo with postings in Manchuria and south-east Asia. As commander of the 25th Army, which invaded Malaya in December 1941, Yamashita captured *Singapore in February 1942 and led his army into Burma. In 1944 he was given command in the Philippines, organizing fierce opposition to US landings at *Leyte and on Luzon, where he continued to fight on until the 'formal' surrender of 2 September. In 1946 he was tried and executed in Manila for atrocities committed by troops under his command.
MALAYAN CAMPAIGNS; BURMA CAMPAIGNS; SINGAPORE, FALL OF

Yan'an (Yen-an)

A town and district in the northern Shaanxi Province in China, which became the headquarters of the Chinese *Communist Party (CCP) after the *Long March in 1935. An initial period of instability ended when hostilities with the *National Revolutionary Army stopped, owing to the formation of the *United Front in 1937. Thereafter, Yan'an Province was developed into a model Soviet through land reforms, rapidly improving social services (more schools and health centres), lower taxation, and political organization. This contrasted sharply with the inefficiency and graft of *Chiang Kai-shek's *Guomindang government, and provided the basis for the CCP's growing popularity. Subsequently, during the *Sino-Japanese war, CCP membership increased from 20,000 to almost three million. The CCP's army, which avoided open warfare and pursued guerilla tactics instead, grew to number 1.5 million in this period. By 1945, more than ninety million people lived under Communist control. The Yan'an period, then, marked a pivotal and successful episode of Communist China, providing the foundation of CCP success in the *Chinese Civil War.

Yeltsin, Boris Nikolaevich (b. 1 Feb. 1931, d. 23 Apr. 2007). President of Russia 1991–9

Early career Born in Butka near Sverdlovsk, he became a construction worker there and in 1955 graduated from the Urals Polytechnic Institute as a construction engineer. He joined the *Communist Party in 1961, and made a name for himself as an energetic promoter of new housing as chief of house construction in the party regional committee (1966–76). Yeltsin became head of the regional party committee in 1976, and in 1981 became a member of the Central Committee of the Soviet Communist Party. In 1985 he was one of the first appointments of the new Party Secretary, *Gorbachev, as first secretary of the Moscow Communist Party committee (effectively Mayor). He became a candidate member of the *Politburo in early 1986. He applied tremendous industry to his Moscow post. Through populist gestures such as declining many of his predecessors' privileges (e.g. the official limousine), as well as through ambitious anti-corruption drives, he became extremely popular among Muscovites.

Yeltsin's success encouraged him to become an increasingly outspoken supporter of *perestroika, outpacing an irritated Gorbachev. His reforms also antagonized most other members of the party hierarchy, and after a heart attack on 9 November 1987, he was 'persuaded' to resign from his offices, and was demoted to become deputy chairman of the state construction committee. He staged a spectacular comeback, however, avoiding oblivion through skilful use of the media. Taking advantage of Gorbachev's recent introduction of multi-candidate elections to the Congress of People's Deputies, he was elected Deputy on 27 March 1989 with 89.6 per cent of the popular vote in Moscow. In this position, he increased his popularity by articulating the general dissatisfaction with the progress of Gorbachev's reforms. By 25 May 1990 he had advanced to become Chairman of the Russian Supreme Soviet, and was thus effectively Russian Prime Minister.

In office On 12 June 1991 Yeltsin called a general election, in which he became the first popularly elected President of Russia, with an overwhelming majority. The authority which resulted from this became evident when he foiled the *August coup of 1991. In the wake of the coup, he outlawed the Soviet Communist Party in Russia, while his creation of the *CIS (Commonwealth of Independent States) on 9 December 1991 heralded the breakup of the Soviet Union.

Yeltsin's economic reforms failed to show early dividends, and he became prone to the same impatient attacks that he himself had formerly directed against Gorbachev. In the *October Putsch, Yeltsin ordered troops to storm the White House and dissolve the obstinate Congress of People's Deputies. Yeltsin pushed through a new constitution with wide presidential powers, which was only narrowly accepted on 12 December 1993.

As the economy deteriorated further, his economic reforms became more erratic, as he frequently switched his allegiances between reformers and conservatives. He also lost increasing control of day-to-day policy, incapacitated by excessive drinking and accumulating health problems, as he suffered from four heart attacks in his period of office. Yeltsin came to resemble more and more an autocratic leader from the Soviet era, a parallelism that became complete with his decision to order the invasion of *Chechnya, in complete disregard of domestic and international opinion. Given this impressive display of incompetence, he fought a remarkable re-election campaign in 1996, recovering his popularity not least through his total control of the media, as well as the lack of a credible challenger. Through promises such as the abolition of conscription, and the drastic reduction in the price of the nation's (and his own) favourite drink, vodka, he did manage to win the elections of 3 July 1996.

Yeltsin became even more corrupt in his second term. In 1998, he presided over a collapse of the country's economic finances and a deep economic recession. Yeltsin's political authority was severely compromised thereafter, as a succession of Prime Ministers he appointed were unable to assert his authority against international financial and political pressure on the one hand, and a rebellious parliament on the other. On 31 December 1999 he handed over power to his Premier, Vladimir *Putin.

Yemen, North

A relatively poor country on the south-western tip of the Arabian peninsula, distinguished by a rich ancient culture.

The area came under the rule of the *Ottoman Empire in 1517. The scene of heavy fighting during World War I between Ottoman troops and the British garrisons in Aden, it became independent in 1918. With British support, Imam Yahya was declared ruler. He established a central government and administration, while satisfying the traditional Muslim tribes through the establishment of Islamic law, the Shariah. He was assassinated in 1948 and succeeded by his son Ahmad, who ruled until his death in 1962. During this period, the country became relatively isolated and cut off from technological and economic developments. In the last decade of his rule, Ahmad faced increasingly strong opposition from those sections dissatisfied with the country's isolation, i.e. urban intellectuals, the army, and commercial groups.

Ahmad's son, Muhammad al-Badr, was immediately opposed by General Abdullah al-Sallal, who proclaimed the **Yemen Arab Republic**. While al-Badr enjoyed the support of Saudi Arabia and the UK, al-Sallal was backed by both Syria and Egypt. Civil war ensued and was not ended until 1970. A fragile republican coalition government was formed, which was replaced in 1974 by a military coup. Under the military government of, first, Hussein al Ghashmi and, from 1978, Ali Abdullah Saleh, the country began to look to Western and Saudi Arabian help and advice, despite the hostility of many of the traditionalist tribal leaders. Given the latter's opposition, progress was relatively modest, which led to the persistence of low rates of literacy and life expectancy. Despite a number of clashes with its neighbour, the Democratic People's Republic of (South) *Yemen, during the 1970s and 1980s, it united with the latter in 1990 to form the Republic of *Yemen.

Yemen, Republic of

A recently unified country on the southern tip of the Arabian peninsula, it has few mineral resources and is the poorest country of the Middle East.

Contemporary history (since 1990) A country on the southern tip of the Arabian peninsula which emerged from the unification of North *Yemen (to the west) and South *Yemen (to the east) in 1990. Unity remained fragile, as it followed decades of strife between the two countries, and was ill-prepared. Insufficient efforts were made to integrate two societies that had developed quite differently, with one still largely based on Islamic traditionalist lines (North Yemen), while Communist egalitarian structures had been imposed on the other (South Yemen).

The President of the more populous North (since 1978), Ali Abdullah Saleh (b. 1942), became President of the new country, with the former President of South Yemen (since 1986), Bakr al-Attas, becoming Prime Minister. The latter's Socialist Party came third in the 1993 elections. Feeling himself more and more sidelined, al-Attas declared South Yemen independent once again on 21 May 1994. Aden was quickly occupied by North Yemenite troops (7 July 1994), so that unity was re-established.

A new constitution was passed on 28 September 1994, which established Islamic law, the Shariah, as the country's legal basis. Saleh was formally elected to a five-year term as President. While the South had thus become totally dominated by the North, traditional border disputes with Saudi Arabia over Yemen's northern border continued, particularly after the discovery of significant oil reserves in the area. The border disputes were formally resolved in 1999, with the creation of a 40 km demilitarized zone between both states. In 2001 Yemeni voters approved a new constitution in a referendum, which allowed Saleh to continue in office as President.

Contemporary politics (since 2000) Although the political dominance of the North continued through the parliamentary strength of the General People's Congress, a growing challenge was presented by *Islamic fundamentalist groups,

some of which had connections to Osama
*Bin Laden. In 2000 two terrorist suicide
bombers sponsored by Bin Laden attacked an
American warship anchoring in Aden, USS
Cole, killing seventeen soldiers. In 2004, a
revolt broke out by supporters of the cleric
Hussein al-Houthi. Al-Houthi was killed in that
year, but his supporters continued sporadic
violent attacks against the government in
subsequent years. In 2006, Saleh was
confirmed in office.

Yemen, South

An Arab country whose strategic port of
Aden brought it to the attention of the world's
large powers.

Aden was occupied by the British in 1839, to
help secure the British passage to India. It was
ruled from India by the presidency of Bombay,
until it was governed directly by the
government of the British colony of India in
1932. Aden itself became a Crown Colony
in 1937, with its surrounding territory
becoming a British protectorate. The latter
became the South Arabian Federation of Arab
Emirates in 1959, which the colony of Aden
joined in 1963. Influenced by the republican
and Arabic nationalist movements in
neighbouring North *Yemen, a National
Liberation Front emerged in a civil war and
was victorious against the rival FLOSY (Front
for the Liberation of Occupied South Yemen).

The civil war resulted in independence in
1967, as the **Democratic People's Republic of
Yemen**. Attempts were made to impose
*Communism upon an Arab society, through
nationalization, collectivization and the
creation of co-operatives, and central
planning. All this was established with
generous help from the USSR, which in return
gained Aden as an important naval base.
Relatively egalitarian income distribution and
a reduction in illiteracy failed to gain
widespread acceptance of the regime. After a
brief civil war in 1986, unity talks with North
Yemen succeeded in the late 1980s,
whereupon a united Republic of *Yemen was
created.

Yen-an, see YAN'AN

Yezhov, Nikolai Ivanovich (b. 1895, d. 1939?). Head of Soviet Secret Police

Born in St Petersburg, he joined the
*Bolsheviks in April 1917 and took part in
the *Russian (October) Revolution of 1917.
During the *Russian Civil War, he was a
political commissar in the *Red Army. He
then worked for the Communist Party's
Central Committee, becoming a member in
1934. Yezhov became the head of the *NKVD
as People's Commissar for Internal Affairs in

1936. In this capacity, he led *Stalin's terror
campaign. By this time a drug addict, he
became the most feared man in the Soviet
Union after Stalin. The *Great Purges are also
known as the Yezhovshchina. Briefly a
member of the *Politburo from 1937, he was
dismissed from the NKVD and replaced by
*Beria in December 1938. He was arrested in
March 1939 and probably executed soon
afterwards.

Yom Kippur War (Oct. 1973)

Known by Arabs as the **October War**. It began
on 6 October, the Day of Atonement (Yom
Kippur), the holiest day of prayer and fasting
in the Jewish year. In their surprise attack
Egypt and Syria won some initial success, as
Egyptian troops advanced over the Suez Canal
while the Syrians reached the *Golan Heights,
which had been occupied by Israel since 1967.
Although caught unawares, Israel forcefully
counter-attacked within two days. On
8 October Israeli forces recrossed the Suez
Canal further west, encircling part of the
Egyptian army and advancing on Cairo; at the
same time other Israeli troops recovered the
Golan Heights, with tanks advancing to
within 35 miles of Damascus. Alarmed by
Israeli successes, oil-rich Saudi Arabia put
pressure on its main customer, the USA, to
persuade Israel to halt its advances and accept
*UN mediation. A cease-fire was arranged on
24 October, followed by disengagement along
the Suez Canal and the establishment of a
*UN peacekeeping force on the Golan
Heights. Even though Israel technically won
the war, the first days of the war had shown
that the Israeli army was not invincible, which
restored Arab pride after their defeat in the
*Six Day War. Furthermore, Israel was only
able to regain the military initiative through
extensive popular mobilization, and at the
expense of heavy casualties.

Yoshida Shigeru (b. 22 Sept. 1878, d. 20 Oct. 1967). Prime Minister of Japan 1946–7, 1948–54

Early career A graduate of Tokyo University,
he entered the Japanese diplomatic service
and held various posts including that of
Japan's minister in Rome and London.
Because he was perceived to favour a less
hostile relationship with Britain and the USA,
his appointment as Foreign Minister in
*Hirota Kôki's Cabinet was blocked. With the
expansion of Japan's war he was excluded
from a role in the government. In the closing
stages of the war, Yoshida fell under the
suspicion of the Japanese authorities for
advocating that Japan sue for peace and he
was detained by the military police.

In power After 1945, Yoshida Shigeru was particularly influential in shaping the idea that Japan would choose to pursue its own economic development while relying on its allies for its foreign and defence policies. He served as Foreign Minister in the early postwar Cabinets. When *Hatoyama Ichiro was purged by the occupation authorities, Yoshida became his successor. He formed a Liberal Party government after the 1946 general election. Although initially distrusted by the US authorities because of his involvement with the prewar establishment, Yoshida the seasoned diplomat proved to be an ideal Prime Minister in the late 1940s, when the main concern of the Japanese government was the negotiation of the postwar settlement and the restoration of sovereignty. With this task concluded in 1952, Yoshida managed to cling on to government for two more years, although he proved to be an increasingly unpopular figure for his domineering style of leadership. He was largely superseded by the politicians who led the *Liberal Democratic Party after 1955, although two of his disciples, *Ikeda Hayato and *Satô Eisaku, went on to be Prime Minister.

Young Maori movement

Once dreams of an independent *Maori state had been shattered by the early 1900s, a new generation of Maori leaders emerged, many of them educated at Te Aute College, such as *Ngata, *Pomare, and *Buck. They believed in the need to accept the benefits of European society, some of them even considering Maori culture to be inferior. They went to live in the towns of the east coast and successfully trained in the professions such as teaching, law, and medicine. They created a political party (the Young Maori Party) which from 1905 represented the four Maori electoral districts which had been created in 1867. For the next three decades, they had a disproportionate influence in New Zealand politics. While perhaps not as influential on Maori culture as *Te Puera Herangi, they were able to achieve important health and educational reforms, thus improving Maori welfare, and encouraging Maori population growth after decades of rapid decline. During the 1930s the movement lost its support to the more radical *Ratana movement.

Young Plan, see REPARATIONS

Young Turks

A loose group of opposition leaders which began to form in the *Ottoman Empire in response to the abrogation of the constitution by Sultan Abdülhamit II in 1878. It was organized clandestinely in 1889 as the Association for the Union of Ottomans, which in 1895 became the Committee for Union and Progress. It called for the removal from power of Abdülhamit II, and the reintroduction of constitutional rule, basing its popular appeal on Islamic *nationalism. Its members became the leaders of a rebellion against Abdülhamit in 1908, who was subsequently forced to establish constitutional rule. He reneged on some of his promises, whereupon a second rebellion removed him from power in 1909. Relations between the Young Turks, many of whom had remained outside the government, and the new Sultan, Muhammad V, remained uneasy until the coup of Enver Pasha (b. 1881, d. 1922) in 1913 finally brought them to power. The Young Turk government entered World War I, and directed the *Armenian genocide from 1915.

Ypres, Battles of (1914–18)

During *World War I a total of four battles took place near the Belgian city of Ypres, representing various attempts by the belligerents to overcome the war of attrition that developed on the Western Front by outflanking their entrenched positions to the south.

1. After the retreat of the *British Expeditionary Force from Mons, between 12 October and 11 November 1914 the Germans attacked and captured the Messines ridge. However, they failed to take Ypres or to reach the Channel ports.

2. Another German attack (22 April–24 May 1915) failed to break the Allied line. This battle represented the first major Canadian involvement in the war, and proved a 'baptism of fire'. Suffering from the first chemical gas attack of the war, the Canadian reputation for bravery was earned by its 1st Division suffering a casualty rate of 46 per cent.

3. An Allied offensive with fundamentally Australian and Canadian support started on 7 June 1917, when they exploded nineteen mines dug under the German positions. It continued into the *Passchendaele offensive, which lasted until November 1917.

4. The last battle was part of the final German *Marne offensive in March–April 1918. The Germans were held at the River Lys and once again failed to capture the devastated city of Ypres. It is estimated that over 500,000 British and Commonwealth troops died fighting around Ypres during World War I.

Yrigoyen, Hipólito (b. 13 July 1850, d. 3 July 1933). Argentine President 1916–22, 1928–30

Under his leadership, the *Radical Party emerged as the principal representative of the Argentinian middle classes from 1893, and he presided over the party's heyday (1916–30). As President he violently repressed riots in 1918–19 caused by the recession and inflation that hit Argentina as part of a worldwide recession. The 1920s were marked by relative calm. From 1929 onwards Argentina was affected by the Great *Depression, though it did not suffer as much as other economies. He was ousted by a military coup of officers deeply suspicious of democracy.

Yuan Shikai (Yuan Shih-k'ai) (b. 16 Sept. 1859, d. 6 June 1916). President of the Republic of China 1912–16

Born in Henan Province into an aristocratic family, he entered military service and went to Korea, where he distinguished himself as commander and army reformer. Returning at the head of a well-organized army, his support was important in the accession to power of the Empress Dowager Cixi in 1898. For this, he was promoted to become Governor of Shandong (1899–1901). He then moved up in government ranks, until he was President of the Ministry of Foreign Affairs (1907–9). Throughout, he was the regime's strongest personality, and carried out substantial army and educational reforms. He was dismissed from office after Cixi's death, but remained an influential figure, particularly because of the size and strength of his army. He was recalled by the royal house to become Prime Minister after the outbreak of the *Wuchang Revolution. In this office, he persuaded the advisers of *Pu Yi that he should abdicate, for which feat he demanded the presidency of the new Republic. However, he betrayed his republican allies by attempting to create a dynasty himself, and expelling other political leaders such as *Sun Yat-sen. His army proved insufficient for him to create a strong government, since he lacked any broader political platform. It had proved strong enough, however, to destroy the Wuchang Revolution, so that his death left a power vacuum which subjected China to an era of *warlordism until *Chiang Kai-shek's *Northern Expedition.

Yudhoyono, Susilo Bambang (SBY) (b. 9 Sept 1949), President of Indonesia, 2004–

Born in Pacitan, East Java, he graduated from the Military Academy in 1973, and rose quickly through the army ranks to become general. Popularly known by his initials, SBY left the army in 2000, serving as minister in the government of Abdurrahman Wahid. He continued to hold a position in the government of *Sukarnoputri, as minister responsible for counter-terrorism. Owing to his rising popularity in that position, SBY was sacked by his jealous President. He founded the Democratic Party, and on the promise of overcoming corruption and graft he won Indonesia's first democratic elections. Although SBY struggled to improve the economy, he did manage to sign a breakthrough peace agreement with the rebels in the Aceh province, ending years of bitter conflict there.

Yugoslavia

A heterogeneous state whose only period of stability (1945–80) was achieved through political repression.

Statehood and early tensions (1918–45) A state created on 1 December 1918 as the Kingdom of Serbs, Croats, and Slovenes. It emerged from the *Corfu Pact of 1917, and was a heterogeneous country consisting of *Slovenia, *Croatia, *Bosnia-Hercegovina, *Serbia, and *Montenegro. The new country's religious and ethnic diversity was expressed in two mutually contrasting ideas about the nature of the new state. Slovenia and Croatia had joined the union with Serbia largely for defensive reasons, to protect their territories against Austrian or Italian revisionist (*irredentist) pretensions. They demanded a federal state, which would leave each component with extensive autonomy. By contrast, Serbia was a relatively homogeneous country which had gained increasing self-confidence since independence in 1878, so that it was interested mainly in increasing its power over other territories in a 'Greater Serbia'.

This latter conception won the day, when a centralized constitution was adopted by a narrow parliamentary majority in 1921. In protest, the Croatian People's Peasants' Party (CPPP) as well as other groups made parliament extremely unstable. After the assassination of the CPPP leader, Stjepan Radić, in 1928, King *Alexander I dissolved parliament and created a royal dictatorship, changing the country's name to Yugoslavia ('Land of Southern Slavs'). His rule strengthened Serbian predominance even further, which motivated the growth of a number of terrorist movements, the most important of which became the *Ustase movement, which carried out Alexander's assassination in 1934.

Despite an agreement on Croatian autonomy negotiated by the Prime Minister, Cvetković, in 1939, emotions against Serbia remained strong. After the German invasion of Yugoslavia in 1941, the Ustase movement was eager to create a *Fascist puppet regime as the Independent State of Croatia. Until 1945 its brutal government was responsible for the expulsion or killing of some 600,000 Serbs. In retaliation, once *Tito's *partisan rebels had established their dominance over the *Chetniks, they vented their wrath on the Croatians, slaughtering many Ustase Fascists, as well as innocent Croatians, in return.

The Tito era (1945–80) With bitterness and hatred between the country's fifteen nationalities at an all-time high, another attempt at unification could only be made by Tito's iron will. He created the Federal People's Republic of Yugoslavia on 31 January 1946, comprising six republics, the autonomous province of *Vojvodina, and the autonomous area of *Kosovo. Unfortunately, the differences between the various ethnicities which had intensified so much during the war were never properly addressed or publicly discussed, and were largely suppressed. As the only Eastern European country (apart from Albania) which had become Communist without Moscow's direct help, Tito enjoyed much freedom of manoeuvre owing to the absence of Soviet troops, and he used this to the full.

To *Stalin's impotent anger, Tito accepted US aid in 1948, from which time Yugoslavia pursued an independent policy as a leading member of the *non-aligned movement. This enabled Tito to play off US against Soviet support, a game at which he excelled. A new constitution for the Federal Socialist Republic of Yugoslavia was introduced in 1963. Growing nationalist aspirations, most notably the Croatian Spring (1967–72), which produced a Croatian cultural and linguistic revival and was ultimately suppressed by Tito, led to the promulgation of the 1974 constitution, which gave the constituent republics and autonomous provinces more powers. After Tito's death, the presidency was shared between the states in rotation.

Dissolution (1980s–2003) While it would be wrong to assume that Yugoslavia was already doomed, there were signs that all was not well in 1981, when street riots in Kosovo were brutally suppressed. Thereafter, its autonomy was severely curtailed and was completely abolished in 1989, following renewed violence. This was accompanied by widespread, increasingly open debate about the nature of the Yugoslav state and the viability of Communist single-party rule. In 1989 the Serbian Communist Party responded to this by ensuring Communist survival through the election of the nationalist *Milošević as leader. Together with the Serbian incorporation of Kosovo, this threatened the other republics, where nationalist movements opposed to the Communists emerged. In some ways it was a repeat of the interwar problem, as the attempt by Serb nationalists to gain control of the Yugoslav state apparatus was met with increasing rejection of the Yugoslav state by its other constituent republics.

The formal breakup of Yugoslavia began with the secession of Slovenia in 1991. By 1992, all that remained within Yugoslavia was Serbia and Montenegro, which on 29 April 1992 formed the Federal Republic of Yugoslavia. In 2003, this was transformed into the Union of Serbia and Montenegro, and at this point Yugoslavia formally ceased to exist.

Yunus, Mohammad (b. 28 June 1940). Nobel Peace Prize winner

Born in Chittagong, he studied economics and won a *Fulbright scholarship to study for a doctorate at Vanderbilt University. After discovering that the poor often needed only small loans to enable them to overcome poverty and start a business, he founded the Grameen Bank. By 2006 this bank had made loans to over five million borrowers who were too poor to qualify for loans from other lenders. Yunus and his bank shared the 2006 *Nobel Prize. As rivalry between the *Awami League and its rival, the Bangladesh Nationalist Party, reached new levels to prevent scheduled elections from taking place, he announced in 2007 the creation of his own political movement to contest the elections.

Yushchenko, Viktor (b. 23 Feb 1954). Ukrainian President 2005–

Born in Choruchivka, he studied economics and joined the Soviet banking sector in 1977. After Ukrainian independence he was appointed President of the Central Bank, and in 1999 he was elected Prime Minister. He introduced a number of successful market-oriented reforms, but in 2001 Yushchenko resigned because of a lack of parliamentary support for his measures. In 2002, his party, 'Our Ukraine', became the largest party in parliament. In the run-up to the 2004 elections, he was poisoned with dioxin, which left permament scars on his face. He lost the rigged elections to his rival, Viktor Yanukovych, whereupon he led the Orange Revolution that paralysed the government, and encouraged the Supreme Court to declare the presidential elections invalid. Yushchenko won the renewed elections, but in order to appease his opponents and allies alike he surrendered some of his vast presidential powers to parliament.

Yushchenko soon fell out with his erstwhile ally, Yulia Tymoshenko, whose political radicalism he criticized. Owing to incessant squabbles among the governing parties, they lost the 2006 elections, forcing Yushchenko to appoint Yanukovich as Prime Minister. A beacon of hope during the Orange Revolution, Yushchenko disappointed many who had hoped for a political shift and policies of Westernization and market reforms.

Z

Zabern Affair (1913)

A German political crisis sparked by unrest in the Alsatian garrison town of Saverne (Zabern). It was caused when, more than four decades after *Alsace's occupation by the Germans, a German army officer openly insulted the local population. This led to popular unrest, which was quelled with brutal means. The crisis was fuelled by the support given by senior army figures and the German Chancellor *Bethmann Hollweg to the behaviour of the military in Saverne. On 4 December the German parliament accepted a vote of no confidence in the Chancellor by a huge majority. This unprecedented move remained without effect as, in the German Empire, the Chancellor was appointed by the Emperor and needed his support only. As with the *Daily Telegraph Affair, the parliament was ultimately half-hearted in its attempts to increase its power against the executive.

Zaghlul, Sa'd, see SAGHLUL, SA'D

zaibatsu

Enormous Japanese prewar trust companies, which exercised extensive influence over key areas of the prewar economy through their ownership of hundreds of businesses. Share ownership of the key holding companies of the zaibatsu was held by a single family alone, although that family was often divided into various branches. In Japan in the late nineteenth century, these families had been able to provide the rare capital necessary for Japan's rapid industrialization. The most prominent zaibatsu, which included famous organizations with a long history such as the Mitsui, Mitsubishi, as well as the so called 'new zaibatsu' which emerged in the twentieth century such as the Nissan, developed interests in areas as diverse as mining, transport, industry, commerce, and finance. After World War II, the US occupation identified the zaibatsu's dominance of the economy as one of the causes of Japanese militarism in the 1920s and 1930s and introduced measures to dissolve them. Ties between some of these companies have endured, although no precise equivalent to the zaibatsu exists today.

Zaïre, see CONGO, DEMOCRATIC REPUBLIC OF

Zambia

A southern African country rich in mineral resources, whose population ranks among the poorest in Africa.

Foreign rule
(up to 1964) Zambia was explored by Livingstone from 1855. In 1890 the *British South African Company (BSAC) established its administrative and economic dominance over the area through contracts with the chiefs of the inhabitant peoples. Known as North-West Rhodesia since 1899, it was united in 1911 with Barotseland (North-East Rhodesia) to form the British Protectorate of Northern Rhodesia, named after the founder of the BSAC, *Rhodes.

The administration of the BSAC ended in 1924, when Northern Rhodesia became a crown protectorate with considerable self-rule. In contrast to Southern Rhodesia (*Zimbabwe), *indirect rule eventually led to the participation of some Blacks in government. To give greater permanence and stability to British rule in an age of growing *decolonization, Northern Rhodesia was united with Southern Rhodesia and Nyasaland (see *Malawi) to form the *Central African Federation in 1953. Demands for independence and an end to White rule grew under *Kaunda's leadership, so that a British government no longer willing to impose its will by force granted Northern Rhodesia independence as the Republic of Zambia on 24 October 1964.

Independence (from 1964)
Kaunda became President, and partially nationalized the country's mining industry, the major earner of foreign currency. He stabilized his position among the ethnically heterogeneous population, and by 1973 his regime was sufficiently strong to allow him to outlaw all opposition and create a one-party state. During the 1970s he emerged as a leading critic of South African *apartheid, as well as *Smith's racist regime in Rhodesia (later Zimbabwe). The capital, Lusaka, served as the headquarters of the respective resistance movements, the *ANC and *ZANU. As Rhodesia was Zambia's

main trading partner, the consequent deterioration of relations between the two was extremely damaging to Zambia's economy. Economic relations improved in the 1980s, but by then its economy was being hit by severe droughts, as well as declining commodity prices for its main exports.

In reaction to growing popular discontent, as well as an abortive coup in 1990, Kaunda lifted the ban on political parties and announced multi-party elections, held on 31 October 1991. They resulted in a devastating defeat for Kaunda's United National Independence Party (UNIP), and a victory for the Movement for Multi-party Democracy (MMD) under *Chiluba. The latter liberalized the economy to stop the economic decline, though he was unable to prevent large-scale inflation (190 per cent in 1993). His privatization plan, imposed by the *IMF, proved a disaster for the country's economy. In 2000 the copper mines, which accounted for 70 per cent of Zambia's exports, were sold for $90 million (Chiluba had rejected an offer of $165 million in 1998). Two years later the buyer, Anglo-American, announced its intention to close the mines altogether, with around 15,000 jobs directly at risk. Chiluba was succeeded by Levy *Mwanawasa in 2002, who benefited from the divisions of the oppositions when he became President with 28 per cent of the vote, which represented a simple majority of votes cast.

Contemporary politics (since 2002) Under Mwanawasa, who was re-elected in 2006, the economy recovered, helped by a growth in world prices for copper. He also benefited from debt relief under the *HIPC scheme. Mwanawana's AIDS prevention schemes were able to stabilize infection rates, but since one in six of the population were infected with HIV, average life expectancy for men and women had declined to 40 years, according to UNAIDS.

ZANU (Zimbabwe African National Union)

A Zimbabwean political party formed in 1963 by disenchanted members of *Nkrumah's Zimbabwe African People's Union (ZAPU) in reaction to its moderate policies towards White minority rule in Southern Rhodesia (now Zimbabwe). Led by *Mugabe, its guerrilla organization, ZANLA (Zimbabwe African National Liberation Army), became the most important oppositional force in the Zimbabwean Civil War during the 1970s. During this time, ZANU managed to rally behind it the overwhelming support of the Shona people, the largest ethnic community in Rhodesia. It cooperated with the ZAPU in the Patriotic Front (PF) from 1976, but

contested separately the 1980 elections leading up to independence, from which it emerged with a large majority. It remained the principal party of government until December 1987, when its integration of *Nkomo's ZAPU to form ZANU-PF effectively transformed it into the single party of the country.

Zanzibar

An island off the East African coast which developed into a trading centre during the nineteenth century. It was coveted by several European powers in the age of *imperialism, but in 1890 Germany gave up its claims to the British in exchange for the North Sea island of Heligoland. The British proceeded to govern through the Sultan and his traditional elites (*indirect rule) and thus entrenched the rule of the privileged Arab minority over the African majority. This continued after independence on 10 December 1963. On 12 January 1964, however, the government was overthrown by the Afro-Shirazi Party under A. Karume. The revolution led to the exodus of around 90 per cent of the Arab population.

Zanzibar was united with Tanganyika to form Tanzania on 26 April 1964, though Zanzibar retained extensive autonomy with a separate legal, executive, and legislative system. President Karume instituted a hardline Marxist regime, but was overthrown by M. A. Jumbe in 1972. The latter continued in power until 1984, when he retired in favour of Ali Hassan Mwinyi (b. 1925). When Mwinyi succeeded *Nyerere as President of Tanzania, his position in Zanzibar was filled by S. S. Hamad (until 1988), Omar Ali Juma (1988–90), and Salmin Amour (1990–2000). Despite Zanzibar's autonomy, there were frequent tensions with the Tanzanian mainland. In 1993 the predominantly Muslim Zanzibar (briefly) entered the Islamic Conference, which caused an uproar in the rest of Tanzania with its religious diversity. Tensions often manifested themselves during the elections, as the ruling Tanzanian Revolutionary Party (CCM) clashed with the opposition Civic United Front (CUF). In 1995, when Amour was re-elected, and in 2000, when Karume's son, Amani, was elected, the CUF accused the CCM of large-scale electoral fraud to ensure its fragile hold over the island. Karume was re-elected in 2005, under renewed allegations of electoral fraud.

Zapata, Emiliano (b. 8 Aug. 1879?, d. 10 Apr. 1919). Mexican revolutionary leader
He organized an army of landless peasants from the poor state of Morelos, who were fighting to regain their lands lost to the large landowning estates under *Díaz. They joined

the opposition of Madero and *Villa against Díaz. However, after Diaz was toppled in 1911, Zapata continued his struggle against the attempts of the moderate Madero and his follower, *Carranza, to consolidate the achievements of the revolution and to prevent it from challenging the social order. In the power vacuum created by the fall of the short-lived Huerta dictatorship (1913–14) his troops entered Mexico City, where he was joined by Villa. He was forced by Carranza's constitutionalist troops to withdraw to the south, where he was killed by government troops in an ambush. A legend in his own time, his name was invoked in the *Chiapas Rebellion.

Zapatero, José Luis Rodríguez (b. 4 Aug. 1960). Prime Minister of Spain, 2004–

Born in Valladolid, he joined the *socialist party (PSOE) in 1979, and studied law at the University of Leon. He was first elected to parliament in 1986, and became secretary general of his party for the Leon region in 1988. After *González vacated the party chairmanship in 1996, the dramatic defeat of the PSOE in the 2000 elections created an opportunity for him to become party leader. Youthful and energetic, he criticized *Aznar's foreign policy, and vowed to recall Spanish troops from Iraq. The *Madrid Bombings unexpectedly brought foreign policy to the top of the political agenda, and focused the electorate on the integrity of the party leaders. Zapatero won a surprise victory at the 2004 elections, and initiated a string of far-reaching social reforms. These included the legalization of same-sex unions, the withdrawal of troops from Iraq, a more supportive attitude towards EU integration, and support for greater regional autonomy. As a result, Catalonia was accepted as a distinct nation with greater domestic powers, though its nationhood was defined in close relation to Spain.

Zeppelins, see AIRSHIPS

Zhdanov, Andrei Aleksandrovich (b. 26 Feb. 1896, d. 31 Aug. 1948). Soviet politician

Born in Mariupol (later Zhdanov), he joined the *Bolsheviks in 1915, and became an active propagandist for the party until the 1917 *Russian (October) Revolution. He became a political officer in the *Red Army, and in 1924 he was responsible for the *Communist Party in Tver and Nizhny Novgorod. In 1934, he succeeded *Kirov as chairman of the Leningrad Communist Party, and was regarded as a likely successor to *Stalin. In that year, he also became a

secretary of the Soviet Communist Party's Central Committee, and in 1939 joined the *Politburo. He took an active part in Stalin's *Great Purge, as well as the ruthless imposition of Soviet rule in the Baltic States (Estonia, Latvia, Lithuania) in 1940–1. He contributed decisively to the organization of the defence of Leningrad, 1941–4. Zhdanov is best remembered for his cultural and ideological influence. He instigated a major educational reform in the Soviet Union in 1934–8, and in 1944 he became responsible for party ideology. He enforced socialist realism in the arts and a Bolshevik historiography. His vicious opposition to any Western, 'decadent' cultural influence led to his country's complete artistic isolation. In 1947, he became the co-founder and leader of Cominform (see *Comintern).

Zhivkov, Todor Christov (b. 7 Sept. 1911, d. 5 Aug. 1998). Secretary-General of the Bulgarian Communist Party 1954–89; President of the State Council 1971–89

Born in Pravec (near Sofia), he became a printer. He joined the Communist Youth League in 1928, and the Communist Party in 1932. He was one of the leading members of the party in Sofia until the outbreak of World War II. During the *Nazi occupation from 1941, he was active as a partisan, linking the activities of the party rank and file with those of Communist guerrillas. After the *coup* of September 1944, he seized the initiative to suppress brutally all potential opposition to a Communist state, through murder, intimidation, and imprisonment. He became a non-voting member of the Communist Central Committee in 1945, and was elevated to full membership in 1949. In 1954, as Secretary-General of the Communist Party he became the effective ruler of his country. Of all political leaders within Communist Eastern Europe, Zhivkov was perhaps the most loyal follower of the Soviet Union, matching each political shift in that country with policy changes of his own. For example, he immediately accepted *Khrushchev's policies of 'de-Stalinization' in 1956, but had no problems accepting the leadership of *Brezhnev after Khrushchev's dismissal. He increased the country's (and his own) cultural, military, and economic dependence on the Soviet Union. This turned against him in 1989, when he tried, for the first time, to oppose the reformist trends of *glasnost and *perestroika coming from Moscow. Nor could he rely on Moscow any longer to ensure his own survival. On 10 November 1989 he was deposed. On 29 February 1992 he was sentenced to seven years' imprisonment and the payment of around $1 million for embezzlement and corruption. He did not have to serve his gaol sentence because of his old age.

Zhou Enlai (Chou En-lai) (b. 1898, d. 8 Jan. 1976). Premier of the People's Republic of China 1949–76

Early career Born in Huaian (Jiangsu Province) into a wealthy Mandarin family, Zhou studied in Japan and France, where he joined the Chinese *Communist Party (CCP) in 1922. After further study in Germany (1923–4), he returned to Guangzhou (Canton), where he was appointed commander of the political department of the Whampoa Military Academy, which was led by *Chiang Kai-shek. He was dismissed by Chiang in 1926, whereupon he became head of the CCP's military department. In this capacity he took part in the first stage of the *Northern Expedition, until the *Guomindang's crackdown on the Communists in 1927. Zhou went to Moscow as the party's representative to *Comintern, but returned and joined the *Jianxi Soviet in 1931. Although initially not an ally of *Mao Zedong, he became his most important aide after Mao's assumption of the CCP leadership during the *Long March in January 1935. In 1936, he led negotiations with *Chang Hsüeh-liang about cooperation with the *National Republican Army and, although not directly involved, he came to Chang's help at the *Xi'an Incident. During the *Sino-Japanese War and the *Chinese Civil War, he emerged as one of the principal political as well as military leaders, and became a chief negotiator with the Nationalists.

In office In the new People's Republic of China, Zhou served as Premier of the Government Administration Council and, from 1954, of the State Council. In these positions, he was responsible for the day-to-day execution of Mao's policies, which he accomplished with great skill. He was Foreign Minister until 1958, though he continued to be a major influence in China's foreign policy until his death. Thus, he brought the *Korean War to an end in 1953, and succeeded in achieving membership of the *UN in 1971, at the height of the *Cultural Revolution. He survived the latter, and even used it to get rid of his closest rival, *Lin Biao. Despite the fact that, as Mao's deputy, he bore substantial responsibility for the excesses of Mao's rule, most notably the *Great Leap Forward and the *Cultural Revolution, he promoted a generation of more moderate leaders to high office, among them *Deng Xiaoping. His

death resulted in large protest demonstrations at *Tiananmen Square.

Zhu De (Chu Teh) (b. 30 Nov. 1886, d. 6 July 1976). Commander-in-Chief of the Chinese Communist army

Born in Yilong, Sichuan Province, Zhu was commissioned into the imperial army and attended the Yunnan military academy. He joined the revolutionary movement, however, and in 1911 participated in the *Wuchang Revolution. He became an officer in the republican Yunnan army, which he left in 1922 to study in Germany. There, he met *Zhou Enlai, joined the *Communist Party, and studied political science at Göttingen University. Expelled for his political activities, he went to Moscow in 1925, and returned to China in 1926. Zhu became commander of an officer's training regiment in the *National Revolutionary Army until the Communist-Nationalist split in 1927. On 1 August 1927, he led the Communist Nanchang uprising, and in 1928, with *Mao Zedong, he founded the 4th Red Army. A loyal supporter of Mao, he was a skilful military leader in defence of the *Jianxi Soviet. After supporting Mao in the *Long March, which took them to *Yan'an, he became overall military commander of the Communist forces in 1936, a position which he retained until the army's final victory in the *Chinese Civil War.

After the foundation of the People's Republic, his practical influence declined. He deputized for *Zhou Enlai as vice-chairman of the Central People's Government Council until 1954, and as vice-chairman of the Republic until 1959. Having been made a Marshall in 1955, his practical influence ended altogether in 1959, when he gave up the formal leadership of the People's Liberation Army. Instead, he was made chairperson of the harmless National People's Congress (1959–76), but he did emerge from the *Cultural Revolution unharmed.

Zhukov, Georgi Konstantinovich (b. 11 Dec. 1896, d. 18 June 1977). Marshal of the Soviet Union

Born in Strelkova (near Moscow), the son of a shoemaker enlisted in the *Red Army in 1918 and fought in the *Russian Civil War, joining the *Bolshevik party in 1919. During the war, he came into close contact with *Stalin. A commander of a cavalry regiment by 1923, he continued his steep rise in the military, and in 1933 was put in charge of the elite 4th Cavalry Division. He filled the post of commander of the 3rd Cavalry Corps, whose previous holder had been removed in the *Great Purge, and defeated the Japanese in their military adventures into Soviet territory in June 1939. A general in 1940, he became Chief of General Staff in 1941.

A great as well as a ruthless commander, he was responsible for most of the major *Red Army operations during World War II. He held Moscow against the German advance, and planned the German defeat at *Stalingrad. He went on to lift the siege of Leningrad and inflict a massive defeat on the German army in Belorussia (*Belarus). He advanced into Poland and led the Soviet capture of *Berlin in April 1945, at a high cost to his own forces. After the war, he was quickly demoted by Stalin, who was unwilling to share the spoils of victory. After Stalin's death, he became deputy minister of defence, and was instrumental in preventing *Beria's succession to the leadership. He thus became Minister of Defence and was then crucial in helping *Khrushchev defeat the 'anti-party group' *coup* of *Molotov, *Malenkov, and *Kaganovich in 1957. In return, Khrushchev relieved him of his duties, fearful of his influence.

Zia, Begum Khaleda (b. 15 Aug 1945).
Prime Minister of Bangladesh, 1991–6, 2001–6
The third of five children, in 1960 she married Ziaur Rahman, an army officer who became Prime Minister of Bangladesh in 1975. Following his assassination in 1981, Khaleda Zia entered politics, and in 1984 she became Chair of the Bangladesh National Party, which her husband had founded. She became the first female Prime Minister, and the first to see out a full term of office. Zia pursued liberal economic policies, and improved general education and health-care provision. Her coalition with Muslim religious parties made it difficult for her to combat the growth of religious fundamentalism, especially in her second full term of office.

Zia-ul-Haq, General Mohammed
(b. 1924, d. 17 Aug. 1988). President of Pakistan 1978–88
Born in Jallundur, Punjab, he was educated at St Stephen's College, Delhi, before entering the British Indian army. He was commissioned in 1945 and joined the Pakistan army in 1947. He rose quickly within its ranks, serving as military adviser in Jordan (1974–5), until he was appointed in 1976 by Zulfikar *Bhutto to become army Chief of Staff, largely for his unpolitical record. Nevertheless, he toppled Bhutto just over a year later, after Bhutto had rigged the general election. He was content to see Bhutto hanged, and took measures to destroy his

party, the Pakistan People's Party (PPP). Meanwhile, he relaxed Bhutto's socialist policies and emphasized his commitment to *Islam, in order to buttress his appeal to the middle classes. He also abandoned Bhutto's neutralist foreign policy in favour of a closer alignment with the USA. He won the 1985 elections, which were boycotted by the PPP now led by Bhutto's widow and his daugher, Benazir *Bhutto. Zia-ul-Haq ruled at the head of a civilian government which was led by Mohammad Khan Junejo. He remained firmly in control, however, until his death in an aeroplane crash. It became evident that the complex political system he had created to overcome the PPP had been built on the weak foundation of his personality alone, for the elections following his death were won by the PPP, with Bhutto's daughter becoming Prime Minister.

Zimbabwe
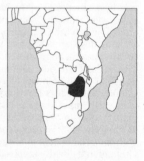
A landlocked country in southern Africa, which turned from a model of a post-colonial state in the 1980s to an international pariah state from the late 1990s.

Colonial history (up to 1965) Zimbabwe originates from Mashonaland (home to the Shona people) and Matabeleland (home to the Ndebele/Matabele people). In a treaty with the Ndebele of 1889, agents of *Rhodes secured exclusive rights for the exploitation of minerals in Matabeleland for Rhodes's *British South Africa Company (BSAC). Declared a British protectorate in 1891, most Matabele and Shona resistance was overcome by 1894 (though sporadic insurrections occurred until 1903). Named **Rhodesia** in 1894, it was administered by the BSAC, which divided the land and gave the fertile half to the White minority (less than 5 per cent of the population), and the infertile half to the Black majority as Tribal Trust Lands (TTL). The TTLs were unable to provide adequate subsistence for the Blacks living on them, who were thus forced to become a cheap labour resource for the Whites managing the fertile farmlands. Economic inequality became reinforced by the spread of the *apartheid ideology transmitted by White immigrants from South Africa. Following a referendum by White settlers against entry into the Union of South

Africa as a fifth state, BSAC rule ended in 1923, whereupon the country essentially gained self-rule as Southern Rhodesia in 1924. In 1953 Southern Rhodesia became part of the *Central African Federation, together with Nyasaland (Malawi) and Northern Rhodesia (Zambia).

UDI (Unilateral Declaration of Independence, 1965–79) When Malawi and Zambia strove for independence from the Federation, the Southern Rhodesian settlers were quick to assert their desire for independence through the racist Rhodesian Front (RF) of Ian *Smith, who was elected (by the Whites) Prime Minister in 1965. Since the British government refused to grant independence unless Blacks were given an appropriate (i.e. majority) share in government, Smith pronounced a UDI. Sanctions imposed by the *UN and Britain were at first largely ineffective, since they were ignored by Rhodesia's main trading partner, South Africa, as well as the neighbouring Portuguese colony of Mozambique. Internal resistance emerged under *Nkomo's *ZAPU (Zimbabwe African People's Union) and *Mugabe's *ZANU (Zimbawe African National Union). Their respective guerrilla movements fought with increasing bitterness, particularly after the breakdown of negotiations with Smith in 1976. Despite continuing rivalries, ZANU and ZAPU united to form the Patriotic Front (PF), which opposed a new settlement in 1978 whereby the Whites would maintain a pivotal role in the political and administrative system. Following the elections of April 1979, *Muzorewa became Prime Minister. After continued international pressure and PF opposition, a final compromise was reached at a British-sponsored agreement at Lancaster House, 21 December 1979.

For four months, Rhodesia reverted to the rule of British authorities, which monitored and ensured fair elections in March 1980. These were won by Mugabe (63 per cent of the popular vote), while Nkomo's ZAPU received 24 per cent. Independence under the name of Zimbabwe followed on 18 April 1980. In the following years, Mugabe's careful and moderate policies produced remarkable racial harmony between the prosperous Whites and the poor Black majority, despite the civil war that had claimed over 30,000 lives during the 1970s. Tensions between ZANU and ZAPU, which sometimes erupted into violence, were finally settled in 1987, when ZAPU joined ZANU to form the ZANU-PF. In accordance with the Lancaster House agreement, parliament voted in June 1987 to end White over-representation in parliament, which for a transitional period of ten years had guaranteed them (1.2 per cent of the population) 20 per cent of the seats.

Nevertheless, most of these seats were filled again by Whites after the 1990 elections under the banner of ZANU-PF, and two White ministers were appointed.

The Mugabe era (from 1980) Under Mugabe's rule, education was made accessible to all, while sanitary provision and health care were improved considerably. Nonetheless, the persistently strong economic performance relied on continued inequality between Blacks and Whites. Because of the differences in agricultural fertility, White farms yielded more than six times more income per head than those owned by Blacks. Four thousand white farmers owned more than 30 per cent of the fertile arable land, obtaining over 40 per cent of the country's exports, and employing over 65 per cent of the workforce. Meanwhile, cheap Black labour continued to guarantee the competitiveness of Zimbabwean agricultural produce. In 1994 the High Court approved an expropriation law (against compensation) originally passed in 1992, though few steps were taken to put it into effect, partly because of the already existing high debt of the state.

In 1997 state debt increased further as 11,000 Zimbabwean troops became involved in the war in Congo, at a cost of over $100 million per year. As the economic problems deepened and unemployment rose to above 50 per cent, Mugabe hoped to restore his popularity by encouraging militant loyalist Blacks to take the law into their own hands and occupy farms owned by Whites from 1998. In that year, the government for the first time expropriated, without compensation, hundreds of White farmers. International aid was frozen as a result. Official and unofficial expropriations continued, despite a High Court ruling in 2000 ordering the return of farms to their White owners. Mugabe's increasing extremism failed to halt the erosion of his popularity, and he ensured re-election in 2002 by electoral fraud and the persecution of opponents.

Contemporary politics (since 2003) By 2003, unemployment had reached 70 per cent and inflation stood at over 500 per cent, while severe droughts had worsened the economic conditions still further. Against this background, Mugabe increased political repression. In 2003, Morgan Tsvangirai, leader of the opposition Movement for Democratic Change, was charged with treason, and foreign reporters were expelled. Aided by these measures, ZANU-PF was returned to parliament with a two-thirds majority in 2005. The economy deteriorated further, with inflation exceeding 1200 per cent by March 2007. According to the UN Office for the Coordination of Humanitarian Affairs, the economic collapse since 2000 has led to an unemployment rate of around 80 per cent, while the industrial base has contracted by one-third.

Zimmermann Note (19 Jan. 1917)

A secret telegram containing a coded message from the German Foreign Secretary Alfred Zimmermann, to the German minister in Mexico City. It instructed the minister to propose an alliance with Mexico if war broke out between the USA and Germany, Mexico being offered the territories lost in 1848 to the USA. The British intercepted and decoded the message, and passed it to the US State Department. It was released on 1 March 1917 as German–US relations were deteriorating over unrestricted submarine warfare. The Note was considered an overt act of German aggression, in blatant disregard of the Monroe Doctrine (1823) which rejected European interference in matters concerning the American hemisphere. Coming after years of debate, it was the final catalyst to propel the USA into World War I, with war being declared on Germany on 6 April 1917.

Zinoviev, Grigori Yevseevich (b. 11 Sept. 1883, d. 25 Aug. 1936). Soviet politician

Born Radomyslsky Apfelbaum in Elizavetgrad, he joined the Russian Social Democratic Party in 1901 and supported the *Bolshevik faction in 1903, becoming a close supporter of *Lenin. Elected to the party's Central Committee in 1907, he left for Western Europe to support Lenin in matters of *propaganda and party organization. He accompanied Lenin over the next five years, but disagreed with his mentor's plans for the October Revolution (*Russian Revolutions, 1917) as premature. He was chairman of the Petrograd Soviet from December 1917. From 1919 until 1926 he was chairman of the external committee of the *Comintern. After Lenin's death, Zinoviev was in contention for the Soviet leadership. He sided with Stalin and *Kamenev against *Trotsky, but then tried to oppose the increasingly powerful Stalin and *Bukharin. His desperate alliance with Trotsky and Kamenev against Stalin proved futile, and he was dismissed from all offices in 1926, and expelled from the party in 1927. He was readmitted (1928), re-expelled (1932), and finally readmitted (1933). After the assassination of *Kirov, in 1935 he was arrested, tried in secret for complicity in the murder, and sentenced to ten years' imprisonment. In 1936, he was retried and, with Kamenev, became the first prominent victim of the show trials which marked Stalin's *Great Purge.

Zionism

A term used to describe the modern movement founded by *Herzl which aimed at establishing a Jewish homeland in *Palestine as the only possible way in which Jews could escape from centuries of discrimination and persecution. The term is derived from Mount Zion in *Jerusalem, which has been used as a symbol for the Jewish homeland in Palestine since the time of the Babylonian captivity, in the sixth century BC. Herzl's idea itself was nothing new, but he gave it an organizational articulation through the World Zionist Organization (WZO), founded in 1897. It sponsored Jewish emigration to Palestine as a prelude to establishing a Jewish state, and lobbied foreign governments to support its aims.

Even though the movement found much support among the less prosperous and persecuted Jews of Eastern Europe (*Pogrom), its reception was more mixed in Western Europe, where Jews were largely assimilated. Even there, however, support grew as a result of increasing waves of *anti-Semitism which demonstrated the futility of assimilation. During the 1920s, it continued to encourage and sponsor Jewish emigration to Palestine, while it successfully persuaded the British government to grant the Jewish community there some self-government, through the creation of the *Jewish Agency. The latter provided a crucial link between the Jewish community in Palestine and the WZO, which continued after the creation of the state of Israel in 1948, itself the realization of the Zionist dream. Since then, the WZO as well as the Israeli government have openly encouraged the Zionist idea of Jewish immigration into Israel, which the WZO supported financially.

( ) SEE WEB LINKS

- The website of the Department for Zionist Activities at the WZO.

Zog I (b. 8 Oct. 1895, d. 9 Apr. 1961). King of Albania 1928–39

A wealthy Albanian landowner born as Ahmed Bey Zogu, he came to lead Albanian popular resistance to Italian occupation during World War I, which eventually forced Italian withdrawal in 1920. He became Prime Minister in 1923 and, after spending seven months in exile, became President in January 1925. Zog proclaimed himself King in 1928 and tried to strengthen his country through promoting education and infrastructural investment. Since capital came primarily from Italy, by 1939 almost the entire Albanian economy was under Italian control. Mussolini invaded Albania in 1939, forcing Zog into exile. The monarchy was formally abolished in 1946.

Maps

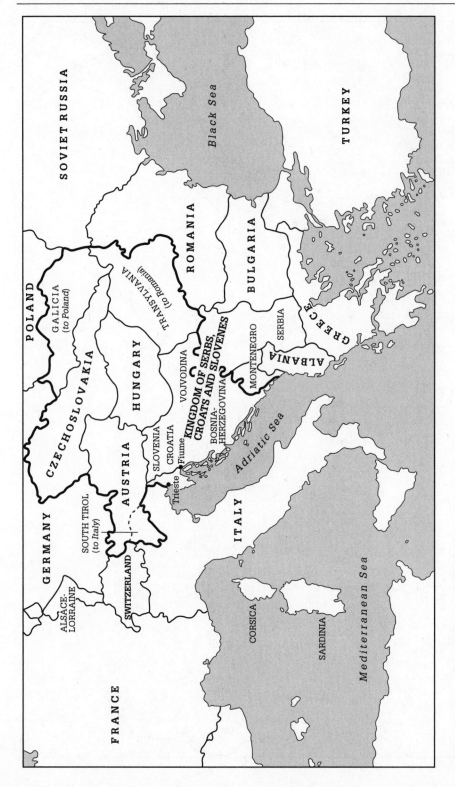

Map 1: Austria–Hungary and its successor states, 1918

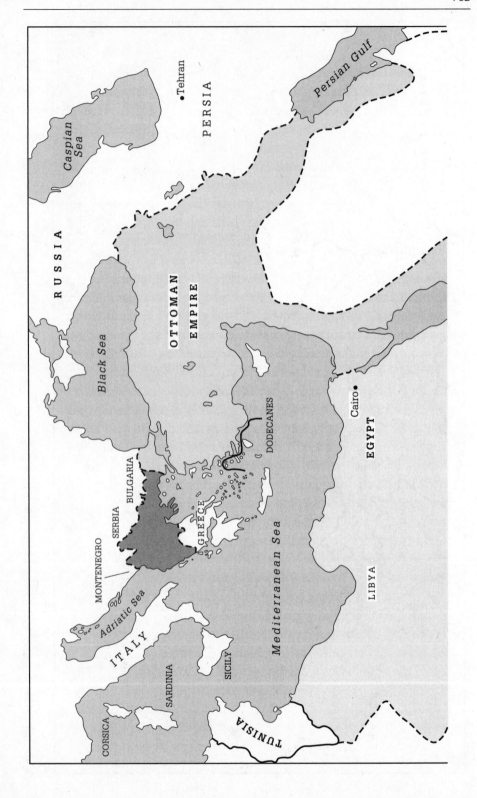

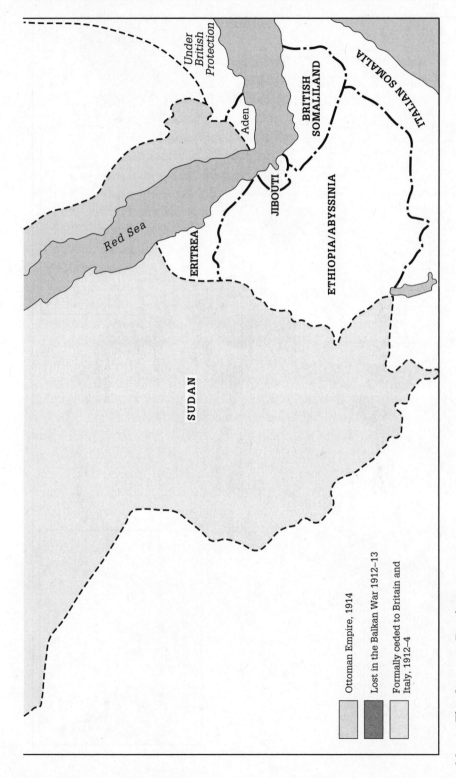

Map 2: The Ottoman Empire, 1912–14

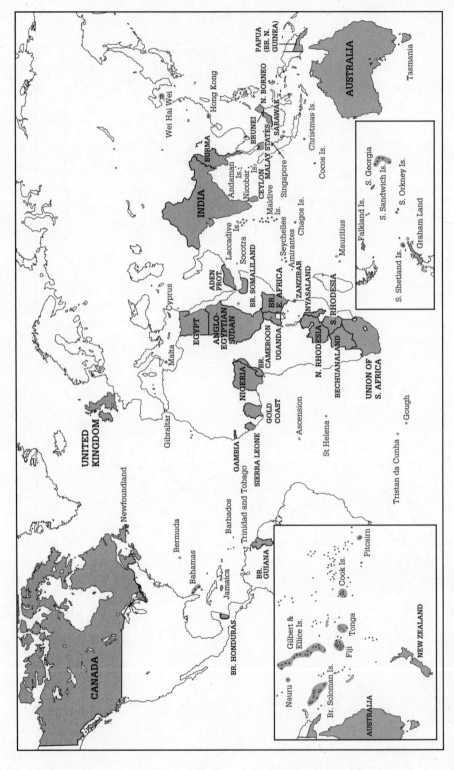

Map 3: The British Empire, 1914

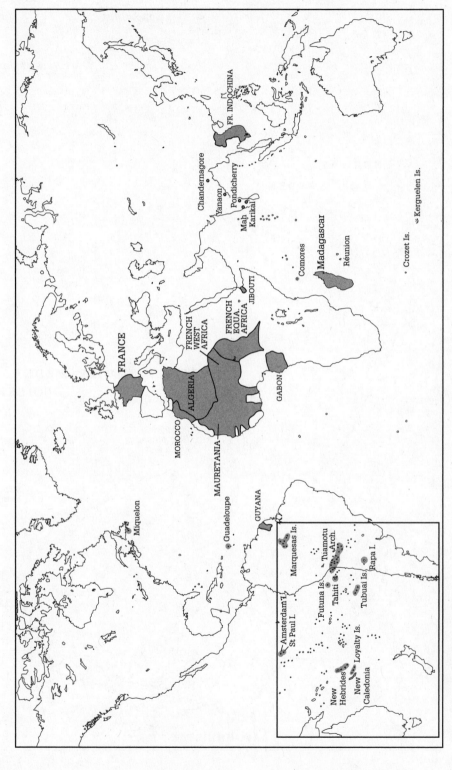

Map 4: The French Empire, 1914

Map 5: The USSR (Union of Soviet Socialist Republics), 1950

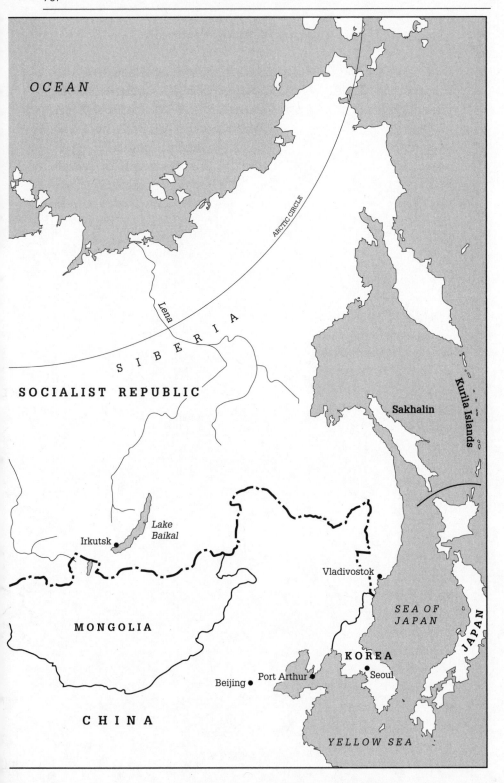